LIST OF THE OFFICERS OF THE BENGAL ARMY

Printed and bound in Great Britain by Antony Rowe Ltd, Eastbourne

LIST OF THE OFFICERS OF THE BENGAL ARMY

1758–1834

Alphabetically Arranged and Annotated with Biographical and Genealogical Notices by

MAJOR V. C. P. HODSON

INDIAN ARMY (RETIRED LIST)
AUTHOR OF 'HISTORICAL RECORDS OF THE VICEROY'S BODY-GUARD'

D - K

NOTICE

I TAKE this opportunity of thanking those correspondents who, in response to my appeal on page vi of the Preface of Part I, have kindly sent me additional particulars relating to that portion of this work. These addenda will be found at the end of the present volume. Especially am I indebted to the Rev. Canon H. B. Swanzy for his valuable notes and references to some of the Irishmen, and to Mr. T. U. Sadleir who, in addition to filling some of the *lacunæ* in Part I, has most kindly looked over the whole of the typescript of Part II, thereby saving me from many errors both of omission and commission.

May I again ask those interested, who may chance to see this volume, to send me, through the Publishers, any corrections or additional matter in their possession.

V. C. P. H.

July 1927.

CONTENTS OF PART II

	PAGE
NOTICE - - - - - - - - - - -	V
DACOSTA, GEORGE—DYSON, JOHN - - - - -	1
EADE, JOHN—EYRES, GEORGE BOLTON - - - -	115
FADDY, SAMUEL BROUGHAM—FYLER, JOHN I'ANSON -	151
GABB, JOHN—GWINNETT, JOHN PRICE - - - -	238
HACKET(T), JAMES—HYSLOP, MAXWELL - - - -	353
IBBETT, HENRY—IVESON, JOHN - - - - -	521
JACK, ALEXANDER—JOWKLEY, HENRY - - - -	534
KAMPTZ, D'OTTAS—KYD, ROBERT - - - - -	572
CORRIGENDA - - - - - - - - - -	614
ADDENDA - - - - - - - - - -	617

D

N.B.—Compound names must be sought under the last element of the compound.

N.B.—An asterisk denotes that the name is omitted from *Dodwell & Miles's List.*

DACOSTA, George (d. 1777). Captain, Infantry. Cadet 1767. Ensign 31 May 1767. Lieut. 4 Apr. 1769. Capt. 2 Apr. 1777. d. Farrukhabad, U.P., 5 Aug. 1777.
Services : N.F.P.

DACRE, Charles (1786-1823). Captain, 12th N.I. *bapt.* Kirklinton, Cumberland, 20 Sept. 1786. Cadet 1803. Arrived in India 14 Aug. 1804. Ensign 8 Sept. 1804. Lieut. 21 Sept. 1804. Capt. 29 June 1815. d. Agra 28 May 1823.
Son of William Dacre, of Kirklinton Hall, Cumberland, and Elizabeth his wife, dau. of Joseph Wilkinson, of Westminster. m. 27 Aug. 1808, Miss Sophia Isabella Assey, sister of Charles Chaston Assey, Surgeon, Bengal Est.
Services : Posted as Lieut. to 12th N.I. (? Second Mahratta War ; siege of Bhurtpore ; Lieut. 12th N.I.) Operations in Oudh 1808 ; Lieut. 12th N.I. Adjt. 1/12th N.I. 25 Oct. 1811 till July 1815. Capt. 1/12th N.I. Fort Adjt. at Agra 1822 till death.
Refs. : Will dated 19 Dec. 1815 ; proved 3 Sept. 1823.

DADE, John (1803-1830). Lieutenant, 56th N.I. b. Denver, Norfolk, 6 July 1803. Cadet 1819. Arrived in India June 1820. Ensign 2 Dec. 1819. Lieut. 30 June 1821. d. Sabathu, Punjab, 30 Oct. 1830.
Son of Rev. Charles Robert Dade, rector of Denver. Addiscombe Cadet 1818-9.
Services : Ensign d.d. Bengal Eur. Regt. July-Oct. 1820. Posted as Ensign to 2/28th N.I. Jan. 1821. Leave to Cape Mar. 1824 till Apr. 1826. Transfd. to 56th N.I. (late 2/28th) May 1824. Leave to Simla Feb. 1830 till death. No record of active service. Victor Jacquemont, the French botanist, who saw him in Simla in 1830,

described him as the young officer " with five or six good reasons for dying."
Refs. : *De Rhé-Philipe.* M.I. at Sabathu.

D'AGUILAR, George Thomas (1783-1839). Lieut. Colonel, Invalid Est. 26th N.I. *b.* London 11 Aug. 1783. Cadet 1798. Arrived in India 24 Nov. 1799. Ensign 19 Nov. 1799. Lieut. 29 May 1800. Capt. 29 Sept. 1811. Major 12 Sept. 1822. Lt. Col. 1 May 1824. Invalided 22 Apr. 1825. *d.* Calcutta 9 Oct. 1839. *bapt.* Marylebone, London, 10 May 1784. Natural son of Benjamin D'Aguilar, of Foley Pl., Marylebone, formerly a merchant at Benares. *m.* Calcutta, 30 Aug. 1814, Miss Catherine Burton, sister of Capt. Joseph Burton, H.M.S. (She died 14 Nov. 1887.)
Services : To be Ensign by purchase H.M. 78th Foot 30 Aug. 1798. Second Mahratta War ; Bundelkhand 1803-4 ; Lieut. 1/13th N.I. Adjt. 1/13th N.I. 1805-7. Operations against Dhundia Khan 1807 ; Komona ; Ganauri ; Lieut. 1/13th N.I. Capt. Lt. 1/13th N.I. 10 Oct. 1810. Capture of Java 1811 ; Lieut. 6th Bengal Vol. Bn. Bareilly insurrection 1816 ; Capt. 1/13th N.I. Transfd. as Lt. Col. to 26th N.I. (late 1/13th) May 1824. First Burma War ; Arakan 1825 ; Lt. Col. comdg. 26th N.I. Comdd. Orissa Provl. Bn. 1825-30 ; afterwards comdd. 2nd Bn. Native Invalids ; subsequently Regulating Or. in Bhagulpur and Tirhut. Leave to Cape 16 Jan. 1837.
Refs. : Will dated 4 Jan. 1836 ; proved 29 Oct. 1839. M.I. in S. Park St. cemetery, Calcutta.

DAINTY, James. (*See* **DENTY.**)

DAKIN, John (1792-?). Ensign. 26th N.I. *b.* Warrington, Lancs., 11 July 1792. Cadet 1811. Ensign 7 Oct. 1814. Resigned in India 7 Feb. 1817.
Son of Edward Dakin, distiller.
Services : Posted as Ensign to 1/26th N.I. 6 Nov. 1815. No record of active service.

DALBY, George Henry Mitford (1802-1834). Captain, 68th N.I. *b.* St. Thomas's, Exeter, 8 Apr. 1802. Cadet 1819. Admitted 14 June 1820. Ensign 14 Nov. 1819. Lieut. 11 July 1823. Capt. 6 Oct. 1832. *d.* Ootacamund, Madras, 13 May 1834.
Son of Thomas Dalby, Capt. R.N.
Services : Posted as Ensign to 1/9th N.I. Transfd. as Lieut. to newly-raised 34th N.I. July 1823 ; to 68th N.I. (late 2/34th) May 1824. D.J.A.G., Presdy. Div., 17 Sept. 1825. Asst. Sec. to Govt., Mily. Board, 12 Feb. 1832. Sailed for Madras with Lord William Bentinck, the G.G., 3 Feb. 1834.

Refs.: *A.J.* N.S. xv. 227. *Bath Chron.*, 27 Nov. 1834. M.I. at Ootacamund.

DALGAIRNS, William (1793-1820). Lieutenant, 3rd N.I. *bapt.* Coupar-Angus, co. Perth, 20 Jan. 1793. Cadet 1810. Ensign 16 Nov. 1813. Lieut. 12 Apr. 1815. *d.* at sea 11 Mar. 1820, on board the licensed ship *Rochester.*
Son of William Dalgairns, of Keithock, and afterwards of Ballentine House.
Services : Posted as Ensign to 2/3rd N.I. Nepal War 1814-5 ; Lieut. 2/3rd N.I., in 1st Div.

DALLAS, Arbuthnot (1814-1848). Bt. Captain, 16th N.I. *b.* Berbice, British Guiana, 14 Aug. 1814. Cadet 1832. Arrived in India 16 Sept. 1833. Ensign 16 Sept. 1833. Lieut. 28 Nov. 1839. Bt. Capt. 17 May 1848. *d.* Calcutta 31 Dec. 1848.
Son of —— Dallas, of the medical service, Berbice, later of Inverness. *m.* Sydney, N.S.W., 30 Dec. 1846, Sophia Elizabeth, eldest dau. of Col. Henry Despard, comdg. H.M. 99th Regt.
Services : Posted as Ensign to 16th N.I. 24 May 1834. With 2nd Inf., Oudh Auxy. Force, Dec. 1837 till 18 Sept. 1838, when he rejoined his Regt. for active service. Offg. S.A.C.G., and attached to Art. Div., Army of the Indus. Posted to Shah Shuja's army. First Afghan War 1838-42 ; Pashut ; Kandahar ; Ghazni ; Kabul ; Lieut. 16th N.I. (Medal). Apptd. Asst. to Paymr. & Comst. Ofr., Shah's army, 27 Feb. 1839. Actg. Asst. to P.A., Kandahar, 3 Nov. 1841. D.C., 2 cl., Saugor & Narbada territories, 31 Mar. 1843. Apptd. 2nd Asst. Sec., Mily. Board, 29 Dec. 1843 ; 1st do. 11 Dec. 1846 till death. On special duty to N.S.W. in 1846.

DALLAS, Charles (1803-1840). Captain, Artillery. *b.* Netley, Salop, 4 June 1803. Cadet 1818. Admitted 27 Sept. 1819. 2nd Lieut. 27 Apr. 1819. Lieut. 16 July 1823. Capt. 11 May 1836. *d.s.p.* Saugor 10 July 1840.
2nd son of Bdr.-Gen. Charles Dallas, of Llymston, co. Montgomery, Govr. of St. Helena 1839, and Jane his wife, dau. of Robert Haldane, of Gleneagles. Nephew of Lt.-Gen. Sir Thomas Dallas, G.C.B., Madras Est. (*D.N.B.*). *m.* 1st, St. Helena, 25 Jan. 1831, Penelope, dau. of Capt. Stephen Long, St. Helena Regt. (She died Chunar 17 Aug. 1834, aged 26.) *m.* 2nd, Calcutta, 14 Nov. 1836, Eliza Helen, dau. of Dr. James Mellis, Bengal Medical Est. Addiscombe Cadet 1818-9.
Services : Adjt. & Qmr. 2nd Bn. Foot Art. 5 Dec. 1828 till 19 Mar. 1835. Leave 2 yrs. to St. Helena 20 July 1829 till 15 Sept. 1831. Offg. Comy. Ord. at Chunar 22 Nov. 1833 ; Dy. Comy. do. 19 Mar.

1835; Comy. Ord. at Dum-Dum 11 Aug. 1835; do. at Saugor 9 Sept. 1839 till death. Posted to 1st Troop 3rd Bde. H.A. 22 Dec. 1836. No record of active service.
Refs. : Burke's *Landed Gentry*, 13th edn., p. 1961, *s.n.* Dallas-Yorke, of Walmsgate, Lincs. *A.J.* N.S. v. 39. Will dated Dum-Dum 29 June 1837; proved 15 June 1841.

DALRYMPLE, James (1771-1804). Capt. Lieutenant, 15th N.I. *b.* Morham 27 Apr. 1771. Cadet 1794. Arrived in India 13 Nov. 1795. Ensign 2 Oct. 1795. Lieut. 3 Oct. 1796. Capt. Lieut. 28 June 1804. *d.* Berhampore, Bengal, 28 Oct. 1804.
Son of Hew Dalrymple, of Nunraw, and Dorothea McCormick his wife.
Services : Ensign H.M. 19th Foot 30 Mar. 1789; Lieut. do. 5 Mar. 1793; resigned 13th June 1795. Ensign 1st Bengal Eur. Regt. in 1796. Operations in Jumna Doab 1803; Sasni; Bijaigarh; Kachaura; Lieut. 15th N.I. Second Mahratta War; battle of Delhi; Agra; Laswari; Lieut. 15th N.I.
Refs. : Burke's *Peerage*, 1923, p. 654, *s.n.* Hamilton-Dalrymple, Bart., of N. Berwick.

DALRYMPLE, Robert (*d.* 1792). Captain, Infantry. Cadet 1770. Ensign 5 Nov. 1771. Lieut. 21 July 1776. Capt. 16 Feb. 1781. *d.* Chapra, B. & O., 29 Dec. 1792.
Services : 2nd Bengal Eur. Bn. in July 1787.

DALRYMPLE, Thomas Richard (1803-1828). Lieutenant, 7th N.I. *b.* Bothwell, co. Lanark, 19 Dec. 1803. Cadet 1824. Ensign 25 Feb. 1825. Lieut. 16 Mar. 1826. *d.* at sea 29 Jan. 1828, on board the *Roxburgh Castle*.
Younger son of Marton Dalrymple, of Cleland, and Frances Ingram Spence his wife. Gt.-grandson of Sir William Dalrymple, 3rd Bart. of Cousland.
Services : Posted to 7th N.I. No record of active service.
Refs. : Burke's *Peerage*, 1923, p. 2075, *s.n.* Earl of Stair. *A.J.* xxv. 568.

DALSTON, Fletcher (*d.* 1836 ?). Captain. 11th N.I. Cadet 1783. Admitted 15 Aug. 1784. Ensign 16 Jan. 1785. Lieut. 7 Feb. 1791. Capt. 27 Jan. 1804. Retired 14 Feb. 1810. *d.* 1836 ?
m. 1st, Catherine. Father of George Dalston, *q.v.* *m.* 2nd, Esther Britain. (She died 18 Dec. 1860, aged 83.)
Services : Lieut. 5th N.I. in June 1798. Adjt. & Qmr. 11th N.I. in 1803. Fur. 23 Feb. till retirement.

THE BENGAL ARMY, 1758-1834 5

DALSTON, George (1812-1848). Bt. Major, 58th N.I. *b.* London 14 Sept. 1812. Cadet 1830. Arrived in India 23 Apr. 1830. Ensign 23 Apr. 1830. Lieut. 16 Apr. 1838. Capt. 3 Mar. 1843. Bt. Major 30 Apr. 1844. *d.* Indore, C.I., 22 July 1848.
Son of Fletcher Dalston, *q.v.*, of Honfleur, France, and Catherine his 1st wife. *m.* Calcutta, 13 Mar. 1840, Margaret Ann, dau. of P. Turnbull.
Services : Cadet d.d. 68th N.I. 7 June 1830. Actg. Ensign 16 July 1832, having been more than 2 yrs. in India. Posted as Ensign to 58th N.I. 20 Aug. 1832. Fur. 1 yr. u.p.a. 24 Mar. 1835 till 21 May 1836. Transfd. to 66th N.I. 24 Sept. 1835 ; to 58th N.I. 24 May 1836. Actg. Adjt. 58th N.I. Feb. 1838. Adjt. 1st Vol. Bn. for service in China 15 Feb. till 6 Nov. 1840. First China War 1840 ; Lieut. 1st Bengal Vol. Bn. (Medal). Rejoined 58th N.I. 22 May 1841. Actg. Adjt. 58th N.I. 4 Oct. 1841. Apptd. Bde. Major to 2nd Bde., 1st Div., Army of Exercise, 17 Nov. 1843. Gwalior campaign ; Paniar ; Bde. Major (Bronze star). Fur. s.c. 1846 till 27 Dec. 1847.

DALTON, Dennis Harman (1771-1828). Lieut. Colonel. 4th N.I. *b.* 1771. Cadet 1783. Admitted 22 Oct. 1783. Ensign 16 Apr. 1785. Lieut. 5 June 1793. Capt. 21 Sept. 1804. Major 16 Dec. 1814. Lt. Col. 14 Jan. 1819. Retired 18 Jan. 1822. *d.* Cheltenham 17 Jan. 1828, aged 56.
Services : On fur. in 1790. Adjt. 2/3rd N.I. in 1803-4. Apptd. to comd. Vol. L.I. Bn. 21 Mar. 1811. Capture of Java 1811 ; Cornelis ; comdg. L.I. Bn. (Gold medal). Capture of Jokyakarta. Apptd. Resdt. and Comdt. at Macassar in 1815. Operations in Celebes 1816 ; Baliangan pass ; Major comdg. the force. Remained on service in the Malay Archipelago until after Java and its dependencies had been restored to the Dutch in Aug. 1816. Transfd. as Major to 2/28th N.I. Fur. s.c. 14 Dec. 1817 till retirement. Transfd. as Lt. Col. to 2/4th N.I.
Refs. : *E.I.M.C.* ii. 348-54. *Misc. Gen. et Her.* N.S. ii. 354. M.I. at Charlton Kings, nr. Cheltenham (where the year of death is incorrectly given as 1827).

DALTON, John (1783-1804). Lieutenant, 12th N.I. *bapt.* St. Peter's, Carmarthen, 26 Sept. 1783. Cadet 1800. Arrived in India 23 Aug. 1801. Ensign 1 Jan. 1802. Lieut. 5 Nov. 1803. *d.* 16 July 1804 : drowned whilst crossing the Chambal R. during the retreat of Col. Monson's detachment.
Younger son of Edward Dalton and Ayliffe his wife and cousin, dau. of James Ormonde Dalton.

Services : Second Mahratta War ; Agra ; Laswari (w.) ; Monson's retreat (kld.) ; Lieut. 1/12th N.I.
Refs. : Burke's *Landed Gentry,* 3rd edn., p. 272, *s.n.* Dalton, of Dunkirk House, Gloucs.

DALY, Frederick (1808-1826). Ensign, 20th N.I. *bapt.* Kilcleagh, co. Westmeath, 1 Jan. 1808. Cadet 1824. Ensign 13 May 1825. *d.* Barrackpore 24 July 1826.

Son of Joseph Morgan Daly, of Castle Daly, co. Westmeath, and Elizabeth his wife, 3rd dau. of Robert Tighe, of South Hill. His cousin *m.* John Kingston Phibbs, *q.v.*

Services: Posted as Ensign to 25th N.I. No record of active service.
Refs. : Burke's *Landed Gentry,* 2nd edn., p. 305, *s.n.* Daly, of Castle Daly, co. Westmeath.

DALYELL, Alexander (1788-?). Lieutenant. 26th N.I. *bapt.* Barncrosh 7 Mar. 1788. Cadet 1804. Arrived in India 1 Sept. 1805. Ensign 15 Oct. 1805. Lieut. 13 Feb. 1806. Resigned in India 7 July 1810.

Son of James Dalyell.

.Services : Posted as Ensign to newly-raised 26th N.I. Operations in Bundelkhand 1807 ; Sehlehuganj ; Lieut. 26th N.I.

DALYELL, Thomas (1806-1857). Bt. Lieut. Colonel, 42nd N.I. *b.* Cupar, co. Fife, 2 Feb. 1806. Cadet 1821. Arrived in India 18 Sept. 1822. Ensign 15 June 1822. Lieut. 1 May 1824. Capt. 6 July 1838. Major 7 May 1855. Bt. Lt. Col. 2 Apr. 1856. *d.* 18 Sept. 1857 : kld. in action at Naraoli, a fort 6 m. N.W. of Saugor, C.P.

3rd son of John Dalyell, of Lingo, co. Fife, and Ticknevin, co. Kildare, Capt. Fifeshire Mil., and Jane his wife, dau. of Major Melville, of Murdocairnie. Cousin-german of Sir John Cheape, *q.v. m.* Cawnpore, 17 Dec. 1844, Margaret, dau. of Robert Andrews, and widow of —— Curty.

Services : Posted as Ensign to 21st N.I. Transfd. to 42nd N.I. (late 2/21st) May 1824. First Burma War ; Arakan 1825 ; Lieut. 42nd N.I. (India medal). Intr. & Qmr. 42nd N.I. 4 Nov. 1828 till 22 Sept. 1838. First Afghan War 1838-42 ; operations around Kandahar ; Ghazni ; re-occupation of Kabul ; Jagdalak pass (s.w. 19 Oct: 1842) (*Lond. Gaz.* 17 Mar. 1843) ; Capt. 42nd N.I. (Medal). Dy. Paymr. at Cawnpore 4 Aug. 1843 till Aug. 1855. First Sikh War ; Sobraon ; Capt. comdg. 42nd N.I. (Medal). Mutiny campaign ; operations in vicinity of Saugor.

Refs. : Burke's *Landed Gentry,* 13th edn., p. 455, *s.n.* Dalyell, late of Lingo and Ticknevin, co. Kildare. *G.M.* 1857, ii. 685 ; 1858, i. 112. Will dated 5 Aug. 1853 ; proved 4 Mar. 1858.

THE BENGAL ARMY, 1758-1834   7

*DALZELL, Arthur Alexander, tenth Earl of Carnwath (1799-1876).
General in H.M. Army, and Colonel 48th Regt. b. 15 Sept. 1799.
Cadet 1818. Resigned his Cadetship on appt. by the Prince
Regent to an Ensigncy in H.M. 45th Regt. d. unm. 28 Apr. 1876.
2nd son of Robert Alexander Dalzell, seventh (or tenth) Earl of
Carnwath, and Andalusia his 2nd wife, dau. of Lt.-Col. Arthur
Browne, of Kinsale, and sister of Marmaduke Williamson Browne,
q.v. Brother of Harry Burrard Dalzell, eleventh Earl, q.v. s. his
nephew, Henry Arthur Hugh Dalzell, ninth Earl, 13 Mar. 1873.
Services : See Hart's A.L. Cornet 13th Light Dgns. 9 Nov. 1819.
Capt. 48th Foot 28 June 1827. Col. 11 Nov. 1851 ; h.p. 13 Dec.
1853. Gen. 14 Apr. 1873.
Refs. : Burke's Peerage, 1923, p. 457, s.n. Carnwath, E.

DALZELL, Harry Burrard, eleventh Earl of Carnwath (1804-1887).
Colonel. Artillery. b. London 10 Nov. 1804. Cadet 1820.
Arrived in India 15 Jan. 1822. 2nd Lieut. 9 June 1821. Lieut.
1 May 1824. Capt. 25 Apr. 1838. Major 16 June 1848. Bt.
Lt. Col. 20 June 1854. Retired 10 Mar. 1854. Hon. Col. 26 Oct.
1855. d. 28 Eaton Pl., London, 1 Nov. 1887, without surviving
issue.
3rd son of Robert Alexander Dalzell, seventh (or tenth) Earl of
Carnwath, and Andalusia his 2nd wife. Brother of Arthur Alexander
Dalzell, tenth Earl, q.v., whom he s. 28 Apr. 1876. m. Dum-Dum,
16 Nov. 1827, Isabella, only dau. of Rev. Alexander Campbell,
grand-niece of Sir Alexander Macleod, q.v., and half-sister of Bannatyne, wife of Richard Horsford, q.v. Addiscombe Cadet 6 Aug. 1819
till 9 June 1821.
Services : A.D.C. to G.G. 30 June 1826 ; tempy. do. 29 Mar.
1828. Adjt. 6th Bn. Foot Art. 31 Dec. 1829 till 2 Dec. 1833. Offg.
Comy. Ord. at Allahabad 15 Oct. 1830. Offg. Dy. Comy. Ord. at
Chunar 9 Feb. 1833 ; permanent do. 22 Nov. 1833 ; do. at Agra
5 Nov. 1834. Comy. Ord. at Agra 18 Mar. 1835 ; do. at Ferozepore
1844. Fur. 15 Jan. 1845 till 11 Nov. 1849. Fur. s.c. 10 Sept. 1851
till retirement. No record of active service.
Refs. : Burke's Peerage, 1923, p. 457, s.n. Carnwath, E. Boase.
The Times, 3 Nov. 1887. I.L.N. 12 Nov. 1887, p. 560. A.J. xxv.
518.

DALZELL, John (d. 1783). Ensign, Infantry. Cadet 1782.
Ensign 10 Jan. 1783. d. Berhampore, Bengal, 30 Nov. 1783.
Services : N.F.P.

DALZELL, William (1801-1825). Lieutenant, 35th N.I. b. Edinburgh 3 Apr. 1801. Cadet 1818. Ensign (?). Lieut. 1 Jan.
1821. d. Singapore 21 Apr. 1825.

Son of Alexander Dalzell, of the Exchequer, writer in Edinburgh.
Services : Lieut. 1/17th N.I. Transfd. to 35th N.I. (late 2/17th) May 1824. Was on sick leave when his death occurred. No record of active service.
Refs. : *S.M.* 1825, ii. 638.

DALZIEL, James (*d.* 1778). Ensign, Infantry. Cadet 1772. Ensign 3 Aug 1776. *d.* 26 Jan. 1778.
Services : N.F.P.

DANA, Charles Patrick (1784-1816). Captain, 23rd N.I. *b.* Wroxeter, Salop, 24 June 1784. Cadet 1800. Arrived in India 23 Aug. 1801. Ensign 5 Jan. 1802. Lieut. 1 Oct. 1803. Capt. 1816. *d.* at sea (? Sept.) 1816, on board the *Sir Stephen Lushington.*
bapt. 9 July 1784. Youngest son of Rev. Edmund Dana, vicar of Wroxeter, and the Hon. Helen his wife, eldest dau. of Charles, sixth Baron Kinnaird. Cousin-german of George William Wiggens, *q.v. m.* (?). Ed. Shrewsbury 1799.
Services : Ensign 17th N.I. Transfd. as Lieut. to newly-raised 1/23rd N.I. in 1803. Operations against Dhundia Khan 1807 ; Komona ; Ganauri ; Lieut. 1/23rd N.I. Adjt. 1/23rd N.I. 20 Mar. 1810 till 1816. Fur. 1816.
Refs. : Burke's *Peerage*, 1923, p. 1302, *s.n.* Kinnaird, B. *Shrewsbury School Register.* *G.M.* 1817, i. 283. Will dated 27 Sept. 1814 ; proved in 1816.

DANCE, Thomas. Ensign. Infantry. Cadet 1782. Ensign 1783. Struck off (?).
Services : N.F.P.

*****DANDRIDGE, Edward** (*d.* 1789 ?). Lieutenant, Engineers. Cadet (?). Ensign 22 Mar. 1781. Lieut. 3 Sept. 1781. *d.* in England 1789 ?
Services : Field Engr. at Cawnpore in 1787. Fur. 15 Dec. 1788 till death.
Refs. : *Philippart MS.*

DANGERFIELD, John (*d.* 1765). Lieutenant, Infantry. Cadet (?). Cornet (?). Lieut. 1 Mar. 1764. *d.* in India 1765.
Son of William Dangerfield.
Services : Served as Cornet and Lieut. in one of the two Troops of Eur. Dgns. War with Mir Muhammad Kasim 1763. Ordered to take rank in the Inf. from the date of his first Commission as Cornet (G.O. of 7 July 1764).
Refs.: Will dated 23 Nov. 1765 ; proved in 1766.

DANIEL, Edward. Captain. Infantry. Cadet 1769. Ensign 1769. Lieut. 28 Jan. 1773. Capt. 12 Nov. 1779. Resigned 20 Nov. 1780.
Services : N.F.P.

*****DANIELL, Averell** (1808-?). Cornet. 3rd L.C. *b.* Bermuda 4 June 1808. Cadet 1825. Never arrived in India. Cornet 20 Dec. 1825. Struck off 28 Dec. 1827.
Son of John Daniell, of the Daresbury family, co. Chester, Col. 49th Foot. Brother of James Townsend Daniell, *q.v.*
Services : Was at the Cape of Good Hope when apptd. Cadet. Posted as Cornet to 3rd L.C. 26 Sept. 1826, but never joined. Ensign H.M. 49th Foot 1 Dec. 1825 ; Lieut. do. 1 Feb. 1829. Retired in 1838.

*****DANIELL, Henry Torrens** (*d.* 1840). Lieutenant, 29th N.I. Cadet 1834. Arrived in India 23 June 1834. Ensign 16 June 1834. Lieut. 12 Aug. 1838. *d.* Banda 14 Feb. 1840.
Brother of John Hinton Daniell, Lieut. H.M. 49th Foot. (*Probably* brother of James Townsend Daniell, *q.v.*)
Services : Ensign d.d. 50th N.I. 7 July 1834. Posted as Ensign to 29th N.I. 5 Nov. 1834. No record of active service.
Refs. : Will dated Banda 14 July 1839 ; proved 16 July 1841.

DANIELL, James Henry (1807-1849). Captain, Artillery. *bapt.* Bovey Tracey, Devon, 26 Feb. 1807. Cadet 1823. Arrived in India 14 June 1824. 2nd Lieut. 18 Dec. 1823. Lieut. 28 Sept. 1827. Capt. 24 Aug. 1842. *d.* Ferozepore 20 June 1849.
Son of Francis Daniell, of Knowle, Devon. *m.* Cawnpore, 4 July 1836, Lucy Anne, youngest dau. of Lt.-Col. George Bristow, and sister of George William Grant Bristow, *q.v.* (*See also* Thomas Dundas.) (She died Ludhiana 10 June 1848.) Addiscombe Cadet 11 May 1821 till 11 Dec. 1823.
Services : Served principally with H.A. First Burma War ; with Sir A. Campbell's force in Burma. Adjt. Nimach Div. Art. 29 May 1835. Adjt. & Qmr. 2nd Bde. H.A. 21 July 1835 till Jan. 1843. Second Sikh War ; Multan ; Capt. comdg. 2nd Coy. 2nd Bn. Foot Art. (Medal).
Refs. : Burke's *Landed Gentry*, 5th edn., p. 146, *s.n.* Bristow, of Broxmore Park, Wilts.

DANIELL, James Townsend (1811-1887). Lieut. Colonel. 7th N.I. *b.* Halifax, Nova Scotia, 29 Sept. 1811. Cadet 1828. Arrived in India 28 June 1829. Ensign 20 Jan. 1829. Lieut. 10 Feb. 1835. Capt. 24 Jan. 1845. Major 1 May 1858. Lt. Col. 31 Dec. 1861. *d.* 27 Mar. 1887.

Son of John Daniell, of the Daresbury family, co. Chester, Col. 49th Foot. Brother of Averell Daniell, *q.v. m.* Kate, dau. of Matthew O'Brien, of Newcastle, co. Limerick. (She died 5 Jan. 1859.)

Services : Ensign 36th N.I. 14 Sept. 1829. Exchanged to 47th N.I. 16 Sept. 1831. Operations against insurgents in Cuttack 1833 ; Ensign 47th N.I. Actg. Intr. & Qmr. 12th N.I. 31 Aug. 1835 ; do. 1st N.I. 28 May 1836 ; do. 29th N.I. 17 May 1837. Fur. s.c. 22 Dec. 1838 till 11 Oct. 1842. Actg. Intr. & Qmr. 11th L.C. 8 Nov. 1843 till 8 Oct. 1844. Gwalior campaign ; Paniar, with 11th L.C. (Bronze star). Offg. D.C. 3 cl., Saugor & Narbada territories, 29 Nov. 1844. Asst. to Comr. & Supt. of Cis-Sutlej territories 26 Dec. 1846 till Mar. 1850. Fur. s.c. 10 Mar. 1850 till Nov. 1853. Fur. 1860 till retirement. Transfd. to 7th N.I. in 1861.

Refs. : *The Times,* 29 Mar. 1887.

DARBY, Charles (1806-1840/41). Lieutenant. 52nd N.I. *b.* Aston, Herts., 27 Mar. 1806. Cadet 1824. Arrived in India 6 May 1825. Ensign 8 Jan. 1825. Lieut. 17 Jan. 1827. Dismissed 20 Nov. 1838. *d.* in England at end of 1840 or beginning of 1841.

bapt. 11 Aug. 1806. 5th son of Edmund Darby, of Aston Hall, Herts., army clothier, and Caroline his wife. *m.* Bath, 5 Jan. 1836, Eliza Harriet, eldest dau. of Major Browne, H.M. 67th Regt., and niece of Col. Fielding Browne, C.B.

Services : Posted as Ensign to 52nd N.I. in 1825. Actg. Adjt. Left Wing 52nd N.I. 4 Dec. 1828. Fur. s.c. 31 Jan. 1835 till 12 Nov. 1836. No record of active service.

Refs. : *G.M.* 1836, i. 199. *A.J.* N.S. xxviii. 217.

DARBY, John (*d.* 1800). Major, 11th N.I. Adjutant General, Bengal. Cadet 1772. Admitted 10 Nov. 1772. Ensign 28 July 1776. Lieut. 14 July 1778. Capt. 25 May 1793. Major 10 Sept. 1798. *d.* Calcutta 21 Aug. 1800.

(*Probably* son of Col. John Darby, and brother of Anne Persode, wife of Rev. John Blair, LL.D. (*D.N.B.*).)

Services : Lieut. 2/3rd Bengal Eur. Regt. in Oct. 1779. Fur. 27 Sept. 1785 till 6 Nov. 1788. Capt. 1st Bengal Eur. Regt. in 1796. Posted as Major to 1/13th N.I. in Oct. 1798. Transfd. to 2/11th N.I. ; to 1/11th N.I. 21 Apr. 1800. At date of death he was A.G., Bengal, with official rank of Lt. Col.

Refs. : Will dated Calcutta 23 June 1800.

Note : The Exors. to his Will in Europe were (Lt. Col.) William John Darby, (Capt.) George Darby, and Anne Persode Blair.

DARE, Hastings (1775-1836). Colonel, 64th N.I. *bapt.* Calcutta 2 Dec. 1775. Cadet 1794. Admitted 2 Nov. 1795. Ensign 5 Nov. 1795. Lieut. 25 Apr. 1797. Capt. 20 July 1805. Major 15 June 1814. Lt. Col. 1 Aug. 1818. Lt. Col. Comdt. 1 May 1824. Col. 5 June 1829. *d.* South Wraxhall House, nr. Bath, 22 Sept. 1836, aged 61.

Son of Lieut. William Dare, *q.v.*, and Melian his wife. Stepson of Samuel Howe Showers, *q.v.*, and godson of Warren Hastings. *m.* Buxton Pl., Edinburgh, 3 Jan. 1806, and in London, Dec. 1806, Harriet, dau. of Col. Daniel Paterson, A.Q.M.G., H.M. Forces, and Comdt. of the Royal Invalids in the Tower garrison (*D.N.B.*).

Services : Minor Cadet till 2 May 1786, when struck off. Was already in India when apptd. a Cadet. Ensign 3rd Bengal Eur. Regt. in 1796. Embarked on the *Europa* for duty in Bencoolen Jan. 1797. Served with a detachment of troops at Fort Marlborough 1799-1802, and 1804-5. Fur. s.c. from Fort Marlborough 18 Nov. 1805 till 2 Oct. 1807. Operations in Bundelkhand against Gopal Singh 1809 ; action at Parari ; Capt. comdg. 5 Coys. 1/7th N.I. Reduction of Kalinjar ; Capt. 1/7th N.I. Nepal War 1814-5 ; Major 1/7th N.I., in 2nd Div. Third Mahratta War ; Major 7th N.I. Transfd. as Lt. Col. to 29th N.I. in 1818 ; to 1/25th N.I. in 1820. Fur. p.a. 5 Feb. 1822 till death. Transfd. to 28th N.I. in 1823 ; as Lt. Col. Comdt. to 64th N.I. May 1824. Col. 64th N.I. June 1829.

Refs. : G.M. 1806, ii. 1167 ; 1836, ii. 557. M.M. xxii. (1806) 596. Grier, p. 315.

*****DARE, William** (*d.* 1774 ?). Lieutenant, Infantry. Cadet (?). Ensign (?). Lieut. (?). *d.* 1774 ? : shipwrecked and drowned off the Coromandel coast.

m. Amelia Ann (Melian). (She *re-m.* Samuel Howe Showers, *q.v.*) Father of Hastings Dare, *q.v.*

Services : N.F.P.
Refs. : Grier, p. 315.

DARELL, Edward (1775-1851 ?). Capt. Lieutenant. Artillery. *b.* Canterbury, Kent, 1775. Cadet 1790. Admitted 30 Aug. 1792. Fireworker 16 Dec. 1790. Lieut. 20 Feb. 1796. Capt. Lt. 28 May 1804. Resigned 24 July 1805. (? *d.* 13 Jan. 1851.)

N.B.—The following is conjectural only : (2nd son of Henry Darell, of Calehill, Kent, and Elizabeth his wife, 2nd dau. of Sir Thomas Gage, Bart. *m.* 10 Feb. 1810, Mary Anne, dau. of Thomas Bullock, of Muscoats, Yorks.)

Services : Fur. 7 Aug. 1802 till resignation. No record of active service.

Refs. : (? Burke's *Landed Gentry*, 12th edn., p. 185, *s.n.* Darell-Blount, of Calehill, Kent.)

DARKE, Charles (*d.* 1775). Lieutenant, Infantry. Cadet 1767. Ensign 29 July 1767. Lieut. 26 Dec. 1769. *d.* 10 Aug. 1775.
Services : N.F.P.

DARKE, Charles (1774-1797). Lieutenant, 3rd Bengal European Regt. *b.* St. Martin's, Ludgate, London, 24 Dec. 1774. Cadet 1794. Arrived in India 26 Sept. 1796. Ensign 16 Nov. 1795. Lieut. 3 Oct. 1796. *d.* Chunar 16 Dec. 1797.
bapt. Overbury, Worcs., 15 Oct. 1778. Son of Thomas Darke and Anne his wife.
Services : Posted as Ensign to 3rd Bengal Eur. Regt. in 1796.

DARLEY, Hugh. Ensign. Engineers. Cadet 1782. Ensign 22 July 1782. Resigned 26 Jan. 1784.
m. Calcutta, 11 Feb. 1784, Ann, widow of James Ogden, sometime a pilot at Calcutta.
Services : N.F.P. After resigning the Service he settled in Calcutta as an architect.
Refs. : *Hickey*, ii. 134.

DARRAH, Thomas (*d.* 1798). Captain, Infantry. Country Cadet 1780. Admitted 20 Apr. 1780. Ensign 1 Mar. 1781. Lieut. 22 Oct. 1781. Capt. 7 Jan. 1796. *d.* Jogi-Ghopa, Assam, 29 May 1798.
Services : Third Mysore War 1790-2 ; Bangalore ; Savandrug ; Lieut. 28th Bn. Sepoys.
Refs. : Will dated Bangalore 4 Dec. 1791 ; proved in 1805.

DARTIQUENAVE, Jacob (*d.* 1778). Ensign, Infantry. Cadet 1777. Ensign 15 Feb. 1778. *d.* in India June 1778.
Services : N.F.P.

DARVALL, Edward (1806-1885). General. 3rd European Inf. *bapt.* Irchester, Northants., 7 Nov. 1806. Cadet 1822. Arrived in India 12 May 1823. Ensign 1 May 1823. Lieut. 6 Jan. 1825. Capt. 4 Aug. 1836. Major 11 July 1853. Lt. Col. 17 Nov. 1857. Bt. Col. 20 June 1857. Maj. Gen. 20 Nov. 1865. Lt. Gen. 20 Feb. 1874. Gen. 1 Oct. 1877. *d.* Acton Place, Suffolk, 20 Oct. 1885.
Eldest son of Edward Darvall, of York, Major 9th Dgns., and Emily his wife. *m.* Thornthwaite, N.S.W., 26 May 1841, Sophia, eldest dau. of Rev. John Docker, vicar of Eastmeon, Hants.
Services : Posted as Ensign to 29th N.I. Transfd. to 57th N.I. (late 1/29th) May 1824. First Burma War ; Assam 1824 ; Lieut. 57th N.I. (India medal). Actg. Adjt. Dinajpur Local Bn. 20 July

THE BENGAL ARMY, 1758-1834   13

1825. Actg. Intr. & Qmr. 57th N.I. 26 Dec. 1827, and 10 Nov. 1828; permanent do. 8 Feb. 1830 till 22 May 1833. Fur. p.a. 16 July 1833 till 30 Aug. 1837. Fur. 18 mos. to N.S.W. 28 Mar. 1840. Mutiny campaign (Medal). Posted as Lt. Col. to 57th N.I. 7 Jan. 1858; transfd. to 3rd Eur. Inf. in 1859.
Refs. : Boase. *The Times,* 4 Nov. 1885.

DASHWOOD, Charles James Augustus (1790-1871). Captain. 2nd L.C. *b.* London 1 July 1790. Cadet 1805. Arrived in India 11 July 1806. Cornet 12 July 1806. Lieut. 23 May 1815. Capt. 27 Sept. 1819. Retired 3 Apr. 1822. *d.* 13 Nov. 1871.
Son of James Dashwood and Sarah his wife.
Services : Posted as Cornet to 2nd N.C. Intr. & Qmr. 2nd N.C. 2 Dec. 1814 till 1818. Nepal War 1814; Cornet 2nd N.C., in 1st Div. Third Mahratta War; Lieut. 2nd N.C., in Reserve Div. Fur. p.a. 7 Mar. 1819 till retirement.

DASHWOOD, Francis (1805-1845). Captain, Artillery. *b.* Portsea, Hants, 13 Feb. 1805. Cadet 1822. Arrived in India 26 Mar. 1824. 2nd Lieut. 6 June 1823. Lieut. 30 Aug. 1826. Capt. 9 June 1840. *d.* Mudki 22 Dec. 1845, of wounds received in the battle of Mudki on 18 Dec.
3rd and youngest son of Sir Charles Dashwood, Vice-Adm. R.N., K.C.B., and Elizabeth his wife, 2nd dau. of John, 26th Baron Kingsale. *m.* Calcutta, 14 Jan. 1836, Jane, dau. of George Skyring, Col. R.A. Addiscombe Cadet 1821-3.
Services : Posted to 7th Coy. 2nd Bn. Art. Apr. 1824. Transfd. to 3rd Troop H.A. in Jan. 1825; to 1st Troop 2nd Bde. July 1825. Siege and capture of Bhurtpore; A.D.C. to Lt. Col. Comdt. Alexander Macleod, *q.v.* Transfd. to 2nd Troop 2nd Bde. May 1826; 3rd Troop 2nd Bde. 1828-32. Adjt. & Qmr. 2nd Bde. H.A. 14 Mar. 1827 till 31 Mar. 1835. Leave s.c. 2 yrs. to N.S.W. 9 Apr. 1832. Actg. Sec. to Mily. Board 20 Feb. 1834; Asst. do. 30 Mar. 1835 till Feb. 1840. Fur. p.a. 22 Feb. 1840 till 5 Nov. 1842. 3rd Coy. 1st Bn. Foot Art.; transfd. to 2nd Coy. 6th Bn. Mar. 1843. Comdd. 1st Troop 1st Bde. H.A. 16 Nov. 1843 till death. First Sikh War; Mudki (mortally w.).
Refs. : Burke's *Peerage,* 1923, p. 1295, *s.n.* Kingsale, B. Foster's *Families of Royal Descent,* ii. 783. *De Rhé-Philipe.* Will undated; proved 9 Mar. 1846. M.I. in St. Andrew's church, Ferozepore.

D'AUVERGNE, Philip (1762/63-1818). Brigadier General. 26th N.I. *b.* 1762/63. Country Cadet 1778. Admitted 9 Mar. 1778. Ensign 4 June 1778. Lieut. 11 Sept. 1779. Capt. 27 Sept. 1796. Major 19 May 1803. Lt. Col. 19 Nov. 1804. Col. 4 June 1813. Brig. Gen. (?). *d.* Calcutta, 31 Mar. 1818, aged 55.

(? *Possibly* son of P. D'Auvergne, Comdr. of the *Scarborough*, East Indiaman, 1747-50.) *m.* 1st, Miss Crane, sister of the wife of Andrew Wilson Hearsey, *q.v.* His reputed dau. *m.* Henry Clapton Barnard, *q.v. m.* 2nd, Monghyr, 22 Sept. 1800, Miss Anna Lowrie. (She re-*m.* 12 June 1821, Lieut. Thomas Francis Smith, H.M. 24th Regt.)
Services : Lieut. 2/2nd Bengal Eur. Regt. in Oct. 1779 ; 1st Bengal Eur. Bn. in July 1787. Major 16th N.I. Fort Adjt. at Monghyr in 1803. Posted as Lt. Col. to newly-raised 1/26th N.I. in 1804. This Regt. was known as " *Duberne-ki-Paltan* " after him. Operations in Bundelkhand 1807 ; Sehlehuganj ; Lt. Col. comdg. 1/26th N.I. Comdg. in Bundelkhand in 1816-7. (Third Mahratta War ; apptd. Bdr. comdg. 1st Inf. Bde., Centre Div., but being on leave he never took up this appointment.)
Refs. : G.M. 1818, ii. 469. *S.M.* 1819, i. 95. Will dated camp Chatterpur, 29 Dec. 1815 ; proved 27 Mar. 1818. M.I. in S. Park St. cemetery, Calcutta.

*D'AUVERGNE, Robert (*d.* 1792). Ensign, Infantry. Cadet 1783. Ensign 6 June 1785. *d.* at sea 1792.
Services : Unposted Ensign in July 1787. N.F.P.

DAVID, Nicholas. Ensign. Infantry. Cadet 1763. Ensign 27 Aug. 1765. Dismissed 16 Aug. 1766.
Services : N.F.P. His dismissal was probably due to implication in the " Batta mutiny " of May 1766.

DAVIDSON, Adam (1793-1824). Lieutenant, 11th N.I. *b.* Kelso, co. Roxburgh, 4 Sept. 1793. Cadet 1809. Arrived in India 3 Oct. 1810. Ensign 1 June 1812. Lieut. 14 June 1817. *d.* nr. Sambalpur, B. & O., 11 Feb. 1824.
Youngest son of Robert Davidson, of Pinnacle Hill, and Helen Elliot his wife. Brother of Cornelius Davidson, *q.v.*
Services : Barasat C.C. Cadet d.d. 19th N.I. 1811. Posted as Ensign to 1/7th N.I. June 1812. Nepal War 1814-5 ; Kalanga (w.) ; Ensign 1/7th N.I., in 2nd Div. Transfd. as Lieut. to 2/11th N.I. in 1817. Third Mahratta War ; Lieut. 2/11th N.I. Adjt. 2/11th N.I. 19 Nov. 1821 till death.
Refs. : S.M. 1824, ii. 639.

DAVIDSON, Alexander (1792-1856). Lieut. Colonel. 2nd Bengal Eur. Regt. *b.* Bengal 10 Aug. 1792. *bapt.* Calcutta 23 Oct. 1792. Cadet 1807. Arrived in India 1 Feb. 1809. Ensign 25 Feb. 1809. Lieut. 31 Jan. 1814. Capt. 13 May 1825. Bt. Major 28 June 1838. Retired 26 Dec. 1842. Hon. Lt. Col. 28 Nov. 1854. *d.* 20 Oct. 1856.

Son of Alexander Davidson, of Calcutta, merchant, and Anne Ellen Mary Isobel his wife. Brother of Charles James Collie Davidson, q.v. m. 1st, Calcutta, 1 Sept. 1825, Miss Diana Wroughton Turner. (She died 28 Sept. 1826, aged 18.) m. 2nd, St. Andrew's, Calcutta, 7 Mar. 1831, Miss Mary Falconer. (*See also* Hugh Campbell Wilson.)

Services: Barasat C.C. for 15½ mos. Posted as Ensign to 7th N.I. Lieut. 2/7th N.I. With Rangpur Local Bn. 1817-8. Fur. s.c. 20 May 1818 till 19 Jan. 1822. Transfd. to 1/7th N.I. To do duty with Rangpur Local Bn. 26 Jan. 1822. Asst. to A.G.G., N.E. frontier, and comd. his escort 6 Dec. 1824. Transfd. to 13th N.I. (late 1/7th) May 1824. Leave s.c. to N.S.W. 31 May 1831 till 22 Mar. 1835. Collector and Mgte. Nowgong district, Assam, 16 May 1835. Senior Principal Asst. to Comr. in Assam, and in charge of Goalpara district. Leave s.c. 2 yrs. to Aust. 20 Dec. 1837. Transfd. to 2nd Bengal Eur. Regt. 8 Oct. 1839. No record of active service.

DAVIDSON, Andrew (*d*. 1793). Captain. Infantry. Pension Est. Cadet 1771. Ensign 21 Feb. 1773. Lieut. 16 Mar. 1778. Capt. 10 Oct. 1781. Pensioned 1 Dec. 1786. *d*. Duns, co. Berwick, 1 Nov. 1793.

Services: Fur. 3 yrs. on h.p. 20 Oct. 1786. N.F.P.

Refs.: *G.M.* 1793, ii. 1056.

DAVIDSON, Charles James Collie (1793-1852). Lieut. Colonel. Engineers. *b*. Calcutta 24 Oct. 1793. Cadet 1812. Ensign 10 Dec. 1814. Lieut. 1 Sept. 1818. Capt. 10 Oct. 1821. Major 22 Jan. 1834. Lt. Col. 31 Mar. 1840. Retired 22 Oct. 1841. *d*. Stockwell Park Rd., London, 31 Mar. 1852.

Son of Alexander Davidson, of Calcutta, merchant, and Anne Ellen Mary Isobel his wife. Brother of Alexander Davidson, *q.v.* m. Calcutta 3 Feb. 1818, Letitia, 5th dau. of —— Crump, of Charlton, Gloucs. Addiscombe Cadet 19 Feb. 1810 till 25 Oct. 1811.

Services: Adjt. Corps of Engineers 27 June 1817. Garr. Engineer at Asirgarh. Siege and capture of Bhurtpore; Capt. Engrs. (India medal). Supt. of canals undertaken by the King of Oudh 13 June 1833. Executive Engr. 6th, Allahabad, Div. P.W.D. 10 Apr. 1838. Fur. 1839-41. Author of "Diary of Travels and Adventures in Upper India, from Bareilly to the Himalaya Mts.," 2 vols., cr. 8vo., 1843.

Refs.: *G.M.* 1818, i. 637; 1852, i. *I.M.* 14 Apr. 1852, p. 244.

DAVIDSON, Cornelius (1786-1804). Lieutenant, Artillery. *b*. Kelso, co. Roxburgh, 30 Mar. 1786. Cadet 1803. Never arrived in India. Lieut. 16 Aug. 1804. *d*. at sea 24 Nov. 1804, on board the *Thomas* on his passage to Bombay.

bapt. Kelso 18 June 1786. Son of Robert Davidson, of Pinnacle Hill, and Helen Elliot his wife. Brother of Robert Davidson (1782-1804), *q.v.*

DAVIDSON, Cuthbert (1810-1862). Lieut. Colonel, C.B., 51st N.I. *b.* Croy, Inverness, 24 May 1810. Cadet 1827. Arrived in India 4 Oct. 1828. Ensign 11 May 1828. Lieut. 4 Jan. 1832. Capt. 8 Sept. 1842. Major 10 May 1852. Lt. Col. 31 May 1857. *d.* 2 Aug 1862.

3rd son of Sir David Davidson, of Cantray, co. Inverness, and Margaret his wife, née Rose, of the Kilravock family. Twin brother of Francis Russell Davidson, *q.v.* *m.* 1st, Benares, 8 Dec. 1834, Anna Maria, 2nd dau. of George Mainwaring, B.C.S., and niece of Edward Henry Mainwaring, *q.v.* *m.* 2nd, Hyderabad, 27 Oct. 1857, Ellen Eliza, dau. of William Hore, *q.v.*

Services : Ensign d.d. 66th N.I. 6 Dec. 1828. Posted to 31st N.I. 4 Mar. 1829. Transfd. to 66th N.I. 22 Apr. 1829. Adjt. 66th N.I. 21 Dec. 1830 till 26 July 1834. A.D.C. to G.G. 5 July 1834. A.D.C. to Sir Robert Grant, Govr. of Bombay, 10 Mar. 1835 till 1 Apr. 1836. Posted to Nizam's 2nd Cav. 7 Dec. 1835. Promoted Capt. in the Nizam's service 11 May 1840. Comdd. Nizam's 3rd Cav. at capture of Kurnool under Bdr. James Blair, *q.v.* Asst. to Resdt. at Hyderabad 28 June 1850. Resdt. at Baroda 14 Nov. 1855. Resdt. at Hyderabad 16 Apr. 1857 till death. Posted as Lt. Col. to 49th N.I. Aug. 1857; to 51st N.I. in 1859. C.B. (Civil) 18 May 1860.

Refs. : Burke's *Landed Gentry*, 13th edn., p. 468, *s.n.* Davidson, of Cantray, co. Inverness. *Boase.*

DAVIDSON, Francis Russell (1810-1848). Ensign. 41st N.I. Subsequently Collector of Saharanpur. *b.* Croy, Inverness, 24 May 1810. Cadet 1827. Arrived in India 4 Oct. 1828. Ensign 11 May 1828. Resigned 1 Mar. 1831. *d. unm.* Landour, U.P., 10 July 1848.

4th and youngest son of Sir David Davidson, of Cantray, co. Inverness. Twin brother of Cuthbert Davidson, *q.v.*

Services : Ensign d.d. 49th N.I. 5 Nov. 1828. Posted to 41st N.I. 4 Mar. 1829. Fur. p.a. 5 Mar. 1830 till resignation. Apptd. to B.C.S. Arrived in India 8 Apr. 1832. Writer 30 Apr. 1832.

Refs. : Burke's *Landed Gentry*, 13th edn., p. 468, *s.n.* Davidson, of Cantray House, co. Inverness. *I.M.* 26 Sept. 1848, p. 556.

DAVIDSON, George Henry (1812-1843). Lieutenant, 72nd N.I. *b.* 22 Dec. 1812. Cadet 1831. Arrived in India 7 Feb. 1833. Ensign 7 Nov. 1832. Lieut. 19 Aug. 1835. *d.* Simla 17 Oct. 1843.

bapt. Westbury, Wilts., 21 June 1813. Son of Leith Alexander

Davidson, of Ostend, formerly of Calcutta, merchant, and Mary his wife, née Burgh. Brother of William Walter Davidson, *q.v.* His sisters *m.* Henry De Budé, *q.v.*, Samuel Boileau Goad, *q.v.*, and George Edward Gowan, *q.v.* Addiscombe Cadet 2 Aug. 1830 till 14 June 1832.
Services : Cadet d.d. 2nd N.I. 21 Feb. 1832; do. 63rd N.I. 7 Dec. 1833. Posted to 16th N.I. 11 Feb. 1834; to 72nd N.I. 8 Apr. 1834. Served at the reduction of the fort of Jhansi 1838-9; Lieut. 72nd N.I. Adjt. 72nd N.I. 9 Jan. 1839 till death. With the Army of Reserve (for Afghanistan) at Ferozepore Oct. 1842 till Jan. 1843. Leave s.c. to Simla Aug. 1843 till death.
Refs. : De Rhé-Philipe. Will dated Karnal 23 Aug. 1843; proved 12 Dec. 1843.

DAVIDSON, Hugh (1786-1825). Captain, 30th N.I. *b.* Dornoch, co. Sutherland, 20 Mar. 1786. Cadet 1804. Arrived in India 29 Apr. 1805. Ensign 17 Mar. 1805. Lieut. 18 Mar. 1805. Capt. 9 Aug. 1816. *d.* Penang, 30 Aug. 1825.
Son of Andrew Davidson, of Overskibo, tacksman. *m.* 5 July 1813, Miss Esther Pearce. His dau. *m.* Clement Read Browne, *q.v.*
Services : Posted as Lieut. to 2/15th N.I. Capture of Mauritius 1810; Lieut. 1st Bengal Vol. Bn. Capt. Lt. 15th N.I. 1 Oct. 1815. Capt. 1/15th N.I. Comdd. Sylhet Sebundy Corps 1 Nov. 1814 till 1823; do. Bencoolen Local Corps 1823 till death. Transfd. to 31st N.I. (late 2/15th) May 1824; to 30th N.I. in 1825.

DAVIDSON, James (*d.* 1802). Major, 18th N.I. Cadet 1775. Admitted 25th July 1776. Ensign 27 Mar. 1777. Lieut. 22 Aug. 1778. Capt. 13 Nov. 1794. Major 31 July 1799. *d.* Monghyr, B. & O., 4 Aug. 1802.
Brother of Harry Davidson, of Edinburgh, W.S. (? of Tulloch), and of Isobel, wife of William Fleeming, shipowner in Dysart, co. Fife. *m.* Edinburgh, 26 Feb. 1798, Grace, 2nd dau. of Duncan Campbell, Lt. Col. 4th Fencible Regt.
Services : Apptd. Cadet 12 Dec. 1775. Sailed for India on the *Prince of Wales* 16 Mar. 1776. Capt. 1/4th N.I. Fur. 21 Jan. 1796 till 24 Dec. 1798. Whilst on fur. he became Comdt. of the Corps of Dysart Vols. Transfd. as Major to newly-raised 1/18th N.I. 29 May 1800.
Refs. : S.M. 1798, p. 213; 1803, p. 291. Will dated Dysart 17 Feb. 1798; codicil dated camp Sirgooja 19 Mar. 1802; proved in 1802.

DAVIDSON, James (1763/64-1825). Major. 2nd N.I. *b.* 1763/64. Cadet 1781. Admitted 21 Dec. 1782. Ensign 1781. Lieut. 24 Sept. 1782. Capt. 29 May 1800. Major 30 Sept. 1808.

Invalided 13 June 1809. Retired 11 Nov. 1812. *d.* Portobello 31 Aug. 1825.

Purchased in Feb. 1820 the estates of Swinton Meikle and Swinton Little from John Swinton, of that Ilk.

Services : Apptd. Cadet on 24 Oct. 1781, aged 17. Lieut. 9th Bn. Sepoys in July 1787. Capt. Lt. 2nd N.I., and Garr. Storekeeper at Chunar in 1798. Capt. 1/2nd N.I. Fur. 18 Feb. 1803 till 6 May 1806. Supt. Lower Orphan School, Calcutta, 1807-9. Fur. 1810 till retirement.

Refs. : S.M. 1825, ii. 512. Will dated Edinburgh 15 Aug. 1823 ; proved 12 June 1827.

DAVIDSON, John Stewart (1809-1848). Captain, Invalid Est. 72nd N.I. *b.* Perth 4 Sept. 1809. Cadet 1828. Arrived in India 4 Dec. 1829. Ensign 17 Feb. 1829. Lieut. 5 Feb. 1835. Capt. 6 July 1844. Invalided 11 Apr. 1845. *d.* Delhi 25 Mar. 1848, whilst proceeding from Simla to Chunar. An open verdict was returned at the Court of Inquest.

Son of Patrick Davidson, of Perth, merchant, and Jean Stewart his wife.

Services : Ensign d.d. 68th N.I. 30 Dec. 1829 ; do. 2nd N.I. Feb.-Oct. 1832 ; do. 48th N.I. 20 Oct. 1832 till July 1833. Posted as Ensign to 72nd N.I. 12 Mar. 1833, and passed the remainder of his service on the active list with that Regt. Offg. Intr. & Qmr. 21 Feb. till Sept. 1835. Intr. & Qmr. 4 Nov. 1835 till Feb. 1845. Reduction of fort of Jhansi 1838-9. With Army of Reserve (for Afghanistan) at Ferozepore Oct. 1842 till Jan. 1843. After transfer to the Invalid Est. he resided at Simla till posted, 11 Feb. 1848, to the Eur. Invalid Coys. at Chunar. He was on his way down to join this appt. when his death occurred, under suspicious circumstances, in the *dak* bungalow at Delhi.

Refs. : De Rhé-Philipe. Will dated Delhi 7 Dec. 1844 ; proved 12 Sept. 1848. M.I. in old cemetery at Delhi.

DAVIDSON, Robert (1742/43- ?). Captain. Infantry. *b.* 1742/43. Cadet 1763. Ensign 21 Jan. 1763. Lieut. 14 Oct. 1763. Capt. 21 Jan. 1766. Resigned 2 Apr. 1773.

A native of Scotland. (*Possibly* father of Adam Davidson, *q.v.*)

Services : Sailed for India in 1761, aged 18. N.F.P.

DAVIDSON, Robert (1782-1804). Lieutenant, 12th N.I. *b.* Roxburgh 16 Mar. 1782. Cadet 1799. Arrived in India 9 Dec. 1800. Ensign 21 Aug. 1800. Lieut. 18 Dec. 1800. *d.* 1804 : taken prisoner on 18 July 1804 during the retreat of Col. Monson's detachment, and subsequently murdered by Holkar (? on 24 Dec. 1804).

bapt. Kelso 26 Mar. 1782. Eldest son of Robert Davidson of Pinnacle Hill, Roxburgh, and Helen Elliot his wife. Brother of Adam Davidson, *q.v.*
Services : Second Mahratta War ; Agra ; Laswari ; Monson's retreat ; Lieut. 1/12th N.I.
Refs. : *S.M.* 1806, p. 78. Intestate ; admon. granted 9 Apr. 1805.

DAVIDSON, Ronald (1742/43-1788). Bt. Ensign, Infantry. *b.* 1742/43. Bt. Ensign 17 Aug. 1781. *d.* Monghyr, B. & O., 3 Aug. 1788, aged 45. *m.* (?).
Services : Commissioned as Bt. Ensign from the ranks.
Refs. : Will. M.I. at Monghyr.

DAVIDSON, William Henry (1813-1835). Ensign, Infantry. *b.* London 19 Apr. 1813. Cadet 1834. Arrived in India 7 June 1835. Ensign 21 Jan. 1835. *d.* 12 July 1835 : drowned in the Ganges off Rajmahal, B. & O.

Son of John Davidson, sometime consul at New Orleans, and Fanny his wife. Brother of Wright Westcott Davidson, *q.v.*
Services : Ensign d.d. 56th N.I. 19 June 1835.
Refs. : *A.J.* N.S. xix. 39.

DAVIDSON, William Walter (1810-1859). Lieut. Colonel. 18th N.I. *b.* Calcutta 9 Nov. 1810. Cadet 1827. Arrived in India 11 Aug. 1828. Ensign 21 Mar. 1828. Lieut. 12 Sept. 1833. Capt. 1 Mar. 1846. Bt. Major 1854. Retired 24 Oct. 1854. Hon. Lt. Col. 28 Nov. 1854. *d.* at his residence, Sussex Terr., Hyde Park, 14 Feb. 1859.

Son of Leith Alexander Davidson, of Bruges, formerly of Calcutta, merchant, and Mary his wife, née Burgh. Brother of George Henry Davidson, *q.v.* *m.* Mussoorie, 2 May 1846, Juliana Catherine, dau. of George Edward Gowan, *q.v.* ; *i.e.* his sister's step-dau.
Services : Ensign d.d. 50th N.I. 8 Sept. 1828. Posted as Ensign to 18th N.I. 4 Nov. 1828. Intr. & Qmr. 18th N.I. 11 July 1835 till May 1842. First China War ; S.A.C.G. (Medal). S.A.C.G. 27 May 1842. First Sikh War ; Ferozshahr ; Sobraon ; S.A.C.G. (Medal with clasp). D.A.C.G. 2 cl., 13 Sept. 1847 ; do. 1 cl., 9 Sept. 1850 ; A.C.G. 2 cl., 9 Nov. 1852. Fur. 1853 till retirement.
Refs. : *G.M.* 1859, i. 334. *The Times,* 16 Feb. 1859. Will dated 31 May 1856 ; proved 18 Nov. 1859.

DAVIDSON, Wright Westcott (1810-1863). Bt. Colonel. 32nd N.I. *b.* St. Mary's, Newington, Surrey, 23 Sept. 1810. Cadet 1827. Arrived in India 10 Jan. 1829. Ensign 19 July 1828. Lieut. 3 Apr. 1835. Capt. 19 July 1843. Major 1 Jan. 1849. Lt. Col.

28 Nov. 1854. Bt. Col. 28 Nov. 1857. *d.* The Sycamore, Balasala, I. of Man, 13 Oct. 1863.

Son of John Davidson, sometime consul at New Orleans, and Fanny his wife. Brother of William Henry Davidson, *q.v. m.* Mussoorie, 20 Sept. 1849, Emma Rose, dau. of William Graham. (She died Murree 1 Sept. 1857.) Addiscombe Cadet 1827.

Services : Ensign d.d. 74th N.I. 26 Jan. 1829. Posted as Ensign to 32nd N.I. 3 June 1829. Actg. Adjt. 32nd N.I. 10 May 1832; permanent do. 15 Feb. 1833 till 18 Nov. 1843. To join Vol. Bn. for China 17 Oct. 1841; Adjt. do. 5 Mar. 1842 till 1 Mar. 1843. First China War 1842 (Medal). Apptd. 2nd in comd. Bhopal Contingent 22nd Sept. 1843. Comdd. 16th Irreg. Cav. 24 Jan. 1846 till 1860. Second Sikh War; Jullundur Doab; Dalla (s.w.); Capt. comdg. 16th Irreg. Cav. (Medal). Against the Hassanzais of the Black Mtn. 1852-3. Against the Mohmands 1854.

Refs. : G.M. 1863, ii. 666. The Times, 21 Oct. 1863.

DAVIE, Frederick. (*See* **DAVY, Frederick.**)

*DAVIE, Thomas. Lieutenant. Infantry. Cadet (?). Ensign (?). Lieut. (?). Resigned (? May) 1766.

Services : Ensign Bengal Eur. Bn. in Feb. 1764.

Probably resigned his Commission during the " Batta mutiny." " Lieut. Thomas Davie, who resigned his Commission in Bengal in 1766 be not Restored " (M.C. of 3 Feb. 1773).

Note : Possibly identical with the following, the above Resolution having been rescinded.

DAVIE, Thomas (*d.* 1794). Captain, Infantry. Cadet 1775. Ensign 1776. Lieut. 26 July 1778. Capt. 8 Dec. 1793. *d.* Calcutta 25 Dec. 1794.

Services : Lieut. 1st Bengal Eur. Bn. in July 1787.

Note : Possibly identical with the foregoing.

DAVIES, Alban Thomas (1803-1860). Captain. 57th N.I. *b.* Hants, 15 Oct. 1803. Cadet 1819. Admitted 14 June 1820. Ensign 10 Jan. 1820. Lieut. 11 July 1823. Capt. 17 Mar. 1830. Resigned 4 Aug. 1836. *d.* 26 Dec. 1860.

Of Ty-glyn, co. Cardigan. Son of Thomas Davies. *m.* Allahabad, 10 Sept. 1828, Ann, dau. of William Wilson, *q.v.* (She died Cheltenham, 9 Mar. 1854, aged 44.)

Services : Ensign 2/22nd N.I. Transfd. to 29th N.I. 11 July 1823; to 57th N.I. (late 1/29th) May 1824. Adjt. 57th N.I. 17 June 1824 till 1831. First Burma War; Assam 1824; Lieut. 57th N.I. (India medal). Fur. p.a. 4 Feb. 1834 till resignation.

Refs. : County Families of Wales, by Thomas Nicholas, London, 1875, i. 192, *s.n.* Davies, of Ty-glyn, co. Cardigan. *G.M.* 1861, i. 230. *The Times*, 4 Jan. 1861.

DAVIES, Arthur (1758/59-1805). Captain. 2nd N.I. *b.* 1758/59. Cadet 1779. Admitted 23 Dec. 1779. Ensign Dec. 1779. Lieut. 6 Feb. 1781. Capt. 30 Oct. 1797. Retired 4 Sept. 1800. *d.* Pulteney St., Bath, 11 June 1805.
Of Forest Hall, nr. Swansea, co. Carmarthen.
Services : Sailed for India on the *Earl Talbot* 7 Mar. 1779, aged 20. Qmr. 6th Bn. Bengal Eur. Inf. in 1787. Lieut. 2nd Bengal Eur. Regt. in 1796. Fur. 3 June 1797 till retirement.
Refs. : G.M. 1805, ii. 680.

DAVIES, Cornelius (1740/41-1788). Major, Artillery. *b.* 1740/41. Cadet 1770. Fireworker 18 Mar. 1771. Lieut. 30 Jan. 1774. Capt. Lieut. 19 Sept. 1779. Capt. 1 Oct. 1781. Major 31 May 1786. *d. unm.* Calcutta, 9 July 1788, aged 47.
Brother of John and Charles Davies.
Services : Apptd. Adjt. to newly-raised Golandaz Coys. in 1777. Major comdg. 2nd Bn. Art. in July 1787.
Refs. : Will dated 25 June 1788. M.I. in S. Park St. cemetery, Calcutta.

DAVIES, Henry Pelham (*d.* 1817). Captain, 11th N.I. Cadet 1797. Arrived in India 1 Dec. 1798. Ensign 10 Oct. 1798. Lieut. 1 Nov. 1798. Capt. 14 Feb. 1810. *d.* Salleia, C.I., 20 Nov. 1817. *m.* Chunar, 28 June 1808, Mary Ann, dau. of Francis Wilford, *q.v.* (*See also* William Baker (1775-1825) and William Pickersgill.) (She died 15 Aug. 1849, aged 58.)
Services : Second Mahratta War ; Lieut. 11th N.I. Capt. Lt. 11th N.I. 17 Aug. 1808. Reduction of Kalinjar 1812 ; Capt. 2/11th N.I. Siege and capture of Hathras 1817 ; Capt. 2/11th N.I.

DAVIES, James Stephens (1805-1859). Colonel. 48th N.I. *bapt.* Merthyr Tydvil, co. Glamorgan, 10 Nov. 1805. Cadet 1823. Arrived in India 19 May 1824. Ensign 17 Jan. 1824. Lieut. 13 May 1825. Capt. 18 July 1837. Major 10 Aug. 1850. Lt. Col. 2 Apr. 1856. Retired 4 Oct. 1857. Hon. Colonel 4 Oct. 1857. *d.* at his father's residence, Lower Hardwick, Chepstow, 15 July 1859.
Son of David Davies, of Merthyr Tydvil, surgeon. *m.* Claudine Collins. (She died 4 Oct. 1877.)
Services : Actg. Adjt. Rt. Wing 32nd N.I. 27 Sept. 1825. Siege and capture of Bhurtpore ; Lieut. 32nd N.I. (India medal). Fur.

s.c. 13 Feb. 1831 till 7 Nov. 1832. Fur. p.a. 1 Mar. 1836 till 26 Feb. 1839. Fur. s.c. 24 Apr. 1842 till 1 July 1845 ; 7 May 1852 till 2 Oct. 1853 ; 7 Mar. 1856 till retirement. Posted as Lt. Col. to 48th N.I. 18 June 1856.

Refs. : *The Times*, 21 July 1859. *G.M.* 1859, ii. 202.

DAVIES, John (1790-1869). Lieut. Colonel. 71st N.I. *b*. Ringwood, Hants, 9 Dec. 1790. Cadet 1805. Arrived in India 19 Sept. 1806. Ensign 4 Oct. 1806. Lieut. 13 Dec. 1809. Capt. 13 May 1825. Major 7th Jan. 1836. Retired 6 Aug. 1839. Hon. Lt. Col. 28 Nov. 1854. *d*. Wellington Villa, Cheltenham. 8 Apr. Son of Rev. Henry Davies. *m*. Cheltenham, 13 Aug. 1835, Mary, widow of Major Thomas Samuel Watson, Madras Est. (She died Cheltenham, 15 Aug. 1882, aged 85.)

Services : Barasat C.C. for 9 mos. Posted as Ensign to 24th N.I. Leave s.c. 6 mos. to sea 1 Aug. 1812. Transfd. to newly-raised 1/28th N.I. in 1815. Intr. & Qmr. do. for a short time in 1815. Third Mahratta War ; Lieut. 1/28th N.I. Fur. s.c. 5 Sept. 1818 till 27 Nov. 1821. Intr. & Qmr. 1/28th N.I. 27 May 1823. Transfd. to 2/32nd N.I. 11 July 1823 ; Intr. & Qmr. do. 1 Oct. 1823 till 17 June 1824. Transfd. to 64th N.I. (late 2/32nd) May 1824 ; as Capt. to newly-raised 3rd Extra Regt. (became 71st N.I.) May 1825. Siege and capture of Bhurtpore ; employed in escorting treasure within Bhurtpore territory ; Capt. 3rd Extra Regt. (India medal). Offg. Fort Adjt. at Fort William 24 June 1826 ; permanent do. 4 Nov. 1826. Offg. Town and Fort Major of Fort William 26 Feb. 1827, 26 Apr. 1828, 10 Nov. 1830, 1 Sept. 1832. Supt. of Gentlemen Cadets. Offg. Supt. Mysore Princes 5 Dec. 1831 till 10 Dec. 1832. Fur. s.c. 24 Dec. 1832 till 26 Nov. 1836 ; fur. p.a. 8 Feb. 1837 till retirement.

Refs. : *Bath Chron.*, Aug. 1835. *The Times*, 10 Apr. 1869.

DAVIES, Philip (*d*. 1778). Ensign, Infantry. Cadet 1778. Ensign 1778. *d*. Cawnpore 21 Oct. 1778.

Services : N.F.P.

DAVIES, Robert (*d*. 1799). Captain, Infantry. Cadet 1779. Admitted 19 Nov. 1779. Ensign 24 July 1779. Lieut. 16 Mar. 1781. Capt. 30 Oct. 1797. *d*. 28 Feb. 1799 : kld. on board the *Sybelle* frigate in action with the French frigate *La Forte*.

3rd son of Robert Farthing Davies, of Farthingville, co. Cork, and Mary his wife, dau. of Col. John Ramsay (of the Dalhousie family). *m*. Jan. 1786 Mrs. Bolton, widow of Col. Bolton. His dau. *m*. Henry Patch, *q.v.*

Services : Lieut. 1st Bengal Eur. Bn. in July 1787. A.D.C. to the Earl of Mornington (afterwards Marquis Wellesley) 1798.

Volunteered his services to comd. a detachment of troops sent on board the *Sybelle* to act as Marines when she sailed to engage the French frigate *La Forte*. " The corpse of the brave and much regretted Capt. Davis, was not committed to the deep, after the engagement in which he fell ; but was preserved in spirits, and brought up to Diamond Harbour ; where his body was interred on the 10th instant (Mar.), with the military honours so justly due to the remains of that gallant officer " (*A.A.R.*).
Refs. : Burke's *Visitation of Seats and Arms*, 1 S. i. 69. *A.A.R.* i. 118.

*DAVIES, Thomas (1734-1761). Lieutenant, Artillery. *b.* 1734. Cadet 1758. Fireworker (?). Lieut. (?). *d.* Patna 6 June 1761, aged 27.
A native of co. Cardigan.
Services : (*Possibly* No. 301 in *Kane's List*. Fireworker (R.A.) 8 June 1757. Broke 1757.) Sailed for India on the *Hardwicke* in 1757, aged 22.
Refs. : *B.* : *P.P.* No. 55, p. 55. M.I. at Patna, in the compound of what was originally the English Factory, was later the Opium Factory, and is now the Government Press, at Gulzarbagh.

LLOYD-DAVIES, Thomas Dolman (1790-1828). Major, 25th N.I. *b.* Bristol 8 Nov. 1790. Cadet 1805. Arrived in India 11 July 1806. Ensign 2 Aug. 1806. Lieut. 14 May 1808. Capt. 19 Apr. 1822. Major 1828. *d. unm.* Titalia, Bengal, 23 Dec. 1828.
Son of Dr. David Lloyd-Davies, of 17 Part St., Bristol.
Services : Posted as Ensign to 20th N.I. in 1807. Supt. of Mily. Works at Fort Marlbro' 1810-3. Intr. & Qmr. 2/20th N.I. 1 July 1814 till 1822. Fur. 1822-4. Transfd. to 25th N.I. (late 1/20th) May 1824. No record of active service.
Refs. : *Bath Chron.*, 11 June 1829. Will dated 15 Sept. 1828; proved 25 Feb. 1829.

DAVINPORT, Edward. Cadet. Infantry. Cadet 1772. Resigned 12 Nov. 1772.
Services : N.F.P.

*DAVIS or DAVIES, Charles (1787-1805). Cadet, Artillery. *bapt.* Newland, Gloucs., 2 Oct. 1787. Cadet 1805. Never arrived in India. *d.* at sea 5 Feb. 1805 : lost in the *Earl of Abergavenny* off Portland.[1]

[1] *Note :* The *Earl of Abergavenny*, East Indiaman, left Portsmouth on 1 Feb. 1805. Bad weather came on, and the pilot, it is said, not being well acquainted with the coast, she struck on the shambles of Portland Bill, about two miles from shore, on 5 Feb., and sank

within a couple of hours in 12 fathoms. About 300 of her crew and passengers, including 7 Bengal Cadets, were drowned, and only some 90 saved.

Son of James Davies and Lucy his wife.

Refs. : Stubbs's List. Philippart MS. G.M. 1805, i. 174-5, 232.

Note : Both Stubbs and Philippart give the name as Davis. His father, however, signed his name "Davies."

DAVIS, Charles (1795-1815). Ensign, 15th N.I. *b.* Somerton, Somerset, 15 Aug. 1795. Cadet 1810. Ensign 18 Nov. 1813. *d.* Bettiah, B. & O., 22 Apr. 1815, of a fever, on return from the Nepal expedition.

bapt. Somerton 4 Oct. 1796. Son of Rev. Henry Davis, vicar of Somerton, and Sarah his wife.

Services : Cadet d.d. 7th N.I. Posted as Ensign to 2/15th N.I. in 1813. Nepal War 1814-5 ; Ensign 2/15th N.I., in 4th Div.

Refs. : Bath Chron., 28 Nov. 1815.

DAVIS, Charles Edmund (1805-1835). Lieutenant, 62nd N.I. *b.* London 8 Aug. 1805. Cadet 1825. Arrived in India 25 June 1826. Ensign 5 Feb. 1826. Lieut. 28 Aug. 1828. *d.* Simla 23 May 1835.

Son of Robert Davis, of Curtain Rd., London, and Wandsworth, and Ann Beaty his wife. (*Possibly* cousin-german of Francis Beaty, *q.v.*)

Services : Ensign d.d. 46th N.I. 8 July 1826. Posted as Ensign to 62nd N.I. 26 Sept. 1826. Was on sick leave at Simla at date of death. No record of active service.

Refs. : A.J. N.S. xviii. 243.

DAVIS, Charles Edward (1791-1843). Major. 58th N.I. *b.* St. Paul, Halifax, Nova Scotia, 2 Dec. 1791. Cadet 1806. Arrived in India 25 Nov. 1807. Ensign 8 Nov. 1807. Lieut. 23 Sept. 1810. Capt. 1 May 1824. Major 1842. Retired 3 Feb. 1843. *d.* Calcutta 8 Mar. 1843.

bapt. 5 Jan. 1792. Son of Joseph Davis and Mary his wife. *m.* (before 1832) Catherine Dorothy Farquhar. (She died 2 Nov. 1861, aged 62.)

Services : Barasat C.C. for 8 mos. Posted as Ensign to 12th N.I. Capture of Java 1811 ; Lieut. 4th Bn. Bengal Vols. Served with Vols. in Java till Nov. 1816. Transfd. to newly-raised 1/29th N.I. in 1815. Siege and capture of Hathras 1817 ; Lieut. 1/29th N.I. Third Mahratta War ; Lieut. 1/29th N.I. Leave u.p.a. 6 mos. to Singapore 1 Nov. 1819. Served in Singapore for the next 8 or 9 years as Cantt. Adjt., and latterly as Principal Asst. to the Govr.

Transfd. to 58th N.I. (late 2/29th) May 1824. Fur. p.a. 12 Feb. 1831 till 6 Feb. 1834. Actg. Bde. Major at Barrackpore 21 Jan. 1837 till 23 Sept. 1840. Comdd. 58th N.I. from 4 Oct. 1842.
Refs. : *I.M.* No. 1, p. 20. Will dated 22 Apr. 1834 ; proved 28 Mar. 1843. M.I. in Circular Rd. cemetery, Calcutta.

DAVIS or DAVIES, Edward (1757/58-1789). Lieutenant. Infantry. *b.* 1757/58. Cadet 1776. Ensign 28 Mar. 1777. Lieut. 21 Aug. 1778. *d.* at sea 1789, on his passage to Europe.

A native of Wales.

Services : Sailed for India on the *Triton*, 19 Apr. 1776, aged 18. N.F.P.

DAVIS, John (*d.* 1770). Ensign, Infantry. Cadet 1768. Ensign 23 Feb. 1769. *d.* Bankipore, B. & O., 11 June 1770.

N.B.—The following is conjectural only : (? Elder son of John Davis, Comy. Gen. in the W.I. Brother of Samuel Davis, *q.v.* " Kld. in action in India.")

Services : N.F.P.

Refs. : (? Burke's *Peerage*, 1859, p. 271, *s.n.* Davis, Bart., of Hollywood, Gloucs.)

DAVIS or DAVIES, Peter (1736/37-1788). Captain, Infantry. *b.* Edinburgh 1736/37. Ensign 4 July 1770. Lieut. 5 July 1776. Capt. 3 Feb. 1781. *d.* Buxar, 24 Mar. 1788, aged 51.

Services : Enlisted as a private in E.I.C.S. in 1761, and was posted to Capt. Henry Somers' Coy. in Bengal Eur. Regt. Promoted Sergt. One of the few survivors of the Patna massacre in Oct. 1763. Campaign against the Nawabs of Bengal and Oudh 1764-5 ; Sergt. in Grenadiers. Refused the offer of a Commission made by Sir Robert Fletcher, *q.v.*, in May 1766 in order to fill one of the vacancies caused by the wholesale resignation of officers. First Mysore War 1767-9 ; Qmr. to 3rd, 4th and 13th Bns. which composed the Bengal detachment. Accepted a Commission in 1770. 4th Bengal Eur. Bn. in July 1787.

Refs. : *Williams*, pp. 131-2. Will. M.I. at Buxar.

DAVIS, Rees. Ensign. Infantry. Cadet 1770. Ensign 23 Dec. 1772. Dismissed by C.M. 4 Mar. 1776.

Services : N.F.P.

*DAVIS, Samuel (1760-1819). Ensign. Engineers. Subsequently Accountant Gen., Bengal. *b.* 1760. Cadet (?). Ensign (?). Resigned 1783. *d.* 16 June 1819.

Younger son of John Davis, Comy. Gen. in W.I., and his wife, née Phillips, of an ancient family in S. Wales. (*Perhaps* brother of

John Davis, *q.v.*) *m.* Burdwan, 24 Sept. 1794, Henrietta, dau. of Solomon Boileau, of Dublin, and sister of John Peter Boileau, *q.v.*

Services : See *D.N.B.* Apptd. a Writer, B.C.S., 7 Aug. 1783. Accompanied Samuel Turner, *q.v.*, on his mission to Tibet, but he himself did not proceed beyond Bhutan. Collector of Burdwan 1 May 1793. Judge and mgte. of Benares 13 July 1795 till May 1800. Third member of board of revenue 1 Apr. 1801. Accountant Gen. 1 May 1804. Resigned 21 Feb. 1806. When attacked in his house at Benares on 14 Jan. 1799 by a fanatical mob, followers of Wazir Ali, the deposed Nawab of Oudh, he successfully defended himself and his family until rescued, standing at the top of a staircase armed only with a hog-spear. An excellent amateur artist. Dir. E.I.C. 10 Oct. 1810 till death.

Refs. : Foster's *Baronetage*, p. 176, *s.n.* Davis, Bart., of Hollywood, Gloucs. *D.N.B. D.I.B.* Pester, p. 449.

*DAVIS, Walter (*d.* 1770). Cadet. *d.* Calcutta 24 Sept. 1770.
Services : N.F.P.
Refs. : Calcutta burial register.

DAVIS, William (*d.* 1780). Captain, Infantry. Cadet (?). Ensign 23 Nov. 1765. Lieut. 5 June 1767. Capt. 2 July 1771. *d.* Chandernagore, Bengal, 25 July 1780.

Services : Adjt. 3rd Eur. Regt. in May 1766. Raised the 34th Bn. Sepoys at Chunar in July 1778. This Bn., called " *Dabi-ki-Paltan* " after him, became 2/8th N.I. in 1796, 24th N.I. in May 1824.
Refs. : Williams, p. 138. Broome, p. 569.

DAVIS, William Bodycott (*or* Bodicote) [1] (*d.* 1842). Lieut. Colonel. 18th N.I. Country Cadet 1772. Admitted May 1772. Ensign 6 Aug. 1776. Lieut. 23 July 1778. Capt. 10 Sept. 1793. Major 1 Nov. 1798. Lt. Col. 19 May 1801. Retired 18 May 1803. *d.* at his residence in Upper Harley St., London, 13 Feb. 1842.

m. in England, 23 May 1803, Maria, dau. of Col. William Blair, of Stratford Pl., London, *q.v.* (She died 11 Sept. 1858, aged 80.)
Services : Lieut. 1/3rd Bengal Eur. Regt. in Oct. 1779. Lieut. 6th Bn. Sepoys in July 1787. Capt. 2nd Bengal Eur. Regt. Major 14th N.I. Posted as Lt. Col. to 18th N.I. Fur. 29 Jan. 1800 till retirement.
Refs. : G.M. 1803, i. 478. A.J. N.S. xxxvii. 263.

[1] *Note :* His second christian name is given in *I.O. Rec.* as Bodicote ; *The Times*, in the obit. notice of his widow, gives it as Bodycott, in that of his eldest son (2 Jan. 1880) as Bodicott.

DAVIS, William Worsley (1784-1833). Lieut. Colonel, 3rd N.I. *b.* Piddletrenthide, Dorset, 11 Aug. 1784. Cadet 1800. Arrived in India 19 Aug. 1801. Ensign 30 Sept. 1801. Lieut. 13 July 1803. Capt. 13 Sept. 1815. Major 1 May 1824. Lt. Col. 25 Dec. 1827. *d.* Cawnpore 15 Sept. 1833.
bapt. Piddletrenthide 16 Aug. 1784. Son of Rev. William Davis, curate of Piddletrenthide, and Frances his wife. *m.* St. John's, Calcutta, 16 Nov. 1822, Miss Letitia Gillanders. (*See also* Charles Farmer, John Frederick Gaitskell, Samuel Swinhoe, and John Robert Talbot.)
Services : Ensign 6th N.I. Nepal War 1814-5 ; Lieut. 1/6th N.I., in 2nd Div. Third Mahratta War ; Capt. 1/6th N.I., in Reserve Div. Comdg. a detachment of Ceylon Vols. in May 1819. Transfd. as Major to 18th N.I. (late 2/6th) May 1824. Siege and capture of Bhurtpore ; Major 18th N.I. Posted as Lt. Col. to 18th N.I. 22 Apr. 1828. Fur. s.c. 4 Dec. 1829 till 16 Nov. 1832. Transfd. to 8th N.I. 7 Sept. 1829 ; to 3rd N.I. ; to 45th N.I. 17 Jan. 1833, but it is doubtful whether he ever joined this last Regt.
Refs. : A.J. N.S. xiii. 205. M.I. at Cawnpore.

DAVISON, Lewis (1780-1801). Lieutenant, 17th N.I. *bapt.* Pontefract, Yorks., 30 Sept. 1780. Cadet 1798. Arrived in India 18 Sept. 1799. Ensign 28 Aug. 1799. Lieut. 28 Oct. 1799. *d.* Kishenganj, Bengal, 17 Sept. 1801.
2nd son of Dr. Robert Davison, formerly of Leeds, and Mary his wife.
Services : N.F.P.
Refs. : M.M. xiii. 393.

DAVISON, William (1787-1829). Captain, 1st Bengal Eur. Regt. *bapt.* East Shefford, Berks., 6 Mar. 1787. Cadet 1807. Arrived in India 21 Mar. 1809. Ensign 15 Feb. 1809. Lieut. 16 Dec. 1814. Capt. 13 May 1825. *d.* at sea 15 Jan. 1829 on board the *Lord Amherst*, proceeding to Kedgeree.
Eldest son of Rev. Thomas Davison.
Services : Posted as Ensign to Bengal Eur. Regt. and served throughout with that Corps. Served in Java 1813-6, afterwards at Macassar. Siege and capture of Bhurtpore (s.w. on 12 Jan. 1826) ; Capt. 1st Bengal Eur. Regt. Fur. s.c. to Cape and Europe 9 Jan. 1829.

DAVOREN, Michael Constance (*d.* 1798). Lieutenant, Infantry. Country Cadet 1782. Ensign 9 May 1783. Lieut. 4 June 1790. *d.* Monghyr, B. & O., 11 Aug. 1798.
(? *Possibly* son of Rev. Michael Davoren, incumbent of Noughaval and Carrane, co. Clare, 1790-1810.)
Services : N.F.P.
Refs. : Will dated 12 June 1798 ; proved 22 Oct. 1800.

DAVY, Frederick (*d.* 1783). Lieutenant. Bengal Eur. Regt. Cadet 1778. Ensign 1778. Lieut. 1778. Struck off (?). bur. Calcutta 22 Feb. 1783.
Services : Originally a Writer on the Bombay Est. Lieut. 1/1st Bengal Eur. Regt. in Oct. 1779.
Refs. : *Cal. Gaz.* 29 Apr. 1784.

DAVY, Leyson Hopkin (*or* **Lyson Hopkyn**) (1782-1872). Captain. 22nd N.I. *b.* 1782. Cadet 1798. Arrived in India 7 Jan. 1801. Ensign 19 Sept. 1799. Lieut. 28 Oct. 1799. Capt. 17 Jan. 1809. Retired 25 Dec. 1817. *d.* Clifton 28 Sept. 1872, in his 91st year. *bapt.* Cardiff 11 Feb. 1783. Son of Jonathan Davy and Mary his wife.
Services : Lieut. 14th N.I. Transfd. to newly-raised 2/22nd N.I. in Nov. 1803. Second Mahratta War ; battle and capture of Deig ; siege of Bhurtpore (w. in 2nd assault on 21 Jan. 1805) ; Lieut. 2/22nd N.I. (India medal). Capt. Lt. 22nd N.I. 22 Nov. 1807. Capt. 1/22nd N.I. Capture of Java 1811 ; Capt. 4th Bengal Vol. Bn. (Medal). Served in Java with 4th Vol. Bn. till 1815. Fur. from Java 1815 till retirement.
Refs. : *The Times,* 2 Oct. 1872.

DAVY, William (*d.* 1784). Major. Infantry. Cadet 1767. Ensign 11 Dec. 1767. Lieut. 19 Oct. 1769. Capt. 31 Mar. 1778. Major 24 Feb. 1782. Resigned 22 Jan. 1784. *d.* at sea in 1784 during his passage to England on the *Dutton.*
Services : Apptd. by Warren Hastings in May 1782 to be confidential asst. to Major William Palmer, *q.v.,* at Lucknow.
Refs. : *Cal. Gaz.* 23 Sept. 1784. *Forrest,* iii. 968.

DAW, William (*d.* 1776). Ensign, Infantry. Cadet 1772. Ensign 3 Apr. 1773. *d.* Calcutta 24 Nov. 1776 ; bur. the following day.
Services : N.F.P.
Refs. : Burial register of St. John's church, Calcutta.

DAWES, George Douglas (1808-1891). Lieutenant. 54th N.I. *bapt.* Halifax, Nova Scotia, 10 Feb. 1808. Cadet 1824. Arrived in India 21 May 1825. Ensign 7 Dec. 1824. Lieut. 11 Feb. 1827. Retired 10 Sept. 1838. *d.* 8 Oct. 1891.
Son of Daniel Butler Dawes, of Winchelsea, Sussex, formerly of Halifax, N.S., a pensioned officer of the Plymouth dockyard, and Elizabeth his wife. Brother of Michael Dawes, *q.v.* Magdalen Hall, Oxon. ; matric. 16 Nov. 1837, aged 29.
Services : Posted as Ensign to 54th N.I. in 1825. Intr. & Qmr. 54th N.I. 31 Jan. 1831 till May 1836. Fur. s.c. 1 May 1836 till

THE BENGAL ARMY, 1758-1834 29

retirement. Retired on h.p., viz. 4/- *p.d.* No record of active service.
Refs. : Alumni Oxon.

DAWES, John Edwin (1799-1822). Ensign, 30th N.I. *b.* Calcutta 7 July 1799. Cadet 1820. Arrived in India June 1821. Ensign 12 Jan. 1821. *d.* 1822 : presumed to have been lost at sea with the ship *Cornwallis.*
bapt. Calcutta 23 Aug. 1799. Son of Walter Dawes, commander of the *Lucy Maria,* and Mary Louisa his wife.
Services : Posted as Ensign to 2/30th N.I. Leave to Madras Dec. 1821.
Refs. : Will dated Calcutta 24 Nov. 1821 ; proved 27 July 1822.

DAWES, Michael (1813-1871). Colonel, C.S.I. Artillery. *bapt.* Halifax, Nova Scotia, 13 Mar. 1813. Cadet 1829. 2nd Lieut. 11 Dec. 1829. Lieut. 12 June 1838. Capt. 3 July 1847. Bt. Major 7 June 1849. Bt. Lt. Col. 28 Nov. 1854. Retired 1 Jan. 1858. Hon. Col. 1 Jan. 1858. *d.* 30 May 1871.
Son of Daniel Butler Dawes, of Winchelsea, Sussex, and Elizabeth his wife. Brother of George Douglas Dawes, *q.v. m.* 1st, Dublin, 17 June 1845, Louisa, 5th dau. of Rev. John Burdett, of Cushcallow, King's Co., rector of Ballygarth, co. Meath. (She died 15 Sept. 1857.) *m.* 2nd, St. Michael's, Chester, 8 May 1862, Harriett Elizabeth, elder dau. of Sir William Fitzroy, K.C.B., Adm. R.N., and grand-dau. of 3rd Duke of Grafton. (She died 14 July 1875.) Addiscombe Cadet 8 Feb. 1828 till 11 Dec. 1829.
Services : Actg. Adjt. & Qmr. 2nd Bn. Art. 29 Jan. 1834. First Afghan War 1838-42 ; capture of Ghazni ; forcing of Khurd Kabul and Jagdalak passes ; taking of Mamu Khel ; defence of Jalalabad ; Mamu Khel ; Jagdalak ; Tazin ; re-occupation of Kabul ; Lieut. 2nd Coy. 6th Bn. (Medals for Ghazni ; Jalalabad, Kabul.) (*Lond. Gaz.* 10 June, 9 Aug., 11 Oct. 1842.) Fur. p.a. 6 Mar. 1843 till 1845. With 1st Troop 1st Bde. H.A. 1842-6. Second Sikh War ; Chilianwala (w.) ; Gujerat ; Capt. comdg. 3rd Coy. 1st Bn. Foot Art. (Medal with clasp). Comdd. 3rd Troop 1st Bde. H.A. 1849-57. Mutiny campaign ; operations in the Punjab, about Delhi ; Agra ; Doab (Medal). C.S.I. 1870.
Refs. : Burke's *Landed Gentry of Ireland,* p. 84, *s.n.* Burdett, of Coolfin, King's Co., and Ballymany, co. Kildare. Burke's *Peerage,* 1923, p. 1015, *s.n.* Grafton, D.

DAWES, Robert (*d.* 1803). Lieut. Colonel. Infantry. Cadet 1768. Ensign 13 Sept. 1768. Lieut. 27 Dec. 1769. Capt. 9 July 1778. Major 27 Jan. 1784. Lt. Col. 1 Mar. 1794. Retired 2 Nov. 1798. *d.* Bath 21 Nov. 1803.

30 LIST OF THE OFFICERS OF

Of Almington Hall, Staffs.
Services : Apptd. in June 1778, on the death of James Crawford, *q.v.*, to comd. 4th Bn. Sepoys. First Mahratta War 1778-84 ; Capt. comdg. 4th Bn. Fur. 28 Nov. 1785 till 19 July 1788, and 15 Mar. 1796 till retirement.
Refs. : Williams, p. 94. *G.M.* 1803, ii. 1255. M.I. in Bath Abbey.

DAWES, Robert John (1783-1821). Major, 19th N.I. *b.* London 1 May 1783. Cadet 1799. Arrived in India 9 Dec. 1800. Ensign 15 Aug. 1800. Lieut. 7 Nov. 1800. Capt. 10 Sept. 1811. Major 25 May 1821. *d.* Cape of Good Hope 21 Oct. 1821.
bapt. St. George's, Hanover Sq., London, 25 May 1783. Son of John Dawes and Harriot his wife.
Services : Posted as Lieut. to 19th N.I. Fur. 25 Dec. 1809 till 1811. Capt. Lt. 19th N.I. 22 Feb. 1811. Capt. 1/19th N.I. Bde. Major at Meerut 24 Oct. 1812 till 1815 ; do. at Benares 1815-9. (? Nepal War 1814-5 ; Capt. 1/19th N.I., Bde. Major.) Bk. Mr. at Fort William 1819. Asst. Sec., Mily. Board, and 1st Asst. in Accounts Dept., 1820. Leave to Cape 1821 till death. Major 1/19th N.I.
Refs. : G.M. 1821, i. 91. Will dated 11 Jan. 1821 ; proved 11 Mar. 1822.

DAWES, Thomas (1763/64-1784). Lieutenant, Infantry. *b.* 1763/64. Cadet 1781. Ensign 20 Mar. 1781. Lieut. 15 July 1782. *d.* Ramgarh, B. & O., 24 Aug. 1784.
A native of London.
Services : Apptd. Cadet on 20 Mar. 1781, aged 18. Sailed for India on the *Northumberland,* 26 June 1781, aged 17 (*sic.*). N.F.P.

DAWES, William (1782-1800). Lieutenant, Infantry. *bapt.* Stoke-on-Tern, Salop, 17 July 1782. Cadet 1797. Arrived in India 22 Dec. 1798. Ensign 1 Oct. 1798. Lieut. 1 Nov. 1798. *d.* Sultanpur, U.P., 21 Aug. 1800.
Son of Andrew Dawes and Margaret his wife.
Services : N.F.P.

DAWKINS, Charles Digby (1800-1846). Bt. Captain, 11th L.C. Comdt. Govr. Gen.'s Body Guard. *b.* 14 Mar. 1800. Cadet 1820. Arrived in India 19 Nov. 1821. Cornet 4 July 1821. Lieut. 1 May 1824. Bt. Capt. 4 July 1836. *d.* Ambala 20 June 1846, from a wound received at the battle of Mudki on 18 Dec. 1845.
bapt. Chipping Norton 13 Apr. 1800. 5th son of Henry Dawkins, Comr. of Woods, Forests, and Land Revenue, M.P. for Aldborough,

THE BENGAL ARMY, 1758-1834

and Augusta his wife, dau. of Gen. Sir Henry Clinton, K.B. Ed. Charterhouse; admitted a scholar 23 Jan. 1812; exhibitioner 2 Apr. 1818. Christ Church Coll., Oxon.; matric. 22 Apr. 1818.
Services : Cornet d.d. 1st L.C. Nov. 1821. Posted as Cornet to 2nd L.C. Apr. 1822. d.d Baddeley's Horse (became 4th Irreg. Cav.) 31 Aug. 1822; Adjt. do. 29 June till 6 Aug. 1824. Adjt. G.G.B.G. 12 Sept. 1825. First Burma War 1825-6; Adjt. G.G.B.G. Bde. Major Mewar F.F. at Nimach 2 Mar. 1827 till 29 Jan. 1834. Tempy. Comdt. G.G.B.G. 6 Feb. 1834; permanent do. 3 Apr. 1834 till 1838. First Afghan War 1838-9; Ghazni (Medal); Kabul; Lieut. 2nd L.C. Comdt. G.G.B.G. 1839 till death. Transfd. to rolls of newly-raised 11th L.C. in Jan. 1842. Gwalior campaign; Maharajpur; Comdt. G.G.B.G. (Bronze star). First Sikh War; Mudki (s.w.); Comdt. G.G.B.G.
Refs. : Burke's *Landed Gentry*, 13th edn., p. 477, *s.n.* Dawkins, of Over Norton. *De Rhé-Philipe. V.B.G. Alumni Carthusiani. Alumni Oxon. G.M.* 1846, ii. 447. M.I. St. Andrew's, Ferozepore.

DAWSON, Edward (1732/33-1785). Lieutenant, Infantry. *b.* York 1732/33. Cadet 1780. Ensign 31 Oct. 1780. Lieut. 13 July 1781. *d.* Chunar, U.P., 23 Mar. 1785.
Services : Sailed for India on the *Ponsborne* 3 Apr. 1780, aged 47. N.F.P.

DAWSON, John (William) (1761/62-1832). Major. 19th N.I. *b.* 1761/62. Country Cadet 1780. Admitted 11 Dec. 1780. Ensign 12 Aug. 1781. Lieut. 9 July 1782. Capt. 29 May 1800. Major 13 May 1806. Retired 22 Feb. 1811. *d.* at his residence in Cheltenham 14 Feb. 1832, aged 70.
m. Mary. (She *re-m.* 6 Apr. 1833, Commodore Thomas Dade Beaty, late Indian Marine.)
Services : Lieut. 5th Bn. Sepoys in 1787. Capt. Lt. 1/5th N.I. (late 5th Bn.) in 1798. Transfd. as Capt. Lt. to 1/8th N.I.; as Capt. to newly-raised 19th N.I. in May 1800. At P.W.I. in 1806. Fur. 17 Feb. 1808 till retirement.
Refs. : A.J. N.S. vii. 166. *G.M.* 1832, i. 284.

DAY, Edward (1779-1851). Lieut. Colonel. 51st N.I. *b.* 8 Sept. 1779. Cadet 1799. Arrived in India 12 Jan. 1801. Ensign 15 Nov. 1800. Lieut. 22 Aug. 1801. Capt. 16 Dec. 1814. Major 1 May 1824. Lt. Col. 28 Nov. 1826. Retired 7 June 1830. *d.* 10 July 1851.
2nd son of John Day, Mayor of Cork 1806, and Margaret Hewson his wife. Uncle of Edward Fitzgerald Day, *q.v.*, and 2nd cousin of James Leslie Day, *q.v. m.* Bishops' Court, Clones, 19 Aug. 1829, Mary, eldest dau. of Patrick Trant, of Dingle.

Services : Lieut. Bengal Eur. Regt. Transfd. to newly-raised 23rd N.I. in Nov. 1803 ; to 26th N.I. in 1805. Operations in Bundelkhand 1807 ; Sehlehuganj ; Lieut. 26th N.I. Capt. Lt. 26th N.I. 16 Jan. 1814. Capt. 1/26th N.I. Fur. 16 Jan. 1816 till 1818. Transfd. to 2/26th N.I. ; as Major to 51st N.I. (late 1/26th) May 1824. Fur. p.a. 9 Jan. 1828 till retirement.

Refs. : Burke's *Landed Gentry of Ireland*, p. 169, *s.n.* Day. Foster's *Families of Royal Descent*, i. 438. *A.J.* xxviii. 382.

DAY, Edward Fitzgerald (1803-1873). Major General. Artillery. *bapt.* Listowel, co. Kerry, 10 Feb. 1803. Cadet 1819. Arrived in India 6 Jan. 1821. 2nd Lieut. 16 June 1820. Lieut. 1 May 1824. Capt. 5 Apr. 1837. Major 3 July 1847. Lt. Col. 23 Jan. 1854. Bt. Col. 28 Nov. 1854. Retired 31 Dec. 1854. Hon. Maj. Gen. 1855. *d. unm.* Tudor Hall, Monkstown, co. Dublin, 15 May 1873.

2nd son of Rev. John Day, rector of Kiltallagh, co. Kerry, and Arabella his wife, dau. of Sir William Godfrey, Bart. Nephew of Edward Day, *q.v.* Addiscombe Cadet 27 Nov. 1818 till 16 June 1820.

Services : Adjt. & Qmr. 2nd Bn. Foot Art. 31 Mar. 1835 till 12 June 1837. A.D.C. to Maj.-Gen. Clements Brown, *q.v.*, comdg. Benares Div., 13 Mar. 1838. Apptd. Comy. of Ord. to force for Afghanistan 28 Aug. 1838. First Afghan War 1838-9 ; Ghazni ; Comy. Ord. (Medal). Leave s.c. to Singapore and China 21 Feb. till Nov. 1843. Gwalior campaign ; Maharajpur ; Comy. Ord. (Bronze star). Comdd. 5th Troop 1st Bde. H.A. 1844-6. First Sikh War ; Ferozshahr ; Sobraon ; Capt. comdg. 5th Troop 1st Bde. (Medal with clasp). Second Sikh War ; Multan (horse shot under him) ; Gujerat ; Major comdg. 3rd Bn. Foot Art. (Medal with clasp). Posted to 1st Bde. H.A. 25 June 1849. Lt. Col. comdg. 9th Bn. Foot Art.

Refs. : Burke's *Landed Gentry of Ireland*, p. 168, *s.n.* Day. Foster's *Families of Royal Descent*, i. 436.

DAY, James Leslie (1789-1838). Major, 8th N.I. *b.* 21 Sept. 1789. Cadet 1805. Arrived in India 7 Apr. 1807. Ensign 8 Apr. 1807. Lieut. 26 Jan. 1809. Capt. 1 May 1824. Major 20 July 1832. *d. unm.* Jermyn St., London, 8 Jan. 1838.

bapt. Kilgobbin, co. Kerry, 23 Sept. 1789. 4th son of Rev. James Day, rector of Tralee, and vicar-general of the diocese of Ardfert and Aghadoe, and Margaret his wife, dau. of M'Gillycuddy, of The Reeks. 2nd cousin of Edward Day, *q.v.*

Services : Barasat C.C. for 15½ mos. Posted as Ensign to 9th N.I. Nepal War 1816 ; Lieut. 2/9th N.I., in 4th Bde., Centre Column. Actg. Adjt. 1/9th N.I. 21 Nov. 1821. Transfd. as Capt.

to 8th N.I. (late 1/9th) May 1824. To survey canal works 22 Nov. 1833. Received charge of Rajputana F.F. 5 Jan. 1835. Comdd. 8th N.I. till 21 Nov. 1836. Fur. p.a. 11 Feb. 1837 till death.
Refs.: Burke's *Landed Gentry of Ireland*, p. 168, *s.n.* Day. Foster's *Families of Royal Descent*, i. 446. *A.J.* N.S. xxv. 127. Will dated Calcutta 4 Jan. 1837 ; proved 27 June 1838.

DAYCOCK, John Thomas (1815-1837). Ensign. Infantry: unposted. Afterwards in the Bank of England. *b.* Clerkenwell, Middlesex, 30 July 1815. Cadet 1832. Arrived in India 23 June 1834. Ensign 13 Dec. 1833. Resigned 16 Oct. 1834. *d.* King Sq., London, 6 May 1837.

Son of John Daycock, H.E.I.C. Home Service, and Elizabeth his wife. Addiscombe Cadet 1 Aug. 1832 till 13 Dec. 1833.
Services: Ensign d.d. 55th N.I. 7 July 1834. After resigning the Service he returned to England, and obtained a post in the Bank of England.
Refs.: *A.J.* N.S. xxiii. 166.

DEA, John. Cadet. Cadet 1783.
Services: N.F.P.

DEAN, Richard (*d.* 1781). Lieutenant, 18th N.I. Cadet 1771. Ensign 4 Mar. 1773. Lieut. 24 Mar. 1778. bur. Cawnpore 25 June 1781.
Services: First Rohilla War 1774 ; battle of St. George ; Ensign 15th Bn. Sepoys.

DEARE, Charles Russell (1749/50-1790). Lieut. Colonel, Artillery. *b.* 1749/50. Cadet 1769. Fireworker Dec. 1769. Lieut. 12 Feb. 1771. Capt. Lieut. 14 May 1777. Capt. 9 Nov. 1779. Major 29 May 1786. Lt. Col. 28 Dec. 1788. *d.* 13 Sept. 1790 : kld. in action at Satyamangalam, Madras, aged 40.

Brother of George Deare, *q.v.*, and of Philip Deare. (*Probably* uncle of Philip Deare, *q.v.*) *m.* Calcutta, 5 June 1779, (Ann) Catherine, dau. of Rev. Thomas Stark, minister of Ballindean, Balmerino, co. Fife. (She died Calcutta, 6 Sept. 1790, aged 34.)
Services: Second Mysore War 1781-5 ; Capt. comdg. 4th Coy. 2nd Bn. Foot Art. Adjt. to the Bde. of Art. (*i.e.* Bde. Major) till Mar. 1786. Apptd. Comy. of Stores in Fort William 27 Oct. 1785. Third Mysore War ; Satyamangalam (kld.) ; Lt. Col. comdg. Art.
Refs.: G.E.C. *Complete Baronetage*, iv. 178, *s.n.* Leman, Bart., of Wisdone and Blachford, Devon. *Hickey*, iv. 4. Will. M.I. on wife's tomb in S. Park St. cemetery, Calcutta.

DEARE, George (1751/52-1823). Lieut. General. Artillery. Commanded the Regt. b. 1751/52. Cadet 1768. Fireworker 12 Sept. 1768. Lieut. 16 Sept. 1770. Capt. Lieut. 4 July 1776. Capt. 6 Oct. 1778. Major 31 Jan. 1785. Lt. Col. 30 May 1786. Col. 1 Mar. 1794. Maj. Gen. 3 May 1796. Lt. Gen. 25 Sept. 1803. d. Baker St., London, 5 Mar. 1823, aged 71. Brother of Charles Russell Deare, q.v.

Services: First Rohilla War; battle of St. George; Lieut. Art. Comdg. 3rd Bn. Art., and Comdt. at Ft. William in July 1787. Comdt. Bengal Art. 16 June 1789 till 1794. Retired on Off-Reckoning Fund 1 Jan. 1803. Fur. 28 Jan. 1805 till death.

Refs.: *G.M.* 1823, i. 284. M.I. St. John's church, St. John's Wood Rd., London (where age at death is given as 70).

DEARE, Philip (1801-1830). Lieutenant, 47th N.I. b. 7 Apr. 1801. Cadet 1818. Admitted 13 Nov. 1819. Ensign 11 July 1819. Lieut. 18 Jan. 1823. d. Arakan, Burma, 29 Dec. 1830.

bapt. Bures, Suffolk, 6 July 1801. Son of Rev. James Russell Deare, minister of Bures. (*Probably* nephew of Charles Russell Deare, q.v.) m. Partabgarh, Oudh, 16 Nov. 1825, Miss Anne Somerset Hughes.

Services: Ensign 2/24th N.I. Transfd. to 47th N.I. (late 1/24th) May 1824. On the disbandment of this Regt. for mutiny in Nov. 1824, he was transfd. the same month to newly-raised 69th N.I. (became 47th N.I. in 1828). Actg. Adjt. 69th N.I. 2 Mar. 1825. Intr. & Qmr. 69th N.I. 29 July 1825. Adjt. 69th N.I. 18 Sept. 1826 till death. No record of active service.

DEAS, Alexander Foulis Cunningham (1811-1842). Lieutenant, 5th N.I. b. Cupar, co. Fife, 29 Aug. 1811. Cadet 1827. Arrived in India 10 June 1828. Ensign (23 Feb. 1828) 4 Nov. 1828. Lieut. 13 Nov. 1835. d. 10 Jan. 1842: kld. in action at Janga Fariki, nr. Kabul.

bapt. Cupar 27 Sept. 1811. Son of Col. Alexander Deas, of Hilton, and Catharine his wife, dau. of Capt. Robert Low. Nephew of Gen. Sir John Low, G.C.S.I. (*D.N.B.*). Addiscombe Cadet 3 Feb. 1826 till 27 Feb. 1828.

Services: Ensign d.d. 46th N.I. 25 July 1828; do. 62nd N.I. 16 Sept. 1828. Posted to 5th N.I. 4 Nov. 1828. Apptd. to 1st Inf., Oudh Auxy. Force (his uncle being at that time Resdt. at Lucknow), 27 Dec. 1837. Rejoined his Regt. proceeding on service Jan. 1840. First Afghan War 1840-2; comdd. 1st Coy. 5th N.I. in a successful attack on the fort of Mohd. Sharif on 6 Nov. 1841; (w.) at Kabul; kld. in retreat from Kabul.

Refs.: Eyre's *Journal*. M.I. in St. Peter's, Fort William, Bengal.

DE BEAUREGARD, John Richard (1785-1820). Captain, 2nd N.I. *bapt.* Cheam, Surrey, 6 Nov. 1785. Cadet 1800. Arrived in India 24 Aug. 1801. Ensign 3 Oct. 1801. Lieut. 15 Aug. 1803. Capt. 12 July 1814. *d.* Calcutta 26 May 1820.

Son of John Michael Charriere De Beauregard and Charlotte his wife. *m.* Calcutta, 26 Aug. 1807, Miss Mary Hickburn. (She *re-m.* —— Ward, and died *c.* 1845.)

Services : Ensign 2nd N.I. Second Mahratta War ; battle of Delhi ; Lieut. 2nd N.I. Capture of Java 1811 ; Lieut. 3rd Bn. Bengal Vols. Served in Java with Vols. till 1815. Capt. Lt. 2nd N.I. 29 Oct. 1812. Capt. 2/2nd N.I. Fur. 14 Sept. 1815 till 1818.

Refs. : Will dated 12 Mar. 1811 ; proved 1 June 1820. M.I. in S. Park St. cemetery, Calcutta.

DE BELART (BELLART or BILLART), Louis (*d.* 1789). Lieutenant. Infantry. Bt. Ensign 1 Feb. 1767. Lieut. 2 July 1770. Resigned 30 Oct. 1772. *d.* Calcutta 2 Nov. 1789.

Services : " Formerly a Lieut. on the Coast Est., and since the year 1761 he commanded the Corps of French Cavalry in Bengal to the time of its being disbanded, and afterwards he was attached to the Sepoy Corps and stationed at the Factories of Chittagong and Luckipore ; but lastly a Private and unfortunate gentleman, after having resigned the service voluntarily. He has left behind him a widow of good morals and character and three helpless children entirely to the mercy of those who have been his friends and benefactors."

Refs. : Cal. Gaz. 5 Nov. 1789.

DEBRETT, George Gibson (1792-1817). Lieutenant, 18th N.I. *b.* London 22 May 1792. Cadet 1807. Arrived in India 14 Aug. 1808. Ensign 19 Sept. 1808. Lieut. 23 May 1811. *d.* Cuttack 24 Dec. 1817, of fever.

2nd son of John Debrett, of Piccadilly, London, bookseller (*D.N.B.*), and Sophia his wife, née Bineford. Brother of John Edward Debrett, *q.v.*

Services : Posted as Ensign to 18th N.I. Nepal War 1816 ; Lieut. 1/18th N.I., in 1st Bde., Rt. Column. Cuttack insurrection 1816 ; Khurda ; Lieut. 1/18th N.I.

Refs.: G.M. 1818, ii. 281. Will dated 6 Jan. 1816 ; proved 14 Mar. 1818.

DEBRETT, John Edward (1789-1835). Captain, Artillery. *b.* London 15 Sept. 1789. Cadet 1806. Arrived in India 23 Nov. 1807. Fireworker 12 June 1807. Lieut. 11 June 1808. Capt. 4 May 1820. *d.* Simla 10 May 1835.

bapt. St. James's, Westminster, 1 Nov. 1789. Eldest son of John Debrett, of Piccadilly, bookseller, and Sophia his wife. Brother of George Gibson Debrett, *q.v.* *m.* Chittagong, 31 Oct. 1825, Martha, youngest dau. of John Burrup, of Brighton, Sussex.
Services : Comdt. detachment of Art. at P.W.I. 1810-2. Nepal War 1814-5; Lieut. 5th Coy. 2nd Bn. Foot Art., with Capt. Barré Latter's force. Nepal War 1816; Lieut. 5th Coy. 2nd Bn., with Sir D. Ochterlony's force. Third Mahratta War; siege of Chanda; Asirgarh; Lieut. 5th Coy. 2nd Bn. (*Lond. Gaz.* 10 Aug. 1819). Fur. 6 Dec. 1821 till 27 Oct. 1824. Offg. Agent army clothing, 1st Div., 13 Dec. 1832 till Feb. 1835. Leave s.c. to Simla 15 Feb. 1835 till death.
Refs. : De Rhé-Philipe. A.J. N.S. xviii. 243. Will dated Simla 8 May 1835; proved 11 Dec. 1835. M.I. in Mall cemetery at Simla.

DEBROSES or DESBROSSES, Richard (*d.* 1778). Lieutenant, Artillery. Cadet (?). Fireworker 13 Mar. 1771. Lieut. 24 Feb. 1773. *d.* Chunar 22 June 1778.
Services : N.F.P.

DE BRUYN, Peter Philip Van Virgilo (1808-1832). Ensign, 58th N.I. *b.* London 11 Oct. 1808. Cadet 1826. Arrived in India 23 Sept. 1827. Ensign (13 May 1827) 31 Jan. 1828. *d.* at sea 15 July 1832.
Son of Philip De Bruyn. Ed. Harrow 1819-23; Westminster 16 Apr. 1823 till Dec. 1825.
Services : Posted as Ensign to 3rd Extra Regt. 3 Jan. 1828. Transfd. to 58th N.I. 31 Jan. 1828. Fur. s.c. 14 July 1832. No record of active service.
Refs. : Harrow School Register. Westminster School Register.

DE BUDÉ, Henry (1800-1843). Major, Engineers. *b.* London, 3 Nov. 1800. Cadet 1815. Admitted 5 Sept. 1818. Ensign 1 Sept. 1818. Lieut. 29 July 1821. Capt. 28 Sept. 1827. Major 31 Mar. 1840. *d.* Calcutta 8 Nov. 1843.
bapt. Marylebone 4 Jan. 1801. Son of Lt.-Gen. Jacob De Budé, of a Swiss family (Govr. of the Princes Edward, Duke of York, and William, Duke of Gloucester), and Mary Lambert his wife. Nephew of Jean Louis De Budé, seigneur de Boisy, Col. in the service of Sardinia. *m.* 1st, Mary Anne. *m.* 2nd, Meerut, 12 July 1825, Miss Jane Anne Royle (*probably* dau. of William Henry Royle, *q.v.*). (She died Calcutta, 27 Feb. 1841, aged 38.) *m.* 3rd, Calcutta, 14 Apr. 1842, Margaret E., dau. of Leith Alexander Davidson, and sister of George Henry Davidson, *q.v.* (*See also* Samuel Boileau Goad, and George Edward Gowan.)

THE BENGAL ARMY, 1758-1834

Services : Operations in Saharanpur district under Capt. Frederick Young, *q.v.*, against Kowar Singh ; capture of fort Kunjawa 3 Oct. 1824. Siege and capture of Bhurtpore ; Lieut. S. & M. Executive Ofr. to conduct alterations and repairs to fortress of Aligarh 23 Feb. 1827. Posted to S. & M. 5 May 1828. Garr. and Executive Engr. at Delhi 8 Apr. 1831. Re-apptd. to comd. S. & M. 5 Sept. 1832. Suptg. Engr. P.W.D., C.P., 18 Mar. 1835 ; do. in Cuttack 9 Jan. 1837. Sec. to Mily. Board 23 June 1841. M.M.B. 1843.
Refs. : *Almanach Généalogique Suisse*, ii. 72. *Dict. Hist. et Biog. de la Suisse* (1921). *I.M.* 6 Jan. 1844, p. 273. M.I. Circular Rd. cemetery, Calcutta.

DE BURGH, Hubert (1790-1833). Major, 2nd L.C. *b.* Bengal 26 Nov. 1790. Cadet 1805. Arrived in India 11 Nov. 1806. Cornet 20 Sept. 1806. Lieut. 22 Sept. 1815. Capt. 30 Jan. 1821. Major 26 Oct. 1827. *d.* in camp at Ghateeara, Rajputana, 30 Dec. 1833, *en route* from Nimach to Agra.

Son of Eliza De Burgh. *m.* Bristol, Dec. 1824, Frances Deborah, youngest dau. of Lt. Col. Cox, R.A. (? and sister of George Hamilton Cox, *q.v.*). (She *re-m.* Sir Frederick Abbot, *q.v.*)
Services : Posted as Cornet to 2nd N.C. With Bengal Vols. in Java 1812-3 ; with Java L.C. 1814-5. Third Mahratta War ; Lieut. 2nd N.C., in Reserve Div. Adjt. 2nd L.C. for a short while till 27 Mar. 1820. Fur. p.a. 5 Feb. 1822 till 6 Sept. 1825.
Refs. : *A.J.* N.S. xiv. 201. Will dated 2 Apr. 1825 ; proved 10 Mar. 1834.

DE BURKE, Thomas (*d.* 1783). Captain, Infantry. Cadet 1769. Ensign 21 June 1770. Lieut. 4 July 1776. Capt. 2 Feb. 1781. *d.* Chandernagore 29 Nov. 1783.
Services : First Rohilla War 1774 ; battle of St. George ; Ensign 8th Bn. Sepoys.

DE CASTRO, Henry (*d.* 1828). Lieut. General. Colonel 53rd N.I. Cadet 1771. Admitted 14 Oct. 1771. Ensign 25 Jan. 1773. Lieut. 31 Dec. 1777. Capt. 2 June 1781. Major 27 July 1797. Lt. Col. 31 July 1799. Lt. Col. Comdt. 21 Sept. 1804. Col. 25 Apr. 1808. Maj. Gen. 4 June 1811. Lt. Gen. 19 July 1821. *d.* London 18 Jan. 1828.
Services : Lieut. 1/3rd Bengal Eur. Regt. in Oct. 1779. Capt. 19th Bn. Sepoys in July 1787. Lt. Col. 5th N.I. Transfd. as Lt. Col. Comdt. to 25th N.I. in 1804 ; to 27th N.I. in 1805. Transfd. as Col. to 19th N.I. in 1808 ; to 25th N.I. in 1808 ; to 24th N.I. in 1816 ; to 53rd N.I. May 1824 ; to 18th N.I. on the day of his death. Fur. 11 Feb. 1812 till death.

*DECKER(S), Adrian (*or* **Ardean**)[1] (*d.* 1762 ?). Lieutenant, Artillery. Lieut. 18 Sept. 1761. *d.* 1762 ?[2]
m. Calcutta 23 Mar. 1760, Mrs. Elizabeth Hamilton, of Calcutta, spinster.

[1] *Note :* The names, as given in the marriage register and in his Will, which is signed " J. A. Decker," are Adrian Decker. Broome and Stubbs give them as Ardean Deckers.

[2] *Note :* Although his name appears on M.I. in Patna city amongst those who were massacred at Patna in Oct. 1763, and both Broome and Stubbs state that he was killed on that occasion, yet it is omitted from the MS. " List of Persons killed in the Massacre at Patna, and at other places during the Troubles, 1763," which is to be found amongst *I.O. Rec.* It is also absent from the diaries of Ensign Walter Mackay, *q.v.*, and of the three Surgeons who were at Patna at the time. In view of the fact that the Will of Adrian Decker was filed in Calcutta on 9 Nov. 1762, and was proved the same day, it may be assumed that he was not, in fact, massacred at Patna. It must be remembered that the memorial was erected many years after the event, and that Gen. Stubbs probably took Broome as his authority. On the other hand, it is, of course, within the bounds of possibility that Ardean Deckers and Adrian (*or* J. A.) Decker may have been two distinct individuals.

Refs. : (? Burke's *Extinct Baronetcies, s.n.* Decker, Bart.) Will dated 14 Mar. 1760 ; proved 9 Nov. 1762.

DECLUZEAU, William (1786-1826). Captain, 6th N.I. *b.* Dublin 29 Nov. 1786. Cadet 1803. Arrived in India 2 Sept. 1804. Ensign 29 Oct. 1804. Lieut. 29 Oct. 1804. Capt. 1 Aug. 1818. *d.* Karnal 21 Nov. 1826.

Son of John Decluzeau, of Dublin, merchant, and Rebecca Sinclair his wife.

Services : Posted as Ensign to 2/3rd N.I. 14 Apr. 1805. Nepal War 1814-5 ; Nalagarh ; Taragarh ; capture of Malaun ; Lieut. 2/3rd N.I., with 1st Div. Insurrection in Ceylon 1818-9 ; Capt. Lt. 1st Bengal Vols. Transfd. to 6th N.I. (late 1/3rd) May 1824. Siege and capture of Bhurtpore ; Capt. 6th N.I. " It is related of him that on the day of the storm (18 Jan. 1826) he was on the sick list and so ill that he was unable to walk ; but his spirit was such that nothing could keep him from his post, and when his regiment advanced to the assault, he actually had himself *carried* up the breach by two sepoys of his company."

Refs. : De Rhé-Philipe.

DE COURCY, John (1760/61-1824). Lieut. Colonel, Invalid Est. 24th N.I. *b.* in Ireland 1760/61. Cadet 1780. Admitted 12 Apr.

THE BENGAL ARMY, 1758-1834

1782. Ensign 1780. Lieut. 16 June 1781. Capt. 1 Nov. 1798. Major 21 Sept. 1804. Lt. Col. 1 Sept. 1809. Invalided 1 May 1813. *d.* Calcutta 10 Dec. 1824, aged 62.

Brother of Rev. Richard De Courcy, sometime of Shrewsbury. Distantly related to Lord Kingsale. His natural dau. *m.* Powell Thomas Comyn, *q.v.*

Services : Sailed for India on the *Mount Stewart* 27 June 1780, aged 20 ; was captured on the voyage by the combined fleets of France and Spain on 9 Aug., taken to Cadiz, and eventually exchanged. He embarked again on the *Northumberland* on 26 June 1781, aged 21, and was captured a second time. Lieut. 25th Bn. Sepoys in July 1787. Capt. 13th N.I. Comdd. escort of Resdt. at Poona 1803-9. Posted as Lt. Col. to 6th N.I. in 1810 ; to 24th N.I. in 1811. Fur. 5 Feb. 1811 till 1812. He afterwards comdd. 1st Bn. Native Invalids.

Refs. : G.M. Nov. 1803. Will dated 27 Mar. 1824 ; proved 14 Dec. 1824. M.I. in S. Park St. cemetery, Calcutta.

DEE, James (*d.* 1783). Captain, Infantry. Cadet 1769. Ensign 1769. Lieut. 29 Mar. 1773. Capt. 25 Jan. 1781. *d.* Fatehgarh 14 Feb. 1783.

Services : N.F.P.

DEE, Robert (1752-1801). Captain, 11th N.I. *b.* 1752. Cadet 1781. Admitted 6 May 1782. Ensign 18 May 1781. Lieut. 1 Sept. 1782. Capt. 21 Apr. 1800. *d.* at the Cape 11 Jan. 1801, on his passage to England.

A native of co. Hereford.

Services : Apptd. Cadet on 3 Jan. 1781, aged 28. Sailed for India on the *Tartar* 26 June 1781, aged 29. Lieut. 2nd Bn. Sepoys in 1787. Capt. 2/11th N.I. Fur. 15 Oct. 1800 till death.

DE FOUNTAIN, Angus (1801-1851). Captain, 40th N.I. *b.* St. Helena 31 Mar. 1801. Cadet 1825. Arrived in India 3 Aug. 1826. Ensign 30 Jan. 1826. Lieut. 27 Apr. 1831. Capt. 24 Jan. 1845. *d.* Allahabad 10 Mar. 1851.

bapt. St. Helena 30 Mar. 1806. Son of John De Fountain,[1] Senior Mercht., St. Helena C.S. Brother of John De Fountain, *q.v. m.* Lucknow, 24 Apr. 1828, Eliza, eldest dau. of James Rainey, *q.v.* (She died Sherghati 7 Apr. 1850.)

[1] *Note. :* His name usually appears as Des Fountain.

Services : Ensign H.M. 66th Foot 13 Mar. 1820. Ensign d.d. 4th N.I. 12 Aug. 1826. Posted to 29th N.I. 26 Sept. 1826. Adjt. Mandleshwar Local Bn. 16 Apr. 1829. Actg. Adjt. Left Wing 29th N.I. 11 Mar. 1832. Transfd. to 40th N.I. 21 Aug. 1832. Actg. Adjt. 40th N.I. 21 Feb. 1837. d.d. Ramgarh L.I. Bn. 14 Dec. 1839

till 1 Nov. 1842, when he rejoined 40th N.I. on service in Bundelkhand. Was in charge of a detachment of Irreg. Cav. attached to Ramgarh L.I. Bn. in 1840.
Refs. : *A St. Helena Who's Who*, p. 71. *A.J.* xxvi. 609. *G.M.* 1851, ii. 217.

DE FOUNTAIN, John (1809-1843). Bt. Captain, 54th N.I. *b.* St. Helena 18 July 1809. Cadet 1825. Arrived in India 2 Aug. 1826. Ensign 30 Jan. 1826. Lieut. 7 May 1827. Bt. Capt. 30 Jan. 1841. *d.* Mussoorie 14 May 1843.
Son of John De Fountain, Senior Mercht., St. Helena C.S. Brother of Angus De Fountain, *q.v.* *m.* 1st, Saugor, 28 Apr. 1831, Frances, 5th dau. of Richard Foquett, and sister of Henry Foquett, *q.v.* (She died Dinapore 15 Aug. 1835.) *m.* 2nd, Calcutta 6 May 1836, Mrs. Adolphina Bell.
Services : Ensign d.d. 50th N.I. 12 Aug. 1826. Posted as Ensign to 56th N.I. 26 Sept. 1826. Transfd. to 54th N.I. 14 Dec. 1842. Leave 12 mos. to Mussoorie 14 Nov. 1842. No record of active service.
Refs. : *I.M.*, No. 4, p. 116.

DE GLOSS, Luis Felix. Major (? Bt. Lieut. Colonel). Engineers. Lieut. Bo. Art. 20 Aug. 1753. Capt. Lt. 27 Dec. 1757. Capt. 13 Apr. 1758. Capt. Bo. Engrs. 8 Feb. 1759. Bt. Capt. Bengal Engrs. 13 Feb. 1764. Bt. Major 15 Jan. 1770. Major 27 Jan. 1773. (? Bt. Lt. Col. 27 Jan. 1773.) Resigned 4 Feb. 1773.
Son of Frederick Daniel De Gloss, of Lublin and Cracow, Poland. Brother of Gottfried Wilhelm de Bernard De Gloss, Capt. in H. Prussian Majesty's Service, and of Susan Conordriade Sparlen, of Warsaw. Cousin of Luis Doupport, of Landow, Alsace. (? *m.* Margaret.)
Services : Bt. Commission or Warrant from C.D. as 1st Lieut. Bo. Art., dated 28 Feb. 1753. Employed on survey work. Clerk of the Works at Bombay 18 Oct. 1757. Made improvements in the manufacture of gunpowder in 1759. Conducted the approaches in the siege of Surat, 1760, and took comd. of the garrison there for nearly 3 yrs. Went to Bengal in 1764. Addl. Surveyor, Bengal Est., 19 Feb. 1765. Employed on survey work. Supt. of bldgs. at Dinapore 1769. Established a foundry nr. Calcutta where he cast cannon and also manufactured gunpowder. A letter from him, dated Calcutta, 30 Nov. 1772, giving a résumé of all his services, will be found in *M.C.* of 17 Dec. 1772. Owing to his nationality the Bengal Govt. would only give him brevet rank until he was about to resign the service. He left India on the *Duke of Grafton* in Feb. 1773.
Refs. : *Spring*, No. 12. Will dated Calcutta 28 Jan. 1773 ; proved 6 Nov. 1778.

DELAFIELD, Philip (*d.* 1783). Captain. 10th Bn. Sepoys. Cadet 1765. Ensign 7 Apr. 1765. Lieut. 7 Aug. 1765. Capt. 14 Sept. 1767. Dismissed by C.M. 24 Feb. 1777. *d.* Kew Green, Surrey, 25 Oct. 1783.

m. Calcutta, 25 July 1772, Mary, sister of Adm. Sir Albemarle Bertie, Bart., K.B., of the ducal house of Ancaster.

Services : Tried by Court Martial and dismissed the Service owing to discontent in his Bn. (10th), due to "intemperate and improper conduct" as C.O. on his part. He was heavily in debt to the Company when he left the country. He was the only officer in 2nd Bengal Eur. Regt. in May 1766 who did not participate in the "Batta mutiny."

Refs. : Williams, p. 59. *Broome*, p. 600. *G.M.* 1783, ii. 979.

DELAFOSSE, Henry (1794-1845). Major, C.B., Artillery. *b.* Richmond, Surrey, 11 Mar. 1794. Cadet 1809. Admitted 13 Nov. 1810. Fireworker 16 Nov. 1810. Lieut. 25 Sept. 1817. Capt. 28 Sept. 1827. Major 2 Jan. 1843. *d.* in camp at Lakki-ki-Dera, 70 m. from Ferozepore, 3 Oct. 1845 : found dead in his *palki*.

Son of Rev. Robert Mark Delafosse, B.C.L. *m.* Islington, 17 Apr. 1827, Miss Shield, of Hornsey Lane, Highgate. (His widow, Louisa Maria, died 29 Oct. 1887, aged 79.) Woolwich Cadet: nominated to R.M.A. 16 Mar. 1808.

Services : Served in Java 1812 ; expeditions to Palembang 1812 ; Sambas 1813 ; Boni 1814 ; with 7th Coy. 1st Bn. Foot Art. Tempy. charge of a detachment of Javanese Corps at Sourabaya 5 Jan. 1813. Transfd. to 6th Coy. 3rd Bn. in 1816. Siege and capture of Hathras 1817. Third Mahratta War. Transfd. to 5th Troop H.A. May 1818. Adjt. & Qmr. of the Art. of Narbada F.F. 20 Oct. 1820 till 24 Dec. 1824. Offg. Bde. Major of Art. at Dum-Dum 7 Nov. 1825 till Apr. 1826. Fur. 4 June 1826 till 13 Oct. 1828. To comd. 1st Coy. 6th Bn. July 1829. Comdd. 3rd Troop 1st Bde. H.A. 5 Nov. 1835 till Jan. 1843. First Afghan War 1842 ; with Gen. Pollock's force ; comdd. Art. of that force from May 1842 ; Mamu Khel ; Jagdalak ; Tazin ; Haft Kotal (Medal). Posted to 2nd Bn. Foot Art. 20 Jan. 1843 ; to 3rd Bn. Jan. 1844. Principal Comy. of Ord. 18 Oct. 1844 till death. C.B. 24 Dec. 1842.

Refs. : De Rhé-Philipe. I.M. 1845, p. 707. *G.M.* 1846, i. 110. M.I. in civil cemetery at Ferozepore.

DELAMAIN, Innis (1759/60-1814). Major, 16th N.I. *b.* 1759/60. Cadet 1782. Admitted 15 Nov. 1782. Ensign 11 Jan. 1783. Lieut. 23 Mar. 1788. Capt. 11 July 1803. Major 4 Apr. 1809. *d.* Cawnpore 2 Mar. 1814.

Son of William Delamain and Mary, née Ackland, his 2nd wife.

Brother of William Maple Delamain, *q.v.* 2nd cousin o Jame⁸ Delamain, *q.v.* *m.* Cawnpore 6 Jan. 1795, Isabella, dau. of Rober Baillie, *q.v.* (She died 6 Sept. 1835, aged 59.) Father of Robert Delamain, *q.v.*, and of William Henry Delamain, *q.v.* His daus. *m.* John William Gibbs, *q.v.*, William Henry Howard, *q.v.*, Arthur Shuldham, *q.v.*, and William Warde, *q.v.*

Services : Sailed for India on the *Worcester*, 6 Feb. 1782, aged 22. Ensign 4th Bengal Eur. Bn. in July 1787. Bt. Capt. 1/1st N.I. in 1798. Adjt. 1/16th N.I. in 1803. Operations in Jumna Doab; attack on Thathia fort 30 Sept. 1803 (w.) ; Capt. Lt. 1/16th N.I. Fur. 11 Jan. 1811 till 1813. Bt. Lt. Col. 4 June 1814, before the report of his death had been received.

Refs. : Family information. Will dated 11 Dec. 1808 ; proved in 1814.

DELAMAIN, James (1779/80-1830). Lieut. Colonel, 61st N.I. *b.* (*probably*) 1779/80. Cadet 1798. Admitted 7 Nov. 1799. Ensign 12 Nov. 1799. Lieut. 21 Apr. 1800. Capt. 5 Jan. 1811. Major 11 July 1823. Lt. Col. 22 Apr. 1825. *d. unm.* at sea 1 Apr. 1830, on board the *Captain Cook*.

Son of Henry Delamain, of 67 Berners St., London, formerly of Ireland, sometime R.N., and Ann his wife, née Nott. Uncle of John Delamain, *q.v.*, and 2nd cousin of Innis Delamain, *q.v.*

Services : Lieut. 7th N.I. Capt. 1/7th N.I. Fur. 15 Feb. 1811 till 4 Sept. 1815. Third Mahratta War ; Capt. 1/7th N.I. Transfd. as Major to newly-raised 33rd N.I. July 1823 ; to 65th N.I. (late 1/33rd) May 1824. Comdd. Malwa Bhil Corps 1822-4. P.A. at Nemawar, C.I., and comdg. Mandleshwar Local Bn. 1824-30. Posted as Lt. Col. to 50th N.I. in 1825 ; to 3rd N.I. in 1826 ; to 61st N.I. in 1828. Fur. from Bombay 1830.

Refs. : Family information. Will dated Bombay 7 Feb. 1830 ; proved 27 Oct. 1832.

DELAMAIN, John (1781 ?-1836). Colonel, C.B., 43rd N.I. *b.* 7 Jan. (? 1781). Cadet 1798. Admitted 7 Nov. 1799. Ensign 11 Nov. 1799. Lieut. 21 Apr. 1800. Capt. 20 July 1808. Major 9 June 1819. Lt. Col. 1 May 1824. Col. 1 Nov. 1830. *d.* Heavitree, Exeter, 30 Apr. 1836, of apoplexy.

Eldest son of John Henry Delamain, of Margaret St., Cavendish Sq., and of East Acton, and Mary his wife, née Woolhouse. Nephew of James Delamain, *q.v.* *m.* Agra, 12 Sept. 1825, Hannah Mary, dau. of T. Norris, of Croom's Hill, Greenwich. (*See also* John Hunter (1781-1836).) (She died Lymington, Hants, 14 Nov. 1894.)

Services : Ensign 2nd Royal Regt. Tower Hamlets Mil. Attd. to Vol. Corps under Major Maclean 21 Dec. 1801. (? Expedition to

Egypt.) Lieut. 19th N.I. Fur. p.a. 15 Feb. 1811 till 28 Jan. 1815. Posted to newly-raised 1/29th N.I. in 1815. Siege and capture of Hathras; Capt. 1/29th N.I. Third Mahratta War; Capt. 1/29th N.I. Major 1/29th N.I. Posted as Lt. Col. to 58th N.I. (late 2/29th) May 1824. Siege and capture of Bhurtpore (*Lond. Gaz.* 4 July 1826). Transfd. from 40th to 3rd N.I. 22 Dec. 1826. Leave s.c. 10 mos. to Mauritius 7 Mar. 1828. Comdt. of fortress of Agra 8 Oct. 1828. Transfd. to 21st N.I. 22 Apr. 1828; to 44th N.I. 29 Dec. 1828; to 5th N.I. 10 June 1830. Col. 43rd N.I. 16 Dec. 1830. Fur. 1832 till death. C.B. 2 Jan. 1827.

Refs. : Family information. *G.M.* 1836, ii. 107. *A.J.* N.S. xx. 205. Will dated 29 Dec. 1830; codicil dated 3 Jan. 1836; proved 29 Nov. 1836. M.I. in Exeter cathedral.

DELAMAIN, Robert (1796-1846). Lieut. Colonel, 66th N.I. *b.* Cawnpore 11 Sept. 1796. Cadet 1813. Admitted 5 Aug. 1814. Ensign 10 Dec. 1814. Lieut. 12 July 1815. Capt. 27 May 1828. Major 13 Mar. 1834. Lt. Col. 7 Nov. 1840. *d.* Exeter 19 Jan. 1846.

bapt. Cawnpore Oct. 1796. Son of Innis Delamain, *q.v.*, and Isabella his wife. Brother of William Henry Delamain, *q.v.* *m.* Barrackpore, 15 Jan. 1833, Jane Amelia, dau. of Col. William Youngson, of Bowscar, Cumberland, late Madras Est., and cousin-german of William Martin (1789-1882), *q.v.* (*See also* Walter Coningsby Erskine, Earl of Kellie, and Richard Charles Lawrence.)

Services : Siege and capture of Hathras 1817; Lieut. 2/1st N.I. Third Mahratta War; Lieut. 1st. N.I. Adjt. 1/1st N.I. 10 Dec. 1818 till 1823. Transfd. to newly-raised 2/33rd N.I. July 1823; to 66th N.I. (late 2/33rd) May 1824. Adjt. 66th N.I. 1 Oct. 1823 till 23 Aug. 1825; Intr. & Qmr. do. 23 Aug. 1825. Supt. of family monies at Barrackpore 21 Oct. 1826. Fur. s.c. 10 July 1827 till 3 May 1830. Magh Sebundy Corps 9 Mar. 1831. Tempy. comdg. Ramgarh L.I. Bn. 7 Dec. 1838 till 19 Feb. 1839. Comdd. 66th N.I. from 30 Apr. 1839. Posted as Lt. Col. to 66th N.I. 19 Feb. 1841. To comd. in Arakan 28 Feb. 1843. Fur. s.c. 14 Jan. 1845 till death.

Refs. : *G.M.* 1846, i. 441.

DELAMAIN, William Henry (1812-1878). Colonel. Artillery. *b.* 1812. Cadet 1830. Arrived in India 20 Sept. 1830. 2nd Lieut. 11 June 1830. Lieut. 20 Oct. 1839. Capt. 16 June 1848. Major 18 Feb. 1856. Lt. Col. 14 Nov. 1858. Col. 1 Sept. 1863. Retired 31 Oct. 1871. *d.* Brighton 19 Oct. 1878, aged 66.

bapt. Kensington, 6 Jan. 1813. Son of Innis Delamain, *q.v.*, and Isabella his wife. Brother of Robert Delamain, *q.v.* *m.* Calcutta, 25 Apr. 1840, Jane, dau. of Henry Lloyd, *q.v.* Addiscombe Cadet 1828-30.

Services : Posted to 1st Coy. 5th Bn. Foot Art. 24 June 1835. Fur. s.c. 11 Feb. 1837 till 20 Jan. 1840. Adjt. & Qmr. 2nd Bn. Art. 13 Apr. 1840 till 21 Sept. 1848. Against the Bori Afridis 29 Nov. 1853 (Medal). Lt. Col. 2nd Bn. Art.
Refs. : *The Times*, 24 Oct. 1878.

DELAMAIN, William Maple (*d.* 1783). Lieutenant, 13th N.I. Cadet, Art., 1782. Transfd. to Inf. Ensign 8 July 1782. Lieut. 11 Jan. 1783. bur. Madras 14 Jan. 1783.

Son of William Delamain and Mary Ackland his 2nd wife. Brother of Innis Delamain, *q.v.* (*N.B.*—Relict of William Maples (*sic.*) Delamain died Tebradon, co. Dublin, 8 Feb. 1837.)

Services : Second Mysore War 1781-3 ; Lieut. 13th N.I.
Refs. : Will dated 13 Jan. 1783 ; proved 24 Jan. 1783.

DELAP, Samuel (1790-1823). Bt. Captain, 24th N.I. *b.* Tullyaughnish, co. Donegal, 4 Dec. 1790. Cadet 1805. Arrived in India 13 Nov. 1806. Ensign 11 Jan. 1807. Lieut. 24 Sept. 1811. Bt. Capt. 24 May 1821. *d.* Calcutta 27 Aug. 1823.

Son of Alexander Delap.

Services : Posted as Ensign to 7th N.I. in 1807. Transfd. to 24th N.I. in 1808. Capt. 1/24th N.I. Third Mahratta War ; Capt. 1/24th N.I. Adjt. 1/24th N.I. 2 Mar. 1821 till death.

DELESSERT or d'ELLERZARTE, Charles L. (*d.* 1763). Lieutenant, European Dragoons. Cornet 22 Sept. 1760. Lieut. 1763. *d.* 19 July 1763 : kld. in action at battle of Katwa.

A native of Switzerland. *m.* Maddalaine.

Note : The name is variously spelt by different authorities as follows : Delassert, Delasart, Delassere.

Services : Apptd. Cornet in 2nd Troop of Eur. Dgns. (M.C. of 22 Sept. 1760). War with Shah Alam 1760-1 ; battle of Suan ; Cornet 2nd Troop. War with Muhammad Kasim 1763 ; battle of Katwa (kld.) ; Lieut. 2nd Troop.

Refs. : *Journal of the United Service Institution of India*, xlii. 112-3. Broome, p. 374. *B. : P.P.*, vi. 247. Will dated 1 July 1763 ; filed 26 Aug. 1763 ; proved 21 Oct. 1763.

DE L'ETANG, Eugene (1803-1829). Ensign, 68th N.I. *b.* Palta, nr. Barrackpore, 5 May 1803. Cadet 1826. Was already in India when apptd. Cadet. Ensign 14 Aug. 1827. *d.* Buxar 15 Nov. 1829.

Son of Le Chevalier Antoine De L'Etang, Kt. of St. Louis, veterinary surgeon and 1st Asst. in H.C. Stud Dept. in India, sometime Supt. of the Stud of Louis XVI of France. Uncle of the third and last Countess Somers.

Services : Ensign H.M. 87th Foot 18 May 1823, and served with that Regt. for nearly 4 yrs. Apptd. Cadet on 5 July 1826. Posted as Ensign to 60th N.I. 10 May 1827. Transfd. to 68th N.I. 1827. Apptd. to Stud Dept., and placed under his father at Buxar in 1827. No record of active service.
Refs. : V.B.G. A.J. N.S. i. 236. M.I. in Ghazipur church.

DE LISLE, Nicholas (1786-?). Lieutenant. 11th N.I. *b.* St. Peter Port, Guernsey, 23 Sept. 1786. Cadet 1805. Arrived in India 19 Aug. 1806. Ensign 24 July 1806. Lieut. 19 Nov. 1807. Resigned 5 Jan. 1810.
Son of Nicholas De Lisle and Elizabeth Carey his wife.
Services : Posted as Ensign to 11th N.I. No record of active service.

DE MATTOS, Charles. Ensign. Infantry. Cadet 1783. Ensign 1783. Struck off before 1790.
Services : N.F.P.

DE MATTOS, Isaac (*d.* 1795.) Lieutenant, Infantry. Cadet 1779. Ensign (?). Lieut. 1 May 1781. *d.* Dinapore June 1795.
Services : Lieut. 6th Bn. Sepoys in July 1787.

DE MONTMORENCY, Reymond Hervey (1808-1847). Major, 65th N.I. *b.* Dorchester 25 Apr. 1808. Cadet 1823. Arrived in India 16 Oct. 1824. Ensign 13 June 1824. Lieut. 13 Oct. 1825. Capt. 1 Aug. 1839. Major 10 June 1845. *d.* at sea, 11 Mar. 1847, on board the *Monarch*, off the Cape.
2nd son of Reymond Hervey Morres (name changed to De Montmorency 5 Apr. 1819), Capt. 13th Light Dgns., Lt. Col. Yorkshire Hussars, M.P., and Letitia his wife, dau. of Rev. Narcissus Charles Proby. Gt. nephew of Lodge Evans, first Viscount Frankfort de Montmorency. *m.* Agra 6 Oct. 1830, Anne Matilda, 3rd dau. of Henry Revell, of Round-Oak, Surrey. (*See also* John Handcock Low.)
Services : Posted as Ensign to 65th N.I. in 1825. Granted 6 mos. leave to Meerut 2 June 1829, to enable him to d.d. with H.M. 16th Lancers, pending confirmation by H.M. of the nomination to a Cornetcy in that Regt. This was cancelled. Fur. p.a. 11 Jan. 1836 till 31 Dec. 1838. Comdd. 65th N.I. 6 Sept. 1841 till 15 Jan. 1842. Fur. 1847. No record of active service.
Refs. : Burke's *Peerage*, 1923, p. 1622, *s.n.* Mountmorres, V. *I.M.* No. 82, p. 453.

DENBY, William (*d.* 1830). Lieut. Colonel. Infantry. Cadet 1768 (1770). Arrived in India 6 Apr. 1770. Ensign 18 Sept. 1769 (12 Apr. 1770). Lieut. 29 June 1771 (17 Mar. 1773). Capt.

9 Jan. 1781. Major 1 Mar. 1794. Lt. Col. 3 Oct. 1796. Retired 7 Aug. 1799. d. London 28 Feb. 1830.
m. in England, 25 Oct. 1787, Miss Bent, of Barnsley.
Services : Fur. Jan. 1786 till 24 July 1788, and 21 June 1798 till retirement.

DENBY, William Charles (1791-1841). Lieut. Colonel, 20th N.I. *bapt.* Leeds 10 Mar. 1791. Cadet 1805. Arrived in India 19 Sept. 1806. Ensign 5 Oct. 1806. Lieut. 23 Aug. 1811. Capt. 1 May 1824. Major 20 May 1834. Lt. Col. 11 Mar. 1841. *d. unm.* Simla, 26 Sept. 1841, " of sheer inanition, having denied himself even *rotee mukhun*," [1] although worth from a lac and a half to two lacs rupees.
Son of John Denby, of Ardwick Green, Manchester. Brother of John, merchant in Rio de Janeiro, and of Mrs. Mary Anne Sale, of Derby.
Services : Barasat C.C. for 10 mos. Posted as Ensign to 5th N.I. Operations in Bundelkhand against Gopal Singh 1810 ; Tirowa ; Lieut. 1/5th N.I. Operations in Baghelkhand 1813-4 ; Entauri ; Lieut. 1/5th N.I. Adjt. 1/5th N.I. 1 Oct. 1823 till 17 June 1824. Transfd. to 20th N.I. (late 2/5th) June 1824. Offg. Intr. & Qmr. H.M. 31st Foot 24 June 1825. Tempy. charge of Kumaon Local Bn. 14 Oct. 1831. Offg. Bde. Major to troops in Oudh 7 Dec. 1831. Comdd. Delhi Palace Guards 17 Oct. 1834 till 29 Mar. 1836. Posted as Lt. Col. to 20th N.I. 27 Apr. 1841.
Refs. : *I.N.* No. 20, p. 454. *A.J.* N.S. xxxvi. *G.M.* 1842, i. 677. Will dated Ludhiana 6 Nov. 1838 ; proved 3 May 1842.

[1] *Note :* Bread and butter.

DENMAN, William (*d.* 1776). Captain, Infantry. Cadet (?). Ensign 29 Oct. 1764. Lieut. 1 Dec. 1766. Capt. 11 Apr. 1769. *d.* Berhampore 11 Oct. 1776.
Services : Bde. Major to Sir Robert Barker, Provincial C.-in-C., *q.v.* N.F.P.
Refs. : *N. & Q.* 12 S. v. 221.

DENNIS, Henry (*d.* 1776). Lieutenant, Infantry. Cadet 1767. Ensign 29 July 1767. Lieut. 26 Dec. 1769. *d.* Belgaum, Bombay, 18 May 1766.
Services : N.F.P.

DENNIS, James. Cadet. Infantry. Cadet 1779.
Services : N.F.P.

THE BENGAL ARMY, 1758-1834

DENNIS, John (*d.* 1780). Cadet. Infantry. Cadet 1774. Dismissed 18 Feb. 1775. *d.* Calcutta 20 Apr. 1780.
Services : N.F.P.

DENNIS, Robert (*d.* 1796). Major, Infantry. Cadet 1768. Admitted 28 Aug. 1768. Ensign 19 May 1769. Lieut. 2 Apr. 1771. Capt. 26 Aug. 1779. Major 17 Mar. 1796. *d.* Kalna, Bengal, 28 May 1796.
Services : Capt. 1/2nd Bengal Eur. Regt. in Oct. 1779. 2nd Bn. Sepoys in July 1787.
Refs. : S.M. 1797, p. 287.

DENNIS, Thomas (1779-1808). Lieutenant, 27th N.I. *bapt.* Burton Leonard, Yorks., 21 Mar. 1799. Cadet 1799. Arrived in India 10 Dec. 1800. Ensign 3 Sept. 1800. Lieut. 17 July 1801. *d. unm.* Agra 2 July 1808.
Son of John Dennis, of Burton Leonard, and Mary his wife. Stepson of Robert Hardcastle, of Burton Leonard.
Services : Ensign 17th N.I. Transfd. to newly-raised 2/27th N.I. in 1804. Adjt. 2/27th N.I. 1805 till death. Operations against Dhundia Khan 1807 ; Komona (s.w.) ; Ganauri ; Lieut. 2/27th N.I.
Refs. : A.A.R. x. 21. Will dated Comona 4 Nov. 1807 ; proved 24 Sept. 1808.

DENNISS, George Gladwin (1792-1856). Lieut. Colonel, C.B., Invalid Est. Artillery. *bapt.* Cashel, co. Tipperary, 8 Feb. 1792. Cadet 1807. Arrived in India 21 Mar. 1809. Fireworker 30 Mar. 1809. Lieut. 29 Aug. 1813. Capt. 6 Apr. 1824. Major 6 Dec. 1839. Lt. Col. 12 July 1844. Invalided 3 July 1847. *d.* Kalka 13 Jan. 1856.
Eldest son of George Denniss, Lt. Col. H.M. 43rd Foot, and Mary his wife, dau. of Francis Gladwin, *q.v. m.* Sikraul, B. & O., 27 July 1815, Anna Ellerker, only dau. of John Macgrath (*d.* 1811), *q.v.* Woolwich Cadet : nominated to R.M.A. 12 Feb. 1806.
Services : Served as Ensign in H.M. 43rd Regt. before entering Woolwich. Minor operations in Oudh 1819-20 ; Lieut. 8th Coy. 4th Bn. Foot Art. Fur. s.c. 8 Jan. 1824 till 21 Oct. 1826. Transfd. to 3rd Troop 2nd Bde. H.A. 6 Jan. 1832. Leave s.c. to Mussoorie Apr. 1834 till Oct. 1836. Fur. s.c. 8 Feb. 1839 till 8 Aug. 1842. Posted to 6th Bn. Foot Art. in Mar. 1841. Gwalior campaign ; Maharajpur ; Major comdg. 6th Bn. (Bronze star). Transfd. to 2nd Bn. in Jan. 1844 ; to 4th Bn. in Aug. 1845. First Sikh War ; Ferozshahr ; Sobraon ; Lt. Col. 4th Bn., Bdr. comdg. Foot Art. (Medal with clasp). After transfer to the Invalid Est. he resided at Kasauli, or in the vicinity, till death. C.B. 3 Apr. 1846.
Refs. : De Rhé-Philipe. I.M. 1856, p. 122. M.I. at Kasauli.

DENNISTOUN, Alexander (1811-1830). Ensign, 11th N.I. *b.* Glasgow 19 Dec. 1811. Cadet 1828. Arrived in India 1 June 1829. Ensign 14 Sept. 1829. *d.* Singapore 11 Dec. 1830.

6th and youngest son of Robert Dennistoun, merchant, and Anne Penelope his wife, dau. of Archibald Campbell, of Jura. Brother of Archibald Campbell Dennistoun, *q.v.*

Services : Ensign d.d. 2nd N.I. 13 July 1829 ; do. 11th N.I. 1830. Leave s.c. 12 mos. to Singapore and China 1 July 1830 ; fur. s.c. from Singapore 18 Nov. 1830.

Refs. : Burke's *Landed Gentry*, 13th edn., p. 489, *s.n.* Dennistoun, of Dennistoun, co. Renfrew. *A.J.* N.S. v. 100.

DENNISTOUN, Archibald Campbell (1800-1882). Lieutenant. 11th N.I. *b.* Glasgow 27 Dec. 1800. Cadet 1821. Arrived in India 2 May 1822. Ensign 3 Dec. 1821. Lieut. 22 Oct. 1824. Retired 7 Aug. 1833. *d.* Carlton-on-Trent, Notts., 22 Sept. 1882.

Of Parkhill, Torquay. 2nd son of Robert Dennistoun, merchant, and Anne Penelope his wife. Brother of Alexander Dennistoun, *q.v. m.* 16 Dec. 1841, Mary, youngest dau. of Peter Vere, of Grosvenor Pl., London. (*See also* Thomas Bradridge Studdy.)

Services : Posted as Ensign to 5th N.I. Transfd. to 11th N.I. (late 1/5th) May 1824. Siege and capture of Bhurtpore ; Lieut. 11th N.I. (India medal). Actg. Adjt. 11th N.I. 31 Oct. 1827. Fur. s.c. 3 Mar. 1831 till retirement. Retired on h.p. of Ensign.

Refs. : Burke's *Landed Gentry*, 13th edn., p. 489, *s.n.* Dennistoun, of Dennistoun, co. Renfrew ; 6th edn., p. 1858, *s.n.* Vere, of Carlton House, Notts. *The Times*, 26 Sept. 1882.

DENNY, James (*d.* 1830). Ensign. Infantry. Afterwards Surgeon, Bengal Est. Cadet 1783. Ensign 12 Mar. 1785. Asst. Surgeon 11 July 1789. Surgeon 5 July 1805. Retired 7 Oct. 1818. *d.* Regent Sq., London, 9 Mar. 1830.

Services : Held the Certificate of the Corporation of Surgeons, now the London Coll., dated 1782.

Refs. : Crawford, i. 238-9. *G.M.* 1830, i. 282.

DENNY, Samuel (1751/52-?). Captain. Infantry. *b.* 1751/52. Cadet 1782. Admitted 15 Nov. 1782. Ensign 16 Jan. 1783. Lieut. 1 Mar. 1789. Capt. 1 Jan. 1796. Retired 22 Jan. 1802. *d.* before 1811.

A native of Suffolk.

Services : Sailed for India on the *Worcester*, 6 Feb. 1782, aged 30. Ensign 1st Bengal Eur. Bn. in July 1787. Bk.Mr. at Dinapore in 1790. Lieut. 2nd Bengal Eur. Regt. in 1796. Fur. 22 Jan. 1798 till retirement.

THE BENGAL ARMY, 1758-1834

DENT, James (*d.* 1782). Ensign, Infantry. Cadet 1781. Ensign 23 Aug. 1781. *d.* Bandel, Bengal, 20 June 1782.
Services : N.F.P.
Refs. : M.I. at Chinsura, Bengal, in the Dutch cemetery.

*DENT, James (1787-1805). Cadet, Artillery. *b.* Thirsk, Yorks., 14 Nov. 1787. Cadet 1805. Never arrived in India. *d.* at sea 5 Feb. 1805 : drowned in the wreck of the *Earl of Abergavenny* off Portland. (See note to Charles Davis or Davies.)
bapt. Thirsk 14 Dec. 1787. Son of Robert Dent, surgeon, and Jane Brignall his wife. Nephew of William Dent.
Services : Woolwich Cadet; nominated to R.M.A. 6 Oct. 1802 ; obtained his certificate 9 Jan. 1805.
Refs. : Philippart MS. Stubbs's List.

DENT, John (1763/64-?). Lieutenant. Infantry. *b.* 1763/64. Cadet 1781. Arrived in India 15 Nov. 1782. Ensign 27 Mar. 1781. Lieut. 13 July 1782. Resigned 23 May 1792.

A native of Yorkshire.
Services : Apptd. Cadet on 31 May 1781. Sailed for India on the *Worcester* 6 Feb. 1782, aged 18. Was Adjt. & Qmr. to Sepoy Corps, 2nd Bde., in 1787. Third Mysore War ; Adjt. & Qmr. to Lt.-Col. John Cockerell's detachment.

DENTY, Henry Francis (1785-1848). Lieut. Colonel. 6th N.I. *b.* 24 Suffolk St., Middlesex Hospital, London, 21 Oct. 1785. Cadet 1800. Arrived in India 24 Aug. 1801. Ensign 11 Nov. 1801. Lieut. 8 Sept. 1803. Capt. 11 May 1816. Major 2 Sept. 1824. Lt. Col. 27 May 1828. Retired 18 July 1829. *d.* 11 Jan. 1848.

Of Exeter : sometime of Hertford St., Fitzroy Sq., London. *bapt.* Percy chapel, London. Son of James Denty, *q.v.*, and Lydia his wife. Cousin-german of Pendock Neale, *q.v. m.* (before 1822). (His widow, Louisa, died 10 Sept. 1853.)
Services : Ensign 3rd N.I. Transfd. as Lieut. to newly-raised 27th N.I. in 1804. Operations against Dhundia Khan 1807 ; Komona (w.) ; Ganauri ; Lieut. 2/27th N.I. Operations in Oudh 1810. Capture of Java 1811 ; Lieut. 4th Bengal Vol. Bn. Fur. 12 Dec. 1813 till 1816. Capt. Lt. 27th N.I. 1 Oct. 1815. Capt. 2/27th N.I. Transfd. to 53rd N.I. (late 1/27th) May 1824 ; as Lt. Col. to 6th N.I. 10 Sept. 1828. Fur. 1828 till retirement.

*DENTY, James (*d.* 1790). Captain, 3rd Bengal Eur. Bn. Cadet 1769. Ensign 1769. Lieut. 29 June 1771. Capt. 9 Sept. 1779. *d.* Cawnpore 20 Apr. 1790.
m. Lydia (who is described in the burial register as " a native ").

(She died St. Helena 9 Mar. 1790.) Father of Henry Francis Denty, *q.v.*
Services : Fur. 1784-7. N.F.P.
Note : Lord Palmerston was an exor. of his Will.

de PEYRON, Charles Adolphus Mary (1781-1807). Captain, 3rd N.C. *b.* 18 Jan. 1781. Cadet 1794. Arrived in India 8 Mar. 1797. Cornet 24 Nov. 1795. Lieut. 25 Apr. 1797. Capt. 11 Mar. 1805. *d.* in England 4 Dec. 1807.
Only son of the Chevalier Charles Adrien de Peyron, in the service of Gustavus, King of Sweden, and Mary his wife, eldest dau. of Sir George Colebrooke, 2nd Bart. Stepson of William Traill.
Services : Lieut. H.M. 80th Foot. Lieut. 3rd N.C. Qmr. 3rd N.C. 29 May 1800 till 1805. Operations in the Jumna Doab 1803 ; Sasni ; Bijaigarh ; Kachaura ; Lieut. 3rd N.C. Capt. Lt. 3rd N.C. 12 Sept. 1803. Second Mahratta War ; Delhi ; Laswari ; Rampura ; battle of Deig ; Capt. Lt. 3rd N.C. Fur. 23 Feb. 1807 till death.
Refs. : Burke's *Peerage*, 1923, p. 554, *s.n.* Colebrooke, Bart., of Crawford, co. Lanark. *G.M.* 1807, ii. 1233. Will dated Bareilly 7 Aug. 1804 ; proved 23 July 1808.

DE PRELAZ, Stephen (*d.* 1792). Lieutenant, Infantry. Cadet 1782. Ensign 2 May 1783. Lieut. 18 May 1790. *d.* Calcutta 1 Oct. 1792.
m. Chandernagore, 9 May 1791, Françoise Boularot, widow, a Frenchwoman. (She re-m. John Hickland, *q.v.*)
Services : Adjt. 16th Bn. Sepoys, in 3rd Bde., 1787-90.

DE RENZY, Annesley (1791-1812). Ensign, 6th N.I. *b.* Clonegall, co. Carlow, 26 Feb. 1791. Cadet 1807. Arrived in India 21 Mar. 1809. Ensign 11 Feb. 1809. *d.* Java 24 Jan. 1812.
Son of John De Renzy, of Clonegall.
Services : Posted as Ensign to 6th N.I. Capture of Java 1811 ; Ensign 6th Bengal Vol. Bn.

*DESPARD, Henry Parnell Moore (1807-?). Cadet. *b.* Dublin 6 Feb. 1807. Cadet 1819. Did not take up his appt. as Cadet.
Son of Philip Pilkington Despard, late director of customs, St. Martins, W.I.

D'ESTERRE, Henry Martin (*d.* 1801). Captain, 17th N.I. Cadet 1780. Ensign 1780. Lieut. 2 Sept. 1781. Capt. 1799. *d.* Malda, Bengal, 12 Jan. 1801.
Eldest son of Norcott D'Esterre, of Limerick, and Anna his wife, younger dau. of Harding Parker, and sister of John Neville Parker, *q.v.* Brother of Norcott Neville D'Esterre, *q.v.*, and cousin-german

of William Neville Parker, q.v. m. Calcutta, 13 Aug. 1800, Elizabeth Grace Charlotte, widow of —— Bateman. (She died Bhagulpur Dec. 1800.)
Services : Lieut. 29th Bn. Sepoys in 1787. Fur. 6 June 1787 till 1791.
Refs. : Burke's *Landed Gentry of Ireland*, p. 551, *s.n.* Parker, of Passage West; p. 594, *s.n.* Roberts, of Ardmore.

D'ESTERRE, Norcott Neville (1762/63-1781). Lieutenant, Infantry. *b.* 1762/63. Cadet 1778. Ensign 1778. Lieut. 18 Sept. 1780. *d.* Bedzegur (? Bijaigarh) Nov. 1781, aged 18.
Son of Norcott D'Esterre, of Killura and Castle Henry, co. Clare (of Limerick), and Anna his wife. Brother of Henry Martin D'Esterre, *q.v.*, and of Anne Louise, wife of Lambert Richard Loveday, *q.v.* Cousin-german of St. Leger Henry Gillman, *q.v.*
Services : Benares insurrection 1781.
Refs. : Burke's *Landed Gentry of Ireland*, p. 551, *s.n.* Parker, of Passage West; p. 594, *s.n.* Roberts, of Ardmore.

DES VOEUX, Thomas (1795-1865 ?). Major. 44th N.I. *b.* 1795. Cadet 1811. Admitted 4 Aug. 1812. Ensign 7 Apr. 1814. Lieut. 13 Dec. 1815. Capt. 14 Mar. 1833. Retired 25 Jan. 1837. Hon. Major 28 Nov. 1854. *d.* 1865 ? (Shown as a casualty in *I.A.L.* for Jan. 1866.)
bapt. Lurgan, co. Armagh, 30 Sept. 1798, aged 3 yrs. Son of Joshua Des Voeux (who was younger son of Anthony Vinchon De Bacquencourt, who assumed the surname of Des Voeux, and the Viscountess de Seden) and Susannah his wife. Nephew of Sir Charles Des Voeux, 1st Bart. of Indiville, Queen's Co., formerly Govr. of Masulipatam, and 2nd in Council at Madras.
Services : Posted as Ensign to 2/22nd N.I. Nepal War 1814-5 ; Lieut. Champaran L.I., in 4th Div. Nepal War 1816 ; Lieut. Champaran L.I., in 1st Bde., Rt. Column (India medal). Served with Champaran L.I. till 1819. With escort to Resdt. at Gwalior 27 Mar. 1819 till 1828 ; comdd. do. from 12 May 1826. Transfd. to 44th N.I. (late 2/22nd) May 1824. Fur. p.a. 21 Dec. 1829 till 24 Nov. 1832. Offg. Bde. Major Malwa F.F. 21 Nov. 1835.
Refs. : Burke's *Peerage*, 1923, p. 709, *s.n.* Des Voeux, Bart., of Indiville.

DE TERRANEAU (various). (*See* **TERRANEAU**.)

DETHICK, Thomas Husky (1761/62-1781). Lieutenant, Infantry. *b.* London 1761/62. Cadet 1778. Ensign 1778. Lieut. 1778. *d.* 1781.
Services : Sailed for India on the *Calcutta*, 27 Apr. 1778, aged 16. N.F.P.

DEVENISH, Christopher (1757/58 ?-1783). Lieutenant, Infantry.
b. 1757/58 ? Cadet 1780. Ensign 2 Feb. 1781. Lieut. 1781.
d. Madras 1783.

(*Possibly* 2nd son of William Devenish, of Rush Hill, co. Roscommon, and Anne his wife, dau. of Francis Fetherston, of Whiterock, co. Longford.) (? T.C.D. Pensioner 1 Nov. 1774, aged 16.)

Services : (? Second Mysore War.)

Refs. : (? Burke's *Landed Gentry of Ireland*, p. 179, *s.n.* Devenish, of Mount Pleasant, co. Roscommon. *Alumni Dub.*)

DEVERELL, Robert (1810- ?). Ensign. 47th N.I. *bapt.* Winchester 8 Feb. 1810. Cadet 1827. Ensign (14 June 1828) 3 June 1829. Resigned in India 17 July 1829.

Son of Samuel Deverell, of Winchester, Hants, solicitor, and Lucy his wife, dau. of Thomas Lechmere.

Services : Ensign d.d. 49th N.I. 11 Feb. 1829. Posted as Ensign to 47th N.I. 3 June 1829.

Refs. : Burke's *Landed Gentry*, 13th edn., p. 493, *s.n.* Deverell, of Rossington, Hants.

DEW, William (1791-1824). Lieutenant, 12th N.I. *bapt.* St. Mary, Newington, Surrey, 27 May 1791. Cadet 1809. Arrived in India 3 Oct. 1810. Ensign 18 Oct. 1811. Lieut. 23 May 1815. *d.* 2 Apr. 1824.

Son of Edward Dew, of the Customs, London.

Services : Posted as Ensign to 1/12th N.I., and served throughout with that Bn. Fur. 10 Feb. 1815 till 1817. No record of active service.

Refs. : Will dated Jubbulpore 1 Sept. 1821 ; proved 7 Apr. 1824.

DE WAAL, John (Peter Lawrence) (1788-1820). Captain, 16th N.I.
b. Cape of Good Hope 5 Sept. 1788. Cadet 1803. Arrived in India 12 Dec. 1804. Ensign 1 Oct. 1804. Lieut. 1 Oct. 1804. Capt. 13 Aug. 1820. *d.* Benares 25 Sept. 1820.

3rd son of —— De Waal, Receiver at the Cape. Brother of Peter Henry De Waal, *q.v.*, and of Jacoba Helena, widow of Col. Henry Erskine, of Maitland, Edinburgh.

Services : Posted as Lieut. to 2/16th N.I. (? Capture of Gohad 1806 ; Lieut. 2/16th N.I. Operations in Bundelkhand 1809-11.) Capture of Java 1811 ; Lieut. 5th Bengal Vol. Bn. Served with Vols. in Java till 1816. Asst. Resdt. at Bantam in 1816. Served with 2nd Ceylon Vol. Bn. 1818-9.

Refs. : Will dated 15 July 1820 ; proved 30 Oct. 1820.

THE BENGAL ARMY, 1758-1834

DE WAAL, Peter Henry (Pieter Hendrick) (1789-1824). Captain, 60th N.I. *b.* Cape of Good Hope 9 Nov. 1789. Cadet 1804. Arrived in India 17 Apr. 1806. Ensign 16 Mar. 1806. Lieut. 2 Feb. 1807. Capt. 11 Sept. 1823. *d.* Charwa, C.P., 30 Oct. 1824.

4th son of —— De Waal, Receiver at the Cape. Brother of John De Waal, *q.v. m.* (before 1817) Jacoba Maria Johanna, 3rd and youngest dau. of Daniel Anthony Overbeek (Overbeck), the last Dutch Govr. of Chinsura, Bengal. (*See also* John Gordon (1787-1822).)

Services : Posted to 4th N.I. Transfd. to newly-raised 2/30th N.I. in 1815; to 60th N.I. (late 2/30th) May 1824. His death occurred whilst he was comdg. a detachment of his Regt. in pursuit of the freebooter Sheik Dallah, S. of the Narbada R.

Refs : Burke's *Colonial Gentry*, ii. 628, *s.n.* Overbeek. *S.M.* 1825, ii. 383. Will dated 19 Jan. 1818; proved 4 July 1825.

DE WAAL, William (1779-1820). Major, 25th N.I. *b.* Cape of Good Hope 8 May 1779. Cadet 1796. Arrived in India 20 Sept. 1797. Ensign 14 Oct. 1797. Lieut. 10 Sept. 1798. Capt. 15 Aug. 1809. Major 10 June 1818. *d.* Nasirabad, Rajputana, 31 Dec. 1820.

Formerly of Edinburgh, later of London. (*Probably* brother of John De Waal, *q.v.*) *m.* 1st, (?). *m.* 2nd, Calcutta, 13 Sept. 1806, Helena, widow of —— Vanheyden.

Services : Lieut. 4th N.I. Transfd. to newly-raised 22nd N.I. in 1803; to 25th N.I. in 1804. Capture of Gohad 1806; Lieut. 25th N.I. With 4th Gren. Bn. in 1816. Siege and capture of Hathras 1817; Capt. 1/25th N.I. Third Mahratta War; Major 1/25th N.I.

DEWAR, Alexander Cumming (1803-1880). Lieut. Colonel. 37th N.I. *b.* Borthwick, Edinburgh, 10 Nov. 1803. Cadet 1824. Arrived in India 9 Aug. 1825. Ensign 11 Apr. 1825. Lieut. 11 Nov. 1833. Capt. 24 Jan. 1845. Major 22 May 1856. Retired 20 Mar. 1857. Hon. Lt. Col. 20 Mar. 1857. *d.* 6 Maitland St., Edinburgh, 12 June 1880.

Of Vogrie, Midlothian, J.P. 4th and youngest son of James Dewar, of Vogrie, J.P. and D.L., and Caroline his wife, 2nd dau. of Sir John Cumming, K.C.B. *m.* Cheltenham, 7 Nov. 1855, Jane Eliza, 2nd dau. of Alexander Cumming, *q.v.* (She died 10 July 1876.)

Services : Posted as Ensign to 15th N.I. in 1826. Actg. Adjt. 15th N.I. 29 Apr. 1829. Fur. s.c. 1 Feb. 1831 till 10 Nov. 1834. Transfd. to 38th N.I. 2 July 1832. Adjt. 38th N.I. 8 May 1839 till 5 Jan. 1843. First Afghan War 1839-42; operations in Sind and

Afghanistan, including the operations of the Kandahar force under Gen. Nott (w.) ; Lieut. 38th N.I. (Medal). Transfd. to 37th N.I. 14 Dec. 1842. Actg. Adjt. 37th N.I. 25 Mar. 1843 ; permanent do. 9 Dec. 1843 till 14 Feb. 1844. Apptd. 2nd in comd. 1st Cav., Gwalior Contingent, 17 Feb. 1844 ; comdd. do. 23 June 1846 till 31 Aug. 1854. Fur. p.a. 12 Sept. 1854 till retirement.

Refs. : Burke's *Landed Gentry*, 13th edn., p. 493, *s.n.* Dewar, of Vogrie, Midlothian. *The Times*, 15 June 1880.

DEWAR, James (*d.* 1824). Lieut. Colonel Comdt., C.B., 23rd N.I. Country Cadet 1781. Arrived in India 15 Oct. 1781. Ensign 17 July 1782. Lieut. 14 Jan. 1785. Capt. 13 July 1803. Major 17 Oct. 1805. Lt. Col. 3 Aug. 1811. Lt. Col. Comdt. 5 Mar. 1823. *d.* at sea, 31 Jan. 1824, on board the *Reliance* : bur. at Cape Town 8 Feb. 1824.

Half-brother of Lieut. James George Thompson, R.N., of Lieut. Thomas Thompson, R.N., and of Elizabeth Margaret Wigmore.

Services : Fur. s.c. to sea 31 Aug. 1785. Lieut. 3rd Bengal Eur. Bn. in July 1787. Capt. Lt. 1/8th N.I. 8 Jan. 1801. Transfd. as Capt. to 20th (Marine) N.I. Served in P.W.I. 1804-6. Transfd. as Lt. Col. to 13th N.I. in 1811. Capture of Java 1811 ; Lt. Col. comdg. 3rd Vol. Bn. Transfd. to 1/25th N.I. in 1815 ; to 24th N.I. in 1816 ; to 13th N.I. in 1818 ; to 1/18th N.I. in 1820. Fur. 1822 till death. C.B. 23 July 1823.

Refs. : *A.J.* xvii. 684. Will dated 18 Jan. 1822 ; proved 12 May 1824.

DIBDIN, Francis (1799-1826). Lieutenant, 3rd L.C. *b.* London 7 Aug. 1799. Cadet 1818. Cornet 16 Aug. 1819. Lieut. 8 May 1821. *d.* Muttra 15 Oct. 1826.

Son of Rev. Thomas Frognall Dibdin, rector of St. Mary's, Marylebone, and vicar of Exning, Suffolk.

Services : Cornet d.d. 8th L.C. Posted as Cornet to 3rd L.C. in 1820. Lieut. d.d. G.G.B.G. 18 Jan. till 20 July 1822. Adjt. 3rd L.C. 17 June 1824 till June 1825. Siege and capture of Bhurtpore ; Lieut. 3rd L.C.

Refs. : *V.B.G. G.M.* 1827, i. 286.

DICK, Alexander (1789-1875). General. 71st N.I. *b.* Logierait, co. Perth, 3 Apr. 1789. Cadet 1803. Arrived in India 3 Dec. 1804. Ensign 5 Oct. 1804. Lieut. 5 Oct. 1804. Capt. 1 Jan. 1819. Major 22 Apr. 1826. Lt. Col. 4 May 1831. Col. 8 Feb. 1843. Maj. Gen. 20 June 1854. Lt. Gen. 4 July 1856. Gen. 3 May 1866. *d.* Dehra Dun, U.P., 25 Nov. 1875.

Son of Robert Dick, of Tullymet, co. Perth. Brother of Robert

THE BENGAL ARMY, 1758-1834   55

Dick, q.v. m. Sydney, N.S.W., 5 June 1824, Louisa, 2nd dau. of Simon Lord, of Sydney.
Services : Second Mahratta War 1805 ; Lieut. 2/17th N.I. Capture of Java 1811 ; Cornelis ; Lieut. 5th Vol. Bn. (Medal). Capt. 2/17th N.I. Leave s.c. to N.S.W. 22 Jan. 1823 till 15 Feb. 1826. Transfd. to 31st N.I. 11 July 1823; to 62nd N.I. (late 2/31st) May 1824. Posted as Lt. Col. to 52nd N.I. Transfd. to 71st N.I. 16 Jan. 1834. Bdr., 2 cl., comdg. at Agra, 5 Dec. 1845 till 1850.
Refs. : Boase. S.M. 1825, i. 254.

DICK, Andrew Edward (1813-1837). Lieutenant, Bengal Eur. Regt. *bapt.* Haslemere, Surrey, 26 June 1813. Cadet 1831. Arrived in India 26 Oct. 1832. Ensign 19 May 1832. Lieut. 25 Feb. 1837. *d.* Agra, 18 Dec. 1837, of smallpox.

Son of John Dick, of Saling Hall, nr. Braintree, Essex, Vice Adm. R.N. (who was cousin of Sir Robert Keith Dick-Cunyngham, 7th Bart.), and Augusta his wife, dau. of Bartlet Goodrich, of Saling Grove, Essex. Addiscombe Cadet 5 Feb. 1830 till 8 Dec. 1831.
Services : Cadet d.d. 6th N.I. 21 Nov. 1832 ; do. 64th N.I. 28 Feb. 1833. Supy. Ensign d.d. 6th N.I. 3 Oct. 1833. Posted to Rt. Wing Bengal Eur. Regt. 19 Dec. 1833. Posted to Revenue Survey, N.W.P., Dec. 1833.
Refs. : A.J. N.S. xxv. 257.

DICK, George (1764/65-1844). Lieut. General. Colonel 72nd N.I. *b.* 1764/65. Cadet 1779. Admitted 12 Feb. 1780. Ensign 4 Aug. 1779. Lieut. 27 Mar. 1781. Capt. 30 Oct. 1797. Major 5 Mar. 1804. Lt. Col. 22 Nov. 1807. Col. 4 June 1814. Maj. Gen. 19 July 1821. Lt. Gen. 10 Jan. 1837. *d.* 4 Catherine Pl., Bath, 13 Mar. 1844, aged 79.

A native of Essex. (*Probably* uncle of Henry Thomas Coggan Kerr, q.v.) *m.* (before 1793) ? His daus. *m.* John Thomas, q.v., and James Sissmore, q.v.
Services : Sailed for India on the *Walpole* 16 June 1779. Formerly a Writer on the Bombay Est. (*Cal. Gaz.* 29 Apr. 1784.) Lieut. 27th Bn. Sepoys in July 1787. On service in Sylhet in 1790. Expedn. to Assam 1792-4. Apptd. Adjt. 12th Bn. Sepoys 1794. Second Rohilla War ; Bitaurah ; Adjt. 12th Bn. Apptd. Adjt. and Qmr. 4th N.I. in 1796. Fur. s.c. 29 Dec. 1799 till 5 Feb. 1802. Operations in Ceylon 1803-4 ; Major comdg. Vol. Bn. In P.W.I. till Dec. 1805. To comd. at Chittagong Oct. 1812. Bdr. 15 Nov. 1814. Nepal War 1814-5 ; Bdr. comdg. 2nd Inf. Bde., 4th Div. Nepal War 1816 ; Lt. Col. 2/9th N.I., 2nd in comd. to Sir David Ochterlony. Third Mahratta War ; Bdr. comdg. 2nd Bde., Centre Div. Bdr. comdg. in Bundelkhand in 1818. Fur. p.a. 14 Dec.

1819 till 10 Oct. 1824. Apptd. to Gen. Staff, Presdy., 19 Nov. 1824; to Benares Div. 20 Nov. 1824; to Dinapore Div. 6 Jan. 1825; to Benares Div. 9 Feb. 1828. Transfd. as Col. from 43rd to 16th N.I. 22 Apr. 1828; to 72nd N.I. in 1828. Tour on Staff expired 7 Nov. 1828. Fur. p.a. 15 Jan. 1829 till death.
Refs. : E.I.M.C. i. 108-9. *G.M.* 1844, i. 556. *The Times*, 18 Mar. 1844.

DICK, Hope (1791-1885). General. 64th N.I. *b.* Logierait, co. Perth, 14 Sept. 1791. Cadet 1807. Arrived in India 14 Sept. 1808. Ensign 28 Sept. 1808. Lieut. 18 Oct. 1812. Capt. 1 May 1824. Major 13 Feb. 1839. Lt. Col. 4 Mar. 1845. Col. 16 Jan. 1855. Maj. Gen. 2 Apr. 1856. Lt. Gen. 10 Nov. 1868. Gen. 28 Apr. 1875. *d.* at his residence in Cheltenham 24 May 1885.

bapt. 20 Sept. 1791. Son of Robert Dick, of Tullymet, co. Perth. Brother of Robert Dick, *q.v.*, and half-brother of Peter Dick, *q.v.*
m. Kinloch, 2 June 1828, Ann Livingston, 3rd dau. of John Campbell, of Kinloch, co. Perth, and sister of Charles Campbell, *q.v.* (She died 1 Nov. 1886.)

Services : Barasat C.C. for 6½ mos. Posted as Ensign to 23rd N.I. Operations in Rewah 1813; Lieut. 2/23rd N.I. Adjt. 7th Gren. Bn. 1815. Transfd. to newly-raised 28th N.I. in 1815. Adjt. 2/28th N.I. 4 May 1815 till 17 June 1824. Third Mahratta War; Dhamoni; Mandala. Transfd. to 56th N.I. (late 2/28th) May 1824. Fur. s.c. 10 Jan. 1825 till 22 Oct. 1828. Comdg. 56th N.I. from 25 June 1840. Gwalior campaign; Maharajpur; Major comdg. 56th N.I. (Bronze star). Posted as Lt. Col. to 48th N.I. June 1845; to 56th N.I. Aug. 1845; to 54th N.I. 17 Sept. 1849; to 42nd N.I. 27 Feb. 1851. Fur. s.c. 10 Apr. 1851 till 6 Jan. 1854. Transfd. to 72nd N.I. Jan. 1853; to 10th N.I. Jan. 1854; to 68th N.I. Nov. 1854. Fur. p.a. 28 Feb. 1854 till death. Posted as Col. to 1st N.I. Apr. 1855; to 4th Bengal Eur. Inf. 1858; to 64th N.I.

Refs. : The Campbells of Kinloch, by E. Dalhousie Login, 1924, chart ii. *A.J.* xxvi. 134. *The Times*, 29 May 1885.

DICK, Peter (1808-1835). Lieutenant. 47th N.I. *b.* Logierait, co. Perth, 5 June 1808. Cadet 1826. Arrived in India 6 Nov. 1827. Ensign 14 June 1827. Lieut. 6 June 1833. Discharged by G.C.M. 10 Feb. 1835. *d.* Calcutta 10 June 1835.

bapt. 17 June 1808. Son of Robert Dick, of Tullymet, co. Perth, and Elizabeth his 2nd wife. Half-brother of Alexander Dick, *q.v.*

Services : Posted as Ensign to 62nd N.I. 22 Jan. 1828. Transfd. to 69th N.I. 20 Feb. 1828; to 47th N.I. 1828. Fur. s.c. 2 Sept. 1831 till 15 Dec. 1834. No record of active service.

Refs. : A.J. N.S. xviii. 255.

THE BENGAL ARMY, 1758-1834   57

DICK, Robert (d. 1770). Cadet, Infantry. Cadet 1769. d. Berhampore 19 Aug. 1770.
Services: N.F.P.

DICK, Robert (1780-1800). Lieutenant, Infantry. b. Logierait, co. Perth, 4 Dec. 1780. Cadet 1794. Arrived in India 2 Feb. 1797. Ensign 21 Nov. 1795. Lieut. 30 Oct. 1797. d. Dinapore 6 Nov. 1800.
bapt. 8 Dec. 1780. Son of Robert Dick, of Tullymet, co. Perth (of Ballekilleure), and Isobel Kennedy his 1st wife. Brother of Alexander Dick, *q.v.*, and half-brother of Peter Dick, *q.v.*
Services: N.F.P.

DICK, Sir William, second baronet (1765-1840). Captain. 14th N.I. b. 8 Dec. 1765. Cadet 1781. Arrived in India 24 May 1781. Ensign 25 Sept. 1781. Lieut. 29 June 1783. Capt. 17 May 1802. Invalided 5 June 1806. Retired 28 Nov. 1815. d. 17 Dec. 1840.
Of Hampton Hill House, Bath. Second Baronet of Braid, N.B. (cr. 1646). Served heir male of his ancestor, Sir William Dick, of Braid, 15 Jan. 1821. Eldest son of Charles Dick of Frackafield, and Martha Montgomerie his wife. Cousin-german of John Petrie Keble, *q.v. m.* St. Paul's, Covent Gdn., London, 26 Apr. 1821, Caroline, dau. of John Kingston, of Rickmansworth, Herts., and widow of Lt. Col. Alexander Fraser, H.M. 76th Regt.
Services: Lieut. 13th Bn. Sepoys in July 1787. Lieut. 14th N.I. Capt. Lt. 14th N.I. 19 May 1801. Returned from fur. 14 Oct. 1801. Second Mahratta War; reduction of Cuttack 1803; Capt. 14th N.I., comdg. a Vol. Bn. of 500 Sepoys. Comdd. 1st Bn. Native Invalids 1806 till retirement.
Refs.: Burke's *Peerage*, 1832, p. 361, *s.n.* Dick, Bart., of Braid, N.B. *Herald and Genealogist*, viii. 268. Will dated 18 June 1833; proved 16 Aug. 1843.

DICKENS, John (1757/58-1810). Lieutenant. Infantry. Subsequently advocate in the supreme court, Calcutta. b. 1757/58. Cadet 1781. Ensign Apr. 1781. Lieut. 27 July 1782. Resigned 23 Feb. 1794. d. Calcutta 22 Sept. 1810, " aged about 50 yrs."
A native of Cambridgeshire.
Services: Apptd. Cadet on 18 Jan. 1781, aged 23. Sailed for India on the *Southampton*, 13 Mar. 1781, aged 23. Lieut. 11th Bn. Sepoys in July 1787.
Refs.: M.I. in N. Park St. cemetery, Calcutta.

DICKEY, Edward John (1804-1883). Major General. 27th N.I. b. Randalstown, co. Antrim, 29 July 1804. Cadet 1822. Ensign 11 July 1823. Lieut. 17 Aug. 1824. Capt. 16 June 1835. Major

27 Oct. 1848. Lt. Col. 15 Apr. 1854. Col. 28 Nov. 1854. Retired 31 Dec. 1861. Hon. Maj. Gen. 31 Dec. 1861. *d.* Parklands, Guildford, Surrey, 19 Sept. 1883.

Son of James Dickey, of Randalstown.

Services : Posted as Lieut. to 16th N.I. May 1824. Transfd. to 14th N.I. Sept. 1824. To comd. escort with P.A. at Bhurtpore 12 Jan. 1827. Adjt. Bareilly Provl. Bn. 27 Aug. 1828 till 1832. Apptd. Sub-Asst. in Stud Dept. 29 June 1835, and remained in that Dept. till retirement. Supt. of Studs 9 May 1853. Posted as Lt. Col. to 57th N.I. 8 May 1854 ; transfd. to 27th N.I. 7 Jan. 1858. No record of active service.

Refs. : Boase. *The Times*, 25 Sept. 1883.

*DICKINSON, John (1725/26- ?). Fireworker. Artillery. *b.* 1725/26. Cadet 1764. (*Probably* transfd. from Bencoolen Est.) Fireworker 10 Oct. 1764.

A native of Yorkshire.

Services : Sailed for Bencoolen as Capt. of Art. on the *Valentine*, 24 June 1762, aged 36. Out of the Service before 1 Feb. 1767.

Refs. : *Stubbs's List*.

DICKINSON, John (1759/60-1779). Lieutenant, Infantry. *b.* London 1759/60. Cadet 1778. Ensign 1778. Lieut. 31 Oct. 1778. *d.* Calcutta Dec. 1779.

Services : Sailed for India on the *Mount Stewart*, 9 Feb. 1778, aged 18. Lieut. 2/3rd Bengal Eur. Regt. in Oct. 1779.

DICKINSON, Samuel (1763/64-1784). Ensign, 3rd Regt., 3rd Bde. *b.* London 1763/64. Cadet 1782. Ensign 26 Jan. 1783. *d.* Chitarpur 5 June 1784 : bur. Cawnpore 6 June 1784.

Services : Sailed for India on the *Earl Talbot* 6 Feb. 1782, aged 18. N.F.P.

DICKINSON, Thomas (1789-1859). Major General. Colonel 10th N.I. *b.* Harrietfield, co. Perth, 22 June 1789. Cadet 1805. Arrived in India 7 Feb. 1807. Ensign 7 Jan. 1807. Lieut. 15 June 1808. Capt. 1 May 1824. Major 11 July 1836. Lt. Col. 3 Oct. 1842. Col. 10 May 1853. Maj. Gen. 28 Nov. 1854. *d.* Tynemouth, Northumberland, 24 Oct. 1859.

Son of George Dickinson, tenant in Harrietfield, and Rebecca his wife. Brother of John Dickinson, of Sunderland, merchant, and nephew of William Ogle Carr, of Stoke, Devon. *m.* 1st, Berhampore, 14 July 1815, Miss Louisa Palmer. (She died Arakan, 25 Oct. 1836, aged 38.) *m.* 2nd, Catherine. (She died Brighton, 3 Dec. 1855, aged 66.)

THE BENGAL ARMY, 1758-1834 59

Services : Barasat C.C. for 7½ mos. Posted as Ensign to 9th N.I. Operations against the Maghs 1814. Transfd. to newly-raised 2/28th N.I. 1815. Adjt. Dacca Provl. Bn. 11 Jan. 1816 till 21 May 1824. Transfd. to 55th N.I. (late 1/28th) May 1824. To comd. Magh Levy 25 June 1824. First Burma War; Arakan 1825; comdg. Magh Levy. Leave s.c. to Cape 20 Feb. 1826 till Dec. 1827. Asst. to Comr. in Arakan 1 Jan. 1828. Local Supt. in Arakan 14 Oct. 1830. Offg. Comr. in Arakan 8 Sept. 1834; permanent do. 7 Mar. 1835 till 20 May 1837. Leave s.c. 2 yrs. to Cape 21 Jan. 1838. Fur. p.a. 5 Feb. 1840 till 10 Sept. 1842. Transfd. to 10th N.I. 15 Nov. 1843; to 55th N.I. 10 Dec. 1844. (? First Sikh War.) Transfd. to 10th N.I. Aug. 1852. Bdr. comdg. 2nd Bengal Bde., Burma Force, 24 Aug. 1852. Second Burma War; Pegu; Bdr. comdg. at Rangoon and comdg. Bengal Bde. Sept. 1853 (Medal). Posted as Col. to 10th N.I. July 1853. Fur. p.a. 17 Mar. 1856 till death.

Refs. : Boase. I.M. 31 Oct. 1859, p. 889. Will dated 28 Apr. 1842 ; admon. 15 June 1860.

DICKSON, Archibald (1788-1846). Major. 60th N.I. *b.* Minto, co. Roxburgh, 23 Oct. 1788. Cadet 1806. Arrived in India 17 Mar. 1808. Ensign 26 Mar. 1808. Lieut. 6 Aug. 1813. Capt. 30 Oct. 1824. Major 7 Jan. 1836. Retired 1 Dec. 1836. *d.* 8 May 1846.

Son of Archibald Dickson. *m.* Dinapore, 22 Oct. 1815, Catherine Jane, dau. of William Bedell, *q.v.* (*See also* Charles Henry Phelips, and Henry Sibley.)

Services : Barasat C.C. for 7½ mos. Ensign d.d. 26th and 16th N.I. Posted as Ensign to 8th N.I. in 1811. Nepal War 1814-5 ; Lieut. 1/8th N.I., in 4th Div. Transfd. to newly-raised 2/30th N.I. in 1815. Actg. Adjt. 2/30th N.I. in 1818. With Gorakhpur L.I. Bn. 1819-24. Actg. Adjt. do. 4 Aug. 1820. Adjt. Dacca Provl. Bn. 11 May 1824. Transfd. to 60th N.I. (late 2/30th) May 1824. To Gorakhpur L.I. Bn. 7 Feb. 1825 ; Actg. Adjt. do. 31 Oct. 1825. Siege and capture of Bhurtpore ; Capt. 60th N.I. Fur. p.a. 24 Mar. 1829 till 29 Nov. 1831.

Refs. : S.M. 1816.

DICKSON, Augustus Keppel (*d.* 1789). Captain, Infantry. Cadet 1768. Ensign 15 Feb. 1769. Lieut. 13 June 1770. Capt. 23 Aug. 1779. *d.* Cawnpore 2 Aug. 1789.

Services : Sometime A.D.C. to Col. Thomas Deane Pearse, *q.v.* 34th Bn. Sepoys in July 1787.

Refs. : Hickey, iii. 350. *G.M.* 1789, ii. 1147.

LIST OF THE OFFICERS OF

DICKSON, Sir Colpoys, fourth baronet (1807-1868). Lieut. Colonel. 51st N.I. *b.* Titchfield, Hants, 21 Aug. 1807. Cadet 1823. Arrived in India 16 June 1824. Ensign 25 Feb. 1824. Lieut. 13 May 1825. Capt. 7 May 1844. Bt. Major 11 Nov. 1851. Retired 5 Jan. 1852. Hon. Lt. Col. 28 Nov. 1854. *d.* Folkestone 21 May 1868.

Fourth Baronet, of Hardingham, Norfolk. *s.* 5 Jan. 1868. 4th son of Sir Archibald Collingwood Dickson, 2nd Bart., Rear Adm. of the Red, and Harriet his wife, dau. of Adm. John Bourmaster. Nephew of Rowland Cotton Dickson, *q.v.*, and cousin-german of William Dickson (1805-1827), *q.v.* His sister *m.* Claud Douglas, *q.v. m.* 1831, Emma, dau. of William Knyvett. (*See* William John Baptist Knyvett.) Addiscombe Cadet 1821.

Services : Posted as Ensign to 51st N.I. Fur. s.c. 11 Apr. 1827 till 21 Sept. 1829. Adjt. 51st N.I. 7 Jan. 1832 till 17 Nov. 1843. Shekhawat expdn. 1834. Bde. Major at Barrackpore in 1841. Actg. A.A.G., Benares Div., 4 Apr. 1842. Apptd. Bde. Major 1st Inf. Bde., Army of Exercise, 17 Nov. 1843. Gwalior campaign ; Paniar ; Bde. Major (Bronze star). Apptd. 2nd in comd. 6th Inf., Gwalior Contingent, 29 Feb. 1844. Bde. Major, Gwalior Contingent, 31 Mar. 1845 till retirement.

Refs. : Burke's *Peerage*, 1923, p. 1238, *s.n.* Islington, B. *Boase. I.L.N.* 13 June 1868, p. 594. *The Times*, 25 May 1868.

DICKSON, Francis (1782-1821). Captain, 26th N.I. *bapt.* Chelsea 15 Aug. 1782. Cadet 1798. Arrived in India 20 Sept. 1799. Ensign 10 Oct. 1799. Lieut. 28 Oct. 1799. Capt. 1 Jan. 1811. *d.* Calcutta, 11 May 1821, of cholera, within 12 hours of being attacked.

2nd son of Thomas Dickson, of Southampton, and Frances his wife. Brother of Henry David Erskine Dickson, *q.v.*

Services : Lieut. 14th N.I. (? Second Mahratta War ; Lieut. 14th N.I.) Transfd. to newly-raised 26th N.I. in 1805. Adjt. 1/26th N.I. 5 Aug. 1805 till 10 Jan. 1810. Operations in Bundelkhand 1807 ; Sehlehuganj ; Lieut. 1/26th N.I. Capt. Lt. 26th N.I. 29 Nov. 1809. Nepal War 1814-5. Suptg. construction of bldgs. at Patna in 1815. Fur. 31 Dec. 1816 till 1818. Third Mahratta War ; Capt. 1/26th N.I. A.D.C. to G.G. 1819 till death.

Refs. : A.J. xxvii. 220. M.I. in S. Park St. cemetery, Calcutta.

DICKSON, Henry David Erskine (1785-1804). Lieutenant, 4th N.I. *b.* Southampton 21 Mar. 1785. Cadet 1799. Arrived in India 13 Jan. 1801. Ensign 25 Oct. 1800. Lieut. 20 Dec. 1801. *d. unm.* 16 Dec. 1804 : kld. in action in the trenches before Deig.

bapt. Holy Rhood, Southampton, 21 June 1785. Son of Thomas

Dickson, of Southampton, and Frances his wife. Brother of William Dickson (1781-1828), *q.v.*
Services : Second Mahratta War ; storm of Aligarh ; siege of Deig (kld.) ; Lieut. 1/4th N.I.
Refs. : Pester, pp. 357-8. *A.J.* xxvii. 220. Will dated camp nr. Secundra 19 Sept. 1804 ; proved 15 Apr. 1805.

DICKSON, James (1744/45-1829). Lieut. General. Colonel 6th N.I. *b.* 1744/45. Country Cadet 1768. Admitted 29 Jan. 1768. Ensign 7 May 1768. Lieut. 23 Dec. 1769. Capt. 29 Mar. 1778. Major 25 Jan. 1784. Lt. Col. 1 Mar. 1794. Col. 1 Jan. 1798. Maj. Gen. 1 Jan. 1805. Lt. Gen. 4 June 1813. *d.* at his residence, Marlbro' Bldgs., Bath, 29 Jan. 1829, aged 84.
m. Edinburgh, 8 Sept. 1787, Rachael, dau. of Henry Lindesay, of Kilconquhar, co. Fife (who assumed the surname of Bethune), and half-sister of David Bethune Lindesay, *q.v.* (She died Bath 1 Jan. 1829.)
Services : Operations against the Bhutias in Cooch Behar 1772-3 ; storm and capture of Cooch Behar (w. in chest and knee) ; Lieut. 6th Bn. Sepoys. Fur. 19 Apr. 1775 till 18 Dec. 1777. First Mahratta War ; Capt. comdg. 1st Bn. Sepoys. Fur. 29 Nov. 1784 till 23 July 1788. 6th Bde. N.I., comdg. Eur. Invalids at Chunar in 1790. Lt. Col. comdg. 2/3rd N.I. Col. 12th N.I. 21 Apr. 1800. A detachment under his comd. of troops from the garrison of Fort William took possession of the Danish settlement of Serampore, without opposition, on 8 May 1801. Fur. 7 Mar. 1802 till death. Transfd. as Col. to 5th N.I. ; to 1st N.I. in 1806. Col. 6th N.I. 1813-9.
Refs. : Burke's *Peerage*, 1923, p. 1403, *s.n.* Lindsay, E. *Williams*, p. 76. *Hickey*, ii. 103. *S.M.* 1787, p. 466. *G.M.* 1829, i. 873. *A.J.* xxvii. 381.

DICKSON, John. Ensign. Infantry. Cadet 1764. Ensign 10 Oct. 1764.
Services : Out of the Service before 1 Feb. 1767. N.F.P.
Note : Possibly identical with John Dixon, *q.v.*

DICKSON, Richard Lothian (1776-1841). Lieutenant. 2nd N.C. Subsequently Major 1st Life Gds. *b.* Nether Lockerwoods 6 Dec. 1776. Cadet 1800. Arrived in India 7 Feb. 1802. Cornet 1 Jan. 1802. Lieut. 3 Apr. 1808. Struck off 22 Oct. 1810. *d.* Bordeaux, France, 20 Mar. 1841.
bapt. Ruthwell, co. Dumfries, 7 Dec. 1776. Youngest son of David Dickson, of Nether Lockerwoods, and Mary Richardson his wife. *m.* Elizabeth. (She died Calcutta, 20 Feb. 1802, aged 20.)
Services : Posted as Cornet to 2nd N.C. Fur. 10 Aug. 1802 till

13 Dec. 1806, and 1810 till struck off in 1812 with effect from 22 Oct. 1810. Entered H.M.S. Capt. 1st Life Gds. 23 Sept. 1812. Capt., h.p., 2nd Dgns. 1815. Major 19 Dec. 1826 ; h.p. 19 Dec. 1826.
Refs. : *G.M.* 1841, ii. 110.

DICKSON, Robert Lowry (1789-1848). Lieut. Colonel. 15th N.I. *b.* Rossinver, co. Leitrim, 3 Nov. 1789. Cadet 1804. Arrived in India 10 July 1805. Ensign 31 Aug. 1805. Lieut. 1 Sept. 1805. Capt. 1 Jan. 1819. Major 20 Dec. 1826. Lt. Col. 1 Oct. 1832. Retired 4 Feb. 1833. *d.* 12 Apr. 1848.

4th son of Thomas Dickson, of Woodville, co. Leitrim, M.P. for Ballyshannon, and Hester his wife, dau. of Rev. James Lowry. *m.* 1st, 1815, (?). (She died in India Mar. 1822.) *m.* 2nd, Kinlough, co. Leitrim, Sept. 1833, Alicia Elizabeth, dau. of Rev. Daniel E. Lucas, rector of Castle Blackney, co. Galway.

Services : Posted as Lieut. to 11th N.I. Reduction of Kalinjar 1812 ; Lieut. 2/11th N.I. Siege and capture of Hathras 1817 ; Lieut. 2/11th N.I. Third Mahratta War ; Lieut. 2/11th N.I. Fur. p.a. 27 Nov. 1818 till 10 Dec. 1821. Transfd. to 17th N.I. (late 2/11th) May 1824 ; to 15th N.I. (late 1/11th) 1826. Apptd. to charge of 5th N.I. 7 Feb. 1828 ; do. 3rd N.I. 10 July 1828. Fur. p.a. 28 Jan. 1832 till retirement.

Refs. : Burke's *Landed Gentry of Ireland*, p. 182, *s.n.* Dickson, of Woodville, co. Leitrim. *A.J. N.S.* xii. 139.

DICKSON, Rowland Cotton (1793-1832). Captain, Artillery. *b.* Kelso, co. Roxburgh, 30 Aug. 1793. Cadet 1809. Admitted 21 Dec. 1810. Fireworker 11 Nov. 1810. Lieut. 25 Sept. 1817. Capt. 25 Mar. 1826. *d.* Calcutta 2 Sept. 1832.

5th son of William Dickson, late of Sydenham, Kelso, Adm. of the Blue, and Elizabeth his 2nd wife, dau. of James Charteris. Uncle of Sir Colpoys Dickson, Bart., *q.v.*, and of William Dickson (1805-1827), *q.v.* *m.* Lucknow, 6 Nov. 1822, Miss Emily Mary Queiros (*probably* sister of Joseph Queiros, *q.v.*). Woolwich Cadet ; nominated to R.M.A. 2 Sept. 1807.

Services : Nepal War 1814-5 ; Lieut. F. 7th Coy. 1st Bn. Foot Art. Nepal War 1816 ; with Capt. Barré Latter's force. Siege and capture of Hathras 1817 ; Lieut. F. 6th Coy. 3rd Bn. Third Mahratta War ; Mandala ; Lieut. 6th Coy. 3rd Bn., afterwards 2nd Coy. 2nd Bn. Siege and capture of Bhurtpore ; Lieut. comdg. 3rd Coy. 2nd Bn.

Refs. : Burke's *Peerage*, 1923, p. 1237, *s.n.* Islington, B.

DICKSON, William (1778-1805). Lieutenant. Infantry. *b.* Downpatrick, co. Down, 12 Jan. 1778. Cadet 1794. Arrived in India 27 Mar. 1797. Ensign 11 Oct. 1795. Lieut. 16 Dec. 1796.

THE BENGAL ARMY, 1758-1834

Resigned 2 Feb. 1802. *d.* 5 June 1805 : bur. at Hillsborough, co. Down.

3rd son of Ven. John Dickson, archdeacon of Down, and Anne his 2nd wife, elder dau. of William Moore, of Moore Hall, Killinchy, co. Down.
Services : N.F.P.
Refs. : M.I. at Hillsborough.

DICKSON, William (1781-1828). Lieut. Colonel, 7th L.C. *bapt.* St. Luke's, Chelsea, 14 Oct. 1781. Cadet 1799. Arrived in India 13 Jan. 1801. Cornet 12 Apr. 1801. Lieut. 11 Mar. 1805. Capt. Lt. 12 Apr. 1817. Major 13 Dec. 1818. Lt. Col. 13 May 1825. *d.* Karnal, 24 July 1828, of a violent fever, due to disease of the liver.

Eldest son of Thomas Dickson, of Southampton, and Frances his wife. Brother of Francis Dickson, *q.v. m.* May 1807, Elizabeth Marianne.

Services : Transfd. from Inf. to Cav. Apr. 1801. Posted as Cornet to 6th N.C. 7 May 1801. Operations in Jumna Doab 1802-3 ; Sasni ; Bijaigarh ; Kachaura (s.w. in thigh 8 Mar. 1803 ; the ball was never extracted) ; Thathia ; Cornet 6th N.C. Second Mahratta War ; Agra ; Laswari (w.) ; relief of Delhi ; pursuit of Holkar ; siege of Bhurtpore ; Cornet 6th N.C. Fur. s.c. 27 June 1805 till 4 Nov. 1808. Asst. to Supt. of Pusa Stud Feb. 1809 till July 1811 ; Sub-Asst. at Pusa 19 Jan. 1816 till Nov. 1819. Leave s.c. to Cape Nov. 1819 till May 1822. Suspended in Sept. 1824. Fur. Dec. 1824 till Oct. 1826. Posted as Lt. Col. to 7th L.C. in May 1825. Restored to the Service without prejudice to his rank in Dec. 1825. Transfd. to 10th L.C. 4 Nov. 1826 ; retransfd. to 7th L.C. in June 1827.

Refs. : De Rhé-Philipe. A.J. xxvii. 220. *G.M.* 1829, i. 373. Will dated 27 Oct. 1824 ; codicils dated 30 Nov. 1826 and 8 July 1828 ; proved 31 Oct. 1828. M.I. in old cemetery at Karnal.

DICKSON, William (1805-1827). Lieutenant, Engineers. *b.* Portsea 24 Jan. 1805. Cadet 1822. Ensign (?). Lieut. 1 May 1824. *d. unm.* Chittagong, 31 Aug. 1827, of jungle fever.

Eldest son of Sir Alexander Dickson, G.C.B., Maj. Gen. R.A. (*D.N.B.*), and Eulalia his wife, dau. of Don Stephen Briones, of Minorca. Nephew of Rowland Cotton Dickson, *q.v.*, and cousingerman of Sir Colpoys Dickson, Bart., *q.v.* Addiscombe Cadet 1820.

Services : After leaving Addiscombe he was detained for some months in England on a trigonometrical survey. Asst. to Supt. of construction of church in Fort William in 1824. First Burma War ; Lieut., Field Engr. On survey duty in S.E. Div. 1826 till death.

Refs. : Burke's *Peerage*, 1905, p. 1312, *s.n.* Dickson-Poynder, Bart. (now Islington, B.), of Hardingham, Norfolk. *G.M.* 1828, i. 478. Will dated Chittagong 26 Aug. 1827 ; proved 15 Oct. 1827. M.I. at Chittagong.

DINGWALL, Arthur Fordyce (1789-1830). Captain, 19th N.I. *bapt.* Forgue, co. Aberdeen, 26 Aug. 1789. Cadet 1806. Arrived in India 25 Nov. 1807. Ensign 3 Nov. 1807. Lieut. 14 Feb. 1812. Capt. 1 May 1824. *d.* Muttra 16 Dec. 1830.
Son of Rev. William Dingwall, minister at Forgue. Christened Arthur after (*probably* nephew of) Arthur Dingwall-Fordyce, of Culsh, advocate in Aberdeen. (*See* Arthur Dingwall-Fordyce.)
Services : Barasat C.C. for 8 mos. Posted as Ensign to 3rd N.I. Intr. & Qmr. 1/3rd N.I. 7 May 1816 till 17 June 1824. Actg. Adjt. 1/3rd N.I. 26 Dec. 1821. Transfd. to 6th N.I. (late 1/3rd) May 1824. Actg. Adjt. 6th N.I. 16 Oct. till 23 Dec. 1824. Transfd. to 19th N.I. 23 Dec. 1824. Fur. s.c. 2 yrs. to Cape 15 Feb. 1827. To comd. a detachment of young officers 19 Sept. 1829. Leave s.c. 6 mos. on the river 4 Nov. 1830.
Refs. : Will dated Muttra 15 Dec. 1830 ; proved 1 Mar. 1831.

DINWOODY, James (*d.* 1776). Ensign, Infantry. Cadet 1771. Ensign 18 Feb. 1773. *d.* in India 3 Feb. 1776.
Services : N.F.P.
Refs. : Will dated 2 Mar. 1775 ; proved 1 Mar. 1776.

DIXON, Charles George (1795-1857). Bt. Colonel, Artillery. *b.* London 30 June 1795. Cadet 1812. Admitted 21 Aug. 1813. Fireworker 14 Aug. 1813. Lieut. 1 Aug. 1818. Capt. 3 Feb. 1830. Major 1 Mar. 1844. Lt. Col. 3 July 1847. Bt. Col. 28 Nov. 1854. *d. unm.* Beawar, Ajmer, 25 June 1857.
bapt. St. Martin-in-the-Fields, Middlesex, 24 July 1795. Son of George Dixon and Sarah his wife, sister of Thomas Hardwicke, *q.v.* Brother of William Hardwick Dixon, *q.v.*, and of Mary, wife of William Sampson Whish, *q.v.* Addiscombe Cadet 1811-2.
Services : Nepal War 1814-5 ; Lieut. F. 5th Coy. 3rd Bn. Foot Art., in 2nd Div. (India medal). Siege and capture of Hathras ; Adjt. Agra Div. Art. Third Mahratta War ; Lieut. 5th Coy. 3rd Bn., Bde. Qmr. in Rt. Div. On service in Merwara 1820-1. Adjt. & Qmr. Rajputana Div. Art. till 2 Apr. 1822. Dy. Comy. Ord. 14 Jan. 1822 ; Comy. Ord. at Ajmer 7 May 1824. Offg. Agent for manufacture of gunpowder at Ichapur 19 Mar. 1835. Actg. P.A. Merwara 1 June 1835 ; Supt. Merwara 12 Jan. 1836 till 1848. Comdg. Merwara Local Bn. 12 Jan. 1836 till death. Mutiny campaign ; operations S. of Jumna ; in Pol. employ. Author of

"Sketch of Mairwara; Origin and Habits of the Mairs: ...,"
32 maps, plans and views, 4to. 1850.
Refs. : Lahore Chron. 9 July 1857. Will dated 20 June 1857 ; proved 8 Apr. 1858.

DIXON, Francis Graham Peter Matthew (1812-?). Ensign. Infantry. *bapt.* Lowestoft, Suffolk, 26 Feb. 1812. Cadet 1828. Arrived in India 10 Sept. 1829. Ensign 12 Apr. 1829. Resigned in India 12 Aug. 1831.

Son of Peter Matthew Dixon, of Rennes, France, and Anna Maria Mary Emily his wife. Addiscombe Cadet 1827.
Services : d.d. 30th N.I. 19 Sept. 1829 ; do. 13th N.I. 10 June 1830 ; do. 2nd N.I. 4 Dec. 1830. No record of active service.

***DIXON, John** (*d.* 1766). 2nd Lieutenant, Artillery. Cadet (?). Fireworker 29 Aug. 1763. 2nd Lieut. 2 Aug. 1765. *d.* 1766.
Services : N.F.P.
Refs. : B.M. Addl. MS. 6050. *Stubbs's List.*
Note : Possibly identical with John Dickson, *q.v.*

DIXON, Thomas (1802-1849). Captain, 43rd N.I. *b.* Dublin 14 Sept. 1802. Cadet 1822. Arrived in India 15 Apr. 1823. Ensign 13 Apr. 1823. Lieut. 13 May 1825. Capt. 26 Sept. 1841. *d.* Moradabad 10 Mar. 1849.

Son of Thomas Dixon.
Services : Posted as Ensign to 22nd N.I. Transfd. to 44th N.I. (late 2/22nd) May 1824. (? First Burma War ; Cachar 1825 ; Ensign 44th N.I.) Transfd. to 43rd N.I. (late 1/22nd) 13 May 1825. Adjt. 43rd N.I. 12 May 1828 till 16 July 1842. First Afghan War 1839-42 ; Kandahar ; Ghazni ; Kabul 1842 ; action nr. Kandahar 29 May 1842 (*Lond. Gaz.* 6 Apr. 1842) ; Capt. 43rd N.I. (Medal). Bde. Major 2nd Inf. Bde. in Afghanistan and Sind 21 July 1842. Fur. s.c. 9 Feb. 1844 till 1846.

DIXON, William Hardwick (1791-1810). Lieutenant, 9th N.I. *bapt.* St. Paul's, Covent Gdn., London, 1 May 1791. Cadet 1805. Arrived in India 11 July 1806. Ensign 20 Aug. 1806. Lieut. 19 Nov. 1807. *d.* 4 Jan. 1810 : kld. in action at the assault of Pragpur, Bahraich district, U.P.

Son of George Dixon and Sarah Hardwicke his wife. Brother of Charles George Dixon, *q.v.*
Services : Settlement of Hariana 1809 ; capture of Bhawani ; Lieut. 1/9th N.I. Operations in Oudh 1809-10 ; assault of Pragpur (kld.) ; Lieut. 1/9th N.I.

DOBBINS, ——. Volunteer.
Services : Apptd. a Volunteer in Calcutta 6 June 1758. N.F.P.
Refs. : Orme MSS. India, xiii. 3639.

DOBBS, Charles (1784-1820). Captain, 21st N.I. *b.* Waterford city 15 Jan. 1784. Cadet 1803. Arrived in India 1 Dec. 1804. Ensign 17 Oct. 1804. Lieut. 17 Oct. 1804. Capt. 22 Sept. 1818. *d.* Banda 13 June 1820.
Son of Charles Dobbs and Grace Hutchinson his wife.
Services : Posted as Lieut. to 1/21st N.I. (? Nepal War 1816 ; Lieut. Rt. Wing 1/21st N.I.)

DOD, George (1805-?). Lieutenant. 71st N.I. *b.* Streatfield-Mortimer, Berks., 24 Feb. 1805. Cadet 1824. Ensign 6 Sept. 1825. Lieut. 13 Sept. 1827. Discharged by G.C.M. 30 Jan. 1830.
Son of John Cowaher Dod.
Services : Posted as Ensign to 3rd Extra Regt. (became 71st N.I.) in 1826. Sick leave to Landour Apr. 1829 till tried by G.C.M. 20 Oct. 1829. No record of active service.
Refs. : A.J. N.S. ii. 156-7.

DODD(S), Charles (1761/62-?). Lieutenant. Infantry. *b.* 1761/62. Cadet 1779. Ensign 12 Feb. 1780. Lieut. 18 Mar. 1781. Resigned 20 Mar. 1783.
A native of Lisbon.
Services : Sailed for India on the *True Briton* 16 June 1779, aged 17. N.F.P.

DODDS, John. Bt. Major. Infantry. Cadet 1769. Ensign 5 Apr. 1770. Lieut. 28 June 1771. Capt. 10 Sept. 1779. Bt. Major Sept. 1781. Resigned on pension 27 Feb. 1782.
Services : Capt. 1/3rd Bengal Eur. Regt. in Oct. 1779.

DODGSON, William Scott (1812-1846). Lieutenant, 31st N.I. *b.* Montrose, co. Forfar, 10 Nov. 1812. Cadet 1833. Arrived in India 7 July 1834. Ensign (4 Mar. 1834) 7 July 1834. Lieut. 20 Dec. 1838. *d.* Hawalbagh, U.P., 17 Aug. 1846.
Son of Rev. John Dodgson and Alexa his wife, younger dau. of William Scott, of Logie, Capt. R.N.
Services : Ensign d.d. 31st N.I. 15 July 1834. Posted to 31st N.I. 5 Nov. 1834. Operations against the Kols 1837-8 ; Ensign 31st N.I. First Afghan War 1838-40. Ghazni ; Kalat ; Lieut. 31st N.I. (Medal). Apptd. Baggage Mr. to Army of Exercise 17 Nov.

1843. Gwalior campaign; Maharajpur; Lieut. 31st N.I. (Bronze star).
Refs. : Burke's *Landed Gentry*, 3rd edn., p. 1071, *s.n.* Scott, of Logie.

DODSWORTH, Francis Alexander (*d.* 1796). Captain, Infantry. Cadet 1770. Admitted 12 June 1770. Ensign 21 Nov. 1771. Lieut. 4 Aug. 1776. Capt. 25 Feb. 1781. *d.* Cawnpore 6 Jan. 1796.
Services : 6th Bengal Eur. Bn. in July 1787.
Refs. : Will dated Cawnpore 1 Jan. 1796.

DOMIT, Nevill. (*See* **DONNETT.**)

DON, Patrick (1756/57-1837). Lieut. Colonel. 15th N.I. *b.* 1756/57. Cadet 1778. Admitted 10 Dec. 1778. Ensign 1778. Lieut. 31 Oct. 1778. Capt. 1 June 1796. Major 29 May 1800. Lt. Col. 30 Sept. 1803. Retired 29 Aug. 1810. *d.* Springfield, co. Fife, 16 Jan. 1837.

Of Springfield, nr. Cupar. *m.* 1st (before 1788), a native of India. His dau. *m.* James Kennedy, *q.v. m.* 2nd, Edinburgh, 19 Dec. 1809, a dau. of David Millie, of Pathhead, co. Fife.

Services : Sailed for India on the *Gatton*, 27 Apr. 1778, aged 21. Lieut. 1st Bengal Eur. Bn. in July 1787. A.D.C. to Maj.-Gen. John Forbes, *q.v.*, comdg. at Dinapore, 1795-7. Capt. 2/7th N.I. Transfd. to 2/8th N.I. in 1799; as Major to newly-formed 2/18th N.I. June 1800. Second Mahratta War; Bundelkhand 1803; Kapsa; capture of Gwalior; .Lt. Col. comdg. 2/18th N.I. Transfd. to 2/8th N.I. Apr. 1804. Taking of Rampura; Lt. Col. 2/8th N.I., comdg. the force of 1 Regt. N.C. and 2 Bns. N.I. Monson's retreat; battle of Deig, comdg. the Reserve; siege of Bhurtpore; comdd. the 3rd assault. D.Q.M.G. June 1805; A.Q.M.G. Feb. 1807. Fur. 18 Feb. 1808 till retirement.

Refs. : *E.I.M.C.* ii. 527-37. *S.M.* 1810, p. 78. *A.J.* N.S. xxii. 205. *Pester, passim.*

DON, William Gilbert (1809-1852). Captain, 43rd N.I. *b.* Forfar 29 Jan. 1809. Cadet 1827. Arrived in India 3 June 1828. Ensign 3 Feb. 1828. Lieut. 10 Dec. 1834. Capt. 25 July 1850. *d.* Bhagulpur, B. & O., 21 Jan. 1852.

Son of William Don, of Forfar, banker, and Mary Ann Hunter his wife. *m.* Lucknow, 8 Feb. 1834, Georgiana King, dau. of George Elliot, and sister of Edward King Elliot, *q.v.* (She died 2 Dec. 1880, aged 72.)

Services : Posted as Ensign to 43rd N.I. 4 Nov. 1828. Adjt. Bhagulpur Hill Rangers 1 Sept. 1831 till 22 Sept. 1838, when he rejoined his Regt. for service in Afghanistan. First Afghan War; Ghazni; Lieut. 43rd N.I. (Medal). The remainder of his life was spent with the Hill Rangers, as Adjt. till 24 Nov. 1849, afterwards as Comdt.

Refs. : *I.M.* 18 Mar. 1852, p. 160. Will dated 19 May 1842; admon. 7 Apr. 1852.

DONALD, Patrick. Ensign. Infantry. Cadet (?). Ensign 29 May 1771.

Services : N.F.P.

DONALDSON, Alexander (1790-1818). Lieutenant, 11th N.I. *b.* Edinburgh 16 Apr. 1790. Cadet 1805. Admitted 13 Dec. 1806. Ensign 16 Oct. 1806. Lieut. 9 Apr. 1809. *d. unm.* Mainpuri, U.P., 4 Sept. 1818.

Eldest son of Capt. Alexander Donaldson, of Heriot Row, Edinburgh, and Helen his wife. Brother of Robert Donaldson, of co. Nairn, and of Allan Donaldson.

Services : Posted as Ensign to 11th N.I. Reduction of Kalinjar 1812; Lieut. 2/11th N.I. Siege and capture of Hathras 1817; Lieut. 2/11th N.I. Third Mahratta War; Lieut. 2/11th N.I.

Refs. : *S.M.* 1819, i. 285. Will dated Mainpuri 3 Sept. 1818; proved 7 Nov. 1818.

DONALDSON, James (1781-1826). Captain, 5th N.I. *b.* Haddington 13 May 1781. Cadet 1804. Arrived in India 10 Sept. 1805. Ensign 13 Sept. 1805. Lieut. 14 Sept. 1805. Capt. 11 June 1823. *d.* Rampur 25 Jan. 1826.

Son of Hay Donaldson, of Haddington, town clerk.

Services : Posted as Lieut. to 1/2nd N.I. in 1806. With 2nd Gren. Bn. 1815-6. Transfd. as Lieut. to 2/2nd N.I. Fur. 15 Mar. 1820 till 1822. Transfd. to 5th N.I. (late 1/2nd) May 1824. Comdd. 1st Narbada Sebundy Corps 1824 till death. No record of active service.

***DONELLAN, John** (*d.* 1781). Captain. Bengal Eur. Bn. Capt. 15 Dec. 1757. Cashiered by C.M. Apr. 1759. *d.* Warwick 1 Apr. 1781 : hanged for poisoning his brother-in-law, Sir Theodosius Boughton, 7th Bart.[1], on 21 Aug. 1780.

Son of Col. Donellan. *m.* June 1777, Theodosia, dau. of Sir Edward Boughton, 6th Bart. (She re-m. twice, and died 14 Jan. 1830.)

[1] *Note* : According to some accounts he was innocent, his mother-in-law subsequently confessing to the crime on her death-bed.

Services : Entered the R.A. at the age of 12 (? No. 237 in *Kane's*

List, where the name is given as James), with part of which Corps he went to India in 1754. Transfd. to Adlercron's Regt.; as Capt. to Bengal Eur. Regt. in 1758. Expedition to the N. Circars 1758-9; Condore (w.); Masulipatam; Capt. Bengal Eur. Regt. Was apptd. one of the four prize agents after the capture of Masulipatam. Tried by C.M. on a charge of receiving bribes from some of the native merchants, to whom part of their effects had been restored, was found guilty, and was sentenced to be cashiered. On the strength, however, of a certificate from the E.I.C., dated 8 July 1772, to the effect that, " during the time of his employment in the Coy.'s Military Service in the East Indies he behaved himself as a gallant Officer," he was eventually placed upon h.p. in H.M. 39th (Adlercron's) Regt.

Refs.: Burke's *Peerage*, 1923, p. 318, *s.n.* Rouse-Boughton, Bart., of Lawford Hall, co. Warwick. *The Patrician*, iii. 36-45. *Innes*, p. 70, n. *Forde*. Portrait—Anon., pub. by J. Walker, 1781.

DONNELLY, Francis Squire (1792-1821). Lieutenant, 27th N.I. *bapt.* Roscommon, Ireland, 10 Sept. 1792. Cadet 1807. Arrived in India 19 Aug. 1808. Ensign 22 Aug. 1808. Lieut. 1 Nov. 1814. *d.* on the Ganges, nr. Benares, 15 Dec. 1821.

Son of Sir Ross Donnelly, K.C.B., Adm. R.N. (*D.N.B.*). Cousin-german of John Donnelly, *q.v.*

Services: Ensign 27th N.I. Lieut. 1/27th N.I. Adjt. Bareilly Provl. Bn. 11 Jan. 1816. Comdg. escort to the Resdt. at Delhi 18 July 1816 till 1818. Comdg. Delhi Najib Bn. 1818 till death. No record of active service.

DONNELLY, John (1790-1826). Lieutenant, 18th N.I. *b.* Athlone, co. Westmeath, Aug. 1790. Cadet 1810. Ensign (13 Nov. 1813) 23 Apr. 1815. Lieut. 9 Sept. 1817. *d.* Liverpool 13 June 1826.

Son of Patrick Donnelly. Cousin-german of Francis Squire Donnelly, *q.v.*

Services: Cadet d.d. 9th N.I. 1811. Fur. 1812 till 11 Jan. 1816. Posted as Ensign to 2/8th N.I. in 1815. Nepal War 1816; Ensign 2/8th N.I., in 4th Bde., Centre Column. Transfd. to 2/6th N.I. in 1816. Operations in Kotah 1821; Mangrol; Lieut. 2/6th N.I. Adjt. 2/6th N.I. 12 Dec. 1821 till Oct. 1824. Transfd. to 18th N.I. (late 2/6th) May 1824. Fur. 1826 till death.

Refs.: *A.J.* xxii. 126.

DONNELLY, Sutton. Lieutenant. Bengal Eur. Regt. Cadet 1778. Ensign 10 Sept. 1779. Lieut. Oct. 1779. Dismissed by C.M. 19 Jan. 1781.

Services: Posted as Lieut. to 2/1st Bengal Eur. Regt. in Oct. 1779.

DONNETT, Nevill (*d.* 1786). Lieutenant, Infantry. Cadet 1778. Ensign 7 May 1779. Lieut. 13 Jan. 1781. *d.* Cawnpore 4 Apr. 1786.
Services : Second Mysore War 1781-5.
Refs. : Will dated Madras 23 Oct. 1783 ; proved 11 Sept. 1786.
Note : The name appears also as Domit and Domett.

DONNITHORNE, James (1800-1819). Ensign, Infantry. *b.* Bengal 9 June 1800. Cadet 1818. Ensign (?). *d.* Calcutta 17 Sept. 1819.
Son of James Donnithorne, of Holmer, Hereford, and St. Agnes, Cornwall, B.C.S., Collector of Calcutta, and sometime Mint Master at Farrukhabad, by his 1st wife.
Refs. : Burke's *Landed Gentry*, 13th edn., p. 508, *s.n.* Donnithorne, of Colne Lodge, Middlesex. M.I. in S. Park St. cemetery, Calcutta.

DOOLAN, Robert Wright Cope. (*See* **COPE, Robert Wright Cope.**)

DORMER, Miles (1800-?). Lieutenant. 16th N.I. *bapt.* Richmond, Yorks., 8 Sept. 1800. Cadet 1818. Ensign (?). Lieut. 1 Jan. 1821. Resigned 2 Nov. 1827.
Younger son of James Dormer and Lucy his wife, youngest dau. of Thomas Fitz-Herbert, of Norbury Manor, co. Derby, and Swynnerton Park, Staffs. Grand-nephew of Charles, 8th Baron Dormer. *m.* 1825, Susan, dau. of W. Randall.
Services : Ensign d.d. Bengal Eur. Regt. 1819. Posted as Ensign to 2/11th N.I. 1820. Fur. 30 Sept. 1820 till 1824. Transfd. to 10th N.I. July 1823 ; to 16th N.I. (late 2/10th) May 1824. Fur. 1825 till resignation. No record of active service.
Refs. : Burke's *Peerage*, 1923, p. 743, *s.n.* Dormer, B.

DORNBUST, Joseph. Ensign. Infantry. Cadet 1770. Ensign 21 Nov. 1771. Resigned 16 Aug. 1773.
Services : N.F.P.

DORRINGTON, William (*d.* 1777). Lieutenant, Infantry. Cadet 1770. Ensign 12 Dec. 1772. Lieut. 11 Mar. 1777. bur. Calcutta 24 Dec. 1777.
Services : N.F.P.

DOUGAL, Alexander (1782-1802). Lieutenant, 1st N.I. *b.* Forres, co. Elgin, 21 Jan. 1782. Cadet 1798. Arrived in India 26 Oct. 1799. Ensign 15 Jan. 1800. Lieut. 29 May 1800. *d.* Midnapore, Bengal, 18 Dec. 1802.
bapt. Forres 5 Feb. 1782. Son of Dr. Hugh Dougal and Jean Seaton his wife.
Services : Lieut. 1/1st N.I. No record of active service.

THE BENGAL ARMY, 1758-1834

DOUGAN, John Crooke (1811-?). Lieutenant. 19th N.I. b. London 2 May 1811. Cadet 1827. Arrived in India 5 July 1828. Ensign 19 Jan. 1828. Lieut. 15 Sept. 1834. Retired 14 Apr. 1837.

Son of John Dougan and Clarissa his wife.

Note : His name appears for the last time in the *India List* for Jan. 1879.

Services : Ensign d.d. 2nd Extra Regt. 25 July 1828. Posted to 19th N.I. 4 Nov. 1828. Intr. & Qmr. 19th N.I. 11 Feb. 1831. Fur. s.c. 14 Oct. 1834 till retirement. Retired on h.p., *viz.* 4/- *p.d.*

DOUGAN, Robert Frederick (1801-1829). Captain, 10th L.C. b. London 26 July 1801. Cadet 1820. Arrived in India July 1821. Cornet 7 Jan. 1821. Lieut. 20 Feb. 1822. Capt. 28 Feb. 1829. d. Mussoorie 30 July 1829.

Son of John Dougan, of Barnsbury St., Islington, merchant. m. Fanny. (She re-m. Dacres Fitz-Herbert Evans, *q.v.*)

Services : Posted as Cornet to 4th L.C. Intr. & Qmr. 4th L.C. 29 June 1824. Transfd. to newly-raised 2nd Extra Regt. (became 10th L.C.) May 1825. Adjt. 10th L.C. 5 Aug. 1825. Siege and capture of Bhurtpore ; Lieut. 10th L.C., extra A.D.C. to G.G. A.D.C. to C.-in-C. 1826. Second in comd. 2nd Local (Gardner's) Horse 1827. Extra A.D.C. to C.-in-C. Comdd. 2nd Local Horse (at that time known as "Dougan's Corps of Irregular Horse") 15 Feb. 1828 till Jan. 1829.

Refs. : Mundy, ii. 15. *A.J.* N.S. i. 156. Will dated Fatehgarh 8 Jan. 1829 ; proved 4 Dec. 1829.

DOUGLAS, Adam (1784-1812). Lieutenant, 6th N.I. b. Shankill, otherwise Lurgan, co. Armagh, 8 Mar. 1784. Cadet 1803. Arrived in India 2 Dec. 1804. Ensign 17 Sept. 1804. Lieut. 21 Sept. 1804. d. Karnal 7 Aug. 1812.

3rd son of William Douglas, of Lurgan, surgeon, and Margaret his wife, dau. of John Cuppage, of Garden Hill, co. Antrim. Related to the Camacs, *q.v.*

Services : Posted as Lieut. to 2/6th N.I. 14 Apr. 1805, and served throughout with that Bn. No record of active service.

Refs. : De Rhé-Philipe. M.I. in old cemetery at Karnal.

DOUGLAS, Alexander (1787-?). Lieutenant. 3rd N.I. b. Bengal 1787. Cadet 1803. Arrived in India 27 Sept. 1804. Ensign 17 Sept. 1804. Lieut. 4 Oct. 1804. Resigned 7 May 1811.

Services : Posted as Lieut. to 6th N.I. Transfd. to 3rd N.I. in 1808. Fur. 24 May 1808 till resignation. No record of active service.

DOUGLAS, Charles (1814-1885). General, Artillery. *b.* London 21 Mar. 1814. Cadet 1833. Arrived in India 7 July 1834. 2nd Lieut. 13 Dec. 1833. Lieut. 12 Jan. 1841. Capt. 20 May 1851. Bt. Major 20 July 1858. Lt. Col. 18 Feb. 1861. Col. 20 Sept. 1865. Maj. Gen. 26 Mar. 1870. Lt. Gen. 1 Oct. 1877. Gen. 1 July 1881. *d.* Calcutta 28 July 1885.

Addiscombe Cadet 3 Feb. 1832 till 13 Dec. 1833.

Services : First Afghan War 1842 ; Tazin ; re-occupation of Kabul ; Lieut. 2nd Coy. 6th Bn. Art., with Pollock's force (Medal). (*Lond. Gaz.* 24 Nov. 1842.) Apptd. to tempy. charge of Agra magazine 3 Apr. 1843. Dy. Comy. Ord. 14 Jan. 1845 ; Comy. Ord. 5 Aug. 1848 ; do. 1 cl., 22 Apr. 1853. From Phillour to Agra magazine 15 Nov. 1854. Fur. 1856 till Sept. 1857. Posted to Delhi magazine Sept. 1857. Mutiny campaign ; with C.I. F.F. under Sir Hugh Rose (Medal). Comdd. Art. of Hyderabad Contingent.

Refs. : The Times, 4 Aug. 1885.

DOUGLAS, Claud (1799-1883). General. 65th N.I. *b.* London 9 Nov. 1799. Cadet 1818. Admitted 10 Feb. 1820. Ensign 16 Aug. 1819. Lieut. 29 Apr. 1823. Capt. 27 Sept. 1828. Major 10 June 1842. Lt. Col. 27 Oct. 1848. Col. 1 May 1858. Maj. Gen. 4 June 1860. Lt. Gen. 25 June 1870. Gen. 1 Oct. 1877. *d.* Bognor, I.W., 11 Apr. 1883.

bapt. St. Pancras, London, 24 Nov. 1799. Son of Patrick Douglas and Ann his wife. *m.* 1st, Titchfield, 7 Dec. 1826, Mary Magdalen, 2nd dau. of Sir Archibald Collingwood Dickson, 2nd Bart., and sister of Sir Colpoys Dickson, Bart., *q.v.* (She died Bideford 14 June 1848.) *m.* 2nd, Marylebone, 22 Nov. 1848, Eliza Harrison, widow of Henry Smith, of Cheshunt. Ed. Eton ; fourth form 1811.

Services : Ensign d.d. 2/9th N.I. 6 Nov. 1820. Posted as Ensign to 2/10th N.I. Transfd. to 14th N.I. (late 1/10th) May 1824. Fur. s.c. 21 Sept. 1824 till 11 May 1827. Second in comd. Rangpur L.I. Bn. 14 Sept. 1827 till 27 July 1829. Fur. s.c. 19 Feb. 1832 till 8 June 1835. In charge of 13th, Rajputana, Div. P.W.D. 23 Oct. 1841 till 1845. Lt. Col. 56th N.I. Fur. 10 Apr. 1848 till 1850. Transfd. to 48th, 60th, 49th, 70th, 56th, 50th, and 32nd N.I. Fur. s.c. 16 Feb. 1855 till death. Col. 55th N.I. 25 July 1858 ; 65th N.I. 1859-70. No record of active service.

Refs. : Burke's *Peerage*, 1923, p. 1237, *s.n.* Islington, B. *Boase.* Eton School Lists. *G.M.* 1826, ii. 556 ; 1849, i. 198. *The Times,* 17 Apr. 1883.

DOUGLAS, David (1780-1802). Ensign, Engineers. *b.* Kinnettles 2 June 1780. Cadet 1796. Ensign 15 Dec. 1798. *d.* Chunar 5 July 1802.

THE BENGAL ARMY, 1758-1834

bapt. 19 June 1780. 4th son of William Douglas, of Brigton, co. Forfar, and Elizabeth his wife, dau. of Robert Graham, 11th of Fintry.
Services : N.F.P.
Refs. : Burke's *Landed Gentry*, 13th edn., p. 512, *s.n.* Douglas, of Brigton, co. Forfar.

DOUGLAS, Henry (*d.* 1803). Bt. Major, Artillery. Cadet 1778. Admitted 17 Dec. 1778. Fireworker 27 Dec. 1778. Lieut. 9 July 1784. Capt. 12 Feb. 1795. Bt. Major 1 Jan. 1798. *d.* Fort Marlborough, Sumatra, 21 Oct. 1803.
m. Calcutta, 16 Jan. 1788, Miss Elizabeth Lee. Father of James William Douglas, *q.v.*
Services : Second Mysore War 1781-5 ; Lieut. 5th Coy. 1st Bn. Foot Art. Third Mysore War ; Bangalore ; Lieut. 2nd Coy. 2nd Bn. Served with detachment of Art. sent from Bengal in Nov. 1793 for service against French cruisers in the Bay of Bengal and E. Archipelago.

DOUGLAS, James (1781-?). Ensign. Infantry. *b.* Aberdeen 1 Mar. 1781. Cadet 1800. Never proceeded to India. Ensign 14 Dec. 1801. Declined the appointment.
Son of James Douglas, Gunner on an East Indiaman, and Euphemia Nicol his wife (*probably* dau. of James Nicol (*d.* 1816), *q.v.*).

DOUGLAS, James (1798-1818). Lieutenant, 9th N.I. *b.* London 4 Jan. 1798. Cadet 1814. Ensign 5 May 1816. Lieut. 1818. *d. unm.* nr. Sambalpur, C.P., 11 Oct. 1818.
Only son of James Douglas, of Berkeley St., London, Adm. of the Red, and Elizabeth his 1st wife, dau. of Capt. Robert Scott, R.N. Grandson of Sir James Douglas, 1st Bart., of Springwood, Adm. R.N. (*D.N.B.*).
Services : Ensign d.d. 4th N.I. 1816. Posted as Ensign to 9th N.I. No record of active service.
Refs. : Burke's *Peerage*, 1923, p. 745, *s.n.* Douglas, Bart., of Springwood, co. Roxburgh.

DOUGLAS, James Dundas (1801-1841). Captain, 53rd N.I. *b.* Edinburgh 13 Sept. 1801. Cadet 1818. Admitted 1 Jan. 1820. Ensign 24 July 1819. Lieut. 15 Dec. 1821. Capt. 13 Sept. 1834.
d. unm. Nazian valley, Afghanistan, 25 Feb. 1841 : kld. in action against the Sangu Khel Shinwaris.
2nd son of Gen. Sir Howard Douglas, 3rd Bart., G.C.B. (*D.N.B.*), and Anne his wife, eldest dau. of James Dundas.

Services : Ensign d.d. Bengal Eur. Regt. Posted as Ensign to 1/27th N.I. Transfd. to 53rd N.I. (late 1/27th) May 1824. Adjt. 3rd Local Horse 13 Nov. 1823 ; 2nd in comd. do. 27 Feb. 1826 till 1 Jan. 1830. Actg. D.A.A.G., Saugor Div., 15 May 1830. Bde. Major at Agra 17 July 1830. D.A.A.G., Saugor, 22 Apr. 1831 till 14 Feb. 1835. D.A.A.G. at Benares 5 June 1835. A.A.G. of Div. at Benares 27 July 1836 ; do. Meerut 13 June 1837 ; do. Benares 6 Oct. 1838 ; do. Meerut Div. 7 Dec. 1839. First Afghan War 1838-41 ; Ghazni ; Nazian valley (kld.) ; Capt. 53rd N.I., A.A.G. Apptd. Dy. Sec. to Govt. of India, Mily. Dept., with official rank of Major, 10 Mar. 1841, before news of his death was received in India.

Refs. : Burke's *Peerage*, 1923, p. 744, *s.n.* Douglas, Bart., of Carr. Will dated 11 Mar. 1838 ; codicil dated 23 Feb. 1841 ; proved 26 May 1841.

DOUGLAS, James Ferdinand (1798-1869). Colonel. 44th N.I. *b.* S. Leith, Midlothian, 28 June 1798. Cadet 1819. Admitted 14 June 1820. Ensign 10 Jan. 1820. Lieut. (11 June 1822) 11 July 1823. Capt. 17 Nov. 1827. Major 11 Apr. 1841. Lt. Col. 19 Mar. 1847. Retired 28 Feb. 1850. Hon. Col. 28 Nov. 1854. *d.* 18 Oct. 1869.

Son of Lieut. Archibald Douglas, of Leith. *m.* 1st, Benares, 23 Sept. 1826, Charlotte Sarah Kelly, widow. (She died Mirzapur, 20 Apr. 1827, aged 42.) *m.* 2nd, Jaunpur, 18 Mar. 1831, Susan, 4th dau. of Thomas Tambs, of Sandwich.

Services : Posted as Ensign to 2/14th N.I. Transfd. to 25th N.I. 11 July 1823 ; to 49th N.I. (late 1/25th) May 1824. First Burma War ; Arakan 1825 ; Lieut. 49th N.I. (India medal). Offg. Intr. & Qmr. 49th N.I. 9 Apr. 1825 ; actg. Adjt. do. 25 Jan. 1826. Fur. s.c. 21 Nov. 1827 till 19 July 1830. Assumed comd. of 49th N.I. 12 Dec. 1840. Fur. s.c. 18 Mar. 1844 till 1846. Posted as Lt. Col. to 49th N.I. 10 Aug. 1847 ; transfd. to 44th N.I. in 1848. Fur. 21 Feb. 1848 till retirement.

Refs. : A.J. N.S. vi. 79.

DOUGLAS, James William (1792-1878). Lieut. Colonel. 52nd N.I. *bapt.* Madras 10 June 1792. Cadet 1807. Arrived in India 19 Aug. 1808. Ensign 21 Aug. 1808. Lieut. 21 Feb. 1814. Capt. 1 May 1824. Bt. Major 28 June 1838. Retired 1 Jan. 1841. Hon. Lt. Col. 28 Nov. 1854. *d.* at his residence, 4 Bays Hill Villas, Cheltenham, 10 Feb. 1878.

Son of Henry Douglas, *q.v.*, and Elizabeth his wife. *m.* Ghazipur 21 Nov. 1826, Fanny Bartholomew, 4th dau. of William Nathan Wrighte Hewett, B.C.S., and sister of James Hewett, *q.v.* (She died 3 May 1893.) (*See also* Frederick Hervey Sandys.)

Services : Barasat C.C. for 13 mos. Wounded in a duel at Barasat (*Cons.* 5 June 1809). Posted as Ensign to 26th N.I. Lieut. 1/26th N.I. Adjt. 2/26th N.I. 21 Dec. 1816 till 17 May 1822. Operations against the Bhattis of Hariana 1818. Actg. Bde. Major at Mhow 6 Jan. 1820. Transfd. to 52nd N.I. (late 2/26th) May 1824. (? First Burma War ; Cachar 1825 ; Capt. 52nd N.I.) In Pol. employment from 1826 till retirement. Third Asst. to Resdt. at Indore ; 2nd do. 19 Feb. 1838 ; offg. 1st cl. do. 23 Jan. 1839 ; permanent do. 5 June 1839 till retirement.
Refs. : *A.J.* xxiii. 856. *The Times*, 15 Feb. 1878.

DOUGLAS, John. Ensign. Infantry. Cadet 1768. Ensign 21 Dec. 1769.
Services : N.F.P.

DOUGLAS, Patrick (1758-1821). Lieut. Colonel. 2nd Bengal Eur. Regt. *b.* 1758. Cadet (?). Ensign (Engrs.) 9 Dec. 1770. Lieut. (Engrs.) 17 Nov. 1773. Lieut. (Inf.) 4 June 1776. Capt. 7 Feb. 1781. Major 1 Mar. 1794. Lt. Col. 6 Dec. 1797. Retired 30 July 1800. *d.* Stratford Pl., London, 16 Mar. 1821, aged 62.

Brother of Isabella Douglas. *m.* Calcutta, 10 Nov. 1787, Jane, dau. of John Fortnom, *q.v.* (*See also* Samuel Cox.) (She died 20 Aug. 1840, aged 73.)
Services : Transfd. as Lieut. from Engrs. to Inf. in 1776. Lieut. 2/3rd Bengal Eur. Regt. in Oct. 1779. Fur. Feb. 1785 till Apr. 1786. 3rd Bengal Eur. Bn. in July 1787. Second Rohilla War ; battle of Bitaurah ; Major comdg. 6th Bn. Sepoys. Posted as Lt. Col. to newly-raised 1/17th N.I. in 1798. Transfd. to 2nd Bengal Eur. Regt. 29 May 1800.
Refs. : *G.M.* 1821, i. 285. *S.M.* 1821, i. 400. M.I. in St. John's church, St. John's Wood Rd., London.

DOUGLAS, Patrick John (1797-?). Cadet. Infantry. *b.* London 27 Sept. 1797. Cadet 1818. Was already in Bengal when apptd. Cadet. Resigned in England 11 Apr. 1820.
Son of Patrick Douglas.
Services : Ensign H.M. 66th Foot 12 Jan. 1815 ; Lieut. do. 28 Sept. 1815.

DOUGLAS, Robert (*d.* 1799). Bt. Captain, Artillery. Country Cadet 1783. Admitted 23 June 1783. Fireworker 25 June 1785. Lieut. 27 Oct. 1794. Bt. Capt. 8 Jan. 1798. *d.* Panjalamcoorchy, Madras (26 m. N.E. of Palamcottah), 5 Sept. 1799 : kld. in action by a pike-thrust in the gateway of the fort.
Services : Fur. 30 Oct. 1786 till 29 Dec. 1789. Served in Ceylon with 5th Coy. 2nd Bn. Art. 1796-9. Operations against the Southern

LIST OF THE OFFICERS OF

Polygars, Madras, Aug.-Sept. 1799; storm of Panjalamcoorchy (kld.); Bt. Capt. comdg. a detachment of Art. (? 1st Coy. 3rd Bn.) with the force under Major John Bannerman, Madras Est.
Refs. : Wilson, iii. 8.

DOUGLAS, William (*d.* 1769). Ensign, Infantry. Cadet 1767. Ensign 5 May 1768. *d.* 1769.
Services : N.F.P.

DOUGLAS, William (*d.* 1827). Lieutenant, 20th N.I. Cadet 1818. Was already in Bengal when apptd. Cadet. Ensign 30 June 1819. Lieut. 1 Aug. 1822. *d.* Akyab, Lower Burma, 2 Sept. 1827.
(*Possibly* son of Patrick Douglas, *q.v.*)
Services : Local Ensign Gorakhpur L.I. Bn. 4 May 1818. Local Lieut. do. Posted as Ensign to 2/5th N.I. 1820. Adjt. Gorakhpur L.I. Bn. 1820-4. Transfd. to 20th N.I. (late 2/5th) May 1824. Adjt. 20th N.I. 22 June 1824 till death. No record of active service.

DOUGLAS, Sir Thomas Monteath (1788-1868). General, K.C.B. Colonel, 35th N.I. *b.* Hanover, Jamaica, 25 Nov. 1788. Cadet 1805. Arrived in India 13 Dec. 1806. Ensign 4 Dec. 1806. Lieut. 9 Sept. 1808. Capt. 1 May 1824. Major 17 Jan. 1829. Lt. Col. 2 Apr. 1834. Col. 7 Sept. 1845. Maj. Gen. 20 June 1854. Lt. Gen. 18 Mar. 1856. Gen. 9 Apr. 1865. *d.* Stone Byres, co. Lanark, 18 Oct. 1868.
Of Douglas-Support, co. Lanark. Son of Thomas Monteath. Nephew of Colin Monteath, *q.v.* Took the additional surname of Douglas 18 Dec. 1850 (*Lond. Gaz.* p. 3477), on succeeding to the estate of Douglas-Support, under the entail of the Duchess of Douglas. *m.* Meerut, 20 July 1826, Mrs. Lucinda Florence Whish. (She died Lucknow, 2 Sept. 1837, aged 39.)
Services : See *D.N.B.* Barasat C.C. for 8 mos. Posted as Ensign to 17th N.I. Served in Bundelkhand 1809-10. Lieut. 4th L.I. Bn. Nepal War 1814-5; Kalanga (w.); Lieut. 1/17th N.I., in 2nd Div. (India medal). Third Mahratta War; against the Pindaris; Lieut. Dromedary Corps. Intr. & Qmr. 1/17th N.I. 4 Dec. 1820 till May 1824. Transfd. as Capt. to 34th N.I. (late 1/17th) May 1824; to 35th N.I. in 1825. Siege and capture of Bhurtpore; Capt. 35th N.I. (Clasp to India medal). First Afghan War 1838-42; Ghazni (Medal); Kabul; defence of Jalalabad, as 2nd in comd. to Sale; Lt. Col. comdg. 35th N.I. (Medal). Fur. 17 Mar. 1844 till 1846. Col. 35th N.I. 7 Sept. 1845. Bdr. 2 cl., comdg. at Ambala, 10 Mar. 1846 till 1851. Fur. p.a. 9 Mar. 1851 till death. Received during his service 3 gunshot wounds, 2 sabre cuts, and one spear wound. C.B. 20 Dec. 1839. Durani 3 cl. 19 Jan. 1841. A.D.C. to the Queen 4 Oct. 1842. K.C.B. 28 Mar. 1865.

Refs. : Foster's *Baronetage*, p. 106, *s.n.* Campbell, Bart., of Blythswood, co. Renfrew. Burke's *Landed Gentry*, 9th edn., p. 418, *s.n.* Douglas, of Mains, and Douglas, of Douglas-Support. *D.N.B. D.I.B. Boase. I.L.N.* vol. 53 (1868), pp. 435, 459, 483.

DOULL, Andrew (*d.* 1801). Captain, 16th N.I. Cadet 1782. Admitted 17 July 1783. Ensign 18 Feb. 1783. Lieut. 8 Feb. 1790. Capt. 7 Jan. 1796. *d.* Sikraul, Benares, 9 Nov. 1801. Son of Susannah Doull, of Turriff, co. Aberdeen.
Services : Adjt. 2/16th N.I. N.F.P.
Refs. : *A.A.R.* iv. 120. Will dated 22 Jan. 1798; proved in 1802.

DOVE, Matthew (*d.* 1793). Lieutenant, Infantry. Cadet 1782. Ensign 2 Jan. 1783. Lieut. 8 Feb. 1788. *d.* Dinapore 9 Nov. 1793.
Services : Adjt. 3rd Bengal Eur. Regt. 1787-90. N.F.P.

DOVETON, Charles Jackson (1784-1832). Lieut. Colonel, 38th N.I. *b.* 1784. Cadet 1799. Admitted 23 Oct. 1800. Ensign 17 Oct. 1800. Lieut. 13 July 1803. Capt. 16 Dec. 1814. Major 21 Oct. 1821. Lt. Col. 1 May 1824. *d.* Midnapore, Bengal, 1 Oct. 1832. *bapt.* St. Helena 8 May 1785. 3rd son of Sir William Webber Doveton, Kt., and Eleanor Beale his wife. Brother of Gen. Sir John Doveton, K.C.B., Madras Est. (*Probably* cousin-german of Richard Doveton, *q.v.*) *m.* 11 Dec. 1807, Maria Ann, dau. of Sir John Arnold, *q.v.* (*See also* William Logie.) His dau. *m.* George Burney, *q.v.*
Services : Ensign 19th N.I. Bde. Major 2nd Inf. Bde. under Col. Gabriel Martindell, *q.v.*, 24 Apr. 1810. Adjt. 1/19th N.I. 1812 till 3 Nov. 1814. Nepal War 1814-5 ; Bde. Qmr. to a Bde. of N.I. in 3rd Div. Third Mahratta War ; storm and capture of Chanda ; Capt. 1/19th N.I., comdg. Light Bn. Nagpur force. Comdd. 1st Berar Inf., Nizam's army, 1819 till 26 Jan. 1822. Posted as Lt. Col. to 38th N.I. (late 1/19th) May 1824. Fur. p.a. 8 Mar. 1829 till 15 May 1830. Comdd. a detachment consisting of Art. and 38th N.I. on service in Sambalpur and Bamanghati, B. & O., 1832.
Refs. : Family information. Will dated 24 Feb. 1829 ; proved 26 Oct. 1832. M.I. at Midnapore.

DOVETON, Henry (1799-1893). Lieut. Colonel. 4th N.I. *b.* London 22 Jan. 1799. Cadet 1818. Admitted 25 Sept. 1819. Ensign 26 May 1819. Lieut. 7 Nov. 1821. Capt. 9 Apr. 1832. Major 31 Mar. 1845. Retired 22 Aug. 1847. Hon. Lt. Col. 28 Nov. 1854. *d.* 30 Norland Sq., Notting Hill, London, 6 Dec. 1893.

LIST OF THE OFFICERS OF

2nd son of Frederick Doveton, of Upper Wimpole St., London, and Mary his wife, dau. of Benjamin Slade, of Deptford. *m.* 1st, Berhampore, 2 June 1832, Augusta, youngest dau. of Wigram Money, B.C.S. (She died Nimach, C.I., 10 Aug. 1835, aged 21.) His dau. *m.* William Maxwell, *q.v.* *m.* 2nd, Calcutta, 14 Nov. 1836, Grace Elizabeth, eldest dau. of Dr. W. W. Hutchinson, of Ripon, and niece of George Hutchinson, *q.v.*

Services: Ensign 1/1st N.I. Actg. Adjt. 1/1st N.I. 25 Jan. 1822. Intr. & Qmr. 1/1st N.I. 25 June 1822. Transfd. to 4th N.I. (late 2/1st) May 1824. Adjt. 4th N.I. 17 June 1824. Intr. & Qmr. 4th N.I. 11 Mar. 1825 till 8 Feb. 1827. Actg. Bde. Major Sirhind frontier 27 Dec. 1825; actg. D.A.A.G. do. 20 July 1826. Supy. S.A.C.G. 30 Dec. 1826. S.A.C.G. 18 Aug. 1827; D.A.C.G., 2 cl., 19 Mar. 1832; A.C.G., 1 cl., 8 Jan. 1844. Fur. s.c. 22 Feb. 1845 till retirement. No record of active service.

Refs.: Walford. The Times, 12 Dec. 1893.

DOVETON, Richard (1763/64-1823). Bt. Colonel, C.B. 3rd N.C. *b.* 1763/64. Cadet 1780. Admitted 3 Mar. 1782. Cornet 1780. Lieut. 29 Aug. 1781. Capt. 29 May 1800. Major 12 Sept. 1803. Lt. Col. 4 Apr. 1807. Bt. Col. 4 June 1814. Retired 30 June 1818. *d.* Regent St., London, 17 Mar. 1823.

A native of St. Helena. (*Probably* son of Frederick Doveton, of London, merchant, brother of Lt.-Gen. Sir John Doveton, G.C.B. (*D.N.B.*), and cousin-german of Charles Jackson Doveton, *q.v.*)

Services: Sailed for India on the *Latham,* 13 Mar. 1781, aged 17. Lieut. 6th Bn. Sepoys in July 1787. With the embassy at Hyderabad in 1790. Lieut. & Qmr. 3rd N.C. in 1800. Operations in Jumna Doab 1803; Sasni; Bijaigarh; Kachaura; Capt. 3rd N.C. Second Mahratta War; battle of Delhi; Laswari; Rampura; battle of Deig; Major 3rd N.C. Fur. 18 Feb. 1806 till 6 Nov. 1809; 1812 till 29 Aug. 1815; and 13 Jan. 1816 till retirement. C.B. 4 June 1815.

Refs.: G.M. 1823, i. 285.

DOW, Adam (1762/63-1784). Lieutenant, Infantry. *b.* 1762/63. Cadet 1779. Ensign 1779. Lieut. 19 Mar. 1781. *d.* 29 May 1784, on service with the Madras Detachment.

A native of co. Berwick.

Services: Sailed for India on the *Ganges,* 7 Mar. 1779, aged 16. Second Mysore War.

DOW, Alexander (1735/36-1779). Lieut. Colonel, Infantry. *b.* Crieff, co. Perth, 1735/36. Cadet 1760. Ensign 14 Sept. 1760.

Lieut. 23 Aug. 1763. Capt. 16 Apr. 1764. Lt. Col. 25 Feb. 1769. d. Bhagulpur, B. & O., 31 July 1779, aged 43.
Son of —— Dow, of the Customs at Dunbar.
Services : See *D.N.B.* Ran away from his apprenticeship at Eyemouth, went out to Bencoolen as a sailor, and became Sec. to the Govr. Apptd. a Cadet on the Bengal Est. Raised at Murshidabad in Mar. 1764 the 19th Bn. Sepoys (became 18th in 1764, 1/11th in 1796, and 15th N.I. in 1824), called after him "*Doo-ki-Paltan.*" Campaign against the Nawabs of Bengal and Oudh 1764; 1st assault on Chunar fort 2 Dec. 1764 (s.w.—skull fractured, subsequently trepanned). Was on leave in England 1768-9 and 1771-2. On receipt of intelligence by the Council in Bengal of the declaration by Gt. Britain of war on France, on 18 Mar. 1778, he was despatched secretly by Warren Hastings, with two Bns. of Sepoys from Barrackpore, to take possession of the French factory of Chandernagore. This mission he accomplished without bloodshed on 10 July 1778. Dramatist : produced at Drury Lane in 1769 *Zingis,* a tragedy, and in 1774 *Sethona,* also a tragedy. Translated Ferishta's *History of Hindostan.*
Refs. : *D.N.B. D.I.B. Williams,* p. 154. *Broome,* p. 489. *Autobiog. of Alexander Carlisle, of Inveresk.* John Macdonald's *Travels,* 1745-79 (1927 edn.). *S.M.* 1780, p. 279. M.I. at Bhagulpur. Portrait by Sir Joshua Reynolds.

DOW, Archibald (1790-1840). Lieutenant. 19th N.I. Pensioner on Lord Clive's fund. *b.* Perth 8 Nov. 1790. Cadet 1808. Arrived in India 27 Oct. 1809. Ensign 22 Mar. 1810. Lieut. 16 Dec. 1814. Pensioned on Lord Clive's fund 17 May 1822. *d.* 12 May 1840.
Son of Archibald Dow, Purser on the *Prince William Henry,* East Indiaman. *m.* (before 1818) ?
Services : Posted as Ensign to 19th N.I. in 1810. Lieut. 2/19th N.I. Fur. s.c. 1812-4 ; 1815-6 ; 1819 till pensioned. No record of active service.

DOWE, Daniel. Ensign. Infantry. Cadet (?). Ensign 8 Nov. 1765. Resigned 16 May 1766.
Services : Resigned his Commission during the " Batta mutiny."

DOWELL, Thomas (1756/57-1831). Major. Artillery. *b.* 1756/57. Cadet 1783. Admitted 2 Sept. 1783. Fireworker 8 Feb. 1785. Lieut. 9 June 1791. Capt. 1 May 1804. Major 15 Sept. 1809. Retired 21 Feb. 1810. *d.* Exeter 11 Nov. 1831, aged 74.
Of Parker's Well, co. Devon. *m.* Calcutta, 28 Aug. 1797, Miss Harriet Cort.
Services : Third Mysore War ; Bangalore ; Lieut. 4th Coy. 2nd

Bn., and 1st Coy. 2nd Bn. Foot Art. Served with the detachment of Art. sent from Bengal in Nov. 1793, for about 12 mos., for service against French cruisers in the Bay of Bengal and E. Archipelago. Fur. 24 Jan. 1809 till retirement.

Refs. : Burke's *Peerage*, 1848, p. 931, *s.n.* Scudamore-Stanhope, Bart., of Stanwell House, Middlesex. *G.M.* 1831, i. 474.

DOWIE, David (1788-1837). Lieut. Colonel, 2nd N.I. *b.* Ayr, Scotland, 13 Mar. 1788. Cadet 1804. Arrived in India 30 Sept. 1805. Ensign 25 Aug. 1805. Lieut. 26 Aug. 1805. Capt. 17 Oct. 1818. Major 28 May. 1829. Lt. Col. 11 Feb. 1835. *d.* Lucknow 24 July 1837.

bapt. Ayr 13 Mar. 1788. Eldest son of Capt. James Dowie, of Camberwell, formerly master of the custom house cutter at Ayr, and Margaret Mackenzie his wife. Brother of Kenneth Dowie, and of Mrs. Mackenzie Forbes, both of Liverpool.

Services : Posted as Lieut. to 1st N.I. Adjt. 1/1st N.I. 28 Dec. 1815 till 1818. Actg. Intr. & Qmr. 1/1st N.I. 1818. Third Mahratta War ; actg. Prize Agent for Centre Div. Capt. 2/1st N.I. Transfd. to 2nd N.I. (late 1/1st) May 1824. Fur. p.a. 15 Dec. 1828 till 5 Oct. 1830. Posted as Lt. Col. to 2nd N.I. 11 Mar. 1835.

Refs. : *G.M.* 1838, i. 221. *A.J.* N.S. xxiv. 277. Will dated Saugor 20 Nov. 1834 ; proved 9 Nov. 1837.

DOWNES, Dennis (1804-1844). Captain, 30th N.I. *b.* Atterbury House, Kilfinaghty, co. Clare, 16 Aug. 1804. Cadet 1825. Arrived in India 20 Mar. 1826. Ensign 25 Oct. 1825. Lieut. 30 Dec. 1828. Capt. 3 Nov. 1843. *d.* Sitapur, U.P., 5 Feb. 1844.

Son of John Downes, surveyor of excise.

Services : Posted as Ensign to 31st N.I. in 1826. Operations against the Bhils 1828 ; Ensign 31st N.I. Transfd. to 30th N.I. in 1830. Adjt. 30th N.I. 18 Mar. 1834 till Sept. 1839. Fur. s.c. 17 Sept. 1839 till 1842. Actg. 2nd in comd. 2nd Oudh Local Inf. 3 Apr. 1843.

DOWNES, John. Lieutenant. Artillery. Cadet (?). Lieut. (Inf.) 1 Aug. 1763. 2nd Lieut. (Art.) 25 Jan. 1765. Lieut. 20 Oct. 1765. Resigned 14 May 1766.

Services : Resigned his Commission during the " Batta mutiny."

DOWNES, Robert (*d.* 1771). Ensign, Infantry. Cadet 1769. Ensign 1769. *d.* Dinapore 15 June 1771.

Services : N.F.P.

Refs. : Will dated 9 June 1771 ; proved 23 Aug. 1771.

THE BENGAL ARMY, 1758-1834   81

DOWNES, Stephen (*d.* 1780). Captain, 2nd Bengal Eur. Regt. Cadet 1768. Ensign 31 Dec. 1768. Lieut. 28 Dec. 1769. Capt. 10 July 1778. *d.* Cawnpore June 1780.
Services : Capt. 2/2nd Bengal Eur. Regt. in Oct. 1779.

DOWNES, William (*d.* 1791 ?). Cadet. Infantry. Cadet 1772. Resigned 1773. (? *d.* Bedale, Yorks., Feb. 1791.)
Services : N.F.P.
Refs. : (? *G.M.* 1791, i. 187.)

DOWNES, William (*d.* 1793 ?). Lieutenant. Infantry. Cadet 1781. Ensign 10 Aug. 1781. Lieut. 2 Sept. 1782. Struck off 1793. (? *d.* Charlotte St., Portland Pl., London, 3 Nov. 1793.)
Services : Granted fur. for 3 yrs. on h.p. 3 Oct. 1786, and was still on fur. in 1790. N.F.P.
Refs. : (? *Eur. Mag.* 1793, ii. 407.)

DOWNIE, George (1760/61-1808). Bt. Major, Bengal Eur. Regt. *b.* 1760/61. Cadet 1782. Admitted 22 Jan. 1783. Ensign 9 May 1783. Lieut. 27 Feb. 1790. Capt. 22 Oct. 1802. Bt. Major 25 Apr. 1808. *d.* Alipore, Calcutta, 4 Dec. 1808, aged 47.

A native of Perth. Brother of Robert Downie, of Calcutta, of the firm of Downie & Maitland, Agents. Nephew of John Downie, of Athentie, Scotland.
Services : 1st Asst. Mily. Auditor Gen. Fur. 14 Mar. 1794 till 1 Apr. 1797. Dy. Mily. Auditor Gen. 10 Oct. 1798 till Sept. 1800. Comdt. Calcutta Native Mil. 4 Sept. 1800 till death.
Refs. : *G.M.* 1809, i. 478. *S.M.* 1809, p. 398. Will dated Alipore 12 Nov. 1803 ; codicil dated 28 Sept. 1804 ; proved 3 Jan. 1809. M.I. in S. Park St. cemetery, Calcutta.

DOWNIE, John (*d.* 1763). Lieutenant, Bengal Eur. Regt. Cadet (?). Ensign (?). Lieut. 7 July 1759. *d.* 25 June 1763 : kld. in action at the assault of Patna.
Services : N.F.P.
Refs. : Broome, p. 365. Innes, p. 169.

DOWNING, David (1802-1888). General. 39th N.I. *bapt.* Ballyscullion, co. Londonderry, 10 Mar. 1802. Cadet 1818. Admitted 10 Feb. 1820. Ensign 16 Aug. 1819. Lieut. 2 Mar. 1822. Capt. 3 July 1832. Major 15 Sept. 1839. Lt. Col. 12 Oct. 1845. Col. 7 May 1855. Maj. Gen. 15 Sept. 1857. Lt. Gen. 23 Aug. 1869. Gen. 23 Aug. 1875. *d.* The Grange, Plaxtol, Kent, 18 Dec. 1888, aged 86.

5th and youngest son of Dawson Downing, of Bellaghy and Rowesgift, co. Londonderry, and Sarah Catherine his 2nd wife, dau. of Hugh Boyd, of Ballycastle. *m.* 1st, Calcutta, 9 Jan. 1833, Margaret Jean Ward. (She died 20 Apr. 1836.) *m.* 2nd, Frances Anne Hamilton, dau. of Levitt Broadley Parkyns, of Notts., and divorced wife of Thomas Henry Shuldham, *q.v.*

Services : Posted as Ensign to 2/6th N.I. Transfd. to 3rd N.I. (late 1/6th) May 1824. Second in comd. 7th Local Horse 28 Dec. 1824 till 1830. Fur. s.c. 12 Mar. 1830 till 11 Dec. 1832. Shekhawat expdn. 1834 ; Capt. 3rd N.I. Comdg. Jodhpur Legion 25 July 1836. Leave s.c. 2 yrs. to Cape 16 Mar. 1839. Comdg. Jodhpur Contingent, and P.A. at Sirohi, 7 Dec. 1840 till 1845. Posted as Lt. Col. to 4th N.I. in 1845. Second Sikh War ; Jullundur and Bari Doabs ; Lt. Col. comdg. 4th N.I., with Bdr. Wheeler's force (Medal). Transfd. to 39th N.I. Mar. 1850. Fur. s.c. 2 Apr. 1850 till 27 Dec. 1852. Transfd. to 2nd N.I. Sept. 1852 ; to 27th N.I. Oct. 1852. Fur. s.c. 20 Mar. 1854 till death. Col. 39th N.I. June 1855.

Refs. : Burke's *Landed Gentry of Ireland*, p. 250, *s.n.* Fullerton, of Ballintoy, co. Antrim. *Boase. A.J.* N.S. xxxvii. 36. *The Times,* 21 Dec. 1888.

DOWSON, Ralph (1816-1851). Captain, 5th N.I. Commandant 4th Punjab Cav. *b.* Reigate, Surrey, 1 Oct. 1816. Cadet 1834. Arrived in India 11 Feb. 1835. Ensign 21 Aug. 1834. Lieut. 15 Dec. 1837. Capt. 13 Jan. 1842. *d.* Bombay 26 Feb. 1851.

Son of William Dalrymple Dowson, of 56 Euston Sq., London, merchant, and Sophie his wife. Addiscombe Cadet 1 Aug. 1832 till 13 June 1834.

Services : Posted as Ensign to 5th N.I. 2 Mar. 1835. First Afghan War 1838-42 ; forcing of Khyber ; Ali Masjid ; apptd. to Shah Shuja's forces 1 Oct. 1839 ; Adjt. Ferris's Jazelchies in 1840 ; comdd. 3rd Jan-baz Cav. ; Kohistan ; Ghorband Pass ; Nazian valley Feb. 1841 ; defence of Jalalabad (Medal) ; actg. Adjt. Ferris's Jazelchies July 1842 ; against Shinwaris ; Tazin ; Haft Kotal ; re-occupation of Kabul (Medal). Rejoined 5th N.I. in 1843. Second in comd. 4th Inf. Gwalior Contingent 6 Feb. 1844 ; do. newly-raised 10th Irreg. Cav. Feb. 1846 (became 11th Irreg. in Sept. 1847).; actg. Comdt. do. 1846-7. Second Sikh War ; Multan ; Gujerat ; pursuit of Sikhs to Rawal Pindi ; 2nd in comd. 11th Irreg. Cav. (Medal with 2 clasps). Apptd. Comdt. 4th Punjab Cav. in May 1849 ; raised and comdd. this Corps till Aug. 1850, when he proceeded on leave to Bombay.

Refs. : De Rhé-Philipe. G.M. 1851, i. 574. *I.M.* 1851, p. 199. M.I. St. Paul's cathedral, Calcutta.

THE BENGAL ARMY, 1758-1834   83

DOXAT, Benjamin (1751/52-1838). Lieutenant. Artillery. b. 1751/52. Cadet 1772. Fireworker 1773. Lieut. 29 Mar. 1778. Resigned 15 Apr. 1783. d. Renens, nr. Lausanne, Switzerland, 10 Feb. 1838, aged 86.
A Swiss from canton Vaud. Brother of Lewis Doxat, q.v.
Services : First Rohilla War ; battle of St. George ; Lieut. F. Art.
Refs. : Livre d'Or. G.M. 1838, i. 670. A.J. N.S. xxv. 300.

DOXAT, Lewis (d. 1781). Captain, comdg. the Company of " Foreign Rangers." [1] Cadet 1768. Ensign 2 Feb. 1769. Lieut. 1 Jan. 1770. Capt. 15 Nov. 1778. d. unm. Ramnagar, opposite Benares, 20 Aug. 1781 : kld. in action during the revolt of the Rajah of Benares.
Brother of Benjamin Doxat, q.v. (*Possibly* uncle of Lewis Doxat—*D.N.B.*)
Services : First Rohilla War ; battle of St. George. Campaign against the Rajah of Benares 1781 ; action at Ramnagar (kld.) ; Capt. comdg. a corps of Foreign Rangers.
Refs. : Forrest, iii. 797. Will dated 12 Mar. 1781.
[1] *Note :* " When the Seven Years War was over, the numerous deserters from the French, and the numerous prisoners who fell into our hands on the capture of Pondicherry, provided so many accessions to our ranks (Madras) that they were formed into the body called the ' Foreign Legion ' comprising both horse and foot ... and were broken up about 12 years later. The Bengal Govt. had done the same, calling their corps the ' Foreign Rangers,' but with no better success ; and in 1786 desired no more deserters to be enlisted at Madras for service in Bengal." (*The Nabobs of Madras*, by Henry Dodwell, p. 77.)

D'OYLY, James Burnell (1790-1809). Ensign, Infantry. Unposted. b. 1790. Cadet 1807. Arrived in India 16 Nov. 1808. Ensign 31 Oct. 1808. d. unm. Barasat C.C. 26 Sept. 1809.
Eldest son of Edward D'Oyly, of Sion Hill, Yorks., J.P. for the N. Riding, and Hannah his wife, 3rd dau. of Richard Marston, of Willenhall, Staffs. Brother of Thomas D'Oyly, q.v., and nephew of William Molyneux Marston, q.v. His sisters m. William Geddes, q.v., and George Twemlow, q.v.
Services : Passed as Cadet on 9 Mar. 1808, aged 17.
Refs. : Burke's *Family Records*, p. 607, s.n. D'Oyly-Twemlow.

D'OYLY, Thomas (1794-1834). Captain, Artillery. b. 12 July 1794. Cadet 1810. Admitted 21 Jan. 1812. Fireworker 13 Jan. 1812. Lieut. 27 Jan. 1818. Capt. 26 Apr. 1828. d. Aug. 1834 :

wrecked in the *Charles Eaton* on Darnley I., Torres Straits, and murdered by the natives.

bapt. Wakefield, Yorks., 7 Aug. 1794. 2nd son of Edward D'Oyly, of Sion Hill, Yorks., and Hannah his wife. Brother of James Burnell D'Oyly, *q.v.* *m.* St. John's, Calcutta, 10 May 1820, Charlotte, dau. of Henry Williams, H.E.I.C.C.S., and grand-dau. of George Burrington, *q.v.* (She also was kld. by the natives of Darnley I. in Aug. 1834.) Addiscombe Cadet 1809/11.

Services : Third Mahratta War ; action at Jubbulpore 19 Dec. 1817 ; Mandala ; Asirgarh ; Lieut. 7th Coy. 2nd Bn. Foot Art. (*Lond. Gaz.* 7 Aug. 1819.) Adjt. & Qmr. 3rd Bn. 12 Jan. 1820 ; do. 1st Bn. 24 Feb. 1823. Adjt. 2nd Bn. 22 July 1825 ; do. 7th Bn. 28 Sept. 1827 till 19 Sept. 1828. Dy. Comy. Ord. at Chunar 22 Aug. 1828. Leave s.c. 2 yrs. to Tasmania 21 Mar. 1833. Apptd. Comy. Ord. at Agra 22 Nov. 1833 ; do. at Delhi 5 Nov. 1834.

Refs. : Burke's *Peerage,* 1848, p. 324, *s.n.* D'Oyly, Bart. Burke's *Landed Gentry,* 2nd edn., iii. 227, *s.n.* Marston, late of Willenhall, Staffs. Burke's *Family Records,* p. 607, *s.n.* D'Oyly-Twemlow. B. : P.P. No. 54, pp. 197-205. *The Times,* 23 Sept. 1836. *A.J.* N.S. xx. 219.

DRAKE, John Minshull (1807-1861). Lieut. Colonel, 65th N.I.
b. Cheriton, Devon, 21 May 1807. Cadet 1824. Arrived in India 5 Mar. 1826. Ensign 14 Aug. 1825. Lieut. 1 Apr. 1828. Capt. 26 Oct. 1844. Major 17 Apr. 1856. Lt. Col. 11 Sept. 1859. *d.* Dinapore 6 July 1861.

Eldest son of John Drake, Comy. Gen., H.M.S. *m.* 1st, St. Leonards, 22 May 1838, Caroline, youngest dau. of G. H. Grimes, Capt. Comy., R.A. (She died Landour 3 Apr. 1848.) *m.* 2nd, Lahore 21 Mar. 1850, Margaret McLean, dau. of John Todd, and widow of R. S. Dring. (She died 13 Oct. 1884.) Ed. Westminster ; admitted 12 Jan. 1818.

Services : Posted as Ensign to 46th N.I. in 1826. Intr. & Qmr. 46th N.I. 22 Apr. 1828 till Apr. 1836. Fur. p.a. 5 Apr. 1836 till 23 Nov. 1838. Intr. & Qmr. 4th L.C. 26 Mar. till 21 Aug. 1839. Actg. Intr. & Qmr. 46th N.I. 17 Aug. 1839 ; permanent do. 13 Feb. 1840 till 19 Dec. 1844. Offg. tempy. D.J.A.G., Presdy., 7 Sept. 1843. Second Sikh War ; Ramnagar ; Sadulapur ; Chilianwala ; Gujerat ; Capt. 46th N.I. (Medal with clasp). D.J.A.G. at Lahore 27 Nov. 1850 till 1856. Author of " An Abstract of the Articles of War for the Native Armies." (*Cal. Gaz.* 12 Aug. 1846.)

Refs. : *Westminster School Register.* *A.J.* N.S. xxvi. 192. *G.M.* 1861, ii. 334. *The Times,* 26 Aug. 1861.

THE BENGAL ARMY, 1758-1834

*DREW, John (1789-1829). Cadet. Artillery. Subsequently B.C.S. Collector at Dacca. *b.* 22 Dec. 1789. Cadet 1805. Did not take up the appointment. *d.* Dacca 30 Jan. 1829.
bapt. St. Leonard's, Shoreditch, London, 3 Feb. 1790. Son of John Crawford Drew, of Charles Sq., London, and Ann his wife. Woolwich Cadet: nominated to R.M.A. 23 Dec. 1803. Nominated student at Coll. of Fort William 8 Apr. 1807; admitted to Coll. Aug. 1808.
Services: Apptd. a Writer, B.C.S., 21 July 1807. Arrived in India 14 Aug. 1808. Apptd. Collector of Land Revenue and Customs, and Supt. of the Eastern Salt Chowkies at Dacca 15 Nov. 1827.
Refs.: A.J. xxviii. 92.

DRING, John. Ensign. 3rd Bengal Eur. Regt. Cadet 1778. Ensign 26 Aug. 1779. Struck off Feb. 1781.
Services: Posted as Ensign to 2/3rd Bengal Eur. Regt. in 1779.

DRINKELL, Francis. Ensign. Infantry. Cadet (?). Ensign 23 May 1766. Resigned (?).
Services: N.F.P. (*Probably* given a Commission in order to fill one of the vacancies caused by the " Batta mutiny.")

DROUGHT, Richard (Graves) [1] (1802-1873). Major General, C.B. 60th N.I. *b.* Claines, Worcester, 11 Nov. 1802. Cadet 1823. Arrived in India 10 Aug. 1824. Ensign 13 Feb. 1824. Lieut. 9 July 1825. Capt. 2 Dec. 1836. Major 25 Feb. 1855. Lt. Col. 17 Mar. 1859. Col. 29 Aug. 1859. Retired 31 Dec. 1861. Hon. Maj. Gen. 31 Dec. 1861. *d.s.p.* at his residence, 23 Upper Brunswick Pl., Brighton, 11 Apr. 1873.
bapt. 30 Nov. 1802. 4th son of Rev. Robert Campbell Drought, M.A., LL.D., and Mary his wife, elder dau. of Major Roger Bristow, of Bristowville, co. Antrim. *m.* Hove, Sussex, 29 Jan. 1856, Mary Anne, eldest dau. of Rev. Henry John Rush, vicar of Hollington, Sussex. (She died Brighton 29 Sept. 1881.)
Services: Siege and capture of Bhurtpore; Lieut. 60th N.I. (India medal). Intr. & Qmr. 60th N.I. 25 Nov. 1831 till 1 Apr. 1837. Reduction of Jhansi 1839; Capt. 60th N.I. First Afghan War 1842; actions in Khyber Pass in Jan., comdg. his Regt.; forcing of Khyber in Apr.; Gandamak; re-occupation of Kabul; Capt. 60th N.I. (Medal). Offg. Fort Adjt. at Chunar 31 Jan. 1848. Fur. 1854 till Dec. 1856. Mutiny campaign; siege of Delhi (s.w. nr. Ludlow Castle on 23 July 1857) (Medal). C.B. 17 June 1858.
Refs.: Family information. *The Times,* 15 Apr. 1873.

[1] *Note:* According to his family, his full name was Richard Graves Drought. The second name, however, does not appear in any official record.

LIST OF THE OFFICERS OF

DRUMMOND, Alpin. (*See* **MACGREGOR, Alpin.**)

DRUMMOND, Charles (*d.* 1766). Ensign, Infantry. Cadet (?). Ensign 1 Jan. 1766. *d.* Calcutta 6 Oct. 1766.
Services : N.F.P.

DRUMMOND, Daniel. (*See* **MACGREGOR, Daniel.**)

DRUMMOND, Francis (1762/63-1823). Lieut. Colonel, Invalid Est. 11th N.I. *b.* 1762/63. Cadet 1783. Admitted 30 Oct. 1783. Ensign 16 Mar. 1785. Lieut. 28 Mar. 1793. Capt. 21 Sept. 1804. Major 7 Jan. 1812. Lt. Col. 5 Aug. 1816. Invalided 20 Sept. 1816. *d.* Calcutta 7 Dec. 1823, aged 60.
Services : Lieut. 1/8th N.I. in 1798. Transfd. to 11th N.I. Capt. Lt. 11th N.I. 30 Sept. 1803. (? Reduction of Kalinjar 1812 ; Capt. 1/11th N.I.) Major 1/11th N.I.
Refs. : Will dated Calcutta 15 July 1823 ; proved 19 Dec. 1823. M.I. in S. Park St. cemetery, Calcutta.

DRUMMOND, Henry (1802-1868). Major General. 1st Eur. L.C. *b.* Edinburgh 7 Dec. 1802. Cadet 1820. Arrived in India Sept. 1821. Cornet 5 May 1821. Lieut. 1 May 1824. Capt. 16 Nov. 1845. Major 3 May 1856. Bt. Lt. Col. 20 June 1854. Bt. Col. 30 May 1859. Retired 31 Dec. 1861. Hon. Maj. Gen. 31 Dec. 1861. *d.* Hunton, Kent, 30 July 1868.
Son of James Drummond, M.P. *m.* (?).
Services : Posted as Cornet to 3rd L.C. (? Operations in Jodhpur 1823 ; capture of Lamba ; Cornet 3rd L.C.) Siege and capture of Bhurtpore ; Lieut. 3rd L.C. (India medal). Adjt. 3rd L.C. 7 June 1825 till 10 June 1826. Fur. s.c. 6 Jan. 1827 till 1 Dec. 1831. Operations against the Kols 1832 ; Lieut. 3rd L.C. Fur. s.c. 21 Nov. 1832 till 3 Oct. 1837. Employed in examining minerals in the Kumaon Hills. First Afghan War 1838-42 ; Ghazni ; Lieut. 3rd L.C. (Medal). Was delivered over as a hostage to Nawab Zeman Khan in Dec. 1841 ; released 21 Sept. 1842. Fur. p.a. 12 Aug. 1843 till 1846. Placed at the disposal of Foreign Office for special employ for 12 mos. in Nov. 1849 ; do. 18 Feb. 1854 till 26 Oct. 1855. Fur. p.a. 1 yr. 21 Mar. 1852, and 16 May 1856 till 31 July 1857. Major and Bt. Lt. Col. 3rd L.C. Posted to newly-raised 1st Eur. L.C. in 1858.
Refs. : *The Times,* 4 Aug. 1868.

DRUMMOND, Hugh (*d.* 1778). Lieutenant, Infantry. Cadet (?). Ensign 24 Sept. 1771. Lieut. 19 July 1776. *d.* Oct. 1778, when on active service with the Bombay detachment.

THE BENGAL ARMY, 1758-1834

(*Possibly* related to Alpin and Daniel Macgregor (formerly Drummond), *q.v.*, who were exors. of his Will.)
Services : First Mahratta War 1778.
Refs. : Will dated 16 May 1778 ; proved 23 July 1779.

DRUMMOND, James (1808-1852). Major, 19th N.I. *b*. Earlston, co. Berwick, 7 Nov. 1808. Cadet 1825. Arrived in India 8 May 1826. Ensign 18 Jan. 1826. Lieut. 9 Jan. 1827. Capt. 8 Oct. 1836. Major 28 Mar. 1850. *d*. Simla 26 Apr. 1852.

Of Balquahandy and Aberuchill, Scotland. *bapt*. 25 Nov. 1808. Son of John Gavin Drummond, *q.v.*, and Euphemia Farmer his wife. *m*. Dehra Dun, 23 Jan. 1851, Ellen Fanshaw Drummond, dau. of Charles Henry Boisragon, *q.v.* (She re-m. 20 Sept. 1858, Charles Simeon Thomason, Bengal Engrs.)

Services : Ensign d.d. 4th Extra Regt. Posted as Ensign to 19th N.I. 26 Sept. 1826. Comdd. Khurda Paik Coy. 1837-8. 2nd in comd. Kumaon Local Bn. 17 Mar. 1839. Rejoined 19th N.I. in Mar. 1842. 2nd in comd. Kumaon Local Bn. Mar. 1843 ; comdd. do. 15 Oct. 1847 till 1 Oct. 1851. Rejoined 19th N.I. in Jan. 1852, and comdd. that Regt. till 7 Apr. 1852, when he proceeded to Simla on sick leave. No record of active service.

Refs. : *De Rhé-Philipe*. *I.M*. 1852, p. 347. Will dated Simla 21 Apr. 1852 ; proved 29 July 1852.

DRUMMOND, James Charles (1807-1827). Lieutenant, 19th N.I. *b*. Bathwick, Somerset, 15 Oct. 1807. Cadet 1824. Ensign 18 Mar. 1825. Lieut. 28 Mar. 1826. *d*. Nasirabad 27 Nov. 1827.

4th son of Sir Adam Drummond, K.C.H., Adm. R.N., of Megginch Castle, co. Perth, and Lady Charlotte Murray his wife, eldest dau. of John, 4th Duke of Atholl. Ed. Westminster ; admitted 22 Sept. 1820.

Services : Posted as Ensign to 19th N.I. No record of active service.

Refs. : Burke's *Landed Gentry*, 13th edn., p. 523, *s.n*. Drummond, of Megginch Castle, co. Perth. *Westminster School Register*.

DRUMMOND, John Gavin (1788-1851). Lieut. Colonel, C.B., 30th N.I. Q.M.G. *b*. Edinburgh 26 Aug. 1788. Cadet 1807. Arrived in India 16 Nov. 1808. Ensign 25 Nov. 1808. Lieut. 11 Mar. 1812. Capt. 13 May 1825. Major 11 Nov. 1837. Lt. Col. 20 Dec. 1843. *d*. Kharian, nr. Jhelum, 11 Dec. 1851.

bapt. St. George's chapel, Edinburgh, 12 Sept. 1788. Son of J. Drummond. *m*. Euphemia Farmer. Father of James Drummond, *q.v.*

Services : Barasat C.C. for 8 mos. Ensign d.d. 1/8th N.I. July

1809 till Apr. 1811. Posted to 2/3rd N.I. 1 Aug. 1809, and joined in 1811. Nepal War 1814-5; Nalagarh; Ramgarh; Malaun; Lieut. 2/3rd N.I., and Staff Ofr. to Reserve of 1st Div. Intr. & Qmr. 2/3rd N.I. 26 Mar. 1816 till Sept. 1822. To officiate in Q.M.G. dept. Sept. 1822. D.A.Q.M.G. 3 cl. 25 Apr. 1823; 2 cl. 7 June 1824. Transfd. to 6th N.I. (late 1/3rd) May 1824. First Burma War; Arakan 1825; D.A.Q.M.G. with Bdr. Morrison's force. D.A.Q.M.G. 1 cl. 17 Jan. 1829; 2nd A.Q.M.G. 10 Apr. 1837 till Apr. 1838. Fur. 28 May 1841 till 11 Nov. 1842. D.Q.M.G. of the Army at Cawnpore 17 Jan. 1843. Gwalior campaign; Maharajpur (Bronze star). D.Q.M.G. Mar. 1844. Posted as Lt. Col. to 61st N.I. 6 Mar. 1844; to 42nd N.I. 18 Dec. 1844. First Sikh War; Sobraon; D.Q.M.G. (Medal). Posted to 30th N.I. in May 1847. Second Sikh War; both sieges of Multan; capture of Multan; Gujerat; D.Q.M.G. (Medal with 2 clasps). Offg. Q.M.G. 1 Dec. 1849; permanent Q.M.G. of the Army 8 Feb. 1850 till death. C.B. 30 Oct. 1844.

Refs. : *De Rhé-Philipe. Boase. I.M.* 1852, pp. 59, 62. *G.M.* 1852, i. 424.

DRUMMOND, John Philip (*d.* 1830). Bt. Major. Artillery. Infantry Cadet 1782. Admitted 1 July 1783. Ensign 16 Mar. 1783. Fireworker 28 Dec. 1788. Lieut. 30 Oct. 1794. Capt. Lt. 15 Nov. 1802. Capt. 17 Sept. 1805. Bt. Major 25 Apr. 1808. Retired 23 Oct. 1811. *d.* Dumfries 29 Dec. 1830.

Of Dumfries. *m.* Mary Harriet Cridland.

Services : Transfd. from Inf. to Art. in 1788. Third Mysore War; Bangalore. Fur. 11 Jan. 1796 till 1 Nov. 1798. Fourth Mysore War; Lieut. & Adjt. Art. Expedition to Egypt 1801; returned sick to India in Sept. 1801. Storm and capture of Broach, Bombay, 29 Aug. 1803; reduction of fort Pawagadh, Panch Mahals, Sept. 1803; Capt. Lt. 5th Coy. 3rd Bn. Art. Comdt. Art., and Adjt. P.W.I. 1804-6. Town Major at P.W.I. 1806-8. Fur. 18 Aug. 1808 till retirement.

Refs. : Will dated 27 June 1820; proved 7 Apr. 1832.

DRUMMOND, Peter (*d.* 1779). Lieutenant, Infantry. Cadet 1771. Ensign 22 Jan. 1773. Lieut. 14 May 1777. *d.* Chittagong Oct. 1779.

Services : N.F.P.

DRUMMOND, Thomas (*d.* 1787). Ensign, Infantry. Cadet 1783. Ensign 16 Mar. 1785. *d.* 31 July 1787 : bur. Calcutta 4 Aug. 1787.

Services : N.F.P.

THE BENGAL ARMY, 1758-1834 89

DRYSDALE, James (1782-1830). Major. 50th N.I. *b.* Kirkcaldy, co. Fife, 14 Oct. 1782. Cadet 1800. Arrived in India 21 Aug. 1801. Ensign 12 Dec. 1801. Lieut. 30 Sept. 1803. Capt. 10 Jan. 1818. Major 23 Aug. 1826. Retired 21 June 1830. *d.* 17 Dec. 1830.
bapt. 15 Oct. 1782. Son of William Drysdale, of Kirkcaldy, town clerk, and Ann Cunnison his wife. *m.* (before 1819) ?
Services : Operations in Jumna Doab 1803 ; Sasni ; Ensign 2/12th N.I. Second Mahratta War ; battle of Delhi ; Laswari ; Bhurtpore (w. in 3rd assault on 20 Feb. 1805) ; Lieut. 2/12th N.I. Transfd. to newly-raised 25th N.I. in 1805. Capture of Gohad 1806 ; Lieut. 1/25th N.I. Fur. 1811 till 29 Aug. 1815. Capt. Lt. 25th N.I. 21 May 1816. Siege and capture of Hathras 1817 ; Capt. Lt. 1/25th N.I. Capt. 2/25th N.I. With 3rd Ceylon Vol. Bn. 1818-9. Transfd. to 50th N.I. (late 2/25th) May 1824. Tempy. comdg. Calcutta Native Mil. 12 Jan. 1827. Fur. s.c. 1 Feb. 1828 till retirement.

DUBOIS, John Hubert Valentia (*d.* 1826). Captain. 9th N.I. Country Cadet 1778. Admitted 9 Mar. 1778. Ensign 31 Mar. 1778. Lieut. 16 Feb. 1779. Capt. 10 June 1796. Retired 19 Mar. 1800. *d.* 1826.
Son of Peter Dubois, a French musician, and Lady Dorothea his wife (*D.N.B.*), dau. of Richard Annesley, 6th Earl of Anglesey, by a dau. of John Simpson, of Meath St., Dublin, clothier. Brother of Simpson Dubois, *q.v.*, and of Frederick Peter Dubois.
Services : Lieut. 1/2nd Bengal Eur. Regt. in Oct. 1779 ; 36th Bn. Sepoys in July 1787. Fur. 11 May 1797 till retirement. The wife of Thomas Whinyates, *q.v.*, writing under date Fatehgarh, 11 Jan. 1787, says, " Valentia de Bois, son of Lady Dorothy, a Lieut. in this Service, is now in irons and was to have been tried some days since for shooting a black man whose wife he was carrying off, but the trial has been deferred till next Sessions."
Refs. : Whinyates Family Records.

DUBOIS, Simpson (1758-1808). Lieut. Colonel, 10th N.I. *b.* in Ireland 1758. Cadet 1778. Admitted 2 Oct. 1778. Ensign 2 Oct. 1778. Lieut. 15 Nov. 1778. Capt. 1 June 1796. Major 10 Aug. 1801. Lt. Col. 27 Jan. 1804. *d.* 20 Nov. 1808 : lost at sea in the *Glory*, and struck off from 24 Jan. 1809.
bapt. Marylebone 1774. Son of Peter Dubois and Lady Dorothea his wife. Brother of John Hubert Valentia Dubois, *q. v. m.* 1st, (before 1789) Mary. *m.* 2nd, Calcutta, 5 Aug. 1805, Miss Bathia Campbell.
Services : Sailed for India on the *Southampton*, 7 Mar. 1778, aged 20. Lieut. 26th Bn. Sepoys in July 1787. Capt. 16th N.I.

Transfd. as Lt. Col. to 21st N.I. in 1805. (? Second Mahratta War ; Lt. Col. 21st N.I.) Transfd. to 10th N.I. in 1808.
Refs. : *N. & Q.* 8S. xii. 349.

DUCAREL, James Coltee (*d.* 1770). Major, Infantry. Capt. 3 Aug. 1765. Major 3 Sept. 1765. *d.* (? Purnea, B. & O.) 8 Sept. 1770.

Son of Adrian Coltee Ducarel, of Cloak Lane, London, merchant and S. Sea director,[1] and Elizabeth his wife. Brother of Gerard Gustavus Ducarel, B.C.S., Supervisor at Purnea, and nephew of James Coltee Ducarel, and of Andrew Coltee Ducarel (*D.N.B.*).

[1] *Note* : Of a Huguenot family which settled in England in 1685. He was naturalized in 1738.

Services : Lieut. H.M. 13th Foot 4 July 1759. Transfd. as Capt. to Bengal army in 1765. Having refused from the first to join the mutinous combination against Lord Clive's new Batta regulations by resigning his Commission in May 1766, was, in consequence, subjected to much annoyance and ill usage from his brother officers.

Refs. : Burke's *Landed Gentry*, 2nd edn., p. 886, *s.n.* Morrice, of Betshanger, Kent ; p. 1037, *s.n.* Phillips, of Garendon Park, Leics. *Broome*, p. 610. *G.M.* 1785, i. 407. Will dated Purnea 24 May 1770 ; proved 23 Oct. 1770.

DUDGEON, Patrick (1789-1825). Captain, 14th N.I. *b.* Athelstaneford, co. Haddington, 27 June 1789. Cadet 1804. Arrived in India 10 Feb. 1805. Ensign 15 Aug. 1805. Lieut. 16 Aug. 1805. Capt. 6 June 1823. *d.* Calcutta 5 Oct. 1825.

bapt. Athelstaneford 27 July 1789. Son of James Dudgeon, tenant in Drem, co. Haddington, and Marion his wife, dau. of George Yule. Brother of Beatrice Dudgeon, and nephew of Udny Yule, *q.v.*

Services : Posted as Lieut. to 1/10th N.I. in 1806. (? Operations in Hariana 1809 ; Bhawani ; Lieut. 1/10th N.I.) Qmr. 6th Bengal Vol. Bn. 22 Mar. 1811 till 1816. Capture of Java 1811 ; Palembang 1812 ; Lieut. 6th Vol. Bn. Fur. 27 Jan. 1817 till 1818. Comdd. 1st Narbada Sebundy Corps 1821-4. Transfd. to 14th N.I. (late 1/10th) May 1824. Comdd. Sylhet Local Bn. 1824 till death.

Refs. : *S.M.* 1826, i. 511. Will dated camp, Banscoondie, 18 Jan. 1821 ; proved 12 Oct. 1825. M.I. in S. Park St. cemetery, Calcutta.

DU FEU, John (1785-1807). Lieutenant, 23rd N.I. *b.* Guernsey 1785. Cadet 1803. Arrived in India 3 Dec. 1804. Ensign 15 Oct. 1804. Lieut. 15 Oct. 1804. *d.* 18 Nov. 1807 : kld. in action in the assault on the fort of Komona.

Eldest son of John Du Feu, of Guernsey.

Services : Posted as Lieut. to 1/23rd N.I. Operations against

Dhundia Khan 1807 ; assault of Komona (kld.) ; Lieut. 1/23rd N.I., d.d. Pioneers.
Refs. : A.A.R. x. 21.

DUFF, John (1751/52-1828). Lieut. Colonel. 24th N.I. *b.* 1751/52. Cadet 1779. Arrived in India 15 Mar. 1780. Ensign 18 July 1779. Lieut. 10 Mar. 1781. Capt. 30 Oct. 1797. Major 30 Sept. 1803. Lt. Col. 10 July 1806. Retired 23 Sept. 1807. *d.* Sidney St., City Rd., London, 17 Nov. 1828, aged 76.

Son of James Duff, of Pitchaish. Brother of Patrick Duff (1742-1803), *q.v. m.* (?).

Services : Sailed for India on the *Walpole* 16 June 1779 (when he gave his age as 23). Lieut. 17th Bn. Sepoys in July 1787. Adjt. 17th Bn. Sepoys in 3rd Bde. in 1790. Capt. 14th N.I. Transfd. to newly-raised 19th N.I. 29 May 1800 ; as Major to newly-raised 24th N.I. Oct. 1804. Fur. 28 Feb. 1805 till retirement.

Refs. : A.J. xxvi. 767. Will dated 16 Sept. 1813 ; proved 18 June 1829.

DUFF, Patrick (1742-1803). Major General. Comdt. Artillery. *b.* 1742. Cadet (?). Arrived in India 1760. Fireworker 12 June 1762. 2nd Lieut. 2 Dec. 1763. Lieut. 28 Mar. 1764. Capt. Lt. 2 Aug. 1765. Capt. 6 Aug. 1768. Major 25 Feb. 1777. Lt. Col. 30 Nov. 1780. Col. 29 May 1786. Maj. Gen. 20 Dec. 1793. *d.* Edinburgh 2 Feb. 1803.

Of Carnousie. 2nd son of James Duff, of Pitchaish. Brother of William Duff, *q.v. m.* 1st, his cousin, Anne Duff. (She died Madras, 27 Apr. 1776, aged 26.) *m.* 2nd, Boruff, 10 Jan. 1794, Dorothea, sister of Gen. Andrew Hay, of Mountblairy. (She died 6 Feb. 1803.)

Services : Went to India in 1760 as a gentleman volunteer in H.M. 89th Regt. (Morris's Highlrs.). Battle of Buxar ; Ensign H.M. 89th. Transfd. to Bengal Art. 4th Coy. Art. at Bankipore in May 1766, when he was implicated in the Batta mutiny, was sent to Calcutta under arrest, was ordered home, but was subsequently restored to the Service without loss of rank. Apptd. to comd. newly-raised Golandaz Coys. in 1777. Comy. of Stores at Fort William till Oct. 1785. Fur. Dec. 6 1788 till 31 Oct. 1790. Third Mysore War ; Bangalore ; Seringapatam. Fur. 13 July 1792 till 13 Feb. 1797. To comd. Art. 29 Mar. 1797 ; to comd. troops at the Presdy. 1 July 1797. Fur. 5 Dec. 1797 till death.

Refs. : Family information. *E.I.M.C.* ii. 250. *Stubbs,* ii. 229-32. *S.M.* 1791 ; 1794, p. 62 ; 1803, p. 220. *G.M.* 1803, i. 197. *N. & Q.* 11S. ix. 98 ; 10S. x. 421. Portrait by G. Romney : engraving by C. H. Hodges pub. in 1791.

*DUFF, Patrick (1751-1785). Captain, Infantry. *b.* 28 Mar. 1751. Cadet (?). Went to India in 1769. Ensign (?). Lieut. (?). Capt. (?). *d.* in India Jan./Apr. 1785.
Son of Patrick Duff, of Whitehill and Crowie, and Clementina his wife, dau. of C. Hay, of Rannes. Related to the Duffs, of Hatton.
Services : Was comdg. a Bn. in the 1st Bde. at date of death. N.F.P.
Refs. : Family information. Burke's *Landed Gentry*, 13th edn., p. 528, *s.n.* Duff, of Hatton, Meldrum and Blyth. Will dated 14 Jan. 1785 ; proved 21 Apr. 1785.

DUFF, Robert (*d.* 1828). Captain. 8th N.I. Cadet 1783. Admitted 26 Sept. 1783. Ensign 5 May 1785. Lieut. 7 Aug. 1793. Capt. 30 Sept. 1803. Retired 25 Jan. 1809. *d.* Elgin 11 Feb. 1828.
Services : Lieut. 8th N.I. Fur. 9 Dec. 1802 till 1 Sept. 1805. Capt. 8th N.I.

DUFF, William (*d.* 1807). Lieut. Colonel, 9th N.I. Country Cadet 1777. Admitted 28 Apr. 1777. Ensign 28 Apr. 1777. Lieut. 5 Oct. 1778. Capt. 18 Mar. 1796. Major 29 May 1800. Lt. Col. 13 July 1803. *d.* 18 Nov. 1807 : kld. in action at the assault of Komona.
Son of James Duff, of Pitchaish. Brother of John Duff, *q.v.*
Services : Returned from fur. 31 Aug. 1785. Lieut. 24th Bn. Sepoys in July 1787. Posted as Capt. to newly-raised 17th N.I. in 1798. Major 1/17th N.I. A.D.C. to Maj.-Gen. Stuart till 2 Oct. 1800. Posted as Lt. Col. to 1/9th N.I. in 1804. Operations against Dhundia Khan 1807 ; Komona (kld.) ; Lt. Col. comdg. 1/9th N.I.
Refs. : A.A.R. x. 21.

DUFFIELD, Vernon. Captain. 6th Bn. Sepoys. Cadet (?). Ensign 12 Sept. 1760. Lieut. 30 Aug. 1763. Capt. 19 Apr. 1764. Cashiered 1766.
Services : " The command of the battalion (6th) was then (Dec. 1764) given to Capt. Duffield who gave an entertainment to the Native officers and Sepoys on joining it, since when it has gone by his name (' *Duffal-ki-Paltan* ')." (*Williams.*) " Threw up his Commission in 1766, and ordered home, went out again in 1775, and was taken in disguise in Patna." (*Dodwell & Miles.*) (*Probably* cashiered as one of the ringleaders of the " Batta mutiny.")
Refs. : Williams, p. 107. *Broome*, p. 604.

DUFFIN, Adam (1789-1838). Lieut. Colonel, 2nd L.C. *b.* Drumglass, co. Tyrone, Mar. 1789. Cadet 1804. Arrived in India 25 Mar. 1806. Cornet 30 Mar. 1806. Lieut. 27 Feb. 1812. Capt.

1 Sept. 1818. Major 13 May 1825. Lt. Col. 26 Dec. 1832. *d.* in camp nr. Bahawalpur, Punjab, 28 Dec. 1838.

Son of Charles Duffin, of Dublin. Brother of Charles Duffin (1791-1831), *q.v.* *m.* Muttra, 10 Aug. 1815, Mary Anne, eldest dau. of Gregory Hickman, *q.v.* His dau. *m.* Edward Garstin, *q.v.*
Services : Posted as Cornet to 7th N.C. 1 Feb. 1807. Served in Oudh 1808, in Hariana 1809-10. Nepal War 1814-5 ; Kalanga ; Lieut. 7th N.C., in 2nd Div. Siege and capture of Hathras 1817. Third Mahratta War ; Dhamoni ; Mandala ; operations against Appa Sahib ; Lieut. 7th N.C. Leave s.c. to Singapore 19 May 1833 till 31 Dec. 1833. Transfd. to 2nd L.C. 24 Dec. 1833, and comdd. this Regt. till death. To comd. Left Column of Cav. proceeding to join Army of the Indus 24 Oct. 1838.
Refs. : *De Rhé-Philipe.* *A.J.* N.S. xxix. 63. Will dated 26 Jan. 1822 ; proved 4 Apr. 1839. M.I. in Bahawalpur cemetery.

DUFFIN, Charles (1747/48-1817). Captain. Infantry. *b.* 1747/48. Cadet 1766. Ensign 14 Oct. 1766. Lieut. 10 Dec. 1767. Capt. 2 July 1771. *d.* 27 Jan. 1817, aged 69.
Services : N.F.P.
Refs. : *G.M.* 1817, i. 184.

DUFFIN, Charles (1791-1831). Captain, 7th L.C. *b.* Drumglass, co. Tyrone, Feb. 1791. Cadet 1810. Admitted 22 Aug. 1811. Cornet 1 Oct. 1815. Lieut. 1 Sept. 1818. Capt. 13 May 1825. *d.* Kaitha, U.P., 26 Aug. 1831.

Son of Charles Duffin, of Dublin. Brother of Adam Duffin, *q.v.* *m.* (before 1821) Olivia Lockhart. (She re-m. William Macgeorge, *q.v.*) T.C.D. Fellow Commoner 2 Nov. 1807, aged 16.
Services : Cadet d.d. 7th N.C. 1811. Posted as Cornet to 7th N.C. in 1815. Siege and capture of Hathras 1817 ; Cornet 7th N.C. Third Mahratta War ; Dhamoni ; Mandala ; Multai (where he made a gallant charge—*Lond. Gaz.* 10 Aug. 1819) ; Harna ; Lieut. 7th N.C. Intr. & Qmr. 7th L.C. 17 June 1824 till 29 July 1825. Siege and capture of Bhurtpore ; Capt. 7th L.C., doing duty with 9th L.C.
Refs. : *Alumni Dub.* Will dated 29 Dec. 1825 ; proved 21 Jan. 1832.

DUFFIN, Charles William (1816-1855). Captain. 26th N.I. *bapt.* Agra 10 July 1816. Cadet 1834. Arrived in India 29 July 1835. Ensign 18 Dec. 1834. Lieut. 12 Jan. 1837. Capt. 1 May 1849. Invalided 1 Sept. 1850. Retired 16 May 1852. *d.* 31 Oct. 1855. Eldest son of Adam Duffin, *q.v.*, and Mary Anne his wife. *m.*

Meerut, 6 Aug. 1838, Louisa, 3rd dau. of Harry Pigou, Capt. 3rd Dgn. Gds. Addiscombe Cadet 3 Feb. 1832 till 12 Dec. 1834.
Services : Ensign d.d. 37th N.I. 19 Aug. 1835. Posted to 40th N.I. 24 Sept. 1835. Transfd. to 26th N.I. 30 Oct. 1835. Intr. & Qmr. 26th N.I. 18 Oct. 1838 till July 1849. First Afghan War 1842 ; Kabul ; Istalif ; Lieut. 26th N.I. (Medal). Apptd. Actg. Bde. Qmr. to Gen. Pollock's force 4 July 1842. Offg. S.A.C.G. Cav. Bde., with troops W. of Indus, 11 July 1842. First Sikh War ; Mudki ; Ferozshahr ; Sobraon ; Lieut. 26th N.I. (Medal with 2 clasps). Fur. 1851 till retirement. Crimean War. Local Major in Turkey 27 Mar. 1855.
Refs. : *I.M.* 1845, pp. 147-51, 308, 498.

DUFFIN, William Clarke (1782-1801). Lieutenant, 6th N.I. *b.* St. Mary, Bungay, Suffolk, 30 Aug. 1782. Cadet 1799. Arrived in India 8 Dec. 1800. Ensign 26 Aug. 1800. Lieut. 30 Jan. 1801. *d.* Ganjam, Madras, 15 Nov. 1801.
bapt. St. Mary, Bungay, 2 Sept. 1782.
Services : Disturbances in Ganjam district 1801 ; Lieut. 2/6th N.I.
Refs. : *A.A.R.* iv. 120.

DUN(N), Andrew (*d.* 1805). Captain, Artillery. Cadet 1783. Admitted 17 Sept. 1783. Fireworker 9 Mar. 1785. Lieut. 17 June 1792. Capt. Lt. 19 Feb. 1802. Capt. 21 Sept. 1804. *d.* Tonk Rampura 2 Oct. 1805.
Brother of James Dun, the father of John Dun, *q.v.*
Services : Third Mysore War ; Bangalore ; Lieut. 5th Coy. 2nd Bn. Art. Second Rohilla War ; battle of Bitaurah ; Lieut. 2nd Coy. 3rd Bn. Fourth Mysore War ; Lieut. 2nd Coy. 3rd Bn. Storm and capture of Broach, Bombay, 29 Aug. 1803 ; reduction of fort Pawagadh, Champaner district, Panch Mahals, Sept. 1803 ; Capt. Lt. 5th Coy. 3rd Bn. Second Mahratta War ; Bhurtpore ; Capt. comdg. 5th Coy. 3rd Bn.
Refs. : Will dated 29 Apr. 1802 ; proved 10 Feb. 1806.

DUN, John (1781-1845). Major General. Colonel 29th N.I. *b.* Selkirk, Scotland, 20 July 1781. Cadet 1799. Arrived in India 9 Dec. 1800. Ensign 12 Nov. 1800. Lieut. 30 Sept. 1803. Capt. 1 Nov. 1815. Major 1 May 1824. Lt. Col. 19 Oct. 1827. Col. 16 Mar. 1838. Maj. Gen. 3 Nov. 1841. *d.* 2 Feb. 1845.
Son of James Dun and Jean Anderson his wife. Nephew of Andrew Dun(n), *q.v. m.* Selkirk, 1 Mar. 1832, Dorothea, eldest dau. of Andrew Henderson, of Midgehope.
Services : (? Second Mahratta War ; Lieut. 11th N.I.) Capture

of Java 1811 ; Lieut. 4th Vol. Bn. Served with Vols. in Java till
1816. Siege and capture of Hathras ; Capt. 2/11th N.I. Third
Mahratta War ; Capt. 2/11th N.I. Fur. p.a. 8 Jan. 1824 till 4 June
1827. Transfd. as Major to 15th N.I. (late 1/11th) May 1824 ; to
17th N.I. (late 2/11th). Posted as Lt. Col. to 35th N.I. 22 Apr.
1828. Transfd. to 53rd N.I. 25 Nov. 1830 ; to 37th N.I. 11 June
1832. Fur. s.c. 14 Feb. 1831 till 4 Jan. 1834. Transfd. to 52nd
N.I. 11 Jan. 1834 ; to 17th N.I. 15 Jan. 1835 ; to 54th N.I. 7 Apr.
1835. Posted as Col. to 29th N.I. 13 Nov. 1838. Fur. s.c. 19 Feb.
1839 till death.

Refs. : *A.J.* N.S. vii. 226.

DUN(N), William (*d.* 1802). Captain, Artillery. Country Cadet
1778. Admitted 17 Sept. 1778. Fireworker 29 Dec. 1778.
Lieut. 19 Oct. 1784. Capt. 8 Jan. 1796. *d. unm.* Monghyr
18 June 1802.

Services : Second Mysore War ; Lieut. F. 4th Coy. 2nd Bn. Art.
Fourth Mysore War ; Capt. comdg. 3rd Coy. 1st Bn.

Refs. : Will dated 1801 ; proved 1802.

DUNBAR, Charles Cumming (1808-1828). Ensign, 59th N.I. *bapt.*
Duffus, co. Elgin, 9 Aug. 1808. Cadet 1825. Ensign 26 Dec.
1825. *d. unm.* Barrackpore 2 July 1828.

5th son of Sir Archibald Dunbar, 5th Bart. of Northfield, and
Helen Penuel his 1st wife, dau. of Col. Sir Alexander Penrose
Cumming-Gordon, Bart., of Altyre.

Services : Posted as Ensign to 59th N.I. in 1826. No record of
active service.

Refs. : Burke's *Peerage*, 1923, p. 772, *s.n.* Dunbar, Bart., of
Northfield. *Annals of Elgin*, 1150-1876, p. 651.

DUNBAR, James (*d.* 1770). Captain, 22nd Bn. Sepoys. Cadet (?).
Ensign 27 Sept. 1764. Lieut. 17 Oct. 1765. Capt. 6 Aug. 1768.
d. Tippera, Bengal, 17 May 1770.

Son of James Dunbar, of Kinkorth. Brother of Robert Dunbar,
surgeon in Banff, and of Margaret Ogilvie Dunbar, wife of James,
4th son of Alexander Duff, of Hatton.

Services : Apptd. A.D.C. to Sir Robert Fletcher, *q.v.*, Aug. 1765,
and was still serving in that capacity during the " Batta mutiny "
in May 1766. (? Operations against the Saniyasis 1770.)

Refs. : *Broome*, pp. 537, ix. Will dated Comilla, Bengal, 9 May
1770 ; proved 28 Aug. 1770.

DUNBAR, James William (1800-1830). Captain. 26th N.I. *b.*
Woolwich 6 Oct. 1800. Cadet 1818. Ensign (?). Lieut. 26 Sept.
1820. Capt. 11 July 1828. Discharged by G.C.M. 30 Jan. 1830.

d. Calcutta 15 July 1830 : committed suicide by shooting himself with a pistol. Verdict—insanity.

Son of James William Dunbar, clerk in the D.A.G.'s office at Woolwich.

Services : Ensign d.d. Bengal Eur. Regt. Posted as Lieut. to 2/13th N.I. in 1820. Transfd. to 27th N.I. (late 2/13th) May 1824 ; to 26th N.I. (late 1/13th) 1825. First Burma War ; Arakan 1825 ; Lieut. 26th N.I.

Refs. : *A.J.* N.S. ii. 155 ; iv. 15.

*DUNBAR, Matthew Charles (1787/88-1819). Bt. Captain, 7th N.I.
b. 1787/88. Cadet 1803. Arrived in India 2 Dec. 1804. Ensign 10 Nov. 1804. Lieut. 10 Nov. 1804. Bt. Capt. 1 Jan. 1818. *d.* Ajmer (? Nasirabad), 21 June 1819, of fever.

Son of William Dunbar, barr.-at-law. Brother of Anne Raymond, wife of George Heath, of Kitlands, Dorking, Serjt.-at-Law.

Services : Apptd. Cadet on 17 May 1803, aged 15. Posted as Lieut. to 7th N.I. in 1805. Adjt. 1/7th N.I. 1808-10. Adjt. & Qmr. 7th N.I. 23 Jan. 1810 till July 1814. Intr. & Qmr. 2/7th N.I. 1 July 1814 till death. Third Mahratta War ; Bt. Capt. 2/7th N.I. (? in Comst. Dept.), Bde. Qmr. 8th Inf. Bde., Reserve Div.

Refs. : Burke's *Landed Gentry,* 13th edn., p. 872, *s.n.* Heath, of Kitlands, Dorking. *G.M.* 1820, i. 186. *A.J.* ix. Will dated 12 June 1819 ; proved 2 Sept. 1819.

DUNBAR, Patrick (*alias* **Peter**) (1777-1864). Lieut. Colonel. 3rd L.C. *b.* 6 Sept. 1777. Cadet 1798. Arrived in India 17 Oct. 1799. Cornet 17 June 1800. Lieut. 11 Mar. 1805. Capt. 1 Sept. 1818. Major 8 May 1821. Retired 26 Apr. 1824. Hon. Lt. Col. 28 Nov. 1854. *d.* Westbourne Terr., Hyde Pk., London, 18 July 1864.

bapt. Auldearn, Nairn, the Tuesday following his birth. 5th and youngest son of Alexander Dunbar, of Boath, co. Nairn, and Jean his wife, 4th dau. of George Burnett, of Kemnay. Younger brother of Sir James Dunbar, 1st Bart., of Boath, Capt. R.N. *m.* St. Andrews, 9 Nov. 1822, Jessy, dau. of Rev. William Leslie, of Balnageith, co. Moray, and niece of the Earl of Caithness. (She died 4 Oct. 1854.)

Services : With 13th N.I. till June 1800. Cornet d.d. newly-raised 6th N.C. June 1800. Posted as Cornet to 3rd N.C. Aug. 1801, and spent the remainder of his service with that Regt. Operations in Jumna Doab 1802-3 ; Sasni ; Bijaigarh ; Kachaura. Second Mahratta War ; Koil ; Aligarh ; Delhi ; Agra ; Laswari ; Rampura ; battle and capture of Deig ; Bhurtpore (India medal with

THE BENGAL ARMY, 1758-1834

5 clasps [1]). Siege and capture of Hathras 1817. Third Mahratta War; Jawad. Fur. 27 Dec. 1821 till retirement.
Refs.: Burke's *Peerage*, 1923, p. 774, *s.n.* Dunbar, Bart., of Boath, co. Nairn. *E.I.M.C.* iii. 413-4. *S.M.* 1822, ii. 751. *G.M.* 1864, ii. 262. *The Times*, 20 July 1864.

[1] *Note*: See note, vol. i. p. xxxii.

DUNBAR, William (*d.* 1774). Captain. Infantry. Cadet 1766. Ensign 14 Sept. 1766. Lieut. 1 Dec. 1767. Capt. 21 Mar. 1773. Resigned 22 Dec. 1773. *d.* Shields 23 Dec. 1774.

3rd son of Sir William Dunbar, 3rd Bart. of Durn, Banff, and Clementina his 1st wife, dau. of Sir James Grant, of Grant.
Services: N.F.P.
Refs.: Burke's *Peerage*, 1923, p. 771, *s.n.* Dunbar, Bart., of Durn, Banff. *S.M.* 1774, p. 679.

DUNCAN, Alexander (*d.* 1789). Lieutenant, Engineers. Cadet (?). Arrived in India 1781. Lieut. 2 Sept. 1781. *d.* Calcutta 28 July 1789, of fever.

Son of Andrew Duncan, of Crail, and later of St. Andrews, merchant and shipmaster. Brother of Andrew Duncan, the elder, physician, and professor Edinburgh University (*D.N.B.*). Uncle of Alexander Duncan, *q.v.*
Services: Was Principal Draughtsman at Fort William in 1787. N.F.P.
Refs.: *G.M.* 1790, ii. 859. *S.M.* 1790, p. 49. Will dated 11 June 1789.

DUNCAN, Alexander (1780-1859). General. Colonel 5th N.I. *b.* Edinburgh 30 Mar. 1780. Cadet 1795. Arrived in India 18 Sept. 1797. Ensign 16 Aug. 1797. Lieut. 31 Aug. 1798. Capt. 22 Nov. 1805. Major 18 Aug. 1814. Lt. Col. 20 Oct. 1818. Lt. Col. Comdt. 1 May 1824. Col. 5 June 1829. Maj. Gen. 10 Jan. 1837. Lt. Gen. 9 Nov. 1846. Gen. 20 June 1854. *d.* Gattonside House, Melrose, 14 May 1859.

bapt. St. Cuthbert's, Edinburgh, 31 Mar. 1780. 3rd son of Andrew Duncan, the elder, physician (*D.N.B.*), and Elizabeth Knox his wife. Brother of John Duncan, *q.v.*, and nephew of Alexander Duncan, *q.v.* *m.* Fatehgarh, 5 Feb. 1802, Miss Mary Mabel Lanigan. (She died 24 Apr. 1857, aged 79.) Father of Andrew Henry Duncan, *q.v.*, Francis Kyan Duncan, *q.v.*, Henry Howard Duncan, *q.v.*, and Elizabeth Mary, wife of Windsor Parker, *q.v.*

Services: Actg. Adjt. 1/2nd N.I. in 1800. On service in Oudh in 1800. Adjt. 2/2nd N.I. 1802-4. Operations in Jumna Doab 1803; Sasni; Bijaigarh; Kachaura. Second Mahratta War; Koil;

Aligarh; battle of Delhi; Agra; Laswari; siege of Bhurtpore (w. and horse killed); Bde. Major 4th Bde., Grand Army (India medal with clasps). Actg. Bde. Major at Fatehgarh 1806. Reduction of Kalinjar 1812; Capt. 2/2nd N.I. Baghelkhand 1813; capture of Entauri; Capt. 2/2nd N.I. On service in Oudh 1815; Major comdg. 1/2nd N.I. Third Mahratta War; with Narbada F.F.; action nr. Sohagpur 13 Jan. 1819 (*Lond. Gaz.* 10 Aug. 1819); Lt. Col. comdg. 1/2nd N.I. Col. 5th N.I. (late 1/2nd) May 1824. Transfd. to 53rd N.I. 18 Jan. 1828. Bdr. comdg. in Rohilkhand 23 Feb. 1828 till 21 Feb. 1829. Comdd. Malwa F.F. 21 Feb. 1829 till 14 June 1834. Comdd. Sirhind Div., as Bdr. Gen. on Gen. Staff, 3 May 1834 till 3 May 1839. Transfd. to 5th N.I. 21 Aug. 1837. Comdd. 2nd Div. of Army of the Indus 13 Sept. till 5 Dec. 1838. Fur. p.a. 5 Jan. 1840 till death.

Refs.: Boase. *The Times,* 21 May 1859. *I.M.* 28 May 1859, p. 467.

DUNCAN, Andrew Henry (1805-1872). Colonel. 3rd Bengal Eur. Inf. *b.* Agra 6 Aug. 1805. Cadet 1825. Arrived in India 18 Mar. 1826. Ensign 28 Sept. 1825. Lieut. 11 Apr. 1828. Capt. 11 Nov. 1847. Major 4 Aug. 1857. Bt. Lt. Col. 11 Sept. 1859. Retired 14 Feb. 1861. Hon. Col. 14 Feb. 1861. *d.* Foxhall, Kirkliston, 16 Apr. 1872.

2nd son of Alexander Duncan (1780-1859), *q.v.*, and Mary Mabel his wife. Brother of Francis Kyan Duncan, *q.v.*

Services: Posted as Ensign to 43rd N.I. in 1826. Adjt. Farrukhabad Local Bn. 22 June 1830. A.D.C. to his father 3 May 1834 till 7 Dec. 1838. A.D.C. to Maj.-Gen. Nott, comdg. 1st Div., Army of the Indus, 28 Feb. 1839. First Afghan War 1839-42; Ghazni; operations in vicinity of Kandahar; advance on Kabul; taking of Istalif; Lieut. 43rd N.I. (Medal). On political duty at Kandahar in 1842. Adjt. 43rd N.I. 11 July 1842 till Jan. 1845. Gwalior campaign; Maharajpur; Lieut. 43rd N.I. (Bronze star). Fur. 24 Jan. 1845 till 1848. Posted to newly-raised 3rd Bengal Eur. Regt. 15 Nov. 1853. Placed at the disposal of the Foreign Office 11 Nov. 1854. Comdd. Bhagulpur Hill Rangers 17 Mar. 1856 till retirement.

Refs.: The Times, 20 Apr. 1872.

DUNCAN, Francis Kyan (1807-1887). Colonel. Artillery. *b.* Barrackpore 24 Nov. 1807. Cadet 1823. Arrived in India 17 Aug. 1824. 2nd Lieut. 18 Dec. 1823. Lieut. 28 Sept. 1827. Capt. 28 Feb. 1842. Major 25 July 1854. Bt. Lt. Col. 1856. Retired 17 Nov. 1856. Hon. Col. 17 Nov. 1856. *d.* 3 Aug. 1887.

3rd son of Alexander Duncan (1780-1859), *q.v.*, and Mary Mabel his wife. Brother of Henry Howard Duncan, *q.v.* Addiscombe Cadet 18 Jan. 1822 till 18 Dec. 1823.

Services : Siege and capture of Bhurtpore ; 2nd Lieut. 1st Coy. 3rd Bn. (Field Battery) ; (India medal). Posted to 1st Troop 1st Bde. H.A. in 1826. First Afghan War 1838-9 ; Ghazni ; Bt. Capt. 2nd Troop 2nd Bde. H.A. (Medal). Comdd. 4th Troop 2nd Bde. H.A. 1845-53. Second Sikh War ; Chilianwala ; Gujerat ; Capt. comdg. 4th Troop 2nd Bde. (Medal with clasp). Fur. 26 Jan. 1855 till retirement.

DUNCAN, Henry Howard (1810-1847). Captain, Engineers. *b.* Jagannath, B. & O., 13 July 1810. Cadet 1828. 2nd Lieut. 12 June 1828. Lieut. 7 June 1836. Capt. 5 May 1846. *d.* Barrackpore 16 June 1847.

Son of Alexander Duncan (1780-1859), *q.v.*, and Mary Mabel his wife. Brother of Andrew Henry Duncan, *q.v.* Addiscombe Cadet 1827-8.

Services : 2nd Lieut. d.d. S. & M. at Aligarh 7 Apr. 1830. Apptd. to P.W.D. 20 Aug. 1832. Offg. Asst. Supt. of Delhi canals 17 Nov. 1835. Transfd. from Mhow to Nimach Div., P.W.D., 26 Sept. 1837. Apptd. Field Engr. 2nd Div., Army of the Indus, 12 Sept. 1838. Offg. Executive Engr., Dinapore Div., P.W.D., 15 Sept. 1841 ; to Dum-Dum Div. 17 Nov. 1843. No record of active service.

Refs. : I.M. 24 Aug. 1847, p. 489. Will dated Barrackpore 27 Aug. 1845 ; proved 29 Dec. 1848.

DUNCAN, James (1783-1815). Lieutenant, 22nd N.I. *b.* Kirkcaldy, co. Fife, 8 May 1783. Cadet 1804. Arrived in India 17 Mar. 1805. Ensign 8 Apr. 1805. Lieut. 9 Apr. 1805. *d.* 1 Jan. 1815 : kld. in action at Samanpur, Nepal.

Son of John Duncan, merchant taylor. *m.* (before 1812) (?).

Services : Posted as Lieut. to 2/22nd N.I. Nepal War 1814-5 ; Samanpur (kld.) ; Lieut. 2/22nd N.I., in 4th Div.

Refs. : Will dated 16 July 1814 ; proved in 1815.

DUNCAN, James (1813-1856). Major. 26th N.I. *b.* Montrose, co. Forfar, 15 May 1813. Cadet 1828. Arrived in India 23 Sept. 1829. Ensign (27 May 1829) 23 Sept. 1829. Lieut. 21 Oct. 1836. Capt. 14 Dec. 1843. Invalided 1 May 1849. Retired 27 Dec. 1855. Hon. Major 27 Dec. 1855. *d.* Montrose 11 Oct. 1856.

Son of James Duncan, mason, and Elizabeth his wife. Nephew of Joseph Hume (*D.N.B.*).

Services : Cadet d.d. 64th N.I. 19 Oct. 1830. Apptd. Actg. Ensign 27 Oct. 1831, having been more than 2 yrs. in India. d.d. 53rd N.I. 24 Nov. 1831. Posted to 26th N.I. 23 Dec. 1832. Intr.

& Qmr. 26th N.I. 22 Feb. 1837 till 2 Mar. 1838. Asst. to A.G.G., Saugor & Narbada territories, 2 Mar. 1838. Offg. 1st Junior Asst. at Betul 24 Aug. 1842. Offg. Intr. & Qmr. 26th N.I. 6 Apr. 1843. Fur. s.c. 20 July 1843 till 1846. Was wrecked in the steam frigate *Memnon* off Cape Guardafui 1 Aug. 1843 on his passage to England. No record of active service.

Refs. : *The Times*, 16 Oct. 1843. *G.M.* 1856, ii. 780.

DUNCAN, John (1787-1856). Colonel. 45th N.I. *b.* Bristo 25 Mar. 1787. Cadet 1802. Arrived in India 31 Aug. 1803. Ensign 2 Sept. 1803. Lieut. 25 Aug. 1804. Capt. 16 Dec. 1814. Major 13 May 1825. Lt. Col. 18 July 1829. Retired 21 May 1830. Hon. Col. 28 Nov. 1854. *d.* Carlton Pl., Edinburgh, 28 Oct. 1856.

Son of Andrew Duncan, the elder (*D.N.B.*), and Elizabeth Knox his wife. Brother of Alexander Duncan (1780-1859), *q.v. m.* Edinburgh, 14 May 1822, Mary, eldest dau. of Robert Hill, of Rosebank, W.S.

Services : Ensign d.d. 2nd N.I. Posted as Lieut. to 2/2nd N.I. Adjt. 2/2nd N.I. 8 May 1806 till May 1815. Reduction of Kalinjar 1812. Operations in Baghelkhand 1813 ; Entauri. Intr. & Qmr. 2/2nd N.I. 1815, for a few weeks. Fur. 14 Dec. 1818 till 1822. Transfd. to 22nd N.I. (late 2/2nd) May 1824 ; as Major to newly-raised 6th Extra Regt. (became 74th N.I.) May 1825. In charge of 41st N.I. 1827-8. Fur. s.c. 27 Nov. 1829 till retirement. Posted as Lt. Col. to 45th N.I. 31 Mar. 1830.

Refs. : *S.M.* 1822, i. 828. *G.M.* 1856, ii. 783.

DUNCAN, Menzies (*d.* 1824). Captain. 12th N.I. Cadet 1782. Admitted 22 Jan. 1783. Ensign 10 Apr. 1783. Lieut. 10 Mar. 1790. Capt. 30 Sept. 1803. Retired 30 Sept. 1807. *d.* Rocke House, Bath, 23 Oct. 1824.

Services : Adjt. 1/12th N.I. 29 May 1800. (? Second Mahratta War ; Agra ; Laswari ; capture of Deig ; Capt. 1/12th N.I.) Fur. 8 Feb. 1805 till retirement.

Refs. : *S.M.* 1824, ii. 767. *Bath Chron.* 28 Oct. 1824.

DUNCAN, Patrick (*d.* 1791). Lieutenant, Invalid Est. Inf. Cadet 1779. Ensign 3 Oct. 1779. Lieut. 14 May 1781. Invalided (?). *d.* Chunar 14 Mar. 1791.

Brother of Mrs. Stephenson, and of Isabella Duncan.

Services : Lieut. 28th Bn. Sepoys in July 1787.

Refs. : Will dated Fatehgarh 27 June 1789 ; proved in 1793.

DUNCAN, William (1746/47-1830). Lieut. Colonel. 3rd Bengal Eur. Regt. *b.* 1746/47. Cadet 1766. Ensign 8 Dec. 1766. Lieut. 2 Apr. 1768. Capt. 2 Aug. 1774. Major 28 Jan. 1781.

Lt. Col. 9 Sept. 1793. Retired 1 June 1796. *d.* Gower St., London, 14 Mar. 1830, aged 83.

Son of Rev. Dr. (? John) Duncan. *m.* London, 26 June 1797, Caroline, 3rd dau. of Robert Milne (or Mylne), of the New River head, Islington.

Services : Major in 1st Bde. in July 1787.

Refs. : *Autobiog. of Sir Walter Scott. S.M.* 1797, p. 503. *G.M.* 1830, i. 282.

DUNCANSON, Duncan (*d.* 1768). Lieutenant, Infantry. Lieut. 16 July 1765. *d.* in India Mar. 1768.

Services : *Probably* transfd. as Lieut. from H.M.S. Lieut. Madras Est. Lent to the Bengal Govt. in June 1766 during the "Batta mutiny." Subsequently transfd. to Bengal Est.

DUNCANSON, William M———. Lieutenant. Infantry. Cadet 1782. Ensign 3 Jan. 1783. Lieut. 9 Feb. 1788. Resigned 8 Oct. 1790.

Services : N.F.P. (*Possibly* to be identified with W. M. Duncanson, of Kensington Sq., London, who was head of a "House of Agency to E.I.Co.," *c.* 1800-6.)

DUNDAS, Sir James Fullerton, third baronet (1786-1848). Major General, Artillery. *b.* 27 Aug. 1786. Cadet 1803. Arrived in India 14 Aug. 1804. Lieut. 15 Aug. 1804. Capt. Lt. 5 Sept. 1806. Capt. 26 Aug. 1813. Major 14 Jan. 1821. Lt. Col. 31 May 1824. Col. 18 Jan. 1837. Maj. Gen. 28 June 1838. *d. unm.* Richmond, Surrey, 16 June 1848.

Third Baronet of Richmond, Surrey. *s.* 13 Nov. 1840. *bapt.* Richmond 24 Sept. 1786. 2nd son of Sir David Dundas, 1st Bart., one of the medical attendants of George III, and Isabella his wife, dau. of William Robertson, of Richmond. Cousin-german of Thomas Graham Dundas, *q.v.*

Services : Fur. s.c. 9 Jan. 1806 till 14 Oct. 1807. Capture of Java 1811 ; Capt. Lt. comdg. 1st Coy. 2nd Bn. Foot Art. In charge of gunpowder factory at Allahabad 14 Nov. 1814 till 2 Oct. 1819. Fur. s.c. 8 Feb. 1823 till 10 Mar. 1826. Posted to 2nd Bn. Art. 14 June 1837. Fur. p.a. 8 Mar. 1838 till death.

Refs. : Burke's *Peerage*, 1859, p. 334, *s.n.* Dundas, Bart., of Richmond, Surrey. Burke's *Family Records*, p. 234. *G.M.* 1848, ii. 263.

DUNDAS, Thomas (*d.* 1769). Captain, Infantry. Capt. 15 Sept. 1767. *d.* Calcutta Sept. 1769.

Son of Robert Dundas, Lord Arniston (1685-1753) (*D.N.B.*), and Anne his 2nd wife, dau. of Sir Robert Gordon, Bart., of Invergordon. Brother of Henry Dundas, 1st Viscount Melville (*D.N.B.*).

Services : Lieut. H.M. 30th Foot 30 Sept. 1757. Transfd. as Lieut. to Bengal Army 2 Aug. 1765.
Refs. : S.M. 1770, p. 287.

DUNDAS, Thomas (1787-1840). Lieut. Colonel, 17th N.I. *b.* Currie, Midlothian, 27 Mar. 1787. Cadet 1803. Arrived in India 3 Dec. 1804. Ensign 18 Oct. 1804. Lieut. 18 Oct. 1804. Capt. 10 Aug. 1816. Major 21 Mar. 1828. Lt. Col. 20 Apr. 1833. *d.* Mussoorie 30 June 1840.

Of Manour. *bapt.* 11 Apr. 1787. Son of Ralph Dundas, Capt. of the *Royal Henry,* East Indiaman, and Elizabeth his wife, dau. of William Wrangham, of St. Helena. 1st cousin once removed of Sir James Fullerton Dundas, Bart., *q.v. m.* St. John's, Calcutta, 22 Aug. 1825, Elizabeth Georgiana, eldest dau. of Lt. Col. George Bristow, and sister of Cerjat Michael Bristow, *q.v.* (*See also* James Henry Daniell.)

Services : Posted as Lieut. to newly-raised 24th N.I. (? Capture of Gohad 1806. Settlement of Hariana 1809 ; Bhawani ; Lieut. 2/24th N.I.) 1st Asst. Sec., Accounts Dept., Mily. Board 7 May 1811 till Mar. 1816. Leave s.c. to sea 9 May till 19 Dec. 1812. Apptd. Bde. Major at Presdy. 11 Mar. 1816. Capt. 2/24th N.I. Leave s.c. to sea 8 Dec. 1818 till 21 Feb. 1821. Fur. s.c. 21 Mar. 1821 till 4 Nov. 1823. Transfd. to 47th N.I. (late 1/24th) May 1824. Offg. Fort Adjt. at Fort William 5 Mar. 1825. Posted as Lt. Col. to 8th N.I. 7 Dec. 1833. Fur. s.c. 11 Feb. 1834 till 5 Feb. 1838. Transfd. to 21st N.I. 19 Feb. 1834 ; to 16th N.I. 27 Sept. 1837 ; to 62nd N.I. 30 Dec. 1837 ; to 17th N.I. 25 Feb. 1840.

Refs. : Burke's *Family Records,* p. 234. Burke's *Landed Gentry,* 5th edn., p. 146, *s.n.* Bristow, of Broxmore Park, Wilts. Will dated 31 Mar. 1833 ; proved 2 Jan. 1841.

DUNDAS, Thomas Graham (1806-?). Lieutenant. 72nd N.I. *b.* Edinburgh 29 Dec. 1806. Cadet 1824. Arrived in India 4 Oct. 1825. Ensign 13 May 1825. Lieut. 19 Oct. 1826. Resigned in England 3 Feb. 1835. (Living in 1851.)

6th and youngest son of James Dundas, of Edinburgh, Clerk to the Signet, and Elizabeth his wife, 3rd dau. of William Graham, of Airth Castle. Cousin-german of Sir James Fullerton Dundas, Bart., *q.v. m.* Berhampore, 14 Aug. 1832, Margaret Maria Louisa, 3rd dau. of Edward Swift Broughton, *q.v.*

Services : Posted as Ensign to 15th N.I. in 1825. Siege and capture of Bhurtpore ; Ensign 15th N.I. (India medal). Transfd. as Lieut. to 4th Extra Regt. (became 72nd N.I.) in 1826. Actg. Intr. & Qmr. do. 1 Mar. 1827. Fur. s.c. 21 Jan. 1828 till 19 Jan.

1831. Actg. Adjt. 72nd N.I. 11 Sept. 1832. Fur. u.p.a. 12 mos.
10 Sept. 1833 till resignation.
Refs. : Burke's *Family Records*, p. 235. *A.J.* N.S. x. 80.

DUNFORD, Nicholas. Lieutenant. Infantry. Cadet 1780. Ensign 27 Jan. 1781. Lieut. 3 Oct. 1781. Resigned 1 Apr. 1783.
Services : N.F.P.

DUNKIN, Edward (*c.* 1774-?). Fireworker. Artillery. *b. c.* 1774. ("Aged about 17 on arrival in India.") Cadet 1790. Arrived in India 14 Aug. 1791. Fireworker 1791. Resigned 16 Apr. 1792.
Son of Sir William Dunkin, Kt., of Clogher, and of Arlington Court, Gloucs., judge of the supreme court in Calcutta, and Eliza his wife, eldest dau. of William Blacker, of Carrickblacker. Cousin-german of George Blacker, *q.v.*, and Edward Olpherts, *q.v.*, and uncle of Arthur Conolly, *q.v.*, and of John Dunkin Macnaghten, *q.v.*
Services : Fur. s.c. 1792. No record of active service.
Refs. : Burke's *Landed Gentry of Ireland*, p. 45, *s.n.* Blacker, of Carrickblacker, Armagh. *Hickey*, iv. 45, 85.

DUNKIN, George Bethune (*d.* 1805). Lieutenant, Invalid Est. 7th N.I. Cadet 1796. Admitted 9 Apr. 1797. Ensign 26 Sept. 1797. Lieut. 10 Sept. 1798. Invalided May 1803. *d.* Serampore, Bengal, 13 Aug. 1805.
Services : N.F.P.

DUNKLEY, Robert (*d.* 1805). Lieut. Colonel, 18th N.I. Cadet 1775. Admitted 4 July 1776. Ensign 18 Aug. 1776. Lieut. 1 Aug. 1778. Capt. 22 Jan. 1794. Major 1 Nov. 1798. Lt. Col. 10 Aug. 1801. *d.* Sultanpur (? Cawnpore) 26 Nov. 1805.
Son of Robert Dunkley.
Services : Lieut. 7th Bn. Sepoys in July 1787. Capt. 7th N.I. Major 16th N.I. Lt. Col. Bengal Eur. Regt. Transfd. to 18th N.I. 4 July 1804.
Refs. : Will dated 2 Aug. 1805 ; proved 14 Dec. 1805.

DUNLOP, John (1786-1840). Lieut. Colonel, 23rd N.I. *b.* 7 June 1786. Cadet 1807. Arrived in India 16 Nov. 1808. Ensign 12 Nov. 1808. Lieut. 16 Dec. 1814. Capt. 1 May 1824. Major 28 July 1833. Lt. Col. 9 July 1840. *d.* Simla 18 July 1840.
bapt. 10 June 1786. Son of John Dunlop, of Drumnagessan, co. Antrim. Brother of Archibald Dunlop, of Bush Mills, nr. Coleraine.
Services : Barasat C.C. for 10 mos. Posted as Ensign to 1/4th N.I. 1 Aug. 1809. d.d. Mirzapur Local Bn. Oct. 1813 till May 1814. Leave s.c. to sea 14 Oct. 1814 till 1817. Posted to 1st Vol. Bn. in Sept. 1818, and served in Ceylon from 1818 till Jan. 1820.

Transfd. to 2/4th N.I. 30 Mar. 1820. Adjt. 1/4th N.I. 29 Jan. 1821 till 17 June 1824. Posted as Capt. to 23rd N.I. (late 2/4th) May 1824. First Burma War 1824-6; Chittagong; Arakan; Capt. 1st Gren. Bn. Offg. Fort Adjt. and Dy. Postmaster at Arakan 1 Feb. 1826. Rejoined 23rd N.I. in 1826. Fur. s.c. 28 Aug. 1828 till 2 July 1832. Comdd. 23rd N.I. 9 Dec. 1836 till death. Leave s.c. to Simla Apr. 1840 till death.

Refs. : *De Rhé-Philipe.* Will dated Simla 18 July 1840; proved 10 May 1841. M.I. in Mall cemetery at Simla.

DUNLOP, William (1785-1841). Major General. Colonel 1st Bengal Eur. Regt. Q.M.G. *b.* Selkirk, Scotland, 16 Mar. 1785. Cadet 1800. Arrived in India 7 Feb. 1802. Ensign 11 Dec. 1801. Lieut. 27 Jan. 1804. Capt. 1 Feb. 1817. Major 1 May 1824. Lt. Col. 8 Feb. 1828. Col. 11 Feb. 1839. Maj. Gen. 23 Nov. 1841. (Promotion gazetted before report of his death was received.) *d.* Allahabad 5 Nov. 1841.

bapt. Selkirk 24 Mar. 1785. Son of Walter Dunlop, of Whilmuir Hall. *m.* Fatehgarh, 9 Aug. 1824, Miss Susan Morton.

Services: Ensign 11th N.I. Transfd. as Lieut. to 19th N.I. 2 Nov. 1803; to newly-raised 26th N.I. in 1804. Adjt. 2/26th N.I. 4 Aug. 1805 till 1816. Operations in Bundelkhand 1807-10; Sehlehuganj; Hirapur; Rajaoli; Ajaigarh. Capt. 1/26th N.I. Bk. Mr., Meerut Div., 12 Apr. 1822. Transfd. as Major to 52nd N.I. (late 2/26th) May 1824. Lt. Col. 52nd N.I. Transfd. to 1st Bengal Eur. Regt. 29 Nov. 1828; from Rt. Wing, Eur. Regt., to 49th N.I. 1 Jan. 1832. Offg. Town and Fort Major of Fort William 14 Nov. 1832. Dy. Comy. Gen. 4 June 1833. D.Q.M.G. 29 Nov. 1833. Q.M.G. 1834 till death. Transfd. to 67th N.I. 11 Jan. 1834; to 50th N.I. 2 Mar. 1835; to 67th N.I. 19 July 1836; to 2nd N.I. 21 Aug. 1837; to 53rd N.I. 13 Nov. 1838. Col. 1st Bengal Eur. Regt. 1839. Received the Auspicious Star of the Punjab from Ranjit Singh on 7 Oct. 1837.

Refs. : Will dated Calcutta 28 Aug. 1841; proved 10 May 1842. M.I. St. Andrew's kirk, Calcutta.

DUNLOP, William (1807-1827). Ensign, 5th Extra Regt. b. Glasgow 11 Nov. 1807. Cadet 1825. Ensign 28 Dec. 1825. *d.* Jubbulpore 13 Nov. 1827.

Services: Ensign d.d. 62nd N.I. 8 July 1826. Posted as Ensign to 5th Extra Regt. 26 Sept. 1826. No record of active service.

Refs. : *A.J.* xxv. 683.

DUNMORE, William Robert (1807-1885). Colonel. 60th N.I. *b.* London 23 Aug. 1807. Cadet 1825. Arrived in India 4 Sept. 1826. Ensign 15 Apr. 1826. Lieut. 14 May 1832. Capt. 3 Apr.

1844. Major 27 July 1851. Lt. Col. 28 Nov. 1856. Retired 3 Aug. 1859. Hon. Col. 3 Aug. 1859. d. 12 Sept. 1885.

Nephew of Thomas Dunmore, Comy. Gen. to H.M. Forces. m. Dromore, co. Down, 14 Feb. 1836, Agnes, 4th dau. of Lt. Col. George Callander, of Craigforth, co. Stirling, and niece of the Earl of Buchan. (She died Calcutta 9 Jan. 1837, aged 26.)

Services: Posted as Ensign to 35th N.I. 5 Oct. 1826. Transfd. to 69th N.I. 3 Jan. 1828; to 38th N.I. 28 Jan. 1828; to 31st N.I. 7 July 1830. Operations against the Chuars 1832. Fur. s.c. 30 July 1833 till 28 Nov. 1836. Operations against the Kols 1836-7; Lieut. 31st N.I. Fur. s.c. 15 July 1837 till 10 Jan. 1840. Offg. D.J.A.G. at Cawnpore 18 Feb. 1842. Gwalior campaign; Maharajpur; Lieut. 31st N.I. (Bronze star). Second Sikh War; Sadulapur; Chilianwala (w.); Gujerat; Capt. 31st N.I. (Medal). Against the Kohat Pass Afridis in Feb. 1850; Capt. 31st N.I. (Medal). Fur. s.c. 30 Dec. 1856 till retirement. Posted as Lt. Col. to 35th N.I. Feb. 1857; to 60th N.I. 17 Dec. 1857.

Refs.: Burke's *Landed Gentry*, 13th edn., p. 265, *s.n.* Callander, of Ardkinglass, co. Argyll. *A.J.* N.S. xix. 309.

DUNN, George (*d*. 1772). Cadet, Infantry. Cadet 1766. Resigned May 1766. Readmitted as Cadet 1770. *d*. Dinapore Sept. 1772.

Services: Resigned his Cadetship during the "Batta mutiny"; subsequently readmitted.

DUNN, James (*d*. 1824). Lieut. General. 17th N.I. Country Cadet 1767. Arrived in India 19 Oct. 1767. Ensign 10 Dec. 1767. Lieut. 10 Oct. 1769. Capt. 27 Mar. 1778. Major 23 Feb. 1782. Lt. Col. 1 Mar. 1794. Col. 1 Jan. 1798. Maj. Gen. 1 Jan. 1805. Lt. Gen. 4 June 1813. *d*. in England 29 Aug. 1824.

m. Margaret. (She died Bath 19 Dec. 1838, aged 84.)

Services: With 12th Bn. Sepoys at Midnapore in 1772. Capt. 2/1st Bengal Eur. Regt. in 1779. To comd. 32nd Bn. 1780. A.D.C. to C.-in-C. 1781. To comd. 23rd Regt. 1783. Major 29th Bn. Sepoys in July 1787. Fur. 4 Mar. 1788 till 3 Mar. 1792. To comd. 3rd Regt. on borders of Assam 1793. Comdd. at Midnapore 1799 till 1802. Col. 1st N.I. 1 May 1800. Fur. 6 Mar. 1802 till death. Transfd. to 8th N.I. in 1804; to 17th N.I. in 1805.

Refs.: *E.I.M.C.* ii. 230-2.

DUNSFORD, Henry Frederick (1817-1887). General, C.B. 59th N.I. *b*. St. Gluvias, Cornwall, 5 Nov. 1817. Cadet 1834. Arrived in India 28 July 1835. Ensign (13 June 1835) 19 Oct. 1835. Lieut. 3 Oct. 1838. Capt. 10 June 1850. Major (11 June 1850) 1 Jan. 1862. Lt. Col. (28 Nov. 1854) 16 July 1864. Col.

18 Dec. 1860. Maj. Gen. 22 Feb. 1868. Lt. Gen. 11 Dec. 1875. Gen. 1 Oct. 1877. *d.* St. Helier, Jersey, 31 Jan. 1887.

Son of Henry Dunsford, of Penzance, agent, and Eleanor his wife. *m.* Bareilly 12 Nov. 1849, Elizabeth, dau. of Samuel Shaw, *q.v.*
Services : Ensign d.d. 34th N.I. 8 Aug. 1835; do. 24th N.I. 6 Nov. 1835. Posted to 59th N.I. 28 June 1836. Adjt. 1st L.I. Bn. 21 Nov. 1840. Adjt. 59th N.I. 27 Feb. 1841 till Apr. 1848. Army of Reserve (for Afghanistan) Oct. 1842 till Jan. 1843. First Sikh War; Sobraon; Bde. Major 7th Bde., 3rd Div. (Medal). Offg. Bde. Major at Barrackpore Nov. 1850. A.D.C. to his father-in-law, comdg. Presdy. Div., Dec. 1852. Fur. p.a. 16 Sept. 1853 till 1 Feb. 1857. Mutiny campaign; siege of Delhi; comdd. troops of Rajahs of Jind and Patiala from 18 July 1857; comdd. Buxar column of Shahabad F.F. Oct.-Nov. 1858; Jagdeshpur 19 Oct. 1858 (s.w.); (Medal with clasp). Operations in Assam 1862-3; comdg. Jaintia F.F. Comdd. columns of Bhutan F.F. Dec. 1864; capture of Dhalimkot. C.B. 17 June 1858. Good Service Pension 11 Jan. 1865.
Refs. : Boase. *The Times,* 4 Feb. 1887.

DUNSMURE, Alexander (Conway) (1782-1825). Captain, Pension Est. 10th N.I. *b.* College Kirk psh., Edinburgh, 8 July 1782. Cadet 1800. Arrived in India 23 Aug. 1801. Ensign 31 Dec. 1801. Lieut. 5 Nov. 1803. Capt. 1 Aug. 1818. Pensioned 6 June 1823. *d.* Serampore 3 Jan. 1825.

bapt. Edinburgh 1 Aug. 1782. Son of John Dunsmure, " teacher of English," and Christian Young his wife.
Services : Ensign 11th N.I. Transfd. to 4th N.I. 15 Feb. 1804. (? Second Mahratta War; Aligarh; Lieut. 4th N.I.) Transfd. to 1/10th N.I. in 1805. (? Operations in Hariana 1809; Bhawani; Lieut. 1/10th N.I.) With 3rd Vol. Bn. in Ceylon 1818-9.
Refs. : *Calcutta Monthly Journal,* Jan. 1825. Will dated Kalinjar 23 Nov. 1816; proved 17 Jan. 1825.

DUNSTALL, Norcross (or Richard) [1] (*d.* 1761). Capt. Lieutenant, Artillery. Cadet (?). Fireworker 4 Oct. 1757. 2nd Lieut. 1758. Capt. Lt. 1760. *d.* Calcutta 4 July 1761.

Brother of Jonathan Dunstall. *m.* Calcutta 9 Feb. 1761, Miss Elizabeth Seaton.
Services : N.F.P.
Refs. : Will dated Calcutta 24 June 1761; proved 7 July 1761.

[1] *Note :* His christian name appears as Norcross in his Will, and in the marriage register; as Richard in the burial register; and as William in *Dodwell & Miles* and *Stubbs's List.*

THE BENGAL ARMY, 1758-1884 107

DUNSTERVILLE, Elias Vivian (1785-1821). Captain, 28th N.I.
b. 27 Feb. 1785. Cadet 1800. Arrived in India 19 Aug. 1801.
Ensign 21 Sept. 1801. Lieut. 7 Oct. 1802. Capt. 23 Nov. 1815.
d. Pakra, nr. Fatehgarh, U.P., 30 June 1821.
bapt. St. Andrew's, Plymouth, Devon, 12 Jan. 1787. Son of Bartholomew Dunsterville and Joan his wife. *m.* Fatehgarh, 18 Sept. 1806, Miss Elizabeth Clara Stuart.
Services : Lieut. 14th N.I. Transfd. to newly-raised 22nd N.I. in 1804 ; to 1/27th N.I. in 1805. Operations against Dhundia Khan 1807 ; Komona (s.w.) ; Lieut. 1/27th N.I. Fur. 3 Apr. 1812 till 1816. Transfd. to newly-raised 2/28th N.I. in 1815. Third Mahratta War ; Dhamoni ; Capt. 2/28th N.I.
Refs. : *A.A.R.* x. 21. *A.J.* xiii. 96.

DUPONT, John (*d.* 1768). Lieutenant, Infantry. Cadet (?). Ensign (?). Lieut. 9 Sept. 1763. *d.* Aug. 1768.
Services : N.F.P. Not in *A.L.* of 1 Feb. 1767.

DUPPA, formerly HANCORN, Baldwin Duppa (1763-1847). Lieutenant. Infantry. *b.* Nov. 1763. Cadet 1782. Ensign 21 Feb. 1783. Lieut. 11 Feb. 1790. Resigned 16 June 1790. *d.* 5 Apr. 1847.
Of Hollingbourne House, Kent, J.P. and D.L. Elder son of Baldwin Duppa (who changed his name from Hancorn) and Martha his wife, *née* Geach. *m.* 29 Nov. 1800, Mary, 5th dau. of Maj.-Gen. Henry Gladwin, of Stubbing Court, Derby. (She died 28 June 1837.)
Services : N.F.P.
Refs. : Burke's *Landed Gentry*, 13th edn., p. 492, *s.n.* Duppa de Uphaugh, of Hollingbourne, Kent. Foster's *Families of Royal Descent*, ii. 643.

DURACK, Lawrence McMahon (1801-1819). Lieutenant, 22nd N.I.
b. Wallingford, Berks., 3 Apr. 1801. Cadet 1817. Ensign (?). Lieut. 1 Nov. 1818. *d.* Puri, B. & O., 20 Oct. 1819.
Eldest son of Lawrence Durack. *m.* St. John's, Calcutta, 25 Mar. 1819, Evelina Jane, sister of Wilton Phipps Madge.
Services : Posted as Lieut. to 22nd N.I. No record of active service.
Refs. : Will dated Puri 29 Sept. 1819 ; proved 10 Jan. 1820.

DURAND, Sir Henry Marion (1812-1871). Major General, K.C.S.I., Engrs. Lieut. Govr. of the Punjab. *b.* 6 Nov. 1812. Cadet 1829. Arrived in India 22 May 1830. 2nd Lieut. 12 June 1828. Lieut. 20 Apr. 1835. Capt. 30 Nov. 1844. Major 8 June 1856. Lt. Col. 13 Aug. 1858. Col. 20 July 1858. Maj. Gen. 1 Mar. 1867.

d. Tonk, Dera Ismail Khan district, 1 Jan. 1871, from injuries received the preceding day when thrown from his elephant howdah.

Birth registered in the Commune de Coulandon, France, 15 Nov. 1812. Son of Col. the Hon. Henry Percy, C.B., 14th Light Dgns., and Jeanne Durand. *m.* 1st, Meerut, 28 Mar. 1843, Anne, 3rd dau. of Maj.-Gen. Sir John McCaskill, K.C.B. (She died Mhow, 28 Aug. 1857, aged 35.) *m.* 2nd, 1859, Emily Augusta, youngest dau. of C. B. Allnut, of Shrewsbury, and widow of Rev. Henry Stedman Polehampton, Bengal Ecclesiastical Est. (She died 29 Mar. 1905.) Addiscombe Cadet 1827-8.

Services : See *D.N.B.* Fur. 23 Feb. 1841 till Feb. 1842 ; Jan. 1847 till Dec. 1848 ; Dec. 1853 till 2 Jan. 1856 ; Jan. 1859 till Aug. 1861. Apptd. Lt. Govr. of the Punjab 1 June 1870. C.B. 24 Mar. 1858. K.C.S.I. 8 Feb. 1867.

Refs. : Burke's *Peerage*, 1923, p. 792, *s.n.* Durand, Bart. *D.N.B. D.I.B.* Boase. De *Rhé-Philipe*. M.I. at Dera Ismail Khan ; inscription on the Durand Gate at Tonk.

DURANT, George (1807-?). Ensign, Pension Est. 32nd N.I. *b.* 23 Mar. 1807. Cadet 1825. Arrived in India 21 Oct. 1826. Ensign 13 June 1826. Pensioned 31 Oct. 1833. *d.* 1863 ? (after which year his name disappears from the *Indian A.L.*).

bapt. London 31 May 1807. Son of George Durant, of Stamford Hill, London, silk broker.

Services : Ensign d.d. 46th N.I. 9 Nov. 1826. Posted as Ensign to 32nd N.I. 8 Jan. 1827. Suspended 17 Sept. 1831 till 16 May 1832. d.d. 39th N.I. 18 Dec. 1832. Fur. s.c. 1 Feb. 1834.

DURANT, James (*d.* 1850). Major General. Colonel 69th N.I. Cadet 1797. Arrived in India 21 Dec. 1798. Ensign 11 Oct. 1798. Lieut. 1 Nov. 1798. Capt. 26 Dec. 1809. Major 1 June 1818. Lt. Col. 11 July 1823. Col. 5 June 1829. Maj. Gen. 28 June 1838. *d.* Brighton 28 Sept. 1850.

Of 7 Hyde Pk. Gate, Kensington. *m.* Sarah Mason.

Services : Lieut. 16th N.I. With Guard of Resdt. at Delhi in 1803. Second Mahratta War ; Gwalior ; Deig ; Bhurtpore (w. on 21 Feb. 1805) ; Bde. Major 3rd Bde. Bde. Major at Fatehpur Sikri 1805-6. Reduction of Kalinjar ; Capt. 2/16th N.I. Against the Bhattis of Hariana 1818. Major 2/16th N.I. Fur. s.c. 5 June 1822 till 15 Oct. 1826. Transfd. to 10th N.I. (late 2/16th) May 1824. Fur. 7 Dec. 1826 till death. Transfd. to 17th N.I. 3 Apr. 1828 ; to 57th N.I. 3 June 1828. Col. 69th N.I. 27 Oct. 1832.

Refs. : *E.I.M.C.* ii. 343. Pester. *G.M.* 1850, ii. 563. Will dated 16 Mar. 1848 ; codicil dated 21 Feb. 1850 ; admon. 10 Aug. 1852.

THE BENGAL ARMY, 1758-1834

DUREY, Robert (d. 1783). Captain, 25th N.I. Cadet (?). Ensign 17 Dec. 1772. Lieut. 17 Mar. 1777. Capt. 17 Mar. 1781. d. Cuddalore, Madras, 13 June 1783 : kld. in action.

Services : Second Mysore War ; siege of Cuddalore (kld.) ; Capt. 25th N.I.

DURHAM, Hercules (1743/44-1776). Ensign. Infantry. Subsequently an Advocate in Calcutta. b. 1743/44. Cadet 1772. Ensign 30 Mar. 1773. Resigned 20 Jan. 1775. d. Calcutta 19 Oct. 1776.

Lineal male representative of the Durhams, of Grange. Only son of John Durham, of Kirkcaldy, co. Fife, surgeon and physician, and an officer in the Customs, and Isabella his wife, dau. of Hercules Smith. Brother of Phoebe, and of Jennet (Jean), mother of Edward Durham Hall, *q.v.* m. Elizabeth, dau. of Adm. (? Sir Joseph) Knight, of Jordanstown. His dau. m. Sir Robert Blair, *q.v.* Brasenose Coll., Oxon.; matric. 14 Dec. 1769, aged 25.

Services : Formerly an officer in H.M.S. Operations against the Bhutias in Cooch Behar 1772-3 ; Ensign 6th Bn. Sepoys, and acted for some months as surgeon to the detachment. Admitted an advocate of the supreme court in Calcutta 7 Jan. 1775. Offg. as Dy. Zemindar in Calcutta. Counsel for the Crown in the Nanda Kumar trial.

Refs. : Douglas's *Baronage of Scotland*, i. 473. *N. & Q.* 11S. ix. 117. *Alumni Oxon.* *B.* : *P.P.* lx. 163-4. *Forrest*, i. 29. Will dated 16 Oct. 1776 ; proved 21 Oct. 1776.

DURHAM, Robert Alexander (1795-1817). Lieutenant, 20th N.I. b. 27 July 1795. Cadet 1811. Ensign (12 Sept. 1814) 25 Apr. 1815. Lieut. 29 Feb. 1816. d. Mullye, Bengal, 27 July 1817.

bapt. Dublin 2 Aug. 1795. 4th and youngest son of Andrew Durham, M.D., of Belvedere, nr. Belfast, formerly Surgeon Bombay Est., and Elizabeth his 2nd wife, dau. of Capt. William Bonner, of Maryport, Cumberland.

Services : Nepal War 1814-5 ; Ensign Champaran L.I., in 4th Div. Nepal War 1816 ; Ensign Champaran L.I. Posted as Ensign to 2/20th N.I. in 1815 ; but owing to the absence from India of that Corps, he never joined, and was still serving with the Champaran L.I. at date of death.

Refs. : Burke's *Landed Gentry*, 13th edn., p. 539, *s.n.* Durham, of Cromer Grange.

DURHAM, Thomas (1759/60-?). Lieutenant. 36th Bn. Sepoys. b. in Scotland 1759/60. Cadet 1781. Ensign 3 Aug. 1781. Lieut. 31 Oct. 1782. Resigned 15 Mar. 1791.

Services: Apptd. Cadet on 31 Jan. 1781, aged 21. Sailed for India on the *Fortitude*, 13 Mar. 1781, aged 21. Adjt. 36th Bn. 1787-90.

DURIE, Alexander (1789-1826). Captain, 15th N.I. *b.* Brechin, co. Forfar, 16 July 1789. Cadet 1808. Arrived in India 27 Oct. 1809. Ensign 30 Oct. 1810. Lieut. 16 Dec. 1814. Capt. 21 Apr. 1824. *d.* Agra 9 Mar. 1826.

Son of Alexander Durie, of Brechin, wright.

Services: Posted as Ensign to 11th N.I. in 1810. Reduction of Kalinjar 1812; Ensign 11th N.I. Siege and capture of Hathras 1817; Lieut. 2/11th N.I. Third Mahratta War; Lieut. 2/11th N.I. Kumaon Local Bn. 1819-25. Transfd. to 15th N.I. (late 1/11th) May 1824. Siege and capture of Bhurtpore; Capt. 15th N.I.

DURIE, Arthur Lee (1803-1829). Lieutenant, 31st N.I. *b.* Clonmel, co. Tipperary, 1 May 1803. Cadet 1820. Arrived in India May 1821. Ensign 16 Jan. 1821. Lieut. 11 July 1823. *d.* 21 Aug. 1829: drowned in the Ganges off Berhampore whilst proceeding to Calcutta.

Son of Sir William Durie, K.H., Asst. Inspector of Ord., Medical Dept.

Services: Posted as Ensign to 1/5th N.I. Transfd. as Lieut. to 15th N.I. July 1823; to 31st N.I. (late 2/15th) May 1824. Siege and capture of Bhurtpore; Lieut. 31st N.I. Adjt. 31st N.I. 25 July 1827 till death. Operations against the Bhils 1828.

Refs.: A.J. N.S. i. 236.

DURIE, Rowley Henry (1806-1834). Lieutenant, 65th N.I. *b.* Tralee, co. Kerry, 13 Mar. 1806. Cadet 1826. Arrived in India 24 Dec. 1827. Ensign 2 Aug. 1827. Lieut. 31 Jan. 1832. *d.* Mhow 18 Aug. 1834.

Son of Charles Durie, British consul for Norway.

Services: Posted as Ensign to 40th N.I. 19 June 1827. Transfd. to 65th N.I. 20 Feb. 1828. No record of active service.

Refs.: A.J. N.S. xvi. 195.

DWYER, Anthony (1785-?). Lieutenant 4th N.I. *b.* Limerick, 13 Jan. 1785. Cadet 1803. Arrived in India 1 Dec. 1804. Ensign 8 Oct. 1804. Lieut. 8 Oct. 1804. Resigned 17 Apr. 1806.

Son of John Dwyer, of Dublin, and Anne his wife.

Services: Posted as Lieut. to 4th N.I. No record of active service.

DWYER, George (1789-1836). Lieutenant, Pension Est. 29th N.I. *bapt.* Gt. Stanmore, Middlesex, 8 May 1789. Cadet 1805. Arrived in India 13 Dec. 1806. Ensign 17 Oct. 1806. Lieut. 26 Nov. 1807. Pensioned 15 Apr. 1815. *d.* Monghyr 17 Mar. 1836.
Son of Dennis Dwyer and Elizabeth his wife. Brother of Henry Dwyer, *q.v.*
Services : Posted as Lieut. to 9th N.I. in 1807. Transfd. to newly-raised 29th N.I. Jan. 1815. Resided at Monghyr 1827 till death. No record of active service.
Refs. : A.J. N.S. xxi. 37. M.I. at Monghyr.

DWYER, Henry (1790-1833). Captain, 42nd N.I. *b.* Gt. Stanmore, Middlesex, 2 Oct. 1790. Cadet 1805. Arrived in India 13 Dec. 1806. Ensign 9 Dec. 1806. Lieut. 8 Sept. 1809. Capt. 1 May 1824. *d. unm.* Saharanpur, U.P., 18 June 1833.
bapt. Gt. Stanmore 4 Nov. 1790. Son of Dennis Dwyer and Elizabeth his wife. Brother of George Dwyer, *q.v.*
Services : Barasat C.C. for 8 mos. Posted as Ensign to 2/21st N.I. Capture of Java 1811 ; Lieut. 4th Bengal Vol. Bn. Served in Java with Vols. till Nov. 1816. Qmr. 4th Vol. Bn. 4 Oct. 1814. Adjt. 2/21st N.I. in 1817. Transfd. to 42nd N.I. (late 2/21st) May 1824. First Burma War ; Arakan 1825 ; Capt. 42nd N.I. Leave s.c. to Cape 23 Dec. 1828 till Dec. 1830. Leave 18 mos. to Cape and N.S.W. 28 Jan. 1831.
Refs. : Will dated Delhi 12 May 1833 ; proved 17 Jan. 1834.

DYCE, David (1764/65-1790). Lieutenant, Infantry. *b.* in Scotland 1764-65. Cadet 1782. Arrived in India 15 Nov. 1782. Ensign 24 Jan. 1783. Lieut. 2 July 1789. *d.* Calcutta 26 Feb. 1790.
His son, by a native woman, the so-called *General* George Alexander David Dyce, Comdt. of Begum Somru's forces, was father of David Ochterlony Dyce-Sombre (*D.N.B.*).
Services : Sailed for India on the *Worcester*, 6 Feb. 1782, aged 17. Ensign 1st Bengal Eur. Regt. in July 1787.
Refs. : M.I. in S. Park St. cemetery, Calcutta (where his age at death is given as 23 yrs.).

DYER, Samuel (1749/50-1802). Colonel, 10th N.I. Q.M.G. *b.* 1749/50. Country Cadet 1769. Admitted 2 June 1769. Ensign 4 Mar. 1769. Lieut. 31 Mar. 1771. Capt. 5 Sept. 1779. Major 1 Mar. 1794. Lt. Col. 1 June 1796. Col. 21 Apr. 1800. *d.* Calcutta, 13 Dec. 1802, aged 52.
Son of William Dyer, of Redcliffe Parade, Bristol. Brother of

Robert Dyer, apothecary, and of Mrs. Eyre, of Reading, and uncle of George Brydges Selwyn, *q.v.* *m.* Calcutta, 22 Jan. 1794, Miss Elizabeth Ann Burdekin.
Services : Sailed for India in 1767. Apptd. D.Q.M.G. (with Bt. rank of Major) 16 May 1786. Was actg. Q.M.G. in 1790. Apptd. Q.M.G., Bengal, before 1800. Col. 10th N.I. 21 Apr. 1800.
Refs. : *G.M.* 1803, i. 478. Will dated 23 Jan. 1796 ; proved 16 Dec. 1802. M.I. in N. Park St. cemetery, Calcutta.

DYER, ——. Captain. Infantry. Capt. 6 June 1758.
Services : N.F.P. Not in Williams's *List of Bengal Officers* in 1760.
Refs. : *Orme MSS.—India*, xiii. 3639.

DYKE, Augustus Hart (1811-1878). Lieut. Colonel. 25th N.I. *bapt.* Lullingstone, Kent, 22 Sept. 1811. Cadet 1828. Arrived in India 4 May 1829. Ensign (8 Jan. 1829) 15 Nov. 1831. Lieut. 25 Feb. 1837. Capt. 24 Jan. 1845. Bt. Major 1855. Retired 18 Jan. 1856. Hon. Lt. Col. 18 Jan. 1856. *d.* 23 Oct. 1878.
9th son of Sir Percival Hart Dyke, 5th Bart., and Anne his wife, eldest dau. of Robert Jenner, of Wenvoe Castle, co. Glamorgan. Brother of George Hart Dyke, *q.v.*, and cousin-german of Birt Wyndham Rous Jenner, *q.v.*
Services : Ensign d.d. 16th N.I. 10 June 1829. Supy. Ensign 56th N.I. 14 Sept. 1829. Posted as Ensign to 13th N.I. 15 Nov. 1831. Transfd. to 56th N.I. 18 Feb. 1832 ; to 25th N.I. 2 Mar. 1835. Adjt. 25th N.I. 19 Aug. 1837 till 2 June 1841. Fur. s.c. 10 Jan. 1845 till 7 Dec. 1847. Second Sikh War ; Sadulapur ; Chilianwala ; Gujerat ; Capt. 25th N.I. (Medal with clasp). Fur. 1854 till retirement.
Refs. : Burke's *Peerage*, 1923, p. 797, *s.n.* Dyke, Bart., of Horeham, Sussex. *The Times*, 25 Oct. 1878.

DYKE, George Hart (1804-1846). Captain, Artillery. *b.* Maidstone, Kent, 5 Dec. 1804. Cadet 1820. Arrived in India 19 Nov. 1821. 2nd Lieut. 9 June 1821. Lieut. 1 May 1824. Capt. 31 Dec. 1838. *d.* Dum-Dum 13 May 1846.
5th son of Sir Percival Hart Dyke, 5th Bart., and Anne his wife. Brother of John Dixon Dyke, *q.v.* Addiscombe Cadet 12 Feb. 1819 till 9 June 1821.
Services : First Burma War ; Arakan 1825 ; comdd. detachment of Art. which occupied Ramri I. in Apr. 1825. Fur. s.c. 4 Nov. 1825 till 6 Aug. 1827. Dy. Comy. Ord. 7 Mar. 1828 ; posted to Saugor 23 Apr. 1828. Comy. Ord. at Allahabad 23 Apr. 1835. Offg. Dy. Principal Comy. Ord. 16 Sept. 1834 ; permanent do.

THE BENGAL ARMY, 1758-1834

4 Mar. 1840. Posted to Delhi magazine 9 Sept. 1842. Supt. Cossipore foundry 8 Aug. 1845 till death.
Refs. : Burke's *Peerage*, 1923, p. 797, *s.n.* Dyke, Bart., of Horeham, Sussex. *G.M.* 1846, ii. 334. Will dated Calcutta 11 Apr. 1846 ; proved 5 May 1847. M.I. at Dum-Dum.

DYKE, John Dixon (1803-1885). Captain. 4th L.C. *b.* Foots Cray, Kent, 9 Jan. 1803. Cadet 1818. Admitted 17 July 1819. Cornet 8 Feb. 1819. Lieut. 17 Mar. 1820. Capt. 10 July 1825. Resigned 18 June 1835. *d.* Glovers House, Sittingbourne, Kent, 1 Aug. 1885.
Of Glovers House, Sittingbourne. J.P. Kent. 3rd son of Sir Percival Hart Dyke, 5th Bart., and Anne his wife. Brother of William Hart Dyke, *q.v.* *m.* 10 Feb. 1836, Millicent, youngest dau. of Isaac Minet, of Baldwyns, Dartford, Kent. (She died 5 Aug. 1901.) Ed. Harrow 1814/15 till 1820.
Services : Posted to 4th L.C. 12 Oct. 1820. Actg. Qmr. 4th L.C. 20 May 1822. Adjt. G.G.B.G. 7 May 1824 till 12 Sept. 1825. First Burma War 1824-6 ; Rangoon ; Kokein ; Lieut. G.G.B.G. (India medal). Apptd. 2nd Asst. to Resdt. at Gwalior 3 Sept. 1825, but remained in Burma with G.G.B.G. till 8 Mar. 1826. Asst. to Resdt. at Gwalior 14 Oct. 1830. Fur. p.a. 10 Jan. 1833 till resignation.
Refs. : Burke's *Peerage*, 1923, p. 797, *s.n.* Dyke, Bart., of Horeham, Sussex. Burke's *Family Records*, p. 432, *s.n.* Minet. *Harrow School List*. *V.B.G.*

DYKE, William Hart (1808-1829). Lieutenant, 60th N.I. *b.* Orpington, Kent, 22 Feb. 1808. Cadet 1823. Arrived in India 30 Mar. 1825. Ensign 10 Sept. 1824. Lieut. 10 Dec. 1826. *d.* Dehra Dun, U.P., 7 Sept. 1829.
7th son of Sir Percival Hart Dyke, 5th Bart., and Anne his wife. Brother of Augustus Hart Dyke, *q.v.* Addiscombe Cadet 1822-4.
Services : Posted as Ensign to 60th N.I. Siege and capture of Bhurtpore ; Ensign 60th N.I.
Refs. : Burke's *Peerage*, 1923, p. 797, *s.n.* Dyke, Bart., of Horeham, Sussex.

DYSART, George (1808-1837). Lieutenant, 2nd N.I. *b.* Londonderry 23 Sept. 1808. Cadet 1826. Arrived in India 1 Feb. 1828. Ensign 16 Aug. 1827. Lieut. 7 Apr. 1831. *d.* Sikandra Rao, nr. Aligarh, 7 Mar. 1837 : accidentally shot himself while out duck shooting.
3rd son of John Dysart, of Londonderry, merchant, and Easter his wife, eldest dau. of George Crookshank Kennedy (who assumed the surname of Skipton), and sister of Thomas Skipton, *q.v.* *m.*

Agra, 4 Feb. 1835, Julia Elizabeth, 3rd dau. of Col. Sir Robert Henry Sale, G.C.B. (*See also* Frederick Brind.)

Services : Posted as Ensign to 2nd N.I. 20 Feb. 1828. Operations against the Kols 1832 ; Lieut. 2nd N.I.

Refs. : Burke's *Landed Gentry*, 7th edn., p. 1678, *s.n.* Skipton, of Beechhill, co. Londonderry. *A.J.* N.S. xxiv. 28.

DYSON, Henry Wilcocks (1793-1818). Lieutenant, 1st N.I. *bapt.* Baughurst, Hants, 15 Sept. 1793. Cadet 1808. Arrived in India 27 Oct. 1809. Ensign 19 Mar. 1810. Lieut. 10 Dec. 1814. *d.* Dungarpur, Rajputana, 20 Dec. 1818.

Son of Rev. Henry Dyson and Elizabeth his wife. Ed. Charterhouse ; admitted a scholar 15 June 1804 ; left before 26 Jan. 1808.

Services : Posted as Ensign to 1st N.I. Lieut. 1/1st N.I. (? Third Mahratta War ; Lieut. 1/1st N.I.)

Refs. : *Alumni Carthusiani.*

DYSON, John (1800-1851). Captain. 21st N.I. *b.* 13 May 1800. Cadet 1821. Arrived in India 19 Aug. 1822. Ensign 10 Mar. 1822. Lieut. 14 Oct. 1824. Capt. 15 Mar. 1841. Retired 1 May 1846. *d.* 23 May 1851.

bapt. Elland, Yorks., 3 Mar. 1801. Son of John Dyson.

Services : Posted as Ensign to 9th N.I. Transfd. to 21st N.I. (late 2/9th) May 1824. Siege and capture of Bhurtpore ; Lieut. 21st N.I. (India medal). Intr. & Qmr. 21st N.I. 8 May 1828. Fur. s.c. 31 Jan. 1832 till 4 Dec. 1834. Actg. D.J.A.G., Sirhind Div., 11 Oct. 1838 ; offg. do. 21 Mar. 1839. D.J.A.G., Cawnpore, 23 Dec. 1840 ; do. Dinapore and Benares Divs., 16 Mar. 1841 ; do. Presdy. Div. 1844 till retirement.

E

EADE, John (1755/56-1828). Captain. Infantry. *b.* 1755/56. Cadet 1780. Ensign 1780. Lieut. 22 July 1781. Capt. 31 July 1799. Retired 23 Oct. 1800. *d.* Bayford, Herts., 17 Oct. 1828, aged 73.
Of Bayford Place, Bayford.
Services : Sailed for India on the *Rochford*, 3 June 1780, aged 23. Adjt. 21st Bn. Sepoys, in 5th Bde., 1787-90. Fur. 25 Jan. 1794 till retirement.
Refs. : *G.M.* 1828, ii. 380.

EAGLE, George (1764-1811). Bt. Major, 3rd N.I. *b.* Nov. 1764. Country Cadet 1782. Admitted 25 Aug. 1782. Ensign 7 May 1783. Lieut. 1 June 1790. Capt. 30 Sept. 1803. Bt. Major 25 July 1810. *d.* Delhi, 29 June 1811, aged 46 yrs. 7 mos.
Eldest son of Dr. Eagle, of Limerick. Brother of Ann, Henry, Edward, and Eyre Massey Eagle. *m.* Ann. (She died Serampore, 19 Dec. 1824, aged 45.)
Services : Posted to 1st Bengal Eur. Regt. in Feb. 1783. Supy. Ensign on h.p. 1786-90. Posted as Ensign to 2nd Eur. Bn. 5 Feb. 1790. Transfd. to 29th Bn. 16 June 1790 ; to 3rd Eur. Bn. in 1792 ; to 35th Bn. 16 Apr. 1793. Posted to 2/5th N.I. (late 23rd Bn.) June 1796 ; transfd. to 2/1st N.I. in Jan. 1799 ; to 2/3rd N.I. in Mar. 1799. Took part with his Bn. in various minor operations against rebellious zemindars.
Refs. : De Rhé-Philipe. *Faulkner's Dublin Journal*, 26 Mar. 1812. *S.M.* 1812, p. 320. *M.M.* 1812, ii. 93. *N. & Q.* 9S. iv. 403. Will dated Amirgaon 5 Nov. 1805 ; proved in 1811. M.I. in old cemetery, nr. the Fort, Delhi.

EALES, John (1760-1819). Major General. Colonel 25th N.I. *bapt.* Liskeard, Cornwall, 14 Nov. 1760. Cadet 1778. Admitted 12 Apr. 1780. Ensign 1778. Lieut. 11 Dec. 1778. Capt. 1 June 1796. Major 8 Dec. 1800. Lt. Col. 30 Sept. 1803. Col. 1 Jan. 1812. Maj. Gen. 4 June 1814. *d.s.p.* Liskeard 3 May 1819.
Of Golden Bank, Liskeard. Eldest son of Alderman William Eales, of Liskeard, and Martha his wife, dau. of Thomas Smerdon.

Uncle of Thomas Eales Soady, *q.v.* *m.* Barbara. (She died Dawlish, 9 Jan. 1842, aged 78.)

Services : Lieut. 24th Bn. Sepoys in July 1787 ; Capt. do. in 1796. Disturbances in Ganjam, Madras, 1801 ; Major 6th N.I. Posted as Lt. Col. to 20th N.I. in 1803. Fur. 17 Feb. 1808 till 1810. Transfd. to 1st N.I. in 1812 ; to Bengal Eur. Regt. 1812. Fur. from Java 1815 till death. Posted as Col. to 25th N.I. in 1816.

Refs. : Burke's *Family Records,* p. 235, *s.n.* Eales. *Howard & Crisp* (Notes), ii. 75. *Hickey,* iv.

EAMER, Charles Samler (1787-1805). Cornet, 8th N.C. *b.* London 2 Feb. 1787. Cadet 1803. Arrived in India 15 Aug. 1804. Cornet 11 Mar. 1805. *d.* Ghazipur, U.P., 8 Oct. 1805, of jungle fever.

bapt. St. Mary Magdalen, Milk St., London, 8 Mar. 1787. 2nd son of Sir John Eamer, Kt., Alderman of London, Col. East London Mil. (originally a wholesale grocer in Wood St.), and Mary his wife.

Services : Cornet d.d. 23rd N.I. Posted as Cornet to 3rd N.C. Second Mahratta War ; battle of Deig (? Bhurtpore) ; Cornet 3rd N.C. Transfd. to newly-raised 8th N.C. in 1805.

Refs. : Pester, p. 436. *G.M.* 1806, i. 181.

EARLE, John Lucas (1791-1845). Lieut. Colonel, 3rd N.I. *b.* Ashburton, Devon, 29 Jan. 1791. Cadet 1805. Arrived in India 7 Apr. 1807. Ensign 12 Apr. 1807. Lieut. 15 June 1809. Capt. 5 Mar. 1823. Major 31 Mar. 1835. Lt. Col. 24 Dec. 1841. *d.* Hoshangabad, C.P., 12 Oct. 1845.

Son of Solomon Earle, *q.v.*, and Rose his wife. Brother of Solomon Earle, *q.v.* *m.* Mary Jane. (She died 18 June 1890.) His daus. *m.* William Young Siddons, *q.v.*, and Robert Christopher Tytler, *q.v.*

Services : Barasat C.C. for 11½ mos. Posted as Ensign to 8th N.I. Expedn. to Mauritius 1810 ; Lieut. 2nd Bn. Bengal Vols. Nepal War 1814-5 ; Lieut. 1/8th N.I., in 4th Div. Nepal War 1816 ; Lieut. 1/8th N.I., in 2nd Bde., Left Column. Leave u.p.a. to Mauritius 15 Nov. 1816 ; fur. s.c. from Cape 27 June 1817 till 11 Sept. 1819. Fort Adjt. at Asirgarh 22 May 1820 till 1825. Transfd. to 9th N.I. (late 1/8th) May 1824. Actg. Bde. Major in Rohilkhand 1 June 1826. Leave u.p.a. to Tasmania 25 Nov. 1831. To comd. 2nd Recruit Depot Bn. at Fatehgarh 7 Sept. 1839. Posted as Lt. Col. to 3rd N.I. 19 Jan. 1842.

Refs. : Will dated Hussingabad 26 Sept. 1845 ; proved 14 Jan. 1846.

EARLE, Solomon. Captain. 30th N.I. Subsequently Paymr. to Coy.'s Depot at Chatham. Cadet 1768. Arrived in India 21 Aug. 1768. Ensign 13 Feb. 1769. Lieut. 15 May 1770. Capt. 21 Aug. 1779. Struck off 1793. (Was living in 1824.)

m. Ashburton, Devon, Aug. 1787, Rose, dau. of Rev. Thomas Rennell, of Stokenham, Devon. Father of John Lucas Earle, *q.v.*, Solomon Earle, *q.v.*, and William Henry Earle, *q.v.*

Services : Apptd. Cadet on 29 Dec. 1767. Posted to 17th Bn. Sepoys in 1769. Transfd. to 2nd Bn. in 1776. First Mahratta War 1778-84 ; succeeded to comd. of 2nd Bn. 21 Aug. 1779 ; siege and capture of Ahmedabad ; action at Pawangarh ; Capt. comdg. 2nd Bn. Resdt. at court of Baroda 1781-3. To comd. 1/30th N.I. 1784. Fur. s.c. 3 yrs. 6 Dec. 1785, and was still on fur. in 1790. Apptd. Capt. and Adjt. of the Coy.'s Recruit Depot in I.W. June 1804 ; Capt. and Paymr. do. Apr. 1814 till 1816, latterly at Chatham. Retired on pension in 1816.

Refs. : *E.I.M.C.* ii. 368-75. *Williams,* p. 88. *G.M.* 1787, ii. 835.

EARLE, Solomon (1797-1858). Lieutenant, Invalid Est. 43rd N.I. *b.* London 26 Jan. 1797. Cadet 1818. Ensign 11 May 1819. Lieut. 8 Jan. 1820. Invalided 11 Apr. 1828. *d.* Intally, Calcutta, 6 June 1858.

Son of Solomon Earle, *q.v.*, and Rose his wife. Brother of William Henry Earle, *q.v.*

Services : Lieut. 2nd Bn. L.I., King's German Legion, 11 Oct. 1813, with which Corps he is said to have served at the battle of Waterloo. Ensign d.d. 30th N.I. 1819. Posted as Lieut. to 2/22nd N.I. in 1820. Fur. 6 Feb. 1821 till 1822. Transfd. to 44th N.I. (late 2/22nd) May 1824 ; to 43rd N.I. in 1825.

Refs. : *I.M.* 27 July 1858, p. 625.

EARLE, Thomas (*d.* 1784). Captain, Infantry. Cadet 1771. Ensign 8 Jan. 1773. Lieut. 2 Apr. 1777. Capt. 28 Mar. 1781. *d.* 21 Jan. 1784, on active service with the Bombay detachment.

Services : First Mahratta War.

EARLE, William Henry (1794-1846). Bt. Lt. Colonel, 39th N.I. *b.* Ashburton, Devon, 27 Jan. 1794., Cadet 1808. Arrived in India 30 July 1809. Ensign 21 Nov. 1809. Lieut. 16 Dec. 1814. Capt. 13 May 1825. Major 18 Mar. 1845. Bt. Lt. Col. 30 Apr. 1844. *d.* Berhampore 18 Nov. 1846.

Son of Solomon Earle, *q.v.*, and Rose his wife. Brother of John Lucas Earle, *q.v.* *m.* Meerut, 12 Feb. 1821, Jane, dau. of John Augustus Shadwell, *q.v.* His dau. *m.* John Charles Haslock, *q.v.*

Services : Barasat C.C. for 10 mos. Posted as Ensign to 19th

N.I. Nepal War 1814-5; Lieut. 1/19th N.I., 3rd Coy. Pioneers, in 1st Div. Served with Pioneers for the next ten years. Nepal War 1816. Siege and capture of Hathras 1817. Third Mahratta War; Mandala (*Lond. Gaz.* 7 Dec. 1818). Operations in Jodhpur 1823; Lamba. First Burma War 1824-5. Adjt. Pioneers 12 June 1823 till 28 Sept. 1825. Transfd. to 39th N.I. (late 2/19th) May 1824. D.A.A.G. to troops for service in Merwara 5 Aug. 1838 till 14 Oct. 1839. Bde. Major at Karnal 5 May 1841 till 14 Apr. 1842. With Army of Reserve (for Afghanistan) Oct. 1842 till Jan. 1843. Gwalior campaign; Paniar (s.w.); Bt. Major 39th N.I. (Bronze star). (*Lond. Gaz.* 8 Mar. 1844.)

Refs.: *A.J.* xii. 290.

EARLES, Joseph. Lieutenant. 3rd Bengal Eur. Regt. Cadet 1778. Ensign 10 May 1779. Lieut. 15 Jan. 1781. Dismissed by C.M. 25 Nov. 1783.

(? *m.* Barbara, who died 9 Jan. 1842, aged 78.)

Services: Posted as Ensign to 2/3rd Bengal Eur. Regt. in Oct. 1779.

EARTIER, James. Lieutenant. Infantry. Cadet (?). Ensign (?). Lieut. 29 Oct. 1763.

Services: N.F.P.

EASSON, James (1793-1820). Ensign, Pension Est. Bengal Eur. Regt. *bapt.* Errol, co. Perth, 4 July 1793. Cadet 1809. Arrived in India 3 Oct. 1810. Ensign 10 Dec. 1811. Pensioned 1 Nov. 1815. *d.* Calcutta 25 May 1820.

Son of Robert Easson, farmer.

Services: (? Lieut. H.M. 24th Regt.) Cadet d.d. 9th N.I. 1811. Posted as Ensign to Bengal Eur. Regt. Served in Java with his Regt. till pensioned.

Refs.: *A.J.* x. 614; xi. 62.

EAST, William. Ensign. Infantry. Cadet 1783. Ensign 1783. Struck off 1788.

Services: N.F.P.

EASTWOOD, William. Ensign. Infantry. Cadet 1778. Ensign 1778.

Services: N.F.P.

EATON, Isaac (*d.* 1789). Major, Infantry. Cadet 1765. Ensign 6 Jan. 1766. Lieut. 28 May 1767. Capt. 26 June 1771. Major 21 Jan. 1781. *d.* in England 20 Feb. 1789.

Ed. Merchant Taylors'; entered the school in 1754.

THE BENGAL ARMY, 1758-1834

Services : Comdt. at Buxar till 16 Nov. 1785. Having been granted fur. s.c. 3 yrs. on 16 Oct. 1785, he returned to England in 1786, and remained to give evidence on behalf of Warren Hastings, an old and close friend, to whom he left a legacy of £1,000.
Refs. : Robinson. Grier. G.M. 1789, i. 185. *Eur. Mag.* 1789, p. 254.

EATON, Robert (*d.* 1804). Captain, Marine Regt. Cadet 1780. Admitted 10 Apr. 1781. Ensign 6 Sept. 1781. Lieut. 18 June 1783. Capt. 8 Jan. 1801. *d.* at sea 24 May 1804, on board the *Lord Eldon.*
Services : Lieut. 16th Bn. Sepoys in July 1787. Bt. Capt. 7th N.I. in 1798. Capt. Lt. 8th N.I. 31 July 1800. Adjt. & Qmr. 8th N.I. Capt. 2/8th N.I. Transfd. to Marine Regt. Fur. 24 Apr. 1803 till death.

EBHART, Bentinck William (1803-1849). Lieutenant. 10th N.I. *b.* Newry, co. Down, 11 Mar. 1803. Cadet 1819. Ensign 14 Nov. 1819. Lieut. 18 Oct. 1822. Retired 13 Apr. 1831. *d.* 26 Sept. 1849.

Son of Frederick Ebhart, Lieut. 9th Light Dgns. Grandson of Andreas Friederich Ebhart. (? Named after Lord William Bentinck.)
Services : Posted as Ensign to 2/27th N.I. in 1820. Transfd. to 7th N.I. 11 July 1823 ; to 10th N.I. (late 2/7th) May 1824. Supy. S.A.C.G. 14 July 1826. S.A.C.G. till Sept. 1828. Fur. s.c. 9 Jan. 1829 till retirement. No record of active service.

ECKFORD, James (1786-1867). Lieut. General, C.B. 56th N.I. *b.* Dunfermline, co. Fife, 5 July 1786. Cadet 1804. Arrived in India 10 July 1805. Ensign 17 Nov. 1805. Lieut. 17 Sept. 1806. Capt. 20 July 1823. Major 18 July 1831. Lt. Col. 11 Mar. 1837. Col. 27 Oct. 1848. Maj. Gen. 28 Nov. 1854. Lt. Gen. 29 Apr. 1861. *d.* 33 Clarendon Rd., St. Helier, Jersey, 2 July 1867.

Son of John Eckford, of Dunfermline, merchant, and Janet Buntein his wife. *m.* 1st, Berhampore, 11 July 1817, Diana Denton Turner, 3rd dau. of George Wroughton, of Newington House, Oxon., and sister of Henry Francis Wroughton, *q.v.* (*See also* William Percival.) (She died 27 May 1819.) *m.* 2nd, Edinburgh, 2 Dec. 1824, Mary, 3rd dau. of James Alexander Haldane, of George St., Edinburgh. (She died Dehra Dun, U.P., 7 Nov. 1857.) *m.* 3rd, Kensington, 13 Apr. 1863, Mary, only dau. of Arthur Forrest, late of Forrest Lodge, Binfield, Berks.
Services : Served as a Midshipman on H.M. Frigate *Greyhound*

with Sir Home Popham's expedn. ; present at bombardment of
Boulogne and Havre, and subsequent destruction of French flotilla.
Posted as Lieut. to 3rd N.I. Operations in Bundelkhand 1807 ;
capture of Chamir. Capture of Java 1811 ; Lieut. & Adjt. 6th Vol.
Bn. (Medal). Capture of Jokyakarta 1812. Served in Java with
Vols. till 1816. Comdd. Amboynese Corps Mar.-Apr. 1816. Fur.
p.a. 25 Nov. 1820 till 18 May 1825. Transfd. to 6th N.I. (late 1/3rd)
May 1824. Siege and capture of Bhurtpore ; Capt. 6th N.I. (India
medal). Posted as Lt. Col. to 6th N.I. 4 May 1838. First Afghan
War 1842 ; Lt. Col. comdg. 6th N.I., with Gen. Pollock's force ;
comdg. at Jalalabad 10 Nov. 1842 (Medal). First Sikh War ; Lt.
Col. comdg. 6th N.I., on escort duty. Transfd. to 7th N.I. 24 July
1847 ; to 56th N.I. 9 May 1848. Bdr., 2 cl., Oct. 1848. Second
Sikh War ; passage of Chenab ; Sadulapur ; Bdr. comdg. 3rd Inf.
Bde. (Medal). Col. 56th N.I. Fur. s.c. 10 Mar. 1850 till 2 Apr.
1854. Bdr., 2 cl., to comd. at Barrackpore 4 Aug. 1854. Maj. Gen.
tempy. comdg. Presdy. Div. 4 May 1855 till 1856. Fur. 1859 till
death. C.B. 9 June 1849.

Refs. : Burke's *Visitation of Seats & Arms*, 1S. ii. 19, *s.n.* Haldane
(now Chinnery-Haldane), of Gleneagles, co. Perth. *Boase. G.M.*
1818, i. 176. *S.M.* 1825, i. 127. *The Times*, 3 July 1867.

EDEN, John (1789-1874). Ensign. 15th N.I. Subsequently
General, C.B. Col. H.M. 34th Regt. *b.* Greenwich 25 Mar. 1789.
Cadet 1805. Arrived in India 7 Feb. 1807. Ensign 2 Jan. 1807.
Resigned 19 Feb. 1807. *d.* Bath 6 Oct. 1874.

2nd son of Thomas Eden, of Wimbledon, dy. auditor of Greenwich
Hospital, and Mariana his wife, dau. of Arthur Jones. Nephew of
William Eden, 1st Baron Auckland. *m.* 1st, 1830, Anne, only dau.
of Sir John Caldwell, Bart., of Castle Caldwell. (She died Montreal
Nov. 1841.) *m.* 2nd, 4 July 1843, Charlotte Carse, dau. of Edmund
Samuel Prentice, of Armagh. Nominated for R.M.A., Woolwich,
29 May 1805. Withdrawn, and apptd. Bengal Inf. Cadet.

Services : Cornet 22nd Light Dgns. 14 Feb. 1807. Capt. 53rd
Foot 26 Dec. 1818. Gen. 25 Aug. 1868. See *Hart's A.L.*

Refs. : Burke's *Peerage*, 1923, p. 809, *s.n.* Eden, Bart., of West
Auckland, Durham. *The Times*, 9 Oct. 1874.

EDGAR, Joseph (1759/60-1782). Lieutenant, Sepoy Corps. *b.*
1759/60. Cadet 1778. Ensign 1778. Lieut. 1778. bur. Cawnpore 5 Jan. 1782 : kld. in a duel.

A native of Dorset.

Services : Sailed for India on the *Gatton*, 27 Apr. 1778, aged 18.
Lieut. 1/3rd Bengal Eur. Regt. in Oct. 1779.

EDMONSON, John (1740/41-1789). Lieut. Colonel, 12th N.I. *b.* 1740/41. Cadet (Bombay) 1762. Ensign (Bombay) (?). Lieut. (Bengal) 25 June 1765. Capt. 10 June 1767. Major 25 Oct. 1779. Lt. Col. 3 Dec. 1782. *d.* on the river 31 Jan. 1789 : bur. Calcutta 2 Feb. 1789.

A native of Liverpool. *m.* Calcutta, 15 Mar. 1787, Miss Sarah Ware. (She *re-m.* James Pearson (1752/53-1826), *q.v.*)
Services : Sailed for Bombay on the *Latham*, 25 Apr. 1763, aged 22. Transfd. to Bengal Est.1765. First Rohilla War; battle of St.George; Capt. comdg. 18th Bn. Sepoys. Second Mysore War 1781-5 ; Major comdg. 12th N.I., and 2nd in comd. to Col. Thomas Deane Pearse's detachment; siege of Cuddalore ; Major comdg. 2nd Bde. Comdg. 3rd Bde. and Sepoy Corps at Barrackpore in July 1787.
Refs. : *Williams*, p. 164. *E.I.M.C.* ii. 218, 247.

EDMONSTONE, Archibald (*d.* 1776). Ensign, Engineers. Cadet 1771. Ensign (Inf.) 17 Jan. 1773. *d.* Bengal Feb. 1776.
" Son of Governor Edmonstone."
Services : Transfd. from Inf. to Engrs. N.F.P.
Refs. : *S.M.* 1777, p. 622.

EDWARDS, Charles (*d.* 1798). Lieutenant, Artillery. Cadet 1783. Admitted 27 Sept. 1783. Fireworker 4 Jan. 1785. Lieut. 26 Dec. 1790. *d. unm.* Calcutta 13 Jan. 1798.
Cousin of Robert Coulson.
Services : Lieut.F. 1st Bn. Art. in July 1787.
Refs. : Will proved in 1798.

EDWARDS, Charles Lloyd (1805-?). Major. 70th N.I. *b.* Dorchester 14 Oct. 1805. Cadet 1826. Arrived in India 22 Sept. 1827. Ensign 8 Feb. 1827. Lieut. 25 Sept. 1837. Bt. Capt. 8 Feb. 1842. Retired 8 Apr. 1850. Hon. Major 28 Nov. 1854. *d.* (?).[1]
bapt. Protestant Dissenters' chapel, Dorchester, 5 Mar. 1806. Son of John Bowditch Edwards and Hannah his wife. Brother of John Edwards, of Dorchester, surgeon. *m.* Dinapore, 25 Sept. 1841, Eliza Anne, dau. of Thomas Ward, *q.v.*
Services : Posted as Ensign to 48th N.I. 19 June 1827. Wahabi rising 1831 ; Ensign 48th N.I. Transfd. to 24th N.I. 11 Oct. 1833 ; to 70th N.I. 22 Apr. 1834 ; to 64th N.I. 24 Sept. 1835 ; to 70th N.I. 10 May 1836. *d.d.* Arakan Local Bn. 8 Sept. 1837 ; Adjt. do. 14 Aug. 1839 till Aug. 1840. Adjt. 70th N.I. 14 May 1847 till June 1849. Crimean War ; Local Major in Turkey 27 Mar. 1855.

[1] *Note :* Name removed from the list of Retired Officers, given in *India List*, after Jan. 1878 ; although it continues to appear in the official *Quarterly Bengal A.L.* down to Jan. 1884.

EDWARDS, Francis (*d.* 1813). Captain, 25th N.I. Cadet 1794. Arrived in India 2 Feb. 1797. Ensign 13 Nov. 1795. Lieut. 6 Aug. 1797. Capt. 25 Mar. 1806. *d. unm.* Barrackpore 25 Oct. 1813.
Of Tooting, Surrey.
Services : Second Mahratta War ; Lieut. 13th N.I. Transfd. to newly-raised 25th N.I. in 1804. Capt. Lt. 25th N.I. 21 Sept. 1804. Capture of Gohad 1806 ; Capt. 25th N.I.

EDWARDS, George Harris (1801-1846). Captain, 13th N.I. *b.* London 14 July 1801. Cadet 1818. Admitted 13 Nov. 1819. Ensign 11 July 1819. Lieut. 29 Oct. 1821. Capt. 18 Feb. 1839. *d.* Midnapore, Bengal, 22 July 1846.
bapt. St. George's, Hanover Sq., London, 21 Jan. 1802. Son of William Jones Edwards, of 5 Amelia Pl., Brompton, and Ellen his wife. *m.* 1st, St. John's, Calcutta, 12 May 1824, Rachel, dau. of William Finch, of Winchelsea. *m.* 2nd, Calcutta, 17 July 1844, Amelia Julia, dau. of Hugh Wrottesley, *q.v.*
Services : Ensign 1/7th N.I. Transfd. to 13th N.I. (late 1/7th) May 1824. Actg. Intr. & Qmr. 13th N.I. 6 Sept. 1824. Adjt. 13th N.I. 14 July 1825 till 19 Jan. 1839. A.D.C. to Maj.-Gen. William Burgh, *q.v.*, comdg. Presdy. Div., 3 Jan. 1839. Executive Ofr. P.W.D., S.E. Provinces, 6 Apr. 1842 till death. No record of active service.
Refs. : Burke's *Peerage*, 1923, p. 2369, *s.n.* Wrottesley, B. Will dated Midnapore 20 July 1846 ; proved 7 Oct. 1846.

EDWARDS, James (1759/60-1804). Lieut. Colonel, 4th N.I. *b.* 1759/60. Cadet 1778. Admitted 2 Oct. 1778. Ensign Oct. 1778. Lieut. 27 Nov. 1778. Capt. 1 June 1796. Major 24 Aug. 1800. Lt. Col. 19 May 1803. *d.* Fatehgarh 22 Sept. 1804.
A native of Kent. Brother of Francis Edwards, of Calcutta, bailiff. *m.* Berhampore 8 Dec. 1793, Catherine, younger dau. of Henry Read, *q.v.* (*See also* Charles Becher.) (She *re-m.* June 1807, John Simpson, of Alsop's Bldgs., London, and died London, 2 May 1838, aged 58.)
Services : Lieut. 1/3rd Bengal Eur. Regt. in Oct. 1779 ; 5th Bn. Sepoys in July 1787. Capt. 4th N.I. Second Mahratta War ; Aligarh ; Lt. Col. 2/4th N.I.
Refs. : Will dated Cheetapur 30 Apr. 1801 ; proved in 1804.

EDWARDS, John. Ensign. Infantry. Cadet 1764. Ensign 27 Dec. 1764. Resigned 2 Jan. 1766.
Services : N.F.P.

EDWARDS, John. Cadet. Infantry. Cadet 1771. Resigned 22 Jan. 1772.
Services : N.F.P.

EDWARDS, John (1806-1831). Lieutenant, Artillery. *b.* London 6 Feb. 1806. Cadet 1821. Arrived in India 21 Feb. 1823. 2nd Lieut. 10 May 1822. Lieut. 16 Dec. 1824. *d.* Calcutta 8 Jan. 1831.
Son of Joseph Edwards. Addiscombe Cadet 1820-2.
Services : Siege and capture of Bhurtpore ; Lieut. comdg. 4th Coy. 1st Bn. Foot Art. Actg. Adjt. Karnal and Sirhind Div. Art. 24 Feb. 1827. Adjt. & Qmr. 1st Bn. Art. 14 Mar. 1827 till death. Leave s.c. 6 mos. to Penang 26 Feb. 1830.
Refs. : A.J. N.S. v. 145. Will dated 30 Nov. 1830 ; proved 21 July 1831. M.I. St. Stephen's, Dum-Dum.

EDWARDS, John William (1782-1815). Captain, 16th N.I. *bapt.* Halifax 22 Dec. 1782. Cadet 1798. Admitted 12 Jan. 1801. Ensign 21 Sept. 1799. Lieut. 28 Oct. 1799. Capt. 16 Mar. 1810. *d. unm.* Meerut 12 Aug. 1815.
Nephew of James Edwards. Brother of Jane, Eliza, and William Edwards.
Services : Lieut. 16th N.I. Operations in Bundelkhand 1809-11 ; Capt. 2/16th N.I. Reduction of Kalinjar 1812 ; Capt. 2/16th N.I. Nepal War 1814-5 ; Kalanga ; Jaithak ; Capt. 2/16th N.I., in 2nd Div.
Refs. : Will dated Dehra Dun 18 Nov. 1814 ; proved in 1816.

EDWARDS, Richard Thomas (1810-1835). Ensign, 28th N.I. *b.* 6 Aug. 1810. Cadet 1831. Arrived in India 12 May 1833. Ensign (9 June 1832) 7 Nov. 1832. *d.* Nimach 24 Sept. 1835. *bapt.* London 29 Aug. 1810. Son of Thomas Edwards (*d.* 1815), *q.v.*, and Margaret his 2nd wife. Brother of William Edwards, *q.v.*
Services : Ensign d.d. 55th N.I. 22 Mar. 1833 ; do. 74th N.I. 5 Sept. 1833. Posted as Ensign to 28th N.I. 11 Feb. 1834. No record of active service.
Refs. : A.J. N.S. xix. 206.

EDWARDS, Thomas (*d.* 1815). Lieut. Colonel. 2nd Bengal Eur. Regt. Cadet 1770. Admitted 6 Nov. 1770. Ensign 25 Sept. 1771. Lieut. 20 July 1776. Capt. 15 Feb. 1781. Major 1 Mar. 1794. Lt. Col. 1 July 1798. Retired 14 May 1799. *d.* at sea 15 Nov. 1815 : lost off Ostend in the wreck of the ship in which he was returning to his family in Brussels.
Son of Rev. Andrew Edwards, rector of Llanrwst, co. Denbigh, by his wife, dau. of Timothy Edwards, of Nanhoron, nr. Pwllheli. *m.* 1st, 14 Sept. 1788, Mary, relict of Hon. George Grimston. *m.* 2nd,

Margaret Minter. (She *re-m*. Dr. E. Black.) Father of Richard Thomas Edwards, *q.v.*, and of William Edwards, *q.v.*

Services : Fur. 22 Jan. 1772 till 26 Oct. 1773. Lieut. 2/2nd Bengal Eur. Regt. in Oct. 1779. Fur. 31 Aug. 1785 till 30 Aug. 1790. Second Rohilla War ; battle of Bitaurah ; Major comdg. 12th Bn. Sepoys. Major 2nd Bengal Eur. Regt. in 1796. " A.D.C. to the late Nabob of Oude, Resident at Lucknow." (*G.M.*) Gave evidence at the trial of Warren Hastings.

Refs. : Burke's *Landed Gentry*, *s.n.* Edwards, of Nanhorn. *Williams*, p. 165. *G.M.* 1788, ii. 836 ; 1815, ii. 569.

EDWARDS, Thomas (1810-1891). Lieutenant. Artillery. *b.* Sutton, Suffolk, 25 Dec. 1810. Cadet 1828. Arrived in India 12 Feb. 1829. 2nd Lieut. 12 June 1828. Lieut. 17 Jan. 1836. Retired 10 Mar. 1836. *d.* June 1891.

Son of Henry Edwards. Addiscombe Cadet 1826-8.

Services : Fur. s.c. 10 Sept. 1833 till retirement. Retired on h.p. as 2nd Lieut., *viz.* 3/- *p.d.* No record of active service.

EDWARDS, Timothy (*d.* 1773). Captain, comdg. 2nd Bn. Sepoys. Capt. 1 Sept. 1768. *d.* Dinajpur, Bengal, 1 Mar. 1773 : kld. in action against the Saniyasis.

Services : Apptd. to comd. 2nd Bn. Sepoys 12 Dec. 1772. Comdd. a detachment operating against the Saniyasis Feb.-Mar. 1773 (kld.).

Refs. : *Forrest*, i. 83. *Cardew*, p. 37. *G.M.* 1773, p. 581.

EDWARDS, William (1809-1875). Lieut. Colonel. 18th N.I. *b.* Baker St., London, 16 May 1809. Cadet 1825. Arrived in India 7 July 1826. Ensign 15 Mar. 1826. Lieut. 13 Dec. 1827. Capt. 24 Jan. 1845. Bt. Major 20 June 1854. Retired 15 Jan. 1855. Hon. Lt. Col. 16 Mar. 1855. *d.* Weston-super-Mare Jan. 1875.

2nd son of Thomas Edwards (*d.* 1815), *q.v.* Brother of Richard Thomas Edwards, *q.v. m.* 1st, Agra, 7 Nov. 1829, Mary Jordon, youngest dau. of John Grimsdick, indigo planter. *m.* 2nd, Dawlish, 30 June 1857, Laura Faith, youngest dau. of T. E. Clarke, of Tremlett House, Wellington, and Chard, Somerset.

Services : Ensign d.d. 45th N.I. 2 Aug. 1826. Posted to 18th N.I. 26 Sept. 1826. Second Sikh War ; Capt. 18th N.I., in garrison at Lahore (Medal).

Refs. : *A.J.* N.S. i. 235.

*****EGERTON, John.** Fireworker. Artillery. Cadet (?). Fireworker 7 Dec. 1764.

Services : N.F.P.

Refs. : *Stubbs's List*.

THE BENGAL ARMY, 1758-1834   125

EGERTON, John Francis (1810-1846). Captain, Artillery. *b.* 10 Aug. 1810. Cadet 1826. Arrived in India Feb. 1827. 2nd Lieut. 16 June 1826. Lieut. 31 May 1833. Capt. 3 July 1845. *d.* Ferozepore, 23 Jan. 1846, of wounds received at the battle of Ferozshahr on 22 Dec. 1845.

3rd son of Rev. Sir Philip Grey-Egerton, 9th Bart., of Egerton and Oulton, rector of Tarporley, and Rebecca his wife, youngest dau. of Josias Du Pré, of Wilton Park, Bucks. Cousin-german of Thomas Lucas Egerton, *q.v.*, and of William Egerton, *q.v.* Addiscombe Cadet 29 Oct. 1824 till 16 June 1826.

Services : Posted to 4th Coy. 2nd Bn. Foot Art. in Apr. 1827. Transfd. to 1st Troop 2nd Bde. H.A. in Dec. 1828 ; to 3rd Troop 2nd Bde. in Nov. 1833. Revenue Surveyor and D.C. in Bhagulpur and Monghyr districts 22 Dec. 1835 till Aug. 1839. Fur. 8 Aug. 1839 till Aug. 1842. Transfd. to 4th Coy. 4th Bn. in Oct. 1841 ; to 4th Troop 3rd Bde. 28 Dec. 1842. D.A.Q.M.G., 2 cl., Dec. 1844 ; posted to Ferozepore in Feb. 1845. Apptd. D.A.Q.M.G. 4th Div., Army of the Sutlej, Dec. 1845. First Sikh War ; Ferozshahr (s.w. 22 Dec. 1845) ; D.A.Q.M.G.

Refs. : Burke's *Peerage*, 1923, p. 818, *s.n.* Grey-Egerton, Bart., of Egerton and Oulton Park, co. Chester. *De Rhé-Philipe.* Will dated Meerut 10 Apr. 1843 ; codicil dated 22 Jan. 1846 ; proved 20 June 1848. M.I. St. Andrew's, Ferozepore. Monument in Oulton Park.

EGERTON, Thomas Lucas (1806-1834). Captain, Invalid Est. 66th N.I. *b.* in America 18 Mar. 1806. Cadet 1823. Arrived in India 13 June 1824. Ensign 19 Feb. 1824. Lieut. 24 Dec. 1825. Capt. 13 Mar. 1834. Invalided 21 Aug. 1834. *d.* on the river, nr. Kistnagarh, 19 Sept. 1834.

(*Probably* son of Thomas Egerton, Major H.M. 29th Foot.) Nephew of Sir John Grey-Egerton, 8th Bart., of Oulton, and cousin-german of John Francis Egerton, *q.v.*, and of William Egerton, *q.v.*

Services : Posted as Ensign to 66th N.I. Adjt. Sylhet L.I. 17 May 1827. Fur. s.c. 10 Jan. 1832 till 15 Dec. 1833. No record of active service.

Refs. : Burke's *Peerage*, 1923, p. 817, *s.n.* Grey-Egerton, Bart., of Oulton Park, Chester. *A.J.* N.S. xvi. 213. Will dated 12 June 1834 ; proved 30 Jan. 1835.

EGERTON, William (1815-1841). Lieutenant, 2nd N.I. *b.* Calcutta 26 Sept. 1815. Cadet 1833. Arrived in India 14 July 1834. Ensign 13 May 1834. Lieut. 3 Oct. 1840. *d.* Sylhet, Assam, 8 June 1841.

Eldest son of William Egerton, of Gresford Lodge, co. Denbigh,

B.C.S., accountant gen., and a director of the Bank of Bengal, and Sibella his wife, dau. of Robert Boswell. Cousin-german of John Francis Egerton, *q.v.*, and of Thomas Lucas Egerton, *q.v.* *m.* Saugor, 10 Oct. 1836, Mary Anne, dau. of Lawford Tronson, of Newry, co. Down. (She *re-m.* Thomas Young (1809-1852), *q.v.*) Addiscombe Cadet 3 Aug. 1832 till 13 Dec. 1833.

Services : Ensign d.d. 19th N.I. 24 Apr. 1834. Posted to 2nd N.I. 5 Nov. 1834. Served with Sylhet L.I. Bn. 20 Feb. till 26 Oct. 1838, when he rejoined 2nd N.I. for service in Afghanistan. As his Regt. did not then proceed on service, he rejoined Sylhet L.I. 22 Jan. 1839, and remained with that Corps till death. Actg. Adjt. Jan. 1839. No record of active service.

Refs. : Burke's *Peerage*, 1923, p. 816, *s.n.* Grey-Egerton, Bart., of Egerton and Oulton Park, co. Chester. Burke's *Colonial Gentry*, ii. 620. *A.J.* N.S. xxii. 268. M.I. at Sylhet.

*EISER, ———. Capt. comdg. Troop of Eur. Hussars in 1761.

Services : Probably accompanied Lt. Col. Eyre Coote from Madras in Apr. 1761. Was comdg. the Troop of Eur. Hrs. which served as Coote's Body Guard in June 1761. N.F.P.

Refs. : Broome, p. 337.

EKINS, Charles (1809-1849). Bt. Major, 7th L.C. *b.* Chiddingfold, Surrey, 7 Oct. 1809. Cadet 1825. Arrived in India 16 May 1826. Cornet 5 Nov. 1825. Lieut. 16 June 1831. Capt. 26 July 1841. Bt. Major 30 Apr. 1844. *d.* 13 Jan. 1849 : kld. in action at the battle of Chilianwala.

Younger son of Rev. Charles Ekins, of Chiddingfold, and Mary his wife, dau. of John Ford, of Queen Anne St., Marylebone. His sister *m.* Edward Revell Eardley-Wilmot, *q.v.* *m.* Kaitha, 27 Mar. 1830, Julia, dau. of William George Maxwell, *q.v.* (*See also* Charles Henry Boisragon and Charles George Ross.) (She died London, 2 July 1882, aged 69.)

Services : Posted as Cornet to 7th L.C. 24 May 1826, and joined 7 Nov. 1826. Offg. Adjt. Sept. 1829 till Feb. 1830, and 30 Oct. 1831 till Nov. 1832. Fur. 13 May 1834 till 20 Feb. 1837. Offg. Adjt. 7th L.C. Aug. 1837 ; permanent do. 24 Mar. 1838 till Apr. 1840. With Army of Reserve (for Afghanistan) at Ferozepore Oct. 1842 till Jan. 1843, as A.A.G. of Cav. 2nd A.A.G. of the Army 10 Nov. 1843. Gwalior campaign ; Maharajpur ; Capt. 7th L.C., A.A.G. (Bronze star). (*Lond. Gaz.* 8 Mar. 1844.) Leave to Cape Jan.-Dec. 1845. Apptd. 1st A.A.G. of the Army 31 Dec. 1845 ; D.A.G. of the Army 1 Mar. 1846. Second Sikh War ; Ramnagar ; passage of the Chenab ; Chilianwala (kld.) ; D.A.G. of the Army, with A.H.Q.

THE BENGAL ARMY, 1758-1834

Refs. : *Howard & Crisp*, xviii. 125, *s.n.* Ekins. *De Rhé-Philipe.* Will dated Cape Town 4 Oct. 1845 ; proved 10 July 1849. M.I. in Salisbury cathedral and St. Luke's, Jullundur.

ELD, Lionel Percy Denham (1808-1863). Colonel. 9th N.I. *b.* 9 Dec. 1808. Cadet 1825. Arrived in India 16 May 1826. Ensign 5 Nov. 1825. Lieut. 15 Sept. 1833. Capt. 1 Jan. 1845. Major 4 Apr. 1857. Bt. Lt. Col. 27 Sept. 1859. Retired 20 Nov. 1860. Hon. Col. 20 Nov. 1860. *d.* Monte Video House, nr. Weymouth, 11 Dec. 1863, from the effects of a wound received in the Mutiny.

Only son of John Eld, of Brighton, Lt. Col. East Local Stafford Mil., and Hon. Louisa Sarah Sidney Smyth his wife, youngest dau. of Lionel, 5th Viscount Strangford. *m.* Calcutta, 19 Sept. 1839, Charlotte Isabella, 4th dau. of Colin Campbell, Member of the Bengal Medical Board. (*See also* Hubert Garbett, Henry Bethune Lindesay, and Hamilton Vetch.)

Services : Posted as Ensign to 26th N.I. in 1826. Transfd. to 9th N.I. in 1827. Actg. Adjt. Wing 9th N.I. 28 Feb. 1830. Intr. & Qmr. 9th N.I. 15 Aug. 1834 till Nov. 1837. Asst. to P.A. in Manipur 13 Nov. 1837. 2nd in comd. Assam L.I. 18 Mar. 1840 till 30 June 1841. Offg. Junior Asst. to Comr. in Assam 11 Nov. 1840 ; permanent do. 2 June 1841. Principal Asst., 2 cl., to Comr. of Assam 15 Jan. 1845 ; do. 1 cl., 20 Aug. 1845 till 1 Jan. 1847. Fur. 1 Jan. 1847 till 17 Jan. 1850. To comd. fort Abazie Mar. 1853. Against the Akka Khel Afridis Mar. 1855 ; Bt. Major 9th N.I. Mutiny campaign (w.). Fur. s.c. 18 May 1858 till retirement.

Refs. : Burke's *Landed Gentry*, 13th edn., p. 554, *s.n.* Eld, of Sleighford Hall, Staffs. *G.M.* 1864, i. 134. *The Times*, 15 Dec. 1863.

ELDE or ELD, Thomas (*d.* 1768). Cadet, Infantry. Cadet 1768. *d.* Calcutta 30 Nov. 1768.

Services : N.F.P.

ELDRIDGE, Ambrose (1785-1846). Captain. 2nd L.C. *bapt.* Abingdon, Berks., 16 June 1785. Cadet 1804. Arrived in India 25 Mar. 1806. Cornet 28 Mar. 1806. Lieut. 23 Oct. 1810. Capt. 15 July 1819. Resigned 21 Feb. 1823. *d.* Cheltenham 6 Mar. 1846, aged 61.

Son of William Eldridge and Ann his wife.

Services : Posted as Cornet to 2nd N.C. and served throughout with that Regt. Nepal War 1814-5 ; Lieut. 2nd N.C., in 1st Div. Fur. 18 Oct. 1816 till 1819.

Refs. : *G.M.* 1856, i. 442.

ELERSON, Frédéric Guillaume (1705/06-?). Lieutenant. 2nd Troop Eur. Dgns. *b.* Eggersdorff (? Switzerland) 1705/06. Cadet (?). Ensign 6 June 1758. Lieut. 27 July 1759. Resigned 12 Oct. 1762.

Services : Sailed for India on the *Fox* in 1756, aged 50. Apptd. to 2nd Troop Eur. Cav. 22 Sept. 1760. Battle of Suan 15 Jan. 1761 ; Lieut. 2nd Eur. Dgns.

ELIOT, Geffery (1815-1835). Ensign, 18th N.I. *bapt.* Peper Harow, Surrey, 3 May 1815. Cadet 1830. Arrived in India 20 Mar. 1832. Ensign (9 June 1831) 29 Dec. 1831. *d.* Betul, C.P., 20 Sept. 1835, aged 20.

2nd son of Rev. Lawrence William Eliot, rector of Peper Harow, J.P. and D.L., Surrey, and Matilda Elizabeth his wife, dau. of Henry Halsey, of Henley Park, Surrey.

Services : d.d. 64th N.I. 12 May 1832. Fur. s.c. 28 May 1832 till 10 July 1833. Posted to 18th N.I. 18 Oct. 1833. No record of active service.

Refs. : Burke's *Landed Gentry*, 4th edn., p. 424, *s.n.* Eliot, formerly of Busbridge, Surrey. *Walford. A.J.* N.S. xix. 206.

ELKIN, Emanuel (1787-?). Lieutenant. 12th N.I. *b.* Aldgate, Middlesex, 19 Oct. 1787. Cadet 1808. Arrived in India 24 July 1809. Ensign 23 July 1809. Lieut. 11 Nov. 1814. Discharged by G.C.M. 14 Sept. 1821.[1]

Son of Judith Elkin.

Services : Posted as Ensign to 12th N.I. Fur. 1814 till 17 Oct. 1815. Nepal War 1816 ; Lieut. 2/12th N.I., in 3rd Bde., Centre Column. Siege and capture of Hathras 1817 ; Lieut. 2/12th N.I. Third Mahratta War ; Dhamoni. Operations against the Bhattis of Hariana 1818 ; Lieut. 2/12th N.I.

[1] *Note :* " Remarks by H.E. the Most Noble the C.-in-C. ' In compliance with the representation of the president and members, application shall be made to the Gov. gen. in council, that an annual allowance equal to what is drawn by a lieut. on the pension list, may be granted to Mr. E., the confirmation of which by the hon. court will be solicited.' "

ELLERKER, Edward (1739/40-1802). Major General. Colonel Marine Regt. *b.* 1739/40. Cadet 1764. Admitted 7 July 1764. Ensign 13 Oct. 1764. Lieut. 26 Oct. 1765. Capt. 4 Apr. 1769. Major 4 Jan. 1781. Lt. Col. 27 May 1786. Col. 1 Mar. 1794. Maj. Gen. 3 May 1796. *d.* Bhagulpur, B. & O., 15 Nov. 1802, aged 62.

Brother of William Ellerker, of Ellerker and North Cave, Yorks.,

and Chilwell, Notts., and of John Ellerker, of Kingston-upon-Hull. *m.* 1st, Calcutta, 3 Apr. 1769, Miss Mary Gascoigne. (She died Chittagong, 18 Oct. 1776, aged 25.) *m.* 2nd, Chittagong, 1777, Miss Ann Rochford. (She died 29 Jan. 1818.)
Services : Resigned his Commission 6 May 1766, during the " Batta mutiny "; readmitted 3 Nov. 1766. Fur. 18 Feb. 1787. Col. 3rd Bengal Eur. Regt. in 1796.
Refs. : Will dated 14 Feb. 1799 ; proved 24 Feb. 1803.

ELLIOT, Edward King (1811-1865). Lieut. Colonel, 43rd N.I. A.G.G. for Rajputana. *b.* Aldermansbury, Middlesex, 11 Oct. 1811. Cadet 1828. Arrived in India 23 May 1829. Ensign 7 Feb. 1829. Lieut. 2 June 1839. Capt. 21 Jan. 1852. Major 28 Nov. 1854. Lt. Col. 18 Feb. 1861. *d.* Nasirabad 11 Oct. 1865.
Son of George Elliot. Ward of Capt. Robert Locke, of 7 Upper Glos. St., Dorset Sq., London. His sister *m.* William Gilbert Don, *q.v.*
Services : Ensign d.d. 32nd N.I. 13 July 1829. Posted as Ensign to 43rd N.I. 14 Sept. 1829. Offg. Intr. & Qmr. 43rd N.I. 8 Apr. 1831. Intr. & Qmr. 43rd N.I. 8 Nov. 1831. Leave s.c. 2 yrs. to N.S.W. 24 July 1834. First Afghan War 1839-42 ; Ghazni ; operations of Kandahar force under Nott ; employed in a political capacity at Kandahar ; Lieut. 43rd N.I. (Medal—Kandahar, Ghazni, Kabul). D.C., 1 cl., Narsinghpur, 1 May 1843. Asst. Resdt. at Nagpur Mar. 1853. D.C., 1 cl., Nagpur, and Comr. and Supt. of Police in province of Nagpur 2 July 1855. Fur. s.c. 18 Sept. 1855 till 6 Oct. 1857. Chief Comr., C.P., 11 Dec. 1861. A.G.G., Rajputana.
Refs. : *D.I.B.*

ELLIOT, George. Lieutenant. Infantry. Cadet 1779. Ensign 21 July 1779. Lieut. 12 Mar. 1781. Resigned 31 Aug. 1782.
Services : N.F.P.

ELLIOT, John (1787-1859). Colonel. 26th N.I. *b.* Plymouth 22 Jan. 1787. Cadet 1803. Arrived in India 2 Dec. 1804. Ensign 9 Oct. 1804. Lieut. 9 Oct. 1804. Capt. 1 Jan. 1816. Major 28 Jan. 1825. Lt. Col. 1828. Retired 28 May 1829. Hon. Col. 28 Nov. 1854. *d.* Burley House, Plymouth, 19 Dec. 1859.
Of Burley House, Plymouth. D.L. co. Devon. 2nd son of James Elliot, of Plymouth. *m.* St. James's, Westminster, 9 Aug. 1832, Catherine Charlotte, dau. of Andrew Tracey, of Gascoyne Pl., Plymouth. (She died 17 June 1882, aged 82.)
Services : Posted as Lieut. to 2/13th N.I. in 1805. Capture of Java 1811 ; Lieut. Pioneers (Medal). Served with Pioneers till

1817. Nepal War 1814-5; Kalanga (s.w.); Lieut. 6th Coy. Pioneers (India medal). Capt. 1/13th N.I. Bk. Mr. 3rd (Dinapore) Div. 6 June 1817 till 1825. Transfd. to 26th N.I. (late 1/13th) May 1824. First Burma War; Arakan 1825; Major 26th N.I. (clasp to India medal). Fur. s.c. 24 Nov. 1826 till retirement.

Refs.: Walford. *Bath Chron.* 23 Aug. 1832. *A.J.* N.S. ix. 51. *The Times,* 21 Dec. 1859.

ELLIOT, William (1740/41-1803). Major General. Artillery. *b.* 1740/41. Cadet 1763. Fireworker 3 Feb. 1764. 2nd Lieut. Jan. 1767. Lieut. 6 Aug. 1768. Capt. Lt. 4 Mar. 1770. Capt. 10 Jan. 1773. Major 29 Jan. 1781. Lt. Col. 9 Dec. 1782. Col. (?). Maj. Gen. (?). Resigned 26 Dec. 1790. *d.* Exmouth, Devon, 23 Apr. 1803, aged 62.

Services: Fireworker 1st Coy. Art. Resigned his Commission 14 May 1766, during the "Batta mutiny"; readmitted 1 Aug. 1766. Second Mysore War 1781-5; Capt. comdg. 4th Coy. 2nd Bn. Fur. Jan. 1785 till 1790.

Refs.: *G.M.* 1803, i. 483.

ELLIOT, William (*d.* 1783). Captain, Infantry. Cadet 1771. Ensign 30 Jan. 1773. Lieut. 4 Jan. 1778. Capt. 6 June 1781. *d.* Madras 18 Apr. 1783.

Services: Second Mysore War.

ELLIOT, William (*d.* 1781). Lieutenant, Infantry. Cadet 1776. Ensign 3 Apr. 1777. Lieut. 29 Aug. 1778. *d.* Dec. 1781.

Services: N.F.P.

ELLIOTT, George Donnithorne (1816-1854). Lieutenant, Invalid Est. 33rd N.I. *bapt.* Bareilly 24 Jan. 1816. Cadet 1834. Arrived in India 23 July 1835. Ensign (24 Feb. 1835) 24 Apr. 1835. Lieut. 12 Feb. 1838. Invalided 7 Sept. 1846. *d.* Naini Tal, U.P., 29 July 1854: drowned in the lake.

Son of Charles Elliott, B.C.S., Senior Member of the Board of Revenue, N.W.P., and Alicia his wife. Addiscombe Cadet 2 Aug. 1833; resigned 2 Jan. 1835.

Services: Ensign d.d. 35th N.I. 8 Aug. 1835. Posted to 33rd N.I. 24 Sept. 1835. Fur. s.c. 14 Jan. 1839 till 6 July 1840. First Afghan War 1842; Khyber Pass; re-occupation of Kabul; Lieut. 33rd N.I., with Gen. Pollock's force (Medal). To do duty with Eur. Invalids at Chunar 11 Feb. 1848.

Refs.: *N. & Q.* 9S. i. 344; ii. 54. *I.M.* 3 Oct. 1854, p. 550.

ELLIOTT, William (1776-1823). Lieut. Colonel, C.B., 4th L.C. *b.* Coventry 26 June 1776. Cadet 1793. Arrived in India 13 Oct. 1794. Cornet 9 Oct. 1794. Lieut. 24 July 1796. Capt. 11 Mar.

1805. Major 29 Aug. 1810. Lt. Col. 27 July 1819. *d.* Diamond Harbour, Bengal, 4 May 1823, on board the *Exmouth*.
bapt. Holy Trinity, Coventry, 5 Mar. 1777. Son of William Elliott and Sarah his wife. Nephew of Richard Frith, *q.v. m.* Cawnpore, 25 Nov. 1813, Mrs. Anne Dawes.
Services : Capt. Lt. 4th N.C. 21 Feb. 1801. Operations in Jumna Doab 1803 ; Sasni ; Bijaigarh ; Kachaura ; Capt. Lt. 4th N.C. Second Mahratta War ; Laswari ; Capt. Lt. 4th N.C. Fur. 17 Nov. 1817 till 1819. Transfd. as Lt. Col. to 7th L.C. 1819 ; retransfd. to 4th L.C. 1823. Fur. s.c. 1823. C.B. 4 June 1815.
Refs. : Will dated 1 Feb. 1813 ; proved 9 May 1823.

ELLIOTT, William (1803-1831). Lieutenant, 27th N.I. *b.* London 6 Mar. 1803. Cadet 1824. Arrived in India 5 Apr. 1825. Ensign 13 Oct. 1824. Lieut. 24 Feb. 1826. *d.* Hoshangabad, C.P., 29 Nov. 1831.
Son of William Elliott.
Services : Ensign d.d. 26th N.I. 21 May 1825. First Burma War ; Arakan 1825 ; Ensign 26th N.I. Fur. s.c. 11 Nov. 1825 till 28 Oct. 1827. Posted as Ensign to 27th N.I. Actg. Adjt. Wing 27th N.I. 28 May 1831.
Refs. : G.M. 1832, i. 575. *A.J.* N.S. viii. 41.

*****ELLIOTT, ——.** Lieutenant. Artillery. Cadet (?). Fireworker 4 Oct. 1757. Lieut. 19 Sept. 1758.
Services : N.F.P.
Refs. : Orme MSS.—India, xiii. 3639. *Stubbs's List.*

ELLIS, Frederick Regent (1810-1843). Bt. Captain, 41st N.I. *b.* Llandilo, co. Monmouth, 4 June 1810. Cadet 1826. Arrived in India 17 June 1827. Ensign 5 Jan. 1827. Lieut. 6 Apr. 1835. Bt. Capt. 5 Jan. 1842. *d.* Gorakhpur, U.P., 12 June 1843.
Eldest son of Capt. Thomas Ellis, of Ty Dee Park, co. Monmouth, late 17th Light Dgns. and Oxford Blues. *m.* Calcutta 28 Oct. 1835, Eliza Clara, dau. of Henry Bean, H.E.I.C.S.
Services : Posted as Ensign to 41st N.I. 19 June 1827. Adjt. 41st N.I. 14 Feb. 1839 till death. No record of active service.
Refs. : G.M. 1843, ii. 670. *The Times,* 4 Nov. 1843. Will dated 19 Apr. 1842 ; proved 8 Sept. 1843. M.I. at Gorakhpur.

ELLIS, George (1806-1843). Captain, Artillery. *b.* Cawnpore 15 Apr. 1806. Cadet 1822. Arrived in India 21 Jan. 1824. 2nd Lieut. 6 June 1823. Lieut. 28 Sept. 1827. Capt. 22 Feb. 1841. *d.* Mussoorie, 26 Nov. 1843, of fever.
4th son of Robert Ellis, of Boulogne, Col. 25th Light Dgns., and

Eliza his wife. Brother of William Ellis (1802-1851), *q.v.* *m.* Benares, 18 Nov. 1834, Anne Charlotte, dau. of Lt.-Gen. Charles Boyé, Bombay Est. (She died 7 Sept. 1887.) Addiscombe Cadet 1 Feb. 1821 till 6 June 1823.

Services : Siege and capture of Bhurtpore ; Lieut. 3rd Coy. 1st Bn. Foot Art. (d.d. 6th Bn.). Posted to 2nd Coy. 4th Bn. 9 Aug. 1830. Actg. Adjt. 7th Bn. 1 Apr. 1835. Revenue survey, Monghyr and Bihar, 21 Jan. 1838 till Oct. 1842. Leave s.c. 2 yrs. to Darjiling 20 Feb. 1841.

Refs. : *G.M.* 1844, i. 334. *The Times*, 9 Feb. 1844.

ELLIS, Henry (1765/66-?). Ensign. Infantry. *b.* 1765/66. Cadet 1782. Ensign 9 Apr. 1782. Struck off 1788.

A native of London.

Services : Sailed for India on the *Brilliant*, 5 May 1782, aged 16. N.F.P.

*****ELLIS, James** (*d.* 1790). Ensign. Infantry. Subsequently Surgeon General, Bengal. Ensign 1760. Resigned combatant Commission on promotion to Surgeon 1 Oct. 1761. *d.* at sea 1790, on board the *Busbridge*, on his passage to England.

Services : Surgeon's Mate of the *Streatham* 1759. Asst. Surg. 1759. Surg. 1 Oct. 1761. War with Mir Muhammad Kasim 1763 ; Katwa ; Gheria ; Udhua Nullah ; capture of Monghyr ; Patna ; Senior Surg. to the army under Major Adams. Second Surg., Calcutta, 25 Nov. 1763 ; Head Surg. 12 Feb. 1771. Resigned and went to England in Apr. 1774. Returned to India in May 1783, and succeeded Daniel Campbell as Surg. Gen. First Presdt. of the Medical Board on its formation 28 Aug. 1786. Resigned 24 Dec. 1789.

Refs. : Crawford.

ELLIS, James (*d.* 1788). Ensign, Infantry. Cadet 1783. Ensign 6 Mar. 1785. bur. Calcutta 9 Oct. 1788.

Services : N.F.P.

ELLIS, James (1793-?). Ensign. 25th N.I. *b.* London 13 Feb. 1793. Cadet 1808. Admitted 27 Oct. 1809. Ensign 22 Mar. 1810. Resigned 4 Apr. 1812.

Son of Samuel Ellis.

Services : Posted as Ensign to 25th N.I. No record of active service.

ELLIS, John Drake Bainbridge (1812-1835). 2nd Lieutenant, Artillery. *b.* 7 Aug. 1812. Cadet 1829. Arrived in India 1 July 1830. 2nd Lieut. 11 Dec. 1829. *d.* Fatehgarh, U.P., 14 Dec. 1835.

bapt. Durham 22 Sept. 1813. Son of Henry James Ellis, Capt. Northumberland Mil. Addiscombe Cadet 1827-9.

Services : Apptd. Actg. 2nd Lieut. 17 July 1832, having been more than 2 yrs. in India. Posted to 3rd Coy. 3rd Bn. Foot Art. 8 Oct. 1834. Was in charge of the Art. at Fatehgarh in Sept. 1835 when a mutiny broke out among the troops of the Baiza Baie.

Refs. : A.J. N.S. xix. 245-6 ; xx. 106. Will dated Cawnpore 7 Aug. 1833 ; proved 15 July 1836.

ELLIS, John Gordon (1807-1827). Ensign, 69th N.I. *b.* London 11 Oct. 1807. Cadet 1824. Ensign 29 Apr. 1825. *d.* at sea, 27 Aug. 1827, on board the *Repulse*, off Macao, China.

bapt. St. Pancras 12 Dec. 1807. Son of Robert Ellis and Eliza his wife. Brother of Richard Rich Wilford Ellis, *q.v.*

Services : Posted as Ensign to 69th N.I. in 1826. Leave s.c. to China 1827. No record of active service.

ELLIS, Richard Rich Wilford (1809-1887). Colonel. 23rd N.I. *b.* London 30 Sept. 1809. Cadet 1825. Arrived in India 16 May 1826. Ensign 5 Nov. 1825. Lieut. 17 Dec. 1832. Capt. 10 Feb. 1846. Major 11 Nov. 1851. Bt. Lt. Col. 21 Sept. 1859. Retired 24 Aug. 1861. Hon. Col. 24 Aug. 1861. *d.* 28 Mar. 1887.

bapt. St. Luke's, Chelsea, 2 Nov. 1809. Son of Robert Ellis and Eliza his wife. Brother of John Gordon Ellis, *q.v. m.* Simla, 22 June 1852, Louisa, dau. of Walker Pearson.

Services : Posted as Ensign to 23rd N.I. in 1826. Actg. Intr. & Qmr. 23rd N.I. 16 Sept. 1829, and 4 Apr. 1831 ; do. 37th N.I. 10 Nov. 1835 ; do. 28th N.I. 9 Dec. 1835 ; do. 26th N.I. 3 May 1838. Offg. Asst. to Resdt. at Gwalior 18 Dec. 1838 ; permanent do. 29 Oct. 1839. To comd. a corps of Najibs raised for service in Sindhia's territories for arresting Thags and Dacoits. Political service in Bundelkhand 30 Sept. 1843 till retirement. Apptd. Comr. of Nagod district, C.I., 31 July 1857. Fur. 14 Apr. 1859 till retirement. No record of active service.

ELLIS, Robert (1786-1814). Lieutenant, 2nd N.I. Pioneers. *b.* Llannor, co. Carnarvon, 22 Dec. 1786. Cadet 1806. Arrived in India 13 Oct. 1807. Ensign 2 Nov. 1807. Lieut. 1814. *d. unm.* 31 Oct. 1814 : kld. in action at the assault of Kalanga.

Son of Thomas Ellis, of Llannor, late of Bodwel, and Elizabeth his wife.

Services : Posted as Ensign to 2nd N.I. in 1808. Capture of Java 1811 ; Ensign Pioneers. Nepal War 1814 ; Kalanga (kld.) ; Lieut. Pioneers, in 2nd Div.

Refs. : Will dated 27 Feb. 1812 ; proved in 1814.

ELLIS, Thomas Powrie (1800-1836). Captain, 52nd N.I. *b.* Woolwich, Kent, 8 May 1800. Cadet 1820. Admitted 31 May 1821. Ensign 13 Jan. 1821. Lieut. 11 July 1823. Capt. 4 Feb. 1833. *d.* Meerut 24 Nov. 1836.

Son of Joseph George Ellis, Comy. of Ord., H.M.S. *m.* St. Pancras, London, 15 July 1834, Catherine Munro, 2nd dau. of Rev. H. Bethune, of Dingwall, co. Ross.

Services : Posted as Ensign to 1/15th N.I. Transfd. as Lieut. to 26th N.I. 11 July 1823 ; to 52nd N.I. (late 2/26th) May 1824. (? First Burma War ; Cachar 1825 ; Lieut. 52nd N.I.) Actg. Adjt. Left Wing 52nd N.I. 14 May 1828. Actg. Intr. & Qmr. 4th N.I. 6 Nov. 1829. Fur. s.c. 31 Jan. 1832 till 10 Feb. 1835.

Refs. : *A.J.* N.S. xiv. 311 ; xxiii. 55.

ELLIS, William (*d.* 1788). Ensign, Engineers. Cadet (?). Ensign 24 Feb. 1774. *d.* Chittagong 18 Aug. 1788.

Services : N.F.P.

ELLIS, William (1802-1851). Captain. 45th N.I. *b.* Cawnpore 8 Dec. 1802. Cadet 1818. Admitted 23 Oct. 1819. Ensign 11 May 1819. Lieut. 15 June 1823. Capt. 3 June 1830. Retired 12 Jan. 1838. *d.* Cadogan Pl., London, 29 July 1851.

Of 46 Cadogan Pl., Chelsea. *bapt.* Cawnpore 16 Dec. 1802. 2nd son of Robert Ellis, of Boulogne, Col. 25th Light Dgns., and Eliza his wife. Brother of George Ellis, *q.v.* *m.* Mary. (She died 13 Oct. 1887.)

Services : Ensign 2/23rd N.I. First Burma War ; operations in Sylhet 1824 ; Bikrampur ; Bhadrapur ; Lieut. 2/23rd N.I. Transfd. to 45th N.I. (late 1/23rd) May 1824. Adjt. Sylhet Local Corps 26 Mar. 1824 till Apr. 1827. Fur. s.c. 27 May 1827 till 9 Oct. 1830. Fur. p.a. 8 Jan. 1834. Entered the Auxy. Corps raised for the service of the Queen of Spain as Major in 1835. Held comd. as Lt. Col. in the Spanish Service. Returned from fur. 28 Nov. 1837. Cross of San Fernando, 2 cl. (*Lond. Gaz.* 18 Apr. 1837.)

Refs. : *A.J.* N.S. xviii. 39. *G.M.* 1851, ii. 333.

ELLIS, William Henry (1811-1831). Lieutenant, 27th N.I. *b.* Fulford, Yorks., 26 Jan. 1811. Cadet 1826. Arrived in India 17 June 1827. Ensign (17 Feb. 1827) 27 June 1827. Lieut. 29 Nov. 1831. *d.* Narsinghpur, C.P., 10 Dec. 1831.

Eldest son of William Joseph Ellis, of Fulford Field House, Fulford, barr.-at-law. Ed. Winchester ; K.S. 1822.

Services : Posted as Ensign to 27th N.I. 19 June 1827. No record of active service.

Refs. : *Kirby.* *G.M.* 1832, i. 648.

ELLISON, Charles (1786-1818). Lieutenant, 22nd N.I. *b.* Castlebar, co. Mayo, 11 Nov. 1786. Cadet 1805. Arrived in India 13 Dec. 1806. Ensign 20 Dec. 1806. Lieut. 30 May 1809. *d. unm.* Calcutta 28 Dec. 1818.

Son of Rev. Thomas Ellison, LL.D., rector of Castlebar, and Florinda Norman his wife. Brother of Frederick Croasdale Ellison, *q.v.*

Services : Barasat C.C. Suspended 14 May 1807 for having, whilst a Cadet at Barasat, "addressed to the O.C. Cadet Coy. a letter intimating his determination not to study the native languages." (G.O. 14 May 1807.) Restored 8 Sept. 1807. Posted as Ensign to 22nd N.I. in 1808. (? Nepal War 1814-5 ; Samanpur ; Lieut. 2/22nd N.I.) Nepal War 1816 ; Lieut. 2/22nd N.I., in 3rd Bde. Centre Column.

Refs. : Burke's *Landed Gentry of Ireland*, p. 430, *s.n.* Ellison-Macartney, of Mountjoy Grange.

ELLISON, Frederick Croasdale (*d.* 1815). Lieutenant, 7th N.C. Cadet 1798. Arrived in India 28 May 1800. Cornet 9 Apr. 1801. Lieut. 11 Mar. 1805. *d. unm.* Muttra 22 Nov. 1815.

3rd son of Rev. Thomas Ellison, LL.D., rector of Castlebar, co. Mayo, and Florinda Norman his wife. Brother of Charles Ellison, *q.v.*

Services : Operations in Jumna Doab 1803 ; Sasni ; Bijaigarh ; Kachaura ; Cornet 3rd N.C. Second Mahratta War ; battle of Delhi ; battle of Deig ; Laswari ; Cornet 3rd N.C. Transfd. as Lieut. to newly-raised 7th N.C. in 1805. Operations in Oudh 1808. Settlement of Hariana 1809-10. Nepal War 1814-5 ; Lieut. 7th N.C., in 2nd Div.

Refs. : Burke's *Landed Gentry of Ireland*, p. 430, *s.n.* Ellison-Macartney, of Mountjoy Grange.

*ELL(I)THORNE, John (1743/44-1771). Lieutenant, Infantry. *b.* 1743/44. Cadet 1764. Ensign (?). Lieut. (?). *d.* Monghyr, B. & O., July 1771.

Son of Mrs. Mary Ell(i)thorne, of Chiswick, Middlesex. Brother of Martha Roberts and Mary Robinson.

Services : Sailed for Bencoolen on the *Earl of Elgin*, 4 May 1764, aged 20. N.F.P. (*Apparently* originally a Bencoolen Cadet who was transfd. to Bengal after Feb. 1767.)

Refs. : Will dated Monghyr 9 July 1771 ; proved 23 July 1771.

ELLMORE, John. Lieutenant. Infantry. Cadet 1781. Ensign 3 Aug. 1782. Lieut. 25 Jan. 1785. Resigned 21 Jan. 1789.

Services : Fur. 26 Jan. 1785. N.F.P.

ELMSLIE, Kenward Wallace (1812-1841). Lieutenant, 62nd N.I. *b.* London 11 Jan. 1812. Cadet 1828. Arrived in India 22 May 1829. Ensign 12 Dec. 1828. Lieut. 23 May 1835. *d.* Nimach 12 Aug. 1841.

Eldest son of Adam Wallace Elmslie, of 10 Fenchurch Bldgs., London, merchant. Addiscombe Cadet 1827-8.

Services : Ensign d.d. 19th N.I. 13 July 1829. Posted to 62nd N.I. 14 Sept. 1829. Suspended from rank, pay, and allowances for 6 mos. by sentence of G.C.M. for having delivered a hostile message from Ensign Bishop to Surgeon Menzies. (G.O. 26 Feb. 1839.) Offg. Qmr. 62nd N.I. Feb. 1840. Actg. Adjt. 62nd N.I. 17 May 1841.

Refs. : *A.J.* N.S. xxix. 133. *G.M.* 1841, ii. 667. *The Times,* 16 Oct. 1841.

ELTON, Robarts William (1808-1861). Lieut. Colonel. 59th N.I. *b.* Little Burstead, Essex, 5 Jan. 1808. Cadet.1828. Arrived in India 21 Mar. 1829. Ensign 12 Sept. 1828. Lieut. 1 Dec. 1837. Capt. 31 Mar. 1848. Bt. Major 20 June 1854. Retired 5 Apr. 1855. Hon. Lt. Col. 15 June 1855. *d.* 5 Nelson Pl., Bath, 12 Mar. 1861.

Son of Jacob Elton, of Clifton, Gloucs., and Charlotte his wife. Nephew of Adm. Sir William Young, G.C.B. (*D.N.B.*). *m.* 1st, Clifton, 5 Nov. 1831, Ashley, eldest dau. of H. Evans Holder, M.D., late of Barbados. (She died London 17 Dec. 1855.) *m.* 2nd, Bathwick, 10 Mar. 1857, Sarah, widow of H. C. Haynes.

Services : Posted as Ensign to 16th N.I. 3 June 1829. Fur. p.a. 8 May 1831 till 5 July 1832. Transfd. to 59th N.I. 13 Feb. 1833. Fur. p.a. 22 Jan. 1841 till 27 Sept. 1843. First Sikh War ; Sobraon ; Bt. Capt. 59th N.I. (Medal). Second in comd. 4th Inf., Gwalior Contingent, 27 Feb. 1846 till retirement.

Refs. : *I.M.* 17 Mar. 1857, p. 194. *G.M.* 1861, i. 473. *The Times,* 16 Mar. 1861.

ELWALL, Frederick Charles (1806-1873). Lieut. Colonel. 49th N.I. *b.* London 2 Dec. 1806. Cadet 1824. Arrived in India 25 July 1825. Ensign 7 Nov. 1824. Lieut. 18 Nov. 1825. Capt. 16 Nov. 1835. Major 9 Nov. 1846. Retired 13 Apr. 1848. Hon. Lt. Col. 28 Nov. 1854. *d.* Tauntfield, Taunton, 27 Sept. 1873.

Son of George Elwall, of London, merchant.

Services : Posted as Ensign to 49th N.I. in 1825. First Burma War ; Arakan 1825 ; Lieut. 49th N.I. Leave s.c. 8 mos. to Mauritius 6 Mar. 1826. Intr. & Qmr. 49th N.I. 10 Apr. 1830 till 24 Jan. 1835. Leave s.c. 6 mos. to Mauritius 2 Sept. 1831. Served in the Dept. for the suppression of Thagi 1835 till retirement.

Refs. : *The Times,* 2 Oct. 1873.

ELWOOD, John (1755/56-1782). Lieutenant, 1st Bengal Eur. Regt.
b. 1755/56. Cadet 1778. Ensign 1778. Lieut. (?). *d.* Calcutta, 1 Mar. 1782, aged 26.
Services : Lieut. 1/1st Bengal Eur. Regt. in Oct. 1779.
Refs. : M.I. in S. Park St. cemetery, Calcutta.

ELWOOD, John (*d.* 1817). Lieutenant, 5th N.I. Country Cadet 1805. Admitted 6 July 1807. Ensign 4 July 1807. Lieut. 11 Mar. 1812. *d.* Saharanpur, U.P., 4 Oct. 1817.
(*Possibly* son of Thomas Moore Elwood, *q.v.*)
Services : Posted as Ensign to 5th N.I. (? Reduction of Kalinjar 1812 ; Ensign 2/5th N.I.) Lieut. 2/5th N.I. With 6th Gren. Bn. 1815-6.

ELWOOD, Thomas Moore (*d.* 1798). Bt. Major, Artillery. Country Cadet 1778. Admitted 11 Aug. 1778. Fireworker 17 Sept. 1778. Lieut. 5 Sept. 1779. Capt. 9 July 1788. Bt. Major 3 May 1796. *d.* Cawnpore 27 Jan. 1798.
m. (?).
Services : Lieut. 1st Bn. Art. in July 1787. Third Mysore War ; Bangalore ; Arikera ; Capt. comdg. 1st Coy. 2nd Bn. Foot Art. To Madras on service in June 1794, for siege of Pondicherry ; Capt. 3rd Coy. 2nd Bn.
Refs. : Will dated 15 Jan. 1798 ; proved in 1798.

EMIN, Joseph (1726-1809). Bt. Ensign, Pension Est. Infantry.
b. Hamadan, Persia, 1726. Bt. Ensign 27 Oct. 1770. *d.* Calcutta 2 Aug. 1809.
Eldest son of Hovsep, or Joseph, Emin, of an ancient Armenian family, and his 1st wife. *m.* 1776, Thangoom-khatoon, dau. of Aga David, of Julfa.
Services : Posted as Bt. Ensign to a Troop of Moghal Horse at Dinapore, under the superintendence of Major Baillie, Oct. 1770, and served with this Troop till its disbandment in 1772. Fur. to Basra 31 Dec. 1772. Subsequently pensioned. Author of " Life and Adventures of Joseph Emin," London, 1792.
Refs. : *Life and Adventures of Joseph Emin*, 2nd edn., edited by Amy Apcar, Calcutta, 1918. *Cal. Gaz.* 1 Jan. 1789. Will dated 26 Dec. 1806 ; proved 9 Aug. 1809. Portrait, by Benjamin Wilson, at Hagley Hall (reproduced in 2nd edn. of his autobiog.).

EMLY, Giles (1795-1868). Major. Artillery. *b.* 14 July 1795. Cadet 1813. Admitted 21 Oct. 1814. Fireworker 24 Mar. 1817. Lieut. 1 Sept. 1818. Capt. 28 Jan. 1832. Retired 31 Jan. 1838. Hon. Major 28 Nov. 1854. *d.* Salisbury 30 Jan. 1868.

bapt. St. Martin's, Salisbury, 4 Oct. 1799. Son of Samuel Emly, of St. Martin's, Salisbury, brewer, and Ann his wife. *m.* St. Martin's, Salisbury, 20 Aug. 1840, Emma Goodenough, 2nd dau. of John Harvey Goddard, of West Woodyates, Dorset, and widow of John Fawson, Capt. H.M. 59th Foot. (She died Salisbury 22 Nov. 1865.) Addiscombe Cadet 1812-4.

Services : Suspended from rank and pay for 3 mos. from 26 Sept. 1815. (? Third Mahratta War ; Lieut. 6th Coy. 1st Bn. Foot Art.) To P.W.I. Oct. 1821. Actg. Engr. at P.W.I. Nov. 1822. Fur. p.a. 5 May 1825 till 24 Nov. 1828. Capt. comdg. 1st Coy. 6th Bn.

Refs. : Howard *& Crisp*, xv. 183, *s.n.* Goddard.

ENANDER, Francis (*d.* 1790). Ensign, Infantry. Cadet 1782. Ensign 30 Apr. 1783. *d.* Calcutta (? Berhampore) 1 June 1790.

Services : N.F.P.

ENGLAND, James. Cadet 1768.

(*Probably* identical with William ENGLISH, *q.v.*)

ENGLEHEART, George (1786-1833). Lieut. Colonel. 2nd N.I. *b.* St. George's, Hanover Sq., London, 9 Oct. 1786. Cadet 1801. Admitted 26 Aug. 1802. Ensign 14 July 1802. Lieut. 4 June 1804. Capt. 16 Dec. 1814. Major 13 May 1825. Lt. Col. 28 May 1829. Retired 14 Nov. 1832. *d.* Bedfont Lodge, nr. Staines, Middlesex, 28 May 1833.

bapt. 9 Dec. 1786. Son of George Engleheart (? the miniature-painter—*D.N.B.*) and Ursula Sarah his wife. Brother of Rev. Henry Engleheart, of Bedfont. *m.* Jaunpur, U.P., 8 Jan. 1813, Miss Elizabeth Murray. (She died 26 Apr. 1863.)

Services : Second Mahratta War ; Monson's retreat. Lieut. 1st N.I. Capt. 1/1st N.I. Third Mahratta War ; Capt. 1st N.I. Transfd. to 2nd N.I. (late 1/1st) May 1824. To act as Bde. Major to troops at Dacca 7 Jan. 1825. Lt. Col. 2nd N.I. Fur. s.c. 21 May 1830 till retirement.

Refs. : G.M. 1833, i. 573. *A.J.* N.S. xi. 203. Will dated 30 Mar. 1833 ; proved 16 Mar. 1835.

ENGLISH, William (*d.* 1769). Major, Infantry. Major 1 Sept. 1768. *d.* Calcutta 6 Sept. 1769.

Services : N.F.P. (*Probably* transfd. as Major from H.M.S.)

ERSKINE, Charles (1808-1827). Lieutenant, 2nd N.I. *b.* Port, co. Perth, 4 Mar. 1808. Cadet 1823. Arrived in India 11 Oct. 1824. Ensign 23 May 1824. Lieut. 20 Oct. 1825. *d. unm.* Kaitha, U.P., 29 Sept. 1827.

3rd son of David Erskine, of Cardross, Ceylon C.S., and Hon.

Keith Elphinstone, 4th dau. of John, 11th Lord Elphinstone. Addiscombe Cadet 1822-4.
Services : Posted as Ensign to 2nd N.I. in 1825. No record of active service.
Refs. : Burke's *Landed Gentry*, 13th edn., p. 576, *s.n.* Erskine, of Cardross, co. Perth.

ERSKINE, Erskine Thomas (1807-1893). Major. 63rd N.I. *b.* London July 1807. Cadet 1823. Arrived in India 11 Oct. 1824. Ensign 23 May 1824. Lieut. 12 Dec. 1825. Capt. 23 May 1839. Invalided 2 Dec. 1849. Retired 9 Mar. 1856. Hon. Major 9 Mar. 1856. *d.* 31 July 1893.

Eldest illegitimate [1] son of Thomas Erskine, 1st Baron Erskine, Lord High Chancellor of Gt. Britain (*D.N.B.*), and Sarah Buck (whom he afterwards *m.* as 2nd wife at Gretna Green).

Services: Siege and capture of Bhurtpore; Lieut. 63rd N.I. (India medal). Fur. s.c. 31 Jan. 1830 till 27 Nov. 1832. Actg. Adjt. 63rd N.I. 28 Dec. 1833. Fur. s.c. 6 Jan. 1836 till 25 Nov. 1838. Actg. A.D.C. to C.-in-C., Sir Jasper Nicolls, 4 Nov. 1842. Second in comd. Kumaon Local Bn. 8 Apr. 1843. Rejoined 63rd N.I. for service in Sind 11 Sept. 1843. First Sikh War; Ferozshahr; Sobraon; Capt. 63rd N.I. (Medal with clasp).

[1] *Note*: Although always treated as legitimate by his father, his application to the Govt. of India, dated 31 July 1826, for permission to prefix the title Honourable to his name was not granted.

ERSKINE, Francis Tell (1783-1853). Lieutenant. 8th N.C. *b.* 8 Oct. 1783. Cadet 1802. Arrived in India 12 Mar. 1803. Cornet 2 Nov. 1803. Lieut. 24 June 1808. Retired 1 Feb. 1814. *d.* 7 Nov. 1853.

bapt. Wootton, Beds., 7 Dec. 1783. Son of Col. James Francis Erskine and Matty Baller, of canton Bern, Switzerland, his wife. Nephew of John Francis Erskine, 7th Earl of Mar, and 1st cousin once removed of John Francis Erskine, *q.v.*

Services : Posted as Cornet to 6th N.C. Second Mahratta War (? Laswari; Cornet 6th N.C.); affair nr. Bhurtpore 23 Jan. 1805 (w.); Cornet 1st N.C. Transfd. to newly-raised 8th N.C. in 1805. Fur. 6 Sept. 1806 till 21 Oct. 1809, and 17 July 1810 till retirement.

Refs. : Burke's *Peerage*, 1923, p. 1511, *s.n.* Mar and Kellie, E.

ERSKINE, George (*d.* 1770). Ensign, Infantry. Cadet 1769. Ensign 1769. *d.* Dinapore 8 Aug. 1770.

2nd son of Rev. John Erskine, D.D., of Carnock, and Hon. Christian Mackay his wife, dau. of George, 3rd Lord Reay. Brother of John Erskine (*d.* 1776), *q.v.*

Services : N.F.P.
Refs. : Burke's *Peerage*, 1923, p. 374, *s.n.* Buchan, E. *G.M.* 1771, p. 378. *S.M.* 1771, p. 390.

ERSKINE, James. Captain, Invalid Est. Infantry. Cadet 1777. Ensign Apr. 1778. Lieut. 3 Oct. 1778. Capt. 17 Mar. 1796. Invalided 1797.
Services : Lieut. 2/1st Bengal Eur. Regt. in Oct. 1779. Lieut. 13th Bn. Sepoys in July 1787. Out of the Service before 1 Jan. 1804.

ERSKINE, John (*d.* 1799). Major General, Infantry. Country Cadet 1764. Admitted 27 Mar. 1764. Ensign 30 Sept. 1764. Lieut. 19 Oct. 1765. Capt. 2 Apr. 1769. Major 2 Jan. 1781. Lt. Col. 11 Dec. 1783. Col. 1 Mar. 1794. Maj. Gen. 3 May 1796. *d.* Chunar, 30 Oct. 1799, of smallpox.
Services : Battle of Buxar 1764 ; Ensign 11th Bn. Sepoys. Capt. 1/2nd Bengal Eur. Regt. in Oct. 1779. Comdd. 34th Bn. Comdg. 5th Bde., and comdg. at Midnapore in July 1787. Apptd. in 1795 to comd. a detachment of four Bns. for service in the N. Circars : this force was countermanded early in 1796. Comdg. at Midnapore in 1796.
Refs. : *Williams*, p. 150. *E.I.M.C.* iii. 107 *n.*

ERSKINE, John (*d.* 1776). Lieutenant, 16th Bn. Sepoys. Cadet 1768. Ensign 1 Feb. 1769. Lieut. 31 May 1770. *d.* 10 June 1776 : kld. in action at the battle of Korah.
Eldest son of Rev. John Erskine, D.D., of Carnock, and Hon. Christian Mackay his wife, dau. of George, 3rd Lord Reay. Brother of George Erskine, *q.v.*
Services : Operations in the Doab against Mahbub Khan 1776 ; battle of Korah (kld.) ; Lieut. 16th Bn., and Intr. to Lt. Col. John Neville Parker, comdg. the force, *q.v.*
Refs. : Burke's *Peerage*, 1923, p. 374, *s.n.* Buchan, E. *Williams*, p. 172. *B. :* *P.P.* ii. 427. *S.M.* 1777, p. 223.

ERSKINE, John (1810-1846). Lieutenant. 40th N.I. *b.* Edinburgh 6 Nov. 1810. Cadet 1827. Arrived in India 3 June 1828. Ensign (3 Feb. 1828) 12 Nov. 1828. Lieut. 20 Oct. 1832. Retired 14 Apr. 1845. *d.* 8 July 1846.
Of Kinneder, Dunfermline, co. Fife. 2nd son of William Erskine, advocate, afterwards Lord Kinneder (*D.N.B.*), and Euphemia Robinson his wife. Nephew of John James Erskine, of Clathick, nr. Crieff, sometime Resdt. Councillor at Singapore. *m.* Aligarh,

9 Sept. 1833, Isabella Christian, dau. of Matthew Alexander Bunbury, *q.v.* (*See also* John Grant Gerrard.)
Services : Posted as Ensign to 40th N.I. 4 Nov. 1828. Actg. Executive Ofr., P.W.D., in Arakan 8 June 1836 till 6 Jan. 1837. Adjt. 40th N.I. 27 Mar. 1837 till Oct. 1842. Fur. s.c. 14 Oct. 1842 till retirement. Was promoted Capt. 2 June 1845, before his retirement was reported in India.
Refs. : *Walford* (1900), p. 337.

ERSKINE, John Francis (1808-1845). Lieutenant. 46th N.I. *b.* Warkworth, Northumberland, 17 Nov. 1808. Cadet 1826. Arrived in India 10 Jan. 1828. Ensign 22 Aug. 1827. Lieut. 1 Mar. 1835. Resigned 1 July 1842. *d. unm.* Broomrig, co. Clackmannan, 29 Sept. 1845.

2nd son of Hon. Henry David Erskine (who was 3rd son of John Francis Erskine, 7th Earl of Mar) and Mary Anne his wife, dau. of John Cooksey. Brother of Walter Coningsby Erskine, 12th Earl of Kellie, *q.v.*
Services : Ensign d.d. 59th N.I. 9 Feb. 1828. Posted to 46th N.I. 1 July 1828. Actg. Adjt. 46th N.I. Apr. 1832, 22 Mar. 1834, and 13 Jan. 1835. No record of active service. Subsequently Capt. Stirlingshire Mil.
Refs. : Burke's *Peerage*, 1923, p. 1511, *s.n.* Mar and Kellie, E. *G.M.* 1845, ii. 663.

ERSKINE, Roger Keys (1793-1825). Lieutenant, 33rd N.I. *b.* York 19 Jan. 1793. Cadet 1808. Arrived in India 15 Dec. 1809. Ensign 4 Aug. 1811. Lieut. 16 Dec. 1814. *d.* Chandernagore, Bengal, 7 Jan. 1825.

2nd son of John Erskine, of York, and Frances Lina his wife, dau. of John Keys, of Lifford, co. Donegal. Uncle of Charles Farquhar Trower, *q.v.*, and of Martina, wife of Alfred Jackson, *q.v. m.* Martha, dau. of —— Thornton.
Services : Barasat C.C. Posted as Ensign to 16th N.I. in 1811. Lieut. 1/16th N.I. Fur. 31 Aug. 1816 till 1818. Transfd. to 33rd N.I. (late 2/16th) May 1824. No record of active service.
Refs. : Family information. *Calcutta Monthly Journal*, Jan. 1825.

ERSKINE, Walter Coningsby, twelfth Earl of Kellie (1810-1872). Lieut. Colonel, C.B. 73rd N.I. Commissioner of Jubbulpore. *b.* Warkworth, Northumberland, 12 July 1810. Cadet 1827. Arrived in India 4 Sept. 1828. Ensign 16 Apr. 1828. Lieut. 3 Oct. 1840. Capt. 21 Dec. 1845. Bt. Major 20 June 1854. Retired 25 Sept. 1861. Hon. Lt. Col. 25 Sept. 1861. *d.* Cannes, France, 17 Jan. 1872.

12th Earl of Kellie and 15th Lord Erskine. *s.* 19 June 1866. Claimed the Earldom of Mar, but died before his claim was allowed by the House of Lords. 3rd son of Hon. Henry David Erskine and Mary Anne his wife. Brother of John Francis Erskine, *q.v. m.* Benares, 11 Sept. 1834, Elise, dau. of Col. William Youngson, of Bowscar, Cumberland, late Madras Est. (*See also* Robert Delamain.) (She died 14 July 1895.)

Services : Ensign d.d. 46th N.I. 5 Nov. 1828. Posted to 73rd N.I. 4 Mar. 1829. Actg. Intr. & Qmr. 73rd N.I. 18 Feb. 1832. Actg. Adjt. 73rd N.I. 14 Nov. 1833. d.d. Assam L.I. 21 Nov. 1836 till 13 Feb. 1837. Adjt. 73rd N.I. 12 Jan. 1837 till Mar. 1844. Second in comd. 2nd Inf., Gwalior Contingent, 6 Mar. 1844 till Apr. 1849. First Sikh War ; Sobraon ; Capt. 73rd N.I. (Medal). Supt. of Jalaun, U.P., 27 Apr. 1849 till Sept. 1853. Comr. of Saugor & Narbada territories 3 Sept. 1853. A.G.G. do. 31 Mar. 1854 till Dec. 1858. Mutiny campaign (Medal). Fur. 16 Dec. 1858 till 30 Jan. 1860. Comr. of Jubbulpore till retirement. C.B. (Civil) 18 May 1860.

Refs. : Burke's *Peerage,* 1923, p. 1512, *s.n.* Mar and Kellie, E. Walford. Boase. The *Times,* 17 Jan. 1872.

EVANS, Dacres Fitzherbert (1807-1856). Colonel. 16th N.I. *b.* Chelsea 26 Oct. 1807. Cadet 1824. Ensign 20 Mar. 1825. Lieut. 5 Aug. 1826. Capt. 28 Nov. 1839. Bt. Major 23 Dec. 1842. Bt. Lt. Col. 20 June 1854. Retired 22 Oct. 1855. Hon. Col. 22 Oct. 1855. *d.* Sion Row, Clifton, 26 Dec. 1856.

bapt. St. Luke's, Chelsea, 4 Jan. 1809. Son of Andrew Fitzherbert Evans, Capt. R.N. *m.* 1st, Mussoorie, 24 Sept. 1832, Fanny, widow of Robert Frederick Dougan, *q.v.* (She died Mhow, 10 July 1834, aged 23.) *m.* 2nd, Mussoorie, 6 Oct. 1836, Hetty Theophila, 2nd dau. of Edward Gwatkin, *q.v.* (*See also* Hon. Robert Barlow Palmer Byng.)

Services : Posted as Ensign to 16th N.I. in 1826. Leave p.a. 9 mos. to Ceylon 4 Nov. 1826. (Leave u.p.a. 18 mos. to Calcutta 22 Jan. 1830.) Adjt. 16th N.I. 3 May 1830 till Dec. 1837. Leave s.c. 1 yr. to Landour 19 Feb. 1832. Fur. s.c. 16 Dec. 1837 till 28 Dec. 1840. First Afghan War 1842 ; recapture of Ghazni ; Capt. 16th N.I. (tempy. comdg. from 5 Sept. 1842), with Gen. Nott's force (Medal). (*Lond. Gaz.* 24 Nov. 1842.) Sub. Asst. in Stud Dept. 14 Aug. 1843 till 31 Jan. 1853. First Sikh War ; Sobraon ; Bt. Major 16th N.I. (Medal). Fur. s.c. 18 Mar. 1853 till retirement. Crimean War ; Local Bdr. Gen. in Turkey 27 Mar. 1855.

Refs. : Burke's *Family Records,* p. 290, *s.n.* Gwatkin. *Howard & Crisp,* ii. 169, *s.n.* Gwatkin. *G.M.* 1857, i. 252.

EVANS, Francis Roberts (1809-1857). Bt. Lieut. Colonel, 26th N.I. *b.* Killaconenagh, co. Cork, 27 Feb. 1809. Cadet 1825. Arrived in India 18 Sept. 1826. Ensign 21 May 1826. Lieut. 14 Feb. 1829. Capt. 8 Feb. 1843. Major 10 Feb. 1856. Bt. Lt. Col. 20 June 1854. *d.* Mussoorie 27 Aug. 1857.
bapt. 2 Mar. 1809. Only son of Robert Evans, Maj. Gen. R.A. *m.* 1st, Bareilly, 20 Nov. 1845, Mary, dau. of William Eccles, of Eccles St., Dublin. (She died Dehra Dun 22 Feb. 1846, aged 36.) *m.* 2nd, Mussoorie, 24 Aug. 1848, Miss Henrietta Turner.
Services : Ensign d.d. 62nd N.I. 7 Oct. 1826. Posted to 21st N.I. 9 Nov. 1826. Transfd. to 26th N.I. 1 Mar. 1828. First Afghan War 1842 ; all engagements leading to the re-occupation of Kabul ; Lieut. 26th N.I., with Gen. Pollock's force (Medal). Apptd. A.D.C. to C.-in-C., Sir Hugh Gough, 11 Sept. 1843. Apptd. Postmaster at H.Q. 2 Nov. 1843. Gwalior campaign ; Maharajpur ; A.D.C. (Bronze star). Apptd. Bde. Major in Rohilkhand 16 Nov. 1844. First Sikh War ; Sobraon ; Capt. 26th N.I. (Medal). Comdd. Sirmoor Bn. 14 Feb. 1846 till 24 Feb. 1857, when he assumed comd. of 26th N.I.
Refs. : Burke's *Landed Gentry of Ireland,* p. 209, *s.n.* Evans, of Carker House, co. Cork. Will dated 14 Aug. 1857 ; proved 13 Mar. 1858.

EVANS, John (1802-1886). Captain. 15th N.I. *b.* Stradbally, co. Limerick, 27 Sept. 1802. Cadet 1819. Admitted 31 July 1820. Ensign 4 Mar. 1820. Lieut. 11 July 1823. Capt. 31 May 1834. Retired 10 Jan. 1838. *d.* Cintra House, Thicket Rd., Anerley, London, 2 July 1886.
Son of George Evans. A near relative of Thomas Montague Black, *q.v. m.* Hennock, Devon, 22 Nov. 1836, Jane Baily, eldest dau. of Rev. John Turner, vicar of Hennock.
Services : Posted as Ensign to 2/25th N.I. Transfd. as Lieut. to 1/11th N.I. July 1823 ; to 15th N.I. (late 1/11th) May 1824. Actg. Intr. & Qmr. 15th N.I. 27 Sept. 1824. Operations in Kotah 1824 ; action at Patan, nr. Kotah, 7 Nov. 1824 ; Lieut. 15th N.I. Siege and capture of Bhurtpore ; Lieut. 15th N.I. (India medal). Actg. Intr. & Qmr. 15th N.I. 22 Nov. 1826. Adjt. 15th N.I. 8 Feb. 1827 till 19 Dec. 1833. Fur. s.c. 6 Feb. 1834 till 9 June 1837.
Refs. : Bath Chron. Dec. 1836. *The Times,* 12 July 1886.

EVANS, Richard. Lieutenant. Infantry. Cadet (?). Ensign (?). Lieut. 27 Aug. 1762.
Services : N.F.P. Casualty on some date after 1 Feb. 1767, when he was the senior Lieut. in the Bengal Army.
Refs. : B.M. Add. MS. 6050, p. 90.

EVANS, Thomas (*d.* 1809). Major, 15th N.I. Cadet 1782. Admitted 7 July 1783. Ensign 19 Apr. 1782. Lieut. 16 Mar. 1790. Capt. 12 Sept. 1803. Major 28 July 1808. *d.* Barrackpore 22 Dec. 1809.

Son of David Evans. Nephew of Higgins Eden, of London, and related to George (Higgins) Raban, *q.v.*

Services : Adjt. 2/15th N.I. till Sept. 1803. Operations in Jumna Doab 1803 ; Sasni ; Bijaigarh ; Kachaura ; Lieut. 2/15th N.I. Second Mahratta War ; battle of Delhi ; Agra ; Laswari ; battle of Deig (? Bhurtpore) ; Capt. 15th N.I. Major 2/15th N.I.

Refs. : Will dated camp Futepore 29 Oct. 1803 ; proved 28 Dec. 1809.

EVANS, Thomas (1776-1812). Captain, 14th N.I. *b.* London 11 Oct. 1776. Cadet 1795. Admitted 30 Jan. 1798. Ensign 9 Aug. 1797. Lieut. 1 July 1798. Capt. 24 Feb. 1807. *d.* Fort Nugent, Borneo, 18 Dec. 1812.

bapt. St. Mary-le-Bow, London, Nov. 1776. Son of Maurice Evans, of London, and Charlotte his wife, 2nd dau. of Thomas Lloyd, of Plas Madoc, and of Wrexham. Brother of Anne, wife of James Nathaniel Rind, *q.v.* Cousin-german of Sir William Lloyd, Kt., *q.v.*, and of Christopher Alderson, formerly Lloyd, *q.v.*

Services : Expedn. to Egypt 1801 ; Lieut. Bengal Vol. Bn. Second Mahratta War ; Lieut 14th N.I. Fur. 18 Feb. 1806 till 21 Mar. 1809. A.D.C. to Maj.-Gen. Francis Fuller, H.M.S., comdg. at Cawnpore, 1809. Capture of Java 1811 ; Capt. 5th Bengal Vol. Bn. Capture of Palembang 1812 ; Capt. 5th Vol. Bn.

Refs. : Burke's *Landed Gentry*, 2nd edn., iii. 207, *s.n.* Lloyd, of Brynestyn, co. Denbigh. Will dated 30 June 1809 ; proved 18 Dec. 1816.

EVANS, William (1762/63-1789). Lieutenant, Infantry. *b.* 1762/63. Cadet 1780. Arrived in India 30 Apr. 1781. Ensign 1780. Lieut. 7 June 1781. *d.* Burdwan, Bengal, 10 Dec. 1789.

A native of Ireland.

Services : Sailed for India on the *Bellmont*, 3 Apr. 1780, aged 17. Lieut. 30th Bn. Sepoys in July 1787.

EVELYN, Charles (1765-1784). Lieutenant, Infantry. *b.* 23 Nov. 1765. Cadet 1780. Ensign 1780. Lieut. 3 Aug. 1781. *d. unm.* at sea 1784, between Basra and Bombay.

bapt. St. James's, Westminster, 16 Dec. 1765. 3rd son of Charles Evelyn, of Totnes, Devon, sometime of Leghorn, Italy, and Philadelphia (Philippa) his wife, dau. of Capt. Fortunatus Wright, of

Liverpool. Brother of Sir John Evelyn, 4th Bart., of Wotton Place, Surrey, and of Sir Hugh Evelyn, 5th Bart.
Services : Sailed for India on the *Bellmont* 3 Apr. 1780, when he gave his age as 18. Campaign against the Rajah of Benares 1781.
Refs. : Burke's *Peerage*, 1848, p. 379, *s.n.* Evelyn, Bart., of Wotton Place, Surrey. *Misc. Gen. et Her.* 2S. v. 226.

EVEREST, Sir George (1790-1866). Colonel, Kt. and C.B. Artillery. Surveyor Gen. of India. *b.* Gwernvale, co. Brecknock, 4 July 1790. Cadet 1805. Arrived in India 11 July 1806. Lieut. 4 Apr. 1806. Capt. Lt. 25 Sept. 1817. Capt. 1 Sept. 1818. Major 25 July 1832. Lt. Col. 7 Mar. 1838. Retired 16 Dec. 1843. Hon. Col. 28 Nov. 1854. *d.* 10 Westbourne St., Hyde Pk. Gdns., London, 1 Dec. 1866.

Of Claybrook Hall, Leics. Eldest son of Tristram Everest and Lucetta Mary his wife. *m.* 17 Nov. 1846, Emma, eldest dau. of Thomas Wing, of Hampstead, and of Gray's Inn, atty.-at-law. Woolwich Cadet; nominated to R.M.A. 11 July 1804; obtained his certificate 13 Jan. 1806.
Services : See *D.N.B.* Chief Asst. Supt. Gt. Trigonometrical Survey of India 25 Nov. 1817. Fur. s.c. 11 Nov. 1825 till 6 Oct. 1830. Apptd. Surveyor Gen. of India 12 Aug. 1829. Mount Everest was named after him. C.B. 26 Feb. 1861. Kt. 13 Mar. 1861. F.R.S. 8 Mar. 1827. F.R.G.S.
Refs. : D.N.B. D.I.B. Boase. *Stubbs*, ii. 251-4. *Ency. Brit.* 11th edn. *The Times*, 5 Dec. 1866.

EVERETT, Thomas Cooper. Lieutenant. Artillery. Cadet (?). Fireworker Sept. 1768. Lieut. 17 Sept. 1770. Resigned 13 Feb. 1771.
Services : N.F.P.

EVERS, Pryse John (1750-1769). Cadet, Infantry. *bapt.* Newtown, co. Montgomery, 9 June 1750. Cadet 1768. *d.* Berhampore, Bengal, 9 Apr. 1769.
Son of David Evers and Diana his wife. Ed. Eton; K.S. 1765.
Services : N.F.P.
Refs. : Austen-Leigh.

EWART, David (1803-1880). Colonel. Artillery. *b.* Camberwell, Surrey, 1 Aug. 1803. Cadet 1818. Admitted 20 Nov. 1819. 2nd Lieut. 13 Apr. 1819. Lieut. 13 Dec. 1820. Capt. 3 Mar. 1835. Major 3 July 1845. Lt. Col. 7 Jan. 1848. Retired 5 May 1849. Hon. Col. 28 Nov. 1854. *d.* Lincluden House, Dumfries, 26 Aug. 1880.
Son of John Ewart, of Carlisle. Brother of William Ewart, *q.v.*

m. 1st, St. Cuthbert's, Carlisle, 12 Aug. 1833, Isabella, dau. of Richard Hodgson, *q.v.* *m.* 2nd, Edinburgh, 15 June 1848, Anne Finlay Anderson, elder dau. of Lt.-Gen. the Hon. John Ramsay, and sister of Hon. Sir Henry Ramsay, *q.v.* Addiscombe Cadet 1817-8.

Services : Actg. Adjt. 1st Bn. Foot Art. 26 Apr. 1820. 2nd Troop H.A. 1821-4. Siege and capture of Bhurtpore ; Lieut. 2nd Troop 1st Bde. H.A. (India medal). Actg. Adjt. 1st Bde. H.A. 14 June 1828, and 15 Apr. 1829. Fur. s.c. 21 Jan. 1831 till 1 Oct. 1834. Offg. Comy. Ord. at Cawnpore 15 Sept. 1835 till 20 Mar. 1837. Comdd. 4th Troop 2nd Bde. H.A. 4 Mar. 1837 till 1844. Comdg. Art. at Ludhiana 7 Jan. 1842. Lt. Col. comdg. 3rd Bn. Foot Art., afterwards comdd. 9th Bn.

Refs. : Burke's *Peerage*, 1923, p. 653, *s.n.* Dalhousie, E. *A.J.* N.S. xii. 63. *The Times*, 30 Aug. 1880.

EWART, James (1792-1820). Lieutenant, Artillery. *b.* Canongate, Edinburgh, 23 Jan. 1792. Cadet 1808. Arrived in India 19 July 1809. Fireworker 25 July 1809. Lieut. 18 Jan. 1816. *d. unm.* Chittagong, 8 Oct. 1820.

2nd son of David Ewart, Depute Clerk of H.M. Chancery, Lieut. Edinburgh Vols., and Janet Fell his 2nd wife. 2nd cousin of John Ewart, *q.v.* Nominated for R.M.A., Woolwich, 13 May 1807, but there being no room at the Academy, was educated privately at Woolwich.

Services : Expedn. to Mauritius 1810 ; Lieut. F. 6th Coy. 1st Bn. Art. ; returned to Bengal with the Coy. in Mar. 1812. Comdg. the Art. at Chittagong in 1816.

Refs. : Burke's *Landed Gentry*, 12th edn., p. 628, *s.n.* Ewart, of Craigcleuch, co. Dumfries.

EWART, James Simon. Captain. Infantry. Cadet 1778. Ensign 22 May 1779. Lieut. 25 Jan. 1781. Capt. (?). Struck off 1793. *m.* 12 Feb. 1790, Catherine, elder dau. of Joseph Skinner, of Aldgate High St., London, and of Wanstead, Essex, and sister of Samuel Skinner, of Shirley Park, Surrey, formerly Madras C.S. (She died 28 Oct. 1855, aged 90.)

Services : Fur. 20 Nov. 1786. N.F.P.

Refs. : Burke's *Landed Gentry*, 2nd edn., p. 1243, *s.n.* Skinner, of Shirley Park, Surrey. *G.M.* 1790, i. 179.

EWART, John (1803-1857). Lieut. Colonel, 1st N.I. *b.* Manchester 24 July 1803. Cadet 1824. Arrived in India 5 Apr. 1825. Ensign 13 Oct. 1824. Lieut. 14 Jan. 1826. Capt. 24 Jan. 1845. Major 14 Apr. 1849. Lt. Col. 24 Nov. 1854. *d.* Cawnpore 27 June 1857 : massacred together with his wife and dau.

Eldest son of Peter Ewart, Chief Engr. H.M. Dockyards, formerly of Manchester, cotton-spinner, and Marianne his wife, dau. of William Kerr, of Kelso, and aunt of Henry Thomas Coggan Kerr, *q.v.* *m.* Nasirabad, 9 Sept. 1841, Emma Sophia, dau. of T. B. Fooks, of Deptford, Kent.

Services : Siege and capture of Bhurtpore; Ensign 37th N.I. (India medal). Transfd. to 55th N.I. A.D.C. to Maj.-Gen. George Dick, *q.v.*, 1 Dec. 1826 till 7 Nov. 1828. Adjt. 6th Local Horse 1 Sept. 1828. Intr. & Qmr. 55th N.I. 21 Feb. 1835 till Oct. 1837. Fur. s.c. 14 Oct. 1837 till 27 Nov. 1840. Intr. & Qmr. 55th N.I. 11 Sept. 1841. Actg. D.J.A.G. 24 Feb. 1843. Offg. D.J.A.G., Meerut Div., 2 July 1844; permanent do. June 1845; do. Saugor Div. (afterwards Meerut and Benares) 12 Sept. 1845 till 1849. Fur. 10 Feb. 1852 till 4 Dec. 1854. Posted as Lt. Col. to 64th N.I. in 1855; to 1st N.I. June 1855.

Refs. : Burke's *Landed Gentry*, 13th edn., p. 590, *s.n.* Ewart, of Craigcleuch, co. Dumfries.

EWART, Richard Sheridan (1806-1885). Colonel. 30th N.I. *b.* Calcutta 19 Dec. 1806. Cadet 1826. Arrived in India 10 Apr. 1827. Ensign 14 Nov. 1826. Lieut. 24 Apr. 1832. Capt. 1 Feb. 1844. Major 9 June 1858. Bt. Lt. Col. 19 Jan. 1858. Retired 31 Dec. 1861. Hon. Col. 31 Dec. 1861. *d.* Clifton 19 July 1885.

bapt. Calcutta 20 June 1807. Son of Simon Ewart and Mary Ann his wife, *née* Bennet. *m.* Mussoorie 1 June 1837, Susan Margaret, eldest dau. of John Hoggan, *q.v.*

Services : Ensign d.d. 46th N.I. 28 May 1827. Posted to 31st N.I. 19 June 1827. Operations against the Bhils 1828. Transfd. to 30th N.I. 7 July 1830. Actg. Adjt. 30th N.I. 11 June 1838; permanent do. 27 Sept. 1839 till Apr. 1844. First Afghan War 1842; retirement through Khyber pass Jan. 1842, actg. Bde. Major to Bdr. Wild's force; forcing of Khyber pass; Lieut. 30th N.I., with Gen. Pollock's force (Medal). First Sikh War; Aliwal; Capt. 30th N.I. (Medal). Second Sikh War; passage of Chenab; Chilianwala (w.); Gujerat; Capt. 30th N.I. (Medal with 2 clasps). Apptd. Bde. Major at Barrackpore 7 Apr. 1852. Actg. D.A.A.G., Peshawar Div., Dec. 1854; permanent do. 20 Feb. 1855. A.A.G., Sirhind Div., 14 Aug. 1857. Mutiny campaign; Badli-ki-Serai 8 June 1857; capture of Delhi; A.A.G. of the Force (Medal).

Refs. : *The Times*, 24 July 1885.

EWART, William (1800-1842). Major, 54th N.I. *b.* Dulwich, Kent, June 1800. Cadet 1816. Admitted 13 Jan. 1818. Ensign (?). Lieut. 1 Aug. 1818. Capt. 3 Sept. 1827. Major 23 July 1838. *d.* 10 Jan. 1842 : kld. in action nr. Kabul.

Son of John Ewart, of Carlisle. Brother of David Ewart, *q.v.*

Services : Posted as Lieut. to 1/27th N.I. Transfd. to 54th N.I. (late 2/27th) May 1824. Intr. & Qmr. 54th N.I. 26 Aug. 1826 till 30 Aug. 1828. Actg. Bde. Major to troops in Assam 25 Nov. 1826. Operations against the Kols in Ramgarh 1832 ; Capt. 54th N.I. Fur. s.c. 15 Mar. 1836 till 15 Dec. 1838. Comdd. 54th N.I. 23 Mar. 1840 till death. First Afghan War 1840-2 ; Kabul disaster ; retreat from Kabul (kld.).

EWINS, Henry. Captain, Pension Est. Infantry. Cadet 1768. Ensign 8 May 1768. Lieut. 24 Dec. 1769. Capt. 6 July 1778. Pensioned 1780.[1]

Brother of Richard Ewins, *q.v.*

Services : First Rohilla War ; battle of St. George.

Refs. : Williams, p. 145.

[1] *Note :* He was present on parade with 16th Bn. Sepoys at Ramgarh on 29 Nov. 1772, and witnessed the murder of his brother. The shock affected his brain, and he eventually died insane at Calcutta early in the nineteenth century.

EWINS, Richard (*d.* 1772). Captain, comdg. 16th Bn. Sepoys. Lieut. 1765. Capt. 28 May 1767. *d.* Ramgarh, B. & O., 29 Nov. 1772 : assassinated on parade by a sepoy of his Bn.

Brother of Henry Ewins, *q.v.*, and of Thomas Ewins, of Burstock, Dorset.

Services : Probably transfd. as Lieut. from H.M.S.

Refs. : Williams, p. 143. Will dated Monghyr 17 Sept. 1772 ; proved 17 Oct. 1773.

EXSHAW, James Robert (*d.* 1803). Captain, Artillery. Country Cadet 1778. Admitted 17 Dec. 1778. Fireworker 30 Dec. 1778. Lieut. 1 Feb. 1785. Capt. Lt. 8 Jan. 1796. Capt. 21 Apr. 1800. *d.* Calcutta 11 Mar. 1803 : bur. there 13 Mar.

m. Calcutta, 17 Dec. 1802, Miss Elizabeth Lowe. (She died Calcutta, 2 Dec. 1826, aged 68.) Father of Sarah, wife of Major Hadden Smith, H.M. Ceylon Rifles, and of Maria Louisa, wife of William Griffiths, of Dublin. (*Possibly* father of John Exshaw, *q.v.*)

Services : Originally apptd. a Cadet for Bombay, but declined the appt., and went out in a private capacity to Calcutta. Second Mysore War 1781-5 ; Lieut. F. 5th Coy. 1st Bn. Art. Third Mysore War ; Bangalore ; Seringapatam ; Lieut. 2nd Coy. 2nd Bn. Posted to 5th Coy. 1st Bn. in Ceylon 8 May 1799.

EXSHAW, John (*d.* 1824). Lieutenant, 20th N.I. Cadet 1810.
Ensign 23 Sept. 1812. Lieut. 1 Oct. 1815. *d.* Tek Naaf, Upper
Burma, 13 Jan. 1824.
(*Possibly* son of James Robert Exshaw, *q.v.*) *m.* St. John's,
Calcutta, 31 Jan. 1823, Miss Louisa Twentyman (*probably* dau. of
J. H. Twentyman, of Calcutta, jeweller.) (She *re-m.* 20 June 1825,
Henry Osborne, of Calcutta, surveyor.)
Services: Cadet d.d. 12th N.I. in 1812. Admitted as one of the
first mily. students at Coll. of Fort William in July 1812. Posted
as Ensign to 2/20th N.I. in 1813. No record of active service.

EYRE, Charles Richard (1805-1826). Lieutenant, 30th N.I. *b.*
Bramshaw, Wilts., Sept. 1805. Cadet 1821. Ensign 3 June
1822. Lieut. 1 May 1824. *d.* Cuttack 23 Nov. 1826.
2nd son of George Eyre, of Warrens, Bramshaw, high sheriff of
Wilts. in 1815, and Frances his 1st wife, 3rd dau. of Sir Edward
Hulse, Bart., of Bracmore, Hants. Ed. Harrow 1817-9.
Services: Posted as Ensign to 24th N.I. in 1822. Transfd. to
15th N.I. in 1823; as Lieut. to 30th N.I. (late 1/15th) May 1824.
No record of active service.
Refs.: Burke's *Landed Gentry*, 6th edn., p. 532, *s.n.* Eyre, of
Warrens, Bramshaw, Wilts. *Harrow School Register*. M.I. at
Cuttack.

EYRE, Giles. Ensign. Infantry. Cadet 1772. Ensign 19 Apr.
1773. Resigned 12 Aug. 1773.
Services: N.F.P.

EYRE, Robert Douglas (1788-1814). Lieutenant, 5th N.I. *bapt.*
Landford, Wilts., 31 Oct. 1788. Cadet 1803. Arrived in India
3 Dec. 1804. Ensign 9 Nov. 1804. Lieut. 9 Nov. 1804. *d.*
Mainpuri, U.P., 31 July 1814.
Son of Rev. Henry Eyre, rector of Landford, and Frances Petti-
ward his 2nd wife.
Services: Posted as Lieut. to 5th N.I. in 1805. Reduction of
Kalinjar 1812; Lieut. 2/5th N.I. Adjt. 2/5th N.I. 1813 till
death.
Refs.: Burke's *Landed Gentry*, 13th edn., p. 594, *s.n.* Eyre, late
of Shaw House, Berks. *G.M.* 1815, ii. 92.

EYRE, Sir Vincent (1811-1881). Major General, K.C.S.I., C.B.
Artillery. *b.* Portsdown, Hants, 22 Jan. 1811. Cadet 1828.
Arrived in India 21 May 1829. 2nd Lieut. 12 Dec. 1828. Lieut.
28 Apr. 1837. Capt. 19 Sept. 1846. Major 4 July 1858. Lt. Col.
27 Aug. 1858. Col. 24 Nov. 1862. Retired 1 Sept. 1863. Hon.

150 LIST OF OFFICERS OF THE BENGAL ARMY

Maj. Gen. 1 Sept. 1863. *d.* Villa des Acacias, Aix-les-Bains, France, 22 Sept. 1881.

bapt. Wimmering, Hants, 20 Feb. 1811. 3rd son of Capt. Henry Eyre and Mary his wife, dau. of J. Concannon, of Loughrea, co. Galway. *m.* 1st, Cawnpore, 6 Sept. 1833, Emily Ahmuty, only dau. of Sir James Mouat, Bart., *q.v.* (She died Calcutta 9 Mar. 1851.) *m.* 2nd, Calcutta, 19 June 1860, his cousin, Catherine Mary, only child of Thomas Eyre, Capt. R.N. Ed. Norwich grammar school. Addiscombe Cadet 7 May 1827 till 12 Dec. 1828.

Services : See *D.N.B.* Leave s.c. 6 mos. to Mauritius 20 Mar. 1837. First Afghan War 1840-2 ; action at Kabul 22 Nov. 1841 (s.w.) ; detained as a hostage by Akbar Khan on retreat from Kabul ; released 21 Sept. 1842. Fur. s.c. 28 Apr. 1855 till 3 Feb. 1857. Mutiny campaign ; comdd. F.F. for relief of Arrah ; first relief of Lucknow ; Bdr. of Art. and Cav. under Sir James Outram at Lucknow and Alam Bagh ; comdd. Art. under Sir Colin Campbell during final operations before Lucknow (Medal with 2 clasps). Supt. Ichapur powder factory 18 Jan. 1858. I.G. Ord. 1862. Pub. in 1843, " The Military Operations at Kabul... " C.B. 5 Feb. 1858. K.C.S.I. 24 May 1867.

Refs. : Burke's *Landed Gentry*, 13th edn., p. 593, *s.n.* Eyre, of Middleton Tyas, Yorks. *D.N.B. D.I.B.* Boase. Foster's *Knightage*, p. 709. *The Times*, 26 and 28 Sept. 1881. *B.* : *P.P.* vi. 87-91 (portrait). *Feudal History of County Derby*, by J. Pym Yeatman, ii. 410.

EYRES, George Bolton (1735/36-1797). Major General. Cavalry.
b. 1735/36. Cadet 1761. Cornet 24 July 1763. Lieut. 1 Sept. 1763. Capt. 4 Aug. 1765. Major 10 Dec. 1771. Lt. Col. 1 Dec. 1781. Col. 30 May 1786. Maj. Gen. 20 Dec. 1793. Retired 1796. *d.* Bath 15 Jan. 1797, aged 61.

m. Calcutta, 18 Nov. 1772, Miss Anna Harris. His son, George Robert, was admitted a Minor Cadet in 1781, and was struck off 2 May 1786.

Services : Lieut. in one of the Troops of Eur. Dgns., and on their disbandment was ordered to take rank in the Inf. from the date of his first Commission as Cornet. (G.O. 7 July 1764.) In 1765 was comdg. 2nd Rissalah of Moghal Horse. Comdg. at Berhampore in July 1787 ; at Cawnpore in 1790. Fur. 3 Dec. 1792.

Refs. : N. & Q. 10S. ii. 38. *G.M.* 1797, i. 84.

F

FADDY, Samuel Brougham (1816-1890). General, 36th N.I. *b.*
Kishangarh, Bengal, 26 July 1816. Cadet 1834. Arrived in
India 21 July 1835. Ensign (24 Feb. 1835) 30 Apr. 1835. Lieut.
1 Feb. 1840. Capt. 14 Nov. 1846. Major 31 May 1857. Lt. Col.
9 Mar. 1861. Col. 24 Feb. 1866. Maj. Gen. 8 Feb. 1877. Lt.
Gen. 1 July 1881. Gen. 1 Dec. 1888. *d.* Ravenswell, Bath,
30 June 1890.

Eldest son of Samuel Faddy, of Kishangarh, indigo manufacturer,
afterwards of Grande rue, Boulogne, and Eliza his wife, *née* Backhouse. *m.* Jullundur, 13 Jan. 1858, Eliza Sophia, eldest dau. of
James Innes, *q.v.*
Services : Ensign d.d. 43rd N.I. 8 Aug. 1835. Posted to 36th
N.I. 24 Sept. 1835. Actg. Adjt. 36th N.I. 31 Mar. 1841. d.d.
tempy. with Sylhet L.I. Bn. 8 Nov. 1841. Intr. & Qmr. 36th N.I.
9 Oct. 1844 till Mar. 1847. First Sikh War ; Aliwal ; Lieut. 36th
N.I. (Medal). Second Sikh War ; Ramnagar ; Sadulapur ; Chilianwala ; Gujerat ; Lieut. 36th N.I., offg. S.A.C.G. (Medal with 2
clasps). Offg. S.A.C.G. at Fort Govindgarh 18 May 1849. Executive Ofr., P.W.D., Govindgarh, 1852 till 21 Apr. 1857.
Refs. : Boase. *The Times*, 3 July 1890.

FAGAN, Christopher (1776-1845). Major General. Colonel 39th
N.I. A.G. Bengal. *b.* Santa Cruz 18 July 1776. Cadet 1794.
Admitted 4 Feb. 1797. Ensign 9 Oct. 1795. Lieut. 3 Oct. 1796.
Capt. 21 Sept. 1804. Major 22 Feb. 1811. Lt. Col. 14 July
1815. Lt. Col. Comdt. 1 May 1824. Col. 5 June 1829. Maj.
Gen. 10 Jan. 1837. *d.* Pau, France, 18 Mar. 1845.

Eldest son of Robert Fagan, of Philadelphia. Brother of Robert
Fagan, *q.v.*, and cousin-german of Christopher Sullivan Fagan, *q.v.*
m. 1st, London, Mar. 1803, Mary Eliza, eldest dau. of John Fagan,
of Kiltallagh, and sister of Christopher Sullivan Fagan, *q.v.* (*See
also* Warren Hastings Leslie Frith, and John Luther Richardson.)
(She died 10 Nov. 1805.) *m.* 2nd, Calcutta, 18 Nov. 1807, Miss
Eliza Lawtie. (*See also* George Hickson Fagan (1778-1821).) *m.*
3rd, 22 Feb. 1833, Maria, 2nd dau. of Rev. Charles Gibbon, of

Lonmay. (She died Pau 5 Nov. 1847.) His dau. *m.* Henry Hall, *q.v.*

Services: Approved as Cadet 16 Mar. 1796. Lieut. 1st Bengal Eur. Regt. in June 1798. Adjt. 2/1st N.I. Apr. 1799 till 1800. Expedn. to Egypt 1801; apptd. Agent for transports on the Nile, and later D.J.A.G. in Alexandria. Fur. p.a. from Egypt May 1802 till 19 Oct. 1803. A.D.C. to Maj.-Gen. Ewen Baillie, *q.v.*, Sept. 1806; Sec. to Maj.-Gen. Baillie, Provincial C.-in-C., July 1807. Capt. 19th N.I. Expedn. to Mauritius 1810; Capt. 2nd Bengal Vol. Bn. D.J.A.G. 19 Mar. 1811 till 26 Nov. 1811. J.A.G. 25 July 1813. Leave s.c. 10 mos. to Cape 28 Oct. 1814. Lt. Col. 2/19th N.I. Fur. s.c. 10 Feb. 1817 till 19 Feb. 1821. To comd. Malwa F.F. 22 Oct. 1821. Transfd. to 24th N.I.; to 22nd N.I. Fur. p.a. 21 Feb. 1824 till 16 Mar. 1826. Transfd. as Lt. Col. Comdt. to 68th N.I. May 1824; to 41st N.I. 12 Oct. 1826. Comdg. Rajputana F.F., with rank of Bdr., 1 Apr. 1827 till 28 Nov. 1827. A.G. 28 Dec. 1827 till 1832. Col. 39th N.I. 15 Aug. 1829. Leave s.c. 14 mos. to Cape 27 Oct. 1829. Fur. p.a. 28 Jan. 1832 till death.

Refs.: Burke's *Landed Gentry of Ireland*, p. 214, *s.n.* Fagan, formerly of Feltrim, co. Dublin. *E.I.M.C.* i. 333-5. *G.M.* 1845, i. 678; ii. 310.

FAGAN, Christopher George (1811-1861). Lieut. Colonel. 8th L.C. *b.* Cawnpore 30 Oct. 1811. Cadet 1827. Arrived in India 2 June 1828. Cornet (3 Feb. 1828) 10 Jan. 1829. Lieut. 20 Feb. 1838. Capt. 1 Sept. 1849. Bt. Major 20 June 1854. Retired 1 Nov. 1854. Hon. Lt. Col. 28 Nov. 1854. *d.* 3 Jan. 1861.

Eldest son of George Hickson Fagan (1778-1821), *q.v.*, and Harriet Sarah his wife. Cousin-german of George Hickson Fagan (1810-1876), *q.v.* *m.* Benares, 30 Jan. 1839, Louisa, 3rd dau. of David Williamson, *q.v.* (*See also* Henry Edward Pearson, and George Ramsay.) Ed. Charterhouse; admitted 1820.

Services: Cornet d.d. 6th L.C. 25 July 1828; do. 8th L.C. 23 Feb. 1829. Posted as Cornet to 1st L.C. 21 Mar. 1829. Transfd. to 8th L.C. in 1829. Intr. & Qmr. 8th L.C. 19 Oct. 1830. Leave s.c. to Cape 9 Sept. 1832 till 28 June 1834. A.D.C. to Actg. G.G., Sir C. Metcalfe, 21 Mar. 1835; do. to G.G. 7 Apr. 1836 till 16 Oct. 1837. Asst. to A.G.G., Saugor & Narbada territories, 9 Oct. 1837 till 5 Feb. 1838. Dy. Paymr. at Benares 7 Sept. 1838 till 1850. Leave s.c. 2 yrs. to Cape 28 Feb. 1842. Cashiered by G.C.M. 19 May 1850. Restored 3 Dec. 1851 (G.G.O. of 20 Feb. 1852.) Returned from fur. 2 Apr. 1852.

Refs.: Burke's *Royal Families*, Ped. lxii. Burke's *Landed Gentry of Ireland*, p. 214, *s.n.* Fagan, formerly of Feltrim, co. Dublin. *I.M.* 1850, pp. 189, 322, 379, 384, 414; 1852, p. 23. *Charterhouse School List.* *G.M.* 1861, i. 231. *The Times*, 10 Jan. 1861.

FAGAN, Christopher Sullivan (1781-1843). Major General, C.B. Colonel 37th N.I. *b.* 22 Mar. 1781. Cadet 1798. Admitted 9 Dec. 1800. Ensign 28 Sept. 1799. Lieut. 28 Oct. 1799. Capt. 18 Feb. 1808. Major 22 Feb. 1811. Lt. Col. 22 Sept. 1821. Col. 5 June 1829. Maj. Gen. 28 June 1838. *d.* Conock Manor House, nr. Devizes, Wilts., 26 May 1843.

Of Hendon House, Hendon. (Of Lichfield House, Richmond.) *bapt.* St. Mary of Shandon, Cork, 30 Mar. 1781. 5th son of John Fagan, of Kiltallagh, co. Kerry, and Elizabeth his wife, only child of George Hickson. Brother of John Fagan (1784-1809), *q.v.*, and cousin-german of Robert Fagan, *q.v.* *m.* 1st, Muttra, 24 July 1809, Agnes, dau. of Christopher Baldock, of New Malton, Yorks., and sister of Christopher Baldock, *q.v.* (*See also* John Howard Kyan.) (She died 19 Apr. 1826, aged 36.) Father of George Hickson Fagan (1810-1876), *q.v.* *m.* 2nd, 29 Mar. 1828, Elizabeth Jane, 3rd dau. of George Moule, of Melksham, and sister of John Moule, *q.v.* (She died 17 Oct. 1882.)

Services : Posted as Ensign to 2/18th N.I. May 1801. Second Mahratta War ; Bundelkhand 1803-4 ; Kapsa ; capture of Gwalior ; defeat of Rajah Ram Singh on 2 July 1804 ; capture of Jaitpur 28 July 1804 (s.w.) ; Lieut. 2/18th N.I. Adjt. 2/18th N.I. July 1804 till Feb. 1808. Capt. Lt. 18th N.I. 14 June 1805. Fort Adjt. and Bk. Mr. at Chunar 14 Nov. 1809. Agent for army clothing at Fatehgarh 11 Sept. 1813 till 15 May 1824. Transfd. as Major to 1/18th N.I. ; as Lt. Col. to 1/6th N.I. Bdr. to comd. 6th Inf. Bde., 2nd Div., 9 Jan. 1826. Siege and capture of Bhurtpore (*Lond. Gaz.* 7 Apr. 1826). Fur. p.a. 4 June 1826 till 9 Nov. 1829. Transfd. as Col. from 44th to 50th N.I. 5 Dec. 1829 ; to 73rd N.I. 13 Jan. 1830 ; to 61st N.I. 30 Nov. 1830. Bdr. 25 Nov. 1830. Comdt. fortress of Agra 1 Jan. 1831. Bdr. on the Est. 13 Oct. 1831. To comd. troops in Rohilkhand 22 Nov. 1831. Comdd. Mewar F.F. 7 Jan. 1833 till 7 Jan. 1835. To comd. 2nd Inf. Bde. for Rajputana 1 Nov. 1834. Transfd. to 37th N.I. 29 July 1833. Fur. p.a. 4 Apr. 1835 till 3 Dec. 1838 ; fur. s.c. 19 Feb. 1839 till death. C.B. 2 Jan. 1827.

Refs. : Burke's *Landed Gentry of Ireland*, p. 214, *s.n.* Fagan, formerly of Feltrim, co. Dublin. *A.J.* xxv. *E.I.M.C.* i. 325-9. *G.M.* 1843, ii. 319. *The Times*, 1 and 2 June 1843. Will dated 30 Apr. 1842 ; proved 21 May 1844.

FAGAN, George Hickson (1778-1821). Lieutenant Colonel, 29th N.I. *b.* 3 Nov. 1778. Cadet 1794. Admitted 4 Feb. 1797. Ensign 10 Oct. 1795. Lieut. 7 Dec. 1796. Capt. 21 Sept. 1804. Major 7 Apr. 1814. Lt. Col. 10 June 1818. *d.* Calcutta 24 May 1821.

bapt. Coreagia (? Correggio, Italy) 8 Sept. 1779. 3rd son of John Fagan, of Kiltallagh, and Elizabeth his wife. Brother of James Patrick Fagan, *q.v.*, and cousin-german of Christopher Fagan, *q.v. m.* Berhampore, 7 Jan. 1811, Miss Harriet Sarah Lawtie. (*See also* Christopher Fagan.) Father of Christopher George Fagan, *q.v.*

Services : Fourth Mysore War ; Seringapatam (s.w.—lost left arm). Transfd. from 2nd N.I. to 2/18th N.I. 29 May 1800. Asst. Sec. Mily. Board 1802. D.A.G. of the Army (with official rank of Major) Mar. 1808. A.G. (with official rank of Lt. Col.)10 Dec. 1811 till 14 Nov. 1816. Major 2/25th N.I. Leave s.c. 10 mos. to Cape 12 Jan. 1816 ; fur. s.c. from Cape 14 Nov. 1816 till 1820. Transfd. as Lt. Col. to 28th N.I. in 1818 ; to 29th N.I. in 1819.

Refs. : Burke's *Landed Gentry of Ireland*, p. 214, *s.n.* Fagan, formerly of Feltrim, co. Dublin. *E.I.M.C.* i. 365-70. *A.J.* xiii. 435. M.I. in S. Park St. cemetery, Calcutta.

FAGAN, George Hickson (1810-1876). Lieut. Colonel. Engineers. *b.* 18 Aug. 1810. Cadet 1830. Arrived in India 8 Mar. 1831. 2nd Lieut. 4 Nov. 1829. Lieut. 20 May 1839. Capt. 5 Dec. 1848. Retired 6 Feb. 1856. Hon. Lt. Col. 6 Feb. 1856. *d.* Lea Grove, Clevedon, Somerset, 23 Nov. 1876.

bapt. Chunar 28 Feb. 1811. Eldest son of Christopher Sullivan Fagan, *q.v.*, and Agnes his first wife. Cousin-german of Christopher George Fagan, *q.v. m.* 1st, Barrackpore, 28 Feb. 1839, Frances Brand, dau. of Francis Hedger, of Prior Lodge, Bath, and Garston Hall, Surrey. (She died Dibrugarh, Assam, 11 Apr. 1847, aged 28.) *m.* 2nd, St. Mary Abbott's, Kensington, 27 Nov. 1849, Mary, eldest dau. of Capt. Thomas Pickering Clarke, R.N., of Perrymead, Bath. Addiscombe Cadet 31 Jan. 1828 till 12 June 1829. Chatham 6 Aug. 1829 till 8 July 1830.

Services : Apptd. Asst. to Supt. of road from Delhi to Allahabad 8 Mar. 1833. Actg. 2nd Lieut. 26 Mar. 1833. Fur. s.c. 27 Jan. 1843 till 21 Jan. 1845. Executive Engr. Upper Assam Div., P.W.D., 28 Mar. 1845. Fur. 10 Sept. 1848 till 8 Feb. 1850. Garr. Engr. at Fort William 11 July 1854 till retirement. No record of active service.

Refs. : Burke's *Landed Gentry of Ireland*, p. 214, *s.n.* Fagan, formerly of Feltrim, co. Dublin. *The Times*, 29 Nov. 1876.

FAGAN, James Patrick (1788-1863). Lieut. Colonel. 9th N.I. *bapt.* St. Mary of Shandon, Cork, 17 Mar. 1788. Cadet 1805. Arrived in India 19 Sept. 1808. Ensign 19 Sept. 1806. Lieut. 17 Oct. 1807. Capt. 1 May 1820. Major 15 Sept. 1833. Retired 31 Mar. 1835. Hon. Lt. Col. 28 Nov. 1854. *d.* St. Servans, nr. St. Malo, France, 16 Apr. 1863.

THE BENGAL ARMY, 1758-1834

8th and youngest son of John Fagan, of Kiltallagh, and Elizabeth his wife. Brother of John Fagan, *q.v.* *m.* (before 1812) Stephanie le Mere. (She died 16 Jan. 1873.)

Services : Barasat C.C. for 7 mos. Posted as Lieut. to 1/8th N.I. Capture of Mauritius 1810 ; Lieut. 2nd Bn. Bengal Vols. Intr. & Qmr. 1/8th N.I. 11 July 1814 till 1817. Apptd. Bde. Major 1st Bde., 4th (Dinapore) Div., for Nepal 15 Nov. 1814. Nepal War 1814-5 ; Bde. Major. Nepal War 1816 ; Lieut. 1/8th N.I., in 2nd Bde., Left Column (India medal). Adjt. Native Invalids at Allahabad 24 June 1817. Dy. Paymr. Rajputana F.F. 23 June 1818 till 4 Apr. 1834. Dy. Postmaster do. 13 Mar. 1819. Transfd. to 9th N.I. (late 1/8th) May 1824. Fur. p.a. 28 Feb. 1835 till retirement. Afterwards a Coolie Stipendiary Mgte. at Trinidad.

Refs. : Burke's *Landed Gentry of Ireland*, p. 215, *s.n.* Fagan, formerly of Feltrim, co. Dublin. *I.N.* 1848, p. 375. *G.M.* 1863, i. 674. *The Times*, 23 Apr. 1863.

FAGAN, John (1784-1809). Lieutenant, 18th N.I. *b.* 20 Nov. 1784. Cadet 1803. Arrived in India 2 Dec. 1804. Ensign 2 Nov. 1804. Lieut. 2 Nov. 1804. *d. unm.* Mallow, co. Cork, 24 Oct. 1809.

bapt. St. Mary of Shandon, Cork, 23 Nov. 1784. 7th son of John Fagan, of Kiltallagh, and Elizabeth his wife. Brother of Patrick Charles Fagan, *q.v.*

Services : Posted as Lieut. to 2/18th N.I. in 1805. Fur. 21 Aug. 1808 till death. No record of active service.

Refs. : Burke's *Landed Gentry of Ireland*, p. 215, *s.n.* Fagan, formerly of Feltrim, co. Dublin. Burke's *Commoners*, iv. 631.

FAGAN, Leonard Cornwall (1807-1832). Lieutenant, Bengal Eur. Regt. *b.* Dublin 6 Oct. 1807. Cadet 1825. Arrived in India 21 Oct. 1826. Ensign 27 June 1826. Lieut. 4 Jan. 1829. *d.* at sea, 11 May 1832, on board the *Royal Sovereign.*

Son of James Fagan, timber merchant, and Catherine his wife.

Services : Ensign d.d. 7th N.I. 9 Nov. 1826. Posted to 11th N.I. 8 Jan. 1827 ; exchanged to 2nd Bengal Eur. Regt. 31 May 1827. Fur. s.c. 27 Mar. 1832. No record of active service.

Refs. : A.J. N.S. ix. 51.

FAGAN, Patrick Charles (1780-1808). Capt. Lieutenant, 12th N.I. *b.* Cork 21 Mar. 1780. Cadet 1797. Admitted 7 Sept. 1798. Ensign 5 Oct. 1798. Lieut. 1 Nov. 1798. Capt. Lt. 1 Oct. 1807. *d.* Patna (? Bankipore) 25 Oct. 1808.

bapt. St. Anne's, Cork, 2 Apr. 1780. 4th son of John Fagan, of Kiltallagh, and Elizabeth his wife. Brother of Christopher Sullivan Fagan, *q.v.*, and cousin-german of Robert Fagan, *q.v.* *m.* Maria

(Mary Anne), dau. of Rev. James Slator, rector of Naas. (She died 16 June 1859, aged 77.)

Services : Second Mahratta War ; Agra ; Laswari ; Monson's retreat ; capture of Deig ; Bhurtpore ; Lieut. 12th N.I. Adjt. 1/12th N.I. 1805 till death. Operations in Oudh 1808 ; Bhadri ; Samanpur ; Gurha ; Capt. Lt. 1/12th N.I.

Refs. : Burke's *Landed Gentry of Ireland*, p. 214, *s.n.* Fagan, formerly of Feltrim, co. Dublin.

FAGAN, Robert (1778-1799). Lieutenant, Infantry. *b.* Santa Cruz 16 Mar. 1778. Cadet 1794. Admitted 4 Feb. 1797. Ensign 8 Oct. 1795. Lieut. 3 Oct. 1796. *d.* Berhampore 27 Jan. 1799.

2nd son of Robert Fagan, of Philadelphia. Brother of Christopher Fagan, *q.v.*, and cousin-german of James Patrick Fagan, *q.v.*

Services : N.F.P.

Refs. : Burke's *Landed Gentry of Ireland*, p. 214, *s.n.* Fagan, formerly of Feltrim, co. Dublin. *A.A.R.* i. 180.

FAIRFAX, John (*d.* 1784). Major, Infantry. Cadet 1767. Ensign 26 July 1767. Lieut. 25 Apr. 1769. Capt. 9 May 1777. Major 27 July 1781. *d.* in England 2 Jan. 1784.

Services : First Rohilla War ; battle of St. George ; Lieut. 8th Bn. Sepoys. Went home with Govt. despatches in 1782.

Refs. : Will dated 19 Feb. 1782.

FAIRFAX, Samuel (1776-1798). Cadet. Infantry. Subsequently Writer, B.C.S. *b.* Burntisland, co. Fife, 1 June 1776. Cadet 1796. Admitted 2 Feb. 1798. Resigned 10 Sept. 1798. *d. unm.* Calcutta 19 Nov. 1798.

2nd son of Sir William George Fairfax, Kt., Vice Adm. of the Red (*D.N.B.*), and Margaret his 2nd wife, dau. of Samuel Charters, solicitor of customs for Scotland. Nephew of Thomas Charters, *q.v.* Elder brother of Sir Henry Fairfax, 1st Bart.

Services : Apptd. a Writer, B.C.S., 9 Oct. 1797. Arrived in India 10 Sept. 1798.

Refs. : Burke's *Peerage*, 1923, p. 1453, *s.n.* Cameron-Ramsay-Fairfax-Lucy, Bart. *A.A.R.* i. 179.

FAIRFIELD or FAIRFULL, Andrew (*d.* 1781). Lieutenant, 29th N.I. Cadet 1779. Ensign 10 Sept. 1779. Lieut. 3 Apr. 1781. *d.* Cawnpore 24 Apr. 1781 ; bur. there 26 Apr.

Brother of Robert Fairfull.

Services : Lieut. 1/29th N.I., in 2nd Bde., at date of death.

Refs. : Will dated 4 Apr. 1781.

Note : Dodwell & Miles and the burial register both give his name as Fairfield ; it appears as Fairfull in his Will.

FAIRHEAD, John Assey (1804-1865). Lieut. Colonel. 2nd Bengal Eur. Regt. b. Norwich 3 July 1804. Cadet 1821. Arrived in India 23 Mar. 1822. Ensign 29 Sept. 1821. Lieut. 11 Sept. 1823. Capt. 26 June 1833. Major 23 Oct. 1845. Invalided 8 Jan. 1847. Retired 10 Aug. 1854. Hon. Lt. Col. 28 Nov. 1854. d. Western Villas, Maida Hill, London, 16 Mar. 1865.

m. Murshidabad, Bengal, 15 Feb. 1826, Maria Frances Corfield. (*See also* Charles Boulton (1806-1860), James Hunter (1808-1867), Alexander Mercer, and Sir Thomas Seaton.) (She died 1869.)

Services : Posted as Ensign to Bengal Eur. Regt. Transfd. to 14th N.I. July 1823 ; to 28th N.I. (late 1/14th) May 1824. Adjt. Magh Levy 11 Dec. 1824 till 18 Nov. 1825. First Burma War ; Chittagong 1825 ; Adjt. Magh Levy (India medal). Adjt. Murshidabad Provl. Bn. 29 Aug. 1826 till 1830. Fur. s.c. 27 Feb. 1836 till 10 Dec. 1838. Posted to newly-formed 2nd Bengal Eur. Regt. 8 Oct. 1839. Operations against the Hill tribes in Sind 1845 ; capture of Trakki fort ; Capt. 2nd Bengal Eur. Regt. To do duty with Eur. Invalids at Chunar 11 Feb. 1848. Fur. 10 Feb. 1852 till retirement.

Refs. : G.M. 1865, i. 534. *The Times,* 18 Mar. 1865.

FAIRLIE, William. Lieutenant. Infantry. Cadet 1779. Ensign 18 Aug. 1779. Lieut. 3 Apr. 1781. Struck off 1781.

Services : N.F.P. (? Of the firm of Fairlie, Gilmore & Co., Calcutta. Sheriff of Calcutta 1808.)

FAIRLY, Edward (d. 1784). Cadet, Infantry. Cadet (?). d. Chunar 29 July 1784.

Services : N.F.P.

FAITHFULL, Alfred (1794-1823). Lieutenant, 20th N.I. b. Warfield, Berks., 22 Sept. 1794. Cadet 1813. Ensign (16 Dec. 1814) 5 June 1815. Lieut. 9 Apr. 1816. d. 11 Sept. 1823.

bapt. 2 Aug. 1795. Son of Rev. John Faithfull, vicar of Warfield, and Patty his wife. Brother of Edward Faithfull, q.v.

Services : Posted as Ensign to 1/20th N.I. Lieut. 1/20th N.I. Fur. 1820 till 1823 (? till death). No record of active service.

FAITHFULL, Charles Complin (1779-1804). Lieutenant, 4th N.I. *bapt.* Winchester 6 Oct. 1779. Cadet 1800. Arrived in India 22 Aug. 1801. Ensign 11 Sept. 1801. Lieut. 13 July 1803. d. 13 Nov. 1804 : kld. in action at the battle of Deig.

Son of Richard Faithfull and Martha his wife. Brother of William Conrad Faithfull, q.v.

Services : Second Mahratta War ; Aligarh ; battle of Deig (kld.) ; Lieut. 1/4th N.I.

Refs. : Pester, p. 346. Will dated Aligarh 28 Oct. 1803 ; proved 26 Feb. 1805.

FAITHFULL, Edward (1784-1806). Capt. Lieutenant, Artillery. *bapt.* St. Thomas's, Winchester, 10 May 1784. Cadet 1800. Arrived in India 9 Feb. 1802. Lieut. 9 Apr. 1802. Capt. Lt. 1 Aug. 1805. *d.* Guna, C.I., 4 Dec. 1806.

Son of Rev. John Faithfull and Patty his wife. Brother of John Faithfull, *q.v.* Woolwich Cadet ; nominated for R.M.A. 20 Sept. 1799 ; obtained his certificate 7 June 1801.

Services : Second Mahratta War ; reduction of Cuttack 1803 ; capture of Barabati (w.) ; Lieut. 7th Coy. 1st Bn. Capture of Gohad 1806 ; Lieut. 2nd Coy. 3rd Bn. Art.

FAITHFULL, Henry (1783-1840). Major General, Artillery. *bapt.* Hertingfordbury, Herts., 11 Mar. 1783. Cadet 1797. Arrived in India 22 Aug. 1801. Fireworker 22 Sept. 1798. Lieut. 23 Feb. 1802. Capt. Lt. 29 Dec. 1804. Capt. 8 Dec. 1810. Major 1 Sept. 1818. Lt. Col. 1 May 1824. Bt. Col. 5 June 1829. Lt. Col. Comdt. 20 Aug. 1831. Maj. Gen. 28 June 1838. *d.* Calcutta, 25 Mar. 1840, " of a spasmodic affection."

Son of John Faithfull and Martha his wife. (*Probably* brother of John Faithfull, *q.v.*) *m.* Calcutta 13 July 1812, Miss Frances Williams. (*See also* Richard Coventry Faithfull.) (She died 5 Feb. 1878, aged 86.) Ed. Winchester 1793 till 15 Sept. 1796. Woolwich Cadet ; nominated for R.M.A. 5 Sept. 1798 ; obtained his certificate 20 Feb. 1801.

Services : Second Mahratta War ; Chaukandi. Capture of Java 1811 ; Capt. comdg. 1st Coy. 2nd Bn. Foot Art. Offg. Asst. Comy. of Stores at Fort William 15 June 1812. Agent for gun carriages at Kasipur 31 July 1813. Principal Comy. of Ord. 10 Nov. 1821 till 28 May 1824. Fur. s.c. 19 Nov. 1824 till 10 Feb. 1829. To comd. Foot Art. at Mhow 6 Oct. 1836. Actg. Comdt. of Art., with rank of Bdr., and a seat at the Mily. Board, 22 Nov. 1836. Comdd. Bengal Art. till 21 Dec. 1838.

Refs. : Kirby. E.I.M.C. iii. 190-1. *G.M.* 1840, ii. 558. *I.N.* vol. i. p. 12. M.I. Dum-Dum burial ground.

FAITHFULL, John (1779-1804). Lieutenant, 15th N.I. *bapt.* East Hendred, Berks., 29 June 1779. Cadet 1794. Admitted 3 Mar. 1797. Ensign 25 Oct. 1795. Lieut. 25 Apr. 1797. *d.* at sea, 13 Mar. 1804, on board the *Windham.*

Son of John Faithfull and Patty his wife. Brother of William Richard Lee Faithfull, *q.v.* Ed. Winchester ; scholar 1792.

Services : Operations in Jumna Doab 1803 ; Sasni ; Bijaigarh ; Kachaura ; Lieut. 15th N.I. Second Mahratta War ; battle of Delhi ; Agra ; Laswari ; Lieut. 15th N.I.

Refs. : Kirby (where he is stated to have been a son of William Faithfull, solicitor in Winchester).

FAITHFULL, Richard Coventry (1787-1835). Lieut. Colonel, 14th N.I. *b.* Overton, Hants, 9 Nov. 1787. Cadet 1804. Arrived in India 6 Apr. 1806. Ensign 22 Mar. 1806. Lieut. 31 May 1807. Capt. 15 Feb. 1824. Major 30 May 1829. Lt. Col. 23 Feb. 1835. *d.* Moradabad, U.P., 13 Aug. 1835.

bapt. St. Peter Cheesehill, Winchester, 1 Feb. 1804. Son of Richard Coventry Faithfull and Martha his wife. Brother of William Conrad Faithfull, *q.v. m.* Calcutta, 8 Jan. 1816, Miss Catherine Williams. (*See also* Henry Faithfull.) (She died Winchester, 5 June 1880, aged 83.)

Services : Posted as Ensign to 2/10th N.I. Lieut. 2/10th N.I. Served with Pioneers 1809-15. Capture of Java 1811 ; Lieut. Pioneers. Reduction of Kalinjar 2 Feb. 1812 (s.w.) ; Lieut. 8th Coy. Pioneers. (*Lond. Gaz.* 30 Oct. 1812.) Nepal War 1814-5 ; Lieut. comdg. 8th Coy. Pioneers, Bde. Major in 3rd Div. Leave s.c. 4 mos. to sea 12 May 1815. Bde. Major Cuttack 2 May 1817. Operations in Cuttack against the Paiks 1817, under Sir Gabriel Martindell, *q.v.* Actg. A.A.G. 13 Mar. 1820. Bde. Major Dinapore ; do. Berhampore 21 Feb. 1822 ; do. to troops in Cuttack 11 Dec. 1822. Transfd. to 14th N.I. (late 1/10th) May 1824. Fur. s.c. 13 Feb. 1827 till 2 June 1831. Comr. with Baji Rao, the ex-Peishwa, 6 Aug. till 1 Nov. 1831. Posted as Lt. Col. to 14th N.I. 25 June 1835.

Refs. : G.M. 1836, i. 444. A.J. N.S. xix. 166. Will dated 18 Jan. 1831 ; admon. 10 June 1836.

FAITHFULL, William Conrad (1782-1838). Colonel, C.B., 29th N.I. *bapt.* St. John's, nr. Winchester, 26 Dec. 1782. Cadet 1798. Admitted 27 Dec. 1799. Ensign 29 Oct. 1799. Lieut. 29 Oct. 1799. Capt. 20 July 1808. Major 7 June 1819. Lt. Col. 1 May 1824. Col. 1 Dec. 1829. *d.* at sea 16 Mar. 1838, on board the *Cornwall*, on his passage from India to the Cape.

Son of Richard Faithfull and Martha his wife. Brother of Charles Complin Faithfull, *q.v. m.* Calcutta, 26 June 1805, Miss Maria Agg. (She died Calcutta, 2 Apr. 1851, aged 65.) His daus. *m.* John Dickson Dyke Bean, *q.v.*, Charles Chester, *q.v.*, Thomas Robert Fell, *q.v.*, James Rutherford Lumley, *q.v.*, John Kennedy McCausland, *q.v.*, and John Moule, *q.v.*

Services : Second Mahratta War ; Aligarh ; battle of Deig ; Lieut. 4th N.I. Adjt. 1/4th N.I. 1805-9. Capture of Java 1811 ;

Capt. 4th Bn. Bengal Vols. Fur. s.c. 12 Feb. 1812 till Nov. 1814. Nepal War 1815; capture of Almora; Capt. 1/4th N.I. (*Lond. Gaz.* 16 Nov. 1815.) Leave s.c. to N.S.W. 21 Feb. 1817. Comdd. Agra Najib Bn. 19 Jan. till 18 Sept. 1819. Major 2/4th N.I. Posted as Lt. Col. to 23rd N.I. (late 2/4th) May 1824. Siege and capture of Bhurtpore (s.w.); Lt. Col. comdg. 23rd N.I. Posted as Col. to 23rd N.I. 18 Nov. 1830; to 49th N.I. 5 Nov. 1831. To comd. Karnal and Sirhind Div. 18 Apr. 1834. Transfd. to 17th N.I. 22 July 1835; to 29th N.I. 28 Nov. 1837. Leave s.c. 2 yrs. to Cape 8 Mar. 1838. C.B. 27 Sept. 1831.

Refs.: *A.J.* N.S. xxvi. 285. *G.M.* 1838, ii. 342. Will dated 9 Feb. 1838; proved 12 Oct. 1838. M.I. in St. John's, Calcutta.

FAITHFULL, William Richard Lee (1792-1836). Captain, Invalid Est. 43rd N.I. *bapt.* Warfield, Berks., 15 July 1792. Cadet 1809. Ensign 6 Aug. 1812. Lieut. 1 Sept. 1815. Capt. 23 Feb. 1827. Invalided 23 Apr. 1830. *d.* Chunar 18 Nov. 1836.

Son of Rev. John Faithfull, vicar of Warfield, and Patty his wife. Brother of Alfred Faithfull, *q.v.*

Services: Cadet d.d. 4th N.I. in 1811. Posted as Ensign to Bengal Eur. Regt. in Java in 1812. Transfd. to 22nd N.I. in 1813. Nepal War 1816; Lieut. 2/22nd N.I., in 3rd Bde., Centre Column. Served with Pioneers 1817-24. Transfd. to 43rd N.I. (late 1/22nd) May 1824. With Pioneers 1825-6, and 7 Nov. 1826 till 1827.

Refs.: M.I. at Chunar.

FALLON, Patrick (*d.* 1786). Lieutenant, Infantry. Cadet 1778. Ensign 1778. Lieut. 1778. *d.* Dacca 7 Nov. 1786.

Brother of Lawrence Fallon, of Bernard St., London.

Services: Lieut. 2/2nd Bengal Eur. Regt. in Oct. 1779. Granted 3 yrs. fur. 20 Oct. 1786.

Refs.: Will dated 5 Nov. 1786.

FALLS, John. Captain. Infantry. Cadet 1771. Ensign 1 Feb. 1773. Lieut. 19 Feb. 1778. Capt. 7 June 1781. Resigned 14 Oct. 1789.

Services: First Rohilla War; battle of St. George. Supy. Capt., unposted, in July 1787.

FALVEY, Dennis Morris (*d.* 1806). Major, 19th N.I. Cadet 1779. Admitted 14 Sept. 1779. Ensign 18 Sept. 1780. Lieut. 27 May 1781. Capt. 31 Aug. 1798. Major 21 Sept. 1804. *d. unm.* Allahabad 27 Oct. 1806.

Services: Fur. 27 Oct. 1785 till 25 Nov. 1788. Capt. 1st N.I. Transfd. to 10th N.I. 29 May 1800; to 19th N.I.

Refs.: Will proved 20 June 1807.

FANE, William John Jarvis (1808-1830). Cornet, 5th L.C. *bapt.* Watlington, Oxon., 6 Aug. 1808. Cadet 1825. Cornet 16 Feb. 1826. *d.* at sea, 13 July 1830, on board the *Mountstuart Elphinstone*, on the voyage to England.

2nd son of John Fane, of Wormsley, high sheriff of Oxfordshire in 1836, and Elizabeth his wife, dau. of William Lowndes Stone, of Brightwell Park. *m.* Allahabad, 24 Nov. 1829, Miss Decima Matthews.
Services : Cornet d.d. 1st L.C. 8 July 1826. Posted as Cornet to 5th L.C. 26 Sept. 1826. Fur. s.c. 5 June 1830 till death. No record of active service.
Refs. : Burke's *Peerage*, 1923, p. 2303, *s.n.* Westmorland, E.

FARIE, Allan Scott (1801-1823). Ensign, Infantry. *b.* Rutherglen, co. Lanark, 25 Sept. 1801. Cadet 1822. Ensign (?). *d.* Calcutta, Apr. 1823, on board the *Marquis of Hastings*.

Son of James Farie, of Farme, co. Lanark, J.P. and D.L., coal merchant, and Jane his wife, dau. of James Scott, of Glasgow.
Services : Ensign R. Lanarkshire Mil. 26 Dec. 1820.
Refs. : Burke's *Landed Gentry*, 13th edn., p. 607, *s.n.* Farie, of Farme, co. Lanark. *S.M.* 1823, ii. 640.

FARINGTON, Edward Fraser (1792-1812). Ensign, 15th N.I. Attached to 3rd Bengal Vol. Bn. *b.* Broxbourne, Herts., 21 Mar. 1792. Cadet 1807. Arrived in India 25 Oct. 1808. Ensign 3 Nov. 1807. *d. unm.* Java 16 Mar. 1812.

Of Cucumber Hall (now Norris Lodge), Hoddesdon, Herts. 4th son of William Farington, H.E.I.C.N.S., and Anne Frances his wife, dau. of William Nash, of Hoddesdon. Nephew of Joseph Farington, the artist (*D.N.B.*).
Services : Posted as Ensign to 15th N.I. in 1809. Capture of Java 1811 ; Ensign 3rd Bn. Bengal Vols.
Refs. : Cussan's *Herts.*, ii. 194-5. Will dated 2 Aug. 1811 ; proved in 1812.

FARIS, Thomas (1791-1816). Lieutenant, 18th N.I. *b.* Dublin 3 Aug. 1791. Cadet 1808. Arrived in India 6 Nov. 1809. Ensign 23 Mar. 1811. Lieut. 16 Dec. 1814. *d.* Ganjpura, Khurda district, 2 Apr. 1816 : kld. in action.

Son of Thomas Faris, of 5 Gardiner's Pl., Dublin, atty., and Elizabeth Elinor Beggs his wife.
Services : Barasat C.C. Posted as Ensign to 18th N.I. in 1811. Nepal War 1816 ; Lieut. 1/18th N.I., in 1st Bde., Rt. Column. Cuttack insurrection 1816 (kld.) ; Lieut. 1/18th N.I.

FARLEY, William Johnson (1791-1831). Lieutenant, Invalid Est. 23rd N.I. *b.* Droitwich, Worcs., Sept. 1791. Cadet 1809. Ensign 23 Oct. 1812. Lieut. 19 Sept. 1816. Invalided 10 July 1823. *d.* Monghyr, B. & O., 28 May 1831.

Son of George Farley, and grandson of Thomas Farley of Worcester. *m.* Calcutta, 17 Aug. 1817, Catherine, eldest dau. of Charles Nicholson, of Jessore, indigo planter, and widow of ―― Kerin, of Sealdah, Calcutta.

Services : Barasat C.C. Cadet d.d. 15th N.I. 1811-2. Posted as Ensign to 1/23rd N.I. in 1813. With 3rd Gren. Bn. 1815-6. Third Mahratta War ; Lieut. 2/23rd N.I.

FARMER, Charles Finch (1800-1852). Major, Invalid Est. 21st N.I. *b.* London 8 Jan. 1800. Cadet 1818. Admitted 4 Sept. 1819. Ensign (?). Lieut. 28 Apr. 1821. Capt. 12 June 1833. Major 27 Aug. 1847. Invalided 1 Dec. 1849. *d.* Mussoorie 4 Feb. 1852.

Son of W. G. Farmer, of Kentish Town, London, a steward. His application to be designated "Charles Finch Palmer" was refused 4 July 1832. *m.* 1st, Agra, 22 Jan. 1829, Miss Eliza Gillanders, aged 14. (*See also* William Worsley Davis.) (She died Delhi 16 Jan. 1836.) *m.* 2nd, Karnal, 13 Sept. 1838, Delia Susan, 2nd dau. of George Weyland Moseley, *q.v.* (*See also* Hugh Johnson and William Ramsey.)

Services : Ensign d.d. Bengal Eur. Regt. Posted as Lieut. to 1/22nd N.I. Transfd. to 9th N.I. 11 July 1823 ; to 21st N.I. (late 2/9th) May 1824. Actg. Adjt. 21st N.I. 8 Sept. 1824. Siege and capture of Bhurtpore ; Lieut. 21st N.I. (India medal). Adjt. 21st N.I. 8 Sept. 1828. Fur. s.c. 1 Mar. 1830 till 10 Dec. 1832. With 1st L.I. Bn. in 1842. Bde. Major at Barrackpore 17 May till 13 Sept. 1844.

Refs. : Will dated 15 Aug. 1850 ; proved 24 June 1852.

FARMER, George (1807-1894). Lieut. Colonel. 66th N.I. *bapt.* The More, Salop, 8 Oct. 1807. Cadet 1823. Arrived in India 9 Feb. 1825. Ensign 12 Sept. 1824. Lieut. 5 May 1826. Capt. 5 May 1834. Bt. Major 9 Nov. 1846. Retired 24 July 1850. Hon. Lt. Col. 28 Nov. 1854. *d.* 7 Jan. 1894.

Son of Richard Farmer. *m.* Ludhiana, 23 May 1842, Anne Maria, dau. of J. Michael, of Ludhiana.

Services : Posted as Ensign to 66th N.I. in 1825. With 2nd L.I. Bn. in 1842. Fur. 1846 till 25 Oct. 1847. No record of active service.

FARMER, John (1809-1830). Lieutenant, 9th L.C. *bapt.* Churchstoke, co. Montgomery, 1 July 1809. Cadet 1825. Cornet 10 Sept. 1825. Lieut. 26 Apr. 1827. *d.* Montgomery 25 Feb. 1830.

THE BENGAL ARMY, 1758-1834   163

Son of Edward Farmer, Capt. Montgomery Yeomanry Cav.
Services : Posted as Cornet to 9th L.C. Fur. s.c. 2 Feb. 1827
till death. No record of active service.

FARMER, Samuel (*d.* 1794). Major, Infantry. Cadet 1768.
Ensign 27 Jan. 1769. Lieut. 15 May 1770. Capt. 20 Sept. 1771.
Major 7 Feb. 1784. *d.* Cawnpore 27 Nov. 1794.
Of London. *m.* Calcutta, 3 Mar. 1789, Miss Susanna Robiniana
Brown.
Services : Capt. 2/1st Bengal Eur. Regt. in Oct. 1779. Major
comdg. 23rd Bn. Sepoys in July 1787.
Refs. : Will dated Apr. 1793 ; proved in 1794.

FARMER, William. Lieutenant. Infantry. Cadet 1764. Ensign
1 Oct. 1764. Lieut. 25 Oct. 1765. Resigned May 1766.
Services : Resigned his Commission during the " Batta mutiny."

FARNABY, Leonard Motley (1792-1811). Fireworker, Artillery.
b. West Wickham, Kent, 13 May 1792. Cadet 1809. Admitted
3 Oct. 1810. Fireworker 6 Nov. 1809. *d.* Java 24 Aug. 1811 :
kld. in action in the attack on Fort Cornelis.
Services : Capture of Java 1811 ; Cornelis (kld.) ; Lt.F. 1st Coy.
2nd Bn. Foot Art.
Refs. : Burke's *Peerage,* 1859, p. 387, *s.n.* Farnaby, Bart., of
Kippington, Kent. *G.M.* 1811, ii. 658. Name on cenotaph " To
the Memory of the Brave " in Barrackpore Park.

FARNWORTH, John Maisterson (1806-1857). Lieutenant. 44th
N.I. *b.* London 27 Oct. 1806. Cadet 1822. Ensign 11 July
1823. Lieut. 13 May 1825. Resigned 25 Jan. 1828. *d.* Calcutta
12 Jan. 1857.
Son of Samuel Farnworth, merchant. *m.* Monghyr, B. & O.,
3 Apr. 1825, Miss Eleanor Gillies. (She died Dacca 1 Mar. 1840.)
Ed. Merchant Taylors' ; entered the school June 1817.
Services : Posted as Ensign to 43rd N.I. in 1824 ; transfd. as
Lieut. to 44th N.I. May 1825. No record of active service.
Refs. : Robinson. *I.M.* 1857, p. 146.

FARQUHAR, Andrew (*d.* 1782). Lieutenant, Infantry. Cadet
1778. Ensign 19 May 1779. Lieut. 23 Jan. 1781. *d.* Berhampore 23 Jan. 1782.
Services : N.F.P.

FARQUHAR, Robert (*d.* 1773). Ensign, Infantry. Cadet 1770.
Ensign 22 Sept. 1770. *d.* Calcutta Aug. 1773.
Services : N.F.P.

FARQUHARSON, Alexander (1794-1837). Major, Invalid Est. 74th N.I. *b.* Edinburgh 4 July 1794. Cadet 1809. Admitted 15 Feb. 1811. Ensign 2 Sept. 1812. Lieut. 16 Dec. 1814. Capt. 2 Sept. 1827. Major 23 May 1836. Invalided 30 Jan. 1837. *d.* Bareilly, U.P., 24 June 1837.

Son of Dr. William Farquharson, of Edinburgh, physician, and Mrs. Margaret Campbell his wife.

Services : Cadet d.d. 15th N.I. Posted as Ensign to 1/3rd N.I. in 1812. Actg. Intr. & Qmr. 2/3rd N.I. 2 Oct. 1823. Transfd. to 6th N.I. (late 1/3rd) May 1824. Intr. & Qmr. 6th N.I. 17 June 1824. Transfd. as Intr. & Qmr. to 6th Extra Regt. (became 74th N.I.) 12 July 1825. Actg. Fort Adjt. at Monghyr 10 Nov. 1826. Actg. D.J.A.G., Dinapore and Benares, 10 Sept. 1829.

Refs. : A.J. N.S. xxiv. 277.

FARQUHARSON, George (1798-1871). Lieut. General. 46th N.I. *b.* Calcutta 4 Dec. 1798. Cadet 1818. Admitted 14 Aug. 1819. Ensign 2 Aug. 1819. Lieut. 11 June 1820. Capt. 20 July 1832. Major 13 Mar. 1844. Lt. Col. 21 June 1850. Col. 29 Aug. 1859. Maj. Gen. 25 Jan. 1861. Lt. Gen. 25 June 1870. *d.* Weston-super-Mare 16 Sept. 1871.

Son of William Farquharson, B.C.S., Mily. Paymr. Gen., and Ann Eliza his wife. Brother of John Peere Farquharson, *q.v.*

Services : Ensign d.d. 9th N.I. Posted as Ensign to 1/9th N.I. Intr. & Qmr. 1/9th N.I. 16 Oct. 1823 till 12 Aug. 1828. Transfd. to 8th N.I. (late 1/9th) May 1824. Fur. s.c. 22 Sept. 1828 till 19 Oct. 1832. Fur. p.a. 17 Jan. 1838 till 24 Dec. 1840. In charge of Bhagulpur Hill Rangers 13 Dec. 1841 till 1843. P.A. at Manipur 1843. Bde. Major at Barrackpore 8 Dec. 1843 till 17 May 1844. Second Sikh War ; Multan ; Gujerat (s.w.) ; Major 8th N.I. (Medal with clasp). Posted as Lt. Col. to 8th N.I. June 1850 ; to 5th N.I. 5 Aug. 1852 ; to 46th N.I. 11 Sept. 1852. Bdr., 2 cl., comdg. at Multan 29 Apr. 1857. Mutiny campaign (w. in two places on outbreak of mutiny at Multan).

Refs. : The Times, 21 Sept. 1871.

FARQUHARSON, John Peere (1805-1862). Major. 8th N.I. *b.* Calcutta 28 Sept. 1805. Cadet 1823. Arrived in India 25 June 1824. Ensign 14 Jan. 1824. Lieut. 13 May 1825. Capt. 23 Feb. 1842. Retired 2 June 1847. Hon. Major 28 Nov. 1854. *d.* Brighton 21 Aug. 1862.

Son of William Farquharson, B.C.S., Commercial Resident at Patna, and Ann Eliza his wife. Brother of George Farquharson, *q.v.*

Services : Posted as Ensign to 8th N.I. Offg. Adjt. Cawnpore

THE BENGAL ARMY, 1758-1834

Provl. Bn. 10 Sept. 1827. Fur. p.a. 17 Jan. 1838 till 24 Dec. 1840. No record of active service.
Refs. : *G.M.* 1862, ii. 374. *The Times,* 21 Aug. 1862.

FARRER, Joseph Liddell (1802-?). Lieutenant, Pension Est. 12th N.I. *bapt.* London 30 June 1802. Cadet 1819. Arrived in India Jan. 1821. Ensign 16 July 1820. Lieut. 11 July 1823. Pensioned in England 9 Aug. 1823.

Eldest son of Rev. Joseph Liddell Farrer, of Lincoln's Inn, and Mary his wife, sister of Sir John Jervis Jervis-White-Jervis, 1st Bart. Cousin-german of Humphrey Jervis-White, *q.v.*

Services : Posted as Ensign to 14th N.I. in 1821. Fur. 1821 till pensioned. Transfd. as Lieut. to 12th N.I. July 1823.

Refs. : Burke's *Peerage,* 1923, p. 1254, *s.n.* Jervis-White-Jervis, Bart.

FARRINGTON, Henry Wortham (1800-1851). Major, Invalid Est. 2nd N.I. *b.* London 12 Sept. 1800. Cadet 1818. Arrived in India May 1819. Ensign 1 Dec. 1818. Lieut. 27 May 1820. Capt. 7 Apr. 1831. Major 26 Dec. 1842. Invalided 1 Jan. 1843. *d.* Ambala 24 Feb. 1851.

bapt. St. Mary's, Lambeth, Surrey, 8 Oct. 1800. Son of John Farrington, merchant, and Elizabeth Charlotte his wife. Brother of John James Farrington, *q.v.* *m.* 1st, Dinapore, 18 July 1831, Hannah Inshaw, widow of John Jones, indigo planter. (She died Dinapore, 23 Aug. 1831, aged 34.) *m.* 2nd, Calcutta, 21 Dec. 1833, Frances, widow of John Turner, solicitor of the supreme court, Calcutta. (She died Sabathu 16 Feb. 1858.)

Services : Ensign d.d. Bengal Eur. Regt. July-Oct. 1819 ; do. 2/14th N.I. Oct. 1819. Posted as Ensign to 2/1st N.I. in June 1820 ; transfd. to 2nd N.I. (late 1/1st) May 1824. Offg. Intr. & Qmr. 2nd N.I. 24 Dec. 1827 till Mar. 1829. First Afghan War ; Ghilzais 1840 (*Cal. Gaz.* 10 Feb. 1841) ; with Nott's force, operations around Kandahar ; Goaine ; recapture of Ghazni ; re-occupation of Kabul ; Capt. 2nd N.I. (Medal).

Refs. : *De Rhé-Philipe.* Will dated 19 Aug. 1850 ; proved 28 June 1851. M.I. at Ambala.

FARRINGTON, John James (1790-1858). Major General, Artillery. *b.* 13 Feb. 1790. Cadet 1807. Arrived in India 28 Oct. 1808. Fireworker 17 Sept. 1808. Lieut. 5 Dec. 1809. Capt. 8 Aug. 1821. Major 18 Jan. 1837. Lt. Col. 23 Nov. 1841. Col. 2 Feb. 1851. Maj. Gen. 28 Nov. 1854. *d.* Leamington 13 Oct. 1858.

bapt. St. Dunstan's-in-the-East, London, 17 Mar. 1790. Son of John Farrington and Elizabeth Charlotte his wife. Brother of

Henry Wortham Farrington, *q.v.* *m.* Agra, 21 Dec. 1820, Miss Jane MacLeod. (She died 4 Mar. 1876.) Woolwich Cadet; nominated to R.M.A. 30 May 1804.

Services : Capture of Java 1811 ; Lieut. 1st Coy. 2nd Bn. Foot Art. (Medal). Capture of Jokyakarta 1812 ; operations in I. of Celebes 1816 ; returned from Java in Dec. 1816. Third Mahratta War ; Lieut. 5th Troop H.A. Operations in Kotah 1821 (*Lond. Gaz.* 20 Mar. 1822). Siege and capture of Bhurtpore ; Capt. comdg. 4th Troop 2nd Bde. H.A. (India medal). Comdd. 3rd Troop 1st Bde. 1828-30. To comd. 3rd Troop 3rd Bde. 9 Mar. 1836. To comd. Nimach Div. Art. 6 Oct. 1838. Comdd. Mewar Div. Art. till 15 Sept. 1839. To comd. 2nd Bde. H.A. 6 Nov. 1840. Posted to 4th Bn. Foot Art. 15 Mar. 1842. Gwalior campaign ; Maharajpur ; Lt. Col. comdg. 4th Bn. (Bronze star). Transfd. to 7th Bn. Actg. Comdt. Bengal Art. May-June 1851. Fur. s.c. 22 July 1851 till death.

Refs. : *G.M.* 1858, ii. 542. *The Times,* 18 Oct. 1858.

FAST, John Wells (*d.* 1849). Major General. Colonel 25th N.I. Cadet 1797. Admitted 8 Feb. 1799. Ensign 4 Oct. 1798. Lieut. 1 Nov. 1798. Capt. 4 Apr. 1807. Major 4 Mar. 1818. Lt. Col. 11 July 1823. Col. 5 June 1829. Maj. Gen. 28 June 1838. *d.* at sea, 19 Mar. 1849, on board the *Prince of Wales*.

m. 1st, in England, Harriott. Father of Thomas Snodgrass Fast, *q.v.* His dau. *m.* Humphrey Howorth (1813-1849), *q.v.* *m.* 2nd, Calcutta, 31 Aug. 1827, Miss Ann Ellis. (She died Bath, 4 Apr. 1850, aged 62.)

Services : Lieut. 17th N.I. Fur. s.c. 23 Mar. 1803 till 30 Oct. 1808. Nepal War 1814-5 ; Kalanga 31 Oct. 1814, comdd. 2nd Column of attack ; Capt. 1/17th N.I., in 2nd Div. (*Lond. Gaz.* 19 Aug. 1815.) Operations against the Mhairs 1821 ; Major 1/17th N.I. Lt. Col. 59th N.I. Fur. p.a. 10 Sept. 1827 till 13 Dec. 1828. Transfd. to 42nd N.I. 3 Apr. 1828 ; to 33rd N.I. 13 Apr. 1829 ; to 24th N.I. 14 Oct. 1831. Tempy. comdg. Benares Div. 6 Nov. till 29 Dec. 1831. Operations against the Chuars 1832 ; Col. comdg. Jungle Mehal F.F. Apptd. Bdr. on the Est. to comd. at Delhi 24 Dec. 1833. Transfd. from 40th to 25th N.I. 4 Apr. 1837. Apptd. to Staff of the Army and posted to Saugor Div. 14 Apr. 1840. Comdd. Sirhind Div. 26 Dec. 1841 till 1845. Fur. s.c. 1849 till death.

Refs. : *G.M.* 1849, ii. 333. Will dated Calcutta 19 Feb. 1849 ; codicil dated 17 Mar. 1849 ; proved 23 June 1849, and 4 Feb. 1850.

FAST, Thomas Snodgrass (1806-1839). Lieutenant. 59th N.I. *b.* St. Mary Newington, Surrey, 27 Jan. 1806. Cadet 1824. Arrived in India 24 Nov. 1825. Ensign 13 May 1825. Lieut.

10 June 1826. Resigned 11 July 1836. *d.* Sukkur, Sind, 20 Aug. 1839.

Son of John Wells Fast, *q.v.*, and Harriott his 1st wife. *m.* Calcutta, 10 Jan. 1831, Miss S. H. Gillespie.

Services: Posted as Ensign to 59th N.I. in 1826. Offg. Intr. & Qmr. 59th N.I. 23 Dec. 1830, and 1 Feb. 1832. Suspended from rank, pay, and allowances for 6 mos. At the date of his death he was comdg. a Troop of Irreg. Cav. with Ross Bell, the Comr. in Upper Sind.

Refs.: Atlas, 23 Nov. 1839.

FAULDER or FOULDER, Thomas (1752/53-?). Lieutenant. Infantry. *b.* 1752/53. Cadet 1781. Ensign 21 July 1781. Lieut. 19 Oct. 1782. Pensioned 21 Oct. 1784.

A native of Cumberland.

Services: Apptd. Cadet on 25 Apr. 1781, aged 28. Sailed for India on the *Blandford,* 26 June 1781, aged 28.

FAWCETT, Walker Dawson (1754-1823). Major General. 5th N.C. *b.* 1754. Cadet 1779. Admitted 12 Feb. 1780. Cornet 12 Feb. 1780. Lieut. 2 Feb. 1781. Capt. 1 Nov. 1798. Major 29 May 1800. Lt. Col. 17 July 1801. Col. 25 July 1810. Maj. Gen. 4 June 1813. *d.* in England, 12 Dec. 1823, aged 70.

Younger son of Gen. Sir William Fawcett, K.B. (*D.N.B.*), and his wife, widow of Dr. George Stenton, chancellor of Lincoln. *m.* (?).

Services: Was a Cadet at the R.M.A., Woolwich, on 7 Sept. 1764, on which date he was " indulged with the Master-General's leave to remain absent from the R.M.A. till he is 12 years of age," he being then aged 10 only. Apparently was never commissioned in the R.A. Apptd. Bde. Major, 5th Bde., 12 June 1786. Bde. Major at Calcutta, with Bt. rank of Capt., in 1790. Capt. 2nd N.C. Transfd. as Major to newly-raised 6th N.C. May 1800; as Lt. Col. to 5th N.C. Second Mahratta War; operations in Bundelkhand 1804; Lt. Col. comdg. the force; superseded on account of the disaster at Bela 22 May 1804. Fur. 12 Dec. 1813 till death. Apptd. Col. of the 3rd Cav. Bde. (3rd and 6th L.C.).

Refs.: Burke's *Colonial Gentry,* i. 16, *s.n.* Fawcett. *Records of the R.M.A.* (1851), p. 16. *Pester,* p. 296. *A.J.* xvii. 112.

FEADE, William (*d.* 1804). Bt. Captain, Artillery. Cadet (Inf.) 1783. Admitted 25 Nov. 1784. Fireworker 1 June 1785. Lieut. 13 July 1794. Capt. Lt. 26 Feb. 1802. Bt. Capt. 8 Jan. 1798. *d.* 22 May 1804 : kld. in action at fort Bela, Bundelkhand.

Services: Transfd. from Inf. to Art. 1785. Third Mysore War; Bangalore; Lieut. 2nd Coy. 2nd Bn. Art. Second Mahratta War; siege of Gwalior; siege of Bela (kld.); Capt. Lt. 1st Coy. 3rd Bn.

FEAKE, Charles (1743-?). Cadet. Infantry. *b.* 1743. Cadet 1763.

Son of Thomas Feake, of Dacca (*d.* Oct. 1750), and grandson of Samuel Feake, Govr. of Fort William, Bengal, 1718-1722. Brother of Samuel Feake, *q.v.*

Services: Sailed for India on the *Hawke*, 2 Jan. 1763, aged 19. N.F.P.

FEAKE, Samuel (1740/41-?). Captain. Infantry. *b.* 1740/41. Cadet 1757. Ensign 18 Sept. 1761. Lieut. 27 Aug. 1763. Capt. 1 Aug. 1764. Resigned 7 Dec. 1772.

Son of Thomas Feake, of Dacca. Brother of Charles Feake, *q.v.*

Services: Sailed for India on the *Prince George* in 1757, aged 16. Campaign against the Nawabs of Bengal and Oudh 1764; battle of Buxar; Capt. comdg. 6th Bn. Sepoys until superseded during the action by Lieut. James Nicol, *q.v.*

Refs.: Broome, p. 476.

FELL, Edward (1790-1824). Captain, 10th N.I. *b.* London 3 Mar. 1790. Cadet 1804. Arrived in India 7 May 1806. Ensign 1 Mar. 1806. Lieut. 1 Feb. 1807. Capt. 11 July 1823. *d. unm.* Bilaspur, 15 Feb. 1824, of fever.

bapt. St. Martin-in-the-Fields, London, 12 Apr. 1790. Son of Edward Fell and Sophia his wife. Brother of Thomas Robert Fell, *q.v.*

Services: Posted as Lieut. to 10th N.I. in 1807. Operations in Rewah 1813-4; Entauri; Lieut. 2/10th N.I. Intr. & Qmr. 2/10th N.I. 1 July 1814 till June 1820. Third Mahratta War; Chanda; Lieut. 2/10th N.I. Sec. to the Hindu Coll. at Benares June 1820 till death. "A noted Oriental scholar" (*A.J.*).

Refs.: *A.J.* xviii. 265. Will dated Benares 28 Aug. 1823; proved 31 May 1824.

FELL, Thomas Robert (1793-1835). Captain, 40th N.I. *b.* London 8 Dec. 1793. Cadet 1809. Admitted 6 Mar. 1811. Ensign 24 Feb. 1812. Lieut. 27 Mar. 1817. Capt. 2 Oct. 1824. *d.* at sea, 1 Apr. 1835, on board the *Orient*.

bapt. St. Martin-in-the-Fields, London, 5 Jan. 1794. Son of Edward Fell and Sophia his wife, "of 97 St. Martin's Lane, tailoress." Brother of Edward Fell, *q.v. m.* Almora, U.P., 26 June 1826, Martha Ann, 2nd dau. of William Conrad Faithfull, *q.v.* (*See also* John Dickson Dyke Bean.)

Services: Cadet d.d. 9th N.I. 1811. Posted as Ensign to 2/10th N.I. 1812. With Pioneers 1815-23. Transfd. as Lieut. to 1/20th N.I. 1817. Apptd. to Cantt. Staff at Hoshangabad 18 Nov. 1817. Third Mahratta War; Nagpur; storm and capture of Chanda

(s.w.); Pioneers. "Comdd. the Pioneers at the storm of Chanda on 20 May 1818, where he received several severe wounds while nobly planting the British standard on the Breach " (*M.I.*). Adjt. Pioneers 1819-23. Sec. and Persian Intr. to O.C. Nagpur Subsdy. Force 9 June 1823. Transfd. to 40th N.I. (late 2/20th) May 1824. Bde. Major to troops on Sirhind frontier 26 Feb. 1825. Bde. Major 3rd Inf. Bde. 3 Dec. 1825. Siege and capture of Bhurtpore; Capt. 40th N.I., Bde. Major. Bde. Major E. frontier 12 June 1826 till 31 July 1826. A.D.C. to Bdr.-Gen. John Withington Adams, *q.v.*, 1 Aug. 1828. Fur. s.c. 30 Mar. 1835.
Refs. : *A.J.* N.S. xviii. 143. M.I. in Winchester cathedral.

FELTHAM, Robert. Lieutenant. Infantry. Cadet 1767. Ensign 13 Aug. 1767. Lieut. 4 Aug. 1769. Resigned 10 Apr. 1773.

Services : Operations against the Saniyasis 1771; comdd. a detachment of Sepoys from Rangpur which surprised the camp of the Saniyasis on 25 Feb. 1771, " and after a short skirmish defeated and dispersed them, taking their camp and baggage and a few prisoners."
Refs. : *B.* : *P.P.* x. 151.

FENDALL, Henry (1802-?). Captain. 20th N.I. *b.* Bengal 31 Oct. 1802. Cadet 1818. Admitted 14 Nov. 1818. Ensign (?). Lieut. 1 May 1820. Capt. 30 July 1828. Resigned 6 Aug. 1834. (Living in 1852.)

Son of John Fendall, B.C.S., salt agent at Tamluk, and Mary his wife, *née* Farquharson. His sister *m.*, as 2nd wife, Sir John Hadley D'Oyly, 8th Bart. *m.* (before 1828) (?).

Services : Allowed to proceed to Bengal as a passenger with a view to his being apptd. a Cadet after 31 Oct. 1818. Mily. Student at Coll. of Fort William in 1819-20. Posted as Lieut. to 2/5th N.I. Leave s.c. 12 mos. to Cape 29 Nov. 1820. To do duty with 1/20th N.I. 1 Jan. 1822. S.A.C.G. 26 Oct. 1822. Transfd. to 11th N.I. (late 1/5th) May 1824; to 20th N.I. (late 2/5th) 16 Aug. 1824. First Burma War; S.A.C.G. (India medal). D.A.C.G., 2 cl., 27 Mar. 1826; 1 cl., 2 July 1828. Fur. p.a. 19 Mar. 1832 till resignation.

FENNEL(L), Richard (*d.* 1774). Lieutenant, Infantry. Cadet 1768. Ensign 19 Jan. 1769. Lieut. 9 May 1770. *d.* Bisauli, U.P., Sept. 1774.

Brother of Frances Fennel(l), and nephew of Mrs. Hester Mexteed.
Services : N.F.P.
Refs. : Will dated 1 Dec. 1772; proved 20 Oct. 1775.

FENNING, Samuel Watson (1806-1894). Lieut. Colonel. Artillery.
b. Mitcham, Surrey, 24 Feb. 1806. Cadet 1821. Arrived in India 2 Jan. 1823. 2nd Lieut. 10 May 1822. Lieut. 14 Jan. 1826. Capt. 25 Mar. 1840. Major 2 Feb. 1851. Retired 10 Mar. 1849. Hon. Lt. Col. 28 Nov. 1854. *d.* Brighton 9 July 1894.

Son of William Fenning, of Stamford St., London, coal merchant. Addiscombe Cadet 1820-2.

Services: First Burma War; 2nd Lieut. Art. (India medal). Fur. s.c. 8 Dec. 1827 till 20 Nov. 1830. Adjt. 7th Bn. Art. 21 Dec. 1833 till 13 Apr. 1840. Offg. Asst. to Agent for manufacture of gunpowder at Ichapur 19 Mar. 1835. Leave s.c. 2 yrs. to Cape and N.S.W. 24 Feb. 1841. Fur. s.c. 10 Sept. 1846 till 1851, when he was retired as Major with effect from 10 Mar. 1849.

Refs.: *The Times*, 11 July 1894.

FENTON, Albert (1802-1849). Captain. 1st N.I. *bapt.* Sheffield 25 Apr. 1802. Cadet 1817. Admitted 11 Aug. 1818. Ensign 29 Mar. 1818. Lieut. 4 Oct. 1818. Capt. 21 Dec. 1827. Retired 18 Aug. 1834. *d.* 14 Sept. 1849.

Son of Francis Fenton, of Wood Hill, Sheffield, merchant, and Ellen his wife. Brother of John Battye Fenton, *q.v. m.* Kensington, 22 Mar. 1843, Mary Elizabeth, eldest dau. of James Wilkinson, of Leeds, merchant.

Services: Posted as Lieut. to 2/12th N.I. in 1818. Actg. Adjt. Left Wing 2/12th N.I. Mar. 1820. Fur. s.c. 20 Aug. 1823 till 29 Oct. 1827. Actg. Subaltern at E.I.C. Chatham Depot 10 May 1826 till Apr. 1827. Transfd. to 1st N.I. (late 2/12th) May 1824. Leave s.c. to China 21 Mar. 1832 till 15 Mar. 1833. Fur. p.a. 8 Jan. 1834 till retirement. No record of active service. Author of "Memoirs of a Cadet, by a Bengalee," post 8vo., 1839.

Refs.: *G.M.* 1849, ii. 551.

FENTON, John Battye (1799-1832). Captain, 67th N.I. *b.* 13 Sept. 1799. Cadet 1817. Admitted 4 Aug. 1818. Ensign 13 Mar. 1818. Lieut. 1 Aug. 1818. Capt. 22 May 1829. *d.* Banda 31 Dec. 1832.

bapt. Sheffield 26 Aug. 1800. Son of Francis Fenton, of Wood Hill, Sheffield, merchant, and Ellen his wife. Brother of Albert Fenton, *q.v.* Ed. Free Grammar School, Sheffield.

Services: Posted as Lieut. to 2/23rd N.I. in 1818. Actg. Adjt. 2/23rd N.I. 14 Dec. 1822. Transfd. to newly-raised 2/34th N.I. 11 July 1823. Actg. Adjt. do. 30 Dec. 1823. Transfd. to 67th N.I. (late 1/34th) May 1824. Adjt. of Major Watson's Levy 14 Apr. 1825; do. 11th Extra Regt. 21 May 1825. Actg. Adjt. 67th N.I.

6 Nov. 1826. Fur. s.c. 9 Dec. 1827 till 10 June 1831. No record of active service.

FENTON, William (1807-1827). Lieutenant, 10th N.I. *b.* Ackworth, Yorks., 11 Jan. 1807. Cadet 1823. Ensign 23 May 1824. Lieut. 4 Sept. 1825. *d.* Nasirabad 1 May 1827.

Son of Thomas Fenton.
Services : Posted as Ensign to 10th N.I. in 1825. No record of active service.

FENWICK, Collingwood Foster (1816-1875). Lieut. Colonel. 30th N.I. *b.* 6 Oct. 1816. Cadet 1834. Arrived in India 7 June 1835. Ensign (21 Jan. 1835) 26 Feb. 1835. Lieut. 13 Oct. 1839. Capt. 26 Dec. 1846. Bt. Major 30 Dec. 1859. Retired 31 Dec. 1861. Hon. Lt. Col. 31 Dec. 1861. *d.* Bath 13 June 1875.

bapt. Walcot, Bath, 14 Dec. 1816. Son of Rev. Collingwood Forster Fenwick, rector of Brooke, I.W., previously Lieut. Gren. Gds., and Eliza his wife, 2nd dau. of Adm. Christie, R.N., of Baberton. *m.* Lucknow, 23 Dec. 1843, Louisa Ann, widow of G. W. Lawrence, and dau. of George Villiers.

Services : Ensign d.d. 34th N.I. 15 June 1835. Posted to 30th N.I. 24 Sept. 1835. First Afghan War 1842 ; actions in Khyber Pass in Jan. ; forcing of Khyber in Apr. ; re-occupation of Kabul ; Lieut. 30th N.I., with Gen. Pollock's force (Medal). First Sikh War ; Aliwal ; Lieut. 30th N.I. (Medal). Second Sikh War ; passage of Chenab ; Chilianwala (s.w.) ; Capt. 30th N.I. (Medal with clasp). Mutiny campaign ; capture of Lucknow (Medal with clasp).

Refs. : Burke's *Landed Gentry*, 13th edn., p. 352, *s.n.* Fenwicke-Clennell, of Harbottle, Northumberland. *The Times*, 16 June 1875.

FENWICK, John (*d.* 1807). Colonel, 5th N.I. Cadet 1770. Admitted 24 Aug. 1770. Ensign 20 June 1771. Lieut. 18 July 1776. Capt. 14 Feb. 1781. Major 1 Mar. 1794. Lt. Col. 1 July 1798. Col. 26 Dec. 1802. *d.* in England 26 Sept. 1807.

m. Berhampore, 9 Mar. 1789, Miss Charlotte Maria Powell, dau. (? sister) of Peregrine Powell, *q.v.* (She died 22 May 1845.)

Services : 5th Bengal Eur. Bn. in July 1787. Col. comdg. at Midnapore 1804-7. Fur. 8 Feb. 1807 till death.

FENWICK, Thomas (*d.* 1765). Captain, Infantry. Capt. 1754. *d.* 1765.

m. Elizabeth.[1] (*Perhaps* father of John Fenwick, *q.v.*)
Services : Capt. Madras Est. Returned from fur. on the *London* in 1757. Was again absent on fur. on 1 Oct. 1759. Transfd. from

Madras Est. to Bengal Eur. Regt. in 1759. War with Shah Alam 1760.

Refs. : Broome, p. 273. *Innes*, p. 109. Will dated Calcutta 1 Aug. 1761 ; filed 23 June 1765 ; proved 24 Jan. 1766.

¹ *Note :* One Captain Thomas Fenwick m. Calcutta, 5 Jan. 1744, Mrs. Elizabeth Badman.

FENWICK, Thomas (1745-?). Ensign. Infantry. (? *bapt.* Calcutta 18 Apr. 1745.) Cadet (?). Ensign 19 May 1759.

(*Probably* son of Capt. Thomas Fenwick and Elizabeth his wife.)

Services : N.F.P. His name appears as Ensign in a list of officers of the Bengal army in the year 1760.

FENWICK, William (*d.* 1776). Captain, Infantry. Cadet (?). Ensign 22 Feb. 1764. Lieut. 27 Feb. 1765. Capt. 7 June 1767. *d.* Barrackpore Oct. 1776.

(? Son of William Fenwick, of St. Andrews, Northumberland.) Brother of John Fenwick, of Newcastle-on-Tyne, atty., of Collingwood Foster Fenwick, of Elizabeth Hindmarsh, of Sarah Fenwick, and of Dorothy, wife of Mark Jobson, of Alnwick. (*Probably* uncle or grand-uncle of Collingwood Foster Fenwick, *q.v.*)

Services : N.F.P.

Refs. : Will dated 19 Mar. 1773 ; proved 24 Oct. 1776.

FERGUSON, Archibald (*d.* 1834). Lieut. General. Colonel 74th N.I. Cadet 1777. Admitted 18 Dec. 1777. Ensign 25 Apr. 1777. Lieut. 5 Sept. 1778. Capt. 11 July 1795. Major 31 July 1799. Lt. Col. 26 Dec. 1802. Col. 4 June 1811. Maj. Gen. 4 June 1814. Lt. Gen. 22 July 1830. *d.* Dunfallandy, Scotland, 29 Nov. 1834.

Of Dunfallandy.

Services : Apptd. Cadet on 2 Apr. 1776. Adjt. 3rd N.I. for 14 yrs. Transfd. as Lt. Col. to 2/7th N.I. in 1803. Second Mahratta War ; Cuttack 1803-4. To comd. at Kishanganj Feb. 1808. Transfd. as Col. to 18th N.I. in 1812. Comdd. the station of Barrackpore. Fur. 2 Jan. 1815 till death.

Refs. : E.I.M.C. i. 180. *A.J.* N.S. xvi. 79.

FERGUSON, George (1778-1849). Lieutenant. 11th N.I. *b.* Ayr 31 May 1778. Cadet 1800. Admitted 15 Feb. 1803. Ensign 21 Nov. 1801. Lieut. 19 Oct. 1803. Retired 31 Dec. 1806. *d.* 20 Sept. 1849.

bapt. Ayr 7 June 1778. Son of James Ferguson, town clerk in Ayr, and Margaret Hutchison his wife.

Services : Posted as Ensign to 11th N.I. Fur. 29 Mar. 1803 till retirement. Transfd. to 6th N.I. in 1805; retransfd. to 11th N.I. in 1806. No record of active service.

FERGUSON, James (1778-1859). Colonel. 23rd N.I. *b.* St. Cuthbert's, Edinburgh, 15 Mar. 1778. Cadet 1798. Admitted 24 Feb. 1799. Ensign 27 Sept. 1799. Lieut. 28 Oct. 1799. Capt. 7 Feb. 1809. Major 13 Feb. 1823. Lt. Col. 1824. Retired 25 Nov. 1824. Hon. Col. 28 Nov. 1854. *d.* 6 Feb. 1859.

Son of Adam Ferguson, LL.D., professor of philosophy at Edinburgh (*D.N.B.*), and Katherine Burnett his wife. Brother of Sir Adam Ferguson, Kt., keeper of the regalia in Scotland (*D.N.B.*), and of Joseph Ferguson, *q.v.*

Services : Lieut. 3rd N.I. Transfd. to newly-raised 23rd N.I. in 1804. Capt. Lt. 23rd N.I. 2 June 1808. Present at the attack by Akalis on Mr. Metcalfe's escort at Amritsar 16 Feb. 1809 (w.); Capt. Lt. 2/23rd N.I. Capt. 1/23rd N.I. Actg. Bde. Major at Calcutta 1810-1. Capture of Java 1811; Capt. 1/23rd N.I., with 1/20th N.I. (Medal). Comdd. escort to Resdt. at Delhi 1812-6. Asst. to Resdt. at Delhi 29 June 1816 till 1822. Transfd. to 2/23rd N.I. First Asst. to Resdt. in Malwa and Rajputana 1822-3. Fur. 1823 till retirement.

FERGUSON, John (*d.* 1773). Lieutenant. Infantry. Cadet (?). Ensign 29 Aug. 1765. Lieut. 13 Jan. 1767. Resigned 24 Jan. 1769. *d.* Cape Town 4 Sept. 1773 : kld. in a duel by Capt. David Roche.

Services : Was employed in settling the Midnapore district in 1767-8.[1] Resigned owing to ill health in order to go home. Sailed on the *Vansittart* from England in May 1773 with the intention of returning to his duty in India. Whilst the fleet was detained at the Cape in Sept., he became involved in a dispute with a Capt. Ro(a)che, who stabbed him in a so-called duel. Roche tried to escape into the country, but was caught and racked on the wheel. According to a later account in *G.M.*, however, he was twice honourably acquitted of murder.

Refs. : *G.M.* 1774, p. 94 ; 1793, ii. 673. *S.M.* 1774, p. 54.

[1] *Note :* A long series of his letters, written during these two years, was published in *B.* : *P.P.*, vols. iii. and iv.

***FERGUSON, Joseph** (1774-?). Cadet. Infantry. *b.* Edinburgh 24 Oct. 1774. Cadet (?). Resigned 30 Nov. 1792.

Son of Adam Ferguson, professor of philosophy at Edin. Univ. (*D.N.B.*). Brother of James Ferguson, *q.v.*

Services : Transfd. to H.M.S. 1st Lieut. H.M. 21st Foot 3 Sept. 1795.

FERGUSON, Rowland Burdon (1790-1825). Captain, 63rd N.I. *b.* Sunderland 5 July 1790. Cadet 1805. Arrived in India 20 July 1807. Ensign 16 July 1807. Lieut. 16 Dec. 1814. Capt. 12 Jan. 1825. *d.* Chittagong 12 Dec. 1825.
Son of William Ferguson, surgeon.
Services : Posted as Ensign to 4th N.I. in 1808. Nepal War 1814-5; Lieut. Ramgarh Bn., in 4th Div. Served with Ramgarh Bn. till 1819. Lieut. 2/4th N.I. To survey line for telegraphic communication between Calcutta and Chunar 21 Oct. 1817. Suptg. the construction of telegraph towers on the new mily. road 1820-2. Transfd. to 32nd N.I. July 1823 ; to 63rd N.I. (late 1/32nd) May 1824. First Burma War ; Arakan 1825 ; Capt. 2nd L.I. Bn.

FERGUSSON, James Alexander Duncan (1812-1864). Lieut. Colonel. 6th L.C. *b.* Dailly, co. Ayr, 30 July 1812. Cadet 1828. Arrived in India 5 Sept. 1829. Cornet 5 Sept. 1829. Lieut. 28 Sept. 1840. Capt. 7 May 1844. Bt. Major 7 June 1849. Retired 19 Aug. 1853. Hon. Lt. Col. 28 Nov. 1854. *d.* Cloncaird Castle, co. Ayr, 8 Nov. 1864.
4th son of Sir James Fergusson, 4th Bart., of Kilkerran, co. Ayr, and Henrietta his 2nd wife, 2nd dau. of Adm. Viscount Duncan. *m.* Wardle Lodge, 15 Nov. 1844, Margaret, 4th dau. of James Hope, W.S. Ed. Edin. Acad. 1824-7.
Services : d.d. 6th L.C. 19 Sept. 1829. Actg. Cornet 27 Oct. 1831. Posted as Cornet to 6th L.C. 9 June 1836. Adjt. 6th L.C. 26 July 1836 till 17 June 1840. Reduction of Jhansi 1838-9 ; Cornet 6th L.C. Adjt. G.G.B.G. 17 June 1840 till 20 Dec. 1842. Offg. A.D.C. to G.G. 6 May 1841 ; permanent do. 24 Nov. 1841. Leave s.c. to Singapore 27 Apr. till 10 Sept. 1842. Fur. s.c. 1 Feb. 1843 till 1846. Bde. Major at Barrackpore 20 Aug. 1847 ; do. Ferozepore Oct. 1847. D.A.A.G., Sirhind Div., 28 Oct. 1848 till retirement. Second Sikh War ; Chilianwala ; Gujerat ; Bt. Capt. 6th L.C., D.A.A.G. (Medal with clasp). Major Argyll and Bute Mil. 27 Mar. 1855.
Refs. : Burke's *Peerage*, 1923, p. 892, *s.n.* Fergusson, Bart., of Kilkerran, co. Ayr. *V.B.G. Edin. Acad. Register. The Times*, 28 Nov. 1864.

FERGUSSON, John Hutcheson. (*See* **FERGUSSON-HOME,** John Hutcheson.)

FERGUSSON, John Tierney (1810-1833). Ensign, 70th N.I. *b.* Calcutta 16 Nov. 1810. Cadet 1825. Arrived in India 26 June 1826. Ensign 5 Feb. 1826. *d.* Banda 2 Nov. 1833.
bapt. Calcutta 5 Dec. 1810. Son of Capt. Benjamin Fergusson,

of Calcutta, mariner, and Eleanor his wife. Brother of Josias Dupré Fergusson, *q.v.* His sisters *m.* John Lealand Mowatt, *q.v.*, and George Newton Prole, *q.v.*

Services : Ensign d.d. 3rd N.I. 8 July 1826. Posted to 2nd Extra Regt. (became 70th N.I.) 26 Sept. 1826. Intr. & Qmr. 70th N.I. 21 Sept. 1833. No record of active service.

Refs. : *A.J.* N.S. xiii. 223. Will dated Banda 28 Oct. 1833 ; proved 3 Feb. 1834.

FERGUSSON, Josias Dupré (1815-1844). Lieutenant, 36th N.I. *b.* 1815. Cadet 1828. Was already in India when apptd. Cadet. Ensign (19 July 1830) 24 Nov. 1830. Lieut. 8 Oct. 1839. *d.* Sabathu 27 Dec. 1844, aged 29.

Son of Benjamin Fergusson. Brother of John Tierney Fergusson, *q.v.*

Services : Passed as Cadet on 7 July 1830, aged 15 ; admitted 20 Dec. 1830. To join 2nd N.I. as Cadet 5 Jan. 1831. Cadet d.d. 33rd N.I. 12 Jan. 1831 ; do. 60th N.I. 11 Oct. 1831. Actg. Ensign 17 Dec. 1832. Ensign 21 June 1833 (subsequently antedated to 19 July 1830). Posted as Ensign to 36th N.I. 18 Oct. 1833. On service in Rajputana ; Jodhpur and Shekhawat 1834-5 ; Ensign 36th N.I. Asst. Revenue Surveyor in Cawnpore district 6 Dec. 1838 till Oct. 1840. Adjt. Bhopal Contingent 14 Oct. 1840. In May 1842 he made a " gallant and most judicious attack on a party of rebels in the Saugor district, when 100 rebels fell." D.C., 2 cl., Saugor Div., and to comd. 2nd Bn. Mily. Police at Damoh 31 Mar. 1843. Leave s.c. to Sabathu Oct. 1844 till death.

Refs. : De Rhé-Philipe. *I.M.* No. 24, p. 111. M.I. at Sabathu.

FERNIE, Robert (1785-1849). Lieut. Colonel, 7th N.I. *b.* Markingall, co. Fife, 4 June 1785. Cadet 1805. Arrived in India 7 Nov. 1806. Ensign 7 Oct. 1806. Lieut. 30 Aug. 1809. Capt. 1 May 1824. Major 7 Feb. 1833. Lt. Col. 8 Oct. 1839. *d.* Theberton St., Islington, 4 Jan. 1849.

Son of John Fernie, tenant in Sythrum, and Mary Grandison his wife. Brother of James Fernie, baker in Southwark. *m.* (?).

Services : Captured by the French off Bombay on the voyage out to India ; released as a prisoner on parole. Barasat C.C. 13½ mos. Posted as Ensign to 13th N.I. Bareilly insurrection 1816 ; Lieut. 1/13th N.I. Actg. Adjt. Left Wing 1/13th N.I. 9 Dec. 1823 till 7 June 1824. Transfd. to 27th N.I. (late 2/13th) May 1824. Bde. Major, 1st Inf. Bde., 4 Jan. 1825. First Burma War ; Arakan 1825 ; capture of Arakan ; Bde. Major (*Lond. Gaz.* 1 Oct. 1825). D.A.A.G. to troops on S.E. frontier 17 Dec. 1825 ; Bde. Major to troops in Arakan 1 Oct. 1826. Fur. s.c. 6 Jan. 1827 till 25 Sept.

1829. Leave s.c. 2 yrs. to Cape 6 Feb. 1836 ; fur. s.c. 13 Jan. 1839 till 7 Jan. 1843. Transfd. to 49th N.I. 30 Oct. 1841 ; to 41st N.I. Apr. 1845. Leave s.c. to Cape 6 Apr. 1845 till 1846. Transfd. to 56th N.I. 17 Sept. 1847 ; to 7th N.I. May 1848. Fur. s.c. 18 Mar. 1848 till death.

Refs. : *G.M.* 1849, i. 326. Will dated 10 July 1841 ; admon. 20 June 1849.

FERNYHOUGH, Francis (1775-1812). Captain, 9th N.I. *b.* Holborn, Middlesex, 15 Oct. 1775. Cadet 1799. Admitted 1 Sept. 1800. Ensign 13 Sept. 1799. Lieut. 28 Oct. 1799. Capt. 26 Jan. 1809. *d.* Java 12 June 1812.

bapt. St. Andrew's, Holborn, 24 Oct. 1775. Son of Francis Fernyhough and Catherine his wife.

Services : Second Mahratta War ; Lieut. 9th N.I. Capt. Lt. 9th N.I. 19 Nov. 1807. Capture of Java 1811 ; Capt. 3rd Bengal Vol. Bn.

FERRER, Edward. Lieutenant. Infantry. Cadet 1761. Ensign 11 Dec. 1761. Lieut. 29 Aug. 1763.

Services : N.F.P. Out of the Service before 1 Feb. 1767.

FERRIER, Alexander (1786-1818). Lieutenant, 12th N.I. *b.* Brechin, co. Forfar, 27 Jan. 1786. Cadet 1804. Arrived in India 25 Mar. 1806. Ensign 21 May 1806. Lieut. 23 Sept. 1806. *d.* 6 Mar. 1818.

Son of James Ferrier, of Broadmyre, New Brechin, farmer in Kintrockal, and Elizabeth Gowan his wife.

Services : Posted as Lieut. to 12th N.I. in 1807. Operations in Oudh 1808 ; Lieut. 12th N.I. Intr. & Qmr. 2/12th N.I. 1 July 1814 till death. Nepal War 1816 ; Lieut. 2/12th N.I., in 3rd Bde., Centre Column. Siege and capture of Hathras 1817 ; Lieut. 2/12th N.I.

FERRIS, James (1786-1824). Bt. Major, Artillery. *bapt.* Battle, Sussex, 2 Feb. 1786. Cadet 1803. Arrived in India 3 Sept. 1804. Lieut. 22 Aug. 1804. Capt. Lt. 15 May 1807. Capt. 17 Jan. 1816. Bt. Major 19 July 1821. *d.* Cawnpore 6 Apr. 1824.

Son of Rev. Thomas Ferris, D.D., dean of Battle, and Mary his wife, dau. of Joseph Dixon, of Whasdyke, Cumberland. *m.* 1st, 10 July 1808, Miss Honorae Ryan. (She died 19 May 1815.) Father of James Henry Ferris, *q.v.*, and of Mary Anne, wife of William Andrew Ludlow, *q.v. m.* 2nd, Cawnpore, 12 Dec. 1818, Miss Caroline Barbara Neale.

Services : Capture of Gohad 1806 ; Lieut. 2nd Coy. 1st Bn. Foot Art. Operations in Bundelkhand 1809 ; Rajaoli ; Ajaigarh. Comy. of Ord. at Cawnpore 9 Oct. 1813 till death.

Refs. : Burke's *Landed Gentry*, 2nd edn., p. 410, *s.n.* Ferris, of Hawkhurst, Kent. Will dated 17 Sept. 1822 ; proved 17 June 1824.

FERRIS, James Henry (1810-1857). Captain, Invalid Est. 12th N.I. *b.* Calcutta 11 May 1810. Cadet 1827. Arrived in India 1 Aug. 1828. Ensign 3 Mar. 1828. Lieut. 21 June 1834. Capt. 23 Feb. 1846. Invalided 1 Jan. 1851. *d.* Gwalior 18 June 1857 : kld. by mutineers.

Son of James Ferris, *q.v.*, and Honorae his 1st wife. *m.* Barrackpore, 25 Nov. 1837, Georgina, 4th dau. of Capt. John Tritton, 24th Light Dgns. (*See also* William Cossart Carleton.)

Services : Ensign d.d. 7th N.I. 8 Sept. 1828. Posted to 7th N.I. 4 Nov. 1828. Transfd. to 12th N.I. in 1829. Actg. Intr. & Qmr. 12th N.I. 30 May 1832. Adjt. 12th N.I. 14 Oct. 1833 till Apr. 1846. First Sikh War ; Ferozshahr ; Bt. Capt. 12th N.I. (Medal).

Refs. : Burke's *Landed Gentry*, 2nd edn., p. 410, *s.n.* Ferris, of Hawkhurst, Kent.

FERRIS, Joseph (1807-1853). Bt. Major, C.B., 20th N.I. Comdt. 2nd Sikh Local Inf. *b.* Penzance, Cornwall, 3 May 1807. Cadet 1823. Arrived in India 3 Apr. 1825. Ensign 25 Aug. 1824. Lieut. 19 July 1825. Capt. 11 Oct. 1834. Bt. Major 23 Dec. 1842. *d.* Dharmsala 14 Aug. 1853.

bapt. 1 June 1807. Son of Richard Jewell Ferris, of Penzance, collector of customs. *m.* Calcutta, 28 Mar. 1826, Georgina Matilda, dau. of William Blanchard, of the Dacca district, indigo planter. (*See also* Stephen Williams.) Addiscombe Cadet 1822-4.

Services : Posted as Ensign to 20th N.I. July 1825. First Afghan War 1839-42 ; raised " Ferris's Jazailchis " 1 Oct. 1839 ; forcing of Khyber Pass ; Ali Masjid ; against the Sangu Khel Shinwaris ; Nazian valley ; Tazin ; Haft Kotal ; re-occupation of Kabul (Medal). Comdd. Bundelkhand Mily. Police from Sept. 1843 till its disbandment in Aug. 1847. Comdd. 2nd (or Hill) Regt. of Sikh Local Inf. from 8 Jan. 1848 till death. Second Sikh War ; Jullundur Doab ; Dinanagar 26 Nov. 1848 (Medal). Durani, 3 cl., 11 Apr. 1843. C.B. 24 Dec. 1842.

Refs. : De Rhé-Philipe. *I.M.* 1853, p. 570. Will dated Kangra 6 Jan. 1849 ; proved 29 Nov. 1853.

FESTING, Thomas Bennet Penwarne (1793-1860). Major. 33rd N.I. *b.* Newnham, Herts., 16 June 1793. Cadet 1810. Admitted 12 Nov. 1811. Ensign 16 Nov. 1813. Lieut. 1 Aug. 1818. Capt.

1 Jan. 1826. Invalided 5 Oct. 1835. Retired 11 Sept. 1839.
Hon. Major 28 Nov. 1854. *d.* 28 Mar. 1860.
Son of Rev. John Festing, vicar of Newnham. *m.* (before 1821)
(?). Woolwich Cadet 1808-9. Addiscombe Cadet 1809-1.
Services : Cadet d.d. 9th N.I. Posted as Ensign to 2/16th N.I.
in 1813. With Champaran L.I. 10 Feb. 1821 till 1824. Transfd.
to 33rd N.I. (late 2/16th) May 1824. Adjt. 33rd N.I. 13 July 1824
till 11 Oct. 1827. Siege and capture of Bhurtpore; Capt. 33rd
N.I. (India medal). Fur. s.c. 27 Sept. 1828 till 8 Aug. 1831, and
11 Jan. 1837 till retirement.
Refs. : *I.M.* 13 Apr. 1860, p. 281. *The Times,* 11 Apr. 1860.

FETHERSTON or FETHERSTONHAUGH,[1] **Thomas** (1754-1832).
Lieut. Colonel. 25th N.I. *b.* 1754. Cadet 1782. Admitted
22 Jan. 1783. Ensign 4 Jan. 1783. Lieut. 19 Feb. 1788. Capt.
13 July 1803. Major 10 Dec. 1811. Lt. Col. 4 June 1814.
Invalided 10 Aug. 1816. Retired 7 May 1823. *d.* Portsmouth,
13 Aug. 1832, aged 78.
Of Shacklewell Green, Middlesex. Only son of Francis Fetherston
or Fetherstonhaugh and Mary Birch his wife. Nephew of Sir
Ralph Fetherston, 1st Bart., of Ardagh, co. Longford. *m.* 10 Feb.
1814, his cousin Elizabeth, eldest dau. of Sir Thomas Fetherston,
2nd Bart. (She died Allahabad 5 June 1820.)
Services : Sailed for India on the *Earl Talbot,* 6 Feb. 1782, aged
26. Apptd. A.D.C. to Col. Arthur Achmuty, *q.v.,* comdg. 3rd Bde.,
5 July 1786. Ensign 6th Bengal Eur. Bn. in July 1787. Bt. Capt.
1/1st N.I. in July 1798. Operations in Jumna Doab 1803; Sasni;
Bijaigarh; Kachaura; Lieut. 2/12th N.I. Second Mahratta War;
Agra; Laswari; Monson's retreat; capture of Deig; Bhurtpore;
Capt. 1/12th N.I. Transfd. to newly-raised 25th N.I. in 1805.
Major 1/25th N.I. Fur. s.c. 1812-4. (? Nepal War 1814-5; Major
25th N.I.) Comdg. 1st Bn. Native Invalids 1816 till retirement.
Refs. : Burke's *Peerage,* 1923, p. 897, *s.n.* Fetherston, Bart., of
Ardagh, co. Longford. Burke's *Landed Gentry of Ireland,* p. 221,
s.n. Fetherstonhaugh, of Carrick. *E.I.M.C.* ii. 439-40. *G.M.* 1832,
ii. 268. Will dated Jan. 1830; proved 20 Aug. 1833.
[1] *Note :* He signs " Thomas Fetherston otherwise Fetherston H."

FIDDES, Thomas (1783-1863). Lieut. General. Colonel 42nd N.I.
b. Wells, Hobkirk, co. Roxburgh, 7 Dec. 1783. Cadet 1803.
Arrived in India 19 Mar. 1805. Ensign 11 Apr. 1805. Lieut.
12 Apr. 1805. Capt. 1 Jan. 1819. Major 16 June 1826. Lt. Col.
19 June 1831. Col. 9 Aug. 1843. Maj. Gen. 20 June 1854. Lt.
Gen. 15 Sept. 1856. *d.* at his residence, Oakfield, Cheltenham,
13 Apr. 1863.

Son of John Fiddes, of an old Scotch family, Fiddes, Futhes, or Fuddes. *m.* (?).
Services : Posted as Lieut. to 1/21st N.I. Second Mahratta War ; Indore 1805-6 ; Lieut. 1/21st N.I. Capture of Java 1811 ; Lieut. 4th Vol. Bn. (Medal). Served with Vols. till 1813. S.A.C.G. in Java 22 May 1813 till June 1817. Capt. 1/21st N.I. Transfd. to 42nd N.I. (late 2/21st) May 1824. Apptd. to general control of Comst. Dept. of combined forces in Ava, with rank of Dy. Comy. Gen., 10 July 1824. First Burma War ; Dy. Comy. Gen. (India medal). A.C.G., 1 cl., 27 Mar. 1826. Fur. p.a. 29 Mar. 1829 till 29 Dec. 1831. Posted as Lt. Col. to 69th N.I. 19 May 1832 ; to 45th N.I. 23 Sept. 1834. Offg. Town and Fort Major, Fort William, 19 Nov. 1838, and 23 Sept. 1842. Transfd. to 53rd N.I. 25 Oct. 1842 ; to 45th N.I. 12 Feb. 1843. Posted as Col. to 45th N.I. 1 Dec. 1843. Fur. p.a. 10 Feb. 1845 till death. Col. 42nd N.I. Mar. 1854.
Refs. : Boase. *N. & Q.* 5S. xii. 95. *G.M.* 1863, i. 673. *Cheltenham Examiner,* 15 Apr. 1863. *The Times,* 15 Apr. 1863.

FIEKINS or FEEKINS, John (*d.* 1790). Lieutenant, 36th Bn. Sepoys. Cadet 1778. Ensign 4 May 1779. Lieut. 10 Jan. 1781. *d.* Barrackpore 30 Oct. 1790.
Of Maidstone, Kent. Brother of Edward Fiekins, formerly of Maidstone.
Services : N.F.P.
Refs. : Will.

FIELD, Charles (1795-1851). Major. 9th N.I. *bapt.* Derby 22 Mar. 1795. Cadet 1810. Admitted 13 Oct. 1811. Ensign 30 July 1813. Lieut. 1 Feb. 1815. Capt. 24 Dec. 1831. Major 24 Dec. 1841. Retired 15 Feb. 1842. *d.* nr. Ilford 26 Nov. 1851.
Of Wangey House, Essex. Son of John Field and Ann his wife. *m.* St. Margaret's, Westminster, 26 Sept. 1839, Miss Georgiana Field.
Services : Posted as Ensign to 1/8th N.I. in 1813. Nepal War 1814-5 ; Lieut. 1/8 N.I., in 4th Div. Nepal War 1816 ; Lieut. 1/8th N.I., in 2nd Bde., Left Column (India medal). Third Mahratta War ; Lieut. 1/8th N.I. With 1st Ceylon Vol. Bn. 1818 till Mar. 1820. Intr. & Qmr. 1/8th N.I. 1 Oct. 1823 till 24 Sept. 1825. Transfd. to 9th N.I. (late 1/8th) May 1824. Adjt. 9th N.I. 24 Sept. 1825 till 23 Dec. 1832. Fur. s.c. 12 Mar. 1839 till 11 Apr. 1841.
Refs. : A.J. N.S. xix. 47 ; xxix. 359. *I.M.* 1852, p. 25.

FIELD, Edmund (1760/61-1786). Lieutenant, Infantry. *b.* Derby 1760/61. Cadet 1780. Ensign 1780. Lieut. 1 July 1781. *d.* Dacca 12 Nov. 1786.
Services : Sailed for India on the *Earl of Dartmouth,* 3 June 1780, aged 19. Granted 3 yrs. fur. 2 Oct. 1786.

FIELD, Francis (*d.* 1768). Lieutenant, Infantry. Cadet (?). Ensign 12 Aug. 1765. Lieut. 22 Dec. 1766. *d.* 4 Sept. 1768.
Services : N.F.P.

FIELD, George Brydges Plantagenet (1789-1861). Captain, Pension Est. 23rd N.I. *b.* Newport, I.W., 17 Dec. 1789. Cadet 1803. Arrived in India 4 Dec. 1804. Ensign 6 Nov. 1804. Lieut. 6 Nov. 1804. Capt. 6 Feb. 1819. Pensioned 15 Apr. 1828. *d.* Calcutta, 2 Apr. 1861, of fever.

Son of Thomas Field and Charlotte his wife. Brother of Ringstead Plantagenet Field, *q.v. m.* 1st, Aletta. (She died Calcutta, 30 Apr. 1840, aged 33.) *m.* 2nd, Calcutta, 20 June 1843, Miss Mary Ann Nyss.

Services : Posted as Lieut. to 14th N.I. in 1805. Transfd. to 4th N.I. in 1806. (? Operations in Bundelkhand 1809 ; Rajaoli ; Ajaigarh ; Lieut. 1/4th N.I.) Nepal War 1816 ; Lieut. 4th N.I. (India medal). Capt. 1/4th N.I. Fur. 1822-4. Transfd. to 23rd N.I. (late 2/4th) May 1824. Siege and capture of Bhurtpore ; Capt. 23rd N.I. (clasp to India medal). Fur. 1828 till Mar. 1831. Fur. s.c. to N.S.W. 5 Mar. 1833. Subsequently settled in Calcutta. Pub. Calcutta, 1827, " View of the Assault on the Fortress of Bhurtpore . . ." One plate, imp. fol., with an Index Sketch.

Refs. : A.J. xxvi. 475.

Note : In the burial register his age at death is given as 64.

FIELD, Ringstead Plantagenet (1784-1837). Captain, Invalid Est. 4th N.I. *b.* London 14 Apr. 1784. Cadet 1800. Admitted 10 Dec. 1801. Ensign 29 Sept. 1801. Lieut. 5 Sept. 1803. Capt. 16 Dec. 1814. Pensioned 19 Jan. 1816. Invalided 1818. *d.* Calcutta 18 Jan. 1837.

bapt. St. Pancras 15 May 1784. Son of Thomas Field and Charlotte his wife. Brother of George Brydges Plantagenet Field, *q.v. m.* 1st, Calcutta, 11 July 1816, Ann Smillie, widow. (*Possibly* widow of Robert Smillie, of Calcutta, cabinet-maker.) (She died Calcutta, 3 Oct. 1817, aged 37.) *m.* 2nd (before 1820), Maria. (She died Bath 25 Mar. 1852.)

Services : Served throughout with 4th N.I. Second Mahratta War. After two years on the Pension List he was transfd. to Invalid Est. with effect from the date on which he was pensioned. Subsequently Fort Adjt. at Buxar for ten yrs.

Refs. : A.J. N.S. xxiii. 161.

FIELDHOUSE, Dennis (1740/41-1768). Lieutenant, Infantry. *b.* 1740/41. Cadet 1764. Ensign 22 Aug. 1765. Lieut. 3 Jan. 1767. *d.* 1768.

THE BENGAL ARMY, 1758-1834   181

A native of Staffordshire.
Services : Sailed for India on the *Anson,* 2 Apr. 1764, aged 23.
N.F.P.

FIELDING, Charles John Johnson (*d.* 1767). Captain, 3rd Bn.
Sepoys. Capt. 10 Nov. 1763. *d.* Allahabad 25 May 1767.
Originally Charles John Johnson : assumed the additional surname of Fielding in 1757 or 1758.
Services : Ensign H.M. 34th Foot 5 Apr. 1757 ; Lieut. do. 1 Mar. 1758. Lieut. H.M. 84th Foot 9 Jan. 1759 ; h.p. do. 24 Nov. 1763. Transfd. as Capt. to Bengal Eur. Regt. Nov. 1763.

FIELDING, William George Augustus (1784-1868). Colonel. 8th
L.C. *b.* London 26 Nov. 1784. Cadet 1799. Admitted 15 Jan.
1801. Cornet 17 Apr. 1801. Lieut. 11 Mar. 1805. Capt. 18 Jan.
1816. Major 13 May 1825. Lt. Col. 17 May 1829. Retired
27 Apr. 1833. Hon. Col. 28 Nov. 1854. *d.* 1868.
bapt. Marylebone 1785. Son of William Robert Fielding and
Mary Magdalene Hartley (or Huntley) his wife.
Services : Transfd. from Inf. to Cav. 5 May 1801. Posted as Cornet to 5th N.C. (? Second Mahratta War ; Bundelkhand 1803-4.) Transfd. as Lieut. to newly-raised 8th N.C. in 1805. Adjt. G.G.B.G. 13 Mar. 1806 till 12 Feb. 1812. Capture of Java 1811 (Medal). Fur. p.a. 12 Feb. 1812 till 28 Mar. 1817. Having been absent from India for over 5 yrs., he was struck off, but was restored to the Service from 28 Mar. 1817. With Roberts's Rohilla Horse 20 June till Sept. 1817. Third Mahratta War ; Jubbulpore ; Capt. 8th N.C. At Sindhia's court in 1819. Comdd. Irreg. Horse of Sindhia's Contingent 1820-3. 1st Asst. to Resdt. at Gwalior 26 Aug. 1825 till 29 Sept. 1830, during part of which period he officiated as Resdt. Siege and capture of Bhurtpore ; affair with the enemy on 18 Jan. 1826 ; Major 8th L.C. (India medal). Posted as Lt. Col. to 8th L.C. 30 Sept. 1829. Resdt. at Katmandu, Nepal, 19 Nov. 1830. Fur. s.c. 28 Dec. 1830 till retirement.
Refs. : V.B.G.

FILEWOOD, William. Lieutenant. Artillery. Cadet 1758. Fireworker 12 Mar. 1758. 2nd Lieut. 1760. Lieut. Nov. 1761.
Resigned 8 Nov. 1763.
m. Calcutta, 22 Feb. 1765, Miss Elizabeth Coker. (She died Calcutta 8 June 1765.)
Services : Was a Corporal in the Bengal Art. in Dec. 1757.

FILMORE, Abraham. (*See* **PHILMORE.**)

FINCH, Henry (1781-1810). Lieutenant, 13th N.I. *bapt.* Watford, Herts., 13 July 1781. Cadet 1800. Admitted 22 Aug. 1801. Ensign 3 Nov. 1801. Lieut. 30 Sept. 1803. *d.* Berhampore 28 Nov. 1810.

Eldest son of John Finch, of Redheath, nr. Watford, and of Ockwells, and Anne his wife, youngest dau. of Ralph Day, of Micklefield Green, Herts. *m.* Bareilly, 2 Nov. 1807, Eliza, dau. of Sir Gabriel Martindell, *q.v.* (*See also* John Stuart Rotton, and William Sivright.)

Services : Served throughout with 13th N.I. (? Second Mahratta War.)

Refs. : Burke's. *Landed Gentry*, 13th edn., p. 639, *s.n.* Finch, of Redheath, Herts. Will dated 14 Oct. 1810; proved 27 Nov. 1812.

FINLAYSON, John. Lieutenant. Infantry. Cadet 1763. Ensign 25 Feb. 1764. Lieut. 10 Aug. 1765. Dismissed 1767.

Services : N.F.P.

FINLAYSON, John Matthew (*d.* 1762). Ensign, Infantry. Cadet 1761. Ensign (?). bur. Calcutta 16 July 1762.

Services : N.F.P.

FINNIS, John (1804-1857). Bt. Colonel, 11th N.I. *b.* Hythe, Kent, 28 Jan. 1804. Cadet 1819. Admitted 3 Aug. 1820. Ensign 4 Mar. 1820. Lieut. 16 Apr. 1822. Capt. 25 Apr. 1836. Major 7 May 1844. Lt. Col. 2 Aug. 1850. Bt. Col. 28 Nov. 1854. *d.* Meerut 10 May 1857 : kld. by mutineers.

Son of Robert Finnis of Hythe, upholsterer. Brother of Stephen Finnis, *q.v.*, and of Thomas Quested Finnis, lord mayor of London in 1857. *m.* Dholi, B. & O., 2 Jan. 1838, Sarah Bridgetta Dorothea, youngest dau. of Robert Roche, *q.v.* (*See also* Samuel Robinson Bagshawe.) (She died 16 Aug. 1890, aged 72.)

Services : Ensign 1/26th N.I. Transfd. to 51st N.I. (late 1/26th) May 1824. Actg. Intr. & Qmr. 51st N.I. 20 Jan. 1825. P.W.D., Saugor Div., 1826-9. Fur. s.c. 4 Feb. 1831 till 16 July 1833. P.W.D. 6 Dec. 1838 till 1844. Second Sikh War ; Multan ; Major 51st N.I. (Medal). Fur. s.c. 17 Mar. 1849 till Mar. 1851. Posted as Lt. Col. to 71st N.I. 2 Aug. 1850 ; to 18th N.I. 3 Feb. 1851 ; to 11th N.I. 6 Dec. 1851 ; to 38th N.I. 1 Apr. 1852 ; to 67th N.I. 7 Mar. 1854 ; to 48th N.I. June 1855 ; to 11th N.I. 18 June 1856. Was comdg. at Allahabad on outbreak of Mutiny.

Refs. : *G.M.* 1857, ii. 225. Will dated 6 Sept. 1848 ; proved 12 Mar. 1858. M.I. in St. Dunstans in the East, London.

FINNIS, Stephen (1798-1819). Lieutenant, 29th N.I. *bapt.* Hythe, Kent, 28 May 1798. Cadet 1817. Lieut. 1 Aug. 1818. *d.* Dinapore 8 Aug. 1819.

Son of Robert Finnis, of Hythe, upholsterer. Brother of John Finnis, *q.v.*, and of Elizabeth, mother of Robert Blosse Lynch, *q.v.*
Services : Posted as Lieut. to 29th N.I. No record of active service.

FISCHER, Christian (*d.* 1781). Lieut. Colonel, Invalid Est. Infantry. Capt. 17 Feb. 1757. Bt. Major 6 June 1765. Bt. Lt. Col. 13 Apr. 1779. Invalided (?). *d.* Calcutta Oct. 1781.

A native of Switzerland. *m.* Calcutta, 19 Apr. 1761, Elizabeth Devril. His dau. was mother of John Gordon (1787-1822), *q.v.*
Services : Transfd. to Madras Est. from the Danish Service. Lieut., Madras, 25 June 1753. Battle of Plassey ; voted against immediate action at the council of war held before the battle, on which occasion he is said to have been new to the country. Expedn. to the N. Circars 1758-9 ; comdd. storming party at storm of Masulipatam ; Capt. Bengal Eur. Regt. War with Shah Alam 1760. Comdg. 2nd Bn. Sepoys at Monghyr in Aug. 1765. Was given brevet rank only on account of his nationality.
Refs. : Broome, p. 135. *Williams,* p. 75. *Forde,* p. 96.

FISHER, Abraham[1] (*d.* 1770). Fireworker, Artillery. Cadet (?). Fireworker 1770. *d.* Calcutta 29 Aug. 1770.
Services : N.F.P.
Note : The christian name is given as James in the bur. register.

FISHER, Andrew (1807-1863). Major. 35th N.I. *b.* Kirk-Hammerton, Yorks., 30 Aug. 1807. Cadet 1823. Admitted 9 Sept. 1824. Ensign 16 Jan. 1824. Lieut. 9 July 1825. Capt. 4 Jan. 1841. Retired 28 Aug. 1847. Hon. Major 28 Nov. 1854. *d.* York 16 Sept. 1863.

bapt. Kirk-Hammerton 5 Sept. 1807. Son of Rev. Henry Fisher, senior chaplain, Bengal Est., formerly P.C. of Kirk-Hammerton, and Mary his wife, eldest dau. of Henry Abbey, of Long Marston, Yorks., brewer. Brother of John Fisher, *q.v.*
Services : Was already in Bengal when nominated Cadet on 6 Jan. 1824. Posted as Ensign to 9th N.I. Transfd. as Lieut. to 34th N.I. July 1825 ; exchanged to 35th N.I. 12 Oct. 1825. Siege and capture of Bhurtpore ; Lieut. 35th N.I. (India medal). Lieut. d.d. Sirmoor Bn. 12 Aug. 1826 till 27 Jan. 1827. Actg. Intr. & Qmr. 35th N.I. 23 Apr. 1828 ; do. 44th N.I. 24 Feb. 1829 ; do. 62nd N.I. 3 Sept. 1829. Intr. & Qmr. 35th N.I. 22 Sept. 1831 till 17 Apr. 1841. First Afghan War 1838-42 ; capture of Ghazni 1839 (Medal) ;

re-occupation of Kabul; Capt. 35th N.I. (Medal). Suspended by G.C.M. 6 Jan. till 9 Apr. 1843. Fur. s.c. 28 Feb. 1845 till retirement.
Refs. : G.M. 1863, ii. 215.

FISHER, Goodricke Armstrong (1814-1881). Lieut. General. 5th N.I. b. London 8 Oct. 1814. Cadet 1831. Arrived in India 29 Dec. 1831. Ensign (9 June 1831) 29 Dec. 1831. Lieut. 1 Feb. 1837. Capt. 31 Oct. 1848. Major 13 Mar. 1859. Lt. Col. 1 Jan. 1862. Col. 18 Feb. 1866. Maj. Gen. 1 Oct. 1877. Lieut. Gen. 14 July 1880. d. Hillersdon House, Dover, 23 Aug. 1881.

Son of James Fisher, of 37 Duke St., London, army clothier, and Susanna his wife. Brother of James Fisher, q.v. m. Calcutta, 16 Dec. 1839, Emily Georgiana, youngest dau. of Metcalfe Stanwix Hogg, q.v. Addiscombe Cadet 1829-31.

Services : d.d. 7th N.I. 1 Feb. 1832. Posted to 17th N.I. 19 Oct. 1833. Transfd. to 1st N.I. 16 Jan. 1834. Fur. 9 Apr. 1838 till 18 Nov. 1839. Adjt. 3rd L.I. Bn. 12 Mar. till Oct. 1842. Adjt. 1st N.I. 8 July 1844 till Nov. 1848. Second Sikh War ; Capt. 1st N.I., in garrison at Fort Govindgarh, Amritsar (Medal). Comdt. of forts Michni and Shabkadar Feb. 1853 till May 1854 (N.W.F. Medal). Fur. p.a. 18 Apr. 1856 till 6 Oct. 1857. d.d. with Gurkha Regt. 23 Oct. 1857. Offg. S.A.C.G. 23 Oct. 1857. Mutiny campaign ; Alambagh ; second relief of Lucknow ; capture of Lucknow (Medal with 2 clasps).

Refs. : The Times, 26 Aug. 1881.

*FISHER, James (1803-1835). Lieutenant, 1st N.I. b. London 22 Sept. 1803. Cadet 1824. Arrived in India 19 May 1825. Ensign 11 Dec. 1824. Lieut. 8 Oct. 1825. d. Fatehgarh, U.P., 3 Jan. 1835.

bapt. St. James's, Westminster, 20 Oct. 1803. Son of James Fisher, of 37 Duke St., London, army clothier, and Susanna his wife. Brother of Goodricke Armstrong Fisher, q.v.

Services : Posted as Ensign to 1st N.I. in 1825. Intr. & Qmr. 1st N.I. 16 Oct. 1826 till death. No record of active service.

Refs. : G.M. 1835, ii. 222. A.J. N.S. xvii. 131.

FISHER, John (1802-1846). Captain, 23rd N.I. Comdt. Sirmoor Bn. of Gurkhas. b. Kirk-Hammerton, nr. Knaresborough, Yorks., 12 July 1802. Cadet 1818. Arrived in India Mar. 1815. Ensign 17 Dec. 1818. Lieut. 9 Jan. 1820. Capt. 4 June 1831. d. 10 Feb. 1846 : kld. in action at the battle of Sobraon.

Son of Rev. Henry Fisher and Mary his wife. Brother of Andrew Fisher, q.v. m. Saharanpur, U.P., 4 June 1825, Lucy, 3rd dau. of Rev. John Vincent, chaplain Bengal Est.

THE BENGAL ARMY, 1758-1834

Services : Was already in India when apptd. 1 Mar. 1817 a Cornet in H.M. 24th Light Dgns. Apptd. Cadet on 12 July 1818, on attaining the age of 16. Admitted 17 Dec. 1818. Ensign d.d. 1/7th, 1/25th, 1/27th N.I. Posted as Ensign to 1/4th N.I. in Mar. 1820. Adjt. Sirmoor Bn. Jan. 1824, and served with that corps till his death. Transfd. to 23rd N.I. (late 2/4th) May 1824, but never joined. Siege and capture of Bhurtpore ; Lieut. comdg. a detachment of 200 of the Sirmoor Bn. 2nd in comd. June 1827. Asst. Pol. Ofr. at Dehra Dun. Comdt. Sirmoor Bn. 2 Jan. 1843. First Sikh War ; Aliwal ; Sobraon (kld.).
Refs. : De Rhé-Philipe. Will dated 28 Jan. 1846 ; proved 16 June 1846. M.I. in St. Andrew's, Ferozepore.

FISHER, Thomas. Ensign. Infantry. Cadet 1781. Ensign 18 Aug. 1781. Dismissed by C.M. 8 Feb. 1783.
Services : N.F.P.

FISHER, Thomas (1798-1847). Major, 48th N.I. Comdt. 2nd Assam L.I. *b.* London 25 Mar. 1798. Cadet 1817. Admitted 4 Aug. 1818. Ensign 13 Mar. 1818. Lieut. 1 Aug. 1818. Capt. 27 June 1835. Major 19 Feb. 1847. *d.* Gauhati, Assam, 24 July 1847.

Eldest son of Thomas Fisher, of Gt. Ryder St., St. James's, London, one of H.M. Messengers. *m.* Comilla, Bengal, 1 Nov. 1823, Miss Emily Maria Terraneau (*probably* sister of Robert Terraneau, *q.v.*). (She died Delhi, 23 June 1837, aged 31.)
Services : Formerly in H.M. Ord. Dept. : pensioned when the various depts. were reduced after the war. Apptd. in 1817 pte. sec. to Sir Edward Thornton, ambassador to the court of Portugal ; but before his departure for Portugal, a cadetship was offered him and accepted. Posted as Lieut. to 1/24th N.I. On survey duty in Sylhet Feb. 1820 till 1823. D.A.Q.M.G., 3 cl., 22 Feb. 1823 ; 2 cl., 7 June 1824. First Burma War ; Sylhet, Cachar, and Assam 1824 ; Bikrampur ; Cachar and Arakan 1825. Transfd. to 48th N.I. (late 2/24th) May 1824. Again employed on survey work in Sylhet 16 Aug. 1826 till 1829. D.A.Q.M.G., 1 cl., 16 Oct. 1828 till 6 Sept. 1833. Operations against the Khasias 1829 ; with Sylhet Local Corps. Principal Asst. to A.G.G., N.E. frontier, 3 Apr. 1833 till 1836. Fur. p.a. 17 Feb. 1838 till 19 July 1839. Actg. A.A.G., Dinapore Div., 18 June 1841. Comdt. 1st Assam Sebundy Corps (became 2nd Assam L.I. Bn. 9 Aug. 1844) 22 Sept. 1841 till death.
Refs. : G.M. 1847, ii. 558. *I.M.* Oct. 1847, p. 610. Will dated 17 July 1847 ; proved 26 Oct. 1847. M.I. at Gauhati.

FITCHER, Jeremiah. (*See* **TITCHER.**)

FITTON, Patrick Bellew (1794-1866). Captain. 27th N.I. *b.* Cork 15 Aug. 1794. Cadet 1811. Admitted 20 Aug. 1812. Ensign 14 Sept. 1814. Lieut. 1 Aug. 1818. Capt. 15 June 1826. Retired 8 Mar. 1834. *d. unm.* in or nr. Cork, 15 Feb. 1866. Son of Richard Fitton, of Cork, barr.-at-law of the Middle Temple, and Brianna his wife, only dau. of Patrick Bellew, of Ballendiness. Cousin-german of Francis John Bellew, *q.v.*
Services : Posted as Ensign to 1/13th N.I. in 1814. Third Mahratta War; Asirgarh; Lieut. 2/13th N.I. With Pioneers 1819-25. Transfd. to 26th N.I. (late 1/13th) May 1824 ; to 27th N.I. (late 2/13th) in 1825. First Burma War ; Arakan 1825 ; attack on Arakan 29 Mar. (s.w.—rt. leg amputated 4 days later) (*Lond. Gaz.* 1 Oct. 1826) ; Lieut. 5th Coy. Pioneers. Received a gratuity of 12 mos. pay for loss of leg. Apptd. Supt. of family pensions, and Paymr. of pensions in Oudh 28 Apr. 1825. Fur. s.c. 11 Feb. 1826 till 4 Aug. 1831. Having been over 5 yrs. absent from India, was struck off, but was readmitted with effect from 4 Aug. 1831. (Letter from C.D. 22 Oct. 1832.) Fur. s.c. 18 Oct. 1831 till retirement. Retired on h.p. owing to ill health due to war service.
Refs. : Burke's *Commoners*, ii. p. xv.

FITZGERALD, Sir Augustine, fourth baronet (1809-1893). Lieut. Colonel. Artillery. *b.* Exeter 12 Mar. 1809. Cadet 1825. Arrived in India 18 Mar. 1826. 2nd Lieut. 28 Sept. 1825. Lieut. 25 July 1832. Capt. 12 July 1844. Bt. Major 11 Nov. 1851. Retired 28 Apr. 1853. Hon. Lt. Col. 28 Nov. 1854. *d.* Carrigoran, Newmarket, co. Clare, 31 Jan. 1893 : bur. Kilnasoolagh church, co. Clare.
4th Bart. of Newmarket-on-Fergus, co. Clare. *s.* 13 Mar. 1865. High sheriff co. Clare 1871. *bapt.* Cornwall 6 Oct. 1809. 2nd son of Sir William Fitzgerald, 2nd Bart., and Emilia Cumming his wife, dau. of William Veale, of Trevaylor, Cornwall. Nephew of Charles FitzGerald (1784-1859), *q.v. m.* 1st, Agra, 10 Dec. 1832, Eliza Margaret, dau. of William Gore. (*See also* Gabriel Napier Christie Campbell.) (She died 31 Aug. 1877.) *m.* 2nd, 19 Apr. 1881, Clara Emma, 2nd dau. of James Whitaker, of Huddersfield. Addiscombe Cadet 1823-5.
Services : Posted to 3rd Troop 3rd Bde. H.A. 9 Aug. 1830 ; to 4th Troop 3rd Bde. 14 Mar. 1833. Actg. Adjt. Mewar Div. Art. 3 Apr. 1835. Posted to 5th Coy. 7th Bn. 11 Sept. 1837. Fur. p.a. 22 Nov. 1837 till 14 Dec. 1840. Posted to 4th Troop 3rd Bde. 13 Apr. 1841. First Afghan War 1842 ; forcing of Khyber ; various operations leading to re-occupation of Kabul ; Bt. Capt. 3rd Troop 2nd Bde., with Gen. Pollock's force (Medal). (*Lond. Gaz.* 24 Nov. 1842.) Adjt. & Qmr. 2nd Bde. H.A. 24 Jan. 1843. Adjt. Meerut

Div. Art. 14 Feb. 1843. Gwalior campaign; Maharajpur; Adjt. 2nd Bde. H.A. (Bronze star). First Sikh War; operations in Kangra; Capt. comdg. 1st Coy. 4th Bn. (12-pdr. Battery). (Medal.) Comdd. 5th Troop 1st Bde. H.A. 1847-52.

Refs. : Burke's *Peerage*, 1923, p. 911, *s.n.* FitzGerald, Bart., of Newmarket-on-Fergus, co. Clare. (Extinct 10 May 1908.) *Boase. The Times*, 2 Feb. 1893, p. 11. *I.L.N.* 29 Apr. 1893, p. 536.

FITZGERALD, Charles (1784-1859). Colonel, C.B. 6th L.C. *b.* Dublin Nov. 1784. Cadet 1800. Arrived in India 15 Sept. 1801. Cornet 5 Jan. 1802. Lieut. 1 Oct. 1806. Capt. 8 Jan. 1816. Major 13 May 1825. Lt. Col. 1 Dec. 1829. Retired 9 Apr. 1833. Hon. Col. 28 Nov. 1854. *d. unm.* at his residence, 15 Regent St., London, 18 Apr. 1859.

7th son of Col. Edward FitzGerald of Carrygoran, M.P. for Clare, and Anne Catherine his 2nd wife, dau. of Major Thomas Burton. His sister *m.* John Robert Leigh, *q.v.* Uncle of Sir Augustine Fitz-Gerald, Bart., *q.v.*

Services : Ensign 13 Nov. 1801. Transfd. to Cav. 1 Apr. 1802. Posted as Cornet to 6th N.C. (? Operations in Jumna Doab 1803; Sasni; Bijaigarh; Kachaura.) Second Mahratta War; Cornet 6th N.C. Actg. Adjt. 6th N.C. in 1806; Adjt. 1807-8. Operations against Dhundia Khan 1807; Komona; Ganauri. Fur. p.a. 12 Feb. 1812 till 26 Aug. 1815. Third Mahratta War; Sitabaldi; Nagpur; Capt. 6th N.C. (India medal). Greatly distinguished himself at the battle of Sitabaldi, when he led 3 Troops of 6th N.C. in a brilliant and decisive charge against overwhelming numbers. (*Lond. Gaz.* 6 May and 9 June 1818.) Apptd. Persian Intr. and Extra A.D.C. to C.-in-C. 1818. Dy. Paymr. Narbada F.F. 5 Dec. 1818. Hon. A.D.C. to G.G. 12 Dec. 1818. Fur. s.c. 17 Feb. 1821 till 7 June 1824. Hon. A.D.C. to G.G. 11 Sept. 1824. To comd. 6th Local Horse, which Corps he raised himself at Bareilly, 19 Nov. 1824. Hon. A.D.C. to G.G. 26 Sept. 1828. Posted as Lt. Col. to 6th L.C. 11 May 1830. Fur. s.c. 21 Oct. 1830 till retirement. Granted a special allowance of £200 p.a. in addition to retired pay for his gallantry at Nagpur. C.B. 27 Sept. 1831.

Refs. : Burke's *Peerage*, 1905, p. 632, *s.n.* FitzGerald, Bart., of Newmarket-on-Fergus, co. Clare. *G.M.* 1859, i. 653. *The Times*, 21 Apr. 1859. *I.M.* 27 Apr. 1859, p. 380.

FITZGERALD, Charles (1796-1865). Lieut. Colonel. 60th N.I. *b.* Salisbury, Wilts., 27 Jan. 1796. Cadet 1811. Admitted 8 Aug. 1812. Ensign (14 May 1814) 1 May 1815. Lieut. 6 July 1818. Capt. 11 Dec. 1826. Major 1 Dec. 1836. Retired 2 Dec. 1836. Hon. Lt. Col. 28 Nov. 1854. *d.* Sidbury, Devon, 25 Feb. 1865.

Of Mount Edgar, nr. Sidmouth, Devon. *bapt.* 10 Feb. 1797. Son of Gerald FitzGerald and Frances his wife. *m.* Calcutta, 25 Aug. 1817, Conradine, dau. of C. H. G. Printzling, judge and mgte. of Serampore. (She died 4 Nov. 1878, aged 80.)

Services : Posted as Ensign to newly-raised 1/30th N.I. in 1815. Nepal War 1816 ; Makwanpur ; Ensign 1/30th N.I., in 4th Bde., Centre Column.[1] Intr. & Qmr. 1st Ceylon Vol. Bn. 1818 till 1 Mar. 1820. Transfd. to 60th N.I. (late 2/30th) May 1824. Siege and capture of Bhurtpore ; Lieut. 60th N.I.[1] D.A.A.G., W. Div., 22 Mar. 1826. Bde. Major Rajputana F.F. 12 June 1826 ; do. Berhampore 30 Apr. 1827 till 25 June 1831. Offg. Bde. Major at Cawnpore 13 May 1832.

Refs. : *G.M.* 1865, i. 529.

[1] *Note :* His name does not appear in the India medal roll.

FITZGERALD, Charles L——. Lieutenant. Artillery. Cadet (?). Fireworker 9 Sept. 1768. Lieut. 16 Mar. 1770. Resigned 6 May 1772.

Services : N.F.P.

FITZGERALD, Dudley (*d.* 1792). Lieutenant, Infantry. Cadet (?). Ensign 26 Jan. 1781. Lieut. 2 Oct. 1781. *d.* Chittagong 1 May 1792.

(*Perhaps* brother of Martin FitzGerald, *q.v.*)

Services : Lieut. 27th Bn. Sepoys in July 1787.

FITZGERALD, Edward (1789-1826). Captain, 59th N.I. *b.* Dublin 19 Jan. 1789. Cadet 1803. Arrived in India 2 Dec. 1804. Ensign 20 Nov. 1804. Lieut. 20 Nov. 1804. Capt. 11 July 1823. *d.* Cawnpore 10 June 1826.

7th son of Rev. Gerald FitzGerald, D.D., rector of Ardstraw, co. Tyrone, sometime Fellow of T.C.D., and Elizabeth his wife, dau. of Rev. Plunket Preston, rector of Duntrileague, co. Limerick. *m.* Dacca, 14 Sept. 1819, Harriet, dau. of Canon Blenkinsop, of Windsor (? and sister of Edward Blenkinsop, *q.v.*). (*See also* Mark Carter Webber.) (She died Southampton 18 Dec. 1834.) T.C.D. ; Pensioner 3 Oct. 1803, aged 15.

Services : Posted as Lieut. to Bengal Eur. Regt. in 1805. Served in Amboyna 1811-4. Fur. 1814-6. Transfd. to newly-raised 2/30th N.I. in 1815. Adjt. 1/30th N.I. 1818-9. Intr. & Qmr. 2/30th N.I. 1 June 1819 till May 1824. Transfd. to 59th N.I. (late 1/30th) May 1824. Fur. 1824-5. No record of active service.

Refs. : *Alumni Dub.* Will dated 14 June 1814 ; proved 22 June 1829. Will dated 14 May 1825 ; proved 29 May 1827.

FITZGERALD, George Fleetwood Charles (1808-1888). Colonel. Artillery. *b.* Buckfastleigh, Devon, 3 Jan. 1808. Cadet 1825. Arrived in India 18 Mar. 1826. 2nd Lieut. 28 Sept. 1825. Lieut. 19 Aug. 1832. Capt. 1 Apr. 1845. Major 20 Feb. 1855. Lt. Col. 14 Jan. 1858. Retired 10 Nov. 1858. Hon. Col. 10 Nov. 1858. *d.* 2 Fauconberg Villas, Cheltenham, 5 Mar. 1888.

Son of Thomas FitzGerald, Purser, R.N. *m.* Hyderabad, 20 May 1850, Matilda, only dau. of Lt.-Gen. Hastings Fraser, H.M.S. (She died 6 Oct. 1887.) Addiscombe Cadet 1823-5.

Services : Served with Nizam's Art. 10 Apr. 1831 till 1853. Adjt. Nizam's Engrs. 20 Apr. 1831 till 25 Sept. 1837. To comd. 4th Coy. Nizam's Art. 21 Aug. 1837. Capt. in Nizam's service 28 Sept. 1837. Fur. s.c. 10 Mar. 1854 till 1857. Crimean War ; Local Lt. Col. in Turkey 27 Mar. 1855. Mutiny campaign ; operations E. of Oudh ; Lt. Col. Gurkha force.

Refs. : The Times, 7 Mar. 1888.

FITZGERALD, John (1796-1851). Bt. Lieut. Colonel, 2nd L.C. *b.* Cawnpore 19 Apr. 1796. Cadet 1811. Admitted 4 Aug. 1812. Cornet 10 June 1816. Lieut. 1 Sept. 1818. Capt. 31 Jan. 1825. Major 5 Jan. 1844. Bt. Lt. Col. 11 Nov. 1851. *d.* Dehra Dun, U.P., 15 Dec. 1851.

Son of Martin FitzGerald, *q.v.*, and Barbara his wife. Brother of William Robert FitzGerald, *q.v. m.* Lucknow, 16 Apr. 1828, Fanny, eldest dau. of Mordaunt Ricketts, B.C.S., Resident at Lucknow. (*See also* Muirson Trower Blake.) (She died 1 Dec. 1891, aged 83.)

Services : Cadet d.d. G.G.B.G. 12 Sept. 1812 till 1815. Offg. Adjt. do. 2 Feb. till 14 May 1813. Posted to 2nd N.C. in 1815. Third Mahratta War ; Lieut. 2nd N.C. in Reserve Div. Adjt. 2nd N.C. 24 May 1819 till 3 May 1822. Employed under the Nagpur Govt. 1822-9. Bde. Major in Oudh 11 Aug. 1829 till 10 June 1831. Fur. s.c. 2 yrs. to Cape 20 Jan. 1832. Fur. p.a. 15 Mar. 1834 till 29 Dec. 1837. First Afghan War ; 1839-42 ; Ghazni ; Bt. Major 2nd L.C. (Medal). On the disbandment of 2nd L.C. for misconduct in Afghanistan, to do duty with 3rd L.C. 6 May 1841. Posted to newly-raised 11th L.C. (became 2nd) in 1842. Gwalior campaign ; Paniar ; Bt. Major 11th L.C., comdg. Rear Guard (*Lond. Gaz.* 8 Mar. 1844). (Bronze Star). Fur. s.c. 14 Mar. 1846 till 1848.

Refs. : Foster's *Peerage*, p. 591, *s.n.* St. Vincent, V. *V.B.G. A.J.* xxvi. 486. *I.M.* 1852, p. 59. Will dated 3 Nov. 1851 ; proved 15 Mar. 1852.

FITZGERALD, Martin (*d.* 1829). Lieut. Colonel Comdt., 10th L.C. Cadet 1782. Admitted 15 Aug. 1783. Ensign 20 Feb. 1783. Lieut. 10 Feb. 1790. Capt. 5 Oct. 1800. Major 15 Aug. 1809.

Lt. Col. 30 June 1818. Lt. Col. Comdt. 1 May 1824. *d.* at his residence, 17 The Circus, Bath, 3 May 1829.

m. Barbara (*probably* sister of John Garstin, *q.v.*). (She died Bath 2 Apr. 1847.) Father of John FitzGerald, *q.v.*, and of William Robert FitzGerald, *q.v.* (*Perhaps* brother of Dudley FitzGerald, *q.v.*)

Services: Posted as Ensign to 3rd Bengal Eur. Regt. in 1783. Became a Supy. Ensign on reduced pay in 1785. Posted as Lieut. to 31st Bn. in Feb. 1790; transfd. to 30th Bn. in 1795. Posted as Bt. Capt. to 1st N.C. 1 June 1796; transfd. to 2nd N.C. in 1800. Capt. Lt. 2nd N.C. 29 May 1800. Second Mahratta War; Agra; Laswari (horse shot under him); Bhurtpore. Offg. Sec. to Board of Suptce. for improving the breed of cattle in 1810; Member of do. in 1812. Major 2nd N.C. Fur. s.c. 1 Jan. 1815 till 1818. Transfd. as Lt. Col. to 1st N.C. Dec. 1818; to 3rd L.C. in 1820. (? Operations in Jodhpur 1823; capture of Lamba; Lt. Col. comdg. 3rd L.C.) Transfd. as Lt. Col. Comdt. to 7th L.C. 1 May 1824. Fur. 1824 till death. Transfd. to newly-raised 10th L.C. in 1825.

Refs.: *E.I.M.C.* iii. 144-6. *G.M.* 1829, i. 556. Will dated Bath 8 Feb. 1827; proved 4 Sept. 1829.

FITZGERALD, Robert (1805-1835). Lieutenant. 6th N.I. *b.* Monkstown, co. Dublin, 23 June 1805. Cadet 1823. Ensign 23 May 1824. Lieut. 24 Feb. 1826. Resigned 5 Dec. 1828. *d.* 1835.

3rd son of Rt. Hon. Maurice FitzGerald, Knight of Kerry, J.P. and D.L., a Privy Councillor and M.P. for Kerry (*D.N.B.*), and Maria his 1st wife, dau. of Rt. Hon. David Digges La Touche, of Marlay, co. Dublin. *m.* Ellen, eldest dau. of Peter Bodkin Hussey, of Farnakilla House, Kerry.

Services: Posted as Ensign to 6th N.I. in 1825. (? Siege and capture of Bhurtpore; Ensign 6th N.I.) Fur. 1826 till resignation.

Refs.: Burke's *Peerage*, 1923, p. 910, *s.n.* FitzGerald, Knight of Kerry.

FITZGERALD, William Robert (1798-1844). Major, Engineers. *b.* Cawnpore 14 Dec. 1798. Cadet 1815. Admitted 26 Sept. 1818. Ensign 1 Sept. 1818. Lieut. 5 July 1822. Capt. 28 Sept. 1827. Major 3 Sept. 1840. *d.* Calcutta 1 Dec. 1844.

Son of Martin Fitzgerald, *q.v.*, and Barbara his wife. Brother of John FitzGerald, *q.v. m.* Calcutta, 18 May 1825, Sarah, eldest dau. of R. Fulcher (*probably* sister of Frederick Page Fulcher, *q.v.*). His dau. *m.* Thomas Mould Edgar Moorhouse, *q.v.* Addiscombe Cadet 1814-6.

Services: Employed on survey duty. Fur. s.c. 22 Feb. 1823 till 5 Oct. 1824. Garr. Engr. and civil architect at Fort William

THE BENGAL ARMY, 1758-1834 191

16 July 1830 till 23 June 1841. Suptg. Engr., S.E. Provinces, 23 June 1841. No record of active service.
Refs. : *I.M.* 8 Feb. 1845, p. 48. M.I. Circular Rd. cemetery, Calcutta.

FITZ SIMONS, Henry (1800-1865). Lieut. Colonel. 29th N.I. bapt. Dublin 4 June 1800. Cadet 1820. Ensign 18 Jan. 1822. Lieut. 1 May 1824. Capt. 6 Apr. 1838. Major 15 Mar. 1851. Invalided 9 Mar. 1855. Retired 16 June 1856. Hon. Lt. Col. 16 June 1856. *d.* 7 Sept. 1865.

Son of Thomas FitzSimon(s). *m.* Calcutta, 4 Sept. 1843, Mary Ann, dau. of Edmund O'Brien.

Services : Posted as Ensign to Bengal Eur. Regt. in 1822. Transfd. to 14th N.I. 1823 ; to 29th N.I. (late 2/14th) May 1824. Fur. s.c. 31 Dec. 1828 till 1831. With 1st L.I. Bn. 1841-3. On leave 1848 till 8 Dec. 1849. (? Operations against the Ranizais and Mohmands 1852 ; Major 29th N.I.)

FLACTION, Caesar (1737/38-1763). Ensign, Infantry. *b.* 1737/38. Cadet 1763. Ensign 1763. *d.* Calcutta 12 May 1763.

A native of Bern, Switzerland.
Services : Sailed for India in May 1762, aged 24.

FLEMING, Browne Jackson (1801-1826). Lieutenant, 11th N.I. *b.* Limerick 14 Apr. 1801. Cadet 1818. Ensign 30 May 1819. Lieut. 6 Oct. 1821. *d.* Calcutta 9 Nov. 1826.

Son of Browne Fleming, of the I. of Man, Capt. 21st Light Dgns., and Elizabeth his wife.

Services : Ensign d.d. Bengal Eur. Regt. 1819. Posted to 1/5th N.I. in 1820. Adjt. Rangpur Local Bn. 1822-3 ; do. Dinajpur Local Bn. 1823-4 ; do. Orissa Provl. Bn. 1824 till death. No record of active service.

Refs. : Will dated 20 Apr. 1820 ; proved 19 Dec. 1826.

FLEMING, George (1760/61-1818). Bt. Colonel, Engineers. Actg. Chief Engr. *b.* 1760/61. Country Cadet 1778. Ensign 25 Dec. 1778. Lieut. 10 May 1781. Capt. 19 Aug. 1793. Major 29 Apr. 1802. Lt. Col. 4 Oct. 1808. Bt. Col. 4 June 1814. *d.* Calcutta 3 July 1818, aged 57.

m. Dacca, 20 Jan. 1794, Margaret, sister of David and Ynyr Burges, and widow of James Ayton. Stepfather of James Alexander Ayton, *q.v.* His dau. *m.* Henry Manley, *q.v.*

Services : Asst. Engr. at Fort William in July 1787. Engr. at Berhampore and Murshidabad 1803-15. Actg. Chief Engr. Jan. 1815 till death.

Refs. : Will dated Berhampore 11 Feb. 1806 ; proved in 1818. M.I. in S. Park St. cemetery, Calcutta.

FLEMING, George (1800-?). Lieutenant. 65th N.I. Pensioner on Lord Clive's fund. *b.* London 6 Mar. 1800. Cadet 1818. Ensign (?). Lieut. 12 Dec. 1820. Pensioned 9 Apr. 1826.

Son of —— Fleming, ordnance store-keeper at Quebec.

Services : Ensign d.d. 10th N.I. 1819. Posted as Ensign to 2/22nd N.I. 1820. Transfd. to newly-raised 33rd N.I. July 1823 ; to 65th N.I. (late 1/33rd) May 1824. Fur. 1824-7, when he was pensioned with effect from 9 Apr. 1826. No record of active service.

FLEMING, James (1783-1830). Major, 38th N.I. *b.* Cavan, Ireland, 15 Dec. 1783. Cadet 1804. Arrived in India 10 July 1805. Ensign 9 Aug. 1805. Lieut. 10 Aug. 1805. Capt. 4 Oct. 1818. Major 22 Apr. 1827. *d.* Barrackpore 8 Mar. 1830.

Son of Thomas Fleming, asst. barr. for co. Leitrim.

Services : Posted as Lieut. to 19th N.I. in 1806. (? Operations in Bundelkhand 1807 ; Sehlehuganj ; Lieut. 1/19th N.I.) Nepal War 1814-5 ; Lieut. 1/19th N.I., in 1st Div. With 3rd Ceylon Vol. Bn. 1818-9. Capt. 1/19th N.I. Fur. 16 Mar. 1821 till 1822. Transfd. to 38th N.I. (late 1/19th) May 1824.

Refs. : *A.J.* N.S. iii. 76. M.I. at Barrackpore.

FLEMING, Peter Joseph (1803-1833). Lieutenant, 55th N.I. *bapt.* Windermere, Westmorland, 27 June 1803. Cadet 1819. Admitted 14 June 1820. Ensign 14 Nov. 1819. Lieut. 6 May 1821. *d.s.p.* Barrackpore 22 July 1833.

4th son of Rev. John Raincock (who assumed in 1779 the surname of Fleming on succeeding to Rayrigg, Westmorland), preby. of Landaff, and rector of Bottle, Cumberland, and Jane his wife, dau. of Peter Taylor, of Whitehaven.

Services : Posted as Ensign to 1/28th N.I. Transfd. to 55th N.I. (late 1/28th) May 1824. Actg. Intr. & Qmr. 55th N.I. 22 Dec. 1824. Actg. Adjt. & Qmr. Div. Art. 19 Dec. 1825. No record of active service.

Refs. : Burke's *Landed Gentry*, 10th edn., p. 557, *s.n.* Fleming, of Rayrigg and Belfield, Westmorland. *A.J.* N.S. xiii. 205.

FLEMING, Robert. Lieutenant. Infantry. Cadet 1780. Admitted 15 Feb. 1780. Ensign 13 Feb. 1781. Lieut. 11 Oct. 1781. Dismissed by C.M. 17 Aug. 1795.

Services : Fur. 31 Oct. 1786 till 26 Oct. 1790. N.F.P.

FLEMING, Robert (1782-1805). Lieutenant, 20th N.I. *b.* St. Thomas's, Dublin, 1 July 1782. Cadet 1802. Arrived in India 29 Aug. 1803. Ensign 14 Sept. 1803. Lieut. 21 Sept. 1804.

d. 21 Nov. 1805 (either at sea on his passage to England, or in Brompton, Middlesex).
Son of Frances Fleming.
Services : Ensign d.d. 12th N.I. 1803. Posted to 20th N.I. 1804. Fur. 29 Jan. 1805 till death. No record of active service.

FLEMING, Thomas (1797-1821). Ensign, 16th N.I. *b*. Kirkcaldy, co. Fife, 22 Dec. 1797. Cadet 1818. Ensign 18 Aug. 1819. *d*. Hingoli, Hyderabad, 9 Feb. 1821.
Son of Rev. Dr. Thomas Fleming, one of the ministers of Edinburgh, formerly minister of Kirkcaldy.
Services : Was already in India as a " Free Merchant " when apptd. a Cadet. Posted as Ensign to 16th N.I. in 1820. Adjt. 1st Bn. Berar Regular Inf. in the service of the Nizam of Hyderabad 1820 till death.
Refs. : S.M. 1821, ii. 394.

FLEMYNG, Thomas Fergusson (1806-1874). Lieut. General. 36th N.I. *bapt*. Dublin 28 Sept. 1806. Cadet 1823. Arrived in India 25 June 1824. Ensign 14 Jan. 1824. Lieut. 6 May 1825. Capt. 12 Jan. 1841. Major 10 July 1852. Lt. Col. 31 May 1857. Bt. Col. 28 May 1854. Maj. Gen. 11 July 1861. Lt. Gen. 25 June 1870. *d*. at his residence, 9 Colville Gdns., Notting Hill, London, 30 Aug. 1874, aged 68.
Son of G. Henry Flemyng,[1] of King's Court, Enniskeen, and of Dublin, atty. *m*. Cawnpore, 9 Jan. 1829, Charlotte, 3rd dau. of John Tritton, Capt. H.M. 24th Dgns., and sister of William Mills Tritton, *q.v.* (*See also* William Cossart Carleton.) (She died 1 June 1892, aged 82.)
Services : Posted as Lieut. to 36th N.I. Siege and capture of Bhurtpore ; Lieut. 36th N.I. (India medal). Actg. Intr. & Qmr. 36th N.I. 25 Apr. 1826, 13 Oct. 1828, 13 July 1829. Fur. s.c. 13 Jan. 1832 till 23 Feb. 1834. Shekhawat expedn. 1834 ; Lieut. 36th N.I. Adjt. 36th N.I. 14 Sept. 1840 till 3 Feb. 1841. First Sikh War ; Aliwal ; Capt. 36th N.I. (Medal). Second Sikh War ; Ramnagar ; Sadulapur ; Chilianwala ; Bt. Major 36th N.I. (Medal with clasp). Posted as Lt. Col. to 36th N.I. 20 Aug. 1857. Fur. 1858 till death.
Refs. : A.J. xxviii. 92. *The Times*, 3 Sept. 1874.

[1] *Note : Probably* Gilbert Henry Flemyng, of St. Stephen's Green, Dublin, and Harriet Bettesworth his wife.

FLEMYNG, William (*d*. 1832). Captain. Artillery. Country Cadet 1781. Admitted 1 Nov. 1781. Fireworker 24 July 1782. Lieut. 25 June 1788. Capt. Lt. 8 Jan. 1796. Capt. 17 Feb. 1802. Retired 2 Dec. 1802. *d*. Dublin 11 Sept. 1832.

m. Calcutta, Jan. 1793, Miss Emilia Price (or Pierce). Father of William Henry Flemyng, *q.v.*

Services : Second Mysore War 1783-5 ; Lieut. F. 5th Coy. 1st Bn. Art. ; joined the force in Mar. 1783. Qmr. 3rd Bn. Art. 1787-90. On service in Madras Aug. 1793 for siege of Pondicherry ; Qmr. to the detachment. Fur. 19 Jan. 1797 till 23 Sept. 1799. Expedn. to Egypt 1801 ; Capt. comdg. Foot Art. Went home from Egypt before Oct. 1801 till retirement. E.I.C. Recruiting Ofr. at Cork 1814-6. Described as " tax collector " on his son's admission to T.C.D. in 1821.

Refs. : *A.A.R.* iv. 87. *A.J.* N.S. ix. 151.

FLEMYNG, William Henry (1805-?). Ensign. 36th N.I. Subsequently P.C. of Milltown, co. Dublin. *bapt.* Dublin May 1805. Cadet 1826. Ensign 29 Oct. 1827. Resigned 15 Jan. 1829. (Living in 1884.)

Son of William Flemyng, *q.v.*, and Emilia his wife. T.C.D. ; Pensioner 5 Nov. 1821, aged 17. B.A. 1833. M.A. 1837. Admitted Oxford, *ad eundem*, 18 Mar. 1852.

Services : Posted as Ensign to 63rd N.I. 19 June 1827. Transfd. to 36th N.I. 1828. No record of active service. Took holy orders.

Refs. : Alumni Dub. Alumni Oxon.

FLETCHER, Daniel. Ensign. Infantry. Cadet 1763. Ensign 24 Oct. 1763.

Services : Out of the Service before 1 Feb. 1767. N.F.P.

FLETCHER, John (1789-1818). Lieutenant, 23rd N.I. *b.* Liverpool 17 Apr. 1789. Cadet 1805. Arrived in India 19 Sept. 1806. Ensign 18 Sept. 1806. Lieut. 1 June 1808. *d.* at sea, Feb. 1818, on board the *Barossa.*

Son of John Fletcher. Grandson of William Allanby, of Flimby.

Services : Posted as Ensign to 23rd N.I. in 1807. (? Operations against Dhundia Khan 1807 ; Komona ; Ganauri ; Ensign 1/23rd N.I.) Lieut. 1/23rd N.I. Fur. 1817 till death.

FLETCHER, Joseph (1765-1810). Major, 12th N.I. *b.* 3 Dec. 1765. Cadet 1783. Admitted 10 Sept. 1783. Ensign 17 Jan. 1785. Lieut. 16 Feb. 1791. Capt. 1 May 1804. Major 8 Sept. 1809. *d.* Calcutta 22 Sept. 1810.

Son of George Fletcher, of Tottenham and Cateaton St., London, and Ruth his wife. *m.* Berhampore, 8 Oct. 1792, Charlotte, dau. of Robert Catts, Dy. Comy. of Ord. at Berhampore. (*See also* John Carige.) (She died 11 Apr. 1854, aged 79.) His dau. *m.* 1st, Anthony Daffy Swinton, *q.v.*, 2nd, John Edward Watson, *q.v.*

Services : Fur. 4 Feb. 1786 till 4 July 1789. Capture of Seringapatam. Lieut. 1st Bengal Eur. Regt, in 1796. Lieut. 1/6th N.I.

in July 1798. Operations in Jumna Doab 1803 ; Sasni ; Bijaigarh ; Lieut. 2/12th N.I. Second Mahratta War ; Aligarh ; battle of Delhi ; Agra ; Laswari (w.) ; Monson's retreat (where he " saved the Colours of his regiment, having wrapped them round his body ") ; Bhurtpore (w. 1st assault on 9 Jan. 1805, and in 3rd assault on 20 Feb. 1805) ; Capt. 2/12th N.I. Fur. 1 Apr. 1807 till 21 Oct. 1809.

Refs. : Family information. *The Times*, 20 May 1854. Will dated camp, Gotta Ghaut, 23 May 1804 ; proved 5 Jan. 1811. M.I. in S. Park St. cemetery, Calcutta.

FLETCHER, Sir Robert (*d.* 1776). Bdr. General, Kt. Afterwards C.-in-C., Madras. Ensign (Madras) Sept. 1757. Lieut. (Madras) (?). Capt. (Madras) 1760. Capt. (Bengal) 3 Aug. 1763. Major 3 May 1764. Lt. Col. 3 May 1765. Dismissed by C.M. 15 Oct. 1766. *d.* Mauritius 24 Dec. 1776.

m. Anne, 2nd dau. of John Pybus, of Bond St., London, banker, formerly Member of Council at Madras.

Services : Apptd. a Monthly Writer at Madras 24 May 1757. Transfd. to Madras army as Ensign in Sept. 1757. Dismissed when a Lieut. for writing an insolent letter to Govt., apologized and was reinstated at Coote's intercession. Capt. 1760. Served in the war of 1760-1. Capture of Manila 6 Oct. 1762 ; Bde. Major to Bdr.-Gen. William Draper. Returned to England 1763. Transfd. to Bengal 1763. Lt. Col. comdg. 1st Bde. at Monghyr Aug. 1765. Implicated in the " Batta mutiny " May 1766. Tried by C.M. and found guilty " of Mutiny and having excited sedition, and after coming to the knowledge of a mutiny having delayed to give information thereof to his Commanding Officer." Dismissed and went to England. M.P. Cricklade, Wilts., 1768. Prevailed on the Directors to reinstate him, and returned to Madras as Col. in 1771. C.-in-C. at Madras Sept. 1772 till 1773. Returned to England and resumed his seat in Parliament. Went out to Madras as Bdr. Gen. and C.-in-C. 1775. C.-in-C. from 1775. Leave s.c. to Cape Oct. 1776. Kt. 29 Dec. 1763.

Refs. : D.I.B. Love. Broome. Holzman. Portrait by Reynolds : engraving pub. by W. Dickinson 24 Nov. 1774.

FLETCHER, Thomas. Ensign. Infantry. Cadet 1776. Ensign 13 Mar. 1777.

Services : N.F.P.

FLETCHER, Walter (1803-1820). Ensign, Infantry. Unposted. *b.* Chesterfield, co. Derby, 28 Mar. 1803. Cadet 1819. Was already in India when apptd. Cadet. Ensign (?). *d.* Monghyr, B. & O., 22 Aug. 1820.

Son of George Fletcher, of Chesterfield.

Refs. : M.I. at Monghyr.

FLINT, George (1786-1811). Ensign. 10th N.I. Subsequently Capt. Lt. 7th Madras N.C. *b.* London 10 Feb. 1786. Cadet 1800. Admitted 17 Sept. 1801. Ensign 31 Oct. 1801. *d.* Jalna, Hyderabad, 6 Sept. 1811.

bapt. St. George's, Hanover Sq., London, 17 Mar. 1786. Son of William Flint and Ann his wife.

Services : Transfd. to Madras Est. Cornet 7th Madras N.C. 4 Mar. 1803. Lieut. 15 Aug. 1804. Fur. 1805-7. Capt. Lt. 6 Sept. 1810.

FLOWER, John Rowe (1808-1841). Captain, 25th N.I. *b.* London 15 Apr. 1808. Cadet 1825. Arrived in India 30 May 1826. Ensign 4 Feb. 1826. Lieut. 3 Aug. 1828. Capt. 5 Jan. 1837. *d.* Barrackpore 16 Nov. 1841.

Son of James Flower. *m.* St. James's, London, 11 June 1839, Julia, eldest dau. of Major Francis Forester, R. Horse Gds., and granddau. of Duke of Cleveland.

Services : Ensign d.d. 57th N.I. 30 June 1826. Posted to 25th N.I. 26 Sept. 1826. Actg. Adjt. Wing 25th N.I. 21 Feb. 1831. Operations against the Chuars 1832 ; Lieut. 25th N.I. Tempy. S.A.C.G. in Arakan 3 July 1834. Actg. Adjt. 25th N.I. 17 Sept. 1834. Apptd. to tempy. charge of Arakan Local Bn. 13 Dec. 1834. Fur. s.c. 26 Oct. 1836 till 24 Dec. 1839. Served with 1st Vol. Regt. for China 15 Feb. 1840 till 1 June 1841. First China War 1840-1 ; Capt. 1st Vol. Regt. (Medal).

Refs. : Burke's *Peerage*, 1923, p. 928, *s.n.* Forester, B. *A.J.* N.S. xxix. 231. M.I. in Barrackpore cemetery.

FLUKER, Thomas Charles Torriano (1784-1804). Lieutenant, 13th N.I. *b.* Wells, Somerset, 4 June 1784. Cadet 1800. Was already in India when apptd. Cadet. Admitted 21 July 1802. Ensign 23 Nov. 1801. Lieut. 30 Sept. 1803. *d.* Bundelkhand district, C.I., 6 Sept. 1804.

bapt. St. Cuthbert's, Wells, 26 June 1784. 2nd son of Capt. Thomas Fluker, H.M. 60th Foot, and Sarah his wife, 2nd dau. of Main Swete Walrond, of the I. of Antigua. Cousin-german of Theodore Lyons, *q.v.*

Services : Second Mahratta War ; operations in Bundelkhand 1803-4 ; Kapsa ; Kalpi ; defeat of Rajah Ram Singh ; Jaitpur ; Lieut. 1/13th N.I.

Refs. : Burke's *Landed Gentry*, 13th edn., p. 1823, *s.n.* Walrond, late of Dulford House, Devon.

FLYTER, James (1811-1848). Captain, 64th N.I. *b.* Gordonsburg, Inverness, 8 May 1811. Cadet 1827. Arrived in India 23 Nov. 1828. Ensign 27 June 1828. Lieut. 28 July 1835. Capt. 24 Jan. 1845. *d.* Tirhut, B. & O., 6 June 1848.

Son of Robert Flyter, of Fort William, Inverness, sheriff substitute, and Mary Campbell his wife. *m.* Dinajpur, Bengal, 21 Oct. 1834, Catherine Louisa, youngest dau. of John French, B.C.S., addl. judge at Tirhut.
Services: Ensign d.d. 27th N.I. 14 Jan. 1829. Posted to 64th N.I. 3 June 1829. Adjt. 64th N.I. 14 Sept. 1840 till Dec. 1844. First Afghan War 1842 ; retreat from Ali Masjid to Jamrud ; forcing of Khyber Pass ; Gen. Pollock's advance on Kabul ; Lieut. 64th N.I. (Medal). Actg. 2nd in comd. 9th Irreg. Cav. 5 June 1844.
Refs.: *I.M.* No. 24, p. 109. Will dated 29 Mar. 1842 ; admon. 20 Apr. 1849.

FOGO, William (1778-1832). Captain. 9th N.I. *b.* Edinburgh 14 Jan. 1778. Cadet 1796. Admitted 22 Sept. 1797. Ensign 28 Sept. 1797. Lieut. 10 Sept. 1798. Capt. 19 Nov. 1807. Pensioned 5 June 1816. Retired 19 June 1821. *d.* Edinburgh 25 Sept. 1832.
bapt. Edinburgh 17 Jan. 1778. Son of James Fogo, of Edinburgh, writer, and Elizabeth Jamieson his wife.
Services: Second Mahratta War ; pursuit of Holkar 1805-6 ; Lieut. 1/9th N.I. Adjt. 1/9th N.I. 1805-7. Operations against Dhundia Khan 1807 ; Komona (s.w.) ; Capt. 1/9th N.I., actg. Bde. Major. Nepal War 1816 ; Makwanpur ; Capt. 2/9th N.I., in 4th Bde. Centre Column.
Refs: *A.A.R.* x. 21. *A.J.* N.S. ix. 151.

FOLEY, John (1804-1821). Ensign, Infantry. Unposted. *b.* co. Pembroke 14 Feb. 1804. Cadet 1820. Ensign (?). *d.* Ghazipur, U.P., 16 Oct. 1821.

Son of John Herbert Foley, of Ridgeway (? Edgeway), co. Pembroke, and Emily Mary Ann his wife, sister of Sir Samuel Chambers, Kt., of Bredgar House, Kent. Twin brother of William Foley, *q.v.*, and nephew of Adm. Sir Thomas Foley, G.C.B. (*D.N.B.*).
Refs.: Burke's *Landed Gentry*, 2nd edn., p. 205, *s.n.* Chambers, of Bredgar House, Kent.

FOLEY, Richard (*d.* 1777). Lieutenant, 5th Bn. Sepoys. Comdg. a Coy. of Art. in the service of Asaf-ud-Dowlah, Nawab-Wazir of Oudh. Cadet 1772. Ensign 3 Nov. 1772. Fireworker 10 Nov. 1772. Lieut. (?). *d.* Mainpuri, U.P., Mar. 1777 : kld. in action.

Son of Mary Foley, late of Newent, Gloucs. Brother of Rev. John Foley, and of Mary Foley. (*Probably* son of Richard Foley, formerly Lieut. 20th Foot, who died at Newent in 1778.)
Services: " He had entered the service of one of the Eastern princes, and was killed in India in his first engagement " (*G.M.*).

Refs. : G.M. 1778, p. 286. Will dated camp nr. Ferochabad (Farrukhabad, U.P.) 1 Nov. 1776 ; codicil dated camp before Mainpoore 24 Feb. 1777 ; proved 8 Aug. 1777.

FOLEY, William (1804-1837). Captain. 10th N.I. *b.* co. Pembroke 14 Feb. 1804. Cadet 1819. Admitted 15 Nov. 1820. Ensign 1 May 1820. Lieut. 11 July 1823. Capt. 4 Feb. 1833. Resigned 1 Jan. 1837. *d.* Moulmein, Burma, 13 Apr. 1837.

Son of Herbert Foley and Emily Mary Ann his wife. Twin brother of John Foley, *q.v. m.* (?). (She died 29 Aug. 1826.)

Services : Posted as Ensign to 2/27th N.I. Fur. s.c. 13 Oct. 1822 till 5 June 1824. Transfd. as Lieut. to 7th N.I. 11 July 1823 ; to 10th N.I. (late 1/7th) May 1824. S.A.C.G. 3 Oct. 1828 ; D.A.C.G., 2 cl., 12 July 1834. No record of active service.

Refs. : Burke's *Landed Gentry,* 2nd edn., p. 205, *s.n.* Chambers, of Bredgar House, Kent. *A.J.* N.S. xxiv. 276. M.I. at Moulmein.

FOLLIOTT, Abraham (1792-1809). Ensign, 7th N.I. *bapt.* Topsham, Devon, 22 Jan. 1792. Cadet 1806. Arrived in India 17 Mar. 1808. Ensign 2 Mar. 1808. *d.* Kishenganj, B. & O., 3 Sept. 1809.

Son of Daniel Folliott.

Services : Posted as Ensign to 7th N.I. No record of active service.

FOORD, William Whiting (1790-1849). Lieut. Colonel, 53rd N.I. *bapt.* Keynsham, Somerset, 28 Feb. 1790. Cadet 1805. Arrived in India 31 July 1807. Ensign 2 July 1807. Lieut. 5 Jan. 1810. Capt. 1 May 1824. Major 18 June 1834. Lt. Col. 15 Mar. 1841. *d.* Guernsey 10 Aug. 1849.

Son of William Foord and Ann his wife.

Services : Posted as Ensign to 9th N.I. (? Operations in Hariana 1809 ; Bhawani. Operations in Oudh 1809-10 ; Pragpur ; Ensign 1/9th N.I.) Actg. Adjt. of a detachment of 1/9th N.I. 11 Nov. 1812. Transfd. to 21st N.I. (late 2/9th) May 1824. Siege and capture of Bhurtpore ; Capt. 21st N.I. Fur. p.a. 4 Jan. 1830 till 6 July 1833. Comdt. 3rd Recruit Depot Bn. at Delhi 7 Sept. 1839 till 5 Oct. 1840. Comdg. 21st N.I. from 26 Oct. 1840. Posted as Lt. Col. to 21st N.I. 28 May 1841. Fur. s.c. 5 June 1847 till death. Transfd. to 53rd N.I. Dec. 1847.

FOQUETT, Henry (1804-1887). Colonel. 35th N.I. *b.* Newport, I.W., 23 Nov. 1804. Cadet 1823. Arrived in India 20 May 1824. Ensign 17 Jan. 1824. Lieut. 11 Feb. 1826. Capt. 11 Dec. 1842. Major 13 Jan. 1849. Lt. Col. 7 Nov. 1854. Retired

11 Nov. 1856. Hon. Col. 11 Nov. 1856. *d.* at his residence, Tezpore, Reading, 20 Mar. 1887.
Sometime of Ilfracombe, Devon. Son of Richard Foquett, of Newport, wine merchant. *m.* Nasirabad, 12 May 1828, Frances, dau. of Rev. George Phillips, rector of New Moat, co. Pembroke.
Services : Posted as Ensign to 11th N.I. in 1824. Transfd. to 4th Extra Regt. in 1825 ; to 56th N.I. in 1826. Adjt. 56th N.I. 14 Mar. 1827 till 20 Oct. 1841. Leave s.c. to Mauritius 28 Sept. 1840 till 28 Jan. 1841. 2nd in comd. Assam Sebundy Corps (became 2nd Assam L.I.) 8 Mar. 1841 till Aug. 1847. Comdt. 2nd Assam L.I. 18 Aug. 1847 till Dec. 1854. Posted as Lt. Col. to 64th N.I. Dec. 1854. Fur. p.a. 19 Jan. 1855 till retirement. Transfd. to 56th N.I. Feb. 1855 ; to 64th N.I. June 1855 ; to 35th N.I. Dec. 1855.
Refs. : A.J. xxvi. 739. *The Times,* 23 Mar. 1887.

FORBES, Alexander (*d.* 1779). Capt. Lieutenant, Artillery. Cadet (?). Fireworker 16 Mar. 1771. Lieut. 2 Nov. 1773. Capt. Lt. 18 Sept. 1779. *d.* 1779, on service with the Bombay detachment.
Services : First Mahratta War 1778-9.

FORBES, Alexander (1775-?). Cadet. Infantry. *b.* Chiry (? Curr), Scotland, 1 May 1775. Cadet 1792. Resigned 1 Feb. 1793.
Services : Transfd. to H.M.S. Ensign H.M. 71st Foot 26 July 1792 ; Lieut. do. 23 May 1795 ; Capt. do. 26 Sept. 1801. Casualty in 1808.

FORBES, Arthur (1812-1834). Ensign, 59th N.I. *b.* Broadstairs, Kent, 25 July 1812. Cadet 1828. Arrived in India 21 Mar. 1829. Ensign 12 Sept. 1828. *d.* Exchange Hotel, Calcutta, 27 Aug. 1834.
Son of —— Forbes, W.I. planter. Nephew of Peter Clutterbuck, of Watford.
Services : Posted as Ensign to 59th N.I. 3 June 1829. Leave to Calcutta preparatory to fur. 2 Aug. 1834. No record of active service.
Refs. : A.J. N.S. xvi. 137.

FORBES, Charles (*d.* 1779). Captain, 2nd Bengal Eur. Regt. Cadet 1765. Ensign Aug. 1766. Lieut. Apr. 1771. Capt. Sept. 1779. *d.* in India 1779.
Services : Capt. 2/2nd Bengal Eur. Regt. in Oct. 1779.

FORBES, George Munro (1804-1822). Ensign, 3rd N.I. *b.* Dornoch, co. Sutherland, 10 Nov. 1804. Cadet 1821. Ensign (?). *d.* Dum-Dum 6 Nov. 1822.
Son of Capt. John Forbes, of Overskibo.
Refs. : M.I. at Dum-Dum.

FORBES, James (*d.* 1769). Lieutenant, Infantry. Cadet 1764. Ensign 9 Mar. 1765. Lieut. 15 Dec. 1766. *d.* 1769.
Services : N.F.P.

FORBES, John (*d.* 1808). Major General. Colonel 10th N.I. Transfd. as Ensign from H.M. 89th Regt. Ensign 9 Mar. 1765. Lieut. 10 July 1765. Capt. 8 June 1767. Major 14 Sept. 1779. Lt. Col. 2 Dec. 1782. Col. 31 Jan. 1793. Maj. Gen. 26 Feb. 1795. Retired 1 Jan. 1803. *d.* at his home, Winterfield, nr. Dunbar, 2 Oct. 1808.
Youngest son of George Forbes, of Lockermick, nr. Aberdeen. Maternal uncle to the wife of Professor Richard Porson (*D.N.B.*) and her brother, James Perry, editor and proprietor of the *Morning Chronicle* (*D.N.B.*). *m.* Cawnpore, 2 Nov. 1787, Mrs. Isabella Hay Bradley (*possibly* widow of Matthew Bradley, *q.v.*). His dau. *m.* his A.D.C., John Paton, *q.v.*
Services : Went out to India in 1761. Ensign H.M. 89th Regt. Resigned during the "Batta mutiny" in May 1766 ; readmitted 2 Dec. 1766. First Mahratta War ; comdg. 1st Bn. Sepoys 1778 till 14 Sept. 1779. Comdg. 1st Bde., and Sepoy Corps at Cawnpore in July 1787. Comdg. 1st Bde. N.I. at Midnapore in 1790. Second Rohilla War ; battle of Bitaurah ; Col. comdg. Right and Left Bdes., and second in comd. to Sir Robert Abercrombie. Comdg. at Dinapore in 1796. Fur. 6 Dec. 1797 till retirement.
Refs. : *Hickey,* iv. 120. *Williams,* p. 76. *M.M.* 1808, p. 396. *S.M.* 1808, p. 800. *G.M.* 1808, ii. 956.

FORBES, John (1782-1804). Lieutenant, 2nd N.I. *b.* Curr, Cromdale, Inverness, 15 July 1782. Cadet 1799. Admitted 22 Aug. 1801. Ensign 24 Sept. 1800. Lieut. 12 Aug. 1801. *d.* 13 Nov. 1804 : kld. in action at the battle of Deig.
bapt. Cromdale 24 July 1782. Son of Capt. Alexander Forbes, late 97th Regt.
Services : Expedn. to Egypt 1801 ; Ensign Bengal Vol. Bn. Operations in Jumna Doab 1803 ; Sasni ; Lieut. 1/2nd N.I. Second Mahratta War ; battle of Delhi ; battle of Deig (kld.) ; Lieut. 1/2nd N.I. He was leading his Coy. when he was struck by a cannon ball and blown to pieces.
Refs. : *Pester,* p. 345.

FORBES, John (1788-1805). Cadet, Infantry. *b.* Aberdeen 26 Mar. 1788. Cadet 1804. Never arrived in India. *d.* at sea 5 Feb. 1805 : drowned in the wreck of the *Earl of Abergavenny* off Portland on the voyage to India. (See note to Charles Davis or Davies.)
bapt. St. Paul's chapel, Aberdeen, 8 Apr. 1788. 2nd son of John

THE BENGAL ARMY, 1758-1834

Forbes of Blackford, J.P., co. Aberdeen, and Anne Margaret Gregory his wife. Brother of William Nairn Forbes *q.v.*

FORBES, John Villiers (1806-1853). Captain, Invalid Est. 15th N.I. *b.* Walcot, Somerset, 19 Aug. 1806. Cadet 1822. Arrived in India 13 May 1823. Ensign 18 Apr. 1823. Lieut. 1 May 1824. Capt. 29 Sept. 1835. Invalided 10 Mar. 1841. *d.* Calcutta 14 July 1853.

Son of Thomas John Forbes, Col. R.A. *m.* 1st (before 1824), Maria Eudoxie, sister of Gaston de Bessy, of Mauritius, planter. *m.* 2nd, Calcutta, 23 Jan. 1849, Anne, dau. of Charles Burgett.

Services : Posted as Ensign to 11th N.I. Transfd. to 15th N.I. (late 1/11th) May 1824. Action at Patan, nr. Kotah, 7 Nov. 1824. Siege and capture of Bhurtpore ; Lieut. 15th N.I. (India medal). Actg. Intr. & Qmr. 3rd N.I. 31 Jan. 1828 ; do. 10th N.I. 12 Mar. 1829. Actg. Adjt. 15th N.I. 28 Apr. 1829. Leave s.c. 18 mos. to Mauritius 12 Dec. 1829. Actg. Intr. & Qmr. 53rd N.I. 22 Feb. 1832. Adjt. 15th N.I. 19 Dec. 1833 till 21 Oct. 1835. Actg. Bde. Major at Cawnpore 4 Jan. 1836. Leave s.c. 2 yrs. to N.S.W. *via* Mauritius 8 June 1838. Was employed for 5 mos. in Mauritius as a Member of a Committee for enquiring into the state and condition of Indian labourers in that island. P.W.D. at Barisal 1 Sept. 1840. Leave s.c. 2 yrs. to Mauritius 11 Apr. 1841.

Refs. : *I.M.* 1853, p. 539. Will dated Patna 2 June 1853 ; proved 1 Aug. 1853.

FORBES, Richard (*d.* 1813). Lieut. Colonel, Invalid Est. 1st N.I. Cadet 1775. Admitted 1776. Ensign 5 Mar. 1777. Lieut. 3 Aug. 1778. Capt. 16 Mar. 1794. Major 26 Nov. 1798. Lt. Col. 5 July 1801. Invalided 26 Jan. 1804. *d.* Chunar 17 Feb. 1813.

Son of Capt. Roderick Forbes. *m.* Rebecca, a native Christian, by the rites of the Church of Rome. As the ceremony did not take place in an English church his children were not regarded as legitimate.

Services : Apptd. Cadet by the C.D. 25 Oct. 1775. Lieut. 2/2nd Bengal Eur. Regt. in Oct. 1779 ; Lieut. 4th Bengal Eur. Bn. in July 1787 ; Capt. 3rd Bengal Eur. Regt. in 1796. Operations in Jumna Doab 1803 ; Sasni ; Bijaigarh ; Kachaura ; Lt. Col. 1/15th N.I. Second Mahratta War ; battle of Delhi ; Agra ; Laswari ; Lt. Col. 1/15th N.I. Transfd. to 1st N.I. Subsequently comdd. 2nd Bn. Native Invalids.

Refs. : Will dated Chunar 15 Feb. 1813 ; proved in 1813.

FORBES, William (1801-?). Lieut. Colonel. 61st N.I. *b.* Shandon, co. Cork, 25 Mar. 1801. Cadet 1817. Admitted 4 Aug. 1818. Ensign 13 Mar. 1818. Lieut. 1 Aug. 1818. Capt. 11 July 1828.

Major 23 Nov. 1841. Invalided 11 Apr. 1845. Retired 10 Oct. 1847. Hon. Lt. Col. 28 Nov. 1854. (*d.* 1877-9 ?)
Son of William Somarsall Forbes, Major 56th Foot.
Services : Posted as Lieut. to 2/23rd N.I. Transfd. to 1/31st N.I. July 1823. Actg. Intr. & Qmr. 1/31st N.I. 21 Oct. 1823. Transfd. to 61st N.I. (late 1/31st) May 1824. Actg. Adjt. Magh Levy 23 Apr. 1826 ; 2nd in comd. do. 1 May 1827. Fur. s.c. 16 Aug. 1830 till 19 Oct. 1833. Shekhawat expedn. 1834 ; Capt. 61st N.I. Fur. s.c. 10 Apr. 1845 till retirement.

FORBES, William Henry (1780-1802). Lieutenant, 14th N.I. *bapt.* St. Mary's, Pembroke, 20 Feb. 1780. Cadet 1798. Admitted 24 Sept. 1799. Ensign 22 Nov. 1799. Lieut. 29 May 1800. *d.* Sultanpur, U.P., 17 May 1802.
Son of William Forbes and Margaret his wife.
Services : No record of active service.

FORBES, William Nairn (1796-1855). Major General, Engineers. Master of the Calcutta Mint. *b.* Auchterless, co. Aberdeen, 3 Apr. 1796. Cadet 1815. Ensign 29 Sept. 1816. Lieut. 1 Sept. 1818. Capt. 7 Feb. 1827. Major 22 Oct. 1841. Lt. Col. 22 Oct. 1841. Col. 15 Sept. 1851. Maj. Gen. 28 Nov. 1854. *d.* at sea nr. Aden 1 May 1855, on board the *Oriental,* on the voyage to England.
Son of John Forbes, of Blackford, and Anne Margaret Gregory his wife. Brother of John Forbes (1788-1805), *q.v. m.* Calcutta, 18 June 1836, Sarah, dau. of Charles Beckett Greenlaw, sec. to the Marine Board, and coroner of Calcutta. Addiscombe Cadet 13 Aug. 1812 till Dec. 1813. LL.D., Aberdeen, 27 Nov. 1822.
Services : Deputed to England to superintend the machinery for the new Calcutta Mint Dec. 1819 till 21 Oct. 1823. Siege and capture of Bhurtpore (w.) ; Lieut. S. & M. (India medal). Mint Master at Calcutta, and Supt. of Govt. machinery, 3 Feb. 1836 till death. On special duty in England Dec. 1847 till June 1849. Architect of St. Paul's cathedral and the Mint, Calcutta.
Refs. : G.M. 1855, ii. 106. Will dated Calcutta 7 Jan. 1837 ; admon. 20 Nov. 1855. M.I. St. Paul's cathedral, Calcutta.

FORD, Matthew Randle (1779-1857). Captain. 12th N.I. *bapt.* Pitcombe, Somerset, 16 Aug. 1779. Cadet 1794. Admitted 27 Sept. 1795. Ensign 21 Oct. 1795. Lieut. 25 Apr. 1797. Capt. 23 Sept. 1804. Retired 1 June 1808. *d.* at his residence, Lansdown Pl., E., Bath, 1 July 1857, aged 77.
Eldest son of John Ford, of Bath, and Margaret his wife. *m.*

16 May 1816, Anne, 2nd dau. of John William Hicks, and sister of John William Hicks, *q.v.*
Services : Sailed for India 24 May 1795. Posted as Ensign to 6th Bn. Bengal Eur. Regt. Transfd. to 3rd N.I. in 1796 ; to newly-raised 13th N.I. in 1797. Fourth Mysore War 1799-1800 ; Malavelli ; storm and capture of Seringapatam ; Lieut. 2nd Bn. Bengal Vols. (Medal). Posted to 1/12th N.I. in 1800. Second Mahratta War ; Agra ; Laswari ; Monson's retreat (s.w. in forehead by a matchlock ball on 27 Aug. 1804) ; Lieut. 1/12th N.I. (India medal). Fur. s.c. 27 June 1805 till retirement.
Refs. : E.I.M.C. iii. 167-9. G.M. 1857, ii. 229. *Bath Chron.*, July 1857.

FORD, Nathaniel (*d.* 1773). Captain, Infantry. Cadet (?). Ensign 30 Oct. 1764. Lieut. 2 Dec. 1766. Capt. 12 Apr. 1769. *d. unm.* Chittagong 24 Nov. 1773.
Son of Elizabeth Ford. Brother of John Ford.
Services : N.F.P.
Refs. : N. & Q. 10s. ix. 46.

FORD, Thomas (*d.* 1782). Captain, Infantry. Cadet 1771. Ensign 11 Dec. 1772. Lieut. 10 Mar. 1777. Capt. 11 Mar. 1781. *d.* Bankipore, B. & O., 9 July 1782.
Brother of Edward Ford, of Golden Sq., London, and of Ann Ford.
Services : N.F.P.
Refs. : Will dated Bankipore 6 July 1782.

FORD, Thomas. Cadet. Infantry. Cadet 1780. Removed to the Madras Est. (?).
Services : N.F.P. Out of the Service before 1787.

FORD, ——. Capt. Lieutenant. Infantry. Capt. Lt. 6 June 1758.
Services : N.F.P. Out of the Service before 1760.
Refs. : Orme MSS.—*India*, xiii. p. 3639.

*FORDE, Francis (*d.* 1770). Colonel. Infantry. Lt. Col. 1758. *d.* at sea 1770 ; lost in the *Aurora* between the Cape and India.
Of Johnstown, co. Meath. 2nd son of Matthew Forde, of Seaforde, co. Down, M.P. for Downpatrick, and Anne his wife, dau. of William Brownlow, of Lurgan. *m.* 1748, Margaret, dau. of Thomas Bowerbank, of Culgaita, Cumberland.
Services : See *D.N.B.* Ensign H.M.S. 5 Dec. 1740. Lieut (?). Capt. Adlercron's Regt. (H.M. 39th) 30 Apr. 1746. Arrived in Madras Sept. 1754. Major 13 Nov. 1755. Joined the Bengal army in 1758 ; arrived in Calcutta 21 Jan. 1758.
Refs. : Burke's *Landed Gentry of Ireland*, p. 238, *s.n.* Forde, of

Seaforde, co. Down. *D.N.B. Forde. D.I.B. Forrest's Clive. N. & Q.* 12 S. ix. 126. *Orme MSS.—India,* xiii. p. 3639.

FORDYCE, Sir John (1806-1877). Lieut. General, K.C.B. Colonel Comdt. Artillery. *b.* 4 Mar. 1806. Cadet 1821. Arrived in India 3 Jan. 1823. 2nd Lieut. 10 May 1822. Lieut. 25 Mar. 1826. Capt. 29 Apr. 1840. Major 2 Feb. 1851. Lt. Col. 8 June 1856. Col. 18 Feb. 1861. Maj. Gen. 29 Apr. 1861. Lt. Gen. 21 Jan. 1872. Col. Comdt. 5 Apr. 1873. *d.* Colne House, Earls Colne, Essex, 26 Feb. 1877.

bapt. Newington, Surrey, 14 Apr. 1806. Eldest son of James D. Fordyce, clerk to Messrs. Reid, Irving & Co., of London, and Margaret his wife, dau. of James McDougal (? Charlotte his wife, dau. of Alexander Macdougall, of the Exchequer, Edinburgh). Nephew of Arthur Dingwall-Fordyce, *q.v. m.* 1st, 1830, Mrs. Bennet. (She died at sea on board the *Warrior* 5 Nov. 1830.) *m.* 2nd, Paris, 16 Mar. 1842, Maria Louisa, youngest dau. of H. G. Alleyne, of Barbados I. (She died Nasirabad, 2 Sept. 1845, aged 29.) *m.* 3rd, Meerut, 14 Apr. 1847, Phoebe, dau. of James Graham, M.D. Addiscombe Cadet 1820-2.

Services : First Burma War ; Arakan 1825. Fur. 19 Jan. 1827 till 29 May 1830. Asst. Revenue Surveyor 4 Apr. 1834 till 1 Oct. 1836. Fur. 4 Dec. 1840 till 2 June 1843. First Sikh War ; Ferozshahr ; Sobraon ; Capt. 3rd Coy. 4th Bn. Foot Art. (Medal with clasp). Comdd. 2nd Troop 2nd Bde. H.A. 1846-52. Second Sikh War ; Chilianwala ; Gujerat ; pursuit of Sikhs and Afghans to Khyber (Medal with 2 clasps). Operations on N.W. frontier 1849-50 ; Yusafzai 30 Nov. 1849 ; Kohat Pass 9 Feb. 1850 ; comdg. the Art. (Medal). Agent for gun carriages at Fatehgarh 9 May 1853. Lt. Col. comdg. 4th Bn. Foot Art. Comdt. Bengal Art. 29 July till 13 Oct. 1860. K.C.B. 24 May 1873.

Refs. : Burke's *Landed Gentry,* 13th edn., p. 664, *s.n.* Dingwall-Fordyce, of Brucklay, co. Aberdeen. *Anderson,* ii. 245. *Boase. D.I.B. Misc. Gen. et Her.* 4S. v. 8. *A.J.* N.S. xxxvii. 380. *The Times,* 6 Mar. 1877.

DINGWALL-FORDYCE, Arthur (1783-1812). Captain, Engineers. Chief. Engr., P.W.I. *b.* 29 Mar. (or June) 1783. Cadet 1797. Ensign 8 Oct. 1798. Lieut. 17 Sept. 1807. Capt. 5 Nov. 1810. *d. unm.* at sea, 22 Dec. 1812, on board the *Fort William,* off the Cape, on his passage to England.

bapt. Aberdeen 12 July 1783. Youngest son of Arthur Dingwall-Fordyce, of Culsh, LL.D., advocate in Aberdeen, and Janet his wife, dau. of James Morrison, of Elsick, provost of Aberdeen. Brother of Thomas Dingwall-Fordyce, *q.v.,* and uncle of Sir John Fordyce,

q.v. Woolwich Cadet: nominated for R.M.A. 25 May 1798; obtained his certificate 2 May 1800.
Services : Second Mahratta War; Gwalior. Operations against Dhundia Khan 1807; Komona (w.). (? Capture of Java 1811.) Chief Engr. in Java 1811-2. Fur. from Java 1812.
Refs. : Burke's *Landed Gentry,* 13th edn., p. 664, *s.n.* Dingwall-Fordyce, of Brucklay, co. Aberdeen. *Anderson,* ii. 245. *Misc. Gen. et Her.* 4 S. v. 8. *A.A.R.* x. 21. *G.M.* 1813, i. 660. Will dated 2 July 1810; proved in 1814.

DINGWALL-FORDYCE, Thomas (1791-1820). Lieutenant, Artillery. *b.* Aberdeen 7 Apr. 1791. Cadet 1808. Arrived in India 19 July 1809. Fireworker 24 July 1809. Lieut. 30 Dec. 1815. *d.* Calcutta 8 Jan. 1820.

Youngest son of Arthur Dingwall-Fordyce, of Culsh, last judge of the consistorial court in Aberdeen. Brother of Arthur Dingwall-Fordyce, *q.v.* *m.* Dum-Dum 17 May 1819, Margaret, dau. of William Hopper, *q.v.* (*See also* Henry Philip Hughes.)
Services : Capture of Mauritius 1810; Lieut.F. 6th Coy. 1st Bn. Foot Art. Returned to Bengal in July 1811. Siege and capture of Hathras 1817; Lieut. 6th Coy. 3rd Bn. Actg. Adjt. & Qmr. Art.
Refs. : Burke's *Landed Gentry,* 13th edn., p. 664, *s.n.* Dingwall-Fordyce, of Brucklay, co. Aberdeen. *Misc. Gen. et Her.* 4S. v. 8. *S.M.* 1820, ii. 190. M.I. in S. Park St. cemetery, Calcutta.

FOREMAN, James (*d.* 1769). Captain, Infantry. Capt. 1 Sept. 1768. *d.* 1769.
Services : Not in *A.L.* of 1 Feb. 1767. *Probably* transfd. as Capt. from H.M.S.

FORREST, Lowther Thomas (1812-1882). Lieut. Colonel. 40th N.I. *bapt.* London 30 May 1812. Cadet 1829. Arrived in India 25 May 1830. Ensign 23 Apr. 1830. Lieut. 18 May 1839. Capt. 18 June 1850. Bt. Major 28 Nov. 1854. Retired 20 Jan. 1857. Hon. Lt. Col. 20 Jan. 1857. *d.* 11 June 1882.

2nd son of Thomas Forrest, of Binfield, Berks., Capt. Warwick Yeomanry, and Mary his wife. *m.* Frankfort, 7 May 1842, Lydia, eldest dau. of Justin McCarty, of Carrignavar, co. Cork. Addiscombe Cadet 1827.
Services : Cadet d.d. 43rd N.I. 7 June 1830; do. 55th N.I. 8 Jan. 1831. Actg. Ensign 16 July 1832. d.d. 39th N.I. 15 Aug. 1832. Posted as Ensign to 40th N.I. 20 Aug. 1833. Transfd. to 41st N.I. 24 Sept. 1835; to 40th N.I. 27 Apr. 1836. Tempy charge of Nepal Escort 27 Nov. 1837. Adjt. Jodhpur Legion 4 Sept. 1838. Operations against the Kols May 1839. Fur. s.c. 21 Feb. 1840 till 5 Nov.

1842. Second in comd. 2nd Oudh Local Inf. 12 June 1847. Comdt. Cav., United Malwa Contingent, 7 Apr. 1848 till retirement. Second Burma War 1852-3 ; Pegu ; Capt. 40th N.I. (Medal).

Refs. : Burke's *Landed Gentry,* 7th edn., p. 1169, *s.n.* McCarty, of Carrignavar. *A.J.* N.S. xxxviii.

FORREST, William (1777-1832). Lieut. Colonel. 2nd N.I. Insp. of Mily. Stores for India. *b.* Haddington 6 Sept. 1777. Cadet 1798. Admitted 24 Feb. 1800. Ensign 26 Sept. 1799. Lieut. 28 Oct. 1799. Capt. 2 Oct. 1808. Major 11 July 1823. Lt. Col. 7 Nov. 1824. *d.* Dundee, 29 July 1832, of cholera.[1]

Of Charlton. *bapt.* 14 Sept. 1777. Son of John Forrest, of Fife, and Janet his wife. *m.* 1st (before 1810) (?). *m.* 2nd, Sunbury, Middlesex, 9 Nov. 1814, Georgiana Christina, younger dau. of James Carmichael-Smyth, M.D., of Charlton House, Sunbury, and sister of Charles Montauban Carmichael-Smyth, *q.v.*

Services : Posted as Ensign to 1/2nd N.I. Operations in Jumna Doab 1803 ; Sasni ; Bijaigarh ; Kachaura ; Thathia ; Lieut. 1/2nd N.I., Asst. Field Engr. Second Mahratta War ; Aligarh ; Delhi ; Agra ; Laswari ; Gwalior ; Rampura ; capture of Deig (s.w.—lost an arm in addition to 22 other wounds) ; Lieut. 1/2nd N.I., with Pioneers. Transfd. as Capt. to 2/2nd N.I. Fur. s.c. 12 Dec. 1813. Retired in England as Capt. on 30 May 1816. Apptd. in 1816 Insp. to E.I.C. of mily. stores for India, and was subsequently promoted Major and Lieut. Col.

Refs. : Burke's *Peerage,* 1859, p. 169, *s.n.* Carmichael, Bart., of Nutwood, Surrey. *E.I.M.C.,* iii. 29-31. *Pester. G.M.* 1814, ii. 600 ; 1832, ii. 190. *Bath Chron.,* Aug. 1832.

[1] *Note :* He was attacked by cholera on 28 July 1832 when on board the *Glasgow,* and died in less than 15 hours.

FORREST, William St. Leger (1810-1839). Lieutenant, 29th N.I. *bapt.* Calcutta 13 Dec. 1810. Cadet 1826. Arrived in India 28 Sept. 1827. Ensign 3 May 1827. Lieut. 12 Oct. 1834. *d.* Hamirpur, U.P., 3 Feb. 1839.

Son of Charles Ramus Forrest, Lt. Col. h.p. 34th Foot, and Ellen his wife, *née* St. Leger (*probably* dau. of Lt. Gen. William St. Leger).

Services : Posted as Ensign to 29th N.I. 3 Jan. 1828. Actg. Adjt. 29th N.I. Aug. 1838. Apptd. Adjt. to the Corps about to be raised for Jalaun, U.P., 7 Jan. 1839. No record of active service.

Refs. : A.J. N.S. xxix. 140.

FORRESTER, John Napier (1783-1860). Captain.[1] Artillery. *b.* Dunipace, co. Stirling, 31 Dec. 1783. Cadet 1804. Arrived in India 25 Mar. 1806. Lieut. 27 Mar. 1806. Capt. Lt. 29 Dec. 1815. Capt. 1 Sept. 1818. Retired 13 Dec. 1820. *d.* 1 July 1860.

Son of Gabriel Forrester, Lieut. of the Independent Coy. of Invalids, of the garrison of Stirling Castle, and Jean Hamilton his wife. Brother of Robert Graham Forrester, *q.v.* *m.* Glasgow, Oct. 1818, a dau. of Alexander Hill, merchant in Stirling.

Services : Adjt. & Qmr. 1st Bn. Foot Art. 1813-6. Fur. 1817 till retirement. No record of active service.

Refs. : *S.M.* 1818, ii. 486.

¹ *Note :* From 1846 onwards he is shown in the list of retired officers as Lt. Col.; previous to that year as Capt. only. The higher rank is probably an error.

FORRESTER, Robert Graham (1785-1810). Ensign, 22nd N.I. *b.* Stirling 21 Sept. 1785. Cadet 1806. Arrived in India 1 Aug. 1807. Ensign 20 Aug. 1807. *d.* Fatehgarh, U.P., 20 July 1810.

Son of Gabriel Forrester, Lieut. of the Independent Coy. of Invalids, and Jean Hamilton his wife. Brother of John Napier Forrester, *q.v.*

Services : Posted as Ensign to 22nd N.I. (? Settlement of Hariana 1809 ; Bhawani ; Ensign 1/22nd N.I.)

FORSTER, George (1798-1834). Captain, 6th L.C. *b.* Brentwood, Essex, 18 Sept. 1798. Cadet 1819. Admitted 14 June 1820. Cornet 10 Jan. 1820. Lieut. 11 Sept. 1821. Capt. 12 Aug. 1831. *d.* in England (? Cheltenham) 23 Apr. 1834.

Son of George Forster, Col. R.A.

Services : Posted as Cornet to 6th L.C. Fur. s.c. 5 June 1822 till 5 Dec. 1826, and 3 Jan. 1831 till death. No record of active service.

FORSTER, James. Captain. Infantry. Cadet (?). Ensign 27 July 1759. Lieut. 18 Sept. 1761. Capt. 13 Oct. 1763. Resigned 25 Jan. 1765.

Services : N.F.P.

FORSTER or **FOSTER, John Hibbard** (*d.* 1811). Lieut. Colonel, 3rd N.I. Cadet 1778. Admitted 9 Mar. 1778. Ensign 4 June 1778. Lieut. 3 Dec. 1779. Capt. 3 Oct. 1796. Major 13 July 1803. Lt. Col. 23 Sept. 1804. *d.* Delhi 11 May 1811.

Son of Thomas Forster or Foster, *q.v.*, and Elizabeth Hibbard his wife. *m.* Jane. (She died in France 7 Mar. 1858, aged 82.)

Services : 1/3rd Bengal Eur. Regt. in 1779. Lieut. 8th Bn. Sepoys in July 1787. Second Mahratta War ; Major 13th N.I. Transfd. as Lt. Col. to 6th N.I. in 1804. Fur. 22 Jan. 1806 till 19 July 1809. Transfd. to 24th N.I. in 1807 ; to 2/3rd N.I. in 1809.

Refs. : Will dated 23 Jan. 1809 ; proved 3 Dec. 1811.

FORSTER, Nicholas. Ensign. Infantry. Cadet 1779. Ensign 5 May 1781. Struck off 1782.
Services : N.F.P.

FORSTER, Ralph (1789-1835). Captain, 72nd N.I. *bapt.* Embleton, Northumberland, 20 May 1789. Cadet 1805. Arrived in India 19 Nov. 1806. Ensign 10 Oct. 1806. Lieut. 11 Apr. 1810. Capt. 13 May 1825. *d.* Monghyr, B. & O., 19 Aug. 1835.
Son of Robert Forster, of High Brunton, and Seaton his wife.
Services : A survivor from the wreck of the *Lady Burges* on the voyage out to India; sailed subsequently on the *Walthamstow.* Barasat C.C. for 13½ mos. Posted as Ensign to 14th N.I. Adjt. 2/14th N.I. 1815. (? Nepal War 1814-5; Lieut. 2/14th N.I. in 3rd Div.) Actg. Intr. & Qmr. 2/14th N.I. in 1816. Actg. Adjt. Farrukhabad Provl. Bn. 26 Oct. 1821. Transfd. to newly-raised 33rd N.I. 11 July 1823; to 66th N.I. (late 2/33rd) May 1824; to 29th N.I. 13 Aug. 1824; to newly-raised 4th Extra Regt. (became 72nd N.I.) May 1825.
Refs. : *A.J.* xxvii. 478.

FORSTER, Richard Wyndham (1791-1822). Bt. Captain, 13th N.I. *b.* Chiswick 25 Sept. 1791. Cadet 1806. Arrived in India 1 Aug. 1807. Ensign 30 Aug. 1807. Lieut. 10 Oct. 1810. Bt. Capt. 1822. *d.* Chittagong 3 June 1822.
bapt. Chiswick 23 Oct. 1791. Son of Robert Forster and Mary his wife.
Services : Posted as Ensign to 13th N.I. in 1808. Lieut. 2/13th N.I. Third Mahratta War 1819; Asirgarh; Lieut. 2/13th N.I. Actg. Adjt. 2/13th N.I. 1819; Adjt. 1820. Intr. & Qmr. 2/13th N.I. 22 June 1821 till death. Leave to N.S.W. 1821-2.

FORSTER or FOSTER, Thomas (*d.* 1776). Lieutenant, Infantry. Cadet 1769. Ensign 18 Aug. 1769. Lieut. 30 Jan. 1773. *d.* Chittagong, Sept. 1776.
Brother of William Forster or Foster, *q.v.* *m.* Elizabeth Hibbard. Father of John Hibbard Forster or Foster, *q.v.*
Services : N.F.P.
Refs. : Will dated 19 Aug. 1775; proved 7 Mar. 1777.

FORSTER or FOSTER, William (*d.* 1782). Captain, Infantry. Cadet 1771. Ensign 3 Feb. 1773. Lieut. 22 Apr. 1778. Capt. 9 June 1781. *d.* Berhampore 12 Sept. 1782.
Brother of Thomas Forster or Foster, *q.v.*, and of William, Lieut. Bo. Est. *m.* (before 1779) Diana.
Services : N.F.P.

FORTNOM, John (*d.* 1779). Colonel, Engineers. Cadet (?). Ensign 6 Sept. 1763. Lieut. 14 Apr. 1764. Capt. 31 Dec. 1766. Major 26 Dec. 1772. Lt. Col. 20 Jan. 1775. *d.* 25 Jan. 1779.

Descended from a branch of the family of Fortnum settled at Erstone, co. Oxford. Brother of Joseph Fortnom, of Horsely Hall, Gresford, co. Denbigh, of Anne, wife of Christopher Green, *q.v.*, and of Sophia, wife of Lawrence Gall, *q.v. m.* Calcutta, 3 Sept. 1767, Miss Jane Yeates. Father of Thomas William Fortnom, *q.v.* His daus. *m.* Samuel Cox, *q.v.*, Patrick Douglas, *q.v.*, Alexander Orme, *q.v.*, and Andrew Pringle, *q.v.*

Services : Civil architect 1765. Director of the Works 1772.

Refs. : Burke's *Landed Gentry*, 9th edn., p. 539, *s.n.* Fortnum, of the Hill House, Middlesex. Will dated 14 Mar. 1778; proved 10 Mar. 1779.

FORTNOM, Thomas William (1772-?). Fireworker. Artillery. *bapt.* Calcutta 28 Oct. 1772. Cadet 1791. Admitted 22 Feb. 1792. Fireworker 9 Mar. 1792. Resigned 28 Aug. 1800.

Younger son of John Fortnom, *q.v.*, and Jane his wife. Godson of Benjamin Wilding, *q.v. m.* Taunton, Aug. 1798, Catherine Leslie, 2nd dau. of Leslie Grove, of Grove Hall, co. Donegal, and sister of Leslie Ralph Grove, *q.v.*

Services : Apptd. a " Minor Cadet " in 1781. (Cons. of 21 May 1781.) Struck off 2 May 1786. Third Mysore War; Seringapatam; joined the army in Jan. 1792. Fur. 19 Jan. 1797 till retirement.

Refs. : Burke's *Landed Gentry*, 9th edn., p. 539, *s.n.* Fortnum, of the Hill House, Middlesex. Burke's *Landed Gentry of Ireland*, p. 281, *s.n.* Grove, of Castle Grove.

FORTUNE, Alexander (1779-1823). Captain, 27th N.I. A.D.C. to the King of Oudh. *b.* Edinburgh 30 Mar. 1779. Cadet 1798. Admitted 13 May 1800. Ensign 16 Jan. 1800. Lieut. 29 May 1800. Capt. 16 Dec. 1814. *d.* Lucknow 20 Aug. 1823.

Son of John Fortune, of New Kirk psh., Edinburgh, vintner, and Ann his wife, sister of William Somers (or Sommers, of Broughton, N.B.). Brother of Major John Fortune, Madras Est., and of Jean, wife of Richard Blackwell, of Haddington, mail contractor.

Services : Lieut. 7th N.I. Transfd. to newly-raised 27th N.I. 1804. Operations against Dhundia Khan 1807; Komona; Ganauri; Lieut. 27th N.I. Capt. 2/27th N.I. Comdd. escort of Resdt. at Lucknow 1811-21. On leave at the Cape in 1816. In the service of the King of Oudh 1821 till death. He bequeathed a gold watch ring, set with diamonds, formerly Tippoo Sultan's, which had been left him by his brother John, to Lt. Col. John Baillie, of Leys, *q.v.*, under whom he had served at Lucknow.

Refs.: *S.M.* 1824, i. 383. Will dated Lucknow 13 Oct. 1820; codicil dated 19 Aug. 1823; proved 12 Sept. 1823.

FOSTER, Charles Thomas (1800-1822). Lieutenant, Bengal Eur. Regt. *b.* Drogheda 14 Oct. 1800. Cadet 1817. Ensign (?). Lieut. 10 Oct. 1818. *d.* Ghazipur, U.P., 7 May 1822.

Services: Posted as Lieut. to Bengal Eur. Regt. in 1819. No record of active service.

FOTHERGILL, Francis (1794-1814). Ensign, 17th N.I. *b.* York 7 Feb. 1794. Cadet 1809. Ensign 31 Oct. 1812. *d.* 31 Oct. 1814: kld. in action in the attack on Kalanga.

bapt. York 20 Mar. 1794. Son of John Fothergill, of Kingsthorpe, Pickering, Yorks., comdg. 5th N. York Local Mil., and Mary his wife, dau. of Francis Bacon. Grandson of Marmaduke Fothergill.

Services: Cadet d.d. 9th N.I. 1811. Posted as Ensign to 1/17th N.I. 1812. Nepal War 1814; Kalanga (kld.); Ensign 1/17th N.I., in 2nd Div.

FOTHERINGHAM, Alexander (*d.* 1784). Ensign. 3rd Bengal Eur. Regt. Cadet 1778. Ensign 9 May 1779. Dismissed by C.M. 8 Nov. 1779. bur. Calcutta 6 Jan. 1784.

Services: Ensign 1/3rd Bengal Eur. Regt. in Oct. 1779.

FOTHERINGHAM, Robert Hamilton (1805-1824). Cadet, Infantry. *bapt.* Trichinopoly, Madras, 22 May 1805. Cadet 1823. Never arrived in India. *d.* Madeira, 18 June 1824, on his passage out to India, aged 19: kld. by a fall from his horse.

Only son of John Fotheringham, Major Madras Engrs., and Margaret his wife.

Refs.: *S.M.* 1824, ii. 382.

FOULIS, Charles (*d.* 1783?). Cadet. Infantry. Cadet 1771. Resigned 12 Mar. 1773. (*d.* Woodford, Essex, 10 July 1783?)

Services: N.F.P. (? Subsequently one of the directors of the Sun Fire Office, London.)

Refs.: (*G.M.* 1783, ii. 629.)

FOULIS, George (1766/67-1805). Major, 4th N.I. *b.* 1766/67. Cadet 1781. Ensign 27 Apr. 1781. Lieut. 15 Aug. 1782. Capt. 29 May 1800. Major 19 Oct. 1803. *d. unm.* Calcutta 18 Dec. 1805.

Son of William Foulis, of Woodhall and Colinton, and his wife, dau. of Campbell, of Cariebank. Brother of Sir James Foulis, 7th

Bart. of Woodhall, and brother-in-law of Alexander Nasmyth, miniature painter (*D.N.B.*).
Services : Apptd. Cadet 10 Oct. 1781, aged 15. Sailed for India on the *Earl Talbot*, 6 Feb. 1782, aged 15. Fur. 27 Sept. 1785 till 1791. Lieut. 4th N.I. Capt. 2/4th N.I. Second Mahratta War; Aligarh; (? defence of Delhi); Major 4th N.I.
Refs. : Burke's *Peerage*, 1923, p. 936, *s.n.* Liston-Foulis, Bart., 'of Colinton and Ravelston. *G.M.* 1806, ii. 776. Will dated Calcutta 11 Nov. 1805.

FOULIS, Henry (*d.* 1783). Lieutenant, Infantry. Cadet 1771. Ensign 23 Mar. 1773. Lieut. 20 Mar. 1778. *d.* Fatehgarh 3 Dec. 1783.
Services : N.F.P.

FOUNTAIN, William Nassau (1776/77-1824). Lieut. Colonel, 8th N.I. *b.* 1776/77. Cadet 1798. Admitted 27 May 1800. Ensign 3 Oct. 1799. Lieut. 28 Oct. 1799. Capt. 5 June 1811. Major 1 Feb. 1820. Lt. Col. 1 May 1824. *d.* Neempoonee, nr. Betul, C.P., 15 Dec. 1824.

Son of Rev. Thomas Fountain, D.D., master of a preparatory school for Westminster, at Marylebone. Ed. Westminster; K.S. 1792, aged 15.
Services : Second Mahratta War; Lieut. 9th N.I. With Ramgarh Bn. 1805 and 1807-9. Capt. Lt. 9th N.I. 26 Jan. 1809. Actg. Fort Adjt. at Fort William in 1809. Expedn. to Mauritius 1810; Capt. Lt. 1st Vol. Bn. Bde. Major at Cawnpore 11 Sept. 1813 till 1820. Major 1/9th N.I. Transfd. to 8th N.I. (late 1/9th) May 1824. On service with the Nagpur Subsdy. Force in 1824.
Refs. : *Alumni Westmon.* Will dated 8 Sept. 1810; proved 24 Feb. 1825.

Note : His name appears in his Will, and occasionally elsewhere, as Fountaine.

FOWEL, James. Cadet. Infantry. Cadet 1783.
Services : N.F.P.

***FOWELL, George** (1744-?). Captain, Infantry. *b.* Black Hall, Devon, 1744. *d. unm.* in Bengal (?).

4th and youngest son of John Fowell, of Black Hall, and Elizabeth his wife, dau. of John Newton, of Crabaton Court, Devon.
Services : N.F.P.
Refs. : Burke's *Landed Gentry*, 2nd edn., p. 438, *s.n.* Fowell of Devon. Foster's *Families of Royal Descent*, ii. 735.

Note : Has not been traced in *I.O. Rec.* : included here on the authority of Burke and Foster.

LIST OF THE OFFICERS OF

FOWLE, Charles (1802-1844). Captain, Invalid Est. 65th N.I. *bapt.* Kintbury, Berks., 29 July 1802. Cadet 1819. Admitted 15 Nov. 1820. Ensign 1 May 1820. Lieut. 11 July 1823. Capt. 16 Mar. 1838. Invalided 1 Feb. 1841. *d.* Liverpool 20 June 1844.

Son of Rev. Fulwar Craven Fowle, vicar of Kintbury and rector of Elkstone, Gloucs., and Elizabeth his wife. Brother of Henry Fowle, *q.v.* *m.* 1st, Calcutta, 2 Oct. 1824, Miss Mary Anne Thomas. (She died Penang 6 May 1826.) *m.* 2nd, Calcutta, 26 Aug. 1841, Mary Anne, dau. of Charles Driscoll. Ed. Winchester; Scholar 1811.

Services: Posted as Ensign to 1/1st N.I. Transfd. as Lieut. to newly-raised 33rd N.I. 11 July 1823; to 65th N.I. (late 1/33rd) May 1824. Fur. 1829 till 13 May 1831. Adjt. 65th N.I. 21 Sept. 1833 till 25 Nov. 1838. Fur. p.a. 18 Mar. 1843 till death. No record of active service.

Refs.: Kirby.

FOWLE, Henry (1820-?). Lieutenant. 44th N.I. *bapt.* Kintbury, Berks., 4 Apr. 1805. Cadet 1820. Arrived in India Nov. 1821. Ensign 4 July 1821. Lieut. 1 May 1824. Dismissed by C.M. 27 Apr. 1830.

Son of Rev. Fulwar Craven Fowle and Elizabeth his wife. Brother of Charles Fowle, *q.v.* *m.* Sylhet, 15 May 1828, Miss Starlina Hayward.

Services: Posted as Ensign to 1st N.I. in 1822. Transfd. to 22nd N.I. in 1823; to 43rd N.I. (late 1/22nd) May 1824; to 44th N.I. in 1825. First Burma War; Arakan 1825; Lieut. 1st L.I. Bn. Fur. 1826 till 31 Oct. 1827.

Refs.: A.J. N.S. iii. 154.

FOWLER, William (*d.* 1783). Captain. Infantry. Cadet 1769. Ensign 1769. Lieut. 13 Nov. 1772. Capt. 6 May 1782. Resigned 13 May 1782. *d.* 1783.

m. a dau. of Richard Huntridge, of the Charterhouse. His dau. *m.* James Wordsworth, B.C.S., cousin-german of the poet laureate.

Services: N.F.P.

Refs.: Will dated Patna 23 Apr. 1780; proved 14 July 1783.

FOX, John (*d.* 1785). Capt. Lieutenant, Artillery. Cadet 1777. Lieut. 30 Sept. 1778. Capt. Lt. 6 July 1784. *d.* at sea, 29 Dec. 1785, on his passage to Europe.

Services: Fur. s.c. 3 yrs. 5 Aug. 1785.

FOY, John (*d.* 1775). Lieutenant, Infantry. Cadet 1769. Ensign 10 Aug. 1769. Lieut. 3 Dec. 1772. *d.* Tellicherry, Madras, Sept. 1775.

Services: N.F.P.

FRAKERNE, John. (*See* **TRAHERNE.**)

FRAMINGHAM, Cozens (1753-1785). Lieutenant, 1st Bengal Eur. Regt. *b.* Swaffham, Norfolk, 1753. Cadet 1777. Ensign 26 Dec. 1777. Lieut. 6 Sept. 1778. *d.* 11 Nov. 1785.
Son of Cozens Framingham, of Swaffham, surgeon. Ed. Lynn. Caius Coll., Camb.: admitted 21 Apr. 1772; B.A. 1776.
Services : Sailed for India on the *Egmont*, 1 Jan. 1777, aged 23. Lieut. 2/1st Bengal Eur. Regt. in Oct. 1779.
Refs. : Graduati Cantab.
Note : His name is given as Framlingham in the embarkation roll, as Frammingham in *Dodwell & Miles*.

FRANCIS, James (*d.* 1773). Captain, Infantry. Cadet 1764. Ensign 8 June 1764. Lieut. 23 Aug. 1765. Capt. 8 Dec. 1767. *d.* Chittagong 27 June 1773.
Services : Lieut. 1st Bengal Eur. Regt. in 1765-6.
Refs. : Broome, pp. lix.-lx.

FRANCIS, Robert (1762/63-1832). Lieut. Colonel, Pension Est. 4th N.I. *b.* 1762/63. Country Cadet 1781. Admitted 10 Oct. 1781. Ensign 13 July 1782. Lieut. 10 Jan. 1785. Capt. 8 Sept. 1802. Major 24 Jan. 1809. Lt. Col. 20 July 1814. Pensioned 1 July 1819. *d.* Calcutta, 29 Sept. 1832, aged 69.
m. 6 Nov. 1810, Miss Anne L'Herondell. (*See also* John Jenkins Bird.) His dau. *m.* Edward Saunders Armigel-Waad Wada Wade, *q.v.*
Services : Lieut. 3rd Bengal Eur. Bn. in July 1787. Capt. Lt. 3rd N.I. 25 Oct. 1800. Major 3rd N.I. Transfd. as Lt. Col. to 9th N.I. in 1815; to 4th N.I. in 1819.
Refs. : G.M. 1833, ii. 190. *A.J.* N.S. x. 157.

FRANCKLIN, William (1763-1839). Lieut. Colonel. 22nd N.I. *b.* 1763. Cadet 1781. Admitted 9 Sept. 1782. Ensign 31 Jan. 1783. Lieut. 20 Dec. 1789. Capt. 30 Sept. 1803. Major 29 Mar. 1810. Lt. Col. 16 Dec. 1814. Invalided 1 Oct. 1815. Retired Dec. 1825. *d.* in England, 12 Apr. 1839, aged 76.[1]
Eldest son of Thomas Francklin, miscellaneous writer (*D.N.B.*), by the dau. of —— Venables, wine merchant. *m.* Calcutta, 9 Mar. 1801, Marian Hastings, dau. of Dr. James Collie, Surgeon, Bengal Est. (*See also* Peregrine Powell.) Ed. Westminster: admitted 6 June 1774; K.S. 1777, aged 14. Trin. Coll., Camb., 1781.
Services : See *D.N.B.* Granted fur. in order to travel in Persia 9 Jan. 1786. Fur. 18 Jan. 1797 till 12 Dec. 1800. Lieut. 19th N.I. in 1803. Capt. and Major 19th N.I. Dy. Paymr. at Chunar 1805-8.

Regulating Ofr. of Invalid Tannah Ests. 1808. Regulating Ofr. at Bhagulpur 1814 till retirement. Transfd. as Lt. Col. to 22nd N.I. Distinguished oriental scholar. Pub. in 1798, "History of the Reign of Shah-Aulum"; in 1803, by authority of the Govt., "The Military Memoirs of Mr. George Thomas," and other works.

Refs. : *D.N.B. D.I.B. Alumni Westmon. A.J.* N.S. xxix. 80.

[1] *Note :* According to *D.N.B.* his death occurred in India ; as, however, it is reported amongst Home Intelligence in *A.J.* for May 1839, this statement is obviously incorrect.

FRANKLIN, James (1783-1834). Major, 1st L.C. *bapt.* Spilsby 6 May 1783. Cadet 1804. Arrived in India 16 May 1806. Cornet 26 Mar. 1806. Lieut. 18 Aug. 1814. Capt. 1 Jan. 1819. Major 7 July 1833. *d.* Greenwich, 31 Aug. 1834, after a long illness, aged 51.

Son of Willingham Franklin and Hannah his wife. Brother of Sir John Franklin, the Arctic explorer (*D.N.B.*). *m.* Cawnpore, 7 Apr. 1818, Margaret Maria Clements, dau. of Sir Thomas Brown, *q.v.* (*See also* William Turner (1791-1827).) (She *re-m.* 10 Feb. 1836, James Evans.)

Services : Lieut. in the Spilsby, Wainfleet and Burgh (Lincs.) Vols. Was present at the capture of C.G.H. on the voyage out to India. Barasat C.C. Posted as Cornet to 1st N.C. in 1808. Sec. to Col. Martindell, on service in Bundelkhand, 1 Jan. 1810. Adjt. 1st N.C. 9 Jan. 1810 till 1816. Operations against Gopal Singh 1810-1; Bichaund; Cornet and Adjt. 1st N.C., and Staff Ofr. to Lt. Col. Thomas Brown, *q.v.* Apptd. to the survey of Bundelkhand 1812. D.A.Q.M.G., 2 cl., 1 Jan. 1817. Third Mahratta War; Jawad; D.A.Q.M.G., 1st Div., and Persian Intr. to his future father-in-law. A.Q.M.G. 25 Feb. 1820 till 22 Feb. 1823. Leave u.p.a. to Singapore 16 Oct. 1821 till 25 Apr. 1822. Fur. p.a. 6 Feb. 1823 till 20 Mar. 1826. Surveyor of iron mines in Saugor and Bundelkhand districts 29 Sept. 1826 till 31 July 1828. Fur. s.c. 1 Apr. 1830 till death.

Refs. : *E.I.M.C.* iii. 96-107. *G.M.* 1834, ii. 554. *A.J.* N.S. xv. 124.

FRANKS, James (*d.* 1786). Ensign, Infantry. Cadet 1782. Ensign 22 Feb. 1783. *d.* Calcutta 21 Jan. 1786.

Services : N.F.P.

FRASER, Alexander (1786-1822). Captain, Artillery. *b.* St. Cuthbert's, Edinburgh, 19 Apr. 1786. Cadet 1803. Arrived in India 19 Mar. 1805. Lieut. 28 Aug. 1804. Capt. Lt. 17 Nov. 1808. Capt. 25 Sept. 1817. *d.* Dinapore 2 Aug. 1822.

Son of Isobel Macdonald. *m.* Calcutta, 16 May 1812, Miss Barbara Henrietta Child. (*See also* Steele Hawthorne, and Æneas Mackintosh.)

THE BENGAL ARMY, 1758-1834   215

Services : Expedn. to Mauritius 1810 ; relieved Allan Graham, *q.v.*, in comd. of 6th Coy. 1st Bn. Foot Art. on 1 Oct. 1811, and returned with it to Bengal in Mar. 1812. Siege and capture of Hathras ; Capt. Lt. comdg. 2nd Coy. 2nd Bn. Third Mahratta War ; Capt. comdg. 2nd Coy. 2nd Bn. Comdd. a Horse Batty. of mixed calibres at Dum-Dum 1821-2.
Refs. : Will dated Dum-Dum 29 Apr. 1821 ; proved 30 Sept. 1822.

FRASER, Alexander (1811-1843). Bt. Captain, 45th N.I. *b.* Forres, co. Elgin, 26 Sept. 1811. Cadet 1827. Arrived in India 24 Oct. 1828. Ensign 7 Apr. 1828. Lieut. 11 Nov. 1831. Bt. Capt. 7 Apr. 1843. *d.* Sikraul, Benares, 20 July 1843, of cholera.

3rd son of Bailie Alexander Fraser, of Forres, merchant, and Jane Warden his wife. Brother of Robert Warden Fraser, *q.v.* Addiscombe Cadet 1824-6.
Services : Ensign d.d. 45th N.I. 20 Nov. 1828. Posted to 45th N.I. 3 June 1829, and served throughout with that Regt. No record of active service.
Refs. : I.M. No. 5, p. 146. *The Times,* 17 Oct. 1843.

FRASER, Alexander John (1802-1842). Captain, 56th N.I. *b.* W.I. 1802. Cadet 1819. Arrived in India 6 Jan. 1821. Ensign 16 July 1820. Lieut. 11 July 1823. Capt. 19 Feb. 1833. *d.* Hazaribagh, B. & O., 11 Dec. 1842.

Related to Affleck Fraser, of Culduthel, Inverness, and to James Fraser (1802-1868), *q.v.* (*Probably* related to George John Fraser, *q.v.*) *m.* Bulwah, nr. Benares, 17 Apr. 1839, Adèle, eldest dau. of J. de Momet, of Benares, indigo planter. (She *re-m.* Hazaribagh, 18 Oct. 1843, James Peter Brougham, M.D., Asst. Surgeon, Bengal.)
Services : Posted as Ensign to 2/13th N.I. Transfd. as Lieut. to 28th N.I. 11 July 1823 ; to 56th N.I. (late 2/28th) May 1824. Actg. Adjt. 56th N.I. 17 Mar. 1828. Fur. p.a. 24 Dec. 1835 till 23 Nov. 1838. Offg. Executive Ofr., Ramgarh Div., P.W.D. 22 May 1841. No record of active service.

FRASER, Andrew (*d.* 1806). Lieut. Colonel, Artillery. Country Cadet 1778. Admitted 11 Aug. 1778. Fireworker 30 Sept. 1778. Lieut. 3 July 1782. Capt. 17 June 1792. Major 1 May 1804. Lt. Col. 21 Sept. 1804. *d. unm.* Fatehgarh 4 Sept. 1806.

Brother of Rev. John Fraser, minister of Libieton, in the presbytery of Biggar, co. Lanark, and of Lily, Ann, and Agatha Fraser, of Shetland. Nephew of Janet Sinclair, of Shetland.
Services : Lieut. 3rd Bn. Art. in July 1787. Comdd. a detachment of Art. sent from Bengal in Nov. 1793 for service against French cruisers in the Bay of Bengal and E. Archipelago : these

operations lasted for about 12 mos. Presented by the merchants of Calcutta with a gold-hilted sword in recognition of his services on this occasion. Expedn. to Macao 1801-2 ; Capt. comdg. 4th Coy. 1st Bn. Art.

Refs. : *S.M.* 1807, p. 477. Will dated 3 June 1805; proved 23 Sept. 1806.

FRASER, Andrew (*d.* 1812). Bt. Major, 25th N.I. Cadet 1783. Admitted 29 Sept. 1783. Ensign 5 Feb. 1785. Lieut. 28 Mar. 1791. Capt. 30 Sept. 1803. Bt. Major 25 July 1810. *d.* Midnapore, Bengal, 12 Aug. 1812.

VIII. of Fairfield, Inverness, which he sold after 1794. Eldest son of Alexander Fraser, VII. of Fairfield. *m.* Ann. (She *re-m.* Henry Chambers Murray Cox, *q.v.*) His dau. *m.* Neville Anbury Parker, *q.v.* His sisters *m.* Allan Macpherson, *q.v.*, and Hiram Cox, *q.v.*

Services : Apptd. Asst. in Secret & Mily. Dept. 9 Aug. 1786. Fur. 12 Nov. 1792 till 6 Mar. 1795. Lieut. 2nd Bengal Eur. Regt. in 1796. Fur. 9 Mar. 1800 till 3 Dec. 1804. Capt. Lt. 17th N.I. Transfd. to newly-raised 25th N.I. in 1804. (? Second Mahratta War 1805 ; Adalatnagar ; Capt. 1/25th N.I.) Capture of Gohad 1806 ; Capt. 1/25th N.I. Fur. 23 Feb. 1807 till 9 Aug. 1810. Bt. Major 1/25th N.I.

Refs. : Frasers of Lovat. Will dated Midnapore 11 Aug. 1812 ; proved in 1813.

FRASER, Archibald William Windham (1806-1841). Lieutenant, Invalid Est. 8th L.C. *b.* Ardersier, co. Inverness, 20 July 1806. Cadet 1823. Arrived in India 20 June 1824. Cornet 20 June 1824. Lieut. 13 May 1825. Invalided 27 Oct. 1831. *d.* 6 Sept. 1841 : drowned in the Ganges above Dinapore.

bapt. Ardersier 3 Aug. 1806. One of the 16 children of Capt. Thomas Fraser, of Leadclune, late Bk. Mr. of Fort George, co. Inverness, and Ann his wife. Brother of Thomas Fraser (1807-1891), *q.v.*

Services : Posted to 8th L.C. in 1825. Fur. s.c. 24 Jan. 1826 till 8 Nov. 1827, and 3 Apr. 1829 till 13 Sept. 1830. No record of active service.

FRASER, Charles (1760/61-1837). Lieut. Colonel. 7th N.C. *b.* Antigua 1760/61. Cadet 1780. Admitted 6 Mar. 1781. Cornet 27 Sept. 1780. Lieut. 15 June 1781. Capt. 29 May 1800. Major 17 July 1801. Lt. Col. 11 Mar. 1805. Retired 15 Aug. 1809. *d.* Paris, 5 Sept. 1837, aged 76 " or thereabouts."

Of the I. of Wight, later of New North St., Red Lion Sq., London. 2nd son of Thomas Fraser, M.D., of Antigua (of the Balnain family), and Elizabeth his wife, dau. of William Mackinnon. *m.* 1st, Cal-

cutta, 27 Jan. 1794, Catherine Charlotte, dau. of —— Raper, and widow of James Browne (1743/44-1792), *q.v.* Father of William Fraser (1800-1825), *q.v.* His daus. *m.* Richard Home, *q.v.*, and Felix Vincent Raper, *q.v.* *m.* 2nd, (?).
Services : Sailed for India on the *Rochford*, 3 June 1780, aged 19. Lieut. 32nd Bn. Sepoys in July 1787. Capt. Lt. 3rd N.C. Transfd. as Capt. to newly-raised 5th N.C. May 1800. A.D.C. to G.G. 1803-5. Garr. Storekeeper at Fort William 1804-5. Transfd. as Lt. Col. to newly-raised 7th N.C. in 1805. Fur. 8 Jan. 1806 till retirement.
Refs. : *Frasers of Lovat.* Will dated 20 Sept. 1827 ; proved 4 Jan. 1839.

FRASER, George John (1800-1842). Captain, 1st L.C. *b.* Inverness 13 May 1800. Cadet 1821. Arrived in India 1 Jan. 1823. Cornet 13 July 1822. Lieut. 13 May 1825. Capt. 12 Nov. 1838. *d.* Aurangabad 27 Aug. 1842.

5th and youngest son of Edward Satchwell Fraser, of Reelig, co. Inverness, and Jane his wife, dau. of William Fraser, of Balnain. Brother of James Baillie Fraser (*D.N.B.*). *m.* Delhi, 12 Sept. 1832, Wilhelmina, youngest dau. of John Moore, of Liverpool.

Services : Posted as Cornet to 1st L.C. Actg. Intr. & Qmr. 1st L.C. 8 July 1825. Asst. Revenue Surveyor at Saharanpur 18 Nov. 1826. Employed on survey work in 1832, and 1834-5. Asst. to Resdt. at Nagpur 15 Feb. 1836 till 15 Apr. 1842. Apptd. to Thagi Dept. June 1837. In pol. charge at Nemawar, C.I. No record of active service.

Refs. : Burke's *Landed Gentry*, 13th edn., p. 683, *s.n.* Fraser, of Reelick, co. Inverness. *Frasers of Lovat.* *G.M.* 1843, i. 554. *The Times*, 24 Nov. 1842. Will dated camp, Budayaon, 12 Oct. 1832 ; proved 18 Feb. 1843.

FRASER, Hugh (1808-1858). Bt. Colonel, C.B., Engineers. Offg. Comr., N.W.P. *b.* Inverness 7 Aug. 1808. Cadet 1827. Arrived in India 11 Aug. 1828. 2nd Lieut. 15 Dec. 1826. Lieut. 28 Sept. 1827. Capt. 12 Aug. 1840. Major 7 Oct. 1851. Lt. Col. 1 May 1855. Bt. Col. 15 Apr. 1857. *d.* Mussoorie, U.P., 12 Aug. 1858.

Younger son of Hugh Fraser, of Stonyfield, afterwards of Ness Side, Inverness, of the family of Phopachy and Torbeck, and Elizabeth Dunbar his wife. Brother of John Wedderburne Fraser, *q.v.* *m.* Calcutta, 4 Nov. 1850, Florena Charlotte, dau. of William Penney, afterwards Lord Kinloch, of the court of session (*D.N.B.*). Addiscombe Cadet 5 Aug. 1825 till 15 Dec. 1826. Chatham 6 May 1827 till 21 Dec. 1827.

Services : Lieut. d.d. S. & M. at Aligarh 8 Sept. 1828. Executive Engr., Kumaon, 13 June 1833 ; do. Nimach 11 May 1835 ; do.

Mhow 26 Sept. 1837 ; do. Cawnpore 10 Apr. 1838. Tempy. charge of King of Oudh's observatory at Lucknow 7 June 1843. Offg. Garr. Engr. and Civil Architect at Fort William Aug. 1847. Second Burma War ; capture of Rangoon and operations in vicinity ; Comdg. Engr. with the expedn. (Medal). Suptg. Engr. P.W.D., Lower Provinces, 3 May 1854. Fur. 1854 till 7 Dec. 1855. Chief Engr., 1 cl., N.W.P., 14 Apr. 1857. Chief Comr., N.W.P., 19 Sept. 1857 till 9 Feb. 1858. C.B. 9 Dec. 1853. Was nominated K.C.B., but died before the Warrant reached India.

Refs. : *Frasers of Lovat.* *D.I.B.* *G.M.* 1858, ii. 646. *I.M.* 1858, p. 798. *The Times*, 9 Oct. 1858. Will dated 9 May 1851 ; proved 21 Sept. 1858. M.I. in St. Paul's cathedral, Calcutta.

FRASER, James (1762/63-1793). Lieutenant, Infantry. *b.* in Scotland 1762/63. Cadet 1779. Ensign 19 Nov. 1779. Lieut. 9 Mar. 1781. *d.* Gauhati, Assam, 1 Aug. 1793.

Services : Sailed for India on the *Ganges*, 7 Mar. 1779, aged 16. Lieut. 16th Bn. Sepoys in July 1787.

FRASER, James (1800-1868). Lieut. Colonel, C.B. 2nd L.C. *b.* 9 Oct. 1800. Cadet 1817. Admitted 3 Oct. 1818. Cornet 10 Apr. 1818. Lieut. 27 Sept. 1819. Capt. 26 Oct. 1827. Bt. Major 23 Nov. 1841. Retired 31 May 1851. Hon. Lt. Col. 28 Nov. 1854. *d. unm.* Edinburgh 2 Jan. 1868.

bapt. Prescot, Lancs., 4 July 1802. 4th and youngest son of James Fraser, of Ravenhead House, Lancs., and of Culduthel, Inverness, formerly in the Line, and afterwards Lt. Col. comdg. Prescot Local Mil., and Millicent his wife, only child of John Mackay, of Ravenhead. Nephew of Roderick Fraser (1763-1818), *q.v.*, and related to Alexander John Fraser, *q.v.* His sister *m.* Sir John Rose, *q.v.*

Services : Posted as Cornet to 8th N.C. Transfd. as Lieut. to 2nd N.C. Actg. Adjt. 2nd L.C. 27 Mar. 1820 till 22 Sept. 1821. Fur. p.a. 31 Jan. 1829 till 20 Oct. 1831. Fur. s.c. 13 Dec. 1834 till 19 Feb. 1838. First Afghan War 1838-42 ; Ghazni (Medal) ; Parwandara (s.w.) ; Capt. 2nd L.C.[1] ; defence of Jalalabad ; d.d. 25th N.I. (Medal) ; Kabul 1842 (Medal). Granted a pension and gratuity of 12 mos. pay for wound. Transfd. to newly-raised 11th L.C. (became 2nd L.C. in 1850). Fur. s.c. 7 Jan. 1843 till 1844. Hon. A.D.C. to G.G. 25 July 1844. C.B. 4 Oct. 1842. Durani, 3 cl., 7 Sept. 1841.

Refs. : *Frasers of Lovat.* Burke's *Landed Gentry*, 7th edn., p. 683. *Scotsman*, Jan. 1868. *G.M.* 1868, i. 260.

[1] *Note :* " Capt. Fraser led a charge of 2 Sqdns. of 2nd L.C. on 2 Nov. 1840 against Dost Mohd. Khan's cavalry. The Troopers

turned about and galloped back, leaving their Officers to their fate. Capt. Fraser had his sword-arm nearly severed. The two offending Sqdns. were immediately sent back to India, and the Regt. was disbanded by G.G.O. No. 38 of 1841 " (*G.M.*).

FRASER, John (1791-1806). Cadet, Cavalry. *b.* St. George, Grenada, W.I., 10 Dec. 1791. Cadet 1804. Arrived in India 6 Apr. 1806. *d.* Barasat C.C. 24 July 1806.

Son of Alexander Fraser of Newington, Surrey.

FRASER, John (1788-1819). Lieutenant, 18th N.I. *bapt.* Inverness 28 Dec. 1788. Cadet 1808. Arrived in India 21 Oct. 1809. Ensign 13 Mar. 1810. Lieut. 16 Dec. 1814. *d.* Midnapore, Bengal, 6 Apr. 1819, of cholera.

Son of Donald Fraser, of Castle Wynd, Inverness, and Mary Davidson his wife. Nephew of Alexander Fraser. Marlow Cadet.
Services : Posted as Ensign to 18th N.I. Nepal War 1816 ; Lieut. 2/18th N.I., in 2nd Bde., Left Column.
Refs. : *A.J.* viii.

FRASER, John Wedderburne (1810-1842). Lieutenant, Engineers. *b.* Inverness 4 Oct. 1810. Cadet 1827. Arrived in India 23 Nov. 1828. 2nd Lieut. (?). Lieut. 28 Sept. 1827. *d. unm.* London 2 Apr. 1842.

Son of Hugh Fraser, of the family of Fraser, of Phopachy and Torbeck, and Elizabeth Dunbar his wife. Brother of Hugh Fraser, *q.v.* Addiscombe Cadet 1826-7.
Services : d.d. S. & M. at Aligarh 14 Jan. 1829. Offg. Executive Engr. Berhampore 22 June 1835. Executive Engr., Balasore Div., 17 Nov. 1835 till 5 Dec. 1836. To suptd. surveys in Cuttack 12 Sept. 1837. Leave s.c. 2 yrs. to Cape 23 Mar. 1838. Fur. s.c. 23 Mar. 1840 till death.
Refs. : *Frasers of Lovat.* *A.J.* N.S. xxxviii. 80.

FRASER, Peter (1759/60-1796). Ensign. Subsequently Lieut., Madras Inf. *b.* Inverness 1759/60. Cadet 1780. Ensign 6 Apr. 1781. Lieut. (Madras) 17 Mar. 1786. *d.* Nov. 1796.

Services : Sailed for India as a private soldier on the *Fox* 7 Mar. 1779, aged 19. Transfd. to Madras Est. 15 Oct. 1781.

FRASER, Richard (1796-1820). Lieutenant, 6th N.I. *bapt.* Inverness 29 May 1796. Cadet 1817. Ensign (?). Lieut. 21 Dec. 1818. *d.* Raipur, C.P., 19 Apr. 1820, of a fever occasioned by fatigue on service.

Eldest son of Donald Fraser, of Inverness, writer, and Mary Oram his wife.

Services : Ensign H.M. 30th Regt. 18 Apr. 1813. Lieut. do. 19 Jan. 1815. Posted as Lieut. to 6th N.I. Third Mahratta War; Lieut. 1/6th N.I., in Reserve Div.

Refs. : S.M. 1820, ii. 479.

FRASER, Robert Warden (1806-1876). Lieut. Colonel. 45th N.I. *b.* Forres, co. Elgin, 3 Jan. 1806. Cadet 1821. Arrived in India 31 Oct. 1822. Ensign 4 Oct. 1822. Lieut. 17 May 1824. Capt. 12 Jan. 1838. Major 17 Apr. 1851. Retired 10 June 1853. Hon. Lt. Col. 28 Nov. 1854. *d.* 17 Napier Rd., Merchiston, Edinburgh, 30 June 1876.

Son of Bailie Alexander Fraser, of Forres, merchant, and Jane Warden his wife. Brother of Alexander Fraser (1811-1843), *q.v. m.* Meerut, 15 Apr. 1852, Caroline Purvis, dau. of Richard Home, *q.v.,* and granddau. of Charles Fraser, *q.v.*

Services : Posted as Ensign to 23rd N.I. Transfd. to 45th N.I. (late 1/23rd) May 1824. Fur. s.c. 10 Jan. 1830 till 14 Jan. 1833. Comdg. 45th N.I. 28 Dec. 1842. Actg. A.A.G., Benares Div., 10 June and 17 Oct. 1843. Fur. s.c. 17 May 1844 till 1846, and 2 Mar. 1847 till 1850. No record of active service.

Refs. : The Times, 5 July 1876.

FRASER, Roderick (1761/62-1846). Major. 9th N.I. *b.* 1761/62. Cadet 1781. Arrived in India 27 Sept. 1783. Ensign 1 July 1781. Lieut. 4 Oct. 1782. Capt. 4 Sept. 1800. Major 28 Aug. 1807. Retired 26 Jan. 1809. *d.* Litchfield Terr., Regent's Pk., London, 7 July 1846, aged 84.

Services : Apptd. Cadet on 30 May 1781, aged 16 (*sic*). Sailed for India on the *Nassau,* 8 Feb. 1782, aged 16. Lieut. 3rd Bn. Sepoys in July 1787. Lieut. 9th N.I. Fur. 4 Dec. 1797 till 10 Sept. 1799. Capt. Lt. 9th N.I. 29 May 1800. Second Mahratta War; pursuit of Holkar 1805-6; Capt. 1/9th N.I. Operations against Dhundia Khan 1807; Komona (w.); Ganauri; Major 1/9th N.I.

Refs. : The Patrician, i. 395. *A.A.R.* x. 21. *G.M.* 1846, ii. 327.

FRASER, Roderick (1763-1818). Lieut. Colonel, 11th N.I. *b.* 5 May 1763. Cadet 1780. Admitted 9 Oct. 1781. Ensign 1780. Lieut. 9 Aug. 1781. Capt. 30 Nov. 1798. Major 21 Sept. 1804. Lt. Col. 22 May 1810. *d.* Midnapore, Bengal, 8 Dec. 1818.

2nd son of Col. Alexander Fraser, of Culduthel, and Lilias his wife, dau. of Roderick Chisholm, the Chisholm. Brother of Simon Fraser, and uncle of James Fraser (1800-1868), *q.v.* His daus. *m.* Harry Nichelson, *q.v.,* and John Walker, *q.v.*

Services : Sailed for India on the *Mount Stewart* 27 June 1780. Lieut. 5th Bengal Eur. Bn. in July 1787. Capt. 11th N.I. Fur.

THE BENGAL ARMY, 1758-1834 221

18 Feb. 1806 till 21 Oct. 1809. Reduction of Kalinjar 1812 ; Lt. Col. 1/11th N.I. Comdg. at Midnapore 1817 till death.
Refs. : Burke's *Landed Gentry*, 13th edn., p. 331, *s.n.* Chisholm, of Erchless Castle. Family information. *Frasers of Lovat.* Will dated 25 May 1817 ; proved 26 Dec. 1818.

FRASER, Simon (1780-1845). Lieut. Colonel. 41st N.I. *b.* Nairn 9 Aug. 1780. Cadet 1798. Arrived in India 7 Jan. 1800. Ensign 31 Aug. 1799. Lieut. 28 Oct. 1799. Capt. 16 Sept. 1807. Major 9 Aug. 1821. Lt. Col. 1 May 1824. Retired 17 Aug. 1824. *d.* Drumduan, Inverness, 24 Sept. 1845.
bapt. 13 Aug. 1780. Son of Capt. James Fraser, of Nairnside, and Isabel Dunbar his wife.
Services : Adjt. 1/6th N.I. 1805-7. Capt. 1/6th N.I. Capture of Java 1811 ; Cornelis (w.) ; Capt. Bengal L.I. Bn. Nepal War 1814-5 ; Capt. L.I. Bn., in 2nd Div. Served with L.I. Bn. till 1816. Comdd. Cuttack Legion 16 May 1817 till 1822. Operations against the Larka Kols in the Singhbhum district 1821. Major 2/6th N.I. Fur. 1822 till retirement. Transfd. as Lt. Col. to 41st N.I. May 1824.
Refs. : *G.M.* 1845, ii. 549.

FRASER, Thomas (1807-1891). Captain. 7th L.C. Member of the Legislative Council of N.Z. *b.* Ardersier, co. Inverness, 27 Dec. 1807. Cadet 1824. Cornet (?). Lieut. 13 May 1825. Capt. 15 May 1840. Invalided 11 Jan. 1842. Retired 27 Mar. 1844. *d.* Wellington, N.Z., 24 June 1891.
bapt. Ardersier 6 Jan. 1808. Son of Capt. Thomas Fraser of Leadclune, Stratherrick, 78th Highlrs., late Bk. Mr. of Fort George, co. Inverness, and Ann his wife. Brother of Archibald William Windham Fraser, *q.v. m.* a dau. of Dr. Macdonald.
Services : Posted as Lieut. to 7th L.C. 1826. Actg. Adjt. 7th L.C. 16 Aug. 1828. Fur. s.c. 24 Mar. 1833 till 2 July 1835. Wrecked in the *Ann and Amelia* nr. Boulogne. Fur. s.c. 4 Dec. 1840 till 28 Aug. 1841, and 11 Jan. 1842 till retirement. No record of active service. Wounded Lieut. John Rose Holden Rose, H.M. 11th Dgns., in a duel at Simla in July 1836.
Refs. : *Frasers of Lovat. A.J.* N.S. xxii. 51. *The Times,* 22 Aug. 1891.

FRASER, William (*d.* 1809). Major, 16th N.I. Country Cadet 1781. Admitted 24 May 1781. Ensign 27 Sept. 1781. Lieut. 1 July 1783. Capt. 13 July 1803. Major 14 Nov. 1805. *d.* at sea 14 Mar. 1809 : lost in the *Calcutta*, which foundered in a gale off Mauritius on the voyage to England.
Brother of Robert Fraser.

Services : Capt. Lt. 16th N.I. 10 Aug. 1801. Supt. of the Coy.'s Stud at Pusa for many years till Nov. 1808, when he was succeeded by William Moorcroft (*D.N.B.*). Fur. 24 Jan. 1809.

Refs. : Hickey, iv. 478. Will proved 11 Aug. 1810.

FRASER, William (1800-1825). Lieutenant, 46th N.I. *b.* Calcutta 13 Mar. 1800. Cadet 1816. Ensign (?). Lieut. 1 Aug. 1818. *d.* Rangpur, Bengal, 2 Nov. 1825.

Son of Charles Fraser, *q.v.*, and Catherine Charlotte his 1st wife. Half-brother of James Edward Browne, *q.v.* Addiscombe Cadet 1816-7.

Services : Ensign d.d. 30th N.I. 1817. Posted as Lieut. to 1/23rd N.I. 1818. (? Third Mahratta War ; Lieut. 1/23rd N.I.) Transfd. to 46th N.I. (late 2/23rd) May 1824. First Burma War ; Assam 1824 ; Lieut. 46th N.I. Adjt. 46th N.I. 17 June 1824 ; Intr. & Qmr. do. 12 July 1825 till death.

FRASER, William (1806-1832). Lieutenant, 61st N.I. *b.* Kiltarlity, co. Inverness, 5 Jan. 1806. Cadet 1823. Arrived in India 2 Nov. 1824. Ensign 20 June 1824. Lieut. 4 Nov. 1825. *d. unm.* Gauhati, Assam, 9 Nov. 1832.

3rd and youngest son of Hugh Fraser, VIII. of Eskadale, and Ann his wife (and cousin), dau. of —— Fraser, of Eskadale.

Services : Posted as Ensign to 61st N.I. in 1825. Actg. Adjt. Tempy. Pioneers 6 July 1826. Adjt. Arakan Provl. Bn. 10 May 1827. Fur. s.c. 15 Jan. 1829 till 23 June 1832. d.d. Sylhet L.I. Bn. 23 Aug. 1832. Offg. Asst. to A.G.G., N.E. frontier, 24 Sept. 1832.

Refs. : Frasers of Lovat.

FRAZER, Hugh. Lieutenant, Infantry. Cadet 1776. Ensign 22 Mar. 1777. Lieut. 18 Aug. 1778. *d.* Berhampore (before July 1787).

Services : N.F.P.

***FRAZER, Simon** (*d.* 1770). Cadet, Infantry. Cadet (?). *d.* Calcutta 19 May 1770.

Services : N.F.P.

Refs. : Calcutta burial register.

FRAZER, Simon (*d.* 1773) Ensign, Infantry. Cadet 1771. Ensign 7 Mar. 1773. *d.* Dinapore May 1773 : drowned.

Services : N.F.P.

FRAZER, Thomas (*d.* 1780). Ensign, Infantry. Cadet 1778. Ensign 1778. *d.* Benares Sept. 1780 : drowned.

Services : N.F.P.

FREAKE or **FREKE, John**[1] (1726/27-?). Captain. Infantry. Subsequently Capt. H.M. 84th Foot. *b.* 1726/27. Capt. 10 Mar. 1762. Resigned 29 June 1763. (Living in 1778.)

A native of London.

Services : Cornet H.M. 3rd Dgn. Gds. 19 July 1759. Sailed for India in 1760, aged 33. Transfd. as Capt. to Bengal Army. He exchanged with George Whichcot or Witchcot, *q.v.*, and became Capt. H.M. 84th Foot 25 June 1763. Capt. h.p. do. 25 June 1765. Living, and still on h.p. 84th Foot, in 1778. Acted as A.D.C. to Major Thomas Adams during the campaign in Bengal in 1763.

[1] *Note :* The name is also given as Freak and Freek.

FREDERICK, Henry Octavius (1806-1851). Lieut. Colonel, 67th N.I. *b.* Sevenoaks, Kent, 13 Apr. 1806. Cadet 1822. Arrived in India 21 Oct. 1823. Ensign 11 July 1823. Lieut. 13 May 1825. Capt. 18 Dec. 1834. Major 3 Nov. 1843. Lt. Col. 28 Feb. 1850. *d. unm.* 3 Oct. 1851, on board the *Benares* off Calcutta.

8th and youngest son of Lt. Col. Thomas Frederick (who was nephew of Sir John Frederick, 4th Bart., of Westminster), comptroller of the lottery, London, and Anne Susannah his wife, dau. of Rev. John Glasse, rector of Pencombe, Hereford. Brother of John Frederick, *q.v.*

Services : Posted as Ensign to 67th N.I. First Burma War; Arakan 1825; Ensign 67th N.I. (India medal). Tempy. charge of escort to Resdt. in Nepal 28 Nov. 1827. Adjt. 67th N.I. 14 Feb. 1832 till 13 Apr. 1835. Fur. p.a. 7 Jan. 1836 till 7 Feb. 1839. Offg. Executive Ofr., Benares Div., P.W.D. 2 Sept. 1840 till 2 Feb. 1842. Posted as Lt. Col. to 67th N.I. Apr. 1850.

Refs. : Burke's *Peerage*, 1923, p. 942, *s.n.* Frederick, Bart., of Westminster. *G.M.* 1851, i. 105. Will dated 14 Jan. 1850; admon. 11 Feb. 1852.

FREDERICK, John (1799-1833). Captain, 67th N.I. *b.* Walcot, Bath, 20 Jan. 1799. Cadet 1819. Admitted 27 Mar. 1820. Ensign 20 Sept. 1819. Lieut. 13 Jan. 1823. Capt. 31 Dec. 1832. *d.* in England 25 Feb. 1833.

3rd son of Lt. Col. Thomas Frederick, of Eastbourne, and Anne Susannah his wife. Brother of William Frederick, *q.v.*

Services : Ensign 1/15th N.I. Transfd. to 34th N.I. 11 July 1823; to 67th N.I. (late 1/34th) May 1824. Supy. S.A.C.G. 17 July 1824. S.A.C.G. 4 Sept. 1824 till 8 July 1825. Asst. to Resdt. at Lucknow 4 June 1825 till 30 June 1830. Fur. s.c. 11 Feb. 1831 till death. No record of active service.

Refs. : Burke's *Peerage*, 1923, p. 942, *s.n.* Frederick, Bart., of Westminster. *A.J.* N.S. x. 179. *G.M.* 1833, ii. 90.

FREDERICK, William (1801-?). Lieutenant. 6th N.I. *b.* 12 Apr. 1801. Cadet 1824. Arrived in India 6 June 1825. Ensign 23 Jan. 1825. Lieut. 21 Nov. 1826. Struck off in England 1827. *d.s.p.* (?).

bapt. Kemsing, Kent, 24 Oct. 1802. 5th son of Lt. Col. Thomas Frederick and Anne Susannah his wife. Brother of Henry Octavius Frederick, *q.v.*

Services : Posted as Ensign to 6th N.I. Fur. 1826 till struck off. No record of active service.

Refs. : Burke's *Peerage*, 1923, p. 942, *s.n.* Frederick, Bart., of Westminster.

FREE, John (1808-1856). Lieut. Colonel, 10th L.C. *b.* Hampstead, Middlesex, 30 July 1808. Cadet 1824. Arrived in India 4 Oct. 1825. Cornet 23 Jan. 1825. Lieut. 10 June 1825. Capt. 12 Apr. 1836. Major 20 Apr. 1849. Lt. Col. 27 May 1853. *d.* Ferozepore, 3 May 1856, of heart disease or apoplexy, during a duststorm.

Page of Honour to George IV. Son of Peter Free, of Portland Pl., London, banker. *m.* Poona, 13 Oct. 1829, Matilda, dau. of Richard Hutt, of Appley, I.W. Ed. Harrow; entered the school 1820/21; left 1823/24.

Services : Cornet d.d. 2nd Extra Cav. (became 10th L.C.). Siege and capture of Bhurtpore; Cornet d.d. 10th L.C. (India medal). Posted as Cornet to 10th L.C. Mar. 1826. Fur. 22 Feb. 1840 till 29 Oct. 1842. Gwalior campaign; Maharajpur; Capt. 10th L.C. (Bronze star). Comdd. 10th L.C. from Mar. 1851 till death. Reposted as Lt. Col. to 10th L.C. 18 June 1853. After his death he was promoted to the rank of Col. by brevet with effect from 9 Apr. 1856.

Refs. : De Rhé-Philipe. Boase. *Harrow School List. G.M.* 1856, ii. 122. *I.M.* 1856, p. 381. Will dated 3 Feb. 1851; proved 18 June 1856.

FREEMAN, Charles Henry Spencer (1800-1833). Lieutenant, 47th N.I. *b.* Barrackpore 12 Feb. 1800. Cadet 1819. Admitted 29 Aug. 1820. Ensign 22 Mar. 1820. Lieut. 11 July 1823. *d.* Bankura, Bengal, 6 June 1833.

Son of Daniel Spencer Freeman, Asst. Surgeon, Bengal, and Charlotte Sophia his wife, widow of Andrew Black, *q.v.*, and sister-in-law of Thomas Hawkins, *q.v. m.* Cuttack, 1 Dec. 1831, Margaret Mary Ann, only dau. of Capt. Hugh Atkins Reid, E.I.C.N.S., and sister of Hugh Atkins Reid, *q.v.* (She *re-m.* in 1854.)

Services : Posted as Ensign to 2/12th N.I. Transfd. as Lieut. to 24th N.I. July 1823; to 48th N.I. (late 2/24th) May 1824; to 47th

THE BENGAL ARMY, 1758-1834

(late 1/24th) 24 June 1824 ; to newly-raised 69th (became 47th) Nov. 1824. Fur. s.c. 5 Nov. 1825 till 6 Oct. 1828. Offg. S.A.C.G. in Arakan 31 Dec. 1828. No record of active service.

Refs. : G.M. 1833, ii. 556. Will dated 22 Mar. 1833 ; proved 11 July 1833.

FREEMAN, Thomas (1762/63-?). Lieutenant, Invalid Pension Est. 12th Bn. Sepoys. *b.* Bengal 1762/63. Cadet 1778. Ensign 25 Aug. 1779. Lieut. 7 Apr. 1781. Invalided and pensioned 9 July 1787.

(*Perhaps* son of Thomas Freeman, bur. Calcutta 21 Feb. 1767.)

Services : Sailed for India on the *Ganges*, 7 Mar. 1779, aged 16. N.F.P.

FREETH, William (1805-1886). Lieut. Colonel. 55th N.I. *b.* 12 Sept. 1805. Cadet 1821. Admitted 17 Dec. 1821. Ensign 12 Sept. 1821. Lieut. 1 May 1824. Capt. 1 Dec. 1836. Bt. Major 9 Nov. 1846. Invalided 15 Feb. 1847. Retired 3 Nov. 1857. Hon. Lt. Col. 3 Nov. 1857. *d.* Upton Park, Slough, Bucks., 20 Dec. 1886.

bapt. Bulwell, Notts., 11 Oct. 1805. Son of John Freeth, of Risley, co. Derby. *m.* Cawnpore, 21 Jan. 1839, Catherine, youngest dau. of Robert Logan, of Edinburgh.

Services : Was already in India when apptd. Cadet. Ensign d.d. 2/23rd N.I. 5 Mar. 1822. Posted as Ensign to 28th N.I. Transfd. as Lieut. to 55th N.I. (late 1/28th) May 1824. Fur. p.a. 15 Jan. 1833 till 1 Mar. 1836. Adjt. 55th N.I. 26 Nov. till 26 Dec. 1836. In charge of Rajputana Div. P.W.D. 23 Oct. 1841. Comdd. 2nd Depot Bn. at Allahabad 4 Mar. 1842 till it was broken up on 1 Mar. 1843. Offg. Bde. Major July 1845. Fur. s.c. 19 Dec. 1856 till retirement.

Refs. : The Times, 23 Dec. 1886.

FRENCH, Frederick. (*See* **TRENCH.**)

FRENCH, John (1804-1859). Major. 14th N.I. *b.* London 13 Apr. 1804. Cadet 1825. Ensign 21 May 1826. Lieut. 30 May 1829. Capt. 1 July 1848. Retired 8 Feb. 1851. Hon. Major 28 Nov. 1854. *d.* Candelo, N.S.W., 4 Aug. 1859.

2nd son of John French, of Wanstead, Essex. *m.* Pontville, Tasmania, 2 Apr. 1846, Mary, eldest dau. of George Brooks Forster.

Services : Ensign d.d. 62nd N.I. 7 Oct. 1826. Posted as Ensign to 57th N.I. 9 Nov. 1826. Transfd. to 14th N.I. 3 Nov. 1828. Fur. p.a. 9 Feb. 1837 till 26 Dec. 1839. Adjt. 14th N.I. 21 May 1842 till 28 Aug. 1848. Gwalior campaign ; Maharajpur ; Lieut.

14th N.I. (Bronze star). Leave s.c. to Tasmania 18 Apr. 1844 till 1846, and 15 Jan. 1849 till retirement.
Refs. : *G.M.* 1859, ii. 541. *The Times*, 13 Oct. 1859.

FRENCH, Luke Henry. (*See* **TRENCH**.)

FRENCH, Patrick (*d.* 1770). Lieutenant, Infantry. Cadet 1766. Ensign 30 May 1766. Lieut. 7 Sept. 1767. *d.* Ghireti, Bengal, 20 Oct. 1770.
Services : N.F.P.

FRENCH, Richard (1739/40-1814). Captain, Invalid Pension Est. 8th N.I. *b.* 1739/40. Cadet 1768. Admitted 28 Aug. 1768. Ensign 8 Feb. 1769. Lieut. 7 June 1770. Capt. 18 Aug. 1779. Pensioned (before July 1787). *d.* Monghyr, 15 Nov. 1814, aged 74. *m.* (?).
Services : Capt. 1/1st Bengal Eur. Regt. in Oct. 1779.
Refs. : Will dated Chunar 27 Mar. 1814 ; proved 16 Feb. 1815. M.I. at Monghyr.

FRENCH, Robert (1777-1811). Captain, 19th N.I. *b.* Vepery, Madras, 27 June 1777. Cadet 1798. Arrived in India 13 Sept. 1800. Ensign 4 Dec. 1799. Lieut. 29 May 1800. Capt. 29 Mar. 1810. *d.* Allahabad 9 Sept. 1811.
bapt. Vepery 17 July 1777. Son of Capt. George French and Anna his wife.
Services : Served throughout with 19th N.I. Capt. Lt. 21 July 1808.
Refs. : Will dated 2 Jan. 1811 ; proved in 1811.

FRENCH, William James (1794-1856). Lieutenant. 21st N.I. *b.* Bow, London, 8 Apr. 1794. Cadet 1808. Arrived in India 22 Feb. 1811. Ensign (1 June 1811) 1 Jan. 1812. Lieut. 3 Jan. 1815. Cashiered 5 July 1816. *d.* Turnham Green, London, 8 May 1856.
Son of William James French.
Services : Posted as Ensign to 1/21st N.I. in 1811. Attached to 8th Gren. Bn. 1815. (? Nepal War 1816 ; Lieut. 8th Gren. Bn., in 2nd Bde., Left Column.)
Refs.: *G.M.* 1856, i. 666.

FRETWELL, Thomas. Ensign. Infantry. Cadet 1770. Ensign 1770. Resigned 26 Sept. 1770.
Services : N.F.P.

FRIELL, Simeon Philip (1780-1804). Lieutenant, 11th N.I. *b.* Dec. 1780. Cadet 1796. Admitted 10 Sept. 1798. Ensign 18 Oct. 1797. Lieut. 10 Sept. 1798. *d.* Cawnpore (? Etah) 9 Sept. 1804.

Son of Peter Friell, formerly of Dublin, later of Guildford, Surrey.
Services : Ensign 76th Foot 18 Feb. 1798 ; 33rd Foot 30 Apr. 1798 ; 19th Foot 12 Sept. 1798. Resigned 23 July 1799. Ensign 2nd Bengal Eur. Regt. Transfd. as Ensign to 2/7th N.I. Oct. 1798 ; as Lieut. to 2/11th N.I. Adjt. 2/11th N.I. in 1803 till death. Second Mahratta War ; Kapsa ; Kalpi ; Gwalior ; Lieut. 2/11th N.I.
Refs. : Pester.

FRIEND, John (*d.* 1788). Captain, Invalid Est. Cadet 1768. Ensign 22 Feb. 1769. Lieut. 2 July 1770. Capt. 30 Aug. 1779. Invalided (before July 1787). *d.* Moradbag, nr. Murshidabad, 3 Jan. 1788.
m. Catharina de Revaro.
Services : N.F.P.
Refs. : G.M. 1788, ii. 658. Will dated Chunar 6 July 1784.

FRITH, Frederick Wollaston (1788-1830). Captain, 47th N.I. *b.* St. Laurence Pountney, London, 17 Apr. 1788. Cadet 1804. Arrived in India 10 Sept. 1805. Ensign 29 Oct. 1805. Lieut. 26 June 1806. Capt. 11 July 1823. *d.* Akyab, Burma, 29 Apr. 1830.

Son of Rev. John Frith. Brother of Henry William Frith, *q.v.*
Services : Lieut. 1/24th N.I. Adjt. 1/24th N.I. 4 May 1815 till 2 Mar. 1821. Third Mahratta War. Transfd. to 47th N.I. (late 1/24th) May 1824. The 47th having been disbanded for mutiny in Nov. 1824, he was posted the same month to newly-raised 69th N.I. (became 47th).
Refs. : A.J. N.S. iii. 158.

FRITH, Henry William (1780-1815). Captain, 8th N.I. *b.* 19 Oct. 1780. Cadet 1798. Arrived in India 24 Feb. 1800. Ensign 12 Sept. 1799. Lieut. 28 Oct. 1799. Capt. 18 Apr. 1810. *d.* Jaunpur, U.P., 31 Jan. 1815.

bapt. Allhallows, London, 17 Nov. 1780. Son of the Rev. John Frith and Mary his wife. Brother of Frederick Wollaston Frith, *q.v.*
Services : Operations in Jumna Doab 1803 ; Sasni ; Lieut. 8th N.I. Second Mahratta War ; Lieut. 8th N.I. Capt. Lt. 8th N.I. Jan. 1809.
Refs. : G.M. 1815, ii. 375.

FRITH, Richard (1756/57-1819). Colonel, 8th N.C. *b.* 1756/57. Cadet 1778. Admitted 12 Feb. 1780. Cornet 14 July 1779. Lieut. 6 Mar. 1781. Capt. 1 Nov. 1798. Major 21 Feb. 1801. Lt. Col. 11 Mar. 1805. Col. 4 June 1813. *d. unm.* 26 July 1819. A native of Ireland. Brother of Robert Frith, *q.v.*, and uncle of William Elliott (1776-1823), *q.v.*

Services : Sailed for India on the *Atlas,* 7 Mar. 1779, aged 22. Lieut. 36th Bn. Sepoys in July 1787. Posted to 1st Regt. Cav. 14 Dec. 1787. Operations in Jumna Doab 1803; Sasni; Bijaigarh; Kachaura; Major 4th N.C. Raised a corps of Irreg. Cav., to be called the "Hindoostany Independent Regt." (G.O. 31 July 1803), and comdd. it throughout the 12 mos. of its existence. Second Mahratta War; Monson's retreat. Posted as Lt. Col. to newly-raised 8th N.C. Mar. 1805. Comdd. Muttra and Agra frontier 2 Jan. 1815 till death. Promoted Bdr. Gen. 12 Aug. 1819, before the report of his death was received.

Refs. : Will dated 14 June 1816; proved 4 Nov. 1819.

FRITH, Robert (*d.* 1800). Lieut. Colonel, 1st N.C. Cadet 1770. Admitted 22 June 1770. Cornet 8 Nov. 1771. Lieut. 23 July 1776. Capt. 17 Feb. 1781. Major 1 Mar. 1794. Lt. Col. 1 Nov. 1798. *d.* Bombay 4 Oct. 1800.

Brother of Richard Frith, *q.v. m.* Elizabeth. Father of Warren Hastings Leslie Frith, *q.v.*

Services : First Rohilla War; battle of St. George. In Feb. 1784 was comdg. a Troop of Cav. which, together with the Body Guard, escorted Warren Hastings from Calcutta to Lucknow. He was left behind at Lucknow in comd. of a portion of the Nawab-Vizier's forces. Capt. 3rd Bengal Eur. Bn. in July 1787. Second Mysore War; Capt. comdg. 1st N.C. "A gallant, active and zealous officer" (*A.A.R.*).

Refs. : V.B.G. Grier, p. 265. *A.A.R.* iii. 104. *G.M.* 1801, i. 576. Will dated 28 June 1794; proved 2 Feb. 1801.

FRITH, Warren Hastings Leslie (1787-1854). Colonel. Lieut. Colonel Comdt. Artillery. *bapt.* Calcutta 23 Apr. 1787. Cadet 1803. Arrived in India 27 Sept. 1804. Lieut. 24 Aug. 1804. Capt. Lt. 14 Feb. 1808. Capt. 21 Apr. 1817. Major 1 May 1824. Lt. Col. 20 Aug. 1831. Lt. Col. Comdt. 6 Dec. 1839. Col. 9 Aug. 1843. *d.* Southampton, 23 Jan. 1854, aged 67.

Son of Robert Frith, *q.v.*, and Elizabeth his wife. *m.* 1 Nov. 1808, Ellen, 4th dau. of John Fagan, of Kiltallagh, and sister of Christopher Sullivan Fagan, *q.v.* (*See also* Christopher Fagan.) (She died nr. Southampton, 7 Nov. 1853, aged 68.) His daus. *m.* George Henry Swinley, *q.v.*, and Sir Archdale Wilson, Bart., *q.v.*

Services : Second Mahratta War; Siege of Bhurtpore. 1st

Troop H.A. 1805-8. Adjt. & Qmr. Agra Div. Art. 1813-5. Comdd. Golandaz at Cawnpore 14 Mar. 1816 till 1818. Leave s.c. 13 mos. to Cape 19 Aug. 1817. Comdd. 3rd Troop H.A. 1818 ; transfd. to 6th Troop 1819. Fur. p.a. 16 Dec. 1819 till 5 July 1822. Fur. s.c. 22 Dec. 1823 till Nov. 1828. To comd. 7th Bn. Foot Art. 1 Aug. 1832. Fur. p.a. 6 Jan. 1835 till 6 May 1839. Transfd. to 6th Bn. 12 Apr. 1836. Comdt. Art., with rank of Bdr., 9 Jan. 1842 till May 1851. Fur. Apr. 1846 till Oct. 1847. 3rd Bde. H.A. 20 Jan. 1843 ; 2nd Bde. 5 Sept. 1846. Fur. 1851 till death.

Refs. : *The Times*, 26 Dec. 1839. *G.M.* 1854, i. 333. *I.M.* 31 Jan. 1854, p. 51.

FROBISHER, Thomas (1789-1863). Major. 51st N.I. *b.* York 5 Feb. 1789. Cadet 1804. Arrived in India 13 May 1806. Ensign 23 Apr. 1806. Lieut. 14 Mar. 1808. Capt. 11 July 1823. Retired 6 May 1833. Hon. Major 28 Nov. 1854. *d.* Cheltenham 8 Jan. 1863.

J.P. and D.L. Gloucs. *bapt.* All Saints upon the Pavement, York, 15 Feb. 1789. 3rd son of Nathaniel Frobisher, of Halifax, Yorks., bookseller, and Mary his wife, dau. of Thomas Spooner, mercer. *m.* 1st, High Harrogate, 11 July 1833, Caroline, 3rd dau. of William Bingley. (She died Cheltenham Nov. 1833.) *m.* 2nd, Cheltenham, 21 Apr. 1836, Rose, 5th and youngest dau. of John Helsham, of Leggetsrath, co. Kilkenny, and Oriel Pl., Cheltenham.

Services : Capture of C.G.H. Jan. 1806, under Sir David Baird. Barasat C.C. , Posted as Ensign to 26th N.I. (? Operations against Gopal Singh in Bundelkhand 1809.) Capture of Java 1811 ; Lieut. 5th Bn. Bengal Vols. (Medal). Served with Vols. in Java till 1814. Nepal War 1814-5 ; Lieut. 8th Coy. Pioneers, in 3rd Div. (India medal). Third Mahratta War ; action with Pindaris 14 Dec. 1817 ; Lieut. 1/26th N.I. 2nd in comd. 3rd Rohilla Cav. 1818-9. Transfd. to 2/26th N.I. Adjt. Ramgarh Bn. 11 July 1820. Served with Nagpur Auxy. Horse 14 May 1821 till 1830. Transfd. to 51st N.I. (late 1/26th) May 1824. Fur. p.a. 9 Jan. 1831 till retirement.

Refs. : Burke's *Landed Gentry*, 9th edn., ii. 196, *s.n.* Helsham, of Leggetsrath, co. Kilkenny. Burke's *Landed Gentry of Ireland*, p. 30, *s.n.* Barton, of Grove. *A.J.* N.S. xii. 62, 284. *G.M.* 1863, i. *The Times*, 12 Jan. 1863.

FROMANTEEL or FROMANTEL, Stephen (*d.* 1771). Cadet. Infantry. Cadet 1771. Resigned 24 Sept. 1771. *d.* Calcutta 17 Nov. 1771.

(*Possibly* son of Rev. Daniel Fromanteel, rector of Alderley, Norfolk, and curate of St. Michael at Thorn, Norwich, who was son of Daniel Fromanteel, mayor of Norwich in 1725.)

Services : N.F.P.

FRUSHARD, James (1789-1847). Bt. Colonel, 1st Eur. Bengal Fus. *b.* Southwick 20 June 1789. Cadet 1804. Arrived in India 26 Mar. 1806. Ensign 11 Mar. 1806. Lieut. 1 Feb. 1807. Capt. 11 July 1823. Major 26 Dec. 1830. Lt. Col. 17 Sept. 1836. Bt. Col. 9 Nov. 1846. *d.* Ambala 11 Nov. 1847.

Son of John Frushard. *m.* Benares, 17 Mar. 1834, Caroline Honoria, widow of Beaumont Dixie Small, Bengal Medical Est.

Services : Barasat C.C. till June 1807. Posted as Ensign to 2/15th N.I. 15 Feb. 1807. Operations in Bundelkhand 1808-9 ; Hirapur ; Rajaoli ; Ajaigarh. Nepal War 1814-5 ; Lieut. 2/15th N.I. ; apptd. Adjt. 5th Gren. Bn. 26 Dec. 1814 ; Ramgarh ; Malaun. Transfd. to 2/29th N.I. 18 Mar. 1815. Operations against the Bhattis of Hariana 1818 ; Lieut. 2/29th N.I. Extra Asst. to Resdt. in Malwa and Rajputana July 1822 till Nov. 1825. Transfd. to 58th N.I. (late 2/29th) May 1824. Siege and capture of Bhurtpore ; D.A.Q.M.G. of Cav. Div. Bde. Major Rajputana F.F. 19 May 1828 till Sept. 1831. Comdd. 58th N.I. Sept. 1831 till Jan. 1840. Comdd. newly-formed 2nd Bengal Eur. Regt. Jan. 1840 till Oct. 1847. With Army of Reserve (for Afghanistan) at Ferozepore Oct. 1842 till Jan. 1843. Against Hill tribes in Sind 1845. To comd. 1st Inf. Bde. Sind F.F. Feb. 1846. Transfd. to 1st Eur. Bengal Fus. 1 Oct. 1847.

Refs. : De Rhé-Philipe. M.I. at Ambala.

FRUSHARD, Peter (1751/52-?). Lieutenant. Infantry. *b.* 1751/52. Cadet 1781. Ensign 16 Apr. 1781. Lieut. 6 Aug. 1782. Resigned 5 Mar. 1788.

A native of London.

Services : Apptd. Cadet on 13 Dec. 1780, aged 29. Sailed for India on the *Latham,* 13 Mar. 1781, aged 29. N.F.P.

FRY, Robert (1778-1816). Captain, 6th N.C. *b.* London 7 Mar. 1778. Cadet 1797. Arrived in India 31 Oct. 1798. Cornet 1 Nov. 1798. Lieut. 29 May 1800. Capt. 1 Oct. 1806. *d.* Cawnpore 14 Apr. 1816.

bapt. St. Dunstan's-in-the-West, London, 8 Apr. 1778. 3rd son of Robert Fry, of Featherstone Bldgs., High Holborn, and Philadelphia his wife. Ed. Eton 1787-95 ; K.S. 1787. Admitted student of Gray's Inn 30 May 1796.

Services : Cornet 2nd N.C. Transfd. as Lieut. to newly-raised 6th N.C. May 1800. Operations in Jumna Doab 1803 ; Sasni ; Bijaigarh ; Kachaura ; Lieut. 6th N.C. Second Mahratta War ; Laswari ; Lieut. 6th N.C. Fur. 27 Mar. 1804 till 4 Nov. 1807. Settlement of Hariana 1809 ; Bhawani ; Capt. 6th N.C. Leave to Cape 1815-6.

Refs. : Austen-Leigh. *G.M.* 1816, ii. 625 ; 1817, i. 189.

FRYE, Charles (1788-1833). Lieut. Colonel, 13th N.I. *b.* London 8 Apr. 1788. Cadet 1803. Arrived in India 14 Aug. 1804. Ensign 1 Sept. 1804. Lieut. 21 Sept. 1804. Capt. 1 Jan. 1818. Major 13 May 1825. Lt. Col. 1 Apr. 1830. *d. unm.* Bareilly, U.P., 19 Sept. 1833.

bapt. Marylebone, Middlesex, 6 May 1788. Son of John Revell Frye, of Charlotte St., Bloomsbury, and Sarah his wife. Brother of Major William Edward Frye, H.M. 4th Foot, and of Rev. Percival Frye, vicar of St. Winnow, Cornwall.

Services : Posted as Lieut. to 7th N.I. Operations in Bundelkhand against Lachman Dawa ; storm of Rajaoli 22 Jan. 1807 (s.w. —lost an arm). Adjt. & Qmr. of Eur. Invalids at Chunar 1809 till 28 Apr. 1817. Bde. Major to troops at Agra and Muttra 5 Sept. 1818 ; do. at Muttra 30 June 1820. Transfd. to 13th N.I. (late 1/7th) May 1824. D.A.A.G. 20 Jan. 1825. D.A.A.G. Benares Div. 22 Feb. till 25 Mar. 1825. To comd. 12th Extra Regt. 11 June 1825. Posted as Lt. Col. to 13th N.I. 4 Aug. 1830.

Refs. : G.M. 1834, i. 454. Will dated 27 Feb. 1817 ; proved 30 Oct. 1833.

***FRYER, George Samuel** (1737/38-?). Cadet 1759.

A native of London.

Services : Sailed for India as a Volunteer on the Bengal Est. on the *Onslow* in 1759, aged 21. He landed in Madras, and in Aug. 1760 accepted a Commission in H.M. 79th Regt. from Col. Monson. For this he was tried by G.C.M. by the Madras Govt. on a charge of desertion. N.F.P.

Refs. : Wilson, ii. 137-40.

FULCHER, Frederick Page (1806-1853). Captain. 67th N.I. *b.* Ipswich 27 June 1806. Cadet 1827. Arrived in India 21 Jan. 1829. Ensign 4 July 1829. Lieut. 22 Sept. 1833. Capt. 24 Jan. 1845. Retired 1 Aug. 1846. *d.* Cravenhill, Hyde Pk., London, 24 Jan. 1853.

Son of Robert Fulcher, of Ipswich, timber merchant. Brother of Robert Page Fulcher, *q.v. m.* All Souls, Langham Pl., London, 29 July 1840, Georgina, youngest dau. of Henry Isaac Moor, of Kirby Hall, Kent, and Cheshunt, Herts. (She died Benares 11 Aug. 1841.)

Services : Posted as Ensign to 67th N.I. 3 June 1829. A.D.C. to Govr. of Agra 22 Aug. 1835 till 13 Apr. 1836. Fur. s.c. 1 Sept. 1837 till 23 Nov. 1840. Apptd. 2nd in comd. Kotah Contingent 2 Dec. 1842. Fur. s.c. 2 Feb. 1844 till retirement. No record of active service.

Refs. : I.M., 1853, p. 51.

FULCHER, Robert Page (1800-1884). Captain. 67th N.I. *b.* Ipswich 26 May 1800. Cadet 1816. Ensign (?). Lieut. 1 Aug. 1818. Capt. 28 May 1829. Retired 8 Apr. 1828. *d.* Green St., Grosvenor Sq., London, 19 Apr. 1884.

Son of Robert Fulcher, of Ipswich, timber merchant. Brother of Frederick Page Fulcher, *q.v.* *m.* Cape of Good Hope, 18 Feb. 1823, the widow of Col. Mackenzie, Madras Est. Addiscombe Cadet 1816-7.

Services: Ensign d.d. Bengal Eur. Regt. in 1817. Posted as Lieut. to 1/20th N.I. in 1818. Mily. student at Coll. of Fort William 1818-20. Intr. & Qmr. 2/20th N.I. 1822. Fur. 1822-4. Transfd. to newly-raised 34th N.I. 11 July 1823; to 68th N.I. (late 2/34th) May 1824; to 67th N.I. in 1824. Fur. 1826 till retirement. No record of active service.

Refs.: *G.M.* 1823, i. 562. *The Times*, 22 Apr. 1884.

FULLARTON, George Alexander Stuart (1804-1832). Lieutenant, 38th N.I. *b.* Kirknewton, Midlothian, 12 Feb. 1804. Cadet 1825. Arrived in India 8 Aug. 1826. Ensign 12 Oct. 1825. Lieut. 31 Dec. 1830. *d.* in camp at Jhangi, nr. Midnapore, 1 June 1832, of fever.

Son of John Fullarton (or Fullerton), Capt. 97th Foot, and Elizabeth Hume his wife. *m.* Dum-Dum, 19 Jan. 1832, Ann Jane, 3rd dau. of Alexander Graham, of Glasgow.

Services: Posted as Ensign to 38th N.I. in 1826. Operations against the Kols 1832; Lieut. 38th N.I.

Refs.: *A.J.* N.S. ix. 186. Will dated camp 5 May 1832; proved 21 Aug. 1832. M.I. at Midnapore.

FULLARTON, John (*d.* 1804). Major General. Colonel 12th N.I. Cadet 1763. Admitted 26 July 1763. Ensign 26 Aug. 1763. Lieut. 17 Apr. 1764. Capt. 29 July 1766. Major 26 Feb. 1778. Lt. Col. 20 Feb. 1782. Col. 2 Feb. 1788. Maj. Gen. 20 Dec. 1793. *d.* Patna 30 June 1804.

Of Nether Skeldon. 2nd son of Patrick Fullarton, of Goldring (afterwards known as Rosemount), and Margaret Harper his wife. Grandson of Patrick Fullarton, younger, of Fullarton. *m.* "Koonden Kuar Bhaije, Mrs. Fullarton, my wife." (She died Buxar 7 Dec. 1827.)

Services: Gave up comd. of 20th Bn. Sepoys on promotion Feb. 1778. First Mahratta War; action with Mahrattas on 19 May 1778. Apptd. to comd. newly-raised 36th N.I. in 1781. Comdg. 2nd Bde. Inf. at Chunar in July 1787; comdg. at the Presdy. in 1790; at Cawnpore in 1796. Fur. 7 Dec. 1792.

Refs.: Paterson's *Ayr and Wigton*, i. 410, 747. *Williams*, p. 68.

THE BENGAL ARMY, 1758-1834

Forrest, ii. 613. *G.M.* 1805, i. 281. Will dated Patna 22 Mar. 1804 ; proved in 1804.

FULLARTON, Robert (1785-1807). Lieutenant, 4th N.I. *b.* Dalry, co. Ayr, 30 May 1785. Cadet 1804. Arrived in India 10 Sept. 1805. Ensign 30 Oct. 1805. Lieut. 17 Sept. 1806. *d.* Calcutta 23 Apr. 1807.

bapt. 16 June 1785. 4th son of Rev. John Fullarton, minister of Dalry. Brother of Gavin Fullarton, of Glasgow, and of Mary, wife of Rev. John Thomson, of Dalry. Cousin-german of John Fullarton, Bengal Medical Est.

Services : Posted as Ensign to 4th N.I. in 1806. No record of active service.

Refs. : S.M. 1807. Will dated 25 Feb. 1807 ; proved 29 Apr. 1807.

FULLARTON, Stewart Murray (1807-1869). Major. 39th N.I. *b.* Edinburgh 8 Oct. 1807. Cadet 1825. Arrived in India 10 Mar. 1826. Ensign 12 Oct. 1825. Lieut. 12 June 1832. Capt. 18 Mar. 1845. Retired 1 Nov. 1849. Hon. Major 28 Nov. 1854. *d.* 5 Apr. 1869.

Son of Stewart Murray Fullarton, of Bartanholm, collector of customs at Irvine.

Services : Posted as Ensign to 39th N.I. in 1826. Actg. Intr. & Qmr. 39th N.I. 14 Jan. 1839. Gwalior campaign ; Paniar (s.w.) ; Lieut. 39th N.I. (Bronze star). (*Lond Gaz.* 8 Mar. 1844.) Fur. 5 May 1847 till retirement.

FULLER, Abraham (1801-1831). Captain, 33rd N.I. *b.* Kilbride, King's Co., Ireland, 6 May 1801. Cadet 1817. Arrived in India Aug. 1818. Ensign 21 Apr. 1818. Lieut. 9 Nov. 1818. Capt. 13 Jan. 1828. *d.* Cawnpore 21 Mar. 1831.

Son of Abraham Fuller, of Gloster Pl., Dublin. *m.* St. John's, Calcutta, 1 Aug. 1823, Anna Amelia, dau. of Paul Kellner, headmaster of the Lower Orphan School, Calcutta. (She died Delhi, 11 May 1857, aged 53.) His dau. *m.* William Thomas Pocklington, *q.v.*

Services : Ensign d.d. Bengal Eur. Regt. Posted as Ensign to 1/16th N.I. Mar. 1819. Served with Narbada F.F. in 1820. To do duty with Rangpur L.I. Bn. July 1823. First Burma War ; Sylhet frontier 1824 ; Bikrampur ; Dudhpatli ; Lieut. Rangpur L.I. Transfd. to 33rd N.I. (late 2/16th) May 1824. Fur. s.c. 15 Dec. 1824 till 8 May 1826.

Refs. : De Rhé-Philipe. M.I. in St. James's, Delhi.

FULLER, George (*d.* 1787). Lieutenant, Infantry. Cadet 1779. Ensign 12 Sept. 1779. Lieut. 29 Apr. 1781. *d.* Dacca 9 May 1787.
Services : N.F.P.

FULLER, George (1756/57-1839). Major. Artillery. *b.* 1756/57. Cadet 1783. Admitted 2 Sept. 1783. Fireworker 24 Feb. 1785. Lieut. 9 Mar. 1792. Capt. Lt. 18 Feb. 1802. Capt. 21 Sept. 1804. Major 8 Dec. 1810. Retired 17 Feb. 1815. *d.* Heathfield, Sussex, 6 Apr. 1839, aged 82.

Of Heathfield. 3rd son of John Fuller, of Hoo and Heathfield, and Mary Duke his wife.

Services : Lieut.F. 2nd Bn. Art. in July 1787. Fur. 18 Jan. 1797 till 11 Dec. 1800. Expedn. to Macao 1801-2 ; Lieut. 4th Coy. 1st Bn. Art. Reduction of Kalinjar 1812 ; Major comdg. the Art. Fur. 14 Feb. 1813 till retirement.

Refs. : Burke's *Landed Gentry*, 2nd edn., p. 452, *s.n.* Fuller, of Rose Hill, Waldron. *G.M.* 1839, i. 557.

FULLER, Richard (*d.* 1786). Lieutenant, Infantry. Cadet 1779. Ensign 12 Feb. 1780. Lieut. 29 Mar. 1781. *d.* Barrackpore 17 Nov. 1786.
Services : N.F.P.

FULLICE, Isaac. Ensign. Infantry. Cadet 1763. Ensign 18 June 1763.
Services : Out of the Service before 1 Feb. 1767. N.F.P.

FULTON, John (1784-1829). Captain. Bengal Eur. Regt. *b.* 1784. Cadet 1804. Arrived in India 10 Sept. 1805. Ensign 10 Sept. 1805. Lieut. 12 Sept. 1805. Capt. 1819. Retired 8 Sept. 1819. *d. unm.* Lisburn, co. Antrim, 17 Mar. 1829.

bapt. Lisburn 5 Sept. 1784. Eldest son of James Fulton, of Lisburn, and Anne his wife, dau. of Henry Bell, of Lambeg. Grandson of John Fulton, of Lisburn and Calcutta, merchant. Brother of Robert Bell Fulton, *q.v.*, and cousin-german of Joseph Hennessey Fulton, *q.v.*, and of Nicholas Graham Fulton, *q.v.*

Services : Posted as Lieut. to Bengal Eur. Regt. in 1806. Adjt. Amboynese Corps 1812-4. Fur. 15 Aug. 1816 till retirement.

Refs. : Burke's *Landed Gentry of Ireland*, p. 252, *s.n.* Fulton, of Braidujle, co. Antrim. Burke's *Colonial Gentry*, p. 340, *s.n.* Fulton, of Napier, N.Z.

FULTON, John (1807-1887). Lieut. Colonel. 5th N.I. *b.* Weeley, Essex, 17 Oct. 1807. Cadet 1823. Arrived in India 12 June 1824. Ensign 19 Feb. 1824. Lieut. 13 May 1825. Capt. 24 Jan.

THE BENGAL ARMY, 1758-1834 285

1845. Bt. Major 11 Nov. 1851. Retired 11 June 1856. Hon. Lt. Col. 11 June 1856. *d.* 161a Piccadilly, London, 23 Mar. 1887.

Son of Robert Fulton, of Hartfield, co. Renfrew, Lt. Col. 79th Highlrs., and Jean (or Jane) his wife and cousin, 4th dau. of John McKerrell, of Hillhouse. Nephew by marriage of Moses Crawfurd, *q.v.*, and of John Reid, *q.v.*, and cousin-german of Robert McKerrell, *q.v. m.* Sikraul, B. & O., 18 Nov. 1830, Rebecca Browne.

Services : Posted as Ensign to 55th N.I. in 1824. Fur. 7 Oct. 1836 till 18 Feb. 1839. Transfd. to 5th N.I. 14 Dec. 1842. Adjt. 5th N.I. 28 Apr. 1843 till Apr. 1845. No record of active service.

Refs. : Burke's *Landed Gentry*, 13th edn., p. 1174, *s.n.* McKerrell, *late* of Hillhouse, co. Ayr. *The Times*, 24 Mar. 1887.

FULTON, Joseph Hennessey (1816-1843). Lieutenant, 3rd N.I. *b.* Calcutta 20 Mar. 1816. Cadet 1834. Arrived in India 7 June 1835. Ensign (21 Jan. 1835) 5 Mar. 1835. Lieut. 25 Jan. 1837. *d.* Doranda, B. & O., 24 May 1843, of fever.

2nd son of John Williamson Fulton, of Calcutta, and 4 Upper Harley St., London, and Anne his wife, dau. of Robert Robertson and widow of John Hunt (*d.* 1804), *q.v.* Cousin-german of Robert Bell Fulton, *q.v.*, and of Nicholas Graham Fulton, *q.v.* His half-sister *m.* Thomas Pottinger, *q.v.*

Services : Ensign d.d. 57th N.I. 12 June 1835. Posted as Ensign to 3rd N.I. 24 Sept. 1835. Actg. Intr. & Qmr. 57th N.I. 21 Apr. till 26 Oct. 1840. Served with Ramgarh L.I. Bn. 22 Feb. 1841 till death. Offg. Junior Asst. to Comr. of Chota Nagpur 14 July 1841. Remanded temporarily to regtl. duty 24 May 1842.

Refs. : Burke's *Landed Gentry of Ireland*, p. 252, *s.n.* Fulton, of Braidujle, co. Antrim. Burke's *Colonial Gentry*, i. 339. *G.M.* 1843, ii. 333. *The Times*, 7 Aug. 1843. M.I. in Trinity church, Marylebone.

FULTON, Nicholas Graham (1781-1804). Lieutenant, 2nd N.I. *b.* Lisburn, co. Antrim, 10 Dec. 1781. Cadet 1799. Arrived in India 9 Dec. 1800. Ensign 11 Aug. 1800. Lieut. 7 Oct. 1800. *d.* Sikandra 24 Aug. 1804 : kld. in action during Col. Monson's retreat.

3rd son of Joseph Fulton, of Lisburn, and Anne his wife, dau. of Francis Graham, of Lisburn. Brother of Thomas Fulton, *q.v.*

Services : Ensign York Fencibles 1798. Operations in Jumna Doab 1803 ; Sasni ; Bijaigarh ; Kachaura ; Lieut. 2/2nd N.I. Second Mahratta War ; battle of Delhi ; Hinglaisgarh ; Monson's retreat (kld.) ; Lieut. 2/2nd N.I.

Refs. : Burke's *Landed Gentry of Ireland*, p. 252, *s.n.* Fulton, of

Braidujle, co. Antrim. Burke's *Colonial Gentry*, p. 339. Intestate; admon. 11 Sept. 1805.

FULTON, Robert Bell (1788-1836). Major, Artillery. *b.* 1788. Cadet 1805. Arrived in India 13 Nov. 1806. Lieut. 11 Apr. 1806. Capt. Lt. 25 Sept. 1817. Capt. 1 Sept. 1818. Major 31 May 1833. *d.* Fatehgarh 11 May 1836.

bapt. Lisburn, co. Antrim, 26 Sept. 1788. 2nd son of James Fulton, of Lisburn, and Anne his wife. Brother of John Fulton (1784-1829), *q.v. m.* Gretna Green 30 Oct. 1817, and at Hillsborough 9 Dec. 1817, Elizabeth Jane, dau. of George Stephenson, of Hillsborough. (She died 5 May 1863, aged 63.)

Services : Fur. s.c. 15 Aug. 1816 till 20 Nov. 1819. Supt. halfwrought material yard at Kasipur 21 Aug. 1820. Tempy. Asst. Agent gun-carriage factory at Kasipur 11 Dec. 1823. Agent guncarriage factory at Fatehgarh 28 May 1824. Actg. Agent for army clothing at Fatehgarh 16 Nov. 1829. Offg. Agent gun-carriage factory at Fatehgarh 16 Feb. 1831. Agent for army clothing, 1st Div., Fatehgarh 25 June 1832. Leave 2 yrs. to Simla 1 Feb. 1833. No record of active service.

Refs. : Burke's *Landed Gentry of Ireland*, p. 252, *s.n.* Fulton, of Braidujle, co. Antrim. Burke's *Colonial Gentry*, i. 340. Will dated 21 Apr. 1836 ; proved 6 Dec. 1836. M.I. at Fatehgarh.

FULTON, Thomas (1780-1849). Lieutenant. Infantry. *b.* 1780. Cadet 1797. Arrived in India 9 Nov. 1798. Ensign (Rank not assigned). Lieut. 1 Nov. 1798. Resigned 15 Feb. 1799. *d.s.p.* Bath 1849.

J.P. cos. Armagh and Antrim. *bapt.* Lisburn, co. Antrim, 14 May 1780. 2nd son of Joseph Fulton, of Lisburn, and Anne his wife. Brother of Nicholas Graham Fulton, *q.v.*, and cousin-german of Robert Bell Fulton, *q.v.*, and of Joseph Hennessey Fulton, *q.v. m.* 1799, Lydia Johnson, grand-dau. of Charles Weston, the Calcutta philanthropist. (She died 5 Sept. 1843, aged 65.)

Services : Ensign 92nd Highlrs. and 78th Foot. Lieut. 78th Foot 26 May 1803. Capt. Armagh Mil. 11 Apr. 1806 ; subsequently Major do.

Refs. : Burke's *Landed Gentry of Ireland*, p. 252, *s.n.* Fulton, of Braidujle, co. Antrim. Burke's *Colonial Gentry*, p. 715.

FURLONG, Walter (*d.* 1763). Lieutenant, Bengal Eur. Regt. Cadet (?). Ensign 8 Sept. 1759. Lieut. 1761. *d.* 2 Aug. 1763 : kld. in action at battle of Gheria.

Services : War with Mir Muhammad Kasim 1763 ; battle of Gheria (kld.) ; Lieut. Bengal Eur. Regt.

Refs. : Innes, p. 152.

FYLER, John I'Anson (1792-1815). Ensign. 5th N.I. b. 1 Jan. 1792. Cadet 1808. Arrived in India 19 July 1809. Ensign 21 July 1809. Resigned in England 19 Mar. 1811. d. 1815.

bapt. Epsom, Surrey, 29 Jan. 1792. 3rd son of Samuel Fyler, of Twickenham, Middlesex, and Dover St., London, barr.-at-law, and Mary his wife, only child of John I'Anson.

Services : Whilst an Ensign at the Barasat C.C. was suspended and ordered to return to Europe on 13 Feb. 1810. His rank was cancelled on resignation.

Refs. : Burke's *Landed Gentry*, 13th edn., p. 697, s.n. Fyler, of Woodlands, Surrey.

G

GABB, John (1783-1823). Captain, 34th N.I. *bapt.* Abergavenny 22 June 1783. Cadet 1800. Arrived in India 24 Aug. 1801. Ensign 2 Oct. 1801. Lieut. 13 July 1803. Capt. 16 Dec. 1814. *d.* Saidabad, U.P., 31 Dec. 1823.

Son of Baker Gabb. *m.* Mary.

Services : Operations in Bundelkhand 1806-7 ; Chamir ; Sehlehuganj ; Lieut. 2/1st N.I. Operations in Bundelkhand 1809 ; Rajaoli ; Ajaigarh ; Lieut. 2/1st N.I. Capt. Lt. 1st N.I. 10 June 1814. Nepal War 1814-5 ; Capt. 2/1st N.I., in 1st Div. Fur. 27 Jan. 1817 till 1818. Transfd. to newly-raised 34th N.I. July 1823.

Refs. : Burke's *Landed Gentry*, 2nd edn., p. 456, *s.n.* Gabb, of Monmouthshire. Will dated 1 July 1820 ; proved 7 Feb. 1824.

GAGE, James (1759/60-1786). (? Cadet, Infantry.) *b.* 1759/60. Cadet 1780. *d.* 1786.

A native of London.

Services : Apptd. Cadet on 8 Dec. 1780, aged 21. Sailed for India on the *Chapman*, 13 Mar. 1781, aged 21. N.F.P.

GAGE, William (1785-1828). Major, 36th N.I. *b.* Hengrave, Suffolk, 19 Nov. 1785. Cadet 1801. Admitted 26 Aug. 1802. Ensign 10 July 1802. Lieut. 23 May 1804. Capt. 16 May 1815. Major 13 May 1825. *d. unm.* Buxar 25 Mar. 1828.

3rd son of Sir Thomas Gage, 6th Bart. of Hengrave, and Charlotte his 1st wife, dau. of Thomas Fitzherbert, of Swinnerton, Staffs.

Services : Posted as Lieut. to 18th N.I. (? Operations in Bundelkhand 1809 ; Rajaoli ; Ajaigarh ; Lieut. 1/18th N.I.) Adjt. 1/18th N.I. 1812. Bk. Mr. at Meerut 7 Aug. 1812 till 1817. Capt. 2/18th N.I. S.A.C.G. 1817-22. Fur. 1822-5. Transfd. to 36th N.I. (late 1/18th) May 1824. Siege and capture of Bhurtpore ; Major 36th N.I.

Refs. : Burke's *Peerage*, 1859, p. 421, *s.n.* Rokewood-Gage, Bart., of Hengrave, Suffolk. M.I. at Buxar.

LIST OF OFFICERS OF THE BENGAL ARMY 289

GAHAGAN, Frederick. Cadet. Infantry. Cadet 1783. Struck off 1786.
Services : N.F.P.

GAHAN, John. Ensign. Infantry. Cadet 1780. Ensign 4 Feb. 1781.
Services : Transfd. to Madras Est. Out of the Service before 1787.

GAHAN, John Beresford Daniel (1803-1847). Major, Invalid Est. 26th N.I. *b.* Waterford 1 Oct. 1803. Cadet 1820. Admitted 31 May 1821. Ensign 13 Jan. 1821. Lieut. 11 July 1823. Capt. 14 Feb. 1829. Major 8 Feb. 1843. Invalided 22 Nov. 1843. *d.* Boulogne, France, 16 Mar. 1847.

Son of Beresford Gahan, Bde. Major of Yeomanry, and Harriet his wife, 2nd dau. of John Townsend, of Shepperton, co. Cork, M.P. Cousin-german of John Townsend Somerville, *q.v.* *m.* Waterford, 1838, Hannah, eldest dau. of Very Rev. Usher Lee, dean of Waterford.

Services : Posted as Ensign to 1/19th N.I. 16 Nov. 1821. Transfd. as Lieut. to 13th N.I. 11 July 1823 ; to 26th N.I. (late 1/13th) May 1824. First Burma War ; Arakan 1825 ; Lieut. 26th N.I. Actg. Adjt. 26th N.I. 26 Jan. 1826. Fur. p.a. 13 Nov. 1835 till 10 Dec. 1838. Actg. Bde. Major at Ferozepore 22 Sept. 1841 till 26 Jan. 1842. First Afghan War 1842 ; forcing of Khyber (*Lond. Gaz.* 7 June 1842). Fur. s.c. 22 Jan. 1844 till death.

Refs. : Burke's *Landed Gentry of Ireland*, p. 699, *s.n.* Townsend, late of Castle Townsend, co. Cork. *A.J.* N.S. xxvi. 192. *I.M.* No. 89, p. 678. Will dated Cape Town 30 May 1845 ; proved 28 Sept. 1847.

GAHAN, Robert (*d.* 1818). Lieut. Colonel, C.B., 6th N.C. Cadet 1780. Admitted 3 Apr. 1780. Cornet 5 Feb. 1781. Lieut. 7 Oct. 1781. Capt. 29 May 1800. Major 11 Mar. 1805. Lt. Col. 29 Aug. 1810. *d.* Jubbulpore 12 Dec. 1818.

(*Probably* brother of Beresford Gahan, of Waterford, who was his residuary legatee, and uncle of John Beresford Gahan, *q.v.*)

Services : Adjt. 1st Bengal Eur. Bn. 1787-90. Second Rohilla War ; battle of Bitaurah. Lieut. 2nd N.C. in 1796. Operations in Jumna Doab 1803 ; Sasni ; Bijaigarh ; Kachaura ; Capt. 4th N.C. Fur. 21 Dec. 1803 till 9 Nov. 1808. Major 4th N.C. Posted as Lt. Col. to 6th N.C. Fur. 11 Feb. 1812 till 1816. Third Mahratta War ; Sitabaldi ; Nagpur ; Lt. Col. 6th N.C. C.B. 14 Oct. 1818.

Refs. : *Williams*, p. 83. Will dated Nagpur 21 Aug. 1818 ; proved 3 Dec. 1819.

GAIRDNER, William John (1789-1861). Major General, C.B. Colonel 63rd N.I. *b.* 6 Sept. 1789. Cadet 1807. Arrived in India 28 Oct. 1808. Ensign 6 Oct. 1808. Lieut. 16 Dec. 1814. Capt. 22 Sept. 1824. Major 16 June 1835. Lt. Col. 12 Jan. 1842. Col. 10 Sept. 1852. Maj. Gen. 28 Nov. 1854. *d.* Strathtyrum House, St. Andrews, Fife, 3 Feb. 1861.

Eldest son of Alexander Gairdner, of Ladykirk, Markton, co. Ayr, and grandson of William Gairdner, of Ayr, writer. Brother of Hon. Alexander Gairdner, of Tobago. *m.* Edinburgh, 1 Aug. 1839, Jane, dau. of Patrick Wishart, W.S.

Services : Barasat C.C. for 13 mos. Posted as Ensign to 10th N.I. Operations against the Bhattis 1809-10 ; Ensign 2/10th N.I. Operations in Oudh 1812 ; in Rewah 1813-4 ; storm of Etah (w.) ; Lieut. 2/10th N.I. Nepal War 1816 ; Lieut. 2/10th N.I., in 2nd Bde., Left Column (India medal). Bareilly insurrection 1816. Adjt. 2/10th N.I. 18 Mar. 1817 till 9 Apr. 1824. Third Mahratta War ; Chanda. Actg. Intr. & Qmr. 2/10th N.I. 29 Nov. 1823. Transfd. to 14th N.I. (late 1/10th) May 1824. Adjt. 14th N.I. 17 June till 26 Oct. 1824. First Burma War 1824-6 ; Rangoon ; Donabyu ; Prome ; tempy. S.A.C.G. with Sir A. Campbell's force (clasp to India medal). S.A.C.G. 2 May 1826 ; D.A.C.G., 2 cl., 26 Aug. 1831. Fur. p.a. 6 Mar. 1836 till 22 Jan. 1840. Comdg. 14th N.I. from 10 Apr. 1842. Gwalior campaign ; Maharajpur ; Lt. Col. comdg. 14th N.I. (Bronze star). First Sikh War ; Ferozshahr ; Lt. Col. comdg. 14th N.I. (Medal). Transfd. to 16th N.I. 1846. Against the Rajah of Sikkim 1850. Fur. s.c. 7 Feb. 1852 till death. Posted as Col. to 63rd N.I. Nov. 1852. C.B. 3 Apr. 1846.

Refs. : Paterson's *Ayr and Wigton,* i. 582. Boase. *A.J.* N.S. xxx. 64. *The Times,* 8 Feb. 1861.

GAITSKELL, Frederick (1806-1901). Major General, C.B. Artillery. *b.* London 26 June 1806. Cadet 1823. 2nd Lieut. 18 Dec. 1823. Lieut. 28 Sept. 1827. Capt. 23 Nov. 1841. Major 17 May 1854. Lt. Col. 14 Sept. 1857. Col. 18 Feb. 1861. Retired 24 Nov. 1862. Hon. Maj. Gen. 24 Nov. 1862. *d.* Lisburn, Torquay, Devon, 8 Feb. 1901.

Son of Thomas Gaitskell, of London, wine and brandy distiller and merchant. *m.* eldest dau. of Major J. Hamilton, H.M. 42nd Foot, and widow of Surgeon-Major Reid, Bengal Medical Est. Addiscombe Cadet 1 Feb. 1822 till 18 Dec. 1823.

Services : Adjt. & Qmr. 4th Bn. Foot Art. 10 Jan. 1838 till 22 July 1840. Apptd. to comd. experimental Camel Field Battery 22 July 1840. Fur. p.a. 1 Feb. 1845 till 1846. Lt. Col. comdg. 8th Bn. Art. Mutiny campaign ; siege and capture of Delhi ;

joined the force on 3 Sept. 1857 (Medal with clasp). C.B. 21 Jan. 1858.
Refs. : The Times, 12 Feb. 1901, p. 6.

GAITSKELL, James Gandy (1813-1885). Lieut. Colonel. 26th N.I. b. Southwark, Surrey, 5 Apr. 1813. Cadet 1829. Arrived in India 7 Aug. 1830. Ensign 7 Aug. 1830. Lieut. 1 Jan. 1837. Capt. 24 Jan. 1845. Major 27 Aug. 1857. Retired 10 Aug. 1858. Hon. Lt. Col. 10 Aug. 1858. d. Waldon House, Cheltenham, 29 Jan. 1885.

Son of Henry Gaitskill, of Abbey Rd., St. John's Wood, London, distiller, and Elizabeth his wife. Brother of John Frederick Gaitskell, q.v., and cousin-german of Thomas Gandy, q.v. m. 1st, Calcutta cathedral, 17 Feb. 1849, Lucy Julia, dau. of John Perfect. (She died Boalia, Bengal, 18 Jan. 1852, aged 27.) m. 2nd, Prestbury, Gloucs., 14 Apr. 1858, Emily Todd, youngest dau. of J. Todd Naylor, of Liverpool.

Services : d.d. 26th N.I. 23 Oct. 1830 ; do. 28th N.I. 16 Nov. 1830. Actg. Ensign 1 Oct. 1832. Posted as Ensign to 8th N.I. 20 Aug. 1833. Transfd. to 26th N.I. 24 Sept. 1835. Fur. s.c. 6 Jan. 1836 till 25 Nov. 1838. Adjt. Mewar Bhil Corps 5 Oct. 1840. Leave s.c. 18 May 1842 till 30 Dec. 1843. Fur. s.c. 20 June 1844 till 1846. Executive Ofr. P.W.D., Purnea Div., 1855. Fur. s.c. 4 Feb. 1856 till retirement. No record of active service.
Refs. : The Times, 4 Feb. 1885.

*GAITSKELL, John Frederick (1811-1833). Cadet. Subsequently B.C.S. b. London 9 May 1811. Cadet 1828. d. Muttra 12 Sept. 1833.

Son of Henry Gaitskell. Brother of James Gandy Gaitskell, q.v. m. Calcutta, 8 Dec. 1831, Miss Harriet Gillanders. (See also William Worsley Davis.) Addiscombe Cadet 1827.
Services : Apptd. Writer 30 Apr. 1830. Arrived in India 7 Aug. 1830. Asst. to the Mgte. and Collector of Agra 27 Dec. 1832.
Refs. : A.J. N.S. xiii. 205.

GALE, Christopher (d. 1806). Captain, Artillery. Cadet 1783. Admitted 27 Sept. 1783. Fireworker 24 Jan. 1785. Lieut. 27 Mar. 1791. Capt. 22 Oct. 1803. d. Chunar 16 Dec. 1806.

Services : Lieut.F. 1st Bn. Art. in July 1787. With the detachment of Art. to Madras in Aug. 1793 for siege of Pondicherry ; Lieut. 2nd Coy. 1st Bn. Art. Dy. Comy. Ord. at Dinapore 26 July 1798 till 1805.

GALE, Curwen (1800-1849). Captain, Invalid Est. 18th N.I. b. London 8 Mar. 1800. Cadet 1819. Arrived in India 10 Jan. 1821. Ensign 22 Apr. 1820. Lieut. 11 July 1823. Capt. 9 Jan. 1833. Invalided 26 June 1837. d. Darjeeling 25 Apr. 1849.

Younger son of John Gale, of Vauxhall, Surrey, and sometime of Petrograd, and Eleanor his 2nd wife, dau. of —— Ethelstone. Half-brother of John Littledale Gale, q.v. m. 1st, 1822, Clementina Diana Ridges. m. 2nd, Agra, 7 Mar. 1827, Eliza Dutton. m. 3rd, May 1841, Ellen, dau. of James Smith.

Services : Posted as Ensign to 2/9th N.I. (? Operations in Oudh 1822 ; capture of Bardgaon ; Ensign 2/9th N.I.) Transfd. as Lieut. to 6th N.I. 11 July 1823 ; to 18th N.I. (late 2/6th) May 1824. Siege and capture of Bhurtpore ; Lieut. 18th N.I. Fur. p.a. 23 Apr. 1831 till 3 July 1833. Leave s.c. to N.S.W. 10 Oct. 1834 till 14 Mar. 1837. Fur. s.c. 10 Mar. 1840 till 5 Mar. 1842. With Invalid Coys. at Chunar from 31 Mar. 1842. Fur. s.c. 1845 till 21 Oct. 1848.

Refs. : Burke's *Family Records*, p. 258, *s.n.* Gale.

GALE, John Littledale (1783-1832). Lieut. Colonel, 37th N.I. *b.* New Broad St., London, 1 Apr. 1783. Cadet 1803. Arrived in India 1 Dec. 1804. Ensign 18 Nov. 1804. Lieut. 18 Nov. 1804. Capt. 5 Mar. 1816. Major 1 May 1824. Lt. Col. 21 Dec. 1827. *d.* Simla, 3 May 1832, of dropsy in the chest.

bapt. St. Peter-le-Poor, London, 12 Apr. 1783. Elder son of John Gale and Catherine his 1st wife, only dau. of Henry Littledale, of Whitehaven. Half-brother of Curwen Gale, q.v. m. 1st, Calcutta, 15 Feb. 1807, Rebecca, dau. of Daniel Brandon, of London. (She died 6 Aug. 1820.) His daus. m. Frederick Wilshire Steer Chapman, q.v., Henry Goodwyn, q.v., and William John Thompson, q.v. m. 2nd, 1 Oct. 1825,[1] Isabella, dau. of Col. Archibald Douglas, of Midshield, N.B., and Adderstone, Northumberland.

Services : Posted as Ensign to 2/12th N.I. 14 Apr. 1805. Operations in Oudh 1807-8 ; Bhadri ; Samanpur ; Gurha ; Pathar-serai ; Lieut. 2/12th N.I. Comdd. Purnea Provl. Bn. 21 May 1813 till 7 June 1824. Transfd. as Major to 1st N.I. (late 2/12th) May 1824. Fur. s.c. 23 Nov. 1824 till 2 Oct. 1827. Posted as Lt. Col. to 42nd N.I. 5 May 1828 ; transfd. to 37th N.I. 24 Sept. 1828. Leave s.c. to Simla Apr. 1832.

Refs. : Howard & *Crisp*, i. 277 ; (Notes) iii. 98. Burke's *Family Records*, p. 258. *De Rhé-Philipe*. A.J. xxiii. 589 ; N.S. ix. 142. Will dated Karnal 3 Dec. 1828 ; proved 4 Aug. 1832. M.I. Mall cemetery, Simla.

[1] *Note* : This is the date of his 2nd marriage according to both *Burke* and *Howard & Crisp* ; the *A.J.* for Apr. 1827, however, has the following : " Feb. 27. At Hastings, Maj. J. L. Gale, Bengal army, to Isabella, dau. of the late Arch. Douglas, Esq., of Edderstone, Roxburghshire."

THE BENGAL ARMY, 1758-1834   243

GALE or **GALL, Matthew** (1759/60-?). Lieutenant. Infantry. *b.* 1759/60. Cadet 1781. Ensign (?). Lieut. 1784. Resigned 23 Feb. 1784.

A native of London.

Services : Sailed for India on the *Latham,* 13 Mar. 1781, aged 21. N.F.P.

GALL, George Herbert (1779-1826). Lieut. Colonel, 8th L.C. *b.* Farrukhabad, U.P., 7 Feb. 1779. Cadet 1795. Arrived in India 8 Mar. 1797. Cornet 9 Oct. 1796. Lieut. 23 June 1799. Capt. 11 Mar. 1805. Major 1 Sept. 1818. Lt. Col. 1 May 1824. *d.* Karnal 26 June 1826.

Son of Lawrence Gall, *q.v.,* and Sophia his wife. *m.* Calcutta, 24 Feb. 1812, Ann, 2nd dau. of J. Wilkinson, of Portman Sq., London.

Services : Posted as Cornet to 3rd N.C. Transfd. as Lieut. to 1st N.C. in 1799. To do duty with G.G.B.G. 12 Dec. 1800 ; Adjt. & Qmr. do. 1 Sept. 1802. Operations in Jumna Doab 1803 ; Sasni ; Bijaigarh ; Kachaura (horse kld. under him) ; Lieut. 1st N.C., having obtained tempy. leave of absence from G.G.B.G. A.D.C. to G.G. (Sir George Barlow, Bart.) 27 Oct. 1805. Comdd. G.G.B.G. Feb. 1806 till 21 June 1818. Capture of Java ; Weltervreden ; Cornelis (w.) ; Capt. comdg. G.G.B.G. (Gold medal). Leave s.c. to Cape 17 Feb. 1817 ; fur. s.c. from Cape Mar. 1818 till Nov. 1821. Posted as Major to 8th L.C. in 1821. Siege and capture of Bhurtpore ; Lt. Col. comdg. 8th L.C.

Refs. : *E.I.M.C.* i. 307-10. *V.B.G.* *G.M.* 1826, ii. 647. Codicil to Will dated Calcutta 14 July 1822 ; proved 16 Dec. 1826.

GALL, Lawrence (1744/45-1806). Captain. Infantry. Subsequently Assessor at Calcutta. *b.* 1744/45. Cadet 1771. Ensign 7 Feb. 1773. Lieut. 26 Feb. 1778. Capt. 3 Oct. 1781. Resigned 23 Feb. 1784. *d.* Calcutta, 27 Apr. 1806, aged 61.

Of Biggleswade, Beds. *m.* Calcutta, 14 Aug. 1777, Sophia, sister of John Fortnom, *q.v.* Father of George Herbert Gall, *q.v.*

Services : After resigning the Service he became assessor to the Justices of the Peace for the town of Calcutta.

Refs. : M.I. in S. Park St. cemetery, Calcutta.

Note : A Bill for the naturalization of one Lawrence Gall passed the House of Commons 10 May 1803.

GALLIEZ, Primrose (1738/39-1819). Colonel. Infantry. *b.* 1738/39. Cadet 1758. Ensign 17 Nov. 1758. Lieut. 28 July 1759. Capt. 11 Oct. 1763. Major 29 Apr. 1766. Lt. Col. 2 Apr. 1768. Col. 18 Jan. 1774. Resigned 11 Nov. 1776. *d.* 18 Edward St.,

Portman Sq., London, 2 Nov. 1819, aged 80 : accidentally burnt to death by falling upon his head in the grate whilst his nurse-attendant was absent from the room.

Services : Apptd. a Vol. at Calcutta 14 June 1758. Obtained comd. of 1st Bn. (became 9th Bn. in 1764, and formed part of 12th N.I. in 1796) in 1763. This Bn., which he comdd. for several years, was called after him " *Gillies-ki-Paltan.*" War with Mir Muhammad Kasim 1763 ; siege and capture of Patna (s.w. on 6 Nov. 1763). First Rohilla War ; battle of St. George ; Col. comdg. 2nd Bde. N.I.

Refs. : E.I.M.C. iii. 301. *Orme MS.—India,* xiii. 3639. *Williams,* p. 166. *Cardew,* p. 23. *G.M.* 1810, ii. 476.

GALLOWAY, Sir Archibald (1780-1850). Major General, K.C.B. Colonel 58th N.I. *b.* 1780. Cadet 1799. Arrived in India 8 Dec. 1800. Ensign 29 Oct. 1800. Lieut. 18 May 1802. Capt. 19 Dec. 1812. Major 1 May 1824. Lt. Col. 6 Mar. 1826. Col. 22 Sept. 1836. Maj. Gen. 3 Nov. 1841. *d.* Upper Harley St., London, 6 Apr. 1850.

Chairman of the E.I.Co. *bapt.* Blairgowrie, co. Perth, 12 Feb. 1780. Son of James Galloway, of Perth, and Margaret Forester his wife. Uncle of Archibald Cowpar, *q.v. m.* Calcutta, 28 Nov. 1815, Adelaide, 3rd dau. of Capt. John Campbell, Madras Art., and grand-dau. of Col. Edward Tanner. (She died at sea on board the *Cornwall* 4 Apr. 1832.)

Services : See *D.N.B.* Operations in Jumna Doab 1803 ; Sasni ; Bijaigarh ; Kachaura ; as a Vol. (Lieut. 2/4th N.I.). Second Mahratta War ; defence of Delhi ; with Reserve under Lake in pursuit of Holkar ; Shamli ; capture of Deig ; Lieut. 2/14th N.I. ; siege of Bhurtpore (w. in windpipe in 2nd assault on 21 Jan. 1805) ; Lieut. Pioneers, whom he led in two assaults. Adjt. & Qmr. 14th N.I. 11 Feb. 1807 till 1811. Leave s.c. to sea 5 mos. 1 Sept. 1807. Sec. and Examiner in Arabic and Persian at Coll. of Fort William 1 Nov. 1811. Agent for manufacture of gunpowder at Allahabad 21 Jan. 1813 till 1821. Leave s.c. to Cape 14 Oct. 1814 till 2 Nov. 1815. Capt. 1/14th N.I. Agent for gunpowder at Ichapur 1821-9. Transfd. as Major to 29th N.I. (late 2/14th) May 1824. Posted as Lt. Col. to 2nd N.I. 7 Dec. 1826 ; transfd. to 10th N.I. 20 Apr. 1830 ; to 55th N.I. 14 Sept. 1833. M.M.B. 1830-5. Fur. p.a. 18 Mar. 1835 till death. Posted as Col. to 6th N.I. 21 Oct. 1836 ; to 58th N.I. 29 Nov. 1836. Director E.I.Co. 24 Sept. 1840 ; Chairman 1849. C.B. 20 July 1838. K.C.B. 25 Aug. 1848. Author of " On Sieges in India," and other works on India.

Refs. : Anderson, ii. 276. *D.N.B. D.I.B. N. & Q.* 6S xii. 435. *G.M.* 1816, i. 562 ; 1850, i. 660-2. *I.M.* 18 Apr. 1850, p. 238.

THE BENGAL ARMY, 1758-1834

Will dated 25 July 1834 ; proved 4 Jan. 1851. Engraved portrait pub. by Dickinson, New Bond St., Aug. 1850.

GAMON, Thomas (1789-1818). Lieutenant, 23rd N.I. *b.* Enfield 9 Aug. 1789. Cadet 1806. Arrived in India 3 Oct. 1807. Ensign 10 Aug. 1807. Lieut. 31 Aug. 1811. *d.* Betul, C.P., 16 Aug. 1818.

bapt. Enfield 13 Dec. 1789. Son of Oliver Gamon and Anne his wife. *m.* 21 Jan. 1812, Miss Eliza Rutledge.

Services : Posted as Ensign to 23rd N.I. in 1808. Fur. 2 Apr. 1813 till 1815. Third Mahratta War ; Lieut. 1/23rd N.I.

GANDY, Thomas (1785-?). Lieutenant. 19th N.I. *bapt.* Kendal, Westmorland, 22 Sept. 1785. Cadet 1804. Arrived in India 12 July 1805. Ensign 27 Aug. 1805. Lieut. 28 Aug. 1805. Resigned in India 30 Aug. 1814. *d.s.p.* (?).

Eldest son of James Gandy and Jane Beck his wife. Nephew of Henry Gaitskell, " of Baragon," and cousin-german of James Gandy Gaitskell, *q.v.*

Services : Posted as Lieut. to 19th N.I. in 1806. (? Operations in Bundelkhand 1807 ; Schlehuganj ; Lieut. 1/19th N.I.) With 5th Vol. Bn. in Java 1813-4.

Refs. : Burke's *Landed Gentry*, 13th edn., p. 701, *s.n.* Gandy, of Skirsgill Park, Cumberland.

GARBETT, Hubert (1803-1858). Bt. Colonel, Artillery. *b.* St. Owen, Hereford, 20 July 1803. Cadet 1818. Arrived in India Oct. 1819. 2nd Lieut. 23 Apr. 1819. Lieut. 19 Sept. 1822. Capt. 17 Jan. 1836. Major 6 Oct. 1846. Lt. Col. 2 Feb. 1851. Bt. Col. 28 Nov. 1854. *d.* Simla, 14 Jan. 1858, of a wound received at the siege of Delhi on 8 Aug. 1857.

Son of Rev. James Garbett, preby. of Hereford. *m.* Karnal, 23 Dec. 1834, Jessy, 2nd dau. of Colin Campbell, M.D., Physician Gen. Bengal. (*See also* Lionel Percy Denham Eld.) Addiscombe Cadet 15 Apr. 1818 till 6 Apr. 1819.

Services : Posted to Foot Art. Operations in Bundelkhand 1821 ; 2nd Lieut. 7th Coy. 1st Bn. Transfd. to 2nd Troop H.A. in Jan. 1824. Siege and capture of Bhurtpore ; Lieut. 4th Troop 2nd Bde., Adjt. 2nd Bde. (India medal). Fur. s.c. 18 Jan. 1829 till 2 Dec. 1831. Adjt. & Qmr. 3rd Bde. H.A. 1 Jan. till 3 June 1836. Capt. Foot Art. First Afghan War 1838-40 ; comdg. 4th Coy. 2nd Bn. ; transfd. to comd. 4th Troop 3rd Bde. H.A. 22 Oct. 1839 ; Bamian ; pursuit of Dost Muhammad Khan over the Hindu Kush (Medal). First Sikh War ; Mudki ; Ferozshahr ; comdg. 4th Troop 3rd Bde. (Medal with clasp). To comd. Art. at Lahore Feb. 1848. Second

246   LIST OF THE OFFICERS OF

Sikh War";"Multan, comdg. Art. throughout the siege ; Gujerat ; comdg. Art. of Gen. Whish's Div. (Medal with 2 clasps). Mutiny campaign ; Delhi F.F. ; apptd. Bdr. comdg. Art. at siege of Delhi 17 July 1857 (w. on 8 Aug. 1857). Leave s.c. to Simla 30 Sept. 1857. Durani, 3 cl. (*Lond. Gaz.* 3 Feb. 1843).

Refs. : De Rhé-Philipe. *A.J.* N.S. xxxii. 2, 305. *The Times*, 9 Mar. 1858. M.I. in new cemetery, Simla.

GARDEN, John (1798-1821). Ensign, 30th N.I. *bapt.* Bandley, Scotland, 15 Jan. 1798. Cadet 1819. Ensign 2 Dec. 1819. *d.* Betul, C.P., 29 Sept. 1821.

Son of Alexander Garden, in Bandley. Brother of William Garden, *q.v.*

Services : Posted as Ensign to 30th N.I. in 1820. No record of active service.

GARDEN, William (1790-1852). Bt. Colonel, C.B., A.D.C., 36th N.I. *bapt.* Alford, co. Aberdeen, 8 Mar. 1790. Cadet 1810. Admitted 21 Jan. 1812. Ensign 29 Nov. 1813. Lieut. 1 Oct. 1815. Capt. 25 Mar. 1828. Major 14 Nov. 1846. Bt. Lt. Col. 20 Apr. 1844. Bt. Col. 2 Aug. 1850. *d.* Glos. Terr., Hyde Pk., London, 29 July 1852.

Son of Alexander Garden, in Bandley, and Grizel McCombie his wife. Brother of John Garden, *q.v.*

Services : Posted as Ensign to 1/18th N.I. Adjt. 1/18th N.I. 1 June 1815. Nepal War 1816 ; Lieut. & Adjt. 1/18th N.I., in 1st Bde., Rt. Column (India medal). D.Q.M.G., 3 cl., 1 Jan. 1817 ; 2 cl. 24 Oct. 1818 ; 1 cl. 16 Oct. 1819. Third Mahratta War. Transfd. to 36th N.I. (late 1/18th) May 1824. Offg. A.Q.M.G. 7 Mar. 1825. Siege and capture of Bhurtpore ; A.Q.M.G. (clasp to India medal). A.Q.M.G. 28 Jan. 1829. A.Q.M.G. of the army 8 June 1832. Offg. A.D.C. to G.G. 27 Aug. 1832. D.Q.M.G. (with official rank of Major) 10 Apr. 1837. First Afghan War 1838-9 ; Ghazni ; D.Q.M.G. (Medal). Q.M.G. of the Army (with official rank of Lt. Col.) 5 Nov. 1841 till 7 Feb. 1850. Gwalior campaign ; Maharajpur ; Q.M.G. (Bronze star). First Sikh War ; Mudki ; Ferozshahr ; Sobraon ; Q.M.G. (Medal with 2 clasps). Second Sikh War ; Chilianwala ; Gujerat ; Q.M.G. (Medal with 2 clasps). Fur. 8 Feb. 1850 till death. C.B. 3 Apr. 1846. Durani, 2 cl., 26 Mar. 1841. A.D.C. to Queen Victoria.

Refs. : Boase. *I.M.* 17 Aug. 1852, p. 467. *G.M.* 1852, ii. 325. Will dated 7 Jan. 1850 ; proved 17 Sept. 1852.

GARDINER, John (*d.* 1813). Major General. Colonel 24th N.I. Cadet 1771. Admitted 23 Oct. 1771. Ensign 24 Jan. 1773. Lieut. 30 Dec. 1777. Capt. 1 June 1781. Major 28 Apr. 1797.

Lt. Col. 31 July 1799. Lt. Col. Comdt. 21 Sept. 1804. Col. 25 Apr. 1808. Maj. Gen. 4 June 1811. d. Devonshire St., London, 31 May 1813.

Services : First Rohilla War ; battle of St. George ; Ensign 15th Bn. Sepoys. Capt. 14th Bn. in July 1787. Fourth Mysore War ; capture of Seringapatam ; Major 10th N.I. (Gold medal). Operations in Jumna Doab 1803 ; Sasni ; Bijaigarh ; Kachaura ; Lt. Col. 15th N.I. Fur. 21 Dec. 1804 till death. Transfd. as Lt. Col. Comdt. to 24th N.I. in 1804 ; Col. 24th N.I. 1808.

Refs. : *A.R.* lv. *G.M.* 1813, i. 592.

GARDINER, Robert (*d.* 1795). Captain. Artillery. Cadet (?). Fireworker 5 Dec. 1771. Lieut. 13 May 1777. Capt. Lt. 23 Sept. 1779. Capt. 1 July 1784. Struck off 1793. *d.* Mountcharles, co. Ayr (? co. Donegal), 11 Sept. 1795.

His widow, Mrs. McRae Smith, died Hanover St., London, 8 Oct. 1819.

Services : Capt. 2nd Bn. Art. in July 1787. Fur. 12 Nov. 1788 till struck off.

Refs. : *G.M.* 1795, ii. 796. *S.M.* 1819, ii.

GARDINER, Thomas (*d.* 1764 ?). Lieutenant, Infantry. Cadet 1763. Ensign 20 June 1763. Lieut. 9 Mar. 1764. (? *d.* May 1764 of wounds received at battle of Patna.)

Services : Battle of Patna 3 May 1764 (s.w.—both legs broken). *Probably* died of his wounds.

Refs. : *Broome*, p. 445.

GARDINER, Thomas. Major. Engineers. Cadet 1767. Ensign 16 Sept. 1767. Lieut. 3 Apr. 1769. Capt. 6 June 1774. Major 25 July 1781. Resigned 22 Jan. 1784.

Services : N.F.P.

GARDINER, Thomas James (1814-1871). Lieut. Colonel. 16th N.I. *bapt.* Mallow, co. Cork, 13 Feb. 1814. Cadet 1829. Arrived in India 29 Dec. 1831. Ensign (9 June 1831) 29 Dec. 1831. Lieut. 30 June 1838. Capt. 2 Nov. 1848. Major 24 Nov. 1858. Retired 10 Feb. 1860. Hon. Lt. Col. 10 Feb. 1860. *d.* 22 Jermyn St., London, 14 Feb. 1871.

Son of John Gardiner, of Mallow, and Elizabeth his wife. Addiscombe Cadet 1829-31.

Services : d.d. 63rd N.I. 1 Feb. 1832 ; do. Bengal Eur. Regt. 30 Apr. 1832 ; do. 2nd N.I. 5 July 1832. Posted as Ensign to 16th N.I. 19 Oct. 1833. First Afghan War 1839-42 ; Ghazni (Medal) ; Kandahar ; Ghazni ; Kabul ; Lieut. 16th N.I., with Gen. Nott's

force (Medal). Gwalior campaign ; Maharajpur ; Lieut. 16th N.I. (Bronze star). Fur. 10 Feb. 1845 till 2 Feb. 1848.
Refs. : *The Times,* 17 Feb. 1871.

GARDINER, William (*d.* 1780). Cornet, Kandahar Horse. Cadet 1778. Cornet 2 May 1779. *d.* 20 Apr. 1780 : kld. in action at the assault of Lahar, whilst leading the forlorn hope.

(*Probably* grandson of Harry Gardiner, whose sister *m.* Rev. Penyston Hastings, the grandfather of Warren Hastings.) *m.* a native wife and left at his death two children, whom he consigned to the care of his kinsman, Warren Hastings.
Refs. : *Grier,* p. 20.

GARDNER, Richard (1791-1874). Lieut. Colonel. 13th N.I. *b.* St. Cuthbert's, Edinburgh, 2 Apr. 1791. Cadet 1806. Arrived in India 25 Nov. 1807. Ensign 1 Nov. 1807. Lieut. 27 Aug. 1811. Capt. 1 May 1824. Major 7 July 1842. Retired 25 Nov. 1842. Hon. Lt. Col. 28 Nov. 1854. *d.* 20 Mar. 1874.

Son of Richard Gardner, of Broughton, Asst. Comptroller of Customs for Scotland, and Mrs. Agnes Maitland, *alias* Pigott. *m.* Aberdeen, 7 July 1835, Charlotte, 5th dau. of William Dyce, M.D., of Cuttlehill.

Services : Posted as Ensign to 7th N.I. Third Mahratta War ; Lieut. 2/7th N.I. Adjt. 2/7th N.I. 27 Sept. 1820 till 17 June 1824. Transfd. to 10th N.I. (late 2/7th) May 1824 ; to 13th N.I. 17 Sept. 1824. Fur. p.a. 9 Jan. 1833 till 29 Nov. 1835. Agent for army clothing, 1st Div., 24 May 1836 till 31 Mar. 1841.
Refs. : *A.J.* N.S. xvii. 279.

GARDNER, Stewart William (1812-1882). Ensign. 28th N.I. *b.* 18 Aug. 1812. Cadet 1827. Arrived in India 10 Jan. 1829. Ensign 19 July 1828. Resigned 30 Jan. 1837. *d.* in India 20 July 1882.

Of Manotha, Etah, U.P. *bapt.* Walcot, Bath, 25 Mar. 1814. 2nd son of Francis Farington Gardner, Rear Adm. R.N., and Catherine his wife, dau. of Charles Van Straubenzee, of Spennethorpe, Yorks. Grandson of Alan Gardner, 1st Baron Gardner. *m.* Agra, 28 Aug. 1834, Harmuzi Begum, younger dau. of Alan Hyde Gardner by his wife the Bibi Sahiba Hinga.[1] (She died 15 June 1869.) His sister *m.* William Henry Rickards, *q.v.* The present Lord Gardner is a grandson of William Stewart Gardner, but has never claimed the barony, which has been dormant since 2 Nov. 1883.

Services : Ensign d.d. 55th N.I. 11 Feb. 1829. Posted to 28th N.I. 3 June 1829. No record of active service.
Refs. : Burke's *Peerage,* 1923, p. 964, *s.n.* Gardner, B.

[1] *Note :* Alan Hyde Gardner was younger son of William Linnæus

Gardner, nephew of 1st Baron Gardner, by his wife Nissa, 2nd dau. of the Nawab of Cambay.

GARNER, James (1781-1825). Lieut. Colonel Comdt., 31st N.I. *b.* Dundonald, co. Down, 1781. Cadet 1797. Arrived in India 21 Sept. 1798. Ensign 13 Sept. 1798. Lieut. 1 Nov. 1798. Capt. 26 Nov. 1805. Major 19 Feb. 1812. Lt. Col. 9 Aug. 1816. Lt. Col. Comdt. 1 May 1824. *d.* at sea 13 Jan. 1825, on board the *Carn Brea Castle*, on his passage to England.

Of Castle Hill, co. Down. *bapt.* Dundonald 1781. *m.* Arrah, 16 Sept. 1823, Dora Louisa, dau. of —— Taylor, and widow of Francis William Ulric Gladwin, *q.v.*

Services : Posted as Ensign to 3rd Bengal Eur. Regt. Oct. 1798. Operations in Jumna Doab 1803 ; Sasni ; Bijaigarh ; Kachaura ; Lieut. 15th N.I. Second Mahratta War ; battle of Delhi ; Agra ; Laswari ; battle of Deig (w.) ; Lieut. 15th N.I. Expedn. to Mauritius 1810-1 ; Capt. 1st Bengal Vol. Bn. Major 1/15th N.I. Comdg. at Fatehgarh in 1812. Fur. 13 Dec. 1814 till 1817. Transfd. as Lt. Col. to 6th N.I. in 1816 ; to 22nd N.I. in 1817 ; to 12th N.I. in 1819 ; to 2/15th N.I. in 1820 ; as Lt. Col. Comdt. to 31st N.I. (late 2/15th) May 1824. Fur. 1824.

Refs. : Pester. *S.M.* 1826, i. 126. *Calcutta Monthly Journal*, xlvii.

GARNER, Joseph (1786-1851). Lieut. Colonel. 29th N.I. *b.* Lisburn, co. Antrim, 15 Sept. 1786. Cadet 1803. Arrived in India 2 Dec. 1804. Ensign 29 Oct. 1804. Lieut. 19 Nov. 1804. Capt. 1 Oct. 1815. Major 1 May 1824. Lt. Col. 1 Nov. 1827. Retired 18 June 1830. *d.* Hamilton Terr., Greenwich, 20 Apr. 1851.

Son of Joseph Garner.

Services : Posted as Ensign to 1/15th N.I. Expedn. to Macao 1808 ; Lieut. Vol. Bn. Expedn. against Mauritius 1810-1 ; Lieut. 1st Bn. Bengal Vols. On service in Rewah 1813 ; Lieut. 15th N.I. Adjt. 2/15th N.I. 1814-5. Nepal War 1814-6 ; Capt. 2/15th N.I., in 4th Bde. Transfd. as Capt. to 1/15th N.I. Fur. s.c. 19 Nov. 1818 till 31 Oct. 1823. Transfd. as Major to 31st N.I. (late 2/15th) May 1824. Siege and capture of Bhurtpore ; Major 31st N.I. Fur. p.a. 17 Feb. 1828 till retirement. Posted as Lt. Col. to 41st N.I. 3 Apr. 1828 ; to 29th N.I.10 Sept. 1828. Retired on a pension of 11/- *p.d.*

Refs. : *E.I.M.C.* iii. 369. *G.M.* 1851, i. 679.

GARNER, Thomas (*c.* 1780-1848). Major General. Colonel 13th N.I. *b. c.* 1780. (Aged 16 and upwards on 18 Mar. 1796.) Cadet 1795. Arrived in India 15 Feb. 1797. Ensign 23 Nov. 1796.

Lieut. 30 Oct. 1797. Capt. 24 Sept. 1805. Major 1 Sept. 1815.
Lt. Col. 14 July 1821. Lt. Col. Comdt. 7 Nov. 1824. Col. 5 June
1829. Maj. Gen. 28 June 1838. *d.* 35 North Bank, Regent's
Pk., London, 27 Oct. 1848.

Services : On the way out to India he took part in the capture of
the Dutch squadron in Saldanha Bay, S.A., under Sir James Craig,
K.C.B., 17 Aug. 1796. Lieut. 1st Bengal Eur. Regt. in June 1798.
Transfd. to 16th N.I. Asst. to the Regulating Ofr. of Tannah
establishments at Bhagulpur 1802-15. Transfd. to newly-raised
22nd N.I. 1804. Nepal War 1816 ; Major 2/22nd N.I., in 3rd Bde.,
Centre Column. Third Mahratta War ; battle of Nagpur ; Major
comdg. 1/22nd N.I. Fur. s.c. 10 Feb. 1820 till 11 Oct. 1824. Posted
as Lt. Col. to 1/7th N.I. ; as Lt. Col. Comdt. to 13th N.I. (late
1/7th) 23 Nov. 1824. Fur. s.c. 21 Nov. 1825 till death.

Refs. : E.I.M.C. i. 193-5. *G.M.* 1848, ii. 664. *I.M.* 2 Nov. 1848,
p. 669.

GARNHAM, Robert Clement (*d.* 1827). Lieut. Colonel, 36th N.I.
Cadet 1797. Arrived in India 22 Dec. 1798. Ensign 7 Oct. 1798.
Lieut. 1 Nov. 1798. Capt. 28 Aug. 1806. Major 14 Jan. 1819.
Lt. Col. 1 May 1824. *d.* at sea 24 Feb. 1827, on board H.C.S.
Fairlie, between Calcutta and the Cape.

Of Oakfield (? Ashfield) Lodge, Suffolk. Son of John Garnham,
late of Thetford, Norfolk. *m.* Hackney, Sept. 1816, Miss Isabella
Mingay Syder.

Services : Lieut. 14th N.I. Fur. 7 Mar. 1803 till 23 July 1807.
Whilst proceeding on fur. on the *Lord Nelson,* was captured by the
French and kept a prisoner in France till 1806. Transfd. to newly-
raised 24th N.I. in 1805. Capture of Java 1811 ; Capt. 3rd Vol.
Bn. Afterwards served in Java with 5th Vol. Bn. Transfd. to
2/29th N.I. 1815. Fur. 1815-9, and 1822-4. Major 2/29th N.I.
Transfd. to 33rd N.I. 11 July 1823 ; as Lt. Col. to 27th N.I. May
1824 ; to 67th N.I. 1825. First Burma War ; Lt. Col. 67th N.I.
Transfd. to 36th N.I. 4 Nov. 1826. Fur. s.c. to Cape 1 Dec. 1826.

Refs. : A.J. ii. 536. *G.M.* 1827, ii. 190. Will dated 12 June
1825 ; proved 10 July 1828.

GARRETT, Charles (1809-1843). Captain, 9th L.C. *b.* Deptford,
Kent, 15 July 1809. Cadet 1825. Arrived in India 9 Mar. 1826.
Cornet 12 Oct. 1825. Lieut. 28 Dec. 1827. Capt. 23 July 1832.
d. 24 Mar. 1843 : kld. in action at the battle of Hyderabad, Sind.

Son of Henry Garrett, Vice Adm. R.N., Govr. of Haslar hospital.
Brother of William Trigge Garrett, *q.v. m.* Nimach, 24 Mar. 1832,
Frances Cordelia, 2nd dau. of Samuel Smith (1783-1852), *q.v.* (She
re-m. W. N. Garrett, and died 13 May 1859, aged 43.)

Services : Posted as Cornet to 9th L.C. in 1826. Operations at Jaipur Dec. 1835. Fur. p.a. 11 Feb. 1837 till 3 Feb. 1840. Campaign in Sind 1843 ; Miani ; Hyderabad (kld.) ; Capt. 9th L.C. (Medal). (*Lond. Gaz.* 6 June and 4 Aug. 1843.)
Refs. : Will dated camp, Scinde, 11 Jan. 1843 ; proved 7 Feb. 1844.

GARRETT, Edward (1810-1842). Bt. Captain, 69th N.I. *bapt.* Magheragall, co. Antrim, 14 Feb. 1810. Cadet 1825. Arrived in India 6 Feb. 1826. Ensign 15 Apr. 1826. Lieut. 15 Oct. 1828. Bt. Capt. 15 Apr. 1841. *d.* Madanpur, C.P., 23 Feb. 1842.

Son of Robert Garrett, of Lisburn, co. Antrim, linen merchant. Brother of Robert Garrett, *q.v.*

Services : Posted as Ensign to 1st Extra Regt. (became 69th N.I.) 5 Oct. 1826. Operations against the Bhils 1827. Actg. Intr. & Qmr. 69th N.I. 26 Aug. 1828. Actg. Adjt. 69th N.I. 27 Oct. 1835. d.d. Ramgarh L.I. Bn. 15 Sept. 1838 ; actg. 2nd in comd. do. 27 Dec. 1838 ; actg. Adjt. do. 28 June 1839 ; permanent do. 7 Nov. 1841 till death.

Refs. : G.M. 1842, i. 677. M.I. at Madanpur.

GARRETT, James Higginson (1807-1836). Ensign, 30th N.I. *b.* 29 Apr. 1807. Cadet 1828. Arrived in India 23 Sept. 1829. Ensign (23 Sept. 1829) 21 Sept. 1832. *d.* Simla 4 Sept. 1836.

bapt. Magheragall, co. Antrim, 1 May 1807. Son of Henry Garrett, of Magheragall, " gentleman farmer."

Services : Before proceeding to India was employed on the Trigonometrical survey of Ireland, under Capt. English, R.E. Cadet d.d. 69th N.I. Nov. 1829. Actg. Ensign 27 Oct. 1831, having been more than 2 yrs. in India. Ensign 69th N.I. 21 Sept. 1832. Posted as Ensign to 30th N.I. 23 Dec. 1832. Apptd. Asst. to A.G.G., Saugor & Narbada territories, 24 Feb. 1835. Apptd. S.A.C.G. at Cawnpore 4 May 1835. Leave s.c. to Simla 10 July 1836. No record of active service.

Refs. : De Rhé-Philipe. A.J. N.S. xxii. 130.

GARRETT, Robert (1801-1864). Bt. Colonel, 64th N.I. *bapt.* Magheragall, co. Antrim, 7 June 1801. Cadet 1818. Admitted 1 Jan. 1820. Ensign 24 July 1819. Lieut. 29 Aug. 1821. Capt. 1 Dec. 1836. Major 31 July 1849. Lt. Col. 28 Nov. 1854. Bt. Col. 20 June 1857. *d.* 3 Aug. 1864.

Son of Robert Garrett, of Lisburn, co. Antrim, linen merchant. Brother of Edward Garrett, *q.v.*

Services : Posted as Ensign to 1/19th N.I. Actg. Intr. & Qmr. 1/19th N.I. 16 Oct. 1823. First Burma War ; Cachar 1824 ; Lieut.

2/19th N.I., with force under Lt. Col. William Innes, C.B., *q.v.* Transfd. to 39th N.I. (late 2/19th) May 1824. Intr. & Qmr. 39th N.I. 17 June 1824. Transfd. to newly-raised 1st Extra Regt. (became 69th N.I.) 1825 ; Intr. & Qmr. do. 12 July 1825 till 14 Mar. 1837. Operations against the Bhils 1827. Fur. s.c. 6 Feb. 1840 till 12 Mar. 1844. S.A.C.G. at Cawnpore and Nasirabad 2 May 1845 till 1849. Posted as Lt. Col. to 69th N.I. 22 Mar. 1855 ; to 64th N.I. Jan. 1856. Fur. s.c. 7 Mar. 1859 till death.

GARRETT, William Trigge (1804-1833). Lieutenant, Artillery. *bapt.* Southampton 12 Feb. 1804. Cadet 1818. Admitted 16 Sept. 1819. 2nd Lieut. 26 Apr. 1819. Lieut. 17 Nov. 1822. *d.* Fatehgarh, 25 July 1833, aged 29.

2nd son of Henry Garrett, Vice Adm. R.N., Govr. of Haslar hospital. Brother of Charles Garrett, *q.v.* *m.* Patna, 3 Apr. 1832, Harriett, dau. of Major Slessor. (She *re-m.* Charles Young Bazett, *q.v.*) Addiscombe Cadet 1818-9.

Services : Siege and capture of Bhurtpore ; Lieut. Art. Apptd. to collect the captured ordnance and stores in the Bhurtpore district 1 Feb. 1826. Actg. Adjt. & Qmr. 1st Bn. Foot Art. 6 July 1826. Adjt. & Qmr. 2nd Bn. 7 Aug. 1827. Fur. s.c. 7 Oct. 1828 till 28 Nov. 1831.

Refs. : A.J. N.S. xiii. 119. *G.M.* 1834, i. 342. M.I. at Fatehgarh.

GARSTIN, Alfred (1799-1826). Captain, 56th N.I. *b.* Walcot, Somerset, 14 Feb. 1799. Cadet 1817. Ensign (?). Lieut. 1 Aug. 1818. Capt. 13 May 1825. *d.* at sea 2 Nov. 1826, on board the *James Sibbald.*

Son of John Garstin, *q.v.*, and Mary his wife. Brother of Edward Garstin, *q.v.*

Services : Posted as Lieut. to 2/28th N.I. Fur. 1822-4. Transfd. to 56th N.I. (late 2/28th) May 1824. First Burma War ; Arakan 1825 ; Capt. 1st Gren. Bn. Fur. 1826 till death.

Refs. : Will dated 16 June 1824 ; codicil dated Port Louis 12 June 1826 ; proved 24 Jan. 1827.

GARSTIN, Edward (1794-1871). General. Colonel Comdt. Royal (Bengal) Engineers. *b.* " either Bankipur or Benares," 6 Feb. 1794. Cadet 1813. Admitted 5 Aug. 1814. Ensign 6 May 1815. Lieut. 1 Sept. 1818. Capt. 5 July 1822. Major 20 Apr. 1835. Lt. Col. 5 Dec. 1848. Col. 17 Mar. 1851. Maj. Gen. 28 Nov. 1854. Lt. Gen. 21 Dec. 1865. Gen. 1 Mar. 1867. *d.* Bangalore, Madras, 13 July 1871.

Son of John Garstin, *q.v.*, and Mary his wife. Brother of Henry Garstin, *q.v.* *m.* Calcutta, 26 July 1836, Mary Anne, dau. of Adam Duffin, *q.v.* Addiscombe Cadet 12 Aug. 1810 till 25 Oct. 1811.

Services: Asst. Surveyor 30 Sept. 1814. Apptd. Asst. Field Engr. 4th (Dinapore) Div. for Nepal 15 Nov. 1814. Nepal War 1814-5 ; Asst. Field Engr. (India medal). P.W.D. at Ludhiana 6 June 1817. Third Mahratta War ; Nagpur ; Taragarh ; Madhurajpura ; Asst. Field Engr. 4th Div. (clasp to India medal). Adjt. Engrs. 9 Dec. 1819 till 27 May 1823. Fur. s.c. 8 Mar. 1827 till 15 Oct. 1831. Leave s.c. to China 1 Oct. 1832 till 14 June 1833. P.W.D. 2nd Div. 30 May 1833. Suptg. Engr., N.W.P., 12 May 1835 ; do. Lower Provinces 6 Dec. 1837. Offg. Chief Engr. 15 Mar. 1844. Offg. Chief Engr., with a seat at Mily. Board, 7 July 1852. Chief Engr. 1852-6.

Refs.: Boase. *A.J.* N.S. xxii. 58. *The Times*, 20 July 1871.

GARSTIN, Fortescue William (1748-1770). Ensign, Infantry. *b.* 1748. Cadet 1769. Ensign 20 Aug. 1769. *d. unm.* Ghireti, Bengal, 15 July 1770.

Son of John Garstin, of Leragh Castle and Ballykerrin, co. Westmeath, and Alethea his 1st wife, niece of Dr. John Farrell, of Carralaragh, co. Longford.

Services: N.F.P.

Refs.: Burke's *Landed Gentry of Ireland*, p. 259, *s.n.* Garstin, of Braganstown, co. Louth.

GARSTIN, Henry (1796-1832). Captain, 10th L.C. *b.* Dinapore 26 Jan. 1796. Cadet 1817. Admitted 23 June 1818. Cornet 11 Jan. 1818. Lieut. 13 Dec. 1818. Capt. 19 July 1828. *d.* Bhagulpur, Bengal, 29 Aug. 1832.

Son of John Garstin, *q.v.*, and Mary his wife. Brother of Alfred Garstin, *q.v. m.* 2 Dec. 1822, Miss Mary Kennedy.

Services: Transfd. from Inf. to Cav. 7 Aug. 1818. To do duty with G.G.B.G. 15 Sept. 1818, but served with that Corps for a few weeks only. Posted as Cornet to 6th N.C. Intr. & Qmr. 6th L.C. 7 Nov. 1823 till 25 Apr. 1825. Actg. Adjt. & Qmr. 2nd L.C. 30 July 1825. Transfd. to newly-raised 2nd Extra Cav. (became 10th L.C.) in 1825. Siege and capture of Bhurtpore ; Lieut. 10th L.C. Actg. Bde. Major at Meerut 20 Apr. 1826. Intr. & Qmr. 8th L.C. 6 Dec. 1828 till 28 Apr. 1829. To take charge of 5th Local Horse 13 Feb. 1831 ; tempy. comdg. do. 29 Apr. 1831.

Refs.: V.B.G. Will dated Bhagulpur 25 Aug. 1832 ; proved 19 Oct. 1832. M.I. at Mhow.

GARSTIN, John (1756-1820). Major General, Engineers. Surveyor Gen., Bengal. *b.* 1756. Country Cadet 1778. Ensign 1778. Lieut. 5 May 1781. Capt. 20 Dec. 1781. Major 25 Apr. 1797. Lt. Col. 1 Jan. 1806. Col. 25 Apr. 1808. Maj. Gen. 4 June 1811. *d.* Calcutta 16 Feb. 1820, aged 63.

Of Manchester Sq., London. A cadet of the family of Garstin, of Braganstown, co. Louth. m. Dinapore, 21 Nov. 1789, Mary, dau. of Rev. John Loftie, vicar of St. Dunstan's, Canterbury, and chaplain, Bengal Est. (She died Calcutta, 28 July 1811, aged 42.) Father of Alfred, q.v., Edward, q.v., and Henry Garstin, q.v.

Services : Given a Commission in Engrs. by George III. Was chiefly employed in the construction of civil works. Architect of the Calcutta town hall. Surveyor Gen. 1809-13. Chief Engr., Bengal, and M.M.B. Fur. 1 Jan. 1815 till 1818.

Refs. : D.I.B. Will dated Calcutta 30 Jan. 1819 ; proved 18 Feb. 1820. M.I. in S. Park St. cemetery, Calcutta.

GASCOIGNE, Peter (1764/65-1814). Bt. Lieut. Colonel, 13th N.I. b. 1764/65. Cadet 1782. Ensign 14 Feb. 1783. Lieut. 5 Feb. 1790. Capt. 13 July 1803. Major 22 Aug. 1810. Bt. Lt. Col. 4 June 1814. d. Port Louis, Mauritius, 6 Aug. 1814, aged 49.

Of Bethnal Green. Brother of George John, Mary Ann, Catherine Penelope, and Emily Gascoigne. Brother-in-law of Charles Boynton Wood. His dau. m. Edward Gwatkin, q.v.

Services : Returned from fur. 28 Nov. 1785. Ensign 5th Bengal Eur. Bn. in July 1787. Apptd. Adjt. 2/13th N.I. 29 May 1800. Fur. 7 Feb. 1803 till 1 Sept. 1805.

Refs. : G.M. 1814, ii. 674. Will dated 22 Mar. 1805 ; proved in 1814.

GASCOYNE, Charles Manners (1806-1872). Major. 5th L.C. bapt. Olveston, Gloucs., 13 Oct. 1806. Cadet 1825. Arrived in India 11 Jan. 1827. Cornet 21 June 1826. Lieut. 1 Sept. 1834. Capt. 13 Jan. 1842. Invalided 1 Dec. 1848. Retired 28 June 1854. Hon. Major 28 Nov. 1854. d. 5 Sept. 1872.

Son of John Gascoyne, Capt. R.N., and Charlotte his wife, dau. of Rev. C. E. De Coetlogon, rector of Godstone, Surrey. Grandson of Bamber Gascoyne (D.N.B.), and nephew of Gen. Isaac Gascoyne (D.N.B.). m. Meerut, 24 Feb. 1835, Isabella Augusta, only dau. of Surg. John Campbell, Madras Est., grand-dau. of Donald Campbell XIV. of Dunstaffnage, and sister of Osborne Campbell, q.v.

Services : Posted to 5th L.C. 8 Jan. 1827. Admitted to Cav. and promoted Cornet 20 Jan. 1827. Actg. Intr. & Qmr. 2nd L.C. 24 Feb. 1834. Intr. & Qmr. 5th L.C. 1 Mar. 1834 till June 1840. Fur. s.c. 2 Jan. 1841 till 28 Sept. 1843. (? Gwalior campaign ; Paniar ; Capt. 5th L.C.—Bronze star). First Sikh War ; Mudki ; Ferozshahr ; Aliwal ; Sobraon ; Capt. 5th L.C. (Medal with 3 clasps).

GASCOYNE, Joseph (1756-1830). Lieut. Colonel. 13th N.I. b. 1756. Cadet 1778. Admitted 10 Feb. 1780. Ensign Dec. 1778. Lieut. 28 Oct. 1778. Capt. 1 June 1796. Major 29 May

1800. Lt. Col. 8 Sept. 1803. Retired 23 June 1809. d. London 21 Mar. 1830.
Son of Joseph Gascoyne, of London. m. 1st, Berhampore, 13 Sept. 1787, Miss Sarah Evance. (*See also* Robert Greene.) m. 2nd, St. George's, Hanover Sq., London, 3 Dec. 1808, Mrs. Sarah Denton, of Tavistock Sq., London. (She died 8 Apr. 1835.) Ed. Westminster; admitted 24 Jan. 1770; admitted a scholar 1771, aged 14. Elected to Cambridge 1774.

Services : Sailed for India on the *True Briton*, 16 June 1779, aged 22. Qmr. 4th Bengal Eur. Bn. 1787-90. Capt. 2/4th N.I. Fur. 11 Oct. 1794 till 19 Nov. 1798. Transfd. to 1st Bengal Eur. Regt. Oct. 1798; retransfd. to 2/4th N.I.; as Major to 1/4th N.I. May 1800. (? Second Mahratta War; Aligarh; Major 1/4th N.I.) Transfd. as Lt. Col. to 26th N.I. 1804; to 21st N.I. 1805. Fur. 19 Sept. 1806 till retirement. Transfd. to 5th N.I. 1808; to 13th N.I. 1809.

Refs. : *Alumni Westmon.* *G.M.* 1808, ii. 1125.

GATLEY, Charles (1777-1806). Lieutenant, 27th N.I. b. Drayton, Oxon., 1777. Cadet 1795. Arrived in India 29 Jan. 1798. Ensign 6 Aug. 1797. Lieut. 30 May 1798. d. Delhi 8 Feb. 1806. Late of Knutsford, co. Chester. m. Azamgarh, U.P., 13 Aug. 1801, Miss Catherine Young.

Services : Second Mahratta War; Lieut. 13th N.I. Transfd. to newly-raised 27th N.I. in 1804.

GATT, Andrew. Ensign. Infantry. Cadet 1778. Ensign 16 May 1779. Struck off 12 Feb. 1781.

Services : N.F.P.

GATTAKER or GATAKER, Edward (1787-1805). Cornet, 1st L.C. b. Hampstead 11 Aug. 1787. Cadet 1803. Arrived in India 2 Dec. 1804. Cornet 11 Mar. 1805. d. Agra 4 Oct. 1805, of fever.

Son of Thomas Gataker, of Dundalk, co. Louth, and Mary his wife.

Services : Posted as Cornet to 1st N.C. No record of active service.

Refs. : *G.M.* 1806, ii. 676.

***GAUPP, George Frederick.** Captain. Infantry. Capt. 3 Aug. 1752.

Services : Capt. of the Swiss Inf. on the Madras Est. Sailed for Bengal from Madras Oct. 1756. Battle of Kasipur 5 Feb. 1757 (w.); comdd. one of the four divisions of Clive's force at the battle of Plassey, having previously voted at the council of war against an immediate action. Returned to Madras. Acted as A.D.C. to Govr. (afterwards Lord) Pigot during the siege of Madras 1758-9.

Refs. : *Orme MSS.*—*India*, xiii. 3639. *Love*, ii. 511. *Hill*. *Wilson*, i.

GAUSSEN, David (1810-1870). Colonel. 5th N.I. *bapt.* Ballyronan, co. Londonderry, 26 Aug. 1810. Cadet 1826. Arrived in India 31 Oct. 1827. Ensign 25 May 1827. Lieut. 24 July 1837. Capt. 15 Feb. 1848. Major 11 May 1860. Retired 31 Dec. 1861. Hon. Col. 31 Dec. 1861. *d.* 28 July 1870.

Son of John Gaussen (of the family of Gaussen, of Shanemullagh, co. Londonderry), of Belfast, merchant, and Jane Macdowell his wife.

Services : Posted as Ensign to 42nd N.I. 3 Jan. 1828. First Afghan War 1839-42 ; defence of Kalat-i-Ghilzai ; Qmr. Shah Shuja's 3rd Inf. (Medal) ; recapture of Ghazni ; 2nd in comd. Shah's 2nd Cav. ; re-occupation of Kabul, with force under Gen. Nott (Medal). Qmr. Regt. of Kalat-i-Ghilzai 4 Oct. 1842 till Mar. 1848. Gwalior campaign ; Maharajpur ; Lieut. Regt. of Kalat-i-Ghilzai (Bronze star). Santhal revolt 1855 ; Capt. 42nd N.I. Offg. Bde. Major 22 June 1855. Offg. Bde. Major at Saugor 9 Apr. 1857. Mutiny campaign ; C.I. 1857-8 ; capture of fort Balabet, Saugor district, June 1857 ; Bt. Major 42nd N.I. (Medal). Served with his Regt. (became 5th N.I. in May 1861) Apr. 1858 till retirement.

Refs. : Burke's *Landed Gentry of Ireland*, p. 261, *s.n.* Gaussen, of Shanemullagh, co. Londonderry.

GAVIN, Alexander (*d.* 1784). Lieutenant, Infantry. Cadet (?). Ensign 21 Sept. 1780. Lieut. 29 May 1781. *d.* Fatehgarh 24 May 1784.
Services : N.F.P.

GAWEN, James (*d.* 1776). Ensign, Infantry. Cadet 1771. Ensign 11 Feb. 1773. *d.* Chunar Sept. 1776.
Services : N.F.P.

GAWEN, John (1755/56-1784). Lieutenant, Infantry. *b.* 1755/56. Cadet 1778. Arrived in India 8 Oct. 1778. Ensign 1778. Lieut. 1778. *d.* Berhampore, Bengal, 7 June 1784.

A native of Salisbury.
Services : Sailed for India on the *Nassau,* 7 Mar. 1778, aged 22. N.F.P.

GEAR, Thomas (1801-1834). Lieutenant, 20th N.I. *b.* 17 Mar. 1801. Cadet 1821. Arrived in India 4 May 1822. Ensign 3 Dec. 1821. Lieut. 16 July 1823. *d.* Chiselborne, Dorset, 11 Oct. 1834.

bapt. Melcombe-Regis, Dorset, 18 Nov. 1807. Son of James Gear and Mary his wife.
Services : Posted as Ensign to 5th N.I. Transfd. to 20th N.I. (late 2/5th) May 1824. First Burma War ; Arakan 1825 ; Lieut.

2nd Gren. Bn. Intr. & Qmr. 2nd Gren. Bn. 17 Dec. 1825. Fur. s.c. 30 Dec. 1826 till 24 Nov. 1829, and 9 Sept. 1832 till death.
Refs. : A.J. N.S. xv. 180. G.M. 1834, ii. 555.

GEARY, Alexander (*d.* 1794). Captain. Infantry. Cadet (?). Ensign 6 Apr. 1764. Lieut. 15 Aug. 1765. Capt. 2 Dec. 1767. Resigned 18 Jan. 1772. *d.* Old Aberdeen 25 Apr. 1794.
Services : N.F.P.
Refs. : S.M. 1794, p. 237. *Eur. Mag.* 1794, i. 327.

GEARY, John (*d.* 1791). Lieutenant, Bengal Eur. Regt. Cadet 1778. Ensign 1778. Lieut. 26 Aug. 1779. *d.* Diamond Harbour 13 Aug. 1791 : lost in the Hooghly R.
Services : Lieut. 1/1st Bengal Eur. Regt. in Oct. 1779 ; 31st Bn. Sepoys in July 1787.

GEDDES, William (1794-1879). Colonel, C.B. Artillery. *b.* Gibraltar 22 Jan. 1794. Cadet 1810. Admitted 21 Jan. 1812. Fireworker 21 Nov. 1811. Lieut. 7 Oct. 1817. Capt. 28 Sept. 1827. Major 8 Oct. 1843. Lt. Col. 6 Oct. 1846. Retired 7 Jan. 1848. Hon. Col. 28 Nov. 1854. *d.* 52 George Sq., Edinburgh, 21 Mar. 1879.

J.P. and D.L. Midlothian. Son of James Geddes, Asst. Surg. E. Garr. Bn. *m.* 15 May 1827, Emma, 3rd dau. of Edward D'Oyly, of Sion Hill, Yorks., J.P., and sister of Thomas D'Oyly, *q.v.* (*See also* George Twemlow.) Father of Sir William Duguid Geddes (*D.N.B.*). Woolwich Cadet ; nominated to R.M.A. 3 Feb. 1808. Addiscombe Cadet 8 Apr. 1809 till 22 Apr. 1811.

Services : Nepal War 1816 ; Lieut.F. 7th Coy. 2nd Bn. (India medal). Third Mahratta War ; Lieut. Rocket Troop H.A. With 2nd Troop H.A. 1819-20 ; 2nd Troop 3rd Bde. 1825-6. Riding Master of Art. at Dum-Dum 22 July 1825 ; designation changed to Supt. of H.A. Depot and Riding Est. at Dum-Dum 5 Aug. 1826. Leave p.a. 6 mos. to Singapore 31 Mar. 1828. Comdg. 3rd Troop 2nd Bde. 1830 ; do. 2nd Troop 3rd Bde. 1831-7. Fur. p.a. 29 Jan. 1838 till 25 Oct. 1840. Comdg. 1st Troop 1st Bde. 1842-3. Posted to 3rd Bde. H.A. 8 Nov. 1843. Gwalior campaign ; Paniar ; Major comdg. 3rd Bde. H.A. (Bronze star). To comd. Art. at Sukkur 17 Apr. 1844. First Sikh War ; Ferozshahr ; Sobraon ; Bt. Lt. Col. 1st Bde. H.A. (Medal with clasp). C.B. 3 Apr. 1846. Comdt. City of Edin. Art. Mil. 6 Nov. 1854.

Refs. : Burke's *Peerage*, 1848, p. 324, *s.n.* D'Oyly, Bart. Burke's *Landed Gentry*, 2nd edn., iii. 227, *s.n.* Marston, late of Willenhall, Staffs. Burke's *Family Records*, p. 697, *s.n.* D'Oyly-Twemlow. *The Times*, 25 Mar. 1879.

GEILS, Joseph Tucker (1808-1871). Major. 60th N.I. *b.* Geilston 22 Nov. 1808. Cadet 1824. Arrived in India 30 June 1825. Ensign 9 Feb. 1825. Lieut. 30 Jan. 1830. Capt. 15 Apr. 1842. Retired 1 Mar. 1851. Hon. Major 28 Nov. 1854. *d.* Geilston 18 Oct. 1871.

Of Geilston, Cardross, co. Dumbarton. Youngest son of Thomas Geils, of Geilston, Col. 3rd Regt. of Foot Gds., and Dorcas Tucker his wife. *m.* 1st, Jessie. (She died Landour, U.P., 6 June 1850.) *m.* 2nd, St. George's, Bloomsbury, 26 Oct. 1853, Hester Elizabeth, dau. of Col. N. Wilson, K.H., and widow of Pierre Armand Bessis, of Boulogne.

Services : Siege and capture of Bhurtpore (w.) ; Ensign 60th N.I. (India medal). (*Lond. Gaz.* 10 June 1826.) Granted on 26 June 1830 a wound pension for permanent injury equivalent to loss of a limb. (? Reduction of Jhansi 1838-9 ; Lieut. 60th N.I.) To raise and comd. Malwa Bhil Corps 24 Feb. 1840, and comdd. from 10 Apr. 1840 till 3 May 1841, when, having failed to embody the Corps, he returned to his Regt. First Afghan War 1842 ; operations in Khyber Pass Jan. ; Tazin 12 Sept. 1842 (w.) ; re-occupation of Kabul ; Capt. 60th N.I. (Medal). (*Lond. Gaz.* 24 Nov. 1842.) Fur. s.c. 7 Apr. 1845 till 1846. Second Sikh War ; Capt. 60th N.I., in Reserve Div.

Refs. : *Walford* (1900). *I.M.* 1850, p. 485. *The Times*, 21 Oct. 1871.

GEORGE, James (1782-1828). Lieut. Colonel, 29th N.I. *bapt.* Lewisham, Kent, 3 Sept. 1782. Cadet 1798. Arrived in India 3 Oct. 1799. Ensign 5 Dec. 1799. Lieut. 29 May 1800. Capt. 13 Aug. 1812. Major 11 June 1822. Lt. Col. 1 May 1824. *d.* Shahjahanpur, U.P., 30 July 1828.

Son of Rev. James Payne George and Dorothy his wife. Grandson of Josiah George, of Birmingham. *m.* Kensington, 8 July 1826, Agnes Charlotte, youngest dau. of Rev. B. Kennett (*probably* sister of Charles Brackley Kennett, *q.v.*).

Services : Lieut. 7th N.I. Transfd. to newly-raised 25th N.I. 1804. Capture of Gohad 1806 ; Lieut. 25th N.I. Capture of Java 1811 ; Supy. A.D.C. to G.G. Supy. A.D.C. 1811-2. Capt. Lt. 25th N.I. 10 Dec. 1811. Capt. 2/25th N.I. Adjt. Calcutta Native Mil. 1812. Comdd. Chittagong Provl. Bn. 31 Oct. 1812 till 1823. Capt. 1/25th N.I. Fur. 1823-6. Transfd. as Lt. Col. to 57th N.I. May 1824 ; to 2nd Bengal Eur. Regt. 1825 ; to 37th N.I. 1825 ; to 60th N.I. 22 Dec. 1826 ; to 29th N.I. 28 Dec. 1826. Several original water-colour drawings of Java, Malacca, and Penang, executed by him whilst on the Java expedn., were recently on sale in London at prices varying from £10 to £20 apiece.

Refs. : *A.J.* xxii. 245 ; xxvii. 221. *G.M.* 1826, ii. 77.

GEORGE, James (1803-1838). Captain, 19th N.I. *bapt.* Middleton-Tyas, Yorks., 22 Apr. 1803. Cadet 1818. Admitted 17 July 1819. Ensign 8 Feb. 1819. Lieut. 7 Oct. 1820. Capt. 6 Jan. 1832. *d.* at sea 8 Aug. 1838, on board the *Abberton*, off the Sandheads.

Son of Sampson George, atty.-at-law.

Services : Ensign d.d. Bengal Eur. Regt. Posted as Ensign to 2/3rd N.I. Transfd. to 19th N.I. (late 2/3rd) May 1824. Actg. Intr. & Qmr. 1st Gren. Bn. 16 Sept. 1824 ; permanent do. 7 Dec. 1824. First Burma War ; Arakan 1825 ; Lieut. 1st Gren. Bn. Leave s.c. 6 mos. to Singapore 9 Jan. 1828. Fur. s.c. 17 Nov. 1828 till 23 Oct. 1832.

Refs. : *A.J.* N.S. xxviii. 78. Will dated 22 Aug. 1836 ; codicil dated Cuttack 30 June 1838 ; proved 18 Jan. 1839.

GEORGE, Robert Griffiths (1807-1839). Ensign, 11th N.I. *b.* St. James's, Bath, 29 Sept. 1807. Cadet 1829. Arrived in India 27 Mar. 1830. Ensign (20 Oct. 1829) 27 Mar. 1830. *d.* Saugor 30 July 1839.

bapt. Bath, 28 Oct. 1807. Son of Thomas Marmaduke George, of Bath, hatter, and Ann his wife. Ed. Winchester ; K.S. 1821 ; left in 1825.

Services : Ensign d.d. 55th N.I. 5 Apr. 1830. Actg. Ensign 3 May 1832. Posted to 7th N.I. 12 Mar. 1833. Exchanged to 11th N.I. 24 Jan. 1834. Actg. Intr. & Qmr. 55th N.I. 21 May 1834 ; do. 11th N.I. 29 Nov. 1834. Intr. & Qmr. 11th N.I. 8 Apr. 1836 till death. No record of active service.

Refs. : *Kirby.* *G.M.* 1839, ii. 666.

GERARD, Alexander (1792-1839). Captain. 27th N.I. *b.* Aberdeen 17 Feb. 1792. Cadet 1807. Arrived in India 14 Aug. 1808. Ensign 9 Sept. 1808. Lieut. 28 Nov. 1814. Capt. 13 May 1825. Retired 15 Feb. 1836. *d.* Aberdeen 15 Dec. 1839.

Son of Gilbert Gerard, D.D., professor of Divinity, King's Coll., Aberdeen (*D.N.B.*), and Helen his wife, dau. of John Duncan, provost of Aberdeen. Brother of Patrick Gerard, *q.v.*, and nephew of John Gerard, *q.v.*

Services : See *D.N.B.* Barasat C.C. for $7\frac{1}{2}$ mos. Posted as Ensign to 13th N.I. Adjt. 2/13th N.I. 27 Oct. 1814 till 12 June 1820. To do duty with Sirmoor Bn. 12 June 1820. Transfd. to 27th N.I. (late 2/13th) May 1824. Employed during a great part of his service in survey work, particularly 1812-7 and 1825-7. Distinguished as a scientific traveller and Himalayan explorer. No record of active service.

Refs. : *Anderson,* ii. 291. *D.N.B.* *D.I.B.* *G.M.* 1840, i. 334.

LIST OF THE OFFICERS OF

GERARD, John (1765-1824). Captain. 14th N.I. *b.* 1765. Cadet 1782. Admitted 5 Sept. 1782. Ensign 15 Jan. 1783. Lieut. 6 Feb. 1790. Capt. 30 Sept. 1803. Retired 13 Jan. 1808. *d.* York Pl., Edinburgh, 17 Apr. 1824.

Of Rochsoles, co. Lanark. 3rd son of Rev. Alexander Gerard, D.D., of King's Coll., Aberdeen (*D.N.B.*), and Jane his wife, eldest dau. of Dr. Wight (or White), of Colnae. Uncle of Patrick Gerard, *q.v. m.* Bruntsfield Links, 21 Mar. 1810, Dorothea Montague, 2nd dau. of Rev. Archibald Alison (*D.N.B.*), and sister of Sir Archibald Alison, 1st Bart.

Services : Sailed for India on the *Worcester*, 6 Feb. 1782, aged 17. Ensign 5th Bengal Eur. Bn. in July 1787. D.A.G. with official rank of Major. Apptd. A.G., with official rank of Lt. Col., 4 Sept. 1800. Second Mahratta War ; A.G. at Army H.Q. with Lord Lake. Persian Intr. to C.-in-C. M.M.B. Fur. 18 Feb. 1806 till retirement.

Refs. : Burke's *Landed Gentry*, 13th edn., p. 716, *s.n.* Gerard, of Rochsoles, co. Lanark. *S.M.* 1810 ; 1824, i. 640. Will dated Tours, France, 3 Nov. 1820 ; proved 29 Dec. 1826.

GERARD, Patrick (1794-1848). Captain, Invalid Est. 9th N.I. *b.* 11 June 1794. Cadet 1809. Arrived in India Feb. 1811. Ensign 19 Aug. 1812. Lieut. 16 Dec. 1814. Capt. 11 Apr. 1828. Invalided 6 Aug. 1832. *d.* Simla 4 Oct. 1848.

Son of Gilbert Gerard, D.D. (*D.N.B.*), and Helen his wife. Brother of Alexander Gerard, *q.v.*

Services : See *D.N.B.* Barasat C.C. till Aug. 1811. Ensign d.d. 1/13th N.I. Posted as Ensign to 2/8th N.I. in 1812. Nepal War 1814-5 ; Ensign 2/8th N.I., in 3rd Div. Transfd. as Lieut. to 1/8th N.I. Nepal War 1816 ; Lieut. 1/8th N.I. Served with 1st Nassiri Bn. 1817 till Sept. 1827. Actg. Adjt. 1 Nov. 1820 till Apr. 1821, and 3 Aug. 1825 till Jan. 1826. Transfd. to 9th N.I. (late 1/8th) May 1824, but did not join till Oct. 1827. Served with 1st Nassiri Bn. 8 Feb. 1828 till 6 Feb. 1832. The remainder of his life was spent in Simla and the vicinity. Geographical writer.

Refs. : *D.N.B. D.I.B. De Rhé-Philipe.* M.I. Simla.

GERRARD, John (1785-1826). Major, 5th N.I. *b.* Drumcondra (? Drumconrath), co. Meath, 16 Oct. 1785. Cadet 1801. Arrived in India 6 Sept. 1802. Ensign 9 Aug. 1802. Lieut. 11 June 1804. Capt. 16 Dec. 1814. Major 25 Nov. 1824. *d.* 25 Apr. 1826.

Of Liscarton Castle, co. Meath. Son of William Gerrard (of the family of Gerrard, of Gibbstown and Boyne Hill, co. Meath) and Anne his wife. *m.* Calcutta, 16 Dec. 1807, Miss Harriet Holt. (She died Calcutta 15 Nov. 1832.) Father of John Grant Gerrard, *q.v.*, of Charlotte Rosina, 2nd wife of Sir Alexander Knox, *q.v.*, and of Louisa Margaret, wife of Nicholas Penny, *q.v.*

Services : Posted to 2nd N.I. in 1803. Second Mahratta War ; Lieut. 2nd N.I. Capt. Lt. 2nd N.I. 22 Sept. 1814. Capt. 1/2nd N.I. Supt. of bldgs. at Gorakhpur 1816-22. Supt. experimental timber agency at Gorakhpur 1822-4. Transfd. to 5th N.I. (late 1/2nd) May 1824. Supt. timber agency at Natpur, Bengal, 1824 till death.

Refs. : Will dated 11 June 1821 ; proved 7 June 1826.

GERRARD, John Grant (1808-1857). Lieut. Colonel, 1st Eur. Bengal Fus. *b.* Calcutta 8 Nov. 1808. Cadet 1825. Arrived in India 14 Dec. 1826. Ensign 21 July 1826. Lieut. 15 Dec. 1830. Capt. 22 Nov. 1843. Major 1 Mar. 1850. Lt. Col. 14 Jan. 1856. *d.* 17 Nov. 1857, of wounds received in action at Narnaul the same day.

bapt. Calcutta 7 Jan. 1809. Son of John Gerrard, *q.v.*, and Harriet his wife. *m.* Dinapore, 7 Oct. 1833, Mary Anne Staphina, 2nd dau. of Matthew Alexander Bunbury, *q.v.* (*See also* John Erskine (1810-1846).)

Services : Ensign d.d. 6th N.I. 23 Dec. 1826. Posted to 1st Bengal Eur. Regt. 10 May 1827. Intr. & Qmr. 1st Eur. Regt. 22 Sept. till 13 Nov. 1829 ; do. Bengal Eur. Regt. 14 June 1832 till Apr. 1840. A.D.C. to Bdr. Abraham Roberts, *q.v.*, comdg. 4th Bde., Army of the Indus, 15 Dec. 1838. First Afghan War 1838-42 ; Ghazni (Medal) ; defence of Jalalabad (w. on 14 Nov. 1841) (Medal) ; defeat of Akbar Khan by Sale's force 7 Apr. 1842 (s.w.) ; Mamu Khel ; re-occupation of Kabul, with Gen. Pollock's force (Medal). To comd. 1st Jezailchie Regt., Shah Shuja's army, June 1841. Against the Hill tribes in Sind 1845. D.A.C.G. 10 Feb. 1848. Second Sikh War ; Ramnagar ; passage of Chenab ; Sadulapur (Medal). In charge of Hissar camel and cattle farm 2 Oct. 1850 till May 1854. Second Burma War 1852-4 ; Pegu ; Major comdg. detachment of Bengal Eur. Fus. (Medal). Posted as Lt. Col. to 34th N.I. 21 Mar. 1856 ; to 14th N.I. May 1856 ; to 27th N.I. Sept. 1857. Mutiny campaign ; Narnaul (kld.) ; comdg. a Bde.

Refs. : Nuncupative Will dated 16 Nov. 1857 ; proved 18 June 1858. Name on 1st Eur. Bengal Fus. M.I. in Winchester cathedral.

GIBB, James (1805-1826). Lieutenant, 34th N.I. *b.* Aberdeen 19 Jan. 1805. Cadet 1820. Ensign 9 Mar. 1821. Lieut. 11 July 1823. *d.* Sitapur, U.P., 22 Aug. 1826.

Son of Robert Gibb, of Aberdeen, merchant, and Mary Smith his wife. Brother of William Gibb, *q.v.*

Services : Posted as Ensign to 2/30th N.I. Transfd. as Lieut.

to 17th N.I. July 1823 ; to 35th N.I. (late 2/17th) May 1824 ; to 34th N.I. 1825. No record of active service.

*GIBB, John (1812-1833). Ensign, 27th N.I. *b.* Auchinleck, co. Ayr, 17 June 1812. Cadet 1828. Arrived in India Sept. 1828. Ensign (27 June 1828) 3 June 1829. *d.* Hansi 21 Aug. 1833.

Son of Andrew Gibb, factor to Sir James Boswell, 2nd Bart. of Auchinleck.

Services : Admitted 2 Jan. 1829. Ensign d.d. 44th N.I. 14 Jan. 1829. Posted to 43rd N.I. 3 June 1829. Offg. Adjt. Left Wing 43rd N.I. 30 Sept. 1831. Transfd. to 27th N.I. 26 Jan. 1833. No record of active service.

Refs. : *A.J.* N.S. xiii. 205. *G.M.* 1835, i. 221.

GIBB, William (1806-1868). Major. 2nd Bengal Eur. Regt. *b.* Aberdeen 21 Feb. 1806. Cadet 1823. Arrived in India 13 June 1824. Ensign 19 Feb. 1824. Lieut. 8 July 1825. Capt. 25 Sept. 1844. Retired 12 July 1847. Hon. Major 28 Nov. 1854. *d.* 23 Apr. 1868.

Son of Robert Gibb, of Aberdeen, clothier, and Mary Smith his wife. Brother of James Gibb, *q.v.*

Services : Posted as Ensign to 35th N.I. in 1824. Exchanged to 34th N.I. 12 Oct. 1824. Operations against the Kols and Chuars 1832 ; Lieut. 34th N.I. Fur. s.c. 17 May 1839 till 12 June 1842. Transfd. to newly-formed 2nd Bengal Eur. Regt. 8 Oct. 1839.

*GIBBONS, William (*d.* 1758/59). Lieutenant, Infantry. Lieut. 29 Sept. 1757. *d.* in India 1758 or 1759.

Services : Shown as Adjt. in a " Muster of the Troops near Calcutta under Major James Kilpatrick." (Fort William Public Cons. of 28 Feb. 1757.)

Refs. : Orme *MSS.—India*, xiii. 3639. *Hill*, ii. 263. Will dated 19 May 1758 ; proved 3 Apr. 1759.

GIBBS, John (1775-1847). Lieut. Colonel, Invalid Est. 16th N.I. *b.* Broadwindsor, Dorset, 31 July 1775. Cadet 1795. Arrived in India 2 Feb. 1797. Ensign 7 Oct. 1796. Lieut. 30 Oct. 1797. Capt. 14 Nov. 1805. Major 19 May 1815. Lt. Col. 5 May 1821. Invalided 14 July 1821. *d.* Buxar 8 Dec. 1847.

bapt. 4 Oct. 1775. Son of Rev. George Gibbs, of Broadwindsor, vicar of Burstock, Dorset, and Jenny his wife. *m.* Purnea, B. & O., 24 June 1798, Miss Mercy Smith. (She died 24 Jan. 1810.) Father of John William Gibbs, *q.v.* (? and of Lucy, wife of Cosmo Macdonald, *q.v.*). Queen's Coll., Oxon. ; matric. 7 Nov. 1793.

Services : Served throughout with 16th N.I. Major 1/16th N.I.

THE BENGAL ARMY, 1758-1834

Comdd. Cawnpore Provl. Bn. from 1822 for over ten yrs. Comdt. of Buxar fort 15 Jan. 1836 till death.

Refs.: Alumni Oxon. I.M. No. 97, p. 165. Will dated Buxar 25 Apr. 1844; proved 28 Dec. 1847.*

GIBBS, John William (1799-1825). Lieutenant, 42nd N.I. *b.* Dinapore 7 Aug. 1799. Cadet 1819. Was already in Bengal when apptd. Cadet. Ensign 12 Apr. 1820. Lieut. 11 July 1823. *d.* Berhampore 23 Nov. 1825.

Son of John Gibbs, *q.v.*, and Mercy his wife. *m.* Anna, youngest dau. of Innis Delamain, *q.v.* (She *re-m.* William Hamilton Halford, *q.v.*) (*See also* William Henry Howard, Arthur Shuldham, and William Warde.)

Services : Ensign H.M. 59th Foot 1 Aug. 1816. Posted as Ensign to 2/5th N.I. in 1821. Transfd. as Lieut. to 21st N.I. July 1823; to 42nd N.I. (late 2/21st) May 1824. Adjt. 42nd N.I. 22 June 1824 till death. First Burma War; Arakan 1825; Lieut. 42nd N.I.

GIBBS, Jonathan Warner (1749/50-1785). Lieutenant, Infantry. *b.* 1749/50. Cadet 1781. Ensign 13 Mar. 1781. Lieut. 10 July 1782. *d.* Chittagong 3 Feb. 1785.

A native of Wilts.

Services : Apptd. Cadet on 19 Dec. 1780, aged 31. Sailed for India on the *Chapman*, 13 Mar. 1781, aged 31. N.F.P.

GIBSON, Gilbert (*d.* 1768). Lieutenant, Artillery. Cadet 1764. Fireworker 7 Oct. 1764. 2nd Lieut. Feb. 1767. Lieut. 15 Sept. 1767. *d.* 1768.

Services : Resigned his Commission during the "Batta mutiny" in May 1766; readmitted 16 June 1766.

GIBSON, John (*d.* 1773). Cadet, Infantry. Cadet 1772. *d.* nr. Mohan, U.P., May 1773.

Services : N.F.P.

GIBSON, Lewis William (1807-1866). Captain, Invalid Est. 27th N.I. *b.* Southampton 13 June 1807. Cadet 1823. Arrived in India 16 June 1824. Ensign 23 Feb. 1824. Lieut. 22 Sept. 1825. Capt. 15 Feb. 1836. Invalided 6 Feb. 1846. *d.* Landour, Mussoorie, 11 July 1866.

Son of William Gibson and Lucy his wife, dau. of Lewis Allsopp. His mother, a widow, was living at Risley, co. Derby, in 1823. *m.* Cape Town, 21 Nov. 1834, Miss Georgiana Peret.

Services : Posted as Ensign to 27th N.I. in 1824. Fur. s.c. 19 Mar. 1832 till 2 Feb. 1835. Comdd. 27th N.I. for a short while till 8 June 1840. Fur. s.c. 12 Feb. 1843 till 1845. No record of active service.

Refs. : *A.J.* N.S. xvi. 202.

GIFFORD, Charles Thomas William Pitt (1807-1834). Ensign, 42nd N.I. *b.* London 26 Aug. 1807. Cadet 1825. Arrived in India 22 Aug. 1826. Ensign 11 Feb. 1826. *d.* Meerut 31 Oct. 1834.

2nd son of John Gifford. Ed. Merchant Taylors'; admitted Oct. 1815.

Services : Posted as Ensign to 2nd N.I. 26 Sept. 1826. Exchanged to 42nd N.I. 12 Mar. 1827. d.d. 65th N.I. 20 Sept. 1832. No record of active service.

Refs. : *Robinson.* *A.J.* N.S. xvi. 272. *G.M.* 1835, i. 558.

GIFFORD, James (1810-1853). Major, Invalid Est. 2nd N.I. *bapt.* Whitechurch, co. Wexford, 29 Apr. 1810. Cadet 1827. Arrived in India 26 Nov. 1828. Ensign 4 July 1828. Lieut. 14 Aug. 1832. Capt. 8 Nov. 1844. Major 22 Mar. 1852. *d. unm.* at sea, 17 May 1853, on board the *Queen of the South.*

7th son of Nicholas Gifford, of Ballysop, and Margaret his wife, dau. of Mitchelbourne Symes, of Coolboy, co. Wicklow. Brother of John Symes Gifford, *q.v.*

Services : Ensign d.d. 1st N.I. 14 Jan. 1829. Posted to 2nd N.I. 3 June 1829. (? Operations against the Kols 1832; Ensign 2nd N.I.) Fur. s.c. 9 June 1839 till 30 Dec. 1841. With 3rd Depot Bn. at Aligarh 20 May 1842 till 3 Mar. 1843. Actg. Adjt. 2nd N.I. 17 Oct. 1843. Gwalior campaign; Maharajpur; Lieut. 2nd N.I. (Bronze star). First Sikh War; Mudki (s.w.—lost an arm); Capt. 2nd N.I. (Medal). Bde. Major at Ferozepore 13 May 1846; do. Barrackpore Oct. 1847 till Feb. 1850. Fur. s.c. 28 Feb. 1850 till Mar. 1853.

Refs. : Burke's *Landed Gentry of Ireland*, p. 265, *s.n.* Gifford, late of Westbrook, co. Wicklow. *I.M.* 1 Aug. 1853, p. 443. Will dated 12 May 1853; proved 7 June 1853.

GIFFORD, John Symes (1803-1867). Major. 1st N.I. *b.* Jan. 1803. Cadet 1822. Arrived in India 5 July 1823. Ensign 11 July 1823. Lieut. 23 Aug. 1824. Capt. 1 Feb. 1837. Retired 16 May 1846. Hon. Major 28 Nov. 1854. *d.s.p.* 27 Aug. 1867.

bapt. New Ross, co. Wexford, 23 Jan. 1803. 4th son of Nicholas Gifford, of Ballysop, and Margaret his wife. Brother of Thomas Gifford, *q.v. m.* 12 Apr. 1845, Beata, dau. of John Glascott, of Killowen, co. Wexford.

Services : Posted as Ensign to 12th N.I. Transfd. to 1st N.I.

THE BENGAL ARMY, 1758-1834   265

(late 2/12th) May 1824. Offg. Adjt. 1st N.I. 3 Oct. 1831. Fur. p.a. 16 Nov. 1843 till retirement. No record of active service.
Refs. : Burke's *Landed Gentry of Ireland*, p. 265, *s.n.* Gifford, late of Westbrook, co. Wicklow.

GIFFORD, Thomas (1807-1837). Lieutenant, 1st N.I. *bapt.* Whitechurch, co. Wexford, 25 Nov. 1807. Cadet 1826. Arrived in India 4 Feb. 1827. Ensign 12 Sept. 1826. Lieut. 18 Aug. 1834. *d. unm.* Saugor 28 June 1837.
6th son of Nicholas Gifford, of Ballysop, and Margaret his wife. Brother of James Gifford, *q.v.*
Services : Ensign d.d. 1st N.I. 20 Feb. 1827. Posted to 1st N.I. 10 May 1827. No record of active service.
Refs. : Burke's *Landed Gentry of Ireland*, p. 265, *s.n.* Gifford, late of Westbrook, co. Wicklow. *A.J.* N.S. xxiv. 277.

GILBERT, Matthew John (1760/61-?). Lieutenant. Infantry. *b.* London 1760/61. Cadet 1779. Ensign 12 Feb. 1780. Lieut. 9 Feb. 1781. Resigned after 1790.
Services : Sailed for India on the *True Briton*, 16 June 1779, aged 18. Fur. 3 yrs. 10 Oct. 1785, and shown as still on fur. in 1790. N.F.P.

GILBERT, Sir Walter Raleigh, first baronet (1785-1853). Lieut. General, G.C.B. Colonel 1st Eur. Bengal Fus. *b.* Bodmin 18 Mar. 1785. Cadet 1800. Arrived in India 24 Oct. 1801. Ensign 26 Sept. 1801. Lieut. 12 Sept. 1803. Capt. 16 Apr. 1810. Major 12 Nov. 1820. Lt. Col. 1 May 1824. Col. 25 June 1832. Maj. Gen. 28 June 1838. Lt. Gen. 11 Nov. 1851. *d.* Stevens' Hotel, Bond St., London, 12 May 1853.
1st Bart. cr. 31 Dec. 1850. *bapt.* Constantine, Cornwall, 26 Apr. 1785. 3rd son of Rev. Edmund Gilbert, vicar of Constantine, and Anne his wife, dau. of Henry Garnett, of Bristol. His sister *m.* William Hickey, *q.v. m.* Calcutta, 1 June 1814, Isabella Rose, dau. of Thomas Ross, Major R.A., and niece of Malcolm Macleod, *q.v.* His dau. *m.* Roderick Norman Maclean, *q.v.*
Services : See *D.N.B.* Posted as Ensign to 15th N.I. Operations in Jumna Doab 1803 ; Sasni ; Bijaigarh ; Kachaura ; Ensign 15th N.I. Second Mahratta War ; Delhi ; Agra ; Laswari ; Deig ; Bhurtpore ; Lieut. 15th N.I. (India medal with 3 clasps). Adjt. & Qmr. 15th N.I. 1807-10. A.D.C. to C.-in-C. 20 June 1812. Bk. Mr. at Cawnpore 14 May 1813. To comd. Calcutta Native Mil. 31 Oct. 1815. Supt. of Mysore Princes 22 Feb. 1821 till 7 Mar. 1822. Comdd. Ramgarh Bn. 26 Feb. 1822 till Mar. 1828. Lt. Col. 27th, 15th, 21st, 14th, 49th, 5th N.I. Fur. p.a. 7 Mar. 1828 till

26 Jan. 1844. Posted as Col. to 35th N.I. 1 Dec. 1832. Offg. Bdr., 2 cl., Agra 12 Apr. 1844 ; Ferozepore 27 Apr. 1844 ; do., 1 cl., to comd. troops and stations on line of R. Sutlej 21 June 1844. First Sikh War ; Mudki ; Ferozshahr ; Sobraon ; Maj. Gen. comdg. a Div. (Medal with 2 clasps). Second Sikh War ; Chilianwala ; Gujerat (Medal with clasp). Mily. Member of the Supreme Council Dec. 1852 till Feb. 1853. Fur. Feb. 1853 till death. K.C.B. 3 Apr. 1846. G.C.B. 9 June 1849.

Refs. : Burke's *Peerage*, 1859, p. 432, *s.n.* Gilbert, Bart. Burke's *Landed Gentry*, 13th edn., p. 724, *s.n.* Gilbert, of The Priory, Bodmin. D.N.B. D.I.B. Boase. *G.M.* 1853, i. 652-3. Will dated 4 Oct. 1852 ; proved 6 Dec. 1853. Portrait, engraved by Thomas Lupton from a painting by G. F. Atkinson, is in the India Office.

GILL, Joseph (1784-1806). Lieutenant, 25th N.I. *b.* 8 Dec. 1784. Cadet 1800. Arrived in India 23 Aug. 1801. Ensign 26 Oct. 1801. Lieut. 30 Sept. 1803. *d.* 22 Feb. 1806 : kld. in action at the capture of Gohad.

bapt. Wilford, Notts., 5 Jan. 1785. Son of Rev. William Gill, of Wilford, schoolmaster, and Elizabeth his wife. Brother of William Gill, *q.v.*, and Francis Gill.

Services : Posted as Ensign to 19th N.I. Transfd. as Lieut. to newly-raised 25th N.I. 1804. Capture of Gohad 1806 (kld.) ; Lieut. 25th N.I.

GILL, William (1774-1806). Captain, 6th N.I. *bapt.* Colston Basset, Notts., 11 Oct. 1774. Cadet 1795. Arrived in India 6 Mar. 1797. Ensign 10 Nov. 1796. Lieut. 30 Oct. 1797. Capt. 21 Sept. 1804. *d.* at sea, 4 Oct. 1806, on board the *Ann* on his passage to England.

Son of Rev. William Gill, of Wilford, Notts., schoolmaster, and Elizabeth his wife. Brother of Joseph Gill, *q.v.*

Services : Capture of Ternate, one of the Dutch Spice Is., 21 June 1801 ; Lieut. comdg. a detachment of 60 men of Bengal Marine Bn., serving as Marines on board the *Swift*, Lt. Comdr. John Hayes (*D.N.B.*). Lieut. 6th N.I.

Refs. : A.A.R. iv. 38. Will dated on board the *Ann* 23 Sept. 1806 ; proved 16 Feb. 1807.

GILLANDERS, Alexander (1808-1837). Lieutenant, 54th N.I. *b.* Allangrange, Black Isle, co. Ross and Cromarty, 20 June 1808. Cadet 1827. Arrived in India 4 July 1828. Ensign 6 Mar. 1828. Lieut. 26 Jan. 1837. *d.* at sea 14 May 1837, on board the *Larkins*, on his passage to England.

4th son of John Gillanders, of Highfield, J.P. and D.L., and Jane Falconer his wife, dau. of John Mackenzie, of Allangrange.

THE BENGAL ARMY, 1758-1834 267

Services : Ensign d.d. 60th N.I. 31 July 1828 ; do. 24th N.I. 31 Oct. 1828. Posted as Ensign to 54th N.I. 4 Nov. 1828. Leave s.c. 2 yrs. to Cape and N.S.W. 18 Mar. 1837. No record of active service.

Refs. : Burke's *Landed Gentry,* 11th edn., p. 667, *s.n.* Mackenzie-Gillanders, of Highfield, co. Ross. *A.J.* N.S. xxiv. 56.

GILLANDERS, John (*d.* 1800). Bt. Lieut. Colonel, 14th N.I. Country Cadet 1771. Admitted 9 Mar. 1771. Ensign 13 Mar. 1773. Lieut. 13 May 1778. Capt. 9 Jan. 1784. Major 30 Oct. 1797. Bt. Lt. Col. (?). bur. Berhampore, Bengal, 4 Feb. 1800.

Services : Capt. 5th Bn. Sepoys in July 1787 ; 1st Bengal Eur. Regt. in 1796.

GILLESPIE, George (1761/62-1793). Lieutenant, Infantry. *b.* 1761/62. Cadet 1780. Ensign 1780. Lieut. 20 June 1781. *d.* Calcutta 29 May 1793.

A native of Ireland.

Services : Sailed for India on the *Contractor,* 3 Apr. 1780, aged 18. Lieut. 25th Bn. Sepoys in July 1787.

GILLESPIE, James (*d.* 1788). Lieutenant, Artillery. Cadet 1778. Fireworker 23 Sept. 1778. Lieut. 15 Apr. 1781. *d.* at sea 15 Apr. 1788.

Services : Campaign against the Rajah of Benares 1781 ; capture of Bijaigarh, in the Kaimur hills.

GILLESPIE, John (1752/53-1838). Bt. Captain. 2nd Bengal Eur. Regt. Subsequently Lieut. Colonel and Comdt. E.I.C. Depot for Recruits at Chatham. *b.* 1752/53. Country Cadet 1781. Admitted 1781. Ensign 6 July 1782. Lieut. 4 Jan. 1785. Capt. 7 Jan. 1796. Retired 12 Feb. 1799. Major 1815. Lt. Col. 1817. *d.* St. James's St., London, 4 Nov. 1838, aged 85.

m. London, 28 Aug. 1813, Georgiana, dau. of G. Hodgson, of Charles St., St. James's Sq., London.

Services : Lieut. 4th Bengal Eur. Bn. in July 1787. Second in comd. E.I.C. recruit depot in I.W. in 1804 ; Comdt. do. 1805-15, in which latter year the depot was removed to Chatham, and he was apptd. Comdt. and promoted Major. He held this appointment, latterly as Lt. Col., for the next five yrs.

Refs. : *M.M.* 1813, ii. 264. *G.M.* 1839, i. 104. *A.J.* N.S. xxvii. 340.

GILLESPIE, John Wood (1785-1804). Lieutenant, 18th N.I. *bapt.* Dumfries 6 July 1785. Cadet 1800. Arrived in India 22 Aug. 1801. Ensign 15 Sept. 1801. Lieut. 13 July 1803. *d.* 22 May

1804 : kld. in action at the siege of fort Bela, nr. Kunch, Bundelkhand.

Son of Capt. Rollo Gillespie and Charlotte his wife, dau. of John Wood, Govr. of I. of Man in 1763.

Services : Second Mahratta War ; operations to S.W. of Delhi 1803 ; Narnaul ; Kanun ; operations in Bundelkhand 1804 ; siege of fort Bela (kld.) ; Lieut. 1/18th N.I.

Refs. : Pester, p. 296. *S.M.* 1805, p. 565.

GILLESPIE, Robert (*d.* 1787). Captain, Infantry. Cadet (?). Ensign 25 Feb. 1773. Lieut. 19 Mar. 1778. Capt. 12 Oct. 1781. *d.* Bhagulpur, B. & O., 21 Jan. 1787.

Services : First Rohilla War ; battle of St. George. Lieut. 2/2nd Bengal Eur. Regt. in Oct. 1779.

Refs. : G.M. 1787, i. 935.

GILLIES, Daniel (*d.* 1802). Captain, 10th N.I. Cadet 1781. Ensign 14 Sept. 1781. Lieut. 22 June 1783. Capt. 21 Feb. 1801. *d.* Calcutta 1 Dec. 1802.

m. (?).

Services : Lieut. 15th Bn. Sepoys in July 1787. Fourth Mysore War ; Seringapatam ; Bt. Capt. 10th N.I. Capt. Lt. 1/10th N.I. 29 May 1800.

Refs. : Will dated 30 Nov. 1802 ; proved 3 Dec. 1802.

GILLMAN, George (1803-?). Captain. 31st N.I. *b.* Galway 12 Nov. 1803. Cadet 1823. Arrived in India 20 May 1824. Ensign 17 June 1824. Lieut. 11 Feb. 1826. Capt. 4 Aug. 1836. Retired 27 Mar. 1837. *d.* 1866 ? [1]

Son of Edward Gillman, Lt. Col., h.p., 15th Foot.

Services : Posted as Ensign to 41st N.I. in 1824. Siege and capture of Bhurtpore ; Ensign 41st N.I. (India medal). Transfd. as Lieut. to 30th N.I. Feb. 1826 ; to 31st N.I. 7 June 1830. Operations against the Chuars 1832. Fur. s.c. 18 Dec. 1833 till 15 Nov. 1836.

[1] *Note :* His name appears for the last time in *A.L.* for July 1866.

GILLMAN, St. Leger Hayward (1758-1795). Bt. Captain, Infantry. *b.* 5 May 1758. Cadet 1777. Admitted 18 Dec. 1777. Ensign 6 Feb. 1778. Lieut. 16 Sept. 1778. Bt. Capt. (?). *d.* Fatehgarh, U.P., 23 Oct. 1795 : bur. next day.

2nd son of Major Hayward St. Leger Gillman, of Gillmanville, co. Cork, and Eliza Anne his wife, elder dau. of Harding Parker, of Hillbrook, co. Cork, and sister of John Neville Parker, *q.v.* Brother of Sir John Gillman, Bart., and cousin-german of Norcott Neville D'Esterre, *q.v.*

Services : Lieut. 2nd Bn. Sepoys in July 1787. At the date of his death was Bde. Major at Fatehgarh, and held the brevet rank of Capt. by virtue of that appt.
Refs. : Burke's *Extinct Baronetcies*, p. 607, *s.n.* Gillman, Bart., of Curriheen, co. Cork. Burke's *Landed Gentry of Ireland*, p. 551, *s.n.* Parker, of Passage West. Burke's *Peerage*, 1904, p. 1049, *s.n.* Martin, Bart., of Lockynge, Berks.

GILMAN, Philip Case (1783-1858). Colonel. 67th N.I. *b.* Hingham, Norfolk, 24 Mar. 1783. Cadet 1803. Arrived in India 8 Dec. 1804. Ensign 1 Nov. 1804. Lieut. 1 Nov. 1804. Capt. 31 Oct. 1816. Major 3 June 1824. Lt. Col. 11 Apr. 1828. Retired 28 Aug. 1831. Hon. Col. 28 Nov. 1854. *d.* Hingham 19 Oct. 1858.

Son of Samuel Gilman.
Services : Posted as Lieut. to 18th N.I. Transfd. to 8th N.I. in 1806. Adjt. 1/8th N.I. 1 July 1814 till 24 Nov. 1817. Nepal War 1814-5; Lieut. 1/8th N.I., in 4th Div. Nepal War 1816 ; Lieut. 1/8th N.I., in 2nd Bde., Left Column (India medal). Capt. 2/8th N.I. In charge of Muttra Inf. Levy 1818-24. Transfd. as Major to 9th N.I. (late 1/8th) May 1824. To comd. 7th Extra Regt. 21 May 1825. To take charge of 67th N.I. 7 Dec. 1826. Posted as Col. to 67th N.I. Fur. p.a. 29 Mar. 1829 till retirement.
Refs. : *G.M.* 1858, ii. 648.

GILMORE, Henry Charles (1806-1859). Captain, Invalid Est. 59th N.I. *b.* Calcutta 11 Dec. 1806. Ensign 9 Jan. 1825. Lieut. 3 Apr. 1826. Capt. 9 Jan. 1840. Invalided 7 July 1845. *d.* Calcutta 25 July 1859.

Son of John Gilmore, of Calcutta, shipbuilder, of the firm of John Gilmore & Co., and Bridget his wife. Brother of Mungo William Gilmore, *q.v.* *m.* 1st, Cape Town, 23 Jan. 1834, Elizabeth Genesa (? Gersina), eldest dau. of Capt. John McKenzie Cameron, H.M. 55th Regt. (She died 31 Aug. 1834, aged 19.) *m.* 2nd, Cawnpore, 12 June 1854, Jena Rosalie, dau. of Emanuel Serguel, and widow of P. A. Johnson.
Services : Posted as Ensign to 59th N.I. in 1825. Leave s.c. to Cape 9 Mar. 1833 till 10 Nov. 1834. Fur. s.c. 13 Feb. 1840 till 11 Sept. 1842. No record of active service.
Refs. : *A.J.* N.S. xiv. 54. *I.M.* 14 Sept. 1859, p. 767.

GILMORE, John (1811-1847). Captain, Engineers. *b.* London 20 July 1811. Cadet 1827. Arrived in India 3 Feb. 1829. 2nd Lieut. (?). Lieut. 28 Sept. 1827. Capt. 29 Dec. 1843. *d.* Mhow 24 Aug. 1847.

Son of Mungo William Alder Gilmore, of Stamford Hill, London, sailmaker. Addiscombe Cadet 1826-7.

Services : Apptd. to Survey Dept. in Burdwan and Bihar 17 Dec. 1829. Brought on the effective strength of Engr. Corps 24 June 1830. Fur. s.c. 27 May 1832 till 26 Sept. 1835. Executive Engr. P.W.D., Ramgarh Div., 5 Feb. till 7 Dec. 1836. Posted to S. & M. at Delhi 13 Dec. 1836. Re-appointed to P.W.D., Barisal Div., 19 Mar. 1838. To raise and organize a Sebundy Corps of S. & M. at Darjeeling for construction of roads in that district 2 July 1838. Leave s.c. 2 yrs. to Cape and N.S.W. 8 Oct. 1839. Executive Engr. Benares Div. 18 Aug. 1842 ; do. Burdwan Div. 31 Oct. 1845 ; do. Mhow and Nimach 28 Nov. 1846.

Refs. : *The Patrician,* iv. 590.

GILMORE, Mungo William (1805-1886). Lieut. Colonel. 39th N.I. *b.* Calcutta 28 Aug. 1805. Cadet 1821. Arrived in India 21 Dec. 1822. Ensign 6 Nov. 1822. Lieut. 11 Sept. 1824. Capt. 22 Apr. 1840. Major 28 Nov. 1849. Retired 21 Feb. 1850. Hon. Lt. Col. 28 Nov. 1854. *d.* 17 St. James's Sq., Bath, 29 Jan. 1886.

Son of John Gilmore, of Calcutta, shipbuilder, and Bridget his wife. Brother of Henry Charles Gilmore, *q.v. m.* All Souls, Langham Pl., London, 26 Oct. 1854, Matilda M., dau. of Charles Beach.

Services : Posted as Ensign to 2nd N.I. Transfd. to 5th N.I. (late 1/2nd) May 1824 ; to newly-raised 2nd Eur. Regt. 11 Sept. 1824. First Burma War ; Lieut. 2nd Eur. Regt. Exchanged to 39th N.I. 4 Sept. 1826. Fur. s.c. 9 Nov. 1826 till 5 Nov. 1829. With Army of Reserve (for Afghanistan) Oct. 1842 till Jan. 1843. (? Gwalior campaign ; Maharajpur *or* Paniar ; Capt. 39th N.I. (Bronze star).)

Refs. : *I.M.* 1854, p. 658. *The Times,* 5 Feb. 1886.

GILPIN, Martin (1743-1824). Major. Infantry. *b.* 1743. Cadet 1765 (?). Ensign (?). Lieut. 7 Sept. 1768. Capt. 8 July 1776. Major 2 Feb. 1781. Resigned 8 Jan. 1785. *d.* Broomhill, nr. Broughton-in-Furness, 20 Dec. 1824, aged 81.

Services : Not in *A.L.* of 1 Feb. 1767. *Possibly* resigned in May 1766 during the " Batta mutiny," being reinstated later.

Refs. : *Forrest,* iii. 969. *A.J.* xix. 108.

GILPIN, Richard (1743/44-1766). Lieutenant, Infantry. *b.* 1743/44. Cadet 1764. Ensign 20 Aug. 1765. Lieut. 1766. *d.* in India 1766. A native of Lancashire.

Services : Sailed for India on the *Fort William,* 17 May 1764, aged 20. N.F.P.

GIRDLESTONE, William Bolton (1789-1853). Lieut. Colonel. 54th N.I. *b.* Wells-next-the-Sea, Norfolk, 24 Mar. 1789. Cadet 1808. Admitted 24 June 1809. Ensign 5 Jan. 1810. Lieut. 25 Sept. 1814. Capt. 13 May 1825. Major 1 Mar. 1838. Lt. Col. 18 Sept. 1844. Retired 12 Sept. 1846. *d.* Southampton 31 Aug. 1853.

Son of Henry Girdlestone. *m.* (before 1828) ?

Services : Barasat C.C. for 10¼ mos. Posted as Ensign to 23rd N.I. Third Mahratta War ; Lieut. 1/23rd N.I. Intr. & Qmr. 1/23rd N.I. 22 Apr. 1817 till 1820. Bde. Major in Nagpur Rajah's service. Comdd. a Bn. of Nagpur Bde. 4 Dec. 1823 till 24 Sept. 1824. Transfd. to 46th N.I. (late 2/23rd) May 1824. Leave s.c. 1 yr. 26 Feb. 1825. With Nagpur force 7 Apr. 1826 till 1830. Fur. s.c. 20 Nov. 1830 till 25 June 1833, and 17 Mar. 1844 till retirement. Posted as Lt. Col. to 54th N.I. 18 Oct. 1844.

Refs. : G.M. 1853, ii. 429.

***GLADSTANES, Charles.** Cadet. Artillery. Apptd. Cadet in India 11 June 1764. Never commissioned.

Refs. : Stubbs's List.

GLADWIN, Charles (1753/54-1826). Major. 4th N.I. *b.* 1753/54. Cadet 1779. Admitted 31 May 1780. Ensign 14 June 1779. Lieut. 8 Feb. 1781. Capt. 30 Oct. 1797. Major 19 Oct. 1803. Retired 2 May 1806. *d.* 13 Nov. 1826.

A native of London. *m.* Calcutta, 14 Oct. 1784, Miss Matilda Denton.

Services : Sailed for India in the *Fox,* 7 Mar. 1779, aged 25. Lieut. 4th Bengal Eur. Bn. in July 1787 ; 2nd Bengal Eur. Regt. in 1796. Was D.J.A.G. in the field in 1803. Fur. 5 Sept. 1803 till retirement.

***GLADWIN, Francis** (*d.* 1812). Commenced his career in the Bengal Army *c.* 1765. Subsequently a Senior Merchant, B.C.S. *d.* Patna 19 or 23 Oct. 1812.

Brother of Thomas Gladwin, *q.v.* *m.* 1st, Patna, 5 Dec. 1769, Ann Proctor. *m.* 2nd, 11 July 1782, Sarah Alexander. Father of Francis William Ulric Gladwin, *q.v.*, and of Mary, mother of George Gladwin Denniss, *q.v.*

Services : See *D.N.B.* Apptd. Writer, B.C.S., in 1766. Apptd. the first Professor of Persian at Coll. of Fort William in 1801. Commercial Resdt. at Patna 1808 till death. Oriental scholar. Pub. in 1788 a " Narrative of Transactions in Bengal " ; also a number of translations of Persian writers. Founder and first editor of the

LIST OF THE OFFICERS OF

Calcutta Gazette and Oriental Advertiser, the first number of which appeared on 4 Mar. 1784.
Refs. : D.N.B. D.I.B. B. : P.P., No. 56, p. 206. *Forrest's Clive*, ii. 339.

GLADWIN, Francis William Ulric (1785-1822). Captain, 13th N.I. *bapt.* Calcutta 5 May 1785. Cadet 1799. Arrived in India 22 Aug. 1801. Ensign 15 Mar. 1801. Lieut. 21 Apr. 1803. Capt. 1 Aug. 1818. *d.* Dacca, 27 Aug. 1822, aged 37.

Son of Francis Gladwin, *q.v.*, and Sarah his 2nd wife. *m.* Calcutta, 10 Nov. 1817, Dora Louisa, dau. of Henry Taylor, Madras C.S. (She *re-m.* James Garner, *q.v.*)

Services : Ensign 13th N.I. Second Mahratta War ; Lieut. 13th N.I. Adjt. Patna Provl. Bn. 1810-5. Capt. Lt. 1/13th N.I. 16 Dec. 1814. Third Mahratta War ; Asirgarh ; Capt. 2/13th N.I.

Refs. : Will dated 27 July 1819 ; codicil dated 27 July 1822 ; proved 30 Dec. 1822. M.I. at Dacca.

GLADWIN, Thomas (1751/52-1790). Captain, Infantry. *b.* 1751/52. Cadet 1771. Ensign 2 Feb. 1773. Lieut. 21 Feb. 1778. Capt. 8 June 1781. *d.* Calcutta, 28 Feb. 1790, aged 38.

Brother of Francis Gladwin, *q.v.*

Services : Lieut. 1/2nd Bengal Eur. Regt. in Oct. 1779. Fur. 3 yrs. 31 Aug. 1785.

Refs. : M.I. in S. Park St. cemetery, Calcutta.

GLASFURD, John (1810-1864). Major General. Engineers. *b.* The Manse, Tillicoultry, co. Clackmannan, 20 Sept. 1810. Cadet 1827. Arrived in India 26 Nov. 1828. 2nd Lieut. 15 June 1827. Lieut. 28 Sept. 1827. Capt. 28 Aug. 1841. Major 1 Aug. 1854. Lt. Col. 8 June 1856. Bt. Col. 26 Jan. 1858. Retired 1 Jan. 1860. Hon. Maj. Gen. 1 Jan. 1860. *d.* 82 George St., Edinburgh, 1 Dec. 1864.

Son of Duncan Glasfurd, of Tillicoultry. *m.* 1st., Hawalbagh, U.P., 30 Mar. 1830, Olive, 7th dau. of Thomas Britten, of Forrest Hill, Kent, and sister of George Ernst Britten, *q.v.* (She died Almora, U.P., 8 Dec. 1834.) *m.* 2nd, Bareilly, 5 Apr. 1841, Agnes Hart, dau. of Andrew Walker, Bengal Medical Est. (She died Bareilly 26 Apr. 1844.) *m.* 3rd, Bareilly, 1 May 1850, Georgiana, dau. of Colin Robertson. Addiscombe Cadet 1826-7.

Services : With S. & M. at Aligarh in 1829. Executive Engr. P.W.D., Kumaon, 11 May 1835 ; do. Bareilly district 20 Jan. 1841 ; do. Lahore 19 Apr. 1850. Second Sikh War ; passage of Chenab ; Chilianwala ; Gujerat (Medal with clasp). Fur. s.c. 21 Feb. 1852

till Dec. 1854. Executive Engr., Bareilly Div., 26 Jan. 1855. Suptg. Engr., 1st Circle, N.W.P., 28 Oct. 1856 till retirement.
Refs. : *Misc. Gen. et Her.* N.S. ii. 464. *G.M.* 1865, i. 121. *The Times,* 6 Dec. 1864.

GLASGOW, William (1800-1841). Captain, Invalid Est. 61st N.I. *b.* Quebec, Canada, 11 July 1800. Cadet 1818. Admitted 7 July 1819. Ensign 5 Feb. 1819. Lieut. 12 June 1820. Capt. 5 June 1829. Invalided 13 June 1833. *d.* Mussoorie 29 Oct. 1841.

Son of George Glasgow, of Greenwich, Lt. Gen. R.A. *m.* Barrackpore, 15 Oct. 1824, Miss Amelia Campbell. Sandhurst Cadet.

Services : Ensign d.d. 10th N.I. Posted as Lieut. to 1/2nd N.I. in 1820. Actg. Adjt. to a detachment of 5 Coys. 1/2nd N.I. 23 Jan. 1822. Transfd. to newly-raised 31st N.I. 11 July 1823 ; to 61st N.I. (late 1/21st) May 1824. No record of active service.

GLASS, Andrew (*d.* 1832). Lieut. Colonel. Artillery. Country Cadet 1778. Admitted 11 Aug. 1778. Fireworker 21 Sept. 1778. Lieut. 29 Jan. 1781. Capt. 14 Sept. 1790. Major 15 Nov. 1802. Lt. Col. 26 July 1804. Retired 15 May 1807. *d.* 29 Sept. 1832.

Of Abbey Park, St. Andrews, co. Fife. *m.* Calcutta, 2 Dec. 1792, Miss Harriet Wynox. (She died 15 May 1851, aged 77.)

Services : Lieut. 1st Bn. Art. in July 1787. Third Mysore War ; Bangalore ; Capt. 5th Coy. 2nd Bn. Art. To Madras in Aug. 1793 for the siege of Pondicherry, returned in Oct. ; Capt. comdg. 4th Coy. 3rd Bn. Fourth Mysore War ; Capt. comdg. 2nd Coy. 3rd Bn. Fur. 2 Dec. 1803 till retirement.

Refs. : *A.J.* N.S. x. 51.

GLASS, John (*d.* 1793). Captain, Artillery. Comdt. of troops at Penang. Cadet 1778. Fireworker 5 Oct. 1778. Lieut. 6 July 1782. Capt. (local rank) 23 Dec. 1786. *d.* Penang 6 Apr. 1793.

Services : (? First Mahratta War ; capture of Sipri Jan. 1781 ; action at Mahatpur ; Lieut.F. 1st Coy. 2nd Bn. Art., with Lt. Col. Jacob Camac's force.) Apptd. Comdt. (with local rank of Capt.) of all troops at P.W.I. 23 Dec. 1786, and held this appt. till death.

Refs. : *G.M.* 1793, ii. 1149. *S.M.* 1793, p. 619.

GLEESON, William (1790-1815). Lieutenant, 12th N.I. *b.* in America May 1790. Cadet 1805. Arrived in India 13 Dec. 1806. Ensign 13 Dec. 1806. Lieut. 10 May 1810. *d.* Natpur, Bengal, 12 July 1815.

Nephew of John P. Dyott.

Services : Posted as Ensign to 12th N.I. in 1807. Operations in Oudh 1808 ; Ensign 12th N.I. Lieut. 1/12th N.I.

GLEGG, Henry Vibart (1796-1874). Captain. 32nd N.I. Subsequently Coy.'s Recruiting Ofr. at Edinburgh. *b.* Calcutta 6 Nov. 1796. Cadet 1816. Admitted 29 July 1817. Ensign (?). Lieut. 1 Aug. 1818. Capt. 30 May 1829. Retired 3 Apr. 1835. *d.* 9 June 1874.

bapt. Calcutta 23 Dec. 1796. Son of Adam Glegg, of Calcutta, master mariner, and Mary his wife. Stepson of Dr. Phillips, of Andover. *m.* Arbroath, 16 Nov. 1839, Mary Gleig, eldest dau. of Patrick Anderson, of Arbroath.

Services : Posted as Ensign to 2/16th N.I. Transfd. to 32nd N.I. (late 1/16th) May 1824. Adjt. 32nd N.I. 23 Aug. 1825 till 24 June 1829. Siege and capture of Bhurtpore ; Lieut. 32nd N.I. (India medal). Fur. s.c. 28 Feb. 1830 till 8 Nov. 1832, and 3 Apr. 1835. Apptd. Coy.'s Recruiting Ofr. at Edinburgh on a Staff pay of 10/- *p.d.*, with an allowance of one guinea per recruit finally approved, 26 Apr. 1839. He held this appt. for over 20 yrs.

Refs. : *G.M.* 1839, ii. 645.

GLEN, William (1805-1827). Lieutenant, 27th N.I. *b.* Falkirk, co. Stirling, 13 Jan. 1805. Cadet 1821. Ensign 5 July 1822. Lieut. 1 May 1824. *d.* Akyab, Burma, 23 Dec. 1827.

4th son of William Glen, of Forgan Hall, co. Stirling, J.P., and Jean his wife, dau. of George Gray, of Aberdeen.

Services : Posted as Ensign to 18th N.I. in 1822. Transfd. to 13th N.I. in 1823 ; to 26th N.I. (late 1/13th) May 1824 ; to 27th N.I. in 1825. First Burma War ; Arakan 1825 ; Lieut. Pioneers. Comdd. Police Corps in Arakan 1826-7 ; do. Arakan Provl. Bn. 1827 till death.

Refs. : Burke's *Landed Gentry*, 7th edn., p. 738, *s.n.* Glen, of Stratton Audley Park, Oxon. Will dated 1 Apr. 1827 ; proved 27 June 1828.

GLENN, William (*d.* 1763). Lieutenant, 9th Bn. Sepoys. Cadet (?). Ensign 28 July 1759. Lieut. 18 Sept. 1761. *d.* 2 Aug. 1763 : kld. in action at the battle of Gheria.

Services : War with Mir Muhammad Kasim 1763 ; greatly distinguished himself by his defence of a convoy, escorted by 9th Bn. Sepoys (eventually the 8th N.I.) under his comd., nr. Katwa, on Adji R., 17 July 1763 ; attacked and captured Katwa the same evening ; battle of Katwa ; battle of Gheria (kld.). For his gallant conduct on 17th July he was apptd. A.D.C. to Major Adams, comdg. the force. " Has been described by a foreign writer, a contemporary of his own, as ' one of the bravest men ever produced in a country so fertile in intrepid men '." (*Broome*).

Refs. : Broome, 370-2. Cardew, 20, 21. B. : P.P. vi. 247.

GLOVER, Charles Halcott (1784-1830). Major. 35th N.I. *b.* Clifton, Gloucs., 14 Jan. 1784. Cadet 1802. Arrived in India 27 Aug. 1803. Ensign 15 Sept. 1803. Lieut. 21 Sept. 1804. Capt. 4 Mar. 1818. Major 1 Jan. 1828. Retired 17 Jan. 1829. *d.* Townsend House, Regent's Pk., London, 15 Aug. 1830.

bapt. 28 Nov. 1784. Son of Joseph Glover and Elizabeth his wife. Brother of Henry Joseph Glover, *q.v.*

Services : Ensign d.d. 2nd N.I. in 1804. Posted as Ensign to 17th N.I. in 1805. Actg. Bde. Major in Bundelkhand 1809-1. Adjt. 1/17th N.I. 1 Aug. 1813 till 1817. Nepal War 1814-5 ; Lieut. 1/17th N.I., in 2nd Div. Operations against the Bhattis of Hariana 1818 ; Capt. 1/17th N.I. Transfd. to 35th N.I. (late 2/17th) May 1824. (? Siege and capture of Bhurtpore ; Capt. 35th N.I.)

Refs. : Farington Diary, ii. 244. *A.J.* N.S. iii. 43.

GLOVER, Henry Joseph (1788-1805). Cadet, Artillery. *b.* Astley 1 Sept. 1788. Cadet 1804. Never arrived in India. *d.* 5 Feb. 1805 : lost at sea in the wreck of the *Earl of Abergavenny,* off Portland. (See note to Charles Davis or Davies.)

bapt. Astley 17 Nov. 1788. Son of Joseph Glover and Elizabeth his wife. Brother of Charles Halcott Glover, *q.v.* Woolwich Cadet ; nominated to R.M.A. 13 Oct. 1802 ; obtained his certificate 22 Dec. 1804.

Refs. : Farington Diary, ii. 244.

GOAD, Charles Elliot (1812-1887). Lieut. Colonel. 67th N.I. *b.* Madras 27 Dec. 1812. Cadet 1828. Arrived in India 23 May 1829. Ensign 7 Feb. 1829. Lieut. 30 Mar. 1837. Capt. 9 July 1852. Bt. Major 1856. Retired 31 Aug. 1856. Hon. Lt. Col. 31 Aug. 1856. *d.* Coningham Rd., Shepherd's Bush, London, 7 June 1887.

Son of Samuel Thomas Goad, B.C.S., and Maria Jane Boileau his wife. Brother of Samuel Boileau Goad, *q.v.,* and nephew of John Fryer Goad, *q.v. m.* Agra, 16 June 1834, Harriet, youngest dau. of Bernard Reilly, Bengal Medical Est.

Services : Ensign d.d. 32nd N.I. 13 July 1829. Posted to 12th N.I. 14 Sept. 1829. Transfd. to 45th N.I. 2 Aug. 1832 ; to 67th N.I. 12 May 1834. Fur. s.c. 26 Oct. 1836 till 24 Dec. 1839. Adjt. 67th N.I. 9 Jan. 1849 till 1852. Second Burma War 1852-3 ; Pegu ; Capt. 67th N.I. (Medal).

Refs. : The Times, 9 June 1887.

GOAD, John Fryer (1788-1816). Lieutenant, 25th N.I. *b.* London 18 Feb. 1788. Cadet 1803. Arrived in India 3 Dec. 1804. Ensign 19 Oct. 1804. Lieut. 19 Oct. 1804. *d.* Ramnagar 14 Nov. 1816.

bapt. St. Thomas the Apostle, London, 26 Mar. 1788. Son of

William Goad and Darling his wife. Uncle of Charles Elliot Goad, *q.v.* m. 19 Mar. 1808, Miss Ann Maria Paul. (She died London 15 May 1850.) Father of Samuel Thomas Alexander Goad, *q.v.*

Services : Posted as Lieut. to newly-raised 2/25th N.I. in 1805. Capture of Gohad 1806 ; Lieut. 2/25th N.I. Adjt. 2/25th N.I. 14 Feb. 1807 till July 1814. Intr. & Qmr. 2/25th N.I. 1 July 1814 till death. Nepal War 1814-5 ; Lieut. 2/25th N.I., in 4th Div. Nepal War 1816 ; passage of Chirriaghati pass 14 Feb. 1816 ; Makwanpur ; Lieut. 2/25th N.I., in 3rd Bde., Centre Column.

Refs. : Will dated 15 Nov. 1815 ; proved 31 Dec. 1816.

GOAD, Samuel Boileau (1809-1876). Major. 1st L.C. *b.* Madras 21 Aug. 1809. Cadet 1824. Arrived in India 24 Feb. 1826. Cornet 6 Sept. 1825. Lieut. 26 June 1826. Capt. 4 Apr. 1844. Retired 16 Nov. 1849. Hon. Major 15 June 1855. *d.* Simla 13 Dec. 1876 : committed suicide.

Son of Samuel Thomas Goad, B.C.S., sometime puisne judge of the court of *sadr diwani* and *nizamat adalat* at Calcutta, and Maria Jane Boileau his wife. Brother of Charles Elliot Goad, *q.v.* m. 1st, Calcutta, 30 Dec. 1833, Emma Gordon, 2nd dau. of Leith Alexander Davidson, and sister of George Henry Davidson, *q.v.* (*See also* Henry De Budé.) m. 2nd, Kasauli, 12 Nov. 1857, Frederica, dau. of Thomas Blood, and widow of Surgeon A. Campbell, H.M. 59th Foot.

Services : Posted as Cornet to 1st L.C. 24 May 1826. Sentenced by G.C.M. to suspension from rank and pay for 1 yr. from 18 Apr. 1833. Fur. p.a. 10 Mar. 1837 till 23 Nov. 1839. First Afghan War 1842 ; forcing of Khyber ; advance to Jalalabad ; actions of Jagdalak ; Tazin ; Haft Kotal ; re-occupation of Kabul ; Lieut. 1st L.C., with Gen. Pollock's advance (Medal). (*Lond. Gaz.* 24 Nov. 1842.) Sub-Asst. in Stud Dept. 30 Jan. 1843 till July 1844. First Sikh War ; Aliwal ; Capt. 1st L.C. (Medal). Second Sikh War ; passage of Chenab ; Chilianwala ; Gujerat ; pursuit of Sikhs and Afghans to Peshawar ; Capt. 1st L.C. (Medal with 2 clasps).

Refs. : *De Rhé-Philipe.* *A.J.* N.S. xi. 127 ; xii. 234 ; xiv. 131 ; xix. 200 ; xx. 101. *The Times*, 19 Dec. 1876. M.I. at Simla.

GOAD, Samuel Thomas Alexander (1817-1847). Lieutenant, 20th N.I. *bapt.* Dinapore 19 Jan. 1817. Cadet 1833. Arrived in India 8 July 1834. Ensign 31 May 1834. Lieut. 23 July 1837. *d.* Barrackpore 10 Oct. 1847.

Son of John Fryer Goad, *q.v.*, and Ann Maria his wife. Addiscombe Cadet 1 Feb. 1832 till 13 Dec. 1833.

Services : d.d. 24th N.I. 15 July 1834. Posted as Ensign to 69th N.I. 5 Nov. 1834 ; to 20th N.I. 7 Apr. 1835. Fur. s.c. 20 Feb.

THE BENGAL ARMY, 1758-1834   277

1839 till 7 Jan. 1842, and 4 Feb. 1844 till 1846. No record of active service.
Refs. : *G.M.* 1848, i. 110. M.I. in Barrackpore cemetery.

GODBY, Christopher (1790-1867). Lieut. General, C.B., A.D.C. Colonel 55th N.I. *b.* St. Leonard's, Shoreditch, London, 28 Jan. 1790. Cadet 1805. Arrived in India 11 July 1806. Ensign 31 July 1806. Lieut. 14 June 1809. Capt. 11 July 1823. Major 14 June 1833. Lt. Col. 1 Feb. 1840. Col. 6 Apr. 1850. Maj. Gen. 28 Nov. 1854. Lt. Gen. 22 Nov. 1862. *d.* South Bank, Batheaston, Somerset, 8 Dec. 1867.
bapt. 28 Feb. 1790. Son of Charles Godby, of Craven St., Strand, London, and Grace his wife. *m.* Calcutta 24 June 1820, Frances Barbara, 3rd dau. of Jacob Vanrenen, *q.v.* (*See also* James Blair.) (She died 1886, aged 86.) His dau. *m.* John Lang, *q.v.*
Services : Barasat C.C. for 9 mos. Posted as Ensign to 18th N.I. Actg. Adjt. 1/18th N.I. 1812-3 ; Adjt. do. 1814. Intr. & Qmr. 1/18th N.I. 1 July 1814 till 1820. Nepal War 1816 ; Lieut. 1/18th N.I., in 1st Bde., Rt. Column (India medal). Cuttack insurrection 1816 ; Khurda. Third Mahratta War ; Jawad. Actg. Adjt. 1/18th N.I. 2 Oct. 1820 ; Adjt. do. 3 Feb. 1821 till 1 Oct. 1823. (? Operations in Jodhpur 1823 ; Lamba.) Transfd. to 36th N.I. (late 1/18th) May 1824. Tempy. charge of Bareilly Provl. Bn. 10 Aug. 1824. Siege and capture of Bhurtpore (s.w.) ; Capt. 36th N.I. (*Lond. Gaz.* 10 June 1825) (clasp to India medal). Granted a wound pension of £100 *p.a.* Fur. s.c. 20 Jan. 1829 till 26 Dec. 1833. Shekhawat expedn. 1834 ; Major comdg. 36th N.I. First Sikh War ; Aliwal ; Lt. Col. comdg. 36th N.I. (Medal). Transfd. to 1st Bengal Eur. Fus. 29 Mar. 1847 ; to 2nd Bengal Eur. Regt. 1 Oct. 1847. Second Sikh War ; Chilianwala ; comdg. a Bde. (Medal). Transfd. to 27th N.I. ; to 38th N.I. 2 Feb. 1850 ; to 15th N.I. 27 Mar. 1850. Fur. s.c. 10 Feb. 1850 till death. Posted as Col. to 58th N.I. 12 June 1850 ; to 55th N.I. 4 Aug. 1853. C.B. 27 June 1846. A.D.C. to Queen Victoria.
Refs. : *De La Ferté. Boase. The Times,* 12 Dec. 1867.

GODDARD, Henry (1739 ?-1770). Lieutenant, Infantry. Lieut. 24 Feb. 1766. *d.* Calcutta Feb. 1770.

N.B.—The remainder is conjectural only :

(*b.* 1739. Elder son of Henry Goddard, an officer in the army, and brother of Thomas Goddard (1740-1783), *q.v.*
Services : Ensign 19th Foot 4 May 1756 ; Lieut. 30 Sept. 1757 ; 66th Foot Apr. 1758 ; 108th Foot 17 Oct. 1761 ; Capt. 17 May 1762.
Refs. : Burke's *Commoners,* iv. 329, *s.n.* Goddard, of Hartham, Wilts.)

GODDARD, Thomas (1740 or 1744-1783). Bdr. General. C.-in-C. of the Bombay Army. b. c. 1740 or 1744. Capt. 24 Oct. 1763. Major May 1766. Lt. Col. Sept. 1768. Col. June 1779. Bdr. Gen. 1781. d. at sea, 7 July 1783, on board the *Pendennis Castle*, off Land's End, Cornwall: bur. at Eltham, Kent.

Younger son of Henry Goddard, an officer in the army. Grandson of Rev. Thomas Goddard, canon of Windsor. (*Possibly* brother of Henry Goddard, *q.v.*)

Services: See *D.N.B.* Ensign H.M. 24th Foot 24 Sept. 1757; Lieut. do. 26 Jan. 1758. Lieut. 84th Foot 8 Jan. 1759; Capt. Lt. do. 10 Nov. 1763; Capt. do. 7 Jan. 1764; Capt. h.p. do. 25 Feb. 1764. Served in H.M. 84th Foot under Coote in Madras 1759-61; capture of Pondicherry. Employed as an Engr. to Major Adams's force 1763; siege of Patna (w. 31 Oct. 1763). Transfd. as Capt. to Bengal Eur. Regt. Raised 18th Bn. Sepoys (afterwards became 17th Bn., 1/7th N.I., and 13th N.I.) at Murshidabad in Jan. 1764. This Bn. was called after him "*Gaurud-ki-Paltan.*" Capture of Burrareah, nr. Chapra, 1770. Against the Mahrattas in Rohilkhand in 1772. First Mahratta War; comdd. the Bengal contingent with the Bombay army in succession to Col. Leslie 1778-81; Ahmedabad; Bassein. Apptd. C.-in-C. of the Bombay army in 1781. Left estate to the value of £106,000.

Refs.: Burke's *Commoners*, iv. 329, *s.n.* Goddard, of Hartham, Wilts. *D.N.B. D.I.B. E.I.M.C.* ii. 414-29. *Williams*, p. 101. *Cardew*, pp. 22, 23. *G.M.* 1783, ii. 628.

GODDARD, Thomas (1811-1880). Major. 44th N.I. b. Cliffe Pypard, Wilts., 4 Aug. 1811. Cadet 1828. Arrived in India 2 Sept. 1829. Ensign 5 June 1829. Lieut. 21 July 1835. Capt. 19 May 1843. Major 2 Aug. 1851. Invalided 29 Feb. 1852. Retired 10 Oct. 1855. d. Cambridge Gdns., Kilburn, 15 Jan. 1880.

5th son of Rev. Edward Goddard, of Clyffe Pypard, vicar of Clyffe Pypard, J.P., and Annica Susan his wife, only dau. of Edward Bayntun, H.M. consul gen. at Algiers. Nephew of Adm. Sir Henry William Bayntun, G.C.B. (*D.N.B.*).

Services: Ensign d.d. 52nd N.I. 10 Sept. 1829. Posted as Ensign to 52nd N.I. 26 June 1830. Transfd. to 44th N.I. 1 Oct. 1832. Fur. s.c. 23 Jan. 1835 till 31 Dec. 1839. First Sikh War; Ferozshahr; operations against Kot Kangra; Capt. 44th N.I. (Medal). D.J.A.G., Cawnpore, 5 Aug. 1848; do. Nimach 1849; do. Meerut Feb. 1850. Fur. 1850 till 5 Feb. 1852. Fur. s.c. 21 Jan. 1853 till retirement.

Refs.: Burke's *Landed Gentry*, 13th edn., p. 734, *s.n.* Goddard (*now* Wilson), of Clyffe Manor, Wilts. *The Times*, 19 Jan. 1880.

GODFREY, John (1783-1805). Lieutenant, Infantry. Unposted. (Really a Cadet only.) *b.* London 26 June 1783. Cadet 1803. Arrived in India 17 Mar. 1805. Ensign 23 Apr. 1805. Lieut. 24 Apr. 1805. *d.* nr. Allahabad June 1805. (Exact date not known.)
Son of Henry Godfrey.
Services : N.F.P.

GODFREY, John (1810-1878). Major. 43rd N.I. *b.* 30 Oct. 1810. Cadet 1826. Arrived in India 23 Sept. 1827. Ensign 13 May 1827. Lieut. 30 Apr. 1834. Capt. 10 Mar. 1849. Retired 25 July 1850. Hon. Major 28 Nov. 1854. *d.* Hyde House, Leamington, co. Warwick, 14 Aug. 1878.
bapt. Tralee, co. Kerry, 5 Nov. 1810. Son of Lt. Col. John Godfrey, of Dublin, and Letitia King his wife, of St. Mary's psh.
Services : Posted as Ensign to 61st N.I. 3 Jan. 1828. Transfd. to 43rd N.I. in 1828. First Afghan War 1838-42 ; Lieut. 43rd N.I. (Kandahar, Ghazni, Kabul medal). Actg. Intr. & Qmr. 43rd N.I. Feb. 1841. Gwalior campaign ; Maharajpur ; Lieut. 43rd N.I. (Bronze star). Fur. 17 May 1844 till 1846. Actg. Adjt. Left Wing 43rd N.I. in 1849.
Refs. : The Times, 23 Aug. 1878.

GODING, Thomas Joseph (1788-?). Lieutenant. Bengal Eur. Regt. *b.* St. George's, Hanover Sq., London, 21 Aug. 1788. Cadet 1807. Arrived in India 14 Aug. 1808. Ensign 24 Sept. 1808. Lieut. 1 July 1814. Retired 2 July 1822. (? *d.* after Jan. 1871.)
bapt. 21 Sept. 1788. Son of Thomas Goding and Margaret his wife.
Services : Posted as Ensign to Bengal Eur. Regt. in 1809, and served throughout with that Corps, principally in Java and Macassar. Fur. 9 Sept. 1818 till retirement.

GOLBORNE, John (*d.* 1791). Lieutenant, Infantry. Cadet 1779. Ensign 19 Aug. 1779. Lieut. 10 Apr. 1781. *d. unm.* Monghyr 3 Aug. 1791.
Uncle of Frances Jane Baptiste.
Services : Lieut. 4th Bengal Eur. Bn. in July 1787.
Refs. : Will dated Barrackpore 20 Apr. 1791.

GOLD, Buckley. (*See* **GOULD, Bulkeley.**)

GOLDFRAP, Frederick William (1790-1838). Lieutenant. Artillery. Subsequently rector of Clenchwarton, Norfolk. *b.* I. of St. Christopher 9 Nov. 1790. Cadet 1807. Arrived in India 16 Nov. 1808. Fireworker 20 Sept. 1808. Lieut. 8 Dec. 1810. Struck off 28 Oct. 1811. *d.* Clenchwarton 26 Nov. 1838.

J.P. for Norfolk. *bapt.* 28 Nov. 1790. Son of John G. Goldfrap and Sarah his wife. (? *m.*¹) Woolwich Cadet; nominated for R.M.A. 11 June 1805.

Services : Fur. 28 Apr. 1809. Remained on fur. till 1814, when he was struck off with effect from the date on which his period of 2½ yrs.' absence from India elapsed. No record of active service.

Took holy orders. Instituted as rector to the living of Clenchwarton, Norfolk, which was in his own patronage, 3 May 1817.

Refs. : Foster's *Index Ecclesiasticus*. *G.M.* 1839, i. 103.

¹ *Note. :* One Frederick William Goldfrap (*possibly* a son) graduated B.A. at Trinity Coll., Camb., in 1847.

GOLDFRAP, James (*d.* 1780). Lieutenant, Infantry. Cadet 1771. Ensign 31 Jan. 1773. Lieut. 18 Feb. 1778. *d.* Chittagong June 1780.

Services : Lieut. 1/3rd Bengal Eur. Regt. in Oct. 1779.

GOLDIE, Andrew (1793-1857). Colonel, 46th N.I. Mily. Auditor Gen. *b.* 21 Mar. 1793. Cadet 1808. Arrived in India 19 July 1809. Ensign 1 Jan. 1810. Lieut. 16 Dec. 1814. Capt. 21 Mar. 1828. Major 8 Oct. 1839. Lt. Col. 22 Dec. 1845. Col. 4 June 1855. *d.* Cawnpore 15 July 1857 : massacred by mutineers.

Son of Rev. William Goldie, minister of Athelstaneford, co. Haddington. *m.* Mary.

Services : Barasat c.c. for 10¼ mos. Posted as Ensign to 24th N.I. Operations in Rewah 1813 ; Ensign 24th N.I. Nepal War 1814-5 ; Lieut. 24th N.I. (India medal). Third Mahratta War 1817. Adjt. Benares Inf. Levy 1818 till 6 Jan. 1823. Paymr. of Native pensioners and Adjt. Native invalids at Allahabad 1 Jan. 1823 till 2 July 1828. Transfd. to 47th N.I. (late 1/24th) May 1824. This Regt. was disbanded for mutiny in Nov. 1824. Apptd. to tempy. charge of 4th Extra Regt. 24 May 1825. Paymr. of invalids at Benares, Dinapore, and Monghyr 12 Mar. 1829 till 27 Mar. 1840. Leave s.c. to Cape and N.S.W. 24 Feb. 1841 till 1842 ; fur. s.c. 3 Feb. 1843 till 1845. Mily. Auditor Gen. 14 Dec. 1846 till death. Lt. Col. 32nd, 20th, 38th, 8th, 65th, 68th, 2nd N.I. Posted as Col. to 47th N.I. July 1855 ; to 46th N.I. 1855.

Refs. : Boase. Will dated 8 Feb. 1856 ; proved 22 Mar. 1858.

GOLDIE, Barré William (1811-1849). Bt. Major, Engineers. *b.* Madras 8 Feb. 1811. Cadet 1827. Arrived in India 22 May 1829. 2nd Lieut. 13 Dec. 1827. Lieut. 20 Oct. 1833. Capt. 19 Feb. 1844. Bt. Major 7 June 1849. *d.* Landour, Mussoorie, 13 Nov. 1849.

Son of John Goldie, of Tunbridge Wells, late of Madras Medical

Board. *m.* St. Mary's, Bryanston Sq., London, 25 May 1836, Julia Harriet, only child of James Gosling, formerly of Clay Hall. Addiscombe Cadet 1826-7.
Services : d.d. S. & M. at Aligarh 13 July 1829. Fur. s.c. 29 Jan. 1834 till 2 Jan. 1837. Executive Engr. P.W.D., Berhampore Div., 27 Feb. 1837. Leave s.c. 2 yrs. to Cape 4 Dec. 1840. Fur. s.c. 5 Feb. 1843 till 1845. Executive Engr. Benares Div. 28 Nov. 1845 till 1848. Second Sikh War; Chilianwala; Gujerat (Medal with clasp).
Refs. : *A.J.* N.S. xx. 131.

GOLDING, Edward (1753/54-1785). Lieutenant, Infantry. *b.* 1753/54. Cadet 1776. Ensign 20 Mar. 1777. Lieut. 15 Aug. 1778. *d.* 6 Oct. 1785.

A native of Ireland.
Services : Sailed for India on the *Duke of Cumberland,* 29 Mar. 1776, aged 22. N.F.P.

GOLDING, George Webb (1810-1841). Lieutenant, 2nd Bengal Eur. Regt. *b.* Loughall, co. Antrim, 27 Dec. 1810. Cadet 1826. Arrived in India 13 Oct. 1827. Ensign 8 May 1827. Lieut. 7 May 1832. *d.* 26 Dec. 1841 : massacred during the mutiny of the Jan-baz nr. Kandahar.

Son of George Richard Golding, of Lime Park Lodge, co. Tyrone, Capt. 4th D.G., and Georgiana his wife, 2nd dau. of Rev. Travers Hume, and sister of George Macartney, of Lissanoure, co. Antrim.
Services : Posted as Ensign to 35th N.I. 3 Jan. 1828. First Afghan War 1838-41; Ghazni; Lieut. 35th N.I.; Bamian (horse shot under him); Nazian valley. Transfd. to 2nd Bengal Eur. Regt. 8 Oct. 1839. Placed at the disposal of the Envoy and Minister at the court of H.M. Shah Shuja 15 Oct. 1839. Apptd. Inspector of 1st Jan-baz Regt.
Refs. : Burke's *Landed Gentry,* 7th edn., p. 1167, *s.n.* Macartney, of Lissanoure, co. Antrim. Will dated Jalalabad 7 Feb. 1841; proved 30 Jan. 1843.

GOLDING, William (*d.* 1796). Captain, Engineers. Country Cadet 1778. Ensign 6 Oct. 1780. Lieut. 27 May 1781. Capt. 7 Jan. 1796. *d.* Calcutta 13 Dec. 1796.

Services : Was Dy. Comy. of Stores at Fort William in 1787, and Asst. Comy. in 1790.
Refs. : B. : *P.P.* iii. 103. *N. & Q.* 12S. vii. 178. Portrait in rt. hand bottom corner of Zoffany's painting "Col. Mordaunt's Cock Fight, Lucknow 1786."

GOLDNEY, Philip (1802-1857). Colonel, 38th N.I. *b.* London 21 Nov. 1802. Cadet 1820. Arrived in India Nov. 1821. Ensign 11 June 1821. Lieut. 30 Jan. 1824. Capt. 3 Mar. 1841. Major 7 July 1848. Lt. Col. 15 Nov. 1853. Col. 1857. *d.* 8 June 1857 : kld. by mutineers at Begumjee, on Gogra R., nr. Fyzabad.

bapt. St. James's, Westminster, 11 Jan. 1803. 2nd son of Thomas Goldney, of Goldney House, Clifton, and of St. James's St., London, goldsmith, and Charlotte his wife, dau. of John Milward. Brother of Thomas Goldney, *q.v.* *m.* Saugor 4 Dec. 1833, Mary Louisa, eldest dau. of John Holbrow, *q.v.*

Services: Ensign d.d. 1/29th N.I. 18 May 1822. Posted as Ensign to 2/14th N.I. Transfd. as Lieut. to 1st N.I. 1 Mar. 1824 ; to 4th N.I. (late 2/1st) May 1824. Operations against the Bhils 1824 ; Lieut. 4th N.I. Actg. Adjt. 4th N.I. 7 May 1827 and 25 July 1828. Intr. & Qmr. 4th N.I. 26 May 1829 till 25 Oct. 1839. Actg. D.C. in Sind 21 June 1844. D.C. in Upper Sind 18 Aug. 1845. Against the Hill tribes in Sind 1845 ; Trakki ; Capt. 4th N.I. D.C. Punjab 19 Oct. 1850 ; do. 1 cl., 10 Feb. 1851. Transfd. as Lt. Col. to newly-raised 3rd Bengal Eur. Regt. 15 Nov. 1853 ; to 35th N.I. 13 Dec. 1853. Comdd. a Bde. for annexation of Oudh. Placed at disposal of Foreign Dept. 1 Dec. 1854. Transfd. to 22nd N.I. Dec. 1854 ; to 38th N.I. 1856. Comr. in Province of Oudh 11 Feb. 1856. Was in charge of Fyzabad Div. on outbreak of the mutiny.

Refs. : Foster's *Baronetage*, p. 257, *s.n.* Goldney, Bart. Burke's *Landed Gentry*, 6th edn., p. 656, *s.n.* Goldney, of Chippenham, Wilts. D.N.B. D.I.B. Boase. G.M. 1857, ii. 685. Will dated 24 May 1857 ; proved 1 Mar. 1858.

GOLDNEY, Thomas (1801-1824). Lieutenant, 1st N.I. *b.* London 17 Mar. 1801. Cadet 1818. Ensign 20 Sept. 1819. Lieut. 23 May 1823. *d.* Narsinghpur, C.P., 23 Aug. 1824.

Eldest son of Thomas Goldney and Charlotte his wife. Brother of Philip Goldney, *q.v.*

Services: Posted as Ensign to 2/14th N.I. in 1822. Transfd. as Lieut. to 12th N.I. in 1823 ; to 1st N.I. (late 2/12th) May 1824. No record of active service.

Refs. : Foster's *Baronetage*, p. 257, *s.n.* Goldney, Bart. Burke's *Landed Gentry*, 6th edn., p. 656, *s.n.* Goldney, of Chippenham, Wilts.

GOODALL, Thomas (1781-1806). Lieutenant, 4th N.I. *bapt.* Andover, Hants, 24 Dec. 1781. Cadet 1798. Arrived in India 26 Aug. 1799. Ensign 8 Oct. 1799. Lieut. 28 Oct. 1799. *d. unm.* Agra 26 Aug. 1806.

Son of Thomas Goodall and Hannah his wife. Brother of Henry Francis Goodall.

Services : Second Mahratta War ; Aligarh ; defence of Delhi ; Lieut. 2/4th N.I.
Refs. : *G.M.* 1807, i. 484. Will dated Delhi 27 Sept. 1804 ; codicil dated 19 July 1806 ; proved 10 Dec. 1807.

GOODDAY, George Christopher Smyth (1808-1880). Lieutenant. Bengal Eur. Regt. *b.* Terling, Essex, 14 Mar. 1808. Cadet 1825. Arrived in India 18 Mar. 1826. Ensign 28 Sept. 1825. Lieut. 13 June 1828. Retired on h.p. 29 July 1836. *d.* 25 Jan. 1880.

Son of Rev. William Goodday, vicar of Terling.
Services : Posted as Ensign to 2nd Bengal Eur. Regt. in 1826 ; to Left Wing, Bengal Eur. Regt., Jan. 1830. Offg. Intr. & Qmr. 52nd N.I. 15 Nov. 1831. Fur. s.c. 29 Jan. 1834 till retirement. No record of active service.

GOODRICK, John (*d.* 1771). Ensign, Infantry. Cadet 1769. Ensign 5 Aug. 1769. *d.* Dinapore 17 Nov. 1771.
Services : N.F.P.

GOODRIDGE, Joseph (*d.* 1771). *d.* Dinapore 17 Nov. 1771.
Note : Appears to be identical with the foregoing.

GOODWIN, Frederick Lumley (1812-1835). 2nd Lieutenant, Artillery. *bapt.* Broughton, Lincs., 10 Dec. 1812. Cadet 1830. Arrived in India 18 Feb. 1831. 2nd Lieut. 11 June 1830. *d.* Mhow 26 Aug. 1835, aged 23.

2nd son of Joseph Goodwin, of Broughton, farmer, later of Hull, and Ann Elizabeth his wife. Addiscombe Cadet 1828-30.
Services : d.d. with H.A. at Meerut 7 Jan. 1832 ; do. 1st Bde. H.A. at Cawnpore 29 Sept. 1832 ; do. 2nd Troop 3rd Bde. 16 Sept. 1834. Actg. 2nd Lieut. 20 Feb. 1833. Posted to 2nd Troop 3rd Bde. 3 June 1835. No record of active service.
Refs. : *G.M.* 1836, i. 566.

GOODWYN, Henry (1807-1886). General, Engineers. Colonel Comdt. Royal (late Bengal) Engineers. *b.* London 18 Jan. 1807. Cadet 1824. Arrived in India 7 May 1825. 2nd Lieut. 18 Dec. 1823. Lieut. 1 Jan. 1826. Capt. 20 May 1839. Major 11 Nov. 1846. Lt. Col. 5 Dec. 1848. Col. 3 Aug. 1855. Maj. Gen. 26 June 1860. Lt. Gen. 1 Mar. 1867. Gen. 14 July 1871. *d.* Selborne, Bournemouth, 8 Nov. 1886.

Son of Henry Robert Goodwyn, of East Smithfield, London, brewer. *m.* Karnal, 15 Oct. 1829, Maria, 3rd dau. of John Littledale Gale, *q.v.* (*See also* Frederick Wilshire Steer Chapman.) (She died 22 May 1862.) Addiscombe Cadet 1822-3.
Services : Posted to S. & M. at Cawnpore 10 June 1825. Siege

and capture of Bhurtpore; Lieut. S. & M. (India medal). Garr. Engr. at Hansi 9 Apr. 1828. Executive Engr. P.W.D., Hansi, 2 July 1828; do. Berhampore 11 May 1835; do. Bareilly 13 Feb. 1837. Fur. 5 Feb. 1840 till 1842. Executive Engr. Cawnpore Div. 29 July 1848. Second Sikh War (Medal). Suptg. Engr. C.P. 6 Aug. 1850; do. S.E. Provinces 17 Mar. 1852. Chief Engr. Lower Provinces 1 May 1854. Comdt. Corps of Engrs. Feb. 1857. Fur. 1857 till death.

Refs.: *Howard & Crisp*, i. 278, *s.n.* Gale. *Boase. A.J. N.S.* i. 235. *The Times*, 13 Nov. 1886.

GOODYAR, William Dinely (1809-1843). Lieutenant, 47th N.I.
b. 9 Oct. 1809. Cadet 1829. Arrived in India 23 Oct. 1830. Ensign (27 June 1830) 23 Oct. 1833. Lieut. 2 Mar. 1838. *d.* Sikraul, Benares, 20 July 1843, of cholera.

bapt. Allhallows, Cumberland, 5 Jan. 1810. Son of Rev. John Dinely Goodyar, of Baggray, rector of Otterden, Kent, sometime Capt. S. Gloucs. Mil., and Harriet his wife, *née* Sanders.

Services: d.d. 54th N.I. 16 Nov. 1830; do. 73rd N.I. 18 Feb. 1833. Actg. Ensign 9 Nov. 1832. Posted as Ensign to 47th N.I. 19 Oct. 1833. Fur. s.c. 22 Dec. 1838 till 5 Mar. 1842. No record of active service.

Refs.: *M.M.* 1805, p. 473. *I.M.* No. 5, p. 146.

GOODYER,[1] **George Dinely** (*d.* 1806 ?). Captain. Infantry. Cadet (?). Ensign 5 Nov. 1765. Lieut. 30 May 1767. Capt. 29 June 1771. Resigned 18 Jan. 1772. (? *d.* Gloucester Dec. 1806.)

Services: N.F.P.

Refs.: (? *M.M.* 1806, p. 609.)

[1] *Note:* The name is variously spelt Goodyar, Goodyer, Goodyear, and Goodyere.

GORDON, Adam Durnford (1796-1857). Lieutenant. 72nd N.I. Subsequently Professor of Oriental languages at Cheltenham Coll.
b. Ardersier, Inverness, 22 Aug. 1796. Cadet 1817. Admitted 19 Sept. 1818. Ensign 26 May 1818. Lieut. 28 Sept. 1819. Resigned 7 Sept. 1831. *d.* Cheltenham 16 June 1857.

bapt. Ardersier 22 Aug. 1796. Eldest son of William Gordon, Capt. R.E. (who was son of Robert Gordon, of Halhead, and Lady Henrietta Gordon his wife, dau. of 2nd Earl of Aberdeen), and Frances Elrington his wife. *m.* Paris, 12 Sept. 1829, Harriet Elizabeth, his cousin-german, only child of Robert Gordon, formerly Govr. of Berbice. Father of Adam Lindsay Gordon (*D.N.B.*).

Services: Ensign 3rd W.I. Regt. 28 July 1814; transfd. as Ensign to 2nd Bn. 47th Foot; h.p. do. 25 Mar. 1816 till 18 Nov.

1831, when he received commuted allowance £300. Ensign 20th
N.I. Transfd. as Lieut. to 1/12th N.I. Mily. student at Coll. of
Fort William 12 June 1820 till 1822. Tempy. D.A.Q.M.G. 1822.
Adjt. 1/12th N.I. 9 Dec. 1822 ; Intr. & Qmr. do. 14 Jan. 1823 till
10 Mar. 1824. Supy. S.A.C.G. 3 Feb. till 16 July 1824. Transfd.
to 12th N.I. (late 1/12th) May 1824 ; to newly-raised 4th Extra
Regt. (became 72nd N.I.) May 1825. Offg. Examiner at Coll. of
Fort William 28 July 1824 ; permanent do. 24 Sept. 1824. Fur.
s.c. 11 Apr. 1827 till resignation. No record of active service.
Professor of Oriental languages at Cheltenham Coll. 1846. Compiled
a Hindustani grammar.
Refs. : Bulloch, No. 110. *N. & Q.* 12S. ix. 128. *The Times*,
23 Aug. 1924, p. 13. *G.M.* 1829, ii. 364.

GORDON, Alexander (1786-1819). Bt. Captain, 5th N.I. *b.* Aberdeen Apr. 1786. Cadet 1804. Arrived in India 16 May 1806.
Ensign 4 Apr. 1806. Lieut. 25 Jan. 1808. Bt. Capt. 1 Jan. 1819.
d. Anupshahr, U.P., 12 Aug. 1819.

Cadet certificate signed by his relative William Gordon.
Services : Barasat C.C. Ensign 5th N.I. Lieut. 2/5th N.I.
(? Reduction of Kalinjar 1812.) Intr. & Qmr. 2/5th N.I. 11 Dec.
1814 till death. Third Mahratta War.
Refs. : Bulloch, No. 200.

GORDON, Charles (1786-1806). Lieutenant, 3rd N.I. *bapt.* Logie
Coldstone, co. Aberdeen, 19 Mar. 1786. Cadet 1804. Arrived
in India 12 Sept. 1805. Ensign 20 Sept. 1805. Lieut. 21 Sept.
1805. *d.* Berhampore, Bengal, 14 Nov. 1806.

Eldest son of Charles Gordon, of Blelack, and Jean Turner his wife.
Services : (*Probably* Ensign Aberdeenshire Mil.) Posted as Lieut.
to 2/3rd N.I. No record of active service.
Refs. : Bulloch, No. 324. *S.M.* 1807, p. 638.

GORDON, George (*d.* 1786). Ensign, Infantry. Cadet 1783. Ensign
2 May 1785. *d.* Calcutta 20 Sept. 1786 : bur. there the following
day.
Services : N.F.P.
Refs. : Bulloch, No. 516.

GORDON, George (1786-1823). Lieutenant, 21st N.I. *b.* 19 May
1786. Cadet 1807. Arrived in India 19 Aug. 1808. Ensign
21 Sept. 1808. Lieut. 16 Dec. 1814. *d. unm.* Chunar 11 Feb. 1823.
bapt. Creich, co. Sutherland, May 1786. Son of William Gordon,
at Spinningdale, and Janet MacIntosh his wife.
Services : Posted as Ensign to 21st N.I. Lieut. 1/21st N.I.

Mily. student at Coll. of Fort William in 1814. Nepal War 1816 ; Lieut. 8th Gren. Bn., in 2nd Bde. Fort Adjt. at Chunar, and in charge of state prisoners, 1819 till death. Transfd. to 2/21st N.I.
Refs. : *Bulloch*, No. 538. *S.M.* 1824, i. 127. Will dated Chunar 14 Feb. 1821 ; proved 10 Mar. 1823.

GORDON, George (1810-1860). Bt. Lieut. Colonel, 50th N.I. *b.* Edinburgh 13 Mar. 1810. Cadet 1825. Arrived in India 7 July 1826. Ensign 15 Mar. 1826. Lieut. 12 Mar. 1829. Capt. 1 Jan. 1849. Bt. Major 20 June 1854. Bt. Lt. Col. 20 July 1858. *d.* Calcutta 7 Mar. 1860.

Son of William Gordon, of Halmyre, co. Peebles (descended from the Gordonstoun Gordons), and Mary Dunn his wife. *m.* Kinblethmont, co. Forfar, 9 Jan. 1845, Mary Elizabeth, eldest dau. of William Fullerton Lindsay-Carnegie, of Spynie and Boysack, and grand-dau. of William, 7th Earl of Northesk. (She died Gt. Malvern, 21 Jan. 1858, aged 37.) Ed. Edinburgh Acad.

Services : Ensign d.d. 14th N.I. 2 Aug. 1826. Posted as Ensign to 50th N.I. 26 Sept. 1826. Fur. s.c. 26 Mar. 1831 till 24 Oct. 1834. Comdd. Resdt.'s escort at Katmandu, Nepal, 28 Nov. 1836 till 14 Mar. 1840. Fur. s.c. 27 Jan. 1843 till 1845. Adjt. 50th N.I. 24 Oct. 1846 till 1849. Second Sikh War ; Gujerat (Medal). 2nd in comd. 1st Sikh Local Inf. 11 July 1849 ; Comdt. do. 17 Nov. 1851. Operations against the Mohmands 1854 and 1855 ; Bt. Major comdg. 1st Sikh Local Inf.

Refs. : Burke's *Landed Gentry*, 13th edn., p. 295, *s.n.* Lindsay-Carnegie, of Spynie. *Bulloch*, No. 551.

GORDON, George Lawrie (1801-1844). Captain, 8th N.I. P.A. at Manipur. *b.* Sorn, co. Ayr, 25 Mar. 1801. Cadet 1818. Admitted 1 Jan. 1820. Ensign 24 July 1819. Lieut. 17 Oct. 1822. Capt. 8 Jan. 1838. *d.* Manipur 30 Dec. 1844.

bapt. Sorn 8 Apr. 1801. Son of Rev. George Gordon, D.D., minister of Sorn, and Ann his wife, dau. of Rev. George Lawrie, of London. Ed. Glasgow.

Services : Posted as Ensign to 2/19th N.I. Attached to Pioneers 28 Dec. 1822. First Burma War ; Lieut. 6th Coy. Pioneers. Adjt. Gambhir Singh's Levy (Manipur), and afterwards 2nd in comd., 12 Nov. 1825 till 11 Feb. 1835. Employed on survey work in Assam in 1832, with Capt. Jenkins and Lieut. Pemberton's mission. To superintend education of young Rajah of Manipur Feb. 1835. Served as the first P.A. in Manipur 25 Feb. 1835 till death. Compiled an "English, Bengali and Muneeporee Dictionary," pub. in 1837.

Refs. : *Bulloch*, No. 589. M.I. outside Residency cemetery at Manipur.

THE BENGAL ARMY, 1758-1834

GORDON, Lord Henry (1802-1865). Major. 5th N.I. b. 31 Aug. 1802. Cadet 1821. Arrived in India 19 Aug. 1822. Ensign 10 Mar. 1822. Lieut. 1 May 1824. Capt. 12 Nov. 1842. Retired 1 May 1846. Hon. Major 28 Nov. 1854. d. 28 Aug. 1865.

bapt. Aboyne, co. Aberdeen, 22 Sept. 1802. 4th son of George, 9th Marquess of Huntly and 5th Earl of Aboyne, K.T., and Catherine his wife, 2nd dau. of Sir Charles Cope, Bart. m. Meerut, 6 Mar. 1827, Louisa, dau. of —— Payne. (She died 17 May 1867.) Ed. Harrow ; entered the school 1814/15 ; left in 1816.

Services : Posted as Ensign to 4th N.I. Transfd. as Lieut. to 23rd N.I. (late 2/4th) May 1824. A.D.C. to G.G. 12 Sept. 1825 till 30 June 1827. Dy. Paymr., Meerut Div., 30 June 1827 till 9 Oct. 1837. Transfd. to newly-formed 2nd Bengal Eur. Regt. 8 Oct. 1839, but never joined. Transfd. as Capt. to 5th N.I. 14 Dec. 1842. Fur. s.c. 11 Feb. 1843 till 7 June 1845. Capt. Aberdeenshire Mil. (with local rank of Major) 27 Feb. 1855 ; retired 12 Nov. 1857.

Refs. : Burke's *Peerage*, 1923, p. 1220, s.n. Huntly, M. *Bulloch*, No. 634. *Harrow School Register*. *G.M.* 1865, ii. 528.

GORDON, Hugh (1800-1829). Captain, 26th N.I. b. Edinburgh 19 Dec. 1800. Cadet 1817. Lieut. 1 Jan. 1819. Capt. 30 Dec. 1826. d. Sandoway, Lower Burma, 14 Feb. 1829.

bapt. St. Andrew's, Edinburgh, 29 Dec. 1817 (sic). Younger son of Thomas Gordon, of Whitburn, W.S., and Letitia McVeagh his wife. Cousin of Thomas Lumsden, q.v., and nephew of Alexander McVeagh, q.v.

Services : Posted as Lieut. to 1/13th N.I. Adjt. 2/13th N.I. 1822-4. Transfd. to 27th N.I. (late 2/13th) May 1824. Asst. Bk. Mr. Cuttack. Transfd. to 26th N.I. 1825. First Burma War ; Chittagong ; Dy. Paymr. to the Chittagong F.F. Asst. to the Comr. in Arakan 8 Sept. 1826 till death.

Refs. : *Bulloch*, No. 668. Will dated Sandoway 7 Jan. 1829 ; proved 6 Apr. 1829.

GORDON, James (d. 1803). Bt. Lieut. Colonel, Artillery. Cadet 1778. Admitted 11 Aug. 1778. Ensign (Inf.) 1778. Lieut. (Art.) 4 Oct. 1778. Capt. 24 Nov. 1786. Major 6 Nov. 1800. Bt. Lt. Col. 1 Jan. 1800. d. 27 Feb. 1803 : kld. by the explosion of a powder magazine at the fort of Bijaigarh, nr. Aligarh, whilst checking the stores after surrender.

Son of James Gordon, at the Laggan of Auchindoun, and Jean MacWilliam his wife.

Services : Capt. 1st Bn. Art. in July 1787. Operations in Jumna Doab 1803 ; Sasni ; Bijaigarh (kld.) ; Bt. Lt. Col. comdg. Art.

Refs. : *Bulloch*, No. 722. *Buckle*, pp. 246-7. *Pester*, p. 59.

GORDON, James (1780-1817). Captain (officially Major), 15th N.I. D.A.G. Bengal. *b.* 1780. Cadet 1799. Arrived in India 10 Dec. 1800. Ensign 9 Oct. 1800. Lieut. 13 July 1803. Capt. 23 Dec. 1809. *d. unm.* Calcutta 12 June 1817.

bapt. Mortlach, co. Banff, 7 Jan. 1781. 2nd son of John Gordon, in Laggan, cadet of Beldorney, and Janet Proctor his wife. Brother of John Gordon, Bt. Lt. Col. 1st Foot (Royal Regt.). Relative of Charles Gordon, of Wardhouse, co. Aberdeen, and of Cosmo Gordon, of H.M. Customs, Liverpool.

Services : Operations in Jumna Doab 1803 ; Sasni ; Bijaigarh ; Kachaura ; Lieut. 1/15th N.I. Second Mahratta War ; battle of Delhi ; Agra ; Laswari ; battle of Deig ; Bhurtpore (w. 23 Jan. 1805) ; Lieut. 1/15th N.I. Adjt. 2/15th N.I. 1806-9. Actg. A.A.G. 1809 ; A.A.G. 1810 ; D.A.G. Bengal, 1811 till death.

Refs. : Bulloch, No. 739. *S.M.* 1818, i. 395. Will dated Calcutta 7 May 1817 ; proved 14 June 1817. M.I. S. Park St. cemetery, Calcutta.

GORDON, James (1807-1875). Lieut. Colonel. 3rd L.C. *b.* Glasgow 25 Nov. 1807. Cadet 1825. Arrived in India 22 Oct. 1826. Cornet 21 May 1826. Lieut. 30 June 1838. Capt. 8 May 1849. Bt. Major 20 June 1854. Retired 10 Mar. 1857. Hon. Lt. Col. 10 Mar. 1857. *d.* Guernsey 15 Sept. 1875.

Son of Alexander Gordon, of Glasgow, merchant, and Elizabeth his wife, dau. of Thomas Buchanan, of Ardoch. *m.* Karnal, 17 Mar. 1842, Mary Harriet, 5th dau. of Henry Loftus Tottenham, of MacMurrough, co. Wexford, and sister of John Loftus Tottenham, *q.v.* (She died 24 Oct. 1869.) Ed. Edin. Univ.

Services : Posted as Cornet to 3rd L.C. 9 Nov. 1826, and remained with that Regt. throughout his service. Operations against the Kols 1832. Fur. p.a. 21 Jan. 1838 till 20 Feb. 1841. Bde. Major 2nd Cav. Bde., Army of Reserve (for Afghanistan), 14 Oct. 1842 till Jan. 1843. First Sikh War ; Badhowal ; Aliwal ; Sobraon (Medal with clasp).

Refs. : Burke's *Landed Gentry,* 13th edn., p. 229, *s.n.* Gray-Buchanan of Scotstown, co. Lanark. Burke's *Landed Gentry of Ireland,* p. 697, *s.n.* Tottenham, of Ballycurry, co. Wicklow. Bulloch, No. 766. *The Times,* 23 Sept. 1875.

GORDON, James Cosmo (1756-1792). Lieutenant, Infantry. Actg. J.A.G., Bengal. *b.* 13 Aug. 1756. Cadet 1781. Ensign 15 June 1781. Lieut. 10 July 1782. *d.* Calcutta 31 Dec. 1792.

Son of John Gordon, of Birkenbush. *m.* Calcutta, 16 Oct. 1792, Christian, dau. of Robert Henry Knox, of Dunbar, merchant, and widow of Robert McLeish, of Dunbar. (She died London 1809.)

THE BENGAL ARMY, 1758-1834

Services : Fur. s.c. to Cape 19 Jan. 1787 till 1790. Actg. J.A.G., Bengal, and Town Major at Fort William. A.D.C. to the Hon. Charles Stuart, Member of the Supreme Council.
Refs. : *Bulloch*, No. 788. *G.M.* 1793, i. 575. *S.M.* 1793, pp. 306-7. M.I. in S. Park St. cemetery, Calcutta.

GORDON, James Gisborne (1804-1825). Lieutenant, 30th N.I. *bapt.* Belfast 12 Sept. 1804. Cadet 1820. Arrived in India June 1821. Ensign 22 Dec. 1820. Lieut. 11 July 1823. *d. unm.* Cuttack, 27 Dec. 1825, aged 21.

2nd son of Alexander Gordon, of Castle Place, Belfast, wine merchant, and Dorothea his wife, dau. of Gen. James Gisborne, C.-in-C. in Ireland, M.P. for Lismore. Ed. Belfast.
Services : Posted as Ensign to 29th N.I. Transfd. as Lieut. to 15th N.I. 11 July 1823 ; to 30th N.I. (late 1/15th) May 1824. No record of active service.
Refs. : Burke's *Landed Gentry of Ireland*, p. 270, *s.n.* Gordon, of Delamont, co. Down. *Bulloch*, No. 797. M.I. at Cuttack.

GORDON, James Innes (1788-1825). Captain, 35th N.I. *b.* Portsoy, co. Banff, 20 June 1788. Cadet 1803. Arrived in India 15 Aug. 1804. Ensign 15 Sept. 1804. Lieut. 21 Sept. 1804. Capt. 25 Oct. 1818. *d.* Meerut 10 Oct. 1825.

3rd son of James Gordon, of Rosieburn, and Janet Mercer his wife. Cousin of James Duff. *m.* 2 Nov. 1824, ——. (She died 6 Mar. 1825, aged 46.)
Services : Posted as Lieut. to 1/17th N.I. Adjt. Murshidabad Provl. Bn. 1811-3. Fur. 1814 till 22 Sept. 1815. 2nd Ceylon Vol. Bn. 1818-9. Capt. 1/17th N.I. Transfd. to 35th N.I. (late 2/17th) May 1824.
Refs. : *Bulloch*, No. 806. *S.M.* 1826, i. 640. Will dated Meerut 2 Oct. 1825 ; proved 1 Nov. 1825.

GORDON, James Thomas (1805-1849). Captain, 15th N.I. *b.* 21 Dec. 1805. Cadet 1824. Arrived in India 31 May 1825. Ensign 8 Jan. 1825. Lieut. 25 Jan. 1826. Capt. 10 Mar. 1841. *d.* Hampstead 12 May 1849.

bapt. Everton, Notts., 17 Feb. 1806. Son of Frederick Gordon, Major R.A., and Elizabeth his wife, 2nd dau. of James Murdoch, of Madeira. *m.* Hampstead, 13 Dec. 1837, Caroline, only dau. of Rev. James Harington Evans, of John St. chapel, London. (She re-m. 5 Feb. 1856, Andrew Steedman.)
Services : Posted as Ensign to 15th N.I. Siege and capture of Bhurtpore ; Ensign 15th N.I. Actg. Intr. & Qmr. 6th N.I. 1 Oct. 1829. Actg. Adjt. Left Wing 15th N.I. 3 Jan. 1830. Actg. Intr. & Qmr. 15th N.I. 28 Apr. 1834 till 13 Jan. 1835. Fur. p.a. 20 June

1835 till 16 July 1838. 2nd in comd. Lower Assam Sebundy Corps 19 Aug. 1839. Junior Asst. to Comr. in Assam 17 Feb. 1840; offg. Principal do., at Tezpur, 22 Sept. 1843. Posted to Nowgong Div. June 1844. Fur. s.c. 21 Oct. 1848 till death.

Refs. : *Bulloch*, No. 818. *G.M.* 1838, i. 205. Will dated 27 Apr. 1849; admon. 25 Jan. 1850. M.I. in Tezpur church.

*GORDON, John (1736/37-1763). Lieutenant, Infantry. *b.* 1736/37. Cadet (?). Ensign (?). Lieut. (?). *d.* 5th, 6th or 11th Oct. 1763 : massacred at or near Patna by order of Nawab Mir Muhammad Kasim.[1]

Son of Gordon of Dundurcus. (*Probably* son of George Gordon, of Fifthpart of Dundurcus.)

Services : Sailed for India on the *Norfolk* in 1760, as a Lieut., aged 23. N.F.P.

Refs. : *Bulloch*, No. 891. MS. list preserved at the India Office entitled " List of Persons killed in the Massacre at Patna, and at other places during the Troubles, 1763," signed " John Graham, Secretary, Fort William, 20 Feb. 1764." *Firminger*. *Forrest's Clive*, 88, 237.

[1] *Note :* " . . . On the nights of the 5th or 6th and 11th of October 1763, brutally massacred near this spot by the troops of Mir Kasim, Nawab Subahdar of Bengal, under command of Walter Reinhardt *alias* Samru, a base renegade." (M.I. in Patna city.)

GORDON, John (1740-1829). Captain. Infantry. *bapt.* Deskford 13 Aug. 1740. Cadet 1771. Ensign 27 Feb. 1773. Lieut. (?). Capt. 13 Oct. 1781. Resigned 1 Dec. 1783. *d.s.p.* Florence 20 July 1829.

Elder son of William Gordon, of Craibstone, and I. of Sheelagreen. *m.* " a dau. to (James Gordon ? of) Clashterim."

Services : N.F.P.

Refs. : *Bulloch*, No. 898.

GORDON, John (1765-1832). Lieut. General. Colonel 10th L.C. *b.* 8 July 1765. Cadet 1778. Admitted 14 Aug. 1778. Cornet 1778. Lieut. 8 Nov. 1778. Capt. 1 June 1796. Major 29 May 1800. Lt. Col. 5 Oct. 1800. Lt. Col. Comdt. 1 May 1804. Col. 25 July 1810. Maj. Gen. 4 June 1813. Lt. Gen. 27 May 1825. *d.* Devonshire St., London, 26 Dec. 1832.

Eldest son of Hon. John Gordon, Lt. Col. H.M. 81st Regt. (who was 2nd son of John, 3rd Earl of Aboyne), and Clementina his wife, dau. of George Lockhart, of Carnwath. *m.* 22 Nov. 1810, Eliza, 3rd dau. of Robert Morris, M.P. for Gloucester. (*See also* Robert Hawkes, and John Lewis Stuart.)

Services : Approved as Cadet 30 Jan. 1778. Sailed for India on the *Calcutta*, 27 July 1778, when he gave his age as 16. Adjt. 4th Bengal Eur. Bn. in 1787. Posted to 2nd Regt. Cav. 14, Dec 1787. Lieut. 2nd N.C. in 1796. Capt. and Major 2nd N.C. Transfd. as Lt. Col. to 1st N.C. Second Mahratta War; Laswari; Lt. Col. 1st N.C., comdg. Reserve Bde. Comdd. 2nd Cav. Bde. 1805-19. Fur. 24 Jan. 1809 till 27 Aug. 1811, and 15 Jan. 1819 till death. Col. 2nd L.C. Transfd. to 8th L.C.; to 2nd L.C. 11 Aug. 1826; to 10th L.C. 27 Oct. 1832.

Refs. : Burke's *Peerage*, 1923, p. 1219, *s.n.* Huntly, M. *Bulloch*, No. 908. *G.M.* 1833, i. 186. M.I. in Marylebone psh. church.

*GORDON, John (1769-?). *b.* Aberdeen Sept. 1769. Cadet 1791.

Services : (? On arrival at Madras from England as an Inf. Cadet in Nov. 1791, was apptd. to do duty with the Bengal Art. at that Presdy., and served with that Corps during third Mysore War.) [1]

Refs. : (? *Stubbs*, i. 131.)

[1] *Note :* This officer is not mentioned in *Bulloch*. The reference in *Stubbs* may possibly be to the following, although, from a comparison of dates, this appears unlikely. (*See* Addenda.)

GORDON, John (1775-?). Cadet. Infantry. *b.* East Florida 2 Aug. 1775. Cadet 1792. Resigned 3 Feb. 1792.

Son of Arthur Gordon, Attorney Gen. of the Province of East Florida, and Harriot Priscilla his wife.

Services : N.F.P.

Refs. : Bulloch, No. 922-3.

GORDON, Sir John, eighth baronet (1776-1804). Lieutenant, Engineers. *b.* Cork 2 July 1776. Cadet 1792. Ensign 8 Nov. 1793. Lieut. 10 Dec. 1800. *d. unm.* Penang 12 Nov. 1804.

8th Baronet, of Embo, co. Sutherland. *s.* 7 Jan. 1804. *bapt.* Cork 17 July 1776. 5th but eldest surviving son of Sir William Gordon, 7th Bart., Capt. 19th Regt., and Sarah his wife, only dau. of Crosby Westfield, R.N. His sisters *m.* William Neville Cameron, *q.v.*, Jabez Mackenzie, *q.v.*, and Charles Stewart (1764-1837), *q.v.*

Services : N.F.P.

Refs. : Burke's *Peerage*, 1923, p. 994, *s.n.* Gordon, Bart., of Embo, co. Sutherland. *Bulloch*, No. 924. *G.M.* 1805, i. 583. Will dated Calcutta 28 Mar. 1803; codicil dated P.W.I. 23 Feb. 1804.

GORDON, John (1787-1822). Captain, 20th N.I. *b.* Calcutta 23 Sept. 1787. Cadet 1803. Arrived in India 12 Dec. 1804. Ensign 2 Oct. 1804. Lieut. 2 Oct. 1804. Capt. 30 June 1818. *d.* Chinsura, Bengal, 18 Apr. 1822.

bapt. Calcutta 16 Jan. 1788. Son of George Gordon, of Calcutta, printer of the *India Gazette*, and Ann his wife, eldest dau. of Christian

Fischer, *q.v.* *m.* Chinsura, 23 May 1815, Johanna Leonora Christiana, 2nd dau. of Daniel Anthony Overbeek (Overbeke or Overbeck), the last Dutch Govr. of Chinsura. (*See also* Peter Dewaal.) (She *re-m.* Alexander Wright, *q.v.*)

Services : Posted as Lieut. to 1/20th N.I. Capture of Java 1811 ; Lieut. 1/20th N.I. Served in P.W.I. 1807-8 ; at Bencoolen in 1816.

Refs. : Burke's *Colonial Gentry*, ii. 828, *s.n.* Overbeek. *Bulloch*, No. 950. *S.M.* 1823, i. 127. Will dated Barrackpore 8 July 1818 ; proved 26 Apr. 1822.

GORDON, John (1811-1853). Ensign. 53rd N.I. Pensioner on Lord Clive's fund. Subsequently Superior of the R.C. Oratory at Birmingham. *b.* St. George, I. of Dominica, 30 Aug. 1811. Cadet 1828. Arrived in India 21 May 1829. Ensign 7 Feb. 1829. Pensioned 2 May 1834. *d.* Bath, 13 Feb. 1853, of pleurisy.

2nd son of John Gordon, of Kethock's Mill, later of Demarara and of 77 Gower St , London, merchant, and Mary Victorie Blanc his wife. Ed. Rugby ; entered the school 1823. Trin. Coll., Camb., B.A. 1837 ; M.A. 1840.

Services : Ensign d.d. 29th N.I. 13 July 1829. Posted as Ensign to 53rd N.I. 14 Sept. 1829. Fur. s.c. 12 Dec. 1831 till pensioned. No record of active service. Took holy orders in 1837. Joined Roman Catholic Church in 1848 (as John Joseph), and eventually became Superior of the Oratory at Birmingham (as Father Joseph), where he was a great friend of Cardinal Newman, who dedicated to him " The Dream of Gerontius." His grave is next to that of Cardinal Newman. His brother, William, was Superior of the Brompton Oratory. Wrote " Reasons of my Conversion."

Refs.: Bulloch, No. 985. *Rugby School Register. Alumni Cantab.*

GORDON, Patrick (1810-1897). Major General. 11th N.I. Raised and comdd. 15th Ludhiana Sikhs (now 2nd Bn. 11th Sikh Regt.). *b.* Cairnfield, co. Banff, 27 Mar. 1810. Cadet 1825. Arrived in India 22 Oct. 1826. Ensign (15 Apr. 1826) 20 Dec. 1826. Lieut. 7 Aug. 1833. Capt. 20 Nov. 1845. Major 12 Oct. 1856. Lt. Col. 13 Apr. 1860. Bt. Col. 20 June 1857. Retired 31 Dec. 1861. Hon. Maj. Gen. 31 Dec. 1861. *d.* 8 Lansdown Cresc., Bath, 27 Apr. 1897.

Of 8 Lansdown Cresc., Bath. *bapt.* Rathven, co. Banff, 13 Apr. 1810. 3rd son of Adam Gordon, of Arradoul and Cairnfield, and Elizabeth his wife, dau. of Patrick Cruikshank, of Strathcaro, co. Forfar. *m.* Meerut, 4 May 1848, Charlotte Mary, only child of Capt. George Mathers, H.M. 59th Foot. (She died Bath, 18 Sept. 1906, aged 73.)

Services : Posted as Ensign to 52nd N.I. 5 Oct. 1826. Transfd. to 11th N.I. 20 Dec. 1826. Wahabi rising 1831 ; Ensign 11th

N.I. Adjt. 11th N.I. 18 Nov. 1840. First Sikh War; Mudki; Ferozshahr; Sobraon; Capt. 11th N.I., Bde. Major 6th Bde., 3rd Div. (Medal with 2 clasps). Raised in 1846 the "Regt. of Ludhiana" (now 2nd Bn. 11th Sikh Regt.), and comdd. it 1 Aug. 1846 till 1857. Comdg. Benares district 1 Dec. 1857. Mutiny campaign; minor operations Nov.-Dec. 1858; comdg. a column. Apptd. to Dinapore Bde. Mar. 1859.

Refs.: Burke's *Landed Gentry*, 13th edn., p. 743, *s.n.* Gordon, of Cairnfield, co. Banff. *Bulloch*, No. 1142. *The Times*, 29 Apr. 1897.

CONWAY-GORDON, William (1798-1882). Captain. 53rd N.I. *b.* Richmond, Surrey, 22 Apr. 1798. Cadet 1815. Admitted 16 Aug. 1816. Ensign 6 Mar. 1816. Lieut. 1 Aug. 1818. Capt. 12 Feb. 1830. Retired 8 Jan. 1840. *d.* Lynwood House, Southsea, 30 June 1882.

bapt. St. Mary Abbott's, Kensington, 7 Oct. 1798. Son of "William and Catherine Conway, of Brompton Row." Assumed by R.L. the surname of Gordon in addition to that of Conway 12 Aug. 1839 (*Lond. Gaz.* p. 1584). Matriculated arms at the Lyon Office 20 Apr. 1846, as "son of the deceased Right Hon. Lord William Gordon" (who was 2nd son of Cosmo, 3rd Duke of Gordon). *m.* Bareilly, 25 Sept. 1828, Louisa, youngest dau. of Jacob Vanrenen, *q.v.* (*See also* James Blair.) (She died 14 Apr. 1877, aged 66.)

Services: Posted as Ensign to Bengal Eur. Regt. Transfd. as Lieut. to 2/27th N.I. Adjt. Left Wing 2/27th N.I. 6 Nov. 1820. Transfd. to 23rd N.I. (late 1/27th) May 1824. Intr. & Qmr. 53rd N.I. 2 Oct. 1824; Adjt. do. 25 July 1827 till 11 June 1830. Fur. s.c. 3 Dec. 1831. Arrived at Madras on return from fur. 11 Oct. 1836, on the staff of Sir Peregrine Maitland, C.-in-C., Madras. A.D.C. to Sir P. Maitland 14 Oct. 1836. Fur. s.c. from Madras 8 July 1837 till retirement. No record of active service.

Refs.: Burke's *Landed Gentry*, 13th edn., p. 745, *s.n.* Conway-Gordon, of Lynwode Manor, Lincs. *Bulloch*, No. 1586. *De La Ferté*, p. 151. *The Times*, 4 July and 8 Sept. 1882.

GORE, Clements (*d.* 1795). Lieutenant, 13th Bn. Sepoys. Cadet 1783. Admitted 4 Aug. 1784. Ensign 16 Feb. 1785. Lieut. 14 Mar. 1792. *d.* 7 Sept. 1795; bur. St. Helena 8 Sept. 1795.

Son of —— Gore and Mary his wife, dau. of John Clements, of Drung, co. Cavan, by his 2nd wife Rachel Parr. Brother of John Arthur Gore, *q.v.*, nephew of John Clements, and cousin of Thomas Parr.

Services: N.F.P.

Refs.: *S.M.* 1797, p. 287. Will dated 5 Sept. 1795; proved in 1796.

GORE, George William Molyneux (1801-1824). Lieutenant, 52nd N.I. *b.* Brislington, Somerset, 23 Dec. 1801. Cadet 1819. Ensign 9 Jan. 1820. Lieut. 13 Jan. 1822. *d. unm.* Chunar 26 Oct. 1824.

2nd son of William Gore, of Bristol, Col. H.M. 33rd Regt. (*Probably* cousin of Ralph Gore Roberts, *q.v.*, who was Exor. of his Will.)
Services : Lieut. 1/26th N.I. Transfd. to 52nd N.I. (late 2/26th) May 1824. No record of active service.
Refs. : Bath Chron. 31 Mar. 1825. Will dated Chunar 16 Oct. 1824; proved 3 Dec. 1824.

GORE, John Arthur (1769-1797/98). Lieutenant, Infantry. *b.* Drung, co. Cavan, 25 Feb. 1769. Cadet 1791. Admitted 17 Aug. 1791. Ensign 14 Mar. 1792. Lieut. 4 Oct. 1794. *d.* at sea in 1797 or 1798 (exact date unknown).

bapt. 20 Mar. 1769. Son of —— Gore and Mary Clements his wife. Brother of Clements Gore, *q.v.*
Services : On arrival at Madras from England as an Inf. Cadet in Aug. 1791, was apptd. to do duty with the Bengal Art. at that Presdy., and served with that Corps during the third Mysore War.
Refs. : Stubbs, i. 131. (? *S.M.* 1797, p. 287.)

GORE, John Escott (1783-1815). Capt. Lieutenant, Invalid Est. 11th N.I. *b.* Tiverton, Devon, 12 June 1783. Cadet 1799. Arrived in India 9 Dec. 1800. Ensign 14 Sept. 1800. Lieut. 12 Jan. 1801. Capt. Lt. 17 Dec. 1814. Invalided 1 Feb. 1815. *d.* Bareilly, U.P., 19 Nov. 1815.

bapt. Tiverton 19 Dec. 1786. Son of Thomas Gore, surgeon and apothecary, and Joan his wife.
Services : Ensign 11th N.I. (? Second Mahratta War ; Lieut. 11th N.I.) Reduction of Kalinjar 1812 ; Lieut. 11th N.I.

GORE, Thomas William (1787-1812). Lieutenant, 23rd N.I. 1st Bengal Vol. Bn. *b.* St. Peter Port, Guernsey, 9 Mar. 1787. Cadet 1804. Arrived in India 13 May 1806. Ensign 18 Feb. 1806. Lieut. 1 Feb. 1807. *d.* at sea 26 Feb. 1812, on board the *Bee*, on the voyage from Java to Malacca.

Son of Anthony Gore (who was younger brother of Sir Ralph Gore, 7th Bart.) and Judith his wife, dau. of Isaac Dobree.
Services : Posted to 23rd N.I. in 1807. Capture of Java 1811 ; Lieut. 6th Bengal Vol. Bn. Afterwards with 1st Vol. Bn.
Refs. : Burke's *Peerage*, 1923, p. 998, *s.n.* Gore, Bart. Will proved in 1813.

GORE, William (1764/65-1793). Lieutenant, Infantry. *b.* in Ireland 1764/65. Cadet 1781. Ensign 18 Apr. 1781. Lieut. 11 July 1782. *d.* Dinapore 2 May 1793.

THE BENGAL ARMY, 1758-1834   295

Services : Apptd. Cadet on 7 Mar. 1781, aged 17. Sailed for India on the *Nassau,* 8 Feb. 1782, aged 17. Fought a duel with William Blacquiere, *q.v.,* at Calcutta in Sept. 1783, in which the latter was killed. For this he was tried at the Calcutta sessions in June 1789, and was honourably acquitted. Lieut. 3rd Bn. Sepoys in July 1787.

Refs. : Cal. Gaz. 25 June 1789.

GOSLING, Robert Hamlet (1790-1814). Lieutenant, 27th N.I. *b.* Southwark, London, 12 Oct. 1790. Cadet 1805. Arrived in India 11 July 1806. Ensign 15 Aug. 1805. Lieut. 1 Jan. 1810. *d.* 31 Oct. 1814 : kld. in action at the storming of Kalanga.

Son of Robert Gosling, surgeon, and Elizabeth his wife.

Services : Posted to 27th N.I. in 1807. Lieut. 1/27th N.I. Nepal War 1814 ; Kalanga (kld.) ; Lieut. L.I. Bn., in 2nd Div.

Refs. : G.M. 1815, ii. 284.

GOTHER, William (1780-1808). Lieutenant, 8th N.I. *bapt.* Shorwell, I.W., 7 Nov. 1780. Cadet 1799. Arrived in India 12 Jan. 1801. Ensign 11 Sept. 1800. Lieut. 10 Apr. 1801. *d.* Cawnpore 23 May 1808.

Son of Rev. Andrew Gother, of Shorwell, vicar of Chesterton, Oxon., and of Thorley, I.W., and Elizabeth his wife.

Services : Posted as Ensign to 8th N.I. Operations in Jumna Doab 1803 ; Sasni ; Bijaigarh ; Kachaura ; Lieut. 2/8th N.I. Second Mahratta War ; Laswari ; Rampura ; Tonk Rampura ; Lieut. 2/8th N.I. Adjt. 2/8th N.I. 1805 till death. Storm of Badekh 1806.

Refs. : Burke's *Visitation of Seats and Arms,* 1S. i. 73, *s.n.* Scott, of I.W. *A.A.R.* x. 298.

GOUCH or GOOCH,[1] **George.** Captain. Infantry. Cadet 1771. Ensign 24 Mar. 1773. Lieut. 21 May 1778. Capt. 15 Jan. 1784. *d.* before 1790.

Services : Fur. 3 yrs. 6 Dec. 1785. N.F.P.

[1] *Note :* The name *possibly* should be Gough.

GOUGH, Christopher (*d.* 1781). Captain, 2nd Bengal Eur. Regt. Cadet (?). Ensign 7 Aug. 1767. Lieut. 29 Sept. 1769. Capt. 14 May 1777. *d. unm.* 12 July 1781.

Son of Sarah Gough. Brother of Hannah Gough.

Services : Capt. 2/2nd Bengal Eur. Regt. in Oct. 1779.

Refs. : Will dated 3 May 1781.

GOUGH, Thomas (1746/47-1780). Captain, 5th Bn. Sepoys. *b.* 1746/47. Cadet 1765. Ensign 26 Aug. 1765. Lieut. 6 Jan. 1767. Capt. 17 Sept. 1770. *d.* 15 Feb. 1780, aged 33, of wounds received in the assault of Ahmedabad two days earlier.

Services : First Mahratta War ; siege of Ahmedabad (kld.) ; Capt. comdg. 5th Bn., with Col. Thomas Goddard's force.
Refs. : Williams, p. 96. *Cardew,* p. 42. M.I. in Protestant cemetery in Ahmedabad city.
Note : One " Thomas Gough, aged 10, son of Thomas G., late of the Inner Temple," was admitted to St. Paul's school on 24 Jan. 1753.

GOUGH, Thomas (1780-1835). Lieut. Colonel, 2nd N.I. *bapt.* Alberbury, Salop, 13 Jan. 1780. Cadet 1800. Arrived in India 21 Aug. 1801. Ensign 5 Sept. 1801. Lieut. 30 Sept. 1803. Capt. 1 June 1813. Major 15 Jan. 1824. Lt. Col. 14 July 1825. *d.* Calcutta, 11 Feb. 1835, aged 55.
Son of Thomas Gough and Ann his wife. *m.* Calcutta 9 Feb. 1808, Miss Arabella Wilkinson.
Services : Lieut. 2nd Regt. Shropshire Mil. Ensign 11th N.I. Posted as Lieut. to newly-raised 23rd N.I. in 1803. Inspecting Ofr. of Irreg. Corps 1 June 1805 till 31 Mar. 1806. Bde. Major at Presdy. 11 June 1807. Reduction of Kalinjar ; Bde. Major (*Lond. Gaz.* 3 Oct. 1812). Siege and capture of Hathras ; Capt. 2/23rd N.I., Bde. Major (*Lond. Gaz.* 12 Oct. 1818). Third Mahratta War ; Madhurajpura ; Bde. Major ; Major comdg. Native Contingents with Reserve under Ochterlony. Bde. Major to troops at Muttra and Agra 3 Mar. 1820. Comdd. newly-raised 5th (Gough's) Local Horse 6 May 1823 till 15 Dec. 1825. Transfd. as Major to 45th N.I. (late 1/23rd) May 1824. Lt. Col. 55th N.I. Tempy. comdg. troops at Delhi 1 Oct. 1828. Transfd. to 10th N.I. 21 Nov. 1828 ; to 15th N.I. 22 Mar. 1829 ; to 2nd N.I. 6 Nov. 1833. Leave s.c. to Tasmania 21 Mar. 1833 till 30 Jan. 1835.
Refs. : A.J. N.S. xvii. 240. Will dated camp before Hatrass 23 Feb. 1817 ; proved 12 May 1835.

GOULD, Bulkeley. Lieutenant. Infantry. Cadet 1779. Ensign 12 Feb. 1780. Lieut. 20 Feb. 1781. Pensioned 23 Jan. 1783. Resigned 8 Feb. 1787.
Services : N.F.P.

GOULD, James (*d.* 1772). Lieutenant, Infantry. Lieut. Sept. 1768. *d.* Moradbag, Bengal, 3 May 1772 : drowned.
Services : N.F.P. *Possibly* transfd. from H.M.S.

GOULD, James (1758/59-1794). Bt. Captain, Infantry. *b.* 1758/59. Cadet 1778. Ensign Oct. 1778. Lieut. 8 Oct. 1778. Bt. Capt. (?). *d.* Fatehgarh, U.P., 26 Oct. 1794.
A native of Middlesex.

THE BENGAL ARMY, 1758-1834   297

Services : Sailed for India on the *Stafford*, 27 May 1778, aged 19. Lieut. 2/2nd Bengal Eur. Regt. in Oct. 1779. Apptd. Bde. Major, 6th Bde., 12 June 1786. Was Bde. Major at Berhampore, with Bt. rank of Capt., in 1790.

GOULD, Robert (*d.* 1772). Cadet, Infantry. Cadet 1771. *d.* Dinapore 22 June 1772.

Services : N.F.P.

GOULD, Thomas (1807-1831). Lieutenant, 11th N.I. *b.* Kirdford, Sussex, 10 May 1807. Cadet 1823. Arrived in India 7 Oct. 1824. Ensign 20 May 1824. Lieut. 20 Oct. 1825. *d.* at sea, 27 Mar. 1831, on board the *Mermaid*, in the Saugor roads.

Son of R. Gould, of E. Clandon, Surrey, farmer.

Services : Siege and capture of Bhurtpore ; Ensign 11th N.I. Intr. & Qmr. 11th N.I. 12 Aug. 1828 till 27 July 1829, and 25 June 1830 till death. Was on 2 mos.' sick leave to the Sandheads at date of death.

Refs. : A.J. N.S. vi. 138.

BARING-GOULD, William (1805-1839). Captain, 42nd N.I. *b.* 7 Dec. 1805. Cadet 1822. Arrived in India 22 Aug. 1823. Ensign 11 July 1823. Lieut. 7 Oct. 1824. Capt. 11 July 1838. *d.s.p.* in camp at Quetta 6 Oct. 1839.

bapt. St. Leonard's, Exeter, 16 Jan. 1806. 2nd son of William Baring-Gould, of Lew Trenchard, Devon, J.P. and D.L., and Diana Amelia his wife, dau. of Joseph Sabine. 2nd cousin of James Drummond Baring, *q.v.* *m.* Delhi, 27 July 1835, Maria Ann, eldest dau. of Joseph Leeson, *q.v.* (She died Delhi, 2 Oct. 1844, aged 25.) Addiscombe Cadet 1820-2.

Services : Posted as Ensign to 21st N.I. Transfd. to 42nd N.I. (late 2/21st) May 1824. First Burma War ; Arakan 1825 ; Lieut. 42nd N.I. Adjt. 42nd N.I. 12 June 1832 till death. First Afghan War ; capture of Ghazni ; Capt. 42nd N.I.

Refs. : Burke's *Landed Gentry*, 13th edn., p. 756, *s.n.* Baring-Gould, of Lew Trenchard, Devon. *Howard & Crisp*, iv. 24, *s.n.* Baring-Gould. Burke's *Peerage*, 1923, p. 1570, *s.n.* Milltown, E. *G.M.* 1840, i. 110.

GOULDHAWKE, James (1790-1839). Captain. 60th N.I. *bapt.* Calcutta 5 May 1790. Cadet 1808. Arrived in India 19 July 1809. Ensign 20 July 1809. Lieut. 16 Dec. 1814. Capt. 13 May 1825. Invalided 2 Oct. 1829. *d.* Cawnpore 23 May 1839.

Son of James Gouldhawke, or Goldhawk, and Mary his wife. *m.* Calcutta, 15 Aug. 1820, Frances, dau. of Isaac Golledge, Asst. Dy. Master Attendant at Calcutta. (She died 1843.)

Services: Ensign 19th N.I. Posted as Lieut. to newly-raised 2/30th N.I. Jan. 1815. On leave to Mauritius in 1816. Adjt. Dacca Provl. Bn. in 1823. Intr. & Qmr. 2/30th N.I. 1 Oct. 1823 till 7 June 1825. Transfd. to 60th N.I. (late 2/30th) May 1824. Siege and capture of Bhurtpore ; Capt. 60th N.I. Fur. p.a. 15 Sept. 1826 till Jan. 1829. Posted to 1st Bn. Native Invalids 26 Jan. 1830. Fur. 18 June 1834 till 7 Mar. 1836.

Refs. : Will dated 4 Oct. 1826 ; proved 4 July 1839.

GOVIN, John. (*See* **GOWEN.**)

GOWAN, Clotworthy. Captain. Infantry. Cadet (?). Ensign 15 Aug. 1764. Lieut. 15 Oct. 1765. Capt. 2 Apr. 1768. Resigned 18 Feb. 1778.

Of Ackton Hall. " Son of Rev. Clotworthy Gowan, rector of Invern, co. Derry " [1] (*Burke*). *m.* 1780, Anne, 3rd dau. of Timothy Mauleverer, of Arncliffe Hall, Yorks. Father of William Mauleverer (*formerly* Gowan), *q.v.*

Services: Comdg. 4th Bn. Sepoys in 1767. This Bn., which eventually became 6th N.I., was known as "*Gowen-ki-Paltan.*" First Mysore War 1767-9 ; Capt. comdg. 4th Bn.

Refs. : Burke's *Landed Gentry*, 6th edn., p. 1081, *s.n.* Mauleverer, of Arncliffe, Yorks. *Williams*, p. 90. *Cardew*, p. 22.

[1] *Note :* Rev. George Gowan, rector of Inver, co. Donegal, in his Will dated 10 Nov. 1759, mentions his eldest son Clotworthy Gowan, and his 2nd son George Gowan.

GOWAN, Edward Parry (1791-1840). Bt. Major, Artillery. *b.* Calcutta 10 July 1791. Cadet 1809. Admitted 9 Oct. 1810. Fireworker 14 Sept. 1810. Lieut. 23 Sept. 1817. Capt. 29 Aug. 1824. Bt. Major 28 June 1838. *d.* Simla 10 Feb. 1840.

Son of George Gowan, *q.v.*, and Mary his wife. Addiscombe Cadet 1809-10.

Services: Reduction of Kalinjar 1812. Nepal War 1814-5 ; Lieut.F. 7th Coy. 3rd Bn. Foot Art., in 2nd Div. Siege and capture of Hathras 1817 ; Lieut.F. 7th Coy. 3rd Bn. Third Mahratta War ; Lieut. 1st Troop H.A. ; transfd. to 3rd Troop Dec. 1817. 4th Troop H.A. 1818-25. Dy. Comy. Ord. 27 Nov. 1823 ; Comy. Ord. 7 June 1824. Asst. Sec. Mily. Board, Ordnance Dept., 8 Nov. 1828. Principal Dy. Comy. Ord. 6 Mar. 1835. Leave s.c. to Cape 4 Nov. 1836 till 25 Aug. 1838. Posted to 4th Troop 3rd Bde. H.A. 4 Feb. 1840.

GOWAN, George. Captain. Infantry. Cadet 1771. Ensign 2 Feb. 1773. Lieut. 20 Feb. 1778. Capt. 7 June 1781. Resigned 9 Oct. 1789.

m. Calcutta, 17 July 1789, Miss Mary Parry. Father of Edward Parry Gowan, *q.v.*

THE BENGAL ARMY, 1758-1834   299

Services : Capt. 11th Bn. Sepoys in July 1787. After quitting the Service he settled in Calcutta as merchant and agent.

Note : One George Gowan was Paymr. at E.I.C. Recruit Depot in I.W. in 1803. He *d.* Medina, nr. Cowes, Jan. 1814.

GOWAN, George Edward (1788-1865). Lieut. General, C.B., A.D.C. Colonel Comdt. Artillery. *b.* 28 May 1788. Cadet 1805. Arrived in India 21 June 1806. Lieut. 28 Mar. 1806. Capt. Lt. 17 Jan. 1816. Capt. 1 Sept. 1818. Major 16 Sept. 1829. Lt. Col. 2 July 1835. Lt. Col. Comdt. 3 July 1845. Col. Comdt. 3 July 1845. Col. 1 Apr. 1846. Maj. Gen. 20 June 1854. Lt. Gen. 27 Sept. 1859. *d.* Pen Hill, nr. Bath, 19 Dec. 1865.

bapt. Calcutta 26 July 1788. Son of Thomas Gowan, sec. to the General Bank of India, and Elizabeth his wife. *m.* 1st, 19 June 1820, Mrs. Margaret Bain. (She died Dinapore 5 Dec. 1840, aged 40.) *m.* 2nd, Meerut, 25 May 1842, Mary, 3rd dau. of Leith Alexander Davidson, and sister of George Henry Davidson, *q.v.* (*See also* Henry De Budé.) Ed. St. Paul's school; admitted 1 May 1797.

Services : Served at capture of Cape of Good Hope in 1806 as a Cadet. 1st Troop H.A. 1810-7. Served in Java 1813-5 with H.A. attached to Java L.C. Comdd. newly-raised 4th (Native) Troop H.A. 1817-29. Siege and capture of Hathras; Capt. Lt. 1st Troop H.A. Third Mahratta War. Against the Bhils 1824. To comd. Art. at Mhow 26 Sept. 1829; to comd. Nimach Div. Art. 1 Oct. 1832. Comr. of Kumaon 22 Mar. 1836 till 15 Sept. 1838. Comdg. 2nd Bde. H.A. 3 Jan. 1839. Gwalior campaign; Maharajpur; Lt. Col. comdg. Art. (Bronze star). First Sikh War; Badhowal; Sobraon; Col. 2nd Bde. H.A., comdg. the Art. (Medal). Comdg. Regt. of Art. 1 July 1852. To Divl. Staff of Army and posted to Lahore 26 July 1853. Fur. 1858 till death. Col. Comdt. "F" Bde. R.H.A. 1864-5. C.B. 2 May 1844. A.D.C. to Queen Victoria 1846.

Refs. : Gardiner. Boase. The Times, 25 Dec. 1865.

GOWAN, William. (*See* **MAULEVERER, William.**)

*****GOWEN or GOVIN,**[1] **John.** Major. Infantry. Major Aug. 1758.

Services : Transfd. from Bombay Est. in 1758. Promoted Major by Lord Clive and apptd. second in comd. of the Bengal army, and Comdt. of the Bengal Eur. Regt. Eight Capts. on the Bengal Est., being thereby superseded by him, resigned their Commissions on 31 Aug. 1758. Retransfd. to Bombay in 1761, and apptd. to comd. the Bombay Eur. Regt.

Refs. : Orme MSS.—India, xiii. 3639. *Broome,* pp. 205-6. *Innes,* pp. 70-1. *Crawford,* i. 168.

[1] *Note :* The name appears as Gowan in *Orme MSS.* and in a list

of officers in 1760 (*Williams*, appendix A). Broome, Innes, and Crawford give the name as Govin, although the last named notes that it appears as Gowen in Fort William Cons. of 27 and 31 Aug. 1758.

GOWING, Rayner (1785-1805). Lieutenant, Artillery. *bapt.* Eye, Suffolk, 3 July 1785. Cadet 1802. Arrived in India 27 Aug. 1803. Lieutenant 30 Aug. 1803. *d.* 21 Feb. 1805 : kld. in action at the siege of Bhurtpore.
Son of Samuel Gowing and Ann his wife.
Services : Second Mahratta War ; battle and capture of Deig ; Bhurtpore (kld.) ; Lieut. 2nd Coy. 1st Bn. Art. (d.d. from 4th Coy. 1st Bn.).
Refs. : Stubbs, i. 258. *E.I. United Service Journal,* ii. 458. Pester, p. 386.

GOWITH, William (*d.* 1798). Captain. Infantry. Cadet 1771. Ensign 19 Jan. 1773. Lieut. 12 Mar. 1777. Capt. 3 Apr. 1781. Resigned 21 Dec. 1784. *d.* Broughton, Lancs., July 1798.
Services : N.F.P.
Refs. : M.M. 1798, p. 152.

GRACE, Henry (1757/58-1820). Major General, Artillery. *b.* 1757/58. Country Cadet 1778. Admitted 17 Dec. 1778. Fireworker 26 Dec. 1778. Lieut. 8 July 1784. Capt. 1 Feb. 1795. Major 21 Sept. 1804. Lt. Col. 28 Feb. 1806. Col. 1 Sept. 1818. Maj. Gen. 12 Aug. 1819. *d.* Calcutta 3 May 1820, aged 62.
Nephew of Mrs. Charlotte Grace, of Dublin. *m.* Dum-Dum 29 June 1791, Ann Helena, dau. of —— Daniel (1), of Canterbury. His dau. *m.* Francis Nicholas Price, *q.v.*
Services : Apptd. A.D.C. to Col. Thomas Deane Pearse, *q.v.,* 24 Aug. 1786. Adjt. (*i.e.* Bde. Major) of Art. Mar. 1786 till Apr. 1787, and 26 Mar. 1788 till Apr. 1806. Lt. Col. comdg. Art. at Cawnpore 3 Nov. 1810 till 1817. Leave s.c. to Cape 1817-9. Compiled in 1792 the first " Code of Regulations for the Bengal Army," known as " Grace's Code." A second vol. appeared in 1799.
Refs. : Stubbs, ii. 240-1. *A.J.* xi. 62. Will dated Dum-Dum 24 Mar. 1819 ; codicil dated 17 Apr. 1820 ; proved 11 May 1820.

GRAHAM, Alexander Park (1807-1834). Lieutenant, 32nd N.I. *b.* Edinburgh 5 Mar. 1807. Cadet 1823. Arrived in India 2 Nov. 1824. Ensign 20 June 1824. Lieut. 14 Dec. 1825. *d.* at his apartments in Piccadilly, London, 5 Sept. 1834.
Son of James Graham, of Underwood.
Services : Posted as Ensign to 32nd N.I. in 1825. (? Siege and

capture of Bhurtpore; Ensign 32nd N.I.) To do duty with 29th
N.I. 18 Feb. 1829. Fur. s.c. 20 Feb. 1834 till death.
Refs. : *A.J.* N.S. xv. 180.

GRAHAM, Allan (1786-1816). Capt. Lieutenant, Artillery. *b.*
Harwich 12 Dec. 1786. Cadet 1803. Arrived in India 11 Dec.
1804. Lieut. 27 Aug. 1804. Capt. Lt. 30 Sept. 1808. *d.* Agra
7 June 1816.
bapt. 13 Sept. 1787. Son of Joseph Graham and Mary his wife.
m. Calcutta, 16 Feb. 1810, Miss Harriet Becher. His dau. *m.*
Charles Montauban Carmichael, *q.v.*
Services : Expedn. to Mauritius Sept. 1810 till Oct. 1811 ; Capt.
Lt. comdg. 6th Coy. 1st Bn. Art. Comy. of Ord. at Agra 23 May
1812 till death.
Refs. : Will dated 2 Oct. 1815 ; proved 5 July 1816.

GRAHAM, Charles (1788-1858). Colonel, C.B. Artillery. *b.*
Hamilton 15 Dec. 1788. Cadet 1806. Arrived in India 11 July
1806. Lieut. 3 Apr. 1806. Capt. Lt. 25 Sept. 1817. Capt.
1 Sept. 1818. Major 20 May 1832. Lt. Col. 28 Apr. 1837.
Retired 1 Jan. 1848. Hon. Col. 28 Nov. 1854. *d.* Suffolk Sq.,
Cheltenham, 26 Feb. 1858.
Son of Lieut. Alexander Graham, H.M. 24th Foot. *m.* Dum-Dum,
11 Oct. 1824, Mary Anne Taylor. Woolwich Cadet ; nominated
for R.M.A. 16 Dec. 1803 ; obtained his certificate 18 Feb. 1806.
Services : Served in Oudh 1808 ; in Malwa 1809-10. Nepal War
1814-5 ; Lieut. 4th Coy. 1st Bn. Foot Art., with 3rd Div. (India
medal). Third Mahratta War ; Taragarh ; Madhurajpura ; Garhakota ; Nasridah ; Capt. 4th Coy. 1st Bn., actg. Adjt. Art.
Reserve. Comdd. "Rocket Troop" 1821-6. First Burma War ;
operations of Sir A. Campbell's force in Burma (*Lond. Gaz.* 25 Apr.
1826) (clasp to India medal). Capt. comdg. 3rd Troop 2nd Bde.
H.A. 1828-30. Against the Wahabis 1831 ; action of 18 and 19
Nov. at Barasat. Fur. s.c. 19 Feb. 1832 till 1 Dec. 1834. Actg.
Dy. Principal Comy. Ord. 25 Oct. 1836 till 30 Dec. 1837. Posted to
1st Bde. H.A. 14 June 1837. Bdr., 2 cl., comdg. Sirhind Div. Art.
13 Sept. 1838 till 1843. Lt. Col. 3rd Bn. Foot Art. Fur. 16 Nov.
1843 till 1845. Principal Comy. Ord. 7 Nov. 1845 till Dec. 1847.
C.B. 20 July 1838.
Refs. : *G.M.* 1858, i. 451. Will dated 6 Nov. 1856 ; admon.
4 Feb. 1859.

GRAHAM, Charles (1805-1857). Major. 55th N.I. *b.* London
11 Dec. 1805. Cadet 1822. Arrived in India 7 July 1823.
Ensign 11 July 1823. Lieut. 29 June 1824. Capt. 3 Oct. 1842.

Retired 30 Dec. 1847. Hon. Major 28 Nov. 1854. *d.* Bath 5 Dec. 1857.

bapt. St. Pancras, London, 8 Feb. 1806. Eldest son of Capt. Charles Graham, of Greigston, co. Fife, E.I.C.N.S., Comdr. of the *Bombay*, and Jane his wife, dau. of Capt. James Brown, E.I.C.N.S., Comdr. of the *Alfred.* Brother of John Graham (1808-1861), *q.v.*, and nephew of William Graham (1778-1806), *q.v.*

Services : Posted as Ensign to 1/28th N.I. Transfd. to 55th N.I. (late 1/28th) May 1824. Fur. s.c. 20 Feb. 1830 till 3 July 1834. Actg. Intr. & Qmr. 55th N.I. 26 Feb. 1836. Adjt. 55th N.I. 3 Jan. 1837 till 2 Jan. 1840. Leave s.c. to Cape and N.S.W. 5 Mar. 1838 till 23 Nov. 1839. Persian Intr. to Sir Jasper Nicolls, C.-in-C., 7 Dec. 1839. P.A. at Bahawalpur 23 Sept. 1843 till 1 Jan. 1844. Leave s.c. to Cape 5 Mar. 1844 till 1845. No record of active service.

Refs. : I.M. 15 Dec. 1857, p. 896. *G.M.* 1858, i. 117.

GRAHAM, Donald (1806-1831). Ensign, 31st N.I. *b.* Snizort, I. of Skye, Feb. 1806. Cadet 1826. Arrived in India 15 Aug. 1827. Ensign 7 Jan. 1827. *d.* Revelganj, B. & O., 18 Nov. 1831.

Son of John Graham, of Snizort. Nephew of John Campbell.

Services : Posted as Ensign to 31st N.I. 19 June 1827. Operations against the Bhils 1828 ; Ensign 31st N.I.

GRAHAM, Edward (1775-1812). Captain, Artillery. *b.* Greigston, co. Fife, 14 Oct. 1775. Cadet 1793. Arrived in India 23 Feb. 1795. Fireworker 8 Oct. 1794. Lieut. 17 Feb. 1802. Capt. Lt. 21 Sept. 1804. Capt. 15 Sept. 1809. *d.* Agra 27 Apr. 1812.

Son of Capt. John Graham, of Greigston. Brother of William Graham (1778-1806), *q.v.*, and uncle of Charles Graham (1805-1857), *q.v. m.* (before 1807) (?).

Services : Came out to India as an Inf. Cadet ; transfd. to Art. in 1795. Posted to 5th Coy. 2nd Bn. Art. in Ceylon 22 Sept. 1796. Fourt Mysore War ; Lieut. F. 5th Coy. 2nd Bn. Operations in Ceylon 1803-4 ; capture of Hangeramkatty 14 Mar. 1803 (s.w.). Comy. of Ord. at Agra 1811 till death.

Refs. : Stubbs, i. 162. Will dated Point de Galle, Ceylon, 15 Jan. 1803 ; proved 3 May 1812.

GRAHAM, George Templer (1806-1870). Captain. Artillery. *b.* Bankipore, B. & O., 1 Apr. 1806. Cadet 1823. Arrived in India 16 Aug. 1824. 2nd Lieut. 18 Dec. 1823. Lieut. 28 Sept. 1827. Capt. 20 Jan. 1842. Retired 1 Nov. 1847. *d.* Newlands, co. Dublin, 1 Aug. 1870.

Of Cossington, Somerset. Son of Robert Graham, B.C.S., judge and mgte. at Dinajpur, Bengal. *m.* 1st, Calcutta, 22 Apr. 1834,

Miss Frances Margaret Golightly. *m.* 2nd, Caroline. (She died 2 Apr. 1885, aged 77.) Addiscombe Cadet 10 Aug. 1822 till 18 Dec. 1823.
Services : To do duty with Art. for service in Ava 26 Sept. 1825. First Burma War ; with Sir A. Campbell's force in Burma (India medal). Posted to 1st Troop 1st Bde. H.A. in 1826. Fur. p.a. 10 Jan. 1827 till 6 Nov. 1831. Apptd. 1st Subaltern of Art., Oudh Auxy. Force, 27 Dec. 1837. Fur. s.c. 20 Dec. 1838 till 11 Apr. 1842. On his way home he took charge of two elephants which were being sent to the Viceroy of Egypt as a present from the Indian Govt. Fur. s.c. 1 May 1845 till retirement.
Refs. : *The Times*, 5 Aug. 1870.

GRAHAM, John. Major. Infantry. Capt. 26 July 1764. Major 1 Dec. 1767. Dismissed 30 Sept. 1769.
Services : N.F.P. *Possibly* transfd. from H.M.S.

GRAHAM, John (*d.* 1774). Ensign, Infantry. Cadet 1770. Ensign 26 Nov. 1771. *d.* Badelganj 1 Feb. 1774.
Son of Capt. John Graham, Duchrie. (*Probably* John Graeme, Capt. of Duchray, heir male special in Over Duchray, co. Stirling, who was brother of Thomas Graham, or Graeme, of Duchray, Lt. Col. H.M. 42nd Regt.)
Services : N.F.P.
Refs. : *Or and Sable*, by L. C. Graeme, Edin., 1903, p. 555. *S.M.* 1774, p. 167.

GRAHAM, John (*d.* 1802). Lieutenant, 6th N.I. Cadet 1795. Arrived in India 14 Feb. 1797. Ensign 25 Oct. 1796. Lieut. 30 Oct. 1797. *d.* Amboina, Moluccas, 24 Sept. 1802.
Of Clement's Lane, London.
Services : Lieut. 1st Bengal Eur. Regt. in June 1798. Transfd. to 6th N.I. (? Disturbances in Ganjam, Madras, 1801 ; Lieut. 6th N.I.)

GRAHAM, John (1777-1816). Captain, 8th N.C. *bapt.* Brednoch House, Port, N.B., 19 Sept. 1777. Cadet 1795. Arrived in India 2 Feb. 1797. Cornet 4 Dec. 1796. Lieut. 29 May 1800. Capt. 27 Feb. 1812. *d.* at sea, 14 Feb. 1816, on board the *Bengal*, on his passage to England.
Youngest son of Capt. John Graham, of Duchray, and Christian his wife, dau. of Robert Murray, of Glencarnock. Brother of Lt. Gen. Alexander Graham (Stirling), of Duchray, and of Sarah, wife of Robert MacGregor, *q.v.*, and kinsman of John Graham (*d.* 1774), *q.v.*
Services : Cornet 3rd N.C. Operations in Jumna Doab 1803 ;

Sasni; Bijaigarh; Kachaura; Lieut. 3rd N.C. Second Mahratta War; battle of Delhi; Laswari; Rampura; battle of Deig; Lieut. 3rd N.C. Transfd. as Capt. Lt. to newly-raised 8th N.C. 11 Mar. 1805. Qmr. 8th N.C. 16 May 1805 till 1812. (? Nepal War 1814; Capt. 8th N.C.) Fur. 1816.

Refs.: *Or and Sable*, by L. C. Graeme, Edin., 1903, p. 555. *S.M.* 1816, p. 557.

GRAHAM, John (1787-1859). Major General. Colonel 67th N.I. *b.* Cumbrae I., co. Bute, 13 Feb. 1787. Cadet 1804. Arrived in India 13 May 1806. Ensign 14 Apr. 1806. Lieut. 1 Feb. 1807. Capt. 13 May 1825. Major 29 July 1834. Lt. Col. 11 July 1841. Col. 17 Mar. 1851. Maj. Gen. 28 Nov. 1854. *d.* Edinburgh 27 Nov. 1859.

Son of Rev. Henry Graham and Jean his wife. *m.* Berhampore 24 July 1811, Miss Margaret Freer.

Services: Ensign 28th (Stirling) Regt. of Mil. 27 Aug. 1804 till 9 Apr. 1805. Capture of C.G.H. Jan. 1806; apptd. by Sir David Baird an Ensign in the Bn. of H.E.I.C. Recruits which served with the army under his comd. Posted as Lieut. to 2/9th N.I. Fur. s.c. 5 June 1814 till 4 Nov. 1817. Adjt. Corps of Hill Rangers 15 Apr. 1820 till 31 May 1824. Transfd. to 21st N.I. (late 2/9th) May 1824; to 4th Extra Regt. (became 72nd N.I.) May 1825. Comdd. Hill Rangers 21 Feb. 1825 till 22 Sept. 1841. Posted as Lieut. Col. to 65th N.I. 29 Sept. 1841. Fur. s.c. 31 Jan. 1842 till 10 Dec. 1844. Transfd. to 55th N.I. 2 Oct. 1844; to 10th N.I. 10 Dec. 1844; to 49th N.I. Feb. 1845; to 39th N.I.; to 40th N.I. Dec. 1849; to 11th N.I. Nov. 1850. Fur. p.a. 16 Feb. 1851 till death. Col. 67th N.I. 20 May 1851.

Refs.: *Bishop Heber's Journal* (2nd edn.), i. 272. *I.M.* 1859, p. 993.

GRAHAM, John (1808-1861). Lieut. Colonel. 3rd Bengal Eur. Regt. *b.* London 6 May 1808. Cadet 1824. Arrived in India 27 May 1825. Ensign 19 Jan. 1825. Lieut. 23 May 1828. Capt. 1 May 1846. Bt. Major 11 Nov. 1851. Retired 1 June 1856. Hon. Lt. Col. 1 June 1856. *d.* Exeter 20 Sept. 1861.

Of Ellerslie, Fremington, Devon. *bapt.* St. Pancras, London, 14 July 1808. Son of Charles Graham, of Greigston, co. Fife, Capt. E.I.C.N.S., and Jane his wife. Brother of William Henry Graham, *q.v.*, and nephew of Edward Graham, *q.v.* *m.* 1st, Heanton, Devon, 3 July 1838, Frances Mervyn, only dau. of ZacharyHammett Drake, of Springfield, Devon. (She died Dacca 19 Oct. 1845.) *m.* 2nd, Dawlish, Devon, 17 Mar. 1860, Jane, dau. of Vice-Adm. Thomas Dick, of Dawlish.

Services : Posted as Ensign to 55th N.I. in 1825. Fur. s.c. 24 Dec. 1835 till 10 Dec. 1838. Transfd. to 5th N.I. 14 Dec. 1842. Offg. Executive Ofr., P.W.D., Dacca Div., 1848 till Dec. 1854. Transfd. to newly-raised 3rd Bengal Eur. Regt. 15 Nov. 1853.
Refs. : *A.J.* N.S. xxvi. 285. *G.M.* 1861, ii. 572. *The Times*, 25 Sept. 1861.

GRAHAM, John Richard (1800-1830). Captain, 5th L.C. *b.* 11 Dec. 1800. Cadet 1817. Cornet (?). Lieut. 26 July 1819. Capt. 26 Mar. 1829. *d.* Landour, Mussoorie, 30 May 1830.
3rd son of James Graham, of Barrock Lodge (Richardby), Hesket, Cumberland.
Services : Posted as Lieut. to 5th L.C. in 1819. (? Operations in Kotah 1821 ; Mangrol ; Lieut. 5th L.C.)
Refs. : *G.M.* 1830, ii. 478. *A.J.* N.S. iii. 210.

GRAHAM, Joseph (1799-1880). Major General. 66th N.I. *b.* Newbury, Berks., 2 Jan. 1799. Cadet 1818. Admitted 24 July 1819. Ensign 20 July 1819. Lieut. 1 Dec. 1820. Capt. 12 Dec. 1833. Major 4 Jan. 1849. Lt. Col. 9 Aug. 1854. Bt. Col. 25 Feb. 1858. Retired 31 Dec. 1861. Hon. Maj. Gen. 31 Dec. 1861. *d.* Cheltenham 10 Jan. 1880.
Son of William Graham, of Newbury, woollen draper. *m.* 1st, Sarah. (She died at sea, 25 Nov. 1829, aged 30.) *m.* 2nd, Barrackpore, 19 Feb. 1834, Harriet Anne, only dau. of Gen. Sir James Watson, K.C.B., of Wendover House, Bucks., Col. 14th Foot, and sister of Edward John Watson, *q.v. m.* 3rd, Calcutta, 13 Sept. 1836, Letitia, dau. of Robert Blackall, *q.v.* (*See also* John William Carter.) (She died Agra, 9 Sept. 1848, aged 33.) *m.* 4th, Landour, U.P., 6 Nov. 1849, Mary Ann, dau. of John Login, and widow of James Davidson. (She died 4 Apr. 1884.)
Services : Ensign d.d. Bengal Eur. Regt. Posted as Lieut. to 2/25th N.I. 8 Jan. 1821. Served in Rajputana 1821. Fur. s.c. 23 Feb. 1822 till 26 Jan. 1824. Transfd. to 50th N.I. (late 2/25th) May 1824. Adjt. Purnea Provl. Bn. 17 June 1824. Fur. s.c. 27 Nov. 1826 till 5 Dec. 1829. Adjt. 50th N.I. 6 June 1831. Operations against the Kols and Chuars 1832-3 ; Lieut. 50th N.I. Mily. Sec. to Provl. C.-in-C. 21 Mar. 1835. Actg. Asst. to Agent to Lt. Govr. at Delhi 10 Oct. 1836 ; permanent do. 26 Apr. 1837. Asst. to Gen. Supt. for suppression of Thagi 2 Dec. 1837 till 12 Mar. 1849 ; Supt. do., N.W.P., 12 Mar. 1849 till 1858. Posted as Lt. Col. to 57th N.I. 1 Dec. 1854 ; to 51st N.I. ; to 29th N.I. 15 Nov. 1855 ; to 66th N.I. (or Gurkha L.I. Regt.) 1858. Lt. Col. 1st Gurkha Regt. (L.I.) 1861 till 14 Nov. 1861.
Refs. : *Boase*. *The Times*, 13 Jan. 1880.

GRAHAM, Richard John (1817-1844). Lieutenant, 72nd N.I. *b.*
Camberwell 23 Nov. 1817. Cadet 1834. Ensign 28 Aug. 1834.
Lieut. 22 Feb. 1836. *d.* Doranda, B. & O., 4 Aug. 1844.
3rd son of Sir Robert Graham, 8th Bart. of Esk, Cumberland
(" of Walbrook, wine merchant "), and Elizabeth his wife, only dau.
of John Young, of Battle, Sussex. His sisters *m.* John Hore
Hatchell, *q.v.*, and John Henry Simmonds, *q.v. m.* Doranda,
28 Nov. 1840, Anna Louisa, dau. of John Gibbs, 42nd Regt. Addiscombe Cadet 3 Aug. 1832 till 13 June 1834.
Services : Posted as Ensign to 72nd N.I. 2 Mar. 1835. Reduction
of Jhansi 1838-9 ; Lieut. 72nd N.I. Served with Ramgarh L.I. Bn.
19 Aug. 1840 till death. Actg. Adjt. Ramgarh L.I. 22 July 1842 ;
permanent do. 1843 till death.
Refs. : Burke's *Peerage*, 1923, p. 1017, *s.n.* Graham, Bart., of
Esk, Cumberland. *G.M.* 1844, ii. 558. Will dated 4 July 1842 ;
proved 12 Aug. 1845.

GRAHAM, Robert Stair (1761/62-1803). Captain, 6th N.I. *b.* in
Scotland 1761/62. Cadet 1782. Admitted 15 July 1783. Ensign
13 Mar. 1783. Lieut. 24 Feb. 1790. Capt. 30 Sept. 1803. *d.*
20 Nov. 1803 : kld. in action at the assault of Chaukandi, Baghelkhand district.
m. Chandernagore, Bengal, 17 Sept. 1800, Maria, dau. of ――――
Fellus, and widow of Francis Hodgson (*d.* 1797), *q.v.* (She died
Chandernagore in 1814.)
Services : Sailed for India on the *Earl Talbot*, 6 Feb. 1782, aged
20. Second Mahratta War ; operations in Baghelkhand 1803 ;
Chaukandi (kld.) ; Capt. 2/6th N.I.
Refs. : Will dated 3 Dec. 1802 ; proved 17 Mar. 1804.

GRAHAM, William (1742/43-1829). Bt. Ensign, Infantry. Invalid
Est. *b.* 1742/43. Bt. Ensign 22 Nov. 1781. Invalided before
1798. *d.* Monghyr, B. & O., 21 Aug. 1829, aged 86.
m. (?).
Services : Arrived in India as a Private in 1766. Commissioned
as Bt. Ensign from the ranks.
Refs. : Will dated 9 Feb. 1829 ; proved 4 Sept. 1829. M.I. at
Monghyr.

GRAHAM, William (1778-1806). Capt. Lieutenant, 23rd N.I. *b.*
St. Andrews, co. Fife, 25 Feb. 1778. Cadet 1795. Arrived in
India 2 Feb. 1797. Ensign 24 Nov. 1796. Lieut. 30 Oct. 1797.
Capt. Lt. 15 Aug. 1805. *d.* Allahabad 14 Jan. 1806.
bapt. 26 Feb. 1778. Son of Capt. John Graham, of Greigston, co.

Fife, and Katharine Gregorie his wife. Brother of Edward Graham, *q.v.*, and uncle of John Graham (1808-1861), *q.v.*
  Services : Lieut. 17th N.I. Transfd. to newly-raised 23rd N.I. in 1804. Adjt. Allahabad Provl. Bn. 1805 till death.

GRAHAM, William Henry (1810-1888). Lieut. Colonel. Engineers.
  b. London 1 July 1810. Cadet 1826. Arrived in India 11 June 1827. 2nd Lieut. (?). Lieut. 28 Sept. 1827. Capt. 20 May 1839. Major 5 Dec. 1848. Retired 15 Jan. 1851. Hon. Lt. Col. 28 Nov. 1854. *d.* 30 Rivers St., Bath, 13 Mar. 1888.

  Son of Charles Graham, of Greigston, co. Fife, Capt. E.I.C.N.S., and Jane his wife. Brother of Charles Graham (1805-1857), *q.v.*, and nephew of Edward Graham, *q.v.* *m.* Meerut, 8 Mar. 1832, Margaret Reid, eldest dau. of George Stedman, of Edinburgh, S.S.C. Addiscombe Cadet 13 Aug. 1824 till 16 Dec. 1825. Chatham 31 Jan. 1826 till 15 Dec. 1826.
  Services : Posted to S. & M. 23 July 1827. Apptd. to 11th Div., P.W.D., 1 Jan. 1831. Executive Engr. Mhow Div. 29 Dec. 1833 till 27 Feb. 1837; do. Burdwan Div. 27 Feb. 1837. Leave s.c. 2 yrs. to Cape 17 Dec. 1838. Executive Engr. Meerut Div. 14 Oct. 1840 till retirement. First Sikh War ; Sobraon ; Capt. Engrs. (Medal).
  Refs. : The Times, 16 Mar. 1888.

GRAMSHAW, Robert Michael Oginski (1786-1829). Major, Artillery.
  bapt. St. James's, Westminster, 27 Oct. 1786. Cadet 1804. Arrived in India 12 July 1805. Lieut. 3 May 1805. Capt. Lt. 8 Dec. 1810. Capt. 25 Sept. 1817. Major 29 Aug. 1824. *d.* Kasipur (Cossipore), Bengal, 16 Sept. 1829, aged 42.

  Son of Samuel Gramshaw, comptroller of H.M. customs at Dover, and Anne Jigon his wife, dau. of Robert Wellard, Capt. R.N. Brother of Joseph George de Hielzen Gramshaw. *m.* Foundling Hospital, Cork, 21 Sept. 1822, Sophia, 2nd dau. of Benjamin Bunn, Paymr. H.M. 39th Regt. (She died 25 July 1826.) Woolwich Cadet ; nominated for R.M.A. 30 Mar. 1803 ; obtained his certificate 19 Jan. 1805.
  Services : Sailed for India on the *Earl of Abergavenny.*[1] Sailed subsequently on the *Walpole.* Capture of Hirapur fort 1808. Operations in Bundelkhand 1809 ; Rajaoli ; Ajaigarh. Served in Java 1812-3. Fur. 27 Dec. 1821 till 1824. Comdg. Sirhind Div. Art. in 1827 ; do. in Rajputana 1828.
  Refs. : G.M. 1795, i. 353 ; ii. 622. *A.J.* xiv. 417. Will dated Nasirabad 16 June 1828 ; admon. 23 Oct. 1829. M.I. in St. Stephen's, Dum-Dum.

  [1] *Note :* See note to Charles Davis or Davies. For an account of his rescue, see *G.M.* 1805, i. 232.

GRAND, George François (1748?-1820). Captain. Bengal Eur. Regt.
b. Lausanne, Switzerland, *c.* 1748. Cadet 1766. Arrived in India June 1766. Ensign 10 Dec. 1766. Lieut. 4 Apr. 1768. Capt. 1773. Resigned 15 Mar. 1773. *d.* Cape Town 17 Jan. 1820, aged 71.

Son of —— Grand (of a family originally from Vullierens, canton Morges, which settled in Lausanne *c.* 1649) and his wife, *née* Clerc de Virly, from Normandy. Brother of John Edmund Grand, *q.v.*, and of Jane, wife of John Peregrine Reed, *q.v. m.* 1st, Chandernagore, 10 July 1777, Noel Catherine, dau. of Pierre Verlée (or Werlée), pilote du Gange, a Dane. (He divorced her 8 Apr. 1798, and she *m.* Tallyrand 9 Sept. 1802 (22 Fructidor An x.). *m.* 2nd, Egberta Sophia Petronella, eldest dau. of Egbertus Bergh, of Oudtshoorn, S.A.

Services : Sailed for India on the *Lord Camden* 21 Feb. 1766. Resigned owing to ill health (rupture) and returned to Europe. No record of active service. Apptd. a Writer on the Bengal Est. 1775/76, and arrived in Calcutta June 1776. Collr. of Tirhut and Hajipur in 1782. Apptd. Judge and Mgte at Patna in 1788. Was at Benares with Warren Hastings when the outbreak occurred in Aug. 1781. Removed from the Service owing to his private operations in indigo. Apptd. in 1802, through the influence of his late wife, Counsellor Extraordinary to the Batavian Govt. at C.G.H. Apptd. Inspector of Woods and Lands at the Cape, under the British, 6 Apr. 1806. Author of " Narrative of the Life of a Gentleman long resident in India," 1814.

Refs. : D.I.B. Busteed's *Echoes from Old Calcutta.* B. : P.P., No. 50, pp. 70-5. *G.M.* 1821, i. 280.

GRAND, John Edmund (*d.* 1793). Lieutenant, Artillery. Cadet 1778. Fireworker 30 Oct. 1778. Lieut. 28 Jan. 1784. *d.* Cawnpore 11 June 1793.

Son of —— Grand, of Lausanne, and his wife, *née* Clerc de Virly. Brother of George François Grand, *q.v.*, and nephew of the Chevalier George Grand, of Amsterdam, who was grandfather of Lt.-Gen. Sir George Prevost, 1st Bart. (*D.N.B.*).

Services : Leave s.c. to sea in the *Nassau* in Apr. 1779. Campaign against the Rajah of Benares 1781. Lieut. 3rd Bn. Art. in July 1787.

Refs. : Hickey, ii. 189.

Note : John James Grand was naturalized in 1748 ; George Grand in 1752.

GRAND, Robert Edward (1757/58-1782). Lieutenant, 1st N.C. (The Kandahar Horse.) *b.* 1757/58. Cadet (?). Cornet 19 Feb. 1778. Lieut. 23 Oct. 1778. *d.* nr. Jaunpur, U.P., 4 Mar. 1782 : kld. in action against rebellious zemindars.

THE BENGAL ARMY, 1758-1834

A native of Surrey. Son of —— Grand, of Lausanne, and his wife, *née* Clerc de Virly. Brother of John Edmund Grand, *q.v.*
Services : Sailed for India on the *Duke of Kingston*, 24 Mar. 1777, aged 19. Apptd. Qmr. to the Kandahar Horse by Warren Hastings in 1781.
Refs. : The *Narrative of George Francis Grand*, ed. for the Calcutta Historical Soc., by the Rev. W. K. Firminger, 1910, p. 115.

GRANGE, Edmund. Ensign. Infantry. Cadet 1783. Ensign 6 Mar. 1785. Resigned 27 Oct. 1790.
(*Perhaps* father of Richard John Grange, *q.v.*)
Services : N.F.P.

GRANGE, Richard George (1804-?). Bt. Captain. 10th N.I. *b.* London 4 Sept. 1804. Cadet 1826. Arrived in India 24 May 1827. Ensign 19 Nov. 1826. Lieut. 5 Nov. 1828. Bt. Capt. 19 Nov. 1841. Retired 8 Sept. 1840. *d.* 1866 ? [1]

Son of Richard George Grange, Capt. Madras Est., subsequently E.I.C. Recruiting Ofr. for Dublin district. Brother of Robert Grange, *q.v.* T.C.D. ; Pensioner 2 June 1823, aged 19.
Services : Ensign d.d. 40th N.I. 2 June 1827. Posted to 10th N.I. 19 June 1827. Intr. & Qmr. 10th N.I. 19 Aug. 1831 till Mar. 1838. Offg. Bk. Mr. at Fort William, and Supt. of Cadets, 10 Apr. till 6 Oct. 1835. Fur. s.c. 8 Mar. 1838 till retirement. Retired in 1843 with effect from 8 Sept. 1840. His promotion to Bt. rank of Capt. was cancelled 24 Nov. 1841 and 3 Mar. 1843, but was subsequently allowed to stand. No record of active service. Capt. 5th R. Elthorne Middlesex Mil. 11 Aug. 1853.
Refs. : Alumni Dub.

[1] *Note :* His name appears in the *Indian A.L.* for July 1866 for the last time.

GRANGE, Richard John (1800-1819). Lieutenant, 12th N.I. *bapt.* Wainsford, co. Dublin, June 1800. Cadet 1817. Ensign (?). Lieut. (?). *d.* Chittagong 24 Aug. 1819.
Eldest son of Edmond Grange, of Dublin, merchant.
Services : N.F.P.

GRANGE, Robert (1806-1869). Bt. Captain. 44th N.I. Of the Hon. Corps of Gentlemen-at-Arms. *b.* Dublin 21 Feb. 1806. Cadet 1827. Arrived in India 26 Nov. 1828. Ensign 4 July 1828. Lieut. 25 Jan. 1837. Bt. Capt. 4 July 1843. Retired 24 Aug. 1843. *d.* Cumberland Pl., Southampton, 24 Aug. 1869, very suddenly.
Son of Richard George Grange, Capt. Madras Est. Brother of

Richard George Grange, *q.v.* *m.* Frederica Helen, youngest dau. of Joseph Brooks, *q.v.*, and grand-dau. of Gerard, 1st Viscount Lake. T.C.D. ; Pensioner 2 June 1823, aged 17.

Services : Ensign d.d. 13th N.I. 14 Jan. 1829 ; do. 10th N.I. 3 Mar. 1829. Transfd. to 44th N.I. 5 Nov. 1832. Actg. Intr. & Qmr. 44th N.I. 18 May 1833 ; permanent do. 18 Nov. 1833 till 15 Apr. 1835, and 6 May 1835 till Feb. 1841. Served against marauders in Jhabua, C.I., Mar. 1836. Fur. p.a. 24 Feb. 1841 till retirement. Capt. 1st R. Surrey Mil. 10 Oct. 1852. Subsequently of the Hon. Corps of Gentlemen-at-Arms, and Adjt. 4th Administrative Bn. Hants Rifle Vols.

Refs. : *Alumni Dub.* *The Times,* 27 Aug. 1869.

*GRANT, Alexander (*d.* 1768). Captain. Infantry. Capt. 1756 ? Resigned 31 Aug. 1758. bur. Calcutta 31 Oct. 1768.

Services : Adjt. Gen. at the siege of Calcutta, and was one of those who escaped to the ships at Fulta with Roger Drake, the Govr., 19 June 1756. His excuse for his desertion, *viz.* that he had endeavoured to induce one of the ships' Captains to return, was accepted, and he was pardoned. Battle of Plassey ; comdg. one of the four divs. of Eur. Inf., having voted at the council of war for immediate action. Resigned owing to supersession by John Gowen or Govin, *q.v.* He subsequently returned to India as a " Free Merchant," and became a contractor for mily. supplies in Bengal.

Refs. : *Orme MSS.—India,* xiii. 3639. *Broome,* pp. 140, 206 *n.* Hill. B. : *P.P.* vi. 102. Calcutta burial register. (*See* Addenda.)

GRANT, Alexander (*d.* 1822 ?). Lieut. Colonel. 16th N.I. Cadet 1777. Admitted 18 Dec. 1777. Ensign 26 Feb. 1778. Lieut. 2 Oct. 1778. Capt. 16 Mar. 1796. Major 21 Apr. 1800. Lt. Col. 13 July 1803. Retired 7 Sept. 1803. *d.* 1822 ? [1]

m. Calcutta, 10 Jan. 1794, Miss Jane Hannay (*probably* sister or dau. of Alexander Hannay, *q.v.*, who was in the same Regt. as Grant).

Services : Lieut. 1/1st Bengal Eur. Regt. in Oct. 1779. A.D.C. to Col. Sir Alexander Mackenzie, Bart., *q.v.*, comdg. 2nd Bde., 5 July 1786 till 1790, or later. Capt. 2nd Bengal Eur. Regt. in 1796. Capt. 2/16th N.I. Major 1/16th N.I. Fur. 20 Feb. 1801 till retirement.

[1] *Note :* His name appears in the list of Retired Officers in *E.I.R.* of 19 Dec. 1821, not in that of 14 Aug. 1822.

GRANT, Alexander (1793-1835). Captain. 52nd N.I. *bapt.* co. Moray 7 Aug. 1793. Cadet 1809. Arrived in India 2 Aug. 1810. Ensign (19 Sept. 1811) 27 Oct. 1811. Lieut. (28 Dec. 1814)

THE BENGAL ARMY, 1758-1834 311

2 Aug. 1818. Capt. 14 June 1828. Retired 6 May 1829. *d.* Edinburgh, 13 Aug. 1835, suddenly.

3rd son of Robert Grant, of Wester Elchies, co. Moray. Woolwich Cadet.

Services : Transfd. as a Cadet from Art. to Inf. Posted as Ensign to 20th N.I. in 1811. Transfd. to 26th N.I. in 1812. With 2nd Gren. Bn. 1815-6. Third Mahratta War; Dhamoni; Lieut. 1/26th N.I. Tried by G.C.M. at Meerut on 5 Nov. 1821 for having sent a written challenge to fight a duel to a brother officer; found guilty, and sentenced to be cashiered. The C.-in-C. commuted the sentence to loss of seniority, and he was placed at the bottom of the list of Lieuts. in 1/26th N.I. Fur. 1823-6. Transfd. to 52nd N.I. (late 2/26th) May 1824. He was promoted Capt. by brevet on 19 Sept. 1826, his loss of seniority in the Army being thus restored to him. Fur. s.c. 8 Dec. 1826 till retirement.

Refs. : *A.J.* N.S. xviii. 41.

GRANT, Andrew (1803-1847). Captain, 2nd Bengal Eur. Regt. *b.* Kilmarnock, co. Ayr, 17 Dec. 1803. Cadet 1823. Arrived in India 12 June 1824. Ensign 7 Jan. 1824. Lieut. 13 May 1825. Capt. 10 July 1844. *d.* Simla 2 June 1847.

4th son of Rev. Andrew Grant, D.D., minister of Kilmarnock, and one of the deans of the Chapel Royal, Scotland. Brother of Rev. James Grant, of Edinburgh, Anne, and Margaret.

Services : Posted as Ensign to 1st Bengal Eur. Regt. in Aug. 1824. Leave to Mauritius Jan. 1825 till Jan. 1826. Transfd. to 36th N.I. 9 Nov. 1826. Shekhawat expedn. 1834; Lieut. 36th N.I. Actg. Intr. & Qmr. 10th L.C. 7 Apr. 1835 till Jan. 1836; do. 36th N.I. Mar.-Nov. 1837. Adjt. & Qmr. of Eur. invalids at Chunar 17 Nov. 1837 till Sept. 1844. Transfd. to newly-formed 2nd Bengal Eur. Regt. in Oct. 1839. With Army of Reserve (for Afghanistan) at Ferozepore Oct. 1842 till Jan. 1843; Capt. 2nd Bengal Eur. Regt. Against the Hill tribes in Sind 1845. Leave s.c. to Simla June 1846 till death.

Refs. : *De Rhé-Philipe.* Will dated Chunar 25 Sept. 1844; proved 24 Sept. 1847. M.I. at Simla.

GRANT, Charles (1756/57-1817). Major. 23rd N.I. *b.* in Scotland 1756/57. Cadet 1781. Ensign 8 May 1781. Lieut. 12 July 1782. Capt. 21 Apr. 1800. Major 15 Aug. 1805. Retired 6 July 1808. *d.* Acharnich, Strathspey, Scotland, 10 July 1817, aged 60.

Services : Apptd. Cadet on 3 Apr. 1781, aged 21 (*sic*). Sailed for India on the *Lord Mulgrave,* 26 June 1781, aged 21. Lieut. 17th Bn. Sepoys in July 1787. Capt. Lt. 4th N.I. 27 Mar. 1800.

Transfd. as Adjt. to 1/13th N.I. Capt. 2/13th N.I. Transfd. to newly-raised 23rd N.I. in 1804. Fur. 18 Feb. 1806 till retirement.
Refs. : S.M. 1817, ii. 98.

GRANT, Charles (1803-1882). General, C.B., Artillery. *b.* Bengal 10 Jan. 1803. Cadet 1818. Admitted 20 Nov. 1819. 2nd Lieut. 22 Apr. 1819. Lieut. 2 Aug. 1822. Capt. 17 Jan. 1836. Major 5 July 1846. Lt. Col. 5 May 1849. Col. 18 Feb. 1861. Maj. Gen. 14 Oct. 1858. Lt. Gen. 14 Dec. 1868. Gen. 1 Oct. 1877. *d.* 3 Suffolk Sq., Cheltenham, 13 Jan. 1882.

Son of Robert Grant, B.C.S., Collector at Cawnpore, and Elizabeth his wife. Brother of William Francis Grant, *q.v. m.* Meerut, 20 Oct. 1842, Frances Eliza, elder dau. of Sir Abraham Roberts, *q.v.*, and half-sister of Earl Roberts. (She died Lahore, 15 Oct. 1853, aged 28.) Addiscombe Cadet 8 Apr. 1818 till 6 Apr. 1819.

Services : Served in Bundelkhand 1821; in Oudh 1822. Posted to 1st Troop H.A. 1823. First Burma War 1824-6; Donabyu; Prome; Paghamyu; Lieut. H.A. (India medal). To comd. 3rd Coy. 5th Bn. Foot Art. 15 Feb. 1836. Offg. Agent for gun carriages at Fatehgarh 30 Aug. 1836. Comdg. Art. of Oudh Auxy. Force 27 Dec. 1837 till 15 Feb. 1838. Comdg. 2nd Troop 2nd Bde. H.A. 25 July 1838 till 1846. First Afghan War 1838-9; Ghazni (Medal). Gwalior campaign; Maharajpur (*Lond. Gaz.* 8 Mar. 1844) (Bronze star). First Sikh War; Sobraon (w.); Capt. comdg. 2nd Troop 2nd Bde. H.A. (Medal). Second Sikh War; Ramnagar; Sadulapur; Chilianwala; Gujerat; Major comdg. 3rd Bde. H.A. (Medal with 2 clasps). Bdr. comdg. at Barrackpore 18 July 1856 till 1858. Fur. s.c. 5 Jan. 1859. Col. Comdt. Royal (Bengal) H.A. 11 Dec. 1868. C.B. 9 June 1849.

Refs. : Burke's *Peerage*, 1923, p. 1884, *s.n.* Roberts, E. *Howard & Crisp*, xi. 8, *s.n.* Roberts. *Boase. The Times*, 18 Jan. 1882, p. 6*d.*

GRANT, Charles (1807/08-?). Cornet. 1st L.C. *b.* 1807/08. Cadet 1825. Cornet 4 Dec. 1825. Struck off in England 10 Feb. 1828.

Services : Apptd. Cadet on 19 Oct. 1825, aged 17. Posted as Cornet to 1st L.C. Fur. p.a. 26 Jan. 1827 till struck off. No record of active service.

GRANT, Charles Alexander (1798-1827). Captain, 7th L.C. *bapt.* co. Bucks., 26 May 1798. Cadet 1817. Cornet (?). Lieut. 1 May 1819. Capt. 16 Sept. 1825. *d.* nr. Karnal, 13 June 1827, of cholera.

Son of James Grant and Harriot his wife.

Services : Posted as Lieut. to 7th L.C. in 1819. Siege and capture of Bhurtpore ; Capt. 7th L.C., d.d. with 9th L.C.
Refs. : *A.J.* xxiv. 792.

GRANT, Charles Edward (1809-1841). Lieutenant, 62nd N.I. *b.* London 15 May 1809. Cadet 1827. Arrived in India 20 May 1828. Ensign 19 Jan. 1828. Lieut. 2 Aug. 1832. *d.* Banda, C.P., 22 June 1841.

2nd son of Alexander William Grant and Mary his wife. Brother of Alexander William Grant, 36 Lincoln's Inn Fields, London.

Services : Posted as Ensign to 62nd N.I. 4 Nov. 1828. Actg. Intr. & Qmr. 62nd N.I. 15 Mar. 1829, 11 Aug. 1829, 28 Feb. 1831. Fur. s.c. 18 Mar. 1834 till 16 Dec. 1837. Intr. & Qmr. 62nd N.I. 20 Mar. till 15 Dec. 1838. Asst. Revenue Surveyor, Allahabad district, 13 Nov. 1838. No record of active service.

Refs. : *G.M.* 1841, ii. 667. *Morning Chron.*, 18 Oct. 1841. Will dated Cawnpore 1 Sept. 1838 ; proved 31 Jan. 1842.

GRANT, Francis John (1787-1843). Lieut. Colonel, 39th N.I. *b.* Peter St., Waterford, 12 Feb. 1787. Cadet 1804. Arrived in India 21 June 1806. Ensign 24 Sept. 1805. Lieut. 25 Sept. 1805. Capt. 1 Jan. 1819. Major 1 Oct. 1832. Lt. Col. 25 July 1839. *d.* Nowgong 21 Aug. 1843.

Son of Stephen Grant, M.D., of Waterford. Nephew of Lawrence Strange. *m.* Calcutta, 15 Mar. 1807, Mary, widow of Joseph Sirrell, of Calcutta, attorney's clerk. (She died 12 July 1837, aged 52.)

Services : Served as a Cadet at the capture of C.G.H. in 1806. Posted as Lieut. to 2/19th N.I. Nepal War 1814-5 ; capture of Malaun ; Lieut. comdg. detachment of 2/19th N.I., in 1st Div. (*Lond. Gaz.* 16 Nov. 1815). Adjt. 2/19th N.I. 21 Oct. 1815 till Nov. 1818. Third Mahratta War. Transfd. to 39th N.I. (late 2/19th) May 1824. With 22nd N.I. on Sylhet frontier July till Sept. 1825. Comdg. Rajah Gambhir Singh's Manipur Levy, and Comr. in Manipur Sept. 1825 till 24 Feb. 1835. Posted as Lt. Col. to 39th N.I. 7 Oct. 1839.

Refs. : *I.M.* No. 6, p. 178.

GRANT, George William Alexander Trapaud (1795-1815). Cadet, Artillery. *b.* 19 Sept. 1795. Cadet 1813. *d.* Bombay, 14 July 1815, on board the *Anne.*

Only son of Rev. Patrick Grant, minister of Duthil, Inverness, and Beatrice his wife,[1] dau. of Neil Campbell, of Duntroon. Uncle of Sir Patrick Grant, *q.v.* Addiscombe Cadet 1812-4.

Refs. : *G.M.* 1816, i. 564.

[1] Author of " Popular Models," Edin. 1815.

314 LIST OF THE OFFICERS OF

*GRANT, Henry (1742/43-1831). Lieutenant. Infantry. Subsequently a Free Merchant in Calcutta. *b.* 1742/43. Transfd. as Lieut. from H.M. 84th Regt. 1763 or 1764 ? Resigned before 1 Feb. 1767. *d.* Portman Sq., London, (? July) 1831, aged 88.

Of The Gnoll, co. Glamorgan. Son of Rev. John Grant, rector of Nolton, and vicar of Roch, co. Pembroke, and Elizabeth his wife, dau. of Gilbert Davies. Brother of Rev. Moses Grant, rector of Nolton from 1767, and uncle of Mary, wife of Charles Ranken, *q.v. m.* Calcutta, 29 Mar. 1779, Miss Alicia Camac (*probably* sister of Jacob Camac, *q.v.*). (She died 1837.)

Services : Ensign H.M. 84th Regt., from Volunteer, 16 Sept. 1763. Ensign, h.p., 84th Regt. 25 June 1764. After resigning the Service he settled in Calcutta as a free merchant. He returned to Europe before 1791.

Refs. : Burke's *Landed Gentry*, 3rd edn., p. 474, *s.n.* Grant, of The Gnoll, co. Glamorgan. *G.M.* 1831, ii. 187.

GRANT, Hugh (*d.* 1822). Colonel. Infantry. Cadet (?). Ensign 13 June 1757. Lieut. 1 Oct. 1758. Capt. 12 Oct. 1763. Major 27 May 1765. Lt. Col. 23 Jan. 1767. Col. 12 Dec. 1773. Resigned 14 Sept. 1774. *d.* Moy, nr. Forres, 31 Mar. 1822.

Of Moy. (? *m.* Calcutta, 27 Dec. 1761, Mary Carvalho.)

Services : Raised 4th Bn. Sepoys (eventually became 5th N.I.) at Chittagong in Sept. 1758. He comdd. this Bn., which was known as " *Grant-ki-Paltan,*" 1761-5. Battles of Suan 1761 ; Gheria 1763 ; Buxar 1764.

Refs. : (? Burke's *Landed Gentry*, *s.n.* Grant, of Glenmoriston, co. Inverness, and Moy House, Forres.) *Broome*, p. 473. *Williams*, p. 85. *S.M.* 1822, i. 695.

GRANT, H—— (*d.* 1775). Cadet, Infantry. Cadet 1772. *d.* 13 Nov. 1775.

Services : N.F.P.

GRANT, James. Bt. Major. Infantry. Cadet 1769. Ensign 1769. Lieut. 21 Nov. 1772. Capt. 20 Sept. 1779. Bt. Major 1782. Resigned 28 Jan. 1782.

Services : N.F.P.

GRANT, James *d.* (1772). Cadet, Infantry. Cadet 1772. *d.* Calcutta 28 Aug. 1772.

Services : N.F.P.

Note : Possibly identical with the last.

THE BENGAL ARMY, 1758-1834 315

GRANT, James (*d.* 1800). Lieutenant, Infantry. Cadet 1783. Admitted 17 Sept. 1783. Ensign 5 Apr. 1785. Lieut. 21 Aug. 1793. *d. unm.* Patna 7 Oct. 1800.
Services : N.F.P.
Refs. : Will proved 3 Jan. 1801.

GRANT, James (1807-1859). Major, Invalid Est. 22nd N.I. *b.* Beaconsfield, Bucks., 15 Dec. 1807. Cadet 1827. Arrived in India 16 Oct. 1828. Ensign 16 Apr. 1828. Lieut. 20 June 1836. Capt. 3 June 1845. Major 15 May 1855. Invalided 1 Dec. 1855. *d.* Barrackpore 12 Nov. 1859.
Son of John Grant, of Edinburgh, late Capt. H.M. 78th Foot. *m.* Ferozepore, 28 June 1850, Mary Charlotte, dau. of Samuel Robinson Bagshawe, *q.v.*
Services : Ensign 10th N. British Mil. 8 Apr. 1822. Ensign d.d. 27th N.I. 20 Nov. 1828. Posted to 2nd Bengal Eur. Regt. 4 Mar. 1829. Transfd. to 22nd N.I. 29 June 1829. Shekhawat expedn. 1834 ; Ensign 22nd N.I. Fur. s.c. 22 Feb. 1839 till 27 Feb. 1842. Second Sikh War ; Capt. 22nd N.I. (Medal). Fur. s.c. 1 Feb. 1856 till 1857.
Refs : I.M. 7 Jan. 1860, p. 12.

GRANT, James Cruikshank (1783/84-1826). Lieut. Colonel, 22nd N.I. *b.* 1783/84. Cadet 1800. Was already in India when apptd. a Cadet. Admitted 8 Oct. 1801. Ensign 22 Oct. 1801. Lieut. 30 Sept. 1803. Capt. 22 Sept. 1814. Major 15 Feb. 1824. Lt. Col. 1826. *d.* London, 2 June 1826, aged 42.
Services : Posted as Ensign to 2nd N.I. Operations in Jumna Doab 1803 ; Sasni ; Ensign 1/2nd N.I. Second Mahratta War ; battle of Delhi ; battle and capture of Deig ; Bhurtpore ; Lieut. 1/2nd N.I. Adjt. 1/2nd N.I. 17 Mar. 1810 till 1 July 1814. With 3rd Vol. Bn. in Java 1812-3. Transfd. to 22nd N.I. (late 2/2nd) May 1824. Fur. 1825 till death.
Refs. : N. & Q. cxlix. 43. M.I. in St. Helen's church, Bishopsgate, transfd. from church of St. Martin, Outwich, in 1874.

GRANT, John. Captain. Infantry. Lieut. 13 July 1764. Capt. 31 July 1766. Resigned Sept. 1775.
Services : N.F.P. *Probably* transfd. from H.M.S.

GRANT, John (*d.* 1770). Captain, Infantry. Cadet 1764. Ensign 3 June 1764. Lieut. 18 Aug. 1765. Capt. 1 Dec. 1767. *d.* 19 Nov. 1770.
Services : N.F.P.

LIST OF THE OFFICERS OF

GRANT, John (1749/50-1782). Captain, Infantry. *b.* 1749/50. Cadet 1768. Ensign 31 Jan. 1769. Lieut. 30 May 1770. Capt. 21 Oct. 1778. *d.* Calcutta, 28 Apr. 1782, aged 32.

Son of Capt. Lewis Grant, of Chelsea Coll. Brother of Lewis Grant (*d.* 1822), *q.v.* *m.* Calcutta, Nov. 1774, Rose, dau. of Domingo D'Cruz (Da Cruz).

Services : Capt. 1/1st Bengal Eur. Regt. in Oct. 1779.

Refs. : Will dated 7 Oct. 1780 ; proved 3 May 1782. M.I. in S. Park St. cemetery, Calcutta.

GRANT, John (*d.* 1778). Ensign, Infantry. Cadet 1772. Ensign 19 July 1776. *d.* Dinapore 19 Nov. 1778.

Services : First Rohilla War ; battle of St. George ; Cadet in the " Select Picket."

GRANT, John (*d.* 1785). Lieutenant, Infantry. Cadet 1772. Ensign 19 July 1776. Lieut. 7 July 1777. *d.* Cawnpore 23 Feb. 1785.

Services : N.F.P.

GRANT, John (1783-1852). Major. 66th N.I. *bapt.* Duthil, co. Moray, 29 June 1783. Cadet 1806. Arrived in India 1 Aug. 1807. Ensign 22 July 1807. Struck off 11 Feb. 1809.[1] Cadet 1811. Ensign 31 Oct. 1812. Lieut. 5 Oct. 1817. Capt. 13 May 1825. Major 8 May 1832. Invalided 13 Mar. 1834. Retired 17 Feb. 1836. *d.* 1 Sept. 1852.

Son of John Grant, of Kinchirdy, Duthil, and Christian his wife. Brother of Lewis Grant (1781-1821), *q.v.*

Services : Ensign Loyal Irish Regt. of Fenc. Inf. ; Lieut. Inverness Mil. Barasat C.C. Posted as Ensign to 2/5th N.I. With Mirzapur Local Bn. in 1816. Third Mahratta War. Leave s.c. 8 mos. to sea 8 Apr. 1819 ; 10 mos. do. 1 Apr. 1822. Intr. & Qmr. 2/5th N.I. 25 Sept. 1819 ; do. newly-raised 1/33rd N.I. 1 Oct. 1823 ; do. 66th N.I. (late 2/33rd) 17 June 1824 till 28 Aug. 1825. Fur. s.c. 28 Nov. 1827 till 30 Sept. 1831. Tempy. comdg. Eur. Invalids at Chunar 8 Apr. 1834. Fur. p.a. 31 Jan. 1835 till retirement.

Refs. : Cal. Gaz. 17 Dec. 1807 and 14 Jan. 1808. *A.A.R.* x. 24-9.

[1] *Note :* For having set fire at Barasat on 24 Oct. 1807 to a hut, the property of his bearer (native servant), he was tried at the supreme court, Calcutta, on 14 Dec. 1807, on a charge of arson, and was found Guilty. He was sentenced to death by Sir Henry Russell, C.J., on 8 Jan. 1808. This sentence was commuted to transportation to Botany Bay for 7 yrs., but in less than two years he obtained a free pardon from the Colonial Govt. of N.S.W. (Mily. Despatch of 13 Jan. 1810).

THE BENGAL ARMY, 1758-1834   317

*GRANT, Lewis (*d.* 1781). Major. Infantry. bur. Calcutta 8 Jan. 1781.
Services : N.F.P.

GRANT, Lewis. Major. Infantry. Cadet 1766. Ensign 12 June 1767. Lieut. 4 Apr. 1769. Capt. 4 Jan. 1781. Major 7 May 1781. Resigned 19 Oct. 1795. *d.* before 1801.
m. (?).
Services : Resigned as Lieut. 3 Dec. 1774, and went home. Restored by C.D. as Capt. from 4 Jan. 1781. Entitled to promotion to rank of Major on his arrival, from 7 May 1781. (Mily. Cons. 12 Sept. 1781.) Major 17th Bn. Sepoys in July 1787. Went home on fur. 12 Nov. 1788.

GRANT, Lewis (*d.* 1822). Lieut. Colonel, Invalid Est. 14th N.I. Country Cadet 1771. Admitted 8 May 1771. Ensign 12 Mar. 1773. Lieut. 12 May 1778. Capt. 8 Jan. 1784. Major 30 Oct. 1797. Lt. Col. 21 Apr. 1800. Invalided 17 Mar. 1803. *d.* Chunar 10 Nov. 1822.
Son of Capt. Lewis Grant, of Chelsea Coll. Brother of John Grant (*d.* 1782), *q.v.* *m.* (before 1780) Agnes.
Services : Lieut. 29th Bn. Sepoys in 1780. Capt. 31st Bn. in July 1787. Major 13th N.I. Posted as Lt. Col. to 1/14th N.I.

GRANT, Lewis (1781-1821). Captain, 7th N.I. *b.* Duthil, co. Moray, 1 Jan. 1781. Cadet 1798. Arrived in India 19 Sept. 1799. Ensign 26 Dec. 1799. Lieut. 29 May 1800. Capt. 31 Jan. 1814. *d.* Lucknow, 29 Oct. 1821, of cholera.
Son of John Grant, of Kinchirdy, Duthil, and Christian his wife. Brother of Robert Grant (1780-1803), *q.v.* *m.* Bath, 20 June 1820, (Eliza) Anne, eldest dau. of Sir George Griffies-Williams, 1st Bart., and cousin of George Griffiths, *q.v.* (She died Forres 7 Apr. 1850.)
Services : (? Second Mahratta War ; Cuttack 1803-4 ; Lieut. 2/7th N.I.) Adjt. 2/7th N.I. 23 Jan. 1810 till 25 June 1813. Capt. Lt. 7th N.I. 5 Jan. 1811. Capt. 2/7th N.I. Fur. 1818-20.
Refs. : Burke's *Peerage*, 1859, p. 1061, *s.n.* Griffies-Williams, Bart. *A.J.* x. 109 ; xiii. 488. Will dated 1 Oct. 1821 ; proved 30 Nov. 1821.

GRANT, Ludovick (1749/50-1830). Lieut. Colonel. 16th N.I. *b.* 1749/50. Cadet 1771. Admitted 15 May 1771. Ensign 21 Dec. 1772. Lieut. 20 Mar. 1777. Capt. 19 Mar. 1781. Major 27 July 1796. Lt. Col. 1 Nov. 1798. Retired 11 Aug. 1802. *d.* Kempsey, co. Worcester, 23 June 1830, aged 80.
His dau. *m.* Chase Bracken, *q.v.*

Services : 6th Bengal Eur. Bn. in July 1787. Comdd. 15th Bn. Sepoys 1788-95. In the latter year this Bn. volunteered to proceed upon foreign service to Malacca by sea. Some days later the Bn. mutinied and refused to proceed overseas. It was accordingly broken with infamy, and its colours burnt at Midnapore. Capt. Grant was completely exonerated, and was directed to raise a new Bn., to be denominated the 37th.

Refs. : M.C., Mily. Dept., 26 Oct. 1795. *Williams,* p. 71. *G.M.* 1830, i. 651. *A.J.* N.S. ii. 185.

GRANT, Ludovick (1786-1818). Captain, 16th N.I. *b.* Duthil, co. Moray, 2 Aug. 1786. Cadet 1800. Arrived in India 7 Feb. 1802. Ensign 17 Oct. 1801. Lieut. 13 July 1803. Capt. 1 June 1818. *d.* Calcutta 30 Aug. 1818.

Son of Ludovick Grant.

Services : Second Mahratta War ; Agra ; Laswari ; Gwalior ; Lieut. 2/16th N.I. Capture of Gohad 1806 ; Lieut. 2/16th N.I. Operations in Bundelkhand 1809-11 ; Lieut. 2/16th N.I. Reduction of Kalinjar 1812 ; Lieut. 2/16th N.I. Capt. Lt. 2/16th N.I. 13 Aug. 1815. In the insane hospital at Calcutta in 1818.

GRANT, Nathaniel Philip (1774-1810). Captain, 15th N.I. *b.* New York 18 Nov. 1774. Cadet 1799. Arrived in India 9 Dec. 1800. Ensign 1 Sept. 1800. Lieut. 13 June 1801. Capt. 19 Nov. 1807. *d. unm.* 15 Apr. 1810 : kld. by banditti nr. the city of Karimabad, Persia, whilst on duty in that country.

Son of Richard Grant, of Russell Pl., Fitzroy Sq., London.

Services : Ensign 15th N.I. Operations in Jumna Doab 1803 ; Sasni ; Bijaigarh ; Kachaura ; Lieut. 15th N.I. Second Mahratta War ; battle of Delhi ; Agra ; Laswari ; battle of Deig ; Lieut. 15th N.I. Capt. Lt. 15th N.I. 5 Mar. 1806. He appears to have gone to Persia on duty in 1808, possibly in connexion with the purchase of remounts.

Refs. : Will dated on board the Sloop *Lucky* in Diamond Harbour 4 May 1808 ; proved 22 Aug. 1810. M.I. on a cenotaph at Barrackpore.

GRANT, Sir Patrick (1804-1895). Field Marshal, G.C.B., G.C.M.G. Colonel Royal Horse Gds. *b.* Duthil, co. Inverness, 23 Apr. 1804. Cadet 1819. Arrived in India 6 Jan. 1821. Ensign 16 July 1820. Lieut. 11 July 1823. Capt. 14 May 1832. Major 15 June 1845. Lt. Col. 29 Aug. 1851. Bt. Col. 2 Aug. 1850. Maj. Gen. 28 Nov. 1854. Lt. Gen. 25 Jan. 1856. Gen. 14 Nov. 1870. F.M. 24 June 1883. *d.* Royal Hospital, Chelsea, 28 Mar. 1895.

2nd son of Major John Grant, of Auchterblair, co. Inverness,

97th Foot, and Anna Trapaud his wife, sister of George William Alexander Trapaud Grant, *q.v.* Brother of William Grant (1803-1842), *q.v.* m. 1st, 1832, Jane Anne, dau. of William Fraser Tytler, of Aldourie, Inverness. (She died Simla 23 Sept. 1838.) m. 2nd, Simla, 17 Sept. 1844, Frances Maria, youngest dau. of F.M. Viscount Gough. (She died Chelsea 20 Jan. 1892, aged 66.)

Services : See *D.N.B.* Posted as Ensign to 2/11th N.I. Transfd. as Lieut. to 30th N.I. July 1823 ; to 59th N.I. (late 1/30th) May 1824. Adjt. 59th N.I. 30 Aug. 1824 till 25 June 1830. Fur. p.a. 24 Jan. 1831 till 8 Nov. 1832. Bde. Major in Oudh 25 Aug. till 20 Dec. 1834. Raised Hariana L.I. Bn. 9 Aug. 1836 ; comdd. do. 1 Oct. 1836 till 22 Feb. 1838. 2nd A.A.G. of the Army 22 Feb. 1838 ; 1st do. 9 Nov. 1842 ; D.A.G. of the Army (with official rank of Major) 27 Oct. 1843. Gwalior campaign ; Maharajpur (Bronze star). First Sikh War ; Mudki (s.w. twice) ; Sobraon (Medal with clasp). A.G. 1846-50. Second Sikh War ; passage of the Chenab ; Chilianwala ; Gujerat (Medal with 2 clasps). Against the Kohat Pass Afridis 9 Feb. 1850 (Medal). Fur. s.c. 10 Jan. 1851. Lt. Col. 14th N.I. Transfd. to 23rd N.I. Jan. 1853 ; to 34th N.I. 4 Aug. 1853 ; to 18th N.I. Dec. 1854. C.-in-C. Madras 10 June 1856. C.-in-C. in India (tempy.) 1857. C.-in-C. and Govr. of Malta 17 June 1867. Govr. of Chelsea Hospital 24 Feb. 1874 till death. Col. Royal Horse Gds. and Gold-Stick-in-Waiting to the Queen 17 Oct. 1885. C.B. 3 Apr. 1846. K.C.B. 2 Jan. 1857. G.C.B. 1 Mar. 1861. G.C.M.G. 23 Apr. 1868.

Refs. : *D.N.B.* *D.I.B.* Boase. *Ency. Brit.* 11th edn. Howard & Crisp, xvii. 152, *s.n.* Gough. Walford. Foster's *Knightage*, p. 711. Portrait in oils by G. F. Watts, R.A., in the possession of the R. Horse Gds.

GRANT, Peter (*d.* 1785). Major. 20th N.I. Cadet 1765. Ensign 2 Sept. 1765. Lieut. 8 Jan. 1767. Capt. 18 Sept. 1770. Major 15 Jan. 1781. Dismissed by C.M. Apr. 1781. *d.* Hadley, nr. Barnet, Herts., 4 Aug. 1785.

Services : Owing to a dispute between him and the men of the Regt. under his commd. (20th N.I.) concerning the distribution of the Chandernagore prize money, a mutiny broke out in the Regt. For this he was tried by C.M. in Feb. 1781 and sentenced to dismissal.

Refs. : Williams, p. 69. *G.M.* 1785, ii. 665. *S.M.* 1785, p. 415.

GRANT, Peter (*d.* 1777). Cadet, Infantry. Cadet 1776. bur. Calcutta, 4 Apr. 1777.

Services : N.F.P.

GRANT, Peter (1764/65-1815). Lieut. Colonel, 13th N.I. *b.* in Scotland 1764/65. Cadet 1781. Admitted 23 Sept. 1781. Ensign 30 May 1781. Lieut. 13 Sept. 1782. Capt. 10 Aug. 1801. Major 22 Nov. 1807. Lt. Col. 3 Jan. 1814. *d. unm.* Bareilly, U.P., 14 May 1815.

Services : Apptd. Cadet on 29 Dec. 1780, aged 16. Sailed for India on the *Chapman*, 13 Mar. 1781, aged 16. Lieut. 17th Bn. Sepoys in July 1787. Fourth Mysore War ; Adjt. 2nd Vol. Bn. Lieut. 16th N.I. Capt. Lt. 2/16th N.I. 29 May 1800. Adjt. 2/16th N.I. 29 May 1800. Expedn. to Egypt 1801 ; Capt. Bengal Vols. Fur. 20 Feb. 1801 till 17 May 1803. Transfd. to newly-raised 22nd N.I. in 1804. Dy. Paymr. at Berhampore 1804-8. Capture of Java 1811 ; Major comdg. 4th Bengal Vol. Bn. Posted as Lt. Col. to 1/13th N.I. in 1814.

Refs. : Will dated Calcutta 22 Feb. 1814 ; proved in 1815.

GRANT, Peter (1787-1878). (*See* **GRANT-PETERKIN, Peter.**)

GRANT, Peter Lewis (1780/81-1819). Major, 12th N.I. *b.* Brooke St., St. Andrew's, Holborn, 1780/81. Cadet 1797. Arrived in India 22 Dec. 1798. Ensign 18 Sept. 1798. Lieut. 1 Nov. 1798. Capt. 24 Sept. 1807. Major 24 Apr. 1816. *d.* Calcutta, 12 June 1819, aged 38.

Brother of Lt. Col. James Grant, 18th Hrs. *m.* Anne, dau. of George Powney, of Grosvenor Sq., London. (She died Calcutta, 2 Sept. 1819, aged 26.)

Services : (? Operations in Jumna Doab 1803 ; Sasni ; Lieut. 2/12th N.I.) Second Mahratta War ; battle of Delhi ; Laswari ; Lieut. 2/12th N.I. Adjt. Benares Provl. Bn. 1804. Capt. 2/12th N.I. Bde. Major at Muttra, afterwards at Chunar and Benares, 1807-12. Fur. 12 Dec. 1813 till 1817. Actg. Town and Fort Major at Calcutta 1818 till death.

Refs. : Burke's *Landed Gentry*, 13th edn., p. 1439, *s.n.* Powney, of Milden Hall, Suffolk. *G.M.* 1820, i. 186. *S.M.* 1820, i. 292. Will dated 21 May 1818 ; proved 28 July 1819. M.I. in S. Park St. cemetery, Calcutta.

GRANT, Peter McAlpin (Macalpine) (1792-1815). Lieutenant, 14th N.I. *b.* Rothiemurcus, co. Inverness, 25 May 1792. Cadet 1809. Ensign 18 June 1812. Lieut. (?). *d.* Dinapore 9 Oct. 1815.

Natural son of Capt. William Grant, 42nd Highlrs., by Jenny Gordon.

Services : Posted as Ensign to 14th N.I. in 1812. (? Nepal War 1814-5 ; Ensign 14th N.I., in 3rd Div.)

GRANT, Peter Warden (1794-1828). Captain, 34th N.I. *b.* Forres, co. Elgin, 2 Dec. 1794. Cadet 1810. Ensign 1 May 1813. Lieut. 3 June 1816. Capt. 13 May 1825. *d.* at sea 7 Apr. 1828.

Son of Alexander Grant, of Forres, merchant. *m.* St. Andrew's, Calcutta, 31 May 1823, Miss Eliza Fraser.

Services : Cadet d.d. 15th N.I. 1811-3. Posted as Ensign to 2/17th N.I. in 1813. Mily. student at Coll. of Fort William 1813-4. Nepal War 1814-5 ; Jitpur ; Ensign 2/17th N.I., in 3rd Div. Lieut. 1/17th N.I. Employed on survey duty 7 Oct. 1817 till 1825, and 1826 till death. Transfd. to 35th N.I. (late 2/17th) May 1824 ; to 34th N.I. in 1825. First Burma War 1825 ; Capt. 34th N.I., D.Q.M.G. Leave s.c. 7 mos. to China 21 Mar. 1828.

Refs. : *A.J.* xxvi. 740. Will dated 23 Dec. 1826 ; proved 2 Sept. 1828.

*GRANT, Robert. Captain. Infantry. Capt. 18 Apr. 1765.

Services : Transfd. as Capt. from H.M.S. Out of the Service before 1 Feb. 1767.

Refs. : G.O. of 15 May 1765.

GRANT, Robert (1750/51-1779). Lieutenant, Infantry. *b.* 1750/51. Cadet 1769. Arrived in India June 1768. Ensign 1769. Lieut. 26 Mar. 1773. *d.* Chittagong 26 Oct. 1779.

2nd son of Alexander Grant and Margaret his wife, dau. of Donald Macbean, of Kinchyle. Brother of Charles Grant (*D.N.B.*), and uncle of Charles Grant, Baron Glenelg.

Services : Went out to India as Midshipman on the Coy.'s ship *Admiral Watson*, which sailed from Plymouth 23 Nov. 1767. Became Sec. and Intr. to the Nawab of Oudh at Lucknow. He fell ill in Jan. 1779, and in Apr. was obliged to leave Lucknow for Chittagong to obtain the benefit of sea air. " Accounted one of the best Persian scholars in the East " (*G.M.*).

Refs. : Burke's *Peerage*, 1859, p. 434, *s.n.* Glenelg, B. *Life of Charles Grant*, by Henry Morris, London, 1904. *G.M.* 1780, p. 394. *S.M.* 1780, p. 446.

GRANT, Robert (1780-1803). Lieutenant, 9th N.I. *bapt.* Duthil, co. Moray, 14 Aug. 1780. Cadet 1800. Arrived in India 17 Sept. 1801. Ensign 4 Sept. 1801. Lieut. 11 Feb. 1803. *d.* Agra 10 Oct. 1803 : kld. in action during the assault of the town.

Son of John Grant, of Kinchirdy, Duthil, and Christian his wife. Brother of John Grant (1783-1852), *q.v.*

Services : Second Mahratta War ; Agra (kld.) ; Ensign 2/9th N.I.

Refs. : *Pester*, p. 200.

*GRANT, William (1768-1794). Fireworker, Artillery. *b.* co. Ross *c.* 24 Mar. 1768. Cadet 1792. Admitted 12 Oct. 1792. Fireworker 7 Apr. 1793. *d.* Madras 26 Sept. 1794.

Services : He left Bengal in June 1794 with the detachment of Art. which proceeded to Madras in order to take part in the proposed expedn. against the French Is. off the E. coast of Madagascar. The design was abandoned, and the detachment returned in Oct.
Refs. : *Stubbs's List. Philippart MS.*

GRANT, William (1787-1837). Major, 67th N.I. *bapt.* Inverness 22 Sept. 1787. Cadet 1804. Arrived in India 6 Apr. 1806. Ensign 11 Mar. 1806. Lieut. 2 Feb. 1807. Capt. 31 Dec. 1823. Major 18 Dec. 1834. *d.s.p.* Little Russell St., Calcutta, 3 Aug. 1837, aged 50.

3rd son of Alpin Grant, of Borlum, co. Inverness, J.P. and D.L., Major Inverness Mil., and Agnes his 2nd wife, dau. of Alexander Shaw, of Woodside, Inverness.

Services : Barasat C.C. Posted as Lieut. to 1/10th N.I. (? Settlement of Hariana 1809 ; Bhawani ; Lieut. 1/10th N.I.) Posted to P.W.D. at Banda 17 May 1816, and spent the following 19 yrs. in that Dept. Transfd. to newly-raised 34th N.I. July 1823 ; to 67th N.I. (late 1/34th) May 1824. Tempy. Bk. Mr., Agra Div., 7 June 1824. Suptg. Engr., C.P., 23 Oct. 1834 till 8 Apr. 1835. Rejoined 67th N.I. at Dinapore in 1835, and afterwards comdd. in Arakan.

Refs. : Burke's *Landed Gentry*, 12th edn., p. 812, *s.n.* Grant, of Glenmoriston, co. Inverness. *G.M.* 1838, i. 222. *A.J.* N.S. xxiv. 277. Will dated Dinapore 19 Sept. 1836 ; proved 8 Aug. 1837. M.I. in Scotch burial ground, Calcutta.

GRANT, William (1803-1842). Captain, 27th N.I. *b.* Auchterblair, co. Inverness, 17 Mar. 1803. Cadet 1818. Admitted 25 Sept. 1819. Ensign 26 May 1819. Lieut. 5 May 1821. Capt. 28 Sept. 1831. *d.* 13 Jan. 1842 : kld. in action at Gandamak, nr. Kabul.

Eldest son of Major John Grant and Anna Trapaud his wife. Brother of Sir Patrick Grant, *q.v. m.* Anne Forbes.

Services : Ensign d.d. Bengal Eur. Regt. Posted as Ensign to 1/13th N.I. Actg. Adjt. Orissa Provl. Bn. 8 Apr. 1824. Transfd. to 26th N.I. (late 1/13th) May 1824. Actg. Adjt. 26th N.I. 23 June 1824 ; Intr. & Qmr. do. 12 Nov. 1824. First Burma War ; Arakan 1825 ; Lieut. 26th N.I. Transfd. to 27th N.I. in 1825. Intr. & Qmr. 27th N.I. 12 July 1825 till 14 Dec. 1827. Fur. s.c. 3 Feb. 1836 till 7 Feb. 1839. Bde. Major to troops at Ferozepore 23 Apr. 1839. Postmaster at Ferozepore 29 Apr. 1840. Bde. Major to force proceeding to Afghanistan 4 Nov. 1840 ; do. 3rd Inf. Bde. in Afghanistan 28 Jan. 1841 ; offg. A.A.G. to troops in Afghanistan

25 Feb. 1841. First Afghan War 1840-2 ; Nazian valley ; Kabul disaster (w. in face at Jagdalak 11 Jan. 1842 ; kld. at Gandamak two days later).
Refs. : Will dated Ferozepore 18 Oct. 1839 ; proved 27 Dec. 1842.
Note : In 1855 a rumour was current in India to the effect that he had escaped the Kabul massacre and had succeeded in making his way to England. This was officially denied.

GRANT, William Francis (1806-1877). Colonel. 63rd N.I. *b.* Cawnpore 18 Apr. 1806. Cadet 1822. Arrived in India 21 Oct. 1823. Ensign 11 July 1823. Lieut. 13 May 1825. Capt. 10 Sept. 1838. Major 5 Dec. 1853. Bt. Lt. Col. 20 June 1854. Retired 19 Jan. 1855. Hon. Col. 16 Mar. 1855. *d.* The Albany, Piccadilly, London, 8 Mar. 1877.
bapt. Cawnpore 28 Feb. 1807. Son of Robert Grant, B.C.S., Collector at Cawnpore, and Elizabeth his wife. Brother of Charles Grant (1803-1882), *q.v.*
Services : Ensign d.d. 1/1st N.I. Posted as Ensign to 1/32nd N.I. Transfd. to 63rd N.I. (late 1/32nd) May 1824. Siege and capture of Bhurtpore ; Lieut. 63rd N.I. (India medal). Actg. Intr. & Qmr. 63rd N.I. 6 Nov. 1828. Actg. Adjt. 63rd N.I. 8 Feb. 1830, 10 Mar. 1831, 16 Dec. 1831. Adjt. 63rd N.I. 17 Nov. 1834 till Dec. 1836. Fur. s.c. 16 Jan. 1837 till 23 Nov. 1839. A.D.C. to Lt. Govr. N.W.P. 26 Dec. 1843. First Sikh War ; Sobraon ; Capt. 63rd N.I., A.D.C. to G.G. (Medal). Hon. A.D.C. to G.G. 26 May 1846, and 12 Jan. 1848. Offg. Pte. Sec. to Lt. Govr. of Agra 2 Mar. 1852. A.D.C. and Pte. Sec. to do. 14 Oct. 1853.
Refs. : *The Times*, 13 Mar. 1877.

GRAVELEY, Thomas Milton (*d.* 1776). Captain, comdg. 15th Bn. Sepoys. Lieut. 17 Oct. 1764. Capt. 29 May 1767. *d.* Belgaum, Bombay, 3 Sept. 1776, of wounds received at the battle of Korah 19 June 1776.
m. Chunar, 8 Apr. 1774, Miss Anna Maria Carter. (She *re-m.* John Haynes (*d.* 1822), *q.v.*)
Services : Lieut. Madras Est. Lent to the Bengal Govt. in June 1766 during the " Batta mutiny," and was subsequently transfd. to Bengal Est. Comdd. 6th Bn. Sepoys (became 15th Bn. in 1775) Dec. 1773 till death. Operations in the Doab against Mahbub Khan ; battle of Korah (s.w.—leg broken, subsequently amputated) ; Capt. comdg. 15th Bn.
Refs. : *Williams*, pp. 110, 115.

GRAVES, Harry Meggs (1803-1861). Major General. 13th N.I. *b.* Ballingarry, co. Limerick, 8 June 1803. Cadet 1821. Arrived in India 25 June 1822. Ensign 19 Jan. 1822. Lieut. 15 Jan.

1824. Capt. 3 May 1833. Major 1 Nov. 1849. Lt. Col. 13 Dec. 1854. Bt. Col. 20 June 1854. Maj. Gen. 27 Aug. 1858. *d.* Gloucester 26 Apr. 1861.

5th son of Rev. John Graves, rector of Ballingarry, and his 2nd wife, *née* Baker. *m.* 1st, Gorakhpur, 22 Jan. 1828, Louisa Seton, 2nd dau. of John Pascal Larkins, B.C.S. (She died Mussoorie, 30 June 1836, aged 31.) *m.* 2nd, Mussoorie, 21 July 1841, Katharine, dau. of William Hugh Dobbie, of Saling Hall, Essex, Capt. R.N.
Services : Posted as Ensign to 10th N.I. First Burma War ; Cachar 1824 ; Bikrampur ; Bhadrapur (w.) ; Lieut. 1/10th N.I. Transfd. to 16th N.I. (late 2/10th) May 1824. Actg. Adjt. 16th N.I. for several short periods 1826-31. First Afghan War 1838-9 ; Ghazni (s.w. 21 July 1839) ; Capt. 16th N.I. (Medal). Gratuity of 18 mos. pay for his wounds. Offg. Agent Army clothing, 1st Div., 22 Apr. 1840. Gwalior campaign ; Maharajpur (s.w.) (*Lond. Gaz.* 8 Mar. 1844) ; Capt. 16th N.I., A.A.G. (Bronze star). Comdd. 3rd Inf. Gwalior Contingent 13 Jan. 1844 till 1 Dec. 1849. First Sikh War ; Sobraon ; Bt. Major comdg. 16th N.I. (Medal). Fur. 1850 till July 1851. Posted as Lt. Col. to 16th N.I. Apr. 1855 ; to 59th N.I. Aug. 1855 ; to 13th N.I. Feb. 1857. Bdr., 2 cl., comdg. at Lahore 21 Mar. 1856 ; do. Delhi 9 Aug. 1856. Mutiny campaign ; Bde. Major Delhi F.F. 8 to 30 June 1857 ; capture of Delhi (Medal). Fur. 1859 till death.
Refs. : Burke's *Landed Gentry of Ireland*, p. 275, *s.n.* Graves, of Cloghan Castle, King's Co. *A.J.* xxvi. 219. *G.M.* 1861, i. 707. *The Times*, 30 Apr. 1861.

GRAVES or GROVES, James (*d.* 1774). Ensign, Infantry. Cadet 1770. Ensign 5 Dec. 1771. bur. Calcutta 20 Jan. 1774.
Services : N.F.P.
Note : The name appears as Graves in the burial register ; as Groves in *Dodwell & Miles.*

GRAY, James Clarke Charnock (1794-1891). General. 48th N.I. *b.* London 19 Aug. 1794. Cadet 1811. Admitted 1 Aug. 1812. Ensign 12 July 1814. Lieut. 5 June 1816. Capt. 1 Aug. 1828. Major 1 Sept. 1841. Lt. Col. 27 Aug. 1847. Col. 27 June 1857. Maj. Gen. 20 July 1859. Lt. Gen. 25 June 1870. Gen. 1 Oct. 1877. *d.* 1 Kildare Terr., Bayswater, London, 15 Mar. 1891.

3rd son of James Gray, Capt. R.N. *m.* Calcutta, 23 July 1822, Miss Arabella Kezia McArthur.
Services : Posted as Ensign to 2/9th N.I. Nepal War 1816 ; Makwanpur ; Ensign 2/9th N.I., in 4th Bde., Centre Column (India medal). Transfd. to 21st N.I. (late 2/9th) May 1824. Adjt. 21st N.I. 12 Nov. 1824 till 8 Sept. 1828. Siege and capture of Bhurtpore ;

THE BENGAL ARMY, 1758-1834   325

Lieut. 21st N.I. (clasp to India medal). Offg. Dy. Paymr. at Muttra 5 Feb. 1829 and 28 Feb. 1831. Comdt. 1st Local Inf., Oudh Auxy. Force, 27 Dec. 1837 till Dec. 1847. Transfd. as Lt. Col. to 35th N.I. in 1848 ; to newly-raised 3rd Bengal Eur. Regt. 13 Dec. 1853 ; to 34th N.I. Dec. 1854 ; to 74th N.I. 21 Mar. 1856. Bdr. comdg. Oudh Irreg. Force 11 Feb. 1856 till 1857. Col. 48th N.I. 1857.

Refs. : Boase. *The Times*, 18 Mar. 1891 ; 20 Mar. p. 3.

GRAY, James Coutts Crawford (1802-1852). Major, 18th N.I. *b.* Carse, co. Forfar, 27 Mar. 1802. Cadet 1822. Arrived in India 22 Aug. 1823. Ensign 11 July 1823. Lieut. 17 May 1824. Capt. 26 June 1837. Major 12 Nov. 1848. *d.* Ferozepore 13 Apr. 1852.

Son of Charles Gray, of Carse Gray, and Ann his wife, dau. of David Hunter, of Burnside, co. Forfar. His sisters *m.* Clements Gillespie Macan, *q.v.*, and Henry Carter (1793-1844), *q.v. m.* Garden Reach, Calcutta, 17 Mar. 1841, Jessie, youngest dau. of William Smith, of Ayr. (She died Nasirabad 22 June 1846.)

Services : Posted as Ensign to 2/6th N.I. 20 Oct. 1823. 1st Gren. Bn. July 1824 ; Adjt. do. 24 Nov. 1824 till its disbandment in May 1826. First Burma War 1824-5 ; Chittagong ; Arakan. Rejoined 18th N.I. (late 2/6th) Nov. 1826. Leave s.c. to N.S.W. 29 Oct. 1827 till Oct. 1829. Fur. s.c. 26 Aug. 1836 till 21 Nov. 1839. Offg. Fort Adjt. at Allahabad 12 May 1843. Fur. p.a. 21 Feb. 1847 till May 1849. Comdd. 18th N.I. from Nov. 1849 till death.

Refs. : Burke's *Landed Gentry*, 13th edn., p. 775, *s.n.* Gray, of Carse, co. Forfar. *De Rhé-Philipe*. M.I. in Civil cemetery, Ferozepore.

GRAY, Thomas (1796-1822). Lieutenant, Artillery. *bapt.* Dumfries 5 Sept. 1796. Cadet 1816. Fireworker 25 Sept. 1817. Lieut. 1 Sept. 1818. *d.* Mhow 27 Oct. 1822, from injuries received on 24 Oct. by his horse falling over upon him.

Son of James Gray, master at the Edinburgh high school. Addiscombe Cadet 1813-6.

Services : Posted to 3rd Troop H.A. in 1820 ; transfd. to 2nd Troop in 1822. No record of active service.

GRAY, Thomas (1810-1830). 2nd Lieutenant, Artillery. *b.* Dundee 6 Jan. 1810. Cadet 1828. Arrived in India 9 Feb. 1830. 2nd Lieut. 12 June 1829. *d.* at sea 30 Nov. 1830.

bapt. Dundee 13 Jan. 1810. Son of George Gray, of Dundee, merchant, and Catherine Balfour his wife. Ward of D. C. Guthrie. Addiscombe Cadet 1827-9.

Services : Fur. s.c. 20 Oct. 1830.

GRAYDON, Robert (1782-1815). Lieutenant, 9th N.I. *b.* Killashee, co. Kildare, 8 Aug. 1782. Cadet 1800. Arrived in India 16 Oct. 1801. Ensign 20 Sept. 1801. Lieut. 18 Mar. 1803. *d.* in U.K. June 1815.

2nd surviving son of Robert Graydon, of Killashee, M.P. in the old Irish Parliament, and Mary his wife, dau. of William Bull, of Dalkey, co. Dublin. Uncle of John William Carter, *q.v.*
Services : Second Mahratta War ; Lieut. 9th N.I. Fur. 1813 till death.
Refs. : Howard & Crisp, ii. 46, *s.n.* Penruddocke.

GREATRAKES, William (*d.* 1771). Lieutenant, Infantry. Cadet 1768. Ensign 4 Feb. 1769. Lieut. 16 May 1770. *d.* Monghyr, B. & O., Jan. 1771.

(*Probably* eldest son of Valentine Greatrakes, of Quarter, co. Waterford, a descendant of Greatrakes the " Stroker " (*D.N.B.*)).
Services : N.F.P.
Refs. : The Patrician, ii. 255.

GREEN, Christopher (*d.* 1805). Major General. Colonel Comdt. Artillery. Cadet 1770. Admitted 6 Nov. 1770. Fireworker 3 Dec. 1771. Lieut. 16 June 1774. Capt. Lt. 21 Sept. 1779. Capt. 2 July 1782. Major 24 Nov. 1786. Lt. Col. 8 Jan. 1796. Col. 21 Apr. 1800. Maj. Gen. 1 Jan. 1805. *d.* Calcutta 31 July 1805.

2nd son of Christopher Green, an officer in the army, kld. at Minden, and Britannia his wife, dau. of Charles Hamilton, of Monaghan. Brother of Sir Charles Green, 1st and last Bart. of Milnrow, Yorks. *m.* Anne, sister of John Fortnom, *q.v.*, and aunt of Sophia, the mother of George Edward Hollings, *q.v.* (She died Sloane St., London, Mar. 1817.) His dau. *m.* Charles Brietzcke, *q.v.*
Services : Apptd. Qmr. to newly-raised Golandaz Coys. in 1777. Second Mysore War ; A.D.C. to Lt. Col. Thomas Deane Pearse, *q.v.* Major comdg. 1st Bn. Art. in July 1787. Second Rohilla War ; battle of Bitaurah ; Major comdg. 3rd Bn. Art. Comdt. Bengal Art. 18 Sept. 1798 till death.
Refs. : Burke's *Extinct Baronetcies*, p. 225, *s.n.* Green, Bart. *S.M.* 1806, p. 318. Will dated 30 July 1805 ; proved 7 Aug. 1805.

GREEN, Henry (1792-1814). Ensign, 12th N.I. *b.* Kelston, Somerset, 28 Dec. 1792. Cadet 1808. Arrived in India 27 Oct. 1809. Ensign 10 May 1810. *d.* Cuttack 12 Apr. 1814.

Son of Rev. John Green.
Services : Posted as Ensign to 1/12th N.I. in 1810. No record of active service.

GREEN, John (*d.* 1780). Lieut. Colonel, Artillery. Cadet (?). Fireworker 11 Nov. 1757. Lieut. (?). Capt. Lt. 4 Jan. 1761. Capt. 6 Sept. 1763. Major 1771. Lt. Col. 15 Sept. 1779. *d.* Calcutta 2 Nov. 1780.

Services : Battle of Udhua Nullah 5 Sept. 1763 ; was promoted the following day by Major Adams for good service on that occasion. Comy. of Stores 1775-8.

GREEN, Patrick (*d.* 1786). Lieutenant, Infantry. Cadet 1778. Ensign 1778. Lieut. 20 Sept. 1780. *d.* Chittagong 27 Dec. 1786.

Brother of Thomas Green (*d* 1797), *q.v.* *m.* Calcutta, 30 Jan. 1779, Eleanor Christian, dau. of —— Moinakin, and widow of William Hartley, *q.v.*

Services : N.F.P.

Refs. : Will dated 28 Apr. 1784.

GREEN, Thomas (*d.* 1797). Captain. 25th Bn. Sepoys. Cadet 1769. Admitted 24 Jan. 1770. Ensign 12 July 1769. Lieut. 6 July 1771. Capt. 19 Nov. 1780. Resigned 19 Oct. 1795. *d.* Craven St., Strand, London, Mar. 1797.

Brother of Patrick Green, *q.v.* (*Probably* related to Thomas Green(e) (*d.* 1819), *q.v.*

Services : Capt. 4th Bengal Eur. Bn. in July 1787. To comd. 25th Bn. Sepoys 31 Oct. 1787.

Refs. : G.M. 1797, i. 358. Will proved in 1797.

GREEN, Valentine Henry Frederick (1800-1821). Lieutenant, 16th N.I. *b.* London 7 Sept. 1800. Cadet 1818. Ensign (?). Lieut. 9 June 1820. *d.* Hoshangabad, C.P., 25 Aug. 1821.

Son of Robert Green and Susannah his wife.

Services : Ensign d.d. 10th N.I. in 1819. Posted as Lieut. to 1/16th N.I. in 1820. Served with his Bn. in the Narbada F.F. in C.I. 1820-1.

Refs. : G.M. 1822, i. 479.

GREEN, William Horatio (*d.* 1820). Major, Invalid Est. Artillery. Cadet 1783. Admitted 16 Oct. 1783. Ensign 30 Jan. 1785. Fireworker 15 Mar. 1789. Lieut. 12 Feb. 1795. Capt. Lt. 10 Mar. 1803. Capt. 7 May 1806. Major 25 July 1810. Invalided 1 Aug. 1814. *d.* Chunar 30 Sept. 1820.

m. in India, 24 Aug. 1792, Miss Mary Neish (*possibly* sister of John Neish, *q.v.*).

Services : Ensign in the Inf. Transfd. to Art. in 1789. Third Mysore War ; Bangalore ; Seringapatam ; Lieut. F. 3rd Coy. 2nd Bn. Art. To Madras Aug. 1793 for siege of Pondicherry ;

Lieut. F. 5th Coy. 3rd Bn. Fourth Mysore War; Lieut. 3rd Coy. 1st Bn. Reduction of Kalinjar 1812. Comdd. Eur. Art. Invalids at Chunar 1815 till death.
Refs. : *A.J.* xi. 393. Will dated Chunar 28 Aug. 1820 ; proved 3 Oct. 1820.

GREENE, Anthony (1765-1814). Bt. Major, 7th N.I. *b.* Greenville, co. Kilkenny, 8 Sept. 1765. Cadet 1783. Admitted 24 Aug. 1785. Ensign 1 May 1785. Lieut. 6 Aug. 1793. Capt. 26 Dec. 1802. Bt. Major 25 July 1810. *d.* Chichester 31 Jan. 1814.

7th son of John Greene, of Greenville, and Olympia his 2nd wife, dau. of Robert Langrishe, and widow of George Birch, of Birchfield, co. Kilkenny. Brother of Robert Greene, *q.v.*, and half-brother of William Greene, *q.v. m.* Calcutta, 29 Sept. 1795, Catharine, dau. of Francis Daniel, and niece of James Daniel, of Herbert Lodge, Roehampton, Surrey. (She died Calcutta 21 Jan. 1811, aged 34.) Father of Godfrey Thomas Green, *q.v.*, and of James Richard Greene, *q.v.*

Services : Lieut. 2nd Bengal Eur. Regt. in 1796. Capt. 7th N.I. Was Sec. to the Mily. Board in Calcutta for over ten yrs. Fur. s.c. 24 Dec. 1812 till death.

Refs. : Burke's *Landed Gentry of Ireland*, p. 277, *s.n.* Greene, late of Greenville. *Greene*, p. 23. *G.M.* 1796, i. 349 ; 1814, i. 408. Will dated 4 Jan. 1813 ; proved in 1814. M.I. Chichester cathedral.

GREENE, George Nuttall (1812-1893). Lieut. Colonel. 70th N.I. *b.* Greenville 11 July 1812. Cadet 1831. Arrived in India 27 Oct. 1832. Ensign (8 Dec. 1831) 19 Dec. 1833. Lieut. 1 July 1836. Capt. 18 Mar. 1847. Bt. Major 11 Sept. 1859. Retired 31 Dec. 1861. Hon. Lt. Col. 31 Dec. 1861. *d. unm.* at his residence, Fairholme, Beckenham, Kent, 2 Aug. 1893.

Of Newtown House, Kilkenny. *bapt.* Kilmacow, Kilkenny, 3 Aug. 1812. 4th son of Joseph Greene, of Low Grange, and Lake View, co. Kilkenny, and Jane his wife, dau. of William Newport. Brother of Joseph Greene (1808-1890), *q.v.* T.C.D. ; Pensioner 19 Oct. 1829, aged 17. Addiscombe Cadet 19 Mar. 1830 till 8 Dec. 1831.

Services : d.d. 48th N.I. 7 Dec. 1832 ; do. 19th N.I. 12 Dec. 1833. Posted as Ensign to 70th N.I. 19 Dec. 1833. Actg. Adjt. Left Wing 70th N.I. 20 Sept. 1842. Actg. Adjt. 70th N.I. 25 Nov. 1843. Gwalior campaign ; Maharajpur ; Lieut. 70th N.I. (Bronze star). Adjt. 70th N.I. 20 Jan. 1844 till May 1847. Second Sikh War ; Ramnagar ; passage of Chenab ; Chilianwala ; Gujerat ; Capt. 70th N.I. (Medal with 2 clasps). Fur. 18 Mar. 1851 till Dec. 1854. Offg. D.J.A.G., Presdy. Div., 23 Oct. 1857.

THE BENGAL ARMY, 1758-1834

Refs. : Burke's *Landed Gentry of Ireland*, p. 278, *s.n.* Greene, late of Greenville. *Greene*, p. 7. *Alumni Dub. The Times*, 5 Aug. 1893.

GREENE, George Philip William (1787-1819). Lieutenant, 15th N.I. *b.* London 15 June 1787. Cadet 1804. Arrived in India 6 Apr. 1806. Ensign 18 Apr. 1806. Lieut. 19 Nov. 1807. *d. unm.* " Ghoca Purchar Nuddee " (? Parsa) 17 Apr. 1819.

Son of William Greene, Sec. to Lord Macartney, and Mary his wife, dau. of Rev. Philip York.

Services : Posted to 1/15th N.I. in 1807. Capture of Java 1811 ; Lieut. 3rd Bengal Vol. Bn. Served with 3rd Vols. till 1816. Third Mahratta War ; Asirgarh ; Lieut. 1/15th N.I.

Refs. : Will dated 2 Mar. 1811 ; proved 24 May 1819.

GREENE, Godfrey (Hayes) (1806-1857). Lieutenant. 48th N.I. *b.* 1806. Cadet 1823. Arrived in India 16 Oct. 1824. Ensign 13 June 1824. Lieut. 17 Jan. 1827. Resigned in England 15 July 1835. *d. unm.* 13 Aug. 1857 : bur. Kilmacow.

Of Rockview, co. Kilkenny. *bapt.* Tallow, co. Waterford, 8 May 1806. 4th son of William Greene, *q.v.*, of Lota, and Jane his wife. Cousin-german of Joseph Greene (1787-1814), *q.v.* T.C.D. ; Fellow Commoner 4 Nov. 1822, aged 17.

Services : Posted as Ensign to 48th N.I. in 1825. Actg. Adjt. to 5 Coys. 48th N.I. 10 Dec. 1827. Actg. Adjt. 48th N.I. 2 Jan. 1830. Wahabi rising 1831 ; Lieut. 48th N.I. Fur. s.c. 15 Jan. 1833 till July 1836, when his resignation was accepted with effect from 15 July 1835. Pensioned on h.p. as Lieut. 14 Dec. 1836.

Refs. : Burke's *Landed Gentry of Ireland*, p. 277, *s.n.* Greene, late of Greenville. *Alumni Dub. Greene*, p. 20.

GREENE, Godfrey Thomas (1807-1886). Colonel, C.B. Engineers. *b.* Calcutta 1 Jan. 1807. Cadet 1824. Arrived in India 21 May 1825. Lieut. 1 May 1824. Capt. 3 Feb. 1839. Major 5 May 1846. Lt. Col. 4 Nov. 1848. Retired 1 May 1849. Hon. Col. 28 Nov. 1854. *d.* 25 Hyde Gdns., Eastbourne, 27 Dec. 1886.

Of Kirby Cane Hall, Norfolk. 3rd son of Anthony Greene, *q.v.*, and Catharine his wife. Brother of James Richard Greene, *q.v. m.* Bareilly, 8 Aug. 1831, Harriett Elliot, 4th dau. of William Wickham Cowell, B.C.S. (She died 5 June 1894.) Addiscombe Cadet 1821-3.

Services : Posted to S. & M. 12 Oct. 1825. Siege and capture of Bhurtpore ; Lieut. S. & M. (India medal). Asst. to Supt. Delhi canal 12 Aug. 1826. Executive Ofr. 8th (Rohilkhand) Div. P.W.D. 16 Apr. 1829 ; do. 7th (Cawnpore) Div. 27 Dec. 1833. Fur. p.a.

4 Feb. 1838 till 6 Jan. 1841. Executive Engr. Benares Div. 20 Jan. 1841 ; do. Dinapore 10 Mar. 1841. Garr. Engr. Fort William, and civil architect Presdy., 18 Aug. 1842. Sec. to Mily. Board 17 Nov. 1843. Offg. for Col. W. N. Forbes, *q.v.*, in charge of Calcutta Mint 26 Nov. 1847 till retirement. Dir. of Dept. of Engineering and Architectural Works to the Admiralty 1850-65. C.B.

Refs. : Burke's *Landed Gentry of Ireland*, p. 278, *s.n.* Greene, late of Greenville. *Greene*, p. 24. *The Times*, 29 Dec. 1886.

GREENE, James Richard (1805-1825). Lieutenant, Artillery. *b.* Calcutta 18 Apr. 1805. Cadet 1820. Arrived in India Nov. 1821. 2nd Lieut. 9 June 1821. Lieut. 1 May 1824. *d. unm.* Garden Reach, Calcutta, 5 Oct. 1825, of Arakan fever.

2nd son of Anthony Greene, *q.v.*, and Catharine his wife. Brother of Godfrey Thomas Greene, *q.v.*, and nephew of Robert Greene, *q.v.* Addiscombe Cadet 1819-21.

Services : Posted as 2nd Lieut. to 5th Coy. 2nd Bn. Art. First Burma War ; Arakan 1824-5.

Refs. : Burke's *Landed Gentry of Ireland,* p. 278, *s.n.* Greene, late of Greenville. *Greene*, p. 24. M.I. in S. Park St. cemetery, Calcutta.

GREENE, Joseph (1787-1814). Lieutenant, 25th N.I. *b.* Dungarvan, co. Kilkenny, 21 Dec. 1787. Cadet 1803. Arrived in India 18 Mar. 1805. Ensign 6 Apr. 1805. Lieut. 7 Apr. 1805. *d. unm.* Calcutta 21 Aug. 1814.

2nd son of Joseph Greene, of Shandon, and of Newtown House, co. Waterford, Major in the army, and Hannah Townsend his 1st wife. Cousin-german of Godfrey Greene, *q.v.*, and 1st cousin once removed of Joseph Greene (1808-1890), *q.v.*

Services : Posted as Lieut. to 25th N.I. in 1806. Expedn. to Mauritius 1810-1 ; Qmr. 2nd Vol. Bn.

Refs. : Burke's *Landed Gentry of Ireland,* p. 277, *s.n.* Greene, late of Greenville. *Greene*, p. 11. *G.M.* 1815, i. 118. M.I. in S. Park St. cemetery, Calcutta.

GREENE, Joseph (1808-1890). 2nd Lieutenant. Artillery. *b.* Derry Lodge, Kilkenny, 14 July 1808. Cadet 1828. Arrived in India 5 May 1829. 2nd Lieut. 8 Jan. 1829. Resigned 7 Aug. 1833. *d. unm.* 8 Blackhall St., Dublin, 24 Jan. 1890.

Of Newtown House, Kilkenny. *bapt.* Derry Lodge 5 Aug. 1808. 3rd son of Joseph Greene, of Low Grange, and Lake View, co. Kilkenny, high sheriff 1808, and Jane his wife. Brother of George Nuttall Greene, *q.v.*, and grand-nephew of William Greene, *q.v.* Addiscombe Cadet 1825-7. Apptd. Cadet in 1824, but permitted to remain in England owing to ill health.

THE BENGAL ARMY, 1758-1834   331

Services : Leave s.c. to China Aug. 1829. Fur. s.c. 15 July 1830 till resignation. Actually resided in India for 3½ mos. only. Distributor of Stamps, Kilkenny, 1848-73.

Refs. : Burke's *Landed Gentry of Ireland*, p. 278, *s.n.* Greene, late of Greenville. *Greene*, p. 7. *The Times*, 1 Feb. 1890.

GREENE, Robert (1761-1818). Lieut. Colonel, 13th N.I. *b.* Greenville 19 Sept. 1761. Cadet 1779. Admitted 19 Nov. 1779. Ensign 1780. Lieut. 5 Aug. 1781. Capt. 31 July 1799. Major 21 Sept. 1804. Lt. Col. 18 Apr. 1810. *d.* Barrackpore 5 Apr. 1818.

6th son of John Greene, of Greenville, and Olympia his 2nd wife. Brother of Anthony Greene, *q.v. m.* Calcutta, 17 Aug. 1788, Miss Lucy Evance. (*See also* Joseph Gascoyne.)

Services : Sailed for India on the *London*, 12 Feb. 1780, aged 18. Lieut. 16th N.I. Apptd. Inspector of victualling horses, Fort William, 15 Mar. 1786. Fort Adjt. at Fort William 1787-90. Operations in Jumna Doab 1803 ; Sasni ; Capt. 8th N.I. Second Mahratta War ; Major 8th N.I. Transfd. as Lt. Col. to 1/16th N.I. in 1810. Suspended from rank and pay for 6 mos. by sentence of G.C.M. 25 Sept. 1815. Transfd. to 30th N.I. in 1816 ; to 13th N.I. in 1817. Translated from the Persian, 1803, a " Chronological, Biographical and Theological History of the Primary and Subsequent Ages of the World."

Refs. : Burke's *Landed Gemtry of Ireland*, p. 277, *s.n.* Greene, late of Greenville. *Greene*, p. 22.

GREENE, Thomas (1761/62-1819). Lieut. Colonel. Artillery. *b.* in Ireland 1761/62. Country Cadet 1778. Admitted 7 Nov. 1779. Fireworker 31 Dec. 1778. Lieut. 2 Feb. 1785. Capt. Lt. 8 Jan. 1796. Capt. 6 Nov. 1800. Major 21 Sept. 1804. Lt. Col. 5 Sept. 1806. Retired 11 Dec. 1810. *d.* London 21 Feb. 1819.

(*Possibly* elder son of Michael Greene, of Kilnamack, co. Waterford, and Greenmount, co. Tipperary, and Jane his wife, eldest dau. of Thomas Bunbury, of Shronell, co. Tipperary. *Probably* related to Thomas Green, *q.v.*, under whose Will he was a beneficiary.) *m.* (before 1792) ?

Services : Second Mysore War 1781-5 ; Lieut. F. 5th Coy. 1st Bn. Art. Lieut. 1st Bn. Art. in July 1787. Third Mysore War ; Bangalore ; Seringapatam ; Lieut. 4th Coy. 2nd Bn., offg. Qmr. Operations in Jumna Doab 1803 ; Sasni ; Bijaigarh ; Kachaura ; Capt. 4th Coy. 2nd Bn. Second Mahratta War ; Aligarh ; battle of Delhi ; Agra ; Laswari ; siege of Gwalior ; Capt. comdg. 1st Coy. 1st Bn. Fur. 17 Feb. 1808 till retirement.

Refs. : (? Burke's *Landed Gentry of Ireland*, p. 276, *s.n.* Greene, late of Greenville. *Greene*, p. 45.)

GREENE, William (1748-1829). Major. Infantry. b. 17 Jan. 1748. Cadet 1769. Ensign 1769. Lieut. 21 Nov. 1772. Capt. 12 Sept. 1779. Major (?). Resigned 3 Jan. 1785. d. Janeville, nr. Tallow, 3 June 1829.

Of Lota, co. Cork, and Janeville, co. Waterford. High sheriff co. Kilkenny 1823 ; M.P. for Dungarvan 1802-6. 4th son of John Greene, of Greenville, and Frances his 1st wife, dau. of Joseph Nicholson, of Richardstown, co. Tipperary. Half-brother of Anthony Greene, q.v., uncle of Joseph Greene (1787-1814), q.v., and grand-uncle of Joseph Greene (1808-1890), q.v. m. Suir Castle, co. Tipperary, Oct. 1789, Hon. Jane, 3rd dau. of Hugh, 2nd Lord Massy. (She died Waterford, 4 Jan. 1848, aged 83.) Father of Godfrey (Hayes) Greene, q.v.

Services : N.F.P.

Refs. : Burke's *Landed Gentry of Ireland*, p. 277, s.n. Greene, late of Greenville. *Greene*, p. 18. Portrait in oils, life size, painted in 1781 at Calcutta, in the possession of the family.

GREENE, William Sheppey (1766-1811). Major, 27th N.I. Mily. Auditor Gen. b. 1766. Cadet 1781. Admitted 9 Oct. 1781. Ensign 22 Apr. 1781. Lieut. 12 Aug. 1782. Capt. 29 May 1800. Major 11 July 1807. d. Calcutta 1 Apr. 1811, aged 44.

Son of Joshua Sheppey Greene, of Dublin, and Elizabeth his wife, dau. of —— Conron. m. Calcutta, 9 Oct. 1800, Miss Charlotte Christiana Corson. (She died Boulogne 27 Oct. 1851.)

Services : Apptd. Cadet on 13 Feb. 1781, aged 16. Sailed for India on the *Essex*, 13 Mar. 1781, aged 16. Lieut. 32nd Bn. Sepoys in July 1787. Lieut. 2nd Bengal Eur. Regt. ; Capt. do. Transfd. as Capt. to Marine Bn. (became 20th N.I.) ; to newly-raised 27th N.I. in 1805. Dy. Mily. Auditor Gen. in 1803 ; Mily. Auditor Gen. 1804 till death.

Refs. : Greene. S.M. 1811, p. 960. Will dated Calcutta 11 Feb. 1808 ; proved 8 Apr. 1811. M.I. in N. Park St. cemetery, Calcutta.

GREENING, Thomas (1785-1807). Ensign. Unposted. b. London. 1 Sept. 1785. Cadet 1804. Arrived in India 13 May 1806. Ensign 20 Apr. 1806. d. Barasat C.C. 14 Jan. 1807.

Son of Thomas Greening and Margaret his wife.

Services : Was an unposted Ensign undergoing instruction at the Barasat C.C. when his death occurred.

GREENSTREET, John (1781-1856). General. Colonel 60th N.I. d. Hitchin, Herts., 1781. Cadet 1795. Arrived in India 4 Mar. 1797. Ensign 22 Nov. 1796. Lieut. 30 Oct. 1797. Capt. 10 Jan. 1805. Major 25 Apr. 1810. Lt. Col. 25 Jan. 1815. Lt. Col. Comdt. 1 May 1824. Col. 5 June 1829. Maj. Gen. 10 Jan. 1837.

Lt. Gen. 9 Nov. 1846. Gen. 20 June 1854. *d.* Frenchay, nr. Bristol, 9 Apr. 1856, aged 74.

Nephew of Thomas Hawkins, *q.v. m.* (before 1821) Sarah. (She died 26 Aug. 1855, aged 64.)

Services : Lieut. 5th N.I. in June 1798. Adjt. 1/15th N.I. 29 May 1800 till 1804. (? Operations in Jumna Doab 1803 ; Sasni ; Bijaigarh ; Kachaura.) Second Mahratta War ; Koil ; Aligarh ; battle of Delhi ; Agra ; Laswari ; battle and capture of Deig (horse kld.—*Cal. Gaz.* 6 Dec. 1804) ; Bhurtpore (India medal with 5 clasps). Adjt. & Qmr. 15th N.I. 1805-6. A.D.C. to V.P. in Council 5 Aug. 1809. Fur. p.a. 12 Nov. 1811 till 23 Oct. 1813. Nepal War 1814-5 ; Lt. Col. comdg. 2/15th N.I., in 4th Div. Nepal War 1816 ; in 4th Bde., Centre Column (6th clasp to India Medal). Siege and capture of Hathras ; Lt. Col. comdg. 2/15th N.I. Third Mahratta War ; apptd. to comd. as Bdr. the Bengal Bde. serving with Bdr.-Gen. Doveton's force ; Asirgarh. Transfd. to 2/30th N.I. ; as Lt. Col. Comdt. to 60th N.I. (late 2/30th) May 1824. Fur. p.a. 15 Jan. 1825 till death. Col. 60th N.I. June 1829.

Refs. : E.I.M.C. iii. 78-80. *Boase. G.M.* 1856, i. 551. *I.M.* 18 Apr. 1856, p. 243 (where age at death is given as 75.)

GREENTREE, John (*d.* 1763). Ensign, Bengal Eur. Regt. Cadet 1760. Ensign 18 Sept. 1761. *d.* 5th, 6th or 11th Oct. 1763 : massacred at or near Patna by order of Nawab Mir Muhammad Kasim. (See note to John Gordon.*)

Services : N.F.P.

Refs. : MS. list in India Office entitled, "List of Persons killed in the Massacre at Patna, and at other places during the Troubles, 1763." *Broome,* p. 365. *Innes,* p. 169. *Firminger,* p. 71. Name on monument in Patna city.

GREENWATER, Weston (*d.* 1765). Ensign, Infantry. Cadet (?). Ensign 29 Oct. 1764. *d.* 1765.

Services : N.F.P.

GREGORY, Robert Bourke (*d.* 1824). Major General, C.B. Colonel 12th N.I. Country Cadet 1778. Admitted 11 Aug. 1778. Ensign 17 Mar. 1779. Lieut. 20 Jan. 1781. Capt. 8 Jan. 1796. Major 13 July 1803. Lt. Col. 23 Sept. 1804. Col. 4 June 1813. Maj. Gen. 12 Aug. 1819. *d.* Benares 7 Nov. 1824.

Eldest son of Robert Gregory, of Coole Park, co. Galway, Chairman E.I.Co., and Maria Nimmo his wife. Nephew of "Aunt Scully, of Tipperary." *m.* Calcutta, 23 Oct. 1822, Mrs. Deborah Matilda Lowe, of Calcutta. His natural son, William McGregor (*see* Appendix), was a Local Lieut. in the Rohilla Cav.

Services : First Mahratta War ; capture of fort Sipri Jan. 1781 (w.) ; with detachment under Lt. Col. Jacob Camac, *q.v.* Lieut. 9th Bn. Sepoys in July 1787. Capt. 1/8th N.I. in Aug. 1798. Operations in Jumna Doab 1803 ; Sasni ; Bijaigarh ; Kachaura ; Capt. 2/12th N.I. Second Mahratta War ; Agra ; Laswari (w.) ; capture of Deig ; Bhurtpore (w. in 1st assault on 9 Jan. 1805) ; Major comdg. 2/12th N.I. Operations in Oudh 1808 ; reduction of forts Bhadri ; Samanpur ; Gurha ; Lt. Col. 1/12th N.I., comdg. the force. Nepal War 1814-5 ; Lt. Col. comdg. 1/12th N.I., in aid of civil authorities in Tirhut, afterwards comdg. Reserve to 3rd Div. Posted as Col. to 12th N.I. 6 Nov. 1818. Apptd. to the Staff in 1822. Maj. Gen. comdg. at Dinapore. C.B. 4 June 1815.

Refs. : Burke's *Landed Gentry of Ireland*, p. 280, *s.n.* Gregory, of Coole Park ; p. 632, *s.n.* 'Scully, of Mantle Hill, Tipperary. Burke's *Landed Gentry*, 14th edn., p. 43, *s.n.* Gregory, of Ashfordbye and West Court, co. Kilkenny. *E.I.M.C.* ii. 441-7. *B. : P.P.* iii. 103. *N. & Q.* 12 S. vii. 478. Will dated Partabgarh 1 Dec. 1818 ; proved 17 Nov. 1824. Portrait in Zoffany's " Cock Fight."

GREGORY, William (1789-1842). Major, Invalid Est. 61st N.I. *b.* Barcelona, Spain, 28 Sept. 1789. Cadet 1804. Arrived in India 11 Dec. 1805. Ensign 10 Mar. 1805. Lieut. 1 Feb. 1807. Capt. 12 Aug. 1820. Major 26 Sept. 1833. Invalided 11 Oct. 1838. *d.* at sea, 7 Jan. 1842, on board the *Lady Macnaghten,* on his passage from Sydney to Calcutta.

bapt. St. Just, Barcelona, 28 Sept. 1789. Eldest son of William Gregory, sometime H.M. consul at Barcelona, and Mary Anne his wife. *m.* Mary Virtue, only dau. of Thomas Browne Evans. (She died 16 June 1859, aged 65.) Marlow Cadet.

Services : Posted as Ensign to 17th N.I. in 1806. Transfd. as Lieut. to 3rd N.I. in 1807. (? Operations in Bundelkhand 1809 ; Rajaoli ; Ajaigarh ; Lieut. 1/3rd N.I.) Fur. s.c. 9 Mar. 1811 till 13 Sept. 1815. Adjt. 2/3rd N.I. 7 May 1816 till 1818. Adjt. Bareilly Provl. Bn. 1819-20 ; tempy. comdg. do. 6 Feb. 1821. S.A.C.G. 7 Mar. 1822. Transfd. to newly-raised 31st N.I. 11 July 1823 ; to 61st N.I. (late 1/31st) May 1824. D.A.C.G., 2 cl., 27 Mar. 1826 ; do. 1 cl., 7 Mar. 1828. A.C.G., 2 cl., 29 Nov. 1833 till 12 July 1834. Leave s.c. to Cape and Tasmania 8 Sept. 1835 till 21 June 1838. Leave s.c. 2 yrs. 10 June 1841.

Refs. : A.J. N.S. xxxviii. 183. *G.M.* 1842, ii. 334. *The Times,* 18 May 1842. Will dated 4 Dec. 1841 ; proved 16 Mar. 1842.

GREIG, Charles (1749/50-1825). Captain. 13th N.I. *b.* 1749/50. Cadet 1781. Arrived in India 10 May 1781. Ensign 23 Sept. 1781. Lieut. 27 June 1783. Bt. Capt. 7 Jan. 1796. Capt. Lt.

THE BENGAL ARMY, 1758-1834   335

21 Feb. 1801. Capt. (?). Retired 11 Feb. 1801. *d.* Newington, Edinburgh, 16 Oct. 1825, aged 75.
m. Edinburgh, 8 Oct. 1800, Miss Mary Anne Anderson. (She died Edinburgh Mar. 1811.)
Services : Lieut. 1st Bengal Eur. Bn. in July 1787. Lieut. 2nd Bengal Eur. Regt. in 1796. Lieut. & Bt. Capt. 13th N.I. Promoted Capt. Lt. 13th N.I. before his retirement had been notified in India. His date of retirement appears to have been subsequently ante-dated to 28 Aug. 1800.
Refs. : G.M. 1800, ii. 1286. S.M. 1825, ii. 640.

GRENIER, Bartholomew Lewis (*d.* 1810). Major, 19th N.I. Country Cadet 1781. Admitted 6 Aug. 1781. Ensign 12 July 1782. Lieut. 9 Jan. 1785. Capt. 13 July 1803. Major 21 July 1808. *d.* in camp at Tehri (Tikamgarh), C.I., 28 Mar. 1810.
(*Probably* a native of canton Vaud, Switzerland. *Possibly* son of David Grenier, Maj. Gen. in the Dutch service.) (? *m.* Louisa, who died 3 Nov. 1829.)
Services : Lieut. 6th Bengal Eur. Bn. in July 1787. Lieut. 1st Bengal Eur. Regt. Bt. Capt. do. 7 Jan. 1796. Capt. 19th N.I. Intr. at C.M. in the field 1803-6.

GRESHAM, Charles (*d.* 1783). Ensign, Infantry. Cadet 1782. Ensign 1782. *d.* Cawnpore Oct. 1783.
Services : N.F.P.

GRESHAM, James (1799-1834). Lieutenant, Pension Est. 34th N.I. *b.* Nottingham 5 Jan. 1799. Cadet 1820. Arrived in India May 1821. Ensign 16 Jan. 1821. Lieut. 17 July 1823. Pensioned 6 Jan. 1825. *d.* Barasat, Bengal, 17 June 1834.
Son of Robert Gresham.
Services : Posted as Ensign to 2/17th N.I. Transfd. to 34th N.I. (late 1/17th) May 1824. No record of active service.

GRESLEY, Francis (1807-1880). Major. 14th N.I. *b.* Kenilworth, co. Warwick, 5 May 1807. Cadet 1822. Arrived in India 8 Oct. 1823. Ensign 11 July 1823. Lieut. 13 May 1825. Capt. 8 Oct. 1839. Retired 1 Mar. 1844. Hon. Major 28 Nov. 1854. *d.* Meriden Hall, nr. Leamington, 10 Dec. 1880.
4th son of Richard Gresley, of Stowe House, Staffs., and Kenilworth Hall, co. Warwick, barr.-at-law, and Caroline his 1st wife, youngest dau. of Andrew Grote. *m.* Ilfracombe, 19 Sept. 1848, Mary, dau. of Rev. Thomas Thorp, rector of Burton-Overy, Leics., and widow of Russell Kendall. (She died 10 Aug. 1894.) Ed. Shrewsbury 1816-7 ; Westminster 14 Jan. 1818 till Whitsun 1822.

Services : Ensign 14th N.I. Served with Nizam's army, in 1st, afterwards 3rd, Cav., 18 Nov. 1826 till retirement. Paymr. Cav. Div., Nizam's army, Feb. 1831. To rank as Capt. in Nizam's service 11 July 1835. Selected as umpire in a boundary dispute on E. frontier of Nizam's territory Feb. 1837. Leave s.c. 20 mos. to Cape 12 Mar. 1839.

Refs. : Burke's *Peerage*, 1923, p. 1036, *s.n.* Gresley, Bart., of Drakelow, co. Derby. *The Gresleys of Drakelow*, by F. Madan (Wm. Salt Soc.), i. 152. *Shrewsbury School Register.* *Westminster School Register.* *The Times*, 13 Dec. 1880.

GREY, John (1760-1837). Lieutenant. 4th Bengal Eur. Bn. Subsequently Lt. Gen. H.M.S. *b.* 1760. Cadet 1778. Ensign Mar. 1778. Lieut. Sept. 1778. Struck off Nov. 1788. *d.* Ruddington, Notts., 29 Jan. 1837, aged 76.

A native of Middlesex.

Services : Sailed for India on the *Nassau*, 7 Mar. 1778, aged 17. First Mahratta War 1779-80. Campaign against the Rajah of Benares 1781 ; Ramnagar (w. in leg); siege of Bijaigarh, C.I. Transfd. to H.M.S. Lieut. 76th Foot (9 July 1783) 1 Nov. 1788. Capt. 113th Foot June 1794 ; Major do. 19 Sept. 1794. This Regt. was disbanded in Aug. 1795, but he continued in receipt of full pay. Apptd. Inspecting Field Ofr. of the Nottingham district 1796. Lt. Col. 1 Jan. 1800. Col. 25 July 1810. Maj. Gen. 4 June 1813. Lt. Gen. 27 May 1825.

Refs. : *Royal Mily. Calendar*, iii. 226. *G.M.* 1837, i. 659.

GREY, Sir John (1780 ?-1856). Lieutenant. Infantry. Subsequently Lt. Gen., K.C.B., H.M.S. C.-in-C., Bombay. *b.* 1780 ? Cadet 1795. Arrived in India 27 Jan. 1798. Ensign 8 Aug. 1797. Lieut. 1 July 1798. Resigned 17 Sept. 1798. *d.* Morwick Hall, Northumberland, 19 Feb. 1856.

bapt. Embleton, Northumberland, 18 Mar. 1782. Son of Charles Grey, of Morwick, and Catherine Maria his wife, dau. of Rev. John Skelley. *m.* 1830, Rosa Josefa Louisa, dau. of Capt. Henry Evelyn Sturt, R.N., and cousin-german of Achmuty Ashley Sturt, *q.v.*

Services : See *D.N.B.* H.M. 75th Foot 1798 (Ensign 28 May 1795). Fourth Mysore War ; Malavelli ; Seringapatam (Medal). Capt. 15th Bn. of Reserve 31 Oct. 1803. Capt. 82nd Foot 23 Aug. 1804. Major 9th Garr. Bn. 27 Nov. 1806. Major 5th Foot 13 June 1811. Peninsula campaign, with 5th Foot ; Ciudad Rodrigo (w. twice). Lt. Col. 6 Feb. 1812. Gwalior campaign, comdg. Left Wing of Army ; Paniar (Bronze star). First Sikh War, comdg. a Div. Apptd. Col. 5th Foot 1849. C.-in-C. Bombay 30 Dec. 1850 till 1852. Lt. Gen. 11 Nov. 1851. K.C.B. 2 May 1844.

THE BENGAL ARMY, 1758-1834

Refs. : Burke's *Peerage*, 1923, p. 1038, *s.n.* Earl Grey. D.N.B. D.I.B. Boase. *Royal Mily. Calendar*, iv. 403. G.M. 1856, i. 424.

*GRIDLAND, John. Cadet. Artillery. Cadet 14 June 1767. Never commissioned.
Refs. : *Stubbs's List*.

GRIER, James (1792-1820). Lieutenant, 2nd N.I. *b.* Dublin 15 Nov. 1792. Cadet 1812. Ensign 1 Nov. 1814. Lieut. 2 Sept. 1817. *d.* Hoshangabad, C.P., 27 May 1820.
Son of James Hawthorn Grier.
Services : Posted as Ensign to 1/2nd N.I. in 1815. No record of active service.

GRIFFIN, Charles (1800-1872). Colonel. 51st N.I. *b.* London 25 Mar. 1800. Cadet 1820. Arrived in India Sept. 1821. Ensign 17 May 1821. Lieut. 15 Dec. 1823. Capt. 7 Feb. 1837. Major 2 Aug. 1850. Bt. Lt. Col. 7 June 1849. Retired 1 Oct. 1852. Hon. Col. 28 Nov. 1854. *d.* 33 Marine Parade, Dover, 27 Sept. 1872.
bapt. St. Martin-in-the-Fields, London, 21 Apr. 1800. Son of John Griffin, of 70 Strand, London, goldsmith, and Mary Ann his wife. Brother of John Griffin, *q.v. m.* 1st, Ryde, I.W., 12 July 1836, Sophia, dau. of Capt. (? Richard Charles) Steele, R.M. (She died Monghyr, 12 Mar. 1838, aged 30.) *m.* 2nd, Calcutta, 4 Jan. 1841, Miss Eliza Kingston.
Services : Posted as Ensign to 26th N.I. Transfd. to 51st N.I. (late 1/26th) May 1824. Actg. Adjt. 51st N.I. 20 Apr. 1829. Actg. Intr. & Qmr. do. 23 Oct. 1832. Shekhawat expedn. 1834 ; Lieut. 51st N.I. Fur. s.c. 19 Feb. 1835 till 21 Dec. 1837. Insurrection in Bundelkhand 1842. (? Gwalior campaign ; Paniar ; Capt. 51st N.I. (Bronze star).) Second Sikh War ; Multan ; Gujerat ; Capt. 51st N.I. (Medal with clasp).
Refs. : A.J. N.S. xx. 275. *The Times*, 2 Oct. 1872.

GRIFFIN, George Nathaniel (1784-1811). Capt. Lieutenant, 5th N.I. *b.* London 10 Jan. 1784. Cadet 1798. Arrived in India 9 Nov. 1799. Ensign 24 Dec. 1799. Lieut. 29 May 1800. Capt. Lt. 30 Aug. 1809. *d.* Cawnpore 15 June 1811.
bapt. St. Bride's, London, 10 Feb. 1784. Son of John Griffin and Honour Pitt his wife. Brother of John Pitt Griffin, *q.v. m.* (?).
Services : (? Second Mahratta War ; Cuttack 1804 ; Khurda ; Lieut. 1/5th N.I.) Adjt. 1/5th N.I. 1 Oct. 1806 till death. Operations in Bundelkhand against Gopal Singh 1810 ; Tirowa ; Capt. Lt. 1/5th N.I.

GRIFFIN, John (1798-1845). Bt. Major, 24th N.I. *b.* London 5 Feb. 1798. Cadet 1817. Arrived in India Apr. 1819. Ensign 23 Aug. 1818. Lieut. 15 Apr. 1820. Capt. 26 Mar. 1830. Bt. Major 23 Dec. 1842. *d.* 21 Dec. 1845 : kld. in action at the battle of Ferozshahr.

bapt. St. Gregory by St. Paul, London, 2 Mar. 1798. Son of John Griffin and Mary Ann his wife. Brother of Charles Griffin, *q.v. m.* Bareilly, 12 Mar. 1825, Elizabeth Margaret, eldest dau. of Major Robert Durie, 11th Light Dgns. (*See also* William Beckett.)

Services : Did duty as Ensign with 1/11th, Bengal Eur. Regt., 2/14th N.I., and Muttra Levy. Posted as Ensign to 1/8th N.I. June 1820. Actg. Adjt. 6 Jan. till May 1824. Intr. & Qmr. 24th N.I. (late 2/8th) 26 July 1824 till 4 Mar. 1830. On service in Hariana Nov.-Dec. 1824, as Staff Ofr. to Lt. Col. Comyn's force. Against the Kols and Chuars 1832-3 ; Capt. 24th N.I. Apptd. A.D.C. to Maj.-Gen. E. H. Simpson, comdg. force raised for Shah Shuja, 9 Nov. 1838. First Afghan War 1838-42 ; Ghazni (Medal) ; Kabul ; apptd. to comd. Shah Shuja's 1st Inf. Oct. 1839-43 ; defence of Quetta June-July 1840 ; Sikandrabad 17 Aug. 1841 ; operations round Kandahar under Nott. First Sikh War ; Mudki ; Ferozshahr (kld.) ; Bt. Major 24th N.I.

Refs. : *De Rhé-Philipe.* M.I. St. John's, Calcutta, and St. Andrew's, Ferozepore.

GRIFFIN, John Pitt (1782-1840). Captain, Invalid Est. 11th N.I. *b.* London 10 Oct. 1782. Cadet 1798. Arrived in India 9 Nov. 1799. Ensign 30 Dec. 1799. Lieut. 29 May 1800. Capt. (7 Jan. 1812) 16 Dec. 1814. Invalided 16 Dec. 1814. *d.* Calcutta 23 Oct. 1840.

bapt. St. Bride's, London, 2 Dec. 1782. Son of John Griffin, of Ludgate Hill, and Honour Pitt his wife. Brother of George Nathaniel Griffin, *q.v. m.* Cawnpore, 23 Aug. 1802, Mary, dau. of James Powell, *q.v.* (*See also* Thomas Newton.) (She died Calcutta, 4 Nov. 1845, aged 64.)

Services : (? Second Mahratta War ; Lieut. 11th N.I.) Adjt. 1/11th N.I. 1807-10. Capt. Lt. 11th N.I. 7 Jan. 1812. Reduction of Kalinjar 1812. After transfer to the Invalid Est. he held for some time the appt. of Supt. of oilcloth manufacture at Monghyr ; afterwards Fort Adjt. at Buxar, then Bk. Mr. in Cuttack. Posted to 2nd Bn. Native Invalids at Chunar 5 Mar. 1827 ; transfd. to 1st Bn. at Allahabad 15 July 1828.

GRIFFIN, Thomas (*d.* 1791). Lieutenant, Artillery. Cadet (?). Fireworker 19 Aug. 1781. Lieut. 25 Nov. 1786. *d.* at sea 7 June 1791.

Services ; Lieut. 1st Bn. Art. in July 1787.

GRIFFITH, Charles Robertson (1808-?). Ensign. 6th Extra Inf. Regt. *b.* Kingston-on-Thames 4 Nov. 1808. Cadet 1824. Ensign (?). Resigned in India 11 Nov. 1825.

Son of Thomas Griffith. Brother of Francis Everard Griffith, *q.v.*

Services : Posted as Ensign to newly-raised 6th Extra Regt. in 1825.

GRIFFITH, Francis Everard (1805-1829). Ensign, 17th N.I. *bapt.* Kingston-on-Thames 2 Nov. 1805. Cadet 1824. Ensign 29 Apr. 1825. *d.* Delhi 24 Sept. 1829.

Son of Thomas Griffith. Brother of Charles Robertson Griffith, *q.v.*

Services : Posted as Ensign to 17th N.I. in 1825. Actg. Adjt. 17th N.I. 15 Feb. 1828. No record of active service.

GRIFFITH, John (*d.* 1780). Captain, Infantry. Lieut. 28 Oct. 1770. Capt. 3 Sept. 1779. *d.* Calcutta July 1780.

" Descended in a direct line from the last monarch of Wales " (Will).

Services : N.F.P.

Refs. : Will dated Farruckabad 2 Sept. 1777.

GRIFFITH, Joseph. Cadet. Infantry. Cadet 1783. Struck off 1784.

Services : N.F.P.

GRIFFITH, Thomas (1788-1813). Lieutenant, 20th N.I. *b.* Mold, co. Flint, 14 Oct. 1788. Cadet 1804. Arrived in India 18 Mar. 1805. Ensign 21 Apr. 1805. Lieut. 22 Apr. 1805. *d. unm.* Barrackpore 14 Aug. 1813.

2nd son of John Wynne Griffith, of Garn, co. Denbigh (of Tower), M.P. for Denbigh boroughs, and Jane his wife, dau. of Robert Wynne, of Garthmeilio and Plas Newydd, co. Denbigh.

Services : Posted as Lieut. to 20th N.I. Capture of Java 1811 ; Lieut. 1/20th N.I. Adjt. & Qmr. 20th N.I. 1812 till death.

Refs. : Burke's *Landed Gentry*, 13th edn., p. 791, *s.n.* Griffith, of Garn, co. Denbigh. *G.M.* 1814, ii. 299. Will proved 25 Feb. 1815. M.I. in old cemetery at Barrackpore.

GRIFFITHS, Charles (1793-1872). Colonel. 26th N.I. *b.* Old Windsor, Berks., 23 Apr. 1793. Cadet 1810. Admitted 3 Dec. 1811. Ensign 25 Aug. 1813. Lieut. 16 May 1815. Capt. 14 Dec. 1826. Major 27 Oct. 1838. Lt. Col. 1 Jan. 1845. Retired 31 Mar. 1851. Hon. Col. 28 Nov. 1854. *d.* 1 June 1872.

Son of Henry Griffiths, of Beaumont Lodge, Berks., and of Bath,

B.C.S., and Anne his wife. Brother of George Griffiths, *q.v.* His sister *m.* Rev. Sir Erasmus Griffies-Williams, 2nd Bart. *m.* Midnapore, 14 Oct. 1819, Anna Grace, 4th dau. of Jacob Vanrenen, *q.v.* (*See also* James Blair.) (She died 12 Jan. 1879, aged 77.) His dau. *m.* Robert Waller, *q.v.*

Services : Cadet d.d. 9th N.I. Posted as Ensign to 1/18th N.I. in 1813. Nepal War 1816; Lieut. 1/18th N.I., in 1st Bde., Rt. Column (India medal). Cuttack insurrection 1816-7; Khurda. Actg. Intr. & Qmr. 1/18th N.I. in 1818. Actg. Adjt. 1/18th N.I. 22 Apr. 1820; actg. Intr. & Qmr. do. 9 Feb. 1821. Actg. Adjt. Bareilly Provl. Bn. 18 Dec. 1822; permanent do. 16 Oct. 1823 till 25 Sept. 1825. Transfd. to 37th N.I. (late 2/18th) May 1824. Actg. Bde. Major 17 Nov. 1825. Siege and capture of Bhurtpore; Lieut. 37th N.I. (clasp to India medal). Actg. Intr. & Qmr. 37th N.I. 17 Aug. 1826; permanent do. 8 Feb. till 2 Oct. 1827. Fur. p.a. 8 Dec. 1827 till 13 Nov. 1829, and 23 Jan. 1836 till 29 Oct. 1837. First Afghan War 1838-42; Ghazni (Medal); comdd. storming party in attack on fort of Mohd. Sharif 6 Nov. 1841; storm of Kikabashee fort; retreat to Jalalabad; Khurd Kabul 8 Jan. 1842 (s.w. in rt. arm); taken prisoner at Gandamak 13 Jan. 1842; released 21 Sept. 1842; Major comdg. 37th N.I. from 21 Dec. 1839. Granted gratuity of 18 mos. pay on account of wound. Posted as Lt. Col. to 46th N.I. 13 Mar. 1845. Fur. s.c. 25 Feb. 1849 till retirement. Durani, 3 cl., 7 Sept. 1841.

Refs. : De La Ferté, p. 59.

GRIFFITHS, Frederick William Stevens (*d.* 1791). Lieutenant, Infantry. Cadet 1776. Ensign 13 Aug. 1776. Lieut. 29 July 1778. *d.* Berhampore 20 Oct. 1791.

m. Elizabeth Jane. (She died Clifton, Aug. 1834, aged 79.)
Services : Lieut. 2/3rd Bengal Eur. Regt. in Oct. 1779. Fur. 3 yrs. h.p. 20 Nov. 1786.
Refs. : Will dated 5 Mar. 1789.

GRIFFITHS, George (1800-1858). Captain. 13th N.I. *bapt.* Old Windsor, Berks., 20 Feb. 1800. Cadet 1818. Admitted 11 Sept. 1819. Ensign 20 May 1819. Lieut. (1 Jan. 1821) 12 July 1822. Bt. Capt. 20 May 1834. Retired 23 July 1838. Capt. (after retirement) 1843. *d.* 4 Sept. 1858.

Son of Henry Griffiths, formerly B.C.S., and Anne his wife. Brother of Charles Griffiths, *q.v.*, and nephew of Sir George Griffies-Williams, 1st Bart. *m.* Clifton, 17 Feb. 1841, Marianne, youngest dau. of W. Rogers Lawrence, of Belle Vue House, nr. Bath, and formerly of Andford, Gloucs.

Services : Ensign d.d. Bengal Eur. Regt. Posted as Ensign to

THE BENGAL ARMY, 1758-1834   341

Eur. Regt. in 1819. Transfd. to 7th N.I. 12 July 1822; to 13th N.I. (late 1/7th) May 1824. Fur. p.a. 9 Aug. 1831 till 16 Nov. 1832. Fur. s.c. 23 Jan. 1836 till retirement. No record of active service.
Refs.: Burke's *Peerage*, 1859, p. 1064, *s.n.* Griffies-Williams, Bart., of Llwyny-Wormwood, co. Carmarthen. *Bath Chron.* Feb. 1841.

GRIFFITHS, Hugh (1780-1856). Colonel. 10th N.I. *b.* 1780. Cadet 1793. Admitted 22 Feb. 1796. Ensign 3 Oct. 1794. Lieut. 8 Jan. 1796. Capt. 21 Sept. 1804. Major 3 Jan. 1814. Lt. Col. 4 Apr. 1818. Invalided 13 Jan. 1823. Retired 16 Oct. 1831. Hon. Col. 28 Nov. 1854. *d.* Burley Lodge, Hants, 31 Dec. 1856, aged 76.

Of Burley, East Woodhay, Hants. *m.* 1st, Berhampore, 4 Sept. 1802, Miss Phillis Augusta Matthews. *m.* 2nd, Cape Town, 7 Apr. 1828, Miss Augusta Wilhelmina Siegruhn. (She died 31 Aug. 1863.)
Services: Lieut. 3rd Bengal Eur. Regt. in 1796. Lieut. 19th N.I. Adjt. 1/19th N.I. in 1803. Transfd. to newly-raised 2/22nd N.I. 1804. Capt. Lt. 30 June 1804. Second Mahratta War; battle and capture of Deig; Bhurtpore (w. in 3rd assault on 20 Feb. 1805); Capt. 2/22nd N.I. (India medal). Capture of Java 1811; Capt. 5th Bengal Vol. Bn. (Medal). Comdd. 5th Vol. Bn. in Java till 1816. Major 1/22nd N.I. Transfd. as Lt. Col. to 2/10th N.I. After transfer to the Invalid Est. he held the appt. of Regulating Ofr., Shahabad. Fur. s.c. 12 mos. to Cape 1 Dec. 1826. Fur. p.a. 26 Dec. 1829 till retirement.
Refs.: *A.J.* xxvi. 384. *I.M.* 17 Jan. 1857, p. 61.

GRIGG, Mark (1794-1824). Lieutenant, 45th N.I. *bapt.* Stoke Damerel, Devon, 18 Mar. 1794. Cadet 1809. Ensign 18 Oct. 1812. Lieut. 15 Sept. 1816. *d.* Ramu, Bengal, 16 May 1824: kld. in action.

Son of Mark Grigg, of Tamerton Foliott, Devon. Ed. Blundell's; admitted 21 Apr. 1808, aged 14; left 29 June 1809.
Services: Cadet d.d. 9th N.I. 1811-2. Posted as Ensign to 1/23rd N.I. in 1812. Third Mahratta War; Lieut. 1/23rd N.I. Intr. & Qmr. 1/23rd N.I. 4 May 1820 till 1823. Adjt. 1/23rd N.I. 1823 till death. Transfd. to 45th N.I. (late 1/23rd) May 1824. First Burma War; Chittagong 1824; Ramu (kld.); Lieut. 45th N.I.
Refs.: *Blundell's School Register.*

GRIMES, Edward Pellew (1815-1837). Lieutenant, 68th N.I. *b.* West Teignmouth, Devon, 13 Jan. 1815. Cadet 1833. Arrived in India 7 July 1834. Ensign 31 May 1834. Lieut. 23 Sept. 1836. *d.* Mhow, 13 Oct. 1837, of fever.

bapt. West Teignmouth 7 Mar. 1815. Only son of Joseph Grimes, Naval Ofr. of H.M. dockyards at Deal, and Mary Ann his wife. Stepson of —— Cartwright. Addiscombe Cadet 1832 till 13 Dec. 1833.

Services : d.d. 46th N.I. 12 July 1834. Posted as Ensign to 68th N.I. 5 Nov. 1834. No record of active service.

Refs. : *A.J.* N.S. xxv. 111. Will dated Sept. 1837 ; proved 3 Aug. 1838.

GRIMES, Henry Stockley (1810-1873). Lieut. Colonel. 46th N.I. *bapt.* Dublin 27 Jan. 1810. Cadet 1825. Arrived in India 22 Oct. 1826. Ensign 27 June 1826. Lieut. 29 Aug. 1833. Capt. 21 Apr. 1848. Major 11 Sept. 1859. Retired 28 Feb. 1861. Hon. Lt. Col. 28 Feb. 1861. *d.* West Brompton, London, 10 May 1873, aged 63.

Son of George Henry Grimes, Capt. Comy. R.A. *m.* 1st, Cheltenham, 17 July 1839, Frances Matilda, eldest dau. of Maj.-Gen. Richard Podmore, Madras Est. (She died Gwalior, Aug. 1845, aged 28.) *m.* 2nd, Gwalior, 19 Feb. 1848, Margaret, dau. of Peter O'Brien, M.D., Surg. 4th Inf., Gwalior Contingent.

Services : Ensign d.d. 32nd N.I. 9 Nov. 1826. Posted to 30th N.I. 8 Jan. 1827 ; to 32nd N.I. 30 Jan. 1827 ; to 46th N.I. 3 Jan. 1828. Comdg. escort to P.A. in Kotah in Oct. 1834. Fur. s.c. 31 Aug. 1837 till 21 Jan. 1840. Paymr. to Gwalior Contingent 14 Feb. 1844 till 1853. Fur. 1853 till Nov. 1856. No record of active service.

Refs. : *A.J.* N.S. xxix. 341. *The Times,* 15 May 1873.

GRISSELL, Charles (1805-1855). Major, 61st N.I. *b.* London 28 July 1805. Cadet 1825. Arrived in India 10 May 1826. Ensign 18 Dec. 1825. Lieut. 2 Mar. 1829. Capt. 13 Jan. 1842. Major 1 Aug. 1851. *d.* Jullundur 3 July 1855 : kld. in a trap accident.

3rd son of Thomas De La Garde Grissell, of Stockwell, Surrey, one of the secs. at the East India House, Capt. 3rd Regt. Royal East India Bde., and Anne his wife, dau. of James Peto, of Effingham, Surrey. Brother of James Grissell, *q.v.* *m.* 1st, Agra, 12 Sept. 1842, Charlotte Julia, only dau. of George Higgins, of Calcutta, atty. and notary public. (She died Lucknow 23 Aug. 1851.) *m.* 2nd, (?). (She died Mussoorie 7 Nov. 1854.)

Services : Posted as Ensign to 61st N.I. 24 May 1826. Fur. s.c. 24 Apr. 1833 till 2 Nov. 1835. Leave s.c. to Mussoorie Mar. 1840 till Nov. 1841. Adjt. 1st Inf. Levy 5 Feb. 1842 till Feb. 1843. Insurrection in Bundelhkand 1843 ; Capt. 61st N.I. Fur. s.c. 22 Nov. 1847 till 1 Jan. 1851. Comdd. 61st N.I. from Apr. 1853 till death.

Refs. : Burke's *Landed Gentry*, 13th edn., p. 794, *s.n.* Grissell, of Redisham Hall, Suffolk. Burke's *Visitation of Seats and Arms*, 2S. ii. 6. *De Rhé-Philipe. G.M.* 1855, ii. 440. *I.M.* 1855, p. 480. Will dated 23 Aug. 1850; admon. 11 Jan. 1856. M.I. in Art. cemetery at Jullundur.

GRISSELL, James (1803-1864). Lieut. Colonel. 46th N.I. *b.* London 28 Apr. 1803. Cadet 1823. Arrived in India 8 Oct. 1824. Ensign 16 Apr. 1824. Lieut. 21 June 1826. Capt. 10 July 1838. Bt. Major 11 Nov. 1851. Retired 31 Dec. 1851. Hon. Lt. Col. 28 Nov. 1854. *d. unm.* Mickleham, Surrey, 30 July 1864.

2nd son of Thomas De La Garde Grissell and Anne his wife. Brother of Charles Grissell, *q.v.*

Services : Posted as Ensign to 2nd Bengal Eur. Regt. in 1824. First Burma War; Arakan 1825; Ensign 2nd Bengal Eur. Regt. Exchanged to 46th N.I. 12 Mar. 1827. Actg. Adjt. Left Wing 46th N.I. 8 Oct. 1827. Fur. p.a. 5 Aug. 1836 till 7 Feb. 1839. Actg. A.D.C. to Maj.-Gen. Edmund Cartwright, *q.v.*, comdg. Presdy. Div., 6 Oct. 1843. Offg. Executive Ofr. P.W.D., Dum-Dum, June 1847. Second Sikh War; Chilianwala; Capt. 46th N.I. (Medal).

Refs. : Burke's *Landed Gentry*, 13th edn., p. 794, *s.n.* Grissell, of Redisham Hall, Suffolk. Burke's *Visitation of Seats and Arms*, 2S. ii. 6. *Walford. G.M.* 1864, ii. 395.

GROAT, Donald (*d.* 1784). Lieutenant, Artillery. Cadet 1778. Fireworker 1778. Lieut. 7 Oct. 1778. *d.* Calcutta 11 July 1784.

Services : Second Mysore War 1781-4; Lieut. 4th Coy. 2nd Bn. Art.

Note : The surname is given in the Calcutta burial register as Grant, and this may possibly be correct, although Gen. Stubbs, who is usually most accurate, gives it as Groat.

GROSE, George (1794-1826). Lieutenant, Pension Est. 35th N.I. *b.* London 19 July 1794. Cadet 1810. Ensign 1 May 1813. Lieut. 1 Sept. 1815. Pensioned 8 July 1825. *d.* Fatehgarh, U.P., 1826.

Eldest son of John Grose, of Bloomfield House, Bath (? formerly B.C.S.), " retired on his private fortune acquired by a long residence in India."

Services : Cadet d.d. 8th N.I. 1811-3. Posted as Ensign to 2/17th N.I. in 1813. Nepal War 1814-5; Jitpur; Ensign 2/17th N.I., in 3rd Div. Served with 2nd Ceylon Vol. Bn. 1818-9. Transfd. to 34th N.I. (late 1/17th) May 1824; to 35th N.I. in 1825.

Refs. : *Bath Chron.* 14 Oct. 1830.

GROTE, Frederick (1807-1828). Lieutenant, Artillery. *b.* Beckenham, Kent, 30 Mar. 1807. Cadet 1822. 2nd Lieut. 6 June 1823. Lieut. 3 Sept. 1827. *d.* Calcutta, 21 Apr. 1828, of typhus fever.

6th son of George Grote, of Beckenham, banker (of Badgemore, Oxon.), and Selina Mary his wife, dau. of Rev. Dr. Peckwell. Brother of George Grote, the historian of Greece (*D.N.B.*), who *m.* a sister of William Charles James Lewin, *q.v.* Addiscombe Cadet 1821-3.

Services : Sailed for India on the *Thomas Grenville* 16 June 1823. Posted to 3rd Troop 2nd Bde. H.A. in 1825. Siege and capture of Bhurtpore ; 2nd Lieut. 3rd Troop 2nd Bde. Supy. A.D.C. to G.G. 1828. Apptd. Junior Asst. to A.G.G., Saugor and Narbada territories, 18 Jan. 1828.

Refs. : Burke's *Landed Gentry*, 2nd edn., p. 510, *s.n.* Grote, of Oxfordshire. *G.M.* 1828, ii. 382. *A.J.* xxvi. 487. M.I. in S. Park St. cemetery, Calcutta.

GROUNDS, Jeremiah Edward (1811-1849). Bt. Captain, 46th N.I. *bapt.* St. Mary, Wisbech, Cambs., 7 Nov. 1811. Cadet 1827. Arrived in India Oct. 1828. Ensign 10 May 1828. Lieut. 26 May 1835. Bt. Capt. 10 May 1843. *d.* Landour, nr. Mussoorie, 25 July 1849, aged 38.

Son of Jeremiah Grounds, of Tholomos Grove, nr. Wisbech, and Alicia his wife.

Services : Ensign d.d. 7th N.I. 20 Nov. 1828 ; do. 63rd N.I. 11 Jan. 1829. Posted as Ensign to 46th N.I. 4 Mar. 1829. Fur. s.c. 19 Feb. 1837 till Nov. 1839. Adjt. 46th N.I. 14 Feb. 1845 till Jan. 1846. Second Sikh War ; Ramnagar ; passage of Chenab ; Sadulapur ; Chilianwala ; Gujerat ; Bt. Capt. 46th N.I. (Medal with 2 clasps). Leave s.c. 9 mos. to Landour 1 Apr. 1849 till death.

Refs. : De Rhé-Philipe. *G.M.* 1850, i. 111. Will dated Landour 23 July 1849 ; admon. 23 Nov. 1850. M.I. in porch of Christ church, Ludhiana.

GROVE, Leslie Ralph (1777-1804). Capt. Lieutenant, Artillery. *b.* Falmouth 26 Oct. 1777. Cadet 1791. Arrived in India 4 Nov. 1793. Fireworker 21 May 1793. Lieut. 6 Aug. 1801. Capt. Lt. 21 Sept. 1804. *d.s.p.* 20 Dec. 1804 : kld. in action at the siege of Deig.

bapt. Falmouth 2 Apr. 1778. Eldest son of Leslie Grove, of Grovehall, co. Donegal, and Sarah his wife, dau. of Samuel Mercer, of Crosby Sq., London. His sister *m.* Thomas William Fortnom, *q.v.*

Services : Fur. 19 Jan. 1797 till 28 Nov. 1799, and 9 Mar. 1800 till 15 Mar. 1804. Second Mahratta War ; siege of Deig (kld. in the mortar battery) ; Lieut. 1st Coy. 1st Bn. Art., d.d. from 6th Coy. 1st Bn.

Refs. : Burke's *Landed Gentry of Ireland,* p. 281, *s.n.* Grove, of Castle Grove, Donegal. *Pester,* p. 360. Will dated camp before Deig, 16 Dec. 1804 ; proved 4 Apr. 1805.

GROVE, Somerset James (1808-1880). Colonel. 68th N.I. *b.* London 29 Jan. 1808. Cadet 1823. Arrived in India 10 Aug. 1824. Ensign 18 Feb. 1824. Lieut. 15 July 1825. Capt. 30 May 1836. Bt. Major 9 Nov. 1846. Bt. Lt. Col. 20 June 1854. Retired 20 Apr. 1855. Hon. Col. 11 May 1855. *d.* Biarritz, France, 15 Apr. 1880.

Son of Henry Grove, Major h.p. 23rd Dgns., sometime A.A.G. on the Staff in Dublin. *m.* Calcutta 12 Dec. 1850, Louisa Eliza, only dau. of George Snowden, of Ramsgate. (She died 18 Jan. 1892, aged 77.) Ed. Eton 1817-23 ; K.S. 1820.

Services : Posted as Ensign to 68th N.I. in 1824. First Burma War ; Arakan 1825 ; Lieut. 68th N.I. (India medal). Intr. & Qmr. 68th N.I. 28 Dec. 1826 till 7 Mar. 1828. Constructed works at Kyaukpyu, Arakan, 1 Nov. 1828 till 16 Feb. 1831. Adjt. 68th N.I. 21 Nov. 1833 till Feb. 1836. Fur. s.c. 27 Feb. 1836 till 23 Nov. 1839. Bde. Major 1st Inf. Bde., Army of Reserve (for Afghanistan), 14 Oct. 1842. Attd. 1st L.I. Bn. till Jan. 1843. Comdd. 6th Inf., Gwalior Contingent, 13 Jan. 1844 till Oct. 1853. Second Burma War ; Pegu ; Bt. Major 68th N.I. (Medal).

Refs. : Eton School Lists. The Times, 20 Apr. 1880.

GROVES, James. (*See* **GRAVES, James.**)

GRUEBER, Nicholas (*d.* 1783). Lieutenant, 24th Sepoy Bn. Cadet 1780. Ensign 22 Feb. 1781. Lieut. 17 Oct. 1781. *d.* 24 June 1783 : kld. in action during the siege of Cuddalore, Madras.

(*Probably* son of Nicholas Grueber, B.C.S., Chief at Dacca, who was killed by a fire-engine at Knightsbridge 11 Dec. 1794. *Probably* brother of Tichbourn Grueber, *q.v.,* and nephew of Richard Grueber, *q.v.*)

Services : Second Mysore War.

GRUEBER, Richard (*d.* 1805). Colonel, 1st N.I. Cadet 1770. Admitted 12 June 1770. Ensign 11 Nov. 1771. Lieut. 26 July 1776. Capt. 19 Feb. 1781. Major 1 Mar. 1794. Lt. Col. 31 Aug. 1798. Col. 1 Jan. 1803. *d.* Lucknow, 19 Oct. 1805, of fever.

Son of Rev. William Grueber, rector of Athboy, co. Meath, whose ancestor emigrated from Frankfort in 1572. Brother of Nicholâs Grueber, B.C.S., Daniel, Arthur, and William. (*Probably* uncle of Tichbourn Grueber, *q.v.*) Father of Richard Grueber (*see* Appendix).

LIST OF THE OFFICERS OF

Services : Capt. 5th Bengal Eur. Bn. in July 1787. Major 1st Bengal Eur. Regt. in 1796. Transfd. as Major to 1/6th N.I. Posted as Col. to 1st N.I. in 1803.

Refs. : Burke's *Colonial Gentry*, p. 244, *s.n.* Grueber. *G.M.* 1806, ii. 775. *Faulkner's Dublin Journal*, 21 Aug. 1806. Will proved 18 Nov. 1805.

GRUEBER, Tichbourn (1766/77-1783). Ensign, Infantry. *b.* 1766/67. Cadet 1781. Ensign 1781. *d.* in India 16 Sept. 1783 : drowned.

(*Probably* son of Nicholas Grueber, B.C.S., Chief at Dacca, and Anna Yates or Yeates his wife.) (*See also* John Fortnom, whose nephew, John Fortnom, of the Bank of England, she *re-m.* 24 Sept. 1794.) (*Probably* brother of Nicholas Grueber, *q.v.*)

Services : Apptd. Cadet on 1 Mar. 1781, aged 15. Sailed for India on the *Nassau*, 8 Feb. 1782, aged 15. N.F.P.

GRUMBY, Robert. (*See* **GUMLEY, Robert.**)

GUILD, John David (1785-?). Lieutenant. 23rd N.I. *b.* Dundee 5 Feb. 1785. Cadet 1799. Arrived in India 8 Dec. 1800. Ensign 11 Nov. 1800. Lieut. 5 Nov. 1802. Resigned in India 9 Oct. 1810.

Son of James Guild, of Dundee, merchant, and Helen Ramsay his wife.

Services : Lieut. 7th N.I. Transfd. to newly-raised 23rd N.I. in 1804.

GUILLOD, Harry Chambers (1806-1823). Cadet, Infantry. *b.* London 25 June 1806. Cadet 1821. Never arrived in India. *d.* at sea 1 Feb. 1823 : drowned on his passage out to India on board the *Thames*.

Son of Thomas Guillod.

GUINAND, Alexander (1786-1813). Lieutenant, Artillery. *b.* Calcutta 18 Sept. 1786. Cadet 1804. Arrived in India 1 Sept. 1805. Lieut. 11 May 1805. *d. unm.* Partabgarh, U.P., 25 June 1813.

bapt. Calcutta 22 Jan. 1787, and Stoke Newington 19 Jan. 1793. 2nd son of John Henry Guinand (of an old Neuchâtel family), of Pondicherry, of the firm of Prinsep, Prinsep & Guinand, chintz manufacturers, and Perretta (? Perette or Mary) Ranby his wife, " said to have been a French creole." Grandson of Henry Guinand, sometime of London, merchant, afterwards B.C.S., and brother of Robert Samuel Guinand, *q.v.*

Services : (? Storm and capture of Chamir fort 1807 ; Lieut. Art.)
Refs. : Misc. Gen. et Her. 4S. iv. 270-1.

THE BENGAL ARMY, 1758-1834   347

GUINAND, Robert Samuel (1788-1810). Lieutenant, Artillery.
b. Calcutta 26 May 1788. Cadet 1805. Arrived in India 11 Nov. 1806. Lieut. 2 Apr. 1806. *d. unm.* Calcutta 15 Oct. 1810.
bapt. Barrackpore 27 July 1788, and Stoke Newington 19 Jan. 1793. 3rd son of John Henry Guinand, of Palta, Bengal, indigo planter, and Perretta or Mary his wife. Brother of Alexander Guinand, *q.v.* Woolwich Cadet; nominated for R.M.A. 16 Nov. 1803; obtained his certificate 25 Mar. 1806.
Services: Sailed for India on the *Lady Burges.* No record of active service.
Refs.: Misc. Gen. et Her. 4S. iv. 270-1. M.I. in S. Park St. cemetery, Calcutta.

GUISE, John (1813-1890). Lieut. Colonel. 24th N.I. *b.* London 8 Mar. 1813. Cadet 1828. Arrived in India 22 Sept. 1829. Ensign 5 June 1829. Lieut. 1 Jan. 1838. Capt. 20 Sept. 1845. Bt. Major 28 Nov. 1854. Retired 31 Dec. 1856. Hon. Lt. Col. 31 Dec. 1856. *d.* 27 Jan. 1890.
Son of John Guise and Maria his wife.
Services: Ensign d.d. 27th N.I. 2 Nov. 1829. Posted as Ensign to 12th N.I. 2 Aug. 1832. Transfd. to 24th N.I. 24 June 1833. (? Rising in Cuttack 1836; Ensign 24th N.I.) Actg. Adjt. Left Wing 24th N.I. 17 Feb., and 28 May 1842; do. Rt. Wing Dec. 1842. Disturbances in Bundelkhand 1842-3; Lieut. 24th N.I. Fur. 1846-8.
Refs.: (? *N. & Q.* 12S. i. 46.)

GUISE, William (1785-1828). Captain, 21st N.I. *b.* Bombay 14 Aug. 1785. Cadet 1804. Arrived in India 10 Dec. 1805. Ensign 16 Oct. 1805. Lieut. 19 Feb. 1806. Capt. 11 July 1823. *d. unm.* Bhurtpore 1 Aug. 1828.
bapt. Bombay 12 Feb. 1786. Son of Samuel Guise, LL.D., Surgeon Bombay Est.
Services: Posted as Lieut. to 9th N.I. in 1806. Operations against Dhundia Khan 1807; Komona; Ganauri; Lieut. 1/9th N.I. Settlement of Hariana 1809; Bhawani; Lieut. 1/9th N.I. Operations in Oudh 1809-10; Pragpur; Lieut. 1/9th N.I. (? Operations in Baghelkhand 1813; Entauri; Lieut. 1/9th N.I.) Fur. 1823-4. Transfd. to 21st N.I. (late 2/9th) May 1824. Siege and capture of Bhurtpore; Capt. 21st N.I.
Refs.: N. & Q. 12S. i. 46. Will dated 21 Oct. 1822; proved 13 Mar. 1829.

GULHAD, Richard (*d.* 1766). Lieutenant, Infantry. Cadet (?). Ensign 20 July 1763. Lieut. 15 Nov. 1764. *d.* 6 Oct. 1766.
Services: N.F.P.

GULLAND, Henry (1779-1803). Ensign, 13th N.I. *b.* Laline 5 Nov. 1779. Cadet 1800. Arrived in India 22 Aug. 1801. Ensign 22 Sept. 1801. *d.* Allahabad 26 Feb. 1803 : struck by lightning.
bapt. 20 Nov. 1779. Son of Andrew Gulland, in Cawsey, and Elizabeth Douglas his wife.
Services : Posted as Ensign to 13th N.I. No record of active service.

GUMLEY, Robert (*d.* 1784). Captain, Infantry. Cadet 1770. Ensign 9 Mar. 1772. Lieut. 14 Aug. 1776. Capt. 4 Mar. 1781. *d.* Ramgarh, B. & O., 1 Dec. 1784.
Services : N.F.P.

GUNN, Robert (1784-1813). Lieutenant, 17th N.I. *b.* Forres, co. Elgin, 23 Oct. 1784. Cadet 1800. Arrived in India 6 Feb. 1802. Ensign 26 Nov. 1801. Lieut. 30 Sept. 1803. *d. unm.* Samarang, Java, 12 Aug. 1813.
bapt. Forres 31 Oct. 1784. Son of John Gunn, of Forres, merchant, and Mary Eddie his wife.
Services : Posted as Ensign to 17th N.I. Capture of Java 1811 ; Lieut. L.I. Bn. Capture of Jokyakarta 1812 ; Lieut. L.I. Bn.
Refs. : Will dated Djokjakarta, Java, 19 May 1813 ; proved 5 Feb. 1814.

GUNNING, William (*d.* 1771). Ensign, Infantry. Cadet (?). Ensign 27 Sept. 1769. *d.* 1771 : drowned.
Services : N.F.P.

GUNSTON, Thomas John Freke (1798-?). Ensign. 16th N.I. *bapt.* Exeter 27 Sept. 1798. Cadet 1819. Ensign 8 June 1820. Resigned in India 8 Nov. 1821.
Son of Francis Freke Gunston, of Exeter, later of Barr, nr. Taunton, and Frances his wife. Exeter Coll., Oxon. ; matric. 25 June 1817, aged 18.
Services : Posted as Ensign to 16th N.I. No record of active service.
Refs. : Alumni Oxon.

GURNELL, Robert Molesworth (1809-1867). Major. 68th N.I. *b.* Pondicherry 13 Sept. 1809. Cadet 1827. Arrived in India 12 Aug. 1828. Ensign (21 Jan. 1828) 4 Nov. 1828. Lieut. 25 Apr. 1833. Capt. 21 Jan. 1843. Invalided 14 Aug. 1846. Retired 15 Nov. 1854. Hon. Major 28 Nov. 1854. *d.* Home Villa, Worthing, Sussex, 4 Feb. 1867.

Son of Lt.-Col. Thomas Gurnell, 15th Madras N.I., and Caroline his wife, only dau. of Robert Molesworth, Capt. H.M. 30th Regt., of the family of Molesworth, V.
Services : Ensign d.d. 7th N.I. 8 Sept. 1828. Posted to 1st Bengal Eur. Regt. 4 Nov. 1828. Transfd. to 12th N.I. 29 June 1829 ; to 68th N.I. 2 Aug. 1832. Demonstration against Jodhpur 1834 ; Lieut. 68th N.I. Actg. Intr. & Qmr. 68th N.I. 10 Dec. 1834 ; do. 44th N.I. Oct. 1837 ; do. 68th N.I. 5 Sept. 1838. Fur. p.a. 10 May 1840 till 7 Feb. 1844. Actg. Intr. & Qmr. 58th N.I. 12 Apr. 1844.
Refs. : Burke's *Peerage*, 1923, p. 1581, *s.n.* Molesworth, V. *G.M.* 1867, i. 401. *The Times*, 16 Feb. 1867.

GURNET, John Price. (*See* **GWINNETT.**)

GUTHRIE, Alexander (1750/51-1785). Lieutenant, Infantry. *b.* 1750/51. Cadet 1778. Ensign 12 May 1779. Lieut. 17 Jan. 1781. *d.* Dinapore, 2 May 1785, aged 34.
Services : N.F.P.
Refs. : M.I. at Dinapore.

GUTHRIE, Charles (1801-1843). Captain, Invalid Est. 46th N.I. *b.* Brechin, co. Forfar, 30 Oct. 1801. Cadet 1819. Admitted 12 Sept. 1820. Ensign 18 Apr. 1820. Lieut. 16 Apr. 1822. Capt. 3 Nov. 1827. Invalided 14 Jan. 1833. *d.* Jangipur, on the Ganges, 18 Mar. 1843, whilst proceeding from Dinapore to Calcutta for the amputation of his leg.
Son of David Guthrie, of Brechin, merchant. *m.* Serampore, Bengal, 30 Oct. 1832, Mrs. Eliza Griffith.
Services : Posted as Ensign to 2/26th N.I. Transfd. as Lieut. to 23rd N.I. 11 July 1823 ; to 46th N.I. (late 2/23rd) May 1824. First Burma War ; Assam 1824. Actg. Adjt. 46th N.I. 8 July 1824. Intr. & Qmr. 46th N.I. 17 Dec. 1825 till 22 Apr. 1828. Invalided owing to his having lost the use of one leg from disease in Assam. Suptg. Ofr. of Burkandaz Gds., Patna Div., 24 Mar. 1835.
Refs. : G.M. 1843, ii. 333. *I.M.* No. 4, p. 116.

GUTHRIE, Charles Seton (1808-1874). Colonel. Engineers. *b.* Calcutta 18 Oct. 1808. Cadet 1827. Arrived in India 11 Aug. 1828. 2nd Lieut. 15 Dec. 1826. Lieut. 28 Sept. 1827. Capt. 30 Sept. 1840. Major 1 Aug. 1854. Lt. Col. 3 Aug. 1855. Retired 1 Oct. 1857. Hon. Col. 1 Oct. 1857. *d.* 107 Gt. Russell St., Bloomsbury, London, 26 Dec. 1874.
Of Scotscalder, co. Caithness. 2nd son of George Dempster Guthrie, B.C.S., Supt. of Police at Calcutta, and Barbara his wife, dau. of Capt. Thomas Dunbar, of Westfield. Cousin of Malcolm

Nicolson (1792-1850), *q.v.* *m.* Sophia, dau. of Frederick George Lister, *q.v.*, and widow of —— Inglis. Addiscombe Cadet 5 Aug. 1825 till 16 June 1826. Chatham 5 Feb. till 21 Dec. 1827.
Services : d.d. S. & M. 8 Sept. 1828. Fur. u.p.a. 11 Jan. 1831 till 16 Oct. 1832. Offg. Executive Engr. P.W.D., Dacca Div., 4 Nov. 1832. Adjt. Corps of Engineers 21 Sept. 1833. Executive Engr., Dacca Div., 27 Apr. 1835 ; do. Allahabad Div. 26 Aug. 1839 ; do. Cawnpore 18 Aug. 1842 ; do. Tenasserim 19 Dec. 1845 ; do. Dum-Dum 25 June 1847. Fur. s.c. 9 Aug. 1851 till Jan. 1855. Suptg. Engr. Nagpur till Mar. 1856. Fur. s.c. 24 Apr. 1856 till retirement. No record of active service.
Refs. : Burke's *Landed Gentry*, 13th edn., p. 800, *s.n.* Guthrie, of Craigie, co. Forfar. *The Times*, 29 Dec. 1874.

GUTHRIE, John (1749-1803). Lieut. Colonel, 16th N.I. *b.* 6 Mar. 1749. Country Cadet 1771. Admitted 20 Mar. 1771. Ensign 15 Mar. 1773. Lieut. 15 May 1778. Capt. 11 Jan. 1784. Major 30 Oct. 1797. Lt. Col. 21 Apr. 1800. *d. unm.* Fatehgarh, U.P., 18 Oct. 1803, of wounds received in the attack on Thathia fort on 30 Sept.

Describes himself in his Will as " a Peer of the Mogul Empire." Son of Hugh Guthrie, of Kilmarnock. Brother of Margaret Cleland, uncle of Helen and Guthrie Cleland, and cousin of Mrs. Jean Armour.[1]
Services : Operations in the Doab against Mahbub Khan 1776 ; battle of Korah. Capt. 33rd Bn. Sepoys in July 1787. Visited Garhwal in company with Thomas and William Daniell, the artists (*D.N.B.*), in 1789. Major 16th N.I. Lt. Col. 1/16th N.I. Operations in the Jumna Doab 1803 ; unsuccessful attack on Thathia fort (kld.) ; Lt. Col. comdg. the force.
Refs. : B. : P.P. No. 49, p. 9. *G.M.* 1804, i. 478. Will dated Sultanpur 16 Mar. 1803 ; proved in 1803.

[1] *Note : Possibly* the wife of Robert Burns.

GUTHRIE, John (*d.* 1791). Lieutenant. Infantry. Cadet 1781. Ensign 28 July 1781. Lieut. 1782. Struck off 1788. *d.* Cullen, co. Banff, 19 Aug. 1791.
Services : Midshipman on the *Valentine* in 1781. Apptd. Cadet on 2 Mar. 1781. Sailed for India on the *Valentine* 13 Mar. 1781.
Refs. : S.M. 1791, p. 467.

GUYON, Henry Joseph (1805-1879). Lieut. Colonel. 31st N.I. *b.* Hampstead 28 Apr. 1805. Cadet 1823. Ensign 16 Apr. 1824. Lieut. 9 July 1825. Capt. 15 Feb. 1836. Major 31 Mar. 1851. Retired 27 July 1851. Hon. Lt. Col. 28 Nov. 1854. *d.* 23 St. James's Sq., Bath, 29 Nov. 1879.

Eldest son of John Guyon, of Richmond, Surrey, Comdr. R.N., and Elizabeth his wife, dau. of Joseph de Beaufre, of Hampstead. *m.* 1st, Lancaster, 1 June 1837, Emma, youngest dau. of John Taylor Wilson, of Lancaster, solicitor. (She died Calcutta 28 Feb. 1851.) *m.* 2nd, Handsworth, Staffs., 10 Aug. 1852, Mary, youngest dau. of William Barrs, of Sutton Coldfield. Addiscombe Cadet 14 Mar. 1823 till 1824, when removed.

Services : Siege and capture of Bhurtpore ; Ensign 31st N.I. (India medal). Operations against the Bhils 1828 ; Lieut. 31st N.I. Adjt. 31st N.I. 28 Sept. 1829 till Aug. 1835. Operations against the Chuars 1832. Fur. p.a. 5 Aug. 1835 till 4 Dec. 1837. First Afghan War 1838-40 ; Ghazni ; Kalat ; Capt. 31st N.I. (Medal). Bde. Major at Cawnpore 24 Nov. 1841 till 27 Oct. 1843. Apptd. D.A.A.G. Left Wing, Army of Exercise, 9 Dec. 1843. Gwalior campaign ; Paniar ; D.A.A.G. (Bronze star). (*Lond. Gaz.* 8 Mar. 1844.) Comdd. Ramgarh L.I. Bn. 31 Jan. 1844 till Mar. 1851.

Refs. : Burke's *Family Records*, p. 287, *s.n.* Guyon. *A.J.* N.S. xxiii. 265. *The Times*, 4 Dec. 1879.

GWATKIN, Charles Robert (1809-?). Major. 60th N.I. *b.* Dinapore 24 Feb. 1809. Cadet 1825. Arrived in India 2 Aug. 1826. Ensign 30 Jan. 1826. Lieut. 31 May 1830. Capt. 5 Feb. 1843. Invalided 21 Nov. 1845. Retired 1 Aug. 1852. Hon. Major 28 Nov. 1854. (Living in Jan. 1895.)

bapt. Dinapore 1 Apr. 1809. 2nd son of Edward Gwatkin, *q.v.*, and Hetty Elizabeth his 1st wife. *m.* 1st, Bareilly, 13 Aug. 1831, Miss Mary Ann Terry. (She died Witham Friary, Somerset, 7 Sept. 1886, aged 75.) *m.* 2nd, Hove, 5 Nov. 1890, Helen, 3rd dau. of William Wright, of Eyston Hall, Sudbury, Suffolk.

Services : Ensign d.d. 60th N.I. 12 Aug. 1826. Posted to 60th N.I. 26 Sept. 1826. Apptd. to Pioneers 22 Jan. 1833. Offg. Intr. & Qmr. 44th N.I. 30 Jan. 1837. Adjt. 60th N.I. 25 Jan. till 1 Apr. 1837. Intr. & Qmr. 60th N.I. 1 Apr. 1837 till Apr. 1843. Reduction of Jhansi 1838-9 ; Lieut. 60th N.I. First Afghan War ; Khyber Pass 23 Jan. 1842 (w.) ; Lieut. 60th N.I., in charge of Comst. of Bdr. Wild's force (Medal). S.A.C.G. 8 Feb. 1843. Fur. 1 Feb. 1850 till retirement.

Refs. : Burke's *Family Records*, p. 290, *s.n.* Gwatkin. *Howard & Crisp*, ii. 167, *s.n.* Gwatkin.

GWATKIN, Edward (1784-1855). Major General. Colonel 31st N.I. *b.* 1 Feb. 1784. Cadet 1804. Arrived in India 10 Sept. 1805. Ensign 12 Sept. 1805. Lieut. 13 Sept. 1805. Capt. 29 Oct. 1821. Major 13 Aug. 1835. Lt. Col. 1 July 1842. Col. 17 Nov. 1853. Maj. Gen. 1855. *d.* at sea 13 Apr. 1855, on board the *Hotspur*, off the coast of England.

bapt. St. Gluvias, Cornwall, 17 Mar. 1785. Elder son of Robert Lovell Gwatkin, of Killiow, Cornwall, and Theophilia his wife, dau. of John Palmer, of Gt. Torrington, Devon. *m.* 1st, Lucknow, 29 May 1806, Hetty Elizabeth, dau. of Peter Gascoigne, *q.v.* (She died Meerut, 8 Oct. 1820, aged 30.) Father of Charles Robert Gwatkin, *q.v. m.* 2nd, Meerut, 21 Sept. 1826, Penelope, dau. of Joseph Smith, and widow of Alexander Bannerman, *q.v.* (She died Mussoorie, 7 Oct. 1854, aged 57.) His daus. *m.* Hon. Robert Barlow Palmer Byng, *q.v.*, and Dacres Fitzherbert Evans, *q.v.*

Services : Ensign 8th Regt. Loyal London Vols. Posted as Lieut. to 1/7th N.I. A.D.C. to G.G. 6 May 1809. Dy. Paymr. Meerut 5 June 1810 till 1827. Transfd. to 13th N.I. (late 1/7th) May 1824. Supt. Hapur Stud 21 May 1827 ; do. C.P. 13 May 1829 ; do. Hapur 30 Jan. 1834 ; do. N.W.P. 14 Feb. 1843. Lt. Col. 45th N.I. Transfd. to 19th N.I. 14 Feb. 1843 ; to 7th N.I. 30 Oct. 1843 ; to 6th N.I. July 1847 ; to 30th N.I. Oct. 1847 ; to 7th N.I. ; to 23rd N.I. Aug. 1850. Posted as Col. to 31st N.I. 2 Feb. 1853. Bdr., 2 cl., on Est. 29 July 1853 ; to comd. at Ambala Sept. 1853 ; at Delhi 1853 till Aug. 1854. Fur. 1855 till death. No record of active service.

Refs. : Burke's *Family Records*, p. 290. *Howard & Crisp*, ii. 166. *Boase. Bath Chron.* 17 May 1855.

GWINNETT, John Price (*d.* 1773). Captain, Infantry. Lieut. (22 June 1765) 10 July 1765. Capt. 9 Sept. 1767. *d.* Berhampore 19 Sept. 1773.

Services : Lieut. H.M. 47th Foot 2 Apr. 1759. Transfd. as Lieut. to Madras army in 1765. Lent to the Bengal Govt. in June 1766 during the "Batta mutiny." Subsequently transfd. to the Bengal Est. Apptd. to comd. 2nd Bn. Sepoys 12 Mar. 1773, having shortly before been passed over for comd. of a Bn. by Henry Bickerton, *q.v.*, "as he had not long before returned from a visit of some years to Europe."

Refs. : Forrest, i. 84, 86. Will, P.C.C. 510, Collier, dated 1 Jan. 1765 ; proved 22 Dec. 1777 by William Wollaston, of Charing Cross, co. Middlesex, Surgeon, the sole legatee and Exor.

H

HACKET(T), James (1759/60-1786). Lieutenant, Infantry. *b.* 1759/60. Cadet 1780. Ensign 1780. Lieut. 14 July 1781. *d.* Cawnpore 15 Dec. 1786.
A native of Ireland.
Services : Sailed for India on the *Neptune*, 3 June 1780, aged 20.

HADAWAY, John (1787-1823). Lieutenant, 24th N.I. *b.* Leith, co. Midlothian, 3 July 1787. Cadet 1808. Arrived in India 27 Oct. 1809. Ensign 27 Oct. 1810. Lieut. 18 Feb. 1815. *d. unm.* Chowringhee, Calcutta, 21 Apr. 1823.
Eldest son of Patrick Hadaway, of Leith, brewer, and Janet his wife. Brother of Cumberland Richard Hadaway, Samuel Maitland Hadaway, and Ann, wife of Dr. John William Watson, of Mauritius.
Services : Posted as Ensign to 24th N.I. in 1810. Lieut. 2/24th N.I. Asst. Surveyor in Rohilkhand 1822 till death. No record of active service.
Refs. : S.M. 1823, ii. 767. *G.M.* 1824, i. 382. Will dated Moradabad 25 Oct. 1822 ; proved in 1823. M.I. in S. Park St. cemetery, Calcutta.

HADDEN, David (1809-?). Ensign. 55th N.I. *bapt.* Nottingham 1 June 1809. Cadet 1827. Ensign (21 Jan. 1828) 21 Nov. 1828. Dismissed 10 Apr. 1832.
Son of John Hadden, of Nottingham, manufacturer, and Violet his wife.
Services : Ensign d.d. 13th N.I. 8 Sept. 1828. Posted as Ensign to 55th N.I. 4 Nov. 1828. Suspended 20 June 1831. Fur. 1 yr. without pay 15 Oct. 1831. No record of active service.
Refs. : A.J. N.S. vii. 37-8.

HADLEY, George (*d.* 1798). Captain. Infantry. Cadet 1763. Ensign 19 June 1763. Lieut. 5 Feb. 1764. Capt. 26 July 1766. Resigned 4 Dec. 1771. *d.* Gloucester St., Queen's Sq., London, 10 Sept. 1798.
Services : See *D.N.B.* Orientalist. Wrote and pub. grammatical

treatises on Hindustani in 1772 and 1796, and Persian, 1776, with vocabularies.

Refs. : D.N.B. D.I.B. G.M. 1798, ii. 816.

HAGART, Charles (1810-1878). Lieut. Colonel. 52nd N.I. *b.* Glasgow 1 July 1810. Cadet 1827. Arrived in India 18 Sept. 1828. Ensign 26 Mar. 1828. Lieut. 1 Jan. 1837. Capt. 30 Sept. 1845. Bt. Major 20 June 1854. Retired 5 Nov. 1855. Hon. Lt. Col. 30 Nov. 1855. *d.* 22 Dec. 1878.

bapt. Episcopal chapel, Glasgow, 21 Aug. 1810. Son of Robert Hagart, of Glasgow and Edinburgh, merchant, and Ann his wife.

Services : Posted as Ensign to 52nd N.I. 4 Nov. 1828. Fur. s.c. 21 Feb. 1837 till 22 Nov. 1840. Actg. Intr. & Qmr. 70th N.I. 17 Mar. 1841 ; do. 45th N.I. 18 Dec. 1841. Intr. & Qmr. 52nd N.I. 11 Aug. 1842 till 2 Dec. 1845. Fur. 26 Feb. 1846 till Feb. 1848. Second Sikh War ; Multan ; Gujerat ; Capt. 52nd N.I. (Medal with clasp). Fur. 1845 till retirement.

HAGE, Daniel. Cadet. Infantry. Cadet 1769. Resigned 15 Mar. 1770.

Services : N.F.P.

HAIG, Alexander James William (1812-1842). Lieutenant, 24th N.I. *b.* Calcutta 29 Sept. 1812. Cadet 1828. Arrived in India 7 Nov. 1829. Ensign 7 Nov. 1829. Lieut. 8 May 1837. *d.* Ferozepore 13 Aug. 1842.

Son of Alexander Haig, Surgeon Bengal Est., afterwards of Marlbro' Bldgs., Bath, and Maria his wife. Brother of Charles William Haig, *q.v.*

Services : Ensign d.d. 74th N.I. 31 Dec. 1829. Actg. Ensign 17 Dec. 1831. d.d. 53rd N.I. 19 Dec. 1831. Posted to 24th N.I. 26 Jan. 1833. Rising in Cuttack 1836 ; Ensign 24th N.I. Actg. Adjt. 24th N.I. 2 Aug. 1836 ; permanent do. 10 Oct. 1836 till 1841. Actg. A.A.G., Saugor Div.,' 11 Nov. 1840. Actg. A.A.G. of the Army 3 Mar. till Dec. 1841. Adjt. 4th Irreg. Cav. 2 Dec. 1841 till death.

Refs. : Bath Chron. 17 Nov. 1842. *G.M.* 1843, i. 110. *The Times,* 16 Nov. 1842.

HAIG, Charles William (1806-1842). Captain, 5th N.I. *b.* Calcutta 1 Jan. 1806. Cadet 1823. Arrived in India 2 June 1824. Ensign (?). Lieut. 7 Nov. 1824. Capt. 15 Dec. 1837. *d.* 13 Jan. 1842 : kld. in action nr. Kabul during the retreat.

bapt. Calcutta 17 Feb. 1806. Son of Alexander Haig, of Bath, and Maria his wife. Brother of Alexander James William Haig, *q.v.*

Services : Posted as Ensign to 2nd N.I. Transfd. to 5th N.I.

(late 1/2nd) May 1824. Fur. s.c. 25 Oct. 1832 till 30 Nov. 1835 A.D.C. to Maj.-Gen. Alexander Duncan, *q.v.*, comdg. 2nd Inf. Div., Army of the Indus, 9 Dec. 1838 till 22 Apr. 1839, when the Div. was broken up. First Afghan War 1840-2 ; Kabul disaster (kld.) ; Capt. 5th N.I.
Refs. : M.I. in St. Peter's, Fort William, Bengal.

*HAILES or HALES, James (*d.* 1766). Capt. Lieutenant, Engineers. Cadet (?). Ensign and Practitioner Engr. (?). Lieut. (?). Capt. Lt. and Sub-Director 25 Mar. 1765. bur. Calcutta 19 Sept. 1766. Brother of Josias, Mary Catherine, and Ruth Hales.
Services : Apptd. Sub.-Director, Engrs., by G.O. of 17 Apr. 1765 N.F.P.
Refs. : Broome, p. 540. *B.M. Add. MSS.* 6050 (where the name is given as Hall). Will dated 16 Sept. 1766 ; proved in 1766.
Note : Broome and the bur. register give the name as Hailes, his Will as Hales.

HAILES, John (1791-1864). Lieut. Colonel. 4th N.I. *b.* Henley, Suffolk, 20 Dec. 1791. Cadet 1807. Arrived in India 21 Mar. 1809. Ensign 14 Feb. 1809. Lieut. 10 Dec. 1814. Capt. 1 May 1824. Bt. Major 28 June 1838. Retired 31 Mar. 1841. Hon. Lt. Col. 28 Nov. 1854. *d.* at his residence, 15 Pitville Lawn, Cheltenham, 21 July 1864.

Son of George Hailes, Lieut. R.N. *m.* 1st, Calcutta, 5 June 1819, Miss Susanna Anne Farrell. (She died Hissar, 17 Dec. 1837, aged 36.) *m.* 2nd, Mary, 3rd dau. of Rev. James Carter Green, of Grimstone, Yorks.

Services : Barasat C.C. for 10 mos. Posted as Ensign to 1st N.I. Nepal War 1814-5 ; Lieut. 2/1st N.I., in 1st Div. (India medal). Siege and capture of Hathras 1817 ; Lieut. 2/1st N.I. Third Mahratta War ; Dhamoni ; Asirgarh ; Lieut. 2/1st N.I. Transfd. to 4th N.I. (late 2/1st) May 1824. Sub-Asst. in Stud Dept. at Pusa 24 July 1819 ; 2nd Asst. do., C.P., 22 June 1829 till 12 Apr. 1837. Leave s.c. 2 yrs. to Cape 7 Feb. 1835. Supervisor of Hissar Stud 12 Apr. 1837 till retirement.
Refs. : G.M. 1864, ii. 262. *The Times,* 25 July 1864.

HAILES, Martin Hunter (1810-1850). Captain, 10th L.C. *b.* Fredericton, New Brunswick, 12 Jan. 1810. Cadet 1825. Arrived in India May 1826. Cornet 18 Jan. 1826. Lieut. 28 Feb. 1829. Capt. 4 Nov. 1839. *d.* 9 Oct. 1850, on board the Ganges steamer *Sir Frederick Currie,* off Berhampore, en route from Karnal to Calcutta.
(? Son of Lt.-Col. Harris W. Hailes, New Brunswick Fenc.) *m.*

Mhow, 10 Oct. 1840, Catherine, 4th dau. of Hugh Bowen, formerly Capt. 41st Foot.

Services : Cornet d.d. 9th L.C. Posted as Cornet to 10th L.C. 26 Sept. 1826. First Afghan War 1842 ; forcing of Khyber ; Capt. 10th L.C., with Gen. Pollock's force (Medal). Gwalior campaign ; Maharajpur ; Capt. 10th L.C. (Bronze star). Supt. Remount depot at Muttra Jan.-Mar. 1846, and 30 May 1846 till death. Leave. s.c. to Mussoorie May 1850. His death took place whilst on his way to Calcutta preparatory to proceeding on leave to sea for his health.

Refs. : *De Rhé-Philipe.* *G.M.* 1851, i. 110. Will dated 28 Aug. 1849 ; proved 12 Nov. 1850. M.I. in St. Luke's, Jullundur.

HAIR, Joseph (1781-1815). Bt. Major, 18th N.I. *b.* British factory, Lisbon, 7 Apr. 1781. Cadet 1795. Arrived in India 31 Jan. 1798. Ensign 10 Aug. 1797. Lieut. 11 July 1798. Capt. 11 Oct. 1804. Bt. Major 4 June 1814. *d. unm.* Calcutta 30 Sept. 1815.

bapt. British factory, Lisbon, 27 July 1781. Son of Patrick Hair and Dorothy his wife. Brother of William Fraser Hair, of the Marine Paymr.'s office, Calcutta.

Services : Lieut. 15th N.I. Transfd. as Lieut. to newly-raised 1/18th N.I. 29 May 1800. Second Mahratta War ; Bundelkhand 1803-4 ; defeat of Rajah Ram Singh 2 July 1804 ; capture of Jaitpur ; Lieut. 18th N.I. Adjt. 2/18th N.I. for a few months before promoted Capt.

Refs. : Will dated 5 Mar. 1815 ; proved in 1815.

HAIR, Thomas F——. Lieutenant. Infantry. Cadet 1779. Ensign 18 Sept. 1780. Lieut. 28 May 1781. Resigned 24 July 1786.

Services : N.F.P.

HALCOMBE, Thomas F——.[1] Lieutenant. Infantry. Cadet 1779. Ensign 28 Sept. 1779. Lieut. 14 May 1781. Struck off Aug. 1781.

Services : N.F.P.

[1] *Note :* There is possibly some confusion between this man and the foregoing.

HALDANE, Charles (1797-1868). Major General. 44th N.I. *b.* Marylebone, London, 9 May 1797. Cadet 1818. Admitted 26 June 1819. Ensign 6 Feb. 1819. Lieut. 26 Aug. 1820. Capt. 23 Feb. 1835. Major 19 Dec. 1842. Lt. Col. 9 Apr. 1849. Col. 13 Mar. 1859. Maj. Gen. 7 Oct. 1860. *d.* Cheltenham 15 Aug. 1868.

Son of Lt.-Col. Henry Haldane, R.E., sometime pte. sec. to Lord Cornwallis when G.G., and Maria Helm his wife. Brother of Radclyffe Haldane, *q.v.*

THE BENGAL ARMY, 1758-1834 357

Services : Ensign d.d. 19th N.I. Posted as Lieut. to 2/16th N.I. Transfd. to 32nd N.I. (late 1/16th) May 1824. Siege and capture of Bhurtpore; Lieut. 32nd N.I. (India medal). Actg. Bde. Major 20 June 1827. Actg. Adjt. 32nd N.I. 5 Aug. 1829, and 16 Mar. 1831. S.A.C.G. 19 Dec. 1831; D.A.C.G., 2 cl., 1 Feb. 1837; 1 cl., 9 Oct. 1838 till 8 Feb. 1843. Fur. 10 Oct. 1846 till Nov. 1849. Lt. Col. 62nd N.I. Transfd. to 39th N.I. Dec. 1849; to 4th N.I. May 1850; to 48th N.I. Oct. 1851. Fur. s.c. 24 Jan. 1852 till 2 Nov. 1854. Transfd. to 68th N.I. 9 Apr. 1852; to 44th N.I. Nov. 1854. Fur. 1859 till death.

Refs. : *The Times*, 18 Aug. 1868.

HALDANE, David (1759/60-1784). Lieutenant, Infantry. *b*. in Scotland 1759/60. Cadet 1780. Ensign 1780. Lieut. 11 July 1781. bur. Calcutta, 19 Nov. 1784, " from the Insane House."

Services : Sailed for India on the *Neptune*, 3 June 1780, aged 20. (? First Mahratta War 1781-4.)

HALDANE, Radclyffe (1808-1849). Captain, 45th N.I. *b*. Croydon, Surrey, 7 Apr. 1808. Cadet 1823. Arrived in India 11 Oct. 1824. Ensign 17 June 1824. Lieut. 14 July 1825. Capt. 10 Nov. 1840. *d*. Lahore, 22 Mar. 1849, of wounds received at the battle of Chilianwala on 13 Jan.

Son of Henry Haldane, Lt. Col. R.E., sometime Q.M.G. of H.M. forces in E.I., and Maria Helm his wife. Brother of Charles Haldane, *q.v. m*. 1st, Muttra, 14 Aug. 1834, Eliza, dau. of William Martin (1789-1882), *q.v.* (She died Agra, 25 June 1835, aged 20.) *m*. 2nd, Delhi, 26 Aug. 1839, Elizabeth, dau. of James Skinner (1778-1841), *see* Appendix. (She *re-m*. 9 Nov. 1853, George Wagentreiber, manager of the Delhi printing press.)

Services : Posted as Ensign to 45th N.I. Mar. 1825. Actg. Intr. & Qmr. 45th N.I. 6 Aug. 1830, for a short time only. To do duty with Hariana L.I. Bn. 15 Nov. 1838; Comdt. do. 14 May till Aug. 1839; Offg. Adjt. do. 9 Apr. till Nov. 1840. 2nd in comd. 1st Irreg. Cav. 11 Nov. 1840 till Oct. 1848. First Afghan War 1840-2; relief of Kalat-i-Ghilzai; Goaine; recapture of Ghazni; reoccupation of Kabul; comdg. detachment of 1st Irreg. Cav. with Gen. Nott's force (Medal) (*Lond. Gaz.* 24 Nov. 1842). Second Sikh War; passage of Chenab; Chilianwala (s.w.); Capt. 45th N.I. (Medal). Leave s.c. to Delhi and Simla Feb. 1849.

Refs. : *De Rhé-Philipe*. M.I. Lahore cemetery.

HALDANE, Robert (1758-1826). Major General, C.B. Colonel 29th N.I. *b*. 10 Sept. 1758. Cadet 1778. Arrived in India 2 Oct. 1778. Ensign Oct. 1778. Lieut. 14 Nov. 1778. Capt. 7 June 1796. Major 13 June 1801. Lt. Col. 27 Jan. 1804. Col.

4 June 1813. Maj. Gen. 12 Aug. 1819. *d.* Stratford Pl., London, 21 June 1826.

bapt. St. Matthew's, Bethnal Green, London, 29 Sept. 1758. Son of Mungo Haldane, of Bethnal Green, and Elizabeth his wife. (*Probably* uncle of Charles Haldane, *q.v.*) Ed. Charterhouse; admitted Scholar 12 June 1769; Exhibitioner 9 Apr. 1776. Pembroke Coll., Oxon.; matric. 18 May 1776.

Services : Sailed for India on the *Southampton* 7 Mar. 1778. Lieut. 3rd Bengal Eur. Bn. in July 1787. Capt. 2nd Bengal Eur. Regt. in 1796. Fur. 6 Dec. 1797 till 5 Feb. 1801. Major 15th N.I. Operations in Jumna Doab 1803; Sasni; Bijaigarh; Kachaura; Major 2/15th N.I. Second Mahratta War; battle of Delhi; Agra; Laswari; battle of Deig; Bhurtpore; Major comdg. 2/15th N.I. Lt. Col. 15th N.I. Fur. 23 Feb. 1807 till 11 Dec. 1810. Transfd. to 19th N.I. in 1808; to Bengal Eur. Regt. in 1810; to 1/14th N.I. in 1812. Comdg. at Allahabad in 1816. Fur. 31 Dec. 1816 till death. Col. 30th N.I. 1816; 26th N.I. 1819; 29th N.I. 1824. C.B. 4 June 1815.

Refs. : Alumni Carthusiani. Alumni Oxon. *G.M.* 1826, i. 646. Will dated 26 Feb. 1825; proved 26 Jan. 1827.

HALDCRAFT or HOLCROFT, James. Ensign. Infantry. Cadet 1781. Ensign 29 Aug. 1781. Resigned 13 May 1782.
Services : N.F.P.

HALDEN, John (*d.* 1767). Lieutenant, Infantry. Cadet (?). Ensign 25 May 1766. Lieut. 1767. *d.* 19 Aug. 1767.
Services : N.F.P.

HALE, John (1804-1832). Lieutenant, 7th N.I. *bapt.* Holton-le-Beckering, Lincs., 9 June 1804. Cadet 1825. Arrived in India 23 Feb. 1826. Ensign 22 Sept. 1825. Lieut. 5 Dec. 1827. *d.* Barrackpore 24 Mar. 1832.

2nd son of Rev. John Hale, rector of Holton-le-Beckering, and of Buslingthorpe, and Margaret his wife.

Services : Posted as Ensign to 7th N.I. in 1826. Fur. s.c. 19 Dec. 1828 till 11 Nov. 1831. *d.d.* 48th N.I. at Barrackpore 18 Mar. 1832. No record of active service.

Refs. : G.M. 1832, ii. 487.

HALES, James (1785-1820). Captain, 21st N.I. *b.* 1 Dec. 1785. Cadet 1802. Arrived in India 14 Dec. 1803. Ensign 18 Dec. 1803. Lieut. 25 Aug. 1804. Capt. 21 Aug. 1818. *d.* Calcutta 18 Dec. 1820.

bapt. St. Nicholas, Deptford, London, 3 Jan. 1786. 3rd son of James Hales, of Butcher Row, Deptford, brewer, and Sophia his

2nd wife, dau. of Richard Waite Cox, of Harwich. Cousin-german of William Hales, *q.v.* *m.* Calcutta, 27 Oct. 1814, Frances Charlotte, eldest dau. of Thomas Blair, of Welbeck St., Marylebone. (She *re-m.* 21 May 1825, James Stilwell, and died 27 Nov. 1871.)
Services : Posted as Ensign to newly-raised 21st N.I. in 1804. Second Mahratta War ; Lieut. 21st N.I. Adjt. 1/21st N.I. 26 Jan. 1810 till 1816. S.A.C.G. 22 Dec. 1815 till death. On fur. in 1819. A.D.C. to G.G. 1820.
Refs. : Howard & Crisp, i. 289 ; (Notes) iii. 105, *s.n.* Hales. Will dated St. Helena 16 June 1819 ; proved 28 Dec. 1820. M.I. in S. Park St. cemetery, Calcutta.

HALES, Robert Unit(t) (1780-1804). Lieutenant, 15th N.I. *b.* London 14 June 1780. Cadet 1798. Arrived in India 26 Mar. 1800. Ensign 5 Jan. 1800. Lieut. 29 May 1800. *d.* 24 Nov. 1804, of wounds received at the battle of Deig on 13 Nov.

bapt. St. Anne's, Middlesex, 14 July 1780. Son of Robert Hales, surgeon, and Martha his wife.
Services : Operations in Jumna Doab 1803 ; Sasni ; Bijaigarh ; Kachaura ; Lieut. 15th N.I. Second Mahratta War ; battle of Delhi ; Agra ; Laswari ; battle of Deig (s.w.) ; Lieut. 15th N.I.
Refs. : Pester, p. 346.

HALES, William (1784-1822). Bt. Captain, 29th N.I. *b.* London 18 June 1784. Cadet 1803. Arrived in India 2 Dec. 1804. Ensign 30 Oct. 1804. Lieut. 30 Oct. 1804. Bt. Capt. 1 Jan. 1818. *d.* Nasirabad 6 Nov. 1822.

Eldest son of William Hales, of Camberwell, and Mary his wife. Cousin-german of James Hales, *q.v.*
Services : Posted as Lieut. to 17th N.I. in 1805. Transfd. to newly-raised 2/29th N.I. in 1815. Intr. & Qmr. 2/29th N.I. 21 Oct. 1815 till death. Operations against the Bhattis of Hariana 1818. Third Mahratta War 1819 ; Asirgarh. Actg. Adjt. 2/29th N.I. in 1822.
Refs. : Howard & Crisp (Notes), iii. 107. *G.M.* 1823, ii. 477. Will dated 20 Dec. 1814 ; proved 28 Dec. 1822.

HALFORD, William Hamilton (1797-1857). Bt. Colonel, 71st N.I. *b.* Upton-on-Severn, Worcs., 1 May 1797. Cadet 1818. Admitted 11 Sept. 1819. Ensign (?). Lieut. 20 Mar. 1821. Capt. 6 Apr. 1835. Major 1 July 1846. Lt. Col. 25 May 1852. Bt. Col. 25 May 1855. *d.* Lucknow 29 July 1857.

Son of J. Halford, " of Windsor Castle." *m.* Calcutta, 9 Jan. 1836, Anna, youngest dau. of Innis Delamain, *q.v.*, and widow of John William Gibbs, *q.v.*

Services : Fur. u.p.a. 20 Nov. 1819 till 8 Oct. 1821. Posted as Lieut. to 2/21st N.I. Operations against Arabs and Mahrattas in C.I. 1822-3 ; Lieut. 1/21st N.I. Transfd. to 41st N.I. (late 1/21st) May 1824. Actg. Adjt. Left Wing 41st N.I. 17 Dec. 1825. Siege and capture of Bhurtpore ; Lieut. 41st N.I. (India medal). Adjt. 41st N.I. 25 July 1827 till 14 Apr. 1835. Fur. p.a. 28 Mar. 1837 till 4 Feb. 1840. Tempy. comdg. Ramgarh L.I. 22 Feb. 1840. With 2nd Vol. Regt. for China 1 Feb. 1842 till 20 Feb. 1843. First China War ; Chin-kiang-Foo ; investment of Nanking ; Capt. 2nd Vol. Regt. (Medal). Offg. D.A.A.G. Presdy. Div. 19 Aug. 1843 ; do. Dinapore Div. 22 Dec. 1843. First Sikh War ; Sobraon (s.w.) ; Capt. 41st N.I. (Medal). Posted as Lt. Col. to 4th N.I. June 1852 ; to 71st N.I. Dec. 1855. Mutiny campaign ; defence of Lucknow Residency.

HALHED, George (1806-1830). Lieutenant, 22nd N.I. *b.* Yateley, Hants, 13 July 1806. Cadet 1822. Arrived in India 5 July 1823. Ensign 20 June 1823. Lieut. 13 May 1825. *d.* Hamirpur, U.P., 17 June 1830.

bapt. Yateley 1 Mar. 1807. Son of John Halhed, of London, underwriter, and of Yateley House (now called Yateley Hall), and Anna Maria his wife, 4th and youngest dau. of John Caswall. Brother of Henry Halhed, *q.v.*, and of Elizabeth, wife of Edward Cairncross Sneyd, *q.v.* Nephew of Nathaniel Brassey Halhed, B.C.S. (*D.N.B.*).

Services : Posted as Ensign to 2nd N.I. Transfd. to 22nd N.I. (late 2/2nd) May 1824. Offg. Intr. & Qmr. 22nd N.I. 29 July 1829. No record of active service.

Refs. : N. & Q. 12S. iii. 255. *A.J. N.S.* iv. 37.

HALHED, Henry (1805-1886). Captain. 7th L.C. *b.* Yateley, nr. Hartford Bridge, Hants, 3 Aug. 1805. Cadet 1821. Arrived in India 4 May 1822. Cornet 3 Dec. 1821. Lieut. 2 Oct. 1824. Capt. 13 Apr. 1837. Retired 23 Apr. 1839. *d.* 28 Mar. 1886.

Son of John Halhed, of Yateley House, and Anna Maria his wife. Brother of Robert William Halhed, *q.v.*, and of Frances Alicia, wife of James Charter, *q.v.*

Services : Posted as Cornet to 7th L.C., and served throughout with that Regt. Actg. Adjt. 11 Dec. 1827, and 27 May 1829. Intr. & Qmr. 9 Dec. 1829. Fur. p.a. 10 Dec. 1832 till 23 Oct. 1835. Actg. Intr. & Qmr. 28 Mar. 1836. Fur. s.c. 23 Oct. 1836 till retirement. No record of active service.

HALHED, Robert William (1803-1831). Captain, 28th N.I. *b.* Yateley, Hants, 25 Apr. 1803. Cadet 1818. Admitted 11 Sept. 1819. Ensign 20 May 1819. Lieut. 25 Aug. 1821. Capt. 27 May 1830. *d.* Jaunpur, U.P., 23 Oct. 1831.

bapt. Yateley 28 May 1803. Son of John Halhed, of Yateley House, and Anna Maria his wife. Brother of George Halhed, *q.v.*, and grandson of William Halhed, of Noke, co. Hereford, director of the Bank of England. *m.* (?).
Services: Ensign d.d. 8th N.I. Posted as Ensign to 2/16th N.I. Transfd. to 14th N.I. in 1823 ; to 28th N.I. (late 1/14th) May 1824. Fur. s.c. 2 May 1825 till 4 Feb. 1829. No record of active service.

HALKERSTON, Robert (1759-1786). Ensign, 3rd Bengal Eur. Regt. *b.* 6 Sept. 1759. Cadet 1782. Ensign 26 Jan. 1783. *d. unm.* Berhampore, Bengal, 14 Nov. 1786.
2nd son of Robert Halkerston, IV, of Carsekerdo, and Christian Johnston his wife.
Services: N.F.P.
Refs.: *Some Old Families*, by H. B. McCall, 1889, p. 47. *S.M.* 1787, p. 206.

HALKET, John. Ensign. Infantry. Cadet 1783. Ensign 1783. Struck off 1788.
N.B.—The following is conjectural only :
(*b.* 1768. 3rd son of Sir John Wedderburne Halkett, 4th Bart., and Mary his 2nd wife, dau. of Hon. John Hamilton. *m.* 1st, Anne, dau. of William Todd. *m.* 2nd, 6 July 1815, Katherine, 5th dau. of Dunbar Douglas Hamilton, 4th Earl of Selkirk.)
Services: N.F.P. (? Govr. of the Bahama Is. 2 Dec. 1801 : do. of Tobago 27 Oct. 1803 till 1806.)
Refs.: (? Burke's *Peerage*, 1904, p. 725, *s.n.* Halkett, Bart., of Pitfirrane, co. Fife.)

*****CRAIGIE-HALKETT, Henry** (1811-1881). Cadet. Afterwards B.C.S. Collector at Nadia, Bengal. *b.* 23 Apr. 1811. Cadet 1825. Never commissioned. *d.* Vernon Terr., Brighton, 13 June 1881.
5th son of John Cornelius Craigie-Halkett, of Hall Hill, Col. 55th Regt., and Margaret his wife, eldest dau. of Robert Davidson, of Revelrig. Brother of John Craigie-Halkett, *q.v. m.* 1850, Emily Elizabeth, dau. of John Wetherall, of Castle Town and Dove Grove, King's Co., J.P. Addiscombe Cadet 1826.
Services: Resigned whilst at Addiscombe, and transfd. to E.I.Co. Civil Coll. Apptd. Writer, B.C.S., 30 Apr. 1829. Arrived in India 20 Dec. 1829. Collector at Nadia in 1859. Retired 20 July 1863.
Refs.: Burke's *Landed Gentry*, 12th edn., p. 857, *s.n.* Craigie-Halkett, of Cramond, co. Edinburgh. *Law Times*, lxxi. 182.

CRAIGIE-HALKETT, John (1805-1870). Major General, C.B. 20th N.I. *bapt.* Inverness 11 June 1805. Cadet 1821. Arrived in India 10 Dec. 1822. Ensign 22 Oct. 1822. Lieut. 22 Oct. 1824.

Capt. 6 Aug. 1834. Major 3 Sept. 1849. Lt. Col. 28 Nov. 1854. Bt. Col. 15 Sept. 1855. Retired 31 Dec. 1861. Maj. Gen. 31 Dec. 1861. *d.* 59 Melville St., Edinburgh, 5 Jan. 1870.

Of Revelrig. Entered the Service as John Halkett-Craigie : name changed to Craigie-Halkett 16 Apr. 1856. 2nd son of John Cornelius Craigie-Halkett, of Hall Hill, Col. 55th Regt., and Margaret his wife. Brother of Henry Craigie-Halkett, *q.v.*, and nephew by marriage of William Sands, *q.v.* *m.* 25 Sept. 1829, Caroline, dau. of William George Maxwell, *q.v.* (*See also* Charles Henry Boisragon.)

Services : Posted as Ensign to 5th N.I. Transfd. to 20th N.I. (late 2/5th) May 1824. First Burma War ; Arakan 1825 ; Lieut. 2nd L.I. Bn. (India medal). Adjt. 20th N.I. 2 Oct. 1827 till 12 Mar. 1836. First Afghan War 1839-42 ; Ghazni (Medal) ; defence of Kalat-i-Ghilzai Nov. 1841 till May 1842 (Medal) ; operations of the Kandahar force under Nott ; Kabul (Medal) ; comdg. Shah Shuja's 3rd Inf. Comdd. Regt. of Kalat-i-Ghilzai (late Shah's 3rd Inf.) from its formation on 4 Oct. 1842 till Jan. 1852. Gwalior campaign ; Maharajpur (Bronze star). Against the Kohat Pass Afridis Nov. 1853. Comdd. force against the Aka Khel Afridis Mar. 1855 ; also against Bussee Khel Afridis 27 Nov. 1855 (India medal, N.W.F.). " He fought in more than 100 battles " (*Boase*). Durani, 3 cl. C.B. 24 Dec. 1842.

Refs. : Burke's *Landed Gentry*, 12th edn., p. 857, *s.n.* Craigie-Halkett, of Cramond. Boase. *The Times,* 8 Jan. 1870.

HALL, Arthur (1809-1879). Major General. 3rd Bengal Eur. L.C. *b.* Oxford 25 Nov. 1809. Cadet 1827. Arrived in India 5 July 1828. Cornet (9 Feb. 1828) 17 May 1829. Lieut. 1 Mar. 1836. Capt. 14 Jan. 1842. Major 14 Nov. 1853. Lt. Col. 5 May 1856. Retired 31 Dec. 1861. Hon. Maj. Gen. 31 Dec. 1861. *d.* at his residence, St. George's Manor, Guernsey, 13 Nov. 1879.

Son of Very Rev. Charles Henry Hall, dean of Christ Church, Oxford, later dean of Durham (*D.N.B.*), and Anna Maria Bridget his wife. *m.* Ghazipur, 3 Oct. 1842, Anne, 2nd dau. of John Mackenzie, *q.v.* Ed. Westminster ; admitted 10 Oct. 1822. (? Clerk to the Indian Board—*Westminster School Register.*)

Services : Cornet d.d. 2nd L.C. 31 July 1828. Posted as Cornet to 5th L.C. 16 July 1829. Actg. Adjt. 5th L.C. 19 Mar. 1834. Sub-Asst. Stud Dept. 24 Apr. 1837 ; 2nd Asst. do. 7 July 1843 till' Dec. 1849. Second Sikh War ; Ramnagar ; Sadulapur ; Chilianwala ; Gujerat ; Capt. 5th L.C. (Medal with 2 clasps). Fur. s.c. 14 Feb. 1850 till 3 Mar. 1853. Posted as Lt. Col. to 5th L.C. May 1856. Fur. s.c. 30 Dec. 1856 till 1859. Transfd. to newly-raised 5th Eur. L.C. in 1858 ; to 3rd Eur. L.C. (became 21st Hrs.) in 1859.

Refs. : Westminster School Register. The Times, 19 Nov. 1879.

THE BENGAL ARMY, 1758-1834

HALL, Charles Bastard (1802-1839). Bt. Captain, 40th N.I. *b.* 26 Oct. 1802. Cadet 1821. Arrived in India 4 May 1822. Ensign 3 Dec. 1821. Lieut. 11 Sept. 1823. Bt. Capt. 3 Dec. 1836. *d.* Calcutta 18 May 1839.

bapt. Georgetown, Penang, 5 Dec. 1802. Son of John Hall, E.I.C.S., dy. collector of customs and land revenue, postmaster, and supt. of convicts at Penang, and Rose Mary his wife. Ed. Tiverton school.

Services : Posted as Ensign to 17th N.I. Transfd. to 1/13th N.I. 23 Oct. 1822 ; to 20th N.I. July 1823 ; to 40th N.I. (late 2/20th) May 1824. Actg. Adjt. Bhagulpur Hill Rangers 7 Jan. 1839. No record of active service.

HALL, Edward (*d.* 1797). Captain, Infantry. Country Cadet 1778. Admitted 11 Aug. 1778. Ensign 8 May 1778. Lieut. 14 Jan. 1781. Capt. 28 Apr. 1797. *d. unm.* Kishanganj, B. & O., 24 Dec. 1797.

Services : Ensign 2/3rd Bengal Eur. Regt. in Oct. 1779. Lieut. 17th Bn. Sepoys in July 1787.

Refs. : Will dated 14 Aug. 1797 ; proved in 1798.

HALL, Edward (1790-1826). Captain, Artillery. *b.* Aughrim, co. Galway, 5 Dec. 1790. Cadet 1806. Arrived in India 15 May 1808. Fireworker 13 June 1807. Lieut. 30 Sept. 1808. Capt. 30 June 1820. *d.* at sea, 14 Jan. 1826, on board the transport *Edward Strettell*, at the entrance of the Talak R., Burma.

3rd son of Ven. Francis Hall, LL.D., rector of Arboe, co. Tyrone, and Christian Trail his wife. Brother of Francis Tipping Hall, *q.v.* Woolwich Cadet ; nominated for R.M.A. 3 Apr. 1805.

Services : Nepal War 1814-5 ; Lieut. 2nd Coy. 3rd Bn. Foot Art., in 2nd Div. Posted to Rocket Troop H.A. in 1819. Fur. 14 Dec. 1818 till 1823. First Burma War ; Arakan 1825.

Refs. : Burke's *Landed Gentry of Ireland*, p. 286, *s.n.* Hall, of Knockbrack, co. Galway. Will dated Dum-Dum 3 Mar. 1824 ; proved 1 Mar. 1826.

HALL, Edward Durham (1786-1806). Lieutenant, 26th N.I. *bapt.* Calcutta 15 Aug. 1786. Cadet 1803. Arrived in India 31 Aug. 1804. Ensign 19 Aug. 1804. Lieut. 21 Sept. 1804. *d.* Partabgarh, U.P., 22 Aug. 1806.

Son of John Hall, B.C.S., P.M.G. Bengal, and Jean his wife, sister of Hercules Durham, *q.v.*

Services : Posted as Lieut. to newly-raised 26th N.I. in 1804. No record of active service.

Refs. : *S.M.* 1807, p. 317.

HALL, Francis Tipping (1794-1855). Ensign. 3rd N.I. *b.* Aughrim, co. Galway, 4 Aug. 1794. Cadet 1810. Ensign 16 Dec. 1812. Resigned in India 15 Jan. 1814. *d.* Brighton 25 Dec. 1855.

4th son of Ven. Francis Hall, LL.D., rector of Arboe, co. Tyrone, and Christian Trail his wife. Brother of Henry Hall, *q.v. m.* Anne Maria Waddington.

Services : Cadet d.d. 25th N.I. 1811-2. Posted as Ensign to 3rd N.I. in 1813. No record of active service.

Refs. : Burke's *Landed Gentry of Ireland*, p. 286, *s.n.* Hall, of Knockbrack, co. Galway. *G.M.* 1856, i. 211.

HALL, George Neville Clayton (1806-1833). Lieutenant, 28th N.I. *b.* Saffron Walden, Essex, 31 July 1806. Cadet 1825. Arrived in India 6 May 1826. Ensign 12 Jan. 1826. Lieut. 6 Nov. 1832. *d.* Agra 24 Mar. 1833.

Son of Thomas Hall, solicitor and atty.

Services : Posted as Ensign to 28th N.I. 26 Sept. 1826. No record of active service.

HALL, Hawkesby (1750/51-1797). Captain. Infantry. *b.* 1750/51. Cadet 1771. Ensign 11 Jan. 1773. Lieut. 5 Apr. 1777. Capt. 30 Mar. 1781. Resigned 22 Jan. 1784. *d.* Langley (Mill), Notts., Aug. 1797, aged 46.

" Son of F. Hall, gent., of Nottingham."

Services : " He had served 16 yrs. as a Capt. of a Grenadier Coy. in the Army in India, and retired for the benefit of his health from a climate unfriendly to his constitution " (*M.M.*).

Refs. : M.M. iv. 157. *G.M.* 1797, ii. 714.

HALL, Henry (1789-1875). General, C.B. 21st N.I. *b.* Aughrim, co. Galway, 11 Sept. 1789. Cadet 1804. Arrived in India 10 Sept. 1805. Ensign 21 Oct. 1805. Lieut. 13 Mar. 1806. Capt. 5 Oct. 1821. Major 13 Jan. 1828. Lt. Col. 9 Jan. 1833. Col. 21 Dec. 1844. Maj. Gen. 20 June 1854. Lt. Gen. 24 Oct. 1858. Gen. 23 July 1866. *d.* Athenry, co. Galway, 22 July 1875.

Of Knockbrack, co. Galway, and Merville, co. Dublin. J.P. 2nd son of Ven. Francis Hall, LL.D., and Christian Trail his wife. Brother of Edward Hall (1790-1826), *q.v. m.* Nasirabad, 3 Oct. 1827, Sara, eldest dau. of Christopher Fagan, *q.v.* (She died 1847.)

Services : Posted as Ensign to 16th N.I. Operations in Bundelkhand 1807 ; Chamir ; Sehlehuganj ; Lieut. 1/16th N.I. Bundelkhand 1809 ; Rajaoli ; Ajaigarh ; Adjt. 4th L.I. Bn. Reduction of Kalinjar 1812. Adjt. 2/16th N.I. 30 Aug. 1811 till Mar. 1817. Bde. Major, Rewari, 1814. To Q.M.G.'s Dept. D.A.Q.M.G., 2 cl., 1 Jan. 1817. Third Mahratta War ; Madhurajpura ; Taragarh ;

THE BENGAL ARMY, 1758-1834 365

Nasridah; D.A.Q.M.G. 4th Div. D.A.Q.M.G., 1 cl., 24 Oct. 1818. A.Q.M.G. Rajputana F.F. 1820. Operations in Kotah 1821; Mangrol, A.Q.M.G. Raised Mhairwara Local Bn. in 1822, and comdd. it from 29 June 1822 till 1835. Transfd. to, 33rd N.I. (late 2/16th) May 1824. Posted as Lt. Col. to 33rd N.I. 14 Sept. 1833; transfd. to 42nd N.I. 24 Dec. 1833. Fur. s.c. 6 Jan. 1836 till 20 Oct. 1840. Transfd. to 52nd N.I. 13 Jan. 1838; to 4th N.I.; to 72nd N.I. 6 June 1844. Fur. s.c. 27 Jan. 1842 till death. Col. 21st N.I. 1845. C.B. 20 July 1838.

Refs. : Burke's *Landed Gentry of Ireland*, p. 286, *s.n.* Hall, of Knockbrack, co. Galway. *Walford. Boase. D.I.B. A.J.* xxv. 517.

HALL, John (1789-1842). Bt. Major, 8th N.I. *b.* London 21 Dec. 1789. Cadet 1807. Arrived in India 21 Mar. 1809. Ensign 23 Feb. 1809. Lieut. 25 Jan. 1815. Capt. 13 May 1825. Bt. Major 28 June 1838. *d.* at sea, 9 Mar. 1842, on board the *St. George.*

Son of Robert Hall. *m.* 1st, Benares, 15 Aug. 1816, Anne Frewen. (She died Barrackpore 3 Sept. 1817.) *m.* 2nd, Cawnpore, 27 Sept. 1822, Miss Harriet Thornton.

Services : Barasat C.C. for 8 mos. Posted as Ensign to 9th N.I. Nepal War 1816; Lieut. 2/9th N.I., in 4th Bde., Centre Column. Intr. & Qmr. 1/9th N.I. in 1817. Adjt. 2/9th N.I. 12 Dec. 1817 till June 1824. Operations in Oudh against Kasim Ali Khan 1822; capture of Bardgaon. Transfd. to 8th N.I. (late 1/9th) June 1824. Adjt. 8th N.I. 17 June 1824 till 23 Aug. 1825. Offg. Bde. Major at Delhi 19 Oct. 1831; do. Rajputana F.F. 4 Dec. 1835; do. Rohilkhand 26 Oct. 1838. Fur. s.c. 27 Jan. 1842.

HALL, Thomas (*d.* 1786). Captain, Infantry. Cadet 1768. Ensign 10 Feb. 1769. Lieut. 9 May 1775. Capt. 19 Aug. 1779. *d.* Cawnpore 2 Dec. 1786.

Services : Capt. 2/3rd Bengal Eur. Regt. in Oct. 1779.

HALL, Thomas (1770/71-1856). Lieut. Colonel. 13th N.I. *b.* 1770/71. Cadet 1797. Arrived in India 7 Sept. 1798. Ensign 19 Sept. 1798. Lieut. 1 Nov. 1798. Capt. 1 Sept. 1809. Major (12 Aug. 1819) 14 Nov. 1819. Invalided 5 May 1821. Retired 18 June 1834. Hon. Lt. Col. 28 Nov. 1854. *d.* Phillimore Terr., Kensington, 21 Dec. 1856, aged 85.

His dau. *m.* James Charles Maclean, *q.v.*

Services : Lieut. 13th N.I. Fur. 9 Oct. 1800 till 18 July 1802. Second Mahratta War; Lieut. 13th N.I. Capt. Lt. 13th N.I. 2 Nov. 1805. Operations against Dhundia Khan 1807; Komona; Ganauri; Capt. 1/13th N.I. Fur. 8 Jan. 1811 till 1813. (? Fur.

11 Sept. 1814 till ?) Comdd. Bareilly Provl. Bn. 1821-32. Leave s.c. 18 mos. to Mauritius and N.S.W. 26 Feb. 1830.

Refs. : *G.M.* 1857, i. 253. *I.M.* 2 Jan. 1857, p. 24.

HALL, William Hughes (1808-1835). Lieutenant, 6th L.C. *b.* Waterford 4 July 1808. Cadet 1825. Arrived in India 7 July 1826. Cornet 15 Mar. 1826. Lieut. 12 Aug. 1831. *d.* Bombay 16 Nov. 1835.

Son of William Hall. *m.* Cawnpore, 1 Mar. 1832, Amelia Margaret, 2nd dau. of Major Benjamin Halfhide, H.M. 44th Regt. (*See also* William John Edward Boys.)

Services : Cornet d.d. 5th L.C. 2 Aug. 1826. Posted to 6th L.C. 26 Sept. 1826. Actg. Adjt. 6th L.C. 9 Apr. 1831. Fur. s.c. *via* Bombay 23 Aug. 1835. No record of active service.

Refs. : *A.J.* N.S. xx. 53.

HALL, William Joseph Osborne (1791-1817). Lieutenant, Engineers. *b.* Acton, Middlesex, 11 Sept. 1791. Cadet 1808. Ensign 4 Nov. 1809. Lieut. 1817. *d. unm.* Hoshangabad, C.P., 14 Dec. 1817.

bapt. 30 Sept. 1791. Son of Rev. Dr. William Hall, of St. Paul's, Shadwell, London, and Frances Eastcourt his wife. Ed. Merchant Taylors' ; admitted Sept. 1805.

Services : At Calcutta 1812-3 ; at Agra 1814-6. Posted as Field Engr. to Nagpur Subsdy. Force 6 Dec. 1816. (? Third Mahratta War.)

Refs. : *Robinson.* Will ; codicil dated 23 July 1817 ; proved 4 May 1818.

HALL, William Lisle (1805-1851). Captain. 2nd Bengal Eur. Regt. *b.* London 19 Sept. 1805. Cadet 1822. Arrived in India 5 July 1823. Ensign 11 July 1823. Lieut. 11 Jan. 1825. Capt. 26 Dec. 1842. Retired 15 Aug. 1847. *d.* Montego Bay, Jamaica, 22 Jan. 1851.

Of Worcester and Roundhill estates, Jamaica. Son of Thomas Delany Hall, of Jamaica, and Hon. Catharine his wife, younger dau. of John Lysaght, 2nd Baron Lisle. *m.* Saidabad, U.P., 7 Oct. 1826, Maria, dau. of Rawson Hart Boddam, Bo. C.S., sometime Govr. of Bombay. Ed. Harrow 1814-8.

Services : Posted as Ensign to 23rd N.I. Transfd. to 36th N.I. 9 July 1825. Siege and capture of Bhurtpore ; Lieut. 36th N.I. In charge of 5 Coys. Pioneers 14 Feb. 1832. Shekhawat expedn. 1834 ; Lieut. 36th N.I. Transfd. to newly-formed 2nd Bengal Eur. Regt. 8 Oct. 1839. Against Hill tribes in Sind 1845 ; capture of

Trakki fort; Capt. 2nd Eur. Regt. Actg. A.D.C. to Maj.-Gen. George Hunter, C.B., *q.v.*, 2 Aug. 1845.
Refs.: Burke's *Peerage*, 1923, p. 1413, *s.n.* Lisle, B. *Harrow School Register. G.M.* 1851, i. 574.

HALLIDAY, Thomas Andrew (1808-1838). Lieutenant, 45th N.I. *b.* London 23 Feb. 1808. Cadet 1828. Arrived in India 6 May 1829. Ensign 4 Dec. 1828. Lieut. 8 June 1832. *d.* Ludhiana 30 Oct. 1838.
Son of Thomas Halliday, of Ewell, Surrey, broker, and Maria his wife. Younger brother of Sir Frederick James Halliday, K.C.B., first Lt. Govr. of Bengal.
Services: Ensign d.d. 7th N.I. 10 June 1829. Posted as Ensign to 45th N.I. 14 Sept. 1829. Fur. s.c. 18 Nov. 1834 till 6 Nov. 1837. Apptd. Adjt. 1st Inf. of the Force being formed for Shah Shuja 17 Aug. 1838. No record of active service.
Refs.: *De Rhé-Philipe. G.M.* 1839, i. 333. M.I. at Ludhiana.

HALLING or **HALDING, William** or **Thomas.** Lieutenant. Infantry. Cadet 1766. Ensign 4 Jan. 1767. Lieut. 6 Aug. 1768. Resigned 15 Dec. 1779.
Services : N.F.P.

HALLOWELL, Benjamin (1802-1832). Lieutenant, 35th N.I. *b.* Eltham, Kent, 7 July 1802. Cadet 1823. Arrived in India 12 June 1824. Ensign (?). Lieut. 25 Feb. 1825. *d.* Markly, Sussex, 7 May 1832.
bapt. 21 Aug. 1802. Son of Adm. Sir Benjamin Hallowell Carew, K.C.B. (*D.N.B.*), who took the name of Carew in 1828, and Ann Inglefield his wife. Ed. Charterhouse ; admitted a Scholar 15 Sept. 1812 ; Exhibitioner 12 May 1821.
Services: Posted to 34th N.I. Transfd. to 35th N.I. in 1825. Siege and capture of Bhurtpore ; Lieut. 35th N.I. Fur. s.c. 2 Jan. 1830 till death.
Refs.: Burke's *Landed Gentry*, 4th edn., p. 211, *s.n.* Carew, of Beddington Park, Surrey. *Alumni Carthusiani. A.J.* N.S. viii. 124.

HAMILTON, Alexander (1762-1824). Ensign. Infantry. *b.* 1762. Cadet 1783. Ensign 13 Mar. 1785. Resigned 6 Oct. 1790. *d.* Liverpool, 30 Dec. 1824, aged 62.
Services: See *D.N.B.* Orientalist. Professor of Sanskrit and Hindu literature at Haileybury Coll. May 1806 till 1818. Pub., London 1815, " Terms of Sanskrit Grammar," and other works. F.R.S. 1808.
Refs.: *D.N.B. D.I.B. G.M.* 1825, i. 189.

HAMILTON, Alexander (1778-1805). Lieutenant, 24th N.I. *b.* Old Church psh., Edinburgh, 22 Feb. 1778. Cadet 1798. Arrived in India 23 Dec. 1799. Ensign 8 Jan. 1800. Lieut. 29 May 1800. *d.* Bhurtpore, 1 Mar. 1805, of wounds received in action on 21 Feb. *bapt.* Edinburgh 28 Feb. 1778. Son of Alexander Hamilton, of Edinburgh, surgeon, and Katherine Reid his wife.
Services : Lieut. Bengal Eur. Regt. Fur. 4 Apr. 1801 till 8 Mar. 1803. Second Mahratta War ; Gwalior ; battle of Deig ; capture of Deig ; Bhurtpore (w. in 1st assault on 9 Jan. 1805 ; s.w. in 4th assault on 21 Feb. 1805) ; Lieut. Bengal Eur. Regt. Transfd. to newly-raised 24th N.I. in Oct. 1804, but never joined, remaining with Bengal Eur. Regt. till death.
Refs. : *S.M.* 1805, p. 726.

HAMILTON, Anthony (1753/54-1830). Lieut. Colonel. 25th N.I. *b.* 1753/54. Cadet 1778. Arrived in India 10 Dec. 1778. Ensign 12 Oct. 1778. Lieut. 7 Nov. 1778. Capt. 1 June 1796. Major 21 Feb. 1801. Lt. Col. 19 Oct. 1803. Retired 23 Dec. 1806. *d.* 29 Dec. 1830.
A native of Cumberland.
Services : Sailed for India on the *Gatton*, 27 Apr. 1778, aged 24. Fur. 9 Mar. 1780 till 19 Nov. 1782. Lieut. 4th Bengal Eur. Bn. in July 1787. Capt. 1/8th N.I. Transfd. as Major to 12th N.I. Feb. 1801. (? Operations in Jumna Doab 1803 ; Sasni. Second Mahratta War ; Laswari ; Major 12th N.I.) Transfd. as Lt. Col. to newly-raised 25th N.I. in 1804. Fur. 18 Dec. 1804 till retirement.

HAMILTON, Charles (1753 ?-1792). Lieutenant, Infantry. *b.* Belfast *c.* 1753. Cadet 1774. Ensign 24 Oct. 1776. Lieut. 10 July 1778. *d.* Hampstead, 14 Mar. 1792, aged 39.
Only son of Charles Hamilton, merchant, and Katherine his wife, *née* Mackay.
Services : See *D.N.B.* Orientalist. First Rohilla War ; battle of St. George ; Cadet in the Select Picket. Lieut. 1/3rd Bengal Eur. Regt. in Oct. 1779. Fur. 11 Jan. 1786. On fur. in 1790. Apptd. Resdt. in Oudh, but died before he could return to India and take up the appt. Pub. 1787 a historical work on the Rohilla Afghans ; translator of the *Hedaya*, or Commentary on Mussulman Laws.
Refs. : *D.N.B. D.I.B. G.M.* 1792, i. 286. *S.M.* 1792, p. 155.

***HAMILTON, Charles** (1782/83-1801). Ensign, Infantry. *b.* St. Helena 1782/83. Cadet 1799. Arrived in India 6 Aug. 1801. Ensign 14 May 1801. *d.* Bhagulpur, B. & O., 18 Nov. 1801.
Services : Apptd. Cadet on 24 Sept. 1799, aged 16.
Refs. : *Philippart MS.*

HAMILTON, Charles (Henry) (1801-1889). General, C.B. 59th N.I. b. at sea, on board H.M.S. *Melpomene*, 30 July 1801. Cadet 1817. Admitted 21 July 1818. Ensign 27 Jan. 1818. Lieut. 1 Aug. 1818. Capt. 2 Oct. 1826. Major 26 Nov. 1836. Lt. Col. 19 Jan. 1843. Col. 14 July 1853. Maj. Gen. 28 Nov. 1854. Lt. Gen. 30 Jan. 1868. Gen. 16 May 1872. d. 19 Sussex Gdns., London, 27 Oct. 1889.

bapt. Antigua 1 Oct. 1801. Son of Sir Charles Hamilton, 2nd Bart., of Iping House, nr. Midhurst, Surrey, Adm. of the Red (*D.N.B.*). *m.* Lucknow, 30 Jan. 1838, Eleanor Hester Maria, eldest dau. of Francis James Thomas Johnston, *q.v.*, and widow of John Nicolson, *q.v.* (*See also* James Mackenzie (1804-1859).) Addiscombe Cadet 8 Feb. 1816 till Dec. 1817.

Services : Posted as Lieut. to 2/2nd N.I. Transfd. to 22nd N.I. (late 2/2nd) May 1824. Adjt. 5th (Gough's) Local Horse 12 June 1823 till 5 Mar. 1829. Actg. Bde. Major to troops in Oudh 4 Aug. 1829. Supt. of family money, and Paymr. of pensions in Oudh and Cawnpore 15 Sept. 1834 till 25 Jan. 1837. Fur. p.a. 11 May 1838 till 12 Dec. 1840. Posted as Lt. Col. to 2nd N.I. (Grenadiers) 21 Apr. 1843. Gwalior campaign ; Maharajpur ; Lt. Col. comdg. 2nd N.I. (Bronze star). First Sikh War ; Mudki ; Ferozshahr ; Lt. Col. comdg. 2nd N.I. (Medal with clasp). Expedn. against Kot Kangra Apr. 1846. Transfd. to 39th N.I. 8 Sept. 1852 ; to 22nd N.I. Apr. 1853 ; to 48th N.I. June 1853. Fur. p.a. 22 Apr. 1853 till death. Posted as Col. to 59th N.I. Sept. 1853. C.B. 2 May 1844.

Refs. : Burke's *Peerage*, 1923, p. 1081, *s.n.* Hamilton, Bart., of Trebinshun, co. Brecon. *Boase*. *The Times*, 29 Oct. 1889.

HAMILTON, Charles William (1783-1866). General. Colonel 40th N.I. b. London 3 Nov. 1783. Cadet 1799. Arrived in India 17 May 1801. Ensign 29 Sept. 1800. Lieut. 20 Sept. 1801. Capt. 16 Dec. 1814. Major 11 July 1823. Lt. Col. 13 May 1825. Col. (18 June 1831) 6 Aug. 1835. Maj. Gen. 23 Nov. 1841. Lt. Gen. 11 Nov. 1851. Gen. 2 Sept. 1861. d. at his residence, Home Mead, Lymington, Hants, 22 July 1866.

bapt. St. Anne's, Westminster, 9 Nov. 1783. Son of William Hamilton and Mary his wife. *m.* Calcutta, 10 Mar. 1807, Miss Charlotte Rozina Hopkins. His daus. *m.* Thomas Vallencey Lysaght, *q.v.*, and Charles Prior, *q.v.*

Services : Second Mahratta War ; operations in Cuttack 1803-4 ; capture of Barabati and Khurda ; Lieut. 2/7th N.I. Capt. Lt. 7th N.I. 15 June 1814. Nepal War 1814-5 ; operations against Amar Singh ; Ramgarh ; Taragarh ; Malaun ; Capt. 2/7th N.I., in 1st Div. (India medal). (*Lond. Gaz.* 16 Nov. 1815.) Third Mahratta

War ; siege of Taragarh ; Baggage Mr. 4th Div. Comdd. Rampura
Local Bn. 4 May 1818 till 9 July 1825. Operations against the Bhils
1820 and 1822-4. Transfd. to 13th N.I. (late 1/7th) May 1824.
Lt. Col. 64th N.I. Transfd. to 27th N.I. 15 Oct. 1833 ; to 61st
N.I. 21 Feb. 1835. Posted as Col. to 61st N.I. 1 Mar. 1836. To
tempy. comd. of Benares Div. 20 Nov. 1839. Bdr., 2 cl., to comd.
garrison of Delhi 29 Apr. 1840. Bdr., 1 cl., to comd. Mewar F.F.
2 June 1841. To comd. Saugor Div. 25 June 1847 ; do. Cis-Jhelum
Div. 3 Sept. 1851. Transfd. from 27th to 40th N.I. Nov. 1849.
Fur. p.a. 9 Apr. 1852 till death.
Refs. : Boase. The Times, 25 July 1866.

HAMILTON, Edward. Captain. Infantry. Capt. 24 Aug. 1765.
Resigned 1765.
Services : Transfd. as Capt. from the Bombay Est.
Refs. : Broome, p. 542.

HAMILTON, Gavin (1809-1838). Ensign. 64th N.I. Pensioner on
Lord Clive's fund. b. Loudon, co. Ayr, 3 Apr. 1809. Cadet
1828. Arrived in India 2 Oct. 1829. Ensign 17 Feb. 1829.
Pensioned 23 June 1833. d. Mauchline Manse 14 Nov. 1838.
Son of John Hamilton, factor to the Duke of Portland and Lady
Hastings.
Services : Posted as Ensign to 64th N.I. 14 Sept. 1829. Transfd.
to 27th N.I. 2 Aug. 1832 ; to 64th N.I. 29 Sept. 1832. Fur. s.c.
4 Feb. 1831 till May 1834, when he was placed on the retired list
with effect from 23 June 1833, and granted a pension of 2/- *p.d.*
with effect from 3 Aug. 1833. No record of active service.
Refs. : A.J. N.S. xxvii. 340.

HAMILTON, Gavin Majer (d. 1776). Ensign, Infantry. Cadet
1771. Ensign 22 Dec. 1772. d. Chunar Sept. 1776.
Of Chertsey, Surrey, where he owned house property and land.
Brother of Mary, of King's Lynn, Norfolk.
Services : N.F.P.
Refs. : Will dated Dinapore 18 Aug. 1776 ; proved 7 Mar. 1777.

HAMILTON, George Dundas (1811-1833). Cadet. Infantry. b.
Coylton, co. Ayr, 12 Dec. 1811. Cadet 1829. Resigned in India
11 June 1830. d. 17 Feb. 1833.
2nd son of John Hamilton, of Sundrum, co. Ayr, and Christian
his wife, eldest dau. of George Dundas, of Dundas. Nephew of
Robert Hamilton (b. 1774), q.v.
Refs. : Burke's Landed Gentry, 13th edn., p. 826, s.n. Hamilton
(now Ames), of Sundrum, co. Ayr.

HAMILTON, George Thomas (1815-1845). Lieutenant, 24th N.I. *b.* 1 Mar. 1815. Cadet 1832. Arrived in India 8 Jan. 1834. Ensign 20 Oct. 1833. Lieut. 8 Oct. 1839. *d. unm.* 18 Dec. 1845 : kld. in action at the battle of Mudki.

bapt. Oakley, Hants, 4 Apr. 1815. 4th and youngest son of John Hamilton, of Tunbridge Wells, later of Dover, and Elizabeth Anna his wife, eldest dau. of John Trayton Fuller, of Ashdown House, Sussex, and grand-dau. of 1st Lord Heathfield. Addiscombe Cadet 1831 till 11 June 1833.

Services : Supy. Ensign d.d. 72nd N.I. 11 Jan. 1834. Posted as Ensign to 24th N.I. 24 May 1834, and passed the rest of his service with that Regt. Intr. & Qmr. 14 Mar. 1839 till death. Insurrection in Bundelkhand 1842-3. First Sikh War ; Mudki (kld.).

Refs. : Howard & Crisp, xi. 72, *s.n.* Hamilton. *De Rhé-Philipe.* M.I. in St. Andrew's, Ferozepore.

HAMILTON, George William (1807-1868). Colonel, C.S.I. 17th N.I. Comr. of Multan. *b.* Edinburgh 17 May 1807. Cadet 1823. Arrived in India 2 Nov. 1824. Ensign 20 June 1824. Lieut. 22 Aug. 1826. Capt. 17 Mar. 1844. Major 5 Aug. 1854. Lt. Col. 19 May. 1858. Col. 1 July 1862. *d.* Park Cresc., Worthing, Sussex, 26 Feb. 1868.

4th son of Daniel Hamilton, of Gilkerscleugh, co. Lanark, and Harriet his wife, 2nd dau. of Walter Campbell, of Shawfield. Brother of John James Hamilton, *q.v. m.* Barrackpore, 18 Jan. 1834, Charlotte, 2nd dau. of William Logie, *q.v.* (*See also* Samuel Athill Lyons.) (She died London 27 Apr. 1893, aged 75.)

Services : Posted as Ensign to 34th N.I. Intr. & Qmr. 34th N.I. 21 Aug. 1829 till 1842. Operations against the Kols and Chuars 1832-3 ; Lieut. 34th N.I. Junior Asst. to Comr. Saugor Div. 30 July 1842. Pol. Ofr. in charge of Levies in the campaign on the Narbada 1842-3, and in the Gwalior campaign 1843. D.C., 3 cl., Saugor and Narbada territories 29 Sept. 1843 ; 2 cl. 27 Oct. 1843 ; 1 cl. 3 Apr. 1847. D.C. Punjab 13 Apr. 1849. D.C. at Multan. Comr. Multan Div. 1 May 1854 till death. Fur. 1855 till 20 Aug. 1856. Mutiny campaign (Medal). Transfd. as Lt. Col. to 17th N.I. Sometime Comr. of Delhi. C.S.I. 17 Sept. 1867.

Refs. : Burke's *Landed Gentry*, 4th edn., p. 630, *s.n.* Hamilton, of Evandale and Gilkerscleugh, co. Lanark. *G.M.* 1868, i. 546. *The Times*, 28 Feb. 1868.

HAMILTON, Gilbert (1808-1856). Major. 53rd N.I. *b.* Glasgow 23 Feb. 1808. Cadet 1824. Arrived in India 6 May 1825. Ensign 8 Jan. 1825. Lieut. 27 May 1828. Capt. 8 Jan. 1840. Retired 8 Apr. 1850. Hon. Major 28 Nov. 1854. *d.* 14 Nov. 1856.

Son of Archibald Hamilton, of Glasgow, rum merchant. *m.* Barrackpore, 24 Dec. 1831, Miss Emma Pickersgill (*probably* dau. of William Pickersgill, *q.v.*). (She died Meerut 5 Oct. 1844.)

Services : Posted as Ensign to 53rd N.I. in 1825. Fur. s.c. 17 Feb. 1829 till 9 Nov. 1831. Actg. Adjt. 53rd N.I. 3 Feb. 1834. First Afghan War ; Kabul ; action in Khyber Pass in Nov. 1842 ; Capt. 53rd N.I. (Medal). Fur. 1846-7. Second Sikh War ; in garrison at Lahore ; Capt. 53rd N.I. (Medal).

HAMILTON, Henry. Ensign. Infantry. Cadet 1782. Ensign 11 Mar. 1783. Transfd. to the Madras Est. Out of the Service before 1787.

Services : N.F.P.

HAMILTON, James (*d.* 1805). Cadet, Artillery. Cadet 1804. Never arrived in India. *d.* at sea 5 Feb. 1805 : lost in the *Earl of Abergavenny,* off Portland. (See note to Charles Davis or Davies.)

Woolwich Cadet : nominated for R.M.A. 4 May 1803 ; obtained his certificate 7 Dec. 1804.

HAMILTON, James (1783-1814). Lieutenant, 12th N.I. *bapt.* 21 Nov. 1783. Cadet 1804. Arrived in India 10 Dec. 1805. Ensign 15 Nov. 1805. Lieut. 24 July 1806. *d.* Jaunpur, U.P., 10 Nov. 1814.

Of Heathlawn, Killimor, co. Galway. Nephew of R. A. Seton.

Services : Posted as Lieut. to 12th N.I. in 1806. Operations in Oudh 1807-8 ; Akbarpur ; Pathar-serai ; Lieut. 2/12th N.I. Expedn. to Mauritius 1810-1 ; Lieut. 2nd Bengal Vol. Bn.

Refs. : M.I. at Jaunpur (where age at death is given as 33 yrs.).

HAMILTON, Sir John, first baronet (1755-1835). Captain. Infantry. Subsequently Lt. Gen., Kt., H.M.S. *b.* 4 Aug. 1755. Cadet 1771. Ensign 2 Mar. 1773. Lieut. 22 Mar. 1778. Capt. 15 Oct. 1781. Transfd. to H.M.S. 1789. *d.* Tunbridge Wells, 24 Dec. 1835.

1st Bart. of Woodbrook, co. Tyrone. *cr.* 21 Dec. 1814. Eldest son of John Hamilton, of Woodbrook and Strabane, and Eleanor his wife, sister of Andrew, Earl of Castle Stewart. *m.* 1 May 1794, Emily Sophia, dau. of George Paul Monck, and grand-dau. of Marcus, 1st Earl of Tyrone. (She died 5 Jan. 1856.)

Services : See *D.N.B.* Operations against the Bhutias in Cooch Behar 1772-3 ; Cadet d.d. 6th Bn. Sepoys. First Mahratta War ; capture of Lahar and Gwalior, with Popham's detachment. Campaign against the Rajah of Benares 1781 ; capture of Bijaigarh, C.I. On leave of absence in Bengal in July 1787. Capt. H.M. 76th Regt. 1 Nov. 1788. Third Mysore War ; Capt. 87th Regt. Lt.

THE BENGAL ARMY, 1758-1834

Col. 61st Foot 1 Feb. 1795. San Domingo 1796-7. At the Cape 1800. Bdr. Gen. on Staff in Ireland 1805. I.G. of Portuguese army Aug. 1809. Albuera; Nivelle (Peninsular medal with clasp). Lt. Gen. 4 June 1814. Col. 2nd Ceylon Regt. 18 Jan. 1813. Govr. of Duncannon fort 10 May 1814. K.T.S. 1813, and subsequently Grand Cross. Kt. 15 July 1813.

Refs.: Burke's *Peerage*, 1859, p. 479, *s.n.* Hamilton, Bart., of Woodbrook, co. Tyrone. *D.N.B. D.I.B. Royal Mily. Calendar,* ii. 329. *G.M.* 1836, i. 315.

HAMILTON, John (1763/64-1803). Captain, 3rd N.I. *b.* London 1763/64. Cadet 1781. Arrived in India 23 Oct. 1781. Ensign 26 Apr. 1781. Lieut. 14 Aug. 1782. Capt. 29 May 1800. *d.* Chittagong 20 Jan. 1803.

Services: Apptd. Cadet on 14 Feb. 1780, aged 17. Sailed for India on the *Southampton*, 13 Mar. 1781, aged 17. Bt. Capt. 5th N.I. in June 1798. Transfd. as Lieut. and Bt. Capt. to 3rd N.I. Capt. 2/3rd N.I.

HAMILTON, John (1808-?). Captain. 9th L.C. *b.* Dublin 15 Jan. 1808. Cadet 1825. Arrived in India 25 June 1826. Cornet 16 Feb. 1826. Lieut. 2 Oct. 1828. Capt. 4 Dec. 1832. Resigned 10 Dec. 1841.

Son of W. S. Hamilton, of Dublin, merchant. (*Probably* son of William Stewart Hamilton and Harriet his wife, dau. of Hon. Hans Blackwood, afterwards 3rd Baron Dufferin.)

Services: Held a Commission in a Regt. of Mil. before entering the Bengal army. Cornet d.d. 9th L.C. 8 July 1826. Posted as Cornet to 9th L.C. 26 Sept. 1826. Adjt. 4th Local Horse 8 Dec. 1829 till 3 Nov. 1831. Adjt. G.G.B.G. 15 Nov. 1831 till 3 Apr. 1834. Offg. Bde. Major Mewar F.F. 3 Feb. 1834; permanent do. 4 Apr. 1834 till Mar. 1839. Bde. Major at Cawnpore 29 Mar. 1839. Fur. s.c. 15 July 1839 till resignation. No record of active service.

Refs.: V.B.G. (? Burke's *Peerage*, 1923, p. 767, *s.n.* Dufferin and Ava, M. Burke's *Landed Gentry of Ireland*, p. 291, *s.n.* Hamilton, of Brown Hall, co. Donegal.)

HAMILTON, John James (1792-1831). Captain, 23rd N.I. *b.* 10 July 1792. Cadet 1808. Arrived in India 19 July 1809. Ensign 19 Dec. 1809. Lieut. 16 Dec. 1814. Capt. 11 Jan. 1825. *d.* Allahabad 28 Jan. 1831.

Son of Rev. George Hamilton, minister of Gladsmuir, co. Haddington. *m.* Calcutta, 13 Jan. 1816, Miss Mary Faithfull.

Services: Barasat C.C. for $10\frac{1}{4}$ mos. Posted as Ensign to 4th N.I. With Pioneers in 1815. Adjt. 2/4th N.I. 4 May 1815 till 1818. Nepal War 1816; Lieut. 2/4th N.I., in 4th Bde., Centre

Column. Leave s.c. 10 mos. to N.S.W. 19 Feb. 1817. Adjt. 1/4th N.I. 1818 till 29 Jan. 1821. Actg. Bde. Major to troops at Agra and Muttra 18 July 1820. D.J.A.G., Dinapore and Benares, 15 Jan. 1821 till 26 May 1825. Transfd. to 23rd N.I. (late 2/4th) May 1824. Actg. A.D.C. to Maj.-Gen. Sir Thomas Brown, q.v., 24 Apr. 1824. Offg. Dy. Paymr. at Dinapore 27 Nov. 1824. Tempy. extra A.A.G. 30 Jan. 1825. Siege and capture of Bhurtpore; A.A.G. Apptd. A.A.G. 9 Nov. 1826. 1st A.A.G. of the Army 5 Dec. 1829 till death. *Refs. : A.J.* N.S. v. 207.

HAMILTON, John James (1805-1874). Colonel. 36th N.I. *b.* Crawfordjohn, co. Lanark, 6 Aug. 1805. Cadet 1823. Arrived in India 9 Oct. 1824. Ensign 23 May 1824. Lieut. 25 Mar. 1828. Capt. 24 Jan. 1845. Bt. Major 7 June 1849. Bt. Lt. Col. 1856. Retired 9 Oct. 1856. Hon. Col. 9 Oct. 1856. *d.* 56 Albany St., Edinburgh, 15 Feb. 1874.

3rd son of Daniel Hamilton, of Gilkerscleugh, co. Lanark, and Harriet his wife. Brother of George William Hamilton, *q.v.*
Services : Posted as Ensign to 36th N.I. in 1825. Siege and capture of Bhurtpore ; Ensign 36th N.I. (India medal). Shekhawat expedn. 1834 ; Lieut. 36th N.I. Actg. Intr. & Qmr. 10th L.C. 27 Mar. 1837 till 3 Feb. 1841. Adjt. 36th N.I. 3 Feb. 1841 till 16 Apr. 1845. First Sikh War ; Aliwal ; Capt. 36th N.I. (Medal). Second Sikh War ; Gujerat ; Capt. 36th N.I. (Medal). Cantt. Mgte. at Jullundur 6 Mar. 1848 till Dec. 1855. Fur. p.a. 28 Dec. 1855 till retirement.
Refs. : Burke's *Landed Gentry*, 4th edn., p. 360, *s.n.* Hamilton, of Evandale and Gilkerscleugh, co. Lanark. *The Times*, 18 Feb. 1874.

HAMILTON, Percy Skeffington (1808-1842). Captain, 5th L.C. *b.* Northampton 31 Dec. 1808. Cadet 1825. Arrived in India 13 Mar. 1826. Cornet 16 Sept. 1825. Lieut. 19 June 1827. Capt. 7 July 1841. *d.* Gandamak, Afghanistan, 13 Jan. 1842 : kld. in action during the retreat from Kabul.

2nd son of Rev. James Hamilton, rector of Drumgoon, co. Cavan, and Margaret his wife, widow of Samuel Black, *q.v.*
Services : Posted as Cornet to 5th L.C. Fur. s.c. 3 Jan. 1831 till 27 Dec. 1833. Adjt. 5th L.C. 9 Apr. 1836 till 17 Sept. 1841. First Afghan War 1840-2 ; Kabul insurrection (kld.) ; Capt. 5th L.C.
Refs. : Will dated Karnal 19 Oct. 1840; proved 9 June 1843. M.I. in St. Peter's, Fort William, Bengal.

*****HAMILTON, Philip** (1743/44-1763). Lieut. Fireworker, Artillery. *b.* 1743/44. Cadet 1759. Fireworker (?). *d.* 5th, 6th or 11th Oct. 1763 : massacred at or near Patna by order of Nawab Mir Muhammad Kasim. (See note to John Gordon.*)

THE BENGAL ARMY, 1758-1834 375

Services : Sailed for India in 1759, aged 15.
Refs. : MS. list in India Office entitled, " List of Persons killed in the Massacre at Patna, and at other places during the Troubles, 1763." *Firminger,* p. 71.

HAMILTON, Robert (*d.* 1802). Lieut. Colonel, 11th N.I. Cadet 1771. Arrived in India 23 Oct. 1771. Ensign 24 Dec. 1772. Lieut. 22 Mar. 1777. Capt. 20 Mar. 1781. Major 14 Sept. 1796. Lt. Col. 26 Nov. 1798. *d.* Amboyna, Moluccas, 7 Sept. 1802 : kld. in a duel by Surgeon William Betty, Madras Est.

Son of Robert Hamilton, formerly laird of Kilbrackmont. Brother of Helen Fotheringham, Anne Fulton, and Mrs. Glegg.

Services : Capt. 3rd Bengal Eur. Bn. in July 1787. Lt. Col. 16th N.I. ; transfd. to 1/15th N.I. 21 Apr. 1800 ; to 11th N.I.
Refs. : Lives of the Lindsays (1849 edn.), iii. 214. *Crawford,* ii. 234. Will dated 17 July 1797 ; proved 30 Nov. 1802.

HAMILTON, Robert (*d.* 1793). Captain, Artillery. Cadet 1772. Fireworker 22 Feb. 1773. Lieut. 7 Mar. 1778. Capt. Lt. 1 Oct. 1781. Capt. 2 Feb. 1785. *d.* Bencoolen, Sumatra, 15 Dec. 1793.

Services : First Mahratta War 1778-84. Comdt. of Art. at Fort Marlborough, Sumatra, 1 Sept. 1786 till death.

HAMILTON, Robert (1774-?). Lieutenant. Infantry. *bapt.* Coylton, co. Ayr, 20 Oct. 1774. Cadet 1794. Arrived in India 14 Mar. 1796. Ensign 2 Dec. 1795. Lieut. 30 Oct. 1797. Resigned 29 Jan. 1801. *d. unm.*

3rd son of John Hamilton, of Sundrum, co. Ayr, and Lillias his wife and cousin, 2nd dau. of Alexander Montgomerie, of Coylsfield, and sister of Hugh, 12th Earl of Eglinton. Uncle of George Dundas Hamilton, *q.v.*

Services : N.F.P.
Refs. : Burke's *Landed Gentry,* 11th edn., p. 756, *s.n.* Hamilton, of Sundrum, co. Ayr.

HAMILTON, William (1779-1818). Major, 18th N.I. *b.* Greenock, co. Renfrew, 31 Oct. 1779. Cadet 1794. Arrived in India 25 Feb. 1796. Ensign 27 Nov. 1795. Lieut. 30 Oct. 1797. Capt. 21 Sept. 1804. Major 17 Feb. 1814. *d.* Jagannath, B. & O., 19 Apr. 1818.

Son of William Hamilton, merchant, of the family of Hamilton, of Grange, co. Ayr, and Jean Donald his wife. Brother of Robert, of Liverpool, Alexander, and Walter. His sister Elizabeth *m.* Thomas Twemlow, uncle of George Twemlow, *q.v.*

Services : Lieut. 3rd N.I. Transfd. to newly-raised 2/18th N.I. 29 May 1800. Comdd. Resdt.'s guard at Poona 1803-5 ; comdd.

escort to Resdt. at Nagpur 1805-9 ; at Poona 1809-10. Fur. from
Bombay 2 June 1810 till 1813. Nepal War 1816 ; Major 2/18th
N.I., in 2nd Bde., Left Column.

Refs. : Burke's *Landed Gentry*, 13th edn., p. 1788, *s.n.* Twemlow,
of Peatswood, Staffs. *G.M.* 1818, ii. 638. Will dated 10 Mar. 1818 ;
proved 28 Apr. 1818.

HAMILTON, Hon. William (1797-1838). Captain, Pension Est.
64th N.I. *b.* co. Lanark 6 Apr. 1797. Cadet 1817. Admitted
19 Sept. 1818. Ensign 26 May 1818. Lieut. 29 Sept. 1819.
Capt. 24 Apr. 1829. Pensioned 13 Mar. 1835. *d.* Serampore
3 July 1838.

Younger son of William Hamilton, 7th Baron of Belhaven and
Stenton, and Penelope his wife, youngest dau. of Ronald Macdonald,
of Clanranald. *m.* Calcutta, 25 Sept. 1834, Marcellina Antonia,
widow of Peter Mendes. (She died Serampore, 22 Oct. 1858, aged
72.) His step-dau. *m.* William Joseph Phillott, *q.v.*

Services : Lieut. 1/12th N.I. Transfd. to newly-raised 32nd N.I.
11 July 1823 ; to 63rd N.I. (late 1/32nd) May 1824 ; to 64th N.I.
24 Aug. 1824. Offg. Adjt. 64th N.I. 19 Nov. 1824. Fur. s.c. 4 Jan.
1830 till 15 Feb. 1834.

Note : He appears to have been wounded, probably in a duel, as
there is no record of his ever having been on active service.

Refs. : Burke's *Peerage*, 1923, p. 247, *s.n.* Belhaven and Stenton,
B.

BAILLIE-HAMILTON, Ker (1804-1889). Ensign. 21st N.I. Subsequently Govr. Gen. of the Leeward Is. C.B. *b.* Hutton Rudby,
Yorks., 13 July 1804. Cadet 1821. Ensign 14 Nov. 1822.
Struck off 1824. *d.* Wood End, Tunbridge Wells, 6 Feb. 1889.

4th son of Ven. Charles Baillie-Hamilton, archdeacon of Cleaveland, and Charlotte his wife, 3rd dau. of Alexander, 9th Earl of
Home. Cousin-german of George, 10th Earl of Haddington. *m.*
Rondebosch, S.A., 19 Apr. 1834, Emma Matilda, only dau. of
Charles Blair, of the Cape. (She died 29 Oct. 1890.)

Services : Clerk of the Council, C.G.H., in 1839. Govr. of Grenada
13 Jan. 1846 till 1852 ; Govr. of Newfoundland 8 Oct. 1852 ; Govr.
Gen. of the Leeward Is. 26 Mar. 1855 till 1867.

Refs. : Burke's *Peerage*, 1923, p. 1061, *s.n.* Haddington, E. *A.J.*
N.S. xiv. 277. *The Times*, 8 Feb. 1889.

HAMMERSLEY, William Frederick (1812-1842). Lieutenant, 41st
N.I. *bapt.* Tipperary 11 Mar. 1812. Cadet 1828. Arrived in
India 5 May 1829. Ensign 8 Jan. 1829. Lieut. 17 Oct. 1838.
d. Quetta 9 Aug. 1842.

Son of Richard Hammersley, of Corolanty, King's Co., and Wilhelmina his wife, dau. of Richard Sadleir, of Tipperary.
Services : Ensign d.d. 48th N.I. 10 June 1829. Posted as Ensign to 3rd N.I. 14 Sept. 1829. Transfd. to 41st N.I. 29 Oct. 1831 ; to 60th N.I. 20 Aug. 1833 ; to 41st N.I. 24 Sept. 1833. Actg. Intr. & Qmr. 31st N.I. 27 Mar. 1837 till 15 Dec. 1838. Apptd. A.D.C. to Maj.-Gen. Nott, comdg. 2nd Inf. Bde., Army of Indus, 6 Jan. 1839. First Afghan War 1839-42 ; Ghazni ; Lieut. 41st N.I., A.D.C. (Medal). P.A. at Shawl 17 Oct. 1839. Offg. Asst. to P.A. at Quetta, and Adjt. Bolan Rangers, 1 Aug. 1840. P.A. at Kalat 28 Apr. 1841. Apptd. to Sind and Baluchistan Agency 10 Jan. 1842. Services placed at disposal of C.-in-C. 29 Apr. 1842. Apptd. Intr. & Qmr. 41st N.I. 30 May 1842, but never rejoined his Regt.
Refs. : Will dated Quetta 1 Aug. 1839 ; proved 3 Jan. 1843.

HAMMOND, George (*d.* 1804). Lieutenant, Bengal Eur. Regt. Cadet 1797. Arrived in India 6 Oct. 1798. Ensign 16 Oct. 1798. Lieut. 1 Nov. 1798. *d.* Kunchanghat 29 May 1804.
(*Probably* nephew of James Hammond, *q.v.*)
Services : Posted as Ensign to 1/5th N.I. Oct. 1798. Transfd. to Bengal Eur. Regt. No record of active service.

HAMMOND, James (*d.* 1805). Lieut. Colonel, 2nd N.I. Country Cadet 1778. Admitted 9 Mar. 1778. Ensign 1778. Lieut. 18 Nov. 1780. Capt. 15 Feb. 1797. Major 12 Aug. 1802. Lt. Col. 21 Sept. 1804. *d.* Bhurtpore, 26 Feb. 1805, of wounds received in the assault of that fortress.
m. Dinapore, 24 Sept. 1793, Sarah, sister of John Shipton, *q.v.* (She died 7 Jan. 1859, aged 86.)
Services : Ensign 2/2nd Bengal Eur. Regt. in Oct. 1779. Fur. 31 Oct. 1786 till 23 July 1788. Capt. 5th N.I. in June 1798. Operations in Jumna Doab 1803 ; Sasni ; Major 2nd N.I. Second Mahratta War ; battle of Delhi ; battle and capture of Deig ; Bhurtpore (s.w. in 4th assault on 21 Feb. 1805) ; Lt. Col. 1/2nd N.I.
Refs. : Pester.

HAMPTON, Joseph Hampton (1800-1878). Colonel. 50th N.I. *b.* 2 Feb. 1800. Cadet 1822. Arrived in India 5 Sept. 1823. Ensign 11 July 1823. Lieut. 18 Nov. 1824. Capt. 7 July 1842. Major 9 Aug. 1854. Lt. Col. 19 May 1858. Retired 31 Dec. 1861. Hon. Col. 31 Dec. 1861. *d.* Brynhyfryd, Beaumaris, co. Anglesey, 5 Oct. 1878.
bapt. Twyning, Gloucs., 30 Oct. 1802. Younger son of John Hampton Hampton-Lewis (who assumed the additional surname of Lewis 1 June 1830), of Henllys, co. Anglesey, high sheriff 1813, and

Mary his wife, dau. of Richard Chambers, of Whitbourn Court, co. Hereford. *m.* Bareilly, 21 Apr. 1824, Ellen, dau. of Major Hall, E.I.C.S.

Services : Posted as Ensign to 25th N.I. Transfd. to 50th N.I. (late 2/25th) May 1824. Operations against the Kols 1832-3 ; Lieut. 50th N.I. Adjt. 50th N.I. 1 July 1836 till 29 Sept. 1842. Fur. s.c. 20 Jan. 1844 till 1846. Second Sikh War ; in garr. at Lahore ; Capt. 50th N.I. (Medal). Offg. Bde. Major at Delhi 16 Sept. 1850. Santhal revolt 1855 ; Major 50th N.I. Apptd. Comr. in Nagode district 31 July 1857.

Refs. : Burke's *Landed Gentry*, 12th edn., p. 1153, *s.n.* Hampton-Lewis, of Henllys and Bodion. *The Times,* 9 Oct. 1878.

Note : It does not appear that he ever assumed the additional surname of Lewis himself.

HAMPTON, Robert (1782-1842). Major General. Colonel 61st N.I. *bapt.* Calcutta 11 June 1782. Cadet 1798. Arrived in India 19 Sept. 1799. Ensign 27 Nov. 1799. Lieut. 29 May 1800. Capt. 3 Jan. 1813. Major 30 June 1818. Lt. Col. 11 July 1823. Col. 5 June 1829. Maj. Gen. 28 June 1838. *d.* Mhow 7 July 1842.

Son of Samuel Hampton, *q.v.,* and Margaret his 2nd wife. *m.* (before 1812) Eliza. Father of Samuel Charles Hampton, *q.v.*

Services : Apptd. a Minor Cadet ; struck off 2 May 1786. Lieut. Marine Regt. 1800. Expedn. to Egypt 1801 ; Lieut. Vol. Bn. Posted to newly-raised 2nd Bn. Marine Regt. (became 2/20th N.I. in 1803) 1802. Adjt. 2nd Bn. Vols. 1805. To Fort Marlbro' 23 Nov. 1807. Served in Bencoolen and Penang till 1820. Capt. Lt. 20th N.I. 3 Aug. 1811. Comst. Dept., Penang, 27 May 1815 till June 1818. To comd. 2/20th N.I. at Penang 27 Mar. 1820. To comd. troops on S. frontier of Chittagong 1823. Reposted to 40th N.I. (late 2/20th) May 1824. First Burma War 1824-5 ; Chittagong ; capture of Ramri I. and Cheduba ; Lt. Col. comdg. 40th N.I. Transfd. to 36th N.I. 3 Oct. 1831 ; to 65th N.I. 9 July 1834 ; to 46th N.I. 12 Jan. 1835. To comd. Mewar F.F. as Bdr., 1 cl., 27 Apr. 1835. Comdg. F.F. for service in Marwar, Jodhpur, 5 Aug. till 14 Oct. 1839. Transfd. to 61st N.I. 1840. Tour on Bde. Staff expired 13 June 1841. Apptd. to Staff of Army, and posted to Saugor Div. 26 Dec. 1841.

Refs. : *G.M.* 1843, i. 554. Will dated Nimach 13 Mar. 1842 ; proved 6 Sept. 1842.

HAMPTON, Samuel (*d.* 1786). Colonel, Infantry. Cadet (?). Ensign 2 Oct. 1759. Lieut. 11 Sept. 1761. Capt. 3 Jan. 1762. Lt. Col. 3 Sept. 1768. Col. 10 June 1779. *d.* Berhampore 7 May 1786.

m. 1st, Calcutta, 1 Sept. 1765, Miss Sarah Hick. *m.* 2nd, Margaret. Father of Robert Hampton, *q.v.*
Services : Battle of Udhua Nullah 5 Sept. 1763 (s.w.). Comdg. 14th Bn. Sepoys in 1764. Resigned his Commission in May 1766, during the " Batta mutiny." His resignation was accepted, but he was ultimately restored to the Service several yrs. later.
Refs. : Williams, p. 76. *Broome,* p. 574. Will dated 30 Aug. 1785.

HAMPTON, Samuel Charles (1812-1838). Ensign, 57th N.I. *b.* Calcutta 3 Nov. 1812. Cadet 1828. Arrived in India 28 Aug. 1829. Ensign 5 June 1829. *d.* Howrah, Calcutta, 18 May 1838.
Son of Robert Hampton, *q.v.,* and Eliza his wife. *m.* Benares, 19 Jan. 1837, Miss Martha Lewis Watson. (She died Torquay 11 Jan. 1851.)
Services : Ensign d.d. 43rd N.I. ; do. 57th N.I. Posted as Ensign to 67th N.I. 26 June 1830. Transfd. to 57th N.I. 21 Aug. 1832. No record of active service.
Refs. : A.J. N.S. xxvii. 208. Intestate ; admon 11 Dec. 1838. M.I. in Howrah cemetery.

HAMPTON, William Philip (1810-1881). Lieut. General. 2nd N.I. *b.* Jalna, Hyderabad, 21 Sept. 1810. Cadet 1827. Arrived in India 1 Aug. 1828. Ensign 3 Mar. 1828. Lieut. 8 May 1834. Capt. 24 Jan. 1845. Major 28 Nov. 1856. Lt. Col. 4 June 1860. Col. 4 June 1865. Maj. Gen. 1 Mar. 1870. Lt. Gen. 1 Oct. 1877. *d.* Haverstock Hill, Hampstead, 23 Jan. 1881.
Son of Capt. James Hampton, 7th Madras N.I.
Services : Ensign d.d. 40th N.I. 9 Sept. 1828. Posted to 30th N.I. 4 Nov. 1828. Transfd. to 31st N.I. 7 July 1830. Operations against the Kols 1836-7 ; Lieut. 31st N.I. Adjt. 31st N.I. 21 Feb. 1839 till 14 Apr. 1840. First Afghan War 1838-40 ; Ghazni ; Kalat ; Lieut. 31st N.I. (Medal). Gwalior campaign ; Maharajpur ; Lieut. 31st N.I. (Bronze star). Second Sikh War ; Sadulapur ; Chilianwala ; Gujerat ; pursuit of Sikhs to Peshawar, under Gen. W. R. Gilbert ; Capt. 31st N.I. (Medal with 2 clasps). Operations against Kohat Pass Afridis Feb. 1850 ; Capt. 31st N.I. (Medal). Santhal revolt 1855 ; Capt. 31st N.I. Comdd. 31st N.I. (one of the few Regts. that was never disarmed and remained loyal at Saugor during Mutiny, and subsequent operations against rebels and mutineers in Saugor district and C.I. 1858-9 (Medal with clasp). Transfd. to 2nd Bengal L.I. (late 31st N.I. ; now 1st Bn. 7th Rajput Regt.) May 1861. Comdt. do. 1 Jan. 1864 till Apr. 1870.
Refs. : Boase. The Times, 27 Jan. 1881.

HANBERS, John. Ensign. Infantry. Cadet 1782. Ensign 18 Mar. 1783. Struck off 1788.
Services : N.F.P.

HANBURY, George (1790-1819). Lieutenant, 25th N.I. *b.* 17 Jan. 1790. Cadet 1809. Arrived in India 3 Oct. 1810. Ensign 31 Aug. 1811. Lieut. 16 Dec. 1814. *d.* Calcutta 8 Aug. 1819.
bapt. London 11 June 1790. 4th son of John Hanbury, of Tottenham, Middlesex (who was eldest son of Capel Hanbury, of Mark Lane and Clapham), and Elizabeth his wife, dau. of Daniel Bell.
Services : (? Ensign H.M. 1st Foot.) Posted as Ensign to 23rd N.I. in 1811. Transfd. to 2/25th N.I. in 1812. Nepal War 1814-5 ; Lieut. 2/25th N.I., in 4th Div. On leave to sea in 1816. Afterwards in the Stud Dept.
Refs. : Burke's *Landed Gentry*, 12th edn., p. 877, *s.n.* Hanbury, of Plough Court, Lombard St., London. Foster's *Families of Royal Descent*, ii. 460. *G.M.* 1820, i. 281.

HANCORN, Baldwin Duppa. (*See* **DUPPA, Baldwin Duppa.**)

HANCORN, Thomas (*d.* 1784). Lieutenant, Infantry. Cadet 1779. Ensign 8 Sept. 1779. Lieut. 26 Apr. 1781. *d.* Barrackpore 29 May 1784.
(? *Probably* son of Baldwin Duppa, previously Hancorn, and Martha Geach his wife.)
Services : N.F.P.
Refs. : (? Burke's *Landed Gentry*, 13th edn., p. 492, *s.n.* Duppa de Uphaugh, of Hollingbourne, Kent.)

HANDSCOMB, Isaac Henley (1805-1857). Bt. Colonel, 72nd N.I. *b.* Newport Pagnell, Bucks., 29 Oct. 1805. Cadet 1821. Arrived in India 24 Sept. 1822. Ensign 12 Sept. 1822. Lieut. 11 Oct. 1824. Capt. 23 Apr. 1834. Major 14 Dec. 1843. Lt. Col. 1 Apr. 1850. Bt. Col. 20 June 1854. *d.* Muriaon, Lucknow, 30 May 1857 : kld. by a mutineer sepoy of 71st N.I.
Of Padbury, Bucks. Son of Isaac Henley Handscomb, of Newport Pagnell, lace merchant, and Anne his wife.
Services : Posted as Ensign to 1/18th N.I. Oct. 1822. Transfd. to 1/13th N.I. Sept. 1823 ; to 27th N.I. (late 2/13th) May 1824 ; to 26th N.I. June 1825. First Burma War ; Arakan 1825 ; Lieut. 26th N.I. (India medal). Comdd. Shah Shuja's 4th Inf. 17 Aug. 1838 till 1 Sept. 1839. First Afghan War 1838-9 ; Kandahar ; Ghazni (Medal) ; Kabul. First Afghan War 1842 ; forcing of Khyber ; Mamu Khel ; Jagdalak ; Tazin ; Haft Kotal ; re-occupation of Kabul ; capture of Istalif ; Capt. 26th N.I., with Gen. Pollock's force (Medal). Comdd. 26th N.I. Dec. 1844 till May

1845, and Sept. 1845 till June 1852. First Sikh War ; Mudki ; Ferozshahr ; Sobraon (Medal with 2 clasps). Transfd. to 19th N.I. June 1852 ; to 40th N.I. Aug. 1852. Second Burma War ; Lt. Col. comdg. 40th N.I. (Medal with clasp). Fur. May 1854 till Mar. 1856. Transfd. to 72nd N.I. 15 June 1854. Apptd. tempy. Bdr. at Thayetmyo 25 Apr. 1856. Bdr. July 1856. To comd. at Saugor Oct. 1856 ; to comd. Lucknow Bde. 12 Jan. 1857.
Refs. : De Rhé-Philipe. *G.M.* 1857, ii. 466. *N. & Q.* 12S. x. 366. M.I. St. Mary Magdalene, Lahore cantt.

HANHAM, Frederick (1783-1804). Lieutenant, 1st N.I. *bapt.* Mere, Wilts., 25 Dec. 1783. Cadet 1798. Arrived in India 9 Dec. 1800. Ensign 6 Nov. 1799. Lieut. 27 Mar. 1800. *d.* Kalpi, U.P., 20 Sept. 1804, of an infectious fever.
Of Salisbury.
Services : Second Mahratta War ; Lieut. 12th N.I.
Refs. : Bath Chron. 24 Apr. 1805.

HANKIN, Cornelius (1790-1819). Lieutenant, 12th N.I. *b.* Stanstead Abbotts, Herts., 24 Apr. 1790. Cadet 1807. Arrived in India 14 Sept. 1808. Ensign 5 Oct. 1808. Lieut. 27 Jan. 1813. *d.* Jubbulpore 27 Dec. 1819.
Son of Michael Hankin and Mary his wife. Brother of Lieuts. James and George Hankin, Madras Est.
Services : Posted as Ensign to 12th N.I. in 1809. Lieut. 1/12th N.I. Nepal War 1816 ; Lieut. 5th Gren. Bn. in 2nd Bde., Left Column.

HANMER, William (1804-1821). Ensign, Infantry. *bapt.* Upton Parva, Salop, 1804. Cadet 1820. Arrived in India May 1821. Ensign (?). *d.* Calcutta 13 June 1821.
Son of William Hanmer, Bk. Mr. in Alderney.

HANNAH, Simon Fraser (1801-1861). Bt. Colonel, 44th N.I. Comdt. 1st Assam L.I. Bn. *b.* Inverness 12 Nov. 1801. Cadet 1819. Admitted 22 Aug. 1820. Ensign 3 Apr. 1820. Lieut. 11 July 1823. Capt. 1 Apr. 1835. Major 26 July 1852. Lt. Col. 8 June 1857. Bt. Col. 20 June 1857. *d.* Dibrugarh, Assam, 25 Jan. 1861.
2nd son of Henry Hannah or Hannay,[1] of Elgin, collector of excise, co. Moray, and his wife, dau. of Capt. Simon Fraser, of Daltulic, co. Inverness. *m.* 1st, St. Andrew's, Calcutta, 4 July 1827, Margaret Campbell, eldest dau. of Alexander Graham, of Glasgow. (She died Gauhati, Assam, 4 July 1841.) *m.* 2nd, Calcutta, 10 Jan. 1844, Mary Florence, dau. of Alexander Campbell. His sister *m.* Charles Cæsar Pigott, *q.v.*

Services : Posted as Ensign to 1/27th N.I. Transfd. as Lieut. to 1/20th N.I. 11 July 1823 ; to 25th N.I. (late 1/20th) May 1824. Served in P.W.I. 1823-6. Adjt. 25th N.I. 11 Oct. 1824. Transfd. to 40th N.I. (late 2/20th) May 1827. Adjt. 40th N.I. 21 May 1827 till 16 Aug. 1833. With the Mission to Assam Nov. 1835 till Nov. 1836. Operations against the Singphos 1836. Second in comd. Assam L.I. Bn. 14 May 1838. Comdd. 1st Assam L.I. 25 Mar. 1839 till death. Posted as Lt. Col. to 44th N.I. in 1857.

Refs. : *G.M.* 1861, i. 583. M.I. in Dibrugarh cemetery.

[1] *Note :* His name appears in *I.O. Rec.* and *E.I.R.* invariably as Hannah ; on his grave and on that of his first wife as Hannay. The former spelling appears to be a not uncommon variant of the latter.

HANNAY, Alexander (1741/42-1782). Lieut. Colonel, 1st Bengal Eur. Regt. *b.* 1741/42. Transfd. from H.M.S. as Capt. 4 Aug. 1765. Major 1 Oct. 1769. Lt. Col. 4 Sept. 1780. *d. unm.* Calcutta, 4 Sept. 1782, aged 40.

Of Kirkdale, co. Kirkcudbright. Eldest son of William Hannay, of Kirkdale, and Margaret his wife, dau. of Rev. Patrick Johnston, of Girthon. Elder brother of Sir Samuel Hannay, of Mochrum and Kirkdale, Bart., and uncle of John Hannay, *q.v.*

Services : Originally in H.M.S. (Lieut. 51st Foot 2 Aug. 1760), and took part in the campaign in Germany (including the battle of Minden 1 Aug. 1759) under the Marquess of Granby. " When the peace came he was a Lieut., and, supported by a splendid testimonial from his C.-in-C., he offered his services to the E.I.Co. They gave him a Captaincy, and he was wrecked in the Bay of Bengal, with the Coy. under his command ; ... In a few years, however, he rose to be A.G. of the Army in India, and Warren Hastings's period found him comdg. the forces of the Nawab of Oudh." Apptd. Field Ofr. of an Inf. Bde. 23 May 1772. First Rohilla War 1774 ; battle of St. George, led the Select Picket and Sepoy Grens. Entered the service of the Nawab of Oudh in 1778, and was placed in charge of the Gorakhpur district. Dismissed by the Nawab in 1781.

Refs. : Burke's *Landed Gentry*, 13th edn., p. 838, *s.n.* Rainsford-Hannay, of Kirkdale. Burke's *Visitation of Seats and Arms*, 1S. ii. 71 ; 2S. i. 183. *Anderson,* ii. 451. *D.I.B.* Will dated 2 Sept. 1782. M.I. in S. Park St. cemetery, Calcutta.

HANNAY, James (1801-?). Lieutenant. 3rd N.I. *b.* Sunbury, Middlesex, 4 Mar. 1801. Cadet 1820. Arrived in India Nov. 1821. Ensign 4 July 1821. Lieut. 11 Sept. 1823. Resigned in England 26 Aug. 1824.

THE BENGAL ARMY, 1758-1834 383

bapt. ptely. 8 Apr. 1801. Son of Andrew Hannay, E.I.C.S., and Maria his wife.

Services : Posted as Ensign to 21st N.I. in 1822. Fur. 1822 till resignation. Transfd. to 6th N.I. July 1823 ; to 3rd N.I. (late 1/6th) May 1824. No record of active service.

HANNAY, John (1780-1805). Capt. Lieutenant, 18th N.I. *bapt.* Walthamstow, Essex, 19 Apr. 1780. Cadet 1797. Arrived in India 17 Sept. 1798. Ensign 6 Oct. 1798. Lieut. 1 Nov. 1798. Capt. Lt. (?). *d. unm.* Gwalior 13 June 1805.

Son of Sir Samuel Hannay, of Mochrum and Kirkdale, Bart., and Mary his wife, dau. of Dr. Robert Meade. Brother of Sir Samuel Hannay, the last Bart., and of William Robert Hannay, *q.v.* Nephew of Alexander Hannay, *q.v.*

Services : Lieut. 10th N.I. Transfd. to newly-raised 1/18th N.I. 29 May 1800. Second Mahratta War ; Bundelkhand 1803 ; Narnaul ; Kanun ; defeat of Rajah Ram Singh 2 July 1804 ; capture of Jaitpur ; Lieut. 1/18th N.I.

Refs. : Burke's *Landed Gentry*, 13th edn., p. 838, *s.n.* Rainsford-Hannay, of Kirkdale. *Holzman,* p. 60 *n.* Intestate ; admon. 7 Oct. 1805.

HANNAY, William Douglas Spalding (1801-1836). Cornet, 8th L.C. *b.* Kelton, co. Kirkcudbright, 10 June 1810. Cadet 1831. Arrived in India 23 June 1832. Cornet (10 Mar. 1832) 23 June 1832. *d. unm.* Landour, Mussoorie, 2 Dec. 1836.

6th and youngest son of James Hannay, of Blairinnie, co. Kirkcudbright, J.P., and Marion Shaw his wife.

Services : Cornet d.d. 3rd L.C. 13 July 1832. He remained unposted till 9 June 1836, when he was posted to 8th L.C. He never joined this Regt., however, being at the time on sick leave at Mussoorie, where he remained until his death. No record of active service.

Refs. : Burke's *Family Records,* p. 295. Burke's *Visitation of Seats and Arms*, 1S. ii. 71. *De Rhé-Philipe. A.J.* N.S. xxii. 268. M.I. St. James's church tower, Karnal.

HANNAY, William Robert (1784-1818). Captain, 17th N.I. *bapt.* St. Giles in the Fields, London, 21 Apr. 1784. Cadet 1799. Arrived in India 1 Sept. 1800. Ensign 7 Jan. 1800. Lieut. 29 May 1800. Capt. 28 June 1813. *d. unm.* Calcutta 24 Oct. 1818.

Son of Sir Samuel Hannay, of Mochrum and Kirkdale, Bart., and Mary his wife. Brother of John Hannay, *q.v.*, and uncle of Frederick Rainsford-Hannay, *q.v.*

Services : Lieut. 17th N.I. (? Operations in Jumna Doab 1803 ; Lieut. 17th N.I.) Second Mahratta War ; Lieut. 17th N.I. Adjt. 2/17th N.I. 1812-3. Capt. Lt. 17th N.I. 6 Nov. 1812. Nepal War 1814-5 ; Jitpur ; Capt. 2/17th N.I., in 3rd Div. Actg. Bde. Major at Benares 1815-7. A.D.C. to Maj.-Gen. John Sullivan Wood, *q.v.,* comdg. at the Presdy., 1817 till death.

Refs. : *G.E.C. Complete Baronetage,* ii. 872, *s.n.* Hannay, Bart., of Mochrum and Kirkdale. *Anderson,* ii. 451. *Pester,* p. 287. Will dated 28 Dec. 1814 ; proved 30 Oct. 1818.

RAINSFORD-HANNAY, Frederick (1810-1884). Major. 67th N.I. *b.* Verdun, France, 3 Mar. 1810, whilst his father was a prisoner of war. Cadet 1827. Arrived in India 11 Aug. 1828. Ensign (21 Jan. 1828) 4 Nov. 1828. Lieut. 25 Feb. 1833. Capt. 3 Nov. 1843. Retired 9 July 1852. Hon. Major 28 Nov. 1854. *d.* Kirkdale 21 Jan. 1884.

Of Kirkdale, co. Kirkcudbright, J.P. and D.L. *s.* his brother (who adopted the surname of Hannay) in 1856. *bapt.* Verdun 25 Mar. 1810. Son of Capt. Thomas Rainsford, 2nd Life Gds., and Jane his wife, sister of Sir Samuel Hannay, Bart., of Mochrum and Kirkdale. Nephew of John Hannay, *q.v.* *m.* Benares, 23 Nov. 1840, Rhoda, dau. of Oliver Charles Johnston. (She died 26 Dec. 1865.) Ed. Edinburgh Univ.

Services : Posted as Ensign to 67th N.I. Nov. 1828. Adjt. 67th N.I. 30 June 1837 till Jan. 1844. Fur. 13 Jan. 1850 till retirement. No record of active service.

Refs. : Burke's *Landed Gentry,* 13th edn., p. 838, *s.n.* Rainsford-Hannay, of Kirkdale, co. Kirkcudbright. *Walford.* *The Times,* 25 Jan. 1884.

HANNYNGTON, John Caulfeild (1807-1885). Major General. 34th N.I. Dy. Mily. Auditor Gen. *b.* Derryloran, co. Tyrone, 8 Mar. 1807. Cadet 1824. Arrived in India 29 June 1825. Ensign 8 Jan. 1825. Lieut. 20 July 1825. Capt. 11 Oct. 1843. Major 6 Oct. 1850. Lt. Col. 9 Apr. 1856. Bt. Col. 1861. Retired 31 Dec. 1861. Hon. Maj. Gen. 31 Dec. 1861. *d.* at his residence, 2 St. Germain's Villas, Honor Oak, London, 4 Mar. 1885.

Son of Thomas Knox Hannyngton, of Belleisle, co. Fermanagh. *m.* (before 1842) (?).

Services : Posted as Lieut. to 24th N.I. in 1825. To comd. escort of Resdt. at Kotah 6 Oct. 1827. Fur. s.c. 23 Jan. 1830 till 15 Nov. 1832. Operations against the Kols in Chota Nagpur 1832-3 ; Lieut. 24th N.I. Adjt. 24th N.I. 5 Mar. 1834 till 4 Aug. 1835. Junior Asst. to A.G.G. at Ramgarh 28 July 1835. Principal Asst. to A.G.G., S.W. frontier, 11 Dec. 1837. D.C. Chota Nagpur 13 Nov.

1843 till 1856. Posted as Lt. Col. to 2nd Eur. Fus. July 1856. Transfd. to 17th N.I. 30 Sept. 1856; to 16th N.I. in 1857; to 63rd N.I. in 1857; to 34th N.I. in 1859. Dy. Mily. Auditor Gen. 22 Feb. 1859 till retirement. Inventor of a slide-rule.
Refs.: Boase. *The Times*, 6 Mar. 1885.

HANSEN, Christian Uldrick (*d.* 1774). Captain, Infantry. Cadet 1764. Ensign 4 June 1764. Lieut. 19 Aug. 1765. Capt. 6 Dec. 1767. bur. Calcutta 24 Sept. 1774.

A native of Lyngby, nr. Copenhagen. *m.* Catherine (or Chatarina). (She *re-m.* Walter Bourke, *q.v.*)
Services: N.F.P.
Refs.: Will dated 22 Sept. 1774; proved 7 Oct. 1774.

HARDING, Ralph (*d.* 1773). Captain, Infantry. Lieut. 3 Aug. 1765. Capt. 12 Sept. 1767. *d.* 20 Mar. 1773.
Services: Transfd. as Lieut. from H.M.S. (G.O. 1 Aug. 1765). Dismissed 26 Dec. 1771; restored to the Service 27 Jan. 1773.

HARDING, Samuel (1791-1815). Ensign, 22nd N.I. *b.* Betley, Staffs., 7 Nov. 1791. Cadet 1810. Ensign 2 Aug. 1813. *d.* Agra 18 July 1815.

Son of William Harding, atty.-at-law, steward to George Tallet, of Betley Hall.
Services: Served for 2 yrs. as Lieut. in the Vols. in which his father was a Capt., and on their disbandment, in Col. Sneyd's North Bn. of Local (Staffs.) Mil. Cadet d.d. 9th N.I. 1811-3. Posted as Ensign to 1/22nd N.I. in 1813. No record of active service.

HARDING, Thomas (*d.* 1794). Major, Infantry. Cadet 1767. Ensign 4 May 1768. Lieut. 21 Dec. 1769. Capt. 28 Mar. 1778. Major 24 Jan. 1784. *d.* Chunar 12 Nov. 1794.

Possessed an estate at Enfield. Nephew of William Brereton, of Bilmore, nr. Bishop's Waltham, and of John and Thomas Brereton, both of Winchester. *m.* Elizabeth Smith.
Services: Capt. 1st Bengal Eur. Regt. in Oct. 1779. First Mahratta War; comdd. 5th Bn. Sepoys for a short while in 1782. Major comdg. 27th Bn. Sepoys in July 1787.
Refs.: Williams, p. 97. Will proved in 1796.

HARDING, William Robert (1791-1820). Lieutenant, 27th N.I. *bapt.* Drayton-in-Hales, Salop, 8 Oct. 1791. Cadet 1807. Arrived in India 14 Sept. 1808. Ensign 8 Oct. 1808. Lieut. 16 Dec. 1814. *d. unm.* Meerut 19 Jan. 1820.

4th son of John Bayley Harding, of Old Springs, Staffs., and Sarah his wife, dau. of —— Booth, of co. Chester.

LIST OF THE OFFICERS OF

Services : Posted as Ensign to 27th N.I. in 1809. Lieut. 1/27th N.I. Third Mahratta War ; Madhurajpura ; Lieut. 1/27th N.I.
Refs. : Burke's *Landed Gentry*, 11th edn., p. 774, *s.n.* Harding, of Old Springs, Staffs. Will dated 15 Jan. 1820 ; proved 28 Feb. 1820.

HARDS, William. Ensign. Infantry. Cadet 1771. Ensign 3 Feb. 1773. Resigned 28 Oct. 1773.
Services : N.F.P.

HARDWICK(E), Champain Addison [1] (1787-1818). Captain, 23rd N.I. *b.* Barrypore (Baruipur), Bengal, at the end of 1787. Cadet 1803. Arrived in India 27 Sept. 1804. Ensign 22 Sept. 1804. Lieut. 22 Sept. 1804. Bt. Capt. 8 Jan. 1818. Capt. 1818. *d.* Hoshangabad, C.P., 16 Dec. 1818.
bapt. Calcutta 8 Feb. 1788. 4th son of Edward Hardwick(e), of Barrypore, and Mary his 2nd wife, widow of —— Porter. Brother of William Richard Hardwick(e), *q.v.*, and half-brother of Edward Hardwick(e), *q.v.*
Services : Posted as Lieut. to 23rd N.I. in 1805. Settlement of Hariana 1809 ; Bhawani ; Lieut. 2/23rd N.I. Capt. Lt. 23rd N.I. 2 Mar. 1818. Third Mahratta War ; Capt. 23rd N.I.

[1] *Note :* The only authority for the second christian name, Addison, is his father's Will. The surname appears sometimes with, sometimes without, the final ' e.'

HARDWICK(E), Edward (1777-1803). Lieutenant, 1st N.I. *bapt.* Calcutta 21 Mar. 1777. Cadet 1794. Arrived in India 16 Oct. 1795. Ensign 30 Oct. 1795. Lieut. 25 Apr. 1797. *d.* Dinapore 30 Nov. 1803.
Eldest son of Edward Hardwick(e), of Barrypore, by his 1st wife. Half-brother of William Richard Hardwick(e), *q.v. m.* Calcutta, 10 Jan. 1801, Miss Mary Barber.
Services : Lieut. 1/1st N.I. No record of active service.

HARDWICK, Frederick Wilson (1804-1866). Major. 10th N.I. *bapt.* Nottingham 16 Mar. 1804. Cadet 1821. Arrived in India 25 Dec. 1822. Ensign 2 Jan. 1823. Lieut. 13 May 1825. Capt. 1 Jan. 1837. Retired 1 Jan. 1851. Hon. Major 28 Nov. 1854. *d.* Leigh Lodge, nr. Worcester, 8 Dec. 1866.
Son of Francis Hardwick, of Nottingham.
Services : Posted as Ensign to 7th N.I. Transfd. to 10th N.I. (late 2/7th) May 1824. Actg. Adjt. 10th N.I. 21 Jan. 1829. Fur. p.a. 15 Jan. 1833 till 12 Nov. 1836. Fur. s.c. 6 Apr. 1841 till 19 Jan. 1844. Offg. Bde. Staff in 1850. No record of active service.
Refs. : *G.M.* 1867, i. 124. *The Times*, 14 Dec. 1866.

HARDWICK(E), William Richard (1789-1813). Lieutenant, 9th N.I. *b.* Calcutta 6 Aug. 1789. Cadet 1805. Arrived in India 13 Dec. 1806. Ensign 15 Oct. 1806. Lieut. 19 Nov. 1807. *d.* Coringa, Madras, 26 Jan. 1813, on board the *Admiral Drury*, from Java.

5th and youngest son of Edward Hardwick(e), of Barrypore, and Mary his 2nd wife. Brother of Champain Addison Hardwick(e), *q.v.*, and half-brother of Edward Hardwick(e), *q.v.*

Services : Posted as Ensign to 9th N.I. in 1807. With Java Vols. in 1812.

HARDWICKE, Thomas (1755/56-1835). Major General. Colonel Comdt. Artillery. *b.* 1755/56. Country Cadet 1778. Admitted 10 Sept. 1778. Fireworker 3 Nov. 1778. Lieut. 16 Feb. 1784. Capt. 20 Aug. 1794. Major 26 July 1804. Lt. Col. 21 Sept. 1804. Col. 21 Sept. 1817. Maj. Gen. 12 Aug. 1819. *d.* the Lodge, South Lambeth, 3 Mar. 1835, aged 79.

Brother of Frances Bull, widow, of Market Deeping, Lincs. Uncle of Charles George Dixon, *q.v. m.* (before 1795) ? His daus. *m.* William Moore, Major H.M. 14th Foot, and Rev. Joseph Parson, of Campsey Ash, Suffolk.

Services : Second Mysore War 1781-5 ; Sholingarh ; relief of Vellore ; siege of Cuddalore ; Lieut. F. 5th Coy. 2nd Bn. Art. Third Mysore War ; Satyamangalam 13 Sept. 1790 (w.) ; Arikera ; Utradrug ; Savandrug ; Lieut. 5th Coy. 2nd Bn. Apptd. Comy. Ord. at Bangalore Dec. 1791. Returned to Bengal in 1793 and was apptd. Adjt. & Qmr. of Art. Second Rohilla War ; Bitaurah ; Capt. comdg. 1st Coy. 3rd Bn. Comy. Ord. at Cawnpore 15 Sept. 1797 till 1803. Fur. p.a. 8 Mar. 1803 till 15 Nov. 1806. Whilst returning from fur. was wrecked in the *Lady Burges* off Bonavista 20 Apr. 1806. Tempy. seat at Mily. Board May 1808. Fur. s.c. 18 Mar. 1811 till 1 Oct. 1815. Apptd. Actg. Comdt. Art., and M.M.B., 15 July 1816. Fur. Feb. 1818 till 1820. Comdt. Art. 26 Feb. 1820. Fur. p.a. 22 Dec. 1823 till death. Author of " Illustrations of Indian Zoology," consisting of coloured figures of Indian animals, from his collection, selected and arranged by J. E. Gray, F.G.S., 2 vols., London, 1830.

Refs. : *E.I.M.C.* i. 178-9. *Stubbs*, ii. 238-9. *A.J.* N.S. xvi. 303. Will dated 11 Dec. 1829 ; proved 21 Nov. 1835.

HARDY, Abraham (1788-1851). Lieut. Colonel. 13th N.I. *bapt.* Wisbech, Cambs., 15 Dec. 1788. Cadet 1803. Arrived in India 5 Dec. 1804. Ensign 23 Nov. 1804. Lieut. 23 Nov. 1804. Capt. 30 June 1821. Major 28 June 1827. Lt. Col. 25 June 1832. Retired 29 June 1835. *d.* Peterborough, 11 Dec. 1851, aged 63.

J.P. for the liberty of Peterborough and I. of Ely. Son of Abraham Hardy.

Services : Posted as Lieut. to 1st N.I. Adjt. 1/1st N.I. 4 Mar. 1809 till 1814. Intr. & Qmr. newly-raised 2/28th N.I. 18 Apr. 1815 till 19 Nov. 1821. Third Mahratta War ; Bde. Qmr. 6th Cav. Bde., 3rd Div. Capt. 1/28th N.I. Junior Asst. to A.G.G. Saugor & Narbada territories 25 Jan. 1823. Transfd. to 56th N.I. (late 2/28th) May 1824. Major 56th N.I. Fur. s.c. 30 Jan. 1830 till 22 Dec. 1832, and 15 Jan. 1833 till retirement. Posted as Lt. Col. to 18th N.I. 2 Mar. 1833 ; to 8th N.I. 15 Oct. 1833 ; to 13th N.I. 7 Dec. 1833.

Refs. : *G.M.* 1852, i. 210.

HARDY, Alexander (1737/38-1799). Major General, Infantry. *b.* 1737/38. Cadet 1766. Ensign 25 May 1766. Lieut. 3 Sept. 1767. Capt. 30 Nov. 1772. Major 24 Jan. 1781. Lt. Col. 1 Feb. 1789. Col. 14 Sept. 1796. Maj. Gen. 1 Jan. 1798. *d.* Barrackpore, 31 Jan. 1799, aged 61.

m. Cawnpore, 13 Mar. 1781, Betty, dau. of Rev. Thomas Blanshard, chaplain 2nd Bde.

Services : Posted as Ensign to 1st Bengal Eur. Regt. May 1766 ; later in 2nd Bengal Eur. Regt. Major in 6th Bde. in July 1787.

Refs. : *G.M.* 1799, ii. 716. Will dated 3 Nov. 1798 ; proved in 1799. M.I. at Barrackpore.

HARDYMAN, George (*d.* 1836). Lieut. General, Cavalry. Cadet 1772. Admitted 10 Oct. 1772. Ensign 27 July 1776. Lieut. 13 July 1778. Capt. 1 Apr. 1793. Major 1 Nov. 1798. Lt. Col. 29 May 1800. Col. 17 June 1801. Maj. Gen. 25 Apr. 1808. Lt. Gen. 4 June 1813. *d.* Heatherwick, E. Lothian, 27 Sept. 1836.

m. 1st, Fatehgarh, 21 Mar. 1787, Gurtruy de Miller. *m.* 2nd, Hopes, co. Haddington, 30 Aug. 1803, Christian, eldest dau. of John Hay, of Hopes, and aunt of Edward Hay, *q.v.*

Services : Apptd. to the Select Picket as a Cadet in 1773. First Rohilla War ; battle of St. George ; Cadet in the Select Picket. Ensign 1776. Posted as Cornet to 1st N.C. in 1777. First Mahratta War 1779-80, under Col. Grainger Muir, *q.v.* Lieut. 34th Bn. Sepoys in July 1787. Capt. 1st Bengal Eur. Regt. in 1796. Fur. 24 Dec. 1802 till death.

Refs. : Burke's *Landed Gentry*, 5th edn., p. 603, *s.n.* Hay, of Hopes, co. Haddington. *E.I.M.C.* i. 271 ; iii. 463-4. *A.J.* N.S. xxi. 192.

HARE, Steuart Bayley (1809-1878). Lieutenant. Engineers. *b.* 9 May 1809. Cadet 1827. 2nd Lieut. 16 June 1826. Lieut. 28 Sept. 1827. Resigned 21 Jan. 1831. *d.* 1878.

Of Calderhall and Handaxwood, J.P. and D.L. *bapt.* Calcutta

19 June 1809. Son of James Hare, M.D., Surgeon Bengal Est., and Harriet his wife, dau. of William Jackson. *m.* 1st, Edinburgh, 4 Feb. 1834, Anne, 3rd dau. of Alexander Maconochie Welwood (Lord Meadowbank), of Meadowbank House, Midlothian. (She died 1854.) *m.* 2nd, 1862, Laura Anne, only dau. of Archibald Trotter, of Bush, and sister of Robert Archibald Trotter, *q.v.* (She died 5 Aug. 1908.) Addiscombe Cadet 1824-6.

Services : After leaving Addiscombe he was detained in England for field instruction under Lt. Col. Pasley, R.E. Posted to S. & M. at Aligarh 25 July 1828. Actg. Adjt. S. & M. 7 Nov. 1828 and 3 Feb. 1829. Fur. p.a. 23 Oct. 1829 till resignation.

Refs. : Burke's *Landed Gentry*, 13th edn., p. 844, *s.n.* Hare, of Calder Hall and Blairlogie.

HARINGTON, Sir Henry Byng (1808-1871). Lieutenant. 37th N.I. Subsequently B.C.S.; Member of the Supreme Council of India; K.C.S.I. *b.* 10 Apr. 1808. Cadet 1823. Ensign 16 Apr. 1824. Lieut. 27 July 1826. Resigned 12 Sept. 1827. *d.* 70 Oxford Terr., London, 7 Oct. 1871.

Eldest son of Henry Hawes Harington, of Madras, merchant and banker, and Martha his wife, dau. of Robert Nicholls, Capt. 87th Regt. Brother of Thomas Lowth Harington, *q.v.*, and of Mary Charlotte, wife of James George Allerton Rice, *q.v. m.* Calcutta, 12 Sept. 1829, Sarah Ann Russell, eldest dau. of Robert Moseley Thomas, of Calcutta, atty.-at-law. (*See also* Edward John Watson.) (She died 11 Dec. 1891, aged 82.)

Services : Posted as Ensign to 37th N.I. Siege and capture of Bhurtpore; Ensign 37th N.I. (India medal). Intr. & Qmr. 37th N.I. 25 Aug. 1826. Fur. s.c. 8 Dec. 1826 till resignation. Apptd. a Writer on Bengal Est. 30 Apr. 1828. Judge of the *Sadr* court at Agra 1852. Member of the Supreme Council 1862. Declined the Lieut. Governorship of the N.W.P. on the retirement of Sir G. F. Edmonstone in Feb. 1863. Retired Mar. 1865. K.C.S.I. 24 May 1866.

Refs. : Howard & Crisp, x. 122, *s.n.* Harington; vi. 46, *s.n.* Thomas. *Misc. Gen. et Her.*, N.S. iv. 275, 291. *D.I.B.*

HARINGTON, James (1784-?). Lieutenant. 14th N.I. *b.* Walcot, Bath, 7 May 1784. Cadet 1799. Arrived in India 6 Dec. 1800. Ensign 31 Aug. 1800. Lieut. 19 May 1801. Dismissed by G.C.M. 15 June 1809.

bapt. Walcot 1 Oct. 1787. Son of Edward Harington and Anne his wife.

Services : Posted as Ensign to 14th N.I. in 1801. Second Mahratta War; Lieut. 14th N.I. (? Resigned in India 7 Nov. 1805 —if so, readmitted without loss of rank shortly afterwards.)

HARINGTON, Thomas Lowth (1811-1860). Bt. Colonel, 5th Bengal Eur. Cav. *b.* Southampton Rd., Reading, 27 Mar. 1811. Cadet 1826. Arrived in India 9 Aug. 1827. Cornet (6 Apr. 1827) 28 Dec. 1827. Lieut. 3 Dec. 1838. Capt. 6 Mar. 1846. Major 5 May 1856. Bt. Lt. Col. 20 June 1854. Bt. Col. 23 Nov. 1858. *d.* Picton Villa, Surbiton Hill, 6 Apr. 1860, suddenly.

2nd son of Henry Hawes Harington, of 35 Hans Pl., Chelsea, formerly of Madras, merchant, and Martha his wife. Brother of Sir Henry Byng Harington, *q.v. m.* Brompton, 2 June 1840, Emily Octavia, 4th dau. of Daniel Hall, of Brompton Sq., London. (She died Bath, 20 Aug. 1906, aged 86.)

Services : Posted as Cornet to 3rd L.C. 4 Feb. 1828. Operations against the Kols 1832 ; Cornet 3rd L.C. Intr. & Qmr. 3rd L.C. 5 Aug. 1834. Transfd. to 5th L.C. 9 June 1836. Fur. p.a. 21 Jan. 1838 till 28 Dec. 1840. First Afghan War 1842 ; forcing of Khyber Pass ; occupation of Kabul ; action at Mamu Khel ; Lieut. 5th L.C. (Medal). Adjt. 5th L.C. 17 Sept. 1841 till 22 Mar. 1843. Intr. & Qmr. 5th L.C. 11 Mar. 1843 till Jan. 1846. Gwalior campaign ; Paniar ; Lieut. 5th L.C. (Bronze star). First Sikh War ; Mudki (w.) ; Sobraon ; Bt. Capt. 5th L.C. (Medal with clasp). Second Sikh War ; Ramnagar ; Sadulapur ; Chilianwala ; Gujerat ; Bt. Major 5th L.C. (Medal with clasps). Transfd. to newly-raised 5th L.C. 1858. Fur. 1858 till death.

Refs. : Howard & Crisp, x. 123, *s.n.* Harington. *Misc. Gen. et Her.* N.S. iv. 275, 291. *A.J.* N.S. xxxii. 291. *G.M.* 1860, i. 532. *The Times,* 10 Apr. 1860.

HARPER, Gabriel (*d.* 1800). Colonel. Infantry. Cadet 1763. Ensign 17 July 1763. Lieut. 3 Feb. 1764. Capt. 25 Aug. 1766. Lt. Col. 2 Dec. 1781. Col. 1 Dec. 1786. Resigned 2 Feb. 1788. *d.* Sidmouth, Devon, Oct. 1800.

m. Anne. (She died Henley-on-Thames 2 Apr. 1820.)

Services : Battle of Buxar 23 Oct. 1764 ; subsequently apptd. Bde. Major to the force for his gallantry on that day. Bde. Major to 2nd Bde. at Allahabad Aug. 1765. Comdd. 19th Bn. Sepoys 1767-73. Resigned in order to go home on fur. in 1773 ; subsequently readmitted. Resdt. at the court of the Nawab of Oudh till 28 Mar. 1772, when he was recalled by Warren Hastings. Resdt. at Lucknow in July 1787.

Refs. : D.I.B. Williams, p. 61. *Broome,* p. 482. *G.M.* 1800, ii. 112.

HARPER, William (1783-1829). Lieut. Colonel, 4th L.C. *b.* Macclesfield, co. Chester, 14 Nov. 1783. Cadet 1798. Arrived in India 9 Nov. 1799. Cornet 18 June 1800. Lieut. 11 Mar. 1805.

Capt. 1 Sept. 1818. Major 16 Aug. 1822. Lt. Col. 13 May 1825.
d. (? Meerut) 17 May 1829.
bapt. Old Church, Macclesfield, 26 Nov. 1783. Son of William
Harper and Lettice his wife.
Services : Operations in Jumna Doab 1803 ; Sasni ; Bijaigarh ;
Kachaura ; Cornet 4th N.C. Second Mahratta War ; Laswari ;
Cornet 4th N.C. Transfd. as Lieut. to newly-raised 7th N.C. in
1805. Operations in Oudh 1808 ; Lieut. 7th N.C. Settlement of
Hariana 1809-10. Capt. Lt. 7th N.C. 27 Feb. 1812. Nepal War
1814-5 ; Capt. Lt. 7th N.C., in 2nd Div. Siege and capture of
Hathras 1817. Third Mahratta War ; Dhamoni ; Mandala ;
Multai ; Harna ; Capt. 7th N.C. Transfd. as Lt. Col. to 4th L.C.
May 1825. Siege and capture of Bhurtpore ; Lt. Col. 4th L.C.

HARRIOTT, David (1788-1851). Colonel, C.B., 6th L.C. *bapt.* Gt.
Stambridge, Essex, 9 Apr. 1788. Cadet 1803. Arrived in India
12 Sept. 1805. Cornet 9 Oct. 1803. Lieut. 2 Feb. 1808. Capt.
1 Jan. 1818. Major 26 Mar. 1829. Lt. Col. 1 Sept. 1834. Col.
30 Jan. 1846. *d.* 13 Royal Parade, Cheltenham, 6 Sept. 1851,
aged 63.
Son of John Harriott and Elizabeth his 2nd wife. Brother of
George Harriott, of N. Waltham, Hants, and of Dorothy Hannah
Pitman, and half-brother of John Staples Harriott, *q.v.* *m.* C.G.H.,
1 July 1823, Miss Anna Margaretta Louw. (She died 4 Mar. 1879,
aged 74.) Marlow Cadet.
Services : Posted as Cornet to 5th N.C. Third Mahratta War ;
Capt. 5th N.C. Leave to Cape 1822-3. Transfd. as Lt. Col. to
10th L.C. 31 Oct. 1835 ; to 6th L.C. 26 Dec. 1835 ; to 8th L.C. in
1839. Apptd. to comd. as Bdr. the three Bdes. of Cav. of the " Army
of the Sutlej " (G.O.C.C. 13 Dec. 1845). First Sikh War ; Ferozshahr ; Lt. Col. 8th L.C. (Medal). Transfd. to 9th L.C. 6 Dec. 1847.
Col. 6th L.C. 30 Oct. 1848. Fur. s.c. 10 Apr. 1849 till death. C.B.
3 Apr. 1846.
Refs. : Boase. *G.M.* 1851, ii. 446. *I.M.* 19 Sept. 1851, p. 564.
Will dated 19 Oct. 1850 ; admon. 24 Apr. 1852.

HARRIOTT, Frederick Joseph (1810-1859). Bt. Major, 4th Bengal
Eur. L.C. D.J.A.G. Meerut Div. *b.* Bengal 2 Nov. 1810. Cadet
1827. Arrived in India 10 June 1828. Cornet (20 Feb. 1828)
10 Jan. 1829. Lieut. 23 Dec. 1839. Capt. 2 Oct. 1851. Bt.
Major 20 June 1854. *d.* Southampton, 6 Apr. 1859, two days
after landing from the *Ripon.*
Son of George Frederick Harriott, *q.v.*, by his 1st wife.
Services : Brought on effective strength of 1st L.C., as Cornet,
2 June 1829. Posted as Cornet to 1st L.C. 9 Sept. 1829. Transfd.

to 9th L.C. 19 Sept. 1832. Intr. & Qmr. 9th L.C. 6 Jan. 1837 till 1843. Fur. s.c. to Cape 6 Mar. 1843 till 26 July 1844. Intr. & Qmr. 9th L.C. 9 Oct. 1844 till 1850. D.J.A.G. at Peshawar 1 May 1850; do. trans-Jhelum 1851; do. Meerut 1852-9. Transfd. to newly-raised 4th Eur. L.C. in 1858. One of the judges who presided at the trial of the ex-King of Delhi. Fur. 1859 till death. No record of active service.

Refs.: *G.M.* 1859, i. 552. *I.M.* 21 Apr. 1859, p. 355. *The Times*, 19 Apr. 1859.

HARRIOTT, George Frederick (1780-1818). Major, 12th N.I. *b.* London 13 June 1780. Cadet 1795. Arrived in India 8 Mar. 1797. Ensign 26 Oct. 1797. Lieut. 30 Oct. 1797. Capt. 14 Nov. 1805. Major 24 June 1815. *d.* nr. Rampura, 24 Aug. 1818, of a fever.

bapt. St. Dunstan's, Stepney, 21 July 1780. Son of Joseph Harriott, of Ratcliffe, London, vintner, and Jane his wife. *m.* 1st (before 1807)? (She died 20 May 1813.) Father of Frederick Joseph Harriott, *q.v. m.* 2nd, Greenwich, 17 Jan. 1815, Matilda Emily Ann, eldest dau. of Thomas Norris, of Greenwich. (? *See also* John Delamain.) (She *re-m.* John Anthony Hodgson, *q.v.*) His dau. *m.* Charles Cheape, *q.v.*

Services: Lieut. 1st Bengal Eur. Regt. in June 1798. Transfd. as Lieut. to 12th N.I. Second Mahratta War; Laswari; Bhurtpore; Lieut. 12th N.I. Operations in Oudh 1808; Capt. 12th N.I. Fur. 1813 till 22 Sept. 1815. Major 1/12th N.I.

Refs.: *G.M.* 1819, i. 376. Will dated 4 Dec. 1817; proved 7 Dec. 1818.

HARRIOTT, John Staples (1780-1839). Major General. Colonel 38th N.I. *bapt.* Gt. Stambridge, Essex, 30 Sept. 1780. Cadet 1796. Arrived in India 30 Jan. 1798. Ensign 13 Oct. 1797. Lieut. 10 Sept. 1798. Capt. 10 Feb. 1807. Major 1 Aug. 1818. Lt. Col. 11 July 1823. Col. 5 June 1829. Maj. Gen. 28 June 1838. *d.* rue Castiglione, Paris, 11 Feb. 1839.

Son of John Harriott and Ann his 1st wife. Brother of Sarah, wife of John Rotton, *q.v.*, and half-brother of David Harriott *q.v.* Mentioned as "a friend" (*probably* cousin-german) in the Will of George Frederick Harriott, *q.v. m.* Brighton, Sept. 1832, Vincenza Ruina Argentini.

Services: Ensign d.d. 1/8th N.I. Mar.-Sept. 1798. Lieut. d.d. 9th N.I. Dec. 1798 till Apr. 1799. Posted as Lieut. to 2nd N.I. Apr. 1799. (? Operations in Jumna Doab 1803; Sasni; Bijaigarh; Kachaura; Lieut. 1/2nd N.I.) Second Mahratta War; Koil; Aligarh; battle of Delhi 11 Sept. 1803 (s.w.—lost a leg); Lieut. 2/2nd N.I. Apptd. Intr. to courts martial at Chunar and Dinapore

19 Jan. 1804. Bk. Mr. at Berhampore 23 Oct. 1806, and served in Bk. dept. till Mar. 1817. Capt. 1/2nd N.I. Major 1/2nd N.I. Fur. p.a. 15 Mar. 1817 ; arrived at Bombay from fur. overland via Russia and Persia 18 Jan. 1822. Apptd. to tempy. charge of Eur. Invalids at Chunar 25 Oct. 1822 ; do. 2nd Bn. Native Invalids 23 Nov. 1822. Transfd. to 22nd N.I. (late 2/2nd) May 1824 ; to 49th N.I. 5 Mar. 1828. Fur. p.a. 10 Mar. 1828 till death. Transfd. as Col. to 22nd N.I. 18 Nov. 1830 ; to 70th N.I. 30 Nov. 1830 ; to 42nd N.I. 28 Dec. 1835 ; to 38th N.I. 11 Aug. 1838.
Refs. : *E.I.M.C.* i. 275. *Pester.* *A.J.* N.S. xxix. 158. Will dated Paris 15 Sept. 1838 ; codicil dated 1 Jan. 1839 ; proved 25 Sept. 1839.

HARRIOTT, Thomas (1752/53-1817). Major. 1st N.I. *b.* 1752/53. Cadet 1779. Admitted 3 May 1780. Ensign 9 June 1779. Lieut. 2 Feb. 1781. Capt. 30 Oct. 1797. Major 25 May 1804. Retired 18 Feb. 1806. *d.* West Hall, Mortlake, Surrey, 19 Apr. 1817, aged 64.

Of West Hall, Mortlake. *m.* Calcutta, 15 Nov. 1788, Mrs. Diana Hill. (She died Twickenham 10 Feb. 1844.)

Services : Apptd. Bde. Major 3rd Bde. 12 June 1786. Bde. Major at Fatehgarh, with Bt. rank of Capt., in 1790. Capt. 1st N.I. Bde. Major at Dinapore 1803-4.
Refs. : *G.M.* 1817, i. 473. *A.J.* iii. 517.

HARRIS, Alfred (1815-1857). Major, 1st L.C. *b.* London 9 Jan. 1815. Cadet 1832. Arrived in India 29 Jan. 1834. Cornet (19 Sept. 1833) 29 Jan. 1834. Lieut. 17 Apr. 1843. Capt. 1 Jan. 1852. Major 1 Jan. 1857. *d.* Mhow 1 July 1857 : kld. by mutineers.

Ward of the Earl of Essex. *m.* Mhow, 30 Sept. 1840, Elizabeth Ann, dau. of David Darling, Asst. Surg. Bengal Est.

Services : Cornet d.d. 3rd L.C. 6 Feb. 1834. Posted to 1st L.C. 9 June 1836. Actg. Adjt. 3rd Local Horse 6 Oct. 1838 till 7 Feb. 1839. Intr. & Qmr. 1st L.C. 5 Feb. till 30 July 1839. 3rd Asst. to Resdt. at Indore 30 July 1839 ; 2nd do. 6 Dec. 1841. Rejoined his Regt. on service 15 Apr. 1842. First Afghan War 1842 ; operations leading to the re-occupation of Kabul ; Cornet 1st L.C., with Gen. Pollock's force (Medal). Resumed charge of his duties at Indore 7 Feb. 1843 till 8 Apr. 1850. Second Sikh War ; passage of Chenab ; Chilianwala ; Gujerat ; Lieut. 1st L.C. (Medal with clasp). Asst. Comr., 1 cl., Leiah Div., 9 Sept. 1853 till 1854. Fur. 1855-6.

HARRIS, Charles (1788-1871). Captain. Artillery. *bapt.* Madras 9 Jan. 1788. Cadet 1804. Arrived in India 12 July 1805. Lieut. 9 May 1805. Capt. Lt. 28 Apr. 1812. Capt. 15 Feb. 1818. Resigned in India 20 Mar. 1819. *d.* 21 Pembridge Sq., London, 30 Jan. 1871, aged 83.

Eldest son of Henry Harris, surgeon, member Madras medical board, and Jane his wife. *m.* Sourabaya, Java (before 1817), Wilhelmina Clara. (She died Sourabaya, Apr. 1825, aged 36.) Father of Charles Harris, *q.v.* Woolwich Cadet; nominated for R.M.A. 1 Dec. 1802; obtained his certificate 17 Jan. 1805.

Services : Operations against Dhundia Khan 1807; Komona; Ganauri; Lieut. 3rd Coy. 1st Bn. Art. Settlement of Hariana 1809; Bhawani. Capture of Java 1811; Lieut. 7th Coy. 1st Bn. (Medal). Expedn. against Sambas 1813. Operations against the Rajah of Boni, in Celebes, 1816.

Refs. : The Times, 2 Feb. 1871.

HARRIS, Charles (1817-1889). General. 27th N.I. *b.* Java 19 Oct. 1817. Cadet 1834. Arrived in India 13 Aug. 1835. Ensign (9 Feb. 1835) 13 Mar. 1835. Lieut. 8 Oct. 1839. Capt. 3 May 1847. Major 4 June 1860. Lt. Col. 15 June 1862. Col. 18 Feb. 1866. Maj. Gen. 1 Oct. 1877. Lt. Gen. 18 May 1881. Gen. 1889. *d.* at his residence, 57 Sutherland Avenue, London, 1 Mar. 1889.

Son of Charles Harris, *q.v.*, and Wilhelmina Clara his wife. *m.* 1st, Mussoorie, 22 May 1840, Anna Auber, only dau. of John Barclay, *q.v. m.* 2nd, Harriett, dau. of W. Harrison, of Leamington.

Services : Ensign d.d. 66th N.I. 25 Aug. 1835. Posted to 27th N.I. 24 Sept. 1835. Intr. & Qmr. 27th N.I. 13 Feb. 1840 till May 1845. First Afghan War 1841-2; operations against the Sangu Khel Shinwaris in the Nazian valley Feb. 1841; defence of Ghazni Nov. 1841 till Mar. 1842; Lieut. 27th N.I. (Medal). A prisoner in the hands of the Afghans at Ghazni and Kabul Mar. till 21 Sept. 1842. S.A.C.G. 2 Dec. 1845 till 1849. First Sikh War; Comst. Ofr. at the bridge of boats over the Sutlej. Fur. 1854 till 19 Jan. 1856. Served with Bdr. F. Wheler's F.F. in Bundelkhand Aug. till Dec. 1859.

Refs. : Boase. The Times, 15 Mar. 1889.

HARRIS, Henry Hamlyn (1782-1804). Lieutenant, 14th N.I. *b.* Exton, co. Rutland, 1 July 1782. Cadet 1798. Arrived in India 14 Oct. 1800. Ensign 14 Dec. 1799. Lieut. 29 May 1800. *d.* Sikandra 29 Aug. 1804 : kld. in action during Monson's retreat.[1]

Son of Rev. Hamlyn Harris, vicar of Exton.

Services : Second Mahratta War; battle of Delhi; Agra; Gwalior; Monson's retreat (kld.); Lieut. 1/14th N.I.

Refs. : Intestate; admon. granted 30 Apr. 1805.

[1] *Note :* (? Taken prisoner by Holkar on 16 July 1804, during Col. Monson's retreat, and subsequently murdered by him nr. Fatehpur Sikri.)

THE BENGAL ARMY, 1758-1834 395

HARRIS, James (d. 1780). Lieutenant, Artillery. Cadet 1772. Fireworker 16 June 1774. Lieut. 30 Mar. 1778. d. 16 Oct. (? 16 Aug.) 1780, on service with the Bombay detachment.
Services: First Mahratta War 1778-80.

HARRIS, James Stanley (1811-1852). Captain, Invalid Est. 30th N.I. b. Wotton-under-Edge, Gloucs., 27 Aug. 1811. Cadet 1827. Arrived in India 12 Dec. 1828. Ensign 12 June 1828. Lieut. 21 June 1833. Capt. 12 June 1843. Invalided 26 Dec. 1846. d. Barrackpore, 7 Mar. 1852, whilst en route to embark for England.
2nd son of George Daniel Harris, of Stanley House, Gloucs. m. St. George's, Hanover Sq., London, 8 July 1835, Susanna Harriot, eldest dau. of James Zinzan, of Brentford Butts. Addiscombe Cadet 1826-8.
Services: Ensign d.d. 44th N.I. 17 Jan. 1829. Posted to 16th N.I. 3 June 1829. Transfd. to 30th N.I. 31 July 1829; to 31st N.I. 7 July 1830; to 30th N.I. 12 Aug. 1830. d.d. Sylhet L.I. 26 Sept. 1832. Actg. Adjt. do. 28 Oct. 1833. Fur. s.c. 22 June 1834 till 4 May 1837, and 8 Nov. 1838 till 9 Oct. 1841. d.d. Recruit Depot Bn. at Bareilly 12 Mar. 1842 till 1 Mar. 1843. Adjt. 30th N.I. 17 Apr. 1844 till Feb. 1845. First Sikh War; Aliwal; Sobraon; Capt. 30th N.I. (Medal with clasp). d.d. with Eur. Invalids at Chunar 4 Apr. 1848. Fur. 1852.
Refs.: *A.J.* N.S. xvii. 279. *I.M.* 4 May 1852, p. 257. *G.M.* 1852, i.

HARRIS, John (1754/55-?). Major. 9th N.I. b. Devon 1754/55. Cadet 1780. Admitted 19 Mar. 1781. Ensign 27 Apr. 1781. Lieut. 7 Aug. 1781. Capt. 30 Oct. 1799. Major 21 Sept. 1804. Retired 9 June 1807. d. before Dec. 1811.
Services: Sailed for India on the *Grosvenor*, 2 June 1780, aged 25. Lieut. 18th Bn. Sepoys in July 1787. Capt. 9th N.I. Bde. Major at Calcutta in 1803-4. Fur. 1805 till retirement.

HARRIS, John (1787-1811). Ensign, 5th N.I. b. Stepney, Middlesex, 25 Mar. 1787. Cadet 1806. Arrived in India 1 Aug. 1807. Ensign 27 Aug. 1807. d. Java 26 Oct. 1811.
Services: Posted as Ensign to 5th N.I. in 1808. Capture of Java 1811; Ensign 3rd Bn. Bengal Vols.
Refs.: Will dated 25 June 1811; proved 15 Sept. 1816.

HARRIS, Joseph (1782-1861). Lieut. General. Colonel 4th Bengal Eur. Inf. b. Northampton 18 Sept. 1782. Cadet 1803. Arrived in India 1 Dec. 1804. Ensign 1 Dec. 1803. Lieut. 13 Nov. 1804. Capt. 1 Jan. 1819. Major 21 Jan. 1829. Lt. Col. 5 Apr. 1834.

Col. 30 Sept. 1845. Maj. Gen. 20 June 1854. Lt. Gen. 29 Aug. 1859. *d.* 14 Carlton Rd., Maida Vale, London, 22 July 1861.

Son of —— Harris and Ann his wife. *m.* (?). (She died 19 May 1815.)

Services : Posted as Lieut. to 21st N.I. Transfd. to 1/2nd N.I. in 1806 ; to newly-raised 32nd N.I. July 1823 ; to 63rd N.I. (late 1/32nd) May 1824. Siege and capture of Bhurtpore ; Capt. 63rd N.I. (India medal). Leave s.c. to Cape and N.S.W. 5 Dec. 1829 till Oct. 1831. Posted as Lt. Col. to 63rd N.I. 10 Sept. 1834. Fur. s.c. 8 Mar. 1838 till 24 Dec. 1839. Transfd. to 3rd N.I. 21 Feb. 1840 ; to 2nd Bengal Eur. Regt. 27 Oct. 1840. Fur. s.c. to Cape 25 Jan. 1841 till 25 Feb. 1843 ; fur. s.c. to Europe 18 Feb. 1843 till death. Col. newly-raised 4th Eur. Inf. 1859.

Refs. : Boase. *G.M.* 1861, ii. 334. *The Times,* 25 July 1861.

HARRIS, Philip (1805-1869). Major General. 1st Bengal Eur. Fus. *b.* Clapham, Surrey, 30 Oct. 1805. Cadet 1823. Arrived in India 10 Aug. 1824. Ensign 18 Feb. 1824. Lieut. 13 May 1825. Capt. 8 Oct. 1839. Major 20 July 1857. Bt. Lt. Col. 20 June 1854. Bt. Col. 8 June 1856. Maj. Gen. 13 June 1865. *d.* Allahabad 31 July 1869.

3rd son of John Harris, of Clapham and Earlswood, Surrey. *m.* 1st, Fatehgarh, 2 Oct. 1827, Ellen, eldest dau. of Thomas Blair, of Lucan, Dublin. (She died 18 Nov. 1843, aged 37.) *m.* 2nd, Nasirabad, 11 Jan. 1847, Ellen Mary, 3rd dau. of Robert Burn, R.N., of Stirling.

Services : Posted as Ensign to 2nd N.I. Exchanged to 2nd Extra Regt. 31 Oct. 1825. Actg. Adjt. Cawnpore Provl. Bn. 13 Mar. 1826 ; do. Left Wing 2nd Extra Regt. 19 Dec. 1827 ; do. Rt. Wing 70th N.I. (late 2nd Extra Regt.) 14 Jan. 1829. Adjt. 70th N.I. 10 Feb. 1831 till 28 Dec. 1839. Fur. p.a. 13 June 1840 till 28 Oct. 1842. Apptd. A.D.C. to Maj.-Gen. John Hunter Littler, *q.v.*, comdg. 3rd Inf. Div., Army of Exercise, 19 Nov. 1843. Gwalior campaign ; Maharajpur ; Capt. 70th N.I., A.D.C. (Bronze star). (Mentioned for " conspicuous gallantry on 30 Dec. 1843 "—*Lond. Gaz.* 8 Mar. 1844.) Actg. D.A.A.G. 3rd Div., Army of Gwalior, 7 Jan. 1844. Comdd. 5th Inf., Gwalior Contingent, 20 Feb. 1844 till 1857. Fur. 1857-9. Bdr. comdg. at Barrackpore 11 Mar. 1862.

Refs. : Foster's *Families of Royal Descent,* ii. 853.

HARRIS, Thomas (1750/51-1786). Lieut. Colonel. Artillery. *b.* 1750/51. Cadet (?). Fireworker 4 Sept. 1768. Lieut. 13 Mar. 1770. Capt. Lt. 30 Jan. 1774. Capt. 31 Mar. 1778. Major 29 Jan. 1784. Lt. Col. 31 Jan. 1785. *d.* Calcutta, 27 Feb. 1786, aged 35.

Brother of William Harris, *q.v. m.* Jane. (She *re-m.* John Howe, *q.v.*)

Services : Apptd. to newly-raised Golandaz Coy. in 1777.

Refs. : *S.M.* 1786, p. 465. Will dated 27 Feb. 1786. M.I. in mily. cemetery at Bhowanipore, Calcutta.

HARRIS, William (d. 1786). Captain, Artillery. Cadet 1771. Fireworker 6 Dec. 1771. Lieut. 14 May 1777. Capt. Lt. 24 Sept. 1779. Capt. 1784. d. Kedgeree, 26 Nov. 1786, on board the *Manship*, on his passage to Europe.
Brother of Thomas Harris, *q.v.*, and brother-in-law of Samuel Wood, *q.v.*
Services : Second Mysore War 1781-5 ; Capt. Lt. with a Coy. of Vols. Fur. 1786.
Refs. : Will.

HARRISON, Charnock Ingleby (1810-1848). Captain, 65th N.I. b. 30 July 1810. Cadet 1829. Arrived in India 27 Mar. 1830. Ensign 27 Mar. 1830. Lieut. 29 Feb. 1836. Capt. 1 Jan. 1844. d. Dacca 6 Nov. 1848.
bapt. Ripon, Yorks., 25 Aug. 1810. 4th son of Charles Harrison, of Newbridge, Nidderdale, Yorks., and Isabella his wife, dau. and heiress of Charles Charnock. *m.* Barrackpore, 10 Mar. 1838, Mary Anne, 5th dau. of Capt. John Tritton, H.M. 24th Dgns. (*See also* William Cossart Carleton.)
Services : Ensign d.d. 55th N.I. 5 Apr. 1830. Actg. Ensign 3 May 1832. Fur. s.c. 27 Mar. 1832 till 12 Feb. 1834. Posted as Ensign to 65th N.I. 14 Mar. 1833. Actg. Intr. & Qmr. 12th N.I. 8 Apr. 1836. Adjt. 65th N.I. 25 Nov. 1838 till 29 May 1839. Intr. & Qmr. 65th N.I. 29 May 1839 till 15 Nov. 1843. Actg. S.A.C.G. 17 Feb. 1841. S.A.C.G. 7 Jan. 1844. S.A.C.G. and Supt. of Police, G.G.'s camp, 15 Aug. 1846 till 1847. S.A.C.G. at Dacca 1848. No record of active service.
Refs. : Burke's *Landed Gentry*, 13th edn., p. 580, *s.n.* Estcourt (*now* Oswald), *formerly* of Pinkney, Wilts. *G.M.* 1849, i. 334. Will dated 21 Oct. 1845 ; proved 21 Dec. 1848.

HARRISON, Francis (1812-?). Bt. Captain. Bengal Eur. L.I. b. London 19 Mar. 1812. Cadet 1828. Arrived in India 5 May 1829. Ensign (4 Dec. 1828) 14 Sept. 1829. Lieut. 2 May 1833. Bt. Capt. 4 Dec. 1843. Retired 13 Nov. 1844. d. 1866 ? [1]
Son of Richard Harrison, of Gray's Inn, atty.-at-law, and Hannah his wife.
Services : Ensign d.d. 44th N.I. 10 June 1829. Posted to 2nd Bengal Eur. Regt. 14 Sept. 1829 ; to Left Wing, Eur. Regt., Jan. 1830. First Afghan War 1839-40 ; Ghazni ; Kabul ; Pashut ; capture of Kajja fort ; Lieut. Bengal Eur. Regt. (Medal). Fur. s.c. 13 May 1842 till retirement.

[1] *Note :* His name appears for the last time in the *Indian A.L.* for July 1866.

HARRISON, James (*d.* 1782). Captain, Infantry. Cadet 1771. Ensign 6 Dec. 1772. Lieut. 19 Aug. 1776. Capt. 8 Mar. 1781. *d.* 4 Jan. 1782.

Brother of Clement Harrison, of Gainsborough, Lincs.

Services : Campaign against the Rajah of Benares 1781 ; capture of Patita ; Capt. Bengal Eur. Regt.

Refs. : Will dated 18 Sept. 1781.

HARRISON, James (1792-1828). Captain, 2nd Bengal Eur. Regt. *b.* Chester 15 Feb. 1792. Cadet 1806. Arrived in India 30 July 1807. Ensign 22 Aug. 1807. Lieut. 10 Mar. 1812. Capt. 1 May 1824. *d. unm.* Chester 6 Oct. 1828.

bapt. 22 Jan. 1796. Son of John Harrison, surgeon, and Sarah his wife. Brother of Edward Spencer Harrison.

Services : Posted as Ensign to Bengal Eur. Regt. in 1808. Served in Amboyna with his Regt. 1811-6. Transfd. to newly-formed 2nd Bengal Eur. Regt. May 1824. Fur. 1824 till death.

Refs. : Will dated 3 Jan. 1815 ; codicil dated 20 Nov. 1824 ; proved 10 Aug. 1829.

HARRISON, John (1758/59-1791). Lieutenant, Infantry. *b.* 1758/59. Cadet 1782. Ensign 2 Apr. 1783. Lieut. 7 Mar. 1790. *d.* Berhampore, Bengal, 27 Mar. 1791.

A native of Yorkshire.

Services : Sailed for India on the *Morse*, 6 Feb. 1782, aged 23. N.F.P.

HARRISON, Robert (1760/61-1788). Lieutenant, Infantry. *b.* London 1760/61. Cadet 1778. Arrived in India 10 Dec. 1778. Ensign 1778. Lieut. 16 Oct. 1778. *d.* Cawnpore 15 Apr. 1788.

Services : Sailed for India on the *Gatton*, 27 Apr. 1778, aged 17. Lieut. 2/2nd Bengal Eur. Regt. in Oct. 1779. Lieut. 34th Bn. Sepoys in July 1787.

HARRISON, Robert Orfeur (1782-1804). Lieutenant, 4th N.I. *b.* Kirkby Stephen, Westmorland, 6 Jan. 1782. Cadet 1799. Arrived in India 10 Dec. 1800. Ensign 23 Aug. 1800. Lieut. 5 Jan. 1801. *d. unm.* Chapra, Bengal, 14 Feb. 1804.

bapt. 12 Apr. 1782. Son of Thomas Harrison, of Kirkby Stephen, surgeon, and Mary his wife.

Services : Second Mahratta War ; Aligarh ; Lieut. 4th N.I.

Refs. : Will dated Cawnpore 27 Jan. 1804 ; proved in 1804.

HARRISON, Samuel. Lieutenant. Infantry. Cadet 1769. Ensign 10 July 1770. Lieut. 26 June 1771. Resigned 7 Jan. 1773.

Refs. : N.F.P.

HART, Robert. 2nd Lieutenant, Artillery. Cadet (?). 2nd Lieut. 1763.
Services : N.F.P.
Refs. : Stubbs's List, No. 36.

HART, Robert (*d.* 1781). Fireworker, Artillery. Cadet 1778. Fireworker 3 Oct. 1778. *d.* Gwalior 28 Oct. 1781.
Services : First Mahratta War ; operations of Camac's detachment 1781 ; capture of Sipri, Jan. 1781.
Refs. : Stubbs, i. 62. *S.M.* 1782, p. 334.

HART, Shepherd (1789-1839). Bt. Major, 43rd N.I. *b.* 11 Nov. 1789. Cadet 1808. Arrived in India 24 July 1809. Ensign 30 Aug. 1809. Lieut. 16 Dec. 1814. Capt. 9 Nov. 1826. Bt. Major 28 June 1838. *d.* Kandahar, Afghanistan, 11 Oct. 1839. *bapt.* S. Shields, co. Durham, 9 Dec. 1789. Son of William Hart.
Services : Posted as Ensign to 22nd N.I. Nepal War 1816 ; Lieut. 2/22nd N.I., in 3rd Bde., Centre Column. Leave s.c. 10 mos. to Cape 18 July 1816. Actg. Adjt. 2/22nd N.I. 26 May 1820. Intr. & Qmr. 2/22nd N.I. 25 Mar. 1822. Transfd. to 43rd N.I. (late 1/22nd) May 1824. Intr. & Qmr. 43rd N.I. 17 June 1824 till 28 Dec. 1826. Offg. D.A.A.G., E. Div., 17 Sept. 1824. Actg. Bde. Major 3rd Bde., E. Div., 13 Dec. 1824. Actg. Dy. Comy. of Ord. to Div. on Chittagong frontier 3 Jan. 1825. First Afghan War 1838-9 ; Ghazni ; 2nd in comd. 43rd N.I.

HARTLE, Anthony (*d.* 1797). Lieut. Colonel, Infantry. Cadet 1768. Ensign (?). Lieut. 13 Sept. 1768. Capt. 30 Mar. 1777. Major 4 Feb. 1781. Lt. Col. 22 Jan. 1794. *d.* Chunar 28 Oct. 1797.

Son of George Hartle and Sarah his wife. *m.* 1st, Calcutta, 14 Sept. 1768, Miss Elizabeth Webber. *m.* 2nd, Calcutta, 1 June 1783, Miss Bridget Hoare.
Services : Fur. 29 Dec. 1777 till Apr. 1782. Major 3rd Bengal Eur. Regt. in June 1783 ; 5th Eur. Bn. in July 1787.
Refs. : Will proved in 1797.

HARTLEY, George Eusebius (1780-1805). Lieutenant, 15th N.I. *bapt.* St. Bridget's, Dublin, 20 Sept. 1780. Cadet 1797. Arrived in India 22 Dec. 1798. Ensign 12 Oct. 1798. Lieut. 1 Nov. 1798. *d. unm.* 21 Feb. 1805 : kld. in action in the fourth assault of Bhurtpore.

Son of John Hartley, of Peter St., Dublin, and Anne Low his wife, of St. John's psh, Dublin.
Services : Operations in Jumna Doab 1803 ; Sasni ; Bijaigarh ; Kachaura ; Lieut. 2/15th N.I. Second Mahratta War ; battle of

Delhi; Agra; Laswari; battle of Deig; Bhurtpore (kld.); Lieut. 2/15th N.I. " He behaved most gallantly, and was shot in the entrance of the Bastion to the right of the Breach " (*Pester*).
Refs.: Pester, p. 386. Will dated 6 Aug. 1804; proved 19 July 1806.

HARTLEY, William (*d.* 1777). Captain, Infantry. Cadet 1766. Ensign 2 Jan. 1767. Lieut. 11 Apr. 1768. Capt. 4 July 1776. *d.* Belgaum, Bombay, 12 Aug. 1777.
Son of Joshua Hartley, of Leeds. *m.* Moradbag, nr. Murshidabad, 28 Oct. 1771, Miss Eleanor Christina Moinakin. (She *re-m.* Patrick Greene, *q.v.*)
Services: N.F.P.
Refs.: Will dated 4 July 1774; proved 8 Dec. 1777.

HARVEY, Edward (1813-1891). Lieut. Colonel. 4th Bengal Eur. L.C. *b.* London 8 Oct. 1813. Cadet 1829. Arrived in India 13 Sept. 1830. Cornet 31 Mar. 1830. Lieut. 4 Nov. 1839. Capt. 8 May 1849. Bt. Major 28 Nov. 1854. Retired 21 Sept. 1861. Hon. Lt. Col. 21 Sept. 1861. *d.* at his residence, 10 Pavilion Sq., Scarborough, 16 Sept. 1891.
Son of Lt. Col. Bissell Harvey, K.H., 1st Foot, Fort Major of Edinburgh, and Mary Jorden his wife. *m.* Banda, 10 Sept. 1845, Julia, dau. of William Morton, *q.v.*
Services: Cadet d.d. 1st L.C. 13 Oct. 1830. Actg. Cornet 1 Oct. 1832. Actg. Adjt. 1st L.C. 3 Sept. 1835. Posted as Cornet to 10th L.C. 9 June 1836. Adjt. 3rd Local Horse 27 Sept. 1838. Fur. s.c. 23 Feb. 1841 till 1844. Adjt. 10th L.C. 29 Mar. 1845 till 12 Aug. 1849. Fur. 3 Apr. 1851 till Dec. 1853. Transfd. to newly-raised 4th Eur. L.C. in 1858. Fur. 1859 till retirement. No record of active service.
Refs.: *The Times*, 23 Sept. 1891.

HARVEY, George Bolton (1812-1833). Ensign, 17th N.I. *b.* Calcutta 6 Jan. 1812. Cadet 1828. Arrived in India 5 May 1829. Ensign 8 Jan. 1829. *d.* Cape Town 31 Jan. 1833.
Son of John Harvey, of Calcutta, merchant, and Isabella his wife.
Services: Ensign d.d. 48th N.I. 10 June 1829. Posted to 17th N.I. 14 Sept. 1829. Fur. s.c. 9 Sept. 1832 till death. No record of active service.
Refs.: *A.J.* N.S. xi. 139.

HARVEY, George Daniel (1807-1826). Lieutenant, 5th Extra Inf. Regt. *b.* Gt. Stanmore, Middlesex, Oct. 1807. Cadet 1823. Ensign (?). Lieut. 21 Sept. 1824. *d.* Benares 29 Aug. 1826.

THE BENGAL ARMY, 1758-1834

Son of George Daniel Harvey, of Saint-Omer, France, commissioner of bankrupts.
Services : Posted as Lieut. to 2nd Bengal Eur. Regt. in 1824. Transfd. to newly-raised 5th Extra Regt. May 1825. No record of active service.
Refs. : A.J. xxiii. 529.

HARVEY, Henry (1747-1811 ?). Captain. Bengal Eur. Regt. *bapt.* Wexford 1 June 1747. Cadet 1768. Ensign 3 Feb. 1769. Lieut. 2 June 1770. Capt. 13 Oct. 1778. Resigned 5 Jan. 1784. *d. c.* 1810/11.
Son of Rev. Ambrose Harvey and Elizabeth his wife, dau. of Rev. Pierce Hughes, of Slad. Nephew of Francis Harvey, of Bargy Castle, one of the six Clerks in Chancery. Cousin-german of Pierce Nixon Hughes, *q.v. m.* Sarah.
Services : Operations against the Bhutias in Cooch Behar 1772-3 ; storm of Dhalimkot ; Lieut. 6th Bn. Sepoys. Capt. 2/1st Bengal Eur. Regt. in Oct. 1779.
Refs. : Burke's *Landed Gentry of Ireland*, p. 299, *s.n.* Harvey, of Bargy Castle, co. Wexford ; p. 328, *s.n.* Hughes, of Ballycross, co. Wexford. Burke's *Landed Gentry*, 5th edn., p. 135, *s.n.* Boxwell, of Sarshill, co. Wexford. *Williams*, p. 109. Will proved 17 Aug. 1811.

HARVEY, John (1753/54-?). Lieutenant. Infantry. *b.* 1753/54. Cadet 1780. Arrived in India 23 Oct. 1781. Ensign 15 July 1781. Lieut. 14 Oct. 1782. Struck off 1793.
A native of Lincolnshire. *m.* in England, 25 Oct. 1786, Miss Harvey.
Services : Apptd. Cadet on 14 Feb. 1781, aged 27. Sailed for India on the *Southampton*, 13 Mar. 1781, aged 27. Fur. 3 yrs. 20 Feb. 1786, and was still on fur. in 1790.
Refs. : G.M. 1786, ii. 995.

HARWOOD, John Terry (1811-?). Lieutenant. 68th N.I. *bapt.* Deane, Hants, 14 Oct.1811. Cadet 1829. Arrived in India 1 May 1830. Ensign 23 Apr. 1830. Lieut. 30 May 1836. Dismissed by G.C.M. 23 Sept. 1836.
Eldest son of Charles Harwood, of Overton, Hants, and Elizabeth his wife. *m.* Calcutta, 1 Dec. 1830, Rebecca, youngest dau. of Clement Johnson, of Colgong, B. & O., indigo planter. Oriel Coll., Oxon. ; matric. 23 June 1829, aged 17.
Services : Cadet d.d. 53rd N.I. 7 June 1830 ; do. 55th N.I. 2 Dec. 1830. Actg. Ensign 16 July 1832. d.d. 63rd N.I. 20 Aug. 1832. Posted as Ensign to 68th N.I. 20 Aug. 1833. No record of active service.
Refs. : *Alumni Oxon.* A.J. N.S. xxii. 127.

HASELL, Christopher (1814-1861). Major, 48th N.I. *b.* Dacre, Cumberland, 29 May 1814. Cadet 1833. Arrived in India 8 July 1834. Ensign 23 May 1834. Lieut. 22 June 1838. Capt. 24 Jan. 1845. Major 4 Oct. 1857. *d.* May 1861.

bapt. Dacre 2 June 1814. 2nd son of Edward Hasell, of Dalemain, Cumberland, and Jane his 2nd wife, dau. of Rev. Robert Whitehead, of Ormside Lodge. Brother of William Lowther Hasell, *q.v. m.* Allahabad, 18 Oct. 1855, Margaret Stuart, dau. of Joseph Orchard, *q.v.* Addiscombe Cadet 1 Feb. 1832 till 13 Dec. 1833.

Services : Ensign d.d. 19th N.I. 17 July 1834. Posted to 48th N.I. 5 Nov. 1834. Adjt. 48th N.I. 1 Jan. 1838 till 8 Mar. 1843. First Afghan War 1839-42 ; capture of Ghazni (Medal) ; operations in Khyber Pass and Waziri Valley ; Lieut. 48th N.I. D.C., 2 cl., Saugor & Narbada territories, at Betùl 13 Feb. 1843 till 1849. To raise a Corps of Manipuris and Cacharis 24 Aug. 1857. Fur. s.c. 2 yrs. to Aust. 5 May 1859.

Refs. : Burke's *Landed Gentry*, 12th edn., p. 908, *s.n.* Hasell, of Dalemain, Cumberland. *I.M.* 1851, p. 223.

HASELL, William Lowther (1816-1849). Captain, 44th N.I. *bapt.* Dacre, Cumberland, 1 Dec. 1816. Cadet 1834. Arrived in India 13 Aug. 1835. Ensign (9 Feb. 1835) 2 Apr. 1835. Lieut. 2 June 1838. Capt. 24 Jan. 1845. *d.* Cairo 13 June 1849.

3rd and youngest son of Edward Hasell, of Dalemain, Cumberland, and Jane his wife. Brother of Christopher Hasell, *q.v.* Ed. Shrewsbury 1830-1.

Services : Ensign d.d. 34th N.I. 25 Aug. 1835. Posted as Ensign to 44th N.I. 24 Sept. 1835. Served against marauders in Jhabua, C.I., Mar. 1836 ; Ensign 44th N.I. Actg. Adjt. Left Wing 44th N.I. 22 Oct. 1838. Adjt. 44th N.I. 3 Aug. 1840 till 18 Oct. 1842. Second in comd. 2nd Regt. Oudh Local Inf. 21 Sept. 1842. Leave s.c. 2 yrs. to Cape 17 May 1843. Fur. s.c. 10 Feb. 1845 till 5 Feb. 1848, and 1849 till death.

Refs. : Burke's *Landed Gentry*, 12th edn., p. 908, *s.n.* Hasell, of Dalemain, Cumberland. *Shrewsbury School Register.* *G.M.* 1849, ii. 328. Will dated on board the *Precentor* in the Red Sea 6 June 1849 ; proved 6 Sept. 1850 ; P.C.C. 26 Dec. 1849.

HASENCLEVER, Christian (1726/27-?). Lieutenant, Infantry. *b.* 1726/27. Lieut. 6 Jan. 1759. *d.* Berhampore before Feb. 1767. A Prussian.

Services : Sailed for India as a Lieut. on the *Bombay Castle* in 1757, aged 30.

Note : A Peter Hasenclever was naturalized in 1763.

HASLAM, Thomas (1790-1832). Captain, 25th N.I. b. London 12 June 1790. Cadet 1808. Arrived in India 27 Oct. 1809. Ensign 25 Aug. 1810. Lieut. 16 Dec. 1814. Capt. 1 May 1824. d. Barrackpore 21 Sept. 1832.

Son of John Haslam, of East side, Bethnal Green. m. Calcutta, 19 Feb. 1811, Miss Eliza Pyefinch.

Services : Barasat C.C. Posted as Ensign to 26th N.I. Transfd. to 20th N.I. 26 Aug. 1811. Offg. Intr. & Qmr. 2/20th N.I. 16 Oct. 1823. Offg. Adjt. 2/20th N.I. 19 Feb. 1824. Actg. Bde. Major to troops on Chittagong frontier 17 Mar. 1824. Transfd. to 40th N.I. (late 2/20th) May 1824. First Burma War ; Chittagong 1824 ; Capt. 40th N.I. Transfd. to 25th N.I. (late 1/20th) in 1827. (? Operations against the Chuars 1832 ; Capt. 25th N.I.)

Refs. : A.J. N.S. x. 157.

HASLOCK, John Charles (1809-1885). Colonel. 65th N.I. b. London 7 May 1809. Cadet 1825. Arrived in India 7 July 1826. Ensign 15 Mar. 1826. Lieut. 9 Sept. 1832. Capt. 15 Aug. 1845. Major 21 Feb. 1850. Lt. Col. 4 June 1855. Retired 21 Aug. 1857. Hon. Col. 21 Aug. 1857. d. Crewkerne, Somerset, 25 June 1885.

Son of Samuel Haslock, of Long Acre, London, silversmith. m. 1st, Karnal, 16 July 1841, Letitia, eldest dau. of William Henry Earle, q.v. m. 2nd, Marianne Shadwell. (She died 1 Dec. 1875, aged 52.)

Services : Ensign d.d. 36th N.I. 2 Aug. 1826. Posted to 39th N.I. 26 Sept. 1826. Actg. Adjt. 39th N.I. 21 Nov. 1835, and 28 Aug. 1837. Operations against the Bhils 1837 ; Lieut. 39th N.I. Adjt. 39th N.I. 17 Dec. 1837 till 16 Oct. 1845. With Army of Reserve (for Afghanistan) Oct. 1842 till Jan. 1843. Postmaster at Nowgong 3 May 1843. Gwalior campaign ; Paniar ; Bt. Capt. 39th N.I. (Bronze star). Posted as Lt. Col. to 65th N.I. Fur. s.c. 22 Jan. 1855 till retirement.

Refs. : The Times, 29 June 1885.

HASSEY, Robert. Captain. Infantry. Cadet 1767. Ensign 8 July 1767. Lieut. 10 Apr. 1769. Capt. 31 Dec. 1772. Resigned 31 Dec. 1772.

Services : N.F.P.

HASTINGS, Henry Cadogan (1813-?). Lieutenant. 55th N.I. Subsequently Chief Constable of Surrey. bapt. Edinburgh 21 July 1813. Cadet 1834. Arrived in India 28 July 1835. Ensign (23 Mar. 1835) 7 May 1835. Lieut. 3 Oct. 1840. Resigned 1 Nov. 1843. Living in 1864.

Eldest son of Sir Charles Holland Hastings, K.C.H., of Dublin, Lt. Col. H.M.S., State Steward to the Lord Lieut. of Ireland. *m.* Edinburgh, 15 May 1838, Mary, 2nd dau. of Henry B. Wood. Ed. Eton ; in Remove 1829.

Services : Ensign d.d. 43rd N.I. 2 Sept. 1835. Posted to 41st N.I. 24 Sept. 1835. Transfd. to 55th N.I. 29 Dec. 1835. Fur. s.c. 3 Apr. 1837 till 20 Jan. 1840. Actg. Adjt. 4th Irreg. Cav. 31 Aug. 1842. With Army of Reserve (for Afghanistan) Oct. 1842 till Jan. 1843 ; Lieut. 55th N.I., tempy. S.A.C.G. No record of active service.

Refs. : Eton School Lists. A.J. N.S. xxvi. 127.

HASTINGS, William (*d.* 1793). Lieutenant, Invalid Est. Infantry. Cadet 1778. Ensign 5 May 1779. Lieut. 11 Jan. 1781. Invalided before 1790. *d.* Calcutta 15 Aug. 1793, insane.

m. Chunar, 21 Feb. 1790, Miss Elizabeth Vickers.

Services : Ensign 1/2nd Bengal Eur. Regt. in Oct. 1779. Lieut. 6th Bengal Eur. Bn. in July 1787. Posted to 22nd Bn. Sepoys 15 Dec. 1787. Adjt. & Qmr. of Eur. Invalids at Chunar in 1790.

HATCH, Thomas (1744/45-1828). Lieutenant. 4th Bn. Sepoys. Subsequently vicar of Washington and Old Shoreham, Sussex. *b.* 1744/45. Cadet 1769. Ensign 6 Sept. 1769. Lieut. 8 Feb. 1773. Resigned 10 Feb. 1775. *d.* Washington, Sussex, 15 Apr. 1828, aged 84.

Son of Rev. John Hatch, of Rudham, Norfolk. Magdalen Hall, Oxon. ; matric. 16 July 1762, aged 17 ; demy Magdalen Coll. 1762-3 ; B.A. 1766 ; M.A. 1769 ; B.D. 1783 ; fellow 1778-86 ; dean of arts 1780-2 ; bursar 1782.

Services : After resigning the Service he took holy orders. Presented by his college in 1784 to the two livings of Washington and Old Shoreham, which he held till death. Noted for his horsemanship. "During the last war he served as a Lieut. in the Corps of Yeomanry Cav. comdd. by Sir Cecil Bisshop " (*G.M.*).

Refs. : Alumni Oxon. G.M. 1828, i. 474.

HATCHELL, John Hore (1806-1844). Bt. Captain, 69th N.I. *b.* Wexford 16 Apr. 1806. Cadet 1824. Arrived in India 5 Sept. 1825. Ensign 9 Feb. 1825. Lieut. 3 July 1827. Bt. Capt. 9 Feb. 1840. *d.* Shikarpur, Sind, 12 Sept. 1844.

Son of N. Christopher Hatchell. (*Probably* son of Nicholas Hatchell, banker.) *m.* Fatehgarh, 21 Jan. 1842, Frances Anne, 3rd dau. of Sir Robert Graham, 8th Bart., of Esk, and sister of Richard John Graham, *q.v.* (*See also* John Henry Simmonds.) (She died 12 Nov. 1894.)

Services : Posted as Ensign to 1st Extra Regt. (became 69th N.I.) in 1825, and served throughout with that Regt. Adjt. 69th N.I. 28 Mar. 1838 till death. Postmaster at Shahjahanpur 28 May 1842. No record of active service.
Refs. : Burke's *Peerage*, 1923, p. 1917, *s.n.* Graham, Bart., of Esk, Cumberland.

HATCHETT, John Charles (1788-?). Ensign. 20th N.I. *b.* London 1 Jan. 1788. Cadet 1806. Arrived in India 1 Aug. 1807. Ensign 23 Aug. 1807. Struck off 1810.
Son of Charles Hatchett.
Services : Suspended for irregularities committed whilst at the Barasat C.C. and sent to Europe 19 Oct. 1807. Posted as Ensign to 20th N.I., but never joined. *Probably* reinstated as Cadet, but resigned and was struck off in England in 1810.

HAUGHTON, Sir Graves Chamney (1788-1849). Lieutenant. 2nd N.I. Subsequently professor of Bengali and Sanskrit at Haileybury Coll., Kt., K.H. *b.* Dublin 17 Mar. 1788. Cadet 1808. Arrived in India 27 Oct. 1809. Ensign 13 Mar. 1810. Lieut. 16 Dec. 1814. Resigned in England 12 Feb. 1819. *d.* St. Cloud, Paris, 28 Aug. 1849, of cholera.
Son of John Haughton, of Dublin, physician, and Jane his wife, dau. of Edward Archer, of Mount John, co. Wicklow. Brother of Richard Haughton, professor of Oriental languages at Addiscombe.
Services : See *D.N.B.* Posted as Ensign to 2nd N.I. Admitted as one of the first Mily. students at Coll. of Fort William May 1812. Lieut. 1/2nd N.I. Fur. s.c. 2 Jan. 1815 till resignation. No record of active service. Held from 1817 till 1828 first the Asst.-Professorship, and afterwards the Professorship of Oriental languages at Haileybury Coll. Pub. 1833, a Bengali-Sanskrit dictionary, "An Inquiry into the Nature of Cholera and the Means of Cure," and other works. Hon. M.A. Oxon. 23 June 1819. F.R.S. 14 Nov. 1821. K.H. 1833. Kt. 18 July 1833.
Refs. : *D.N.B. D.I.B. Alumni Oxon. N. & Q.* 11 S. iii. 4. *Life of Lt. Col. John Haughton*, by Major A. C. Yate, 1900. *G.M.* 1833, ii. 76 ; 1849, ii. 420.
Note : His second christian name is incorrectly given as Champney in both *D.N.B.* and *D.I.B.*

HAUTENVILLE, Alexander Jaffray (1787-1806). Cadet, Infantry. *b.* 10 Nov. 1787. Cadet 1805. Never arrived in India. *d.* Dec. 1806, on his passage to India, in the wreck of the *Skelton Castle*. Struck off with effect from 5 Nov. 1806. (See note to David Allan.)

bapt. Dublin 1 Dec. 1787. Son of Rawdon Hautenville and Abigail his wife, dau. of Robert Jaffray, of Kingswell. Cousin of Thomas Jaffray, *q.v.*
Services : Lieut. H.M. 7th Fus. 26 Feb. 1804. Retired 14 Mar. 1805.
Refs. : Family information. *Hickey,* iv. 346.

HAVEN, Stephen (*d.* 1772). Cadet, Infantry. Cadet 1771. *d.* Benares 25 May 1772.
(*Probably* son of Stephen Haven, of Belfast, who died 1775.)
Services : N.F.P.

HAWES, George (1788-1879). Colonel. 17th N.I. *b.* Southampton 26 Mar. 1788. Cadet 1803. Arrived in India 14 Aug. 1804. Ensign 6 Sept. 1804. Lieut. 21 Sept. 1804. Capt. 6 Apr. 1818. Major 28 Nov. 1826. Lt. Col. 3 Nov. 1831. Retired 10 Apr. 1836. Hon. Col. 28 Nov. 1854. *d.* 7 Jan. 1879.
Son of Herbert Hawes, of Holy Rhood, Southampton, and Ann his wife. *m.* 1st, Calcutta, 29 May 1811, Miss Anna Frederica Thomasin Johnston. *m.* 2nd, St. John's, Calcutta, 2 Jan. 1824, Miss Eliza Sophia Templeton. (She died 18 Apr. 1865, aged 60.)
Services : Posted as Lieut. to 26th N.I. Operations in Bundelkhand 1807 ; Sehlehuganj ; Lieut. 26th N.I. Leave s.c. to Cape 29 July 1814 till 1817. Capt. 2/26th N.I. Fur. p.a. 17 Feb. 1821 till 13 Nov. 1823. Transfd. to 51st N.I. (late 1/26th) May 1824. First Burma War ; Assam 1824 (*Lond. Gaz.* 22 Mar. 1825). Fur. p.a. 10 Feb. 1827 till 10 Jan. 1828. Posted as Lt. Col. to 51st N.I. 27 Oct. 1832. Bdr., 2 cl., comdg. 2nd Inf. Bde. for Shekhawat expedn. 18 Nov. 1834 till 25 Jan. 1835. Transfd. to 17th N.I. 7 Jan. 1836.

HAWKES, Robert (1791-1876). General. 4th Bengal Eur. Cav. *b.* Okehampton, Devon, 30 Jan. 1791. Cadet 1807. Arrived in India 16 Nov. 1808. Cornet 30 July 1806. Lieut. 9 Nov. 1811. Capt. 13 May 1825. Major 10 Oct. 1836. Lt. Col. 23 Dec. 1839. Col. 4 Feb. 1859. Maj. Gen. 28 Nov. 1854. Lt. Gen. 17 Aug. 1864. Gen. 25 June 1870. *d.* 52 York Terr., Regent's Pk., London, 18 Dec. 1876.
Son of John and Mary Hawkes. *m.* Cawnpore, 1 Nov. 1812, Caroline, dau. of Robert Morris, M.P. for Gloucester 1806. (*See also* John Gordon (1765-1832.).) Divorced 18 June 1828. Marlow Cadet.
Services : Barasat C.C. 10½ mos. Posted as Cornet to 5th N.C. in 1809. Adjt. 5th N.C. 4 Nov. 1816 till 1824. Third Mahratta War ; storm and capture of Chanda ; pursuit of Pindaris ; actg. A.D.C. to Bdr. J. W. Adams, *q.v.* (*Lond. Gaz.* 7 Dec. 1818) (? Medal).

A.D.C. to C.-in-C. 11 Feb. 1824. To raise and comd. 7th Local Horse 19 Nov. 1824. Transfd. as Capt. to newly-raised 1st Extra Regt. (became 9th L.C.) May 1825. Offg. 2nd A.A.G. of the Army 12 Mar. 1833 till 31 Jan. 1834. Comdd. 3rd Local Horse 13 Mar. 1835 till 19 Feb. 1838. Comdd. 9th L.C. 25 Dec. 1838 till 6 Oct. 1841. Posted as Lt. Col. to 9th L.C. 14 Mar. 1840; to 1st L.C. 22 Sept. 1841. Fur. s.c. 31 Jan. 1842 till 25 Nov. 1844. Transfd. to 9th L.C. 5 Dec. 1844; to 8th L.C. 6 Dec. 1847; to 1st L.C. Fur. s.c. 10 Apr. 1849 till Dec. 1851. Transfd. to 4th L.C. 22 Sept. 1851; to 8th L.C. Oct. 1851; to 7th L.C.; to 9th L.C. 14 Apr. 1852. Bdr., 2 cl., comdg. Ambala 26 Jan. 1852; comdg. Lucknow 1852-4. Fur. p.a. 6 March 1854 till death. Col. 4th Eur. L.C.
Refs.: Boase. *A.J.* xxvi. 131. *The Times*, 28 Dec. 1876.

HAWKES, Walter (1761-1808). Major, 2nd N.I. *b.* 1761. Cadet 1780. Admitted 5 Nov. 1782. Ensign 1781. Lieut. 13 Aug. 1782. Capt. 31 July 1799. Major 21 Sept. 1804. *d.* 20 Nov. 1808 : lost at sea, together with his wife, on his passage to England *via* China, in the *Experiment*.

Son of Jeremy Hawkes, of London. Brother of Joseph Hawkes, and uncle of Walter Cracroft. *m.* Chunar, 18 Aug. 1797, Sarah, sister of John Staples Harriott, *q.v.*, and widow of John Rotton, *q.v.* Ed. Westminster; admitted 14 Jan. 1771; K.S. 1776, aged 14; elected to Cambridge 1780.

Services: Fur. 26 Aug. 1785 till 28 Apr. 1788. Capt. 1/8th N.I. in Aug. 1798. D.J.A.G., Dinapore and Chunar, till 1804. Second Mahratta War; battle and capture of Deig; Bhurtpore (s.w. in 4th assault on 21 Feb. 1805); Major 1/2nd N.I. Fur. 28 Sept. 1808 till death.

Refs.: *Alumni Westmon. Pester*, p. 386. Will dated Deegah, nr. Patna, 2 Aug. 1804; codicil dated Sept. 1808; proved 28 May 1810. Monument in Westminster Abbey, erected by William Francklin, *q.v.*

HAWKINS, Alexander William (1813-1857). Captain, Artillery. *b.* Dublin 11 Jan. 1813. Cadet 1831. Arrived in India 21 Jan. 1833. 2nd Lieut. 14 June 1832. Lieut. 29 July 1840. Capt. 23 Sept. 1850. *d.* Gwalior 15 June 1857 : kld. by mutineers.

Son of John Hawkins and Ellen (? Walker) his wife. *m.* Gwalior, 25 Apr. 1848, Georgina Rebecca, 7th dau. of Nuttall Greene, of Kilmanahan Castle, co. Waterford, and niece by marriage of James Parsons, *q.v.* (She died Edgbaston, 21 Mar. 1886, aged 62.) Addiscombe Cadet 6 Aug. 1830 till 14 June 1832.

Services: Posted to 4th Troop 3rd Bde. H.A. 12 Mar. 1836. First Afghan War 1839-42; Lieut. Shah Shuja's H.A. (Medal).

LIST OF THE OFFICERS OF

Adjt. Shah's H.A. at Kandahar 24 May 1839. Transfd. from 1st Troop 1st Bde. to Supplementary Troop 20 Jan. 1843. Actg. Adjt. Art. Div., Ferozepore, 8 Dec. 1843. Comdd. 4th Coy. Art., Gwalior Contingent, 14 Feb. 1844 till Feb. 1852 ; do. 1st Coy. Feb. 1852 till death.

Refs. : I.M. 1848, p. 361. Burke's *Landed Gentry*, 3rd edn., p. 479, *s.n.* Greene, of Kilmanahan Castle. *Greene*, p. 53.

HAWKINS, Edward Simeon (1796-1840). Major, 38th N.I. *b.* Cawnpore 5 Dec. 1796. Cadet 1812. Admitted 25 Sept. 1813. Ensign (?). Lieut. 17 Apr. 1815. Capt. 1 Nov. 1829. Major 30 Mar. 1837. *d.* Ferozepore 18 Feb. 1840.

Son of Thomas Hawkins, *q.v.*, and Maria Magdalen his 1st wife. Brother of Francis Spencer Hawkins, *q.v.* *m.* 1st, St. George's, Bloomsbury, 8 June 1826, Alicia Isabella, 3rd dau. of John Lumsden, of Cushnie, co. Aberdeen, Director E.I.Co. (She died 13 May 1828, aged 22.) *m.* 2nd, Calcutta, 10 June 1830, Miss Elizabeth Amelia Goodwyn. (She died 15 Mar. 1837, of cholera.)

Services : (? Nepal War 1814-5 ; Ensign 1/19th N.I., in 1st Div.) Third Mahratta War ; Lieut. 19th N.I. Intr. & Qmr. 1/19th N.I. 23 Dec. 1816 till Dec. 1823. Fur. p.a. 9 Jan. 1824 till 23 Oct. 1826. Transfd. to 38th N.I. (late 1/19th) May 1824. Actg. Fort Adjt., Fort William, 4 June 1827. Offg. Executive Ofr. P.W.D., 14th (Saugor) Div., 11 Apr. till 5 July 1828. Fur. s.c. 28 Aug. 1828 till 30 May 1830. Actg. D.J.A.G., Benares, 17 Feb. 1835. In charge of Hariana L.I. Bn. 16 Oct. 1838 till 14 May 1839.

Refs. : Burke's *Landed Gentry*, 4th edn., p. 913, *s.n.* Lumsden, of Cushnie, co. Aberdeen. *G.M.* 1826, i. 560. Will dated 14 June 1838 ; proved 10 Mar. 1840.

HAWKINS, Francis Spencer (1798-1860). Major General, C.B. Colonel 2nd N.I. *b.* 27 Feb. 1798. Cadet 1817. Was already in India when apptd. Cadet. Ensign (?). Lieut. 1 Aug. 1818. Capt. 1 Dec. 1830. Major 18 Feb. 1840. Lt. Col. 26 Feb. 1846. Col. 17 Mar. 1851. Maj. Gen. 28 Nov. 1854. *d.* 32 Sussex Gdns., Hyde Pk., London, 3 June 1860.

bapt. Cawnpore 18 July 1798. Son of Thomas Hawkins, *q.v.*, and Maria Magdalen his 1st wife. Brother of Edward Simeon Hawkins, *q.v.* *m.* 1st, Benares, 17 Sept. 1823, Miss Mary Loveday. *m.* 2nd, Calcutta, 9 July 1831, Emily, 2nd dau. of Henry Kellett, of Morrison's I., Cork. (She died London 11 June 1856.)

Services : Ensign H.M. 24th Foot 3 Aug. 1815. Third Mahratta War ; Nagpur. Posted as Ensign to 1/19th N.I. Offg. Intr. & Qmr. 1/19th N.I. 20 Nov. 1821. Adjt. 1/19th N.I. 28 Oct. 1822 till 19 Oct. 1825. Transfd. to 38th N.I. (late 1/19th) May 1824.

Tempy. comdg. Pioneer detachment at Almora 19 Jan. 1825. Supy. S.A.C.G. 3 Oct. 1825; attd. to Cav. Div. Dec. 1825. Siege and capture of Bhurtpore (India medal). S.A.C.G. 27 Mar. 1826; D.A.C.G., 2 cl., 5 Apr. 1831; 1 cl., 29 Nov. 1833; A.C.G., 2 cl., 12 Apr. 1837; Dy. Comy. Gen. with force for China 11 Mar. 1840. First China War 1840-2; Chusan; Canton; Amoy; Chin-kiang-Foo; Dy. Comy. Gen., Bengal (Medal). (*Lond. Gaz.* 8 Oct. 1841 and 6 Sept. 1842.) Dy. Comy. Gen. 17 Nov. 1843; Comy. Gen. 10 Feb. 1848 till 1852. M.M.B. 5 Feb. 1848. Lt. Col. 31st N.I. Posted as Col. to 43rd N.I. 17 June 1851; to 60th N.I. Aug. 1852. Fur. s.c. 5 Oct. 1852 till death. Col. 2nd N.I. June 1856. C.B. 24 Dec. 1842.

Refs.: Boase. *A.J.* N.S. vi. 190. *G.M.* 1860, ii. 97. *The Times*, 6 June 1860. Will dated 28 May 1860; proved 20 Nov. 1860.

HAWKINS, Henry (*d.* 1812). Major. Infantry. Cadet 1767. Ensign Dec. 1767. Lieut. 17 Oct. 1769. Capt. 25 Mar. 1778. Major 21 Feb. 1782. Struck off 1793. *d.* Lawrence End, Herts, 20 Sept. 1812.

Elder brother of Thomas Hawkins, *q.v.*

Services: First Mahratta War, under Col. Thomas Goddard, *q.v.* Fur. 3 yrs. 9 Oct. 1785, and was still on fur. in 1790.

Refs.: *E.I.M.C.* ii. 467. *G.M.* 1812, ii. 402.

HAWKINS, James Zachariah (1787-1814). Lieutenant, 3rd N.I. *b.* Kingston-on-Thames, Surrey, 25 Nov. 1787. Cadet 1804. Arrived in India 12 July 1805. Ensign 26 Aug. 1805. Lieut. 27 Aug. 1805. *d.* Berhampore 29 Sept. 1814.

bapt. 26 Dec. 1787. Son of Zachariah Hawkins and Susannah his wife. *m.* 17 Apr. 1808, Miss H. Rutledge.

Services: Posted as Lieut. to 3rd N.I. in 1806. Adjt. & Qmr. 3rd N.I. 1811-2.

HAWKINS, Samuel (*d.* 1782). Fireworker, Artillery. Cadet 1781. Fireworker 16 Aug. 1782. *d.* Sept. 1782.

Services: N.F.P.

HAWKINS, Thomas (1757/58-1818). Colonel, 4th N.I. *b.* 1757/58. Cadet 1778. Admitted 10 Dec. 1778. Ensign 1778. Lieut. 24 Nov. 1778. Capt. 1 June 1796. Major 30 June 1802. Lt. Col. 25 May 1804. Col. 4 June 1813. *d.* Camden Pl., Bath, 1 Mar. 1818.

A native of Bedfordshire. Brother of Henry Hawkins, *q.v.*, of Ann Hawkins, and of Mrs. Hannah Beaumont. Uncle of John

Greenstreet, *q.v.* *m.* 1st, Berhampore, 14 Nov. 1792, Maria Magdalena, dau. of Simon Droz(e), B.C.S. (*See also* Andrew Black.) Father of Edward Simeon Hawkins, *q.v.*, and of Francis Spencer Hawkins, *q.v.* (*Probably* father of Harriet, wife of George Hunter (1785-1819), *q.v.*) (She died Barrackpore 10 Aug. 1799.) *m.* 2nd, Calcutta, 2 Feb. 1801, Elizabeth Friell, his deceased wife's sister. Brother-in-law of Charlotte Sophia, wife of Daniel Spencer Freeman.
Services : Lieut. 2/1st Bengal Eur. Regt. in Oct. 1779. Lieut. 5th Bn. Sepoys in 1787. Capt. 5th N.I. in 1798. Major 1st N.I. Operations in Bundelkhand 1806-7 ; capture of Chamir fort ; capture of Sehlehuganj fort ; Lt. Col. 2/1st N.I., comdg. the force. D.A.G. Jan. 1808. Transfd. to 10th N.I. in 1811 ; to 1/22nd N.I. in 1815. Fur. 16 Jan. 1816 till death.
Refs. : E.I.M.C. ii. 467. *G.M.* 1818, i. 644. *Bath Chron.* 5 Mar. 1818. Will dated Calcutta 16 Nov. 1815 ; proved 21 July 1818.

HAWKS, John Shaftoe (1809-1844). Lieutenant, 7th N.I. *b.* Gateshead, co. Durham, 16 Oct. 1809. Cadet 1828. Arrived in India 24 Nov. 1829. Ensign 24 Nov. 1829. Lieut. 3 Oct. 1840. *d.* Delhi, 13 June 1844, of consumption.

Son of John Hawks, of 6 Ducksfoot Lane, London, and Gateshead-on-Tyne, ironmerchant, and Jane his wife, eldest dau. of Thomas Longridge, of Gateshead-on-Tyne.

Services : Ensign d.d. 7th N.I. 1 Dec. 1829 ; do. 38th N.I. 19 Oct. 1831 ; do. 47th N.I. Dec. 1831. Posted as Ensign to 22nd N.I. 12 Mar. 1833 ; transfd. to 7th N.I. 18 Oct. 1833. Actg. Intr. & Qmr. 19th N.I. 7 June 1839 till Dec. 1841. Actg. 2nd in comd. 2nd Irreg. Cav. Apr. 1842 till Jan. 1843. Insurrection in Bundelkhand 1842 ; Lieut. 2nd Irreg. Cav. Actg. Adjt. 7th N.I. 3 Dec. 1843 ; permanent do. Mar. 1844 till death.

Refs. : Herald & Genealogist, vii. 142. *De Rhé-Philipe.* G.M. 1844, ii. 558. I.M. No. 17, p. 528. Will dated Fort of Petora Ghur 13 Dec. 1835 ; codicil dated Nimach 19 July 1842 ; proved 7 July 1845. M.I. in Rajpura cemetery, Delhi.

HAWKSHAW, Thomas (1755-1819). Major General. Colonel 22nd N.I. *b.* 1755. Cadet 1772. Admitted 3 Feb. 1772. Ensign 6 Feb. 1773. Lieut. 25 Feb. 1778. Capt. 2 Oct. 1781. Major 25 Oct. 1797. Lt. Col. 31 July 1799. Col. 25 Apr. 1808. Maj. Gen. 4 June 1811. *d.* Middlesex Pl., London, 30 June 1819, suddenly, aged 63.

Only son of Thomas Hawkshaw, of Dublin, timber merchant, and Margaret his wife, dau. of Hugh Gordon. *m.* 1st, Calcutta, 13 July 1791, Gertruida Christina, sister of Jacob Vanrenen, *q.v.*, and widow of Freiheer Hatfeldt. *m.* 2nd, Marylebone, Nov. 1807, Anne, eldest dau. of Robert Percival, of Knightsbrook, co. Meath, and Laricor and Carrickmakcegan, co. Leitrim.

Services : Supy. Capt., unposted, in July 1787. Lt. Col. 8th N.I. Fur. 25 Nov. 1802 till death. Transfd. to 19th N.I. in 1803 ; as Lt. Col. Comdt. to newly-raised 22nd N.I. 28 Sept. 1804. Col. 22nd N.I. Apr. 1808.

Refs. : Burke's *Colonial Gentry,* ii. 819, *s.n.* Percival, of N.Z. *De La Ferté,* p. 167. *M.M.* xxiv. *G.M.* 1819, ii. 90. *S.M.* 1819, ii. 200.

HAWTHORNE, Robert John (1808-1889). General. 2nd Bengal Eur. Cav. *b.* Northwood, Hants, 14 Sept. 1808. Cadet 1827. Arrived in India 23 Mar. 1829. Cornet 12 Sept. 1828. Lieut. 13 Apr. 1837. Capt. 11 Dec. 1848. Major 13 Apr. 1855. Lt. Col. 1 Jan. 1862. Col. 18 Feb. 1866. Maj. Gen. 1 May 1872. Lt. Gen. 18 July 1879. Gen. 1 Dec. 1888. *d.* London 2 Dec. 1889.

Son of Robert Hawthorne, Major 4th Garr. Bn., and Jane his wife. *m.* 1st, Calcutta, 15 Dec. 1834, Eliza, eldest dau. of Antoine Louis D'Olivier, Capt. h.p. York L.I. *m.* 2nd, 19 May 1848, Sarah S., dau. of Capt. D'Olivier.

Services : Cornet d.d. 4th L.C. 10 June 1829. Actg. Cornet 14 Oct. 1831. Posted as Cornet to 7th L.C. 28 Feb. 1832. (? Shekhawat expedn. 1834 ; Cornet 7th L.C.) Served with Sind F.F. 1845-6 ; Lieut. 7th L.C. Second Sikh War ; Jullundur and Bari Doabs ; Capt. 7th L.C. with Bdr. Wheeler's force (Medal). Fur. 1857 till 11 Sept. 1857. Transfd. to newly-raised 2nd Eur. L.C. in 1858. Fur. 1859.

Refs. : I.M. 22 Aug. 1848, p. 495.

HAWTHORNE, Steele (1789-1853). Lieut. Colonel. 32nd N.I. *b.* Killinchy co. Down 26 Feb. 1789. Cadet 1803. Arrived in India 17 Mar. 1805. Ensign 27 Apr. 1805. Lieut. 27 Apr. 1805. Capt. 1 Aug. 1818. Major 19 Oct. 1827. Lt.. Col 15 Oct. 1832. Retired 28 Feb. 1840. *d.* 25 Feb. 1853.

Nephew of Charles Stewart Hawthorne. *m.* Calcutta, 28 Nov. 1813, Miss Elizabeth Anna Child.

Services : Posted as Lieut. to 11th N.I. Reduction of Kalinjar 1812 ; Lieut. 1/11th N.I. Adjt. 2/11th N.I. in 1817. Capt. Lt. 1/11th N.I. 27 Nov. 1817. Third Mahratta War ; Capt. 2/11th N.I. Fur. p.a. 8 Nov. 1822 till 4 Oct. 1825. Transfd to 15th N.I. (late 1/11th) May 1824. Siege and capture of Bhurtpore ; Capt. 15th N.I. (India medal). Posted as Lt. Col. to 17th N.I. 9 July 1833. Fur. s.c. 27 Feb. 1835 till 20 Oct. 1838. Transfd. to 52nd N.I. 15 Jan. 1835 ; to 53rd N.I. 29 Apr. 1836 ; to 15th N.I. 1 July 1837; to 62nd N.I. 18 Nov. 1837; to 32nd N.I. 22 Oct. 1838.

HAWTREY, Frederick Hill (1812-1842). Lieutenant, 37th N.I. *bapt.* West Meon, Hants, 18 Mar. 1812. Cadet 1830. Admitted 7 June 1831. Ensign 7 June 1831. Lieut. 26 Mar. 1839. *d.* Gandamak, Afghanistan, 13 Jan. 1842 : kld. in action during the retreat from Kabul.

Son of Rev. Charles Sleech Hawtrey, of Wells St., Hackney, vicar of Wilston, co. Monmouth, and minister of the Episcopal Jews' chapel, Bethnal Green, and Harriet his wife. Nephew of Henry Hawtrey, *q.v.*

Services : Cadet d.d. 54th N.I. 28 June 1831 ; do. 73rd N.I. 10 Feb. 1833. Actg. Ensign 25 June 1833. Posted as Ensign to 37th N.I. 19 Oct. 1833. Fur. s.c. 4 Feb. 1837 till 12 July 1838. First Afghan War 1838-42 ; Kabul insurrection (kld.) ; Lieut. 37th N.I.

HAWTREY, Henry (1783-1833). Lieut. Colonel, 3rd L.C. *bapt.* Bampton, co. Oxford, 5 June 1783. Cadet 1798. Arrived in India 15 Dec. 1799. Cornet 12 June 1800. Lieut. 11 Mar. 1805. Capt. 1 Sept. 1818. Major 7 Mar. 1823. Lt. Col. 10 July 1825. *d.* Ghazipur, 7 July 1833, aged 49.

2nd son of Rev. Charles Hawtrey, vicar of Bampton, and Grace his wife, 2nd dau. of Rt. Hon. Sir Robert Deane, 5th Bart., P.C. Uncle of Frederick Hill Hawtrey, *q.v.* *m.* Kaitha, U.P., 23 June 1813, Miss Margaret Chamberlayne. Ed. Eton between 1796 and 1798.

Services : Operations in Jumna Doab 1803 ; Sasni ; Bijaigarh ; Kachaura ; Cornet 4th N.C. Second Mahratta War ; Laswari ; Cornet 4th N.C. Actg. Adjt. 4th N.C. 27 Feb. 1813. Actg. Qmr. 4th N.C. 5 Apr. 1817. Bde. Major 3rd Cav. Bde. till 2 Feb. 1818. Third Mahratta War ; Capt. 4th N.C., Bde. Major. (? Operations in Kotah 1821 ; Mangrol.) Posted as Lt. Col. to 9th L.C. Leave s.c. to Cape 4 Nov. 1825 till Sept 1827. Transfd. to 8th L.C. 4 Nov. 1826 ; to 3rd L.C. in 1828. Operations against the Kols 1832 ; surprised a body of insurgents at Baloonagar on 25 Feb. 1832 ; Lt. Col. comdg. 3rd L.C.

Refs. : Burke's *Peerage*, 1923, p. 1641, *s.n.* Muskerry, B. *Hist. of the Hawtrey Family*, by Florence M. Hawtrey (1903), i. 117-9. *Eton School Lists.* G.M. 1833, ii. 556. Will dated 9 Mar. 1829 ; proved 31 Dec. 1833. M.I. St. John's church, Calcutta.

HAY, Archibald (*d.* 1772). Cadet, Infantry. Cadet 1770. *d.* Calcutta 2 Mar. 1772.

Services : N.F.P.

HAY, Charles (1746/47-1778). Captain, Infantry. *b.* 1746/47. Cadet 1766. Ensign 15 Sept. 1766. Lieut. 5 Dec. 1767. Capt. 1 Apr. 1773. *d. unm.* Patna, 26 Nov. 1778, aged 31.

Son of —— Hay and Elizabeth his wife. Brother of John, William, and Elizabeth Hay, Mrs. Mary Forbes, and Mrs. Jean Robertson.
Services : First Rohilla War ; battle of St. George.
Refs. : Will dated 28 Oct. 1770 ; codicil dated 12 May 1775 ; proved 25 Feb. 1779. M.I. in Patna cemetery.

HAY, Charles Peter (1780-1820). Major, 22nd N.I. Comdt. Champaran L.I. *b.* (? Dunbar) 2 Mar. 1780. Cadet 1795. Admitted 14 Mar. 1798. Ensign 15 Aug. 1797. Lieut. 12 Aug. 1798. Capt. 9 Sept. 1806. Major 4 Apr. 1818. *d.* Mullye, B. & O., 27 July 1820.

Son of Major Hay, Elgin Regt. of Fenc. Inf. *m.* 1st, Esk Grove, Midlothian, 1 July 1812, Helen, eldest dau. of Sir David Rae, of Esk Grove, 1st Bart. (She died Calcutta, 20 Feb. 1813, aged 25.) *m.* 2nd, Calcutta, 22 Nov. 1817, Miss Clementina Stuart. (She died 18 May 1858.)

Services : Second Mahratta War ; Laswari ; Lieut. 12th N.I. Transfd. to newly-raised 22nd N.I. in 1804. Adjt. 1/22nd N.I. 1804. Adjt. & Qmr. 22nd N.I. 1805-6. Settlement of Hariana 1809 ; Bhawani ; Capt. 1/22nd N.I. Fur. 1811-3. Comdd. Champaran L.I. 11 Sept. 1813 till death. Nepal War 1814-5. Nepal War 1816. Comdt. of the Nepal frontier post of Mullye.
Refs. : *G.M.* 1812, ii. 81 ; 1821, i. 185. *S.M.* 1821, i. 398. Will dated Mullye 1 June 1818 ; proved 6 Sept. 1820.

HAY, David. Cadet. Infantry. Cadet 1769. Resigned 1 Feb. 1770.
Services : N.F.P.

HAY, Edward (1806-1842). Bt. Captain, 35th N.I. *b.* Aston, nr. Birmingham, 20 Nov. 1806. Cadet 1825. Arrived in India 24 Jan. 1827. Ensign 8 Aug. 1826. Lieut. 21 Aug. 1831. Bt. Capt. 8 Aug. 1841. *d.* 13 Jan. 1842 : kld. in action nr. Gandamak during the retreat from Kabul.

bapt. Aston 16 Jan. 1809. 2nd son of John Hay, of Buckingham St., Strand, London, merchant, afterwards of Inverleith Row, Edinburgh, and Anne Walker his wife. Brother of John Hay (1802-1839), *q.v.*, and nephew by marriage of George Hardyman, *q.v.*
Services : Ensign d.d. 35th N.I. 20 Feb. 1827. Posted to 35th N.I. 10 May 1827. Adjt. 35th N.I. 8 Oct. 1829 till Mar. 1841. First Afghan War ; Ghazni ; retreat from Kabul (kld.) ; Bt. Capt. 35th N.I., Shah's service. Bde. Major 4th Bde. 9 Dec. 1840. Apptd. to Shah Shuja's army 10 Mar. 1841. Inspector 1st Regt. of Kazil Bash.
Refs. : Burke's *Landed Gentry*, 5th edn., p. 603, *s.n.* Hay, of Hopes, co. Haddington. *G.M.* 1842, ii. 446. *The Times*, 13 Sept. 1842.

HAY, George. Captain. Comdt. Troop of Eur. Cav. Cadet (?). Ensign 1759. Lieut. 23 Sept. 1760. Capt. Lt. 17 Mar. 1763. Capt. 19 Oct. 1763. Resigned 17 Feb. 1765.
Services : Apptd. as Lieut. to 1st Troop of Eur. Dgns. 22 Sept. 1760. Battle of Suan 15 Jan. 1761 ; Lieut. 1st Troop. Apptd. to comd. the Body Guard, which Col. Coote brought with him from Madras, 17 Mar. 1763. To comd. the Troop of Eur. Cav. formed by amalgamating the Hrs. and Body Guard Mar. 1764. Battle of Buxar ; comdd. the Reserve, consisting of the Eur. Cav. and the Gren. Coys. of Bengal Inf.
Refs. : Broome, p. 473. *Journal of the U.S. Institution of India,* xlii. (Jan. 1913), p. 113.

HAY, George Charles Ker (1808-1828). Ensign, 13th N.I. *b.* Edinburgh 21 Oct. 1808. Cadet 1826. Ensign 8 Feb. 1827. *d.* Dinapore 25 May 1828.

4th son of John Hay, Capt. 9th Regt., Bk. Mr. at Sunderland (who was half-brother of Sir Thomas Hay, 5th Bart., of Alderston), and his wife, dau. of —— Ker, of Broadmeadows, co. Berwick. Grand-nephew of Patrick (Peter) Hay, *q.v.*
Services : Posted as Ensign to 13th N.I. 19 June 1827. Exchanged to 46th N.I. 21 Mar. 1828. This exchange was apparently cancelled. No record of active service.
Refs. : Burke's *Peerage,* 1923, p. 1136, *s.n.* Hay, Bart., of Alderston.

HAY, Humphrey (1800-1860). Lieut. Colonel. 11th L.C. *b.* Spott, E. Lothian, 10 Oct. 1800. Cadet 1817. Admitted 3 Oct. 1818. Cornet (?). Lieut. 15 July 1819. Capt. 15 Sept. 1825. Bt. Major 28 June 1838. Retired 21 Aug. 1847. Hon. Lt. Col. 28 Nov. 1854. *d.* 13 Rutland St., Edinburgh, 30 Aug. 1860.

3rd son of Robert Hay, of Spott, and Catherine Babington his wife. Addiscombe Cadet 1817-8.
Services : Posted as Lieut. to 2nd L.C. in 1819. Offg. Intr. & Qmr. 2nd L.C. 14 Dec. 1822. Extra A.D.C. to C.-in-C. 14 Jan. 1823. Bde. Major in Bundelkhand 25 June 1825 ; do. in Rohilkhand 27 Sept. 1825 ; do. Rajputana F.F. 6 Oct. 1838. D.A.Q.M.G., Cav., Army of the Indus, 8 Dec. 1838 till 31 Dec. 1839. First Afghan War 1838-9 ; Ghazni ; Bt. Major 2nd L.C., D.A.Q.M.G. (Medal). Posted to newly-raised 11th L.C. on the disbandment for misconduct of 2nd L.C. in Mar. 1841. Bde. Major in Rohilkhand ; do. at Sukkur 16 Nov. 1844. Fur. s.c. 21 Feb. 1845 till retirement.
Refs. : The *Times,* 4 Sept. 1860.

THE BENGAL ARMY, 1758-1834   415

HAY, James (1758/59-?). Lieutenant. Infantry. *b.* in Scotland 1758/59. Cadet 1781. Ensign (?). Lieut. 1782. Struck off 1788.
Services : Sailed for India on the *Hinchinbrooke,* 13 Mar. 1781, aged 22. N.F.P.

HAY, James (1800-1832). Lieutenant, 40th N.I. *b.* Madras 20 Dec. 1800. Cadet 1819. Admitted 30 May 1820. Ensign 10 Jan. 1820. Lieut. 13 Mar. 1823. *d.* Perth 20 Oct. 1832.
bapt. Vepery, Madras, 31 Dec. 1800. Son of George Hay, of the firm of Hunter & Hay, Madras. *m.* Barrackpore, 2 Nov. 1822, Miss Isabella Helen Porteous (*probably* dau. of Charles Porteous, *q.v.*). (*See also* William Innes (1803-1832).)
Services : Apptd. originally a Cadet for Madras ; transfd. as Cadet to Bengal Est. Ensign 2/20th N.I. (? First Burma War ; Chittagong 1824 ; Lieut. 2/20th N.I.) Transfd. to 40th N.I. (late 2/20th) May 1824. Actg. Adjt. 5 Coys. 25th N.I. (late 1/20th) 23 Aug. 1826. Adjt. Bundelkhand Provl. Bn. 4 Aug. 1827 ; do. Benares Provl. Bn. 28 Dec. 1827. Fur. s.c. 10 Oct. 1831 till death.
Refs. : A.J. N.S. ix. 197.

*HAY, James (1803-1819 ?). Cadet, Infantry. *b.* Edinburgh 9 May 1803. Cadet 1819. Never arrived in India. *d.* in England (? 1819) before his ship sailed.
Son of James Hay, W.S., of Edinburgh, and Matilda Clark his wife. Brother of Robert Hay (1813-1846), *q.v.*

HAY, John (*d.* 1773). Lieutenant, Infantry. Cadet 1768. Ensign 28 Jan. 1769. Lieut. 16 May 1770. *d.* Berhampore May 1773.
Services : N.F.P.

HAY, John (1784-1839). Lieut. Colonel. 17th N.I. *b.* Yester, co. Haddington, 4 Oct. 1784. Cadet 1800. Arrived in India 22 Aug. 1801. Ensign 4 Jan. 1802. Lieut. 30 Sept. 1803. Capt. 8 Jan. 1816. Major 1 May 1824. Lt. Col. 13 Jan. 1828. Retired 21 Jan. 1829. *d.* Musselburgh 22 Oct. 1839.
Son of John Hay, of Duncanlaw, and Elizabeth Begbie his wife. *m.* Winter Hill, 15 Nov. 1836, Margaret, eldest dau. of James Howden.
Services : Ensign 16th N.I. Served with the Pioneer Corps 1808-24. Adjt. Pioneers 1 Aug. 1809 till 1818. Lieut. 1/16th N.I. Nepal War 1814-5 ; Lieut. 5th Coy. Pioneers, in 2nd Div. Capt. 1/16th N.I. Capt. comdg. 4th Coy. Pioneers. Transfd. as Major to 33rd N.I. (late 2/16th) May 1824. Fur. 1824 till Aug. 1828. Posted as Lt. Col. to 17th N.I. 3 June 1828.
Refs. : A.J. N.S. xxii. 68 ; xxx. 359.

HAY, John (1792-?). Ensign. 18th N.I. *b.* Edinburgh 20 May 1792. Cadet 1808. Arrived in India 1 June 1810. Ensign 13 July 1811. Resigned in India 30 Sept. 1814.

Son of Lewis Hay, of Edinburgh, banker.

Services : On fur. 1810-1. Posted as Ensign to 18th N.I. in 1811. No record of active service. Sailed from India on the *Europe* in Jan. 1815.

HAY, John (1802-1839). Bt. Major, 35th N.I. *b.* Aston, nr. Birmingham, 24 Nov. 1802. Cadet 1819. Admitted 27 Mar. 1820. Ensign 20 Sept. 1819. Lieut. 1 Jan. 1823. Capt. 17 Jan. 1829. Bt. Major 23 July 1839. *d.* Kabul, Afghanistan, 13 Oct. 1839.

bapt. St. Peter & St. Paul, Aston, 3 June 1803. Elder son of John Hay, of Sculcoates, Yorks., Liverpool merchant, afterwards of Inverleith Row, Edinburgh, and Anne Walker his wife, of Hull. Brother of Edward Hay, *q.v.* Ed. Shrewsbury 1814-9.

Services : Ensign 2/17th N.I. Actg. Adjt. 2/17th N.I. 26 Dec. 1822. Transfd. to 34th N.I. (late 1/17th) May 1824 ; to 35th N.I. (late 2/17th) 26 June 1824. Intr. & Qmr. 35th N.I. 5 Aug. 1825 till 3 Feb. 1829. Siege and capture of Bhurtpore ; Lieut. 35th N.I. Apptd. to tempy. charge of Calcutta Native Mil. 28 Oct. 1831. Offg. D.J.A.G. at Presdy. 28 Feb. 1832. Persian Intr. to C.-in-C. 14 Nov. 1836 till 1 Mar. 1839. Attd. to Staff of Army of the Indus 13 Sept. 1838. First Afghan War 1839 ; Ghazni (*Lond. Gaz.* 30 Oct. 1839) ; Bt. Major 35th N.I. Durani, 3 cl. (*Cal. Gaz.* 15 Aug. 1840).

Refs. : Burke's *Landed Gentry*, 5th edn., p. 603, *s.n.* Hay, of Hopes, co. Haddington. *Shrewsbury School Register. G.M.* 1840, i. 223.

HAY, John Thompson (1812-1832). Acting Ensign, Infantry. *b.* Londonderry 9 Mar. 1812. Cadet 1830. Arrived in India 9 Mar. 1831. Actg. Ensign 30 Sept. 1830. *d.* in India 15 Oct.1832.

Son of Rev. George Hay, Presbyterian minister of Londonderry.

Services : d.d. 2nd N.I. 7 Apr. 1831.

HAY, Patrick (1806-1860). Colonel. 54th N.I. *b.* Seggieden, co. Perth, 29 Sept. 1806. Cadet 1824. Arrived in India 21 Dec. 1825. Ensign 26 Mar. 1825. Lieut. 4 Mar. 1828. Capt. 24 Jan. 1845. Bt. Lt. Col. 20 June 1854. Retired 31 May 1855. Hon. Col. 10 Aug. 1855. *d.* Edinburgh 11 Aug. 1860.

4th son of James Hay, of Seggieden, and Margaret his 1st wife, dau. of John Richardson, of Pitfour. Distantly related to William Edmund (Maule Ramsay) Hay, *q.v.*

THE BENGAL ARMY, 1758-1834   417

Services : Posted as Ensign to 42nd N.I. in 1826. Actg. Adjt. 42nd N.I. 17 Dec. 1828, and 22 Oct. 1834. Adjt. 42nd N.I. 5 Oct. 1839 till 7 Apr. 1843. First Afghan War 1839-42 ; Kandahar ; Ghazni ; Kabul ; operations of Kandahar force under Gen. Nott ; Lieut. 42nd N.I. (Medal). Transfd. to 54th N.I. 14 Dec. 1842. Adjt. 54th N.I. 21 Apr. 1843 till 1844. First Sikh War ; Ferozshahr ; Capt. 54th N.I. (Medal). Fur. 10 Mar. 1847 till 7 Mar. 1850.

Refs. : Burke's *Landed Gentry*, 12th edn., p. 914, *s.n.* Drummond-Hay, of Seggieden, co. Perth. *The Times*, 15 Aug. 1860.

HAY, Patrick (Peter) (1748/49-1822). Colonel. Infantry. *b.* 1748/49. Cadet 1768. Admitted 1768. Ensign 12 Jan. 1769. Lieut. 9 Jan. 1770. Capt. 16 July 1778. Major 3 Feb. 1784. Lt. Col. 1 Mar. 1794. Col. (?). Retired 2 Jan. 1799. *d.* Ensham Hall, Oxon., 1 Apr. 1822, aged 73.

4th son of Thomas Hay, a senator of the Coll. of Justice by the title of Lord Huntingdon, and Margaret his wife, dau. of Sir David Murray, of Stanhope, Bart. *m.* 24 June 1782, Sarah, 4th dau. of Robert Dashwood, of Vallow Wood, Stogumber, Somerset. (She died 19 Jan. 1850, aged 88.) Father of Patrick Martin Hay, *q.v.*, and grand-uncle of George Charles Ker Hay, *q.v.*

Services : Capt. 2/2nd Bengal Eur. Regt. in Oct. 1779. Major comdg. 22nd Bn. Sepoys in July 1787. Fur 18 Jan. 1796 till retirement.

Refs. : Burke's *Peerage*, 1923, p. 1136, *s.n.* Hay, Bart., of Alderston. *G.M.* 1822, i. 381. *S.M.* 1822, i. 695.

HAY, Patrick Martin (1786-1845). Colonel, 70th N.I. *b.* Calcutta 24 Feb. 1786. Cadet 1802. Arrived in India 27 Aug. 1803. Ensign 16 Sept. 1803. Lieut. 25 Aug. 1804. Capt. 8 Jan. 1817. Major 24 Dec. 1825. Lt. Col. 26 June 1830. Col. 26 Aug. 1842. *d.* Milton St., Dorset Sq., London, 23 Oct. 1845.

2nd son of Patrick (Peter) Hay, *q.v.*, and Sarah his wife. *m.* 9 Sept. 1819, Mary Susan, 2nd dau. of Richard Clarke, *q.v.* His dau. *m.* Thomas Sewell, *q.v.*

Services : Ensign d.d. 9th N.I. 1804. Posted as Lieut. to 9th N.I. 1804. Adjt. 2nd L.I. Bn. 1809. Adjt. 1/4th N.I. 21 Sept. 1809 till 4 May 1815. Capture of Java 1811 ; Lieut. 4th Vol. Bn. Transfd. as Adjt. to newly-raised 1/28th N.I. 4 May 1815. Fur. 16 Jan. 1817 till 1 Sept. 1820. Tempy. comdg. Benares Provl. Bn. 7 Nov. 1820 ; do. Cawnpore 26 Feb. 1821. A.D.C. to Maj.-Gen. Lewis Thomas, *q.v.*, 2 Jan. 1822. Tempy. comdg. Chittagong Provl. Bn. 25 Jan. 1823 till 29 Mar. 1824. Transfd. to 33rd N.I. 11 July 1823 ; to 66th N.I. (late 2/33rd) May 1824. Bk. Mr. Purnea Div. 29 Mar. 1824 ; do. Rohilkhand 7 June 1824 till 1826. Apptd.

to charge of 69th N.I. 17 Oct. 1827 ; do. 21st N.I. 22 Apr. 1828 ; do. 29th N.I. 9 Aug. 1828. Posted to 56th N.I. 1 Oct. 1833 ; to 24th N.I. 26 Dec. 1833. Fur. s.c. 6 Jan. 1835 till 6 Sept. 1839. Transfd. to 70th N.I. 17 Sept. 1839. Fur. p.a. 11 Feb. 1843 till death.

Refs. : Burke's *Peerage*, 1923, p. 1136, *s.n.* Hay, Bart., of Alderston. *G.M.* 1819, ii. 368 ; 1845, ii. 657.

HAY, PHILIP (1780-?). Lieutenant. 9th N.I. *b.* Edinburgh 14 Nov. 1780. Cadet 1800. Arrived in India 26 Oct. 1801. Ensign 28 Dec. 1801. Lieut. 11 Oct. 1803. Struck off 14 Aug. 1815.

bapt. College church psh., Edinburgh, 30 Nov. 1780. Son of William Hay, of Newhall, and Helen Gray his wife. (? *m.* Edinburgh, 13 Mar. 1815, Elizabeth Wellwood, dau. of Bdr.-Gen. French.)

Services : Ensign 9th N.I. Second Mahratta War ; Agra ; Laswari ; Gwalior ; Monson's retreat ; Bhurtpore ; Lieut. 2/9th N.I. Fur. 14 Feb. 1813. Struck off in 1818 with effect from 14 Aug. 1815, *i.e.*, after 2½ yrs. absence from India.

HAY, Richard (*d.* 1825). Major. 18th N.I. Cadet 1782. Admitted 19 Nov. 1782. Ensign 27 Jan. 1783. Lieut. 3 July 1789. Capt. 30 Sept. 1803. Major 25 Apr. 1808. Retired 21 Apr. 1809. *d.* Rye, 16 Mar. 1825, of a lingering consumption.

m. Calcutta, 15 Dec. 1793, Miss Maria Hannay. (*See also* Alexander Grant (Cadet 1777).) (She died 25 Sept. 1827.)

Services : Ensign 4th Bengal Eur. Regt. in July 1787. Lieut. 3rd N.I. Transfd. to newly-raised 2/18th N.I. 29 May 1800. Capt. Lt. 18th N.I. 5 Aug. 1802. Adjt. & Qmr. Rangpur district in 1803. Second Mahratta War ; Capt. 18th N.I. Fur. 20 Sept. 1806 till retirement.

Refs. : *A.J.* xix. 721.

HAY, Robert (*d.* 1771). Cadet, Infantry. Cadet 1770. *d.* Dinapore 9 June 1771.

Services : N.F.P.

HAY, Robert (1813-1846). Lieutenant, 50th N.I. *b.* Edinburgh 29 Oct. 1813. Cadet 1831. Arrived in India 26 Oct. 1832. Ensign 19 May 1832. Lieut. 29 Oct. 1838. *d.* 10 Feb. 1846 : kld. in action at the battle of Sobraon.

Son of James Hay, of Edinburgh, W.S., and Matilda Clark his wife. Brother of James Hay,* *q.v.* Addiscombe Cadet 15 Feb. 1830 till 8 Dec. 1831.

Services : Ensign d.d. 35th N.I. 21 Nov. 1832. Posted as Ensign

to 50th N.I. 19 Dec. 1833. Fur. s.c. 15 Aug. 1834 till 14 Jan. 1839. Adjt. Nassiri Bn. 30 Apr. 1841 ; offg. 2nd in comd. do. May-Oct. 1842. Insurrection in Bundelkhand 1842-3 ; Lieut. 50th N.I. Adjt. Nassiri Bn. Apr. 1843 till death. First Sikh War; Aliwal, Adjt. Nassiri Bn.; Sobraon (kld.) ; Bde. Major 2nd Bde. 1st Div.
Refs. : *De Rhé-Philipe.* M.I. St. Andrew's, Ferozepore.

HAY, Samuel Sinclair (1779-1816). Bt. Major, Artillery. *b.* Tron kirk psh., Edinburgh, 2 Apr. 1779. Cadet 1794. Arrived in India 22 Feb. 1796. Fireworker 8 Dec. 1795. Lieut. 19 Feb. 1802. Capt. Lt. 21 Sept. 1804. Capt. 5 Dec. 1809. Bt. Major 4 June 1814. *d.* 57 George St., Edinburgh, 1 Oct. 1816.

2nd son of Dr. Thomas Hay, of Edinburgh, surgeon, and Jean Graham his wife.

Services : Fur. 18 Jan. 1797 till 19 Aug. 1799. Second Mahratta War ; Agra ; Laswari ; siege of Gwalior ; Lieut. 1st Coy. 2nd Bn. Art. ; battle and capture of Deig ; Bhurtpore ; Lieut. 3rd Coy. 2nd Bn. Comdd. Golandaz Bn. 8 July 1808 till 1816. Fur. 1816 till death.

Refs. : *G.M.* 1816, ii. 466. *S.M.* 1816, p. 377.

HAY, Thomas (1790-?). Cadet. Infantry. *b.* Calcutta Dec. 1790. Cadet 1805. Arrived in India 1 Sept. 1806. Resigned in India 22 Jan. 1807.

Son of T. Hay. Marlow Cadet.

HAY, William Edmund (Maule Ramsay) (1805-1879). Captain. 1st Bengal Eur. L.I. *b.* Bathwick, Somerset, 31 Jan. 1805. Cadet 1821. Arrived in India 12 Aug. 1822. Ensign 19 July 1822. Lieut. 9 May 1825. Capt. 10 Nov. 1843. Retired 1 Nov. 1844. *d.* Upper Norwood 12 Dec. 1879.

Only son of James Hay, of Collipriest, Devon, and Lady Mary Ramsay his first wife, 4th dau. of George, 8th Earl of Dalhousie. Of the same family as Patrick Hay, *q.v.* Cousin-german of Andrew Ramsay, *q.v. m.* Agra, 15 June 1835, Elizabeth Margaret, eldest dau. of Joseph Taylor (1790-1835), *q.v.* (*See also* Johnson Phillott.)

Services : Posted as Ensign to 1/1st N.I. Transfd. to 19th N.I. ; to 39th N.I. (late 2/19th) May 1824. Leave s.c. 12 mos. to Singapore and Penang 19 Nov. 1824. Did duty with Penang Local Corps. Actg. Bde. Major at Berhampore 2 Aug. 1826. Exchanged to 2nd Bengal Eur. Regt. 4 Sept. 1826. Actg. A.D.C. and Mily. Sec. to Govr. of P.W.I. in 1828. Fur. s.c. from P.W.I. 15 Sept. 1828 till 29 Nov. 1830. Posted to Left Wing of Eur. Regt. Jan. 1830. Bde. Major at Agra 7 Jan. 1832. Leave to Cape 19 Feb. 1837. First Afghan War 1838-9 ; Ghazni (w.) (*Lond. Gaz.* 30 Oct.

1839); Lieut. Eur. Regt. (Medal). Comdd. a Bn. of Shah Shuja's Gurkhas in Afghanistan. With Army of Reserve (for Afghanistan) Oct. 1842 till Jan. 1843 ; tempy. S.A.C.G.
Refs. : Burke's *Landed Gentry*, 12th edn., p. 914, *s.n.* Drummond-Hay, of Seggieden, co. Perth. Burke's *Peerage*, 1923, p. 653, *s.n.* Dalhousie, E. *I.N.* 1848, p. 223. *The Times*, 18 Dec. 1879.

HAYES, William Henry (1789-1825). Captain, 54th N.I. *b.* Cork 18 Apr. 1789. Cadet 1805. Arrived in India 7 Feb. 1807. Ensign 29 Dec. 1806. Lieut. 7 Nov. 1811. Capt. 1 May 1824. *d.* Chittagong 18 June 1825.

Maternal nephew of Atwell Hayes, of Cork. *m.* (before 1813) Caroline Hinds.

Services : Posted as Ensign to 27th N.I. in 1807. (? Operations against Dhundia Khan 1807 ; Komona ; Ganauri ; Ensign 27th N.I.) Operations in Oudh 1809-10 ; Ensign 2/27th N.I. Adjt. 2/27th N.I. 17 Aug. 1819 till May 1824. Transfd. as Capt. to 54th N.I. (late 2/27th) May 1824. First Burma War ; Arakan 1825 ; Capt. 2nd Gren. Bn.

Refs. : *Howard & Crisp's Ireland*, ii. 45, *s.n.* Macartney, formerly of Rosebank, co. Armagh.

*****HAYNES, John** (*d.* 1762). Ensign, Infantry. Cadet (?). Ensign (?). *bur.* Calcutta 23 Dec. 1762.

m. Elizabeth, of the psh. of St. James's (? London).

Services : Described himself in his Will as Ensign and Adjt. Described in the burial register as " Lieut. John Hynes."

Refs. : Will dated 11 Nov. 1762 ; proved 29 Mar. 1763.

HAYNES, John (*d.* 1822). Lieut. General. Colonel Bengal Eur. Regt. Cadet 1772. Admitted 27 Sept. 1772. Ensign 31 Mar. 1773. Lieut. 30 May 1778. Capt. 24 Jan. 1784. Major 11 Mar. 1794. Lt. Col. (1 Jan. 1798) 29 May 1800. Col. 25 Apr. 1808. Maj. Gen. 4 June 1811. Lt. Gen. 19 July 1821. *d.* Cheltenham 26 Aug. 1822.

Son of Bartholomew Haynes, of Tubber, co. Galway. Brother of Bartholomew Haynes, of Gort, co. Galway, of Elizabeth Haynes, and of Bridget Haynes. *m.* Calcutta, 21 Dec. 1778, Anna Maria, widow of Thomas Milton Gravely, *q.v.*

Services : Capt. 17th Bn. Sepoys in July 1787. Fur. 8 Mar. 1789 till 15 Aug. 1791. Major and Bt. Lt. Col. 3rd N.I. Posted as Lt. Col. to 2/3rd N.I. May 1800. Fur. 22 Jan. 1810 till death. Posted as Col. to Bengal Eur. Regt. in 1811.

Refs. : *G.M.* 1822, ii. 285. Will.

THE BENGAL ARMY, 1758-1834   421

HAYS, William (*d.* 1765). Capt. Lieutenant, Artillery. Cadet (?).
Fireworker 1762. 2nd Lieut. 1 Jan. 1763. Lieut. 3 Dec. 1763.
Capt. Lt. 28 Mar. 1764. *d. unm.* 1765.
Of Neston, co. Chester. Step-brother of John and Samuel Hays, ironmongers.
Services : N.F.P.
Refs. : Will dated Calcutta 7 Oct. 1764 ; proved 11 June 1765.

CURTIS-HAYWARD, Frederick Thomas (1809-1831). Ensign, 29th N.I. *b.* 28 Oct. 1809. Cadet 1827. Arrived in India 29 Sept. 1828. Ensign (22 May 1828) 22 Apr. 1829. *d.* Karnal 20 Nov. 1831.
bapt. Bitton, Gloucs., 23 Mar. 1810. 2nd son of Rev. John Adey Curtis, vicar of Bitton, and Albinia Frances his wife, eldest dau. and heir of William Hayward, of Quedgeley, Gloucs.
Services : Ensign d.d. 43rd N.I. 5 Nov. 1828 ; 73rd N.I. 4 Mar. 1829. Posted as Supy. Ensign to 37th N.I. 22 Apr. 1829 ; to 66th N.I. 1 Oct. 1831 ; to 29th N.I. 12 Nov. 1831. No record of active service.
Refs. : Burke's *Landed Gentry*, 12th edn., p. 917, *s.n.* Curtis-Hayward, of Quedgeley, Gloucs. *A.J.* N.S. viii. 41.

HEALY, (Benjamin) William (*d.* 1794). Lieutenant, Infantry.
Cadet 1780. Ensign 7 Mar. 1781. Lieut. 23 Oct. 1781. *d.* at sea 25 Aug. 1794.
m. (?). His dau. Jane *m.* Capt. Robert Perry, Marines.
Services : Lieut. 9th Bn. Sepoys in July 1787. N.F.P.
Refs. : Will proved in 1794.

HEALEY, James (1794-1815). Cadet. Infantry. Subsequently Lieut. H.M. 14th Foot. *b.* London 10 Feb. 1794. Cadet 1812. Resigned 20 Nov. 1813. *d.* Calcutta 28 Aug. 1815.
bapt. St. Luke's, Chelsea, 31 May 1794. Son of Anthony Healey, Page to George III, and Ann his wife. Ed. Charterhouse ; admitted Scholar 18 Feb. 1804 ; Exhibitioner 23 Apr. 1811.
Services : Ensign H.M. 14th Foot 1 Nov. 1813. Lieut. 1st Bn. 14th Foot 2 Apr. 1815.
Refs. : *Alumni Carthusiani.* M.I. in N. Park St. cemetery, Calcutta.

HEARD, EDWARD (*d.* 1810). Captain. Infantry. Cadet 1769.
Ensign 8 Aug. 1769. Lieut. 1 Dec. 1772. Capt. 13 Sept. 1779.
Resigned (?). *d.* at his seat, Patna, co. Cork, May 1810.
Of Ballintubber, co. Cork. Eldest son of Bickford Heard, of Ballintubber, and Susan his wife, dau. of John Maunsell, of Limerick.

Uncle of St. John Heard, *q.v.* *m.* Margaret, 2nd dau. of Francis Drew, M.D., of Mocollop Castle, co. Waterford.

Services: Capt. 1/1st Bengal Eur. Regt. in Oct. 1779. First Mahratta War. " Particularly distinguished himself on the Staff of Gen. Goddard in the reduction of the province of Guzerat." (*M.M.*). (? Fur. 14 Dec. 1783.) Was on fur. in 1790.

Refs.: Burke's *Landed Gentry of Ireland*, p. 305, *s.n.* Heard, of Kinsale. *Bath Chron.* 30 May 1810. *M.M.* 1810, ii. 290.

HEARD, George (1763-1793). Lieutenant, Infantry. *b.* 1763. Cadet 1780. Ensign 24 Aug. 1781. Lieut. 24 Aug. 1781. *d.* Palta, Bengal, 14 Nov. 1793, aged 29 : drowned through the upsetting of his boat.

A native of Ireland. *m.* Berhampore, 2 July 1790, Elizabeth Williams. (She *re-m.* Thomas Jaffray, *q.v.*)

Services: Fur. 24 Jan. 1786. 1st Eur. Bn. 31 Oct. 1787.

Refs.: Will dated 7 Jan. 1792. M.I. at Barrackpore.

HEARD, St. John (1785-1834). Lieut. Colonel. 10th N.I. *b.* Dublin 24 June 1785. Cadet 1803. Arrived in India 18 Mar. 1805. Ensign 29 Apr. 1805. Lieut. 30 Apr. 1805. Capt. 1 Aug. 1818. Major 30 July 1824. Lt. Col. 10 May 1828. Retired in India 13 Apr. 1830. *d.* 9 Park St., Bath, 28 July 1834.

Son of John Heard, of Grafton St., Dublin, atty.-at-law, and Margaret his wife, dau. of —— Doyle, of Dublin. Nephew of Edward Heard, *q.v.*

Services: Lieut. Royal E. Middlesex Mil. Posted as Lieut. to 8th N.I. Nepal War 1814-5 ; Lieut. 1/8th N.I., in 4th Div. Nepal War 1816 ; Lieut. 1/8th N.I., in 2nd Bde., Left Column. Capt. Lt. 8th N.I. 19 Nov. 1817. Third Mahratta War ; Capt. 2/8th N.I. Fur. 26 Dec. 1821 till 1823. Transfd. to 24th N.I. (late 2/8th) May 1824 ; as Lt. Col. to 15th N.I. in 1828 ; to 10th N.I. 22 Mar. 1829. Fur. s.c. 10 mos. to Mauritius 17 Jan. 1829.

Refs.: Burke's *Landed Gentry of Ireland*, p. 306, *s.n.* Heard, of Kinsale. *Bath Chron.* 31 July 1834. *G.M.* 1834, ii. 445. *A.J.* N.S. xv. 65.

HEARSEY, Andrew Wilson (1752-1798). Lieut. Colonel, 9th N.I. *b.* 1752. Cadet 1765. Admitted 3 Nov. 1769. Ensign 11 Sept. 1769. Lieut. 6 Mar. 1773. Capt. 18 Jan. 1781. Major 1 Mar. 1794. Lt. Col. 25 Nov. 1797. *d.* Allahabad, 10 July 1798, aged 46, from the effects of an accident whilst riding an unbroken horse.

Only son of Andrew Hearsey, Capt. of an East Indiaman, and Jane his wife. *m.* Walton-on-Thames, 1787, Miss Charlotte Crane. (*See also* Philip D'Auvergne.) (She died Addlestone, nr. Chertsey,

2 June 1835.) Father of Sir John Bennet Hearsey, K.C.B., *q.v.*
His daus. *m.* Paris Bradshaw, *q.v.*, and William Broome Salmon, *q.v.*
Services : First Mysore War 1768-70. Held the rank of Ensign in India for nearly five yrs. before he was gazetted Ensign in England. First Mahratta War 1780 ; capture of Lahár and Gwalior ; Lieut. with Popham's detachment. Second Mysore War 1781-5, first as Baggage Mr. to Col. T. D. Pearse's column, later as Baggage Mr. and " Grain Keeper " to the whole army ; Pollilur ; Sholingarh ; relief of Vellore ; siege of Cuddalore. Fur. 1786-9. Third Mysore War ; Coimbatore 21 July 1790 ; Dindigul 22 Aug. 1790 ; Palaghat ; Calicut 8 Dec. 1790 ; Bangalore ; Arikera ; Seringapatam. Major comdg. 8th Bn. Sepoys. Comdt. Allahabad fort 1797 till death.
Refs. : *The Hearseys. Misc. Gen. et Her.,* 4S. i. 278. *A.A.R.* i. 178. Will. M.I. at Allahabad.

HEARSEY, Sir John Bennet (1793-1865). Lieut. General, K.C.B. 6th L.C. Colonel 21st Hussars. *b.* Midnapore 21 Jan. 1793.[1] Cadet 1807. Arrived in India 14 Sept. 1807. Cornet 20 Sept. 1808. Lieut. 1 Nov. 1809. Capt. 31 Aug. 1819. Major 19 Nov. 1835. Lt. Col. 28 Dec. 1838. Col. 4 Nov. 1852. Maj. Gen. 28 Nov. 1854. Lt. Gen. 1863. *d.* 24 Rue Marquetra, Boulogne-sur-Mer, 23 Oct. 1865, of bronchitis.
Son of Andrew Wilson Hearsey, *q.v.* *m.* 1st, Nasirabad, 7 Jan. 1832, Harriet, dau. of his kinsman Major Hyder Hearsey. (She died London 27 Dec. 1847.) *m.* 2nd, Chertsey, Surrey, 22 May 1854, Emma, dau. of Thomas Rumball, of Friday Hall, Woodford, Essex.
Services : Barasat C.C. 1 Oct. 1807 till 15 Apr. 1808. Posted as Cornet to 8th N.C. ; transfd. to 6th N.C. Dec. 1809. Bundelkhand 1809-10. Rewah 1812-3. Nepal War 1814-5 ; comdg. mounted police escort of his brother-in-law, Major Paris Bradshaw, *q.v.* (India medal). Adjt. 6th N.C. 27 Aug. 1815 till 1820. Third Mahratta War ; Sitabaldi (s.w.) ; Nagpur (clasp to India medal). Siege and capture of Bhurtpore (w.) ; Capt. 6th N.C. (clasp to India medal). Commd. 2nd Local Horse 22 Jan. 1829 till 3 Sept. 1839. Lt. Col. 6th L.C. Fur. s.c. 22 Dec. 1840. Transfd. to 10th L.C. 24 July 1847 ; to 2nd L.C. Second Sikh War ; Gujerat ; comdg. a Cav. Div. (Medal). Transfd. to 10th L.C. Mar. 1851. Col. 6th L.C. Jan. 1853. Bdr. comdg. at Sialkot. Fur. 1854 till Dec. 1855. Was comdg. at Barrackpore on the outbreak of the mutiny. Col. 21st Hrs. 4 Nov. 1862. C.B. 9 June 1849. K.C.B. 3 July 1856.
Refs. : *The Hearseys* (portrait). *Walford. Boase. D.I.B. I.M.* 1854, p. 305. *N. & Q.* 8S. vii. 128. *The Times,* 27 Oct. 1865.

[1] *Note :* This is the date given in his birth certificate ; he himself, in his Autobiog., gives the date as 21 Sept. 1793. This latter is possibly the date of baptism.

*HEATH, Joseph Barnaby. Cadet. Artillery. Cadet 1783. Never commissioned.
Services : Apptd. in England a Cadet for the Art. Declined coming out.
Refs. : Stubbs's List.

HEATHCOTE, George Deare (1786-1831). Lieut. Colonel, 32nd N.I. *b.* London 28 Mar. 1786. Cadet 1800. Arrived in India 24 Oct. 1801. Ensign 27 Sept. 1801. Lieut. 13 July 1803. Capt. 16 Dec. 1814. Major 26 Aug. 1823. Lt. Col. 13 May 1825. *d.* London 31 Aug. 1831.
Of the Oriental Club, and of 2 University St., London. *bapt.* Marylebone 24 Apr. 1786. 2nd son of Robert Heathcote, of Fleet St., London, of the family of Heathcote of Hursley, and Elizabeth his wife, dau. of Philip Deare. Brother of William Samuel Heathcote, *q.v.*
Services : Second Mahratta War ; Laswari (w.) ; Gwalior ; Lieut. 2/16th N.I. Adjt. 1/16th N.I. 1804. Transfd. to newly-raised 1/24th N.I. in 1805. Adjt. do. 1805-8. Fur. p.a. 15 Mar. 1812 till 7 Oct. 1815. Third Mahratta War ; Capt. 1/24th N.I., Bde. Major 3rd Inf. Bde., 1st Div. Transfd. to 48th N.I. (late 2/24th) May 1824. First Burma War ; Arakan 1825 ; Major comdg. 1st Gren. Bn. Posted as Lt. Col. to 33rd N.I. Transfd. to 61st, 69th, 60th, 53rd, 37th, 15th, 9th N.I. Leave s.c. 2 yrs. to N.S.W. 13 Jan. 1827. Transfd. to 32nd N.I. 10 Dec. 1828. Fur. s.c. 17 Jan. 1829 till death.
Refs. : The Family of Heathcote, by E. D. Heathcote, M.A., ptely. printed, Winchester 1899. *Pester,* p. 252. *G.M.* 1831, ii. 282. Will dated 9 Aug. 1831 ; proved 11 Jan. 1832 and 9 Oct. 1832.

HEATHCOTE, William Samuel (1781-1841). Major General. Colonel 71st N.I. *b.* London 11 Mar. 1781. Cadet 1796. Arrived in India 4 May 1798. Ensign 4 Oct. 1797. Lieut. 10 Sept. 1798. Capt. 19 Mar. 1807. Major 1 Mar. 1816. Lt. Col. 18 Jan. 1822. Col. 5 June 1829. Maj. Gen. 28 June 1838. *d.* Chandos St., Cavendish Sq., London, 11 Mar. 1841.
bapt. Marylebone 8 Apr. 1781. Eldest son of Robert Heathcote and Elizabeth his wife. Brother of George Deare Heathcote, *q.v. m.* Bareilly, 17 July 1806, Miss Harriet Amelia Armstrong. (She died 1865, aged 80.)
Services : Adjt. 2/14th N.I. 3 Dec. 1800 till 1807. Second Mahratta War ; operations in the Karnal district 1803 ; defence of Delhi Oct. 1804 ; pursuit of Holkar 1805-6 (*Cal. Gaz.* 31 Oct. and 15 Nov. 1804). Fur. s.c. 24 Jan. 1809 till 12 Nov. 1811. (? Nepal War 1814-5 ; Capt. 2/14th N.I., in 3rd Div.) Major 2/14th N.I. Posted as Lt. Col. to 2/25th N.I. 4 Oct. 1822. Fur. s.c. 20 Feb. 1824 till

death. Transfd. to newly-raised 3rd Extra Regt. (became 71st
N.I.) in 1825. Col. 71st N.I. 1829.
Refs. : *The Family of Heathcote.* *G.M.* 1841, i. 442. Will dated
30 June 1825 ; proved 21 Apr. 1841.

HEATLY, Patrick (1753-1834). Cadet. Subsequently B.C.S. *b.*
New England Jan. 1753. Cadet 1772. Transfd. to B.C.S. 1776.
d. London 22 July 1834.
Of Hertford St., Mayfair, London. Son of Andrew Heatly, of
Newport, R.I., and Mary his wife, dau. of Suetonius Grant and
Temperance Talmage. His maternal ancestry was a branch of the
ancient family of Talmash. Brother of Suetonius Grant Heatly,
B.C.S., and of Mary, mother of James Tod, *q.v.* *m.* Anne Carey.
Services : First Rohilla War ; battle of St. George ; Cadet in the
Select Picket. Apptd. a Writer in 1776. At home in 1790. For
the last 36 yrs. of his life was a member of the Committee of By-Laws
of the India Direction.
Refs. : *G.M.* 1834, ii. 219, 543. *A.J.* N.S. xiv. 308. *B.* : *P.P.*,
No. 52, p. 164. Portrait by Zoffany in the possession of his descendant, Capt. C. D. M. Blunt, of Adderbury Manor, Banbury.

HEAVER, James (1795-1826). Lieutenant, Invalid Est. 16th
N.I. *b.* Lewes 10 Feb. 1795. Cadet 1810. Ensign 21 Aug.
1813. Lieut. 1 Oct. 1815. Invalided 1 July 1825. *d. unm.*
Barrackpore 7 Jan. 1826.
Son of John Heaver, of Chapel Yard, Spital Sq., silk manufacturer.
Services : Cadet d.d. 9th N.I. 1811-3. Posted as Ensign to 10th
N.I. in 1813. Operations in Baghelkhand 1813-4 ; Entauri ;
Ensign 2/10th N.I. Third Mahratta War ; Chanda ; Lieut. 2/10th
N.I. Actg. Intr. & Qmr. 2/10th N.I. in 1818. Transfd. to 16th
N.I. (late 2/10th) May 1824.

HEFFERNAN, John. Ensign. Infantry. Cadet 1782. Ensign 23
May 1783. Struck off before 1790.
(*Probably* son of Denis Heffernan and Sarah Owens his wife.)
Services : N.F.P.

HEFFERNAN, Michael (1756/57-1811). Lieut. Colonel, 17th N.I.
b. 1756/57. Cadet 1778. Admitted 10 Dec. 1778. Ensign Dec.
1778. Lieut. 28 Oct. 1778. Capt. 1 June 1796. Major 29 May
1800. Lt. Col. 8 Sept. 1803. *d.* Haverfordwest, co. Pembroke,
4 Sept. 1811.
A native of Ireland.
Services : Sailed for India on the *Stafford* 27 May 1778, aged 21.
Lieut. 2/2nd Bengal Eur. Regt. in Oct. 1779 ; 4th Bengal Eur. Bn.

in July 1787. Fur. 19 Jan. 1797 till 18 Dec. 1800. Capt. 2/6th N.I. Disturbances in Ganjam, Madras, 1801 ; Major 1/6th N.I. Lt. Col. 6th N.I. Transfd. to 4th N.I. in 1808 ; to 17th N.I. in 1810. Fur. 25 Jan. 1809 till death.
Refs. : G.M. 1811, ii. 595.

HELE, John Selby (1793-1824). Lieutenant, Artillery. *b.* Eltham, Kent, 8 Mar. 1793. Cadet 1809. Fireworker 14 Nov. 1810. Lieut. 25 Sept. 1817. *d.* Natal, Sumatra, 11 Aug. 1824.
bapt. Blunham, Beds., 7 Apr. 1793. Son of Rev. Robert Hele Selby (who assumed the additional surname of Hele 17 May 1791), rector and patron of Brede. Brother of William Selby Hele, *q.v. m.* Calcutta, 2 June 1820, Miss Susanna Conyers. (*See also* Joseph Gilbert Balcetti, and Edward Rushworth.)
Services : Served in Java with 1st Coy. 2nd Bn. Art. 1813-6. Siege and capture of Hathras 1817 ; Lieut. F. 3rd Coy. 2nd Bn.

*****HELE, William Selby** (1797-1851). Cadet. Artillery. Subsequently Captain Madras Art. *b.* Roxton, Beds., 9 Jan. 1797. Cadet 1813. Transfd. to Madras 1814. *d.* 4 Sussex Gdns., Hyde Pk., London, 27 Nov. 1851.

Son of Rev. Robert Hele Selby Hele, rector of Brede. Brother of John Selby Hele, *q.v.* Addiscombe Cadet 1811-4.
Services : Transfd. as Cadet to Madras Art. Fireworker 4 July 1814. Lieut. 1 Sept. 1818. Capt. 12 Dec. 1825. Retired 5 Aug. 1835.
Refs. : I.M. 1851, p. 792.

HELLIER, Thomas. Cadet before 1790.
Services : N.F.P. Given in *Dodwell & Miles* ("Not to be traced."). No mention of this officer has been found elsewhere. *Probably* identical with Thomas Hely, *q.v.*

HELM, William (1778-1804). Lieutenant, 18th N.I. *bapt.* Kensington, London, 6 Dec. 1778. Cadet 1798. Arrived in India 20 Sept. 1799. Ensign 19 Oct. 1799. Lieut. 28 Oct. 1799. *d.* Bundelkhand 13 Dec. 1804.
Son of Richard Helm and Rebecca his wife.
Services : Second Mahratta War ; Bundelkhand 1803 ; defeat of Rajah Ram Singh 2 July 1804 ; capture of Jaitpur ; Lieut. 18th N.I.
Refs. : Intestate ; admon. granted 24 June 1805.

HELY, Thomas. Captain. Infantry. Cadet 1769. Ensign 1769. Lieut. 11 Mar. 1773. Capt. 8 Jan. 1781. Dismissed by C.M. 3 June 1782.
Services : N.F.P. *Probably* identical with Thomas Hellier, *q.v.*

HEMMING, Henry. (*See* **HIMING, Henry.**)

HEMMINGS, William (1764/65-1810). Major, 1st N.I. *b*. Feriglassin, Ireland, 1764/65. Cadet 1781. Admitted 4 June 1782. Ensign 23 Apr. 1781. Lieut. 13 Aug. 1782. Capt. 29 May 1800. Major 19 Feb. 1806. *d*. Hyderabad 30 June 1810.

Son of Mrs. Mary Hemmings.[1] Brother of Mather, Eliza, and Ann Hemmings; half-brother of Graham and Delia Contes.

Services: Apptd. Cadet on 2 May 1781, aged 16. Sailed for India on the *Lord Mulgrave* 26 June 1781, aged 16. Lieut. 18th Bn. Sepoys in July 1787. Capt. 2/1st N.I. Was comdg. the Guard of the Resdt. at Hyderabad in 1803, and held this post till death.

Refs.: Will dated 10 Aug. 1809; codicil dated Hyderabad 30 June 1810; proved 24 Sept. 1810.

[1] *Note:* A William Hemings, of Folliot's Regt., *m*. Mary Domvill 1747.

HENCHMAN, Henry (1807-1848). Captain, 57th N.I. *b*. London 17 Feb. 1807. Cadet 1827. Arrived in India 10 June 1828. Ensign 20 Feb. 1828. Lieut. 13 Jan. 1834. Capt. 12 Apr. 1845. *d. unm*. Doranda, Chota Nagpur, 28 Sept. 1848.

Son of Francis Henchman, of 38 Gt. Ormond St., London, solicitor, and Lucretia his wife.

Services: Ensign d.d. 57th N.I. 25 July 1828. Posted to 66th N.I. 4 Nov. 1828. Transfd. to 57th N.I. 11 Aug. 1829. Actg. Intr. & Qmr. 57th N.I. 11 Apr. 1835; permanent do. 22 June 1836 till 12 Feb. 1844. Fur. s.c. to Aust. 18 Aug. 1840 till 8 Oct. 1842. Fur. s.c. 1 May 1844 till 1846. Apptd. Comdt. of Irreg. Cav. attached to Ramgarh L.I. Bn. July 1848. No record of active service.

Refs.: Will dated 23 Sept. 1848; admon. 12 Feb. 1849.

HENDERSON, George (1776-1799). Lieutenant, 14th N.I. *b*. London 11 Feb. 1776. Cadet 1794. Arrived in India 3 Nov. 1795. Ensign 4 Nov. 1795. Lieut. 25 Apr. 1797. *d*. Barrackpore 7 June 1799.

Son of John Henderson, of Cornhill, London.

Services: Lieut. 2/14th N.I. No record of active service.

Refs.: *G.M.* 1800, i. 385.

HENDERSON, Henry Barkley (1793-1862). Lieut. Colonel. 8th N.I. *b*. St. Mary, Newington, Surrey, 1 Aug. 1793. Cadet 1809. Arrived in India 3 Oct. 1810. Ensign 13 Jan. 1812. Lieut. 16 Dec. 1814. Capt. 2 Nov. 1825. Bt. Major 28 June 1838. Retired 18 Feb. 1841. Hon. Lt. Col. 28 Nov. 1854. *d*. Spring Grove, nr. Isleworth, Middlesex, 3 Dec. 1862.

Son of James Henderson. *m.* St. John's, Calcutta, 1 July 1822, Miss Elizabeth Magdalene Hawkins. (She died 14 Mar. 1886, aged 84.) His dau. *m.* Keith Young, *q.v.*

Services : Cadet d.d. 25th N.I. Posted as Ensign to 2/9th N.I. in 1812. Nepal War 1816 ; Lieut. 2/9th N.I., in 4th Bde., Centre Column (India medal). Third Mahratta War. S.A.C.G. 29 Feb. 1820; D.A.C.G., 2 cl., 28 May 1825; 1 cl., 27 Mar. 1826. Transfd. to 8th N.I. (late 1/9th) May 1824. Fur. p.a. 10 Jan. 1828 till 5 June 1830. Offg. 2nd Asst. Mily. Auditor Gen. 14 Mar. 1831 ; 2nd Asst. and actg. 1st Asst. do. 1 Oct. 1831 ; offg. Dy. Mily. Auditor Gen. 18 Feb. 1832 ; 1st Asst. do. 23 Oct. 1832 ; Dy. Mily. Auditor Gen. 8 Dec. 1835 till retirement. Shortly after retirement was admitted a partner in the firm of Carr, Tagore & Co., Calcutta. Pub. in 1829 " The Bengalee ; or Sketches of Society and Manners in the East."

Refs. : *I.N.* vol. i. 263. *G.M.* 1863, i. 131. *The Times*, 10 Dec. 1862.

HENDERSON, John (*d.* 1795). Lieut. Colonel. Infantry. Cadet 1766. Ensign 29 Dec. 1766. Lieut. 8 Apr. 1768. Capt. (?). Major 30 Jan. 1781. Lt. Col. (?). Struck off 1793. *d.* Campsey, nr. Musselburgh, 7 Mar. 1795.

Services : Fur. 6 Nov. 1786, and was still on fur. in 1790. N.F.P.

Refs. : *G.M.* 1795, i. 350. *S.M.* 1795, p. 206.

HENDERSON, Robert (*d.* 1784). Lieutenant, 3rd N.I. (? 3rd Bengal Eur. Regt.) Cadet 1778. Ensign 1778. Lieut. 22 Nov. 1778. bur. Cawnpore 22 June 1784.

Services : N.F.P.

HENDERSON, Samuel. Lieutenant. Infantry. Cadet 1773. Ensign 12 Aug. 1776. Lieut. 28 July 1778. Resigned 25 Apr. 1779.

Services : N.F.P.

HENDERSON, William (*d.* 1782). Captain, Engineers. Cadet (?). Ensign 15 Aug. 1775. Lieut. (?). Capt. 5 Apr. 1781. *d.* Cawnpore 7 June 1782.

Services : N.F.P.

HENDERSON, William (1756/57-?). Lieutenant. Infantry. *b.* in Scotland 1756/57. Cadet 1779. Ensign 12 Feb. 1780. Lieut. 7 Mar. 1781. Resigned after 1790.

m. Rose-bank, nr. Montrose, 8 Apr. 1788, Henrietta, eldest dau. of Alexander Smith, of Rose-bank.

Services : Sailed for India on the *Neptune* 3 June 1780, aged 23. Granted fur. for 3 yrs. 6 Dec. 1785, and was still on fur. in 1790.

Refs. : *G.M.* 1788, i. 365. *S.M.* 1788, p. 206.

HENDY, Gerard John (1787-1820). Bt. Captain, 16th N.I. b. Southwark, Surrey, 6 Jan. 1787. Cadet 1804. Arrived in India 16 July 1806. Ensign 21 Apr. 1806. Lieut. 2 Feb. 1808. Bt. Capt. 1 Jan. 1819. d. Lohargaon, Ajaigarh, C.I., 6 Oct. 1820.
Son of — Hendy and Elizabeth his wife.
Services: Posted as Ensign to 16th N.I. in 1807. Operations in Bundelkhand 1809-11 ; Lieut. 2/16th N.I. Capture of Java 1811 ; Lieut. L.I. Bn. Nepal War 1814-5 ; Lieut. L.I. Bn., in 2nd Div.
Refs.: *G.M.* 1821, i. 647.

HENLEY, William (1783-1823). Major, 24th N.I. Resident and P.A. in Bhopal. b. Rendlesham, Suffolk, 22 Dec. 1783. Cadet 1798. Arrived in India 24 Feb. 1800. Ensign 30 Oct. 1799. Lieut. 30 Oct. 1799. Capt. 23 June 1809. Major 30 June 1819. d. Sehore, Bhopal, 26 Aug. 1823.
Son of Rev. Samuel Henley, rector of Rendlesham, and Susan his wife. *m.* Eugenia.
Services: Posted as Lieut. to 1/7th N.I. Apr. 1800. Transfd. to 2/6th N.I. July 1801. Disturbances in Ganjam, Madras, 1801 ; Lieut. 2/6th N.I. Adjt. 2/6th N.I. Sept. 1802. Operations in Baghelkhand 1803 ; Chaukandi ; Lieut. & Adjt. 2/6th N.I. Adjt. & Qmr. 6th N.I. Jan. 1804 ; do. newly-raised 24th N.I. Feb. 1805. Comdg. 2/24th N.I. Mar. 1805 till Oct 1806. Second Mahratta War 1805-6 ; Adalatnagar ; capture of Gohad. Apptd. to 2nd L.I. Bn. Nov. 1808, and comdd. the Bn. from Feb. 1809 till its disbandment in May 1809. From Dec. 1809 till June 1812 was occupied in the compilation of a code of the standing orders and regulations of the Bengal Army. This work, known as "Henley's Code," superseded that prepared by Henry Grace, *q.v.* Comdd. 1/24th N.I. July 1812 till Jan. 1813. Comdg. a detachment on service in Rewah Jan.-June 1813. Fur. Nov. 1813 till 14 Nov. 1815. Offg. A.A.G. of the Army Jan.-May 1816. A.A.G. Nagpur Subsdy. Force Nov. 1816. Third Mahratta War ; Supt. of the Bhopal Contingent from Dec. 1817. Resdt. and P.A. in Bhopal Feb. 1818 till death. Transfd. as Major to 2/24th N.I. 1819.
Refs.: *E.I.M.C.* ii. 354-8. *G.M.* 1824, i. 382. Will dated Hoshangabad 26 Aug. 1807 ; proved 3 Nov. 1823.

HENNESSY, Atty (1761/62-1831). Lieut. Colonel. 21st N.I. b. 1761/62. Cadet 1782. Admitted 28 Dec. 1782. Ensign 12 Jan. 1783. Lieut. 15 Apr. 1788. Capt. 17 July 1801. Major 2 Apr. 1811. Lt. Col. 1 Oct. 1815. Retired 11 June 1822. *d. unm.* Clifton, 11 June 1831, aged 69.
Younger son of James Hennessy and —— his wife, née Nagle.
Services: Ensign 5th Bengal Eur. Bn. in July 1787. Lieut.

2/13th N.I. in Aug. 1798. Adjt. 1/17th N.I. Adjt. & Qmr. 17th
N.I. 29 May 1800. Capt. Lt. 17th N.I. 13 Jan. 1801. Transfd. to
newly-raised 27th N.I. in 1805. Fur. 1806-8. A.D.C. to G.G.
1810-3. Town Major of Fort William 1 May 1813 till 1819. Posted
as Lt. Col. to 1/6th N.I. in 1816 ; to 13th N.I. in 1818 ; to 4th N.I.
in 1819 ; to 2/21st N.I. in 1820. Fur. 27 Feb. 1819 till retirement.
A director of the Bank of Bengal.

Refs. : Burke's *Landed Gentry of Ireland*, p. 310, *s.n.* Hennessy,
of Ballymacmoy, co. Cork. *G.M.* 1831, i. 573. *A.J.* N.S. v. 178.

*HENNESSY, John (1807/08-1872). Major General. 11th N.I.
b. 1807/08. Cadet 1827. Was already in India when apptd. a
Cadet. Ensign 3 Feb. 1828. Lieut. 10 Apr. 1836. Capt. 24 Jan.
1845. Bt. Major 20 June 1854. Bt. Lt. Col. 7 Apr. 1860. Col.
18 Feb. 1866. Retired 7 Jan. 1870. Hon. Maj. Gen. 7 Jan. 1870.
d. 28 Oct. 1872.

m. Mussoorie, U.P., 17 May 1831 (aged 23), Miss Sophia Maria
Stedman (aged 16). (She died 18 Nov. 1872.)

Services : Served as a Volunteer with H.M. 59th Foot at siege
and capture of Bhurtpore (India medal). Apptd. Cadet 28 Dec.
1827 ; admitted 16 Aug. 1828. Ensign d.d. 20th N.I. 5 Sept. 1828.
Posted as Ensign to 34th N.I. 4 Nov. 1828. Transfd. to 20th N.I.
21 Nov. 1828 ; to 60th N.I. 27 Aug. 1831 ; to 70th N.I. 10 Nov.
1832. Actg. Adjt. 70th N.I. 15 Feb. 1834 and 29 Aug. 1835. Adjt.
70th N.I. 28 Dec. 1839 till 13 Jan. 1844. Bde. Major 6th Bde.,
Army of Exercise, 17 Nov. 1843. Gwalior campaign ; Maharajpur ;
Bde. Major (Bronze star). Second in comd. 1st Inf., Gwalior Contingent, 13 Jan. 1844 till May 1849 ; Comdt. do. 23 May 1849 till
1857. Comdd. Agra Police Bn. Transfd. to 11th Bengal N.I.
(late 70th N.I. ; now 5th Bn. 7th Rajput Regt.) in 1861. Fur. 1868
till retirement.

HENRY, James Thomas [1] (*d.* 1776). Ensign, Engineers. Cadet
1776. Ensign 1776. bur. Calcutta 1 Aug. 1776.
Services : N.F.P.

[1] *Note :* Christian names given in *Dodwell & Miles* as James
Thomas, as John in the burial register.

HENRY, Richard (1765-1807). Major, 26th N.I. *b.* Kent 1765.
Cadet 1781. Admitted 10 Mar. 1783. Ensign 3 Apr. 1781.
Lieut. 26 July 1782. Capt. 29 May 1800. Major 28 Feb. 1805.
d. Bundelkhand 29 Dec. 1807.

Only son of David Henry, editor and printer of the *Gentleman's
Magazine*, by his 2nd wife, widow of William Newell, master of the
Jerusalem tavern, Clerkenwell. His daus. *m.* Henry Philipps, *q.v.*,
and Augustus Thomas Watson, *q.v.*

Services : Apptd. Cadet on 18 Jan. 1781, aged 15. Lieut. 10th Bn. Sepoys in July 1787. Fur. 18 Mar. 1794 till 10 Apr. 1798. Capt. Lt. 2/16th N.I. 21 Apr. 1800. Operations in Jumna Doab 1803 ; Thathia (w.) ; Capt. 1/16th N.I. Transfd. as Major to newly-raised 26th N.I. in 1805. Operations in Bundelkhand 1807 ; Sehlehuganj ; Major 26th N.I.
Refs. : G.M. 1808, ii. 851. Will dated 18 Dec. 1807 ; proved 1 Mar. 1808.

HEPBURN, David (1788-1851). Lieut. Colonel. 29th N.I. *b.* Whitekirk, co. Haddington, 21 Apr. 1788. Cadet 1807. Arrived in India 14 Sept. 1808. Ensign 1 Oct. 1808. Lieut. 1 Aug. 1814. Capt. 13 May 1825. Major 30 July 1839. Lt. Col. 7 Apr. 1845. *d.* Plymouth, Devon, 11 Apr. 1851, insane.[1]

bapt. 30 Apr. 1788. Son of David Hepburn and Elizabeth Skirving his wife. Brother of George Hepburn, and cousin of George Miller, of Syderserfe, and of William Skirving, merchant.

Services : Barasat C.C. for 9½ mos. Posted as Ensign to 5th N.I. (? Reduction of Kalinjar 1812 ; Ensign 2/5th N.I.) Lieut. 2/5th N.I. Operations against the Bhils 1821 ; Lieut. 1/5th N.I. Transfd. to 11th N.I. (late 1/5th) May 1824. Actg. Adjt. 2nd L.I. Bn. 1 Sept. 1824. First Burma War ; Arakan 1825 ; Lieut. 2nd L.I. Bn. Served with Pioneers in Arakan 7 May 1825 till 8 Sept. 1826. Wahabi rising 1831. Disturbances in Bundelkhand 1842 ; Major 11th N.I. Posted as Lt. Col. to 38th N.I. 11 June 1845 ; to 56th N.I. ; to 29th N.I. 1849. Fur. 1850 till death.

Refs. : I.M. 1851, p. 448. G.M. 1851, i. 682. Will dated 21 Jan. 1846 ; proved 11 July 1851.

[1] *Note :* The loss of about Rs 90,000 owing to the failure of the Union Bank in 1847 affected his brain. " A rough diamond, but a good soldier." (*I.M.*).

HEPBURNE, Cosmo Alexander (1816-1878). Ensign. 51st N.I. Pensioner on Lord Clive's fund. *b.* Edinburgh 26 May 1816. Cadet 1834. Arrived in India 7 June 1835. Ensign (21 Jan. 1835) 24 Feb. 1835. Pensioned on Lord Clive's fund 28 Feb. 1838. *d.* London 11 Dec. 1878.

Youngest son of Robert Hepburne, of Clarkington, N.B., head of the stamp office for Scotland, and Catharine his wife, 3rd dau. of Hon. Alexander Gordon, Lord Rockville. Brother of William Henry Hepburne, *q.v.*, and of Catherine Gordon, wife of James Peckett, *q.v. m.* Brit. Embassy, Paris, 18 Feb. 1841, Jane Seymer, dau. of Rev. William Chester, Chaplain Madras Est. (She died 15 Nov. 1882.)

Services : Ensign d.d. 34th N.I. 15 June 1835. Posted to 51st

N.I. 24 Sept. 1835. Fur. s.c. 13 Dec. 1835 till his resignation on 20 May 1837. Granted a pension of 2/- *p.d.* from Lord Clive's fund with effect from 28 Feb. 1838. Apptd. a Writer on the Home Est. 28 Mar. 1838.
Refs. : The *Times*, 10 and 11 May 1843 ; 17 Dec. 1878.

HEPBURNE, William Henry (1812-?). Cornet. 5th L.C. *b.* Clarkington, N.B., 26 June 1812. Cadet 1827. Arrived in India 10 Jan. 1829. Cornet (19 July 1828) 10 Jan. 1829. Resigned 20 May 1837.

Son of Robert Hepburne, of Clarkington, and Catharine his wife, grand-dau. of William, 2nd Earl of Aberdeen. Brother of Cosmo Alexander Hepburne, *q.v.*, and nephew of Hon. Hugh Lindsay, an E.I. director.

Services : Cornet d.d. 3rd L.C. 11 Feb. 1829. Fur. u.p.a., without pay, 21 Dec. 1829 till 25 Oct. 1830. Cadet d.d. 3rd L.C. 25 Nov. 1830. Actg. Cornet 27 Oct. 1831. Posted as Cornet to 5th L.C. 28 Feb. 1832. Suspended 25 Sept. 1835 for absence without leave since 16 July 1835. Fur. u.p.a. 13 Dec. 1835 till 8 Nov. 1836. Suspension removed from date of return to India. No record of active service.

HEPTINSTALL, Douglas Hughes (1788-1828). Major, 31st N.I. *bapt.* Llandebie, co. Carmarthen, 21 Dec. 1788. Cadet 1806. Arrived in India 1 Aug. 1807. Ensign 1 Dec. 1806. Lieut. 30 June 1809. Capt. 13 Jan. 1823. Major 8 June 1827. *d.* nr. Bhurtpore 30 Dec. 1828.

Son of John Heptinstall and Eliza his wife. Brother of John Marshall Heptinstall, *q.v.*

Services : Ensign 15th N.I. Actg. Adjt. 1/15th N.I. 1810-3. Adjt. 1/15th N.I. 29 June 1813 till 1818. Third Mahratta War ; Asirgarh. Transfd. to 30th N.I. (late 1/15th) May 1824 ; to 31st N.I. 1825. Siege and capture of Bhurtpore ; Capt. 31st N.I. Comdd. 1st Narbada Sebundy Corps 1826-8. Apptd. to charge of 57th N.I. 20 Dec. 1828.

Refs. : A.J. xxviii. 92.

HEPTINSTALL, John Marshall (1798-1836). Captain, 31st N.I. *bapt.* Llandebie, co. Carmarthen, 4 Nov. 1798. Cadet 1817. Admitted 5 Dec. 1818. Ensign 12 June 1818. Lieut. 25 Nov. 1819. Capt. 13 Apr. 1827. *d.* Meerut 4 Aug. 1836.

Son of John Heptinstall and Eliza his wife. Brother of Douglas Hughes Heptinstall, *q.v.* Ed. Shrewsbury ; entered the school in 1806.

Services : Ensign d.d. 20th N.I. in 1819 ; Lieut. d.d. 1/13th N.I.

12 Aug. 1820. Transfd. as Lieut. to 2/15th N.I. Actg. Adjt. Ramgarh Bn. 28 Dec. 1822. Transfd. to 31st N.I. (late 2/15th) May 1824. Siege and capture of Bhurtpore; Lieut. 31st N.I. Operations against the Bhils 1828. Fur. s.c. 17 Nov. 1828 till 5 Nov. 1832. Actg. Bde. Major 17 Sept. 1833. D.A.A.G. at Meerut 25 Mar. 1835 till death. Dy. Postmaster at Meerut 17 Feb. 1836.
Refs.: *Shrewsbury School Register*. *A.J.* N.S. xxii. 58. Will dated Meerut 30 July 1836; proved 14 Oct. 1836.

HEPWORTH, Thomas Alexander (1788-1829). Captain, 61st N.I. *b.* London 26 Nov. 1788. Cadet 1804. Arrived in India 12 Sept. 1805. Ensign 8 Nov. 1805. Lieut. 17 Sept. 1806. Capt. 11 July 1823. *d.* Allahabad, 5 June 1829, of a malignant fever.

bapt. St. Clement Danes 15 July 1800. Eldest son of Capt. Brodie Hepworth, of the *Mansfield*, East Indiaman, and Ann his wife. Stepson of —— Taylor. *m.* Calcutta, 4 Nov. 1810, Jane Sophia, sister of Frederick Mullins, *q.v.* (She died Allahabad 18 June 1854.) (*See also* John Oakes and Arthur Wortham.)

Services: Posted as Ensign to 4th N.I. Served with Pioneers in 1808, and 1810-2. With Java Inf. Vols. in 1813. Intr. & Qmr. 1/4th N.I. Fur. 12 Dec. 1815 till 1818. Transfd. to 31st N.I. 11 July 1823; to 61st N.I. (late 1/31st) May 1824. A.D.C. to Maj.-Gen. George Dick, *q.v.*, 1825-6. Offg. Bde. Major to troops in Assam 9 Oct. 1826 till 1828.

Refs.: *G.M.* 1829, ii. 651. *A.J.* xxviii. 734. Will dated 17 May 1818; admon. 17 Nov. 1829.

HERBERT, George (1778/79-1813). Captain, Invalid Est. 6th N.I. *b.* 1778/79. Cadet 1797. Admitted 12 Nov. 1798. Ensign 23 Sept. 1798. Lieut. 1 Nov. 1798. Capt. 8 May 1806. Invalided 12 Dec. 1809. *d.* Calcutta, 25 Jan. 1813, aged 34.

Services: Apptd. Cadet on 6 Mar. 1798. Disturbances in Ganjam, Madras, 1801; Lieut. 6th N.I. Served in P.W.I. 1804-5. Capt. Lt. 6th N.I. 22 Aug. 1805.

Refs.: M.I. in N. Park St. cemetery, Calcutta.

HERBERT, George Edward (1809-1891). Lieut. Colonel. 9th L.C. *b.* Penstrowed, co. Montgomery, 3 Jan. 1809. Cadet 1826. Arrived in India 8 June 1827. Cornet 23 Jan. 1828. Lieut. 16 June 1829. Capt. 10 Dec. 1841. Bt. Major 20 June 1854. Retired 12 July 1856. Hon. Lt. Col. 12 July 1856. *d.* 30 Dec. 1891.

Of Upper Helmsley, and Westow, Yorks., and Glan Hafren and Llanllugan, co. Montgomery. J.P. co. Montgomery; J.P. and D.L. for the N. Riding of Yorks.; high sheriff co. Montgomery 1879. 2nd son of George Arthur Herbert, of Glan Hafren and Llanllugan, and Elizabeth his wife, dau. and heir of Athelstan Hamer, of Glan Hafren. Brother of Richard Athelstan Herbert, *q.v. m.* 13 Apr. 1869, Anna Maria, eldest dau. and heir of Joshua Francis Whittell, of Upper Helmsley and Westow.

Services : Posted as Cornet to 9th L.C. 23 Jan. 1828, and remained with that Regt. throughout his service. Actg. Adjt. 9th L.C. 19 Aug. 1840. Fur. s.c. 27 Feb. 1841 till 10 Dec. 1843. Fur. 1854 till retirement. No record of active service.

Refs. : Burke's *Landed Gentry,* 13th edn., p. 880, *s.n.* Herbert, of Glan Hafren, co. Montgomery. *History of the Wilmer Family,* p. 151. *I.M.* 1848, p. 359. *The Times,* 1 Jan. 1892.

HERBERT, James Dowling (1791-1833). Captain, 9th N.I. Astronomer to H.M. the King of Oudh. *b.* Dublin Aug. 1791. Cadet 1806. Arrived in India 17 Mar. 1808. Ensign 18 Mar. 1808. Lieut. 18 Mar. 1813. Capt. 3 June 1824. *d.* Lucknow 25 Sept. 1833.

Son of Joseph Dowling Herbert. *m.* St. John's, Calcutta, 28 Apr. 1823, Miss Mary Manson (*probably* sister of James Manson, *q.v.*). (She died 2 Feb. 1888, aged 88.)

Services : Ensign d.d. 15th and 10th N.I. Posted as Ensign to 1/8th N.I. in 1811. Nepal War 1814-5 ; Lieut. 1/8th N.I., in 4th Div. Nepal War 1816 ; Lieut. 1/8th N.I., in 2nd Bde., Left Column. Actg. Intr. & Qmr. 1/8th N.I. in 1815. Asst. Surveyor in Kumaon 15 Nov. 1816. Intr. & Qmr. 1/8th N.I. 1820 till Sept. 1821. Asst. to Surveyor Gen. of India 17 Sept. 1821 till 6 Mar. 1823. Employed on a geological survey of the Himalayas 1823-8, and first discovered graphite in those mountains. Transfd. to 9th N.I. (late 1/8th) May 1824. Re-appointed Asst. to Surveyor Gen. of India 30 May 1828 ; Dy. Surveyor Gen. of Bengal 14 Sept. 1829. Permitted to enter the service of the King of Oudh in order to erect and superintend an observatory at Lucknow 26 Dec. 1831. His widow was granted the sum of Rs. 40,000 by the King of Oudh. Pub. Calcutta, 1830, " Report on Dargeeling in the Sikhim Mountains," 8vo.

Refs. : A.J. N.S. xiii. 205. Will dated Lucknow 28 Aug. 1833 ; proved 22 Feb. 1834.

HERBERT, Philip (*d.* 1782). Lieutenant, Artillery. Cadet 1772. Fireworker 5 July 1774. Lieut. 31 Mar. 1778. *d.* Madras 27 Dec. 1782.

Services : Second Mysore War 1781-2 ; Qmr. to the Art.
Refs. : Will dated 26 Dec. 1781.

HERBERT, Richard Athelstan[1] (1811-1848). Bt. Captain, 46th N.I. 1st Sikh Local Inf. *b.* 1811. Cadet 1828. Arrived in India 28 June 1829. Ensign 20 Jan. 1829. Lieut. 1 Mar. 1838.

Bt. Capt. 20 Jan. 1844. *d.* Jullundur 16 Nov. 1848 : committed suicide by shooting himself.

3rd son of George Arthur Herbert, of Glan Hafren and Llanllugan, co. Montgomery, and Elizabeth his wife. Brother of George Edward Herbert, *q.v.*

Services : Posted as Ensign to 46th N.I. Sept. 1829. Actg. Intr. & Qmr. 2nd L.C. 24 Sept. till Dec. 1834 ; do. 46th N.I. Nov. 1835 till Apr. 1836 ; do. 9th L.C. Apr.-Aug. 1836. Intr. & Qmr. 46th N.I. 10 Aug. 1836 till Jan. 1840. Junior Asst. to Comr., Saugor Div., Jan. 1840 till Mar. 1843. Qmr. and Staff Ofr. to Bundelkhand Legion 4 Mar. till Sept. 1843. Fur. s.c. 17 Jan. 1844 till Dec. 1846. Offg. 2nd in comd. 1st Sikh Local Inf. 23 Sept. 1848 till death. Defeat of Ram Singh at Basu, nr. Nurpur, Sept. 1848.

Refs. : Burke's *Landed Gentry*, 13th edn., p. 880, *s.n.* Herbert, of Glan Hafren, co. Montgomery. *De Rhé-Philipe.* M.I. in Art. cemetery, Jullundur.

[1] *Note :* His second christian name appears as Athelustan in the *A.L.* and in official documents throughout his service.

HERIOT, Charles William (1792-1824). Lieutenant, Pension Est. 4th L.C. *b.* Marylebone, London, 15 June 1792. Cadet 1812. Resigned as Cadet 5 July 1816. Readmitted 15 Nov. 1816. Cornet 30 Nov. 1816. Lieut. 1 Nov. 1818. Pensioned 4 Dec. 1823. *d.* Nimach 16 Apr. 1824.

Son of John Heriot. *m.* Cawnpore, 18 Mar. 1814, Mary M'Ginniss. (She *re-m.* Edward Horsley, *q.v.*)

Services : Posted as Cornet to 3rd N.C. in 1816. Siege and capture of Hathras 1817 ; Cornet 3rd N.C. Third Mahratta War ; Jawad. Transfd. as Lieut. to 4th N.C. (? Operations in Kotah 1821 ; Mangrol ; Lieut. 4th L.C.)

HERON, Francis (1782-1866). Captain. 8th N.I. *b.* Killyleagh, co. Down, 9 Dec. 1782. Cadet 1805. Arrived in India 19 Aug. 1806. Ensign 25 July 1806. Lieut. 22 July 1807. Capt. 1 Jan. 1819. Retired 17 Jan. 1821. *d.* 7 Dec. 1866.

Son of —— Heron and Jane his wife. *m.* (before 1817) ?

Services : Posted to 8th N.I. in 1807. (? Expedn. to Mauritius 1810-1 ; Lieut. 2nd Vol. Bn.) Adjt. 2/8th N.I. 28 Nov. 1811 till 1817. Nepal War 1816 ; Lieut. 2/8th N.I., in 4th Bde., Centre Column (India medal). Fur. 16 Nov. 1817 till retirement. Capt. 2/8th N.I.

HERON, John (*d.* 1779). Lieutenant, Infantry. Cadet 1776. Ensign 16 Mar. 1777. Lieut. 13 Aug. 1778. *d.* Cawnpore 29 Sept. 1779.
Services : N.F.P.

HERON, William (*d.* 1770). Cadet, Infantry. Cadet 1770. *d.* Berhampore 9 Sept. 1770.
Services : N.F.P.

HERRING, Edmund (1793-1852). Major. 57th N.I. *b.* Saltash, Cornwall, 21 Feb. 1793. Cadet 1807. Arrived in India 21 Mar. 1809. Ensign 21 Feb. 1809. Lieut. 1 June 1813. Capt. 6 Jan. 1825. Major 28 June 1838. Invalided 21 July 1841. Retired 19 Dec. 1845. *d.* Rose Clift, Saltash, 2 Apr. 1852.

Son of Edmund Herring (? Rev. Edmund Herring, rector of North Petherwin, Devon). *m.* South Brent, 11 May 1826, Anne Mary, eldest dau. of William Lee, of Glazebrook House, Devon. (She died 12 Mar. 1850.)

Services : Posted as Ensign to 23rd N.I. Transfd. to newly-raised 2/29th N.I. in 1815. Operations against the Bhattis of Hariana 1818. Third Mahratta War 1819 ; Asirgarh ; Lieut. 2/29th N.I. Fur. s.c. 10 Jan. 1823 till 21 Jan. 1827. Transfd. to 57th N.I. (late 1/29th) May 1824. Fur. p.a. 24 Feb. 1838 till 15 Feb. 1841.

Refs. : *A.J.* xxi. 817. *I.M.* 14 Apr. 1852, p. 244.

HERRING, John (1789-1839). Lieut. Colonel, C.B., 37th N.I. *bapt.* Uttoxeter, Staffs., 24 Mar. 1789. Cadet 1804. Arrived in India 10 Sept. 1805. Ensign 3 Nov. 1805. Lieut. 8 July 1806. Capt. 11 July 1823. Major 4 Apr. 1832. Lt. Col. 27 Oct. 1838. *d.* Haidar Khel, Afghanistan, 3 Sept. 1839 : murdered by tribesmen whilst escorting 5 lacs of treasure for the army at Kabul : bur. Kabul 5 Sept. 1839.

Son of Rev. Athanasius Herring and Mary his wife. Stepson of —— Phillips. *m.* 1st, Cawnpore, 20 May 1824, Miss Maria Ann Wright. (She died 15 Feb. 1825.) *m.* 2nd, Nasirabad, 12 Feb. 1834, Eliza Anne, 3rd dau. of Lambert Loveday, *q.v.* (*See also* John Inglis, and Arthur Cole Spottiswood.)

Services : Posted as Lieut. to 2/18th N.I. Nepal War 1814-5 ; Lieut. Ramgarh Bn., in 4th Div. Leave s.c. 6 mos. to China 7 July 1818. Adjt. 2/18th N.I. 24 Oct. 1817 till 3 Feb. 1821. A.D.C. to Maj.-Gen. Lambert Loveday, *q.v.*, 11 Jan. 1821 till 13 Oct. 1824 ; do. to Maj.-Gen. Sir Gabriel Martindell, *q.v.*, comdg. at Cawnpore 27 Oct. 1824. Transfd. to 37th N.I. (late 2/18th) May 1824. Siege and capture of Bhurtpore ; Capt. comdg. L.I. Coy. 37th N.I. Tempy. charge of Bareilly Provl. Bn. 1 Oct. 1827. Actg. D.J.A.G., Sirhind, 27 May 1829. Actg. Bde. Major to troops at Delhi 3 Oct. 1831. Offg. D.J.A.G., Meerut Div., 5 Mar. 1832. Posted as Lt. Col. to 37th N.I. 3 Dec. 1838. First Afghan War 1838-9 ; Ghazni ;

THE BENGAL ARMY, 1758-1834

comdd. garrison at Kandahar. C.B. 20 July 1838. Durani, 3 cl. (*Cal. Gaz.* 15 Aug. 1840).
Refs. : *Seaton*, i. 162-4. *G.M.* 1840, i. 109. Will dated 5 Apr. 1839 ; proved 13 Apr. 1843.

HERVEY, Andrew (1790-1862). Lieut. General, C.B. Colonel 52nd N.I. *b.* St. George's Fields, Surrey, 25 Sept. 1790. Cadet 1805. Arrived in India 11 July 1806. Ensign 15 Sept. 1806. Lieut. 2 Jan. 1811. Capt. 1 May 1824. Major 31 Jan. 1832. Lt. Col. 16 Mar. 1838. Col. 8 Mar. 1849. Maj. Gen. 28 Nov. 1854. Lt. Gen. 23 July 1861. *d.* Darjeeling, 14 June 1862, of dropsy.

Son of Margaret Millar (formerly Margaret Coghlan), of Coal Harbour Lane, psh. of St. Mary, Lambeth, Surrey, and Andrew Barnard.[1] Uncle of Gerald Augustus Frederick Hervey, *q.v.* *m.* 1st, Cawnpore, 1 Sept. 1810, Miss Sophia Francis. *m.* 2nd, Darjeeling, 9 Oct. 1855, Rose Emeline, dau. of George Hoare Swaine.

Services : Nominated to a Cadetship by the Lord Lieut. of Ireland. Posted as Ensign to 4th N.I. S.A.C.G. 22 Dec. 1815. Nepal War 1816 ; Lieut. 2/4th N.I., S.A.C.G., 4th Bde. (India medal). Third Mahratta War ; Nagpur ; Mandala ; S.A.C.G., Bdr.-Gen. Hardyman's Div. (clasp to India medal). S.A.C.G., 2 cl., 2 Oct. 1819 ; 1 cl. 12 Dec. 1823 till 18 Mar. 1826. Transfd. as Lieut. to 1/4th N.I. ; to newly-raised 33rd N.I. 11 July 1823 ; to 65th N.I. (late 1/33rd) May 1824. Fur. p.a. 9 Dec. 1829 till 14 May 1831. Posted as Lt. Col. to 65th N.I. 13 Nov. 1838. Transfd. to 30th N.I. 20 Jan. 1844 ; to 65th N.I. Sept. 1845 ; to 46th N.I. Apr. 1846. Second Sikh War ; Multan ; Gujerat ; comdg. 1st Inf. Bde. (Medal with 2 clasps). Col. 52nd N.I. Mar. 1849. C.B. 9 June 1849.
Refs. : *Boase*. M.I. at Darjeeling.

[1] *Note* : Her son was born whilst she was " a prisoner in the custody of the Marshal of the King's Bench," and was bapt. " by the names of Andrew Hervey by the Rev. Mr. Siddons, rector of Stratford-on-Avon, then a prisoner in the said prison."

HERVEY, Gerald Augustus Frederick (1816-1891). Captain, Invalid Est. 3rd N.I. *b.* 9 June 1816. Cadet 1834. Arrived in India 7 June 1835. Ensign 12 Dec. 1834. Lieut. 19 Apr. 1839. Capt. 12 Oct. 1845. Invalided 7 Jan. 1853. *d.* Hammersmith, London, 2 May 1891.

2nd son of Hervey Augustus Frederick Hervey, Capt. 13th Bo. N.I. Nephew of Andrew Hervey, *q.v.*, and ward of Hon. Hugh Lindsay (son of James, 5th Earl of Balcarres). *m.* Christ church, Lucknow, 6 Oct. 1846, Fanny Elizabeth, 2nd dau. of Frederick

Moule, of Melksham, Wilts., and niece of John Moule, *q.v.* Addiscombe Cadet 8 Feb. 1833 till 12 Dec. 1834.
Services : Ensign d.d. 65th N.I. 19 June 1835. Posted as Ensign to 34th N.I. 24 Sept. 1835. Transfd. to 3rd N.I. 28 June 1836. Actg. Intr. & Qmr. 3rd N.I. 28 Jan. 1840. d.d. Ramgarh L.I. 19 Aug. 1840 till 22 Feb. 1841. First China War June-Sept. 1842 ; capture of Chin-kiang Foo ; Lieut. 2nd Bengal Vol. Bn. (Medal). Served with 2nd Vol. Bn. 1 Feb. 1842 till 1 Mar. 1843. Fur. s.c. 30 Sept. 1843 till 1845. Second Sikh War ; Jullundur Doab ; Capt. 3rd N.I., with Bdr. Wheeler's Force (Medal). Fur. 1854 till Mar. 1856.
Refs. : The Times, 7 May 1891.

*HESSMAN, William (1737/38-1779). Major, Infantry. *b.* Stevenage, Oxon., 1737/38. *d.* Oct. or Nov. 1779 : kld. in a duel by Gilbert Ironside, *q.v.*
m. Calcutta, 15 Sept. 1768, Miss Elizabeth Mills.
Services : Sailed for Madras as Quartermaster on the *Chesterfield* in 1760, aged 23. *Probably* transfd. from Madras Est. Lieut. in one of the two Troops of Eur. Dgns., and on their disbandment in 1764 was ordered (G.O. 7 July 1764) to take rank in the Inf. from the date of his first Commission as Cornet. Promoted Capt. before Feb. 1767.

HESTER, William Chicheley (1794-1818). Cornet, 3rd N.C. *b.* Islington, London, 26 Dec. 1794. Cadet 1810. Cornet (15 Apr. 1816) 2 Aug. 1816. *d.* Souard (? Suadi, B. & O.) 3 Nov. 1818.
Son of Theodore John Hester and Harriot Catherine Chicheley his first wife. Cousin-german of James Chicheley Hyde, *q.v.*, and related to the Plowdens, *q.v.*
Services : Posted as Cornet to 3rd N.C. in 1816. Siege and capture of Hathras 1817 ; Cornet 3rd N.C. Third Mahratta War ; Jawad ; Cornet 3rd N.C.
Refs. : Will proved 2 Dec. 1818.

HETZLER, George Berners Barbut (1803-1827). Captain, 56th N.I. *b.* Calcutta 12 Aug. 1803. Cadet 1817. Ensign (?). Lieut. 17 Oct. 1818. Capt. 2 Nov. 1826. *d.* Nasirabad, 7 May 1827, of cholera.
bapt. Calcutta 16 Nov. 1803. Only son of Robert Hetzler, *q.v.*, and Eliza Maria his 1st wife.
Services : Posted as Lieut. to 2/28th N.I. in 1819. On fur. in 1823. Transfd. to 56th N.I. (late 2/28th) May 1824. No record of active service.
Refs. : A.J. xxiv. 792.

HETZLER, Robert (*d.* 1834). Lieut. Colonel Comdt., C.B., Artillery. Cadet 1783. Admitted 25 Nov. 1784. Fireworker 2 June 1785. Lieut. 20 Aug. 1794. Capt. Lt. 7 May 1802. Capt. 10 July 1805. Major 1 Sept. 1818. Lt. Col. 5 June 1829. Lt. Col. Comdt. 1 May 1824. *d.* Axminster 1 Dec. 1834.

m. 1st, Jaffna, Ceylon, Oct. 1802, Eliza Maria, dau. of T. B. Plestow, of Watlington, Norfolk. Father of George Berners Barbut Hetzler, *q.v.* *m.* 2nd, Chardstock, Dorset, 2 Apr. 1832, Elizabeth Langdon, eldest dau. of William Loveridge, of Paradise Lodge.

Services : Served in Ceylon with 5th Coy. 2nd Bn. Foot Art. Sept. 1796 till Nov. 1802. Fourth Mysore War ; Lieut. 5th Coy. 2nd Bn. Posted as Capt. Lt. to 4th Coy. 3rd Bn. Second Mahratta War ; operations in Cuttack 1803 ; capture of Barabati fort (*Cal. Gaz.* 22 Oct. 1803). Operations against Dhundia Khan 1807 ; Komona ; Ganauri ; Capt. comdg. 3rd Coy. 1st Bn. Dy. Comy. Ord. Leave s.c. 6 mos. to sea 3 Oct. 1808. Third Mahratta War ; Dhamoni ; Mandala (not personally engaged) ; Garhakota ; Asirgarh ; Major comdg. Art., Left Div., and Saugor F.F. To comd. W. Div. Art. 23 Dec. 1823. Jaipur 1824. To comd. Meerut Div. Art. 5 Oct. 1825. To comd. Art. with battering train at Bhurtpore, with rank of Bdr., 2 cl., 3 Dec. 1825. Siege and capture of Bhurtpore. To comd. Art. at Agra 20 Feb. 1826. Fur. p.a. 26 Jan. 1827 till 28 May 1830, and 9 Aug. 1830 till death. C.B. 23 July 1823.

Refs. : *M.M.* xv (1803), 390. *A.J.* N.S. viii. 58 ; xvi. 70. *G.M.* 1835, i. 107.

HEWETT, James (1802-1842). Captain, 52nd N.I. *b.* Hooton Pagnell, Yorks., 14 Sept. 1802. Cadet 1818. Admitted 13 Nov. 1819. Ensign 11 July 1819. Lieut. 30 Oct. 1821. Capt. 6 May 1829. *d.* at sea, 8 Apr. 1842, on board the *Plantagenet*, nr. Table Bay.

bapt. ptely. 19 Sept. 1802 : publicly at Hooton Pagnell 6 June 1804. Son of William Nathan Wrighte Hewett, of Weston Green, nr. Thames Ditton, and Sarah Bartholomew his 2nd wife. Brother of William Hewett, *q.v.*, and half-brother of Peter Selwood Hewett, *q.v.* *m.* Meerut, 20 Sept. 1832, Miss Elizabeth Waller. (She died 22 Nov. 1887, aged 73.)

Services : Posted as Ensign to 26th N.I. Lieut. 2/26th N.I. Transfd. to 52nd N.I. (late 2/26th) May 1824. Adjt. 52nd N.I. 17 June 1824 till 3 Apr. 1830. First Burma War ; Cachar 1825. Actg. Bde. Major Meerut Div. 13 July till 29 Oct. 1835. Fur. s.c. 2 Feb. 1842 till death.

HEWETT, Peter Selwood (1792-1834). Cadet. Infantry. Subsequently Lieut. in H.H. Nizam's 7th Regt. of regular Inf. *b.* Calcutta 27 Nov. 1792. Cadet 1811. Resigned 12 July 1813. *d.* Coonoor, Madras, 9 July 1834, of a paralytic stroke.

Son of William Nathan Wrighte Hewett, B.C.S., of Bilham Hall, Yorks., and Martha Tuting his 1st wife. Half-brother of William Hewett, *q.v.* His sister *m.* James William Douglas, *q.v.* (*Probably* nephew by marriage of Edward Rowland Jackson, *q.v.*) *m.* Sarah. (She died Coonoor 20 Sept. 1831.) Ed. Westminster ; left in 1806.
Services : After resigning his Cadetship he entered the service of the Nizam of Hyderabad.
Refs. : *Westminster School Register. A.J.* N.S. xvi. 137.

HEWETT, William (1801-1818). Ensign, Infantry. Unposted.
b. Hooton Pagnell, Yorks., 8 Oct. 1801. Cadet 1817. Ensign (?).
d. Calcutta 21 Oct. 1818.
bapt. 10 Nov. 1801. Son of William Nathan Wrighte Hewett, of Bilham Hall, Yorks., formerly B.C.S., and Sarah Bartholomew his 2nd wife. Brother of James Hewett, *q.v.* His sister *m.* Frederick Hervey Sandys, *q.v.*
Refs. : M.I. in S. Park St. cemetery, Calcutta.

HEWIT, Henry (*d.* 1807). Major, 9th N.I. Country Cadet 1780. Admitted 1780. Ensign 28 Jan. 1781. Lieut. 4 Oct. 1781. Capt. 29 May 1800. Major 21 Sept. 1804. *d.* Gorakhpur, U.P., 27 Aug. 1807.
Services : Originally a Minor Cadet. Lieut. 22nd Bn. Sepoys in July 1787. Capt. 2nd Bengal Eur. Regt. Second Mahratta War ; Major 9th N.I.

HEWITT, Francis (1800-1846). Major, 33rd N.I. *b.* Cork 28 Nov. 1800. Cadet 1821. Arrived in India 17 May 1822. Ensign 1 Dec. 1821. Lieut. 10 Sept. 1823. Capt. 13 May 1833. Major 23 Mar. 1840. *d.* at sea, 29 Jan. 1846, on board the *Bucephalus*.
(*Probably* son of Francis Hewitt.)
Services : Posted as Ensign to 1/24th N.I. Transfd. to 2/29th N.I. 23 Oct. 1822 ; to 2/16th N.I. 29 Nov. 1823 ; to 33rd N.I. (late 2/16th) May 1824. Actg. Intr. & Qmr. 33rd N.I. 10 July 1824. First Burma War ; Arakan 1825 ; Lieut. 1st L.I. Bn. Fur. s.c. 5 May 1829 till 16 May 1832. First Afghan War ; forcing of Khyber ; occupation of Kabul ; Capt. 33rd N.I., with Gen. Pollock's force (Medal). Was on leave when his death occurred.

HEWITT, William Henry (1790-1863). Lieut. General. Colonel 27th N.I. *b.* London 31 Dec. 1790. Cadet 1806. Arrived in India 15 May 1807. Ensign 19 Mar. 1808. Lieut. 23 Sept. 1812. Capt. 23 May 1823. Major 13 Apr. 1830. Lt. Col. 9 Nov. 1835. Col. 11 Mar. 1847. Maj. Gen. 20 June 1854. Lt. Gen. 30 Dec. 1859. *d.* Westfield House, Old Wells Rd., Bath, 16 Apr. 1863.
Son of Thomas Hewitt. *m.* 1st, (?). (She died Penang 27 June

1825.) His dau. *m.* George Pengree, *q.v. m.* 2nd, Patna, 1 June 1843, Sophia Maria, dau. of Robert Baynes.
Services : Ensign d.d. 7th N.I. Posted as Ensign to 1/20th N.I. in 1810. Capture of Java 1811 ; Ensign 1/20th N.I. (Medal). Served at Fort Marlbro' Mar. 1812 till Apr. 1814 ; in Penang 1816. Actg. Adjt. 1/20th N.I. 16 Nov. 1821. Transfd. to 40th N.I. (late 2/20th) May 1824. First Burma War ; Chittagong 1824 ; Capt. 40th N.I. (India medal). Comdd. 40th N.I. Jan. 1835 till Mar. 1837. Posted as Lt. Col. to 40th N.I. 15 Feb. 1836. Transfd. to 25th N.I. 11 Feb. 1837 ; to 63rd N.I. 10 Jan. 1840 ; to 40th N.I. 10 Sept. 1841. Col. 27th N.I. Nov. 1849. Bdr., 2 cl., comdg. at Multan 7 Dec. 1850 till 4 May 1853. Maj. Gen. comdg. Peshawar Div. 15 Nov. 1853 ; comdd. Meerut Div. Jan. 1855 till June 1857. G.O.C. at Meerut on outbreak of the Mutiny. Fur. 1858 till death.
Refs. : Boase. *The Times,* 18 Apr. 1863. *G.M.* 1863, i. 674.

HEYLAND, Arthur (1807-?). Lieutenant. 12th N.I. *b.* Coleraine, Londonderry, 11 May 1807. Cadet 1824. Ensign 9 Sept. 1825. Lieut. 8 Sept. 1828. Resigned 5 Mar. 1830. *d.* before 1858.

2nd son of Arthur Rowley Heyland, Major 40th Regt. (who was kld. at Waterloo), and Mary his wife, née Kyffin.
Services : Posted as Ensign to 12th N.I. in 1826. No record of active service.
Refs. : Burke's *Landed Gentry,* 6th edn., p. 780, *s.n.* Heyland, of Glendaragh, co. Antrim, and Tamlaght, co. Derry.

HEYLAND, William (*d.* 1769). Lieutenant, Artillery. Cadet (Inf.) (?). Fireworker 6 Oct. 1764. Lieut. 2 Apr. 1769. *d.* Calcutta 22 May 1769 : kld. in a duel.
Services : Fireworker 1st Coy. Art. ; resigned 14 May 1766 during the " Batta mutiny " ; readmitted 19 Oct. 1766.

Note : Both *Dodwell & Miles* and *Stubbs's List* give two separate individuals, William Hyland and William Heyland. These are evidently the same person. In the *A.L.* of 1 Feb. 1767 the name appears as William Heylan.

HEYSHAM, Edmund (1778-1819). Captain, Pension Est. 11th N.I. *b.* Little Munden, Herts., 10 Apr. 1778. Cadet 1799. Arrived in India 9 Dec. 1800. Ensign 22 Oct. 1800. Lieut. 13 July 1803. Capt. (?). Pensioned 1819. *d.* Kishnagur (? Kishunnagar, B. & O.) 20 Dec. 1819.

bapt. 19 May 1778. Son of Rev. Edmund Heysham, of Little Munden, and Sarah his wife. Exeter Coll., Oxon. ; matric. 11 May 1796, aged 19.
Services : Second Mahratta War ; Shikohabad 4 Sept. 1803

(w.); Ensign 1/11th N.I. Cashiered 26 Nov. 1811. Restored to the Service as Capt. in 11th N.I. Mar. 1817.

Refs. : *Alumni Oxon.* *Pester,* p. 161.

HEYSHAM, William (1796-1825). Lieutenant, 53rd N.I. *b.* 27 Sept. 1796. Cadet 1813. Ensign 16 Dec. 1814. Lieut. 1 Oct. 1815. *d.* Karnal 13 Oct. 1825.

bapt. Carlisle 27 Oct. 1796. 3rd son of John Heysham, M.D., J.P., of the family of Heysham, formerly of Heysham, nr. Lancaster. His sister *m.* a nephew of George Stevenson Mounsey, *q.v.*

Services : Posted as Ensign to 1/27th N.I. in 1815. Third Mahratta War; Madhurajpura; Lieut. 1/27th N.I. Adjt. 1/27th N.I. 4 Aug. 1818 till death. Transfd. to 53rd N.I. (late 1/27th) May 1824.

Refs. : Burke's *Landed Gentry,* 11th edn., p. 819, *s.n.* Mounsey-Heysham, of Castletown, Cumberland. *G.M.* 1826, i. 478.

HEYWOOD, Daniel Ananias (1809-1831). Ensign 63rd N.I. *b.* London 20 Feb. 1809. Cadet 1828. Arrived in India 5 May 1829. Ensign 4 Dec. 1828. *d.* Berhampore 12 Sept. 1831.

Son of Daniel Heywood, of 18 Thames St., London, fish factor, and Jane his wife.

Services : Ensign d.d. 33rd N.I. 10 June 1829. Posted to 63rd N.I. 14 Sept. 1829. No record of active service.

Refs. : *A.J.* N.S. vii. 159.

HIATT, William (1780-1825). Major, 28th N.I. Dy. Sec. to Govt. in the Mily. Dept. *bapt.* Celbridge, co. Kildare, 20 Oct. 1780. Cadet 1800. Arrived in India 9 Feb. 1802. Ensign 29 Dec. 1801. Lieut. 30 Sept. 1803. Capt. 2 Feb. 1816. Major 1825. *d. unm.* Calcutta 15 June 1825.

Son of Love Hiatt and Elizabeth his wife.

Services : Second Mahratta War; Lieut. 14th N.I. A.D.C. to Maj.-Gen. J. S. Wood, comdg. Benares Div., 1811-5. Nepal War 1814-5; A.D.C. to Maj.-Gen. Wood, comdg. 3rd Div. Actg. A.A.G. 1 June 1815. Capt. Lt. 2/14th N.I. 26 Aug. 1815. Fur. 1816-9. Capt. 2/14th N.I. Dy. Sec. to Govt., Mily. Dept., 1822 till death. Transfd. to 28th N.I. (late 1/14th) May 1824.

Refs. : *Calcutta Monthly Journal,* xlvii. Will dated 28 May 1824; proved 28 June 1825. M.I. in S. Park St. cemetery, Calcutta.

HICKEY, John (1805-1839). Lieutenant, 10th L.C. *b.* Nisbett's Town, Ireland, 1805. Cadet 1825. Arrived in India 9 Mar. 1826. Cornet 12 Oct. 1825. Lieut. 19 July 1828. *d.* Muttra, 19 Jan. 1839, suddenly.

Son of a widow, of 38 Upper Rutland St., Dublin. *m.* Mussoorie,

THE BENGAL ARMY, 1758-1834 443

17 Oct. 1837, Ann, eldest dau. of George Playfair, Suptg. Surg., Bengal, and niece of Sir Hugh Lyon Playfair, *q.v.*
Services : Posted as Cornet to 10th L.C. in 1826, and remained with that Regt. throughout his service. No record of active service.
Refs. : A.J. N.S. xxv. 180 ; N.S. xxix. 63.

HICKEY, William (1794-1841). Lieutenant. 2nd N.I. Subsequently a Free Merchant in Calcutta. *b.* Dublin 27 May 1794. Cadet 1818. Ensign (?). Lieut. 5 May 1821. Resigned in India 22 May 1829. *d.* Calcutta, 5 Nov. 1841, of cholera.

Nephew of Lt.-Gen. William Thomas, Lt. Govr. of Tynemouth and Cliff fort. *m.* Exmouth, Feb. 1819, Frances Isabella, youngest dau. of Rev. Edmund Gilbert, vicar of Constantine, and sister of Sir Walter Raleigh Gilbert, Bart., *q.v.*
Services : Lieut. H.M. 41st Foot 7 Jan. 1813 ; h.p. 25 Mar. 1817. Apptd. in 1819, whilst still an unposted Ensign, Adjt. of the Calcutta Native Mil., and held this post till 1828. He was, in addition, from 1820 till retirement, Sec. to the Board of Superintendence for improving the breed of cattle. Posted as Lieut. to 1/16th N.I. Transfd. to 1st N.I. 11 July 1823 ; to 2nd N.I. (late 1/1st) May 1824. He appears to have done no regtl. duty at any period of his service. After quitting the Service he joined the firm of Moore, Hickey & Co., Calcutta, till *c.* 1840, when he joined Tulloh & Co., a Calcutta firm of auctioneers.
Refs. : Burke's *Landed Gentry*, 13th edn., p. 722, *s.n.* Gilbert, of the Priory. A.J. vii. 461. M.I. Circular Rd. cemetery, Calcutta.

HICKLAND, John (1756/57-1806). Captain, 5th N.I. *b.* 1756/57. Cadet 1781. Admitted 10 Mar. 1784. Ensign 27 June 1781. Lieut. 30 Sept. 1782. Capt. 17 Nov. 1799. *d.* Midnapore, 14 Aug. 1806, aged 49.

A native of Denmark. *m.* Calcutta, 19 Feb. 1799, Françoise Boularot (*b.* Marsillac, in Provence (?), 1760 ; died Midnapore 4 Apr. 1803), widow of Stephen De Prelaz, *q.v.*
Services : Lieut. 21st Bn. Sepoys in July 1787. (? Second Mahratta War ; Cuttack 1804 ; Khurda ; Capt. 1/5th N.I.)
Refs. : Will dated Midnapore 13 Aug. 1806 ; proved 6 Sept. 1806. M.I. at Midnapore.

HICKMAN, George William Jones (1797-1871). Major. 70th N.I. *b.* Cawnpore district 2 Jan. 1797. Cadet 1811. Admitted 4 Aug. 1812. Ensign 29 Jan. 1814. Lieut. 16 Dec. 1814. Capt. 7 June 1830. Retired 25 Sept. 1837. Hon. Major 28 Nov. 1854. *d.* 14 Oct. 1871.

bapt. Cawnpore 19 Apr. 1797. Son of Gregory Hickman, *q.v.*, and Gertrude Henrietta his wife. Brother of John Palliser Hickman, *q.v. m.* Calcutta, 20 Mar. 1819, Miss Mary Anne Judah (*possibly* dau. of Abraham Judah, index keeper in the mily. dept.). (She died Calcutta, Dec. 1856, aged 61.) Ed. Headlam Hall, co. Durham.

Services : Posted as Ensign to 1st N.I. in 1814. Nepal War 1814-5; Lieut. 2/1st, N.I., in 1st Div. (India medal). Third Mahratta War; Mahidpur 21 Dec. 1817 (clasp to India medal). With 2nd Bn. Ceylon Vols. 1818-20. Transfd. to 2nd N.I. (late 1/1st) May 1824 ; to 2nd Extra Regt. (became 70th N.I.) in 1825. Adjt. 70th N.I. 6 Jan. 1826 till Feb. 1831. Actg. Intr. & Qmr. 70th N.I. 29 Nov. 1833. Leave s.c. 12 mos. to Singapore and China 2 Aug. 1806.

HICKMAN, Gregory (*d.* 1828). Lieut. Colonel, Invalid Est. 1st N.I. Cadet 1783. Admitted 16 Oct. 1783. Ensign 14 Mar. 1785. Lieut. 1 June 1793. Capt. 21 Sept. 1804. Major 25 Aug. 1811. Lt. Col. 5 Dec. 1815. Invalided 1 Oct. 1818. *d.* Fatehgarh 14 May 1828.

(*Probably* son of Hugh Hickman, of Fenloe, co. Clare, and Bridget his wife, dau. of John Bury, of co. Cork.) *m.* 10 Nov. 1791, Gertrude Henrietta, dau. of William Vanas, *q.v.* Father of George William Jones Hickman, *q.v.*, John Palliser Hickman, *q.v.*, and Mary Anne, wife of Adam Duffin, *q.v.*[1]

Services : Adjt. 5th Bengal Eur. Bn. 1787-90 ; do. 1st Bengal Eur. Regt. in 1796. Adjt. & Qmr. 1st N.I. 1803-5. Capt. Lt. 1st N.I. 25 May 1804. Lt. Col. 1/1st N.I. After transfer to the Invalid Est. was Supt. of Invalids at Hapur, later at Chittagong. Comdd. Farrukhabad Provl. Bn. 1825 till death.

Refs. : (? Burke's *Landed Gentry of Ireland*, p. 320, *s.n.* Hickman, of Fenloe, co. Clare.)

[1] *Note :* Thus four generations are represented in these pages.

HICKMAN, John Palliser (1794-1853). Captain, Invalid Est. 69th N.I. *bapt.* Dinapore 19 Apr. 1794. Cadet 1810. Ensign 25 June 1813. Lieut. 16 Dec. 1814. Capt. 3 July 1827. Invalided 15 Oct. 1828. *d.* Allahabad 6 Oct. 1853.

Son of Gregory Hickman, *q.v.*, and Gertrude Henrietta his wife. Brother of Thomas Hickman (1801-1838), *q.v.*

Services : Cadet d.d. 1st N.I. 1811-3. Posted as Ensign to 1st N.I. in 1813. Third Mahratta War ; Rampur ; Jawad ; Lieut. 1/1st N.I. Adjt. Delhi Najib Bn. 1822-8. Transfd. to 4th N.I. (late 2/1st) May 1824 ; to 1st Extra Regt. (became 69th N.I.) in 1825. Fort Adjt. at Monghyr from 18 Sept. 1829 ; do. at Allahabad from 1834 till 14 May 1843.

THE BENGAL ARMY, 1758-1834 445

HICKMAN, Thomas (*d.* 1824). Captain. 3rd N.I. Country Cadet 1781. Admitted 26 Feb. 1781. Ensign 22 Aug. 1781. Lieut. 7 June 1783. Capt. 25 Oct. 1800. Retired 31 Aug. 1803. *d.* 21 June 1824.

3rd son of Hugh Hickman, of Fenloe, co. Clare, and Bridget his wife, dau. of John Bury, of co. Cork. (*Probably* brother of Gregory Hickman, *q.v.*) *m.* 1803, Jane, dau. of Thomas Cosby.

Services : Lieut. 5th Bengal Eur. Bn. in July 1787. Fur. 26 Jan. 1790 till 15 Aug. 1791. Lieut. 1st Bengal Eur. Regt. in 1796. Capt. Lt. 3rd N.I. 2 Oct. 1800. Fur. 21 Mar. 1801 till retirement.

Refs. : Burke's *Landed Gentry of Ireland*, p. 320, *s.n.* Hickman, of Fenloe, co. Clare.

HICKMAN, Thomas (1801-1838). Captain, Artillery. *b.* Bengal towards the end of 1801. Cadet 1818. Admitted 22 Jan. 1819. 2nd Lieut. 15 Sept. 1818. Lieut. 18 Dec. 1819. Capt. 15 Oct. 1833. *d.* Nasirabad, 22 Aug. 1838, whilst en route to Mhow.

Son of Gregory Hickman, *q.v.* Brother of George William Jones Hickman, *q.v.* Addiscombe Cadet 1816-8.

Services : Served with 3rd Troop H.A. 1820-4 ; 4th Troop 1st Bde. 1825-7 ; 4th Troop 3rd Bde. 1827-9 ; 4th Troop 2nd Bde. 1829-30. Fur. p.a. 19 Mar. 1832 till 3 Nov. 1835. Posted to 3rd Coy. 2nd Bn. Foot Art. 11 Sept. 1837 ; to 1st Coy. 3rd Bn. 18 Apr. 1838. No record of active service.

Refs. : A.J. N.S. xxvii. 335.

HICKS, George (1791-1873). Lieut. General, C.B. Colonel 70th N.I. *b.* London 12 Feb. 1791. Cadet 1807. Arrived in India 9 Aug. 1808. Ensign 7 Sept. 1808. Lieut. 14 Sept. 1813. Capt. 9 Nov. 1824. Major 8 Jan. 1838. Lt. Col. 13 Mar. 1844. Col. 7 May 1854. Maj. Gen. 18 Feb. 1856. Lt. Gen. 18 Nov. 1868. *d.* Jersey 24 Oct. 1873.

Son of William Hicks. *m.* Calcutta, 21 Oct. 1818, Miss Jane Hennessy.

Services : Posted as Ensign to 9th N.I. Lieut. 1/9th N.I. Adjt. Saharanpur Provl. Bn. 1820 till 12 June 1822. Transfd. to 2/9th N.I. Adjt. Agra Najib Bn. 12 June 1822 till 14 Sept. 1824. Transfd. to 8th N.I. (late 1/9th) May 1824. Actg. Adjt. 8th N.I. 16 Sept. 1829. Fur. s.c. 20 Jan. 1833 till 17 Dec. 1835. Lt. Col. 8th N.I. Transfd. to 47th N.I. June 1845. First Sikh War ; Badhowal ; Mudki ; Ferozshahr ; Aliwal ; Lt. Col. 47th N.I., comdg. a Bde. (Medal with 2 clasps). Transfd. to 37th N.I. in Sept. 1851 ; to 21st N.I. in Aug. 1852. Fur. s.c. 21 Mar. 1852 till death. Col. 70th N.I. 20 May 1854. C.B. 3 Apr. 1846.

Refs. : Boase.

HICKS, Henry Wilkins (1761-1812). Major, 11th N.I. *b.* 1761. Cadet 1782. Admitted 7 Jan. 1783. Ensign 11 Feb. 1783. Lieut. 2 Feb. 1790. Capt. 13 July 1803. Major 31 Aug. 1810. *d. unm.* Calcutta 6 Jan. 1812.

Brother of Thomas Hicks, of Enborne, Berks. Uncle of John Rawlins, *q.v.*, and of John Padbury.

Services : Ensign 4th Bengal Eur. Bn. in July 1787. A.D.C. to Col. Christian Knudson, *q.v.*, in 1790. Fur. 18 Jan. 1796 till 8 Nov. 1799. Capt. Lt. 11th N.I. 12 Jan. 1801. Fur. 6 Mar. 1802 till 12 Sept. 1805. (? Capture of Gohad 1806 ; Capt. 2/11th N.I.)

Refs. : Will dated 13 Jan. 1810 ; proved 23 Jan. 1812 (the sole executrix being Frances, widow of Thomas Higgins, *q.v.*). M.I. in S. Park St. cemetery, Calcutta.

HICKS, John (*d.* 1781). Captain, Infantry. Cadet 1771. Ensign 28 Jan. 1773. Lieut. 2 Jan. 1778. Capt. 4 June 1781. *d.* Bahadurpur, nr. Gwalior, C.I., Nov. 1781.

Services : (? First Mahratta War.)

Refs. : Mundy, ii. 54.

HICKS, John (1791-1841). Bt. Major. 17th N.I. *b.* Aylesbury, Bucks., 3 Apr. 1791. Cadet 1808. Arrived in India 24 July 1809. Ensign 26 Aug. 1809. Lieut. 16 Dec. 1814. Capt. 19 Oct. 1827. Bt. Major 28 June 1838. Retired 1 Oct. 1841. *d.* Ghazipur, 27 Nov. 1841, on board a river boat, on his way to Calcutta.

Son of James Hicks. Brother of Mrs. Henry Williamson, of Harefield, nr. Uxbridge.

Services : Posted as Ensign to 11th N.I. Reduction of Kalinjar 1812 ; Ensign 2/11th N.I. Siege and capture of Hathras 1817 ; Lieut. 2/11th N.I. Third Mahratta War ; Lieut. 2/11th N.I. Transfd. to 17th N.I. (late 2/11th) May 1824. Adjt. 17th N.I. 5 Mar. till 1 May 1827.

Refs. : G.M. 1842, i. 566. Will dated Cawnpore 14 Nov. 1841 ; proved 10 Feb. 1843.

HICKS, John William (1806-1880). Major General. 69th N.I. *b.* London 25 May 1806. Cadet 1823. Arrived in India 22 May 1824. Ensign 17 Jan. 1824. Lieut. 13 May 1825. Capt. 15 Feb. 1836. Major 28 Feb. 1850. Lt. Col. 10 Nov. 1855. Bt. Col. 15 Feb. 1858. Retired 31 Dec. 1861. Hon. Maj. Gen. 31 Dec. 1861. *d.* 6 Claverton St., London, 4 Apr. 1880.

Son of John William Hicks, of Ilfracombe and Lincoln's Inn, later of Cheltenham. Brother of William Charles Hicks, *q.v. m.*

Dinapore, 15 June 1835, Mary Roza, eldest dau. of Richard Clements Walker, q.v. Ed. Rugby ; admitted midsummer 1818.
Services : Posted as Ensign to 67th N.I. First Burma War ; Arakan 1825 ; Lieut. 67th N.I. (India medal). Adjt. 67th N.I. 13 Apr. 1835 till 4 Mar. 1836. Attached to 3rd L.I. Bn. at Cawnpore in 1842. Fur. 16 Feb. 1851 till Feb. 1853. Transfd. as Lt. Col. to 69th N.I. in Feb. 1856, and was comdg. that Regt. at Multan on the outbreak of the Mutiny.
Refs. : Rugby School List. The Times, 7 Apr. 1880.

HICKS, William Charles (1809-1882). Colonel. 3rd N.I. *b.* Hadbury (?), Worcs., 8 Jan. 1809. Cadet 1824. Arrived in India 5 June 1825. Ensign 23 Jan. 1825. Lieut. 8 May 1826. Capt. 19 Apr. 1839. Major 3 Oct. 1851. Lt. Col. 26 Oct. 1855. Retired 10 Sept. 1855. Hon. Col. 10 Sept. 1855. *d.* Boulogne-sur-Mer, France, 9 Jan. 1882.

bapt. 22 Feb. 1809. 3rd son of John William Hicks, of Ilfracombe and of Lincoln's Inn, sometime of Lansdown Cresc., Bath, and of I. of Jamaica. Brother of John William Hicks, *q.v. m.* Walcot, Bath, 31 Aug. 1854, Catherine, youngest dau. of John Stedman, of Royal Cresc., Bath.
Services : Posted as Ensign to 67th N.I. in 1825. (? First Burma War ; Arakan 1825 ; Ensign 67th N.I.) Transfd. to 3rd N.I. in 1826. d.d. 67th N.I. 30 May 1826 ; do. 15th N.I. 30 Sept. 1829. Shekhawat expedn. 1834 ; Lieut. 3rd N.I. Actg. Intr. & Qmr. 8th L.C. 19 May 1836. Adjt. 3rd N.I. 19 Feb. 1837 till 6 July 1839. Fur. s.c. 23 Jan. 1840 till 12 Oct. 1842. Second Sikh War ; Jullundur Doab 1848-9 ; assault of the heights of Dalla ; Capt. 3rd N.I., with Bdr. Wheeler's force (Medal). Fur. 1854 till retirement.
Refs. : The Times, 12 Jan. 1882.

HIGGINS, Charles Thomas (1785-1827). Lieut. Colonel, 25th N.I. *b.* Bengal 23 Dec. 1785. Cadet 1799. Arrived in India 18 Dec. 1800. Ensign 27 Aug. 1800. Lieut. 21 Feb. 1801. Capt. 3 Jan. 1814. Major 14 July 1821. Lt. Col. 1 May 1824. *d.* Ashburton, Devon, 29 June 1827.

Sometime of Queen's Pl., Knightsbridge, later of Taunton. *bapt.* Calcutta 27 Apr. 1786. Son of Thomas Higgins, *q.v.,* and Frances his wife. Brother of Edmund Buttall Higgins, *q.v. m.* Calcutta, 20 Dec. 1810, Emma Maria, dau. of Thomas Raban, and sister of Richard Raban, *q.v.* (She died Bristol 4 May 1861.)
Services : Posted as Lieut. to Bengal Eur. Regt. Aug. 1801. Second Mahratta War ; capture of Gwalior ; Lieut. Bengal Eur. Regt. Transfd. to newly-raised 22nd N.I. Apr. 1804. On service in June 1805 (s.w. in rt. elbow). Settlement of Hariana 1809 ;

Bhawani; Lieut. 1/22nd N.I. Capture of Java 1811. On Pol.
duty in Amboyna 1812-3, and in Java 1811. Capt. Lt. 25 July 1813.
Third Mahratta War; Nagpur; Capt. 1/22nd N.I., Bde. Major to
Cav. Bde. Major 1/22nd N.I. Offg. Fort and Town Major of Fort
William in 1822. Agent for army clothing, 2nd Div., in 1823.
Transfd. as Lt. Col. to 25th N.I. May 1824. Comdg. troops at
Penang 1824-5. Fur. from Singapore, *via* China, 26 Nov. 1825 till
death.

Refs. : Family information. *E.I.M.C.* ii. 354-8. *G.M.* 1827,
ii. 92; 1828, i. 369. Will dated 26 June 1827; proved 18 July 1829.
M.I. in Ashburton church.

HIGGINS, Edmund Buttall (1787-1828). Major, 62nd N.I. *b.*
Bengal 23 Feb. 1787. Cadet 1799. Arrived in India 18 Dec.
1800. Ensign 5 Oct. 1800. Lieut. 8 Apr. 1802. Capt. 16 Dec.
1814. Major 13 May 1825. *d.* Clifton 8 Aug. 1828.

bapt. Calcutta 27 Mar. 1787.· Son of Thomas Higgins, *q.v.*, and
Frances his wife. Brother of Charles Thomas Higgins, *q.v.*

Services : Lieut. Bengal Eur. Regt. Transfd. to newly-raised
25th N.I. 1805. Adjt. & Qmr. 25th N.I. 18 Jan. 1805 till 1814.
Capture of Gohad 1806. Capt. Lt. 25th N.I. 7 Apr. 1814. Capt.
1/25th N.I. With 4th Gren. Bn. 1815-6. Leave to sea in 1818. Supt.
of Cadets at Fort William 1820-4. Transfd. to 31st N.I. 11 July
1823; to 62nd N.I. (late 2/31st) May 1824. Fur. Dec. 1823 till death.

Refs. : Family information. *G.M.* 1828, ii. 189.

HIGGINS, J—— T——. Captain. Infantry. Cadet 1767. Ensign 1 Dec. 1767. Lieut. 10 Oct. 1769. Capt. 23 Feb. 1778.
Dismissed by C.M. 9 Apr. 1779.

Services : N.F.P.

HIGGINS, Thomas (1754-1800). Lieut. Colonel, 4th N.I. *b.* 1754.
Country Cadet 1769. Arrived in India Dec. 1766. Admitted 6
Nov. 1769. Ensign 20 Jan. 1770. Lieut. 30 Mar. 1773. Capt.
26 Jan. 1781. Major 1 Mar. 1794. Lt. Col. 30 Oct. 1797. *d.* at
sea, 24 May 1800, between the Cape and St. Helena.

Son of Thomas Higgins, Dy. Comy., Bengal Est., and Mary
Stokoe his wife. *m.* Frances, dau. of Edward Ironside, of Twicken-
ham, and niece of Gilbert Ironside, *q.v.* Father of Charles Thomas
Higgins, *q.v.*, and of Edmund Buttall Higgins, *q.v.*

Services : First Rohilla War; battle of St. George; Lieut. 8th
Bn. Sepoys. 6th Bengal Eur. Bn. in July 1787. Comdd. 4th N.I.
with detachment under Maj.-Gen. Erskine in Madras Presdy. 1797-8.
Leave s.c. 6 mos. to St. Helena 27 Feb. 1800.

Refs. : Family information.

THE BENGAL ARMY, 1758-1834   449

HIGGINSON, George (d. 1796). Lieutenant, Infantry. Cadet 1783. Admitted 27 Sept. 1783. Ensign 19 Feb. 1785. Lieut. 15 Mar. 1792. d. Dinapore 6 Sept. 1796.
Services : N.F.P.

HIGGINSON, Sir James Macaulay (1805-1885). Bt. Captain. 58th N.I. Governor of Mauritius. K.C.B. b. Gibraltar 15 Aug. 1805. Cadet 1823. Arrived in India 7 June 1824. Ensign 21 Feb. 1824. Lieut. 21 Jan. 1826. Bt. Capt. 21 Feb. 1839. Resigned 17 Aug. 1840. d. Tulfaris, co. Wicklow, 28 June 1885.
Eldest son of James Higginson, Major H.M.S., late 10th Foot, and Mary his wife, dau. of Alexander Macaulay, of Glenville, co. Antrim. m. 1st, Calcutta, 25 Nov. 1835, Louisa Mary Ann, dau. of Henry Shakespear, B.C.S. m. 2nd, 11 Feb. 1854, Olivia Nichola, eldest dau. of Conway Dobbs, of Castle Dobbs, co. Antrim. (She died Oct. 1906.) T.C.D. ; Pensioner, 4 Nov. 1822, aged 17.
Services : (? Siege and capture of Bhurtpore ; Ensign 55th N.I.[1]) A.D.C. to G.G. 11 June 1828. Offg. Mily. Sec. to V.P. and Dy. Govr. 11 Nov. 1830. Paymr. at the Presdy., and to King's troops, 23 Jan. 1832. Extra A.D.C. to V.P. 23 Feb. 1832. Town and Fort Major at Allahabad 6 Feb. 1835. Pte. Sec. to Lord Metcalfe, offg. G.G., 20 Mar. 1835 till 4 Mar. 1836. Pte. Sec. and A.D.C. to Lord Metcalfe, Lt. Govr. N.W.P., 13 Apr. 1836 till 1838. Fur. p.a. 17 Feb. 1838 till resignation. Sec. to Lord Metcalfe in Jamaica, 1838, and Canada 1843. Govr. of the Leeward Is. 26 June 1846 ; of Mauritius 1 Oct. 1850 till 11 Sept. 1857. K.C.B. 2 Jan. 1857.
Refs. : Burke's *Landed Gentry of Ireland,* p. 184, *s.n.* Dobbs, of Castle Dobbs, co. Antrim. *Alumni Dub. Walford. Boase.* Foster's *Knightage. List of Pte. Secs. to the Governors General and Viceroys.*
[1] *Note :* His name is not included in either the India medal roll or the Bhurtpore P.R.

HIGGOTT, Richard (1782-1816). Captain, Bengal Eur. Regt. *bapt.* Uttoxeter, Staffs., 18 Feb. 1782. Cadet 1799. Arrived in India 5 Jan. 1801. Ensign 8 Aug. 1800. Lieut. 4 Sept. 1800. Capt. 2 July 1813. d. *unm.* at sea, 27 July 1816, on board the *Exmouth,* between the Cape and England.
Son of Thomas Higgott, of Uttoxeter, and Penelope his wife. Brother of Thomas Lee Higgott, John Higgott, and Mary Anne Burwell.
Services : Posted as Lieut. to Bengal Eur. Regt. Second Mahratta War ; capture of Sambalpur ; Lieut. Ramgarh Bn. Served with Ramgarh Bn. till 1806. Fur. 22 Sept. 1806 till 18 Oct. 1809. With Ramgarh Bn. 1811-5. Capt.Lt. Bengal Eur. Regt. 22 Jan.

1812. Nepal War 1814-5; Capt. Ramgarh Bn., in 4th Div. Fur. 1816.

Refs. : *G.M.* 1816, ii. 465. Will dated 22 Mar. 1813; codicil dated 20 Feb. 1816; proved in 1816.

HIGHMORE, George (1789-1805). Ensign, Infantry. Unposted. *b.* Beaconsfield, Bucks., 8 June 1789. Cadet 1803. Arrived in India 18 Mar. 1805. Ensign 19 Apr. 1805. *d.* Delhi 4 Nov. 1805.

Son of William Highmore.

HILL, Douglas (*c.* 1740-1777). Major. Comdt. 19th N.I. *b. c.* 1740. Capt. 12 Nov. 1763. Major 2 Apr. 1767. *d.* 1777 : drowned at sea on the voyage from Madras to Calcutta.

Son of an Irish gentleman.

Services : Ran away from school in 1754, being then about 14 yrs. of age, and joined a recruiting party of H.M. 39th Regt., comdd. by Col. John Adlercron. With this Regt. he arrived at Fort St. David, Madras, in Sept. 1754 as a Drummer. Went home in 1758 with Col. Coote, who, on arrival in England, procured his discharge. Apptd. Qmr. to newly-raised 84th Regt.; Warrant dated 7 Feb. 1759. Arrived Madras towards the close of 1759, and in the following year secured an Ensign's Commission in H.M. 84th. Ensign H.M. 84th 11 Sept. 1760; Lieut. do. 1 Sept. 1761. Capture of Pondicherry 1761. Went to Bengal with Coote. War with Mir Muhammad Kasim 1763. Transfd. to Bengal army as Capt. when the 84th went home in Oct. 1763. h.p. 84th Foot 25 Dec. 1764. Comdd. newly-raised 19th Bn. Sepoys 1764-7. Resigned in 1767 owing to super-cession by Grainger Muir, *q.v.* After remaining a few yrs. in England he was restored to the Service, but was drowned coming from Madras.

Refs. : *Williams,* pp. 61, 67.

HILL, George Mytton (1810-1883). Lieut. General. 17th N.I. *b.* 25 May 1810. Cadet 1825. Arrived in India 22 Oct. 1826. Ensign 13 June 1826. Lieut. 28 Aug. 1833. Capt. 31 Oct. 1849. Major 27 Dec. 1859. Lt. Col. 18 Feb. 1861. Col. 18 Feb. 1866. Maj. Gen. 1 Oct. 1877. Lt. Gen. 3 Nov. 1878. Retired list 1882. *d.* Lee, Kent, 13 Jan. 1883.

bapt. London 12 June 1812. Younger son of Richard Hill, of Chester, merchant, and Anne his wife, dau. of Richard Mytton, of Garth. Cousin-german of Rowland Hill, *q.v. m.* Simla, 23 Oct. 1841, Harriet Mary Benyon, eldest dau. of Martin Thomas Whish, B.C.S. (She died 10 Jan. 1908.)

Services : Ensign d.d. 2nd Extra Regt. (became 70th N.I.) 9 Nov.

1826. Posted to 2nd Extra Regt. 8 Jan. 1827. Transfd. to 17th N.I. 3 Nov. 1829. Intr. & Qmr. 17th N.I. 2 Aug. 1833 till 22 Feb. 1840. A.D.C. to G.G. 8 Nov. 1839 till 24 Dec. 1841. Offg. Mily. Sec. to G.G. (Lord Auckland) 6 May 1840 till Feb. 1842. Paymr. of Native pensioners in Oudh and Cawnpore 24 Nov. 1841. Dy. Paymr. at Agra 17 Oct. 1842 ; do. at Jullundur 1848 till Oct. 1858. Fur. 1855-6. Paymr. at Presdy. 1 Oct. 1858. Mily. Accountant, Bengal, 31 Jan. 1861 till Mar. 1871. Fur. 29 Mar. 1871 till retirement. No record of active service.

Refs. : Burke's *Peerage*, 1923, p. 1169, *s.n.* Hill, V. *List of Mily. Secs. to the Governors General and Viceroys.* The *Times*, 16 Jan. 1883.

HILL, Hugh Harrison (1805-1830). Lieutenant, 40th N.I. *bapt.* Larne, co. Antrim, June 1805. Cadet 1824. Arrived in India 12 June 1825. Ensign 25 Jan. 1825. Lieut. 27 Mar. 1826. *d.* Sehore, Bhopal, 15 Nov. 1830.

Son of David Hill, of Larne, and Margaret his wife.

Services : Posted as Ensign to 36th N.I. in 1825. Siege and capture of Bhurtpore ; Ensign 36th N.I. Transfd. as Lieut. to 40th N.I. in 1826. Leave s.c. 6 mos. 6 Nov. 1830, and died on the way from Mhow to Calcutta.

Refs. : Will dated camp before Bhurtpore 17 Jan. 1826 ; proved 7 Mar. 1831.

HILL, John Lewis (1781-1813). Lieutenant, 6th N.I. *bapt.* Carew, co. Pembroke, 29 Jan. 1781. Cadet 1799. Arrived in India 8 Jan. 1801. Ensign 7 Oct. 1800. Lieut. 26 Mar. 1803. *d.* Ludhiana, 25 Apr. 1813, aged 32.

Son of John Hill and Elizabeth his wife.

Services : Posted as Ensign to 2/6th N.I. 17 Apr. 1801, and served throughout with that Regt. On service in Ganjam, Madras, July 1801. Second Mahratta War ; operations in Baghelkhand 1803 ; reduction of Chaukandi fort. On service in Bundelkhand 1804-6.

Refs. : *De Rhé-Philipe.* M.I. at Ludhiana.

HILL, Justly. Major. Artillery. Cadet (R.A.) 3 Jan. 1763. Fireworker, from R.A., 7 Sept. 1768. Lieut. 15 Mar. 1770. Capt. Lt. 31 Jan. 1774. Capt. 4 Oct. 1778. Major 1 July 1784. Struck off 1793.

Of Walsingham Hall, Norfolk. *m.* 1st, Calcutta, 10 Apr. 1779, Miss Wilhelma (sic) Carter. (She died Cawnpore 13 Oct. 1781.) *m.* 2nd, Calcutta, 9 Nov. 1784, Miss Dorothea Grifiths. (She died 1 Jan. 1788.) *m.* 3rd, I.W., Nov. 1788, Mrs. Tees, of Pidford, I.W.

Services : Apptd. as Capt. Lt. to comd. newly-raised Golandaz

Coy. in 1777. Campaign against the Rajah of Benares 1781;
Patita; Bijaigarh; Capt. comdg. 1st Coy. 2nd Bn. Art. Shown as
on fur. in 1790, although his name does not appear in *A.L.* of 1 July
1787.

Refs. : *Kane*, No. 441. *G.M.* 1788, ii. 1124.

HILL, Lawrence (1812-1844). Lieutenant, Engineers. *b.* Edinburgh 2 Mar. 1812. Cadet 1830. Arrived in India 15 July 1831.
2nd Lieut. (11 Dec. 1829) 22 Jan. 1834. Lieut. 20 May 1839.
d. Jhalokatty, nr. Barisal, 24 Sept. 1844.

Son of Robert Hill, of York Pl., Edinburgh, W.S., and Barbara
Geddes his wife. Nephew of Thomas Hill (*d.* 1821), *q.v.* Addiscombe Cadet 8 Aug. 1828 till 11 Dec. 1829. Chatham 5 Feb. till 23
Sept. 1830.

Services : d.d. S. & M. 30 Aug. 1831. Shekhawat expedn. 1834;
Asst. Field Engr. Survey Dept. 1835. Asst. Supt. Delhi-Allahabad
road 1836-42. Fur. p.a. 13 Feb. 1841 till 20 Apr. 1844. P.W.D. at
Barisal 2 Aug. 1844.

Refs. : M.I. at Barisal.

HILL, Rowland (1807-1854). Lieut. Colonel. 70th N.I. *b.* co.
Chester 12 Dec. 1807. Cadet 1823. Arrived in India 25 June
1824. Ensign 14 Jan. 1824. Lieut. 9 July 1825. Capt. 1 July
1839. Bt. Major 19 June 1846. Retired 9 Aug. 1851. Hon. Lt.
Col. 28 Nov. 1854. *d. unm.* Colton House, nr. Rugeley, Staffs.,
12 Dec. 1854.

3rd son of John Hill, of Standish Hall, Wigan (of Ashley Hall,
co. Chester), barr.-at-law, and Elizabeth his wife, dau. of Thomas
Wilkinson. Cousin-german of George Mytton Hill, *q.v.*

Services : Posted as Ensign to 54th N.I. in 1824. Transfd. as
Lieut. to newly-raised 2nd Extra Regt. (became 70th N.I.) July
1825. Adjt. 5th Local Horse 5 Mar. 1829 till Dec. 1836. Fur. s.c.
8 Dec. 1836 till 24 Dec. 1839. Bde. Major in Oudh 22 Sept. 1841.
2nd in comd. 4th Irreg. Cav. 11 July 1842. Bde. Major at Lucknow
1 Oct. 1844. Comdd. 4th Irreg. Cav. 28 Feb. 1845 till Sept. 1850.
First Sikh War; Aliwal; Capt. 70th N.I., comdg. 4th Irreg. Cav.
(Medal). Extra A.D.C. to G.G. 11 Jan. 1851.

Refs. : Burke's *Peerage*, 1923, p. 1169, *s.n.* Hill, V. Will dated
21 Mar. 1849; proved 2 Aug. 1856.

HILL, Rowley John (1806-1850). Captain, 4th N.I. Comdt. 5th
Irreg. Cav. *b.* Lower Moville, co. Donegal, 1 Sept. 1806. Cadet
1827. Arrived in India 8 June 1828. Ensign 23 Feb. 1828.
Lieut. 3 Oct. 1840. Capt. 16 May 1848. *d.* Bombay 12 Nov.
1850.

2nd son of Rev. John Beresford Hill, rector of Langfield and Moville, and Letitia his wife, 2nd dau. of Dominick M'Causland, of Daisy Hill, co. Derry. Brother of Sir George Hill, 3rd Bart. of St. Columbs, co. Derry. *m.* Karnal, 23 Jan. 1836, Caroline Catherine, 2nd dau. of Sir Robert Henry Sale, G.C.B. (*See also* Frederick Brind.) (She died 1 Aug. 1890.)

Services : Ensign d.d. 2nd N.I. 25 July 1828. Posted to 4th N.I. 4 Nov. 1828. Actg. Intr. & Qmr. 4th N.I. 20 Nov. 1829. Actg. Adjt. 4th Local Horse 23 Sept. 1833. Apptd. to 1st Inf., Oudh Auxy. Force, 18 Dec. 1837. Transfd. to 1st Cav., Oudh Auxy. Force, 19 Feb. 1838 ; 2nd in comd. do. (became 5th Irreg. Cav.) 17 Jan. 1840 till Apr. 1849. Comdt. 5th Irreg. Cav. 16 Apr. 1849 till death. No record of active service.

Refs. : Burke's *Peerage*, 1923, p. 1172, *s.n.* Hill, Bart., of St. Columbs, co. Londonderry.

HILL, Thomas (*d.* 1821). Lieut. Colonel, Artillery. Cadet 1783. Admitted 27 Sept. 1783. Fireworker 16 Feb. 1785. Lieut. 6 Jan. 1792. Capt. Lt. 16 Feb. 1802. Capt. 26 July 1804. Major 22 Feb. 1810. Lt. Col. 21 Apr. 1817. *d.* Edinburgh 14 Jan. 1821.

Brother of Robert Hill, of Edinburgh, W.S., and of Ninian Hill. Nephew of Thomas Hill, and uncle of Lawrence Hill, *q.v.*

Services : Lieut. F. 3rd Bn. Art. in July 1787. Third Mysore War ; Bangalore ; Nandidrug (w.) ; Lieut. 5th Coy. 1st Bn. Head Asst. to Sec. to Govt., Mily. Dept., 1804-6. Garr. storekeeper at Fort William 12 Mar. 1807 till 1818. Fur. 1819 till death.

Refs. : *S.M.* 1821, i. 191. Will dated Edinburgh 9 Jan. 1821 ; proved 13 Aug. 1821.

HILL, Thomas (1781-1803). Lieutenant, 12th N.I. *bapt.* Errol, co. Perth, 17 Sept. 1781. Cadet 1799. Arrived in India 7 Dec. 1800. Ensign 4 Oct. 1800. Lieut. 18 Oct. 1801. *d.* 11 Sept. 1803 : kld. in action at the battle of Delhi.

Son of Peter Hill, of Inchmichael, Errol, farmer, and Agnes Hunter his wife.

Services : Operations in Jumna Doab 1803 ; Sasni ; Lieut. 2/12th N.I. Second Mahratta War; battle of Delhi (kld.); Lieut. 2/12th N.I.

Refs. : *Pester*, p. 170.

HILL, Thomas William (1806-1869). Lieutenant. 44th N.I. *b.* Houghton-le-Spring, co. Durham, 14 Mar. 1806. Cadet 1824. Arrived in India 24 Feb. 1826. Ensign 6 Sept. 1825. Lieut. 4 Mar. 1828. Retired 1 Aug. 1839. *d.* 11 Jan. 1869.

2nd son of Robert Hill. *m.* Cawnpore, 21 Jan. 1835, Jane Augusta Graham.

Services : Posted as Ensign to 44th N.I. in 1826. Operations against marauders in Jhabua, Malwa, C.I., May 1836 ; Lieut. 44th N.I. Fur. p.a. 1 Feb. 1837 till Jan. 1840, when he was placed on the retired list with effect from 1 Aug. 1839.

HILL, William (1758/59-1800). Captain, 3rd N.I. *b.* in Ireland 1758/59. Cadet 1781. Arrived in India 1781. Ensign 22 June 1781. Lieut. 26 Sept. 1782. Capt. 2 Oct. 1800. *d. unm.* Barrackpore 24 Oct. 1800.

Brother of Miss Letitia Hill, of Ringville, nr. Waterford. Nephew of Richard Devereux, of Ringville, and cousin of John Hill, of Kilkenny, physician.

Services : Apptd. Cadet on 6 Apr. 1781, aged 22. Sailed for India on the *Northumberland* 26 June 1781, aged 22. Fur. 3 yrs. on h.p. 23 Mar. 1787. Capt. Lt. 2/3rd N.I. 29 May 1800.

Refs. : A.A.R. iii. 104. Will dated 20 May 1800 ; proved 29 Oct. 1800. M.I. in old cemetery at Barrackpore.

HILLIARD, George (1783-?). Cornet. 1st N.C. *b.* Lamb's Conduit St., London, 3 May 1783. Cadet 1807. Arrived in India 14 Sept. 1808. Cornet 17 Sept. 1808. Resigned 13 Mar. 1813.

bapt. St. George the Martyr, Queen's Sq., London, 31 May 1783. Son of Edward Hilliard, of Lamb's Conduit St., and Elizabeth Stafford his wife. *m.* Chunar, 10 Nov. 1809, Miss Louisa Ann Anstruther (*probably* dau. of Hon. David Anstruther, *q.v.*). Woolwich Cadet ; nominated for R.M.A. 6 June 1798 ; resigned 10 June 1799. Christ Church Coll., Oxon. ; matric. 24 Nov. 1801, aged 18.

Services : Posted as Cornet to 1st N.C. in 1809. Operations in Bundelkhand 1810-1 ; Bichaund ; Cornet 1st N.C.

Refs. : Alumni Oxon.

HILLIARD, John (*d.* 1801). Lieut. Colonel, Infantry. Cadet 1770. Admitted 17 Oct. 1770. Ensign 2 Dec. 1771. Lieut. 11 Aug. 1776. Capt. 2 Mar. 1781. Major 1 Mar. 1794. Lt. Col. 1 Nov. 1798. *d. unm.* Chunar 9 Aug. 1801.

Brother of Elizabeth Hilliard and Mary Hilliard.

Services : Returned from fur. 16 June 1786. 6th Bengal Eur. Bn. in July 1787. Major 1st Bengal Eur. Regt. in 1796.

Refs. : Will dated 13 Sept. 1797 ; proved 29 Dec. 1801.

HIMING, Henry (1756/57-1784). Lieutenant, Infantry. *b.* Essex 1756/57. Cadet 1776. Ensign 1777. Lieut. 10 Aug. 1778. *d.* Berhampore, Bengal, 2 Sept. 1784.

Son of Isaac Himing and Mary his wife.

Services : Sailed for India on the *Duke of Cumberland* 29 Mar. 1776, aged 19. N.F.P.

Refs. : Will dated 18 July 1784.

HINCHMAN, John. Lieutenant. Infantry. Cadet 1779. Ensign 12 Apr. 1780. Lieut. 10 Feb. 1781. Resigned 1781.
Services : N.F.P.

HINCKSMAN, William (1760/61-1794). Lieutenant, 13th N.I. *b.* Gloucester 1760/61. Cadet 1779. Arrived in India 12 Feb. 1780. Ensign 12 Feb. 1780. Lieut. 11 Mar. 1781. *d.* 26 Oct. 1794 : kld. in action at the battle of Bitaurah, nr. Bareilly, U.P.
Services : Sailed for India on the *Norfolk* 7 Mar. 1779, aged 18. Lieut. 8th Bn. Sepoys in July 1787. Second Rohilla War ; battle of Bitaurah (kld.).
Refs. : Will dated 4 Feb. 1791 ; proved in 1795. Name on cenotaph in St. John's churchyard, Calcutta.

*****HINCLES, William** (*d.* 1763). Ensign, Bengal Eur. Regt. Cadet (?). Ensign (?). *d.* 5th, 6th or 11th Oct. 1763 : massacred at or near Patna by order of Nawab Mir Muhammad Kasim. (*See* note to John Gordon*.)
Services : N.F.P.
Refs. : Broome, p. 365. *Innes*, p. 169. M.I. in Patna city.

HIND, Alexander (*d.* 1828). Bt. Colonel. Artillery. Country Cadet 1779. Admitted 19 Aug. 1779. Fireworker 30 Sept. 1780. Lieut. 28 May 1786. Capt. Lt. 8 Jan. 1796. Capt. 14 Feb. 1802. Major 12 Nov. 1804. Lt. Col. 16 Sept. 1807. Bt. Col. 4 June 1814. Retired 15 Feb. 1818. *d.* 25 May 1828.

m. 1 Mar. 1814, Clara Wilkin, dau. of —— Nash, of Finsbury Sq., London, and widow of Joseph Thornton, *q.v.* (She died Highbury 8 Nov. 1852, aged 68.)
Services : Campaign against the Rajah of Benares 1781 ; Patita ; Bijaigarh.[1] Lieut. 1st Bn. Art. in July 1787. Third Mysore War ; Bangalore ; Savandrug ; Seringapatam ; Lieut. 5th Coy. 1st Bn. Foot Art. With detachment of Art. sent from Bengal (Nov. 1793, for about 1 yr.) for service against French cruisers in the Bay of Bengal and E. Archipelago. Expedn. to Macao 1801-2 ; Capt. Lt. 4th Coy. 1st Bn. Second Mahratta War ; siege of Bhurtpore ; Major Art. Lt. Col. comdg. 1st Bn. Foot Art. Fur. 19 Feb. 1814 till retirement.
Refs. : E.I.M.C. i. 397-8. *G.M.* 1815, i. 370. Will dated 14 Apr. 1827 ; admon. 7 Sept. 1830.

[1] *Note :* Name omitted from the list given in Stubbs (i. 70) of the Ofrs. of Art. who took part in these operations.

HINDSON, John (1802-1826). Lieutenant, 66th N.I. *bapt.* Penrith, Cumberland, 2 Aug. 1802. Cadet 1821. Ensign 18 Jan. 1822. Lieut. 1 May 1824. *d. unm.* Barrackpore 5 May 1826.

Son of John Hindson, of Penrith, Cumberland, and Charlotte his wife.
Services : Posted as Ensign to 19th N.I. in 1822. Transfd. to 33rd N.I. 11 July 1823 ; as Lieut. to 66th N.I. (late 2/33rd) May 1824. No record of active service.
Refs. : Will dated 23 Mar. 1826 ; proved 6 June 1828.

HINES, John (*d.* 1786). Lieutenant, Infantry. Cadet 1780. Ensign 24 Feb. 1781. Lieut. 19 Oct. 1781. *d.* Cawnpore 21 Sept. 1786.
Services : N.F.P.

HINTZ, George (*d.* 1771). Cadet, Infantry. Cadet 1770. *d.* Dinapore May 1771.
Services : N.F.P.
Note : The name appears also as Haynes and Hyndes.

HISKETH, Robert. Lieutenant. Infantry. Cadet 1770. Ensign 27 Sept. 1770. Lieut. 18 Mar. 1773. Resigned 21 Apr. 1774.
Services : N.F.P.

HISLOP, William (*d.* 1829). Lieutenant, 39th N.I. Cadet 1823. Ensign 15 Jan. 1824. Lieut. 13 May 1825. *d.* Kotah, Rajputana, 29 Aug. 1829.
Son of Sir Thomas Hislop, 1st Bart., G.C.B. (D.N.B.).
Services : Cornet 13th Light Dgns. 26 Nov. 1818. (? Lieut. 16th Light Dgns.) Served in the "Russell Cavalry" in Hyderabad, which was disbanded in 1822. Was at Madras when apptd. Cadet. Posted as Ensign to 39th N.I. Extra Asst. to Resdt. at Delhi 1825-6. Re-entered Nizam's service in 1826. Asst. to Resdt. at Delhi 1827 till death, and actg. P.A. in Haraoti.
Refs. : Burton, pp. 82-3 *n.* A.J. N.S. i. 236.

HITCHCOCK, Peter (*d.* 1770). Lieutenant, Infantry. Cadet 1768. Ensign 7 Jan. 1769. Lieut. 19 Dec. 1769. *d.* Calcutta 15 Apr. 1770.
Services : N.F.P.

HOARE, James Griffith (*d.* 1798). Bt. Captain, Infantry. Cadet 1782. Admitted 10 June 1783. Ensign 15 Jan. 1783. Lieut. 2 Feb. 1789. Bt. Capt. 7 Jan. 1796. *d.* Barrackpore 9 Aug. 1798.
Services : Ensign 3rd Bengal Eur. Bn. in July 1787. Asst. in the office of the Surveyor Gen.
Refs. : A.A.R. i. 178. Will proved in 1798. M.I. at Barrackpore.

HOARE, John (1800-1823). Lieutenant, 20th N.I. *bapt.* Derby 23 Nov. 1800. Cadet 1816. Ensign (?). Lieut. 1 Aug. 1818. *d.* Barrackpore 22 Sept. 1823.

Son of John Hoare, of Derby, farmer.
Services : Posted as Lieut. to 2/20th N.I. in 1818. No record of active service.

HOBKIRK, William (1785-?). Lieutenant. 16th N.I. · *b.* London 18 Oct. 1785. Cadet 1803. Arrived in India 3 Dec. 1804. Ensign 25 Oct. 1804. Lieut. 25 Oct. 1804. Resigned in India 2 Feb. 1808.
Son of Adam Hobkirk.
Services : Posted as Lieut. to 16th N.I. in 1805.

HODGES, Alexander (1800-1841). Captain, 29th N.I. *bapt.* Bromfield, Salop, 24 Aug. 1800. Cadet 1819. Admitted 31 July 1820. Ensign 4 Mar. 1820. Lieut. 11 Feb. 1823. Capt. 12 Oct. 1834. *d.* Lucknow 6 Sept. 1841.
Son of Rev. Thomas Hodges, of Ludlow, Salop, and Mary his wife. *m.* Everton, 9 Aug. 1838, Hessy, dau. of William Huffington, of Fayham cottage, co. Donegal.
Services : 2nd Lieut. 3rd Ceylon Regt. of Foot 15 July 1814. Ensign 2/21st N.I. Transfd. to 14th N.I. in 1823 ; to 29th N.I. (late 2/14th) May 1824. Asst. Revenue Surveyor at Saharanpur 18 Nov. 1826. Surveyor to the Comrs. of the Sundarbans, Bengal, 11 Jan. 1828 till 30 Apr. 1835. Fur. p.a. 7 Oct. 1836 till 30 Jan. 1840. Bde. Major to troops in Oudh 25 Nov. 1840. No record of active service.
Refs. : *A.J.* N.S. xxvii. 68. *G.M.* 1842, i. 115. *The Times,* 4 Dec. 1841.

HODGES, Charles Alexander Crickett (1802-?). Ensign, Infantry. Unposted. *b.* Embleton, Northumberland, 11 Nov. 1802. Cadet 1818. Ensign (?). Dismissed 9 May 1821.
Son of Rev. H. Hodges, vicar of Embleton.
Services : Ensign d.d. Bengal Eur. Regt. 1819. Dismissed in England by order of the C.D.

HODGES, Charles Wyndham (1792-1875). Lieut. Colonel. 5th L.C. *b.* Charles St., Berkeley Sq., London, 8 Oct. 1792. Cadet 1812. Arrived in India Aug. 1813. Cornet 15 Sept. 1816. Lieut. 1 Sept. 1818. Capt. 19 June 1827. Major 5 Aug. 1839. Invalided 7 July 1841. Retired 10 Mar. 1842. Hon. Lt. Col. 28 Nov. 1854. *d.* 7 Apr. 1875.
Son of either Anthony Hodges, of Hertford St., Mayfair, London, and Anna Sophia Ashton his wife (whom he afterwards divorced), or of Mr. Wyndham, by the same mother. His sister, Caroline Wyndham, was mother of Charles Wyndham Stanhope, 7th Earl of Harrington. Applied to Govt. of India in 1819 for permission to

drop the name of Hodges and to be borne in future in the *A.L.* as Charles Wyndham. This application was refused, but in 1832 he announced his intention of designating himself " Charles Wyndham." His name, however, figures regularly in the *A.L.* down to the date of his death as Charles Wyndham Hodges.

Services : Posted as Cornet to 5th N.C. in 1816. Third Mahratta War ; Cornet 5th N.C. Actg. Adjt. 5th L.C. Dec. 1820 ; actg. Intr. & Qmr. do. Jan. 1821. Second in comd. 6th Local Horse 20 Apr. 1825 till 20 Dec. 1827. Fur. p.a. 20 Feb. 1830 till 6 July 1833. Offg. Bde. Major at Cawnpore 31 Aug. till 2 Dec. 1837.

Refs. : Cons. 24 Apr. 1819. *The Times,* 23 July 1832. M.C. 22 Aug. 1832.

HODGES, Nathaniel (1783-1818). Captain, 3rd N.C. *b.* 28 Jan. 1783. Cadet 1798. Arrived in India 20 Aug. 1799. Cornet 11 June 1800. Lieut. 12 Sept. 1803. Capt. 25 May 1816. *d.* Sonara (?), 22 Oct. 1818.

bapt. St. Mary's, Rotherhithe, Surrey, 1 Mar. 1783. Son of Nathaniel Hodges and Elizabeth his wife. *m.* (?).

Services : (? Operations in Jumna Doab 1803 ; Sasni ; Bijaigarh ; Kachaura ; Cornet 3rd N.C.) Second Mahratta War ; battle of Delhi ; Laswari ; Rampura ; battle of Deig ; pursuit of Holkar ; Lieut. 3rd N.C. (? Operations against Dhundia Khan 1807 ; Komona ; Ganauri. Operations in Bundelkhand 1809 ; Rajaoli ; Ajaigarh ; Lieut. 3rd N.C.) Capt. Lt. 3rd N.C. 12 Apr. 1810. Dy. Paymr. to troops in Kumaon 3 Aug. 1815 till 1816. Siege and capture of Hathras 1817 ; Capt. 3rd N.C. Third Mahratta War ; Jawad ; Capt. 3rd N.C.

HODGES, Walter (1791-1809). Ensign, 7th N.I. *b.* Dulish, Dorset, Feb. 1791. Cadet 1806. Arrived in India 21 July 1807. Ensign 26 July 1807. *d.* at sea, 11 May 1809, on board the *Monarch,* on his passage to England.

Son of Walter Hodges, of Shipton, Dorset, and Mary his wife.

Services : Posted as Ensign to 7th N.I. in 1808. Fur. 29 Apr. 1809 till death. No record of active service.

HODGSON, Francis (*d.* 1797). Major, Infantry. Cadet 1770. Admitted 24 Aug. 1770. Ensign 19 Dec. 1772. Lieut. 18 Mar. 1777. Capt. 18 Mar. 1781. Major 1 Mar. 1794. *d.* Fatehgarh 27 Apr. 1797.

m. Calcutta, 26 Aug. 1778, Miss Maria Fellus, of Chandernagore. (She *re-m.* Robert Stair Graham, *q.v.*) Father of Francis Hodgson, *q.v.,* and of William Hodgson (1790-1828), *q.v.*

Services : Capt. 3rd Bengal Eur. Bn. in July 1787.

HODGSON, Francis (1786-1831). Captain, 35th N.I. *b.* Bengal 2 Sept. 1786. Cadet 1806. Arrived in India 25 Nov. 1807. Ensign 8 Oct. 1807. Lieut. 6 Nov. 1812. Capt. 1 May 1824. *d.* Calcutta 21 Aug. 1831.

Son of Francis Hodgson, *q.v.*, and Maria his wife. Brother of William Hodgson (1790-1828), *q.v. m.* Chitarpur, B. & O., 31 Dec. 1819, Miss Phoebe Macnamara.

Services : Barasat C.C. for 11 mos. Posted as Ensign to 17th N.I. Nepal War 1814-5 ; Jitpur ; Lieut. 2/17th N.I., in 3rd Div. Actg. Intr. & Qmr. 2/17th N.I. 1 June 1820. Adjt. 2/17th N.I. 28 Jan. 1823 ; do. 34th N.I. (late 1/17th) 17 June 1824 till 23 Mar. 1825. Transfd. to 35th N.I. Mar. 1825. Siege and capture of Bhurtpore ; Capt. 35th N.I. Leave u.p.a. 6 mos. to Calcutta 18 Sept. 1828.

Refs. : A.J. N.S. vii. 104. M.I. in Mily. cemetery at Bhowanipore, Calcutta.

HODGSON, Henry (1781-1855). Lieut. General. Colonel 12th N.I. *b.* 24 Feb. 1781. Cadet 1798. Arrived in India 6 Sept. 1799. Ensign 10 Dec. 1799. Lieut. 29 May 1800. Capt. 31 July 1810. Major 25 Aug. 1818. Lt. Col. 4 Sept. 1823. Col. 5 June 1829. Maj. Gen. 28 June 1838. Lt. Gen. 11 Nov. 1851. *d.* Passy, Paris, 8 Mar. 1855.

bapt. Congleton, co. Chester, 4 Apr. 1781. Son of Robert Hodgson and Mildred his wife. Brother of Adm. Brian Hodgson, and of Very Rev. Robert Hodgson, dean of Carlisle. Nephew of Rt. Rev. Beilby Porteous, bishop of London (*D.N.B.*). *m. c.* 1811, Emilie, eldest dau. of Jacques Grand-Jean de Fouchy, of Chandernagore. (*See also* John Oliver, Vincent Shortland, and David Williamson.) (She died Paris 1844.) Ed. Charterhouse ; scholar 7 Apr. 1793 ; left in 1798.

Services : Posted as Ensign to 2/9th N.I. Dec. 1799. Transfd. as Lieut. to 2/12th N.I. in 1802. Operations in Jumna Doab 1802-3 ; Sasni ; Bijaigarh ; Lieut. 2/12th N.I. Leave s.c. to sea Sept. 1803 ; fur. s.c. 31 May 1804 till Mar. 1808. Operations in Oudh 1808 ; Patharserai ; Lieut. 2/12th N.I. Capture of Mauritius 1810-1 ; Capt. 1st Bn. Bengal Vols. Leave s.c. 8 mos. to Mauritius and Cape 3 July 1813 ; fur. s.c. from Cape 5 Apr. 1815 till 2 June 1818. Transfd. as Lt. Col. to 1st N.I. (late 2/12th) ; to 12th N.I. 7 Dec. 1826. Leave s.c. 18 mos. to Mauritius and Cape 2 Mar. 1827. Transfd. to 33rd N.I. 24 Dec. 1827 ; to 10th N.I. 3 Apr. 1828. Lt. Col. Comdt. 51st N.I. Fur. s.c. 24 Jan. 1829 till death. Col. 12th N.I. 11 Jan. 1838.

Refs. : Burke's *Royal Families*, ped. lxii. *Boase. E.I.M.C.* i. 312-3. *Alumni Carthusiani. G.M.* 1855, i. 544.

HODGSON, James (1763/64-1825). Bt. Colonel. 5th N.I. *b.* 1763/64. Cadet 1781. Admitted 31 Mar. 1782. Ensign 2 May 1781. Lieut. 19 Aug. 1782. Capt. 29 May 1800. Major 11 July 1805. Lt. Col. 12 May 1811. Bt. Col. 19 July 1821. Retired 11 June 1822. *d.* Carlisle, 28 Mar. 1825, aged 61.

A native of Cumberland. (*Probably* brother of Richard Hodgson, *q.v.*) *m.* Cawnpore, 17 Mar. 1799, Miss Maria Theresa Hardwicke. His daus. *m.* Sir Gerald George Aylmer, 8th Bart., and the Hon. John Henry Roper-Curzon.

Services: Apptd. Cadet on 8 Dec. 1780, aged 16. Sailed for India on the *Latham* 13 Mar. 1781, aged 16. Lieut. 14th Bn. Sepoys in July 1787. Fur. 14 Jan. 1793 till 22 Feb. 1796. Lieut. 1st Bengal Eur. Regt. in 1796. Disturbances in Ganjam, Madras, 1801 ; Capt. 2/6th N.I. Second Mahratta War ; Baghelkhand 1803 ; Chaukandi ; Capt. 2/6th N.I. Fur. 17 Jan. 1808 till 14 Nov. 1810. Lt. Col. 6th N.I. Transfd. to 1/5th N.I. in 1815. Fur. 1819 till retirement.

Refs. : *G.M.* 1825, i. 573.

HODGSON, John Anthony (1777-1848). Major General. Colonel 14th N.I. *bapt.* St. Andrew's, Bishop Auckland, 4 July 1777. Cadet 1798. Arrived in India 26 Mar. 1800. Ensign 19 Jan. 1800. Lieut. 29 May 1800. Capt. 16 Dec. 1814. Major 3 Oct. 1824. Lt. Col. 11 July 1828. Col. 22 Jan. 1834. Maj. Gen. 3 Nov. 1841. *d.* Ambala 28 Mar. 1848.

Of Sheraton, co. Durham. Son of George Hodgson, of Bishop Auckland, co. Durham. *m.* Calcutta, 6 Feb. 1822, Matilda Emily Ann, widow of George Frederick Harriott, *q.v.* (She died Calcutta, 28 Nov. 1828, aged 32.) Ed. Durham.

Services : Ensign d.d. 1/4th N.I. Posted as Ensign to 2/10th N.I. Apr. 1801. Served in Ceylon 1803-5 ; Lieut. 2nd Bengal Vols. Second Mahratta War 1805-6 ; Lieut. 2/10th N.I. Surveyor Gen.'s Dept. Oct. 1813 till 1818. Transfd. to 1/10th N.I. Mar. 1821. Surveyor Gen. of India May 1821. Transfd. to 2/31st N.I. Sept. 1823. Revenue Surveyor Gen. Oct. 1823. Transfd. to 61st N.I. (late 1/31st) May 1824. Surveyor Gen. of India Mar. 1826 till Jan. 1829. Transfd. as Lt. Col. to 42nd N.I. 29 Nov. 1828. Fur. s.c. 13 Jan. 1829 till 15 Dec. 1833. Transfd. to 49th N.I. 3 Jan. 1834 ; to 68th N.I. 16 May 1834. Fur. s.c. 28 Jan. 1835 till 1 Jan. 1840 ; p.a. 4 Jan. 1841 till 13 Nov. 1844. Bdr. 20 Dec. 1844 ; to comd. at Delhi 24 Jan. 1845 ; at Ferozepore June 1846 ; at Delhi Sept. 1846 ; the Rohilkhand district Jan. 1847. Died whilst on his way to Simla on sick leave.

Refs. : Burke's *Peerage*, 1859, p. 410, *s.n.* Ford, Bart. *De Rhé-Philipe. Durham School Register.* Will dated Bareilly 13 May 1847 ; proved 8 June 1848. M.I. at Ambala.

THE BENGAL ARMY, 1758-1834

HODGSON, John Studholme (1805-1870). Major General. 12th N.I. *b.* Blake St., York, 24 Apr. 1805. Cadet 1821. Arrived in India 12 July 1822. Ensign 3 Feb. 1822. Lieut. 1 May 1824. Capt. 21 June 1834. Major 28 Aug. 1853. Lt. Col. 25 Apr. 1858. Bt. Col. 28 Nov. 1854. Maj. Gen. 25 July 1861. *d.* Stanhope Terr., Hyde Pk., London, 14 Jan. 1870.

2nd son of Gen. John Hodgson, Col. 4th King's Own Regt. (*D.N.B.*), and Catherine Krempion, of Petrograd, his wife.

Services : See *D.N.B.* Posted as Ensign to 12th N.I. Actg. Adjt. 12th N.I. 26 Oct. 1824. Actg. Adjt. Mhairwara Local Bn. 25 Nov. 1828. Fur. s.c. 12 Mar. 1838 till 7 Oct. 1842. First Sikh War ; Sobraon (w.) ; Capt. 12th N.I. (Medal). Raised 1st Regt. of Sikh Local Inf. 14 Dec. 1846. Second Sikh War ; Capt. comdg. 1st Sikh Local Inf. (Medal). Bdr. Punjab Irreg. Force 23 Nov. 1850 till July 1854. Comdd. a force against the Hassanzais and Shiranis Mar. 1853 (Medal). Lt. Col. 12th N.I. Fur. s.c. 16 Jan. 1855. Posted as Col. to 12th N.I. 24 July 1858. Pub. in 1857, " Opinions on the Indian Army."

Refs. : *D.N.B.* *D.I.B.* *Boase.* *I.M.* No. 15, p. 451. *The Times*, 18 Jan. 1870.

HODGSON, Richard (1760-1830). Major. 11th N.I. *b.* 1760. Cadet 1781. Admitted 31 Mar. 1782. Ensign 8 July 1781. Lieut. 9 Oct. 1782. Capt. 29 May 1800. Major 17 Aug. 1808. Retired 31 Aug. 1810. *d.* Moorhouse Hall, nr. Carlisle, 21 May 1830, aged 70.

Of Moorhouse Hall. J. P. Cumberland. (*Probably* brother of James Hodgson, *q.v.*) *m.* Brampton, Cumberland, Dec. 1809, ——, only dau. of John Hetherington, of Intack, Cumberland. His dau. *m.* David Ewart, *q.v.*

Services : Apptd. Cadet on 6 Dec. 1780, aged 20. Sailed for India on the *Latham*, 13 Mar. 1781, aged 20. On the voyage out the *Latham* was in action against the French fleet under Suffren in Porto Praya bay 16 Apr. 1781. On arrival at Bombay on 31 Mar. 1782 was posted as Ensign to 7th Bn., and served during the latter part of the First Mahratta War under Goddard. Transfd. to 29th Bn. Capt. 5th N.I. in June 1798. Capt. Lt. 1/11th N.I. 21 Apr. 1800. Operations in Jumna Doab 1803 ; Sasni ; Bijaigarh ; Kachaura ; Capt. comdg. Lord Lake's escort, consisting of 1 Troop 3rd N.C. and 4 Coys. Grens. Apptd. to raise and comd. Cawnpore Provl. Bn. in 1803. Fur. 18 Feb. 1808 till retirement.

Refs. : *E.I.M.C.* ii. 232-8. *M.M.* 1809, p. 536. *G.M.* 1810, i. 280. *A.J.* N.S. ii. 185.

HODGSON, William (*d.* 1772). Cadet, Infantry. Cadet 1771. bur. Calcutta 14 Nov. 1772.
Services : N.F.P.
Refs. : Calcutta burial register.
Note : The christian name appears as Henry in *Dodwell & Miles.*

HODGSON, William (1790-1828). Captain, Invalid Est. 26th N.I. *b.* Bengal 7 Mar. 1790. Cadet 1806. Arrived in India 15 May 1808. Ensign 22 Feb. 1808. Lieut. 29 Sept. 1811. Capt. 11 Oct. 1824. Invalided 11 July 1828. *d.* Lucknow 25 Oct. 1828. *bapt.* Cawnpore 19 Sept. 1791. Son of Francis Hodgson, *q.v.,* and Maria his wife. Brother of Francis Hodgson, *q.v. m.* St. John's, Calcutta, 21 Oct. 1820, Anne M., dau. of Col. Johan Frederick Meiselback. (*See also* George Byron.) (She died 3 Aug. 1828, aged 28.) His dau. *m.* Peter William Luard, *q.v.*
Services : Ensign d.d. 9th N.I. 1810. Posted as Lieut. to 1/13th N.I. in 1811. Bareilly insurrection 1816 ; Lieut. 1/13th N.I. (? Third Mahratta War ; Asirgarh ; Lieut. 2/13th N.I.) Adjt. 2/13th N.I. 22 June 1821 ; Intr. & Qmr. do. 1822-4. Transfd. to 26th N.I. (late 1/13th) May 1824. Intr. & Qmr. 26th N.I. 17 June 1824 till 1825. (? First Burma War ; Arakan 1825 ; Capt. 26th N.I.)
Refs. : A.J. xxvii. 622.

HODGSON, William Edward John (1805-1838). Bt. Captain, Artillery. *b.* Prestbury, co. Chester, 17 Dec. 1805. Cadet 1822. Arrived in India 16 May 1824. 2nd Lieut. 6 June 1823. Lieut. 28 Sept. 1827. Bt. Capt. 6 June 1838. *d.* Mhow 12 June 1838.
2nd son of Brian Hodgson, of Colchester, and Catherine his wife, dau. of William Houghton, of Manchester and Newton Park, Lancs. Brother of Brian Houghton Hodgson, B.C.S. (*D.N.B.*). *m.* Dinapore, 14 July 1835, Mary Rose, only dau. of Samuel Tickell, *q.v.,* and sister of Samuel Richard Tickell, *q.v.* (She re-*m.* 1 Jan. 1840, Lumsden Strange, M.C.S.) Addiscombe Cadet 1820-3.
Services : Siege and capture of Bhurtpore ; 2nd Lieut. 2nd Troop 1st Bde. H.A. The greater part of his service was with H.A.
Refs. : Life of Brian Houghton Hodgson, by Sir W. W. Hunter. *A.J.* N.S. xxvii. 208. M.I. at Mhow.

HOGAN, John (*d.* 1767). Cadet, Infantry. Cadet 1765. *d.* 1767.
Services : N.F.P.

HOGAN, Thomas (*d.* 1793). Captain, Infantry. Cadet 1769. Ensign 15 Feb. 1770. Lieut. 6 Feb. 1773. Capt. 23 Nov. 1780. *d.* Buxar 20 Mar. 1793.

Services : Lieut. 1/3rd Bengal Eur. Regt. in Oct. 1779. Campaign against the Rajah of Benares ; outbreak of the insurrection at Benares on 21 Aug. 1781 ; A.D.C. to Warren Hastings. 6th Bengal Eur. Bn. in July 1787.

HOGARD, Thomas (*d.* 1794 ?). Lieutenant. Infantry. Cadet (?). Ensign (?). Lieut. 1775. Dismissed Aug. 1775. (? *d.* Deeping St. James, Lincs., 31 May 1794.)
Services : N.F.P.
Refs. : (? *G.M.* 1794, i. 578.)

HOGARTH, John (1787-1819). Lieutenant, 2nd N.I. *bapt.* Berwick-on-Tweed 20 Jan. 1787. Cadet 1807. Admitted 19 Aug. 1808. Ensign 16 Sept. 1808. Lieut. 1 Nov. 1814. *d.* Colombo, Ceylon, 23 Apr. 1819.
3rd son of James Hogarth.
Services : Posted as Ensign to 2nd N.I. in 1809. Lieut. 1/2nd N.I. Served with 2nd Ceylon Vol. Bn. 1818 till death.
Refs : *S.M.* 1819, ii. 581.

HOGG, Metcalf Stanwix (1790-1824). Captain, Invalid Est. Bengal Eur. Regt. *b.* Southwark, Surrey, 27 Jan. 1790. Cadet 1804. Arrived in India 1 Mar. 1806. Ensign 1 May 1806. Lieut. 11 Apr. 1807. Capt. 11 July 1823. Invalided 1 Jan. 1824. *d.* Nagpur 27 Oct. 1824.
bapt. St. John's, Southwark, 16 May 1790. Son of Jonah Hogg and Mary his wife, née Simpson, grand-niece of Gen. John Stanwix (*D.N.B.*). Uncle of Robert William Hogg, *q.v. m.* Berhampore, 10 Nov. 1819, Mary Anne, dau. of John Borthwick Gilchrist, LL.D., professor of Oriental languages in the Coll. of Fort William (*D.N.B.*), and widow of Charles Burton, *q.v.* (She died Calcutta, 20 June 1828, aged 35.)
Services : Posted to Bengal Eur. Regt. in 1807, and served throughout with that Corps. Actg. Adjt. & Qmr. to the detachment at Dinapore 1810-2 ; do. to the detachment in Java 1812-4. Qmr. 4 Nov. 1816 till 1823.
Refs : Family information.

HOGG, Robert William (1807-1840). Captain, 8th L.C. *bapt.* Dinapore 22 Dec. 1807. Cadet 1823. Arrived in India 25 June 1824. Cornet 14 Jan. 1824. Lieut. 13 May 1825. Capt. 24 July 1838. *d.* Cawnpore 8 Nov. 1840.
Son of Jonah John Hogg, of Calcutta, merchant, formerly Surgeon Bengal Est., and Ann his wife, née Bishop. Nephew of Metcalf Stanwix Hogg, *q.v.* His sister *m.* Thomas Moore, *q.v.*

Services : Posted as Cornet to 8th L.C. Siege and capture of Bhurtpore ; Lieut. 8th L.C. Actg. Intr. & Qmr. 8th L.C. 2 Mar. 1827 ; permanent do. 25 July 1827 till 14 Apr. 1829.
Refs. : Family information.

HOGG, Roger (*d.* 1776). Captain. Infantry. Capt. 15 Nov. 1768. Resigned 30 Nov. 1775. *d.* St. Helena, Mar. 1776, on his passage to England : bur. there 27 Mar. 1776.
Services : Probably transfd. as Capt. from H.M.S. N.F.P.
Refs. : S.M. 1776, p. 566.

HOGGAN, George. Captain. Infantry. Cadet (?). Ensign 10 Aug. 1765. Lieut. 20 Dec. 1766. Capt. 1769. Resigned 19 Aug. 1769.
Services : Apptd. Qmr. 1st Bengal Eur. Regt. in Aug. 1765.
Refs. : Broome, p. 537.

HOGGAN, John (1789-1861). Major General, C.B. Colonel 45th N.I. *b.* 29 May 1789. Cadet 1807. Arrived in India 14 Aug. 1808. Ensign 13 Sept. 1808. Lieut. 16 Dec. 1814. Capt. 1 May 1824. Major 8 Oct. 1836. Lt. Col. 22 Dec. 1842. Col. 14 July 1853. Maj. Gen. 28 Nov. 1854. *d.* Mussoorie, U.P., 13 Nov. 1861.

Of Hampton House, Mussoorie ; formerly of Stranfasket, co. Galloway. 4th son of Major George Hoggan, of Waterside, Keir, co. Dumfries. Brother of William Hoggan, *q.v. m.* 1st, Bareilly, 12 Oct. 1816, Frances Kennaway, eldest dau. of Rev. Robert Palk Welland, rector of Shillingford, Devon, and niece of Sir John Kennaway, Bart., *q.v.* His dau. *m.* Richard Sheridan Ewart, *q.v. m.* 2nd, Aligarh, 14 Apr. 1832, Jane, dau. of Samuel Long (*probably* sister of Richard Long, *q.v.*). His sister *m.* George Anderson Vetch, *q.v.*

Services : "First served in the English Army at home." Barasat C.C. for 13 mos. Posted as Ensign to 27th N.I. Nepal War 1814-5 ; Lieut. Eur. Flank Bn. (India medal). Insurrection at Bareilly 1816 ; Lieut. 2/27th N.I. Third Mahratta War. Intr. & Qmr. 2/27th N.I. 18 Mar. 1817 till 1822. Fort Adjt. at Delhi 1822. Adjt. Native Invalids, and Paymr. Native pensioners at Meerut and Hapur, 28 Oct. 1822 till 13 Feb. 1837. Transfd. to 53rd N.I. (late 1/27th) May 1824. Tempy. comdg. 5th Bde., Army of the Indus, 24 Nov. 1838. First Afghan War 1842 ; comdd. 53rd N.I. on retreat from Ali Masjid to Jamrud ; operations of Gen. Pollock's force ; forcing of Khyber ; comdd. rearguard of Bdr. Wild's force on march through Khyber to Ali Masjid Nov. 1842 (Medal). Posted as Lt.

THE BENGAL ARMY, 1758-1834

Col. to 53rd N.I. 14 Feb. 1843 ; to 45th N.I. 26 Nov. 1847. Second Sikh War ; Ramnagar ; Sadulapur ; Chilianwala ; Gujerat ; Lt. Col. 45th N.I., comdg. 8th Inf. Bde. (Medal with clasp). Posted as Col. to 45th N.I. Sept. 1853. Bdr., 2 cl.,.comdg. Lucknow 15 Nov. 1853 ; comdg. Ferozepore Feb. 1855 till 1856. C.B. 9 June 1849.
Refs. : Boase. *G.M.* 1862, i. 237. *The Times,* 14 Jan. 1862.

HOGGAN, William (1799-1860). Lieut. Colonel. 63rd N.I. *b.* Waterside, co. Dumfries, 12 Mar. 1799. Cadet 1819. Admitted 9 Oct. 1820. Ensign 17 Apr. 1820. Lieut. 12 Sept. 1822. Capt. 5 Apr. 1834. Major 19 June 1846. Invalided 1 Oct. 1848. Retired 8 July 1853. Hon. Lt. Col. 28 Nov. 1854. *d.* 21 Mar. 1860.

Youngest son of Major George Hoggan, of Waterside. Brother of John Hoggan, *q.v.*

Services : Ensign 1/13th N.I. Transfd. to newly-raised 32nd N.I. 11 July 1823 ; to 63rd N.I. (late 1/32nd) May 1824. Actg. Adjt. Rt. Wing 63rd N.I. 28 Dec. 1825. Siege and capture of Bhurtpore ; Lieut. 63rd N.I. (India medal). Adjt. Ramgarh Bn. 8 Mar. 1830 till 1835. Operations against the Kols 1832 ; against the Chuars 1834-5. First Sikh War ; Ferozshahr ; Sobraon ; Capt. 63rd N.I. (Medal with clasp). Fur. 8 Jan. 1851 till retirement.

HOGGE, Charles (1813-1865). Colonel, C.B., Artillery. *b.* Southacre, Norfolk, 7 Dec. 1813. Cadet 1829. Arrived in India 30 May 1830. 2nd Lieut. 11 Dec. 1829. Lieut. 1 Dec. 1838. Capt. 1 Jan. 1848. Bt. Major 7 June 1849. Lt. Col. 27 Sept. 1858. Col. 20 Feb. 1863. *d.* Erith, Kent, 18 Sept. 1865.

Son of Rev. Martin Hogge, rector of Southacre, afterwards rector of West Winch, and Elizabeth his wife. *m.* Emma Marianne Birch. (She died 1 June 1889.) Addiscombe Cadet 1828-9.

Services : Cadet d.d. H.A. at Meerut 7 Jan. 1832. Actg. 2nd Lieut. 16 July 1832. Posted to 1st Bde. H.A. 15 Sept. 1832 ; to 1st Troop 3rd Bde. 8 Nov. 1834 ; to 2nd Troop 1st Bde. 29 June 1836. Actg. Adjt. & Qmr. Mewar Div. Art. 9 Dec. 1838. Intr. & Qmr. 7th Bn. Foot Art. 10 July 1840. Fur. s.c. 12 Aug. 1843 till Sept. 1845. Dy. Comy. Ord. at Ferozepore 21 Aug. 1846. Second Sikh War ; passage of Chenab ; Chilianwala ; Gujerat ; Comy. of Ord. (Medal with 2 clasps). Dy. comy. of Ord. at Peshawar 1849 ; do. at Dum-Dum 21 Dec. 1850. Comy. of Ord., 2 cl., 22 Apr. 1853. Director of Art. Depot of Instruction 1854-60. Mutiny campaign ; Delhi ; relief of Lucknow ; Director of Ord. (Medal with 2 clasps). Member of the Ordnance Select Committee at Woolwich. C.B. 18 June 1858.

Refs. : Boase. *G.M.* 1865, ii. 655. *The Times,* 23 Sept. 1865.

HOHNEY (*recte* **HÖHNE**), Christian (1808-1844). Cadet, Infantry. Subsequently an indigo planter. *b.* Cape Town 8 Apr. 1808. Cadet 1825. *Probably* never joined the Service. *d.* Chowringhee, Calcutta, 24 Feb. 1844, of cholera.
Son of Christian Gottlob Höhne, of the Cape of Good Hope. *m.* Calcutta, 4 Jan. 1841, Emma Louisa, dau. of William Bensley Walker, *q.v.*
Refs. : *I.M.* No. 13, p. 401. Will dated 15 Mar. 1843 ; proved 1 Mar. 1844. M.I. in Circular Rd. cemetery, Calcutta.

HOLBROW, John (1790-1849). Colonel, 30th N.I. *b.* 15 Nov. 1790. Cadet 1805. Arrived in India 11 July 1806. Ensign 1 Sept. 1806. Lieut. 4 Sept. 1808. Capt. 27 May 1820. Major 25 June 1826. Lt. Col. 23 Aug. 1831. Col. 3 Nov. 1843. *d.* Kent 16 July 1849.
bapt. Stonehouse, Devon, 29 Nov. 1790. Son of Samuel Holbrow and Sarah his wife. *m.* 1st, Meerut, 14 Sept. 1812, Charlotte Eliza Preston, dau. of John Jenkins Bird, *q.v.* (*See also* Aynott Chitty.) His dau. *m.* Philip Goldney, *q.v.* *m.* 2nd, Monmouth, 27 Nov. 1842, Mary Anne, eldest dau. of C. Hough, of Monmouth, and niece of Rev. George Hough, senior chaplain, C.G.H.
Services : Barasat C.C. 9½ mos. Posted as Ensign to 1st N.I. (? Operations in Bundelkhand 1809 ; Rajaoli ; Ajaigarh ; Lieut. 2/1st N.I.) Nepal War 1814-5 ; Lieut. 2/1st N.I., in 1st Div. Siege and capture of Hathras ; Lieut. 2/1st N.I. Third Mahratta War ; Lieut. 1st N.I. Capt. 1/1st N.I. A.D.C. to Maj.-Gen. Gabriel Martindell, *q.v.*, 1820-1. Transfd. to 4th N.I. (late 2/1st) May 1824. (? Operations against the Bhils 1824.) Posted as Lt. Col. to 4th N.I. 11 June 1832 ; to 44th N.I. 15 Aug. 1834. Comdd. 44th N.I. when engaged in expulsion of marauders from Jhabua, Malwa, C.I., Mar. 1836. Transfd. to 1st N.I. 9 Dec. 1840 ; to 46th N.I. Fur. s.c. 12 Feb. 1842 till death. Posted as Col. to 30th N.I. 15 Jan. 1844.
Refs. : *A.J.* N.S. xl. 99.

HOLCROFT, James. (*See* **HALDCRAFT.**)

*****HOLLAND, Dennis.** Fireworker. Artillery. Cadet (?). Fireworker 12 Aug. 1763.
Services : N.F.P.
Refs. : *Stubbs's List.*

HOLLAND, George Freer (1788-1857). Lieut. Colonel. 3rd N.I. *bapt.* Birmingham 4 Aug. 1788. Cadet 1805. Arrived in India 13 Dec. 1806. Ensign 21 Dec. 1806. Lieut. 27 Nov. 1811. Capt. 1 May 1824. Major 10 Jan. 1837. Retired 25 Jan. 1837. Hon. Lt. Col. 28 Nov. 1854. *d.* Southsea, 16 Dec. 1857, aged 72.

Son of Thomas Holland and Margaret his wife. *m.* Meerut, 18 Jan. 1819, Eliza, dau. of William George Maxwell, *q.v.* (*See also* Charles Henry Boisragon.)

Services : Posted as Ensign to 6th N.I. Served with Pioneers 1814-16. Nepal War 1814-5 ; Lieut. 1/6th N.I., 5th Coy. Pioneers, in 2nd Div. (India medal). On service in Merwara ; action on 1 Jan. 1821 (*Lond. Gaz.* 24 Mar. 1823) ; Lieut. 2/6th N.I. (? Operations in Kotah 1821 ; Mangrol.) Actg. Adjt. 2/6th N.I. 17 Apr. 1823. Transfd. to 3rd N.I. (late 1/6th) May 1824. First Burma War ; Arakan 1825 ; Capt. 2nd Gren. Bn. (clasp to India medal). To do duty with 29th N.I. 26 Oct. 1828.

Refs. : G.M. 1858, i. 118.

HOLLAND, Thomas (1762/63-1804). Colonel, Artillery. *b.* 1762/63. Cadet 1777. Admitted 12 July 1777. Fireworker 28 Sept. 1777. Lieut. 27 Sept. 1778. Capt. Lt. 4 July 1784. Capt. 28 May 1786. Major 25 Apr. 1797. Lt. Col. 1 July 1801. Col. 26 July 1804. *d.* at his residence, Axford Bldgs., Bath, 11 Nov. 1804, aged 41.

A native of Essex. *m.* Calcutta, 16 Nov. 1793, Miss Anne Frances Clarke. His grand-dau. *m.* Crawford Crossman, *q.v.*

Services : Sailed for India on the *Egmont,* 1 Jan 1777, when he gave his age as 15. Second Mysore War 1781-5 ; Lieut. 4th Coy. 2nd Bn. Art. Fur. 20 Mar. 1785 till 12 July 1787, and 30 Sept. 1802 till death.

Refs. : Bath Chron. 27 Nov. 1804.

HOLLINGBURY or HOLLINGBERRY, John (*d.* 1782). Fireworker, Artillery. Cadet 1778. Fireworker 6 Nov. 1778. *d.* Madras 1782.

m. (?).

Services : Second Mysore War 1781-2.

HOLLINGS, George Edward (1811-1857). Bt. Major, 38th N.I. *b.* Calcutta 24 July 1811. Cadet 1826. Arrived in India 24 Dec. 1827. Ensign 4 Aug. 1827. Lieut. 1 June 1832. Capt. 8 Oct. 1843. Bt. Major 20 June 1854. *d.* Landour, U.P., 9 May 1857.

Son of William C. Hollings, of Calcutta, merchant and agent, and Sophia his wife, niece of Anne, wife of Christopher Green, *q.v.* (and *probably* dau. of Lawrence Gall, *q.v.*). Brother of Henry Hollings, *q.v. m.* Calcutta, 3 Sept. 1832, Harriet Mary, youngest dau. of Hugh Augustus Boscawen (*d.* 1820), *q.v.*

Services : Ensign d.d. 51st N.I. Posted as Ensign to 5th Extra Regt. (became 73rd N.I. in 1828) 20 Feb. 1828. Transfd. to 51st N.I. 8 Jan. 1829 ; to 38th N.I. 17 Jan. 1831. Actg. Intr. & Qmr. 38th N.I. 20 June 1832 ; permanent do. 21 May 1833 till 15 Jan.

468   LIST OF THE OFFICERS OF

1838. Apptd. to 2nd Inf., Oudh Auxy. Force (became 2nd Oudh Local Inf.), Jan. 1838 ; 2nd in comd. do. 17 Jan. 1840 till 21 Sept. 1842. Asst. to Resdt. at Lucknow Sept. 1840. Asst. to Supt. of operations for suppression of *thagi* Dec. 1842 till 1846. Supt. Oudh Frontier Police Feb. 1846. D.C. at Leiah Apr. 1849 ; at Shahpur Dec. 1852 till May 1856. Rejoined 38th N.I. in 1856. Author of " Some Remarks on the Proposed Articles of War for the Indian Armies . . .," 1845 ; reprinted from the *Calcutta Courier*.

Refs. : De Rhé-Philipe. M.I. at Kasauli.

HOLLINGS, Henry (1812-1847). Captain, 66th N.I. *b.* Calcutta 3 Sept. 1812. Cadet 1828. Arrived in India 27 Aug. 1829. Ensign 5 June 1829. Lieut. 23 July 1832. Capt. 16 May 1844. *d.* Lucknow 23 Feb. 1847.

Son of William C. Hollings, of Calcutta, merchant, and Sophia his wife. Brother of William Charles Hollings, *q.v.* His sister *m.* Hugh Augustus Boscawen (1805-1881), *q.v. m.* Calcutta, 29 Sept. 1842, Fanny Louisa, dau. of Arthur John Fraser. (She died 12 Aug. 1860.)

Services : Ensign d.d. 51st N.I. 19 Sept. 1829. Posted as Ensign to 66th N.I. 26 June 1830. Offg. Intr. & Qmr. 3rd L.C. 14 July 1834 ; do. 25th N.I. 7 Feb. 1835 ; do. 1st N.I. 21 Mar. 1838. Intr. & Qmr. 66th N.I. 2 Mar. 1841 till Aug. 1844. Junior Asst. to Comr. in Arakan 19 Sept. 1843 till 1844. No record of active service.

Refs. : G.M. 1847, ii. 558. M.I. in S. Park St. cemetery, Calcutta.

HOLLINGS, William Charles (1810-?). Captain. 47th N.I. *b.* Calcutta 27 Mar. 1810. Cadet 1825. Arrived in India 23 Oct. 1826. Ensign 23 May 1826. Lieut. 16 Feb. 1835. Capt. 22 Dec. 1845. Cashiered Mar. 1850.

Son of William C. Hollings, of Calcutta, merchant, and Sophia his wife. Brother of George Edward Hollings, *q.v.*

Services : Posted as Ensign to 53rd N.I. 9 Nov. 1826. Transfd. to 51st N.I. in 1827. Offg. Intr. & Qmr. 38th N.I. 7 Feb. 1831 ; do. 63rd N.I. 7 June 1831 ; do. 47th N.I. 24 Sept. 1831. Transfd. to 47th N.I. 30 May 1832. Intr. & Qmr. 47th N.I. 5 July 1832 till 21 Feb. 1839. Actg. Adjt. 1st Inf., Oudh Auxy. Force, 27 Jan. till 23 Mar. 1839. Asst. to Gen. Supt. for suppression of *thagi* 18 Jan. 1840 till 28 Apr. 1843. Offg. Intr. & Qmr. 63rd N.I. Apr. 1845. No record of active service.

Refs. : I.M. 1850, p. 256.

HOLLINS, Edward (1788-1808). Ensign, Infantry. Unposted. *b.* Nottingham 16 July 1788. Cadet 1805. Arrived in India 11 July 1806. Ensign 29 July 1806. *d.* Barasat C.C. 18 Jan. 1808.

Son of Henry Hollins, a member of the High Pavement Society of Nottingham.[1]
Services : His death occurred whilst he was still under instruction as an unposted Ensign at the Barasat C.C.

[1] *Note* : A community of Dissenters.

HOLLOND, Richard (1742-1763). Lieutenant, Bengal Eur. Regt. *b.* Madras 1742. Cadet 1760. Ensign 5 Feb. 1760. Lieut. 11 Dec. 1761. *d. unm.* 5th, 6th or 11th Oct. 1763 : massacred at or near Patna by order of Nawab Mir Muhammad Kasim. (See note to John Gordon*.)
Eldest son of Major John Hollond, formerly Madras, later Bengal Est., and Sophia his wife, dau. of Randall Fowke, M.C.S., and sister of Edward Fowke, of Hawley, Kent.
Services : Sailed for India on the *Suffolk* in 1758, aged 16.
Refs. : Burke's *Landed Gentry*, 13th edn., p. 913, *s.n.* Hollond, of Benhall Lodge, Suffolk. *Love*, ii. 352, 384. *Broome*, p. 365. *Innes*, p. 169. *Firminger*, p. 71.

HOLLOWAY, George (1810-1832). Ensign, 44th N.I. *b.* Kingston-on-Thames, Surrey, 16 May 1810. Cadet 1825. Arrived in India 26 Oct. 1826. Ensign 23 May 1826. *d.* Bareilly 7 Oct. 1832.
Son of Charles Holloway. Nephew of Lady Popham, wife of Adm. Sir Home Riggs Popham, K.C.B. (*D.N.B.*).
Services : Posted as Ensign to 69th N.I. 9 Nov. 1826. Exchanged to 44th N.I. 25 Nov. 1826. No record of active service.
Refs. : *A.J.* N.S. x. 157.

HOLMES, Edward (*d.* 1770). Ensign, Infantry. Cadet 1769. Ensign 1769. *d.* Monghyr 18 Aug. 1770.
Services : N.F.P.

HOLMES, Griffiths (1788-1850). Lieut. Colonel, C.B., 56th N.I. *b.* London 2 Jan. 1788. Cadet 1808. Arrived in India 19 July 1809. Ensign 30 Aug. 1809. Lieut. 16 Dec. 1814. Capt. 13 May 1825. Major 14 June 1842. Lt. Col. 21 Nov. 1848. *d.* Kalka 1 Mar. 1850.
Son of Thomas Holmes. *m.* Coolbereah, Bengal, 24 June 1818, Margaret Haldane, dau. of Dr. James Robertson, Suptg. Surg. Bengal Est. His dau. *m.* Stephen Moody, *q.v.*
Services : Barasat C.C. for 3½ mos. Posted as Ensign to 2/4th N.I. 11 Nov. 1809. Nepal War 1816 ; Lieut. 2/4th N.I., in 4th Bde., Centre Column. Third Mahratta War ; Rewah and Sambalpur frontier ; Lieut. 2/4th N.I. Leave s.c. 6 mos. to sea 24 Feb. 1818.

Transfd. to 7th N.I. (late 1/4th) May 1824. Adjt. 7th N.I. 17 June 1824 till 29 July 1825. First Burma War 1824-5 ; Sylhet frontier ; Lieut. 7th N.I. Fur. s.c. 9 Jan. 1831 till 28 Dec. 1833. Offg. Bde. Major at Cawnpore 25 Nov. 1837 till 2 Feb. 1838. Comdd. 7th N.I. Mar. 1843 till 23 Jan. 1849. Posted as Lt. Col. to 56th N.I. 23 Jan. 1849. Second Sikh War ; Gujerat ; pursuit of Sikhs and Afghans to Peshawar ; Lt. Col. comdg. 56th N.I. (Medal with clasp). Died whilst in comd. of escort to G.G.'s camp proceeding from Lahore to Kalka. C.B. 9 June 1849.

Refs. : De Rhé-Philipe. Will dated Nimach 15 Mar. 1843 ; proved 16 Sept. 1851. M.I. at Kasauli.

HOLMES, Henry (1784-1808). Lieutenant, 24th N.I. *bapt.* Edmonton, Middlesex, 28 Mar. 1784. Cadet 1803. Arrived in India 3 Dec. 1804. Ensign 14 Nov. 1804. Lieut. 14 Nov. 1804. *d.* in England 8 Oct. 1808.

Son of Joseph Holmes.

Services : Posted as Lieut. to newly-raised 24th N.I. in 1805. Fur. 24 Feb. 1807 till death.

HOLMES, John Addison (1786-1819). Bt. Captain, 13th N.I. *b.* Thirsk, Yorks., 22 Mar. 1786. Cadet 1804. Arrived in India 13 May 1806. Ensign 26 Apr. 1806. Lieut. 16 Mar. 1808. Bt. Capt. 1 Jan. 1819. *d.* Saugor 25 June 1819.

Son of Rev. Jonathan Holmes and Mary Addison his wife.

Services : Posted as Ensign to 13th N.I. in 1807. Actg. Adjt. 2/13th N.I. 1816 till death. Third Mahratta War ; Asirgarh ; Bt. Capt. 2/13th N.I.

HOLMES, Joseph (1798/99-1836). Captain, 23rd N.I. *b.* 1798/99. Cadet 1818. Was already in India when apptd. Cadet. Ensign 7 July 1819. Lieut. 1 Sept. 1822. Capt. 17 Dec. 1832. *d.* 10 Grafton St., London, 23 Feb. 1836.

(*Probably* brother of Griffiths Holmes, *q.v.*).

Services : Apptd. by Lord Hastings, the G.G., a Local Ensign d.d. 1st Rampura Bn. in Aug. 1818. Apptd. Cadet on 23 June 1819, aged 20. Posted as Ensign to 1/4th N.I. Transfd. to 23rd N.I. (late 2/4th) May 1824. Actg. Adjt. Rt. Wing 23rd N.I. 1 Aug. 1825. Siege and capture of Bhurtpore ; Lieut. 23rd N.I. Adjt. 23rd N.I. 29 May 1826 till 27 Jan. 1833. Fur. s.c. 28 Jan. 1835 till death.

Refs. : A.J. N.S. xix. 232.

HOLMES, William Burvill (1805-1846). Captain, 12th N.I. *bapt.* Dover 3 Mar. 1805. Cadet 1824. Arrived in India 29 June 1825. Ensign 8 Jan. 1825. Lieut. 12 Sept. 1825. Capt. 10 Apr. 1843.

THE BENGAL ARMY, 1758-1834   471

d. Ferozepore, 23 Feb. 1846, of wounds received at the battle of Ferozshahr on 21 Dec. 1845.

Son of James Holmes, of Dover, shipowner. *m.* Elizabeth Allen. (She died Lucknow 12 May 1842.) Brother-in-law of William Malston Cavell.

Services : Posted as Ensign to 12th N.I. 23 July 1825, and remained with that Corps throughout his service. Offg. Adjt. for short periods in 1829, 1831, and 1832. Fur. s.c. 16 July 1837 till 16 July 1840. Offg. Adjt. 11 Dec. 1840 till Mar. 1842, and July-Aug. 1842. Leave s.c. to Mussoorie Feb. 1844 till Nov. 1845. First Sikh War ; Ferozshahr (s.w.) ; Capt. 12th N.I. (Medal).

Refs. : *De Rhé-Philipe.* Will dated 24 Jan. 1840 ; proved 2 June 1846. M.I. St. Paul's cathedral, Calcutta, and St. Andrew's, Ferozepore.

HOLROYD, George Chaplin (1790-1871). Bt. Captain. 57th N.I. *b.* London 9 Sept. 1790. Cadet 1809. Arrived in India 3 Oct. 1810. Ensign 2 Dec. 1811. Lieut. 5 Sept. 1815. Bt. Capt. 2 Dec. 1826. Retired 18 July 1828. *d.* Southernhay, Exeter, 25 Nov. 1871.

Eldest son of Sir George Sowley Holroyd, Kt., one of the justices of the Court of King's Bench (*D.N.B.*), and Sarah his wife, dau. of Amos Chaplin. *m.* 1st, Hyderabad, 2 Apr. 1818, Virginie, dau. of Gen. Mottet de la Fontaine, govr. of Pondicherry. (She died 1 Aug. 1845.) *m.* 2nd, 14 Aug. 1848, Fanny, dau. of Rev. Edward Harington, of I. of Mona. (She died 25 Mar. 1874.) Ed. Harrow ; admitted 1803, left 1808/9. Trin. Coll., Camb.

Services : On the voyage out to India on board the *Astell*, was in action, together with the *Windham* and *Ceylon*, against two large French frigates and a corvette on 3 July 1810. During this action, in which he was wounded, he comdd. two guns on the gun-deck, and was reported by the Capt. as having particularly distinguished himself. Posted as Ensign to 13th N.I. in 1812. Served with the escort to the Resdt. at Hyderabad 1813-25 ; Comdt. from 25 Nov. 1817. Transfd. to newly-raised 2/29th N.I. in 1815 ; to 57th N.I. (late 1/29th) May 1824. Fur. 1825 till retirement.

Refs. : Burke's *Colonial Gentry*, i. 26. *Harrow School Register. The Times*, 29 Nov. 1871.

HOLT, Thomas (1782-1805). Lieutenant, 26th N.I. *bapt.* St. Anne's, Manchester, 28 June 1782. Cadet 1799. Arrived in India 9 Dec. 1800. Ensign 7 Nov. 1800. Lieut. 13 July 1803. *d.* Hautgong (? nr Benares) 16 July 1805.

Son of John Holt and Anne his wife.

Services : Ensign 19th N.I. Transfd. to newly-raised 26th N.I. in 1805. No record of active service.

HOLWELL, John W——. Fireworker. Artillery. Cadet (?). Fireworker 9 Jan. 1764. Resigned 2 Feb. 1764.
Services : N.F.P.

HOLYOAKE, John (1794-1833). Captain, 18th N.I. *b.* Aston Cantlow, co. Warwick, 9 Apr. 1794. Cadet 1809. Admitted 17 Nov. 1810. Ensign 7 May 1812. Lieut. 16 Dec. 1814. Capt. 25 Dec. 1827. *d. unm.* Betul, C.P., 12 Sept. 1833.
Son of Francis Edward Holyoake, of Morton Bagot, co. Warwick, farmer. Brother of Francis Holyoake, of Hollowfield, Hanbury, Worcs., and of Thomas Holyoake, of Morton, co. Warwick. Nephew of Rev. Henry Holyoake, vicar of Bedford.
Services : Cadet d.d. 9th N.I. Posted as Ensign to 6th N.I. Nepal War 1814-5 ; Lieut. 2/6th N.I., in 1st Div. Operations in Kotah 1821 ; Mangrol ; Lieut. 2/6th N.I. Transfd. to 18th N.I. (late 2/6th) May 1824. Actg. Intr. & Qmr. 18th N.I. 18 Aug. 1824. Siege and capture of Bhurtpore ; Lieut. 18th N.I. Apptd. Station Staff Ofr. at Bhurtpore 20 Apr. 1826.
Refs. : (*See* Burke's *Commoners,* ii. 597, *s.n.* Holyoake, of Tetenhall, Staffs., and Studley Castle, co. Warwick.) Will dated Seonee 27 Aug. 1832 ; proved 5 Nov. 1833.

HOME, Gabriel Murray (1795-1826). Lieutenant, 2nd Extra Regt. *b.* 15 Sept. 1795. Cadet 1811. Ensign 1 Sept. 1814. Lieut. 24 May 1816. *d.* St. Helena 3 May 1826.
Son of Rev. Robert Home, minister of Polwarth, Duns, co. Berwick.
Services : Posted as Ensign to 1/22nd N.I. in 1815. Adjt. 1/22nd N.I. 27 June 1816 till May 1824. Third Mahratta War ; Nagpur ; Lieut. 1/22nd N.I. Transfd. to 43rd N.I. (late 1/22nd) May 1824. Adjt. 43rd N.I. May 1824 till 1825. Transfd. to newly-raised 2nd Extra Regt. May 1825. Adjt. do. 12 July 1825 till death. Fur. 1826.

HOME, James (*d.* 1793). Major. Infantry. Cadet (?). Ensign 23 Apr. 1765. Lieut. (?). Capt. 17 Nov. 1769. Resigned 29 Dec. 1777. *d.* Jersey, 1 Oct. 1793, suddenly.
N.B.—The following is conjectural only : (? Grandson of Sir John Home, Bart., of Blackadder, co. Berwick. *m.* Marguerite Perchard. Father of William Home, *q.v.*) His widow died in Jersey 6 July 1817.
Services : As his name is not in the *A.L.* of 1 Feb. 1767, it is probable that he resigned during the " Batta mutiny," being subsequently readmitted. " Many years an officer in the service of the E.I.C., formerly on the Bombay Est., but latterly of Bengal. He went to India about the year 1753, and, after many vicissitudes, returned to Europe about 15 years ago. After which he *m.* a lady of

THE BENGAL ARMY, 1758-1834 473

the island of Jersey, whom he has left with two children, a son and a dau. He was a native of Ireland, and of good family. He was a good officer, and a man of strict honour and probity." (*G.M.*).
Refs. : *G.M.* 1793, ii. 1051. *S.M.* 1817, ii.

HOME, John (1763/64-1816). Major, Invalid Est. 12th N.I.
b. 1763/64. Cadet 1780. Ensign 12 Apr. 1780. Lieut. 15 Aug. 1781. Capt. 21 Apr. 1800. Major 23 Sept. 1804. Invalided 14 Nov. 1805. *d.* Hooghly, nr. Calcutta, 1816.

Son of William Home, of Broomhouse, co. Berwick, and Jane his wife, dau. of James Hunter. Brother of Lt.-Gen. James Home, of Broomhouse.

Services : Sailed for India on the *Neptune*, 3 June 1780, aged 16. Lieut. 29th Bn. Sepoys in July 1787. Operations in Jumna Doab 1803 ; Sasni ; Capt. 2/12th N.I. (? Second Mahratta War ; battle of Delhi ; Laswari ; Bhurtpore ; Major 12th N.I.)

Refs. : Burke's *Landed Gentry*, 13th edn., p. 916, *s.n.* Logan-Home, of Broomhouse. Will dated 27 Feb. 1810 ; codicil dated 17 Jan. 1813 ; proved 15 Jan. 1817.

Note : He devised his house and grounds at Hoogly, together with the sum of Rs. 15,100, for the keep of a favourite mare, " Khooshie Khan." His Will also contained elaborate instructions as to the manner in which this animal's food was to be prepared, and fed to her off a wooden table.

HOME, John (1787-1860). Major General. Colonel 57th N.I.
b. Gt. Britain St., Dublin, 18 Sept. 1787. Cadet 1803. Arrived in India 14 Aug. 1804. Ensign 3 Sept. 1804. Lieut. 21 Sept. 1804. Capt. 31 May 1820. Major 31 May 1830. Lt. Col. 7 Jan. 1836. Col. 19 Mar. 1847. Maj. Gen. 20 June 1854. *d.* at his residence, The Retreat, Weston Lane, Bath, 12 Apr. 1860.

bapt. Dublin 25 Sept. 1787. Son of Robert Home, sometime of Calcutta, portrait painter (*D.N.B.*), and Susannah Peterson his 1st wife. Brother of Richard Home, *q.v.*, and nephew of Anne Hunter. *m.* Weston, Somerset, 24 Apr. 1838, Susan, eldest dau. of Charles Batsford, of Weston.

Services : Posted as Lieut. to 21st N.I. Transfd. to newly-raised 1/30th N.I. in 1815. Intr. & Qmr. 1/30th N.I. 1818-20 ; actg. Adjt. do. in 1819. In the service of the King of Oudh at Lucknow, as Equerry and European A.D.C., 26 Apr. 1820 till 1825. Transfd. to 60th N.I. (late 2/30th) May 1824. Bde. Major at Cawnpore 25 June 1825. Siege and capture of Bhurtpore ; Capt. 60th N.I., Bde. Major 5th Inf. Bde. (India medal). Bde. Major 2nd Inf. Bde., 2nd Inf. Div., 4 Feb. 1826 till 27 Oct. 1829. Major 60th N.I. Fur. s.c. 21 Feb. 1835 till 10 Dec. 1838. Posted as Lt. Col. to 17th N.I. 29

Apr. 1836; to 5th N.I. 26 Dec. 1838; to 50th N.I. 17 Jan. 1839; to 37th N.I. 30 Oct. 1841. Fur. s.c. 1 Mar. 1842 till 1846, and 10 Feb. 1847 till death. Transfd. to 44th N.I. 13 Mar. 1845; to 50th N.I. Col. 57th N.I. Dec. 1853.

Refs.: Burke's *Peerage*, 1859, p. 527, *s.n.* Home, Bart., of Well Manor Farm, Hants. *Boase.* Bishop Heber's *Journal*, ii. 77. *G.M.* 1838, i. 654; 1860, i. 640. *The Times*, 16 Apr. 1860. Will dated 8 Feb. 1858; codicil dated 5 Nov. 1859; admon. 17 Aug. 1860.

HOME, Richard (1789-1862). Major General. Colonel 43rd N.I. *b.* London 17 Mar. 1789. Cadet 1804. Arrived in India 10 July 1805. Ensign 1 Jan. 1804. Lieut. 29 Aug. 1805. Capt. 10 Nov. 1821. Major 29 Nov. 1834. Lt. Col. 17 Sept. 1841. Col. 7 Apr. 1851. Maj. Gen. 28 Nov. 1854. *d.* 8 Vernon Terr., Brighton, 19 Apr. 1862.

bapt. St. James's, Westminster, 25 Apr. 1789. Son of Robert Home and Susannah his 1st wife. Brother of John Home (1787-1860), *q.v.*, and nephew of Sir Everard Home, 1st Bart. (*D.N.B.*). *m.* Lucknow, 4 Oct. 1822, Frances Sophia, dau. of Charles Fraser, *q.v.* (*See also* Felix Vincent Raper.) Father of Lieut. Duncan Charles Home, V.C., Bengal Engrs., and of Caroline Purvis, wife of Robert Warden Fraser, *q.v.*

Services: Posted as Lieut. to 4th N.I. Leave s.c. 6 mos. to sea 11 July 1808. Transfd. to newly-raised 1/28th N.I. in 1815. Third Mahratta War; Lieut. 1/28th N.I. Comdd. escort of Resdt. at Lucknow 4 June 1818 till 18 June 1825. Leave s.c. 12 mos. to P.W.I. 19 Jan. 1824. Transfd. to newly-raised 5th Extra Regt. (became 73rd N.I.) June 1825. Fur. s.c. 8 Mar. 1829 till 5 Nov. 1832. Offg. Sec. to Clothing Board 10 Oct. 1833; permanent do. 5 July 1834. Fur. p.a. 21 Feb. 1835 till 24 Nov. 1836. Offg. Presdy. Paymr. 25 Sept. 1837 and 9 Apr. 1838; permanent do. 6 May 1839 till Oct. 1841. Posted as Lt. Col. to 65th N.I. 30 Oct. 1841; to 22nd N.I. 21 Apr. 1843; to 47th N.I. 15 Aug. 1843; to 29th N.I. 13 Dec. 1844; to 2nd Bengal Eur. Regt. Jan. 1845. Fur. s.c. 10 Jan. 1845 till 1846. Posted as Col. to 43rd N.I. 17 June 1851. Bdr. on Est. 26 June 1852; to comd. Benares Bde. Sept. 1852; to comd. at Barrackpore Apr. 1854. Fur. s.c. 10 Jan. 1855 till death.

Refs.: Burke's *Peerage*, 1859, p. 527, *s.n.* Home, Bart., of Well Manor Farm, Hants. *Boase.* *G.M.* 1862, i. 658. *The Times*, 22 Apr. 1862.

HOME, William (1784-1815). Captain, Bengal Eur. Regt. *bapt.* St. Helier, Jersey, 2 Oct. 1784. Cadet 1799. Arrived in India 2 Dec. 1800. Ensign 27 Oct. 1800. Lieut. 22 Aug. 1801. Capt. 31 Aug. 1813. *d.* Macassar 12 Aug. 1815.

Son of James Home, *q.v.*, and Marguerite Perchard his wife.
Services : (? Second Mahratta War ; Gwalior ; battle and capture of Deig ; Bhurtpore ; Lieut. Bengal Eur. Regt.) Fur. 26 June 1805 till 10 Dec. 1810. Served with the detachment of Bengal Eur. Regt. in Java 1812 till death.
Refs. : Burke's *Landed Gentry*, 13th edn., p. 760, *s.n.* Graham, of Airth. *S.M.* 1816, p. 557. Will dated Macassar 3 Dec. 1814 ; proved in 1816.

FERGUSSON-HOME, John Hutcheson (1813-1881). Major. 33rd N.I. *b.* Edinburgh 18 Aug. 1813. Cadet 1830. Arrived in India 6 June 1831. Ensign 11 May 1831. Lieut. 11 Feb. 1837. Capt. 4 Jan. 1847. Retired 1 Oct. 1853. Hon. Major 28 Nov. 1854. *d.s.p.* Edinburgh 27 May 1881.

Of Bassendean, co. Berwick, J.P. & D.L. Son of James Fergusson, of Crosshill, co. Ayr, barr.-at-law, and Mary his wife, dau. of Capt. John Home, of Bassendean. Assumed the additional surname and arms in 1860, on succeeding his maternal uncle, Lt.-Gen. John Home Home. *m.* 1st, 5 June 1851, Jane Anne, eldest dau. of James Walker, of Dalry, Midlothian, one of the principal clerks of session in Scotland. (She died Benares, 12 June 1852, aged 26.) *m.* 2nd, 1861, Dorothea, dau. of Hugh Veitch, of Stuartfield. Addiscombe Cadet 1829-30.

Services : Against the Kols in Chota Nagpur 28 Jan. till 9 May 1832 ; Cadet d.d. 34th N.I. Did duty with several Regts. before posted as Ensign to 33rd N.I. 19 Dec. 1833. Transfd. to 63rd N.I. 24 Sept. 1835 ; to 33rd N.I. 10 May 1836. First Afghan War 1842 ; Kabul ; Lieut. 33rd N.I., with Gen. Pollock's force (Medal). First Sikh War ; Ferozshahr ; Sobraon ; Lieut. 33rd N.I. (Medal with clasp). Fur. 1850 till 20 Dec. 1851.

Refs. : Burke's *Landed Gentry*, 7th edn., p. 915, *s.n.* Home of Bassendean, co. Berwick. *The Times*, 30 May 1881.

HOMER, Arthur Aston (1790-?). Lieutenant. 27th N.I. *bapt.* Newington, Surrey, 27 Sept. 1790. Cadet 1805. Arrived in India 11 July 1806. Ensign 25 July 1806. Lieut. 3 July 1808. Retired 8 Jan. 1820.

Son of Richard Homer.

Services : Posted as Ensign to 27th N.I. in 1807. (? Operations against Dhundia Khan 1807 ; Komona ; Ganauri ; Ensign 1/27th N.I.) Lieut. 1/27th N.I. Capture of Java 1811 ; Lieut. 6th Bengal Vol. Bn. Served in Java with Vols. till 1816. Fur. 9 June 1816 till retirement.

Note : His name appears in the list of Retired Officers given in the *Indian A.L.* for the last time in July 1866.

HONE, Leland (1806-1840). Captain, 57th N.I. *bapt.* Dublin 29 June 1806. Cadet 1823. Arrived in India 19 May 1824. Ensign 17 Jan. 1824. Lieut. 22 Mar. 1825. Capt. 11 Aug. 1840. *d.* Cherrapunji, Assam, 11 Nov. 1840.

Son of William Hone, of Dublin, merchant. T.C.D. Pensioner 5 July 1821, aged 15.

Services : Posted as Ensign to 57th N.I. Fur. s.c. 17 Oct. 1824 till 5 Dec. 1826. Adjt. 57th N.I. 30 July 1833 till 22 June 1836. Fur. p.a. 26 Aug. 1836 till 6 Sept. 1839. Was on leave when his death occurred. No record of active service.

Refs. : Alumni Dub. M.I. in Cherrapunji cemetery.

HONYWOOD, Edward John (1790-1867). Colonel. 7th L.C. *b.* Honiton, Devon, 26 June 1790. Cadet 1807. Arrived in India 16 Nov. 1808. Cornet (20 Nov. 1808) 4 Nov. 1810. Lieut. 30 Nov. 1816. Capt. 16 Aug. 1822. Major 26 Dec. 1832. Lt. Col. 13 Apr. 1837. Retired 1 Nov. 1838. Hon. Col. 28 Nov. 1854. *d. unm.* at his residence, Whimple, nr. Exeter, 12 Dec. 1867.

Of Woodhayes, Devon. *bapt.* Honiton 18 Sept. 1791. Only son of Rev. Edward Honywood, LL.D., rector of Honiton and preby. of Exeter, and Sophia his wife, dau. of Rev. John Long. Nephew of Sir John Honywood, 4th Bart. Ed. Winchester ; K.S. 1800-7.

Services : Barasat C.C. for 4 mos. Posted as Cornet to 7th N.C. in Nov. 1810. Nepal War 1814-5 ; Cornet 7th N.C., S.A.C.G. in 1st Div. (India medal). Actg. Qmr. 7th N.C. 1816 ; Adjt. do. 13 Dec. 1816 till 1819. Siege and capture of Hathras. Third Mahratta War. Actg. Intr. & Qmr. 7th L.C. 1820. Fur. p.a. 18 Oct. 1820 till 30 Oct. 1822. To do duty with G.G.B.G. 16 Dec. 1822. A.D.C. to C.-in-C. 14 Jan. 1823 till 11 Feb. 1824. Bde. Major Malwa F.F. 12 Dec. 1823 ; do. Mewar F.F. 12 July 1824 till 10 Mar. 1827. Comdd. G.G.B.G. 3 Mar. 1827 till 3 Apr. 1834. Supt. Mysore Princes 4 Apr. 1834 till 5 June 1836. A.D.C. to G.G. 21 Mar. 1835. Fur. p.a. 1 May 1836 till retirement.

Refs. : Burke's *Peerage,* 1923, p. 1190, *s.n.* Honywood, Bart., of Evington, Kent. *Kirby. V.B.G. Walford. The Times,* 14 Dec. 1867.

HOOK, Lionel (*d.* 1808). Captain, 1st N.I. Cadet 1783. Admitted 16 Oct. 1783. Ensign 3 Jan. 1785. Lieut. 23 June 1790. Capt. 1803. *d.* Osborne's Hotel, Adelphi, London, 30 Apr. 1808.

Brother of Charles Hook, of Calcutta, of the firm of Campbell and Hook, merchants. Nephew of Dr. Lionel Campbell, of Campbeltown. *m.* (?). Father of Lionel Hook, Lt. Col. H.M. 19th Foot.

THE BENGAL ARMY, 1758-1834

Services: Sec. to Govt., Mily. Dept., c. 1803-6. Fur. 8 Dec. 1807 till death.
Refs.: *G.M.* 1808, i. 466. Will dated 21 Feb. 1806; codicil dated 13 Sept. 1807; proved 29 June 1810.

HOOKE, Archibald (1750/51-1826). Major. Infantry. *b.* 1750/51. Cadet 1763. Ensign 6 Feb. 1769. Lieut. 5 May 1770. Capt. 5 Jan. 1779. Major 8 Feb. 1784. Struck off 1793. *d.* Ham St., Ham Common, Nov. 1826, aged 75.
m. (?).[1]
Services: Major comdg. 32nd Bn. Sepoys in July 1787. On fur. in 1790.
Refs.: *G.M.* 1826, ii. 572.

[1] *Note*: "Being entitled to an annuity *whilst his wife was above ground*, he embalmed her body and placed it in a glass case in a chamber in his house, where it remained for 30 years." (*G.M.*)

HOPE, John Cooper (1770-1796). Fireworker, Artillery. *b.* Dublin 17 Sept. 1770. Cadet 1790. Admitted 22 Oct. 1791. Fireworker 27 June 1791. *d.* Fatehgarh 10 July 1796.
bapt. St. Nicholas Without, Dublin, 20 Oct. 1770.
Services: N.F.P.
Refs.: *S.M.* 1797, p. 287.

HOPE, Thomas (*d.* 1772). Lieutenant, Infantry. Transfd. as Lieut. from H.M.S. Lieut. 1 Aug. 1765. *d.* Apr. 1772.
Services: Lieut. H.M. 11th Foot 20 Dec. 1759. N.F.P.

HOPE, Sir William, third baronet (1727/28-1763). Lieutenant, Bengal Eur. Regt. *b.* 1727/28. Cadet (?). Ensign 28 Jan. 1758. Lieut. 1 May 1759. *d.s.p.* 5th, 6th or 11th Oct. 1763: massacred at or near Patna by order of Nawab Mir Muhammad Kasim. (See note to John Gordon*.)

3rd and last Bart. of Kirklistoun. *s.* 20 Nov. 1729. Of Balcomie, co. Fife. Only son of Sir George Hope, 2nd Bart., a Capt. of Foot, and Anne his wife, dau. of Sir John Mackenzie, Bart., of Coul. *m.* Margaret ——, a Dutch lady. (She *re-m.* 27 Apr. 1764, William Lambert, Mily. Paymr. Gen., Bengal.)
Services: Lieut. R.N. 1749. Subsequently Lieut. H.M. 31st Foot. Sailed for Madras on the *Grantham* in 1756, aged 28.
Refs.: Burke's *Peerage*, 1923, p. 1406, *s.n.* Linlithgow, M. Burke's *Extinct Baronetcies*, p. 626, *s.n.* Hope, Bart., of Kirklistoun. Walter Wood's *E. Neuk of Fife*, 2nd edn., p. 447. *Swinton of Kimmerghame Records*, pp. 83,84. *Broome*, p. 365. *Innes*, p. 169. M.I. in Patna city.

HOPE, William (1806-?). Lieutenant. 57th N.I. *b.* Hundon, Suffolk, 9 Sept. 1806. Cadet 1823. Arrived in India 16 Aug. 1824. Ensign 29 Mar. 1824. Lieut. 13 May 1825. Struck off in England 27 Feb. 1829. (Living in 1851 when the India medal was awarded.)
Son of John Fisher Hope.
Services : Ensign d.d. 46th N.I., and proceeded with a detachment of that Regt. to Assam 29 Nov. 1824. Posted as Ensign to 57th N.I. First Burma War ; Assam 1824-5 ; Lieut. 57th N.I. (India medal). Fur. s.c. 4 Aug. 1826 till struck off.

HOPKINS, John Wadel(l) (*d.* 1801). Major, 2nd Bengal Eur. Regt. Cadet 1776. Admitted July 1776. Ensign 11 Mar. 1777. Lieut. 8 Aug. 1778. Capt. 26 Sept. 1794. Major 29 Apr. 1799. *d.* Berhampore 21 Oct. 1801 : bur. there 22 Oct.
Services : Lieut. 36th Bn. Sepoys in July 1787. Capt. 7th N.I. in June 1798.
Refs. : A.A.R. iv. 119.

HOPKINS, Perin (1804-1842). Captain, 27th N.I. *b.* New Alresford, Hants, 7 Oct. 1804. Cadet 1823. Arrived in India 25 June 1824. Ensign 14 Jan. 1824. Lieut. 13 May 1825. Capt. 8 Mar. 1834. *d.* nr. Jalalabad 13 Jan. 1842 : kld. during the retreat from Kabul.[1]
bapt. New Alresford 10 Oct. 1804. Son of Edward Hopkins and Betty his wife.
Services : Posted as Ensign to 27th N.I. Intr. & Qmr. 27th N.I. 9 Feb. 1829 till 20 Nov. 1830 ; offg. do. 5 Apr. 1831. Fur. s.c. to N.S.W. 26 Sept. 1832 till 19 Jan. 1835. Apptd. Bde. Major 3rd Bde., 1st Div., Army of the Indus 10 Sept. 1838. First Afghan War 1838-42 ; to comd. 27th N.I. 8 Feb. 1830 ; placed at the disposal of the Envoy and Minister at the Court of Shah Shuja 12 Nov. 1839 ; Bamian (*Lond. Gaz.* 9 Jan. 1841) ; Nazian valley ; comdg. Shah Shuja's 6th Inf. at Kabul ; Kabul insurrection (kld.).

[1] *Note :* His body was found on the Kabul road, about 3 m. from Jalalabad, on the morning of 14 Jan.

HOPPE, John (1805-1842). Bt. Captain, 16th N.I. *b.* London 5 Sept. 1805. Cadet 1826. Arrived in India 17 May 1827. Ensign 18 Jan. 1827. Lieut. 18 Sept. 1833. Bt. Capt. 18 Jan. 1842. *d.* on the Indus R., between Sukkur and Sewan, 4 (or 12) Nov. 1842.
3rd son of Charles Edgeley Hoppe, of New Bridge St., London, coal merchant, later of Withycombe, Devon.
Services : Ensign d.d. 16th N.I. 28 May 1827. Posted to 16th N.I. 19 June 1827. Actg. Intr. & Qmr. 16th N.I. 18 Sept. 1827.

Leave s.c. 12 mos. to hills 11 May 1830. Adjt. 2nd Inf., Oudh Auxy. Force, 29 Jan. 1838. Rejoined his Regt. for service in Afghanistan 18 Sept. 1838. Apptd. to Shah Shuja's army 14 Nov. 1838. First Afghan War 1838-42 ; Ghazni (Medal) ; Kandahar ; Bt. Capt. 16th N.I., 2nd in comd. Shah's 2nd Inf.
Refs : *G.M.* 1843, i. 555. *The Times*, 18 Mar. 1843.

HOPPER, Arthur Quin (1811-1857). Major. 24th N.I. *b*. London 16 Oct. 1811. Cadet 1827. Arrived in India 9 June 1828. Ensign 10 Feb. 1828. Lieut. 19 Sept. 1833. Capt. 1 Apr. 1845. Retired 1 May 1852. Hon. Major 28 Nov. 1854. *d*. Sydney St., Chelsea, London, 24 Nov. 1857.

bapt. Hammersmith Dec. 1811. Son of William Hopper, *q.v.*, and Margaret his wife. Brother of William McDowell Hopper, *q.v.*, and cousin-german of Edward Keene Hopper, *q.v. m*. Calcutta, 15 Aug. 1835, Louisa, youngest dau. of "the late Lieut. Cunningham, Bengal Est." (*See also* Patrick John Chicne.) Ed. Charterhouse ; admitted 1823. Addiscombe Cadet 1827.

Services : Ensign d.d. 57th N.I. 25 July 1828. Posted as Ensign to 57th N.I. 4 Nov. 1828. Transfd. to 24th N.I. 2 Dec. 1829. Operations against the Kols and Chuars 1832-3 ; Ensign 24th N.I. Leave s.c. 18 mos. to Mauritius 16 Oct. 1833. Offg. Fort Adjt. at Fort William 23 Sept. 1835. Actg. Intr. & Qmr. 9th N.I. 20 Nov. 1837 ; do. 71st N.I. 21 Apr. 1840 ; do. 73rd N.I. 1 Mar. 1842. Fur. 1 Nov. 1849 till retirement.

Refs. : *Charterhouse School List. G.M.* 1858, i. 114. *I.M.* 1 Dec. 1857, p. 846.

HOPPER, Edward Keene (1809-1843). Bt. Captain, 73rd N.I. *bapt*. St. Paul's, Cork, 21 May 1809. Cadet 1824. Arrived in India 21 Nov. 1825. Ensign 16 Aug. 1825. Lieut. 22 Sept. 1826. Bt. Capt. 13 May 1840. *d*. Delhi, 17 Oct. 1843, aged 34.

Son of Edward Jervoise Hopper and Margaret his wife. Nephew of William Hopper, *q.v.*

Services : Allowed to proceed as a passenger to India with his uncle 13 Apr. 1824. Ensign d.d. 57th N.I. Jan. 1826. Posted as Ensign to 5th Extra Regt. (became 73rd N.I.) Mar. 1826. Fur. s.c. 8 Sept. 1829 till 5 Nov. 1832, and 4 Jan. 1841 till 22 Apr. 1843. No record of active service.

Refs. : *De Rhé-Philipe. I.M.* No. 8, p. 240. M.I. in Rajpura cemetery, Delhi.

HOPPER, William (1765-1843). Major General, Artillery. *b*. Aug. 1765. Cadet 1783. Admitted 20 Sept. 1783. Ensign (Inf.) 6 Apr. 1785. Fireworker 16 Mar. 1790. Lieut. 12 Jan. 1796. Capt. Lt. 22 Oct. 1803. Capt. 17 Dec. 1806. Major 25 Sept.

1817. Lt. Col. 4 May 1820. Lt. Col. Comdt. 30 May 1824. Col. 5 June 1829. Maj. Gen. 10 Jan. 1837. *d.* Calcutta, 6 July 1843, aged 77 yrs. and 11 mos.

Brother of Lieut. George Hopper, and half-brother of Thomas Hopper, of Dublin. Uncle of Mrs. Warren, of Castle Warren, co. Cork, and of Edward Keene Hopper, *q.v. m.* Calcutta, 16 Nov. 1792, Miss Margaret Quin. (She died Calcutta Mar. 1848.) Father of Arthur Quin Hopper, *q.v.*, William McDowell Hopper, *q.v.*, Margaret, wife of Thomas Dingwall-Fordyce, *q.v.*, and Eleanor, wife of Henry Philip Hughes, *q.v.*

Services : Transfd. from Inf. to Art. in 1790. Second Rohilla War ; battle of Bitaurah ; Lieut. F. 2nd Coy. 3rd Bn. Art. Operations against the Rana of Gohad 1806 ; capture of Gohad ; Capt. Lt. comdg. 2nd Coy. 3rd Bn. Storm and capture of Chamir fort 1807 ; Capt. Lt. comdg. 2nd Coy. 3rd Bn. Comy. Ord. at Cawnpore 9 July 1807 till 1810. Fur. p.a. 11 Jan. 1811 till 30 Sept. 1815 ; s.c. 24 Jan. 1822 till 11 Oct. 1824 ; p.a., via Cape, 2 Jan. 1830 till 17 June 1832. Presdt. of Arsenal Committee 13 Nov. 1834. Leave s.c. 2 yrs. to Cape 15 Jan. 1836. Fur. p.a. 20 Jan. 1838 till 5 Nov. 1840.

Refs. : Will dated Grove House, Roeland St., Cape Town, 4 Oct. 1841 ; codicil dated 31 Dec. 1842 ; proved 5 Feb. 1844. M.I. S. Park St. burial ground, Calcutta.

HOPPER, William McDowell (1803-1841). Captain, 57th N.I. *b.* Bengal 19 Nov. 1803. Cadet 1819. Admitted 29 Aug. 1820. Ensign 20 Apr. 1820. Lieut. 11 July 1823. Capt. 17 July 1832. *d.* at sea, 7 Jan. 1841, on board the *Reliance.*

Son of William Hopper, *q.v.*, and Margaret his wife. Brother of Arthur Quin Hopper, *q.v. m.* Calcutta, 20 Feb. 1839, Rose Amelia, widow of Andrew Liddell. (She died Barrackpore, 9 Aug. 1840, aged 27.)

Services : Posted as Ensign to 2/28th N.I. Transfd. as Lieut. to 29th N.I. 11 July 1823 ; to 57th N.I. (late 1/29th) May 1824. (? First Burma War ; Assam 1824 ; Lieut. 57th N.I.) Intr. & Qmr. 57th N.I. 24 Oct. 1825 till 1830. Fur. p.a. 10 Sept. 1830 till 7 Jan. 1832. Leave s.c. 2 yrs. to Cape 27 Nov. 1840.

Refs. : A.J. N.S. xxxiv. 363.

HORE, Walter. (*See* **HORE-RUTHVEN, Hon. Walter.**)

HORE, William (1809-1845). Bt. Captain, 18th N.I. A.D.C. to Sir Henry Hardinge. *b.* Dinapore 6 May 1809. Cadet 1826. Arrived in India 9 June 1833. Ensign 14 Feb. 1827. Lieut. 9 Jan. 1833. Bt. Capt. 14 Feb. 1842. *d.* 21 Dec. 1845 : kld. in action at the battle of Ferozshahr.

bapt. Calcutta 9 Aug. 1809. Only son of William Hore, Major

67th Foot, and Sarah Ker his wife. Cousin-german of Hon. Walter Hore-Ruthven, *q.v.* *m.* Bray, 24 June 1834, Ellen, youngest dau. of Thomas Oxley, of Killiney, co. Kerry. His dau. *m.* Cuthbert Davidson, *q.v.* T.C.D. Pensioner 18 Oct. 1824.
Services : Ensign d.d. 67th N.I. 23 June 1827. Posted as Ensign to 18th N.I. 1 Dec. 1827. Fur. s.c. 14 June 1832 till 19 Dec. 1834. Actg. Intr. & Qmr. 8th L.C. 24 Feb. 1837 till Jan. 1839. Junior Asst. to Comr. of Saugor Div. at Hoshangabad 13 Feb. 1839 till Sept. 1842. Intr. & Qmr. 18th N.I. 16 May 1843. Offg. 2nd Asst. Sec. Govt. of India, Mily. Dept., 1 Mar. 1845. Offg. Dy. Sec., Mily. Dept., Oct. 1845. First Sikh War ; Mudki ; Ferozshahr (kld.) ; A.D.C. to G.G.
Refs. : Burke's *Commoners*, iv. 720, *s.n.* Hore, of Harperstown. *De Rhé-Philipe.* *A.J.* N.S. xiv. 311. M.I. in St. Andrew's, Ferozepore. *Alumni Dub.*

HORNBY, Henry (1741/42-1794). Captain. Infantry. *b.* 1741/42. Cadet 1766. Ensign 21 Aug. 1766. Lieut. 15 Sept. 1767. Capt. 27 Mar. 1773. Resigned 28 Oct. 1773. *d.* Halton Hall, the seat of W. B. Bradshaw, 2 Aug. 1794, aged 52.

Sometime of Norwich. *m.* Rebecca Mary, dau. of Morris Doran, and widow of John Darrell, of Scotney, Kent. Father of Robert Hornby, *q.v.*
Services : N.F.P.
Refs. : *G.M.* 1794, ii. 770.

HORNBY, Robert (1788-1836). Major, 29th N.I. *bapt.* Norwich 14 June 1788. Cadet 1803. Arrived in India 17 Mar. 1805. Ensign 5 May 1805. Lieut. 6 May 1805. Capt. 16 Aug. 1822. Major 27 Apr. 1831. *d.* Banda 4 July 1836.

Son of Henry Hornby, *q.v.*, and Rebecca Mary his wife. *m.* Midnapore, 24 Apr. 1811, Sarah Arabella, dau. of Rev. Henry Peter Stacy, chaplain Bengal Est., and sister of Henry Peter Stacy, *q.v.* (She died the Vicarage, Hornchurch, May 1850, aged 55.)
Services : Posted as Lieut. to 1/14th N.I. (? Nepal War 1814-5 ; Jitgarh ; Lieut. 1/14th N.I., in 3rd Div.) Third Mahratta War ; Dhamoni ; Mandala ; Garhakota ; Lieut. 1/14th N.I. Actg. Intr. & Qmr. 1/14th N.I. 2 Oct. 1821, and 8 Jan. 1823. Transfd. to 29th N.I. (late 2/14th) May 1824.
Refs. : *A.J.* N.S. xxi. 267.

HORNE, Alexander (1808-1834). Lieutenant, 62nd N.I. *b.* St. Vincent, W.I., 18 Dec. 1808. Cadet 1824. Arrived in India 7 May 1825. Ensign 8 Jan. 1825. Lieut. 6 Sept. 1825. *d.* Barh, nr. Simla, 23 May 1834.

bapt. St. Vincent 4 May 1809. Son of John Horne, of St. Vincent,

Services : Ensign d.d. 67th N.I. 21 May 1825. Posted as Ensign to 62nd N.I. July 1825, and joined that Regt. in Arakan in Nov. 1825. First Burma War ; Arakan 1825 ; Ensign 62nd N.I. Fur. s.c. 2 May 1826 till 28 Sept. 1828. Actg. Intr. & Qmr. 62nd N.I. Oct. 1833 till Mar. 1834. Leave s.c. to the Hills W. of the Jumna 21 May till 1 Dec. 1834, and died whilst on his way to Simla.
Refs. : De Rhé-Philipe. M.I. in old cemetery, Sabathu.

HORNE, Francis Woodley (1810-1858). Ensign. Infantry. Subsequently Major 7th Hrs. *b.* London 3 Jan. 1810. Cadet 1829. Arrived in India 23 Apr. 1830. Ensign 3 Jan. 1830. Resigned 8 Aug. 1833. *d.* Oudh 31 Dec. 1858.

3rd son of Sir William Horne, Kt., of Epping House, Herts., and Upper Harley St., London, Atty. Gen. (*D.N.B.*), and Ann his wife.
Services : Cadet d.d. 13th N.I. 7 June 1830 ; do. 2nd N.I. 10 Dec. 1830 ; do. 33rd N.I. 25 Jan. 1831 ; do. 10th N.I. 22 Oct. 1831. Actg. Ensign 16 July 1832. d.d. 52nd N.I. 24 Oct. 1832. Cornet 11th Light Dgns. 31 Aug. 1832 ; Lieut. do. 6 Sept. 1833 ; Lieut. 15th Light Dgns. (Hrs.) July 1839 ; Capt. do. 19 Aug. 1842 ; Bt. Major do. 20 June 1854.
Refs. : G.M. 1859, i. 438.

HORNE, William (1760/61-1792). Lieutenant, Infantry. *b.* in the W.I. 1760/61. Cadet 1779. Ensign 12 Feb. 1780. Lieut. 4 Feb. 1781. *d.* Calcutta, 5 July 1792, in the lunatic asylum.

Services : Sailed for India on the *True Briton*, 16 June 1779, aged 18. Lieut. 30th Bn. Sepoys in July 1787.

HORNE, William Gelston (1811-1843). Lieutenant, 55th N.I. *b.* Stoke Damerel, Devon, 2 Oct. 1811. Cadet 1827. Arrived in India 12 Feb. 1829. Ensign 23 Aug. 1828. Lieut. 4 Aug. 1836. *d.* Sukkur, Sind, 28 June 1843, drowned by the upsetting of a boat.

Son of Crichton Horne and Ann his wife. Nephew of Andrew John Nash.
Services : Ensign d.d. 44th N.I. 3 Mar. 1829. Posted to 55th N.I. 3 June 1829. Actg. Adjt. 55th N.I. 1 Dec. 1837 ; permanent do. 2 Jan. 1840 till death. With Army of Reserve (for Afghanistan) Oct. 1842 till Jan. 1843 ; Lieut. 55th N.I. No record of active service.

HORNER, Thomas (1759/60-1789). Ensign. Infantry. Subsequently Ensign 7th Madras N.I. *b.* 1759/60. Cadet 1781. Ensign 17 July 1781. *d.* Trichinopoly, Madras, 22 Oct. 1789.
A native of Yorks.
Services : Apptd. Cadet on 24 Oct. 1781, aged 21. Transfd. to Madras Est. Ensign 5 Dec. 1782.

THE BENGAL ARMY, 1758-1834 483

HORNIDGE, William Henry (1784-1816). Lieutenant, Invalid Est. 13th N.I. *b.* London 24 Sept. 1784. Cadet 1803. Arrived in India 17 Mar. 1805. Ensign 16 Apr. 1805. Lieut. 17 Apr. 1805. Invalided 29 Aug. 1809. *d.* Chunar 14 Aug. 1816.

Son of John Hornidge. *m.* Cawnpore, 24 Feb, 1806, Melesina Elwood, widow (*possibly* widow of Thomas Moore Elwood, *q.v.*). (She died Chunar 15 May 1831.)

Services : Posted as Lieut. to 13th N.I. in 1806. (? Operations against Dhundia Khan 1807 ; Komona ; Ganauri ; Lieut. 1/13th N.I.)

HORSBRUGH, Alexander (1788-1865). Lieut. Colonel. 46th N.I. *b.* Inverleithen 10 Apr. 1788. Cadet 1804. Arrived in India 10 Dec. 1805. Ensign 29 Sept. 1805. Lieut. 17 Oct. 1805. Capt. 11 July 1823. Major 29 Aug. 1833. Retired 1 Mar. 1838. Hon. Lt. Col. 28 Nov. 1854. *d.* 3 Coote's Cresc., Edinburgh, 26 Jan. 1865.

Of Horsbrugh, co. Peebles. 2nd son of Alexander Horsbrugh, of that ilk, and Violet his wife, dau. and heir of Thomas Turnbull, of Know, co. Selkirk. Brother of Samuel Mitchelson Horsbrugh, *q.v.* *m.* 1st, Calcutta, 5 Apr. 1817, Emily, dau. of Charles Hodgkinson. (She died Calcutta, 3 June 1825, aged 25.) *m.* 2nd, Edinburgh, 3 Sept. 1829, Helen Hay, youngest dau. of John Maclaren, of Leith.

Services : Posted as Lieut. to 2/23rd N.I. Settlement of Hariana ; assault and capture of Bhawani 29 Aug. 1809 (w.) ; Lieut. 2/23rd N.I. Capture of Java 1811 ; Lieut. 5th Bn. Bengal Vols. (Medal). Served with 5th Vol. Bn. in Java till 1816. Third Mahratta War ; Lieut. 2/23rd N.I. Transfd. to 46th N.I. (late 2/23rd) May 1824. First Burma War ; Assam 1824 (*Lond. Gaz.* 22 Feb. 1825) ; Capt. 46th N.I. (India medal). Served with Rangpur L.I. Bn. 26 June till 1 Nov. 1826. Fur. p.a. 22 Jan. 1827 till 15 May 1830. Comdd. 46th N.I. for a few weeks in 1835. Fur. s.c. 27 Feb. 1836 till retirement.

Refs. : Burke's *Landed Gentry*, 10th edn., p. 807, *s.n.* Horsbrugh, of Horsbrugh, co. Peebles. *E.I.M.C.* ii. 355. *The Times*, 28 Jan. 1865.

HORSBRUGH, James (*d.* 1791). Lieutenant, Artillery. Cadet 1778. Fireworker 28 Sept. 1778. Lieut. 1 July 1782. *d.* Bangalore, 6 Sept. 1791, of wounds received at the battle of Satyamangalam on 13 Sept. 1790.

Brother of John Horsbrugh. *m.* (?).

Services : Second Mysore War 1781-5 ; Lieut. 5th Coy. 2nd Bn. Art. Third Mysore War ; Satyamangalam (w.) ; Bangalore ; Lieut. 1st Coy. 2nd Bn.

Refs. : Will dated 5 Mar. 1790.

HORSBRUGH, Samuel Mitchelson (1789-1833). Captain, 38th N.I. *b.* Inverleithen 4 Sept. 1789. Cadet 1806. Arrived in India 25 Nov. 1807. Ensign 24 Oct. 1807. Lieut. 24 Sept. 1812. Capt. 13 May 1825. *d.* Benares 11 Nov. 1833.

3rd and youngest son of Alexander Horsbrugh, of that ilk, and Violet his wife. Brother of Alexander Horsbrugh, *q.v. m.* 1st, 12 Feb. 1814, Miss Skinner (*probably* dau. of either Hercules Skinner, *q.v.*, or James Skinner, *see* Appendix). (She died Hansi 18 June 1814.) *m.* 2nd, Calcutta, 15 Jan. 1816, Eliza, dau. of John Meller, *q.v.*

Services : Posted as Ensign to 19th N.I. Nepal War 1814-5 ; Lieut. 1/19th N.I., in 1st Div. Third Mahratta War ; Lieut. 19th N.I. Transfd. to 39th N.I. (late 1/19th) May 1824. Operations against the Kols 1832 ; comdd. a detachment in a successful attack on the insurgents on 26 Feb. 1832.

Refs. : Burke's *Landed Gentry*, 10th edn., p. 807, *s.n.* Horsbrugh, of Horsbrugh, co. Peebles. *A.J.* N.S. xiv. 131.

HORSBURGH, Charles Bell (1814-1842). Lieutenant, 5th N.I. *b.* Kilmany, co. Fife, 10 Jan. 1814. Cadet 1834. Arrived in India 5 June 1835. Ensign (21 Dec. 1834) 24 Feb. 1835. Lieut. 3 Oct. 1840. *d.* Gandamak, Afghanistan, 13 Jan. 1842 : kld. in action during the retreat from Kabul.

Son of Boyd Horsburgh, of Lochmalony, co. Fife, late Major H.M. 39th Regt., and Jean Hay Scott his wife. Brother of Thomas Scott Horsburgh, *q.v.*

Services : Ensign d.d. 32nd N.I. 15 June 1835. Posted to 5th N.I. 24 Sept. 1835. Actg. Adjt. Left Wing 5th N.I. 30 Dec. 1840. First Afghan War 1840-2 ; Kabul insurrection (kld.) ; Lieut. 5th N.I.

HORSBURGH, Thomas Scott (1812-1863). Bt. Major. 32nd N.I. *b.* 1 Feb. 1812. Cadet 1828. Arrived in India 2 Oct. 1829. Ensign 17 Feb. 1829. Lieut. 19 Sept. 1836. Capt. 9 Apr. 1849. Bt. Major 28 Nov. 1854. Retired 31 Dec. 1861. *d.* Norwood Green, Middlesex, 29 Jan. 1863.

2nd son of Boyd Horsburgh, Major H.M. 39th Regt., and Jean Hay Scott his wife. Brother of Charles Bell Horsburgh, *q.v.*

Services : Posted as Ensign to 32nd N.I. 19 Sept. 1829. Actg. Adjt. Wing 32nd N.I. 25 May 1833. Shekhawat expedn. 1834 ; Ensign 32nd N.I. Fur. s.c. 28 July 1836 till 10 Feb. 1840. P.W.D. at Dacca 9 Nov. 1840 till 1843. Fur. s.c. 10 Apr. 1851 till 2 Apr. 1854. Fur. 3 yrs. 16 Apr. 1858.

Refs. : *G.M.* 1863, i. 395. *The Times*, 2 Feb. 1863.

THE BENGAL ARMY, 1758-1834   485

HORSFORD, Sir John (1751-1817). Major General, K.C.B. Colonel Comdt. Artillery. *b.* 2 May 1751. Country Cadet 1778. Admitted 9 Mar. 1778. Fireworker 31 Mar. 1778. Lieut. 5 Oct. 1778. Capt. 28 Nov. 1786. Major 1 July 1801. Lt. Col. 1 May 1804. Lt. Col. Comdt. 1 Aug. 1805. Col. 25 July 1810. Maj. Gen. 4 June 1813. *d. unm.* Cawnpore 20 Apr. 1817.

Son of John Horsford, of St. George's, Middlesex. Brother of James Horsford. Ed. Merchant Taylors'; entered the school in 1759. St. John's Coll., Oxon.; matric. 30 June 1768, aged 17.

Services : See *D.N.B.* Enlisted in E.I.C. Art. as a private under the name of John Rover. Sailed for India in the *Duke of Grafton* 1 Apr. 1772. Rose to the rank of Sergt., and was apptd. Cadet of Art., under his real name, 9 Mar. 1778. Capt. 2nd Bn. Art. in July 1787. Third Mysore War; Bangalore; Arikera; Seringapatam; Capt. comdg. 3rd Coy. 2nd Bn. Sent to Madras in Aug. 1793 for siege of Pondicherry; Capt. comdg. 1st Coy. 2nd Bn. Second Mahratta War; Aligarh; Delhi; Agra; Laswari; Major comdg. Art.; battle and capture of Deig; Bhurtpore; Lt. Col. comdg. Art. Operations against Dhundia Khan 1807; Komona; Ganauri; Lt. Col. comdg. Art. Comdt. Bengal Art. 25 May 1808 till 28 June 1816. Siege and capture of Hathras; Maj. Gen. comdg. Art. K.C.B. 7 Apr. 1815.

Refs.: *D.N.B.* *E.I.M.C.* ii. 309-12. *Stubbs*, ii. 234-8. *D.I.B. Robinson. Alumni Oxon. G.M.* 1817, ii. 561. Will dated 3 July 1816; proved 7 May 1817. M.I. at Cawnpore.

HORSFORD, Richard (1801-1869). Major General. Commandant Artillery. *b.* Antigua, W.I., 28 Dec. 1801. Cadet 1818. Admitted 2 Oct. 1819. 2nd Lieut. 29 Apr. 1819. Lieut. 27 Sept. 1823. Capt. 7 Oct. 1836. Major 31 Mar. 1847. Lt. Col. 21 July 1851. Col. 18 Feb. 1861. Maj. Gen. 6 Feb. 1861. *d.* Clifton 13 Sept. 1869.

Son of Valentine Horne Horsford, of Antigua, and Jane his wife, 3rd dau. of Thomas Ottley, of Antigua. Stepson of James O'Brien, 3rd Marquis of Thomond (*D.N.B.*). Cousin-german of George O'Bryen Ottley, *q.v. m.* 1st, Dum-Dum, 23 Oct. 1830, Ann Louisa, youngest dau. of Charles Pattenson, B.C.S. (She died Dum-Dum, 16 July 1831, aged 21.) *m.* 2nd, Agra, 5 Oct. 1838, Bannatyna Wilhelmina, dau. of Alexander Macleod, of View Field, and half-sister of Isabella, wife of Harry Burrard Dalzell, *q.v.* (She died 30 Nov. 1892, aged 75.) Addiscombe Cadet 1818 till 6 Apr. 1819.

Services : Actg. Adjt. & Qmr. Div. Art. 24 Dec. 1824. Adjt. & Qmr. 4th Bn. Art. 22 July 1825 till 3 Jan. 1837. Siege and capture of Bhurtpore; Lieut. 4th Bn. Foot Art. (India medal). Posted to 4th Coy. 4th Bn. 22 Dec. 1836. To comd. No. 9 Light Field Battery

5 Nov. 1842. First Sikh War; Mudki; Ferozshahr; Sobraon; Capt. comdg. 4th Coy. 6th Bn. (Medal with 2 clasps). Second Sikh War; Sadulapur; Chilianwala; Gujerat; Major comdg. 4th Bn. (Medal with 2 clasps). Lt. Col. comdg. 3rd Bn. Art. Fur. s.c. 15 Jan. 1856 till 6 Oct. 1857. Tempy. Bdr., 2 cl., comdg. at Raniganj 5 Nov. 1857. Mutiny campaign; minor services. Bdr., 2 cl., comdg. at Meerut, 4 Nov. 1859. Comdt. Bengal Art. 27 Oct. 1859 till 28 July 1860.

Refs.: Burke's *Extinct Peerage*, 1883 edn., p. 407, *s.n.* O'Brien, Earl of Inchiquin. *The Times*, 17 Sept. 1869.

HORSLEY, Edward (1803-1829). Captain, 9th L.C. *bapt.* Harbledown, Kent, 31 July 1803. Cadet 1820. Arrived in India Oct. 1821. Cornet 21 Mar. 1821. Lieut. 4 Dec. 1823. Capt. 3 Jan. 1829. *d.* Nimach 1 Oct. 1829.

Son of John Horsley, of Canterbury. *m.* Meerut, 23 Mar. 1825, Mary, widow of Charles William Heriot, *q.v.*

Services: Posted as Cornet to 4th L.C. Transfd. to newly-raised 9th L.C. in 1825. Siege and capture of Bhurtpore; Lieut. 9th L.C.

HOSSACK, John (*d.* 1769). Lieutenant, Infantry. Cadet 1766. Ensign 26 Dec. 1766. Lieut. 7 Apr. 1768. *d.* 1769.

Services: N.F.P.

HOTHAM, John (1805-1881). Bt. Captain. Artillery. *b.* Bishop Burton, Yorks., 29 Jan. 1805. Cadet 1821. Arrived in India 3 Jan. 1823. 2nd Lieut. 10 May 1822. Lieut. 28 Dec. 1824. Bt. Capt. 10 May 1837. Retired 19 Aug. 1837. *d.* 9 St. Leonard's Pl., York, 11 Feb. 1881.

Of Scaptworth. *bapt.* 3 Feb. 1805. 4th son of Lt.-Col. George Hotham and Caroline his 1st wife, dau. of Roger Gee, of Bishop Burton. Grand-nephew of Beaumont, 2nd Baron Hotham and 12th Bart. *m.* 1st, 9 Apr. 1842, Maria Elizabeth, youngest dau. of Henry Thompson, of Burton, Yorks. (She died 3 June 1853.) *m.* 2nd, 11 Jan. 1855, Mary Anne, dau. of Rev. Danson Richardson Roundell, of Gledstone, Yorks. (She died 20 June 1898.) Addiscombe Cadet 1820-2.

Services: First Burma War; Arakan 1825; Lieut. Foot Art. (India medal). Posted to 2nd Troop 3rd Bde. H.A. in 1826; transfd. to 3rd Troop 3rd Bde. 1826. Fur. s.c. 9 May 1831 till 3 Dec. 1834, and 19 Feb. 1835 till retirement. Retired on h.p., *viz.* 4/- *p.d.*

Refs.: Burke's *Peerage*, 1923, p. 1199, *s.n.* Hotham, B. *The Times*, 14 Feb. 1881.

HOTSON, Campbell George (1800-1818). Cadet, Infantry. *b.* St. Helena 28 July 1800. Cadet 1817. Never arrived in India. *d.* at sea, 29 May 1818, on board the *Castle Huntley*, on his passage out to India.

Son of John Hotson, purser H.E.I.C.N.S.

HOUGH, William (1789-1865). Lieut. Colonel. 48th N.I. *bapt.* London 22 May 1789. Cadet 1805. Arrived in India 11 July 1806. Ensign 7 Aug. 1806. Lieut. 9 Oct. 1808. Capt. 26 Aug. 1823. Major (10 Jan. 1837) 1 Mar. 1840. Invalided 1 Oct. 1840. Retired 15 Feb. 1850. Hon. Lt. Col. 28 Nov. 1854. *d.* Tenterden St., Hanover Sq., London, 3 Jan. 1865, aged 75.

Son of Stephen Hough and Sarah his wife. *m.* Saharanpur, 19 Feb. 1835, Sophia, eldest dau. of Thomas Raikes, of London, banker. (He divorced her in 1838.)

Services : Barasat C.C. Posted as Ensign to 24th N.I. Intr. & Qmr. 8th Gren. Bn. 1815-6. Nepal War 1816 ; Lieut. 8th Gren. Bn., in 2nd Bde., Left Column (India medal). Third Mahratta War ; Lieut. 1/24th N.I. Fur. p.a. 30 Dec. 1821 till 10 Oct. 1825. Transfd. to 48th N.I. (late 2/24th) May 1824. Actg. D.J.A.G., Cawnpore Div., 17 Jan. 1826. D.J.A.G., Cawnpore, 31 Oct. 1827 ; do., Sirhind, 12 Feb. 1829 ; Benares 29 Dec. 1835. Attached to Staff of Army of the Indus 13 Sept. 1838, as D.J.A.G. Bengal Column ; D.J.A.G., Saugor Div., 11 Mar. 1839. First Afghan War 1838-40 ; Ghazni ; Bt. Major 48th N.I. (Medal). Ceases to be D.J.A.G. on promotion 21 Oct. 1840. Pub. Calcutta, 1840, "Narrative of the March and Operations of the Army of the Indus . . ." "The Practice of Courts-Martial," London, 1835 ; "Political and Military events in British India," 2 vols., 1853 ; etc.

Refs. : *Boase. A.J.* N.S. xxvii. 245. *G.M.* 1865, i. 259. *The Times*, 9 Jan. 1865. Burke's *Landed Gentry*, 11th edn., p. 1395.

HOUGH, William Henry (1777-?). Lieutenant. 2nd Bengal Eur. Regt. *b.* Berry-Pomeroy, Devon, 23 Aug. 1777. Cadet 1793. Never arrived in India. Ensign 25 Sept. 1794. Lieut. 1 June 1796. Struck off *c.* 1796.

Son of William Hough and Mary his wife.

Services : Although he never was in India, yet he was promoted Lieut. in 2nd Bengal Eur. Regt. in 1796, shortly before being struck off.

HOUGHTON, Richmond (1804-1880). Major General. 16th N.I. *b.* Liverpool 8 Jan. 1804. Cadet 1819. Admitted 21 Aug. 1820. Ensign 21 Apr. 1820. Lieut. 11 July 1823. Capt. 25 Sept. 1834.

Major 1 Oct. 1848. Lt. Col. 5 Dec. 1853. Bt. Col. 28 Nov. 1854. Retired 31 Dec. 1861. Hon. Maj. Gen. 31 Dec. 1861. *d.* Weston-super-Mare, Somerset, 10 June 1880.

Son of Edward Houghton. *m.* 1st, Dinapore, 12 Dec. 1833, Anna Matilda, eldest dau. of Charles William Brooke, *q.v.* (*See also* Henry Augustus Morrieson.) (She died Cawnpore 15 Mar. 1854.) *m.* 2nd, Mussoorie, 22 July 1857, Eliza Louisa, dau. of John Angelo, *q.v.* (*See also* John Abercrombie.)

Services : Ensign 2/8th N.I. Transfd. to newly-raised 32nd N.I. 11 July 1823 ; to 63rd N.I. (late 1/32nd) May 1824. Siege and capture of Bhurtpore ; Lieut. 63rd N.I. (India medal). Adjt. 63rd N.I. 17 Jan. 1826 till 17 Nov. 1834. Fur. s.c. 8 Jan. 1835 till 16 Dec. 1837. With 2nd L.I. Bn. in 1842. Bde. Major at Ambala 4 June 1844. A.D.C. to Maj.-Gen. W. R. Gilbert, *q.v.*, 11 Jan. 1845. First Sikh War ; Mudki ; Ferozshahr ; A.D.C. to Gilbert ; Sobraon ; A.A.G. of 2nd (Gilbert's) Div. (Medal with two clasps). D.A.A.G., Sirhind Div., 4 Mar. 1846 ; A.A.G. do. 6 Aug. 1847 till Oct. 1848. Major 63rd N.I., comdg. 1st Inf. Recruit Depot in 1849. Posted as Lt. Col. to 63rd N.I. 2 Feb. 1854 ; to 16th N.I. in 1857.

Refs. : *A.J.* N.S. xiv. 131. *The Times*, 14 June 1880.

HOULTON, Samuel (1787-1827). Captain, 11th N.I. *bapt.* Carmarthen 20 June 1787. Cadet 1803. Arrived in India 10 Mar. 1805. Ensign 15 Apr. 1805. Lieut. 16 Apr. 1805. Capt. 1 Aug. 1822. *d.* Dinapore 8 Sept. 1827.

5th son of Joseph Houlton, of Farley Castle, Somerset, Capt. in the army, and Dorothea Sarah his wife, dau. of Charles Torriano, Capt. R.A. *m.* Dinapore, 24 Oct. 1823, Madelina Edward. His dau. *m.* William Eastfield Colebrooke, *q.v.*

Services : Posted as Lieut. to 5th N.I. in 1806. Reduction of Kalinjar 1812 ; Lieut. 2/5th N.I. Third Mahratta War ; Lieut. 2/5th N.I. Fur. 18 Jan. 1819 till 1821. Transfd. to 11th N.I. (late 1/5th) May 1824. First Burma War ; Arakan 1825 ; Capt. 2nd Gren. Bn.

Refs. : Burke's *Landed Gentry*, 11th edn., p. 760, *s.n.* Houlton, of Farley Castle, Somerset. *A.J.* xxv. 378. Will dated Dinapore 31 Aug. 1827 ; proved 16 Oct. 1827.

HOUSTON, Henry (1764/65-1795). Lieutenant, Infantry. *b.* in Ireland 1764/65. Cadet 1781. Arrived in India 23 Oct. 1781. Ensign July 1781. Lieut. 11 Oct. 1782. *d.* Dinapore 12 Jan. 1795.

Services : Apptd. Cadet on 13 Feb. 1781, aged 15. Sailed for India on the *Essex*, 13 Mar. 1781, aged 16. Lieut. 16th Bn. Sepoys in July 1787.

THE BENGAL ARMY, 1758-1834   489

HOUSTON, Sir Robert (1779-1862). General, K.C.B. Colonel 4th Eur. L.C. *b.* Renfrew 2 Dec. 1779. Cadet 1794. Arrived in India 26 Feb. 1796. Cornet 5 Dec. 1795. Lieut. 1 Nov. 1798. Capt. 22 Dec. 1803. Major 1 Nov. 1809. Lt. Col. 13 Dec. 1818. Lt. Col. Comdt. 1 Mar. 1824. Col. 5 June 1829. Maj. Gen. 10 Jan. 1837. Lt. Gen. 9 Nov. 1846. Gen. 20 June 1854. *d.* Torquay 5 Apr. 1862.

D.L. co. Haddington. 5th son of Col. Andrew Houston, of Jordanhill, co. Renfrew, and Margaret his wife, dau. of Hugh Wallace, of Cairnhill, co. Ayr. *m.* Cawnpore, 23 Nov. 1802, Frances, dau. of Capt. (? Daniel) Folliott, R.N. (She died 16 Nov. 1864.)

Services : Posted as Cornet to 2nd N.C. Transfd. as Lieut. to 4th N.C. Nov. 1798 ; as Adjt. to newly-raised 6th N.C. 29 May 1800. Operations in Jumna Doab 1803 ; Sasni ; Bijaigarh ; Kachaura. Second Mahratta War ; battle of Delhi ; Agra ; Laswari ; capture of Deig ; Bhurtpore ; Afzalgarh ; Bde. Major to Cav. Bde., and Prize Agent for Native Cav. (India medal with 3 clasps). Comdd. 6th N.C. 1805-14. Operations against Dhundia Khan 1807 ; Komona ; Ganauri. Settlement of Hariana 1809 ; Bhawani. Fur. s.c. 2 Jan. 1815 till Sept. 1817. Third Mahratta War ; in charge of Guide and Intelligence Dept. from 12 Nov. 1817. Comdd. a Cav. Depot 1818-9. Fur. p.a. 20 Oct. 1821 till death. The first Lieut. Govr. of Addiscombe 18 Mar. 1824 till 26 Mar. 1834. C.B. 3 Feb. 1817. K.C.B. 10 Mar. 1837.

Refs. : Burke's *Landed Gentry*, 13th edn., p. 931, *s.n.* Houston, of Mayshiel, Duns. *Walford. E.I.M.C.* ii. 232-3. *Boase. Vibart*, pp. 87-8. *G.M.* 1862, i. 656. *D.I.B. The Times*, 8 Apr. 1862.

HOWARD, John. Lieutenant. Infantry. Cadet 1781. Ensign 16 Aug. 1782. Lieut. 26 Jan. 1785. Resigned Apr. 1789.

Services : Fur. 25 Oct. 1785 till resignation. N.F.P.

HOWARD, Thomas Ward (1765-1807). Captain, 19th N.I. *b.* 1765. Cadet 1783. Admitted 5 Dec. 1784. Ensign 6 Jan. 1785. Lieut. 10 Nov. 1790. Capt. 27 Jan. 1804. *d.* Calcutta, 24 Dec. 1807, aged 42.

Only son of Thomas Howard, Col. 1st Regt. of Foot Gds. (who was elder brother of John, 15th Earl of Suffolk), who was kld. on his passage from America on board the *Eagle* packet in an engagement with the American privateer *Vengeance* on 21 Sept. 1778.[1] *m.* Cawnpore, 3 Aug. 1797, Sophia, dau. of Edward Rawstorne, *q.v.* (*See also* William Innes (1771/72-1850).) (She died 19 Dec. 1808.)

Services : Fur. 16 Jan. 1786 till 12 Mar. 1788. Adjt. & Qmr.

14th N.I. Transfd. to newly-raised 19th N.I. 29 May 1800. Adjt. & Qmr. 19th N.I. till 1803.
Refs. : Will dated 19 Aug. 1805 ; proved 5 Jan. 1808. M.I. in S. Park St. cemetery, Calcutta.

¹ *Note* : As Col. Howard's marriage could not be proved, Thomas Ward Howard was presumed to be illegitimate.

HOWARD, William Henry (1795-1835). Captain, Bengal Eur. Regt. *b.* Westminster, London, 4 July 1795. Cadet 1810. Admitted 21 Jan. 1812. Ensign 17 Dec. 1813. Lieut. 28 July 1816. Capt. 15 Jan. 1829. *d.* Dinapore, 8 Sept. 1835, of fever.

Son of William Howard. *m.* Berhampore, 14 Oct. 1817, Jane, dau. of Innis Delamain, *q.v.* (*See also* John William Gibbs.) (She *re-m.* Parker Duckworth Bingham, Comdr. R.N., Nov. 1838.)

Services : Posted as Ensign to Bengal Eur. Regt. in 1813 ; to 1st Bengal Eur. Regt. May 1824. Intr. & Qmr. 1st Bengal Eur. Regt. 23 Sept. 1824 till 22 Aug. 1827. Siege and capture of Bhurtpore ; Lieut. 1st Eur. Regt. Tempy. charge of escort to P.A., Haraoti, 4 May 1827. Intr. & Qmr. 1st Eur. Regt. 6 Dec. 1827 till Sept. 1829.

Refs. : *A.J.* N.S. xix. 149.

HOWE, George (*d.* 1772). Ensign, Infantry. Cadet 1769. Ensign 1770. *d.* Dinapore 6 Sept. 1772.

Services : N.F.P.

HOWE, John (*d.* 1828). Captain. Infantry. Cadet 1771. Ensign 27 Mar. 1773. Lieut. 24 May 1778. Capt. 18 Jan. 1784. Resigned after 1790. *d.* Bath 28 May 1828.

m. Calcutta, 28 Nov. 1787, Jane, widow of Thomas Harris, *q.v.*

Services : Supy. Capt., unposted, in July 1787. Fur. 3 Oct. 1788 till resignation.

Refs. : *A.J.* xxvi. 134.

HOWELL, Edward (1785-1815). Lieutenant, 12th N.I. *bapt.* Southwark 11 May 1785. Cadet 1803. Arrived in India 17 Mar. 1805. Ensign 18 Apr. 1805. Lieut. 18 Apr. 1805. *d.* Natpur, Bengal, 29 June 1815.

Son of Edward Howell, slop merchant, and Elizabeth his wife.

Services : Posted as Lieut. to 1/12th N.I. in 1806. Operations in Oudh 1808 ; Bhadri ; Samanpur ; Gurha ; Lieut. 1/12th N.I.

Refs. : Will dated Dinapore 8 Jan. 1815 ; proved in 1816.

HOWELL, George (*d.* 1794). Captain, Artillery. Cadet 1772. Fireworker 17 July 1776. Lieut. 15 July 1778. Capt. Lt. 29 Jan. 1784. Capt. 26 May 1786. *d. c.* Aug. 1794 : lost at sea on the voyage to Bencoolen.

THE BENGAL ARMY, 1758-1834   491

Services : Fur. s.c. to China 13 Mar. 1786. 3rd Bn. Art. in July 1787. A.D.C. to Col. George Deare, *q.v.*, in 1790. Third Mysore War ; Seringapatam ; Capt. comdg. 5th Coy. 2nd Bn. Art.

HOWISON, John. Cadet. Infantry. Cadet (?). Resigned 13 June 1781.
Services : N.F.P.

HOWLEY, Richard (*d.* 1820). Ensign. Infantry. Subsequently Lt. Col. Madras Art. Cadet 1781. Ensign 25 Feb. 1781. *d.* Paris 6 Apr. 1820.
Services : Transfd. to Madras Art. Fireworker 29 Nov. 1780. Lt. Col. 4 Apr. 1804. Retired 13 May 1806.
Refs. : Leslie.

HOWLEY, Thomas. Ensign. Infantry. Cadet (?). Ensign 5 Mar. 1781.
Services : N.F.P.

HOWORTH, Humphrey (1778-1817). Captain, 6th L.C. *b.* London 4 Oct. 1778. Cadet 1795. Arrived in India 6 Feb. 1797. Cornet 1 Mar. 1799. Lieut. 29 May 1800. Capt. 1 Nov. 1809. *d.* Lohargaon, Ajaigarh, C.I., 11 Apr. 1817 : kld. by Pindaris.

bapt. the Temple, London, 4 Oct. 1778 : received into the Church 6 July 1783. Son of Counsellor Henry Howorth, K.C., M.P. for Abingdon (who was related to Thomas Chippendale, the furniture maker), and Mary his wife. *m.* 1st, Ghazipur, Dec. 1801, Miss Cecilia Stewart. *m.* 2nd, Chunar, 17 May 1809, Miss Selina Cecilia Rider. (*See also* Francis James Thomas Johnston.) (She died Marseilles 9 Apr. 1820.) Father of Humphrey Howorth, *q.v.*

Services : Lieut. 1st Bengal Eur. Regt. in June 1798. Cornet 4th N.C. Transfd. as Lieut. to newly-raised 6th N.C. May 1800. Operations in Jumna Doab 1803 ; Sasni ; Bijaigarh ; Kachaura ; Lieut. 6th N.C. Second Mahratta War ; Laswari ; pursuit of Holkar ; Lieut. 6th N.C. Capt. Lt. 6th N.C. 31 Jan. 1807. (? Settlement of Hariana 1809 ; Bhawani ; Capt. Lt. 6th N.C.) Being on sick leave at Lohargaon in Apr. 1817 when a Sqdn. of 4th N.C., under Capt. Edward Jervoise Ridge, *q.v.*, moved out from that post to attack the Pindaris, he joined this Sqdn. as a volunteer. " In the *mêlée* he was obliged to take shelter under the shade of some trees near a village. He had only his servant with him, also on horseback, when he was surrounded by a party of Pindaris and murdered." (*The Hearseys.*) According to another account (*A.J.*), " He fell off his horse from illness, fatigue, and sunstroke and died immediately.

He was speared in two places when dead by the Pindaris. He was bur. at Poryah on the banks of the Cain R."

Refs. : *The Hearseys*, pp. 236-7. *A.J.* v. 325-6. *G.M.* 1817, ii. 637. *N. & Q.* 12S. x. 228, 258, 354. Will dated 25 Feb. 1817 ; proved 8 Dec. 1817.

HOWORTH, Humphrey (1813-1849). Captain, 39th N.I. *b.* Bengal 16 Sept. 1813. Cadet 1829. Arrived in India 1 Sept. 1830. Ensign 1 Sept. 1830. Lieut. 13 Nov. 1837. Capt. 30 Jan. 1846. *d.* Bhadrachalam, on the banks of R. Godaveri, 11 June 1849, of heat apoplexy.

Son of Humphrey Howorth, *q.v.*, and Selina his 2nd wife. *m.* Delhi, 5 Dec. 1835, Louisa Catherine, 2nd dau. of John Wells Fast, *q.v.* (She died 6 June 1892, aged 74.) Ed. Charterhouse ; admitted 1826.

Services : Cadet d.d. 29th N.I. 19 Oct. 1830 ; do. 43rd N.I. 1 Jan. 1831 ; do. 29th N.I. 23 Feb. 1831. Actg. Ensign 1 Oct. 1832. Posted as Ensign to 39th N.I. 20 Aug. 1833. Actg. Adjt. 39th N.I. 24 Mar. till 21 Nov. 1835. Served with Nizam's army, first in 8th, afterwards in 3rd Inf., 1 Sept. 1836 till death. Attack and capture of Bhadrachalam, Madras, 10 June 1849.

Refs. : Burton, pp. 134-5. *Charterhouse School List.*

*****HOZEE** (? **HOSEA), William.** Lieutenant. Infantry. (? Subsequently B.C.S.) Cadet (?). Ensign (5 Mar. 1765) 15 Aug. 1765. Lieut. 31 Dec. 1766.

N.B.—The following is conjectural only : (Nephew of Robert Orme, the historian. *m.* Calcutta, 17 Sept. 1772, Miss May Browne. Wrecked in the *Grosvenor* off Durban 3 Aug. 1782, together with his wife, and subsequently murdered by the natives.)

Services : N.F.P. (? Transfd. to B.C.S. Asst. to the Council of Revenue of Bihar 7 Feb. 1771. Collector of Hooghly 1772-3. Second in Council of Murshidabad.)

Refs. : *B.M. Add. M.S.* 6050 (where the name is given as Hozee. The Bengal civilian was Hosea.)

HUDLESTON, Henry (1803-1858). Lieut. Colonel. 7th N.I. *b.* Holy Walton, Leics., 1 Feb. 1803. Cadet 1819. Admitted 3 Aug. 1820. Ensign 4 Mar. 1820. Lieut. 11 July 1823. Capt. 8 Oct. 1839. Bt. Major 9 Nov. 1846. Retired 1 Mar. 1851. Hon. Lt. Col. 28 Nov. 1854. *d.* Caundle-Purse, Dorset, 25 Oct. 1858.

Son of Edward Hudleston, of Caundle-Purse.

Services : Posted as Ensign to 1/5th N.I. Transfd. as Lieut. to 4th N.I. July 1823 ; to 7th N.I. (late 1/4th) May 1824. (? First Burma War ; Cachar 1825 ; Lieut. 7th N.I.) Intr. & Qmr. 7th

N.I. 29 July 1825 till 1838. Actg. Bde. Major at Berhampore 11 Aug. 1826. Offg. Asst. Comr. in Kumaon 2 Mar. 1838. Senior Asst. Comr. in Kumaon 19 Feb. 1839 till 1845. Fur. 1846-8.

Refs. : (*See* Burke's *Landed Gentry*, 13th edn., *s.n.* Huddleston, of Sawston and Caundle-Purse.) G.M. 1858, ii. 650.

HUDSON, George Isaac (1811-1864). Captain. 67th N.I. *b.* Aston, Herts., 24 Oct. 1811. Cadet 1828. Arrived in India 2 Sept. 1829. Ensign 5 June 1829. Lieut. 10 Apr. 1834. Capt. 1 Aug. 1846. Retired 20 Feb. 1852. *d.* Tunbridge Wells 8 Feb. 1864.

Son of William Henry Hudson, of Frogmore Lodge, and Margaret his wife. *m.* Buscot rectory, Gloucs., 30 Mar. 1853, Catherine Sarah, eldest dau. of Rev. C. A. Brock.

Services : Ensign d.d. 52nd N.I. 19 Sept. 1829 till 15 Oct. 1830. Posted as Ensign to 67th N.I. 7 Jan. 1830. Fur. s.c. 22 Nov. 1837 till 27 Oct. 1840 ; p.a. 18 Dec. 1846 till 1849 ; s.c. 1849 till retirement. No record of active service.

Refs. : *The Times*, 10 Feb. 1864.

HUDSON, Luke. Lieutenant. Infantry. Cadet (?). Ensign (?). Lieut. 11 Feb. 1764. Resigned 14 Jan. 1766.

Services : N.F.P.

HUDSON, Watson (1785-1807). Lieutenant, 13th N.I. *bapt.* Brampton, Cumberland, 28 Feb. 1785. Cadet 1803. Arrived in India 27 Sept. 1804. Ensign 18 Sept. 1804. Lieut. 21 Sept. 1804. *d.* Bareilly 12 June 1807.

Son of John Hudson, surgeon, and Ann his wife.

Services : Posted as Lieut. to 13th N.I. in 1806. No record of active service.

*****HUGGIN, Henry.** Captain. Engineers. Capt. 25 Mar. 1765.

Services : Battle of Udhua Nullah 5 Sept. 1763. Promoted from Capt. Lt. and Sub-Director Engineers to be Capt. and Director. (G.O. 17 Apr. 1765.)

Refs. : *B.M. Add. MS.* 6050. *Broome*, pp. 386, 389.

HUGGINS, Gilbert (*d.* 1783). Lieutenant, Infantry. Cadet 1779. Ensign 11 Oct. 1779. Lieut. 21 May 1781. *d.* Hyderabad 12 Oct. 1783.

Services : (? Second Mysore War 1781-3.)

HUGHES, Edward Cumberland Thomas Bostock (1803-1837). Captain, Artillery. *b.* Killinick, co. Wexford, 8 July 1803. Cadet 1819. Arrived in India Feb. 1821. 2nd Lieut. 16 June

1820. Lieut. 21 Apr. 1824. Capt. 18 Jan. 1837. *d.* Karnal, 16 Oct. 1837, of a wound received the previous evening in a duel with Lieut. James Keating, H.M. 13th L.I.

Only son of Rev. William Hughes, rector of Killinick, and Elizabeth Shaw his wife. Addiscombe Cadet 1818-20.

Services : Posted to 4th Coy. 2nd Bn. Foot Art. Mar. 1821. Transfd. to 1st Coy. 2nd Bn. May 1822 ; to 3rd Coy. 2nd Bn. Apr. 1823. Comdg. Art. in Cuttack 3 Mar. 1823 till 1824. Posted to 2nd Coy. 2nd Bn. July 1825. Transfd. as Capt. to 4th Coy. 2nd Bn. June 1837. No record of active service.

Refs. : Foster's *Families of Royal Descent*, i. 390. *De Rhé-Philipe. A.J.* N.S. xxv. 144. Intestate ; admon. 16 July 1838. M.I. St. James's church tower, Karnal.

HUGHES, Henry Philip (1795-1871). Major. Artillery. *b.* Hounslow, Middlesex, 20 Oct. 1795. Cadet 1812. Admitted 16 Aug. 1813. Fireworker 15 Aug. 1813. Lieut. 1 Sept. 1818. Capt. 26 Sept. 1830. Retired 18 Mar. 1840. Hon. Major 28 Nov. 1854. *d.* Bridge Villa, Christchurch, Hants, 14 May 1871.

Son of Philip Hughes, dockmaster E.I. docks, and Ann his wife. *m.* Dum-Dum, 24 Oct. 1835, Eleanor, dau. of William Hopper, *q.v.* (*See also* Thomas Dingwall-Fordyce.)

Services : Served in Bencoolen 19 Aug. 1814 till 4 July 1817. Third Mahratta War ; Lieut. 6th Coy. 3rd Bn. Foot Art. Actg. Adjt. & Qmr. 2nd Coy. 1st Bn. 27 Jan. 1820. Fur. s.c. 14 Mar. 1821 till 8 Oct. 1824. Siege and capture of Bhurtpore ; Lieut. 1st Coy. 3rd Bn. (? India medal). Fur. p.a. 26 Dec. 1830 till 15 Dec. 1833. Leave s.c. 2 yrs. to Cape 28 Feb. 1837.

Refs. : The Times, 17 May 1871.

HUGHES, John (1759/60-?). Lieutenant. Infantry. *b.* London 1759/60. Cadet 1780. Arrived in India 30 Apr. 1781. Ensign 1780. Lieut. 1 Aug. 1781. Struck off after 1790.

Services : Sailed for India on the *Bellmont*, 3 Apr. 1780, aged 20. Granted fur. for 3 yrs. 28 Dec. 1785, and was still on fur. in 1790.

HUGHES, Michael (1793-1879). Major. 44th N.I. *b.* Llansamlet, co. Glamorgan, 9 Nov. 1793. Cadet 1813. Admitted 12 Oct. 1814. Ensign 16 Dec. 1814. Lieut. 16 June 1816. Capt. 21 Jan. 1835. Retired 1 Aug. 1843. Hon. Major 28 Nov. 1854. *d.* 6 Princes St., Hanover Sq., London, 11 Aug. 1879.

Son of John Hughes, of Swansea.

Services : Posted as Ensign to 1/22nd N.I. Third Mahratta War ; Nagpur ; Lieut. 1/22nd N.I. Leave s.c. 16 mos. to Cape 24 July 1819. Intr. & Qmr. 1/22nd N.I. 25 Feb. 1822 ; actg. Adjt. do. 30

Jan. 1824. Transfd. to 44th N.I. (late 2/22nd) May 1824. Intr. & Qmr. 44th N.I. 17 June 1824. Fur. s.c. 21 Mar. 1826 till 26 Oct. 1829. Leave s.c. to Cape 5 Feb. 1840 till 6 Nov. 1841.
Refs.: The Times, 18 Aug. 1879.

HUGHES, Pierce Nixon (1758/59-1792). Lieutenant, Infantry. *b.* 1758/59. Cadet 1777. Ensign 20 Feb. 1778. Lieut. 26 Sept. 1778. *d.* Madras 21 Sept. 1792.

Son of Benjamin Hughes, of Wexford, and Euphemia his wife, dau. of George Nixon, of Belmont. Cousin-german of Henry Harvey, *q.v.*

Services : Sailed for India on the *Duke of Portland*, 30 Apr. 1777, aged 18. Lieut. 28th Bn. Sepoys in July 1787. (?Third Mysore War.)

Refs. : Burke's *Landed Gentry of Ireland*, p. 328, *s.n.* Hughes, of Ballycross, co. Wexford.

HUGHES, Richard Radford (1796-1862). Lieut. Colonel. 62nd N.I. *bapt.* Worcester 16 Oct. 1796. Cadet 1817. Admitted 3 Oct. 1818. Ensign 3 May 1818. Lieut. 24 Apr. 1819. Capt. 4 May 1831. Major 22 Mar. 1844. Invalided 5 July 1844. Retired 12 Jan. 1850. Hon. Lt. Col. 28 Nov. 1854. *d.* at his residence, 37 Kensington Pk. Gdns., London, 29 Nov. 1862, aged 67.

Son of Henry Hughes. *m.* (before 1831) Mary. (She died 26 Apr. 1862, aged 64.) His dau. *m.* James Ruthven Pond, *q.v.*

Services : Posted as Lieut. to 25th N.I. in 1819. Transfd. to 2/11th N.I. 2 Dec. 1820. Fur. s.c. 17 Aug. 1821 till Apr. 1823. Transfd. to newly-raised 31st N.I. 11 July 1823. Adjt. 1/28th N.I. 21 Oct. 1823. Transfd. to 62nd N.I. (late 2/31st) May 1824. Fur. s.c. 24 Dec. 1824 till 13 June 1827. Fur. p.a. 5 Dec. 1835 till 17 Sept. 1838. No record of active service.

Refs. : G.M. 1863, i. 130. The Times, 2 Dec. 1862.

HUISH, Mark (1808-1867). Captain. 74th N.I. *b.* Nottingham 9 Mar. 1808. Cadet 1823. Arrived in India 26 July 1824. Ensign 23 Mar. 1824. Lieut. 24 Aug. 1825. Capt. 30 Jan. 1837. Resigned 8 July 1837. *d.* at his residence, Combe Wood, Bonchurch, I.W., 18 Jan. 1867.

Elder son of Mark Huish, of Nottingham, hosier, D.L. Notts., and Eliza his wife, dau. of John Gainsford, of Worksop. *m.* St. Michael's, Derby, 12 Aug. 1841, his cousin-german Margaret, 2nd dau. of John Huish, of Smalley Hall, co. Derby.

Services : Posted as Ensign to 67th N.I. in 1824. Transfd. to newly-raised 6th Extra Regt. (became 74th N.I.) July 1825. Actg.

Intr. & Qmr. 74th N.I. 11 July 1829 ; permanent do. 20 Jan. 1830 till Jan. 1835. Fur. p.a. 8 Jan. 1835 till resignation. No record of active service.
Refs. : Burke's *Commoners*, iv. 417, *s.n.* Huish, of Nottingham. Burke's *Landed Gentry*, 6th edn., p. 846, *s.n.* Hewish, of Doniford, Somerset. *The Times*, 22 Jan. 1867.

HULL, Edward Anthony (1801-1817). Ensign, Infantry. *b.* Gt. Baddow, Essex, 14 Mar. 1801. Cadet 1816. Ensign (rank unadjusted). *d.* Calcutta 23 Dec. 1817.
bapt. 15 Jan. 1802. Son of James Watson Hull, of Belvidere, co. Down, afterwards of Gt. Baddow, J.P. and D.L., high sheriff co. Down in 1789, and Sophia his wife. Brother of John Watson Hull, *q.v.* Brother-in-law of Sir Thomas Stamford Raffles, Kt. (*D.N.B.*), and kinsman of John Popham Watson, Lt. Col. H.M. 75th Foot.
Services : Ensign d.d. 2/10th N.I.
Refs. : Burke's *Landed Gentry*, 14th edn. (1925), p. 51, *s.n.* Hull, of The Crossways, Ewell, Surrey. Family information. M.I. in S. Park St. cemetery, Calcutta.

HULL, John Watson (1792-1842). Captain. 14th N.I. *b.* Belvidere 25 July 1792. Cadet 1813. Admitted 6 Jan. 1815. Ensign (16 Dec. 1814) 5 June 1815. Lieut. 30 Oct. 1817. Capt. 28 Feb. 1827. Retired 13 Apr. 1831. *d.* at his residence, Mount Ida, Dromore, 10 Nov. 1842.
bapt. Drumbo, co. Down, 29 July 1792. Called for his granduncle Commodore John Watson, Bombay Marine. Son of James Watson Hull, of Belvidere, Drumbo. Brother of Lawrence Nilson Hull, *q.v.*, and cousin of James Watson Wakefield, *q.v. m.* Pannal, Yorks., 15 Oct. 1835, Martha, dau. of John Younghusband, of Ballydrain, Belfast. (She died 6 May 1844.)
Services : Ensign East Essex Mil. 28 Jan. 1813. Posted as Ensign to 1/10th N.I. in 1815. With 4th Gren. Bn. in 1816. Third Mahratta War ; Lieut. 1/10th N.I. Actg. Intr. & Qmr. 2/10th N.I. 22 May 1820. On duty to Bencoolen 11 Sept. 1822. In charge of the spice plantations at Bencoolen from 1822. Transfd. to 14th N.I. (late 1/10th) May 1824. Leave s.c. 10 mos. to Penang and Singapore 19 Feb. 1828 ; fur. s.c. 13 Dec. 1828 till retirement. Apptd. S.A.C.G. 16 Oct. 1828.
Refs. : Burke's *Landed Gentry*, 14th edn., p. 51, *s.n.* Hull, of The Crossways, Ewell, Surrey. Family information. *A.J.* N.S. xxxix. 451. *The Times*, 21 Nov. 1842.

HULL, Lawrence Nilson (1799-1845). Major, 16th N.I. *b.* Gt. Baddow, Essex, 7 Jan. 1799. Cadet 1814. Arrived in India

THE BENGAL ARMY, 1758-1834   497

Sept. 1815. Ensign (16 Dec. 1814) 21 Aug. 1815. Lieut. 21 July 1818. Capt. 7 Mar. 1826. Major 28 Nov. 1839. *d.* Ferozepore, 23 Dec. 1845, of wounds received the previous day at the battle of Ferozshahr.

Son of James Watson Hull, of Gt. Baddow. Brother of Robert Redman Hull, *q.v.*

Services : Was in early life on the personal staff of his brother-in-law, Sir Stamford Raffles, in Sumatra, and was wrecked with him in the *Fame.* Posted as Ensign to 1/12th N.I. Oct. 1815. Served with 4th Gren. Bn. Nov. 1815 till June 1816. Nepal War 1816 ; Ensign 4th Gren. Bn., in 2nd Bde. Transfd. to 2/10th N.I. 1 Mar. 1816. Third Mahratta War 1817-8 ; in Nagpur and Narbada territories ; Ensign 2/10th N.I. Adjt. Fort Marlbro' (Bencoolen) Local Corps 1 Jan. 1820 till Jan. 1824. Fur. s.c. 12 Feb. 1824 till 16 May 1827. S.A.C.G. 26 Dec. 1828 ; Cawnpore ; Meerut ; Dinapore. Bde. Major Dacca 18 Mar. 1831 ; do. Cawnpore 8 Aug. 1831. D.A.A.G. 25 June 1832 ; Meerut ; Cawnpore. A.A.G. 27 July 1836 till 10 Feb. 1840. Rejoined 16th N.I. (late 2/10th) 6 Dec. 1838. First Afghan War 1838-9 ; Ghazni ; Capt. 16th N.I. (Medal). Fur. s.c. 1 Dec. 1841 till 7 June 1845. First Sikh War ; Mudki ; Ferozshahr (s.w.) ; Major 16th N.I.

Refs. : Burke's *Landed Gentry,* 14th edn., p. 51, *s.n.* Hull, of The Crossways, Ewell, Surrey. Family information. *De Rhé-Philipe.* M.I. St. Andrew's, Ferozepore.

HULL, Robert Redman (1789-1820). Bt. Captain, 10th N.I. *b.* Belvidere, co. Down, 12 Sept. 1789. Cadet 1804. Arrived in India 6 Apr. 1806. Ensign 8 Apr. 1806. Lieut. 16 July 1807. Bt. Capt. 1 Jan. 1819. *d. unm.* Fort Marlborough, Sumatra (where he was staying with his sister, Lady Raffles), 21 Oct. 1820.

Son of James Watson Hull, of Belvidere, Drumbo. Brother of Edward Anthony Hull, *q.v.*

Services : Posted as Ensign to 10th N.I. in 1807. Operations in Baghelkhand 1813 ; Entauri ; Lieut. 2/10th N.I. Intr. & Qmr. 4th Gren. Bn. 1815-6. Dy. Postmaster to Nagpur Subsdy. Force 1816 ; Qmr. do. 12 Aug. 1817 till 1819. Third Mahratta War. Bk. Mr. 15th (Narbada) Div. 1819. Leave s.c. 1820.

Refs. : Burke's *Landed Gentry,* 14th edn., p. 51, *s.n.* Hull, of The Crossways, Ewell, Surrey. Family information. Will dated Calcutta 12 Jan. 1820 ; proved 4 Apr. 1821.

HUME, Edmund Kent (1809-1849). Lieutenant. 64th N.I. *b.* London Mar. 1809. Cadet 1825. Ensign 5 Feb. 1826. Lieut. 24 Apr. 1827. Resigned in India 7 Nov. 1829. *d.* Dacca 18 Sept. 1849.

Son of James Hume. *m.* 1st, Dacca, 3 Apr. 1829, Mary, dau. of —— Stephanos, an Armenian, and widow of Michael Aratoon. *m.* 2nd, Pheannah Norrah.
Services : Ensign d.d. 16th N.I. 8 July 1826. Posted to 64th N.I. 26 Sept. 1826. No record of active service.
Refs. : A.J. N.S. xix. 239. Will dated 26 Aug. 1846 ; proved 5 Oct. 1849.

HUME, John (1761/62-1815). Lieut. Colonel. 3rd N.I. *b.* in Scotland 1761/62. Cadet 1778. Admitted 21 Oct. 1778. Ensign Oct. 1778. Lieut. 22 Oct. 1778. Capt. 1 June 1796. Major 20 May 1800. Lt. Col. 30 Sept. 1803. Retired 7 Sept. 1803. *d.* 27 July 1815.
Services : Sailed for India on the *Mount Stewart,* 9 Feb. 1778, aged 16. Lieut. 1/2nd Bengal Eur. Regt. in Oct. 1779. Adjt. and Qmr. at Midnapore 1787-90, or later. Capt. 3rd N.I. Major 2/3rd N.I. Fur. 20 Feb. 1801 till retirement.

HUME, Peter Bearsley (1778-1823). Captain. 16th N.I. *b.* the Close, Salisbury, 31 July 1778. Cadet 1796. Admitted 18 Sept. 1797. Ensign 7 Oct. 1797. Lieut. 10 Sept. 1798. Capt. Lt. 14 Nov. 1805. Capt. (?). Retired 25 Dec. 1809. *d.* 2 Jan. 1823.
bapt. 14 Sept. 1778. Son of Rev. Nathaniel Hume, canon residentiary of Salisbury cathedral, and Mary his wife. *m.* Sandila, Oudh, 22 Feb. 1802, Mary, dau. of St. George Ashe, *q.v.* (*See also* John Lumsdaine (1782-1805).) Ed. Westminster ; K.S. 1792, aged 13. Trin. Coll., Camb., 1796.
Services : Posted as Ensign to 16th N.I. Fur. 20 Sept. 1806 till retirement.
Refs. : Alumni Westmon.

HUMFRAYS (HUMPHREYS or HUMPHRAYS [1]**), Alexander** (1806-1846). Captain, Artillery. *b.* Allahabad 1806. Cadet 1824. Arrived in India 18 Mar. 1826. 2nd Lieut. 16 Dec. 1824. Lieut. 28 May 1829. Capt. 1 Mar. 1844. *d.* Delhi 19 Aug. 1846.
bapt. Dinapore 13 Oct. 1806. Youngest son of Richard Humfrays or Humphreys, *q.v.,* and Margaret Ursula his wife. Brother of Samuel Peter Crockat Humfrays, *q.v.,* and cousin-german of Charles Wyndham Humphreys, *q.v. m.* 1st, Madeline. (She died 12 Apr. 1839.) *m.* 2nd, Calcutta, 8 Feb. 1842, Louisa, dau. of James Sutherland, sometime Principal of the Hooghly coll., Calcutta. (She *re-m.* Simla, 5 June 1851, Thomas Tudor Tucker, *q.v.*) Addiscombe Cadet 1823-5.
Services : Posted to 2nd Troop 3rd Bde. H.A. May 1826. Transfd. to 1st Troop 1st Bde. Oct. 1827 ; to 2nd Troop 3rd Bde. Sept. 1832.

Fur. s.c. to China, Cape, and England, 5 Dec. 1833 till 1 Aug. 1836. Leave to England 4 Jan. till 30 Dec. 1841. Offg. Bde. Major H.A., Army of Exercise, 14 Dec. 1843. Gwalior campaign; Paniar; Lieut. 3rd Troop 3rd Bde. (Bronze star). Posted as Capt. to 5th Coy. 7th Bn. Foot Art. Aug. 1844.

Refs.: Burke's *Landed Gentry*, 13th edn., p. 1352, *s.n.* Humphreys-Owen, of Glansevern, co. Montgomery. *De Rhé-Philipe.* M.I. in Rajpura cemetery, Delhi.

[1] *Note*: The name is given as Humphreys by Burke; as Humfrays by Stubbs, *E.I.R.*, and official records; as Humphrays in *Gen. Mily. Register*, 1795-1810, and Addiscombe List; as Humfray in the marriage register.

HUMFRAYS or HUMPHREYS, Richard (1762-1806). Bt. Lieut. Colonel, Engineers. *b.* 28 Jan. 1762. Cadet 1778. Ensign 2 Oct. 1778. Lieut. 1 May 1781. Capt. 31 May 1786. Bt. Major 6 May 1796. Bt. Lt. Col. 1 Jan. 1800. *d.* Allahabad 14 Apr. 1806.

3rd son of Charles Gardiner Humphreys, of Bank House, Montgomery, and Martha his wife, dau. of Edward Bright. Uncle of Charles Wyndham Humphreys, *q.v. m.* Calcutta, 4 Feb. 1786, Margaret Ursula, dau. of Thomas Kearnan, of the city of London, and sister of Thomas Kearnan, *q.v.* (*See also* Alexander Nowell.) (She died London 20 June 1837.) Father of Alexander Humfrays, *q.v.*, Samuel Peter Crockat Humfrays, *q.v.*, Margaret Marian, wife of William Fergusson Beatson, *q.v.*, Emma, wife of William Stewart Beatson, *q.v.*, and Eliza, wife of Gavin Young, *q.v.*

Services: Asst. Engr. at Budge-Budge in July 1787.

Refs.: Burke's *Landed Gentry*, 13th edn., p. 1352, *s.n.* Humphreys-Owen, of Glansevern, co. Montgomery. Will dated Monghyr 4 Feb. 1792; proved 9 May 1806.

HUMFRAYS, Samuel Peter Crockat (1791-1839). Bt. Major, 36th N.I. *b.* Monghyr 4 Sept. 1791. Cadet 1807. Arrived in India 1 Nov. 1808. Ensign 4 Nov. 1808. Lieut. 16 May 1813. Capt. 13 May 1825. Bt. Major 28 June 1838. *d.* Sylhet, Assam, 27 May 1839.

bapt. 10 Oct. 1791. Son of Richard Humfrays, *q.v.*, and Margaret Ursula his wife. Brother of Alexander Humfrays, *q.v.*

Services: Barasat C.C. for 10 mos. Posted as Ensign to 18th N.I. Nepal War 1816; Lieut. 1/18th N.I., in 1st Bde., Rt. Column. Cuttack insurrection 1816; Khurda; Lieut. 1/18th N.I. A.D.C. to Maj.-Gen. Gabriel Martindell, *q.v.*, Mily. Comr. in Cuttack, 14 May 1817. S.A.C.G. 17 July 1819. Leave s.c. to sea 11 Sept. 1819 till 16 Feb. 1822. D.A.C.G., 2 cl., 19 Dec. 1823; 1 cl. 3 Oct. 1825. Transfd. to 36th N.I. (late 1/18th) May 1824. Leave s.c. 14 mos. to

China and N.S.W. 15 Oct. 1825. Fur. s.c. 6 Jan. 1827 till 23 Oct. 1830. Shekhawat expedn. 1834 ; Capt. 36th N.I., Bde. Major. Actg. Bde. Major at Agra 9 Dec. 1836 till 6 Oct. 1837. Bde. Major to troops on E. frontier 9 Jan. 1838 till death.
Refs. : M.I. in Sylhet cemetery.

HUMFREY, Henry (1803-1842). Captain, Invalid Est. Artillery. *b.* St. Helier, Jersey, 24 Mar. 1803. Cadet 1819. Admitted 19 Feb. 1821. 2nd Lieut. 16 June 1820. Lieut. 1 May 1824. Capt. 27 Apr. 1837. Invalided 22 Feb. 1841. *d.* Malvern 18 Sept. 1842.
2nd son of John Humfrey, of Reading, Maj. Gen. R.E. Brother of William Henry Humfrey, *q.v.* Addiscombe Cadet 1818-20.
Services : Served throughout with Foot Art. Fur. p.a. 17 Jan. 1836 till 1 Dec. 1838. Fur. s.c. 28 May 1841 till death. No record of active service.
Refs. : *G.M.* 1842, ii. 557. Will dated Bareilly 1 Nov. 1832 ; proved 13 Oct. 1843.

HUMFREY, William Henry (1809-1827). 2nd Lieutenant, Artillery. *b.* St. Helier, Jersey, 27 May 1809. Cadet 1826. 2nd Lieut. 3 Sept. 1827. *d.* Calcutta 23 Sept. 1827.
Son of John Humfrey, of Rugby, Maj. Gen. R.E. Brother of Henry Humfrey, *q.v.* Addiscombe Cadet 1825-6.
Refs. : *A.J.* xxv. 378. M.I. in mily. cemetery at Bhowanipore, Calcutta.

HUMPHREYS, Charles Wyndham (1806-1825). 2nd Lieutenant, Artillery. *b.* Bombay 9 Nov. 1806. Cadet 1822. 2nd Lieut. 10 May 1822. *d. unm.* at sea, 21 Apr. 1825, on board the *Euphrates*, on the voyage to England.
Younger son of Samuel Humphreys, of Bombay, atty. and clerk of the small causes, and Anne his wife, dau. of Joseph Popham, of Cork, and half-sister of Sir Home Riggs Popham, K.C.B. (*D.N.B.*). Nephew of Richard Humfrays (1762-1806), *q.v.*, and of William Popham, *q.v.* Addiscombe Cadet 1821-2.
Services : No record of active service.
Refs. : Burke's *Landed Gentry*, 13th edn., p. 1352, *s.n.* Humphreys-Owen, of Glansevern, co. Montgomery.

HUMPHREYS, Christopher (1786-1853). Ensign, Pension Est. 10th N.I. *b.* 6 Feb. 1786. Cadet 1806. Arrived in India 25 Nov. 1807. Ensign 9 Nov. 1807. Pensioned 1 Sept. 1812. *d.* Moradabad 12 June 1853.
bapt. St. Michan's, Dublin, 15 Feb. 1786. Eldest son of William Humphreys, of Ballyhaise, co. Cavan, high sheriff co. Cavan 1822,

sometime of Pill Lane, Dublin, woollen draper, and Letitia Kennedy his wife. *m.* Ann.
Services : Served for 18 mos. in a Corps of Irish Mil. or Fenc., part of the time as Adjt. Posted as Ensign to 10th N.I. in 1808. No record of active service.
Refs. : Burke's *Landed Gentry of Ireland,* p. 330, *s.n.* Humphreys, of Ballyhaise. *I.M.* 16 Aug. 1853, p. 480. Will dated 17 Aug. 1852 ; proved 18 May 1855.

HUMPHREYS, Edward (*d.* 1783). Major, Infantry. Cadet 1767. Ensign 8 July 1767. Lieut. 7 Apr. 1769. Capt. 3 Apr. 1777. Major 7 May 1781. *d.* Chunar 6 May 1783.
Brother of Henry Humphreys, of Trumpington, Cambs. Uncle of William Humphreys, *q.v.*
Services : N.F.P.
Refs : Will.

HUMPHREYS, Isaac (1751/52-1801). Captain, Infantry. *b.* in Ireland 1751/52. Cadet 1779. Admitted 19 Nov. 1779. Ensign 16 July 1779. Lieut. 8 Mar. 1781. Capt. 30 Oct. 1797. *d. unm.* Calcutta, 27 Oct. 1801, aged 49.
Services : Sailed for India on the *Ganges,* 7 Mar. 1779, when he gave his age as 24. Second Mysore War ; Pte. Sec. and A.D.C. to Col. Thomas Deane Pearse, *q.v.* Apptd. Sec. and Accomptant to the Board of Ord. 9 Nov. 1785. Apptd. on 23 May 1786 Sec. to the newly-constituted Mily. Board, which held its first consultation two days later. Was Head Asst. to the Mily. Board in 1790, and at the date of his death was Sec. to that Board.
Refs. : Hickey, iii. 98. *A.A.R.* iv. 119. Will dated 19 Oct. 1801. M.I. in S. Park St. cemetery, Calcutta.

HUMPHREYS, Richard (*d.* 1803). Bt. Captain, Artillery. Cadet 1783. Admitted 11 July 1784. Fireworker 23 Feb. 1785. Lieut. 9 Mar. 1792. Capt. Lt. 17 Feb. 1802. Bt. Capt. 8 Jan. 1798. *d.* Kandy, Ceylon, Sept. 1803 : murdered whilst a prisoner of war.
Services : Lieut. F. 2nd Bn. Art. in July 1787. Fur. 8 Dec. 1788 till 15 Aug. 1790. Served with the detachment of Art. sent from Bengal in Nov. 1793 for service against French cruisers in the Bay of Bengal and E. Archipelago. Went to Ceylon in Sept. 1795 with 5th Coy. 1st Bn. Art. Capture of Ceylon 1795-6. Operations in Ceylon, against the King of Kandy, 1803.
Refs. : Stubbs, i. 163. *G.M.* 1817, ii. 24, 119.

HUMPHREYS, WILLIAM (1781-1811). Lieutenant, Invalid Est. 16th N.I. *bapt.* Trumpington, Cambs., 7 Jan. 1781. Cadet 1799.

Arrived in India 10 Jan. 1801. Ensign 21 Sept. 1800. Lieut. 10 Nov. 1801. Invalided 30 May 1808. *d.* Bhowanipore, Calcutta, 11 Feb. 1811.

Son of Henry Humphreys and Martha his wife. Nephew of Edward Humphreys, *q.v.*

Services : Served throughout with 16th N.I.

*HUMPHRIES or HUMPHREYS, Isaac (1726/27-1763). Ensign, Bengal Eur. Regt. *b.* in Ireland 1726/27. Cadet 1760. Ensign (?). *d.* 1 July 1763 : kld. in action at the battle of Manjhi ; or *d.* 5th, 6th or 11th Oct. 1763 : massacred at or near Patna by order of Nawab Mir Muhammad Kasim. (See note to John Gordon.*)

Services : Sailed for India in 1759, aged 32. N.F.P.

Refs. : Broome, p. 366. Innes, p. 169. M.I. in Patna city.

HUMPHRIES, Thomas (*d.* 1789). Ensign. Infantry. Afterwards Lieut. Madras Art. Cadet 1780. Ensign 2 Feb. 1781. *d.* 18 May 1789.

Services : Transfd. to Madras Art. Fireworker 30 Nov. 1780. Lieut. 18 Feb. 1782.

Refs. : Leslie.

HUNGERFORD, Townsend James William (1814-1859). Lieut. Colonel, C.B., Artillery. *b.* Bombay 18 June 1814. Cadet 1830. Arrived in India 4 June 1831. 2nd Lieut. 10 Dec. 1830. Lieut. 31 Dec. 1839. Capt. 15 Jan. 1849. Bt. Major 12 Oct. 1857. Lt. Col. 12 Jan. 1859. *d.* Melbourne, N.S.W., 5 Dec. 1859, of disease contracted during the Mutiny.

Younger son of John Townsend Hungerford, of Bombay, solicitor, and Mary Anne his wife, dau. of J. Payne. *m.* Simla, 28 July 1855, Harriet Georgina, dau. of George Heorald Railton Willoughby. Addiscombe Cadet 1829-30.

Services : Actg. 2nd Lieut. 25 June 1833. Fur. s.c. 28 Jan. 1835 till 26 May 1838. Mutiny campaign ; minor operations (Medal). Fur. s.c. 1858 till death. C.B. 16 May 1859.

Refs. : Burke's *Landed Gentry of Ireland*, p. 332, *s.n.* Hungerford, of Cahirmore, co. Cork. *The Times*, 15 Feb. 1860. Will dated 19 Dec. 1856 ; admon. 3 Apr. 1860.

HUNT, John (*d.* 1804). Capt. Lieutenant, 17th N.I. Cadet 1783. Admitted 27 Sept. 1783. Ensign 11 Mar. 1785. Lieut. 6 May 1793. Capt. Lt. 1804. *d.* Cawnpore 8 Mar. 1804.

m. Anne, dau. of Robert Robertson, a scion of the family of Robertson, of Inshes, co. Inverness. (She *re-m.* 1 Feb. 1806, John Williamson Fulton, and became mother of Joseph Hennessy Fulton, *q.v.*)

Services: Lieut. 1st Bengal Eur. Regt. in June 1798. Transfd. as Lieut. to 17th N.I. Adjt. 2/27th N.I. in 1803. Operations in Jumna Doab 1803. (? Second Mahratta War; Aligarh; battle of Delhi; Lieut. 2/17th N.I.)
Refs.: Burke's *Colonial Gentry*, ii. 715, *s.n.* Fulton.

HUNT, John (1806-1883). Lieut. Colonel. 22nd N.I. *b.* 3 Nov. 1806. Cadet 1823. Arrived in India 10 Aug. 1824. Ensign 18 Feb. 1824. Lieut. 25 Nov. 1825. Capt. 27 June 1842. Major 15 Sept. 1854. Retired 15 May 1855. Hon. Lt. Col. 21 Sept. 1855. *d. unm.* at his residence, Stoke-Doyle, Oundle, Northants, 16 Mar. 1883.

5th and youngest son of Rev. Edward Hunt, rector of Benefield, Northants, and Bridget his wife, dau. of Rev. John Hawkins.

Services: Posted as Ensign to 22nd N.I. in 1824. First Burma War; Cachar 1825-6; Lieut. 22nd N.I. (India medal). Actg. Intr. & Qmr. 22nd N.I. 2 Nov. 1831. Shekhawat expedn. 1834; Lieut. 22nd N.I. Fur. s.c. 20 Jan. 1837 till 3 Feb. 1840. Attached to 2nd L.I. Bn. in 1842. Second Sikh War; Capt. 22nd N.I. (Medal).

Refs.: Burke's *Landed Gentry*, 12th edn., p. 1002, *s.n.* Hunt, of Boreatton, Salop. *The Times*, 19 Mar. 1883.

HUNT, Samuel (*d.* 1787). Captain, comdg. 4th Bn. Sepoys. Cadet 1768. Ensign 22 Feb. 1769. Lieut. 19 May 1770. Capt. 29 Jan. 1779. *d. unm.* Calcutta 20 Aug. 1787.

Brother of Ann, wife of Lucas Jackson, and uncle of Thomas Clegg, of Dublin.
Services: Capt. 1/2nd Bengal Eur. Regt. in Oct. 1779.
Refs.: *Hickey*, i. 237-9. Will dated 11 Aug. 1787.

HUNTER, Charles (1802-1833). Lieutenant, Pension Est. 50th N.I. *b.* Dunino, co. Fife, 6 July 1802. Cadet 1823. Ensign 23 Feb. 1824. Lieut. 23 Aug. 1826. Pensioned 27 June 1828. *d.* Calcutta 10 Mar. 1833.

Son of Rev. Dr. James Hunter, professor of logic at St. Andrews Univ. Brother of Francis Hunter, *q.v.*
Services: Posted as Ensign to 50th N.I. in 1824. No record of active service.

HUNTER, Francis (1805-1831). Lieutenant, 53rd N.I. *b.* St. Andrews, co. Fife, 11 Apr. 1805. Cadet 1820. Admitted 8 Oct. 1821. Ensign 5 May 1821. Lieut. 1 May 1824. *d.* Rothesay, Bute, 31 May 1831.

Son of Rev. Dr. James Hunter, professor at St. Andrews Univ. Brother of James Hunter (1808-1867), *q.v.*

Services : Posted as Ensign to 27th N.I. Transfd. to 53rd N.I. (late 1/27th) May 1824. Actg. Adjt. Rt. Wing 53rd N.I. 17 Apr. 1826. Actg. Intr. & Qmr. 53rd N.I. 7 May 1827. Actg. Adjt. 53rd N.I. 6 Sept. 1827. Fur. s.c. 17 Feb. 1829 till death. No record of active service.

Refs. : A.J. N.S. v. 178.

HUNTER, George (1784-1854). Lieut. General, C.B. Colonel 1st Eur. Bengal Fus. *bapt.* Monifieth, co. Forfar, 16 Sept. 1784. Cadet 1800. Arrived in India 22 Aug. 1801. Ensign 6 Jan. 1802. Lieut. 27 Jan. 1804. Capt. 8 Jan. 1816. Major 6 Jan. 1825. Lt. Col. 2 Aug. 1828. Col. 17 Jan. 1841. Maj. Gen. 23 Nov. 1841. Lt. Gen. 11 Nov. 1851. *d.* Bridge of Allan, co. Stirling, 10 Nov. 1854, of apoplexy.

Son of Charles Hunter, of Burnside, and Elizabeth Gray his wife. *m.* Christian Elizabeth, dau. of Abraham Bunbury, of Kilfeacle, co. Tipperary, Capt. 62nd Foot. (*See also* Hamilton George Maxwell.) (She died 27 Sept. 1866.)

Services : Ensign 17th N.I. Transfd. as Lieut. to newly-raised 21st N.I. Jan 1804. Fur. s.c. 30 Mar. 1805 till 19 July 1807. Served in Rohilkhand 1807-8. Capture of Java ; Cornelis 26 Aug. 1811 (w.) ; Lieut. 4th Vol. Bn. (Medal). Capture of Jokyakarta 1812. Served with Vols. till Dec. 1813. Fur. p.a. 12 Dec. 1813 till 4 Sept. 1815. Nepal War 1816 ; Hariharpur ; Lieut. 2/21st N.I., in 1st Bde., Rt. Column (India medal). Third Mahratta War. Sub-Asst. Stud Dept., Ghazipur, 9 July 1821. Transfd. to 41st N.I. (late 1/21st) May 1824. Actg. Supt. Stud, Lower Provinces, 12 Nov. 1825. Siege and capture of Bhurtpore (s.w.—sabre wound left arm on 18 Jan. 1826) ; Major comdg. 41st N.I. (*Lond. Gaz.* 4 July 1826) (clasp to India medal). Supt. Stud, Lower Provinces, 27 May 1826 till 13 May 1829. Lt. Col. 43rd N.I. Transfd. to 74th N.I. 16 Jan. 1834. Fur. s.c. 23 May 1834 till 11 Mar. 1839. Transfd. to 47th N.I. 8 Sept. 1835 ; to 49th N.I. 15 Dec. 1838 ; to 5th N.I. 1 Mar. 1839. Bdr., 2 cl., to comd. troops at Ferozepore 9 Apr. 1839. Fur. s.c. 31 Jan. 1840 till 14 Mar. 1841. Col. 19th N.I. 27 Apr. 1841. Bdr., 2 cl., to comd. garr. at Delhi 9 June 1841 ; to comd. troops at Sukkur 4 Apr. 1844. Against the Hill tribes in Sind 1845. Col. 1st Eur. L.I. 14 Feb. 1843. Fur. 10 Nov. 1849 till death. C.B. 2 Jan. 1827.

Refs. : Boase. *G.M.* 1855, i. 106. *I.M.* 18 Nov. 1854, p. 658.

HUNTER, George (1785-1819). Captain, 1st N.I. *b.* Lisburn, co. Antrim, 7 Sept. 1785. Cadet 1803. Arrived in India 14 Aug. 1804. Ensign 13 Sept. 1804. Lieut. 21 Sept. 1804. Capt. 5 Dec. 1815. *d.* at sea 5 Mar. 1819.

THE BENGAL ARMY, 1758-1834 505

Son of —— Hunter and Jane his wife. Brother of Edward Hunter, H.M.S. *m.* Harriet (*probably*) dau. of Thomas Hawkins, *q.v.*). Father of George Hunter, *q.v.*, Emma, wife of Edward Touchet Milner, *q.v.*, Louisa, wife of Ferdinand Charles Milner, *q.v.*, and Harriet Jenny, wife of John Scott (1801-1848), *q.v.*

Services : Posted as Lieut. to 1st N.I. in 1805. Operations in Bundelkhand against Lachman Dawa 1806-7 ; Chamir ; Sehlehuganj ; Lieut. 2/1st N.I. Adjt. & Qmr. 1st N.I. 8 Aug. 1810 till July 1814. Adjt. 1/1st N.I. 1 July 1814 till Dec. 1815. 2nd Asst. Sec. and 1st Asst. Accountant, Mily. Board, 21 Jan. 1817. S.A.C.G. 1818 till death.

Refs. : Will dated 25 Dec. 1818 ; proved 4 Aug. 1819.

HUNTER, George (1811-1831). Ensign, 15th N.I. *b.* Rewari 20 July 1811. Cadet 1826. Arrived in India 10 Jan. 1828. Ensign (22 Aug. 1827) 1 July 1828. *d.* Moradabad 19 Oct. 1831.

Son of George Hunter, *q.v.*, and Harriet his wife.

Services : Ensign d.d. 59th N.I. 31 Jan. 1828. Posted to 15th N.I. 1 July 1828. No record of active service.

HUNTER, Henry (1801-1842). Captain, 58th N.I. *b.* London 26 Apr. 1801. Cadet 1822. Arrived in India 22 Oct. 1823. Ensign 11 July 1823. Lieut. 13 May 1825. Capt. 15 Apr. 1840. *d.* Meerut 10 Aug. 1842.

Son of William Hunter, King's Messenger.

Services : Posted as Ensign to 58th N.I. Siege and capture of Bhurtpore ; Lieut. 58th N.I. Fur. s.c. 9 Dec. 1826 till 5 Nov. 1830. Actg. Adjt. Left Wing 58th N.I. 29 Jan. 1834. With 3rd L.I. Bn. at Meerut in 1842.

HUNTER, James (1754/55-1812). Bt. Colonel, 24th N.I. *b.* 1754/55. Cadet 1776. Admitted July 1776. Ensign 5 Apr. 1777. Lieut. 29 Aug. 1778. Capt. 28 June 1795. Major 31 July 1799. Lt. Col. 14 Dec. 1802. Bt. Col. 4 June 1811. *d.* Saharanpur, U.P., 11 Oct. 1812.

A native of Surrey. Brother of Benjamin Hunter, of Hadleigh, Suffolk.

Services : Sailed for India on the *Duke of Cumberland*, 29 Mar. 1776, aged 21. Lieut. 18th Bn. Sepoys in July 1787. Major 1/6th N.I. Fur. 24 Jan. 1798 till 20 Aug. 1802. Transfd. to newly-raised 19th N.I. 29 May 1800. Fur. 23 Oct. 1804. Transfd. as Lt. Col. to 3rd N.I. in 1804 ; to Bengal Eur. Regt. in 1805. Struck off 31 Dec. 1809, having exceeded 5 yrs. absence from India. Restored to the Service and returned to India in 1810. Posted to 2/24th N.I. in 1811.

Refs. : Will dated 1 Jan. 1810 ; proved in 1812.

HUNTER, James (1777-1817). Captain, 4th N.I. *b.* Edinburgh 29 Sept. 1777. Cadet 1798. Arrived in India 22 Dec. 1799. Ensign 23 Jan. 1800. Lieut. 29 May 1800. Capt. 2 Jan. 1811. *d. unm.* Hapur, nr. Meerut, 8 Dec. 1817.

bapt. Edinburgh 3 Oct. 1777. Son of James Hunter, of Abbeyhill, and Mary Muir his wife.

Services : Second Mahratta War ; Aligarh ; battle of Deig (w.) ; Lieut. 1/4th N.I. Supt. of Invalids at Hapur 1 Apr. 1806 till death. Capt. Lt. 4th N.I. 19 Dec. 1809. Capt. 2/4th N.I.

Refs.: Will dated 20 July 1817 ; proved 24 Jan. 1818.

HUNTER, James (1808-1867). Lieut. Colonel. 53rd N.I. *b.* St. Andrews, co. Fife, 24 July 1808. Cadet 1827. Arrived in India 9 June 1828. Ensign 23 Feb. 1828. Lieut. 13 Nov. 1834. Capt. 23 June 1843. Bt. Major 20 June 1854. Retired 4 June 1855. Hon. Lt. Col. 10 Aug. 1855. *d.* St. Andrews 22 Jan. 1867.

Son of Rev. Dr. James Hunter, professor at St. Andrews Univ., and Jane Wilson his wife. Brother of Charles Hunter, *q.v. m.* 1st, Ludhiana, 15 June 1839, Miss Anna Margaretta Corfield. (*See also* John Assey Fairhead.) *m.* 2nd, Perth, 24 July 1860, Alexa, eldest dau. of Rev. John Dodgson, of Comely Bank, Perth, and sister of William Scott Dodgson, *q.v.*

Services : Posted as Ensign to 53rd N.I. 4 Nov. 1828. Fur. s.c. 17 Feb. 1829 till 9 Nov. 1831. Actg. Adjt. Left Wing 53rd N.I. 4 Mar. 1835 till 1837. Adjt. 53rd N.I. 9 Nov. 1837 till 10 Sept. 1842. First Afghan War 1842 ; forcing of Khyber Pass ; Ali Masjid ; operations of Bdr. Wild's Bde. ; re-occupation of Kabul ; Lieut. 53rd N.I., with Gen. Pollock's force (Medal). Intr. & Qmr. 53rd N.I. 10 Sept. 1842. Bde. Qmr. to Bdr. Wild's force 28 Sept. 1842. Offg. Bde. Major at Meerut 3 Dec. 1844. Second Sikh War ; in garrison at Lahore ; Capt. 53rd N.I. (Medal). Offg. Bde. Major at Delhi Dec. 1853. Fur. 1854 till retirement.

Refs. : G.M. 1867, i. 395. *The Times,* 26 Jan. 1867.

*__HUNTER, John__ (*d.* 1771). Cadet, Infantry. Cadet (?). bur. Calcutta 2 June 1771.

Services : N.F.P.

Refs. : Calcutta burial register.

HUNTER, John (*d.* 1786). Ensign, Infantry. Cadet 1783. Ensign 1783. *d.* 19 May 1786.

Services : N.F.P.

HUNTER, John (1781-1836). Lieut. Colonel, 29th N.I. *b.* Virginia 6 May 1781. Cadet 1800. Arrived in India 24 Aug. 1801. Ensign 25 Nov. 1801. Lieut. 30 Sept. 1803. Capt. 8 Jan. 1816.

Major 11 Feb. 1826. Lt. Col. 26 Dec. 1830. d. Banda 17 Sept. 1836.

4th and youngest son of John Hunter, of Virginia, and Jane his wife, dau. of Col. Broadwater. Cousin-german of Patrick Hunter, *q.v. m.* Allahabad, 2 Apr. 1817, Louisa Maria, 2nd dau. of Thomas Norris, of Croom's Hill, Greenwich. (*See also* John Delamain.)

Services : Posted as Ensign to 16th N.I. Second Mahratta War ; Agra ; Laswari ; Gwalior ; Lieut. 2/16th N.I. Leave s.c. 3 June 1804 till 4 Mar. 1805. Transfd. to 1/16th N.I. July 1805. (? Operations in Bundelkhand 1807 ; Chamir ; Lieut. 1/16th N.I.) Fur. s.c. 25 Aug. 1807 till 21 Jan. 1812. Adjt. Calcutta Native Mil. 6 July 1812 till 1815. Transfd. to newly-raised 1/29th N.I. in 1815. Actg. Intr. & Qmr. 2/29th N.I. 1815. Sub-Asst. Stud Dept., Pusa, 19 Jan. 1816 till Apr. 1819. Transfd. to 58th N.I. (late 2/29th) May 1824. Siege and capture of Bhurtpore (s.w. 18 Jan. 1826), "behaved with great gallantry" (*Lond. Gaz.* 4 July 1826) ; Capt. 58th N.I. Granted as a special case an addition of £50 to his wound pension. Regulating Ofr. of Invalids and Thannahs in Bihar 13 Dec. 1827 till 1 Jan. 1832. Posted as Lt. Col. to 71st N.I. 24 Sept. 1831. Transfd. to 56th N.I. 11 Jan. 1834 ; to 17th N.I. 8 June 1835 ; to 51st N.I. 8 Jan. 1836 ; to 29th N.I. 19 July 1836.

Refs. : Burke's *Landed Gentry*, 12th edn., p. 1002, *s.n.* Hunter, of Thurston, co. Haddington. *A.J.* N.S. xxii. 191. *G.M.* 1817, ii. 465. Will dated Agra 25 Apr. 1836 ; proved 22 Oct. 1836.

HUNTER, Patrick (*d.* 1826). Captain. Infantry. Cadet 1771. Ensign 29 Mar. 1773. Lieut. 26 May 1778. Capt. 20 Jan. 1784. Struck off 1793. d. Edinburgh 29 Aug. 1826.

Son of James Hunter, of Ayr, banker, and Sarah his wife, dau. of Patrick Ballantine, of Ayr. Cousin-german of John Hunter (1781-1836), *q.v. m.* Edinburgh, 31 Mar. 1795, Hon. Jane (Jean), 2nd dau. of James, 7th Lord Rollo. (She died 18 Sept. 1838.)

Services : Granted fur. 3 yrs. 2 Nov. 1785, and remained on fur. till struck off.

Refs. : Burke's *Landed Gentry*, 12th edn., p. 1002, *s.n.* Hunter, of Thurston, co. Haddington. Burke's *Peerage*, 1923, p. 1897, *s.n.* Rollo, B. *A.J.* xxi. 499.

HUNTER, Robert. Cadet. Infantry. Cadet 1766. Dismissed 11 Oct. 1766.

Services : (*Probably* dismissed owing to implication in the "Batta mutiny" in May 1766.)

HUNTER, Robert (*d.* 1784). Ensign, 3rd N.I. Cadet 1782. Ensign 31 Jan. 1783. bur. Cawnpore 8 Dec. 1784.

Services : N.F.P.

HUNTER, Robert Mackellar (1807-1845). Captain, 73rd N.I. *b.* Halifax, Nova Scotia, 15 Mar. 1807. Cadet 1822. Arrived in India 20 Oct. 1823. Ensign 11 July 1823. Lieut. 13 May 1825. Capt. 30 June 1842. *d.* 21 Dec. 1845 : kld. in action at the battle of Ferozshahr.

3rd son of Gen. Sir Martin Hunter, G.C.M.G., of Medomsley, co. Durham (*D.N.B.*), and Jean his wife, only dau. of James Dickson, of Anton's Hill, co. Berwick. Brother of Thomas Harvey Hunter, *q.v.* Addiscombe Cadet 1821-3.

Services : Posted as Ensign to 2/7th N.I. Jan. 1824. First Burma War ; Arakan 1825 ; Ensign 2nd L.I. Bn. Transfd. as Lieut. to 5th Extra Regt. (became 73rd N.I.) July 1825. Pioneers 16 Oct. till Dec. 1833. Assam Sebundy Corps 12 May 1835 till Sept. 1836. Fur. s.c. 3 Jan. 1837 till 20 Jan. 1840. First Sikh War ; Mudki ; Ferozshahr (kld.) ; Capt. 73rd N.I.

Refs. : Burke's *Landed Gentry*, 13th edn., p. 951, *s.n.* Hunter, *formerly* of Medomsley. *De Rhé-Philipe*. M.I. St. Andrew's, Ferozepore.

HUNTER, Samuel Orby (1799-1825). Lieutenant, 9th L.C. *bapt.* Limerick 15 Apr. 1799. Cadet 1819. Cornet 4 Mar. 1820. Lieut. 16 Oct. 1823. *d.* Cawnpore 15 Nov. 1825.

Son of Samuel Hunter, of Catherine St., Limerick.

Services : Posted as Cornet to 7th L.C. in 1820. Adjt. 7th L.C. 7 Mar. 1822 till 1825. Transfd. to newly-raised 9th L.C. 1825. Adjt. 9th L.C. 12 July 1825 till death. No record of active service.

Refs. : Will dated 1 Nov. 1825 ; proved 21 Dec. 1825.

HUNTER, Thomas (1787-1806). Cadet, Infantry. *b.* Hoddam, co. Dumfries, 12 Aug. 1787. Cadet 1805. Never arrived in India. *d.* Dec. 1806, on his passage to India, in the wreck of the *Skelton Castle*. Struck off with effect from 5 Nov. 1806. (See note to Alexander Jaffray Hautenville.)

Son of Robert Hunter, in Mainfool, Hoddam.

HUNTER, Thomas Harvey (1812-1860). Lieutenant, Invalid Est. 26th N.I. *bapt.* St. John's, New Brunswick, 7 June 1812. Cadet 1828. Arrived in India 21 May 1829. Ensign 7 Feb. 1829. Lieut. 7 May 1835. Invalided 3 Nov. 1841. *d.* Mussoorie, U.P., 7 Apr. 1860.

6th and youngest son of Gen. Sir Martin Hunter, G.C.M.G., and Jean his wife. Brother of Robert Mackellar Hunter, *q.v. m.* Dehra Dun, U.P., 16 Nov. 1853, Eliza, dau. of James Swetenham, *q.v.*

Services : Ensign d.d. 5th N.I. 13 July 1829 ; do. 55th N.I. 15 Aug. 1829. Posted to 26th N.I. 14 Sept. 1829. Assam Sebundy

Corps 1835. d.d. Eur. Invalids at Chunar 11 Feb. 1848. No record of active service.
Refs. : Burke's *Landed Gentry*, 13th edn., p. 951, *s.n.* Hunter, *formerly* of Medomsley, co. Durham. *G.M.* 1860, ii. 98. *I.M.* 22 May 1860, p. 384.

HUNTER, Watson (1776-1826). Lieut. Colonel, Invalid Est. 27th N.I. *b.* Hexham, Northumberland, 8 June 1776. Cadet 1794. Arrived in India 30 Oct. 1795. Ensign 15 Oct. 1795. Lieut. 15 Feb. 1797. Capt. 21 Sept. 1804. Major 16 Dec. 1814. Lt. Col. 24 Jan. 1819. Invalided 18 Jan. 1823. *d.* Benares 18 Oct. 1826.
Son of Richard Hunter and Jane his wife. Brother of Jane Hunter, of Cumberland Pl., Marylebone.
Services : Disturbances in the Ganjam district, Madras, 1801 ; Lieut. 6th N.I. Capt. Lt. 6th N.I. 21 Nov. 1803. Transfd. as Capt. to newly-raised 27th N.I. in 1805. Operations against Dhundia Khan 1807 ; Komona ; Ganauri ; Capt. 27th N.I. Fur. 22 Jan. 1810 till 1812. Transfd. as Major to newly-raised 29th N.I. in 1815. Siege and capture of Hathras 1817 ; Major 1/29th N.I. Transfd. as Lt. Col. to 1/27th N.I. in 1819. Comdd. 1st Bn. Native Invalids 1823 till death.
Refs. : Will dated in 1826 ; proved 13 Sept. 1828.

HUNTER, William (1800-1874). Lieut. Colonel. 15th N.I. *b.* Cavendish Sq., London, 4 June 1800. Cadet 1821. Arrived in India 21 Aug. 1822. Ensign 14 June 1822. Lieut. 1 May 1824. Capt. 26 Feb. 1835. Major 5 Oct. 1846. Retired 15 Sept. 1848. Hon. Lt. Col. 28 Nov. 1854. *d.* Mount Severn, Llanidloes, co. Montgomery, 11 Dec. 1874.
Of Mount Severn, co. Montgomery, J.P. Eldest son of Robert Hunter, of Kew, Surrey, and Elizabeth (? Charlotte) his wife, dau. of Capt. Hansford, R.N. *m.* 1854, Emily Jane, dau. of Robert Wood, of Bath. Ed. Harrow 1812/13 till 1814/15.
Services : Posted as Ensign to 11th N.I. Transfd. to 17th N.I. (late 2/11th) May 1824 ; to 15th N.I. (late 1/11th) 2 Aug. 1824. Siege and capture of Bhurtpore ; Lieut. 15th N.I. (India medal). Intr. & Qmr. 15th N.I. 12 July 1825 till 30 May 1835. Fur. p.a. 25 Nov. 1835 till 20 Dec. 1839. Comdd. Khurda Paik Coy. at Balasore 13 Jan. till 1 Aug. 1840. Comdt. Mewar Bhil Corps 15 July 1840 till May 1848, and, in addition, from 9 Aug. 1841 was Asst. to P.A. Mewar. J.P. co. Montgomery 1859.
Refs. : Burke's *Landed Gentry*, 10th edn., p. 829, *s.n.* Hunter, of Mount Severn, co. Montgomery. *County Families of Wales*, by Thomas Nicholas, ii. 824. *Harrow School Register*. *The Times*, 16 Dec. 1874.

HURRING, Thomas (*d.* 1806). Captain, 15th N.I. Cadet 1782. Admitted 15 Aug. 1783. Ensign 8 Jan. 1783. Lieut. 21 Mar. 1788. Capt. 13 July 1803. *d.* at sea, 4 May 1806, on board the American ship *Rising Sun*, on his passage to England.

Brother of John, Benjamin; Susan, wife of Joseph Francis; Rose, wife of Samuel Jay; Ann, wife of John Poole; and Mary, wife of William Draper.

Services : Ensign 4th Bengal Eur. Bn. in July 1787. Capt. Lt. 15th N.I. 13 June 1801. Operations in Jumna Doab 1803; Sasni; Bijaigarh; Kachaura; Capt. 15th N.I. Second Mahratta War; battle of Delhi; Agra; Laswari; battle of Deig; Capt. 15th N.I. Fur. 21 Feb. 1806 till death.

Refs. : Will dated 18 Nov. 1805; proved 16 Oct. 1807.

HURST, William (*d.* 1792). Lieutenant, Infantry. Cadet 1779. Ensign 1779. Lieut. 24 May 1781. *d.* Tangepore (? Tangi, Bengal) 6 Oct. 1792.

Services : Lieut. 3rd Bn. Sepoys in July 1787.

HUSSEY, Vere Warner (1746/47-1823). Lieut. General. Comdt. Artillery. *b.* 1746/47. Cadet 1769. Admitted 6 Oct. 1770. Fireworker 12 Mar. 1771. Lieut. 10 Jan. 1773. Capt. Lt. 28 Sept. 1777. Capt. 5 Jan. 1779. Major 17 Apr. 1786. Lt. Col. 14 Sept. 1790. Col. 8 Jan. 1796. Maj. Gen. 1 Jan. 1798. Lt. Gen. 1 Jan. 1805. Retired on off-reckonings 1 July 1801. *d.* Gt. Cumberland Pl., London, 29 Apr. 1823, aged 76.

Of Wood Walton, co. Huntingdon. Only son of Thomas Hussey, of Wrexham, co. Denbigh.

Services : First Rohilla War; battle of St. George. Second Mysore War (s.w. in 1781, which rendered him lame for life); Capt. comdg. 5th Coy. 1st Bn. Art. Comy. Ord. 1784, and to comd. Art. in province of Benares and the garr. of Chunar. Fur. 28 Nov. 1785 till 23 July 1788. To comd. Bengal Art. Oct. 1797. Fur. 15 Feb. 1799 till retirement.

Refs. : Burke's *Landed Gentry*, 2nd edn., p. 623, *s.n.* Hussey, of Wood Walton, Hunts.; 13th edn., p. 1280, *s.n.* Moubray, of Cockairnie and Otterston, co. Fife. *E.I.M.C.* i. 49. *S.M.* 1823, i. 648. *G.M.* 1823, i. 475. *A.R.* 1823.

HUTCHINGS, George (1806-1840). Lieutenant, 69th N.I. *b.* Bristol 5 Dec. 1806. Cadet 1826. Arrived in India 22 Sept. 1827. Ensign 8 Feb. 1827. Lieut. 29 June 1835. *d.* on the river nr. Kishnaghur 22 Apr. 1840.

Eldest son of John Hutchings, of Bristol (of Sandford Orcas). *m.* Muttra, 8 Jan. 1830, Mary Ann Milligan, eldest dau. of George

Gwilt, F.S.A., of Southwark, architect (*D.N.B.*), and widow of William Leman Dunlap, Asst. Surg. Bengal Est. Wadham Coll., Oxon. ; matric. 31 May 1824.
Services : Posted as Ensign to 1st Extra Regt. (became 69th N.I.) 19 June 1827. Offg. Intr. & Qmr. 31st N.I. 27 Sept. 1830 ; do. 71st N.I. 8 Jan. 1834 ; do. 2nd N.I. 20 Feb. 1836. Intr. & Qmr. 69th N.I. 14 Mar. 1837. Fur. p.a. 8 Feb. 1838 till 28 Oct. 1839. No record of active service.
Refs. : Foster's *Baronetage*, p. 396, *s.n.* Medlycott, Bart. *Alumni Oxon*. *G.M.* 1830, ii. 364.

HUTCHINS, George Henry (1792-1844). Major. 30th N.I. *b.* London 22 Aug. 1792. Cadet 1807. Admitted 29 Aug. 1808. Ensign 17 Sept. 1808. Lieut. 12 Jan. 1813. Capt. 1 May 1824. Major 30 Dec. 1828. Retired 17 Apr. 1832. *d.* 15 Pittville Villas, Cheltenham, 10 Mar. 1844.

Son of Rev. John Hutchins. *m.* 1st, Calcutta, 8 Mar. 1811, Miss Mary Ann Haigs. *m.* 2nd, Catherine. (She died 16 Aug. 1871.)
Services : Barasat C.C. for 10½ mos. Posted as Ensign to 15th N.I. Fur. s.c. 18 Nov. 1812 till 5 Aug. 1814. Nepal War 1814-5 ; Lieut. 2/15th N.I., in 4th Div. Nepal War 1816 ; Lieut. 2/15th N.I., in 4th Bde., Centre Column. Siege and capture of Hathras 1817 ; Lieut. 2/15th N.I. (? Third Mahratta War ; Asirgarh.) Tempy. comdg. Jubbulpore Najib Corps 22 May 1821. To comd. escort of A.G.G., Saugor & Narbada territories, 22 Feb. 1823 and 21 May 1827. Transfd. to 30th N.I. (late 1/15th) May 1824. Leave s.c. 18 mos. to N.S.W. 22 Jan. 1830.
Refs. : *G.M.* 1844, i. 442. *The Times*, 14 Mar. 1844.

***HUTCHINS, William** (*d.* 1769). Ensign, Infantry. Cadet (?). Ensign (?). *d.* in India 1769.

m. Elizabeth.
Services : N.F.P.
Refs. : Will dated 19 Feb. 1769 ; proved 20 Dec. 1769.

HUTCHINSON, Alfred Cooper (1813-1857). Captain. Artillery. *bapt.* Ripon, Yorks., 19 Jan. 1813. Cadet 1828. Arrived in India 4 Nov. 1829. 2nd Lieut. 12 June 1829. Lieut. 20 Apr. 1838. Capt. 1 July 1847. Invalided 26 Oct. 1848. Retired 28 July 1856. *d.* in England 24 Jan. 1857.

Son of William Walker Hutchinson, of Rotherham, Yorks., M.D., and Grace his wife. *m.* Simla, 30 Sept. 1854, Sophy Croome, dau. of Charles Mabey. (She *re-m.* 1864.) Addiscombe Cadet 1827-9.
Services : Rank as 2nd Lieut. cancelled, and reduced to Cadet (G.G.O. 31 May 1830). Actg. 2nd Lieut. (G.G.O. 27 Feb. 1832). Service afterwards allowed to count for brevet rank. Served

throughout with Foot Art. Fur. s.c. 28 Oct. 1839 till 1844. No record of active service.

Refs. : *I.M.* 30 Jan. 1857, p. 97.

HUTCHINSON, Charles (1768/69-1805). Captain, Artillery. *b.* Somerset 1768/69. Country Cadet 1781. Admitted 5 Nov. 1781. Fireworker 30 July 1782. Lieut. 15 Jan. 1789. Capt. Lt. 8 Jan. 1796. Capt. 20 Sept. 1802. *d.* Tonk Rampura, 16 Sept. 1805, aged 36.

Son of an officer in H.M.S. Brother-in-law of John Davidson, of Newcastle-on-Tyne. *m.* Alnwick, Northumberland, Feb. 1801, a dau. of Anthony Lambert (1759/60-1800), *q.v.* (She died Kendal Dec. 1801.)

Services : Lieut. F. 2nd Bn. Art. in July 1787. The greater part of his service was spent at Fort Marlbro', Bencoolen. Apptd. Adjt. at Fort Marlbro' 26 Nov. 1790. Fur. s.c. for 3 yrs. Second Mahratta War ; Aligarh ; battle of Delhi ; Agra ; with Col. Monson's force ; operations in Rampura district 1805 ; Khataoli ; Bhamangaon ; Karawal ; Dhalra ; Capt. comdg. 2nd Coy. 2nd Bn. Art.

Refs. : *Stubbs,* i. 246. *G.M.* 1806, i. 180. *M.M.* 1801, p. 184 ; 1806, p. 194. Will dated Tonk Rampoora 29 June 1805.

HUTCHINSON, Charles (1804-1825). Lieutenant, 42nd N.I. *b.* Dunnottar, co. Kincardine, 10 Mar. 1804. Cadet 1823. Ensign 21 Feb. 1824. Lieut. 1825. *d.* Arakan, Burma, 14 July 1825.

Youngest son of John Hutchinson, R.N., Comdr. of H.M. revenue cutter *Nepean.*

Services : First Burma War ; Arakan 1825 ; Lieut. 42nd N.I.

Refs. : *S.M.* 1826, i. 255.

HUTCHINSON, George (*d.* 1828). Lieut. Colonel. 27th N.I. Country Cadet 1778. Admitted 9 Mar. 1778. Ensign 4 June 1778. Lieut. 13 Nov. 1780. Capt. 3 Oct. 1796. Major 30 Sept. 1803. Lieut. Col. 19 Oct. 1805. Retired 1 Aug. 1810. *d.* Edinburgh 24 July 1828.

Services : Lieut. 21st Bn. Sepoys in July 1787. Fur. 29 Dec. 1799 till 15 Feb. 1803. Capt. Marine Regt. Second Mahratta War ; reduction of Cuttack 1803 ; Capt. comdg. detachment of 20th N.I. (late Marine Regt.). " The conduct of Capt. Hutchinson was most steady, able, and highly meritorious." (Lt.-Col. Harcourt's despatch of 24 Oct. 1803.) Major 20th N.I. Transfd. as Lt. Col. to newly-raised 27th N.I. Operations against Dhundia Khan 1807 ; Komona ; Ganauri ; Lt. Col. 27th N.I. Fur. 25 Dec. 1809 till retirement.

Refs. : *A.J.* xxvi. 389.

THE BENGAL ARMY, 1758-1834   513

HUTCHINSON, George (1793-1852). Lieut. Colonel. Engineers.
bapt. Knaresborough, Yorks., 23 July 1793. Cadet 1810. Ensign 23 Dec. 1812. Lieut. 4 July 1818. Capt. 29 July 1821. Major 10 July 1832. Lt. Col. 31 Mar. 1840. Retired 28 Aug. 1841. *d.* Cheltenham 28 Aug. 1852.
   Son of Thomas Hutchinson, of Harrogate, M.D. Brother of Thomas Frederick Hutchinson, *q.v.* *m.* 1st, Calcutta, 20 Mar. 1823, Miss Martha Williams. (She died at sea 1 Apr. 1826.) *m.* 2nd, Calcutta, 20 Jan. 1830, Eliza Harington, 2nd dau. of Rev. Thomas T. Thomason, of Calcutta, senior chaplain. (*See also* William George Stephen.) Addiscombe Cadet 20 Feb. 1809 till 22 Oct. 1810.
   Services : Apptd. Asst. Field Engr. 3rd Div., for Nepal, 15 Nov. 1814. Nepal War 1814-5 ; capture of Malaun (*Lond. Gaz.* 16 Nov. 1815) ; in 1st Div. (India medal). Garr. Engr. and Executive Ofr. at Delhi 5 Dec. 1816 till 16 Dec. 1822. Built the church at Meerut. Siege and capture of Hathras 1817. Operations against the Bhattis of Hariana 1818 ; Asst. Field Engr. to Bdr.-Gen. J. Arnold's force from 12 Aug. 1818. Third Mahratta War. Fur. s.c. 26 Feb. 1826 till 24 May 1829. Supt. Kasipur foundry 1829-39. Fur. s.c. 28 Feb. 1839 till retirement. Apptd. Resident Dir. of the new Coll. of Civil Engrs. in England 12 Mar. 1840 ; resigned in Feb. 1842. F.R.S.
   Refs. : G.M. 1852, ii. 436. *Bishop Heber's Journal,* ii. Will dated 10 Apr. 1849 ; proved 20 Dec. 1852.

HUTCHINSON, James (*d.* 1790). Lieutenant, Bengal Eur. Regt. Cadet 1778. Ensign 30 May 1779. Lieut. 1 Feb. 1781. *d.* Korea, C.P., 4 Jan. 1790.
   Services : Lieut. 1/2nd Bengal Eur. Regt. in Oct. 1779. Lieut. 14th Bn. Sepoys in July 1787. Apptd. to 3rd Eur. Bn. 15 Dec. 1787. Was Adjt. 3rd Bn. Bengal Eur. Regt. at death.

HUTCHINSON, John (1751/52-1801). Lieut. Colonel, 5th N.I. *b.* 1751/52. Country Cadet 1771. Admitted 15 Mar. 1771. Ensign 14 Mar. 1773. Lieut. 14 May 1778. Capt. 10 Jan. 1784. Major 30 Oct. 1797. Lt. Col. 21 Apr. 1800. *d. unm.* Bhagulpur, B. & O., 18 May 1801, aged 49.
   Of Antrim. Son of Martha Hutchinson. (*Probably* son of Rev. James Hutchinson, and uncle of James Rainey, *q.v.*, and of James Garner, *q.v.*)
   Services : Capt. 9th Bn. Sepoys in July 1787. Capt. 2nd Bengal Eur. Regt. Major 15th N.I. Posted as Lt. Col. to 2/3rd N.I. Transfd. to 1/18th N.I. 29 May 1800 ; to 5th N.I. For many yrs. Regulating Ofr. of the Jaghirdar Invalid Institution.
   Refs. : A.A.R. iv. 117. Will dated 10 Jan. 1800 ; proved 13 June 1801. M.I. at Bhagulpur.

LIST OF THE OFFICERS OF

HUTCHINSON, Joseph Horsley (d. 1803). Captain, 6th N.I. Country Cadet 1778. Admitted 13 July 1778. Ensign 25 Apr. 1779. Lieut. 6 Jan. 1781. Capt. 1797. d. in England 5 May 1803.
Services: Lieut. 3rd Bengal Eur. Bn. in July 1787. Capt. 7th N.I. in June 1798. Transfd. to 6th N.I. Fur. 3 Jan. 1801 till death. Promoted Major 30 Sept. 1803, before the report of his death had reached India.

HUTCHINSON, Robert (d. 1774). Ensign, Infantry. Cadet 1772. Ensign 23 Jan. 1773. d. Bisauli, U.P., 28 Oct. 1774.
Services: N.F.P.

HUTCHINSON, Thomas (d. 1777). Ensign, Invalid Est. Infantry. Cadet (?). Ensign 1772. Invalided (?). d. Chunar 19 June 1777.
Services: N.F.P.

HUTCHINSON, Thomas Frederick (1788-1831). Major, 20th N.I. bapt. Knaresborough, Yorks., 20 May 1788. Cadet 1803. Arrived in India 29 Apr. 1805. Ensign 29 Mar. 1805. Lieut. 30 Mar. 1805. Capt. 30 Dec. 1820. Major 30 July 1828. d. Cape Town 22 Apr. 1831.
Son of Thomas Hutchinson, of Harrogate, M.D. Brother of George Hutchinson (1793-1852), q.v. m. Edinburgh, 25 Nov. 1817, Isabella, 3rd dau. of Archibald Hepburn Mitchelson, of Middleton.
Services: Posted as Lieut. to 1/5th N.I. Operations in Bundelkhand against Gopal Singh 1810; Tirowa; Lieut. 1/5th N.I. (? Operations in Baghelkhand 1813; Entauri; Lieut. 1/5th N.I.) Fur. s.c. 14 Apr. 1815 till 28 July 1818. Fort Adjt. at Delhi 3 July 1819. Capt. 1/5th N.I. Comdd. Delhi Najib Bn. 4 Sept. 1821 till 1828. Transfd. to 20th N.I. (late 2/5th) May 1824. Leave s.c. 2 yrs. to Cape 7 Feb. 1831.
Refs.: S.M. 1817, ii. 498. G.M. 1831, ii. 382. A.J. N.S. vi. 25. Will dated 1 July 1829; proved 2 Aug. 1831. M.I. St. George's Rd. cemetery, Cape Town.

HUTHWAITE, Charles Joseph (1803-1824). Lieutenant, 27th N.I. b. Nottingham 24 Sept. 1803. Cadet 1819. Ensign 4 Mar. 1820. Lieut. 11 July 1823. d. Chittagong 11 Nov. 1824.
Son of Cornelius Huthwaite, of Nottingham, wine merchant, and Catherine his wife, dau. of Lewis Allsop, of Nottingham.
Services: Posted as Ensign to 2/18th N.I. in 1820. Transfd. as Lieut. to 13th N.I. July 1823; to 27th N.I. (late 2/13th) May 1824. First Burma War; Chittagong 1824; Lieut. 27th N.I.

THE BENGAL ARMY, 1758-1834   515

HUTHWAITE, Sir Edward (1793-1873). Lieut. General, K.C.B. Artillery. *bapt.* St. Peter's, Nottingham, 24 June 1793. Cadet 1809. Admitted 13 Nov. 1810. Fireworker 12 Nov. 1810. Lieut. 25 Sept. 1817. Capt. 30 Aug. 1826. Major 20 Jan. 1842. Lt. Col. 3 July 1845. Col. Comdt. 23 Jan. 1854. Col. 20 June 1854. Maj. Gen. 14 Mar. 1857. Lt. Gen. 6 Mar. 1868. *d.* Naini Tal, U.P., 5 Apr. 1873, aged 79.

Son of William Huthwaite, of Nottingham, draper, alderman and mayor, and Lucy his wife. Nephew of Henry Huthwaite, *q.v.* Woolwich Cadet; nominated to R.M.A. 19 Aug. 1807.

Services : See *D.N.B.* Nepal War 1814-5; Lieut. F. 2nd Coy. 1st Bn. Foot Art., with Col. Gregory's detachment in Tirhut. Nepal War 1816; Lieut. F. 7th Coy. 2nd Bn. Third Mahratta War; Lieut. 7th Coy. 2nd Bn., d.d. 7th Coy. 3rd Bn. First Burma War; Assam frontier. Siege and capture of Bhurtpore; Lieut. 2nd Coy. 3rd Bn., d.d. 6th Bn. (India medal with clasps for Nepal and Ava). Bde. Major Art. for service in Rajputana 18 Nov. 1834. Comdd. Mewar Div. Art. Nov. 1836 till 29 Jan. 1837, and Oct. 1837 till 2 Jan. 1839. 2nd Bde. H.A. 15 Mar. 1842. To comd. Art. of Mewar F.F. 30 Dec. 1842. First Sikh War; Ferozshahr; Sobraon; Lt. Col. comdg. 3rd Bde. H.A. (Medal with clasp). Second Sikh War; passage of Chenab; Chilianwala; Gujerat; Bdr. comdg. Foot Art. (Medal with 2 clasps). Comdd. Art. with force under Sir W. R. Gilbert, *q.v.*, in pursuit of Sikhs across Jhelum R. 1849. C.B. 3 Apr. 1846. K.C.B. 2 June 1869.

Refs. : *D.N.B.* *D.I.B.* Boase. *The Times,* 6 May 1873. *I.L.N.* vol. 62 (1873), p. 475.

HUTHWAITE, Henry (1774-1853). Lieut. General. Colonel 42nd N.I. *bapt.* Chapel on the High Pavement, Nottingham, 20 Feb. 1774. Cadet 1795. Arrived in India 1 Feb. 1797. Ensign 9 Nov. 1796. Lieut. 30 Oct. 1797. Capt. 31 Mar. 1807. Major 3 May 1819. Lt. Col. 1 May 1824. Col. 1 Dec. 1829. Maj. Gen. 28 June 1838. Lt. Gen. 11 Nov. 1851. *d.* Hoveringham, Notts., 5 Dec. 1853.

Son of William Huthwaite, of Nottingham, chief mgte., and Elizabeth his wife. Grandson of Cornelius Huthwaite, of Nottingham, and uncle of Sir Edward Huthwaite, *q.v.* *m.* Gedling, Notts., 10 Apr. 1828, Miss Ann Eliza Beaumont, niece of Rev. Thomas Beaumont, of Bridgeford Hill.

Services : With Marine Bn. 1800-1. Transfd. to 2/5th N.I. 1803. Adjt. & Qmr. 5th N.I. 1805. Asst. teacher of Persian and Hindustani at Barasat C.C. 1 Jan. 1806 till its abolition in Sept. 1811. Capt. Lt. 5th N.I. 14 Aug. 1806. Capt. 1/5th N.I. Persian Intr. and A.D.C. to C.-in-C. 1816-7. Third Mahratta War; Persian Intr

To comd. Gorakhpur L.I. Bn. 20 Jan. 1818. Comdd. Calcutta Native Mil. 22 Feb. 1821 till 7 Mar. 1822. Supt. Mysore Princes 7 Mar. 1822 till Feb. 1827. Supy. A.D.C. to G.G. 7 Mar. 1822, 14 Jan. 1823, and 11 Aug. 1823. Posted as Lt. Col. to 30th N.I. 1 May 1824. Fur. s.c. 13 Feb. 1827 till death. Transfd. to 19th N.I. ; to 34th N.I. 30 Oct. 1826 ; to 61st N.I. 9 July 1830. Posted as Col. to 18th N.I. 4 Aug. 1830 ; to 29th N.I. 2 Mar. 1833 ; to 15th N.I. 29 Nov. 1836 ; to 42nd N.I. Oct. 1852.
Refs. : Boase. *A.J.* xxv. 709. *G.M.* 1854, i. 109. *I.M.* 1853, p. 730.

Note : Boase gives year of birth as 1769, and *I.M.* gives age at death as 85.

HUTTON, Charles (1808-?). Lieutenant. 20th N.I. *b.* London 3 Nov. 1808. Cadet 1825. Arrived in India 3 Aug. 1826. Ensign 30 Jan. 1826. Lieut. 30 July 1828. Resigned 31 July 1839.

Son of William Charles Hutton. Brother of Thomas Hutton (1806-1824), *q.v.*

Services : Ensign d.d. 20th N.I. 17 Aug. 1826. Posted as Ensign to 20th N.I. 26 Sept. 1826. Fur. p.a. *via* N.S.W. 30 Jan. 1837 till resignation. No record of active service.

HUTTON, Thomas (1806-1824). Ensign, Infantry. Unposted. *b.* London 26 Dec. 1806. Cadet 1823. Ensign 23 May 1824. *d.* Calcutta 3 Dec. 1824.

Son of William Charles Hutton. Brother of Charles Hutton, *q.v.*

Refs. : M.I. in S. Park St. cemetery, Calcutta.

HUTTON, Thomas (1807-1874). Captain, Invalid Est. 37th N.I. *b.* Penang 4 Mar. 1807. Cadet 1824. Arrived in India 18 Mar. 1826. Ensign 28 Sept. 1825. Lieut. 12 Sept. 1827. Capt. 27 Oct. 1838. Invalided 24 Dec. 1841. *d.* Rajpur, nr. Mussoorie, 19 Dec. 1874.

Son of Thomas Hutton, of Calcutta, agent, and of Notton Lodge, Wilts. *m.* 1st, Edinburgh, 10 June 1831, Mary Dundas, eldest dau. of John Jardine, advocate, sheriff of Ross and Cromarty. (She died Nimach 4 Sept. 1834.) *m.* 2nd, Delhi, 25 Feb. 1836, Georgiana Fortesque, dau. of John Brown, Surg. Bengal Est.

Services : Posted as Ensign to 37th N.I. in 1826. Fur. s.c. 28 Nov. 1828 till 2 Dec. 1831. Apptd. to the Revenue Survey Dept. Dec. 1837. First Afghan War 1839-40 ; Ghazni ; Capt. 37th N.I., with Shah Shuja's army (Medal).

Refs. : *A.J.* N.S. v. 178. *The Times*, 23 Jan. 1875.

HUYSHE, Alfred (1811-1880). General, C.B. Artillery. *b.* 8 Aug. 1811. Cadet 1827. Arrived in India 10 June 1828. 2nd Lieut. 13 Dec. 1827. Lieut. 28 Sept. 1835. Capt. 5 Sept. 1845. Major 25 Sept. 1857. Lt. Col. 27 Aug. 1858. Col. 29 Apr. 1861. Maj. Gen. 31 Oct. 1867. Lt. Gen. 1 Oct. 1877. Gen. 1 Oct. 1877. *d.* 46 Onslow Sq., London, 25 Feb. 1880.

bapt. 10 Oct. 1811. 4th son of Rev. John Huyshe (sometime Huish), of Sand and Clisthydon, Devon, and Milborough Anne his wife, dau. of Thomas Harris, of Hereford. Brother of George Huyshe, *q.v. m.* Mussoorie, 15 July 1836, Julia Maria, dau. of Rev. George Hagar, of Lonmay, Elgin. (She died 1890.) Addiscombe Cadet 1826-7.

Services : 4th Troop 3rd Bde. H.A. 1830-6. Transfd. to 4th Troop 1st Bde. 15 Feb. 1836 ; to 2nd Troop 1st Bde. 29 June 1836 ; to 2nd Troop 3rd Bde. Oct. 1837. Adjt. & Qmr. 3rd Bde. H.A. 12 Sept. 1842. Bde. Major Foot Art., Army of Exercise, 18 Nov. 1843. Gwalior campaign ; Maharajpur ; Bde. Major (Bronze star). Comdd. 1st Troop 2nd Bde. H.A. 1848-53. Second Sikh War ; Sadulapur ; Chilianwala ; Gujerat (Medal with 2 clasps). Fur. 1854 till 3 Jan. 1857. Mutiny campaign ; minor operations ; Lt. Col. comdg. 5th Bn. Foot Art. Col. 2nd H.A. Bde. 1862 ; "A" Bde. 1867. I.G. of Art. for India. Good Service Pension 11 Jan. 1865. C.B. 2 June 1877.

Refs. : Burke's *Landed Gentry*, 13th edn., p. 962, *s.n.* Huyshe, of Sand and Clisthydon, Devon. *Boase. D.I.B. The Times*, 3 Mar. 1880, 11 *f. Graphic*, vol 22 (1880), p. 196 (portrait).

HUYSHE, George (1804-1881). General, C.B. Colonel, 3rd Bengal Eur. Inf. *b.* 2 Feb. 1804. Cadet 1819. Admitted 29 Aug. 1820. Ensign 22 Mar. 1820. Lieut. 3 June 1822. Capt. 21 Jan. 1829. Major 12 Jan. 1837. Lt. Col. 8 Feb. 1843. Col. 15 Nov. 1853. Maj. Gen. 28 Nov. 1854. Lt. Gen. 12 Feb. 1867. Gen. 19 Feb. 1872. *d.* Guernsey 6 Oct. 1881.

bapt. Talaton, Devon, 25 Feb. 1804. 3rd son of Rev. John Huyshe and Milborough Anne his wife. Brother of Alfred Huyshe, *q.v. m.* 1st, Sikraul, Benares, 2 Nov. 1830, Harriette Matilda Lightfoot. (She died 1844.) *m.* 2nd, Kensington, 21 Aug. 1862, Rosa, dau. of John Savery Brook, of Detroit, Guernsey, and widow of Rev. W. H. Barnes. (She died 3 Apr. 1892.)

Services : Posted as Ensign to 1/13th N.I. Transfd. to 26th N.I. (late 1/13th) May 1824. Actg. Adjt. Left Wing 26th N.I. 7 June 1824. Supy. S.A.C.G. 4 Sept. 1824. First Burma War ; S.A.C.G. (India medal). S.A.C.G. 28 May 1825 ; D.A.C.G., 2 cl., 2 July 1828 ; 1 cl. 14 Sept. 1831 ; A.C.G., 2 cl., 12 July 1834 till 1 Feb. 1837. To comd. G.G.'s escort 19 Nov. 1839. First Afghan War 1842 ; opera-

tions of Gen. Pollock's force; Khyber (*Lond. Gaz.* 7 June 1842);
Mamu Khel (s.w.); Jagdalak; Tazin; Kabul; Istalif; Major
comdg. 26th N.I. (Medal). Fur. p.a. 1 Mar. 1843 till 1846. Posted
as Lt. Col. to 71st N.I. 18 May 1843; to 45th N.I. in 1846; to 1st
Eur. Bengal Fus. Nov. 1847; to 69th N.I.; to 37th N.I. 21 Nov.
1849; to 47th N.I. Sept. 1851; to 37th N.I. Aug. 1852; to 71st N.I.
Aug. 1853; to 45th N.I. Sept. 1853. Fur. s.c. 16 May 1853 till
death. Col. newly-raised 3rd Bengal Eur. Regt. 15 Nov. 1853. C.B.
27 Sept. 1843.

Refs. : Burke's *Landed Gentry*, 13th edn., p. 962, *s.n.* Huyshe, of
Sand and Clisthydon, Devon. Boase. *The Times*, 10 Oct. 1881,
p. 9.

HYDE, Arthur (*d.* 1775). Lieutenant, Infantry. Cadet 1769.
Ensign 1769. Lieut. 25 Nov. 1772. *d.* Dinapore 23 Sept. 1775.
Services : N.F.P.

HYDE, George (1768/69-1827). Lieutenant, Invalid Est. Infantry.
b. 1768/69. Cadet 1783. Admitted 27 Nov. 1784. Ensign 1
Apr. 1785. Lieut. 10 Aug. 1793. Invalided before 1798. *d.
unm.* Monghyr, B. & O., 18 Oct. 1827, aged 58.

Brother of Saville John, Thomas, William, Sarah, Mary Redford,
and Elizabeth King.

Services : Fur. 3 yrs. h.p. 2 Oct. 1786. With Eur. Invalids at
Chunar in Aug. 1798.

Refs. : Will dated Monghyr 28 Dec. 1826; proved 10 Nov. 1827.
M.I. at Monghyr.

HYDE, James (1783-1821). Captain, Engineers. *b.* psh. of St.
Peter & St. Paul the Apostle, Marlborough, Wilts., 21 Oct. 1783.
Cadet 1802. Ensign 1 Sept. 1803. Lieut. 9 Oct. 1806. Capt.
1 July 1812. *d.* Aligarh 29 July 1821.

3rd son of John Hyde, of Marlborough, and afterwards of Hyde
End, Brimpton, Berks., and Charlotte his wife, dau. of Capt. Jelfe,
R.N. Brother of John (Francis) Hyde, *q.v. m.* (?). (She died 16
Nov. 1817.)

Services : Served as Engr. in Bundelkhand 1806-14. Asst. Engr.
at Chunar 1815-6. Field Engr., Kumaon, 6 June 1817.

Refs : Burke's *Landed Gentry*, 6th edn., p. 847, *s.n.* Hyde, of Hyde
End, Berks. Will dated Aligarh 27 Feb. 1821; proved 6 Sept.
1821.

HYDE, James Chicheley (1789-1867). Lieut. Colonel. Artillery.
b. Islington, Middlesex, 2 Apr. 1789. Cadet 1805. Arrived in
India 13 Dec. 1806. Lieut. 15 Dec. 1806. Capt. Lt. 25 Sept.

THE BENGAL ARMY, 1758-1834   519

1817. Capt. 1 Sept. 1818. Major 10 Feb. 1834. Retired 5 Apr. 1837. Hon. Lt. Col. 28 Nov. 1854. *d*. Timbercombe Lodge, Bridgwater, Somerset, 10 May 1867.

bapt. Islington 8 May 1789. Son of James Chicheley Hyde, of the accountant's office, E.I. House, and Dorothy Fryer his wife. Grand-nephew of Henry Chicheley Plowden, *q.v.*, and cousin of William Chicheley Hester, *q.v.*

Services : 3rd Troop H.A. 1809-18. Siege and capture of Hathras 1817. Third Mahratta War ; Capt. comdg. 3rd Troop. A.D.C. to Maj.-Gen. Thomas Hardwicke, *q.v.*, 6 May 1820 till 1823. Comdd. 2nd Troop H.A. 1823-31. Siege and capture of Bhurtpore ; Capt. comdg. 1st Troop 2nd Bde. H.A. (India medal). Comdd. 3rd Troop 1st Bde. 1832-3. Posted to 3rd Bde. H.A. 8 Oct. 1834. Fur. p.a. 22 Dec. 1834 till retirement.

Refs. : *G.M.* 1867, i. 831. *The Times*, 16 May 1867.

HYDE, John. Ensign. Infantry. Cadet (?). Ensign 22 Dec. 1783. Resigned 7 Nov. 1785.

Services : N.F.P.

HYDE, John Fleming (1785-1846). Captain. 30th N.I. *b*. Dublin 28 Sept. 1785. Cadet 1805. Arrived in India 5 July 1807. Ensign 3 July 1807. Lieut. 23 Dec. 1809. Capt. 1 May 1824. Struck off 11 Mar. 1826. *d*. Calcutta 12 May 1846. *m*. 15 Feb. 1813, Miss Eliza Pearson. (She died Calcutta 17 Nov. 1817.)

Services : Posted as Ensign to 15th N.I. in 1808. Lieut. 1/15th N.I. Asst. to Surveyor Gen. 1814-20. On leave to Bencoolen in 1818. Leave to Cape 1820 ; fur. from Cape 17 Mar. 1821 till struck off after 5 yrs. absence from India. Transfd. to 30th N.I. (late 1/15th) May 1824. No record of active service. He afterwards settled in Calcutta, and was at one time Sec. to the lottery committee.

Refs. : Will dated 12 May 1846 ; proved 15 May 1846.

HYDE, John (Francis) (1780-1803). Lieutenant, 7th N.I. *b*. 16 July 1780. Cadet 1798. Arrived in India 8 Dec. 1800. Ensign 1 Oct. 1799. Lieut. 28 Oct. 1799. *d. unm.* Midnapore, Bengal, 3 Nov. 1803.

bapt. St. Peter & St. Paul the Apostle, Marlborough, 1 Jan. 1784. Eldest son of John Hyde and Charlotte his wife. Brother of James Hyde, *q.v.*

Refs. : Burke's *Landed Gentry*, 6th edn., p. 847, *s.n.* Hyde, of Hyde End, Berks.

HYDE, William (*d*. 1787). Captain, 24th Bn. Sepoys. Cadet (Art.) 2 July 1768. Ensign (Inf.) 20 Feb. 1769. Lieut. 17 May 1770. Capt. 28 Jan. 1779. *d*. Cawnpore 21 Oct. 1787.

Son of —— Hyde and Mary his wife. Brother of David Hyde, and nephew of Thomas Lewis, of Tottenham High Cross.
Services : Capt. 2/1st Bengal Eur. Regt. in Oct. 1779.
Refs. : Will.

HYNDMAN, Henry (*d.* 1803). Colonel, 6th N.I. Country Cadet 1769. Admitted 18 Dec. 1769. Ensign 19 Jan. 1770. Lieut. 3 July 1776. Capt. 1 Feb. 1781. Major 1 Mar. 1794. Lt. Col. 30 Oct. 1797. Col. 14 Dec. 1802. *d.* at sea, 4 Nov. 1803, on board the *Lord Eldon*, on his passage to England.
m. Buxar, 13 Feb. 1795, Sarah, 2nd dau. of Rev. John Blair, preby. of Westminster (*D.N.B.*), and niece of William Blair, *q.v.*
Services : 1st Bengal Eur. Bn. in July 1787. A.D.C. to Col. John Fullarton, *q.v.*, in 1790. Third Mysore War; Capt. comdg. a Vol. Bn. Apptd. to comd. 14th Bn. Sepoys in 1793. Second Rohilla War; battle of Bitaurah; Major comdg. 14th Bn. Fourth Mysore War; comdd. a detachment sent from Bengal to disarm the Nizam's troops, officered by Frenchmen, in Hyderabad Oct. 1798; Seringapatam; Lt. Col. comdg. 2/10th N.I. (late 14th Bn.). Transfd. to 2/6th N.I. 21 Apr. 1800. Fur. 29 Aug. 1799 till 15 Feb. 1803, and 24 Mar. 1803 till death.
Refs. : *Williams*, pp. 81, 148. *G.M.* 1795, ii. 877; 1803, ii. 1186.

HYNDS, Martin. Fireworker, Artillery. Cadet 1764. Fireworker 27 Dec. 1764.
Services : N.F.P.

HYSLOP, Maxwell (1808-1878). Lieut. Colonel. 59th N.I. *b.* London 30 June 1808. Cadet 1823. Arrived in India 3 Jan. 1825. Ensign 26 July 1824. Lieut. 2 Sept. 1825. Capt. 23 Dec. 1844. Major 11 Nov. 1851. Retired 5 Feb. 1854. Hon. Lt. Col. 28 Nov. 1854. *d.* 11 Cavendish Pl., Bath, 19 June 1878.

4th and youngest son of John Hyslop, of London, surgeon, and of Lochend (now Lotus), co. Kirkcudbright, and Margaret his wife, eldest dau. of Archibald Geddes, of Hermitage Park, Edinburgh. *m.* 23 July 1846, Mary, 3rd dau. of Robert Robertson, of Auchlecks, co. Perth. Ed. Charterhouse; entered the school in 1820.
Services : Posted as Ensign to 59th N.I. in 1825. Actg. Intr. & Qmr. 53rd N.I. 3 Sept. 1829; do. 11th N.I. 18 Apr. 1831; do. 59th N.I. 12 Nov. 1833. Intr. & Qmr. 59th N.I. 23 Jan. 1834 till 1842. Tempy. S.A.C.G., 3rd Inf. Bde., Army of Reserve (for Afghanistan) 2 Nov. 1842. Fur. s.c. 1 Nov. 1843 till 1846, and 21 Feb. 1852 till retirement. No record of active service.
Refs. : Burke's *Landed Gentry*, 13th edn., p. 964, *s.n.* Hyslop, *formerly* of Lotus. *Charterhouse School List. The Times*, 24 June 1878.

I

IBBETT, Henry (*d.* 1794). Lieutenant, Invalid Pension Est. Infantry. Cadet 1778. Ensign 12 Aug. 1779. Lieut. 4 Apr. 1781. Invalided before 1787. *d.* Chunar 30 June 1794.
Services : N.F.P.

ILIFFE, George (1802-1837). Captain, 67th N.I. *bapt.* Higham, Kent, 4 July 1802. Cadet 1818. Admitted 7 May 1819. Ensign 8 Nov. 1818. Lieut. 12 May 1820. Capt. 10 Jan. 1832. *d.* Kyaukpyu, Arakan, 30 Mar. 1837, of Arakan fever, aged 35.
Son of —— Iliffe and Sarah his wife.
Services : Ensign d.d. 10th N.I. 1819. Posted as Lieut. to 2/12th N.I. Actg. Adjt. & Qmr. 2/12th N.I. 15 June 1821. Transfd. to newly-raised 34th N.I. 11 July 1823 ; to 67th N.I. (late 1/34th) May 1824. First Burma War ; Arakan 1825 ; Lieut. 67th N.I. Intr. & Qmr. 67th N.I. 5 Aug. 1825 ; Adjt. do. 4 June 1828 till 14 Feb. 1832. Actg. Executive Ofr., P.W.D., 6 Jan. 1837.
Refs. : *A.J.* N.S. xxiii. 317.

IMLACH, Henry (1760-1830). Colonel, 54th N.I. Military Auditor Gen., Bengal. *b.* in Scotland 31 May 1760. Cadet 1781. Admitted 15 May 1782. Ensign 12 Apr. 1781. Lieut. 16 Oct. 1782. Capt. 19 May 1801. Major 16 Sept. 1807. Lt. Col. 1 May 1813. Lt. Col. Comdt. 11 July 1823. Col. 5 June 1829. *d.* Calcutta 8 Mar. 1830.

Son of Rev. Alexander Imlach, minister of Murroes, co. Forfar, for 47 yrs., and Susan Ogilvy his wife. His natural dau., Susan, *m.* Patrick Ogilvy Carnegy, *q.v.*
Services : Apptd. Cadet on 2 May 1781. Sailed for India on the *Earl of Chesterfield,* 26 June 1781, aged 21. Lieut. 9th Bn. Sepoys in July 1787. Lieut. and Bt. Capt. 1/6th N.I. Capt. Lt. 1/14th N.I. 29 May 1800. Capt. 14th N.I. Apptd. Sec. to the Board of Superintendence for the breed of cattle 31 July 1802. Dy. Mily. Auditor Gen. 25 June 1804. Mily. Auditor Gen. 11 July 1811 till death. Lt. Col. 1/21st N.I. Transfd. to 2/9th N.I. ; as Lt. Col.

Comdt. to 27th N.I. July 1823 ; to 54th N.I. (late 2/27th) May 1824.
Col. 54th N.I. in 1829.

Refs.: Family information. *A.J.* N.S. iii. 28, 210. Will dated 16 Feb. 1824 ; proved 18 Mar. 1830. M.I. in S. Park St. cemetery, Calcutta. Portrait in possession of the family.

IMPEY, Elijah Pattle (1817-1837). Ensign, 18th N.I. *bapt.* Calcutta 7 Jan. 1817. Cadet 1834. Arrived in India 21 July 1835. Ensign 21 Jan. 1835. *d.* in camp at Kasur, nr. Lahore, 30 Mar. 1837, of confluent smallpox, aged 20.

Son of Edward Impey, B.C.S., of Cheltenham, and Julia his wife, eldest dau. of the Chevalier Antoine de L' Etang, Kt. of St. Louis, and sister of Eugene de L'Etang, *q.v.* Grandson of Sir Elijah Impey (*D.N.B.*), and cousin-german of Henry Raleigh Impey, *q.v.* Addiscombe Cadet 8 Feb. 1833 till 12 Dec. 1834.

Services : Ensign d.d. 38th N.I. 12 Aug. 1835. Posted to 22nd N.I. 24 Sept. 1835. Transfd. to 18th N.I. 17 Nov. 1835. Was on escort duty with the C.-in-C. when his death occurred. No record of active service.

Refs. : A.J. N.S. xxiii. 317. *G.M.* 1837, ii. 214.

IMPEY, Henry Raleigh (1794-1835). Captain, 50th N.I. *b.* St. Lucia, W.I., 8 July 1794. Cadet 1811. Admitted 4 Aug. 1812. Ensign 16 Jan. 1814. Lieut. 24 June 1817. Capt. 10 Jan. 1829. *d.* at sea, 14 July 1835, on board the *Sherburne*, off Kedgeree, Bengal.

Son of Michael Impey, Major H.M. 6th Foot (who was kld. in a duel at Quebec in 1801), and Henrietta Matilda his wife. Brother of Michael Elisha Impey, and cousin-german of Elijah Pattle Impey, *q.v.* Nominated to Woolwich for Art. or Engrs., but as there was no room at R.M.A. he went to Marlow instead, thence to Addiscombe.

Services : Having failed to qualify for Art., was nominated to Inf. 12 Feb. 1812. Posted as Ensign to 2/25th N.I. Nepal War 1814-5 ; Ensign 2/25th N.I., in 4th Div. Nepal War 1816 ; Chiriaghati Pass ; Makwanpur (*Lond. Gaz.* 12 Aug. 1816) ; Ensign 2/25th N.I. Third Mahratta War ; Lieut. 2/25th N.I. Intr. & Qmr. 2/25th N.I. 25 Sept. 1819 till May 1824. Transfd. to 50th N.I. (late 2/25th) May 1824. Intr. & Qmr. 50th N.I. May 1824 till 3 Feb. 1829. Operations against the Kols in Chota Nagpur 1832 ; action with insurgents at Tekoe 8 and 9 Feb. 1832 ; Capt. comdg. 6 Coys. 50th N.I. Leave s.c. to Singapore and China 26 Mar. till 31 July 1834. Fur. s.c. 7 July 1835.

Refs. : A.J. N.S. xix. 39. *I.M.* 1848, p. 729. Will dated 9 July 1835 ; proved 28 Aug. 1835.

THE BENGAL ARMY, 1758-1834   523

INCELL, Thomas Weaman (1791-1827). Captain, 28th N.I. *bapt.* Worcester 18 Jan. 1791. Cadet 1808. Arrived in India 27 Oct. 1809. Ensign 22 Mar. 1810. Lieut. 10 Dec. 1814. Capt. 13 May 1825. *d.* Barrackpore 8 Apr. 1827.
Son of Thomas Incell.
Services : Posted as Ensign to 14th N.I. in 1810. Lieut. 1/14th N.I. (? Nepal War 1814-5 ; Jitgarh ; Lieut. 1/14th N.I., in 3rd Div.) Fur. 1816-7. Transfd. to 2/14th N.I. ; to 28th N.I. (late 1/14th) May 1824.
Refs. : A.J. xxiv. 499.

INGLE, Henry (1793-1824). Lieutenant, 31st N.I. *b.* Bury St. Edmunds 1 Mar. 1793. Cadet 1809. Arrived in India 3 Oct. 1810. Ensign 24 Feb. 1812. Lieut. 16 Dec. 1814. *d.* Jaunpur, U.P., 15 Sept. 1824.
Son of Samuel Ingle. *m.* St. John's, Calcutta, 2 June 1820, Miss Helen Smith.
Services : Cadet d.d. 19th N.I. in 1811. Posted as Ensign to 15th N.I. in 1812. Lieut. 2/15th N.I. (? Nepal War 1814-5 ; Lieut. 2/15th N.I., in 4th Div.) Leave s.c. to sea 1815-6. Siege and capture of Hathras 1817 ; Lieut. 2/15th N.I. Third Mahratta War ; Asirgarh ; Lieut. 2/15th N.I. Transfd. to 31st N.I. (late 2/15th) May 1824.
Refs. : M.I. at Jaunpur.

INGLIS, Hempbel (*d.* 1773). Ensign, 6th Bn. Sepoys. Cadet 1769. Ensign 1771. *d.* Cooch Behar, Bengal, 26 Feb. 1773 : drowned.
Services : Operations against the Bhutias in Cooch Behar 1772-3 ; Ensign 6th Bn. Sepoys.

INGLIS, John (1805-1849). Captain, 11th L.C. *b.* London 26 Dec. 1805. Cadet 1821. Arrived in India 24 June 1822. Cornet 19 Jan. 1822. Lieut. 7 Oct. 1824. Capt. 21 Aug. 1847. *d.* Multan 16 Feb. 1849.
bapt. St. Olave's, Hart St., London, 27 Feb. 1806. Son of James Inglis and Mary Jane his wife. *m.* Nimach, 3 Nov. 1835, Louisa Maria, 2nd dau. of Lambert Loveday, *q.v.* (*See also* John Herring.) (She *re-m.* Calcutta, 7 Feb. 1855, Rev. J. Powrie.)
Services : Posted as Cornet to 1st L.C. Oct. 1822. Transfd. to 2nd L.C. Nov. 1822. Jodhpur demonstration 1834 ; Lieut. 2nd L.C. First Afghan War 1838-9 ; Ghazni (Medal) ; Kabul ; Lieut. 2nd L.C. Transfd. to newly-raised 11th L.C. Jan. 1842. Fur. s.c. 28 Feb. 1842 till 8 Dec. 1843. A.D.C. to Maj.-Gen. Horatio Thomas Tapp, *q.v.*, Sept. 1847 till 14 Feb. 1848. Second Sikh War ; both sieges of Multan ; Capt. comdg. 11th L.C.
Refs. : De Rhé-Philipe. M.I. at Multan.

INGLIS, Robert (1813-1841). Lieutenant, 37th N.I. *b.* Calcutta 18 Apr. 1813. Cadet 1831. Arrived in India 16 Oct. 1832. Ensign 19 May 1832. Lieut. 30 Jan. 1840. *d.* 20 Apr. 1841 : drowned in the Ganges nr. Allahabad, in attempting to save Ensign George Eardley Norton, 59th N.I.

Son of Robert Inglis, of Kirkmany House, Crail, N.B., formerly of Calcutta, merchant, of the firm of Inglis & Dalton, and Mary his wife. Addiscombe Cadet 1828 till 8 Dec. 1831.

Services : Ensign d.d. 33rd N.I. 9 Dec. 1832. Posted to 37th N.I. 19 Dec. 1833. Fur. s.c. 12 Jan. 1838 till 6 Jan. 1841. Was on recruiting duty at Allahabad when his death occurred, his Regt. at that time being on service in Afghanistan.

Refs. : G.M. 1841, ii. 447.

INGRAM, John William (1794-1838). Captain. 19th N.I. *bapt.* Halifax, Yorks., 11 Aug. 1794. Cadet 1809. Admitted 15 Feb. 1811. Ensign 22 Aug. 1812. Lieut. 16 Dec. 1814. Capt. 11 Feb. 1826. Retired 21 Sept. 1835. *d.* Cheltenham, 14 Feb. 1838, of apoplexy.

Son of William Ingram, of Halifax, banker. *m.* Dum-Dum, 26 Aug. 1823, Miss Marian Isabella Scott.

Services : Barasat C.C. for 5½ mos. Cadet d.d. 15th N.I. Posted as Ensign to 1/3rd N.I. in 1812. With 3rd Gren. Bn. 1815-6. Actg. Cantt. Adjt. & Bk. Mr. at Ghazipur 21 Aug. 1817 till 1819. Actg. tempy. Bk. Mr. Ghazipur Div. 31 July 1819. Fur. p.a. 16 Mar. 1821 till 3 May 1823. Intr. & Qmr. 2/3rd N.I. 1 Oct. 1823 till 27 Nov. 1826. Transfd. to 19th N.I. (late 2/3rd) May 1824. No record of active service.

Refs. : A.J. N.S. xxv. 300.

INNES, Alexander (1808-1830). Lieutenant, 3rd L.C. *b.* Auldearn, co. Nairn, 28 July 1808. Cadet 1825. Arrived in India 9 Mar. 1826. Cornet 12 Oct. 1825. Lieut. 14 Oct. 1826. *d.* Cawnpore 8 Oct. 1830.

bapt. Auldearn 6 Aug. 1808. Son of William Innes, of Garbliss, and Ann McRitchie his wife. Brother of John Innes, *q.v.*

Services : Posted as Cornet to 3rd L.C., and served throughout with that Regt. Actg. Adjt. 1 June 1828, and 14 Apr. 1830. No record of active service.

Refs. : A.J. N.S. iv. 215.

INNES, James Charles (1811-1885). Lieut. General. 17th N.I. *b.* Lucknow 30 May 1811. Cadet 1827. Arrived in India 21 Nov. 1828. Ensign 14 June 1828. Lieut. 26 Sept. 1833. Capt. 26 Dec. 1844. Major 3 July 1855. Lt. Col. 15 July 1859. Col. 15

July 1864. Maj. Gen. 2 Jan. 1870. Lt. Gen. 1 Oct. 1877. d. 13 Dunsford Pl., Bath, 5 May 1885.

Son of William Innes (1771/72-1850), q.v. Brother of William Innes (1803-1832), q.v. m. Nimach, 30 Sept. 1834, Anna, eldest dau. of Henry Clapton Barnard, q.v. (See also John Bontein.)

Services : Ensign d.d. 43rd N.I. 14 Jan. 1829. Posted to 61st N.I. 3 June 1829. Shekhawat expedn. 1834 ; Lieut. 61st N.I. Intr. & Qmr. 61st N.I. 16 July 1833 till Mar. 1845. Fur. s.c. 20 Feb. 1839 till Feb. 1841. On service in Bundelkhand 1843-5. Second Sikh War ; Capt. 61st N.I., with Reserve Div. Fort Adjt. Govindgarh 9 June 1849. Offg. Bde. Major in Oudh Sept. 1850. Supt. of family money, and Paymr. of Native pensioners at Lucknow Dec. 1851. Subsequently comdd. 17th N.I., late Loyal Poorbeah Regt.

Refs. : Boase. *The Times,* 9 May 1885.

INNES, John (1810-1886). Major. Artillery. b. Auldearn, co. Nairn, 8 Mar. 1810. Cadet 1827. Arrived in India 10 Jan. 1829. 2nd Lieut. 12 June 1828. Lieut. 11 May 1836. Capt. 23 Jan. 1846. Retired 7 July 1853. Hon. Major 28 Nov. 1854. d. 18 Torrington Sq., London, 2 Apr. 1886.

Son of William Innes, of Bogside, Auldearn, and Ann McRitchie his wife. Brother of Alexander Innes, q.v. m. St. Pancras, 12 Jan. 1837, Sarah Eugenia, eldest dau. of Samuel Ferrar.

Services : Served throughout with Foot Art. Fur. u.p.a. 3 Jan. 1831 till 6 Aug. 1832. Fur. s.c. 19 Aug. 1834 till 16 June 1837. Operations against the Singphos in Upper Assam Mar. 1839 ; comdg. Art. with the detachment of Assam L.I.

Refs. : A.J. N.S. xxii. 135. *The Times,* 5 Apr. 1886.

INNES, Peter (1804-1871). Lieut. General. 14th N.I. Comdt. 2nd Punjab Vol. Rifles. b. Wick, co. Caithness, 20 May 1804. Cadet 1823. Arrived in India 19 May 1824. Ensign 16 Jan. 1824. Lieut. 28 Aug. 1825. Capt. 12 June 1842. Major 15 Apr. 1854. Lt. Col. 4 May 1858. Bt. Col. 20 June 1854. Maj. Gen. 13 July 1858. Lt. Gen. 22 Mar. 1870. d. Simla, 10 May 1871, from injuries sustained in an accidental fall.

bapt. Wick 29 May 1804. 9th son of Major James Innes, of Thrumston, J.P. and D.L. co. Caithness, and Margaret Clunes his wife.

Services : Ensign d.d. 61st N.I. May 1824. Posted as Ensign to 14th N.I. Aug. 1824. First Burma War ; operations on Sylhet-Cachar frontier 1824-5. Adjt. 14th N.I. 31 Oct. 1828 till 21 May 1842. Gwalior campaign ; Maharajpur ; Capt. 14th N.I., Bde. Major 4th Bde. (Bronze star). Apptd. D.A.A.G. 4th Div., Army of the Sutlej, 13 Dec. 1845. First Sikh War ; Ferozshahr ; D.A.A.G.

(Medal). Fur. s.c. 10 Feb. 1847 till Feb. 1849. Offg. A.A.G.
Dinapore Div. Aug. 1850 till Feb. 1851. Comdd. 14th N.I. Jan.
1852 till 1856. Bdr. 14 Feb. 1856 ; to comd. Multan Bde. 21 Mar.
1856 ; do. Ferozepore Apr. 1857, and assumed comd. 13 May, the
day before the mutiny broke out at that station. Resided at Simla
for the rest of his life. Comdt. 2nd Punjab Vol. Rifles Nov. 1865
till death.
Refs. : *De Rhé-Philipe. The Times*, 13 June 1871.

INNES, William (1771/72-1850). Major General, C.B. Colonel
39th N.I. *b.* 1771/72. Cadet 1794. Arrived in India 8 Oct.
1795. Ensign 2 Nov. 1795. Lieut. 25 Apr. 1797. Capt. 13
Mar. 1806. Major 16 Dec. 1814. Lt. Col. 18 Feb. 1820. Col.
5 June 1829. Maj. Gen. 28 June 1838. *d.* at his residence,
Grosvenor Pl., Bath, 2 Aug. 1850, aged 78.

Of Ealing, Middlesex. *m.* Berhampore, 17 June 1799, Eliza
Helen, dau. of Edward Rawstorne, *q.v.* (*See also* Thomas Ward
Howard.) (She died 8 Jan. 1857.) Father of James Charles Innes,
q.v., and of William Innes (1803-1832), *q.v.*

Services : Adjt. 2/19th N.I. 1801-4. Adjt. & Qmr. 19th N.I.
1805-6. Nepal War 1814-5 ; taking of Malaun Apr. 1815 ; Major
2/19th N.I., in 1st Div., comdg. a column (*Lond. Gaz.* 9 Dec. 1815).
Third Mahratta War ; Major 2/19th N.I. First Burma War ;
Cachar 1824 ; Lt. Col. 2/19th N.I., comdg. troops in Cachar. Lt.
Col. Comdt. 39th N.I. (late 2/19th) May 1824. To comd. 4th Bde.
on Sylhet frontier 25 Oct. 1824. Fur. p.a. 2 Jan. 1827 till death.
Posted as Col. to 56th N.I. 15 Aug. 1829. Col. 39th N.I. 6 June
1845. C.B. 8 Dec. 1815.

Refs. : G.M. 1850, ii. 341. *Bath Chron.* 8 Aug. 1850.

INNES, William (1803-1832). Lieutenant, 12th N.I. *b.* Berhampore 10 Feb. 1803. Cadet 1820. Arrived in India Oct. 1821.
Ensign 15 Apr. 1821. Lieut. 11 Sept. 1823. *d.* Buxar 28 Aug.
1832.

Son of William Innes, *q.v.*, and Eliza Helen his wife. Brother of
James Charles Innes, *q.v.* *m.* Calcutta, 5 Mar. 1827, Eliza Ann, 3rd
dau. of Charles Porteous, *q.v.* (*See also* James Hay.)

Services : Ensign d.d. 2/19th N.I. Posted as Ensign to 2/15th
N.I. Transfd. as Lieut. to 12th N.I. 11 July 1823 ; to 12th N.I.
(late 1/12th) May 1824. Intr. & Qmr. 12th N.I. 9 Feb. 1829 till
death. No record of active service.

Refs. : A.J. xxiv. 498 ; N.S. x. 80.

INNES, William (1806-1872). Lieut. Colonel. 15th N.I. *b.* Edinburgh 1 Jan. 1806. Cadet 1823. Arrived in India 6 Oct. 1824.

Ensign 20 May 1824. Lieut. 13 May 1825. Capt. 1 Apr. 1838. Major 15 Sept. 1848. Retired 20 Sept. 1849. Hon. Lt. Col. 28 Nov. 1854. d. 26 Aug. 1872.
Son of Major John Innes and Margaret Liddle his wife. m. Edinburgh, 29 Jan. 1839, Jemima R., 2nd dau. of Capt. Thomas Hamilton, and grand-dau. of Sir George L. A. Colquhoun, of Tillycolquhoun, Bart.
Services : Siege and capture of Bhurtpore ; Ensign 15th N.I. (India medal). Fur. p.a. 28 Jan. 1835 till 2 Aug. 1839. Served with 2nd Vol. Bn. from 1 Feb. 1842 till 1 Mar. 1843. First China War 1842 ; Chin-kiang-Foo ; Capt. 2nd Vol. Bn. (Medal). Second Sikh War ; Chilianwala ; Gujerat ; Major 15th N.I. (Medal with clasp).
Refs. : A.J. N.S. xxviii. 249.

INSLY, John (d. 1775). Capt. Lieutenant, Artillery. Cadet 1768. Fireworker 11 Sept. 1768. Lieut. 12 July 1770. Capt. Lt. 14 July 1774. d. Madras 18 Sept. 1775.
Services : N.F.P.

IRONSIDE, Charles (d. 1790). Lieut. Colonel. Infantry. Cadet 1763. Ensign 20 Aug. 1763. Lieut. 13 Apr. 1764. Capt. 27 July 1766. Major 24 Feb. 1778. Lt. Col. 3 Dec. 1781. Resigned 28 Jan. 1782. d. Charlotte St., Rathbone Pl., London, 4 May 1790.
m. in England, 26 Aug. 1784, Miss Neil.
Services : Major 2/3rd Bengal Eur. Regt. in Oct. 1779.
Refs. : G.M. 1790, i. 478.

IRONSIDE, Edmund (1805-1840). Lieutenant. 62nd N.I. b. 18 Aug. 1805. Cadet 1825. Arrived in India 30 June 1826. Ensign 28 Dec. 1825. Lieut. 10 May 1828. Pensioned on Lord Clive's fund 25 July 1837. d. 14 Oct. 1840.
Only son of Ralph Anthony Ironside, of Tennockside, co. Lanark, *jure uxoris,* and Judith his wife, dau. of John Dunn, of Tennockside. m. Marianne Lloyd, 2nd dau. of Wolfe Murray, Lord Cringletie, of Cringletie, co. Peebles, a lord of session.
Services : " Was for a time, before entering the service, in the office of Mr. Kinderley, an attorney of repute in London, where his father also had been." (*Memoirs of a Highland Lady.*) Ensign d.d. 62nd N.I. 8 July 1826. Posted to 62nd N.I. 26 Sept. 1826. Fur. s.c. 5 Feb. 1830 till July 1834, when his resignation was accepted to date from 2 Aug. 1832. Pensioned 2 June 1839, with effect from 25 July 1837.
Refs. : Burke's *Landed Gentry,* 12th edn., p. 1029, *s.n.* Bax-Ironside, of Heronden House, Kent.

IRONSIDE, Gilbert (1737-1802). Colonel. 3rd Bengal Eur. Regt.
b. 12 Dec. 1737. Cadet 1758. Ensign 14 Dec. 1758. Lieut. 19
Sept. 1759. Capt. 13 Oct. 1763. Major 1 May 1766. Lt. Col.
2 Apr. 1768. Col. 12 Sept. 1774. Resigned 13 Feb. 1786. *d.* at
his residence, Upper Brook St., Grosvenor Sq., London, 7 Oct.
1802.

bapt. St. George's, Hanover Sq., 19 Dec. 1737. 2nd son of Edward
Ironside, of Twickenham and London, banker, alderman, and lord
mayor. Grandson of Gilbert Ironside, the younger, bishop of Bristol
and Hereford (*D.N.B.*), brother of Edward Ironside (*D.N.B.*), and
uncle of Frances, wife of Thomas Higgins, *q.v. m.* Calcutta 13
May 1765, Loetitia, dau. of Rev. Robert Roberts, Vicar of Aldford,
co. Chester. Ed. Winchester; scholar 1751.

Services : Sailed for India on the *Prince George* in 1757, as Ensign
in an Independent Coy. comdd. by Capt. Robert Delaval. Returned
to England shortly after his arrival in India. Returned to India in
1759. Raised at Calcutta in Aug. 1763 the 14th Bn. (became 10th
in 1764, 1/5th in 1796, 11th in 1824), which was called after him
" *Runseet-ki-Paltan.*" Promoted Bt. Major by Lord Clive in May
1766 in order to secure a sufficiency of Field Officers for the trial by
C.M. of officers during the " Batta mutiny." Comdd. 3rd Bde.
1774. Fur. 14 Sept. 1774. Left India 13 Feb. 1786. Col. of 3rd
Bengal Eur. Regt. for 17 yrs. Author of " Rudiments of War."

Refs. : Kirby. Broome, p. 575. Williams, p. 95. Cardew, pp.
22, 23. *E.I.M.C.* ii. 452-3. *G.M.* 1802, ii. 981. *A.A.R.* iv. (1802)
43.

IRVINE, Alexander (1791-1816). Lieutenant, Bengal Eur. Regt.
b. Redbrae, nr. Edinburgh, 24 June 1791. Cadet 1807. Arrived
in India 14 Aug. 1808. Ensign 1 Sept. 1808. Lieut. 16 Apr.
1814. *d. unm.* Fort Rotterdam, Macassar, 16 Aug. 1816.

Eldest son of Maj.-Gen. Charles Irvine and Diana his wife, 2nd
dau. of Sir Alexander Gordon, Bart., of Lesmore. Brother of
George Nugent Irvine, *q.v.*, and cousin-german of Francis Irvine, *q.v.*

Services : Posted as Ensign to Bengal Eur. Regt. in 1809. Served
with his Regt. in Java 1812-6. Was Qmr. with H.Q. of Bengal Eur.
Regt. at Fort Rotterdam at date of death.

Refs. : Burke's *Landed Gentry*, 12th edn., p. 1030, *s.n.* Irvine, of
Drum Castle, co. Aberdeen. *G.M.* 1817, i. 182. *S.M.* 1817, i. 239.
Will dated Fort Rotterdam 15 Aug. 1816; proved 19 Feb. 1817.

IRVINE, Archibald (1797-1849). Lieut. Colonel, C.B. Engineers.
Subsequently Director of Engineering and Architectural Works
of the Admiralty. *b.* Hawcleugh, Hawick, co. Roxburgh, 10 Nov.
1797. Cadet 1815. Ensign 6 May 1817. Lieut. 1 Sept. 1818.

THE BENGAL ARMY, 1758-1884 . 529

Capt. 28 Sept. 1827. Major 20 May 1839. Lt. Col. 19 Feb. 1844. Retired 5 May 1846. *d*. Highgate, Middlesex, 29 Dec. 1849, as the result of a fall at Portsmouth when on duty.

Son of Thomas Irvine, of Hawcleugh, farmer. *m*. Allahabad, 27 Mar. 1835, Marianne Eliza Sparks, dau. of John Talbot Shakespear, B.C.S., and sister of Sir Richmond Campbell Shakespear, *q.v.* (She died 13 July 1891.) Addiscombe Cadet; admitted 27 Apr. 1812.

Services : Third Mahratta War; Mandala (*Lond. Gaz.* 7 Dec. 1818); Asirgarh; Asst. Field Engr., Centre Div. Superintended the destruction of fort Dhamoni in 1819. Siege and capture of Bhurtpore (s.w.—blown up by a mine); Bde. Major Engrs. Executive Engr., Allahabad Div., P.W.D. 6 Oct. 1826. Fur. s.c. 12 Jan. 1827 till 11 Nov. 1831. Posted to S. & M. 5 May 1828. Suptg. Engr., P.W.D., C.P. 20 Aug. 1832. M.M.B. 5 Mar. 1835. Supt. of Marine, Calcutta, Sept. 1843 till 1846. First Sikh War; Sobraon; Bdr. Engrs. (Medal). Director of Works to the Admiralty Nov. 1846 till death. C.B. 27 Sept. 1831.

Refs. : *Thackeray*, pp. 35-8. *I.M.* 1850, p. 190. *G.M.* 1850, i. 212. Will dated 13 Jan. 1846; proved 21 Feb. 1850.

IRVINE, Francis (1786-1855). Captain. 15th N.I. *bapt.* Drumoak, co. Aberdeen, 8 Feb. 1786. Cadet 1804. Arrived in India 10 Sept. 1805. Ensign 28 Sept. 1805. Lieut. 17 Oct. 1805. Capt. 12 July 1820. Retired 25 Nov. 1822. *d.* Edinburgh, 16 Dec. 1855, aged 69.

4th and youngest son of Alexander Irvine, of Drum Castle, Drumoak, and Jean his wife, dau. of Hugh Forbes, of Schivas. Cousin-german of Alexander Irvine, *q.v. m.* Calcutta, 29 Sept. 1815, Frances Sophia, dau. of John Herbert Harington, B.C.S., Member of the Supreme Council.

Services : Posted as Lieut. to 11th N.I. in 1806. Reduction of Kalinjar 1812; Lieut. 1/11th N.I. Sec. to the Madrassa (School) committee in Calcutta 1819-22. Leave s.c. to sea in 1822, and afterwards went home on fur. Retired in England 4 Aug. 1824, his date of retirement being ante-dated to 25 Nov. 1822. Transfd. to 15th N.I. (late 1/11th) May 1824.

Refs. : Burke's *Landed Gentry*, 12th edn., p. 1030, *s.n.* Irvine, of Drum Castle, co. Aberdeen. *I.M.* 2 Jan. 1856, p. 19. *G.M.* 1856, i. 210.

IRVINE, George (1800-1866). Captain. 33rd N.I. *bapt.* St. Michael's, Trory, co. Fermanagh, 8 Feb. 1800. Cadet 1819. Admitted 3 Aug. 1820. Ensign 4 Mar. 1820. Lieut. 11 July 1823. Capt. 9 Jan. 1833. Retired 30 May 1834. *d.* 1866.

5th son of Gerard Irvine, of Rockfield, co. Fermanagh, Capt. 47th

Regt., and Catherine his wife, dau. of Robert Hassard, of Skea, co. Fermanagh. Brother of Robert Irvine, *q.v.*
Services : Posted as Ensign to 2/2nd N.I. Transfd. as Lieut. to 16th N.I. July 1823 ; to 33rd N.I. (late 2/16th) May 1824. Siege and capture of Bhurtpore ; Lieut. 33rd N.I. (India medal). Adjt. Bundelkhand Provl. Bn. 8 Apr. 1825. Adjt. Kumaon Local Bn. 12 July 1825 till 9 Aug. 1831. Fur. p.a. 28 Jan. 1832 till retirement.
Refs. : Burke's *Landed Gentry of Ireland*, p. 345, *s.n.* Irvine, of Killadeas, co. Fermanagh.

IRVINE, George Nugent (1801-1827). Lieutenant, 29th N.I. *b.* Montrose, co. Forfar, 10 Oct. 1801. Cadet 1819. Was already in India when apptd. Cadet. Ensign 25 May 1820. Lieut. 11 July 1823. *d. unm.* Sawar, nr. Nimach, 3 Dec. 1827.
Son of Maj.-Gen. Charles Irvine and Diana his wife. Brother of Alexander Irvine, *q.v.*
Services : Posted as Ensign to 2/11th N.I. in 1820. Transfd. to 14th N.I. July 1823 ; to 29th N.I. (late 2/14th) May 1824. Second in comd. 4th Local Horse 1825 till death. No record of active service.
Refs. : Burke's *Landed Gentry*, 12th edn., p. 1030, *s.n.* Irvine, of Drum Castle, co. Aberdeen. *A.J.* xxv. 684. Will dated 1 Sept. 1827 ; proved 9 Feb. 1828.

IRVINE, Robert (1790-1823). Ensign. 5th N.I. *bapt.* Trory 20 July 1790. Cadet 1805. Arrived in India 13 Nov. 1806. Ensign (?). Resigned in India 20 July 1807. *d.* 1823.
2nd son of Gerard Irvine, of Rockfield, co. Fermanagh, Dy. Govr. of co. Fermanagh, high sheriff 1803, Capt. 47th Regt., and Catherine his wife. Brother of George Irvine, *q.v.*
Services : Posted as Ensign to 5th N.I.
Refs. : Burke's *Landed Gentry of Ireland*, p. 345, *s.n.* Irvine, of Killadeas, co. Fermanagh.

IRVING, James. Ensign. Infantry. Cadet 1770. Ensign 14 Nov. 1771. Resigned 27 Jan. 1782.
Services : N.F.P.

IRVING, James (1807-?). Major. 1st L.C. *b.* Holywood, co. Dumfries, 21 Nov. 1807. Cadet 1827. Arrived in India 22 Mar. 1829. Cornet 22 Mar. 1829. Lieut. 27 Aug. 1842. Capt. 31 Mar. 1851. Retired 1 Jan. 1852. Hon. Major 28 Nov. 1854.
Of Barwhinnock, co. Kirkcudbright. J.P. for the Stewartry of Kirkcudbright. Son of William Irving, of Edinburgh, later of Gribston, co. Dumfries, and Jane his wife, eldest dau. of David

THE BENGAL ARMY, 1758-1834 531

Currie, of Newlaw, co. Galloway. *m*. 1845, Margaret, only child of Peter Laurie MacMillan, of Barwhinnock.
Services : Transfd. from Inf. to Cav. 3 Dec. 1828 (G.O. 30 May 1829). Cornet d.d. 9th L.C. 10 June 1829. Actg. Cornet 27 Oct. 1831. Posted as Cornet to 1st L.C. 6 Oct. 1832. First Afghan War 1842 ; re-occupation of Kabul ; Lieut. 1st L.C., with Gen. Pollock's force (Medal). To do duty with 3rd Irreg. Cav. 23 Apr. 1842. Fur. s.c. 18 Apr. 1843 till 1846. Second Sikh War ; passage of the Chenab ; Ramnagar ; Chilianwala ; Gujerat ; Lieut. 1st L.C. (Medal with clasps).
Refs. : Burke's *Landed Gentry*, 7th edn., p. 978, *s.n.* Irving, of Barwhinnock, co. Kirkcudbright.
Note : His name appears in the *India List* amongst Retired Officers down to Jan. 1878, and in the *Quarterly Bengal Army List* down to Jan. 1884.

IRVING, James Alexander. (*See* **IRWIN.**)

IRVING, John (*d*. 1763). Major, Bengal Eur. Regt. Capt. (?). Major 27 Oct. 1763. *d*. Patna, 10 Nov. 1763, of wounds received in action on 6 Nov.
Services : Ensign 2nd Bn. 34th Foot 31 Aug. 1756 ; Lieut. 34th Foot 4 Oct. 1757. Lieut. 84th Foot 28 Dec. 1758 ; Capt. Lt. do. 4 Oct. 1761 ; Capt. do. 23 Oct. 1761. Transfd. as Capt. to Bengal Army in 1763. Battle of Udhua Nullah ; Capt. Bengal Eur. Regt., comdd. the storming party. Comdd. one of the two columns of attack at the assault of Patna 6 Nov. 1763 (s.w.—thigh shattered by a rocket) ; Major Bengal Eur. Regt.
Refs. : *Broome*, pp. 384, 398. *Innes*, pp. 157, 171.

IRVING, Thomas (1804-1825). Lieutenant, 1st N.I. *b*. Edinburgh 6 Mar. 1804. Cadet 1823. Ensign (?). Lieut. 23 May 1824. *d*. Gadarwara, C.P., 3 Aug. 1825.
Eldest son of James Irving, of Chessell's Court, Edinburgh, Lt. Col. R. Irish Art.
Services : Posted as Lieut. to 1st N.I. in 1825. No record of active service.
Refs. : *S.M.* 1826, i. 255.

IRWIN, James (*d*. 1769). Fireworker, Artillery. Cadet (?). Fireworker Sept. 1768. *d*. Calcutta 3 Sept. 1769.
Services : N.F.P.

IRWIN, James (*d*. 1805). Captain, 13th N.I. Cadet 1783. Ensign 1 Mar. 1785. Lieut. 1 Apr. 1793. Capt. 1804. *d*. in camp nr. Jhansi 1 Nov. 1805.

Services : Adjt. 1/13th N.I. 29 May 1800 till Jan. 1804. Capt. Lt. 13th N.I. 27 Jan. 1804. Second Mahratta War ; Bundelkhand 1803-4 ; Kapsa ; Kalpi ; defeat of Rajah Ram Singh ; Jaitpur ; Capt. 1/13th N.I.

IRWIN, James Alexander (1759/60-1813). Lieut. Colonel, 23rd N.I. *b.* 1759/60. Cadet 1779. Admitted 12 Feb. 1780. Ensign 16 Aug. 1779. Lieut. 8 Apr. 1781. Capt. 19 Dec. 1797. Major 21 Sept. 1804. Lt. Col. 24 Jan. 1809. *d.* in the U.K. 25 Mar. 1813. Of George St., Portman Sq., London. Brother of Edward Irwin, of Waterford, and of Mary Irwin. *m.* (?).

Services : Sailed for India on the *True Briton,* 16 June 1779, aged 19. Lieut. 16th Bn. Sepoys in July 1787. Capt. 3rd N.I. Major 3rd N.I. Transfd. as Lt. Col. to 23rd N.I. in 1809. (? Settlement of Hariana 1809 ; Bhawani ; Lt. Col. 2/23rd N.I.) Fur. 22 Jan. 1810 till death.

Refs. : G.M. 1813, i. 392. Will dated 15 Jan. 1813 ; proved in 1814.

IRWIN, John (1790-1824). Captain, 2nd Bengal Eur. Regt. *bapt.* St. Bees, Cumberland, 12 Dec. 1790. Cadet 1805. Arrived in India 19 Sept. 1806. Ensign 28 Sept. 1806. Lieut. 15 Dec. 1808. Capt. 1 May 1824. *d.* Kamptee, nr. Nagpur, 21 Sept. 1824.

2nd son of Thomas Irwin, of Justicetown, Cumberland, and Jane his wife, 2nd dau. of John Senhouse, of Calder Abbey. *m.* Berhampore, 2 July 1818, Mary, dau. of Thomas Charters, *q.v.*, and cousin-german of Samuel Fairfax, *q.v.* (She *re-m.* James Auriol, *q.v.*)

Services : Posted as Ensign to Bengal Eur. Regt. in 1807. Served with his Regt. in Java 1812-6, at Macassar in 1816. Adjt. Bengal Eur. Regt. Apr. 1823 till May 1824. Transfd. to newly-formed 2nd Bengal Eur. Regt. May 1824.

Refs. : Burke's *Landed Gentry,* 13th edn., p. 976, *s.n.* Irwin, of Justicetown, Cumberland.

ISAAC, Baptist Edward (1799-1822). Lieutenant, 7th N.I. *b.* Brookheath, Hants, 4 Mar. 1799. Cadet 1817. Ensign (?). Lieut. 25 Oct. 1818. *d.* Cuttack 28 Mar. 1822.

Son of Edward Isaac.

Services : Posted as Lieut. to 1/7th N.I. in 1819. No record of active service.

Refs. : M.I. in Cuttack cemetery.

ISAAC, Elias Edward (1792-1831). Captain, 63rd N.I. *bapt.* Marshfield, Gloucs., 4 Jan. 1792. Cadet 1810. Admitted 22 Oct. 1811. Ensign 24 July 1813. Lieut. 25 Jan. 1815. Capt. 21 Jan. 1829. *d.* Berhampore 28 Mar. 1831.

Son of Nicholas Isaac, of Marshfield, banker. *m.* Calcutta, 14 Nov. 1829, Miss Mary Willis. (She *re-m.* Calcutta, 27 Nov. 1832, G. H. Huttmann.)

Services : Cadet d.d. 12th N.I. Posted as Ensign to 1/15th N.I. in 1813. Third Mahratta War ; action nr. Boordah Feb. 1819 (w.) ; Lieut. 1/15th N.I. (*Lond. Gaz.* 20 Jan. 1821). Adjt. Wing 1/15th N.I. 20 Jan. 1821. Transfd. to 32nd N.I. 11 July 1823 ; to 63rd N.I. (late 1/32nd) May 1824. Fur. s.c. 21 Feb. 1824 till 2 Nov. 1827. Refs. *: A.J.* N.S. i. 236 ; vi. 138. *G.M.* 1831, ii. 573.

IVESON, James (1803-1831). Lieutenant, 7th N.I. *b.* Hedon, Yorks., 10 Nov. 1803. Cadet 1823. Arrived in India 3 May 1824. Ensign 9 Jan. 1824. Lieut. 13 May 1825. *d.* Singapore 30 Sept. 1831.

Son of William Iveson, atty.-at-law. Brother of John Iveson, *q.v.*

Services : Posted as Ensign to 7th N.I. (? First Burma War ; Cachar 1825 ; Lieut. 7th N.I.) Fur. s.c. 23 Feb. 1827 till 20 Feb. 1830, and 24 July 1831 till death.

IVESON, John (1805-1841). Bt. Captain, 7th N.I. *bapt.* Hedon, Yorks., 11 Mar. 1805. Cadet 1825. Arrived in India 8 May 1826. Ensign 18 Jan. 1826. Lieut. 24 Mar. 1832. Bt. Capt. 18 Jan. 1841. *d.* Nimach 27 Oct. 1841.

Son of William Iveson, atty.-at-law. Brother of James Iveson, *q.v.*

Services : Posted as Ensign to 7th N.I. 26 Sept. 1826, and served throughout with that Regt. No record of active service.

J

JACK, Alexander (1805-1857). Bt. Colonel, C.B., 31st N.I. Brigadier comdg. at Cawnpore. *b.* Old Machar, Aberdeen, 19 Oct. 1805. Cadet 1823. Arrived in India 6 Oct. 1824. Ensign 23 May 1824. Lieut. 28 Sept. 1825. Capt. 2 Dec. 1838. Major 19 Jan. 1846. Lt. Col. 11 Dec. 1851. Bt. Col. 20 June 1854. Bdr. 8 Aug. 1856. *d.* Cawnpore 27 June 1857 : massacred at the Ghaut.

5th son of Rev. William Jack, Principal of King's Coll., Aberdeen, 1815-1854, and Grace his wife, dau. of Andrew Bolt, of Lerwick. Ed. King's Coll., Aberdeen.

Services : See *D.N.B.* Posted as Ensign to 30th N.I. Leave s.c. to China and Mauritius 31 Jan. 1834 till 14 Oct. 1835. Fur. p.a. 15 Dec. 1835 till 11 Apr. 1839. First Sikh War ; Aliwal ; Capt. comdg. 30th N.I. (Medal). Second Sikh War ; passage of Chenab ; Chilianwala ; Gujerat (Medal with 2 clasps). Posted as Lt. Col. to 30th N.I. Jan. 1852. Transfd. to 33rd N.I. Aug. 1852 ; to 41st N.I. 1 Dec. 1852 ; to 42nd N.I. Jan. 1853. Returned from fur. Feb. 1856. Transfd. to 34th N.I. May 1856 ; to 31st N.I. 1856. Bdr. on the Est. and posted to Cawnpore 9 Aug. 1856. C.B. 9 June 1849. *Refs. :* *D.N.B.* *D.I.B.* *G.M.* 1857, ii. 565.

JACKSON, Alfred (1806-1839). Captain, 30th N.I. *bapt.* Southampton 21 Jan. 1806. Cadet 1821. Arrived in India 3 Jan. 1823. Ensign 2 Jan. 1823. Lieut. 13 May 1825. Capt. 24 Apr. 1832. *d.* Nasirabad 13 Oct. 1839.

Son of Josiah Jackson. *m.* Calcutta, 3 Sept. 1838, Martina, youngest dau. of William Lewis Grant, Surgeon Bengal Est., and niece of Roger Keys Erskine, *q.v.* (She *re-m.* Capt. Charles Bowles, 10th Hrs.) Addiscombe Cadet 1820-2.

Services : Posted as Ensign to 15th N.I. Transfd. to 30th N.I. (late 1/15th) May 1824. Actg. Adjt. & Qmr. Eur. Invalids at Chunar 22 Apr. 1829 till July 1830. Actg. Adjt. Kumaon Local Bn. 13 Feb. till 18 May 1832. Fur. p.a. 13 Dec. 1833 till 3 Jan. 1837. Offg. Paymr. of Native pensioners at Meerut and Hapur 5 June 1837.

LIST OF OFFICERS OF THE BENGAL ARMY, 535

Offg. Agent for family money and Paymr. of Native pensioners at Barrackpore 20 Nov. 1837. No record of active service.
Refs. : Burke's *Landed Gentry*, 6th edn., p. 175, *s.n.* Bowles, of N. Aston, Oxon.

JACKSON, Augustus Henry Ernest (1783-1819). Captain, 16th N.I. *b.* London 5 July 1783. Cadet 1798. Arrived in India 23 Dec. 1799. Ensign 25 Nov. 1799. Lieut. 29 May 1800. Capt. 17 Oct. 1810. *d.* Calcutta 18 Jan. 1819.
bapt. St. George's, Hanover Sq., 6 Aug. 1783. Eldest son of Sequin Henry Jackson, M.D., of Hanover St., London, and Augusta Elizabeth his wife.
Services : Operations in Jumna Doab 1803 ; Thathia ; Lieut. 1/16th N.I. Adjt. 1/16th N.I. 1805-10. Operations in Bundelkhand 1807 ; Chamir ; Sehlehuganj. Operations in Bundelkhand against Gopal Singh 1810-1 ; Capt. 1/16th N.I.
Refs. : G.M. 1819, ii. 281.

JACKSON, Charles. Captain. Infantry. Cadet 1769. Ensign 1769. Lieut. 15 Nov. 1772. Capt. 1 Jan. 1781. Casualty after 1790.
Services : Fur. 3 yrs. 27 Sept. 1785. N.F.P.

JACKSON, Charles Alexander (1819-1846). Lieutenant, 31st N.I. *b.* Calcutta 6 Jan. 1819. Cadet 1834. Arrived in India 28 July 1835. Ensign (13 June 1835) 2 Nov. 1835. Lieut. 17 Aug. 1839. *d.* London 12 Mar. 1846.
bapt. Calcutta 20 Mar. 1819. Son of James Nesbitt Jackson, *q.v.*, and Augusta Katharine his 1st wife. Brother of Henry Colvin Jackson, *q.v.*, and nephew of Thomas Charles Jackson, *q.v.*
Services : Ensign d.d. 12th N.I. 19 Aug. 1835. Posted to 31st N.I. 28 June 1836. Operations against the Kols 1837-8. First Afghan War 1838-42 ; Ghazni 1839 ; Kalat ; Lieut. 31st N.I. (Medal). Apptd. to charge of Comst. duties with 2nd Bde., Bengal column, Army of the Indus, May 1839. Posted to Shah Shuja's army Apr. 1840. Asst. to P.A. at Kandahar 3 June 1840. Offg. S.A.C.G. with Army of Exercise 15 Dec. 1843. Gwalior campaign ; Maharajpur ; Lieut. 31st N.I., S.A.C.G. (Bronze star). Fur. s.c. 15 Nov. 1844 till death.

JACKSON, Edward (1805-1834). Captain, 68th N.I. *b.* Walthamstow, Essex, 26 July 1805. Cadet 1821. Arrived in India 19 Aug. 1822. Ensign (10 Mar. 1822) 11 July 1823. Lieut. 1 May 1824. Capt. 13 May 1834. *d.* Sikraul, Benares, 23 May 1834, of apoplexy.
bapt. 4 Aug. 1805. Youngest son of John Jackson, of Dowgate iron wharf, iron merchant, and Sarah his wife. Brother of William

Jackson (1801-1822), *q.v.* *m.* Dinapore, 5 Sept. 1829, Susan Elizabeth, 4th dau. of Johan Frederick Meiselback, sometime Col. in the Mahratta service. (*See also* George Byron.)

Services : Posted as Ensign to 1/29th N.I. 14 Dec. 1822. Transfd. to newly-raised 34th N.I. July 1823 ; as Lieut. to 68th N.I. (late 2/34th) May 1824. Served in Arakan Nov. 1825 till Sept. 1826. Fur. s.c. 5 Oct. 1826 till 11 Nov. 1828.

Refs. : *A.J.* N.S. xv. 227. *G.M.* 1835, i. 221.

JACKSON, Edward Rowland (1751/52-?). Lieutenant. Infantry. *b.* 1751/52. Cadet 1778. Arrived in India 10 Dec. 1778. Ensign Oct. 1778. Lieut. 3 Dec. 1778. Struck off 1793.

Of Castleview, co. Cork. Son of Dr. Rowland Jackson, of Ballyboy, M.R.C.P., London, sometime " Medical Attendant to the Civil and Military Servants of the Company, when called upon," and physician to the Calcutta jail, and Frances Perreau his wife, of co. Carmarthen.[1] Brother of John Jackson (1752/53-?), *q.v.* *m.* 1st, Calcutta, 28 Jan. 1779, Miss Phoebe Tuting. (*See also* Peter Selwood Hewett, George Urquhart Lawtie, and Peter Murray.) (She died Calcutta, 20 Nov. 1785, aged 24.) His dau. *m.* Robert Turton, *q.v.*, and his grandson *m.* a dau. of Sir John Rose, *q.v.* *m.* 2nd, Anne, dau. of William Beere, of Ballyboy, nr. Clogheen, co. Tipperary. *m.* 3rd, Margaret Cole.

Services : Sailed for India on the Gatton, 27 Apr. 1778, aged 26. Lieut. 2/2nd Bengal Eur. Regt. in Oct. 1779. Granted fur. 3 yrs. 28 Oct. 1785, and was still on fur. in 1790.

Refs. : Burke's *Landed Gentry*, 8th edn., p. 1056, *s.n.* Jackson, of Ahanesk, co. Cork. Mrs. Eliza Fay's *Original Letters from India* (1925 edn.), p. 188.

[1] *Note :* According to Mrs. Fay, she was a native of Jamaica. It appears more probable, however, that she was related to the twin brothers, Robert and Daniel Perreau, for whom see Hickey's *Memoirs*, iv.

JACKSON, George (1812-1889). General. 2nd Bengal Cav. *b.* Doncaster 1 July 1812. Cadet 1827. Arrived in India 10 Jan. 1829. Cornet 19 July 1828. Lieut. 26 Mar. 1838. Capt. 30 July 1849. Major (20 June 1854) 18 Feb. 1861. Lt. Col. (18 Feb. 1861) 18 Feb. 1863. Col. 18 Feb. 1866. Maj. Gen. 1 Oct. 1877. Lt. Gen. 17 Nov. 1879. Gen 1889. *d.* St. Helen's, Preston, nr. Brighton, 26 Apr. 1889.

Of St. Helen's, Lancaster. *bapt.* Doncaster 28 Sept. 1812. 7th son of James Jackson, of Doncaster, J.P., banker and alderman of the borough of Doncaster, mayor in 1803 and 1814, and Henrietta Priscilla his wife, dau. of Freeman Bower, of Maltby Hall, Yorks.,

J.P. and D.L. *m*. Karnal, 9 Feb. 1839, Phillis Sophia, dau. of
Nathaniel Nugent Strode, Capt. H.M. 16th Regt. Ed. Durham.
Services : Cornet d.d. 3rd L.C. 11 Feb. 1829. Posted to 4th L.C.
26 June 1830. Fur. u.p.a. 17 Jan. 1834 till 8 June 1835. Actg.
Adjt. 4th L.C. Sept. 1839. Actg. 2nd in comd. 2nd Local Horse
14 Aug. 1840 ; do. 7th Irreg. Cav. 18 Feb. 1842. Adjt. 2nd Irreg.
Cav. 14 Apr. 1842 ; 2nd in comd. do. 11 July 1842 till Feb. 1848.
Operations in Bundelkhand 1842-3. Apptd. Comdt. 2nd Irreg. Cav.
24 Feb. 1848, and comdd. this Corps (which became 2nd Bengal Cav.
in 1861, and now forms part of 2nd Lancers (Gardner's Horse)) for
over 22 yrs. Second Sikh War (Medal). Operations on N.W.F. ;
Mohmands 1851-2 (medal with clasp). Mutiny campaign (w. twice).
Refs. : Burke's *Colonial Gentry*, i. 162, *s.n.* Jackson. *Boase.
Durham School Register. The Times*, 30 Apr. 1889.

JACKSON, Gregory Haldane (1802-1828). Lieutenant, 42nd N.I.
b. Calcutta 31 May 1802. Cadet 1818. Ensign (?). Lieut. 9
Nov. 1820. *d.* Sardhana, Meerut, 4 Mar. 1828.

bapt. Calcutta 25 June 1802. Son of Gregory Jackson, Coy.'s
agent for loading and unloading H.C.'s ships at Kedgeree, and
Elizabeth his wife.
Services : Ensign d.d. Bengal Eur. Regt. in 1819. Posted as
Lieut. to 1/21st N.I. in 1820. Transfd. to 42nd N.I. (late 2/21st)
May 1824. First Burma War ; Arakan 1825 ; Lieut. 42nd N.I.
Intr. & Qmr. 42nd N.I. 27 Feb. 1826 till death.

JACKSON, Henry Colvin (1812-1842). Lieutenant, 45th N.I. *b.*
Calcutta 26 May 1812. Cadet 1828. Arrived in India 25 June
1829. Ensign 12 Dec. 1828. Lieut. 12 Jan. 1838. Capt. (in
Nizam's army) 17 Mar. 1841. *d.* Hyderabad 9 Apr. 1842.

Eldest son of James Nesbitt Jackson, *q.v.*, and Augusta Katharine
his 1st wife. Brother of Charles Alexander Jackson, *q.v.*, and nephew
of William Hill Jackson, *q.v.*, and of James Colvin, of Manchester
Sq., London. Addiscombe Cadet 1826-8.
Services : Posted as Ensign to 45th N.I. 14 Sept. 1829, but did
not join till May 1833, serving in the meantime with 59th N.I.
Served with 1st Inf., Nizam's army, 17 June 1836 till death. No
record of active service.

JACKSON, James Nesbitt (1788-1832). Major, C.B., 45th N.I.
D.Q.M.G., Bengal. *b.* Calcutta 16 Aug. 1788. Cadet 1803.
Arrived in India 10 Mar. 1805. Ensign 27 Apr. 1805. Lieut. 28
Apr. 1805. Capt. 17 Dec. 1818. Major 2 June 1830. *d.* Calcutta
8 June 1832.

bapt. Calcutta 18 Nov. 1788. Son of William Jackson, register
of the supreme court of judicature at Calcutta, and Margaret his

wife. Brother of Thomas Charles Jackson, *q.v.*, and of Elizabeth Amelia, wife of Alexander Binny, *q.v. m.* 1st, Cawnpore, 26 Feb. 1811, Augusta Katharine, dau. of Col. Wade, of Leatherhead, Surrey, 25th Light Dgns. (She died Calcutta, 5 Apr. 1831, aged 42.) Father of Charles Alexander Jackson, *q.v.*, and of Henry Colvin Jackson, *q.v. m.* 2nd, Calcutta, 10 Apr. 1832, Mary, sister of Malcolm Nicholson (1792-1850), *q.v.* (She died 13 Jan. 1870.)
Services : Posted as Lieut. to 1/23rd N.I. Leave s.c. 6 mos. to sea 1 Apr. 1807. With Ramgarh Bn. 1811-6. Employed on survey duty 8 Jan. 1814 till 6 Jan. 1815. Nepal War 1814-5 ; Lieut. 1/23rd N.I., with Ramgarh Bn., in 4th Div. On survey duty from 19 Apr. 1816. D.A.Q.M.G., 2 cl., 1 Jan. 1817 ; do., 1 cl., 24 Oct. 1818. Capt. 2/23rd N.I. Transfd. to 45th N.I. (late 1/23rd) May 1824. First Burma War ; capture of Rangoon ; D.A.Q.M.G. (*Lond. Gaz.* 22 Feb. 1825). Tempy. A.D.C. to G.G. 29 Mar. 1828. Actg. D.Q.M.G. 10 June 1829. A.Q.M.G. at the Presdy. C.B. 27 Sept. 1831.
Refs. : Burke's *Landed Gentry*, 10th edn., p. 1366, *s.n.* Rose, of The Ferns, Wivelsfield, Sussex. Will dated 13 Apr. 1832 ; proved 15 June 1832.

JACKSON, John (1752/53-?). Lieutenant. Infantry. *b.* 1752/53. Cadet 1778. Arrived in India 10 Dec. 1778. Ensign Oct. 1778. Lieut. 4 Dec. 1778. Struck off 1793.
Younger son of Dr. Rowland Jackson, of Ballyboy, and Frances his wife. Brother of Edward Rowland Jackson, *q.v.*
Services : Sailed for India on the *Gatton*, 27 Apr. 1778, aged 25. Lieut. 2/3rd Bengal Eur. Regt. in Oct. 1779. Granted fur. 3 yrs. 5 Dec. 1785, and was still on fur. in 1790.
Refs. : Burke's *Landed Gentry*, 8th edn., p. 1056, *s.n.* Jackson, of Ahanesk, co. Cork.

JACKSON, John (1789-?). Lieutenant. 3rd N.I. *b.* Leicester 8 June 1789. Cadet 1806. Arrived in India 1 Aug. 1807. Ensign 26 Aug. 1807. Lieut. 30 June 1811. Struck off in England 28 June 1821. (Living in Mar. 1855.)
Of Charlton Kings, Cheltenham. Son of John Jackson. *m.* Leicester, 6 Jan. 1820, Miss Anna Maria Gossett, of Gt. George St., London. (She died Charlton Kings, 31 Mar. 1855, aged 57.)
Services : Posted as Ensign to 3rd N.I. in 1808. (? Operations in Bundelkhand 1809 ; Rajaoli ; Ajaigarh ; Ensign 1/3rd N.I.) Lieut. 1/3rd N.I. Adjt. 3rd Gren. Bn. 1815-6. Fur. 24 Dec. 1818 till struck off in 1823 (C.D. Mily. Letter of 8 Oct. 1823, para. 27) with effect from 28 June 1821, after 2½ yrs. absence from India.
Refs. : *A.J.* ix. 205.

JACKSON, John (1805-1825). Lieutenant, 4th L.C. *b.* Houghton-le-Spring, co. Durham, 27 Oct. 1805. Cadet 1821. Cornet 10 Mar. 1822. Lieut. 1825. *d.* Karnal 9 June 1825.

4th son of Capt. James Jackson, of Richmond, Yorks., late Comdr. E.I.C.N.S., and Harriot Goodchild his wife. Brother of Philip Jackson (1802-1879), *q.v.*

Services: Posted as Cornet to 5th L.C. in 1822. Transfd. to 4th L.C. in 1824. No record of active service.

JACKSON, Julian (1790-1853). Lieutenant, Artillery. *b.* London 30 Mar. 1790. Cadet 1807. Arrived in India 16 Nov. 1808. Fireworker 26 Sept. 1808. Lieut. 28 Apr. 1812. Resigned in India 28 Aug. 1813. *d.* 16 Mar. 1853.

Son of William Turner Jackson and Lucille his wife. *m.* Calcutta, 6 Dec. 1808, Miss Margaret Isabella Gordon. Woolwich Cadet; nominated for R.M.A. 1 May 1805.

Services: No record of active service.

Refs.: G.M. 1853, i. 562.

JACKSON, Philip (1760-?). Ensign. Infantry. *b.* 1760. Cadet 1781. Ensign 21 May 1781. Struck off 1788.

A native of Ireland.

Services: Apptd. Cadet on 3 Jan. 1781, aged 20. Sailed for India on the *Hinchinbrooke*, 13 Mar. 1781, aged 20. N.F.P.

JACKSON, Philip (1802-1879). Captain. Artillery. *b.* Bishop Wearmouth, co. Durham, 24 Sept. 1802. Cadet 1818. Admitted 1 Jan. 1820. 2nd Lieut. 11 Apr. 1819. Lieut. 1 Oct. 1820. Capt. 1 Dec. 1834. Invalided 23 Nov. 1835. Retired 4 Jan. 1836. *d.* 1879.

2nd son of Capt. James Jackson, of Bishop Wearmouth, late Comdr. E.I.C.N.S., and Harriot Goodchild his wife. Brother of William Jackson (1804-1822), *q.v.* Addiscombe Cadet 1818-9. Magdalen Hall, Oxon.; matric. 18 June 1838, aged 35.

Services: Executive Ofr. at Singapore 18 Dec. 1824. Surveyor of public lands at Singapore 27 May 1826. Actg. Asst. to Ofr. in charge of Residency at Singapore 3 Aug. 1826. Fur. from P.W.I. 1 July 1827 till 9 June 1831. Leave s.c. 2 yrs. to N.S.W. 27 Mar. 1832. No record of active service.

Refs.: Alumni Oxon.

JACKSON, Randle (1798-1831). Lieutenant, Artillery. *b.* London 21 July 1798. Cadet 1816. Admitted 9 Sept. 1817. 2nd Lieut. 25 Sept. 1817. Lieut. 1 Sept. 1818. *d. unm.* at sea, 16 Apr. 1831, on board the *James Sibbald*, off St. Helena.

bapt. St. Pancras, London, 21 Feb. 1800. 2nd son of John Jackson, of Pulteney St., St. James's, London, leather merchant, formerly

H.E.I.C.S., and Mary Page his wife. Nephew of Randle Jackson. His sister *m.* James Patrick M'Dougall, *q.v.* Ed. Charterhouse; entered the school 1812. Addiscombe Cadet 1815-7.

Services : A.D.C. to G.G. 8 May 1819. Offg. Garr. Storekeeper at Fort William 17 Apr. 1820. Dy. P.M.G. 19 June 1820 till 9 Oct. 1823. Leave s.c. to Mauritius 11 Feb. 1822 till 28 Dec. 1823. Comdg. Art. in Sylhet 13 July 1825. Posted to Nizam's army 18 Nov. 1826; took over comd. of the battery of four 6-pdrs. at Hingoli 14 Apr. 1827. Fur. p.a. 24 Jan. 1831. No record of active service.

Refs.: Burke's *Landed Gentry*, 12th edn., p. 1035, *s. n.* Jackson, of Swordale, co. Ross. *Charterhouse School List.* Burton, p. 103. *G.M.* 1831, i. 650. Will dated 14 Jan. 1831; proved 16 Aug. 1831.

JACKSON, RICHARD C—— (*d.* 1805). Captain, 7th N.C. Cadet 1783. Admitted 5 Dec. 1784. Cornet 28 Mar. 1785. Lieut. 3 May 1792. Capt. 1 May 1804. *d.* Ghazipur, U.P., 23 Oct. 1805.

Services : Adjt. 2nd N.C. 29 May 1800 till 1803. Capt. Lt. 2nd N.C. 5 Oct. 1800. (? Operations in Jumna Doab 1803; Capt. Lt. 2nd N.C.) Fur. 1803-5. Transfd. to newly-raised 7th N.C. Apr. 1805.

JACKSON, Samuel (1787-?). Ensign. 13th N.I. *bapt.* Wyke Regis, Dorset, 12 Jan. 1787. Cadet 1805. Arrived in India 11 July 1806. Ensign 10 Aug. 1806. Resigned in India 2 Feb. 1808.

Son of Samuel Jackson and Honor his wife.

Services : Posted as Ensign to 13th N.I. in 1807. No record of active service.

JACKSON, Thomas Charles (1786-1815). Lieutenant, 1st N.I. *bapt.* Calcutta 22 July 1786. Cadet 1802. Admitted 4 Sept. 1804. Ensign 25 Aug. 1804. Lieut. 21 Sept. 1804. *d.* Langa, Macassar, 12 June 1815 : kld. in action during the attack on a fortified village.

Son of William Jackson, atty.-at-law, register of the supreme court of judicature at Calcutta, and Margaret his wife. Brother of William Hill Jackson, *q.v.*

Services : Posted as Lieut. to 1st N.I. in 1805. Operations in Bundelkhand 1806; Lieut. 1st N.I. (? Operations in Bundelkhand 1809; Rajaoli; Ajaigarh; Lieut. 2/1st N.I.) Capture of Java 1811; Lieut. 6th Bengal Vol. Bn. Served in the Malay Archipelago with 6th Vol. Bn. till death.

Refs. : Will dated Macassar 28 Mar. 1814; proved 20 Oct. 1815.

JACKSON, Verney (1760/61-1784). Lieutenant, Infantry. *b.* 1760/61. Cadet 1780. Ensign 1780. Lieut. 26 Aug. 1781. *d.* Buxar 18 Feb. 1784.

A native of London.
Services : Sailed for India on the *Earl of Dartmouth,* 3 June 1780, aged 19. N.F.P.

JACKSON, William. Ensign. Infantry. Cadet 1770. Ensign 27 Dec. 1772. Resigned 2 June 1775.
Services : N.F.P.

JACKSON, William (1801-1822). Ensign, 1st N.I. *b.* Walton, Lancs., 27 Dec. 1801. Cadet 1819. Ensign 22 Mar. 1820. *d.* Agra 25 Oct. 1822.

bapt. Walthamstow, Essex, 17 Apr. 1802. Son of John Jackson, iron merchant, and Sarah his wife. Brother of Edward Jackson, *q.v.*
Services : Posted as Ensign to 2/1st N.I. No record of active service.

JACKSON, William (1804-1822). Ensign, 4th N.I. *b.* Houghton-le-Spring, co. Durham, 19 Mar. 1804. Cadet 1819. Ensign 15 Apr. 1820. *d.* Jubbulpore 30 Sept. 1822.

3rd son of Capt. James Jackson, of Richmond, Yorks., late Comdr. E.I.C.N.S., and Harriot Goodchild his wife. Brother of John Jackson (1805-1825), *q.v.*
Services : Posted as Ensign to 1/4th N.I. No record of active service.

JACKSON, William Hill (1785-1813). Capt. Lieutenant, 24th N.I. *bapt.* Calcutta 5 Feb. 1785. Cadet 1799. Admitted 13 Jan. 1801. Ensign 16 Aug. 1800. Lieut. 14 Nov. 1800. Capt. Lt. 29 Apr. 1812. *d.* Cawnpore, 4 Mar. 1813, " of a violent fever."

Son of William Jackson, of Calcutta, atty.-at-law, and Margaret Stewart his wife. Brother of James Nesbitt Jackson, *q.v. m.* in England, 23 July 1810, Albinia, 3rd dau. of Rev. Sydenham Teast Wylde, of Barrington, nr. Bristol, rector of Ubley, Somerset. (She was drowned in the wreck of the *Elizabeth,* off Dunkirk, 27 Dec. 1810.)

Services : Second Mahratta War ; Cuttack 1803-4 ; Lieut. 2/7th N.I., with 1st Vol. Bn. ; (? Adalatnagar ; Lieut. 2/24th N.I.). Transfd. to newly-raised 24th N.I. Oct. 1804. Capture of Gohad 1806 ; Lieut. 2/24th N.I. Fur. 29 Sept. 1808 till 1811. He sailed for India in Nov. 1810, at the end of his fur., in the *Elizabeth,*

which was totally lost off Dunkirk 27 Dec. 1810. His wife was drowned, and he was taken a prisoner on landing at Dunkirk. He was released by Napoleon's order and returned to England 30 Jan. 1811.
Refs. : *A Master Mariner*, an autobiog. of Capt. R. W. Eastwick, edited by Herbert Compton, 1891, chap. xiii. *S.M.* 1810. Will dated Cawnpore 28 Nov. 1812 ; proved in 1813.

JACOB, John (1783-1818). Lieutenant, 23rd N.I. *bapt.* St. Clement Danes, London, 20 Sept. 1783. Cadet 1804. Arrived in India 21 June 1806. Ensign 7 Mar. 1806. Lieut. 1 Feb. 1807. *d.* Narsinghpur, C.P., 9 Oct. 1818.
Son of Joseph Jacob and Sarah his wife.
Services : Posted as Lieut. to 2/23rd N.I. in 1807. Settlement of Hariana 1809 ; Bhawani ; Lieut. 2/23rd N.I. Adjt. 2/23rd N.I. 29 May 1810 till death. Third Mahratta War.

JACOB, Vickers (1788-1836). Lieutenant. 3rd N.I. Subsequently an indigo planter. *b.* 9 Nov. 1788. Cadet 1808. Admitted 6 Nov. 1809. Ensign 20 Mar. 1811. Lieut. 31 Aug. 1814. Resigned 11 July 1822. *d.* Calcutta 11 June 1836.
bapt. Aghadoe, Queen's Co., 17 Nov. 1788. Son of John Jacob, M.D., of Maryborough, Queen's Co., and Grace his wife, dau. of Jerome Alley, of Donaghmore, Queen's Co. (*See* George Holroyd Alley.) *m.* Barrackpore, 9 Aug. 1817, Miss Anne Watson. (She died Hobart, Tasmania, 3 Oct. 1836.) T.C.D. ; Pensioner 7 July 1806, aged 17.
Services : Barasat C.C. Posted as Ensign to 3rd N.I. in 1811. Nepal War 1814-5 ; Lieut. 2/3rd N.I., in 1st Div. Transfd. to 1/3rd N.I. Fur. to N.S.W. 1821 till resignation. He appears to have settled in N.S.W. till *c.* 1831, when he returned to Bengal and engaged in the manufacture of indigo at Jessore.
Refs. : *Alumni Dub.* *A.J.* N.S. xxi. 189 ; xxii. 272.

JACQUES, Henry (*d.* 1813). Bt. Major, 22nd N.I. Cadet 1783. Ensign 23 Mar. 1785. Lieut. 2 July 1793. Capt. 30 June 1804. Bt. Major 25 July 1810. *d.* Agra 28 July 1813.
(*Probably* father-in-law of James Bourdieu, *q.v.*)
Services : Lieut. 31st Bn. Sepoys in 1796. Lieut. 10th N.I. Transfd. as Capt. to newly-raised 22nd N.I. June 1804. Settlement of Hariana 1809 ; Bhawani ; Capt. 1/22nd N.I. Reduction of Kalinjar 1812 ; Bt. Major 1/22nd N.I.
Refs : Will dated Comillah, nr. Agra, 9 Apr. 1812 ; proved in 1813.

THE BENGAL ARMY, 1758-1834   543

JACQUES, Leonard. Captain. 27th Bn. Sepoys. Cadet 1769. Ensign 6 Aug. 1769. Lieut. 30 Nov. 1772. Capt. 3 Jan. 1781. Dismissed by C. M. 31 May 1784.

His dau., Anne, was bapt. at Fatehgarh 27 Apr. 1780.

Services: N.F.P.

Note: One Leonard Jacques, of Bombay, merchant and proprietor of the library and commission warehouse, died there Mar. 1807, aged 45.

JAFFRAY, Thomas (d. 1807). Captain, Invalid Est. Comdg. 1st Bn. Native Invalids. Cadet 1772. Admitted 11 Oct. 1772. Ensign 14 June 1774. Lieut. 4 June 1778. Capt. 7 Oct. 1792. Invalided before 1798. d. at sea, 6 Feb. 1807, on board the *Phoenix*, on his passage to England.

Son of Thomas Jaffray or Jaffrey, of the family of Jaffray of Kingswell. Cousin of Alexander Jaffray Hautenville, *q.v.* *m.* Monghyr, 19 May 1798, Elizabeth, dau. of —— Williams, and widow of George Heard, *q.v.* (She died 27 Nov. 1845, aged 77.)

Services: First Rohilla War; battle of St. George; Cadet in the Select Picket. Lieut. 18th Bn. Sepoys in July 1787. Was comdg. 1st Bn. Native Invalids at Monghyr in 1798, and held this comd. till 1803. Fur. 24 Sept. 1806 till death.

Refs.: Family information.

JAMES, Henry (1789-1833). Captain, 20th N.I. *b.* London 28 Sept. 1789. Cadet 1808. Arrived in India 24 July 1809. Ensign 24 Oct. 1809. Lieut. 13 Aug. 1814. Capt. 19 July 1825. d. Sitapur, U.P., 18 June 1833.

bapt. St. Mary's, Islington, 27 Dec. 1789. Son of Thomas James and Hannah his wife. *m.* Meerut, 17 July 1822, Miss Maria Cordelia Gane. (She died 18 Dec. 1863.) His dau. *m.* William Tritton, *q.v.*

Services: Posted as Ensign to 5th N.I. (? Operations in Baghelkhand 1813; Entauri; Ensign 1/5th N.I.) Lieut. 1/5th N.I. Transfd. to 20th N.I. (late 2/5th) May 1824. First Burma War; Arakan 1825; Capt. 2nd Gren. Bn. Offg. Supt. of Cadets at Fort William 6 Oct. 1820 and 10 Feb. 1827. Actg. Bde. Major to troops in Bundelkhand 19 Oct. 1827.

JAMES, John Arthur (1808-1882). Major. 69th N.I. *b.* London 3 Oct. 1808. Cadet 1825. Arrived in India 6 May 1826. Ensign 12 Jan. 1826. Lieut. 25 Oct. 1827. Capt. 24 Jan. 1845. Retired 15 Aug. 1850. Hon. Major 28 Nov. 1854. d. Sheen Lodge, Leamington, 14 June 1882.

Son of Charles James, of Glos. Pl., New Rd., London. *m.* Mussoorie, 28 June 1849, Caroline, dau. of Richard Bignell, of Middleton-

Stoney, and sister of William Phillips Bignell, *q.v.* (She died 20 Feb. 1888, aged 70.)
Services : Posted as Ensign to 1st Extra Regt. (became 69th N.I.) 26 Sept. 1826, and served throughout with that Regt. Operations against the Bhils 1827. Actg. Adjt. 5 Oct. 1844. Against the Hill tribes in Sind 1845. Second Sikh War ; Chilianwala (s.w.) ; Capt. 69th N.I. (Medal).
Refs. : *The Times*, 16 June 1882.

JAMES, Richard (1785-1813). Lieutenant, Invalid Est. 24th N.I. *b.* 16 Aug. 1785. Cadet 1799. Arrived in India 12 Jan. 1801. Ensign 16 Nov. 1800. Lieut. 16 Nov. 1801. Invalided 4 Oct. 1812. *d.* Monghyr 25 May 1813.
bapt. Narberth, co. Pembroke, 14 Sept. 1789. Son of William James, of Pantsaison, co. Pembroke, and Rebecca his wife, sister and heir of John Bateman, of Robeson-Wathen, co. Pembroke.
Services : Lieut. Marine Regt. (became 20th N.I.). Served in P.W.I. 1804-6. Transfd. to newly-raised 24th N.I. in 1805.
Refs. : Burke's *Landed Gentry*, 13th edn., p. 983, *s.n.* James, late of Pantsaison, co. Pembroke.

JAMES, Thomas (*d.* 1768). Lieutenant, Artillery. Cadet (?). Fireworker 3 Dec. 1763. 2nd Lieut. 1 Nov. 1765. Lieut. 31 Mar. 1767. *d.* Calcutta 23 Nov. 1768 : bur. the following day.
Services : Lieut. 1st Coy. Art. ; resigned 14 May 1766 during the " Batta mutiny " ; readmitted 19 Oct. 1766.

JAMES, Thomas (1807-1871). Lieut. Colonel. 21st N.I. *b.* Carlow 23 Jan. 1807. Cadet 1827. Arrived in India 18 Mar. 1828. Ensign 4 Nov. 1827. Lieut. 12 June 1833. Capt. 24 Jan. 1845. Bt. Major 20 June 1854. Retired 28 Feb. 1856. Hon. Lt. Col. 28 Feb. 1856. *d.* 1 Kildare Terr., Bayswater, London, 17 May 1871.

Son of Thomas James, of Ballycrystal, co. Wexford. *m.* 23 July 1837, Marie Dolores Eliza Rosanna (" Lola Montez "—*D.N.B.*), dau. of Ensign Edward Gilbert, H.M. 44th Regt., and step-dau. of Patrick Craigie, *q.v.* He divorced her 15 Dec. 1842. (She died New York 17 Jan. 1861.)
Services : Ensign d.d. 48th N.I. 18 Apr. 1828 till 15 Oct. 1829. Posted as Ensign to 21st N.I. 4 Nov. 1828. Fur. s.c. 8 July 1829 till 16 Sept. 1833, and 4 Nov. 1836 till 26 Jan. 1839. Apptd. 2nd in comd. Kotah Contingent 27 Oct. 1841 ; Comdt. do. 28 Oct. 1842 till 15 Jan. 1856. No record of active service.
Refs. : *Autobiog. of Lola Montez*. *The Times*, 20 May 1871.

THE BENGAL ARMY, 1758-1834 545

JAMES, William (*d.* 1765). Ensign, Infantry. Cadet 1764. Ensign 1 Oct. 1764. *d.* in India 1765.
Services : N.F.P.

JAMES, William (1785-1855). Major. 66th N.I. *b.* Radstoke, Somerset, 11 Feb. 1785. Cadet 1803. Arrived in India 17 Mar. 1805. Ensign 30 Mar. 1805. Lieut. 31 Mar. 1805. Capt. 12 Sept. 1822. Major 26 Nov. 1830. Retired 4 Jan. 1832. *d.* Saltford House, nr. Bath, 6 Apr. 1855.
Eldest son of Rev. Samuel James, of Radstoke. *m.* Meerut, 30 Nov. 1811, Mary, 2nd dau. of Sir Dyson Marshall, K.C.B., *q.v.*, and widow of John Winston, *q.v.* (*See also* Christopher D'Oyly Aplin.) (She died 31 Jan. 1820.)
Services : Posted as Lieut. to 2/13th N.I. Actg. A.D.C. to Maj.-Gen. Dyson Marshall, *q.v.*, 1812-3 ; permanent do. 1814-8. Siege and capture of Hathras (*Lond. Gaz.* 12 Oct. 1818). D.A.A.G. Gen. Marshall's Div. of Grand Army Sept. 1817. Third Mahratta War ; Mandala ; Asirgarh ; D.A.A.G. 3rd (Marshall's) Div. (*Lond. Gaz.* 7 Dec. 1818 and 30 Aug. 1820). D.A.A.G. Saugor F.F. 1819. Bde. Major 16 Sept. 1820. Transfd. to newly-raised 33rd N.I. 11 July 1823 ; to 66th N.I. (late 2/33rd) May 1824. D.A.A.G. Saugor Div. 28 Jan. 1825 ; A.A.G. do. 29 Dec. 1829 till 15 May 1830. Fur. p.a. 21 Jan. 1831 till retirement.
Refs. : *G.M.* 1855, i. 550. *I.M.* 17 Apr. 1855, p. 211. Will dated 27 Nov. 1854 ; proved 4 Dec. 1855.

JAMES, William (1803-1833 ?). Lieutenant. 68th N.I. *b.* Dublin 24 Feb. 1803. Cadet 1824. Admitted 8 Aug. 1825. Ensign 11 Dec. 1824. Lieut. 7 Apr. 1826. Retired 27 Aug. 1832. *d.* 1833 ?
bapt. St. Bridget's, Dublin, 26 Feb. 1803. Son of Thomas James, of Stephen St., Dublin, and Marianne his wife.
Services : Acted as Lieut. and Adjt. of the Bencoolen Corps before he was apptd. a Cadet. (Letter from C.D. of 24 Nov. 1824, and G.O. of 9 May 1825.) Actg Adjt. Sylhet Local Bn. 18 May 1826. Actg. Intr. & Qmr. 68th N.I. 11 June 1828. Fur. s.c. via Penang and China 30 June 1829 till Aug. 1833, when, in consideration of his having served 9 yrs. in the unhealthy climate of Sumatra and Arakan, he was retired on a special pension of £40 *p.a.* with effect from 27 Aug. 1832.

JAMIESON, James William Henry (1807-?). Major General. 52nd N.I. *bapt.* Woodbridge, Suffolk, 1 July 1807. Cadet 1823. Arrived in India 19 May 1824. Ensign 16 Jan. 1824. Lieut. 13 May 1825. Capt. 4 Sept. 1839. Major 15 Sept. 1851. Lt. Col.

10 May 1857. Bt. Col. 28 Nov. 1857. Retired 31 Dec. 1861. Hon. Maj. Gen. 31 Dec. 1861. (Apparently still living in 1895.)

Son of James Jamieson, R.H.A., (? Asst. Surg.).

Services : First Burma War ; Arakan 1825 ; Ensign 26th N.I. (India medal). Transfd. as Lieut. to 52nd N.I. in 1825. Actg. Adjt. 52nd N.I. 26 Sept. 1827. Fur. s.c. 17 Nov. 1828 till 18 Oct. 1831. Adjt. 52nd N.I. 17 Mar. 1837 till 9 Apr. 1839. Disturbances in Bundelkhand 1841 ; Chirgaon ; with Bundelkhand Legion. (*Cal. Gaz.* 12 May 1841.) To officiate as Capt. of Inf. with Bundelkhand Legion 27 July 1841. Second Sikh War ; both sieges of Multan ; Gujerat (w.) ; Capt. comdg. 52nd N.I. (Medal with clasp). Posted as Lt. Col. to 52nd N.I. 4 July 1857.

JAMIESON or JEMMISON, William (*d.* 1775). Ensign, Infantry. Cadet 1772. Ensign 30 Mar. 1773. *d.* Gourah (? Gura, Rajputana) 28 May 1775.

Services : N.F.P.

JAMIESON or JAMISON, William (1784-1809). Lieutenant, 19th N.I. *b.* Glasgow 17 Dec. 1784. Cadet 1803. Arrived in India 18 Mar. 1805. Ensign 24 Apr. 1805. Lieut. 25 Apr. 1805. *d.* Ajaigarh, Bundelkhand, 2 Feb. 1809, of wounds received in action at the storm of Rajaoli on 22 Jan. 1809.

Son of James Jamieson or Jamison, of Glasgow, merchant, and Alexis Snodgrass his wife.

Services : Posted as Lieut. to 1/19th N.I. in 1806. Operations in Bundelkhand 1807 ; Sehlehuganj ; Lieut. 1/19th N.I. Operations in Bundelkhand against Lachman Dawa 1809 ; Rajaoli (s.w.) ; Lieut. 1/19th N.I., serving with L.I. Bn.

JARDINE, Edward Raleigh (1800-1825). Lieutenant, 1st N.I. *b.* East Stonehouse, Devon, 5 Oct. 1800. Cadet 1817. Ensign (?). Lieut. 1 Aug. 1818. *d.* Hoshangabad, C.P., 8 Oct. 1825.

Son of James Jardine, Capt. R.M.

Services : Posted as Lieut. to 2/12th N.I. in 1819. Transfd. to 1st N.I. (late 2/12th) May 1824. No record of active service.

JARRETT, John (*d.* 1800). Captain, 3rd N.I. Country Cadet 1778. Admitted 20 Mar. 1778. Ensign 4 June 1778. Lieut. 19 Nov. 1780. Capt. 15 Feb. 1797. *d.* Fatehgarh, U.P., 2 Oct. 1800.

Services : Ensign 2/1st Bengal Eur. Regt. in Oct. 1779. Lieut. 26th Bn. Sepoys in July 1787.

Refs. : *A.A.R.* iii. 104.

JARVIS, John Henry (1799-1832). Lieutenant, Artillery. *b.* 3 Nov. 1799. Cadet 1817. Admitted 21 July 1818. 2nd Lieut. 15 July 1818. Lieut. 3 Nov. 1818. *d.* at sea, 19 Aug. 1832, on board the *Leda*, between Mauritius and the Cape.
bapt. Naas, co. Kildare, 10 Dec. 1799. Son of John Jarvis, Essex Light Dgns., and Paymr. R. Montgomeryshire Mil. Addiscombe Cadet 1816-8.
Services : Intr. to Art. at Dum-Dum 29 July 1823. Intr. & Qmr. 7th Bn. Foot Art. 28 Sept. 1827. Leave s.c. 2 yrs. to Cape 16 Apr. 1832. No record of active service.

JAYNE, Alfred (1793-1812). Cadet, Infantry. *b.* Rendcombe, Gloucs., 9 Jan. 1793. Cadet 1810. *d.* Berhampore, Bengal, 30 Oct. 1812.
Son of Rev. Thomas Jayne, vicar of Rendcombe.
Services : Cadet d.d. 21st N.I.

JEFFERSON, John. Ensign. Infantry. Cadet 1769. Ensign 1769. Resigned 1773.
Services : N.F.P.

JEFFERY, Joseph White. (*See* **ORCHARD, Joseph.**)

JEFFREYS, Edward (1789-1863). Lieut. Colonel. 43rd N.I. *bapt.* Layston, Herts., 24 June 1789. Cadet 1805. Arrived in India 11 July 1806. Ensign 30 July 1806. Lieut. 17 Jan. 1809. Capt. 1 May 1824. Major 30 Apr. 1834. Retired 10 Dec. 1834. Hon. Lt. Col. 28 Nov. 1854. *d.* Malvern 21 Oct. 1863.
Son of Rev. Richard Jeffreys and Sarah his wife. Brother of Francis Jeffreys, *q.v. m.* Elizabeth Margaret. (She died 10 Dec. 1848, aged 55.)
Services : Barasat C.C. Posted as Ensign to 22nd N.I. Lieut. 2/22nd N.I. Operations against Gopal Singh in Bundelkhand 1810; distinguished himself in an attack on Lachman Singh at Bhamori 19 Nov. 1810. With Rangpur Local Bn. 1814-6. Fur. s.c. 2 May 1817 till 25 Sept. 1820. Transfd. as Lieut. to 1/22nd N.I.; to 43rd N.I. (late 1/22nd) May 1824. With Rangpur Local Bn. 27 Sept. 1820. Fort Adjt. at Chunar 22 Feb. 1823. Offg. Adjt. & Qmr. Eur. Invalids 1 Oct. 1824. In charge of 2nd Bn. Native Invalids 11 June 1825. Fur. p.a. 11 Jan. 1832 till 2 Dec. 1834.
Refs. : *G.M.* 1863, ii. 806. *The Times*, 24 Oct. 1863.

*JEFFREYS, Francis (1809-1839). Lieutenant, 70th N.I. *b.* Fatehgarh, U.P., 27 June 1809. Cadet 1824. Admitted 13 July 1825. Ensign 13 May 1825. Lieut. 13 Mar. 1834. *d.* North Bank, Regent's Pk., London, 16 Apr. 1839.
bapt. Fatehgarh 29 July 1809. Son of Rev. Richard Jeffreys,

chaplain Bengal Est., and Sarah his wife. Brother of Edward Jeffreys, q.v.

Services : Allowed to proceed to Bengal as a passenger on the *Woodford* with a view to being apptd. a Cadet on attaining his 16th yr. Posted as Ensign to 2nd Extra Regt. (became 70th N.I.) in 1826. Intr. & Qmr. 70th N.I. 14 Nov. 1833. Fur. p.a. 15 Sept. 1836 till death. No record of active service.

Refs. : A.J. N.S. xxix. 80.

JELF, Charles (1806-1829). Ensign, 24th N.I. *b.* Oaklands, nr. Newnham, Gloucs., 5 Aug. 1806. Cadet 1826. Ensign 9 Sept. 1826. *d.* Calcutta 1 Nov. 1829.

4th son of Sir James Jelf, Kt. Bach., alderman and mayor of Gloucester (who was distantly related to the Earls of Denbigh), and Mary his wife. Brother of Rev. Dr. Richard William Jelf (*D.N.B.*). Ed. Rugby; admitted in 1816. Oriel Coll., Oxon.; matric. 26 June 1824, aged 17.

Services : Ensign d.d. 7th N.I. 12 Mar. 1827. Posted as Ensign to 7th N.I. 10 May 1827 ; transfd. to 24th N.I. 3 Jan. 1828. No record of active service.

Refs. : Rugby School Register. Alumni Oxon.

JELLAND, John. Fireworker. Artillery. Cadet (?). Fireworker 27 Dec. 1764. Dismissed 3 Apr. 1766.

Services : N.F.P.

JELLICOE, Anthony Highmore (1799-1849). Major, 55th N.I. *b.* Walworth, Newington, Surrey, 19 Dec. 1799. Cadet 1818. Admitted 30 Oct. 1819. Ensign 10 June 1819. Lieut. 1 Jan. 1821. Capt. 11 July 1836. Major 15 June 1848. *d.* Benares 14 Apr. 1849.

Son of Adam James Jellicoe, of Highbury Pl., and of Wandsworth, Surrey, atty., and Elizabeth his wife. His sister *m.* 23 Oct. 1798, Anthony Highmore, junr., of Bury Court, St. Mary Axe, London, and of Dulwich, atty. *m.* Barrackpore, 27 June 1833, Georgiana Olivia, 2nd dau. of Lewis Wiggins or Wiggens, *q.v.* (*See also* Andrew Gildart Reid and Francis Edward Manning.)

Services : Ensign d.d. 18th N.I. Posted as Ensign to 1/28th N.I. Transfd. to 55th N.I. (late 1/28th) May 1824. Actg. Intr. & Qmr. 55th N.I. 29 Aug. 1826. Actg. Adjt. 55th N.I. 28 Mar. 1827. Adjt. 55th N.I. 15 Jan. 1831 till 26 Nov. 1836. Actg. Paymr. and Supt. of Native pensioners, Oudh and Cawnpore, 21 Sept. 1838. With Army of Reserve (for Afghanistan) 1842. With 2nd L.I. Bn. 1842. Major comdg. 3rd Inf. Recruit Depot in 1849. No record of active service.

Refs. : G.M. 1849, ii. 110.

JEMMISON, William. (*See* **JAMIESON.**)

JENKIN, Charles Coles (1808-1827). Lieutenant, 18th N.I. *b.* London 25 Jan. 1808. Cadet 1823. Ensign 23 May 1824. Lieut. 24 July 1826. *d.* Agra 26 July 1827.
Son of George Hatch Jenkin, East and West India broker.
Services : Sailed for India on the *Cornwall* 23 May 1824. Siege and capture of Bhurtpore ; Ensign 18th N.I.

JENKINS, Charles Edward Orlando (1789-1823). Captain, Artillery. *b.* 19 Jan. 1789. Cadet 1805. Arrived in India 13 Nov. 1806. Lieut. 8 Apr. 1806. Capt. Lt. 25 Sept. 1817. Capt. 1 Sept. 1818. *d. unm.* Aurangabad, Bombay, 16 July 1823.
Younger son of Richard Jenkins, of Bicton Hall, Salop, and Harriet Constantina his wife, dau. of George Ravenscroft, of Wrexham, co. Denbigh. Brother of Sir Richard Jenkins, G.C.B. (*D.N.B.*), and cousin-german of Richard Boycott Jenkins, *q.v.*
Services : Served throughout with Foot Art. Commd. the Art. at Partabgarh 1815-6. At Nagpur 1821 till death. No record of active service.
Refs. : Burke's *Landed Gentry*, 13th edn., p. 989, *s.n.* Jenkins, of Cruckton Hall, Salop.

JENKINS, Charles Howard (1812-1841). Lieutenant, 35th N.I. *b.* London 11 Jan. 1812. Cadet 1828. Arrived in India 22 May 1829. Ensign 7 Feb. 1829. Lieut. 8 Oct. 1839. *d.* Afghanistan 20 Oct. 1841 : shot in the spine during a night attack on the camp at Butkhak on 17 Oct.
Son of Feilder Jenkins, of Woburn Pl., Russell Sq., London, underwriter, and Sarah his wife.
Services : Ensign d.d. 31st N.I. 13 July 1829. Posted to 35th N.I. 14 Sept. 1829. First Afghan War 1838-41 ; Ghazni 1839 ; Lieut. 35th N.I. (Medal). Actg. Adjt. Wing 35th N.I. 16 Dec.1840. To conduct Comst. duties at Kabul 23 Mar. 1841. Apptd. Actg. Asst. to Lieut. Sturt, Executive Engr., P.W.D., Kabul.
Refs. : G.M. 1842, i. 341. *The Times*, 8 and 16 Jan. 1842.

JENKINS, Francis (1793-1866). Major General. 61st N.I. *b.* Truro, Cornwall, 4 Aug. 1793. Cadet 1809. Arrived in India 8 Oct. 1810. Ensign 2 Dec. 1811. Lieut. 11 May 1816. Capt. 29 Apr. 1830. Major 22 Dec. 1845. Lt. Col. 16 Oct. 1851. Bt. Col. 28 Nov. 1854. Retired Feb. 1861. Hon. Maj. Gen. 31 Dec. 1861. *d.* Gauhati, Assam, 28 Aug. 1866.
Son of Rev. Francis Jenkins, vicar of St. Clements, Truro.
Services : Cadet d.d. 15th N.I. Posted as Ensign to 1/24th N.I. Nepal War 1816 ; Ensign 8th Gren. Bn., in 2nd Bde., Left Column

(India medal). A.D.C. to V.P. 8 July and 30 Oct. 1817. Bk. Mr. at Cawnpore 30 June 1818 ; do. Cawnpore Div. 3 June 1819 ; do. Nagpur Div. 29 Sept. 1821. Transfd. to 47th N.I. (late 1/24th) May 1824. Asst. Sec. to Mily. Board in P.W.D. 14 Aug. 1826 till 29 Dec. 1830. Apptd. to Pol. Dept. in Arakan. Comr. and A.G.G. in Assam and N.E. parts of Rangpur 23 Jan. 1834 till retirement. Posted as Lt. Col. to 19th N.I. Jan. 1852 ; to 26th N.I. July 1852 ; to 1st Eur. Fus. ; to 2nd N.I. 26 Sept. 1857 ; to 61st N.I. in 1858.
Refs. : M.I. at Gauhati.

JENKINS, George (1786-1853). Major. 63rd N.I. *b.* Tiverton 2 Oct. 1786. Cadet 1805. Arrived in India 11 July 1806. Ensign 16 Aug. 1806. Lieut. 6 Aug. 1809. Capt. 1 May 1824. Major 25 Sept. 1834. Retired in India 20 Jan. 1835. *d.* Ryde, I.W., 25 Aug. 1853.

Son of William Jenkins, of Tiverton (? exciseman), and Mary his wife.

Services : Barasat C.C. Posted as Ensign to 7th N.I. Reduction of Kalinjar 1812 ; Lieut. 1/7th N.I. Nepal War 1814-5 ; Lieut. 1/7th N.I., in 2nd Div. (India medal). Third Mahratta War ; Lieut. 1/7th N.I. Transfd. as Capt. to 32nd N.I. 11 July 1823 ; to 63rd N.I. (late 1/32nd) May 1824. Fur. s.c. 25 Dec. 1823 till 20 Oct. 1826.

Refs. : *G.M.* 1853, ii. 428. *I.M.* 20 Sept. 1853, p. 563.

JENKINS, Jason (*d.* 1773). Lieutenant, Infantry. Cadet 1769. Ensign 1769. Lieut. 11 Nov. 1772. *d.* Berhampore 25 Dec. 1773.

Services : N.F.P.

JENKINS, Richard Boycott (1788-1843). Colonel, 44th N.I. *b.* Coleraine, co. Londonderry, 22 Feb. 1788. Cadet 1802. Arrived in India 6 Sept. 1803. Ensign 7 Sept. 1803. Lieut. 31 Aug. 1804. Capt. (8 Jan. 1817) 1 Aug. 1818. Major 3 Mar. 1826. Lt. Col. 27 Apr. 1831. Col. 19 Jan. 1843. *d.* Calcutta 11 Nov. 1843.

Eldest son of Edward Jenkins and Elizabeth his wife, eldest dau. of George Ravenscroft, of Wrexham. Cousin-german of Charles Edward Orlando Jenkins, *q.v.* *m.* 22 Nov. 1820, Miss Eliza Ord.

Services : Ensign d.d. 2nd N.I. Posted as Lieut. to 2/14th N.I. Nepal War 1814-5 ; Lieut. 2/14th N.I., Baggage Mr. 3rd Div. Adjt. of a Bn. of Irreg. Inf. in Nagpur service 15 Nov. 1816. Adjt. of a Regular Bn. in Nagpur service 3 Jan. 1817. Capt. Lt. 14th N.I. 4 Nov. 1817. Third Mahratta War ; Nagpur (*Lond. Gaz.* 16

THE BENGAL ARMY, 1758-1834 551

July 1818). To comd. Nagpur Bde. 4 Dec. 1823. Transfd. to 29th N.I. (late 2/14th) May 1824. Comdt. Nagpur Auxy. Force 29 July 1825. Fur. p.a. 20 Nov. 1830 till 20 Oct. 1833. Posted as Lt. Col. to 39th N.I. 29 Nov. 1831 ; to 16th N.I. 6 Nov. 1833. To comd. Malwa F.F. 18 Jan. 1835. Transfd. to 46th N.I. 15 Apr. 1835 ; to 61st N.I. 23 Nov. 1839 ; to 44th N.I. Dec. 1840. Comdg. in Kumaon 7 Oct. 1842. Posted as Col. to 44th N.I. 14 Feb. 1843.
Refs. : Burke's *Landed Gentry*, 13th edn., p. 989, *s.n.* Jenkins, of Cruckton Hall, Salop. *I.M.* No 9, p. 273. Will dated 21 Feb. 1839 ; proved 25 Apr. 1844. M.I. in Circular Rd. cemetery, Calcutta.

JENKINS, Robert Castle (1803-?). Lieutenant. 61st N.I. Subsequently a Calcutta merchant. *b.* Chepstow, co. Monmouth, 27 Mar. 1803. Cadet 1819. Ensign 5 June 1820. Lieut. 11 July 1823. Resigned 23 Nov. 1827.

Son of Richard Jenkins, of co. Gloucs. *m.* Calcutta, 4 Apr. 1825, Anna Bazett Catherine, dau. of John Palmer, of Calcutta, merchant, and sister of Francis Charles Palmer, *q.v.* (*See also* Llewellyn Conroy.) (She died 1885, aged 84.)
Services : Posted as Ensign to 1/21st N.I. in 1820. Transfd. to 31st N.I. July 1823 ; to 61st N.I. (late 1/31st) May 1824. Intr. & Qmr. 61st N.I. 17 June 1824 till resignation. To officiate as Supt. of Cadets in Fort William 15 Sept. 1826 ; to officiate as Supt. of works at Sulkea until further orders 28 Sept. 1826. No record of active service. After resigning the service he founded the firm of R. C. Jenkins, Fergusson & Co., of Fairlie Pl., Calcutta, merchants and agents. He left India in 1837.

JENNER, Birt Wyndham Rous (1810-1863). Bt. Captain. 64th N.I. *b.* 1810. Cadet 1826. Arrived in India 31 Oct. 1827. Ensign 25 May 1827. Lieut. 10 May 1834. Bt. Capt. 25 May 1842. Retired 11 Dec. 1843. *d.* at his residence, Llanblethian cottage, co. Glamorgan, 12 Dec. 1863.

Of Llanblethian, co. Glamorgan, J.P. and D.L. *bapt.* Wenvoe, co. Glamorgan, 9 Dec. 1810. 6th and youngest son of Robert Jenner, of Wenvoe Castle, co. Glamorgan, and Frances his wife, eldest dau. of Maj.-Gen. Francis Lascelles. Cousin-german of Augustus Hart Dyke, *q.v. m.* Stringston, 14 Oct. 1847, Anne, eldest dau. of Langley St. Albyn, of Alfoxton, Somerset. Ed. Eton ; admitted 1823.
Services : Posted as Ensign to 2nd N.I. 3 Jan. 1828. Transfd. to 64th N.I. 16 Feb. 1828. Fur. u.p.a. 7 Jan. 1832 till 1 Dec. 1833. Attached to Ramgarh Bn. 27 Jan. 1834. Adjt. do. 9 Sept. 1835. Operations in Singhbhum 1836. Pol. Asst. to A.G.G., S.W. frontier,

1 June 1840. Offg. Junior Asst. to Comr. in Chota Nagpur 12 Aug. 1840. Fur s.c. 7 July 1841 till retirement.
Refs. : Burke's *Landed Gentry*, 13th edn., p. 990, *s.n.* Jenner, of Wenvoe Castle, co. Glamorgan. *Eton School Lists. Bath Chron.* 17 Dec. 1863.

JENNINGS, George. Ensign. Infantry. Cadet 1774. Ensign 16 Aug. 1776. Resigned 9 Apr. 1777.
Services : N.F.P.

JENNINGS, William (1718/19-1766). Major, Artillery. Comdt. Bengal Art. *b.* 1718/19. Cadet (Madras Art.) 1753. Fireworker (Madras) (15 June 1754) 21 July 1754. Lieut. (Madras) 2 May 1756. Capt. Lt. (Bengal) 25 May 1757. Capt. 29 June 1758. Major 11 Feb. 1765. *d.* Mar. 1766.
Son of Joseph Jennings, of High Wycombe, Bucks., and Mary his wife. *m.* Harriot.
Services : Sailed for Madras on the *Essex* in 1753, aged 34. Came to Bengal from Madras at end of 1756 in comd. of a detachment of Art. Action at Budge-Budge 29 Dec. 1756 ; capture of Hooghly 10 Jan. 1757. Transfd. to Bengal Art. 1757. Battle of Kasipur ; capture of Chandernagore ; battle of Plassey (when he voted against coming to an immediate action). Comdt. Bengal Art. 29 June 1758 till death. War with Mir Muhammad Kasim 1763 ; Gheria ; Udhua Nullah. Succeeded Major Randfurlie Knox, *q.v.*, in comd. of the army in the field in Jan. 1764.
Refs. : Leslie, No. 23. *Broome*, p. 139. Will dated 12 Mar. 1763 ; proved in 1766.

JENNINGS, William (1809-1854 ?). Lieutenant. 68th N.I. *bapt.* Hartford, Hunts., 16 Apr. 1809. Cadet 1828. Arrived in India 3 May 1829. Ensign 8 Jan. 1829. Lieut. 23 May 1834. Dismissed by G.C.M. 13 Nov. 1836. (? *d.* Evershot, Dorset, 20 Jan. 1854.)
Son of Midgeley John Jennings and Margaret his wife.
Services : Ensign d.d. 6th N.I. 10 June 1829 ; do. 55th N.I. 19 Aug. 1829. Posted as Ensign to 54th N.I. 14 Sept. 1829. Transfd. to 68th N.I. 20 Aug. 1833. Operations against marauders in Jhabua, C.I., Mar. 1836.
Refs. : A.J. N.S. xxiii. 50. (? *G.M.* 1854, i. 333.)

JENNINGS, William Robert (1786-1837). Lieutenant. 9th N.I. Subsequently B.C.S. *b.* Calcutta 18 Sept. 1786. Cadet 1802. Arrived in India 15 Feb. 1804. Ensign 15 Dec. 1803. Lieut. 21 Sept. 1804. Resigned 22 May 1805. *d.* Patna 31 Mar. 1837.

bapt. Calcutta 16 Oct. 1786, and St. Mary's, Lambeth, Surrey, 31 Mar. 1796. Son of Ross Jennings, sometime of Caldbeck, Cumberland, later of Jessore and Chinsura, indigo manufacturer and factor to Lord Denbigh in Bengal, and Sarah his wife.
Services : Apptd. a Writer, B.C.S., 27 Sept. 1804. Arrived in India 27 Sept. 1805. Admitted to Coll. of Fort William June 1806. Mgte. at Patna 13 Dec. 1831 till death.
Refs. : N. & Q. 3S. xi. 10.

JERASMALL, Charles (*d.* 1765). Capt. Lieutenant, Artillery. Cadet (?). Fireworker (?). Lieut. 18 Sept. 1761. Capt. Lt. 2 Dec. 1763. *d.* 1765.
Services : N.F.P.

JEREMIE, Peter (1786-1831). Captain, Invalid Est. 3rd Extra Regt. Subsequently Asst. Opium Agent in Bihar. *b.* St. Peter Port, Guernsey, 28 Dec. 1786. Cadet 1803. Arrived in India 1 Dec. 1804. Ensign 14 Oct. 1804. Lieut. 14 Oct. 1804. Capt. 20 Oct. 1819. Invalided 7 Apr. 1826. *d.* Patna 29 July 1831.

Son of John Jeremie and Mary Durell his wife. *m.* Calcutta, 20 May 1807, Miss Ann Eliza Thompson. His daus. *m.* Henry Walter Bellew, *q.v.*, and John Turner, *q.v.*
Services : Posted as Lieut. to 1/2nd N.I. in 1805. Served with Pioneers 1808. Adjt. & Qmr. 2nd N.I. 8 July 1809 till July 1814. Adjt. 1/2nd N.I. 1 July 1814 till 1816. Fur. 1816. Capt. 2/2nd N.I. Asst. to Resdt. in Malwa and Rajputana 1822 till invalided. Transfd. to 5th N.I. (late 1/2nd) May 1824 ; to 3rd Extra Regt. May 1825. Asst. to Opium Agent in Bihar, with a salary of Rs. 500 *p.m.* in addition to his mily. pay and allowances, 17 Nov. 1826 till death.
Refs. : A.J. N.S. vii. 42. Will dated 13 May 1831 ; proved 14 Sept. 1831. M.I. at Patna.

JERVIS, John (1796-1849). Lieut. Colonel, 5th N.I. *bapt.* Uxbridge, Middlesex, 27 Nov. 1796. Cadet 1813. Admitted 5 Aug. 1814. Ensign 16 Dec. 1814. Lieut. 1 Aug. 1818. Capt. 25 Apr. 1826. Major 10 Jan. 1842. Lt. Col. 8 July 1848. *d.* at sea, 3 Sept. 1849, on board the *Precursor*, on his passage to England.

Son of William Jervis. Brother of Mary, wife of Maj.-Gen. Sir George Adam Wood, Kt., R.A. (*D.N.B.*). *m.* Lucknow, 22 May 1822, Miss Catherine Jane Fraser.
Services : Posted as Ensign to 2/2nd N.I. Lieut. 2/2nd N.I. Adjt. 2/2nd N.I. 27 Oct. 1823. Transfd. to 5th N.I. (late 1/2nd) May 1824. Adjt. 5th N.I. 17 June 1824 till 25 Aug. 1826. Fur. s.c. 17 Dec. 1826 till 4 Feb. 1828. Tempy. comdg. Delhi Provl. Bn. 20 Dec. 1828. Actg. Bde. Major Rajputana F.F. 7 Jan. 1832. Fur.

p.a. 13 Jan. till 1 Dec. 1834. Supt. of family monies and Paymr. Native pensioners, Oudh and Cawnpore, 25 Jan. 1837. Bde. Major 5th Inf. Bde., Army of the Indus, 17 Sept. 1838. Offg. D.A.A.G. Sirhind Div. 8 Dec. 1838 till 25 Feb. 1839. Supt. of family pensions and Paymr. Native pensioners at Barrackpore 24 Nov. 1841 till 19 Dec. 1842. Rejoined 5th N.I. in 1843. Posted as Lt. Col. to 5th N.I. 21 July 1848. Fur. s.c. 10 Aug. 1849.
Refs. : G.M. 1849, ii. 559. Will dated 10 Sept. 1848 ; proved 29 July 1850.

JERVIS, Thomas Septimus (1810-1885). Captain, Invalid Est. 71st N.I. *b.* 13 Holland St., Kensington, London, 24 July 1810. Cadet 1827. Arrived in India 18 Mar. 1828. Ensign 4 Nov. 1827. Lieut. 31 Jan. 1835. Capt. 4 Nov. 1842. Invalided 1 May 1847. *d.* Mussoorie, U.P., 23 Nov. 1885.

4th son of Swynfen Jervis, of Netherseal, Leics., and Maria Anne his wife, dau. of William Anderson. Brother of William Jervis, *q.v. m.* Landour, Mussoorie, 10 Oct. 1855, Annie ——. Ed. Merchant Taylors' ; admitted Apr. 1820.

Services : Ensign d.d. 42nd N.I. 1 May 1828. Posted as Ensign to 71st N.I. 4 Nov. 1828, and served throughout with that Regt. Fur. s.c. 19 June 1840 till 12 Dec. 1842. Posted to Eur. Invalids at Chunar May 1848. No record of active service.

Refs. : Burke's *Landed Gentry*, 13th edn., p. 993, *s.n.* Jervis (*now* Gooch), of Chatcull, Staffs. *Robinson* (where date of birth is given as 1 Apr. 1810).

JERVIS, William (1806-1891). Lieut. Colonel. 3rd Bengal Eur. Regt. *b.* Mitcham, Surrey, 28 Mar. 1806. Cadet 1824. Arrived in India 15 May 1825. Ensign 14 Nov. 1824. Lieut. 23 Nov. 1825. Capt. 18 July 1844. Major 1856. Retired 21 Jan. 1857. Hon. Lt. Col. 21 Jan. 1857. *d.* Chatkyll, Sydenham, 8 June 1891.

Of Chatkyll, Laurie Park, Sydenham. 3rd son of Swynfen Jervis, of Netherseal, Leics., and Maria Anne his wife. Brother of Thomas Septimus Jervis, *q.v. m.* 1st, Cawnpore, 29 Dec. 1828, Paulina Sophia, eldest dau. of John Swinton, *q.v.* (She died Nimach 6 Dec. 1830.) *m.* 2nd, St. Pancras, 20 Dec. 1838, Mary Amelia, 2nd dau. of Capt. William Hugh Dobbie, R.N., of Saling Hall, Essex. (She was divorced 19 May 1844.) *m.* 3rd, St. John's, Calcutta, 11 June 1850, Helen Martin Ann, dau. of Francis Pemble Strong, Asst. Surg. Bengal Est. (She died 1864.)

Services : First Burma War ; Arakan 1825 ; Ensign 42nd N.I. (India medal). Fur. p.a. 9 Jan. 1836 till 17 May 1839. d.d. with Recruit Depot at Aligarh 26 Aug. 1839 ; Adjt. do. 29 Nov. 1839. First Afghan War 1840-2 ; operations of Kandahar force ; advance

on Kabul; Haft Kotal 15 Oct. 1842 (w.); Lieut. 42nd N.I., with Gen. Nott's force (Medal). (*Lond. Gaz.* 10 Jan. 1843.) Paymr. & Supt. of Native pensioners at Barrackpore 1 Mar. 1844 till retirement. Posted to newly-raised 3rd Bengal Eur. Regt. 15 Nov. 1853.
Refs.: Burke's *Landed Gentry*, 13th edn., p. 993, *s.n.* Jervis (*now* Gooch), of Chatcull, Staffs. *A.J.* xxvii. 754. *I.M.* No. 102, p. 344. *The Times*, 15 June 1891.

JESSUP, John Henry Bowes (1789-?). Lieutenant. 5th N.C. *bapt.* London 25 Nov. 1789. Cadet 1805. Arrived in India 11 July 1806. Cornet 16 July 1806. Lieut. (?). Resigned in India 5 Nov. 1811.
Son of Henry James Jessup and Lady Anna Maria his wife, younger dau. of John, 9th Earl of Strathmore.
Services: Posted as Cornet to 5th N.C. in 1807. No record of active service.
Refs.: Burke's *Peerage*, 1923, p. 2113, *s.n.* Strathmore, E.

JEWEL, F——. Lieutenant. Infantry. Lieut. 17 Feb. 1765.
Services: Probably transfd. from H.M.S. Not in A.L. of 1 Feb. 1767.
Refs.: *B.M. Add. MS.* 6050.

JOECHER, Charles Ernest (*d.* 1763). Captain, Bengal Eur. Regt. Lieut. 16 June 1757. Capt. 1 Sept. 1758. *d.* 5th, 6th or 11th Oct. 1763: massacred at or near Patna by order of Nawab Mir Muhammad Kasim. (See note to John Gordon.*)
Services: Probably transfd. as Lieut. from Madras Eur. Regt.
Refs.: See John Greentree. Will dated Patna 15 Dec. 1760; proved 13 Dec. 1763.

JOHNSON, Alexander. Lieutenant. Infantry. Cadet 1778. Never arrived in India. Ensign 1778. Lieut. 29 Nov. 1778. Struck off (?).

JOHNSON, Arthur (1804-1867). Cadet. Subsequently lecturer of St. Vedast, Foster Lane, and St. Michael le Querne, London. *b.* Bristol 2 Apr. 1804. Cadet 1825. Did not proceed to India. *d.* 36 Canonbury Sq., Islington, London, 30 Sept. 1867.
5th son of Rev. William Moor Johnson, of St. James's, Bristol. Christ Church Coll., Oxon.; matric. 14 Dec. 1822. B.A. 1826. Took holy orders; deacon 1831; priest 1832.
Refs.: *Alumni Oxon. Crockford. The Times*, 4 Oct. 1867.

JOHNSON, Charles John. (*See* **FIELDING, Charles John Johnson.**)

JOHNSON, Hugh (1805-1874). Lieut. Colonel. 26th N.I. *b.* Alnwick, Northumberland, 22 Aug. 1805. Cadet 1823. Arrived in India 16 Aug. 1824. Ensign 29 Mar. 1824. Lieut. 13 May

1825. Capt. 1 Jan. 1837. Major 6 Apr. 1850. Retired 18 June 1850. Hon. Lt. Col. 28 Nov. 1854. *d.* Beaumont, Cheltenham, 26 Feb. 1874.

2nd son of Hugh Johnson. *m.* 22 Jan. 1844, Hetty Betsey Harriet, eldest dau. of George Weyland Moseley, *q.v.* (*See also* Charles Finch Farmer.) (She died 10 Jan. 1888.)

Services : Posted as Ensign to 26th N.I. in 1824. First Burma War ; Arakan 1825 ; Ensign 26th N.I. (India medal). Intr. & Qmr. 26th N.I. 27 Nov. 1826 till 30 June 1837. S.A.C.G. 1 Mar. 1837. Posted to the Hissar Stud 16 Oct. 1837. In the Pay & Comst. Dept. of Shah Shuja's army 28 Aug. 1838 till 17 June 1840. S.A.C.G. 8 Nov. 1838. First Afghan War 1839-42 ; Ghazni 1839 (Medal) ; Kabul insurrection ; handed over as one of the hostages to Mahomed Akbar 11 Jan. 1842 ; released 21 Sept. 1842. Re-appointed S.A.C.G. 21 Dec. 1842 ; D.A.C.G., 2 cl., 8 Jan. 1844 ; do. 1 cl., 3 Feb. 1846. Fur. s.c. 28 Jan. 1849 till retirement. Durani, 3 cl., 15 Aug. 1840.

Refs. : The Times, 28 Feb. 1874.

JOHNSON, James (1794-1844). Captain. Artillery. *b.* 14 June 1794. Cadet 1810. Admitted 27 Aug. 1811. Fireworker 19 Aug. 1811. Lieut. 25 Sept. 1817. Capt. 28 Sept. 1827. Retired 17 Jan. 1836. *d.* Willow Bank, nr. Ryde, I.W., 10 Sept. 1844.

bapt. London 13 July 1794. Son of Magnus Johnson, of Red Lion St., Wapping, London, mariner, and Henrietta Elizabeth his wife. Woolwich Cadet.

Services : Third Mahratta War ; Lieut. 4th Coy. 1st Bn. Foot Art. Posted to 4th Troop H.A. in 1819 ; 1st Troop 1819-20. Adjt. & Qmr. Malwa Div. Art. 2 Apr. 1822 ; do. 1st Bn. Foot Art. 23 Nov. 1824. Actg. Bde. Major 14 Apr. 1825 ; do. 2nd Bde. H.A. 22 July 1825. Siege and capture of Bhurtpore ; Adjt. 2nd Bde. H.A., and Bde. Major Foot Art. and Battering Train. Adjt. & Qmr. 2nd Bde. H.A. till Feb. 1827. Fur. p.a. 2 Feb. 1827 till 30 June 1828. Offg. Supt. H.A. Depot and Riding Est. at Dum-Dum 24 July 1828. Comdg. 1st Troop 1st Bde. 1828 ; do. 4th Troop 2nd Bde. 1829-34.

Refs. : G.M. 1844, ii. 443. *The Times*, 17 Sept. 1844.

*****JOHNSON, Jeremiah Martin** (*d.* 1833). Colonel, 30th N.I. Cadet 1783. Admitted 25 Aug. 1785. Ensign 28 May 1785. Lieut. 14 Oct. 1793. Capt. 21 Sept. 1804. Major 1 June 1813. Lt. Col. 1 Feb. 1818. Lt. Col. Comdt. 1 May 1824. Col. 5 June 1829. *d.* in France 10 Jan. 1833.

m. Mary Ann Breeze. Father of William Thompson Johnson, *q.v.*
Services : Fur. 12 Mar. 1800 till 30 June 1802. Raised at Cawnpore in July 1803 the 2/21st N.I., called after him "*Jansin-ki Paltan.*" Fort Adjt. at Fort William Jan. 1804. Adjt. Calcutta

Eur. Mil. 1 Nov. 1804. Actg. Garr. Storekeeper at Fort William 30 Jan. 1806. To act as Agent for Stores 6 Mar. 1806. Fur. p.a. 24 Feb. 1807 till 27 Oct. 1809. Bk. Mr. at Fort William 30 Sept. 1810. Apptd. Paymr. to troops proceeding to Java 22 Feb. 1811. Capture of Java 1811. Capture of Jokyakarta 1812. Dy. Paymr. at Java 1812-4. Served with Bengal Vol. Bn. 1815-6. Major 2/21st N.I. Transfd. as Lt. Col. to 1/15th N.I. Fur. s.c. 19 Nov. 1818 till 1 Jan. 1823. Transfd. as Lt. Col. Comdt. to 30th N.I. (late 1/15th) May 1824. Fur. 31 Aug. 1825 till death.
Refs. : *E.I.M.C.* ii. 230. *A.J.* N.S. xi. 203.

JOHNSON, John (1781-1852). Captain. 30th N.I. *bapt.* Walthamstow, Essex, 24 Apr. 1781. Cadet 1800. Arrived in India 30 Sept. 1801. Ensign 10 Sept. 1801. Lieut. 12 June 1802. Capt. 16 Dec. 1814. Retired 5 Apr. 1820. *d.* Bath 9 Apr. 1852. Son of Richard Johnson and Elizabeth his wife.
Services : Lieut. Bengal Eur. Regt. Transfd. to newly-raised 21st N.I. in 1804. Second Mahratta War ; Lieut. 21st N.I. Fur. 1811 till 22 Sept. 1815. Transfd. to newly-raised 30th N.I. in 1815. Nepal War 1816 ; Makwanpur ; Capt. 1/30th N.I. in 4th Bde., Centre Column (India medal). Fur. 13 Sept. 1817 till retirement. (? Author of " A Journey from India to England, through Persia, Georgia, Poland and Prussia in 1817," coloured and plain aquatint plates, 4to, 1818.)
Refs. : *G.M.* 1852, i. 633. *I.M.* 9 Apr. 1852, p. 276.

JOHNSON, Richard Courtenay (1801-1869). Major. 50th N.I. *b.* London 13 Sept. 1801. Cadet 1817. Admitted 21 July 1818. Ensign (?). Lieut. 1 Aug. 1818. Capt. 12 Mar. 1829. Invalided 29 Oct. 1838. Retired 29 July 1841. Major 1850. *d.* Arcachon, France, 7 Jan. 1869.
Son of Richard Johnson. Addiscombe Cadet 1816-8.
Services : Posted as Lieut. to 2/25th N.I. in 1818. Actg. Adjt. detached Wing of 2/25th N.I. 2 Apr. 1821. Transfd. to 50th N.I. (late 2/25th) May 1824. Fur. s.c. 22 Jan. 1827 till 19 Jan. 1831. Operations against the Kols in Chota Nagpur 1832 ; Capt. 50th N.I., comdg. Centre Column. Operations against the Chuars 1832-3 ; Capt. 50th N.I., in Jungle Mehal F.F. Leave s.c. 2 yrs. to Tasmania 9 Mar. 1836. Fur. s.c. 29 Jan. 1839 till retirement.
Refs. : *The Times*, 29 Jan. 1869.

JOHNSON or JOHNSTONE, Robert Grotts Wallace (*d.* 1784). Captain, Engineers. Cadet (?). Ensign 23 Feb. 1774. Lieut. 13 June 1776. Capt. 11 Feb. 1781. *d.* Calcutta 27 Mar. 1784.
Services : N.F.P.

JOHNSON, William. Captain. Artillery. Cadet (?). Fireworker 20 June 1766. 2nd Lieut. 23 July 1769. Lieut. 7 Mar. 1770. Capt. Lt. 11 Jan. 1773. Capt. 1 Mar. 1778. Resigned 1 Mar. 1778.
Services : N.F.P.

JOHNSON, William Thompson[1] (1807-1828). Lieutenant, 62nd N.I. *b.* Bengal 20 Sept. 1807. Cadet 1823. Ensign 7 Jan. 1824. Lieut. 13 May 1825. *d.* Sitapur, U.P., 16 May 1828, of smallpox. *bapt.* Calcutta 21 Nov. 1807. Son of Jeremiah Martin Johnson, *q.v.,* and Mary Ann his wife.
Services : Posted as Ensign to 62nd N.I. First Burma War; Arakan 1825 ; Lieut. 62nd N.I. Actg. Intr. & Qmr. 62nd N.I. 1 Apr. 1828.
Refs. : A.J. xxvi. 740.

[1] *Note :* Although apparently baptized as William Jeremiah, he is invariably called William Thompson Johnson in official documents.

JOHNSTON, D'Arcy (1807-1830). Lieutenant, 2nd Bengal Eur. Regt. *b.* 1807. Cadet 1824. Ensign 26 Feb. 1825. Lieut. 26 Apr. 1827. *d.* Aligarh 30 Sept. 1830, of fever.
bapt. Crawley, Hants, 17 Oct. 1807. 2nd son of Sir William Johnston, 7th Bart., of that ilk, and Maria his 2nd wife, only dau. of John Bacon, of Fryern House, Middlesex.
Services : Posted as Ensign to 2nd Bengal Eur. Regt. in 1826. On the amalgamation of 1st and 2nd Bengal Eur. Regts. in Jan. 1830, he was posted to Left Wing of Bengal Eur. Regt., and was on his way from Landour to join at Agra when his death occurred. No record of active service.
Refs. : Burke's *Peerage,* 1923, p. 1260, *s.n.* Johnston, Bart., of that ilk. *G.M.* 1831, i. 285. *A.J.* N.S. iv. 145.

JOHNSTON, Francis James Thomas (1776-1844). Major General, C.B. Colonel 11th L.C. *b.* 26 Aug. 1776. Cadet 1796. Arrived in India 3 Aug. 1797. Cornet 7 Aug. 1797. Lieut. 29 May 1800. Capt. 15 Aug. 1809. Major 30 June 1818. Lt. Col. 12 Dec. 1823. Lt. Col. Comdt. 10 July 1825. Col. 5 June 1829. Maj. Gen. 28 June 1838. *d.* London 5 Jan. 1844.
Of 21 Holles St., Cavendish Sq., London. *bapt.* London 15 Sept. 1776. Youngest son of Samuel Johnston, E.I.C.C.S., and Hon. Hester Napier his wife, 3rd dau. of Francis, 5th Lord Napier. Brother of Rt. Hon. Sir Alexander Johnston, Kt., C.J. of Ceylon (*D.N.B.*). *m.* Ghazipur, 5 July 1808, Miss Sally Rider. (*See also* Humphrey Howorth (1778-1817).) Father of Samuel Gardner Johnston, *q.v.*

THE BENGAL ARMY, 1758-1834

Services : Cornet 6th Inniskilling Dgns. Jan. 1792 ; Lieut. do. 24 Oct. 1794. Served with his Regt. during the Duke of York's campaign in the Low Countries 1794-5 ; present at the battles of Willems and Tournay as well as the various actions in Apr. and May 1794, and during the Duke's retreat through Holland. Posted as Cornet to 2nd N.C. Dec. 1797. Operations in Jumna Doab 1803 ; Sasni ; Bijaigarh ; Kachaura. Second Mahratta War ; Aligarh ; battle of Delhi ; Agra ; Laswari ; battle and capture of Deig ; Bhurtpore. Adjt. 2nd N.C. Apr. 1804 till Feb. 1807. Capture of Gohad Feb. 1806 ; Lieut. comdg. a detachment of 3 Troops 2nd N.C. Qmr. 2nd N.C. Feb. 1807 till Apr. 1810. Served in the Bhatti country under Lt. Col. J. W. Adams, *q.v.*, Nov. 1810 till Jan. 1811 ; Capt. comdg. 2 Sqdns. 2nd N.C. Nepal War 1814-5 ; Capt. 2nd N.C., in 1st Div. Comdd. 2nd N.C. Aug. 1815 till Feb. 1827. Third Mahratta War ; with Reserve. On service in Bundelkhand 1821-2. Transfd. as Lt. Col. Comdt. to 8th L.C. 11 Aug. 1826, and joined in Feb. 1827. Tempy. comdg. Rajputana F.F. Jan.-June 1829. To comd. Benares Div., with rank of Bdr., 27 Dec. 1833 till Dec. 1834. Bdr. on Est., to comd. troops in Oudh 11 Feb. 1835. Transfd. to 2nd L.C. 19 Sept. 1838. This Regt. was disbanded in Mar. 1841 owing to misconduct in Afghanistan, and he was posted in 1842 as Col. to newly-raised 11th L.C. which replaced it. Comdd. Cawnpore Div. 29 Dec. 1838 till 27 Nov. 1840. Fur. p.a. 27 Jan. 1842 till death. C.B. 20 July 1838.

Refs. : *G.M.* 1844, ii. 92. *The Times*, 11 Jan. 1844. Will dated 9 Dec. 1843 ; proved 6 Sept. 1844.

JOHNSTON, Gabriel (1742-1820). Lieut. General. Colonel 12th N.I. *b.* 1742. Cadet 1764. Admitted 1 Sept. 1764. Ensign 27 Dec. 1764. Lieut. 6 Dec. 1766. Capt. 16 Apr. 1769. Major 6 Jan. 1781. Lt. Col. 29 May 1786. Col. 3 May 1796. Maj. Gen. 3 May 1796. Lt. Gen. 25 Sept. 1803. Retired on the Off-Reckoning fund 9 Oct. 1799. *d.* Kingston, Surrey, 28 Mar. 1820, aged 78.

A native of Ireland. *m.* Calcutta, 17 June 1785, Miss Félicieuse Georgette Marie Kaulie. (She died Norbiton Hall, Kingston, Feb. 1816.)

Services : Sailed for India on the *Vansittart*, 4 Mar. 1764, aged 21. Comdg. 5th Eur. Bn., and Comdt. at Berhampore in July 1787. Comdg. 1st Bde. N.I. at Cawnpore in 1796.

Refs. : *G.M.* 1820, i. 378. *S.M.* 1820, i. 487.

JOHNSTON, George (1760/61-1815). Major. Artillery. *b.* London 1760/61. Cadet 1781. Admitted 17 Sept. 1782. Fireworker 18 Aug. 1781. Lieut. 24 Nov. 1786. Capt. Lt. 8 Jan. 1796. Capt.

16 Feb. 1802. Major 1 Aug. 1805. Retired 13 May 1807. *d.*
London 7 Apr. 1815.
Services : Apptd. Cadet on 17 Oct. 1781, aged 21. Sailed for
India on the *Worcester,* 6 Feb. 1782, aged 21. Adjt. 2nd Bn. Art.
1787-90, or later. Third Mysore War ; Bangalore ; Adjt. & Bde.
Major Art. Fur. 28 Jan. 1805 till retirement.
Refs. : G.M. 1815,'i. 471.

JOHNSTON, George (1805-1881). Lieut. Colonel. 46th N.I. *b.*
London 12 Aug. 1805. Cadet 1825. Arrived in India 16 May
1826. Ensign 5 Nov. 1825. Lieut. 14 Jan. 1833. Capt. 24 Jan.
1845. Bt. Major 3 Apr. 1846. Retired 1 Nov. 1853. Hon.
Lt. Col. 28 Nov. 1854. *d.* 102 Rue du Faubourg St. Honoré, Paris,
31 July 1881.
Son of Charles Johnston, of Dublin.
Services : Posted as Ensign to 46th N.I. Fur. s.c. 1 Apr. 1828
till 4 Aug. 1831. Actg. Intr. & Qmr. 51st N.I. 10 Feb. 1834 ; do.
2nd L.C. 14 July 1834, and 24 Aug. 1835. Intr. & Qmr. 46th N.I. 8
Apr. till 10 Aug. 1836. Actg. Intr. & Qmr. 1st N.I. 17 May 1837.
S.A.C.G. 6 Sept. 1837. First Afghan War 1842 ; S.A.C.G., with
Gen. Pollock's force (Medal). Gwalior campaign ; Maharajpur
(w.) ; S.A.C.G. (Bronze star). (*Lond. Gaz.* 8 Mar. 1844.) Supt. of
Police in G.G.'s camp 19 Jan. 1844. First Sikh War ; Mudki ;
Ferozshahr ; Sobraon ; S.A.C.G. (Medal with 2 clasps). D.A.C.G.,
2 cl., 3 Feb. 1846. Apptd. Mily. Sec. Hyderabad Residency 19 May
1846, and served with Nizam's army till retirement.
Refs. : The Times, 5 Aug. 1881.

JOHNSTON, George Joseph Bidmead (1789-1867). Lieut. Colonel.
65th N.I. *b.* Hampstead, London, 15 July 1789. Cadet 1806.
Arrived in India 21 July 1807. Ensign 17 Aug. 1807. Lieut. 18
May 1810. Capt. 22 Apr. 1825. Major 16 Mar. 1838. Retired
1 Aug. 1839. Hon. Lt. Col. 28 Nov. 1854. *d.* St. Helier, Jersey,
29 July 1867.
bapt. St. John's, Hampstead, 7 Nov. 1789. Son of George Johnston and Jane his wife.
Services : Posted as Ensign to 9th N.I. Leave s.c. 1 yr. to
Mauritius 21 Apr. 1815. Adjt. 2/9th N.I. 6 Nov. 1815. Intr. &
Qmr. 1/9th N.I. 12 Dec. 1817 ; do. newly-raised 2/33rd N.I. 1 Oct.
1823 ; do. 65th N.I. (late 1/33rd) 17 June 1824 till July 1825. To
Penang on service 29 July 1825.
Refs. : G.M. 1867, ii. 402. *The Times,* 13 Aug. 1867.

JOHNSTON, John. Ensign. Infantry. Cadet 1770. Ensign 14
Nov. 1771. Resigned 22 Mar. 1776.
Services : N.F.P.

THE BENGAL ARMY, 1758-1834 561

JOHNSTON, John Campbell (1817-?). Captain. 29th N.I. *bapt.* London 14 Feb. 1817. Cadet 1834. Arrived in India 5 June 1835. Ensign (21 Dec. 1834) 2 Feb. 1835. Lieut. 3 Feb. 1839. Capt. 10 Nov. 1850. Resigned 10 Apr. 1853.

Son of David Johnston, of London, merchant, and Lindsay his wife.
Services : Ensign d.d. 57th N.I. 12 June 1835. Posted to 29th N.I. 24 Sept. 1835. Adjt. Inf., Bundelkhand Legion, 30 Jan. 1840 till 18 Aug. 1841. Disturbances in Bundelkhand 1840-1 ; Chirgaon. Actg. Adjt. 29th N.I. 21 Oct. 1841. Adjt. do. 28 Mar. till Sept. 1845. Fur. 9 Sept. 1845 till 1846. Fur. 1848. Actg. Adjt. 29th N.I. 4 Jan. 1849. Second Sikh War ; Jullundur Doab 1849 ; Lieut. 29th N.I. (Medal). Comdt. 2nd Punjab Inf. 18 May 1849 ; do. 1st Sikh Local Inf. 23 Nov. 1850 ; do. 5th Punjab Inf. 5 Nov. 1851 ; do. 2nd Punjab Inf. 22 Oct. 1852.

JOHNSTON, Joseph (1785-1827). Captain, 46th N.I. *bapt.* 17 Jan. 1785. Cadet 1804. Arrived in India 21 June 1806. Ensign (?). Lieut. 2 July 1805. Capt. 1 Jan. 1819. *d.* Hajipur, B. & O., 3 Nov. 1827.

Son of Rev. Alexander Johnston, minister of Monquhitter. *m.* (?).
Services : A survivor from the wreck of the *Earl of Abergavenny* off Portland 5 Feb. 1805. Posted as Lieut. to 23rd N.I. in 1806. Settlement of Hariana 1809 ; Bhawani ; Lieut. 2/23rd N.I. With 7th Gren. Bn. 1815-6. Third Mahratta War ; Lieut. 2/23rd N.I. First Burma War ; Assam 1824 ; Dudhpatli (w.) ; Capt. 2/23rd N.I. Transfd. to 46th N.I. (late 2/23rd) May 1824. Sub-Asst. in Stud Dept. 1824 till death.

JOHNSTON, Samuel Gardner (1809-1843). Lieutenant, Pension Est. 26th N.I. *b.* Bengal 22 Apr. 1809. Cadet 1824. Arrived in India 3 Oct. 1825. Ensign 13 May 1825. Lieut. 30 Dec. 1826. Pensioned 23 July 1832. *d.* Intally, Calcutta, 26 Sept. 1843.

bapt. Chunar 27 Apr. 1809. Only son of Francis James Thomas Johnston, *q.v.*, and Sally his wife. *m.* Calcutta, 12 July 1841, Louisa, dau. of Charles Isaac Levade, *q.v.* (She *re-m.* Calcutta, 1 Mar. 1845, Henry Kyte.)
Services : Posted as Ensign to 26th N.I. in 1826. Lieut. d.d. 11th N.I. 12 Feb. 1827 ; do. 12th N.I. 3 Oct. 1828. No record of active service.
Refs. : M.I. in Circular Rd. cemetery, Calcutta.

*JOHNSTONE, Benjamin. Cadet. Artillery. Cadet 1783. Declined coming out.
Services : N.F.P.
Refs. : Stubbs's List.

JOHNSTONE, George Dempster (1805-1867). Captain. 25th N.I.
Subsequently rector of Creed. *b.* Alva, co. Clackmannan, 13 Mar.
1805. Cadet 1821. Arrived in India 2 July 1822. Ensign 19
Jan. 1822. Lieut. 22 Sept. 1823. Capt. 21 Sept. 1832. Retired
7 Aug. 1834. *d.* Creed rectory, Cornwall, 8 Sept. 1867.
4th son of James Raymond Johnstone, of Alva, and Mary Elizabeth his wife, sister of Sir Montague Cholmeley, 1st Bart., of Easton,
Lincs. *m.* 1 Sept. 1842, Mary Anne, dau. of John Hawkins, of
Bignor, Sussex. (She died 16 Apr. 1890.) Trin. Coll., Camb. ;
B.A. 1836 ; M.A. 1839.
Services : Posted as Ensign to 11th N.I. Transfd. to 20th N.I.
July 1823 ; to 25th N.I. (late 1/20th) May 1824. Lieut. d.d. 1/23rd
N.I. 1 Mar. 1824. First Burma War ; Chittagong 1824 ; Cachar
1825 ; Lieut. 25th N.I., d.d. 45th N.I. (India medal). Fur. s.c. 22
Jan. 1827 till 23 Nov. 1829. Fur. s.c. 28 Aug. 1830 ; returned overland *via* Persia 28 May 1834. Took holy orders. Deacon and
priest 1834. Rector of Creed 1858.
Refs. : Burke's *Peerage*, 1923, p. 1261, *s.n.* Johnstone, Bart., of
Westerhall, co. Dumfries. Burke's *Landed Gentry*, 13th edn.,
p. 1001, *s.n.* Johnstone, of Alva, co. Clackmannan. *Graduati Cantab.*
Crockford. The Times, 14 Sept. 1867.

JOHNSTONE, George Home (1790-?). Lieut. Colonel. 26th N.I.
b. Foulden, co. Berwick, 17 May 1790. Cadet 1808. Arrived in
India 27 Oct. 1809. Ensign 29 Nov. 1810. Lieut. 5 Sept. 1815.
Capt. 28 Jan. 1825. Major 1 Jan. 1837. Invalided 12 Jan. 1837.
Retired 31 Mar. 1840. Hon. Lt. Col. 28 Nov. 1854. (*d.* after 1864.).
Son of William Johnstone.
Services : Posted as Ensign to 13th N.I. Nepal War 1814-5 ;
Ensign 13th N.I. (India medal). Bareilly insurrection 1816 ; Lieut.
1/13th N.I. Actg. Adjt. 1/13th N.I. 1817-9. Intr. & Qmr. 1/13th
N.I. 17 Aug. 1819 till 1824. Leave s.c. 1 yr. to China 14 June 1821.
Actg. Adjt. 1/13th N.I. 15 Apr. 1824. Transfd. to 27th N.I. (late
2/13th) May 1824. Intr. & Qmr. 27th N.I. 17 June 1824 till 12 July
1825. Actg. Adjt. 27th N.I. 13 Jan. 1825. Transfd. as Capt. to
26th N.I. (late 1/13th) in 1825. Fur. s.c. 2 Jan. 1828 till 29 Nov.
1830, and 13 Jan. 1839 till retirement.

JOHNSTONE, Henry. Ensign. Infantry. Cadet 1782. Ensign
27 Feb. 1783. Struck off 1788.
Services : N.F.P.

JOHNSTONE, James (1789 ?). Major. 74th N.I. *b.* Coldstream,
co. Berwick, 23 Feb. 1789. Cadet 1806. Arrived in India 1 Aug.
1807. Ensign 30 July 1807. Lieut. 28 Apr. 1812. Capt. 13

May 1825. Major 15 Dec. 1835. Retired 23 May 1836. (d. apparently between 1871 and 1877.)

Son of Wynne Johnstone, of Hawkslaw. Brother of Peter Johnstone, q.v.

Services : Barasat C.C. for 8 mos. Posted as Ensign to 24th N.I. Actg. Adjt. 1/24th N.I. in 1815. Third Mahratta War; Lieut. 1/24th N.I. Transfd. as Capt. to 48th N.I. (late 2/24th) May 1824 ; to newly-raised 6th Extra Regt. (became 74th N.I.) May 1825. Employed on survey work in Bhopal, and comdd. Bhopal Contingent 1825-8. Junior Asst. to A.G.G., Saugor and Narbada territories, 26 June 1828. Fur. p.a. 18 Apr. 1834 till retirement.

JOHNSTONE, Peter (1785 ?). Lieut. Colonel. 5th N.I. *b.* Coldstream, co. Berwick, 18 Nov. 1785. Cadet 1806. Arrived in India 1 Aug. 1807. Ensign 27 July 1807. Lieut. 29 Oct. 1812. Capt. 7 Nov. 1824. Major 1837. Retired 15 Dec. 1837. Hon. Lt. Col. 28 Nov. 1854. (*d.* apparently between 1864 and 1867.)

Son of Wynne Johnstone, of Hawkslaw. Brother of James Johnstone, q.v.

Services : Barasat C.C. for 8 mos. Posted as Ensign to 2nd N.I. Actg. Adjt. 1/2nd N.I. in 1817. With the escort to Resdt. at Indore from 6 Apr. 1821. Transfd. to 5th N.I. (late 1/2nd) May 1824. Apptd. to a civil situation in Indore 26 Oct. 1827. Third Asst. to Resdt. at Indore 21 Feb. 1828, 2nd do. 10 June 1831 till retirement. No record of active service.

JOHNSTONE, Robert Grotts Wallace. (*See* **JOHNSON**.)

JOLLIFFE, George (*d.* 1771). Ensign, Infantry. Cadet 1771. Ensign 15 Jan. 1771. *d.* Calcutta 6 Nov. 1771.
Services : N.F.P.

JOLLIFFE, John (1787-1815). Lieutenant, 21st N.I. *bapt.* Chale, I. W., 30 Dec. 1787. Cadet 1808. Arrived in India 24 July 1809. Ensign 27 Sept. 1809. Lieut. 16 Dec. 1814. *d.* Malacca 2 June 1815.

Son of William Jolliffe and Elizabeth his wife.

Services : Posted as Ensign to 21st N.I. in 1809. Served with Java Inf. Vols. 1814 till death.

*JOLLY or JOLLIE, James (*d.* 1803). Captain. Infantry. Cadet 1783. Admitted 27 Jan. 1784. Ensign 12 Mar. 1785. Lieut. 25 May 1793. Capt. (?). Retired 5 Mar. 1802. *d.* Dalkeith, Midlothian, Apr. 1803.

Services : Second Rohilla War ; battle of Bitaurah (w.) ; Lieut. Bengal Eur. Regt. Fur. 11 Mar. 1798 till retirement.

Refs. : Innes, p. 276. *S.M.* 1803, p. 362.

JOLLY, William (1789-1809). Lieutenant, 11th N.I. *bapt.* Kirriemuir, co. Forfar, 17 Dec. 1789. Cadet 1804. Arrived in India 13 May 1806. Ensign 15 Apr. 1806. Lieut. 12 June 1807. *d.* 8 Apr. 1809 : kld. in action at Mainpuri, U.P.
Son of Rev. William Jolly, Episcopal minister of Kirriemuir, and Elizabeth his wife.
Services : Posted as Lieut. to 11th N.I. in 1807.

JONES, George (*d.* 1790). Fireworker, Artillery. Cadet (Inf.) 1783. Ensign 17 Jan. 1785. Fireworker 17 Jan. 1785. *d.* Negapatam, Madras, 9 Nov. 1790.
Services : Transfd. from Inf. to Art. in 1789. Third Mysore War ; Lieut. 5th Coy. 2nd Bn. Art.

JONES, Griffith. Fireworker. Artillery. Cadet 1781. Fireworker 28 Sept. 1781. Resigned 5 Aug. 1784.
Services : N.F.P. (? Settled in Calcutta, where he was living in 1808, being then accountant to the Bank.)

JONES, Henry (*d.* 1764). Ensign, Infantry. Cadet 1763. Ensign 22 Oct. 1763. *d.* May 1764.
Services : N.F.P.

JONES, Isaac (1812-?). Captain. 58th N.I. *bapt.* Drakestown, co. Meath, 30 Jan. 1812. Cadet 1827. Arrived in India 8 June 1828. Ensign 23 Feb. 1828. Lieut. 1 Jan. 1837. Capt. 3 Feb. 1843. Cashiered by G.C.M. 4 Feb. 1844.
Son of Rev. Francis Jones, of Fermoy.
Services : Ensign d.d. 46th N.I. 25 July 1828. Posted to 58th N.I. 4 Nov. 1828. Fur. s.c. 23 Aug. 1839 till 10 Aug. 1842. Gwalior campaign ; Paniar ; Capt. 58th N.I.
Refs. : I.M. No. 12, p. 362.

JONES, James (*d.* 1763). Lieutenant, Infantry. Cadet (?). Ensign 11 Dec. 1759. Lieut. 11 Dec. 1761. *d.* 5th, 6th or 11th Oct. 1763 : massacred at or near Patna by order of Nawab Mir Muhammad Kasim. (*See* note to John Gordon.*)
Services : N.F.P.
Refs. : MS. list at the India Office entitled "List of Persons killed in the Massacre at Patna, and at other places during the Troubles, 1763." *Firminger,* p. 71. *Forrest's Clive,* ii. 237.

JONES, John (*d.* 1773). Captain, comdg. 6th Bn. Sepoys. Lieut. 2 Nov. 1764. Capt. 27 May 1767. *d.* Cooch Behar 24 May 1773.
Services : Comdd. 6th Bn. Sepoys from 1768 till death. Operations against the Bhutias in Cooch Behar 1772-3 ; storm and capture

of Cooch Behar 21 Dec. 1772 (w.) ; capture of Dhalimkot Apr. 1773 ;
Capt. comdg. the force.
Refs. : D.I.B. Williams, pp. 107, 110. *Cardew*, p. 37.

JONES, John. Lieutenant, Infantry. (? *bapt.* Wilts. 23 Sept. 1764.)
Cadet 1777. Ensign (?). Lieut. 6 Oct. 1778. *d.* (?).
(? Son of Catherine Jones.)
Services : N.F.P.

JONES, John (1782-1819). Captain, 7th N.C. *b.* 8 Oct. 1782.
Cadet 1798. Arrived in India 5 Sept. 1799. Cornet 7 June 1800.
Lieut. 4 Aug. 1801. Capt. 27 Feb. 1812. *d.* Husainabad, B. & O.,
30 Apr. 1819, of cholera.

3rd son of Robert Jones, of Fonmon Castle, co. Glamorgan, and
Joanna his 2nd wife, dau. of Edmund Lloyd, of Cardiff. *m.* 7 June
1807, Miss Cordelia Ferguson. (She died 24 Jan. 1845.)
Services : Cornet 5th N.C. Second Mahratta War ; Lieut. 5th
N.C. Transfd. to newly-raised 7th N.C. in 1805. Adjt. 7th N.C.
1807 till May 1809. Operations in Oudh 1808. Settlement of
Hariana 1809-10. Capt. Lt. 7th N.C. 4 Nov. 1810. Nepal War
1814-5 ; Capt. 7th N.C., in 2nd Div. Siege and capture of Hathras
1817. (? Third Mahratta War ; Dhamoni ; Mandala ; Multai ;
Harna ; Capt. 7th N.C.)
Refs. : Burke's *Landed Gentry*, 12th edn., p. 1060, *s.n.* Jones, of
Fonmon Castle, co. Glamorgan. *A.J.* ix. Will dated Muttra July
1816 ; proved 9 Aug. 1819.

JONES, John (1801-1875). Captain. 46th N.I. *b.* Walcot,
Somerset, 18 Mar. 1801. Cadet 1818. Admitted 10 Feb. 1820.
Ensign 16 Aug. 1819. Lieut. 18 July 1823. Capt. 20 Apr. 1826.
Resigned 1 Mar. 1835. *d.* Torquay, Devon, 7 Apr. 1875.

Son of John Jones, of 63 Harley St., London, formerly in the army.
m. Cheltenham, 1 Aug. 1831, Mary, widow of Richard Carpenter, of
Monkton House, Somerset. (She died at sea off the Cape 23 Aug.
1835.)
Services : Posted as Ensign to 2/23rd N.I. Actg. Adjt. Rt. Wing
2/23rd N.I. 11 Mar. 1823. Transfd. to 46th N.I. (late 2/23rd) May
1824. First Burma War ; Assam 1824 (*Lond. Gaz.* 19 Apr. 1825) ;
Lieut. 46th N.I. (India medal). Actg. Adjt. 46th N.I. 23 Dec.
1824 ; permanent do. 12 July 1825 till 25 Aug. 1826. D.A.Q.M.G.
in Assam. Offg. in Q.M.G. Dept. 13 Mar. 1829. Fur. s.c. 5 May
1829 till 15 Apr. 1834. Granted the h.p. of a Capt. 25 Dec. 1843.
Capt. R. North Gloucs. Mil. 15 Apr. 1853. F.R.A.S. 8 May
1835.
Refs. : Boase.

JONES, John Heming (1782-1807). Lieutenant, Engineers. *b.* London 27 Aug. 1782. Cadet 1799. Ensign 10 Dec. 1800. Lieut. 1 Jan. 1806. *d.* 14 Nov. 1807 : kld. in action in the assault of Komona fort.

bapt. Marylebone 24 Sept. 1782. Son of Lt.-Col. John Jones, of East Wickham, Kent, and Elizabeth Heming his 1st wife. Cousin-german of Priscilla Martha, dau. of Capt. William Belford, and wife of Lt.-Col. Hon. Christopher Carleton, 3rd son of first Baron Dorchester. Woolwich Cadet ; nominated for R.M.A. 18 July 1798 ; obtained his certificate 31 Mar. 1800.

Services : Second Mahratta War ; siege and capture of Gwalior, serving with Pioneers. Operations against Dhundia Khan 1807 ; siege of Komona ; kld. by the enemy springing a mine which destroyed the head of the approach, burying him in the ruins.

Refs. : Stubbs, i. 304. *Pester*, pp. 256, 417. *A.A.R.* x. 21. Will dated 13 Oct. 1807 ; proved 1 Jan. 1808.

JONES, John Landon (1790-1843). Bt. Major. 5th N.I. *bapt.* London 9 Sept. 1790. Cadet 1808. Arrived in India 24 July 1809. Ensign 7 Aug. 1809. Lieut. 16 Dec. 1814. Capt. 5 Feb. 1826. Bt. Major 28 June 1838. Retired 31 Dec. 1840. *d.* Bury, nr. Alverstoke, Hants, 20 Apr. 1843.

Eldest son of John Jones, of Ely Pl., London, and of Alverstoke, Hants, and Anna his wife, sister of Rev. Charles Richard Landon. Cousin-german of Charles Ginkell Landon, *q.v. m.* 6 Sept. 1818, Miss Sarah Jacques. (*See also* James Bourdieu.)

Services : Barasat C.C. Posted as Ensign to 2nd N.I. (? Reduction of Kalinjar 1812. Operations in Baghelkhand 1813 ; Entauri ; Ensign 2/2nd N.I.) Lieut. 2/2nd N.I. Actg. Adjt. 2/2nd N.I. 24 Oct. 1823. Transfd. to 5th N.I. (late 1/2nd) May 1824. Adjt. Left Wing 5th N.I. 28 June 1825. Fur. s.c. 20 Jan. 1829 till 11 Nov. 1831. Shekhawat expedn. 1834 ; Capt. 5th N.I.

Refs. : Foster's *Families of Royal Descent*, ii. 863. *The Times*, 26 Apr. 1843.

JONES, John Weldon (*d.* 1779). Ensign, Infantry. Cadet 1777. Ensign 24 Sept. 1777. *d.* Dinapore 4 Mar. 1779.

Services : N.F.P.

JONES, John William(s) (1786-1833). Major, 17th N.I. *bapt.* Llanbeblig, co. Carnarvon, 24 Oct. 1786. Cadet 1805. Arrived in India 11 July 1806. Ensign 19 Aug. 1806. Lieut. 2 Feb. 1808. Capt. 20 Feb. 1821. Major 9 Jan. 1833. *d. unm.* at sea, at the mouth of the Ganges, 28 Aug. 1833.

Of Tyddyn Einddu, nr. Carnarvon, Son of David Jones and

Margaret his wife. Brother of William Jones, of Carnarvon, atty.
Services : Barasat C.C. for $9\frac{1}{2}$ mos. Posted as Ensign to 11th N.I. Reduction of Kalinjar 1812 ; Lieut. 2/11th N.I. Siege and capture of Hathras 1817 ; Lieut. 2/11th N.I. Intr. & Qmr. 2/11th N.I. 20 Nov. 1815 till 1820. Third Mahratta War ; Bde. Qmr. 3rd Inf. Bde., 1st Div. Actg. Adjt. 2/11th N.I. 25 Feb. 1820. Fur. p.a. 8 Jan. 1824 till 4 June 1827. Transfd. to 17th N.I. (late 2/11th) May 1824. Leave s.c. 2 yrs. to Tasmania 17 July 1833.
Refs. : *A.J.* N.S. xiv. 59. Will dated Fatehgarh 23 July 1831 ; proved 15 Oct. 1833.

JONES, Nathaniel (1800-1869). Major General. 49th N.I. *b.* Lambeth, Surrey, 20 Nov. 1800. Cadet 1816. Arrived in India Sept. 1817. Ensign 2 Sept. 1817. Lieut. 1 Aug. 1818. Capt. 21 Sept. 1828. Major 21 July 1841. Lt. Col. 12 Aug. 1847. Col. 31 May 1857. Maj. Gen. 30 May 1859. *d.* Murree 21 July 1869.

Son of Benjamin Scott Jones, of Manor Place, Walworth, Surrey, one of the principal clerks to the commissioners for the affairs of India. Brother of William Cabell Jones, *q.v.* *m.* Cawnpore, 29 Jan. 1836, Mary Anne Drake Mouat, eldest dau. of John Andrew Biggs, *q.v.* Addiscombe Cadet 1816-7.

Services : Ensign d.d. 1/20th N.I. till July 1819. Posted as Ensign to 1/29th N.I. Sept. 1818. Asst. Bk. Mr. Dacca Div. Feb. 1824. Transfd. to 57th N.I. (late 1/29th) May 1824. Asst. Executive Ofr. P.W.D. July 1824. First Burma War ; Assam 1824-5 ; Rangpur ; Lieut. 57th N.I. (India medal). Offg. D.J.A.G. to force in Assam 25 Mar. 1825 till Mar. 1828. Asst. Executive Ofr. P.W.D., Dacca, Mar. 1828 ; do. Dinapore Nov. 1828. D.J.A.G. Cawnpore Div. 29 Nov. 1830 till 19 Mar. 1835. Dy. Paymr. Nasirabad 19 Mar. 1835 till 15 Sept. 1841. Rejoined 57th N.I. Feb. 1842, and comdd. a detachment on service in Bundelkhand in 1842. Fur. p.a. 7 Mar. 1843 till Feb. 1846. Posted as Lt. Col. to 58th N.I. Dec. 1847. Transfd. to 17th N.I. Mar. 1850 ; to 49th N.I. 23 Sept. 1853 ; to 64th N.I. Aug. 1855 ; to 49th N.I. 20 Oct. 1855, and was comdg. when the Regt. was disarmed at Mian Mir 13 May 1857. Posted as Col. to 49th N.I. Aug. 1859. Fur. p.a. June 1859 till Nov. 1860.

Refs. : *De Rhé-Philipe.* *Boase.* M.I. in new cemetery at Murree.

JONES, Richard (1785-1802). Cornet, 1st N.C. *b.* Criccieth, co. Carnarvon, 18 July 1785. Madras Cadet 1798. Transfd. to Bengal Cav. Cornet 21 June 1800. *d.* in camp nr. Kanauj, U.P., 31 Dec. 1802.

bapt. Criccieth 4 Oct. 1785. Son of John Jones, of Brynhir, and Elizabeth his wife.
Services : Was on his way from Madras to join his Regt. when his death occurred.

JONES, Richard Elliston (1806-1828). Ensign, 25th N.I. *b.* Edinburgh 20 May 1806. Cadet 1825. Ensign 4 Dec. 1825. *d.* at sea 3 Aug. 1828.
Son of Richard Jones, of the Customs.
Services : Posted as Ensign to 25th N.I. in 1826. Fur. s.c. 29 Feb. 1828 till death. No record of active service.
Refs. : A.J. xxvi. 517.

JONES, Samuel (1761/62-1802). Lieut. Colonel, 1st Bengal Eur. Regt. *b.* 1761/62. Cadet 1776. Admitted 7 July 1776. Ensign 10 Mar. 1777. Lieut. 7 Aug. 1778. Capt. 2 Sept. 1794. Major 1 Feb. 1799. *d.* Sherghati, Bengal, 29 June 1802, aged 40.
Brother of Amelia Cole, wife of —— Jackson, of 8 Chapel Row, Spa Fields, London. Cousin of Mrs. Ann Shepherd, *née* Ovington.
Services : 1/2nd Bengal Eur. Regt. in Oct. 1779. Was Adjt. 15th Sepoy Bn. in July 1787. Adjt. 15th Bn., in 6th Bde., in 1790. Capt. 1/13th N.I. in Aug. 1798.
Refs. : Will dated Hazaribagh 7 Apr. 1801 ; proved 15 July 1802.

JONES, Samuel Giffin (1793-1820). Lieutenant, 22nd N.I. *b.* Calcutta 28 June 1793. Cadet 1808. Arrived in India 15 Dec. 1809. Ensign 13 Aug. 1811. Lieut. 2 Jan. 1815. *d.* between Cuttack and Nagpur 11 Dec. 1820.
bapt. Calcutta 18 Nov. 1793. Son of Samuel Jones, head asst., G.P.O., Calcutta, and Mary Ann his wife.
Services : Barasat C.C. Posted as Ensign to 22nd N.I. in 1811. (? Reduction of Kalinjar 1812 ; Ensign 1/22nd N.I.) Third Mahratta War ; Nagpur ; Lieut. 1/22nd N.I.

JONES, Sidney Caesar (*d.* 1809). Major, 23rd N.I. Cadet 1782. Admitted 9 July 1783. Ensign 17 Jan. 1783. Lieut. 2 Mar. 1789. Capt. 30 Sept. 1803. Major 2 June 1808. *d. unm.* Delhi 6 Feb. 1809.
Services : Ensign 1st Bengal Eur. Regt. in July 1787. Bt. Capt. 2/1st N.I. in July 1798. Capt. Marine Regt. Transfd. to newly-raised 23rd N.I. in 1804. Major 1/23rd N.I.
Refs. : Will dated 1 Nov. 1803 ; proved 22 Mar. 1809.

*JONES, Thomas. 2nd Lieutenant. Artillery. Cadet 1763. Fireworker (?). 2nd Lieut. 1766. Resigned (?).
Services : N.F.P.
Refs. : Stubbs's List, No. 55.

THE BENGAL ARMY, 1758-1834 569

JONES, Thomas. Ensign, Infantry. Cadet 1770. Ensign 14 Nov. 1771. d. Madras (?).
Services : N.F.P.

JONES, Thomas (1784-1812). Captain, 2nd N.I. *bapt.* St. Clement Danes, London, 23 May 1784. Cadet 1798. Arrived in India 24 Feb. 1800. Ensign 11 Jan. 1800. Lieut. 29 May 1800. Capt. 24 Jan. 1809. *d. unm.* Malacca 28 Oct. 1812.
Son of Joseph Jones and Ann his wife.
Services : Operations in Jumna Doab 1803 ; Sasni ; Bijaigarh ; Kachaura ; Lieut. 2/2nd N.I. Second Mahratta War ; battle of Delhi ; Hinglaisgarh ; Monson's retreat ; action on banks of Banas R. 24 Aug. 1804 (w.), " the only surviving officer " (*Pester*) ; Lieut. 2/2nd N.I. Adjt. 1/2nd N.I. 1807 till Mar. 1810. Capture of Java 1811 ; Capt. 3rd Bengal Vol. Bn.
Refs. : Pester, pp. 169, 314. Will dated 31 Aug. 1812 ; proved 5 Jan. 1813.

JONES, William (1740/41-1818). Lieut. General. 1st N.I. *b.* 1740/41. Bencoolen Cadet 1763. Transfd. to Bengal as a Lieut. from the Bencoolen Est. 1765. Lieut. 31 Aug. 1765. Capt. 1 Apr. 1768. Major 4 Sept. 1780. Lt. Col. 6 Dec. 1782. Col. 1 Sept. 1793. Maj. Gen. 26 Feb. 1795. Lt. Gen. 29 Apr. 1802. Retired 24 July 1799. *d.* Walden, Herts., 6 Nov. 1818.
Of St. Paul's, Walden, Herts., and of Gt. Cumberland Pl., Marylebone, London. A native of co. Glamorgan. Brother of Elizabeth Jones. *m.* Elizabeth Ann.
Services : Sailed for Bencoolen on the *Duke of Richmond*, 20 Feb. 1764, aged 23. Resigned his Commission 8 May 1766 during the " Batta mutiny " ; readmitted in 1766. Operations in the Doab against Mahbub Khan 1776 ; battle of Korah ; Capt. comdg. 16th Bn. Sepoys. Fur. 9 Dec. 1782 till 5 Sept. 1788. Lt. Col. 4th Bn. Eur. Inf. in 1790. Fur. 5 Dec. 1797 till retirement. Placed on the list of officers retired on the Off-Reckoning Fund from 1 Jan. 1803.
Refs. : Williams, pp. 111, 172. S.M. 1818, ii. 588. Will dated 12 June 1813 ; proved 30 Nov. 1821.

JONES, William. Fireworker. Artillery. Cadet 1782. Fireworker Jan. 1783. Resigned 10 Sept. 1785.
Services : N.F.P.

JONES, William (1812-1871). Major. Engineers. *b.* Houghamby-Dover, Kent, 9 Oct. 1812. Cadet 1832. Arrived in India 16 Sept. 1833. 2nd Lieut. 8 Dec. 1831. Lieut. 20 May 1839. Capt.

1 Jan. 1854. Retired 19 Nov. 1855. Hon. Major 19 Nov. 1855. d. 11 Feb. 1871.

Son of John Edward Jones, Maj. Gen. R.A., and Louisa his wife. Addiscombe Cadet 5 Feb. 1830 till 8 Dec. 1831. Chatham 13 Feb. 1832 till 12 Feb. 1833.
Services: 2nd Lieut. d.d. S. & M. at Delhi 3 Oct. 1833. Apptd. to Survey Dept. at Cawnpore May 1834. Shekhawat expedn. 1834, with S. & M. 2nd Asst. Gt. trig. survey 4 May 1835 ; 1st do. 1 Feb. 1837. Supt. canals in Rohilkhand 17 Oct. 1844. Fur. s.c. 10 Feb. till 12 Dec. 1849. Supt. embankments and watercourses in Rohilkhand 3 Jan. 1850 till retirement.

JONES, William Cabell (1796-1818). Ensign, Engineers. *b.* St. Mary, Newington, Surrey, 19 June 1796. Cadet 1815. Ensign 4 July 1818. *d.* Calcutta 18 Dec. 1818.

Son of Benjamin Scott Jones, of Manor Place, Walworth, Surrey. Brother of Nathaniel Jones, *q.v.* Addiscombe Cadet 1814-6.
Services : No record of active service.
Refs. : M.I. in S. Park St. cemetery, Calcutta.

JONES, William Ponsonby (1807-1849). Captain, 22nd N.I. *bapt.* Cork 1 June 1807. Cadet 1825. Arrived in India 21 Sept. 1826. Ensign 2 Mar. 1826. Lieut. 12 Nov. 1830. Capt. 24 Jan. 1845. *d.* Ludhiana 23 Apr. 1849.

Son of John Townsend Jones and Elizabeth his wife.
Services : Posted as Ensign to 22nd N.I. 26 Sept. 1826. Actg. Adjt. 22nd N.I. 13 Sept. 1830. Shekhawat expedn. 1834 ; Actg. Adjt. 22nd N.I. Adjt. 22nd N.I. 23 June 1836 till 11 Dec. 1839. Fur. s.c. 12 Mar. 1840 till 10 Sept. 1842. Adjt. 22nd N.I. 5 Apr. 1844 till Sept. 1845. Second Sikh War ; Capt. 22nd N.I. (Medal).
Refs. : Will dated 28 Sept. 1846 ; admon. 9 Apr. 1850.

JONES, William Wynne (1806-1835). Lieutenant, 3rd N.I. *b.* Aber, co. Carnarvon, 4 Feb. 1806. Cadet 1824. Arrived in India 8 May 1825. Ensign 9 Jan. 1825. Lieut. 11 Dec. 1825. *d.* Nasirabad 11 Sept. 1835.

Son of Rev. Hugh Wynne Jones, of Friorwerth, Anglesey.
Services : Posted as Ensign to 3rd N.I. in 1825. Actg. Intr. & Qmr. 3rd N.I. 13 June 1827, and 11 Jan. 1828 ; permanent do. 9 Feb. 1829. S.A.C.G. 19 Dec. 1831. (? Shekhawat expedn. 1834 ; Lieut. 3rd N.I.)
Refs. : *A.J.* N.S. xix. 206. Will dated Lucknow 1 Jan. 1827 ; proved 26 Apr. 1836.

JORDEN, Charles (1803-1861). Captain, Invalid Est. 1st Bengal Eur. L.I. *b*. Birmingham 4 Nov. 1803. Cadet 1822. Arrived in India 5 July 1823. Ensign 1 July 1823. Lieut. 27 May 1824. Capt. 16 Dec. 1835. Invalided 23 July 1844. *d*. Meerut 15 Nov. 1861.
Son of John Jorden, Lieut. h.p. H.M. 91st Foot. *m*. Calcutta, 6 Jan. 1830, Miss Margaret Gillies.
Services : Posted as Ensign to Bengal Eur. Regt. ; as Lieut. to 1st Bengal Eur. Regt. May 1824. Siege and capture of Bhurtpore ; Lieut. 1st Eur. Regt. (India medal). Apptd. 20 Sept. 1838 to comd. the Depot at Agra during the absence of his Regt. on service in Afghanistan. To comd. Depot of 1st Bengal Eur. L.I. 16 Dec. 1843. Apptd. Postmaster at Simla in May 1850.

JOVER, William George Thomas (1789-1827). Captain, 64th N.I. *b*. London 28 Feb. 1789. Cadet 1806. Arrived in India 1 Aug. 1807. Ensign 14 Aug. 1807. Lieut. 16 Dec. 1814. Capt. 13 May 1825. *d*. Commercial Rd., London, 24 Apr. 1827.
Son of William Jover.
Services : Barasat C.C. Posted as Ensign to 4th N.I. in 1808. (? Operations in Bundelkhand 1809 ; Rajaoli ; Ajaigarh ; Ensign 1/4th N.I.) Served with Java Inf. Vols. 1812-5 ; with 5th Vol. Bn. 1815-6. Lieut. 1/4th N.I. At Bencoolen in 1819. Transfd. to 32nd N.I. 11 July 1823 ; to 64th N.I. (late 2/32nd) May 1824. Fur. 1826 till death.
Refs. : A.J. xxiii. 889.

*****JOWKLEY, Henry.** Ensign. Infantry. Cadet 1765. Ensign 5 Mar. 1765.
Services : " To be Ensign from 5 Mar. 1765 till his Rank is settled by the date of his Commission." Not in A.L. of 1 Feb. 1767.
Refs. : B.M. Add. MS. 6050.

K

KAMPTZ, D'Ottas. Ensign. Infantry. Cadet 1772. Ensign 30 Mar. 1773. Dismissed by C.M. 20 Nov. 1773.
Services : N.F.P.

KAY, Robert Duncan (1810-1848). Captain, 2nd N.I. *b.* Kinclaven, co. Perth, 13 May 1810. Cadet 1827. Arrived in India 15 Oct. 1828. Ensign 15 Apr. 1828. Lieut. 28 June 1831. Capt. 4 Oct. 1844. *d.* at sea, 8 Dec. 1848, on board the *Essex.*
Son of Rev. Robert Kay, minister of Kinclaven, and Louisa Stewart his wife. *m.* Benares, 7 Apr. 1846, Caroline Alice, dau. of Nathaniel John Halhed.
Services : Ensign d.d. 2nd N.I. 20 Nov. 1828. Posted to 2nd N.I. 4 Mar. 1829. (? Operations against the Kols 1832 ; Lieut. 2nd N.I.) Adjt. 2nd N.I. 28 May 1835 till 13 July 1842. To officiate as Asst. in Dept. of A.G. of the Army, and accompany D.A.G. on service. First Afghan War 1838-9, and 1841-2 ; Kandahar ; Ghazni ; Kabul ; Lieut. 2nd N.I. (Medal). (*Lond. Gaz.* 24 Nov. 1842.) Apptd. D.J.A.G. Cawnpore 10 Nov. 1841, but to continue to act as Adjt. to his Regt. in Afghanistan. D.J.A.G. to troops at Kandahar under Nott 11 June 1842. Offg. J.A.G. to the Force 13 July 1842. D.J.A.G. Sirhind Div. 19 Oct. 1842. D.A.A.G. Dinapore Div. 9 Feb. 1843. A.A.G. Dinapore 4 Dec. 1843. Fur. s.c. to Cape 12 Feb. 1844 till 1845. First Sikh War ; Sobraon ; Capt. 2nd N.I., actg. extra A.D.C. (Medal). 2nd Asst. D.A.G. of the Army 28 Mar. 1846. Fur. 1848 till death.

KAYE, Sir John William (1814-1876). Lieutenant. Artillery. Subsequently Sec., Pol. and Secret Dept., India Office. K.C.S.I. *b.* 1814. Cadet 1832. Arrived in India 16 Sept. 1833. 2nd Lieut. 14 Dec. 1832. Lieut. 19 Aug. 1840. Resigned 1 Apr. 1841. *d.* Rose Hill, Forest Hill, Kent, 24 July 1876.
bapt. St. Pancras, London, 30 June 1814. 2nd son of Charles Kaye, of Purbrook, Hants, and of Acton, Middlesex, sometime solicitor to the Bank of England, and Eliza his wife. *m.* Calcutta, 16 Jan. 1839, Mary Catherine, dau. of Thomas Puckle, chairman of

quarter sessions for Surrey. (She died 23 Dec. 1893, aged 80.) Ed. Eton ; left before 1826. Addiscombe Cadet 4 Feb. 1831 till 14 Dec. 1832.

Services : See *D.N.B.* Fur. s.c. 15 Aug. 1834 till 27 Nov. 1837. Leave s.c. 6 mos. to sea 3 Sept. 1838. No record of active service. Joined the staff of the *Bengal Harkaru* Apr. 1841. Established the *Calcutta Review* in 1844 and edited the first five numbers. Returned to England in 1845. Entered E.I.C. Home Service 1856 ; retired 1874. Author of " The History of the Sepoy War in India, 1857-8," 3 vols., 1864-76, and numerous other works. Edited Buckle's "Memoir of the Services of the Bengal Art." K.C.S.I. 20 May 1871. F.R.S., F.R.G.S., etc.

Refs. : *D.N.B. D.I.B.* Plaster replica of a bust by Alexander Brodie, in the possession of the family, in the India Office. *Ency. Brit.* 11th edn.

KAYLOR, George Frederick. (*See* **KOEHLER.**)

KEANE, Lionel Richard (1808-1850). Captain, Invalid Est. 32nd N.I. *b.* London 8 July 1808. Cadet 1827. Arrived in India 2 June 1828. Ensign 3 Feb. 1828. Lieut. 23 Feb. 1835. Capt. 3 Feb. 1843. Invalided 1 Jan. 1849. *d.* Ferozepore 13 Dec. 1850.

bapt. Marylebone 16 June 1809. Youngest son of Hugh Perry Keane, of Spring Gdns., London, and of the I. of St. Vincent, barr.-at-law, and Susannah his wife, youngest dau. of Sir Gillies Payne, 2nd Bart., of St. Christophers. Ed. Harrow 1820-4.

Services : Posted as Ensign to 32nd N.I. 4 Nov. 1828. (? Shekhawat expedn. 1834 ; Ensign 32nd N.I.) Fur. s.c. 10 Feb. 1840 till 11 Oct. 1842.

Refs. : Burke's *Peerage*, 1859, p. 784, *s.n.* Payne, Bart., of St. Christophers. Burke's *Landed Gentry*, 4th edn., p. 1146, *s.n.* Palmer, of Clifton Lodge, Beds. *Harrow School Register. G.M.* 1851, i. 334.

KEARNAN, Thomas (1750/51-1803). Lieut. Colonel, 5th N.I. *b.* 1750/51. Cadet 1772. Admitted 3 Oct. 1772. Ensign 4 Apr. 1773. Lieut. 1 June 1778. Capt. 26 Jan. 1784. Major 1 Mar. 1794. Lt. Col. 1 Jan. 1798. *d.* Calcutta, 3 Feb. 1803, aged 52.

Son of Thomas Kearnan, of the City of London. His sisters *m.* Richard Humfrays or Humphreys, *q.v.*, and Alexander Nowell, *q.v. m.* Calcutta, 26 Aug. 1802, Miss Lilias Craig.

Services : Capt. 16th Bn. Sepoys in July 1787. Capt. 1/9th N.I. in Aug. 1798.

Refs. : Burke's *Landed Gentry*, 13th edn., p. 1328, *s.n.* Nowell, of Netherside, Yorks. Will dated Calcutta 1 Jan. 1803 ; proved 17 Feb. 1803. M.I. in S. Park St. cemetery, Calcutta.

KEARNEY, Brydges (1752/53-1783). Lieutenant, Infantry. *b.* in Ireland 1752/53. Cadet 1782. Ensign 1782. Lieut. 1782. bur. Calcutta 14 Dec. 1783.
Services: Apptd. Cadet on 8 May 1782, aged 29. Ensign 19th Foot 14 Mar. 1766; Lieut. do. 25 Dec. 1770; resigned 20 Mar. 1779.

KEASBERRY, William (1759/60-1797). Captain, Infantry. *b.* 1759/60. Cadet 1778. Arrived in India 8 Oct. 1778. Ensign 2 Oct. 1778. Lieut. 2 Nov. 1778.˚ Capt. 1 June 1796. *d.* Chittagong 15 Apr. 1797.
Eldest son of William Keasberry, of St. James's St., Bath, sometime manager, subsequently one of the proprietors of the Bath theatre, by his wife, a Bath actress. Cousin-german of Capt. Peach, city treasurer of Bath.
Services : Lieut. 1/3rd Bengal Eur. Regt. in Oct. 1779. Lieut. 19th Bn. Sepoys in July 1787.
Refs. : The Bath Stage.

KEATING, George (*d.* 1771). Lieutenant, Infantry. Cadet 1768. Ensign 10 Jan. 1769. Lieut. 19 Dec. 1769. *d.* Patna 25 Oct. 1771.
Services : N.F.P.

KEATING, Michael (D.) (1775-1829). Major, C.B. 27th N.I. *b.* Kilkenny Aug. or Nov. 1775. Cadet 1794. Arrived in India 20 Feb. 1796. Ensign 20 Nov. 1795. Lieut. 30 Oct. 1797. Capt. 11 July 1807. Major 1 Oct. 1815. Struck off 17 May 1816. *d.* nr. Dublin 7 Sept. 1829.
Of Tinny Park, co. Kilkenny. Nephew of Patrick Den, to whose extensive property he succeeded in 1811. *m.* Gertrude, only dau. of Francis Kyan, *q.v.*
Services : Fourth Mysore War 1797-1800 ; operations in Hyderabad ; (? Seringapatam) Lieut. 1/10th N.I. Transfd. to 17th N.I. Adjt. 1/17th N.I. in 1803. Operations in Jumna Doab 1803 ; Sasni. (? Second Mahratta War 1803.) Transfd. as Capt. Lt. to newly-raised 27th N.I. 21 Sept. 1804. Bde. Major at Delhi Oct. 1804 till 1808. Settlement of Hariana 1809 ; Bhawani ; Bde. Major Rewari. Bde. Major at Meerut 1809 ; at Cawnpore 1810 ;. at Meerut 1811-2. Major 2/27th N.I. Fur. 24 Oct. 1812 till struck off for having exceeded the period of his fur. C.B. 4 June 1815.
Refs. : Burke's *Landed Gentry*, 5th edn., p. 744, *s.n.* Kyan, of Ballymurtagh, co. Wicklow. *G.M.* 1829, ii. 477 ; 1830, i. 370.

KEBLE, John Petrie (1772-1823). Lieut. Colonel, Invalid Est. 28th N.I. *b.* Bloomsbury, London, 30 Dec. 1772. Cadet 1791. Admitted 4 Nov. 1791. Ensign 23 Feb. 1792. Lieut. 2 Oct.

1794. Capt. 21 Sept. 1803. Major 10 June 1814. Lt. Col. 1 Aug. 1818. Invalided 6 July 1820. d. Benares 23 July 1823. bapt. St. George's, Bloomsbury, 25 Jan. 1773. Son of Page Keble, sometime Master Attendant and Marine Paymr. at Calcutta, and Christian his 1st wife. Cousin-german of Sir William Dick, Bart., q.v. m. London, Sept. 1807, Elizabeth Ann Doigly (sic), of Southrop, Gloucs.

Services : Apptd. a Minor Cadet ; struck off 2 May 1786. Fur. 19 Jan. 1797 till 1 Sept. 1799. Lieut. 1st N.I. Fur. 8 Feb. 1803 till 17 Mar. 1808. (? Operations in Bundelkhand 1809 ; Rajaoli ; Ajaigarh ; Capt. 2/1st N.I.) Capture of Java 1811 ; Capt. 5th Bengal Vol. Bn. Transfd. as Major to newly-raised 1/28th N.I. 16 Dec. 1814. Fur. 28 Dec. 1816 till 1818. Comdd. Benares Provl. Bn. 1821 till death.

Refs. : Burke's Landed Gentry, 8th edn., p. 2212, s.n. Wilkinson, of Upper Hare Park, Cambs. M.M. 1807, p. 291. Will dated 27 Nov. 1808 ; codicil dated 23 July 1823 ; proved 17 Sept. 1823.

KEENE, Thomas Berkeley Parker (1799-1821). Ensign, 25th N.I. b. Burdwan, Bengal, 22 Feb. 1799. Cadet 1818. Ensign 15 Sept. 1819. d. Allahabad 1 (? 16) Sept. 1821.

Son of James Hanson Keene, coroner of Calcutta.

Services : Posted as Ensign to 25th N.I. No record of active service.

KEILLER, David Cabel (1802-1850). Bt. Major, 6th N.I. Comdt. 2nd Punjab Cav. b. Dundee 25 June 1802. Cadet 1821. Arrived in India 26 June 1822. Ensign 19 Jan. 1822. Lieut. 29 Jan. 1824. Capt. 11 Nov. 1837. Bt. Major 7 June 1849. d. Peshawar 17 Nov. 1850.

Son of James Keiller, of Dundee, shipmaster and wood merchant. Brother of James, Alexander, and Mary, wife of Richard Gleadhill Holden, of Dundee.

Services : Ensign d.d. 2/31st N.I. July 1822. Posted as Ensign to 1/14th N.I. Oct. 1822. Transfd. to 19th N.I. (late 2/3rd) May 1824 ; to 6th N.I. (late 1/3rd) Sept. 1825. Siege and capture of Bhurtpore ; Lieut. 6th N.I. Fur. s.c. 25 Jan. 1828 till 8 Mar. 1831. First Afghan War 1842 ; Capt. 6th N.I., on line of communications (Medal). First Sikh War ; Capt. 6th N.I., on escort duty. Bde. Major Lahore Mar. 1846. Bde. Major 8th Inf. Bde. Nov. 1848. Second Sikh War ; passage of Chenab ; Sadulapur ; Chilianwala ; Gujerat ; Bde. Major (Medal with 2 clasps). Comdt. 2nd Punjab Cav. July 1849 till death.

Refs. : De Rhé-Philipe. I.M. 1851, p. 3. Will dated 30 Nov. 1848 ; admon. 9 Sept. 1851. M.I. Sudder Bazaar cemetery, Peshawar.

KEIR, Archibald. Captain. Infantry. Lieut. 1756. Capt. 4 Oct. 1757. Resigned Aug. 1758. Readmitted as Capt. 18 May 1766. Resigned 1 Sept. 1768.

Services : Came out to India as Surgeon of the *Godolphin* in 1752, and served for about three yrs. in the Madras Presdy. After the capture of Calcutta in 1756 he accompanied the relieving force under Major Kilpatrick, sent from Madras to Fulta, as Surgeon. Whilst at Fulta he also acted as Sec. to the Council, and accepted a Commission as Lieut., being shortly afterwards apptd. Qmr. to the force. *Probably* present at battle of Plassey. Resigned his Commission in 1758 owing to supercession by John Gowen, *q.v.* He went home, but afterwards returned to India as a free merchant, settled at Patna, and engaged in transactions in salt. At the time of the Batta mutiny he rejoined the army as Capt. in Sir Robert Barker's Bde. at Patna. Purchased the mines of Ramgarh from the Rajah of that district in 1769. In 1785 he unsuccessfully sought to re-enter the Medical Dept. Author of a pamphlet " Thoughts on the Affairs of Bengal," London, 1772.

Refs. : Crawford, i. 167-9. Broome, p. 583.

KEITH, Robert (*d.* 1770). Lieutenant, Infantry. Cadet 1768. Ensign 5 Jan. 1769. Lieut. 19 Dec. 1769. *d.* nr. Rangpur, Bengal, Jan. 1770 : kld. in action against the Saniyasis.

Services : Operations against the Saniyasis Jan. 1770 ; Lieut. comdg. a detachment which was disgracefully defeated and almost totally destroyed.

Refs. : Cardew, p. 37.

KEITH, William (1785-1803). Ensign, 13th N.I. *b.* Kildonan, Scotland, 27 July 1785. Cadet 1800. Arrived in India 7 Feb. 1802. Ensign 13 Dec. 1801. *d.* Allahabad 21 Aug. 1803.

Son of Rev. William Keith, minister of Kildonan.

Services : Posted as Ensign to 13th N.I. No record of active service.

KELLER, Robert (*d.* 1763). Lieutenant, Infantry. Lieut. 1763. *d.* Aug. 1763.

Services : N.F.P.

KELLETT, William Napier (1792-1818). Lieutenant, 8th N.C. *b.* Milliken, co. Renfrew, 23 Nov. 1792. Cadet 1808. Arrived in India 25 Sept. 1809. Cornet 14 Nov. 1812. Lieut. 1 Sept. 1818. *d.* Chhapara, C.P., 4 Nov. 1818.

2nd son of William Augustus Kellett, Capt. H.M. 39th Regt. (who was younger brother of Sir Richard Kellett, 1st Bart., of Lota, co.

THE BENGAL ARMY, 1758-1834

Cork), and Jane McDowell his 1st wife, only dau. of Col. Napier, of Culcreuch and Milliken.
Services : Barasat C.C. Cadet d.d. 22nd N.I. 1811-2. Posted as Cornet to 8th N.C. in 1812. Leave s.c. to sea 1815-6. Third Mahratta War ; Jubbulpore ; Lieut. 8th N.C. ; comdg. Auxy. Horse with Bdr.-Gen. Hardyman's Div.
Refs. : Burke's *Peerage*, 1923, p. 1271, *s.n.* Kellett, Bart., of Lota, co. Cork. *S.M.* 1819, i. 480.

KELLY, Anthony (*d.* 1772). Cadet, Infantry. Cadet 1772. *d.* Benares June 1772.
Services : N.F.P.

KELLY, Bartlett Hugh (*d.* 1818). Lieut. Colonel, 27th N.I. Country Cadet 1781. Admitted 10 Apr. 1781. Ensign 4 Sept. 1781. Lieut. 17 June 1783. Capt. 21 Dec. 1801. Major 2 Jan. 1810. Lt. Col. 16 June 1814. *d.* Mirzapur, U.P., 19 Oct. 1818.
Son of Hugh Kelly, of Gough Sq., Fleet St., London, barr.-at-law, playwright and author (*D.N.B.*), and Eliza his wife. Stepson of Samuel Davis. *m.* (?).
Services : Lieut. 15th Bn. Sepoys in July 1787. Lieut. & Bt. Capt. 1/1st N.I. in July 1798. Transfd. to 7th N.I. Capt. Lt. 1/7th N.I. 4 Jan. 1801. Comdd. 4th L.I. Bn. 1808-9. Operations in Bundelkhand against Lachman Dawa 1809 ; Rajaoli ; Ajaigarh ; Capt. comdg. 4th L.I. Bn. (? Reduction of Kalinjar 1812 ; Major 1/7th N.I.) Transfd. as Lt. Col. to 1/27th N.I. in 1815. (? Third Mahratta War ; Madhurajpura ; Lt. Col. comdg. 1/27th N.I.)
Refs. : *Stubbs*, i. 313. *G.M.* 1819, i. 585. *S.M.* 1819, ii. 95. Will dated Muttra 1 Oct. 1817 ; proved 31 Oct. 1818.

KELLY, Christopher (1758-1791). Lieutenant, Infantry. *bapt.* St. Martin-in-the-Fields, London, 13 Jan. 1758. Cadet 1781. Ensign 15 Mar. 1781. Lieut. 11 July 1782. *d.* Jaunpur, U.P., 28 Sept. 1791.
Son of Dr. Christopher Kelly. Brother of John and Frances Kelly. Ed. Winchester ; K.S. 1771 ; left in 1772.
Services : Apptd. Cadet on 19 Dec. 1780, aged 23. Sailed for India on the *Chapman*, 13 Mar. 1781, aged 23. Lieut. 10th Bn. Sepoys in July 1787.
Refs. : *Kirby*. Will.

KELLY, Edward (1805-1828). Lieutenant, 59th N.I. *b.* Dublin barracks 25 Nov. 1805. Cadet 1823. Ensign 17 Jan. 1824. Lieut. 13 May 1825. *d.* at sea, 5 Mar. 1828, on board the *Lady Flora*.
Son of Lt.-Col. Edward Kelly, of Portarlington, Queen's Co.,

sometime 2nd Life Gds., later H.M. 6th Foot, on the Staff of the C.-in-C. in India.

Services : Posted as Ensign to 59th N.I. in 1824. Siege and capture of Bhurtpore ; Lieut. 59th N.I., with 33rd N.I. Adjt. 8th Local Horse 1825 ; do. 3rd Local Horse 1826-8. Fur. s.c. 9 Jan. 1828 till death.

Refs. : A.J. xxvi. 134.

KELLY, James (*d.* 1808). Captain. 12th N.I. Country Cadet 1781. Admitted 4 May 1781. Ensign 21 Sept. 1781. Lieut. 25 June 1783. Capt. 16 Jan. 1803. Retired 9 Sept. 1807. *d. unm.* Belhaven, nr. Dunbar, 6 Sept. 1808.

Grandson of James Kelly. Brother of John and Janet Kelly, and of Martha Kelly, of Dunbar.

Services : Lieut. 22nd Bn. Sepoys in July 1787. Capt. Lt. 12th N.I. 21 Feb. 1805. Second Mahratta War ; Agra ; Laswari ; capture of Deig, comdg. rt. column of storming party ; Capt. 2/12th N.I. Fur. 28 Jan. 1805 till retirement.

Refs. : Pester, p. 365. *S.M.* 1808, p. 720. Will dated Chunar 6 Oct. 1800 ; proved 13 Dec. 1808.

***KELLY, Patrick** (*d.* 1792). Lieutenant, Infantry. Cadet (?). Ensign (?). Lieut. (?). *d.* in the Carnatic 1 Apr. 1792.

Services : (? Third Mysore War.)

Refs. : MS. A.L. dated 30 June 1792 (*I.O. Rec.*).

KELLY, Samuel (1764/65-1811). Lieut. Colonel, Bengal Eur. Regt. *b.* 1764/65. Cadet 1781. Admitted 9 Oct. 1781. Ensign 13 Apr. 1781. Lieut. 4 Aug. 1782. Capt. 29 May 1800. Major 20 Oct. 1805. Lt. Col. 4 Sept. 1811. *d.* Amboyna, 21 Dec. 1811, of malaria.

Son of Mrs. Jane Kelly, of Ireland. (*Probably* son of Thomas Kelly, of Armagh.) Brother of Rev. Daniel Kelly, William Kelly, Lt. Col. H.M.S., Dawson Kelly, Capt. H.M.S., Arthur Irwin Kelly, and Mrs. Alicia Campbell. *m.* Queen St. chapel, Bath, 25 Apr. 1809, Maria, eldest dau. of John Robinson, of Cumberland, and niece of Alexander Jaffray, of Marlbro' Bldgs., Bath.

Services : Apptd. Cadet on 13 Feb. 1781, aged 16. Sailed for India on the *Essex,* 13 Mar. 1781, aged 16. Lieut. 18th Bn. Sepoys in July 1787. Bt. Capt. 7th N.I. in June 1798. Transfd. as Lieut. & Bt. Capt. to 1st Bengal Eur. Regt. A.D.C. to Maj.-Gen. William Dowdeswell, comdg. at Cawnpore, in 1805. Fur. 12 Feb. 1806 till 5 Nov. 1809.

Refs. : Bath Chron. 27 Apr. 1809. Will dated 14 Nov. 1810 ; proved 19 June 1812.

THE BENGAL ARMY, 1758-1834 579

KELSHA, Richard. (*See* **KILSHA, Richard.**)

KELSO, Fleming (1794-1825). Cadet. Infantry. Subsequently Lieut. 13th Light Dgns. *b.* Symington, co. Ayr, 28 June 1794. Cadet 1812. Resigned 22 Jan. 1814. *d. unm.* Hyderabad Residency 14 Nov. 1825.

3rd and youngest son of William Kelso, of Dankeith, Major 23rd Light Dgns., Col. of the Ayrshire Mil., J.P. and D.L., and Susanna his wife, dau. of William Fergusson, of Doonholm. His uncle, Archibald Kelso, of Sauchrie, *m.* a sister of James Macharg, *q.v.*
Services : Cornet H.M. 8th Light Dgns. 11 Nov. 1813. Lieut. do. 20 July 1825. Transfd. to 13th Light Dgns. in 1825.
Refs. : Burke's *Landed Gentry*, 12th edn., p. 1071, *s.n.* Kelso, of Kelsoland, Essex. M.I. Hyderabad Residency cemetery.

*****KEMBLE, Peter** (*d.* 1837). Cadet. Infantry. *b.* New Brunswick, N. America. Cadet 1790. Resigned 12 Nov. 1792. *d.* 29 Jan. 1837.
Services : Was an Ofr. in H.M. 46th Regt. *c.* 1787-90. Retransfd. to H.M.S. 1792. Ensign 75th Foot 23 May 1792 ; Lieut. 1 Jan. 1797. Lieut., h.p., French's Recruiting Corps till 1811. Town Adjt. at Cape Breton 1806-9. Lieut. 11th R. Veteran Bn. Retired on full pay 1 Feb. 1812.

KEMM, William Henry (1783-1859). Lieut. General. Colonel 25th N.I. *bapt.* Lawrenny, co. Pembroke, 19 Mar. 1783. Cadet 1799. Admitted 15 Jan. 1801. Ensign 3 Oct. 1800. Lieut. 20 July 1801. Capt. 7 Apr. 1814. Major 1 May 1824. Lt. Col. 23 Aug. 1826. Bt. Col. 18 June 1831. Maj. Gen. 3 Nov. 1841. Lt. Gen. 11 Nov. 1851. *d.* at his residence, 9 Terrace, St. Helier, Jersey, 25 May 1859, aged 76.

Son of Henry Kemm and Janet his wife. *m.* St. George's, Hanover Sq., London, 12 Aug. 1834, Charlotte, dau. of John Dolbel, of Jersey. (She died 15 May 1884, aged 87.)
Services : Lieut. 11th N.I. Transfd. to newly-raised 25th N.I. in 1804. Capture of Gohad 1806 ; Lieut. 1/25th N.I. Expedn. to Mauritius 1810 ; Lieut. 1st Vol. Bn. Fur. s.c. 12 Dec. 1813 till 7 Mar. 1817. Third Mahratta War ; Capt. 2/25th N.I., Baggage Mr. to G.G. and C.-in-C. Bk. Mr. at Meerut 23 June 1818 ; do. Rohilkhand Div. 3 June 1819 ; do. Burdwan Div. till 7 June 1824. Transfd. as Major to 50th N.I. (late 2/25th) May 1824. Comdd. 2nd L.I. Bn. Sept. 1824 till 11 Mar. 1826. First Burma War ; Arakan 1825 (w. on 29 Mar. 1825) ; Major comdg. 2nd L.I. Bn. (*Lond. Gaz.* 1 Oct. 1825) (? India medal). Tempy. comdg. Light Bde., S.E. Div., 22 Oct. 1825. Posted as Lt. Col. to 50th N.I. 22

Dec. 1826. Fur. p.a. 21 Jan. 1832 till 12 Feb. 1835. Transfd. to 31st N.I. 2 Mar. 1835. Fur. s.c. 8 Sept. 1836 till death. Posted as Col. to 62nd N.I. 4 May 1838 ; to 25th N.I. 1849.
Refs. : Boase. *A.J.* N.S. xv. 65. *G.M.* 1859, ii. 90. The *Times,* 28 May 1859.

KEMPE, Richard Russell (1794-1827). Lieutenant. Artillery. *b.* South Malling, Sussex, 22 Jan. 1794. Cadet 1811. Fireworker 5 Aug. 1812. Lieut. 14 July 1818. *d.* Brompton, London, 5 Aug. 1827.

Son of William Kempe (Mr. Serjeant Kempe), formerly Russell, of Malling, who assumed his mother's family name of Kempe in 1760, and Mary his wife. Brother of William Russell Kempe, *q.v.* Addiscombe Cadet 1809-11.

Services : Nepal War 1814-5 ; Lieut. F. 6th Coy. 2nd Bn. Foot Art., in 1st Div. Nepal War 1816 ; Lieut. F. 6th Coy. 2nd Bn. Third Mahratta War ; Jawad ; Lieut. 6th Coy. 2nd Bn., afterwards 5th Troop H.A. Served with H.A. till 1824. Fur. 1824 till death.
Refs. : N. *& Q.* 11S. v. 35. *A.J.* xxiv. 402.

KEMPE, William Russell (1792-1814). Ensign, 24th N.I. *bapt.* South Malling, Sussex, 16 Apr. 1792. Cadet 1807. Arrived in India 16 Nov. 1808. Ensign 27 Nov. 1808. *d.* Cawnpore 6 Oct. 1814.

Son of William Kempe (Mr. Serjeant Kempe) and Mary his wife. Brother of Richard Russell Kempe, *q.v.*
Services : Barasat C.C. Posted as Ensign to 2/24th N.I. in 1809. (? Settlement of Hariana 1809 ; Bhawani ; Ensign 2/24th N.I.)

KEMPEL, George Augustus (1784-1806). Cadet, Infantry. *b.* 21 July 1784. Cadet 1805. Never arrived in India. *d.* Dec. 1806, on his passage to India, in the wreck of the *Skelton Castle.* Struck off with effect from 5 Nov. 1806. (See note to David Allan.)

bapt. German chapel, St. James's, London, 10 Aug. 1784. Son of Charles Frederick Kempel (? of Leipzig) and Jane Catherine his wife.

KEMPLAND, George Arthur (1789-1850). Major. 8th L.C. *b.* 13 Feb. 1789. Cadet 1806. Arrived in India 3 Oct. 1807. Cornet 29 July 1807. Lieut. 2 Feb. 1814. Capt. 14 Apr. 1822. Retired 21 July 1836. Major 5 Oct. 1836. *d.* Leamington 19 Sept. 1850.

bapt. Walmer, Kent, 11 Apr. 1789. Son of Arthur Kempland and Hannah his wife. *m.* (before 1820) Amelia. (She died 5 Oct. 1855.) Nominated for Woolwich 17 Aug. 1804, but did not enter the R.M.A. Apptd. a Cav. Cadet in 1804.

Services : Barasat C.C. for 8 mos. Posted as Cornet to 8th N.C.

Actg. Adjt. 8th N.C. 1812. Served with Java L.C. 1814-5. Actg. Adjt. 8th N.C. in 1817. Third Mahratta War; Jubbulpore; Mandala Apr. 1818 (slight spear wound in chest); Lieut. 8th N.C. (*Lond. Gaz.* 7 Dec. 1818). Fur. s.c. 4 Feb. 1819 till 17 Oct. 1820. Adjt. 8th L.C. 4 Dec. 1820 till 26 Jan. 1825. Siege and capture of Bhurtpore; Capt. 8th L.C. Fur. s.c. 21 Jan. 1833. Retired owing to ill health on a pension of 10/6 *p.d.*
Refs. : *G.M.* 1850, ii. 563. *I.M.* 24 Sept. 1850, p. 561.

KEMPT(Z), James (*d.* 1784). Capt. Lieutenant, Artillery. Cadet 1772. Fireworker 18 May 1772. Capt. Lt. 18 Sept. 1780. *d.* Dinapore 24 July 1784.

Son of James Kempt(z), of the Canongate, Edinburgh, merchant, and Sarah his wife. Brother of Gavin, Francis, and Magdalen Kempt(z).
Services : First Mahratta War 1778-84; Capt. Lt. Art., with the Bombay detachment.
Refs. : *G.M.* 1785, i. 403. *S.M.* 1785, p. 206. Will dated 13 Oct. 1778.

Note : Stubbs and *Dodwell & Miles* give his name as Kemptz; it appears as Kempt in his Will and in *S.M.*; as Kemp in *G.M.*

KENDALL, Bernard (1811-1846). Bt. Captain, 1st Bengal Eur. L.I. *bapt.* Lanlivery, Cornwall, 15 Sept. 1811. Cadet 1828. Arrived in India 1 June 1829. Ensign 1 Jan. 1829. Lieut. 13 Mar. 1835. Bt. Capt. 1 Jan. 1844. *d.* Ferozepore, 6 Feb. 1846, of wounds received in action at the battle of Ferozshahr on 21 Dec. 1845.

2nd son of Rev. Nicholas Kendall, vicar of Lanlivery, and Susan Goodwin his wife. *m.* 1 Aug. 1838, Melloney Grace Schobel Trood.
Services : Ensign d.d. 33rd N.I. 13 July 1829. Posted as Supy. Ensign to 2nd Bengal Eur. Regt. (became Left Wing, Bengal Eur. Regt.) Sept. 1829. Fur. 22 Dec. 1835 till 4 Mar. 1839. First Sikh War; Ferozshahr (s.w.); Bt. Capt. 1st Bengal Eur. L.I. (Medal).
Refs. : Burke's *Landed Gentry*, 11th edn., p. 940, *s.n.* Kendall, of Pelyn, Cornwall. *De Rhé-Philipe*. Will dated 15 Mar. 1839; admon. 1 May 1848. M.I. in St. Andrew's, Ferozepore, and Winchester cathedral.

KENNAN, Robert. Captain. Infantry. Afterwards Lt. Col. in H.M.S. Cadet 1772. Ensign 1 July 1776. Lieut. 22 June 1778. Capt. 20 Apr. 1781. Transfd. to H.M.S. 1789.

3rd son of Thomas Kennan, of Diswellstown, co. Dublin, and Emilia Jones his wife.
Services : Returned from fur. 16 June 1786. Capt. H.M. 75th

Foot (9 July 1783) 1 Nov. 1788; do. 57th Foot 28 Oct. 1795. Exchanged into 57th Regt. from 75th Regt. 8 July 1796. Major in the army 1 Mar. 1794; Lt. Col. do. 1 Jan. 1798. Major 70th Foot 8 Mar. 1801. Out of the Service in 1803.

KENNAWAY, Glass (1801-1889). Captain. 5th. L.C. *b.* Exeter 10 Mar. 1801. Cadet 1820. Arrived in India 5 Nov. 1821. Cornet 4 July 1821. Lieut. 13 May 1825. Capt. 1 Mar. 1836. Invalided 3 Dec. 1838. Retired 17 Aug. 1842. *d.* 15 July 1889.

Son of Thomas Kennaway, of Exeter, merchant, sometime of Oxford, and Ann his wife. Brother of Richard Kennaway, *q.v.*, and nephew of Sir John Kennaway, Bart., *q.v.*

Services : Cornet d.d. 1st L.C. Posted as Cornet to 5th L.C. Adjt. 7th Local Horse 28 Dec. 1824 till 1829. Fur. p.a. 5 Jan. 1833 till 17 Dec. 1835. Fur. s.c. 20 Jan. 1840 till retirement. No record of active service.

KENNAWAY, Sir John, first baronet (1758-1836). Major. Infantry. *b.* Exeter 6 Mar. 1758. Cadet 1772. Admitted 1 Aug. 1772. Ensign 5 Apr. 1773. Lieut. 2 June 1778. Capt. 27 Jan. 1784. Major 1 Mar. 1794. Retired 14 Jan. 1801. *d.* Escot Lodge, Ottery St. Mary, Devon, 1 Jan. 1836.

1st Bart., of Escot, Devon. cr. 25 Feb. 1791. 3rd son of William Kennaway and Frances his wife, dau. of Aaron Tozer, of Exeter. Uncle of Thomas Kennaway, *q.v. m.* 18 Feb. 1797, Charlotte, 2nd dau. of James Amyatt, M.P. for Southampton. (She died 1845.) Ed. Exeter grammar school.

Services : See *D.N.B.* Served as Cadet in the Select Picket. Second Mysore War 1781-5; Persian Sec. to Col. Thomas Deane Pearse, *q.v.*, comdg. the detachment. A.D.C. to Lord Cornwallis, the G.G., 4 Apr. 1787. The first Resdt. at Hyderabad from 28 Apr. 1788 till 1794. Fur. 1794 till retirement. Granted in Nov. 1796 an annuity of £500 *p.a.* in consideration of the important services which he had rendered to the E.I. Co. Apptd. Col. East Devon Legion, Yeomanry Cav., in 1805, and of 7th, or East Devon Local Mil., of both of which he held simultaneous comd.

Refs. : Burke's *Peerage,* 1923, p. 1274, *s.n.* Kennaway, Bart., of Escot, Devon. *D.N.B. E.I.M.C.* i. 87-90. *D.I.B. G.M.* 1836, i. 313. *A.J.* N.S. xix. 232. M.I. in Escot churchyard. Portrait, presented by H.E.H. the Nizam, in the Victoria Memorial Hall, Calcutta.

KENNAWAY, Richard (1788/89-1807). Lieutenant, 10th N.I. *b.* 1788/89. Cadet 1804. Arrived in India 10 Dec. 1805. Ensign 5 Sept. 1805. Lieut. 6 Sept. 1805. *d.* Rewari, 30 May 1807, of abscess on the liver.

2nd son of Thomas Kennaway, of Exeter, merchant, and Ann his wife. Brother of Thomas Kennaway, q.v.
Services : Apptd. Cadet on 18 Apr. 1804, aged 15. Posted as Lieut. to 10th N.I. in 1806. No record of active service. Apptd. a Writer on the Madras Est. 29 July 1807, before news of his death had been received in England.
Refs. : G.M. 1809, i. 982.

KENNAWAY, Thomas (1792-?). Cornet. Cavalry. Unposted. *b.* Exeter 8 June 1792. Cadet 1807. Arrived in India 17 Mar. 1808. Cornet (?). Resigned 29 Apr. 1808.
Son of Thomas Kennaway, of Exeter, merchant, and Ann his wife. Brother of Glass Kennaway, q.v. Balliol Coll., Oxon.; matric. 15 May 1811, aged 18.
Refs. : *Alumni Oxon.*

KENNEDY, Archibald (1806-1834). Lieutenant, 67th N.I. *b.* Cork 4 Apr. 1806. Cadet 1826. Arrived in India 23 Sept. 1827. Ensign 13 May 1827. Lieut. 22 May 1829. *d.* Cawnpore 10 Apr. 1834.
Son of Rev. Alexander Kennedy, curate of Holy Trinity, Cork, afterwards rector of Leighmoney, co. Cork, and Sarah his wife, dau. of —— O'Callaghan.
Services : Posted as Ensign to 3rd N.I. 3 Jan. 1828. Transfd. to 67th N.I. 14 Apr. 1828 ; to 22nd N.I. 8 May 1828 ; to 67th N.I. 21 Aug. 1828. No record of active service.
Refs. : *A.J.* N.S. xv. 172.

KENNEDY, Charles Pratt (1789-1875). Lieut. Colonel. Artillery. Pol. Agent at Sabathu. *b.* Holywood, co. Down, 15 Nov. 1789. Cadet 1805. Arrived in India 7 Apr. 1807. Fireworker 3 May 1807. Lieut. 13 May 1807. Capt. Lt. 15 Feb. 1818. Capt. 1 Sept. 1818. Major 3 Mar. 1835. Retired 17 Jan. 1836. Hon. Lt. Col. 28 Nov. 1854. *d.* Cheltenham 25 May 1875.
Of Cheltenham. 8th son of John Kennedy, of Cultra, co. Down, J.P., and Elizabeth his wife, dau. of Rev. Henry Cole, of Brookville, co. Fermanagh. Brother of William Kennedy (*d.* 1836), q.v., and uncle of John Kennedy McCausland, q.v. *m.* Sutton Michael, 20 Dec. 1838, Charlotte, 3rd dau. of Henry Unett, of Freen's Court, co. Hereford. Ed. Shooter's Hill Acad. Woolwich Cadet; nominated for R.M.A. 25 Nov. 1803 ; obtained his certificate 8 July 1806.
Services : Served with 1st Troop H.A. 1808-16. Nepal War 1814-5 ; Kalanga ; Lieut. 1st Troop, with 2nd Div. (India medal). Leave s.c. 6 mos. to sea 16 Dec. 1816. Adjt. & Qmr. 1st Bn. Foot Art. 11 July 1816. Fur. s.c. 28 Mar. 1818 till 24 Mar. 1821.

Assumed charge of 1st Nassiri Bn. 29 Sept. 1821. Asst. to Dy. Supt. of Sikh and Hill affairs 11 Feb. 1822. To comd. 1st Nassiri Bn. 25 May 1822. P.A. at Sabathu 30 July 1832 till 2 Nov. 1835.

Refs. : Burke's *Landed Gentry of Ireland*, p. 366, *s.n.* Kennedy, of Cultra, co. Down. Burke's *Landed Gentry*, 5th edn., p. 1429, *s.n.* Unett, of Freen's Court, co. Hereford. *Stubbs*, ii. 240. *The Times*, 27 May 1875.

KENNEDY, James (1778-1859). Lieut. General, C.B. Colonel 5th Eur. L.C. *b.* St. Peter's, London, 24 July 1778. Cadet 1797. Arrived in India 6 Nov. 1798. Cornet 1 Nov. 1798. Lieut. 29 May 1800. Capt. 16 Sept. 1815. Major 1 Oct. 1819. Lt. Col. 13 May 1825. Col. 26 Dec. 1832. Maj. Gen. 3 Nov. 1841. Lt. Gen. 11 Nov. 1851. *d.* Benares, 25 Sept. 1859, after 60 yrs. of continuous residence in India.

Of Benares. Son of John Kennedy and Ann his wife, dau. of John Hadfield. *m.* Partabgarh, U.P., 1804, Anna, dau. of Patrick Don, *q.v.*, by his 1st wife. (She died Benares, 1 Nov. 1884, aged 96.) Father of James Don Kennedy, *q.v.*, and of the wives of William Alexander, William Charles Birch, Edward Macleod Blair, James Duncan Macpherson, Robert Augustus Master, William Minto, *q.v.*

Services : Posted as Cornet to 1st N.C. Transfd. as Lieut. to newly-raised 5th N.C. 29 May 1800. Second Mahratta War; Bundelkhand 1804 ; Lieut. 5th N.C. Adjt. 5th N.C. 16 May 1805 till 1816. Capt. Lt. 27 Feb. 1812. Third Mahratta War ; storm and capture of Chanda (when he led a dismounted Sqdn.) and in the various operations of Bdr. J. W. Adams's force ; Capt. 5th N.C. Operations in Kotah 1821 ; Mangrol ; Major comdg. 5th L.C. Posted as Col. to 7th L.C. 26 Dec. 1833. Shekhawat expedn. 1834 ; Bdr., 2 cl., comdg. Cav. of the force. Transfd. to 5th L.C. 20 Aug. 1835. Bdr. on Est. to comd. Rajputana F.F. 4 Dec. 1838. Comdd. Cav. of Jodhpur force on service in Marwara 5 Aug. till 14 Oct. 1839. Tour on Staff expired on 20 Jan. 1844. Comdd. Benares Div. 20 Mar. 1847 till Mar. 1852. Apptd. Col. of newly-raised 5th Eur. L.C. in 1858. C.B. 20 July 1838.

Refs. : *S.M.* 1805. *G.M.* 1859, ii. 654. *The Times*, 10 Nov. 1859.

KENNEDY, James Don (1806-1898). Major General. 70th N.I. *b.* Calcutta 11 Feb. 1806. Cadet 1827. Admitted 4 Sept. 1828. Ensign 19 Jan. 1828. Lieut. 2 July 1833. Capt. 5 July 1837. Major 26 Dec. 1846. Lt. Col. 10 Sept. 1852. Bt. Col. 28 Nov. 1854. Retired 31 Dec. 1861. Hon. Maj. Gen. 31 Dec. 1861. *d.* 38 Green Park, Bath, 23 Apr. 1898.

Son of James Kennedy, *q.v.*, and Anna his wife. Nephew of John Hadfield Kennedy. *m.* Cawnpore, 24 Jan. 1840, Eliza Madelina, dau. of William Turner (1791-1827), *q.v.*

Services : Was already in India when conditionally apptd. Cadet on 2 Jan. 1828. Ensign d.d. 43rd N.I. 12 Sept. 1828 ; do. 1st N.I. 25 Sept. 1828. Posted as Ensign to 65th N.I. Transfd. to 25th N.I. 4 Mar. 1829. d.d. 37th N.I. 5 Mar. 1831 ; do. 69th N.I. 15 Apr. 1832. Actg. Adjt. 25th N.I. 16 Nov. 1833 ; actg. Intr. & Qmr. 25th N.I. 13 June 1834. Adjt. 25th N.I. 16 Sept. 1834 till 19 Aug. 1837. S.A.C.G. 20 Sept. 1838. Gwalior campaign ; Maharajpur ; S.A.C.G. (Bronze star). First Sikh War ; Sobraon ; Capt. 25th N.I., S.A.C.G. (Medal). D.A.C.G., 2 cl., 1 Aug. 1846. Fur. 3 Feb. 1847 till 4 Dec. 1849. Posted as Lt. Col. to 5th N.I. 10 Dec. 1852. Transfd. to 70th N.I. in 1856.

Refs. : *The Times*, 23 Apr. 1898.

KENNEDY, James Thomas (1794-1846). Captain. 11th N.I.
b. Calcutta 16 Aug. 1794. Cadet 1809. Admitted 15 Dec. 1810. Ensign 11 June 1812. Lieut. 5 Nov. 1816. Capt. 20 Oct. 1825. Retired 1 Dec. 1836. *d.* 18 July 1846.

bapt. Calcutta 10 Dec. 1794. Eldest son of James Thomas Kennedy, "a gentleman of fortune, residing at Summer Hill, Dublin," formerly of the firm of Lee & Kennedy, of Calcutta, merchants, and Mary his wife, née Wilkins. Brother of Thomas Lee Kennedy, *q.v.*

Services : Barasat C.C. for 7½ mos. Cadet d.d. 25th N.I. Posted as Ensign to 1/5th N.I. in 1812. (? Operations in Baghelkhand 1813 ; Entauri ; Ensign 1/5th N.I.) Third Mahratta War ; Lieut. 5th N.I. In Ceylon with 2nd Ceylon Vol. Bn. 7 Dec. 1818 till 22 May 1819. Attd. to Champaran L.I. 16 Apr. 1821 ; tempy. Adjt. do. 11 Jan. 1823 ; permanent do. 25 June 1823. Transfd. to 20th N.I. (late 2/5th) May 1824 ; to 11th N.I. (late 1/5th) 16 Aug. 1824. Fur. p.a. 27 May 1827 till 9 Jan. 1831.

***KENNEDY, John** (*d.* 1765). bur. Calcutta 23 Dec. 1765.

Services : Was Adjt. at date of death. N.F.P.

Refs. : Calcutta burial register.

KENNEDY, Thomas Lee (1803-1827). Lieutenant, 37th N.I.
b. Booterstown, nr. Dublin, 2 May 1803. Cadet 1819. Ensign 14 Feb. 1820. Lieut. 11 July 1823. *d. unm.* Bishnath, Assam, 22 Oct. 1827 : accidentally shot himself whilst after elephant.[1]

Son of James Thomas Kennedy, of Summerhill, Dublin. Brother of William Kennedy (1809-1883), *q.v.*

Services : Posted as Ensign to 1/11th N.I. in 1820. Transfd. as

Lieut. to 18th N.I. 11 July 1823; to 36th N.I. (late 1/18th) May 1824; to 37th N.I. in 1825. Adjt. Rangpur L.I. Bn. 1824 till death. First Burma War; Assam 1824; Lieut. Rangpur L.I. *Refs.: A.J.* xxv. 511. Will dated Bishnath 27 May 1826; proved 23 Jan. 1828. M.I. at Bishnath.

[1] *Note :* "He and Lieut. Veitch (Hamilton Vetch, *q.v.*) had gone out to hunt elephants, and Mr. Kennedy's gun, by some accident or other, went off and its contents were lodged in his body. He expired almost immediately." (*A.J.*)

KENNEDY, William (1784-1836). Lieut. Colonel, 16th N.I. Dy. Mily. Auditor Gen. *b.* Holywood, co. Down, 14 Feb. 1784. Cadet 1802. Arrived in India 11 July 1803. Ensign 30 July 1803. Lieut. 25 Aug. 1804. Capt. 8 Jan. 1817. Major 25 Nov. 1826. Lt. Col. 18 June 1830. *d.* Calcutta, 8 Jan. 1836, on board the *Cornwall,* off the botanical gdns.

6th son of John Kennedy, of Cultra, co. Down, J.P., high sheriff 1769, and Elizabeth his wife. Brother of Charles Pratt Kennedy, *q.v. m.* Calcutta, 20 Dec. 1822, Charlotte, 2nd dau. of Sir Robert Blair, *q.v.* (*See also* Henry Clayton.) (She died Dover 11 Sept. 1846.)

Services : Ensign d.d. 15th N.I. 1804. Posted as Lieut. to 9th N.I. in 1804. (? Second Mahratta War; Bhurtpore; Lieut. 2/9th N.I.) Adjt. 2/9th N.I. 16 May 1805 till 1809. Actg. Adjt. & Qmr. 9th N.I. in 1809. Adjt. 1/9th N.I. 1810-18. Additional Asst. Mily. Auditor Gen. 2 Jan. 1819; 1st Asst. do. 27 Sept. 1823. Transfd. to 8th N.I. (late 1/9th) May 1824. Mily. Auditor Gen. 10 Apr. 1829. Posted as Lt. Col. to 11th N.I. 1 Mar. 1831. Leave s.c. 18 mos. to Cape 22 Dec. 1831. Transfd. to 46th N.I. 22 July 1833; to 16th N.I. 15 Apr. 1835. Fur. s.c. 8 Dec. 1835.

Refs. : Burke's *Landed Gentry of Ireland,* p. 366, *s.n.* Kennedy, of Cultra, co. Down. *G.M.* 1823, i. 562; 1836, i. 678. *A.J.* N.S. xx. 106. Will dated 3 Apr. 1829; proved 9 Jan. 1836. M.I. in S. Park St. cemetery, Calcutta.

KENNEDY, William (1809-1883). Major. 5th N.I. *b.* Dublin 2 Dec. 1809. Cadet 1825. Arrived in India 10 May 1826. Ensign 18 Dec. 1825. Lieut. 22 Sept. 1836. Capt. 8 July 1848. Retired 15 Feb. 1851. Hon. Major 28 Nov. 1854. *d.* London 29 Apr. 1883.

Son of James Thomas Kennedy, of Summerhill, Dublin. Brother of James Thomas Kennedy, *q.v.*

Services : Posted as Ensign to 3rd N.I. Transfd. to 2nd Extra Regt. (became 70th N.I.) 18 Oct. 1826. Fur. s.c. to Mauritius and N.S.W. 21 Sept. 1831 till 25 May 1833. Transfd. to 38th N.I. 2 July 1832. Intr. & Qmr. 38th N.I. 16 Feb. 1838 till 14 Dec. 1842.

Placed at the disposal of P.A. in Upper Sind. To reside at court of H.H. Mir Rustam Khan at Khairpur 23 Dec. 1840. Transfd. to 5th N.I. 14 Dec. 1842. No record of active service.
Refs. : *The Times*, 1 May 1883.

KENNEDY, William Drummond (1806-1827). Lieutenant, 6th Extra Regt. *b.* London 25 Nov. 1806. Cadet 1822. Ensign 11 July 1823. Lieut. 2 Oct. 1824. *d.* Calcutta 3 Dec. 1827.
Son of Patrick Kennedy and Mary Ann his wife.
Services : Posted as Ensign to 25th N.I. in 1824. Transfd. to newly-raised 6th Extra Regt. in 1825. No record of active service.
Refs. : *A.J.* xxv. 684.

KENNEDY, William Scott (1794-1821). Lieutenant, 6th L.C. *b.* Inverness 17 Apr. 1794. Cadet 1809. Cornet 26 Feb. 1814. Lieut. 1 Sept. 1818. *d.* Mhow 11 Sept. 1821.
Son of William Kennedy, M.D., of Inverness. *m.* Calcutta, 7 June 1817, Miss Emma Lydia Gardiner. (She *re-m.* Lucius Horton Smith, *q.v.*)
Services : Barasat C.C. Cadet d.d. 8th N.C. 1811-3. Posted as Cornet to 5th N.C. in 1814. Transfd. to 6th N.C. in 1815. Mily. student at Coll. of Fort William in 1815. Third Mahratta War ; Sitabaldi ; Nagpur ; Cornet 6th N.C. With escort to Comr. at Poona 1818-9. Adjt. 6th L.C. 1820 till death.

KENNETT, Charles Brackley (1807-1827). Lieutenant, 64th N.I. *bapt.* Michelmersh, Hants, 1 Aug. 1807. Cadet 1822. Ensign (14 Feb. 1823) 11 July 1823. Lieut. 13 May 1825. *d.* Agra 21 May 1827.
Son of Rev. Brackley Charles Kennett and Emilia his wife. Related to Charles Robert Kennett, *q.v.*
Services : Posted as Ensign to 32nd N.I. July 1823. Transfd. to 64th N.I. (late 2/32nd) May 1824. No record of active service.
Refs. : Burke's *Landed Gentry*, 7th edn., p. 1028, *s.n.* Kennett-Barrington, of the Manor House, Dorchester.

KENNETT, Charles Robert (1783-1845). Lieut. Colonel. 68th N.I. *b.* New Bond St., London, 11 Aug. 1783. Cadet 1800. Arrived in India 14 Oct. 1801. Ensign 23 Dec. 1810. Lieut. 13 Oct. 1803. Capt. 16 Dec. 1814. Major 1 May 1824. Lt. Col. 23 Feb. 1827. Retired 27 May 1830. *d. unm.* Hans Cresc., Sloane St., London, 29 Jan. 1845 : found dead in his bed : " died by the visitation of God "—verdict at the inquest.
3rd and youngest son of Robert Kennett and Anne his wife.
Services : Ensign 18th N.I. Second Mahratta War ; Bundelkhand 1803 ; defeat of Rajah Ram Singh 2 July 1804 ; Jaitpur ;

Lieut. 18th N.I. Fur. 17 Aug. 1806 till 13 Sept. 1808. (? Operations in Bundelkhand 1809; Rajaoli; Ajaigarh; Lieut. 1/18th N.I.) Capt. Lt. 18th N.I. 19 Feb. 1814. Nepal War 1816; Capt. 1/18th N.I., in 1st Bde. Rt. Column. Cuttack insurrection 1816; Khurda. Third Mahratta War; Jawad. Operations in Jodhpur 1823; Lamba; Capt. 1/18th N.I. Transfd. as Major to 37th N.I. (late 2/18th) May 1824. Siege and capture of Bhurtpore; Major 37th N.I. Lieut. Col. 37th N.I. Transfd. to 3rd Extra Regt. (became 71st N.I.) 18 Feb. 1828; to 68th N.I. 28 Aug. 1829. Fur. 1828 till retirement.

Refs. : Burke's *Landed Gentry*, 7th edn., p. 1028, *s.n.* Kennett-Barrington, of the Manor House, Dorchester. *G.M.* 1845, i. *I.M.* No. 22, p. 63.

KENT, Arthur Brown Sober (1803-1837). Lieutenant. 66th N.I. Pensioner on Lord Clive's fund. *b.* Edinburgh 7 Feb. 1803. Cadet 1819. Ensign 26 Oct. 1819. Lieut. 11 July 1823. Pensioned in England 4 Aug. 1827. *d.* Stonehouse, Devon, 14 Apr. 1837.

Son of Rodolphus Kent, Capt. R.M.

Services : Posted as Ensign to 1/3rd N.I. in 1820. Transfd. as Lieut. to 33rd N.I. July 1823; to 66th N.I. (late 2/33rd) May 1824. Fur. 1825 till 1829, when he was transfd. to the Pension list with effect from Aug. 1827. No record of active service.

Refs. : *A.J.* N.S. xxii. 75.

KENT, Robert (1791-1848). Lieut. Colonel. 18th N.I. *bapt.* St. Petrox, Dartmouth, Devon, 21 Oct. 1791. Cadet 1808. Arrived in India 19 July 1809. Ensign 13 Dec. 1809. Lieut. 1 Nov. 1814. Capt. 17 May 1824. Major 15 Apr. 1840. Lt. Col. 1 Mar. 1846. *d.* Lahore, 3 Oct. 1848, from a paralytic stroke whilst riding.

Son of Thomas Kent. His dau. *m.* Arthur Broome, *q.v.*

Services : Barasat C.C. Aug. 1809 till Nov. 1810. Posted as Ensign to 1/6th N.I. 30 Dec. 1809. Nepal War 1814-5; Kalanga; Nahan; Jaithak; Lieut. 1/6th N.I., in 2nd Div. Third Mahratta War; Lieut. 1/6th N.I., in Reserve Div. Actg. Intr. & Qmr. 1/6th N.I. 24 Mar. 1824. Transfd. to 18th N.I. (late 2/6th) May 1824. Siege and capture of Bhurtpore; Capt. 18th N.I. Posted to Vol. Regt. for service in China 20 Jan. 1840. First China War 1840-1; Chusan. Returned to India May 1841. Posted to newly-formed Vol. Regt. 29 Jan. 1842. First China War 1842; capture of Chinkiang Foo (Medal). Returned to India Feb. 1843 and rejoined 18th N.I., which he comdd. till death. Reposted as Lt. Col. to 18th N.I. July 1846.

THE BENGAL ARMY, 1758-1834   589

Refs. : *De Rhé-Philipe. Mundy,* i. 191. *I.M.* 1848, p. 710. Will dated 20 June 1842 ; admon. 3 Apr. 1849. M.I. at Lahore.

KENT, William Streat (1785-1808). Capt. Lieutenant, Artillery. *bapt.* Little Bedwyn, Wilts., 11 Feb. 1785. Cadet 1804. Arrived in India 27 Sept. 1804. Lieut. 17 Aug. 1804. Capt. Lt. 5 Dec. 1806. *d.* Berhampore 30 Mar. 1808.

Son of William Kent and Elizabeth his wife. Woolwich Cadet ; nominated for R.M.A. 18 Apr. 1800 ; obtained his certificate 13 Mar. 1804.

Services : No record of active service.

KENYON, Edward (1785-1856 ?). Lieutenant. 19th N.I. *b.* 27 June 1785. Cadet 1800. Arrived in India 15 Sept. 1801. Ensign 17 Sept. 1801. Lieut. 13 July 1803. Resigned in England 7 Dec. 1808. (? *d.* at his house in Vienna 20 Nov. 1856.)

bapt. Rivington, Lancs., 24 July 1785. Son of John Kenyon and Milborough his wife. (? Brother of John Kenyon, of Devonshire Pl., Marylebone.) Nephew of Samuel Kenyon.

Services : Posted as Ensign to 19th N.I. Fur. 12 Mar. 1806 till resignation. No record of active service.

Refs. : (? *G.M.* 1857, i. 121.)

KER, George (*d.* 1770). Captain, Infantry. Cadet 1765. Ensign 23 Feb. 1765. Lieut. 12 Dec. 1766. Capt. 11 Oct. 1769. *d.* Calcutta 12 June 1770.

Services : N.F.P.

KER, Hugh Inglis (1788-1818). Captain, 7th N.C. *b.* Peebles 29 Nov. 1788. Cadet 1804. Arrived in India 1 Oct. 1805. Cornet 29 May 1804. Lieut. 1 May 1829. Capt. 1818. *d.* Bourdah, Betul, C.P., 20 Dec. 1818.

Youngest son of William Ker, of Kerfield, bailie in Peebles, and Robina Wightman his wife. Brother of William Ker, *q.v.* Marlow Cadet 1804.

Services : Posted as Cornet to 7th N.C. in 1806. Operations in Oudh 1808. Adjt. 7th N.C. 1 May 1809 till 1816. Settlement of Hariana 1809-10. Adjt. Java L.C. 1813-5. Intr. & Qmr. 7th N.C. 13 Dec. 1816 till death. Siege and capture of Hathras 1817. Third Mahratta War.

Refs. : *S.M.* 1819, ii. 294. M.I. on his brother's tomb in S. Park St. cemetery, Calcutta.

KER, James (*d.* 1773). Ensign, Infantry. Cadet (?). Ensign 20 Sept. 1770. *d.* Sultanpur 1 Aug. 1773.

Services : N.F.P.

KER, John Baker (1784-1832). Lieutenant. 8th N.I. Subsequently Capt. 7th D.G. *b.* Dundonald, co. Ayr, 3 Oct. 1784. Cadet 1804. Arrived in India 10 Sept. 1805. Ensign 2 Sept. 1805. Lieut. 3 Sept. 1805. Resigned 15 July 1808. *d.* Paris, 28 Apr. 1832, of cholera.

Son of Hugh Ker, of Newfield, later of Hull, and Sarah Baker his wife. *Services :* Posted as Lieut. to 8th N.I. in 1806. Cornet H.M. 9th Light Dgns. 8 June 1809 ; Lieut. do. 4 June 1811 ; Capt. do. 2 Jan. 1817 ; h.p. 1821.

Refs. : G.M. 1832, i. 649.

KER, William (1772-?). Ensign. Infantry. Unposted. *b.* Peebles 11 May 1772. Cadet 1794. Never arrived in India. Ensign 22 Nov. 1795. Struck off (?).

bapt. Peebles 14 May 1772. Son of William Ker and Robina Wightman his wife. Brother of Hugh Inglis Ker, *q.v.*

KERIE, Jedediah (1789-1875). Lieutenant. 20th N.I. *b.* St. Mary, Cayon, I. of St. Kitts, W.I., 14 Nov. 1789. Cadet 1804. Arrived in India 10 Dec. 1805. Ensign 2 Nov. 1805. Lieut. 17 Sept. 1806. Retired 16 Apr. 1817. *d.* at his residence, 8a Gloucester Pl., Portman Sq., London, 30 Oct. 1875.

Son of Jedediah Kerie. *m.* Emma. (She died 23 Dec. 1877, aged 85.)

Services : Posted to 20th N.I. in 1806. Actg. Adjt. 1/20th N.I. at different periods 1810-2. Capture of Java 1811 ; Lieut. 1/20th N.I. (Medal). Transfd. to 2/20th N.I. Fur. 17 Feb. 1814 till retirement.

Refs. : The Times, 2 Nov. 1875.

KERIN, Donat Vaughan (1758/59-1823). Lieut. Colonel, Invalid Est. 5th N.I. Comdt. Farrukhabad Provl. Bn. *b.* 1758/59. Country Cadet 1781. Admitted 14 Oct. 1781. Ensign 14 July 1782. Lieut. 11 Jan. 1785. Capt. 23 Jan. 1803. Major 25 Jan. 1808. Lt. Col. 4 June 1814. Invalided 29 Aug. 1809. *d. unm.* Patna, 3 Dec. 1823, aged 64.

Services : Lieut. 3rd Bengal Eur. Bn. in July 1787. Lieut. 1st Bengal Eur. Regt. in 1796. Capt. 5th N.I. Comdd. Invalids at Patna 1803-8. Comdd. Fatehgarh Provl. Bn. 1820-2 ; do. Farrukhabad Provl. Bn. 1822 till death.

Refs. : Will dated Fatehgarh 11 Mar. 1822 ; proved 7 Apr. 1824. M.I. at Patna.

KERNS, James (1789-?). Lieutenant. 3rd N.I. *b.* Dublin 10 Jan. 1789. Cadet 1805. Arrived in India 13 Nov. 1806. Ensign 9 Jan. 1807. Lieut. 1810. Dismissed 19 Mar. 1811.

THE BENGAL ARMY, 1758-1834   591

Son of James Kerns.
Services : Suspended 14 May 1807 for having, whilst at Barasat C.C., " addressed to the O.C. Cadet Coy. a letter intimating his determination not to study the native languages." (G.O. 14 May 1807.) Restored 28 Sept. 1807. Posted as Ensign to 3rd N.I. in 1807.

*KERR, Bernard. Cadet. Artillery. Was never commissioned. Cadet 24 Feb. 1780. Never arrived in India.
Refs. : Stubbs's List.

KERR, George (1746/47-1770). Captain, Infantry. *b.* 1746/47. Cadet 1764. Ensign 23 Feb. 1765. Lieut. 12 Dec. 1766. Capt. 11 Oct. 1769. *d.* Calcutta 12 June 1770.
A native of Ireland.
Services : Sailed for India on the *Fort William*, 17 May 1764, aged 17. N.F.P.

KERR, Henry Thomas Coggan (1800-1845). Lieutenant. 39th N.I. *b.* Corsham, Wilts., 9 May 1800. Cadet 1817. Ensign (?). Lieut. 22 Oct. 1818. Retired 19 Mar. 1830. *d.* 25 Sept. 1845.
4th son of Maj.-Gen. James Kerr, Bombay Est., and Anne his 2nd wife, dau. of Thomas Dick, of Stratford-le-Bow. Brother of Russell Edward James Kerr, *q.v.* (*Probably* nephew of George Dick, *q.v.*) *m.* 21 July 1828, Louisa Anne, 2nd dau. of Hugh Blaydes, of High Paull, Yorks., and Ranby Hall, Notts. (She died 7 Apr. 1872, aged 68.)
Services : Posted as Lieut. to 1/19th N.I. in 1819. Fur. 21 Dec. 1821 till 1824. Transfd. to 39th N.I. (late 2/19th) May 1824. (? First Burma War ; Cachar 1824-5 ; Lieut. 39th N.I.) A.D.C. to Maj.-Gen. George Dick, comdg. Dinapore Div., 1825-6. Supt. of Cadets in Fort William 1826-7. Fur. 1828 till retirement.
Refs. : Burke's *Landed Gentry*, 13th edn., p. 1023, *s.n.* Kerr, of The Haie, Gloucs. *Howard & Crisp*, i. 55, *s.n.* Blaydes, of Bedford.

KERR, John (1783-1805). Lieutenant, 8th N.I. *b.* Edinburgh 17 Apr. 1783. Cadet 1797. Arrived in India 30 Oct. 1798. Ensign 25 Sept. 1798. Lieut. (1 Nov. 1798) 1 Mar. 1799. *d.* 20 Feb. 1805, of wounds received in action the same day during the third assault of Bhurtpore.
2nd son of James Kerr, of Blackshiels, Midlothian, and Mary Bruce his wife.
Services : Posted as Lieut. to 8th N.I. Mar. 1799. Adjt. & Qmr. 8th N.I. 8 Jan. 1801 till death. Operations in Jumna Doab 1803 ;

Sasni ; Lieut. 1/8th N.I. Second Mahratta War ; capture of Deig ;
Bhurtpore (s.w. in 1st assault on 9 Jan. 1805 ; s.w. in 3rd assault on
20 Feb. 1805) ; Lieut. 1/8th N.I.
Refs. : *Pester*, pp. 377, 384. *S.M.* 1805, p. 726. Intestate ;
admon. granted 30 July 1805.

KERR, John (1787-1827). Captain, 54th N.I. *b.* Durisdeer, co.
Dumfries, 25 Aug. 1787. Cadet 1808. Admitted 15 Dec. 1809.
Ensign 13 Aug. 1811. Lieut. 16 Dec. 1814. Capt. 18 Jan. 1825.
d. unm. " on the river," 11 Feb. 1827.
Son of David Kerr.
Services : Barasat C.C. Posted as Ensign to 27th N.I. in 1811.
Lieut. 2/27th N.I. With 6th Gren. Bn. 1815-6. Adjt. Kumaon
Provl. Bn. 1818-25. Transfd. to 54th N.I. (late 2/27th) May 1824.
Refs. : Will dated Hawalbagh, U.P., 11 Sept. 1825 ; proved 24
Aug. 1827.

KERR, Loraine Macdowall (1807-?). Lieutenant. 65th N.I. *b.*
Galle, Ceylon, 11 July 1807. Cadet 1823. Ensign 17 Jan. 1824.
Lieut. 13 May 1825. Resigned in England 5 July 1826.
Son of Maj.-Gen. Thomas William Kerr, H.M. 2nd Ceylon Regt.,
sometime Comdt. at Colombo.
Services : Posted as Ensign to 65th N.I. in 1824. Fur. 1825 till
resignation. No record of active service.

KERR, Robert (*d.* 1794). Captain, Infantry. Cadet 1770. Ensign
26 Jan. 1773. Lieut. 23 Mar. 1777. Capt. 21 Mar. 1781. *d.*
Chittagong 16 Feb. 1794.
Services : Capt. 3rd Bengal Eur. Regt. in July 1787.

KERR, Russell Edward James (1803-1825). Lieutenant, 57th N.I.
b. 26 Dec. 1803. Cadet 1818. Arrived in India 1818. Ensign
7 July 1819. Lieut. 29 Oct. 1822. *d. unm.* in Assam 23 Sept.
1825.

7th and youngest son of Maj.-Gen. James Kerr, Bombay Est.,
and Anne his 2nd wife, dau. of Thomas Dick. Brother of Henry
Thomas Coggan Kerr, *q.v.*
Services : Went out to India as a Midshipman, E.I.C.N.S., in
1818. Local Cornet 4th (Sneyd's) Horse 28 Nov. 1818. Transfd.
as Cornet to 1st Rohilla Cav. 21 Aug. 1819. Posted as Ensign to
1/29th N.I. in 1820. Transfd. to 57th N.I. (late 1/29th) May 1824.
First Burma War ; Assam 1824 ; Lieut. 57th N.I.

KERR, William (1794-1819). Lieutenant, 12th N.I. *b.* I. of St.
Vincent 18 Mar. 1794. Cadet 1809. Ensign 5 May 1812. Lieut.
14 June 1815. *d.* Muttra 18 Nov. 1819.

Son of Maj.-Gen. Kerr, H.M.S. Grandson of Dr. William Kerr, of Northampton.
Services : Barasat C.C. Cadet d.d. 9th N.I. 1811. Posted as Ensign to 12th N.I. in 1812. Nepal War 1816 ; Lieut. 2/12th N.I., in 3rd Bde., Centre Column. Siege and capture of Hathras 1817 ; Lieut. 2/12th N.I. Third Mahratta War ; Dhamoni. Operations against the Bhattis of Hariana 1818 ; Lieut. 2/12th N.I.

KERR, William (1810-1831). Lieutenant, 7th L.C. *b.* London 12 Jan. 1810. Cadet 1825. Arrived in India 6 July 1826. Cornet 15 Mar. 1826. Lieut. July 1831. *d.* Kaitha, U.P., 18 Aug. 1831. Son of William Kerr. Nephew of Mrs. Eliza de Pontcarré.
Services : Cornet d.d. 1st L.C. 2 Aug. 1826. Posted to 7th L.C. 26 Sept. 1826. No record of active service.

KEWNEY, Henry (1810-1838). Lieutenant, 50th N.I. *b.* Nottingham 19 May 1810. Cadet 1827. Arrived in India 10 Oct. 1828. Ensign 10 May 1828. Lieut. 22 Apr. 1836. *d.* Karnal 4 Nov. 1838 : committed suicide in a fit of temporary insanity brought on by overwork.

Son of Jonas Kewney, of Nottingham and Grantham, hosier, and Charlotte his wife.
Services : Ensign d.d. 48th N.I. 5 Nov. 1828. Posted as Ensign to 50th N.I. 4 Mar. 1829. Operations against the Kols and Chuars 1832-3 ; Ensign 50th N.I. Offg. D.A.Q.M.G. 2 cl., Presdy. Div., 17 Mar. 1835 ; D.A.Q.M.G., Malwa F.F., 25 Apr. 1836. Employed on survey duty in the valley of the Narbada R. 1836-8. D.A.Q.M.G., 1 cl., 24 Apr. 1838. Apptd. D.A.Q.M.G. 1st Div., Army of the Indus, Sept. 1838.
Refs. : De Rhé-Philipe. *G.M.* 1839, i. 333. *A.J.* N.S. xxviii. 142.

KEY, Alexander Maxwell (1805-1832). Captain, 9th L.C. *b.* London 25 Mar. 1805. Cadet 1821. Arrived in India 21 Aug. 1822. Cornet 17 Mar. 1822. Lieut. 1 May 1824. Capt. 1 Oct. 1829. *d.* Sultanpur, Benares, 4 Dec. 1832.

bapt. St. Anne's, Westminster, 16 May 1805. 2nd son of Alexander Key, of Golden Sq., London, wine merchant, and Sarah his wife. Ed. Cheam school.
Services : Posted as Cornet to 6th L.C. Exchanged to 4th L.C. 14 Feb. 1825. Transfd. to newly-raised 1st Extra Regt. (became 9th L.C.) May 1825. Actg. Adjt. do. 13 Dec. 1825. Siege and capture of Bhurtpore ; Lieut. 9th L.C. Fur. p.a. 14 Mar. 1828 till 11 Feb. 1830.
Refs. : *A.J.* N.S. xi. 82.

KIELY, William Bagwell (1805-?). Cornet. 7th. L.C. *b.* psh. of Innislonnagh, or Abbey, 2 m. from Clonmel, co. Tipperary, Nov. 1805. Cadet 1825. Cornet 26 Sept. 1826. Struck off in India 26 Jan. 1827.

Son of John Kiely, " a private gentleman of Strancally, co. Waterford," and Margaret his wife, dau. of John Bagwell, of Marlfield, co. Tipperary.

Services : Cornet d.d. 1st L.C. 8 July 1826. Posted to 7th L.C. 26 Sept. 1826. No record of active service.

KIERNANDER, Charles (1787-1834). Captain, Invalid Est. 15th N.I. *b.* Bengal 5 Feb. 1787. Cadet 1807. Arrived in India 19 Aug. 1808. Ensign 24 Aug. 1808. Lieut. 7 Jan. 1812. Capt. 1 May 1824. Invalided 25 Jan. 1826. *d.* Chinsura, Bengal, 3 July 1834.

bapt. 21 Sept. 1787. Son of Robert William Kiernander and Jane Lucy his wife, dau. of F. Morris, the Coy.'s standing counsel. Brother of John Samuel William Kiernander, *q.v.*, and grandson of Rev. John Zachariah Kiernander (a Dane, *b.* in Sweden), sent out to India by the S.P.C.K. from England in 1740. *m.* (before 1816) ?

Services : Barasat C.C. Posted as Ensign to 11th N.I. in 1809. Reduction of Kalinjar 1812 ; Lieut. 1/11th N.I. With 3rd Gren. Bn. 1815-6. Intr. & Qmr. 1/11th N.I. 4 Nov. 1816 till May 1824. Transfd. as Capt. to 15th N.I. (late 1/11th) May 1824. Action at Patan, nr. Kotah, 7 Nov. 1824. Siege and capture of Bhurtpore ; Capt. 15th N.I. In Jan. 1826 he was adjudged by a Court of Enquiry to have behaved irregularly during a disturbance which took place on 10 Jan. in his Regt., and he was sent out of camp. Subsequently invalided from 25 Jan.

Refs. : *The Hearseys,* p. 303. *A.J.* N.S. xvi. 66.

KIERNANDER, John Samuel William (1784-1806). Ensign, Infantry. Unposted. *b.* Bengal May 1784. Cadet 1805. Arrived in India 14 Mar. 1806. Ensign 12 July 1806. *d.* Barasat C.C. 6 Dec. 1806.

bapt. Calcutta, 13 June 1784, aged 1 month. Son of Robert William Kiernander and Jane Lucy his wife. Brother of Charles Kiernander, *q.v.*, and of Jane Charlotte, wife of George Waite, *q.v.*

KILKELLY, Francis (*d.* 1771). Cadet, Infantry. Cadet 1770. *d.* Dinapore May 1771.

Services : N.F.P.

KILPATRICK, Samuel (*d.* 1781). Major, 24th N.I. Cadet 1766. Ensign 16 Sept. 1766. Lieut. 3 Dec. 1767. Capt. 30 Mar. 1773.

THE BENGAL ARMY, 1758-1834   595

Major 26 Jan. 1781. *d.* Madras 24 Aug. 1781 : kld. in a duel with Capt. Richard Scott, *q.v.*
Of Campbeltown, co. Argyll. Son of —— Kilpatrick and Ann his wife, née White. Stepson of Archibald Fleming, of Campbeltown. Brother of Margaret, wife of William Clarke, of Campbeltown, and half-brother of John Porter, *q.v.*
Services : First Rohilla War. Raised a Bn. of N.I. at Cawnpore in July 1778. This Bn., which was called after him, became 24th Regt. in 1781, and formed part of 7th N.I. by the re-organization of 1796. Second Mysore War 1781 ; Major comdg. 24th N.I.
Refs. : Williams, pp. 116, 198. Will dated camp, Nellore, 22 July 1781 ; filed 17 Oct. 1781 ; proved 20 Dec. 1781. M.I. in Tripasore cemetery, Chingleput district, Madras.

KILSHA, Richard (1777-1794). Fireworker, Artillery. *bapt.* Stoke, co. Warwick, 15 Oct. 1773. Cadet 1791. Fireworker 20 Aug. 1792. *d. c.* Aug. 1794 : lost at sea on his passage to Bencoolen. Son of Rev. Richard Kilsha, rector of Barkston, Lincs., 1801-29.
Services : N.F.P.

KIMBER, Edward (1790-1808). Ensign, 21st N.I. *bapt.* North Cerney, Gloucs., 9 Mar. 1790. Cadet 1805. Arrived in India 20 July 1807. Ensign 15 July 1807. *d.* Kumarkhali (Comercolly), Bengal, 21 May 1808, whilst proceeding to join his Regt.
Son of William Kimber.
Services : Barasat C.C. Posted as Ensign to 21st N.I. in 1808, but never joined.
Refs. : A.A.R. x. 298.

KINCH, John (*d.* 1763). Captain, Artillery. Fireworker (Bombay) Dec. 1755. Lieut. (Bengal) 11 Nov. 1757. Capt. Lt. 19 Sept. 1758. Capt. 26 Sept. 1760. *d.* 5th, 6th or 11th Oct. 1763 : massacred at or near Patna by order of Nawab Mir Muhammad Kasim. (See note to John Gordon.*)
Services : Commissioned as Lieut. F. in Bo. Art., from Sergt., Dec. 1755. Went to Bengal to serve under Clive. (? Expdn. to N. Circars 1758 ; Condore ; Masulipatam ; Capt. Lt. 2nd Coy. Bengal Art.)
Refs. : Spring, No. 22. *Stubbs,* i. 25, 36. MS. list in India Office. *Broome,* p. 365. *Firminger,* p. 71.

KINDERSLEY, Nathaniel (*d.* 1769). Lieut. Colonel Comdt., Artillery. Transfd. from R.A. May 1764. Fireworker, R.A., 19 Apr. 1758. 2nd Lieut., R.A., 31 Jan. 1764. Capt. (Bengal) 27 July 1764. Major 1 Apr. 1767. Lt. Col. 28 July 1769 (ante-dated to 8 Nov. 1768). *d.* Calcutta 24 Oct. 1769 : bur. the following day.

Only son of Rev. John Kindersley (the first to spell his name with an 's') and Sarah Raining his wife. *m.* in England *c.* 1762, Miss Jemima Wicksted or Wickstead.[1] (She died in 1809, aged 68.)
Services : Comdt. Bengal Art. 9 Nov. 1768 till death.
Refs. : Burke's *Landed Gentry*, 13th edn., p. 1026, *s.n.* Kindersley, of Clyffe, Dorset. *Kane's List*, No. 328. *Love*, ii. 616 *n.* Will dated Calcutta 18 Oct. 1769 ; proved 27 Oct. 1769.

[1] *Note :* She pub. in 1777, "Letters from the I. of Teneriffe, Brazil, The Cape of Good Hope, and the East Indies." Known to her friends as 'Pulcherrima.'

KING, Arnold (1759/60-1833). Major. 13th N.I. *b.* 1759/60. Cadet 1782. Admitted 3 July 1783. Ensign 1782. Lieut. 11 Mar. 1790. Capt. 30 Sept. 1803. Bt. Major 25 Apr. 1808. Major 1810. Retired 10 Oct. 1810. *d.* 5 Lodge Rd., Regent's Pk., London, 7 Dec. 1833, aged 73.
Services : Lieut. & Bt. Capt. 5th N.I. Capt. Lt. 13th N.I. (? Second Mahratta War ; Capt. 13th N.I.) Fur. 8 Feb. 1807 till retirement.
Refs. : A.J. N.S. xiii. 67.

KING, Charles Prager (1788-1846). Lieut. Colonel. 4th L.C. *b.* London 2 Jan. 1788. Cadet 1805. Arrived in India 11 July 1806. Cornet 13 July 1806. Lieut. 17 May 1816. Capt. 27 July 1819. Major 10 July 1825. Lt. Col. 9 Apr. 1833. Invalided 23 Dec. 1839. Retired 6 Jan. 1841. *d.* Hans Pl., London, 19 Mar. 1846.

Only son of E. King, of Pangbourne, Berks. *m.* Bombay, 12 June 1819, Jane Margaretta, 2nd dau. of R. C. Brownell, of Surrey. (She died Chelsea, 5 Dec. 1860, aged 65.)
Services : Posted as Cornet to 4th N.C. Third Mahratta War ; Jawad ; Lieut. 4th N.C. Fur. p.a. 28 Nov. 1819 till 25 June 1822. Siege and capture of Bhurtpore ; Major 4th L.C. Posted as Lt. Col. to 4th L.C. 1 Aug. 1833. Shekhawat expedn. 1834 ; Lt. Col. comdg. 4th L.C. Transfd. to 10th L.C. 26 Dec. 1835. Leave s.c. 2 yrs. to Cape 14 Apr. 1836. Retransfd. to 4th L.C. 12 May 1837. To comd. Bde. of Cav. and Troop H.A. at Ranjit Singh's interview with Lord Auckland, the G.G., in 1838.
Refs. : G.M. 1819, ii. 562 ; 1846, i. *The Times*, 21 Mar. 1846.

KING, James. Ensign. Infantry. Cadet 1772. Ensign 7 Jan. 1773. Resigned 1774.
Services : N.F.P.

KING, John (1806-1833). Lieutenant, Bengal Eur. Regt. *b.* Dover 11 May 1806. Cadet 1824. Arrived in India 10 June 1825. Ensign 8 Feb. 1825. Lieut. 26 Sept. 1826. *d. unm.* Dacca 2 May 1833.

Son of John King, of Dover, merchant. Addiscombe Cadet 1821-5.

Services : Posted as Ensign to 13th N.I. in 1825. Transfd. to 62nd N.I. 4 Aug. 1826 ; to 5th Extra Regt. 26 Sept. 1826. d.d. 61st N.I. 30 Jan. 1828. Exchanged to 2nd Bengal Eur. Regt. 9 Mar. 1828. No record of active service.

KINGLY, Charles. Lieutenant. Engineers. Cadet (?). Ensign 2 July 1770. Lieut. 13 Sept. 1773. Resigned 19 Sept. 1775.
Services : N.F.P.

KINGSTON, George (1789-1844). Lieut. Colonel, 52nd N.I. *bapt.* Cork 25 Sept. 1789. Cadet 1804. Arrived in India 13 May 1806. Ensign 10 Apr. 1806. Lieut. 30 Dec. 1807. Capt. 13 Jan. 1822. Major 4 Feb. 1833. Lt. Col. 4 Sept. 1839. *d.* Calcutta 23 Dec. 1844.

Son of Isaac and Mary Kingston. *m.* St. John's, Calcutta, 16 Mar. 1820, Miss Elizabeth Barton. (She died 26 Oct. 1864, aged 79.)

Services : Capture of C.G.H. Jan. 1806 under Sir David Baird. Barasat C.C. for 13½ mos. Posted as Ensign to 1/26th N.I. Third Mahratta War ; Dhamoni ; Lieut. 1/26th N.I. Adjt. 1/26th N.I. 27 Sept. 1820 till 28 Jan. 1822. Transfd. to 52nd N.I. (late 2/26th) May 1824. First Burma War ; Cachar 1824-5 ; Capt. 52nd N.I. Fur. p.a. 7 Jan. 1836 till 12 Nov. 1837. Occupation of fortress of Jodhpur 28 Sept. 1839 ; Lt. Col. comdg. 52nd N.I. Fur. s.c. 13 Dec. 1844, but did not live to embark.

Refs. : *I.M.* No. 23, p. 86. Will dated Calcutta 9 Dec. 1844 ; proved 25 Mar. 1845. M.I. Circular Rd. cemetery, Calcutta.

KINLESIDE, Robert Raikes (1810-1871). Major General. Artillery. *b.* Angmering, Sussex, 30 Dec. 1810. Cadet 1827. Arrived in India 30 Jan. 1828. 2nd Lieut. 28 Sept. 1827. Lieut. 25 Sept. 1834. Capt. 3 July 1845. Major 25 June 1857. Lt. Col. 27 Aug. 1858. Col. 18 Feb. 1861. Maj. Gen. 14 July 1867. *d.* Landour, Mussoorie, 27 Aug. 1871.

Son of Rev. William Kinleside, vicar of Angmering and of Poling, Sussex, and Martha his wife, 2nd dau. of William Raikes, of Valentines, Essex. 2nd cousin of Charles Lewis Napier Raikes, *q.v.* *m.* Cawnpore, 14 Aug. 1838, Isabella Barbara, 2nd dau. of Major Samuel George Carter, H.M. 16th Foot. Addiscombe Cadet 1825-7.

Services : Posted as Lieut. to 1st Coy. 3rd Bn. Foot Art. 29 Dec.

1834. Transfd. to 2nd Troop 3rd Bde. H.A. 18 Nov. 1835. Actg. Adjt. & Qmr. 3rd Bde. H.A. June 1838 and 28 Jan. 1841. Comdd. 2nd Troop 3rd Bde. 1 Dec. 1841 till 12 Feb. 1842. Bde. Qmr. of Art., Army of Reserve (for Afghanistan) 5 Dec. 1842. Fur. p.a. 30 Dec. 1843 till 1846. Transfd. to 4th Coy. 3rd Bn. Comdd. 3rd Troop 2nd Bde. 1849-57. Second Sikh War; Sadulapur; Gujerat; Capt. comdg. 3rd Troop 2nd Bde. (Medal with 2 clasps). Mutiny campaign; Agra; Doab; operations about Delhi; Bt. Col. 2nd Bde. H.A. (Medal). Fur. s.c. 15 mos. 24 June 1859.

Refs. : Burke's *Landed Gentry*, 13th edn., p. 1473, *s.n.* Raikes, of Treberfydd, co. Brecon. Boase. *The Times*, 7 Oct. 1871.

KINLOCH, Alexander. Lieutenant, Infantry. Cadet 1780. Ensign 1780. Lieut. 13 June 1781. Struck off 1793.

Services : Apptd. Sub-Sec., Mily. Board, 24 July 1786. Fur. 3 yrs. on h.p. 1 Mar. 1787 till struck off.

KINLOCH, Charles (*d.* 1770). Ensign, Infantry. Cadet 1767. Ensign 15 Sept. 1767. *d.* Patna 10 Sept. 1770.

Son of David Kinloch, of Kilrie, and Isabel his wife, 2nd dau. of George Oliphant, of Clashbenie. Brother of George Kinloch (*d.* 1768), *q.v.*

Services : (? "afterwards took service with the Dutch, was imprisoned by them in the Dutch Factory, and was eventually released by order of the Patna Council.") (*B. : P.P.*)

Refs. : Foster's *Baronetage*, p. 362, *s.n.* Kinloch, Bart., of Kinloch, co. Perth. *B. : P.P.*, No. 55, p. 63. Will dated Bankipore 3 Sept. 1770 ; proved 19 Oct. 1770.

KINLOCH, Francis Peregrine (1747/48-1806). Lieutenant. Infantry. *b.* 1747/48. Cadet 1778. Ensign 1778. Lieut. 30 Aug. 1779. Resigned 1 Jan. 1792. *d.* Calcutta, 24 Aug. 1806, aged 58.

4th son of Sir James Kinloch, 3rd Bart., of that ilk, and of Nevay, co. Forfar, and Janet Duff his wife, sister of the Earl of Fife.

Services : Lieut. 2/2nd Bengal Eur. Regt. in Oct. 1779. Apptd. Sub-Sec., Board of Ord., 28 Nov. 1785. On fur. in 1790. He returned to India and resided in Calcutta till death.

Refs. : Burke's *Peerage*, 1923, p. 1298, *s.n.* Kinloch, Bart., of Kinloch, co. Perth. *S.M.* 1807. M.I. in S. Park St. cemetery, Calcutta.

KINLOCH, George (*d.* 1768). Captain, Infantry. Capt. 23 May 1764. *d.* Patna 10 May 1768.

Son of David Kinloch, of Kilrie, and Isabel his wife. Brother of Charles Kinloch, *q.v.*

THE BENGAL ARMY, 1758-1834   599

Services: Lieut. H.M. 70th Foot 4 Feb. 1760. Having raised from amongst the King's troops at Madras a party of 65 men for H.E.I.C.S., 44 of whom volunteered for service in Bengal, he was sent to that Presdy. in May 1764, after being given a Commission as Capt. on the Madras Est., dated 11 Apr. 1764. Resigned his Commission during the " Batta mutiny " in May 1766 ; afterwards restored. " Commanded the abortive expedn. to Nepal in 1767, his objective being to assist the Raja of Khatmandu to repel the Gurkha invasion from western Nepal." (*B. : P.P.*)

Refs. : Foster's *Baronetage*, p. 362, *s.n.* Kinloch, Bart., of Kinloch, co. Perth. *Broome*, p. 574. *Wilson*, i. *B. : P.P.* No. 55, p. 63. *S.M.* 1769, p. 279. Will dated Patna 1 Aug. 1767 ; proved 25 Oct. 1768.

KINLOCH, George (1801-1829). Lieutenant, 71st N.I. *b.* London 3 May 1801. Cadet 1818. Ensign 10 June 1819. Lieut. 1 Jan. 1821. *d.* Benares, 28 Oct. 1829, of fever.

bapt. St. Pancras 1 June 1801. Eldest son of James Kinloch, of Brunswick Sq., London, banker and merchant, and Helen his wife. Brother of James John Kinloch, *q.v.*

Services: Ensign d.d. Bengal Eur. Regt. in 1819. Posted as Ensign to 1/30th N.I. in 1820. Transfd. to 59th N.I. (late 1/30th) May 1824 ; to 3rd Extra Regt. (became 71st N.I.) May 1825. Intr. & Qmr. 71st N.I. 25 Aug. 1826 till death. No record of active service.

Refs. : A.J. N.S. i. 236.

KINLOCH, James John (1804-?). Ensign. 27th N.I. *b.* London 15 May 1804. Cadet 1827. Arrived in India 30 May 1828. Ensign 19 Jan. 1828. Resigned 6 Feb. 1833.

Son of James Kinloch, of Brunswick Sq., London, and Helen his wife. Brother of George Kinloch (1801-1829), *q.v.*

Services: Ensign Renfrew Mil. 8 Dec. 1826. Ensign d.d. 7th N.I. ; do. 27th N.I. 25 Sept. 1828. Posted to 27th N.I. 4 Nov. 1828. Fur. s.c. 9 Aug. 1829 till resignation. No record of active service.

KIRBY, Gravenor (1811-1892). Colonel. Artillery. *b.* Woolwich, Kent, 30 Aug. 1811. Cadet 1830. Arrived in India 4 Aug. 1831. 2nd Lieut. 10 Dec. 1830. Lieut. 6 Dec. 1839. Capt. 1 Sept. 1848. Bt. Major 3 Oct. 1857. Lt. Col. 21 Nov. 1858. Retired 11 Mar. 1860. Hon. Col. 11 Mar. 1860. *d.* Beltie House, Aberdeen, 9 Sept. 1892.

Son of Stephen Kirby, Lt. Gen. R.A., of Ballincollig, co. Cork, and Martha his wife. Brother of John Ancrum Kirby, *q.v. m.*

Peshawar, 8 Sept. 1853, Mary, dau. of John Ross. Addiscombe Cadet 8 May 1829 till 10 Dec. 1830.

Services : Actg. Adjt. & Qmr. 2nd Bn. Foot Art. 18 Sept. 1835, and 12 June 1837. Actg. Dy. Comy. of Ord. at Ajmer 16 Oct. 1837. Actg. Adjt. & Qmr. 2nd Bn. 9 Mar. 1839 ; permanent do. 12 Nov. 1839 till 1845. Fur. s.c. 14 Dec. 1847 till 6 Dec. 1850. Mutiny campaign ; minor operations (Medal).

Refs. : The Times, 15 Sept. 1892.

KIRBY, James (*d.* 1769). Lieutenant, Infantry. Cadet 1766. Ensign 2 Oct. 1766. Lieut. 1 Dec. 1767. *d.* in India 1769.

Services : N.F.P.

KIRBY, John Ancrum (1807-1842). Bt. Captain, 54th N.I. *b.* Woolwich 19 May 1807. Cadet 1825. Arrived in India 9 Mar. 1826. Ensign 12 Oct. 1825. Lieut. 18 May 1833. Bt. Capt. 12 Oct. 1840. *d.* 10 Jan. 1842 : kld. in action nr. Kabul during the retreat from that place.

Eldest son of Stephen Kirby, of Ballincollig, co. Cork, Lt. Gen. R.A., and Martha his wife. Brother of Gravenor Kirby, *q.v.*

Services : Posted as Ensign to 54th N.I. in 1826. (? Operations against the Kols 1832 ; Ensign 54th N.I.) Apptd. tempy. to Comst. Dept. 18 Oct. 1835. Intr. & Qmr. 54th N.I. 27 May 1836 till death. Offg. Asst. Agent & Comr. at Delhi 6 Dec. 1838 till 9 Feb. 1839. Offg. S.A.C.G. in Afghanistan 13 Nov. 1841. First Afghan War 1840-2 ; Kabul insurrection (kld.) ; Bt. Capt. 54th N.I.

Refs. : G.M. 1843, i. 554. *The Times,* 21 Oct. 1842.

KIRBY, John Stupart (1795-1851). Captain. Artillery. *b.* Greenwich 28 May 1795. Cadet 1810. Admitted 21 Jan. 1812. Fireworker 14 Jan. 1812. Lieut. 15 Feb. 1818. Capt. 27 Aug. 1828. Retired 31 Dec. 1838. *d.* London 23 Oct. 1851.

Son of John Kirby. Ed. Eton 1808-9. Addiscombe Cadet 1810-1.

Services : Offg. as Engr. at Malacca 21 Sept. 1814 till Sept. 1816. Third Mahratta War ; Mandala ; Lieut. 3rd Coy. 1st Bn. Foot Art., afterwards 6th Coy. 2nd Bn., and from June 1818 2nd Coy. 2nd Bn. 2nd Troop H.A. in 1820. Adjt. & Qmr. to Capt. Curphy's detachment 8 Oct. 1822. Adjt. Chittagong Div. Art. 27 Oct. 1824. First Burma War ; Arakan 1825 (India medal). Fur. s.c. 4 Feb. 1826 till 14 Nov. 1828.

Refs. : Eton School Lists. G.M. 1851, ii. 668. *I.M.* 1 Nov. 1851, p. 659.

KIRCHOFFER, Thomas (1801-1822). Captain, Bengal Eur. Regt. *bapt.* St. Mary's, Dublin, 30 Apr. 1786. Cadet 1801. Arrived in

THE BENGAL ARMY, 1758-1834   601

India 18 July 1802. Ensign 13 July 1802. Lieut. 30 May 1804. Capt. 28 July 1816. d. Monghyr 22 Feb. 1822.

Son of Francis Kirchoffer, of Dublin, cabinet-maker, and Sarah his wife, dau. of Robert Brooke, of Rantavan, co. Cavan. His sister m. Joseph Orchard, q.v.

Services : Served throughout with Bengal Eur. Regt. Served for several yrs. at Amboyna. Fort Adjt. at Ternate, Moluccas, 1814-5. Comdd. Amboynese Corps 1815-6.

KIRK, David (1785-1815). Lieutenant, 27th N.I. b. Perth 23 Apr. 1785. Cadet 1804. Arrived in India 21 June 1806. Ensign 3 Sept. 1805. Lieut. 4 Sept. 1805. d. Almora, U.P., 16 May 1815.

Son of James Kirk, of Perth, merchant, and Margaret Simpson his wife.

Services : Posted as Lieut. to 27th N.I. in 1806. Operations against Dhundia Khan 1807 ; Komona ; Ganauri ; Lieut. 27th N.I.

KIRK, William (d. 1772). Cadet, Infantry. Cadet 1771. d. Dinapore 17 July 1772.

Services : N.F.P.

KIRKE, Henry (1806-1857). Bt. Major, 12th N.I. b. 1806. Cadet 1822. Arrived in India 6 Oct. 1823. Ensign 11 July 1823. Lieut. 13 May 1825. Capt. 30 Apr. 1842. Bt. Major 11 Nov. 1851. d. Mahoba, nr. Nowgong, C.I., 19 June 1857.[1]

bapt. E. Retford, Notts., 6 Nov. 1806. 4th son of John Kirke, of Markham and Retford, J.P., sometime Capt. 24th Light Dgns., and afterwards Col. of the Sherwood Rangers, and Ann Mervyn his 1st wife, eldest dau. of Sir William Richardson, 1st Bart. of Augher, co. Tyrone. m. Dehra Dun, 10 July 1830, Margaret, dau. of Col. Blair.

Services : Ensign 1st N.I. Transfd. to 12th N.I. May 1824. Siege and capture of Bhurtpore (w. 18 Jan. 1826) (*Lond. Gaz.* 4 July 1826) ; Lieut. d.d. 1st Nassiri Bn. (India medal). Served with Sirmoor Bn. 16 Feb. 1826 till 26 Sept. 1827, when he rejoined 12th N.I. Adjt. Sirmoor Bn. 16 Apr. 1828 till 1 June 1842. Supt. of watercourses in the Dun 1 Nov. 1841. P.W.D., in charge of the Dun canals, 24 Dec. 1842 till 1848.

Refs. : Burke's *Landed Gentry*, 10th edn., p. 899, s.n. Kirke, of Mirfield Hall, Notts. *I.M.* 1857, p. 591. *G.M.* 1857, ii. 466.

[1] *Note :* While seeking refuge from the mutineers at Nowgong, he fell from his horse nr. Mahoba, and died shortly after.

KIRKMAN, Nathaniel (1792-1821). Lieutenant, 19th N.I. bapt. Chenies, Herts., 18 Feb. 1792. Cadet 1806. Arrived in India

25 Nov. 1807. Ensign 9 Oct. 1807. Lieut. 10 Sept. 1811. *d.* at sea, 29 Aug. 1821, on board the *Mangles*.

Son of Nathaniel Kirkman, of Hales Hall (? Capt. h.p. 92nd Foot), and Augusta his wife, younger dau. of Philip Bulkeley, of Huntley Hall.

Services : Barasat C.C. Posted as Ensign to 19th N.I. in 1808. Nepal War 1814-5; Lieut. 2/19th N.I. With 3rd Ceylon Vol. Bn. 1818-9. Fur. 17 Mar. 1821 till death.

Refs. : Burke's *Landed Gentry*, 2nd edn., iii. 48, *s.n.* Bulkeley, of Stanlow, Staffs. *N. & Q.* 11S. xii. 9.

KIRKPATRICK, William (1754-1812). Major General. Colonel 6th N.I. Resident at Poona. *b.* 1754. Cadet 1771. Admitted 26 Sept. 1771. Ensign 18 Jan. 1773. Lieut. 9 Apr. 1777. Capt. 3 Apr. 1781. Major 25 Apr. 1797. Lt. Col. 31 July 1799. Lt. Col. Comdt. 30 June 1804. Col. 25 Apr. 1808. Maj. Gen. 4 June 1811. *d.* in England, 22 Aug. 1812, aged 58. His death was occasioned by his taking a large dose of laudanum in mistake for a black draught.

Eldest son of Col. James Kirkpatrick, Madras Est., of Keston, Kent, by his 1st wife. Half-brother of James Achilles Kirkpatrick, Lt. Col. Madras Est., Resdt. at Hyderabad, and cousin of Major James George Graham, Madras Est. *m.* Calcutta, 26 Sept. 1785, Maria Seaton, dau. of George Pawson, of London, wine merchant, and sister of William Pawson, B.C.S. His dau. *m.* Sir John Louis, Bart., K.C.B., Adm. R.N.

Services : See *D.N.B.* Persian Intr. to Gen. Stibbert, C.-in-C. Fur. 18 Dec. 1783 till 10 Sept. 1786. A.D.C. to G.G., and Resdt. at court of Sindhia July 1787. D.J.A.G. in 1790. Third Mysore War; Persian Intr. to Lord Cornwallis. Resdt. at Hyderabad 15 Nov. 1797 till 18 Sept. 1798. Mily. Sec. to the Earl of Mornington (Marquess Wellesley), G.G., 7 Sept. 1798 till 31 Oct. 1799; Actg. Pte. Sec. to do. 1 Nov. 1799. Fourth Mysore War; Seringapatam; Persian Intr. to Gen. Harris. Resdt. at Poona Jan. 1801. Fur. 18 May 1802 till death. Pub. "Diary and Letters of Tippoo Sultaun," London, 1804, as well as several translations from the Persian.

Refs. : *D.N.B.* *E.I.M.C.* ii. 454-5. *D.I.B.* *S.M.* 1786, p. 206. *G.M.* 1812, ii. 297; 1786, i. 351. *M.M.* 1812, ii. 266-8. *A.R.* liv. Will dated 15 Oct. 1811; proved 5 July 1824. Portrait, by Thomas Hickey, in Victoria Memorial Hall, Calcutta.

KITCHEN, Henry (*d.* 1767). Ensign, 3rd Bn. Sepoys. Cadet 1766. Ensign 17 Sept. 1766. *d.* Allahabad 10 June 1767.

Services : N.F.P.

Refs. : *Williams*, p. 156 *n.*

THE BENGAL ARMY, 1758-1834   603

KITCHIN or **KITCHEN, William Wilby** (1773-1812). Major, 15th
N.I. *b.* 1773. Cadet 1795. Arrived in India 22 Oct. 1796.
Ensign 6 Oct. 1796. Lieut. 30 Oct. 1797. Capt. 29 Oct. 1804.
Major 23 Dec. 1809. *d.* Calcutta 18 Feb. 1812.
bapt. St. Giles-in-the-Fields, London, 28 Mar. 1773. Son of
William Kitchin and Ann Rhodes his wife. *m.* (?).
Services : Posted as Ensign to 3rd Bengal Eur. Regt. in 1796.
Lieut. 15th N.I. Fur. 9 June 1802 till 12 Dec. 1804. No record of
active service.
Refs. : M.I. in S. Park St. cemetery, Calcutta.

KITSON, Charles Andrew (1812-1860). Lieut. Colonel. 10th L.C.
bapt. Denbury, Devon, 17 Oct. 1812. Cadet 1828. Arrived in
India 27 Aug. 1829. Cornet 27 Aug. 1829. Lieut. 19 Jan. 1839.
Capt. 20 Apr. 1849. Bt. Major 28 Nov. 1854. Retired 20 Sept.
1855. Hon. Lt. Col. 20 Sept. 1855. *d.* 19 Apr. 1860.
Of Werescote, Wellington, Somerset. Son of Rev. Walter Kitson,
of Chilton Foliat, Wilts., and Mary Anne his wife. *m.* Exeter, 10
Sept. 1846, Juliana Speke, younger dau. of Samuel Barnes, of Gt.
Duryard, Exeter. (She died 2 July 1873.)
Services : Cornet d.d. 3rd L.C. 19 Sept. 1829. Actg. Cornet
14 Oct. 1831. Posted as Cornet to 10th L.C. 9 June 1836. Actg.
Adjt. 10th L.C. Jan. 1839, and Apr. 1840 ; permanent do. 30 Dec.
1840 till Feb. 1845. First Afghan War 1842 ; operations leading
to the re-occupation of Kabul ; Lieut. 10th L.C., with Gen. Pollock's
force (Medal). Gwalior campaign ; Maharajpur ; Lieut. 10th L.C.
(Bronze star). Fur. 10 Feb. 1845 till 1846.
Refs. : Burke's *Landed Gentry*, 7th edn., p. 87, *s.n.* Barnes, of
Gt. Duryard, Devon. *G.M.* 1860, i. 534. *The Times*, 21 Apr.
1860.

KITTOE, Markham (1808-1853). Major, 6th N.I. *b.* Woolwich,
Kent, 16 Nov. 1808. Cadet 1824. Arrived in India 3 Oct.
1825. Ensign 13 May 1825. Lieut. 12 Sept. 1827. Capt. 24
Jan. 1845. Major 5 May 1851. *d.* Coddenham, Suffolk, 18 Apr.
1853.
Of Coddenham. Son of Robinson Kittoe, late a Naval Ofr.
m. Calcutta, 12 Nov. 1835, Emily, dau. of Robert Chalmers,
q.v.
Services : Posted as Ensign to 6th N.I. in 1825. Dismissed by
G.C.M. 12 Dec. 1837. Restored to his rank and standing from 21
Jan. 1839. Fur. s.c. 5 Jan. 1842 till 16 Oct. 1844. Apptd. to
P.W.D. Asst. to Executive Ofr. in charge of Benares road 6 Dec.
1844. On special duty conducting archaeological inquiries in Bihar
and Benares 15 Feb. 1848 till 1853. Superintended erection of coll.

at Benares 1849-50. Fur. 1853 till death. No record of active service. Author of " Architecture of Hindustan."
Refs. : *A.J.* N.S. xxv. 250 ; xxix. 54. *I.M.* 29 Apr. 1853, p. 242. *G.M.* 1853, i. 676.

KNATCHBULL, Reginald Edward (1812-1885). Lieut. General. Artillery. *b.* Mersham, Kent, 11 May 1812. Cadet 1828. Arrived in India 23 Mar. 1829. 2nd Lieut. 12 June 1828. Lieut. 17 Jan. 1836. Capt. 21 Dec. 1845. Major 28 Sept. 1857. Lt. Col. 27 Aug. 1858. Col. 29 Apr. 1861. Maj. Gen. 28 Aug. 1871 (ante-dated to 6 Mar. 1868). Retired 1 Aug. 1872. Hon. Lt. Gen. 1 Aug. 1872. *d.* Claremont Court, St. Helier, Jersey, 12 Apr. 1885.

Of Claremont Court. 8th and youngest son of Sir Edward Knatchbull, 8th Bart., of Mersham Hatch, Kent, and Mary his 3rd wife, dau. of Thomas Hawkins, of Nash Court, Kent. *m.* 1st, 11 July 1845, Lucy Eleanor, 2nd dau. of Capt. William Bowen. (She died Ludhiana, 20 Sept. 1847, aged 18.) *m.* 2nd, Sialkot, 21 Oct. 1852, Sarah Emma, eldest dau. of Owen Lomer, *q.v.* (She died 23 Nov. 1907.) Addiscombe Cadet 1826-8.

Services : Posted to 3rd Troop 3rd Bde. H.A. 14 Mar. 1833. Transfd. to 1st Troop 3rd Bde. 18 June 1836 ; to 1st Troop 2nd Bde. 1840. Fur. 17 May 1844 till 1846. Served with 7th Bn. Foot Art. for over ten yrs. Fur. 1858-60. No record of active service.

Refs. : Burke's *Peerage*, 1923, p. 329, *s.n.* Brabourne, B. *The Times*, 17 Apr. 1885.

KNIGHT, George (1779-?). Lieut. Colonel. 22nd N.I. *bapt.* Loders, Dorset, 1 May 1779. Cadet 1798. Arrived in India 6 Nov. 1799. Ensign 31 Dec. 1799. Lieut. 29 May 1800. Capt. 23 Sept. 1810. Major 13 June 1819. Lt. Col. 1 May 1824. Pensioned 6 Jan. 1825. Retired 1828. *d.* 1837/38 ?

Son of George Knight and Lydia his wife.

Services : Second Mahratta War ; Laswari ; Bhurtpore ; Lieut. 12th N.I. Operations in Oudh 1808 ; Lieut. 12th N.I. Capt. 1/12th N.I. Capture of Java 1811 ; Cornelis (w.) ; Capt. 4th Bengal Vol. Bn. Served with Vols. in Java till 1816. Posted as Lt. Col. to 22nd N.I. May 1824. Fur. 12 Jan. 1827 till retirement.

KNIGHT, John. Lieutenant. Infantry. Cadet 1780. Ensign (?). Lieut. 1 Feb. 1781. Struck off 1788.

Services : N.F.P.

KNIGHT, John Rogers (1790-1825). Captain, 49th N.I. *b.* Conyers, Somerset, 3 June 1790. Cadet 1804. Arrived in India 13 May 1806. Ensign 5 Apr. 1806. Lieut. 23 Sept. 1807. Capt. 11 July 1823. *d.* Calcutta, 19 Dec. 1825, of fever.

2nd son of Rev. Robert Knight, vicar of Tewkesbury, and Ann his wife.
Services : Barasat C.C. Posted as Ensign to 25th N.I. in 1807. Lieut. 2/25th N.I. Served with Java Inf. Vols. 1812-5; with L.I. Vol. Bn. 1816. Third Mahratta War; Lieut. 2/25th N.I. Transfd. to 49th N.I. (late 1/25th) May 1824. First Burma War; Arakan 1825; Capt. 49th N.I.
Refs. : *G.M.* 1826, ii. 191.

KNOTT, George. Captain. Infantry. Cadet 1762. Ensign Aug. 1763. Lieut. 17 Mar. 1764. Capt. 8 July 1766. Resigned 18 Nov. 1788.
Services : N.F.P.

KNOWLES, Samuel (*d.* 1797). Major, Infantry. Country Cadet 1769. Admitted 8 Aug. 1769. Ensign 11 Oct. 1769. Lieut. 2 Apr. 1773. Capt. 29 Jan. 1781. Major 1 Mar. 1794. *d. unm.* Barrackpore 24 July 1797.
Brother of George Knowles, and of Mrs. Ursula Martin, of Thetford, Norfolk.
Services : 5th Bengal Eur. Bn. in July 1787. Second Rohilla War; battle of Bitaurah; Major comdg. 21st Bn. Sepoys.
Refs. : *Williams*, p. 173. Will proved in 1797.

KNOX, Sir Alexander (1759/60-1834). Major General, K.C.B. Colonel 5th L.C. *b.* London 1759/60. Cadet 1780. Admitted 6 Oct. 1780. Cornet 6 Oct. 1780. Lieut. 4 Aug. 1781. Capt. 29 May 1800. Major 1 May 1804. Lt. Col. 15 Aug. 1809. Col. 12 Aug. 1819. Maj. Gen. 22 July 1830. *d.* Barrackpore 1 Sept. 1834.
Brother of William Hunter Douglas Knox, *q.v. m.* 1st, Rewari, 22 Nov. 1817, Miss Maria Becher. (She died 28 May 1822.) *m.* 2nd, Dinapore, 8 July 1829, Charlotte Rosina, eldest dau. of John Gerrard, *q.v.* (*See also* Nicholas Penny.)
Services : Sailed for India on the *Ponsbourne*, 3 Apr. 1780, aged 20. Campaign against the Rajah of Benares 1781; capture of Bijaigarh. Lieut. 14th Bn. Sepoys in July 1787. Third Mysore War; Bangalore; Savandrug; Utradrug; Seringapatam; Lieut. 1st N.C. Second Rohilla War; battle of Bitaurah; Lieut. 1st N.C. Qmr. 2nd N.C. Apr. 1799 till May 1800. Operations in Jumna Doab 1803; Sasni; Bijaigarh; Kachaura. Second Mahratta War; Aligarh; battle of Delhi (horse kld. under him); Agra; Laswari; battle and capture of Deig; Bhurtpore; Major 2nd N.C. Third Mahratta War; Lt. Col. comdg. 4th Cav. Bde., 4th Div.; siege and capture of Taragarh; Bdr. comdg. the force. To comd. troops in Rajputana 26 Dec. 1818. Operations in Jodhpur 1823;

capture of Lamba ; Bdr. comdg. Rajputana F.F. Apptd. to Gen. Staff with rank of Bdr. 1 Apr. 1827. Comdd. Rajputana F.F. till 31 Dec. 1827. To comd. Dinapore Div. 1 Oct. 1828. Col. 7th L.C. 22 Aug. 1833 ; transfd. to 5th L.C. 24 Dec. 1833. K.C.B. 27 Sept. 1831.

Refs. : *E.I.M.C.* iii. 202-9. *D.I.B.* *A.J.* N.S. xvi. 137. Will dated Barrackpore 7 Sept. 1833 ; proved 9 Sept. 1834. M.I. Barrackpore cemetery.

KNOX, John Samuel (1808-1891). Lieut. Colonel. 42nd N.I. *bapt.* Aghadowey, co. Londonderry, 13 Mar. 1808. Cadet 1827. Arrived in India 9 June 1828. Ensign 23 Feb. 1828. Lieut. 6 July 1838. Capt. 17 Feb. 1850. Bt. Major 20 June 1854. Retired 9 Aug. 1854. Hon. Lt. Col. 11 May 1855. *d.* Rozel, St. John's Park, Ryde, I.W., 23 Nov. 1891, aged 83.

Son of John Knox, of Rushbrooke, co. Londonderry, linen merchant. *m.* Biggleswade, Beds., 15 Apr. 1846, Alice Caroline Catherine, 2nd dau. of Robert Lindsell, of Fairfield and Holme, Beds., J.P. and D.L., high sheriff. (She died Dunbar, nr. Enniskillen, 24 Mar. 1853.)

Services : Posted as Ensign to 42nd N.I. 4 Nov. 1828. Actg. Intr. & Qmr. 42nd N.I. 10 Dec. 1832 ; do. 39th N.I. 29 May 1833 ; do. 27th N.I. 18 Sept. 1834. Intr. & Qmr. 42nd N.I. 22 Sept. 1838 till Mar. 1843. First Afghan War 1839-42 ; operations in vicinity of Kandahar ; Ghazni ; various engagements leading to re-occupation of Kabul ; Lieut. 42nd N.I. (Medal). Fur. p.a. 1 Apr. 1843 till Apr. 1846. Intr. & Qmr. 42nd N.I. 12 Apr. 1848 till 2 Nov. 1849. Fur. s.c. 9 Feb. 1852 till retirement.

Refs. : Burke's *Landed Gentry*, 13th edn., p. 1097, *s.n.* Lindsell, of Fairfield, Beds. *The Patrician*, i. 83. *The Times*, 25 Nov. 1891.

KNOX, Randfurlie (1730 *or* 1734-1764). Major, Bengal Eur. Regt. *b.* Sligo 1730 *or* 1734—probably the latter. Ensign (Madras) (17 June 1754) 16 June 1755. Lieut. (Madras) 7 Feb. 1757. Capt. (Bengal) 1 Sept. 1758. Major 2 Aug. 1763. *d.* Patna, 28 Jan. 1764, aged 34 : bur. at Bankipore, B. & O.

Son of John Knox and Rebecca his wife. Brother of Lieut. John Knox, of the Marines, and of Lucy Foster(Forster or Forester). Cousin of Capt. Mitchelburne Knox, E.I.C.S., previously in Maj.-Gen. Barrington's (8th) Regt.

Services : Sailed for India on the *Denham* in 1753, aged 19. Transfd. from Madras Eur. Bn. to Bengal Est. in Sept. 1758. Expedn. to the N. Circars 1758-9 ; Condore ; Rajamundry ; Masulipatam ; Capt. comdg. 1st Sepoy Bn. War with Shah Alam 1760 ;

comdd. the detachment which relieved Patna ; Birpur. War with Mir Muhammad Kasim 1763 ; Katwa ; Gheria ; Udhua Nullah ; Monghyr ; siege and capture of Patna. Apptd. Q.M.G. to Major Adams's force July 1763. Succeeded Major Adams in comd. of the army in the field 9 Dec. 1763, but being in ill health was obliged to hand over the comd. to Major William Jennings, *q.v.*, the following month.

Refs. : Major Randfurlie Knox : *Dilawar Jang Bahadur*, by Mr. S. C. Hill, in the *Journal of the Bihar & Orissa Research Soc.* for Mar. 1917. Forde. Broome. Will dated 22 and 27 Jan. 1764 ; proved 29 June 1764 ; proved *P.C.*, Ireland, 1765. M.I. at Patna.

KNOX, Robert Trotter (1807-1841). Bt. Captain, 6th L.C. *b.* Charlemont Fort, co. Armagh, Nov. 1807. Cadet 1825. Arrived in India 7 July 1826. Cornet 15 Mar. 1826. Lieut. 30 Oct. 1837. Bt. Capt. 15 Mar. 1841. *d.* Sultanpur, Benares, 20 Nov. 1841.

Son of Francis Arthur Skene Knox, Bt. Major R.A. Related to the Trotters, of Ballindean, co. Perth, and directly descended from William Knox, of Gifford, the father of John Knox, the reformer. *m.* Edinburgh, 7 Mar. 1839, Charlotte Knox, dau. of William Trotter, of Ballindean.

Services : Cornet d.d. 1st L.C. 17 Aug. 1826. Posted to 4th L.C. 26 Sept. 1826. (? Shekhawat expedn. 1834 ; Cornet 4th L.C.) Transfd. to 6th L.C. 9 June 1836. Fur. p.a. 27 Jan. 1837 till 31 Dec. 1839.

Refs. : Burke's *Landed Gentry*, 2nd edn., p. 1436, *s.n.* Trotter, of Ballindean, co. Perth. *A.J.* N.S. xxviii. 348. *G.M.* 1842, i. 566.

KNOX, Thomas Saunders (1780-1818). Captain, Pension Est. 7th N.C. *b.* Christ church, Cork, 10 June 1780. Cadet 1795. Arrived in India 22 Oct. 1796. Cornet 14 Nov. 1796. Lieut. 29 May 1800. Capt. 24 Oct. 1805. Pensioned 1 May 1809. bur. Calcutta 6 Jan. 1818.

Son of George Knox and Ann his wife.

Services : Posted as Ensign to 2nd Bengal Eur. Regt. in 1796. Transfd. as Cornet to 4th N.C. (? Operations in Jumna Doab 1803 ; Sasni ; Bijaigarh ; Kachaura. Second Mahratta War ; Laswari ; Lieut. 4th N.C.) Transfd. as Capt. to newly-raised 7th N.C. in 1805. (? Operations in Oudh 1808 ; Capt. 7th N.C.) Pensioned owing to insanity, and died in the insane hospital in Calcutta.

KNOX, William (1762/63-1782). Lieutenant, Infantry. *b.* 1762/63. Cadet 1781. Ensign 1781. Lieut. Aug. 1782. *d.* Cawnpore, 15 Sept. 1782, aged 19 : kld. in a duel.

3rd son of James Knox, of Moyne Abbey, co. Mayo, high sheriff 1758, and Dorothea his wife, dau. of Peter Ruttledge, of Cornfield.

Kinsman (*probably* cousin-german) of Francis Rutledge (1760/61-1817), *q.v.*
Services : Apptd. Cadet on 16 Jan. 1781, aged 19. Sailed for India on the *Southampton*, 13 Mar. 1781, aged 19.
Refs. : Burke's *Landed Gentry of Ireland*, p. 374, *s.n.* Knox, of Brittas Castle, co. Tipperary. Will dated Cawnpore 1 Sept. 1782.

KNOX, William Hunter Douglas (1762/63-1829). Colonel, 5th L.C. *b.* London 1762/63. Cadet 1781. Admitted 6 May 1782. Cornet 10 May 1781. Lieut. 20 Sept. 1782. Capt. 13 Nov. 1800. Major 11 Mar. 1805. Lt. Col. 27 Feb. 1812. Lt. Col. Comdt. 12 Dec. 1823. Col. 5 June 1829. *d.* Edinburgh 1 Dec. 1829.
Of Athol Cresc., Edinburgh. Brother of Sir Alexander Knox, *q.v. m.* Edinburgh, 29 Nov. 1826, Jane, eldest dau. of John Waite, of London. (She *re-m.* 24 July 1835, C. E. Wylde.)
Services : Apptd. Cadet on 8 Mar. 1781, aged 18. Sailed for India on the *Blandford*, 26 June 1781, aged 18. Lieut. 35th Bn. Sepoys in July 1787. Lieut. 3rd N.C. Capt. Lt. 3rd N.C. 29 May 1800. Capt. 3rd N.C. Resdt. in Nepal 1803-5. Transfd. as Major to newly-raised 7th N.C. in 1805. Operations in Oudh 1808. Settlement of Hariana 1809-10. Nepal War 1814-5 ; Lt. Col. 7th N.C., in 2nd Div. Siege and capture of Hathras ; Lt. Col. 7th N.C. Transfd. to 1st N.C. in 1817. Third Mahratta War. Fur. 1819-23. Transfd. to 8th N.C. in 1819 ; to 4th L.C. in 1820 ; to 7th L.C. in 1823. Posted as Lt. Col. Comdt. to 5th L.C. in 1824. Fur. 1824 till death.
Refs. : *N. & Q.* 4S. v. 227, 350. *G.M.* 1826, ii. 556 ; 1829, ii. 651. *A.J.* N.S. i. 58.

KNUDSON, Christian (*d.* 1792). Colonel, Infantry. Comdt. at Chunar. *b.* Wendelbor, Denmark. Lieut. 12 Oct. 1763. Capt. 8 Aug. 1765. Lt. Col. 2 Jan. 1781. Col. 29 May 1786. *d.* Chunar 31 Aug. 1792.
A Dane. Brother of " Lady Bergetta Maria Mazar, wife of F. De Mazar, Esq." (*Probably* brother of Peter Knudson, *q.v.*) *m.* (?). His dau., Cecilia, *m.* 1800, John Berkeley Deane, of Berkeley, co. Wexford.
Services : Ensign H.M. 84th Foot 27 June 1762 ; h.p. do. 25 Dec. 1764. Transfd. as Lieut. to Bengal army in 1763. Battle of Buxar ; Lieut. 11th Bn. Sepoys. Major 1/3rd Bengal Eur. Regt. in Oct. 1779. Second Mysore War. Comdg. at Fatehgarh in July 1787 ; do. Dinapore in 1790.
Refs. : *Williams*, p. 150. Burke's *Landed Gentry of Ireland*, p. 170, *s.n.* Deane, late of Glendaragh, co. Wicklow. Will dated 4 June 1790. M.I. at Chunar.

THE BENGAL ARMY, 1758-1834   609

KNUDSON, Peter (*d.* 1768). Lieutenant. Infantry. Cadet 1762. Ensign 16 May 1763. Lieut. 1 Feb. 1764. Resigned 25 May 1766. *d.* Calcutta 4 July 1768.

(*Probably* brother of Christian Knudson, *q.v.*)
Services : Resigned his Commission during the " Batta mutiny " in May 1766, and was not re-admitted.

KNYVETT, Arthur (1804-1886). Colonel. 1st Eur. Bengal Fus. *b.* London 3 Dec. 1804. Cadet 1820. Arrived in India Sept. 1821. Ensign 4 Apr. 1821. Lieut. 4 Sept. 1823. Capt. 13 Mar. 1835. Major 26 Oct. 1848. Lt. Col. 1 Feb. 1854. Retired 24 Apr. 1855. Hon. Col. 11 May 1855. *d.* Sonning, Berks., 18 Apr. 1886.

4th son of Charles Knyvett, of Sonning, organist of St. George's, Hanover Sq. (*D.N.B.*), and Jane his wife, dau. of John Laney, of Shorwell, I.W. Brother of John Knyvett, *q.v.*, and cousin-german of Frederick Knyvett, *q.v.* Ed. Westminster ; admitted 27 Mar. 1818 ; left Xmas 1818.

Services : Posted as Ensign to 1/1st N.I. Transfd. to 1/27th N.I. 5 Mar. 1822. To do duty with 1/29th N.I. 3 May 1822. Transfd. to newly-raised 32nd N.I. July 1823 ; to 64th N.I. (late 2/32nd) May 1824. Asst. to Agent for timber at Natpur, Bengal, 21 Oct. 1826. Fur. s.c. 14 mos. to Cape 30 Sept. 1828. Intr. & Qmr. 64th N.I. till 1 Sept. 1829. In charge of 14th (Saugor) Div. P.W.D. 16 Oct. 1837 till 1841. First Afghan War 1842 ; Khyber ; Capt. 64th N.I., with Gen. Pollock's force (Medal). Fur. 12 Apr. 1843 till 12 Nov. 1844. (? Operations against the Hill tribes in Sind 1845 ; Capt. 64th N.I.) Posted as Lt. Col. to 74th N.I. Apr. 1854 ; to 64th N.I. Oct. 1854 ; to 1st Eur. Fus. Dec. 1854.

Refs. : Burke's *Family Records*, p. 364. *Westminster School Register. The Times*, 21 Apr. 1886.

KNYVETT, Frederick (1805-1857). Bt. Lieut. Colonel, 64th N.I. *b.* London 18 Dec. 1805. Cadet 1821. Arrived in India 25 June 1822. Ensign (19 Jan. 1822) 11 July 1823. Lieut. 13 May 1825. Capt. 8 Oct. 1839. Major 1 Feb. 1854. Bt. Lt. Col. 28 Nov. 1854. *d.* Burhie 10 July 1857.

bapt. Marylebone 26 June 1808. 2nd son of William Knyvett, gentleman and composer of the Chapel Royal (*D.N.B.*), and Sarah his wife, dau. of John Laney. Brother of William John Baptist Knyvett, *q.v.*, and cousin-german of John Knyvett, *q.v. m.* Dacca, 25 July 1831, Helen Maria, dau. of Henry Williams, B.C.S., and sister of George Walter Williams, *q.v.* (*See also* Henry John McGeorge.) Ed. Burlington House, Fulham.

Services : Ensign d.d. 1/5th N.I. 24 Dec. 1822. Posted as Ensign to 32nd N.I. July 1823. Transfd. to 64th N.I. (late 2/32nd) May 1824. Actg. Intr. & Qmr. 64th N.I. 13 Sept. 1828 till 22 June 1829. Leave s.c. to Cape 6 Apr. 1832 till 18 Nov. 1833. Bde. Major to troops at Ferozepore 11 Nov. 1840 till 1 Dec. 1841. First Afghan War; retreat from Ali Masjid to Jamrud Jan. 1842; Capt. 64th N.I. Fur. s.c. 3 Mar. 1842 till 12 Nov. 1844. Offg. in P.W.D. Apptd. to Grand Trunk Road Div., P.W.D., 30 Jan. 1846; Executive Ofr. do. 30 May 1854 till death.

Refs. : Burke's *Family Records*, p. 364. *I.M.* 1857, p. 587.

KNYVETT, John (1803-1854). Captain. 66th N.I. *b.* London 29 Aug. 1803. Cadet 1820. Arrived in India Sept. 1821. Ensign 4 Apr. 1821. Lieut. 29 Aug. 1823. Capt. 4 Jan. 1832. Invalided 25 Nov. 1842. Retired 23 Mar. 1854. *d.* the Rectory, Heslerton, Yorks., 24 Oct. 1854.

3rd son of Charles Knyvett, of Sonning, Berks., and Jane his wife. Brother of Arthur Knyvett, *q.v.*

Services : Posted as Ensign to 1/27th N.I. Transfd. to newly-raised 33rd N.I. July 1823; to 66th N.I. (late 2/33rd) May 1824. Fur. s.c. 4 Nov. 1825 till 24 Oct. 1828. Offg. Adjt. 66th N.I. 11 June 1832. Leave s.c. 2 yrs. to Tasmania 18 Mar. 1835; fur. s.c. 8 Feb. 1839 till 4 Mar. 1842, and 21 Feb. 1847 till 28 Jan. 1850. No record of active service.

Refs. : Burke's *Family Records*, p. 364. *G.M.* 1854, ii. 644. *I.M.* 30 Oct. 1854, p. 629.

KNYVETT, William John Baptist (1803-1863). Major General. 38th N.I. *b.* London 30 Sept. 1803. Cadet 1821. Arrived in India 20 Aug. 1822. Ensign 28 Mar. 1822. Lieut. 13 May 1825. Capt. 30 Mar. 1837. Major 6 Jan. 1852. Lt. Col. 25 May 1857. Retired 31 Dec. 1861. Hon. Maj. Gen. 31 Dec. 1861. *d.* Dehra Dun, 6 Jan. 1863, of apoplexy.

Eldest son of William Knyvett (*D.N.B.*) and Sarah his wife. Brother of Frederick Knyvett, *q.v. m.* 1st, Cawnpore, 10 Mar. 1828, Elizabeth Dobree, 5th dau. of J. Morris, of Staines, Middlesex. *m.* 2nd, Calcutta, 1 Sept. 1831, Fanny Agnes, dau. of Nathaniel Cumberlege, *q.v.* (She died Dehra Dun, 10 Dec. 1879, aged 70.)

Services : Posted as Ensign to 19th N.I. Transfd. to 38th N.I. (late 1/19th) May 1824. Offg. Adjt. 6th Local Horse 26 Feb. 1825. Actg. Adjt. Bundelkhand Provl. Bn. 17 Mar. 1826. Second in comd. 6th Local Horse 1 Sept. 1828. Adjt. 38th N.I. 17 Jan. 1831. Operations against the Bhils in Sambalpur and Bamanghati, B. & O., 1832; Lieut. 38th N.I. Fur. s.c. 19 Sept. 1832 till 26 Dec. 1835. Offg. Adjt. Calcutta Native Mil. 16 Feb. 1836. Asst. to P.A. in

THE BENGAL ARMY, 1758-1834   611

Upper Sind 20 May 1840. Asst., 1 cl., to P.A. in Sind and Baluchistan 10 Jan. 1842. Posted as Lt. Col. to 38th N.I. July 1857.
Refs.: Burke's *Family Records*, p. 364. *A.J.* xxvi. 486; N.S. vii. 158.

KOEHLER, George Frederick (*c* 1730-1763). 2nd Lieutenant, Artillery. *b. c.* 1730. Cadet 1758. Fireworker 8 Jan. 1759. 2nd Lieut. 16 Oct. 1761. *d.* 2 Aug. 1763 : kld. in action at the battle of Gheria.

A native of Frankfurt, Prussia.
Services : Was a Corporal in Capt. Thomas Smith's Coy. of 2nd Bn. R.A. when given a Bengal cadetship in May 1758. Sailed for India on the *Bombay Castle* in 1758, aged 27. Battle of Gheria (kld.).
Refs. : M.I. in Patna city (where the name is incorrectly given as "George Hockler ").
Note : Stubbs's List gives two individuals, " G. F. Kaylor " (No. 14) and " George F. Hockler " (No. 17). This is manifestly wrong.

***KRAFT, —— ** (*d.* 1763). Ensign, Infantry. Cadet (?). Ensign (?). *d.* 1 July 1763 : kld. in action at the battle of Manjhi.
Services : N.F.P.
Refs. : MS. list in India Office entitled, " List of Persons killed in the Massacre at Patna, and at other places during the Troubles, 1763." *Firminger*, p. 71.

KYAN, Dennis (1778-1812). Lieutenant, Invalid Pension Est. 5th N.I. *b.* Carlow 1778. Cadet 1798. Arrived in India 17 Sept. 1799. Ensign 29 Sept. 1799. Lieut. 28 Oct. 1799. Invalided 28 Aug. 1806. *d. unm.* Calcutta 9 Aug. 1812.

Eldest son of James Kyan, of Carlow, and Ellen his wife, dau. of Thomas MacCarthy. Brother of John Howard Kyan, *q.v.*, nephew of Francis Kyan, *q.v.*, and cousin-german of Thomas Sutton Kyan, *q.v.*
Refs. : Burke's *Landed Gentry*, 5th edn., p. 744, *s.n.* Kyan, of Ballymurtagh, co. Wicklow.

KYAN, Francis (1752-1814). Bt. Colonel, 22nd N.I. *b.* 1752. Cadet 1778. Admitted 10 Dec. 1778. Ensign Dec. 1778. Lieut. 20 Oct. 1778. Capt. 1 June 1796. Major 29 May 1800. Lt. Col. 15 Aug. 1803. Bt. Col. 1 Jan. 1812. *d.* in U.K. 18 Aug. 1814.

4th and youngest son of Howard Kyan, of Mount Howard and Ballymurtagh, co. Wicklow, and Frances his wife, dau. of Laurence Esmonde, of Ballynastray, co. Wexford. Uncle of Dennis Kyan, *q.v.*, John Howard Kyan, *q.v.*, and Thomas Sutton Kyan, *q.v. m.* 1798, Jane, dau. of James Blackney, of Ballycormuck, co. Carlow, and sister of James Blackney, *q.v.* (She died Tinny Park, nr. Kilkenny, 27 Mar. 1836.) His only dau. *m.* Michael (D.) Keating, *q.v.*

Services : Lieut. 3rd Bn. Sepoys in July 1787. Returned from fur. 20 Sept. 1799. Capt. 2nd N.I. Major 2/2nd N.I. Second Mahratta War ; battle of Delhi ; Major comdg. 1/2nd N.I. ; battle and capture of Deig ; Bhurtpore ; Lt. Col. comdg. 2/22nd N.I. Fur. 1813 till death.

Refs. : Burke's *Landed Gentry*, 5th edn., p. 744, *s.n.* Kyan, of Ballymurtagh, co. Wicklow. *G.M.* 1814, ii. 294. Will dated 25 Jan. 1814 ; proved in 1815.

KYAN, John Howard (1779-1844). Captain, Pension Est. 2nd L.C. *b.* 1779. Cadet 1799. Arrived in India 11 Jan. 1801. Cornet 14 Apr. 1801. Lieut. 11 Mar. 1805. Capt. 1 Jan. 1819. Pensioned 30 Jan. 1821. *d.* 17 Jan. 1844.

2nd son of James Kyan, of Carlow, and Ellen his wife. Brother of Dennis Kyan, *q.v. m.* Muttra, 27 Oct. 1809, Mary, dau. of Christopher Baldock, and sister of Christopher Baldock, *q.v.* (*See also* Christopher Sullivan Fagan.)

Services : Posted as Cornet to 2nd N.C. and served throughout with that Regt. Operations in Jumna Doab 1803. Second Mahratta War ; battle of Delhi ; Laswari ; battle of Deig. Qmr. 2nd N.C. 20 Mar. 1810 till Dec. 1814. Nepal War 1814, in 1st Div. Third Mahratta War, in Reserve Div. Fur. 29 Dec. 1818 till pensioned.

Refs. : Burke's *Landed Gentry*, 5th edn., p. 744, *s.n.* Kyan, of Ballymurtagh, co. Wicklow. *A.J.* 3S. ii. 445.

KYAN, Thomas Sutton (1785-1813). Lieutenant, 9th N.I. *b.* 1785. Cadet 1806. Arrived in India 25 Nov. 1807. Ensign 10 Oct. 1807. Lieut. 5 June 1811. *d. unm.* Calcutta 13 Sept. 1813.

bapt. Rathdrum, co. Wicklow, 20 Dec. 1785. Younger son of John Howard Kyan, of Mount Howard and Ballymurtagh, co. Wicklow, and Phillis his wife, dau. of Thomas Sutton, Comte de Clonard. Nephew of Francis Kyan, *q.v.*, cousin-german of Dennis Kyan, *q.v.*, and uncle of William Carleton Ormsby, *q.v.* Brother of John Howard Kyan (*D.N.B.*).

Services : Barasat C.C. Posted as Ensign to 9th N.I. in 1808. Fur. s.c. 1809-13. No record of active service.

Refs. : Burke's *Landed Gentry*, 5th edn., p. 744, *s.n.* Kyan, of Ballymurtagh, co. Wicklow.

KYD, Alexander (1754-1826). Lieut. General, Engineers. Chief Engr. at Calcutta. *b.* in Scotland 14 Mar. 1754. Cadet 1775. Ensign 11 Dec. 1775. Lieut. 9 Oct. 1778. Capt. 13 Feb. 1781. Major 23 Feb. 1793. Lt. Col. 25 Apr. 1797. Col. 1 Jan. 1805. Maj. Gen. 25 July 1810. Lt. Gen. 12 Aug. 1819. *d.* Albemarle St., London, 25 Nov. 1826.

Son of James Kyd, Capt. R.N. Brother of Anne, widow of William Elmsall, of Brierly Manor, Yorks., and of Helen, widow of Dr. James Nairne, of Pittenweem, co. Fife. Related to Robert Kyd, *q.v.*, whose heir he was. *m.* Clifton, Somerset, 13 Nov. 1804, Eliza, dau. of —— Wagstaff, and widow of Edward Hay, B.C.S., Sec. to the Bengal Govt. (She died 22 Jan. 1819, aged 56.)

Services : Was Town Major at Fort William in July 1787. Constructed fortifications on the Andamans. Surveyor Gen. and Comdt. at Budge-Budge in 1790. Third Mysore War. Engr. in the field at Allahabad in 1803. Fur. 1804-7. Chief Engr. at Calcutta, and M.M.B., Sept. 1807. Fur. 22 Jan. 1810 till death. F.R.S. Author of " Tidal Observations in the Hooghly."

Refs. : *Hickey*, iii. 362. *Thackeray*, p. 6. *Bath Chron.* *G.M.* 1804, ii. 1070; 1826, ii. 570. Will dated 18 Dec. 1823; proved 16 June 1827. M.I. in St. John's Wood church, London.

KYD, John Bevis (1787-1806). Cadet, Infantry. *b.* in India 20 June 1787. Cadet 1805. Never arrived in India. *d.* at sea 20 Apr. 1806: lost in the wreck of the *Lady Burges* off Bonavista I. (? Tinian I., Ladrones.)

bapt. Thornhill, Yorks., 23 Feb. 1797. Natural son of A. Kyd by a European woman. Nephew of Anne Elmsall.

KYD, Robert (1746-1793). Lieut. Colonel, Infantry. *b.* 1746. Cadet 1764. Ensign 27 Oct. 1764. Lieut. 16 Oct. 1765. Capt. 3 Apr. 1768. Major 4 Sept. 1780. Lt. Col. 7 Dec. 1782. *d.* Calcutta 26 May 1793.

Descended from an old Forfarshire family, and related to Alexander Kyd, *q.v.*, to whom he bequeathed the bulk of his property.

Services : See *D.N.B.* Apptd. Adjt. of Sepoy Bns. in 1st Bde. at Monghyr Aug. 1765. Returned from fur. 3 Apr. 1786. Sec. to the Supreme Council, in the Mily. Dept. of Inspection, 24 Aug. 1786 till death. Proposed the formation of the Botanical Gdns. nr. Calcutta, which he laid out in 1786. Hon. Supt. of the Gdns. till death.

Refs. : *D.N.B.* *D.I.B.* Memorial marble urn, by Banks, in the Botanical Gdns., Calcutta.

CORRIGENDA

Vol. i. page xxxii, footnote : *for* 1824 *read* 1924.

Vol. i. page xxxiii, footnote : *for* 1809 *read* 1909.

Vol. i. page xliii, line 29 : *for* May 14 (Battle of Arikera) *read* May 15.

ANSTRUTHER, Hon. David.

Vol. i. page 41, lines 17-20 : *for* 3rd son . . . Newark *read* 3rd son of Alexander Anstruther, titular Lord Newark, a merchant at Boulogne, by his wife, dau. of Capt. Price, E.I.C.S. Younger brother of John Anstruther, who assumed the title of Lord Newark on his father's death in 1791.

Line 23 : *for* Nawab Wazir of Oudh's Body Guard *read* Nawab Nazim's bodyguard at Murshidabad.

ANSTRUTHER, Robert Lindsay.

Vol. i. page 41, lines 29 and 30 : *for* 1789 *read* 1787.

ASHE, Benjamin.

Vol. i. page 55, line 4 : *delete* ' Probably.'

ASHHURST, James Henry.

Vol. i. page 56, line 25 : *for* 1715 *read* 1815.

BAILLIE, Lamington.

Vol. i. page 73, line 5 from bottom : *for* 1805 *read* 1806.

BAINES, Charles Henry.

Vol. i. page 76, line 22 : *for* (? dau. of Thomas Raban, of Calcutta.) *read* dau. of Robert Raban, and niece of Thomas Raban, of Calcutta.

BAUGH, James.

Vol. i. page 105, line 9 : *for* Robert Walker Baugh *read* Job Walker Baugh and Elizabeth his wife.

BELLEW, Edmund.

Vol. i. page 126, line 3 from bottom : *for* 1 Feb. *read* 5 Feb.

CORRIGENDA

BIRCH, Sir Richard James Holwell.
Vol i. page 145, line 9 : *for* William Rider, sheriff of Calcutta 1757 *read* Jacob Rider, B.C.S.

BIRCH, Robert.
Vol. i. page 145, line 19 : *for* Robert *read* Robert Johnston. Lines 22 and 27 *delete* ' ?.'

BIRD, Henry Frederick.
Vol. i. page 146, line 8 from bottom : *for* 1799 *read* 1779.

BLACK, Peter (*alias* Patrick).
Vol. i. page 154, line 16 : *for* (She died 23 Dec. 1859, aged 74.) *read* (She died London 23 Mar. 1860, aged 75).

BLAGRAVE, George.
Vol. i. page 158, line 32 : *delete* ' Probably.'
Line 35 : *delete* ' ?.'

BLAIR, Charles Devaynes.
Vol. i. page 159, line 2 : *for* Ramsay *read* Ramsey.

BOWE, William.
Vol. i. page 185, lines 23 and 27 : *for* Harworth, Notts. *read* Hurworth-upon-Tees, co. Durham.

BRERETON, William Bolton.
Vol. i. page 200 : *Note :* This biography is possibly incorrect. There appears to be some confusion with one Boulter Brereton, sometime Lieut. H.M. 68th Foot. Corrected biographies of both officers will appear at the end of Part III.

BREWER, Philip.
Vol. i. page 201, line 6 from bottom : *for Services read Refs.*

BROOKS, James.
Vol. i. page 217, line 10 : *for* Brooke *read* Brooks.

BROWN, Samuel.
Vol. i. page 227, line 15 : *for* England *read* Belfast.

BURROWES, Alexander.
Vol. i. page 261, line 23 : *for* Berhampore, Bengal *read* nr. Farrukhabad, U.P.

CAMAC, Jacob.
Vol. i. page 277, lines 4 and 3 from bottom : *for* 1744/45 *read* 1745.

CORRIGENDA

CAMERON, Hugh Stronach.
   Vol. i. page 278, line 30 : *for* Stronack *read* Stronach.

CAMPBELL, James (1789-1806).
   Vol. i. page 289, line 6 : *for* Infantry *read* Artillery.

CAREW, Henry Holdsworth.
   Vol. i. page 301, line 8 : *for* Infantry *read* Artillery.

CARNAC, John.
   Vol. i. page 305, line 33 : *for* b. 1716 *read* b. London c. 1720.
   Line 38 : *delete* ' Possibly.'

CASEMENT, Hugh.
   Vol. i. page 317, line 8 from bottom : *for* 6 *read* 26.

CHAIGNEAU, Christopher Theophilus.
   Vol. i. page 325, line 18 : *for* Thomas *read* Theophilus.

CHITTY, Richard.
   Vol. i. page 340, line 5 : *for* 1836 *read* 1736.

CRAIG, William.
   Vol. i. page 403, line 4 from bottom : *for* 1 Feb. *read* 5 Feb.

CRICHTON, Charles.
   Vol. i. page 412, line 9 : *delete* Parentheses and ' Probably.'

CRICHTON, David.
   Vol. i. page 412, line 19 : *delete* Parentheses and ' Probably.'

DALYELL, Alexander.
   Vol. ii. page 6, line 15 : *for* bapt. Barncrosh *read* bapt. Tongland, nr. Kirkcudbright.

DAVIE, Thomas.
   Vol. ii. page 20, line 28 : *for* Dec. *read* Sept.

DE MATTOS, Isaac.
   Vol. ii. page 45, line 18 : *for* June 1795 *read* 27 Apr. 1795.

DENBY, William Charles.
   Vol. ii. page 46, line 7 : *for* bapt. *read* b.

ADDENDA

Add to Bibliography, pp. xvii-xx.

Austen-Leigh. The Eton College Register, 1753-1790, by R. A. Austen-Leigh. Eton, 1921.

De La Ferté. A Notable Record : the descendants of Daniel Van Renen, by E. Joubert de la Ferté. London, 1926.

Greene. Pedigree of the Family of Greene, by Lt.-Col. J. J. Greene, R.A.M.C. Dublin, 1899.

Holzman. The Nabobs in England, by James M. Holzman, Ph.D. New York, 1926.

Wilson. History of the Madras Army, by Col. W. J. Wilson. 5 vols., Madras, 1882-9.

Vol. i. page 1, between lines 3 and 4 from bottom : *add* (*Fortescue*, vol. xii. pp. 32-289).

Vol. i. page lii, between lines 3 and 4 from bottom : *add* (*Fortescue*, vol. xii. pp. 302-24).

Vol. i. page liii, between lines 11 and 12 : *add* (*Fortescue*, vol. xii. pp. 281-300).

Between lines 18 and 19 : *add* (*Fortescue*, vol. xii. pp. 327-40).

Between lines 26 and 27 : *add* (*Fortescue*, vol. xii. pp. 343-90).

Between lines 32 and 33 : *add* (*Fortescue*, vol. xii. pp. 420-69).

Vol. i. page liv, between lines 1 and 2 : *add* (*Fortescue*, vol. xii. pp. 475-98).

ACHMUTY, Arthur Forbes.

Vol. i. page 6 : *add* b. c. 1737/38. Sailed for Madras on the *Chesterfield* in 1758/59, aged 21. Ensign H.M. 84th Regt. 24 June 1762 ; Lieut. do. 16 Nov. 1763 ; h.p. do. 25 Dec. 1764.

ADNETT, Joseph.

Vol. i. page 10, line 3 from bottom : *add* Transfd. from Madras Eur. Bn. to Bengal Est. in 1758.

AFTON, John.

Vol. i. page 11, line 6 : *add* bur. Calcutta 30 May 1782.

ALEXANDER, James (1780-1847).

Vol. i. page 19, line 26 : *add* m. Harriet, 8th dau. of George Bowles, of Mountprospect, co. Cork.

Bottom line : *add* to *Refs.* Burke's *Landed Gentry of Ireland*, p. 67, *s.n.* Bowles, of Ahern, co. Cork.

ALLEN, Andrew.

Vol. i. page 23, bottom line : *add* bapt. 18 May 1787.

ADDENDA

ALLEN, James.
Vol i. page 24, line 5 : *add* Cadet 1763.
Line 7 : *add* Apptd. Cadet 28 Nov. 1763.
Line 9 : *add* to *Refs.* " Journal of the Army under the command of Major Adams in Bengal from 26 June 1763 to 23 March 1764." (*Orme MSS.* vii.)

ALLEN, James (1793-1859).
Vol. i. page 24, line 16 : *add* 4th and youngest son of Thomas Allen, of Crane Hall, Suffolk, and Jane his wife, youngest dau. of William Watts.

ANDERSON, David Dalrymple.
Vol. i. page 29, line 34 : *add* bapt. 5 Oct. 1789. Son of John Anderson, of Windygard, and Jean Dalrymple his wife.

ANDERSON, George.
Vol. i. page 30, line 6 : *add* and Frances Mitchell his wife, of St. Michael's psh:., Dublin.

ANDERSON, James (1784-1811).
Vol. i. page 30, line 2 from bottom : *add* bapt. Cupar 22 Dec. 1784. Son of Bailie James Anderson and Janet Lister his wife.

ANDERSON, John (d. 1812).
Vol. i. page 31, line 16 : *add* (She died Blackheath 21 Feb. 1837).

ANDERSON, John (1787-1806).
Vol. i. page 32, line 5 : *add* bapt. 9 Aug. 1787. Son of John Anderson.

ANDREWS, William Eyre.
Vol. i. page 37, line 9 : *add* His sister m. George Powell Thomas, *q.v.*

ANSTICE, Frederick.
Vol. i. page 40, line 6 from bottom : *add* 2nd dau. of Francis Harvey.

ARABIN, Alfred.
Vol. i. page 45, line 5 : *add* and Henrietta his wife, 3rd dau. of Rt. Hon. Sir Capel Molyneux, 3rd Bart.
Add to *Refs.* Burke's *Peerage*, 1923, p. 1582, *s.n.* Molyneux, Bart.

ARMSTRONG, Alexander (1782-1817).
Vol. i. page 48, line 10 from bottom : *add* 6th son of Robert Armstrong, Capt. 50th Foot, of Hackwood, co. Cavan, and Dorothy his wife, dau. of Mathew Young, of Lahard, co. Cavan.

ADDENDA

ARMSTRONG, Richard.
Vol. i. page 51, line 6 : *add* Son of Ann Armstrong.

ARNAUD, Henry Hawker.
Vol. i. page 52, line 4 : *add* Capt. 7th R. Lancs. Mil. 4 Apr. 1855.

ASHE, Benjamin.
Vol. i. page 55, line 4 : *add* Lieut. 8th (or King's) Foot 27 Jan. 1760.

BABINGTON, William.
Vol. i. page 65, line 16 : *add* Eldest son of Murray Babington.

BAGSHAW, Stephen.
Vol. i. page 70, line 29 : *add* bur. Calcutta 9 Sept. 1786. After resigning the Service he became an attorney in Calcutta, where he acted as sheriff during part of 1784.

BAGSHAWE, Samuel Robinson.
Vol. i. page 70, line 2 from bottom : *add* His sister m. Charles Herbert White, *q.v.*

BAILLIE, William (1752/53-1799).
Vol. i. page 74, line 31 : *add* Started the *Calcutta Chronicle* as a weekly newspaper in Jan. 1786. Artist; executed views of Calcutta.

BAILLIE, William (1786-1806).
Vol i. page 75, line 13 : *add* bapt. Musselburgh 20 Jan. 1787.

BAKER, Henry Minson.
Vol. i. page 78, line 19 : *add* bapt. Bromley St. Leonard 2 Sept. 1785.

BALDOCK, John.
Vol. i. page 83, line 2 : *add* (*See also* Hugh Atkins Reid).

BALDWIN, Philip Homan.
Vol. i. page 83, line 27 : *add* 2nd son of Henry Baldwin, of Mountmellick, Queen's Co., and Margaret his wife, dau. of Philip Homan, of Surock, co. Westmeath. m. Eleanor, dau. of Edward O'Brien, of Ballinacloonagh, Westmeath.

BALDWIN, Thomas James.
Vol. i. page 84, line 6 : *add* and Frances his wife, dau. of John Kearney, D.D. Nephew of Henry John Kearney.

BALFOUR, Francis.
Vol. i. page 84, line 4 from bottom : *add* m. (before 1779) Amelia or Emily.

ADDENDA

BARKER, Sir Robert.
Vol. i. page 92, line 15 : *add* b. St. Anne's, Soho.
Line 18 : *add* Son of Robert Barker, M.D., sometime of Hammersmith. m. Bolsover, co. Derby, 1780.
Line 28 : *add* to *Refs. Holzman.*

BARLAND, Walter.
Vol. i. page 92, line 32 : *add* to *Services* 2nd Lieut. H.M. 87th (Highland Vol.) Regt. 27 Aug. 1759.

BARNARD, Henry Clapton.
Vol. i. page 93, line 13, after *q.v.* : *add* and cousin-german of Sir John Bennet Hearsey, K.C.B., *q.v.*

BARNES, Walter Richard.
Vol. i, page 94, line 27 : *add* Capt. 2nd Royal Surrey Mil. 6 Oct. 1852.

BATEMAN, John (1790-1819).
Vol. i. page 103, line 14 : *add* Uncle of Frederick Colthurst Maitland, *q.v.*

BAUMGARDT, Francis Robert.
Vol. i. page 105, line 22 : *add* Son of John Pieter Baumgardt, of Breslau, Receiver Gen. of revenue at the Cape, and Johanna Elizabeth his wife, sister of Jacob Vanrenen, *q.v.* Uncle of John Laughton, *q.v.*, and brother of Johanna Elizabeth, wife of William White Moore, *q.v.*
Line 28 : *add* to *Refs. De La Ferté.*

BAYLEY, Brook William.
Vol. i. page 106, line 25 : *add* b. Crane Court, London, 9 Mar. 1788. Son of John Bayley and Sarah his wife. Nephew of Folliot Smith.

BAYLISS, William.
Vol. i. page 107, line 1 : *add* and Ann his wife.

BECHER, Samuel John.
Vol. i. page 117, line 1 from bottom : *add* (*See also* George Timins.)

BEDINGFIELD, John George.
Vol. i. page 121, line 20 : *add* d. Upper Sind, 7 Aug. 1841.

BELL, Charles Hamilton.
Vol. i. page 123, line 12 : *add* (She died Nasirabad 19 May 1827, of cholera).

ADDENDA

BELL, William.
Vol. i. page 125, line 23, after ' merchant ' *add* by his wife, dau. of Charles Robertson, of Edinburgh, and sister of James Robertson (1775-1810), *q.v.*

BELLASIS, Joseph Harvey.
Vol. i. page 126, line 13 : *add* Ensign Berks. Mil. 1779.

BELLEW, Francis John.
Vol. i. page 127, line 9 : *add* m. 2nd, Miss Shout.

BURLTON-BENNETT, Francis Edward.
Vol. i. page 130, line 1 from bottom : *add* His sister m. James Ramsay (1808-1868), *q.v.*

BERNARD, William Owen.
Vol. i. page 134, line 10 : *add* bapt. Sutton 20 Jan. 1789.

BETTSWORTH, William Henry Robin.
Vol. i. page 136, line 29 : *add* bapt. Marylebone 13 June 1788. Son of John Bettsworth and Frances his wife.

BICKERTON, Henry.
Vol. i. page 137, line 19 : *add* Apptd. to comd. 22nd Bn. Sepoys 26 Feb. 1773.

BIRCH, Robert Johnston.
Vol. i. page 145, line 21 : *add* d. of a bilious fever.
Line 22 : *add* Son of Rev. George Birch, vicar of Comber, co. Down, and Anne his wife, dau. of Adam Blair Johnston.
Line 27 : *add* to *Refs. Belfast Newsletter*, 4 Feb. 1826.

BIRRELL, George.
Vol. i. page 150, line 7 from bottom : *add* His youngest dau. Maria m. David Simpson, *q.v.*

BIRRELL, James Ramsay.
Vol. i. page 151, line 3 : *add* (She died Centre Villa, Wardie, Edinburgh, 27 Dec. 1854).

BLACK, Andrew.
Vol. i. page 153, line 3 from bottom : *add* (She re-m. Daniel Spencer Freeman, and became mother of Charles Henry Spencer Freeman, *q.v.*)

BLACK, Robert.
Vol. i. page 154, line 28 : *add* of a fever caught in the expedn. under Col. Monson.
Line 29 : *add* Son of Rev. Robert Black, D.D., of Derry, Presbyterian minister.
Line 32 : *add Refs. : Faulkner's Dublin Journal*, 29 Aug. 1805.

ADDENDA

BLACK, Samuel.
Vol. i. page 154, line 5 from bottom : *add* m. St. Mary's, Dublin, 20 Jan. 1788.
Line 3 from bottom : *add* (She re-m. and became mother of Percy Skeffington Hamilton, *q.v.*).

BLACKALL, Robert.
Vol. i. page 155, line 29 : *add* b. 5 Oct. 1787.

BLAGDON, Edward.
Vol. i. page 158, line 25 : *add* bapt. Meeting House, Puddington, 16 Oct. 1788. Son of Peter Blagdon and Elizabeth his wife.

BLAGRAVE, George.
Vol. i. page 158, line 28 : *add* b. 14 Dec. 1786.

BLAIR, Thomas.
Vol. i. page 161, line 21 : *add* bur. Calcutta 1 July 1783.

BLAIR, William.
Vol. i. page 162, line 6 : *add* His dau. m. William Bodycott Davis, *q.v.*

BLAKE, Benjamin.
Vol. i. page 162, line 17 : *add* bapt. Portsmouth 28 Sept. 1788. Son of George Blake and Ann his wife.

BLANE, George Rodney.
Vol. i. page 165, line 23 : *add* bapt. St. James's, Westminster, 9 Feb. 1791.

BLANSHARD, John Henry.
Vol. i. page 166, line 17 : *add* Ed. Durham ; left the school in 1822.
Line 21 : *add Refs. : Durham School Register.*

BLENKINS, Frederick Augustus.
Vol. i. page 167, line 7 : *add* Reduction of Kalinjar 1812 ; Ensign 2/16th N.I.

BLENKINSOP, Edward.
Vol. i. page 167, line 14 : *add* (? His sister m. Edward FitzGeràld, *q.v.*).

BLISSET, Robert.
Vol. i. page 167, line 37 : *add* bapt. St. George the Martyr, Middlesex, 23 Feb. 1787.

ADDENDA

BLUETT, William Henry Clarke.
Vol. i. page 169, line 9 : *add* Ed. Blundells 23 Aug. 1813 till 29 June 1816.

BLUNT, Henry James.
Vol. i. page 170, line 7 : *add* His dau. m. David Edward Brewster-Macpherson, *q.v.*

BOILEAU, John Peter (1787-1838).
Vol. i. page 173, line 6 : *add* His sister m. Samuel Davis, *q.v.*

BOISRAGON, Charles Henry.
Vol. i. page 175, line 4 : *add* of smallpox.

BOYD, Mossom.
Vol. i. page 192, line 18 : *add* His dau. m. Francis Elliot Voyle, *q.v.*

BRADBY, Edward Taylor.
Vol. i. page 195, line 33 : *add* and Sarah his wife.

BRADSHAW, Paris.
Vol. i. page 197, line 4 from bottom : *add* Son of John Bradshaw. His sister m. William Harden Bradshaigh, of Kapnagorran, co. Tipperary.
Page 198, line 6 : *add* to *Refs.* Burke's *Landed Gentry*, 4th edn., p. 145, *s.n.* Bradshaigh.

BRADSHAW, William Rigby.
Vol. i. page 198 : *add* b. 8 Apr. 1784. bapt. Fitzroy chapel, St. Pancras, Middlesex, 19 June 1784. Son of Robert Halden Bradshaw and Cornelia Thornhill his wife.

BRICE, James.
Vol. i. page 201, bottom line : *add* (*Probably* son of Edward Brice, of Berners St., London, whose dau. m. Rt. Hon. Sir John Anstruther, 4th and 1st Bart., C.J. of Bengal).
Page 202, line 3 : *add* to *Refs.* (? Burke's *Peerage*, 1923, p. 120, *s.n.* Carmichael-Anstruther, Bart.).

BRIDGEMAN, Simeon.
Vol. i. page 203, line 2 : *add* d. 28 Mar.

BRIGGS, William Thomas.
Vol. i. page 204, line 18 : *add* of cholera.

BRITTEN, George Ernst.
Vol. i. page 208, line 26 : *for* P. Goullet *read* Peter Goullet.

BROOKS, James.
Vol. i. page 217, line 10 : *add* bapt. St. Giles-in-the-Fields 7 May 1790. Son of William Brooks and Mary his wife.

ADDENDA

BROWN, Samuel (*c.* 1774-1805).
Vol. i. page 227, line 16 : *add* Eldest son of Samuel Brown, of Belfast.
Line 18 : *add* to *Refs.* : *Faulkner's Dublin Journal*, 2 Jan. 1806.

BROWNE, Henry Cumming Ayscough.
Vol. i. page 231, line 29 : *add* His sister m. Edward Simons, *q.v.* Ed. Blundells 18 Feb. 1810 till 29 June 1814.

BRUCE, William (d. 1783).
Vol. i. page 239, line 8 : *add* A. G. Bengal army 1780-3.

BUREAU, Alexander William.
Vol. i. page 249, line 5 : *add* b. 1783/84.
Line 6 : *add* d. aged 24.
Line 10 : *add* Brother of Julia Bureau.
Line 14 : *add* to *Refs.* M.I. church of St. John Baptist, Kentish Town.

BURRINGTON, George.
Vol. i. page 259, line 6 from bottom : *add* Lieut. H.M. 71st Foot 9 Oct. 1757. Served in the Madras army 1777-83.

BURROWES, Alexander.
Vol. i. page 261, line 24 : *add* d. nr. Farrukhabad, U.P., 29 June 1792.
Add to *Services* : " Extract of a letter from Cawnpore, dated 4th July (1792). 'A very melancholy circumstance has lately happened about 13 coss from Furruckabad ; Lieut. Burrows was sent from Futtyghur with his Coy. of Sepoys, accompanied by Lieut. Loveday with his Coy., to apprehend a Zemindar who had stopped some boats belonging to Col. Stuart's detachment. Lieut. B., in his zeal to perform the service, exposed himself imprudently, and was shot in the Zemindar's compound, where he had pushed his way.'"
Add Refs. : *Cal. Gaz.* 19 July 1792.

BUSH, James Tobin.
Vol. i. page 265, line 4 from bottom : *add* Ed. Blundells 2 Feb. 1824 till 2 May 1825, when he " eloped."

BUSHBY, Ewen.
Vol. i. page 266, line 29 : *add* to *Services* Second Mysore war ; prisoner for 2 yrs. in Bangalore and Savandrug. Third Mysore war ; in Comst. Dept.
Line 30 : *add* to *Refs.* : *Cal. Gaz.* 7 Feb. 1793.

BYERS, John Lawson.
Vol. i. page 270, line 19 : *add* and Elizabeth his wife, *née* Lawson.

ADDENDA

CAESAR, Julius.
Vol. i. page 274, line 3 : *add* Lieut. (Madras) 6 Dec. 1765. Sent to Bengal in June 1766 during the " Batta mutiny."

CAMAC, Jacob.
Vol. i. page 278, line 2 : *add* and Elizabeth Turner his wife, of Killfallart (m. 8 Sept. 1744).
Line 4 : *add* and of Letitia, wife of Richard Scott, *q.v.*
Line 6 : *add* Was an Ensign in H.M. 84th in June 1763 ; h.p. do. 25 Dec. 1764.
Line 12 : *add* to *Refs.* Portrait, by Romney, sold at Christie's in May 1926.

CAMPBELL, James (1805-1850).
Vol. i. page 289, line 18 : *add d.s.p.* Tandridge, Surrey, 25 Sept, 1850.
Line 25 : *add* Joined John Cockburn, wine merchant, Edinburgh, in 1832, when the firm became Cockburn & Campbell, its present designation.
Line 27 : *add* to *Refs. G.M.* 1850, ii. 563.

CAMPBELL, James Hunter.
Vol. i. page 290, line 15 : *add* b. Calcutta 6 Oct. 1811.

CAMPBELL, Osborne.
Vol. i. page 294, line 27 : *add* His sister m. Charles Manners Gascoyne, *q.v.*

CARDEW, Ambrose.
Vol. i. page 300, line 1 from bottom : *add* His sister m. Sir Henry Edward Landor Thuillier, *q.v.*

CARLETON, Charles William.
Vol. i. page 302, line 22 : *add* bapt. Coolock 29 Nov. 1789.

CARLETON, Henry Peter.
Vol. i. page 303, line 26 : *add* bapt. Coolock 16 Dec. 1787.

CARNAC, John.
Vol. i. page 305, line 38 : *add* Son of Capt. Peter Carnac.
Line 2 from bottom : *add* T.C.D. ; Pensioner 15 May 1736, aged 15.
Page 306, line 2 : *add* to *Refs* : *Alumni Dub. Holzman.*

CARNAC, Scipio.
Vol. i. page 306, line 6 : *add* to *Services* Lieut. H.M. 3rd Foot (Buffs) 29 Aug. 1756.

CARNEGIE, Nicholas.
　Vol. i. page 307, line 8 : *add* His dau. m. James Roxburgh, *q.v.*

CARROLL, Christopher.
　Vol. i. page 310, line 15 : *add* d. 20 Sept.

CARRUTHERS, David Alexander.
　Vol. i. page 310, line 25 : *add* d. Warmanbie 25 Oct. 1872.

CARTER, John William.
　Vol. i. page 313, line 22 : *add* Son of Benjamin Carter, Capt. R.N., and Anne his wife, elder dau. of Robert Graydon, of Killashee, co. Kildare, M.P. Nephew of Robert Graydon, *q.v.*

CHAIGNEAU, Christopher Theophilus.
　Vol. i page 325, line 20 : *add* Was *probably* a Volunteer in H.M. 84th Regt. before transfer to the Bengal army. Reverted to H.M. 84th in 1761. Ensign 30 Aug. 1761 ; Lieut. do. 1 Nov. 1761. Wounded in action in July or Aug. 1763. h.p. 24 Dec. 1764. Capt. (Madras) 7 July 1765. Was Fort Major at Madras in 1769 ; removed in 1777.
　Line 22 : *add* to *Refs.* : *Wilson*, i. 389.

CHAMBERS, John.
　Vol. i. page 327, line 4 : *add* Bt. Ensign 4 Nov. 1782.

CHAMBERS, Robert Ewbank.
　Vol. i. page 327, line 31 : *add* bapt. All Saints, Newcastle-on-Tyne, 1 June 1790.

CHARTERS, Thomas.
　Vol. i. page 333, line 5 from bottom : *add* Uncle of Samuel Fairfax, *q.v.*

CHRISTIE, Andrew.
　Vol. i. page 341, line 26 : *add* 2nd dau. of Cathcart Dempster, of Scotland.

CLARKSON, James Oram.
　Vol. i. page 348, line 13 : *add* dau. of James Price (d. 1842), *q.v.*

CLAYTON, Thomas William.
　Vol. i. page 350, line 13 : *add* (She died Chunar 1793).

CLELAND, David.
　Vol. i. page 350, line 34 : *add* Ensign 3rd Bn. Sepoys. d. Allahabad 10 June 1767.

ADDENDA

CLEWLOW, Charles.
　Vol. i. page 350, line 2 from bottom : *add* (*Possibly* son of Rev. James Hamilton Clewlow, incumbent of Bangor, co. Down, and Ismay Jane his wife (m. in 1756), only dau. of George Mathews, of Springvale, co. Down.)

COLEBY, Richard L——.
　Vol. i. page 362, line 23 : *add* Bt. Ensign 1 Aug. 1782.

COLLINS, James.
　Vol. i. page 365, line 10 : *add* Son of Samuel Collins, of Dublin, ribbon weaver, and Rachel Darragh his wife.

COOKE, William Percy.
　Vol. i. page 378, line 2 from bottom : *add* Son of Ann Cooke.

COOKSON, George Bryan.
　Vol. i. page 379, line 22 : *add* bapt. Petersfield 24 June 1789. Son of Rev. James Cookson and Sarah his wife.

COOKSON, William.
　Vol. i. page 380, line 11 : *add* His sister m. Auchmuty Tucker, *q.v.*

CORBET, Samuel.
　Vol. i. page 385, line 4 from bottom, after 'Komona' *add* (w.); Lieut. 1/27th N.I.

CORFIELD, Alfred Henry.
　Vol. i. page 386, line 33 : *add* Ed. Blundells 29 Jan. 1821 till 29 June 1823.

CORFIELD, Charles.
　Vol. i. page 387, line 3 : *add* Ed. Blundells 16 Aug. 1819 till 16 Dec. 1822.

CORFIELD, Frederick Brooke.
　Vol. i. page 387, line 26 : *add* Ed. Blundells 14 Aug. 1815 till 16 Dec. 1818.

COWLISHAW, Elias.
　Vol. i. page 396, line 8 from bottom : *add* Bt. Ensign 4 Mar. 1782.

CRABBE, William Joseph.
　Vol. i page 402, line 7 : *add* Ensign H.M. 84th Regt. 26 June 1761 ; Lieut. do. 6 Oct. 1761 ; h.p. do. 25 Mar. 1765.
　Line 11 : *add Note :* His christian names are variously given as William, Joseph William, and Joshua William.

ADDENDA

CRAIG or CRAIGIE, John.
Vol. i. page 403, line 22 : *add* A Mr. John Craigie was bur. in Calcutta 20 Aug. 1783.

CRAIG, Thomas.
Vol. i. page 403, line 34 : *add* bapt. 10 Jan. 1786.

CRAWFORD, James (d. 1787).
Vol. i. page 409, line 11 : *add* 3rd son of James Crawford, of Crawfordsburn, co. Down, and Mabel his wife, dau. of Hugh Johnston, of Rademan, co. Down. Brother-in-law of James Alexander, 1st Earl of Caledon.
Line 16 : *add* to *Refs.* Burke's *Peerage*, 1923, p. 422, *s.n.* Caledon, E.

CRAWFURD, Moses.
Vol. i. page 410, line 9 from bottom : *add* (*See also* John Fulton (1807-1887), Robert McKerrell, and John Reid).

CRICHTON, Charles.
Vol. i. page 412 : *add* b. Colvend, co. Kirkcudbright, 31 Oct. 1787. Son of Robert Crichton and Agnes Wilson his wife.

CRICHTON, David.
Vol. i. page 412, line 20 : *add* bapt. Colvend, co. Kirkcudbright, 18 May 1782.

CULLEY, Thomas.
Vol. i. page 422, line 18 : *add Refs.* : *A.J.* N.S. v. 39.

CUMMING, Sir John.
Vol. i. page 426, line 29 : *add* Ensign H.M. 84th Regt. 31 Aug. 1761 ; Lieut. do. 16 Nov. 1761 ; h.p. do. 24 Dec. 1764.

CUMMING, Robert.
Vol. i. page 427, line 4 : *add* bapt. Edinburgh 2 Feb. 1788.

CUMMINGS, David.
Vol. i. page 427, line 20 : *add* A Mr. Cummins, Volunteer in H.M. 84th Regt., was transfd. as Ensign to the Bengal army 26 July 1763. *Refs.* : *Orme MSS.*, vii.

CUNINGHAME or CUNNINGHAM, John (1788-1814).
Vol. i. page 429, line 16 : *add* bapt. St. Cuthbert's, Edinburgh, 2 Oct. 1788.

CUNNINGHAM, William.
Vol. i. page 431, line 8 from bottom : *add* bapt. Irvine 9 Apr. 1787.

ADDENDA

CURRAN, James.
Vol. i. page 433, line 3 from bottom : *add* bapt. Newmarket 31 Jan. 1787. Son of Rt. Hon. John Philpot Curran, Master of the Rolls in Ireland (*D.N.B.*), and Sarah Creagh his wife. *Refs.* : Brady's *Clerical Records of Cork, Cloyne and Ross*, ii. 132.

CURTIS, Robert Ruddock.
Vol. i. page 435, line 29 : *add* d. on board the *Norma* transport (? on the voyage from W.I. to England) 18 May 1838.
Line 33 : *add* Ensign H.M. 84th, by purchase, 10 Sept. 1829. *Refs.* : *Roll of Officers 84th York & Lancaster Regt.*, by Raikes and Key.

DALYELL, Alexander.
Vol. ii. page 6, line 18 : *add* Son of James Dalyell, in Barncrosh.

DASHWOOD, Charles James Augustus.
Vol. ii. page 13, line 11 : *add* bapt. Marylebone 9 Feb. 1791.

D'AUVERGNE, Robert.
Vol. ii. page 14, line 19 : *add* d. at sea 16 Aug. 1792.

DELAP, Samuel.
Vol. ii. page 44, line 18 : *add* Son of Rev. Alexander Delap, of Ray.

DENBY, William Charles.
Vol. ii. page 46, line 13 : *add* bapt. psh. church, Leeds, 4 Apr. 1791.

DENNISS, George Gladwin.
Vol. ii. page 47, line 29 : *add* Uncle of Norman Chester Macleod, *q.v.*

DICKINSON, Thomas.
Vol. ii. page 58, line 6 from bottom : *add* bapt. 5 July 1789.

DONALDSON, James.
Vol. ii. page 68, line 26 : *add* and Janet McCaull his wife.

DOUGLAS, Alexander.
Vol. ii. page 71 : *add* Nephew of Patrick Heatly, *q.v.*

GALL, Lawrence.
Vol. ii. page 243, line 33 : *add* Father of Marian, mother of Charles George Ross, *q.v.*

*GORDON, John.
   Vol. ii. page 291, line 18 : *add Note :* Possibly Gen. Stubbs has confused this man with John Arthur Gore, *q.v.*, although he states that the former was apptd. to do duty with the Bengal Art. in Nov., the latter in Aug. 1791.

*GRANT, Alexander.
   Vol. ii. page 310 : *add* Was living in Bedford Row, London, in Apr. 1765, when he made his Will. Brother of Patrick Grant, of Lochlater, Scotland. m. Margaretha Henrietta.
   Add to *Refs.* Will dated London 2 Apr. 1765 ; filed in Calcutta 1768.

HUTCHINSON, Thomas Frederick.
   Vol. ii. page 514, line 21 : *add* Son of Thomas Hutchinson, of Harrogate, M.D., and Jane his wife.

www.ingramcontent.com/pod-product-compliance
Lightning Source LLC
Chambersburg PA
CBHW061922220426
43662CB00012B/1771